3rd Annual International Conference on Information Technology and Applications (ITA 2016)

ITM Web of Conferences Volume 7 (2016)

Hangzhou, China
29 - 31 July 2016

Editors:

Tao Gong
Ting Yang
Juan Xu

ISBN: 978-1-5108-3280-0

Printed from e-media with permission by:

Curran Associates, Inc.
57 Morehouse Lane
Red Hook, NY 12571

Some format issues inherent in the e-media version may also appear in this print version.

Printed by Curran Associates, Inc. (2017)

For additional information, please contact EDP Sciences – Web of Conferences
at the address below.

EDP Sciences – Web of Conferences
17, Avenue du Hoggar
Parc d'Activité de Courtabœuf
BP 112
F-91944 Les Ulis Cedex A
France

Phone: +33 (0) 1 69 18 75 75
Fax: +33 (0) 1 69 28 84 91

contact-edps@webofconferences.org

Additional copies of this publication are available from:

Curran Associates, Inc.
57 Morehouse Lane
Red Hook, NY 12571 USA
Phone: 845-758-0400
Fax: 845-758-2633
Email: curran@proceedings.com
Web: www.proceedings.com

TABLE OF CONTENTS

Aims & scope

ITM Web of Conferences is an open-access journal devoted to the publishing of conference proceedings dealing with all areas related to information technology, computer science and mathematics.

ITM Web of Conferences aims to make conference proceedings visible, citable and widely usable by the scientific community. It offers outstanding services for the publication and dissemination of contents in order to ensure long-term archiving and maximum exposure of scientific events.

Coverage includes the whole spectrum of pure and applied mathematics, as well as all domains related to computer science such as programming, operating systems, databases, software engineering, web technologies, human-computer interaction, etc.

Why publish with ITM Web of Conferences?

- **Open access:** conference papers available worldwide.
- **Fast publication:** less than 3 months.
- **Total flexibility:** no page restrictions, free unlimited use of colour in the online version, any kind of scientific document welcomed (traditional articles, posters, abstracts and slideshows).
- **High visibility:** all documents indexed in main databases and easily found online.
- **Fair author rights:** CC-BY Creative Commons license.
- **Range of additional publishing options:** printed proceedings, CD-ROMs, copy-editing, etc.

ISSN (electronic edition): pending

Contact: Isaline Augusto
itm@webofconferences.org

www.itm-conferences.org

edp open Open Access Publishing from EDP Sciences

DOI: 10.1051/itmconf/20160700001

Preface

ITA 2016

3rd Annual International Conference on Information Technology and Application (ITA 2016) was held in Hangzhou, China, from 29-31 July 2016. ITA 2016 is to offer scholars, professionals, academics and graduate students to present, share, and discuss their studies from various perspectives in the aspects of Information Technology and Applications. These proceedings tend to collect the up-to-date, comprehensive and worldwide state-of-art knowledge on information technology and application. All accepted papers were subjected to strict peer-reviewing by expert referees. The papers have been selected for this proceedings based on originality, significance, and clarity for the purpose of the conference. The selected papers and additional late-breaking contributions to be presented will make an exciting technical program on conference. The conference program is extremely rich, featuring high impact presentation. We hope this conference will not only provide the participants a broad overview of the latest research results on information technology, but also provide the participants a significant platform to build academic connections.

The Technical Program Committee worked very hard to have all papers reviewed before the review deadline. The final technical program consists of 99 papers. There is four keynote speech and nine invited sessions. The keynote speakers are internationally recognized as a leading expert in the research field of information technology who has demonstrated outstanding proficiency and has achieved distinction in his profession. The proceedings were published as a volume in by EDP science.

We would like to express our sincere gratitude to all the members of Technical Program Committee and organizers for their enthusiasm, time, and expertise. Our deep thanks also go to many volunteers and staffs for the long hours and hard work they have generously given to ITA 2016. Finally, we would like to thank all the authors, speakers, and participants of this conference for their contributions to ITA 2016, and also looks forward to welcoming you to ITA 2017.

Prof. Ting Yang

General Chair

Prof. Kingsum Chow, University of Washington USA

Co-Chair

Prof. Li Zhou, National University of Defense Technology, China

Prof. Junli Zhao, Qingdao University China

Editor

Prof. Tao Gong, Donghua University, China

Prof. Ting Yang, Tianjin University, China

Prof. Juan Xu, Hefei University of Technology China

Technical Program Committee

Dr. Imran Memon, College of Computer Science and Technology, Zhejiang University

Dr. Jianzhou Zhao, Cadence Design System, San Jose, United States

Dr. Malka N. Halgamuge, Department of Electrical & Electronic Engineering, Melbourne School of Engineering, The University of Melbourne, Melbourne, Australia

Dr. Ximing Fu, Department of Computer Science and Technology, Tsinghua University

Dr. NoranAzizan Bin Cholan, Faculty of Electrical and Electronics Engineering, UniversitiTun Hussein Onn Malaysia, BATU PAHAT, Malaysia

Dr. Krzysztof Gdawiec, Institute of Computer Science, University of Silesia, Sosnowiec, Poland

Dr. Tigang Jiang, University of Electronic, Science and Technology of China

Prof. Huamin Wang,Wuhan University, Wuhan, hubei, China

Dr. Ray-Hwa Wong, Department of Mechanical Eng., Hwa-Hsia University of Technology, Taiwan, R.O.C, Taiwan

Dr.Nongqing Yang, Northwest University for Nationalities, China

Dr. Cao Danyang, North industry China University, Beijing , China

Dr.Weilong He, Henan Normal University, China

Dr. Pingping Liu, Beijing Wuzi University Beijing , China

Dr.Xiaodong Wang, East China Jiaotong University, China

Dr. An Bao-Ran, School of Astronautics, Harbin Institute of Technology, Harbin, China

Dr.Yan Shi, Hohai University, China

Dr. Sunwei, College of Information and Control, China

Dr.Xiongkai Shao, Anhui University of Technology, China

Prof. Zhiting Lin, Anhui University, Anhui, China

Dr. Xiang Li, Yunnan University, China

Dr. Tongliang Fan, China Maritime Police Academy, China

Keynote I

Software Hardware Co-optimization

Prof .Kingsum Chow
Chief Scientist, Technology Infrastructure
Alibaba Infrastructure Service

Abstract

Hardware and software configuration parameters directly impact the performance of computer systems in the data center. This presentation describes how to approach the performance co-optimization problem from three viewpoints: the CPU clock-ticks, the cycles per instruction, and the number of instructions to complete a task. It suggests the roles that can be played by hardware developers, software developers, compiler writers, and managed runtime systems. It also introduces a large-scale performance data monitoring and analysis system that can set directions for system optimizations.

Speaker's Bio

Kingsum is currently a Technology Infrastructure Chief Scientist at Alibaba Infrastructure Services. Before joining Alibaba in May 2016, he was a Principal Engineer and Chief Data Scientist in the System Technology and Optimization (STO) division of the Intel Software and Services Group (SSG). He joined Intel in 1996 after receiving Ph.D. in Computer Science and Engineering from the University of Washington. Since then, he has been working on performance, modeling and analysis of software applications. At the Oracle Open World in October 2015, Intel and Oracle CEO's announced the joint Cloud lab called project Apollo led by Kingsum in the opening keynote in front of tens of thousands of software developers. He has been issued more than 20 patents. He has presented more than 80 technical papers. In his spare time, he volunteers to coach multiple robotics teams to bring the joy of learning Science, Technology, Engineering and Mathematics to the K-12 students in his community. His teams appeared in national and world championships three times, taking home best programming in 2010 and best sensor technology and machine learning for robotics in both 2014 and 2015.

 DOI: 10.1051/itmconf/20160700003

Keynote2

Intelligent Information Processing and Visual Net Logo-Based Simulations of Immune Computation (IC)

Prof. Tao Gong
College of Information Science and Engineering,
Donghua University

Abstract

Immune system is a complex defending system for the health of a body, and the modeling of this immune system is as complex as that of the brain. This immune system is of natural parallel nonlinear recognition ability, and it can discriminate selfs and nonselfs in normal immune responses. This immune system is based on some complex pattern recognition mechanism in its models and functions. One of the difficult problems in understanding this immune system is how to generate the simulation results in biological shapes, which are similar to cells and molecules. We propose a visual simulation approach of the tri-tier immune system against the viruses with Java Applet technique. The immune network is built on the normal model, the tri-tier immune model and the parallel computing of the immune cells against the viruses. The embedded immune medical system is a artificial intelligent immune system with adaptive learning and parallel computing. SARS patients' lungs show different degree of flake or patchy ground glass density shadow. The shadow shows a trend of progress, because in some cases a small shadow may quickly grows into a large shadow. The super-resolution reconstruction can help us to detect more shadows, so we can use this method for decrease early lesions. Though these single images have low resolutions, we can use the super-resolution reconstruction approach to break through the resolution limits of the medical images, in order to generate the high-resolution image for better disease analysis. We use the chest CT sequence images of the SARS patient for the reconstruction experiments, and the experiments are simulated in Matlab. When the simulation was completed, the simulation model was viewed on both the NetLogo client and the remote web browser, after the model was saved as the Java Applet and embedded into the web pages.

Speaker's Bio

Prof. Tao Gong received the MS degree in Pattern Recognition and Intelligent Systems and PhD degree in Computer Science from the Central South University respectively in 2003 and 2007. He is an associate professor of immune computation, Vice Head of Automation Department, Assistant Director of Research Department at Donghua University, China, and he was a visiting scholar at Department of Computer Science and CERIAS, Purdue University, USA. He is the Editors-in-Chief of the journal Immune Computation, and an editorial board member of some international journals. He was a Technical Committee Chair of ISEEIP 2012, and a Publicity Chair of ISA 2012 and ICSI3 2015. He was Invited Speaker for some conferences such as SecTech 2012 and ICAMR 2014. He was also a program committee member of some international conferences such as IEEE ICNC 2011, IEEE BMEI 2011, WMSE 2011, ICARIS 2012, AITS 2012, CCA 2012, ASP 2012, IST 2012, ISA 2012 and SIS2013 etc. He is a Life Member of Sigma Xi, The Scientific Research Society, a Vice-Chair of IEEE Computer Society Task Force on Artificial Immune Systems, and Chen Guang Scholar of Shanghai. His research has been supported by National Natural Science Foundation of China, Shanghai Natural Science Foundation, Shanghai Educational Development Foundation and Shanghai Education Committee etc. He has published over 100 papers in referred journals and international conferences, and over 20 books such as Artificial Immune System Based on Normal Model and Its Applications, and Advanced Expert Systems: Principles, Design and Applications etc. His current research interests include computational immunology and immune computation. He is also a committee member of intelligent robots committee and natural computing committee in the Association of Artificial Intelligence of China.

DOI: 10.1051/itmconf/20160700003

Keynote3

Bio-Inspired Information Technique

Prof. Xin Ma
School of Information Science and Engineering,
Shandong University

Abstract

The goal of our activity is to propose bio-inspired mechanisms to solve complex problems such as distributed resource allocation in cognitive radio, self-syncronization, distributed detection and estimation in wireless sensor networks. A modern trend in the design of complex engineering systems is to endow the system with self-organization and self-healing capabilities. Nature is full of examples of biological systems capable of accomplishing extremely complex tasks, even if constituted by simple components, in many cases without the intervention of any central entity having full control of what is going on.An example is the design of radio access mechanism for cognitive networks mimicking the behavior of a flock of birds swarming in search for food in a cohesive fashion without colliding with each other. Another example is bats navigation and location system. Bats have good navigation and locationing capabilities by sound which can give inspiration for radar, which mainly depend on the coordination of organs of Larynx, Vocal tract and Face construct and ears.. Bioinspired technique leverage this knowledge to develop new technologies and translate them into products that meet real world challenges.

Speaker's Bio

Xin Ma received his Ph.D. degree from Institute of Acoustics, China Academy of Sciences, Beijing in 2005. He is currently a Professor in the School of Information Science and Engineeringat Shandong University. He is the inventor or co-inventor of 20 patents, the author or co-author of 80 papers and 2 books intheareasof digital signal process and electronic devices design.He has been undertaken a number of national research projects and provincial or ministerial research topics.Now his research workmainly focuses on the Bioinspired Signal Process and its Applicaiton.

ITM Web of Conferences 7, 00003 (2016) DOI: 10.1051/itmconf/20160700003
ITA 2016

Keynote4

Cyber physical systems in Smart Grid

Prof. Ting Yang
Key Laboratory of Smart Grid of Ministry of Education
School of Electrical Engineering and Automation
Tianjin University

Abstract

Cyber physical systems (CPS) refer to the class of systems which offer close integration of computation, networking, and physical processes. In the real world, CPS range from miniscule such as pacemakers to large-scale such as power grid. Among them, since mutual coupling between energy flow and information flow is an important feature of Smart grid (SG), SG becomes a typical cyber physical system. In order to realize the SG, we will have to heavily depend on CPS that will be able to seamless integration and interaction of the power network infrastructure as the physical systems, and information sensing, processing, intelligence, and control as the cyber systems. This lecture covers the introduction of CPS in Smart Grid: 1) CPS architectures, which are designed specifically for interfaces between power networks and cyber systems. 2) Communication technologies, which are vital for efficient and effective interaction between the physical systems and the cyber systems. 3) Modeling and simulation tools, which are critical to ensure that the large-scale network CPSs of SGs can operate seamlessly and components. 4) Reliability and Security technologies, which are the basement for CPS and trustworthy SG to detect, prevent, and mitigate the cyber-attacks. In summary, this lecture focuses on effective and efficient interaction between and integration of physical systems and cyber systems, and presents CPS technologies in SG to make electrical power system more efficient in operations, more economically viable, and environmentally sustainable.

Speaker's Bio

Dr. Ting Yang is currently a Chair professor of Theory and Advanced Technology of Electrical Engineering, at the School of Electrical Engineering and Automation, Tianjin University, China. He was the cooperative research staff of Imperial College London (2008), University of Sydney, Australia (2011, 2015). Prof. Yang is the winner of the “New Century Excellent Talents in University Award” from Chinese Ministry of Education. He is the leader of tens of research grant projects, including the International S&T Cooperation Program of China, the National High-Tech Research and Development Program of China (863 Program), the National Natural Science Foundation of China, and so on. Prof. Yang is the chairman of two workshops of IEEE International Conference (the 6th IEEE International Conference on Cloud Computing Technology and Science–IEEE Cloud Com, the 18th IEEE International Conference on Parallel and Distributed Systems–IEEE ICPADS), and the editor in Chief of the Special Issues “Ubiquitous Data-Centric Sensor Networks” of the international journal of DSN. He is the author/co-author of four books, more than one hundred publications in internationally refereed journals and conferences (such as IEEE Trans. on Instrumentation and Measurement, IEEE Trans. on Cloud Computing, Journal of Applied Energy, Journal of Network and Computer Applications). Prof. Yang is a senior member of the Chinese Institute of Electronic, the fellow of Circuit and System committee, the fellow of Theory and Advanced Technology of Electrical Engineering, and the member of International Society for Industry and Applied Mathematics. Professor Yang’s research effort is focused on information and communication technologies in industrial application, big data and cloud computing.

edp sciences

ITM Web of Conferences

Statement of Peer review

In submitting conference proceedings to ITM Web of Conferences, I certify to the Publisher that I adhere to the **Policy on Publishing Integrity** of the journal in order to safeguard good scientific practice in publishing.

1. All articles have been subjected to peer review administered by the proceedings editors.
2. Reviews have been conducted by expert referees, who have been requested to provide unbiased and constructive comments aimed, whenever possible, at improving the work.
3. Proceedings editors have taken all reasonable steps to ensure the quality of the materials they publish and their decision to accept or reject a paper for publication has been based only on the merits of the work and the relevance to the journal.

Title, date and place of the conference

The 3rd International Conference on Information Technology and Application (ITA 2016)

Hangzhou, China, July 29-31, 2016

Proceedings editor(s):

prof Tao Gong prof. Ting Yang prof. Juan Xu

9/15/16 9/15/2016 9/15/16

Date and editor's signature

17, avenue du Hoggar - PA de Courtabœuf – BP 112 - 91944 Les Ulis Cedex A (France)

A Smart phone Identification Method Based on Gesture

Di XU[1], Quan ZHANG[2]

[1]*School of Electronic Science and Engineering, National University of Defense Technology, China*
[2]*School of Electronic Science and Engineering, National University of Defense Technology, China*

Abstract. In order to promote the practicality of smart phone identification based on gesture, we introduce weighted morphological characteristics and early termination of authentication into dynamic time warping (DTW) algorithm, which based on characteristic moving data captured by in-built accelerometer and gyroscopes, and put forward an effective identification algorithm (ME-DTW) for smartphone. The algorithm controls the contribution made by the difference between the latitudes to the total Euclidean distance by smartphone morphological characteristics. It also introduces restricted areas touch trigger gesture acquisition scheme and authentication gesture length selection scheme based on normal distribution, which effectively improve the identification accuracy and efficiency. Experimental results show that: when others imitate gestures attack false acceptance rate tends to 0%, the personal identification false rejection rate remained at 3.29%, which can meet most practical security needs

1. Introduction

With the development of mobile information technology, smart phones are widely used to manage personal information, mobile payments, etc. as data processing terminals. These applications require high smart phone security, because the loss and disclosure of user privacy information will bring great security risk. Thus a more flexible, safer identification mechanism on the smart phone has become a hot issue of common concern.

Subscriber identity is verifying the legal status of the users before they enter the system or an application. It prevents the system from abusing by illegal users and privacy information from leaking. The traditional identification methods are insecure, including password, PIN-code, etc., which may be stolen or cracked easily. Biometrics complement or substitute the traditional methods which benefits from its features of safety, reliability and convenience. However, current biometric identification methods, such as face recognition [1], fingerprint identification [2], iris recognition [3] and handwritten signatures [4], have the drawbacks of requiring high cost of technology or specific hardware, or being affected by the surrounding environment easily. Meanwhile, the face, fingerprint, iris and signature are significant features that determine someone uniquely and cannot be changed or replaced anymore. The leak of these features would cause irreversible identity fake threat. This article puts forward a gesture-based identification method using characteristic moving data captured by in-built accelerometer and gyroscope. This method uses biometrics to ensure the safety and avoid the leak of privacy features.

Currently, smart phones are generally equipped with 3-axis accelerometers and 3-axis gyroscopes, with the advantages of low price, high sensitivity, small size and low power consumption. Gesture-based identification means that the users hold the smart phones in hand and make signatures in air, meanwhile the in-built accelerometer and gyroscope collect the 3-axis acceleration and rotation data of each time frame, as the biometric characteristic to identify users. Motion gesture trail can be seen as a special form of handwriting in space. Because of individual organisms mechanism structures (muscle length, arm length, etc.) and behavior traits difference, when different people wave the same gesture, the final size, shape and intensity of the tracks will be different. However for the same person it will be relatively stable over a period of time.

At present, international and domestic academics have achieved some results on gesture-based identification. The most representative method are Dynamic Time Warping (DTW) technology and Hidden Markov Models (HMMs) model. In [5] accelerometer data are quantized to reduce the computational burden, noise and extrinsic changes, then similarity between sequences is measured by DTW. In [6] the Sliding Window and Bottom-up (SWAB) method is applied to segment gesture data, and then HMMs is used to identify the user. The identification in smartphones has special request of small samples, timeliness and accuracy. The learning-based methods (such as HMM, etc.) are not suitable resource-constrained smartphones since they need a lot of training samples while the DTW-based method is more suitable for it demands less samples and has good identification effect. However the practical use is restricted by its efficiency and accuracy. In [7] an improved Half

DOI: 10.1051/itmconf/20160701001

Dynamic Time Warping (HDTW) algorithm is put forward to reduce the time complexity effectively. In [8] the bending slope of matching path is constrained to reduce the amount of calculation and improve the efficiency. In [9] the endpoint alignment restriction is canceled to improve the identification accuracy. In order to further increase the efficiency and accuracy of the DTW, we introduce restricted areas touch trigger gesture acquisition scheme to collect accelerometer and gyroscope data. After pre-processing and authentication gesture length selection based on normal distribution, we put forward an effective identification algorithm ME-DTW which combines weighted morphological characteristics and early termination of authentication to measure the similarity. Finally, we compare the matching result with threshold.

The rest of the paper is organized as follows: Section 2 describes the identification procedure. Then, section 3 explains the details of gestures acquisition and pre-processing including smoothing and normalization. The proposed algorithm ME-DTW is detailed in Section 4, in which firstly an overview of traditional DTW algorithm is introduced, followed by detailed descriptions of weighted morphological characteristics, early termination of authentication and pseudo-code of ME-DTW. Section 5 presents experimental results including the pre-processing effect, threshold setting and simulation results by MATLAB. Finally, the conclusions and future work are presented in Section 6.

2. Identification Procedure

The overall identification process takes place in two phases: registration phase and authentication phase, as shown in Fig.1.

In registration phase, a certain number of registration gestures are collected. After pre-processing, an optimal gesture is selected as a template. The selection method is calculating the distance between any two registration gestures, and the template is the one which has the minimum distance with all the other gestures. The threshold is determined by the maximum distance between the template and other registration gestures.

In authentication phase, after pre-processing and length screening, the authentication gesture matches the template using ME-DTW algorithm which is proposed in this paper. Finally, we give the identification result.

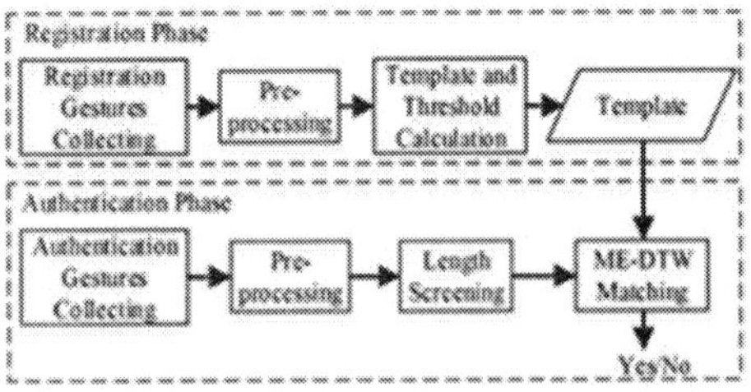

Figure 1. Flowchart of Identification Using Gestures

3. Gesture Acquisition and Pre-Processing

3.1. Gesture Acquisition

In order to improve the security and accuracy of the software, we present a restricted area touch trigger gesture acquisition scheme. The touch trigger refers to that when a user holds the smartphone with his thumb touching the designated area of screen, the sensors begin to collect gesture data. Once the thumb left designated area, the gesture data collection finishes. This way can not only intercept effective period of gesture, save the time and space of endpoint detection, but also make user collect the gesture with almost similar holding manner, so the gestures have a better consistency and it increases the difficulty for attacker to trigger program.

While we touch the screen, the in-built accelerometers and gyroscopes begin to collect the 3-axis acceleration and 3-axis rotation data in every time frame as the original gesture data. The data are stored in a matrix of n rows 6 columns, where the stand for the time point, the first three columns represent the changes of accelerometer in 3-axis, and the rest represent the changes of gyroscope in 3-axis. Therefore, a gesture can be represented as

$$A=\begin{bmatrix} a_{x1} & a_{y1} & a_{z1} & g_{x1} & g_{y1} & g_{z1} \\ a_{x2} & a_{y2} & a_{z2} & g_{x2} & g_{y2} & g_{z2} \\ \vdots & \vdots & \vdots & \vdots & \vdots & \vdots \\ a_{xn} & a_{yn} & a_{zn} & g_{xn} & g_{yn} & g_{zn} \end{bmatrix} \tag{1}$$

where a stands for accelerometer data and g stands for gyroscope data.

3.2 Smoothing

When collecting the data, sensors always suffer from two kinds of noises, one of which is the accuracy of the sensors themselves, the other is tiny shake of the hand. Taking into account of the resource-constrained of the smartphones, we introduce Simple Moving Average (SMA) to smooth the noise. Just from the start point of a gesture, we calculate the average of m consecutive sensor data for each incoming data as

$$\begin{aligned} \overline{a}_i &= \left(a_{i-m+1}+a_{i-m+2}+\cdots+a_i\right)/m \\ &= \overline{a}_{i-1}+\left(a_i-a_{i-m}\right)/m \end{aligned} \tag{2}$$

where m denotes the window size of the data segment and this paper m is set to 5. The processing of the rotation data is similar to this.

3.3 Normalization

In this paper we introduce z-score standardization method to normalize acceleration and rotation data in order to

DOI: 10.1051/itmconf/20160701001

make them have the same influence in subsequent similarity measure. It is obtained as

$$a'_{di} = \frac{a_{di} - \overline{a}_d}{\sigma a_d}, d = x, y, z \quad (3)$$

$$g'_{di} = \frac{g_{di} - \overline{g}_d}{\sigma g_d}, d = x, y, z \quad (4)$$

where $a'_{xi}, a'_{yi}, a'_{zi}, g'_{xi}, g'_{yi}, g'_{zi}$ stand for the normalized 3-axis acceleration and rotation data at time of, $\overline{a}_x, \overline{a}_y, \overline{a}_z, \overline{g}_x, \overline{g}_y, \overline{g}_z$ stand for the average of the 3-axis acceleration and rotation data and $\sigma a_x, \sigma a_y, \sigma a_z, \sigma g_x, \sigma g_y, \sigma g_z$ stand for the standard deviation respectively.

4 Identification Algorithm ME-DTW

In this paper we propose ME-DTW algorithm which combines weighted morphological characteristics and early termination of authentication to calculate the similarity between the authentication gestures and template. Before that, authentication gesture length should be filtered to reduce calculation.

We introduce an authentication gesture length selection scheme based on normal distribution. For one gesture track, gesture length of the same person will be in a certain range, meanwhile different people will be different.

For m registration data, of which lengths are respectively, with length mean value and standard deviation which is defined as

$$\sigma_L = \sqrt{\frac{1}{m}\sum_{i=1}^{m}(L_i - \mu_L)^2} \quad (5)$$

the probability distribution function is defined as

$$\begin{aligned} &P(\mu_L - k\sigma_L < L < \mu_L + k\sigma_L) \\ &= \Phi(k) - \Phi(-k) = 2\Phi(k) - 1 \end{aligned} \quad (6)$$

Since the normal distribution 3σ criteria that the probability of distribution of values in the interval is 0.9974, the authentic user gestures length are almost entirely contained in the interval. So we can rule out most invalid authentication data to make a preliminary screening.

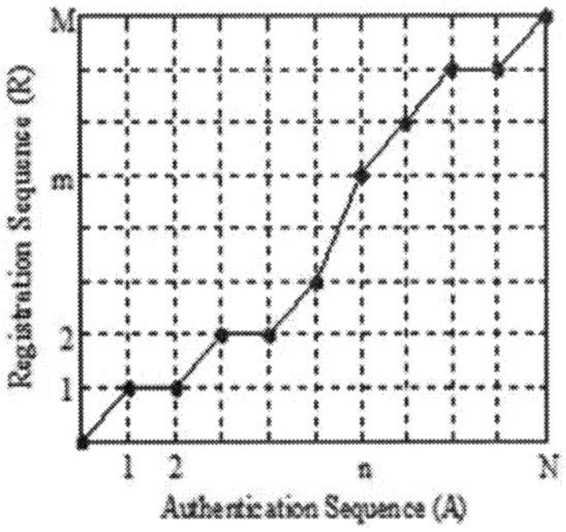

Figure 2.DTW Optimal Path

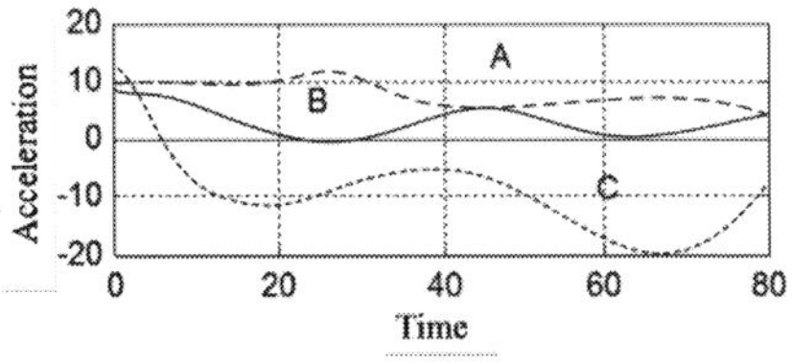

Figure 3.Schematic Diagram of Morphological Weighted Euclidean Distance.

4.1 DTW Algorithm

Dynamic Time Warping is an algorithm that combines time alignment and distance measurement together, with excellent effect on non-linear time normalization. It has been widely utilized in the field of speech recognition [8].

DTW can adjust the correspondence between the different elements of two time series to obtain an optimal matching curved path. Hence it can measure the distance between two time series with different length and obtain a minimum cumulative distance. DTW optimal path seeking is shown in Fig. 2.

When measuring the similarity between registration sequence with the length of M and authentication sequence with the length of N, we firstly construct a cumulative distance matrix D of. The value stands for accumulated value of the minimum distance distortion of each matching points from to if the and match. In order to control the slope of the match path, we set it in the range of 0 to 2. Theis finally calculated as

$$\begin{aligned} &D(i,j) = d(R_i, A_j) + \\ &\min(D(i,j-1), D(i-1,j-1), D(i-2,j-1)) \end{aligned} \quad (7)$$

where denotes the Euclidean distance between at moment and at moment, which is computed as

$$d(R_i, A_j) = \sqrt{\Sigma_{k=1}^{6}(R_{ik} - A_{jk})^2} \quad (8)$$

Ultimately, the matching path begins at and finishes at, and theis the final shortest cumulative distance between and.

 DOI: 10.1051/itmconf/20160701001

4.2ME-DTW Algorithm

4.2.1Weighted Euclidean distance base on Morphology

In DTW, the Euclidean distance-based similarity measure cannot reflect the trend of the time series. As shown in Fig. 3, the gestures A and B have substantially opposite shape, while gestures B and C have substantially similar shape. However, the distance between the gestures A and B will be less than the distance between the gestures B and C, which does not meet the people's visual and intuitive judgment.

Therefore, we introduce weighted morphological characteristics into DTW. It controls the difference between the latitudes contributing to the total Euclidean distance by morphological characteristics. Hence the morphological differences play a certain role in the similarity metric. For registration and authentication sequence R and, firstly we calculate corresponding slope sequences in each axis. For, the slope of the point in - axis is given as

$$SR_{ik} = R_{ik} - R_{(i-1)k} \cdot \tag{9}$$

The slope can be discretized to as

$$SR'_{ik} = \begin{cases} 1, & SR_{ik} > 0 \\ 0, & SR_{ik} = 0 \\ -1, & SR_{ik} < 0 \end{cases} . \tag{10}$$

It is same to authentication sequence. When and match, and are the discretized slope values in the -axis, so the divergence can be defined as

$$S_{ijk} = \left| SR'_{ik} - SA'_{jk} \right| + 1 . \tag{11}$$

It means if two points of two sequences in current axis have the same morphology, divergence gets the minimum value of 1, and if opposite it gets the maximum value of 3.

The divergence is used as the weighted factor of Euclidean distance as

$$d\left(R_i, A_j\right)' = \sqrt{\Sigma_{k=1}^{6} S_{ijk}\left(R_{ik} - A_{jk}\right)^2} . \tag{12}$$

The greater the morphological difference between two points of two gestures is, the greater the weighting factor will be, so the distance between the matching points will also be greater, which stresses the importance of morphological characteristics to some extent.

In our algorithm, in order to reduce the computational complexity of the algorithm and prevent pathological match that a short segment of one sequence match with a large segment of another sequence, we restrict the distance between two matching points in different sequence. The matching point in the curved path must satisfies $M / N \times j - r \leq i \leq M / N \times j + r$, where is the maximum length difference between the template and the other registration gestures.

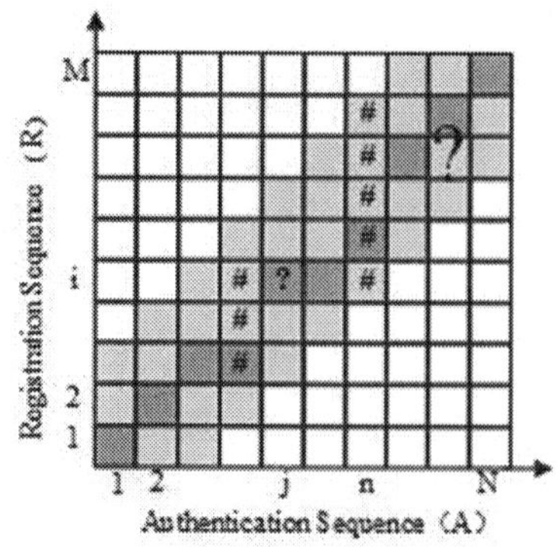

Figure 4. Early Termination of Authentication (If "#"overflow, "?"must overflow)

4.2.2Early termination algorithm

DTW needs to calculate the accumulative distortion values of all the point in limited matching region. In fact, there is no sense to do subsequent calculation when the distortion exceeds a certain threshold. Therefore, we further introduce early termination algorithm. If a column points of authentication gesture in the cumulative distance matrix are greater than the threshold as the column *n* of in Fig. 4, the final shortest cumulative distance must be greater than the threshold, so there is no need to calculate the cumulative distances in following "?" area. The authentication is failure. By this way we can exit calculation process rapidly once the data distortion is large, thereby the calculation is reduced in authentication phase.

Meanwhile, in the column) of in Fig. 4, if ,, are all overflowing when we calculate , the calculation of and can be omitted for must overflow. We assign the maximum value to directly.

4.2.3ME-DTW algorithm description

We design ME-DTW based on the above ideas as shown in Algorithm 1. The algorithm uses two arrays of length M to store the current needed cumulative distance matrix column vector whose space complexity limits in.

Row 1 is the screening of the authentication sequence length. If the length meets the requirement, we initialize the cumulative distance vector of based on row 2 to row 12. Then we calculate the cumulative distance per column in the limit match region based on rows 13 to 41. If ,, can be omitted as rows 19 to 22. We use the divergence weighted Euclidean distance to calculate the distance between two points, as shown in rows 24 and 28. If any column of cumulative distance sequence overflow, early termination can be shown in rows 35 to 36. After a column of cumulative distance calculation, we replace the old array by new array and repeated rows13 to 41 to calculate the next column cumulative distance. If there is no intermediate exit, it returns authentication success.

DOI: 10.1051/itmconf/20160701001

Algorithm 1. ME-DTW algorithm

```
Input: registration data R = {R_i|1 ≤ i ≤ M},authentication data A = {A_j|1 ≤ j ≤ N},the maximum difference between registration gestures and template r,authentication sequence length interval[L_min, L_max],threshold τ;
Output: when optimal matching path cumulative distance is less than the threshold valuer,return true, else return false;
if(N < L_min)||(N > L_max)return false.
else new oldD[ ] and newD[ ],initialize
oldD[1,...,M] ← ∞, newD[1,... M] ← ∞;
oldD[1] ← d(R_1,I_1);
  //initialize the cumulative distance sequence of j=1.
j ← 1;
fori ← 2 tor.
ifoldD[i − 1] > τ,then.
oldD[i] ← ∞;
else
oldD[i] ← oldD[i − 1] + d(R_i, A_1);
endif.
endfor.
forj ← 2 toNdo
overflow ← true;
i_max ← min(M/N * j + r), M);
i_min ← max(1,(M/N * j − r));
fori ← i_min toi_max
ifi > 2.
v ← min(oldD[i],oldD[i − 1],oldD[i − 2]);
    //if voverflow, omit the calculation of D(i,j).
    ifv > τthen.
newD[i] ← ∞;
    //d(R_i, A_j)' is weighted Euclidean distance based
on divergence.
elsenewD[i] ← v + d(R_i,A_j)';
    elseifi = 1.
newD[i] ← oldD[i] + d(R_i, A_j);
elseifi = 2.
newD[i] ← min(oldD[i],oldD[i − 1]) + d(R_i, A_j)';
endif.
ifnewD[i] < τthen.
overflow ←false;
endif.
endfor.
  //early termination if one column overflow.
  ifoverflow then.
   return flase.
  else.
oldD[ ] ← newD[ ];
newD[ ] ← ∞;
  endif
endfor.
endif.
return oldD[M] ≤ τ.
```

5 Experiment and Evaluation

5.1Data acquisition and Pre-processing

The gesture-based identification method is designed for usage on smartphones. We choose Samsung N9100 to collect sensor data, because it fulfils the requirements and is available on the market. It came to market in September 2014 with the CPU of Qualcomm snapdragon 805, RAM of 3GB, operating system version of Android 5.0.1 and has built-in accelerometer, gyroscope and linear accelerometer. The linear accelerometer is more suitable for this experience for it can measure the acceleration without gravity.

There are four grades of sensor sampling rates: FASTEST, GAME, NORMAL and UI, of which the sampling rate and power consumption are reduced accordingly. We choose GAME level which can reduce the power dissipation as much as possible without the loss of the gesture information.

False Rejection Rate (FRR) and False Acceptance Rate (FAR) are used to verify the security of the algorithm. FRR represents the possibility of authentic rejection. FAR represents the probability of attacker acceptance. The smaller the FRR and FAR are, the higher the security of the algorithm has. Eight gesture tracks were designed as shown in Fig. 5. The database I is the gestures that collected by author for 10 consecutive days of each track 15 times. At last we obtain a database of 1200 samples to calculate the FRR. The database II is the gestures collected from 5 volunteers for each track 50 times that imitating the author. At last we obtain a database of 2000 samples to calculate the FAR.

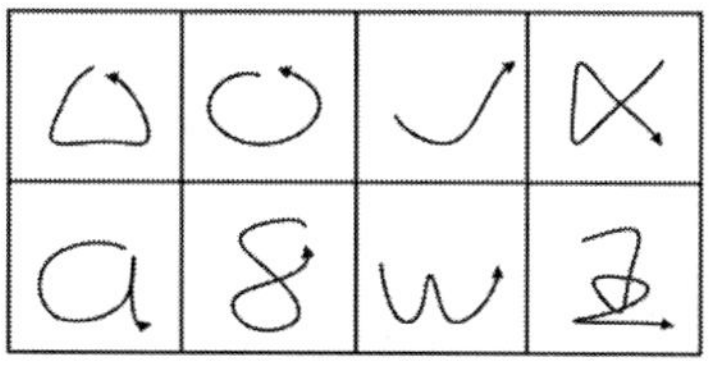

Figure 5. Gestures Track Samples

The original 3-axis acceleration waveform of one of the author gestures is shown in Fig. 6. After smoothing by SMA is shown in Fig. 7 and after normalization is showed in Fig. 8. It can be concluded that SMA smooth the data well and the normalization constraint the size of accelerometer well, thus reduce the calculation and ultimately improve the efficiency.

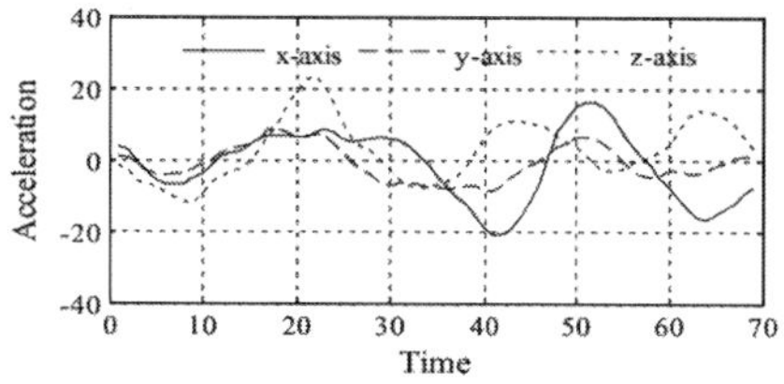

Figure 6. Original Gesture Data

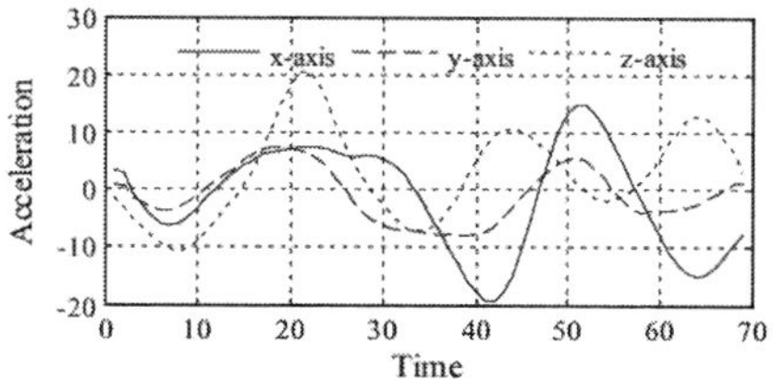

Figure 7. Gesture Data afterDenoising

 DOI: 10.1051/itmconf/20160701001

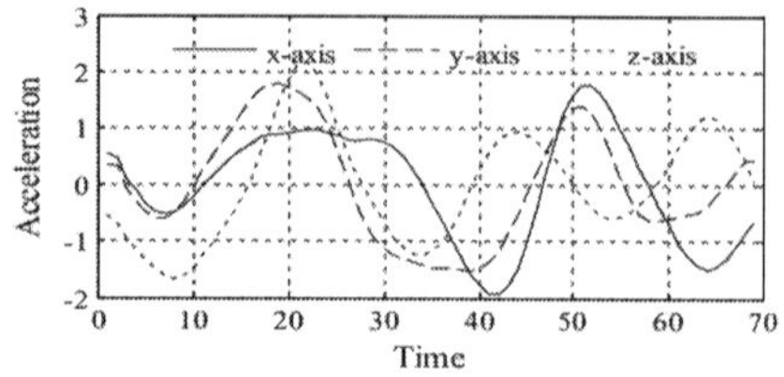

Figure 8. Gesture Data after Normalization

5.2Parameter Setting

We collect 10 registration gestures on account of the actual operation and user experience. The gestures taken by the author on the first day are used as registration gesture samples, wherein the maximum distance between the template and other registration gestures is. The threshold is multiplying a parameter since the one-time collected registration gestures have large similarity. Threshold has great influence on recognition accuracy, so optimizing the is needed. For the eight gesture tracks shown in Fig. 5, FRR and FAR have sensitive changes with different as shown in Fig. 9. When we attach more importance in identification security, the FAR must tends to 0%. The of eight gesture tracks are 1.25, 1.1, 1.35, 1.2, 1.35, 1.25, 1.2, 1.15, concentrating in the vicinity of 1.2. Sois set to 1.2 approximately in the condition of high security requirement. Therefore, when it is used just for general occasions, Equal Error Rate (EER) is used to evaluate the security. When FRR equals to FAR, the θ of corresponding eight gesture tracks are 1.4, 1.4, 1.4, 1.45, 1.4, 1.35, 1.4, 1.45, concentrating in the vicinity of 1.4. So is set to 1.4 approximately in condition of general applications.

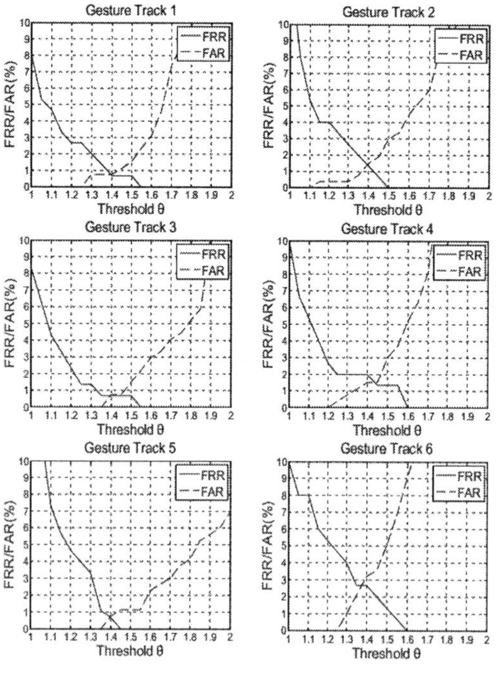

Figure 9. The Relationship between Misjudgment Rate and Threshold of Eight Gesture Tracks

5.3Simulation Analysis

5.3.1Compare ME-DTW with DTW

In the following, the performance of ME-DTW proposed in this paper and traditional DTW are compared. We primarily measure the impact of weighted Euclidean distance to the matching precision. We verify the validity of the two algorithms respectively based on the database I and II. The experimental results are shown in Tab. 1.

Table 1. Compare with ME-DTW and DTW

Gesture track	FRR/%		FAR/%	
	ME-DTW	DTW	ME-DTW	DTW
1	2.67	4.00	0	6.75
2	4.00	3.33	0.38	3.76
3	2.33	1.33	0	3.70
4	2.67	3.33	0	6.72
5	4.67	6.00	0	2.23
6	5.33	5.33	0	5.46
7	3.33	2.00	0	0.37
8	1.33	1.67	0.37	1.35
mean	3.29	3.37	0.09	3.79

As shown in Tab. 1, the mean FRR of ME-DTW is 3.29% and FAR is 0.09%, showing that the ME-DTW has high security.

ME-DTW has little impact on FRR compared with DTW, because for the registration and authentication gestures from one user, the ME-DTW will increase their distance a bit, but the threshold will also have a corresponding increase. However, ME-DTW presents significantly better FAR values of eight gesture tracks in varying degrees, with the mean of 3.70% less. ME-DTW greatly increase the distance between gestures from authentic user and attacker based on the morphological Euclidean distance. In summary, ME-DTW reduce the FAR under the premise of protecting FRR, which improves the security of the identification system.

5.3.2Compare Collecting Gyroscope Data or Not

Most domestic and international surveys about motion gesture-based identification collect acceleration as raw data. In the following, the performance of collecting both accelerometer and gyroscope data and only acceleration data are compared. We use ME-DTW and both database I and II. The results shown in Tab. 2.

As shown in the Tab. 2, when using both accelerometer and gyroscope have nearly equal FRR with only accelerometer, the FAR of the former is greater than the latter in different degrees of eight gesture tracks, with the average increase of 14.86%. The conclusion is that the rotation information as a biological characteristic enlarges the distance between template and authentication gesture especially for the attacker. It makes it possible to distinguish the intruders better, so the rotation information can be an effectively biological characteristic to improve the security of identification system.

Table 2. Compare with Collect Accelerometer and Gyroscopes And Only Accelerometer Data

Gesture track	FRR/%		FAR/%	
	A+G	A	A+G	A
1	2.67	8.67	0	16.4
2	4.00	5.33	0.38	7.89
3	2.33	1.33	0	22.2
4	2.67	2.00	0	13.4
5	4.67	8.67	0	13.3
6	5.33	1.33	0	23.8
7	3.33	0	0	20.4
8	1.33	0	0.37	1.50
mean	3.29	3.41	0.09	14.86

5.3.3ME-DTW Identification Efficiency

In the following, we test the influence of identification efficiency by introducing weighted morphological characteristics and early termination of authentication into DTW. ME-DTW is the algorithm proposed in this article, and M-DTW only introduces weighted morphological characteristics into DTW. MATLAB R2014a is used to simulate the actual running time of the identification. The results are shown in Tab. 3.

Table 3. The Total Time For 270 Times Gesture Identification Of Three Algorithms

Gesture track	ME-DTW/s	M-DTW/s	DTW/s
1	1.123	1.052	0.972
2	0.920	1.072	0.996
3	0.723	0.748	0.670
4	1.120	1.144	1.024
5	1.094	1.151	1.088
6	1.163	1.107	1.027
7	1.035	1.144	1.032
8	1.220	1.601	1.498
mean	1.050	1.127	1.038

As shown in Tab. 3, for ME-DTW, the average time of 270 times gesture identification for eight gesture tracks is 1.050s shown in Fig. 5, while for S-DTW is1.127s and for DTW is 1.038s. S-DTW consume slightly more than DTW due to the introduction of weighted morphological characteristics, while the early termination makes amends on the efficiency that the time cost of ME-DTW is substantially flat with DTW. In order to obtain better system security, ME-DTW sacrifice a small amount of computing time, but is redeemed by the early termination. Finally, the average cost of a single identification is about 3.89ms simulated by MATLAB, so the ME-DTW features good real-time performance.

6. Conclusion and Future Work

In this paper, we presented MD-DTW that controls the difference between the latitudes contributing to the total Euclidean distance by smartphone morphological characteristics to enhance identification accuracy and introduces early termination to guarantee the efficiency. Meanwhile, we proposed restricted areas touch trigger gesture acquisition scheme and authentication gesture length selection scheme to improve the accuracy and efficiency. Experimental results show that: when FAR tends to 0%, the FRR remained at 3.29%, which can meet most practical security needs.

In part of our future work, we plan to expand our dataset by acquiring more samples of gestures per user and also, by increasing the number of users in our databases. Besides, we plan to test the identification in the real smartphone of the time-consuming.

References

1. Ijiri Y, Sakuragi M, Lao S. Security Management for Mobile Devices by Face Recognition[C]// Proceedings of the 7th International Conference on Mobile Data Management. IEEE Computer Society, 2006:49-49.
2. Yong J C, Ong T S, Goh M K O, et al. Integrating Palmprint and Fingerprint for Identity Verification[C]// Proceedings of the 2009 Third International Conference on Network and System Security. IEEE Computer Society, 2009:437-442.
3. Jeong D S, Park H A, Kang R P, et al. Iris recognition in mobile phone based on adaptive gabor filter[J]. Lecture Notes in Computer Science, 2005, 3832:457-463.
4. Argones R E, Alba Castro J L. Online Signature Verification Based on Generative Models[J]. IEEE Transactions on Systems Man & Cybernetics Part B Cybernetics A Publication of the IEEE Systems Man & Cybernetics Society, 2012, 42(4):1231-1242.
5. Liu J, Zhong L, Wickramasuriya J, et al. uWave: Accelerometer-based personalized gesture recognition and its applications[J]. Pervasive & Mobile Computing, 2009, 5(6):657-675.
6. Junker H, Amft O, Lukowicz P, et al. Gesture spotting with body-worn inertial sensors to detect user activities[J]. Pattern Recognition, 2008, 41(6):2010-2024.
7. Zhou Z, Miao M. Gesture Authentication Research Based on Improved Dynamic Time Warping and Mutual Information De-Noising (In Chinese) [J], Chinese Journal of Sensors and Actuators, 2014(8):1070-1076.
8. Hu J, Chen R, Li Z. Discussion of DTW algorithm in speech recognition (In Chinese) [J]. Image

DOI: 10.1051/itmconf/20160701001

Processing and Multimedia Technology, 2011, 30(3):30-32.

9. Gao H, Cao X, Wang L,et al. An Identity Authentication Method Based on Dynamic Gesture and Its Application in Mobile Phone (In Chinese) [J]. Acta Electronica Sinica, 2014(9):1857-1862.

ITM Web of Conferences 7, 01002 (2016) DOI: 10.1051/itmconf/20160701002
ITA 2016

A Novel Logic for Analyzing Electronic Payment Protocols

Yi LIU[1, a], Xing-Tong LIU[1, b] and Chao-Jing TANG[1]

[1]*College of Electronic Science and Engineering, National University of Defence Technology, Changsha, China*
[a]*louis0121@126.com,* [b] *liuxingtong@nudt.edu.cn*

Abstract. A novel formal method which can be used to analyze security properties such as accountability, fairness and timeliness in electronic payment protocols is proposed. The novel method extends Qing-Zhou approach based on logic reasoning by adding a simple time expression and analysis method. It increases the ability to describe the event time, and extends the time characteristics of the logical inference rules. An anonymous electronic cash payment protocol is analyzed by the novel logic, and the result shows that the fairness of the protocol is not satisfied due to the timeliness problem in protocol. The novel logic method proposed in this paper has a certain theoretical and practical significance for the design and formal analysis of electronic payment protocols. At the same time, its idea has a certain guiding value for improving the security of other security protocols.

1 Introduction

Electronic payment has made unprecedented progress in recent years, and the security problems in electronic payment activities are increasingly being valued by everyone. Electronic payment protocol is the technical basis for the security of electronic commerce activities, and all kinds of security services are provided by electronic payment protocols for consumers. The analysis and research of electronic payment security protocol has become an important issue in the field of information security [1]. However, the electronic payment protocol is the same as other cryptographic protocols. Even though electronic protocols are carefully designed, there are still security vulnerabilities. Secure and reliable electronic payment protocols are important guarantees for the security of electronic payment activities. In order to ensure the correctness and security of electronic payment protocols, it is necessary to analyze protocols accurately and find out defects and vulnerabilities in protocols through formal analysis method. The results obtained can be used to guide the design of the protocol or make up for the defects of the original protocol. Therefore, it has important theoretical significance and application value to research the formal analysis method of electronic payment protocol.

Nowadays, the main formal analysis methods of electronic payment protocol are logic reasoning, model checking, and theorem proving method. The method of model checking cannot analyze some special security properties like accountability, fairness and anonymity due to lack of the ability of logical reasoning. Approach based on logic is a kind of important formal analysis method of electronic payment protocol in recent years. Kailar logic [2] can analyze the accountability in protocol, but it can't analyze the fairness; Qing-Zhou logic[3][4] can be used for the analysis of accountability and fairness in protocol. The common properties of protocols are described by the ATL logic (alternating time temporal logic) based on game theory in paper [5]. The fairness and timeliness are analyzed through the model checking tool MOCHA. However, most of the current logic methods can only be used to analyze some secure properties. Therefore, it is a hotspot and trend to improve the analysis ability of existing typical electronic payment security protocol logic methods in current formal method research.

In this paper, a novel logic is proposed for the analysis of electronic payment protocols by adding simple time expression and time analysis method. The ISI protocol is analyzed using the proposed novel logic and the analysis result shows that ISI protocol does not provide timeliness. Therefore, the novel logic has the ability to describe and analyze the timeliness of electronic payment protocols.

2 Concepts and Definitions

The definitions and symbols used in the novel logic are defined as follows:

2.1 Basic Symbol

A, *B*: Parties participate in protocol;

TTP: Trust third party;

M: Message transferred in protocol;

(M, n): Indicates that message m is combined with message n;

K_a : The public key of the party A, which is used to verify the digital signature of A. K_a^{-1} is the secret key that corresponds to K_a ;

$\tilde{K}$: Dual key of K. If K is an asymmetric key, then $\tilde{K}=K^{-1}$. If K is a symmetric key, then $\tilde{K}=K$;

$\{m\}_K$: Cipher text of message m encrypted with the secret key K;

T: Time of occurrence;

EOO (evidence-of-origin): It is non-repudiation evidence that is provided to the receiver in electronic payment protocol, which is used to prove that the sender has sent the message;

EOR (evidence-of-receipt): It is non-repudiation evidence that is provided to the sender in electronic payment protocol, which is used to prove that the receiver has received the message sent by the sender.

2.2 Time System

We describe the time when event occurs by adding a condition in the formula language of formal logic, like $A \rightarrow m$ at T. m is a message, and A is one of the parties in protocol. T is a time expression. This definition increases the description of the occurrence time of sending and receiving message.

Set $I = \{0,1,2,3,...\} \cup \{-1,-2,-3,...\}$, stands for integers, then the time expression defines as follows:

1. x is constant time element, while $x \in I$.

2. X is variable time element, while X is an variable element in I.

3. $X|TS$ is time binding expression, while X is an variable time element and $TS \subseteq I$.

4. $[T]$ is time expression, while T is a time binding expression.

The constant time element is represented by a lower case t with a subscript, and the variant time element is represented by a capital letters T with a subscript.

Time binding expression is a variable time element X with a certain value of constant time element as $t(t \in TS)$. Once the value of the variable time element is bound by a time binding expression, its function is the same as the time constant. It can't be bound again before the binding value is released. In logical formulas, the time expression [X|I] can be abbreviated to [X], and [X|{x}] can be abbreviated to [x], where x is a constant time element or a variable time element with bound value. The value of the variable time element is bound to the first appearance of operations in its formula.

2.3 Protocol and Environment

Protocol party set Principle={TTP,A,B,C,...,P,Q,R...}, where A,B,Q,R,..., are participants in protocol. They can either be honest or dishonest. That is, they can obey the execution of the protocol, and also can not obey the implementation of the protocol. In general, we assume that these parties are dishonest and that they may be able to interrupt the execution of the protocol at will. TTP(Third trust party) is a special party, which is regarded as a fair trusted third party by other parties participate in protocol. It can be served as the TTP role by the bank or the arbitration organization.

Another important part of the environment is the communication channel. Communication channels can be both reliable and unreliable, depending on the specific operating environment. Usually, the communication channel between general parties is unreliable, while the communication channel between the *TTP* and other parties is recoverable. That is the communication channel may not be always paralyzed, the message can be transmitted finally.

Protocol statement defines what messages should be sent and received by parties in the current round , which is described as follows :

$A \rightarrow B$: m at T : represents A sent message m to B at T.

2.4 Possession Sets in Protocol

Assuming the protocol begins to run at T_0 , A is an arbitrary party participate in protocol. At the beginning of protocol, the initial possession sets of A is $O_a(T_0)$. When protocol execution to T_x , the possession sets of A becomes $O_a(T_x)$. Besides, we defines $O_a(T_e)$ is the final possession sets of A at the end of protocol. When the protocol runs to any time, the possession sets of A contains the information that is not deleted in the possession sets before and the message which is received and sent at this time. The possession sets of A changes constantly with execution of protocol, until $O_a = O_a(T_e)$.

When the protocol runs at T_x, the possession sets of A changes from $O_a(T_y)$ to $O_a(T_x)$ $\wedge$ $(T_y \leq T_x)$, which means T_y is the moment before T_x . It follows the following rules :

(1) If the execution of the protocol statement is $A \rightarrow B$: m at T_x. m is a new message generated by A, which means $m \notin O_a(T_y)$. Then $O_a(T_x) = O_a(T_y) \cup \{m\}$. If m is not a new message generated by A, we get $m \in O_a(T_y)$.

(2) If the execution of the protocol statement is $B \rightarrow A$: m at T_x , while $m \notin O_a(T_y)$, then $O_a(T_x) = O_a(T_y) \cup \{m\}$.

(3) Otherwise, $O_a(T_x) = O_a(T_y)$.

3 Logic Analysis Methods

3.1 Logic Component

Our method consists of the following 5 logical components :

(1) $A \succ x$: For any party B, A can make B believe in formula x by performing a series of operations without leaking any secret $y \neq x$;

(2) $A \to m$ at T : A sent message m at T. The following implication was established in the process of analysis :

$$A \to (m \quad n) \text{ at } T \Rightarrow A \to m \text{ at } T \qquad (1)$$

That means, if A sends messages (m, n) at T, then A sends message m at T.

(3) $A \ni m$: A possesses message m.

(4) $A \leftarrow m$ at T : A received message m at T. The following implication was established in the process of analysis :

$$A \leftarrow (m \quad n) \text{ at } T \Rightarrow A \leftarrow m \text{ at } T \qquad (2)$$

That means, if A received messages (m, n) at time T, then A received message m at T.

(5) $\xrightarrow{K_a} A$: K_a is the public key of A, which is used to verify the message signed by K_a^{-1}.

3.2 Axiom System

The axiom system consists of 1 inference rule and 6 axioms. Inference rule is as follows :

$$(\vdash \varphi) \wedge (\vdash (\varphi \Rightarrow \psi)) \Rightarrow \vdash \psi \qquad (3)$$

The inference rule illustrates $\vdash \psi$ can be obtained from $\vdash \varphi$ and $\vdash (\varphi \Rightarrow \psi)$. $\vdash$ is a meta language symbol. $\Gamma \vdash \psi$ represents ψ can be deduced from the formula sets Γ. $\vdash \varphi$ indicates φ is a theorem, which means φ can be deduced from axioms. Therefore, the inference rule above indicates that ψ is theorem when φ is theorem and φ contains ψ.

The 6 axioms in the axiom set are as follows :

A1. $A \succ x \wedge A \succ y \Rightarrow A \succ (x \wedge y)$

A2. $A \succ x \wedge (x \Rightarrow y) \Rightarrow A \succ y$

A3. $A \ni \{m\}_{K_b^{-1}}$ at T_x $\wedge$ $A \succ \xrightarrow{K_b} B$ at $T_x \Rightarrow A \succ B \to m$ at $[T_Y \mid T_Y \le T_X]$

A4. $A \succ B \to \{m\}_k$ at T_x $\wedge$ $A \succ B \to k$ at T_Y $\Rightarrow$ $A \succ B \to m$ at $\max(T_X, T_Y)$

A5. $A \leftarrow m$ at $T \Rightarrow A \ni m$ at T

A6. $A \leftarrow \{m\}_K$ at $T \wedge A \ni \tilde{K} \Rightarrow A \leftarrow m$ at T

When the time of events is not analyzed, all time expressions in the above axioms use [X|I], and the operation at can be omitted. The steps of using the novel logic to analyze protocols are as follows :

(1) Before giving the basic assumption of the protocol, we have to give all the constant and variable time elements that are used in the process of protocol reasoning. The actual value of the constant element may not be given, but if there is a constraint relationship between the different time constant, the constraint relationship should be pointed out. It is required to describe the time dependence of the events in protocol using the formula apparently, while giving the basic assumptions and the target of the protocol.

(2) The proof procedure of protocol target is divided into two steps. The first step is called logical reasoning, which proves the first part of the protocol target. The second step is called time calculus, which proves the latter half of the protocol target. The function of this procedure is to prove that the result obtained in the logic reasoning satisfies the time constraints specified in the protocol target. The method used in this procedure is the proof approach of algebraic equation and inequality, so it is easy to grasp and use. If the formula is established at any time of the protocol, the time description at T can be omitted.

3.3 Protocol Analysis Procedure

Protocol analysis consists of the following 5 steps.

(1)List the initial possession sets of the parties in protocol.

(2)List the initial assumptions of the protocol :

(a)The basic assumptions

(b)The credible assumptions

(c) The protocol comprehension assumptions

(3)List EOO and *EOR*, and analyze whether the design of *EOO* and *EOR* meets the requirements of accountability.

(4)Analyze whether $EOO \in O_b(T_e) \wedge EOR \in O_a(T_e)$ is set up at the end of the protocol.

(5) Analyze whether the protocol is to achieve the target of fairness, which means whether the protocol meets $EOO \in O_b(T_e)$ if and only if $EOR \in O_a(T_e)$ at the end of the execution time T_e.

4 ISI Protocol Analyses

ISI protocol[6] is an anonymous electronic cash payment protocol proposed by Medvinsky and Neuman, including three participants : customer A, merchant B and the currency server CS trusted by both parties. The purpose is customer A pay the merchant B through the currency server CS, while B provides payment receipt to A. Throughout the payment process, the customer A remain anonymous, and CS play a role as TTP. Protocol steps are as follows :

(1) $A \to B : K_{ab}$ at T_0

(2) $B \to A : \{K_b\}_{K_{ab}}$ at T_r

(3) $A \to B : \{\{coins\}_{K_{cs}^{-1}}, SK_a, K\_ses, S\_id\}_{K_b}$ at T_s

(4) $B \to CS : \{\{coins\}_{K_{cs}^{-1}}, SK_b, transaction\}_{K_{cs}}$ at T_k

(5) $CS \to B : \{\{new\_coins\}_{K_{cs}^{-1}}\}_{SK_b}$ at T_c

(6) $B \to A : \{\{amount, Tid, date\}_{K_b^{-1}}\}_{SK_a}$ at T_d

In the ISI protocol, K_{ab} represents the session key between A and B. K_a and K_b respectively stand for the public key of customer A and merchant B, while K_{cs} and K_{cs}^{-1} stand for the public key and private key of currency server CS. $\{coins\}_{K_{cs}^{-1}}$ represents electronic currency of A.

DOI: 10.1051/itmconf/20160701002

All currency is issued by CS. SK_a and SK_b represent the shared key of A and B. K_ses represents the key to a service that would like to be obtained. S_id is an identifier for the service to be obtained. Transaction represents specific transaction processing.

The analysis procedure of the protocol is as follows :

(1)List the initial possession sets. At the initial time of the protocol operation, the initial state of the A and B is

$$O_a(T_0) = \{K_{cs}\}$$

$$O_b(T_0) = \{K_{cs}\}$$

$$A \succ \xrightarrow{K_{cs}} CS$$

$$B \succ \xrightarrow{K_{cs}} CS$$

(2)List the credible assumptions of the protocol are as follows :

$$\text{T1: } A \succ CS \rightarrow m_1 \Rightarrow A \succ P \rightarrow m_1'$$

Assume that the currency server is fully in accordance with the provisions of the protocol and will not do anything that is harmful to any party in the protocol. If A can prove that CS has sent message m_1 to him, then A can prove some other party P has sent the message m_1' to CS which made CS send m_1 to A.

(3)List the evidence of origin (EOO) and the evidence of receipt(EOR) as follows :

$$EOR = \{new\_coins\}_{K_{cs}^{-1}}$$

$$EOR = \{amount, Tid, date\}_{K_b^{-1}}$$

Assume that the equation $EOO \in O_b(T_e)$ satisfied at the end of the protocol T_e. According to axiom A3 and the credible assumption T1, we will get :

$$B \succ CS \rightarrow new\_coins \text{ at } [T_a \mid T_a \leq T_e] \qquad (4)$$

According to the credible assumption T1, we can obtain :

$$B \succ A \rightarrow k \text{ at } [T_a \mid T_a \leq T_e] \qquad (5)$$

Because it is a protocol for anonymous payment, B only needs to prove the payment of someone is effective, without the need to prove who the payer is. So the equation (5) can meet the requirement of accountability.

Assume that the equation $EOR \in O_a(T_e)$ satisfied at the end of the protocol, which means $A \ni \{amount, Tid, date\}_{K_b^{-1}}$ satisfied. Since we can't prove $A \succ \xrightarrow{K_b} B$, $A \succ B \rightarrow \{amount, Tid, date\}_{K_b^{-1}}$ can not be derived. Therefore the evidence of receipt EOR in protocol can not achieve the target of non-repudiation. It is proved by the novel logic that ISI payment protocol does not meet the accountability.

(4) After all the steps of the protocol are completed, there will be $A \ni EOR$ and $B \ni EOO$. Therefore, $EOO \in O_b(T_e) \wedge EOR \in O_a(T_e)$ is set up at the end of the protocol.

(5)Then analyze the fairness of the protocol. The fairness objective is:

$$EOO \in O_b(T_e) \text{ if and only if } EOR \in O_b(T_e) \qquad (6)$$

That is two parties obtain the evidence of each other for non-repudiation at the same time.

Because CS is completely believable, so we can obtain $CS \rightarrow B : \{new\_coins\}_{K_{cs}^{-1}}$ at T_c and $\{new\_coins\}_{K_{cs}^{-1}} \in O_b(T_c) \Rightarrow EOO \in O_b(T_c)$.

Only after the sixth step is completed, $\{amount, Tid, date\}_{K_b^{-1}} \in O_a(T_d)$ is established. According to the steps of the protocol, the relationship between T_c and T_d is $T_c < T_d$. So $EOO \in O_b(T_c) \wedge EOR \in O_b(T_e) \wedge (T_c < T_d)$, which can not achieve fairness.

The main reason is that the implementation of the protocol does not have specific constraints on the relevant event time in the process. After the completion of the third step of the protocol, B is required to perform the fourth step in certain time delay t_b . And it's also required to perform the sixth step operation within a certain time delay t_c after receipt of $\{new\_coins\}_{K_{cs}^{-1}}$.

If A did not receive $\{amount, Tid, date\}_{K_b^{-1}}$ after the certain period of time, the protocol is terminated. Due to CS is completely believable, $(T_c\text{-}T_k) \leq t_s$ must be satisfied. t_s is processing delay of CS. So in order to make A received EOR at the end of the protocol, $t_b + t_s + t_c \leq t_a$ must be established. It means the behavior delay of B must be constraint to satisfy $t_b + t_c \leq t_a\text{-}t_s$, in order to ensure the fairness of the protocol.

5 Conclusions

In this paper, the analysis of ISI protocol specifically illustrates how the novel logic analyzes the temporal relations between events in the electronic payment protocol. The novel logic is not a simple logic method, but an integrated approach. The logic reasoning in the process of the objective proof of protocols is based on the proof method in Qin-Zhou logic approach, but the time calculus part uses the method of algebra and set theory. It is suitable for analyzing the timeliness of electronic payment protocols. Further more, this idea can be introduced to other formal methods to analyze the security of cryptographic protocols.

DOI: 10.1051/itmconf/20160701002

References

1. P. McCorry, S.F. Shahandashti, F Hao, 20th Financial Cryptography and Data Security, (2016)
2. Kailar R, IEEE Trans. on Software Engineering, 22, 313-328,(1996)
3. DC Zhou, SH Qing, ZF Zhou, Journal of Software, 12, 1318-1328(200l)
4. SH Qing, Journal of Software, 16, 1758-1765(2005)
5. Kremer S, Universit'e Libre de Bruxelles Facult'e des Sciences(2003-2004)
6. G. Medvinsky, C. Neuman, Proc of the 1st ACM Conference on Computer and ComAnications Security, 102-106(1993)

Research of the Communication Middleware of the Yacht Supervision Management System Based on DDS

Yan-Ru WANG [1], Yi-Kun ZHANG [2], Song-Yuan GU [2], Wei-Feng XU [3]

[1] *Economics School of Jilin University, Jilin University, 2699 Qianjin Street, Changchun, 130012, China*
[2] *College of Computer Science and Technology, Jilin University, 2699 Qianjin Street, Changchun, 130012, China*
[3] *School of Control and Computer Engineering, North China Electric Power University, 619 Yonghua North Street, Baoding, 071003, China*

Abstract. The communication middleware of the yacht supervision management system (YSM) which is based on the DDS is the communication management software of the yacht supervision center system and the ship monitoring system .In order to ensure the high efficiency and high reliability of communication middleware, the paper for the first time introduced DDS communication framework to the yacht supervision system in the process of software design and implementation, and designed and implemented more flexible and reliable communication management interface for the DDS communication framework. Through practical test, each performance index of DDS communication middleware software of the yacht supervision management system has reached the design requirements.

1 Introduction

Currently, marine resources have been vital bases for the further development of countries in the world. China is also at a crucial period of the development strategy of marine resources. The strategic objective of building maritime power which proposed at the report to Eighteenth CPC National Congress, offered a golden development opportunity and political guarantee to research, exploit and utilize the marine resources of China's marine related industries. China's marine related industries cover many trades including energy, scientific research, resources and tourism etc. The marine tourism plays an important role in marine related industry, which based on plentiful travel resources, various types and high-grade tourism products, broad and comfortable tourism activities, and unique content of tourism culture. Currently, since enormous advantages the yacht tourism takes in consumption levels and brand effect, it is gradually turning into a new jumping-off point for marine tourism, and have been proven to be an important segment of China's marine strategy at the meanwhile[1].

The communication middleware of the yacht supervision management system (YSM) which based on the DDS is the communication management software of the yacht supervision center. In supervision center, this software complete functions including information sending, receiving and recording, replaying, transferring in different means of communication and trafficking statistics between supervision center and ships[2-4]. The software also offers timing services and the management function of various communication devices for yacht supervision center and the ship monitoring system. The software can make one communication device serves multiple business systems, and lay a foundation for the forming of the distributed internal system for supervision center or larger yacht.

The communication middleware of the yacht supervision management system (YSM) based on DDS that we research and implement will build on RTI-DDS communication middleware, to design and implement the communication interface which is fit for the application of this software, to implement the functions of transmitting-receiving information, switching different communication mode, forwarding information, recording and replaying information, trafficking statistics, managing devices, configuring software, selecting channels, issuing logs and displaying the transmitted-received information.

2 DDS Theoretical Model

2.1. Publish/subscribe Model

Publish/subscribe model was a messaging communication middleware proposed by OMG (Object Management Group) based on real-time communication of distributed system[5]. This is the only messaging communication mode so far which able to meet the time, space, and loosely coupled of data transmission at the meanwhile. OMG has been issued a latest standard based on publish/subscribe communication mode called Data Distribution Service (DDS). The specification carries out data distribution completely based on data-centric, meanwhile, define and implement QoS strategy, achieve a unified description of resources state, the level of resources expectation and network state. Thus enable the control to system, and satisfy the flexibility and timeliness of the real-time communication[6-7].

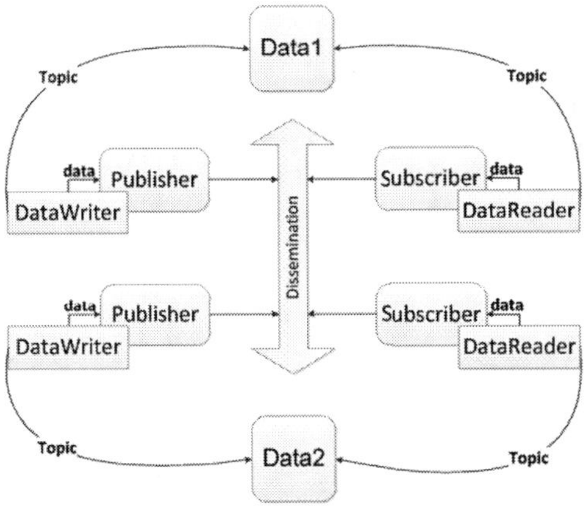

Figure 1 Basic Implementation Architecture of Dds Model

There are many data transmit system software achieved by publish/subscribe mechanism. Currently, perfect DDS products are RTI-DDS, ZHDDS, OpenDDS and Opensplice-DDS[8-10]. The paper implement the improvement of data transmit mechanism mainly based on RTI-DDS open source, and also introduce the important architecture and implementation mechanism of OpenDDS. OpenDDS has the advantage of single-node control and easy to configuration, which can significantly reduce the workload of environment configuration before use. Yet DCPSInfoRepo has to run on a separate node because of the internal implementation mechanism, so it is easy to have the problem of single point failure, and then get to performance bottleneck.

Data Distribution Service(DDS) model is a data communication standard with high real-time performance and high reliability, including two part, Data-Centric Publish-Subscribe(DCPS) layer and Data Local Reconstruction layer(DLRL) respectively. DCPS layer is the basic layer, constraint to the QoS policy strictly, and establish the application programming interface. DLRL layer built on the top of DCPS layer, and it is optional, allows local object to share transmission data like to share local data.

The basic implementation architecture of DDS data distribution service model is shown in Figure 1, which mainly involves the following members: Publisher which is responsible for data publish, Subscriber which is responsible for data subscriptions, DataWriter which is responsible for data writing and DataReader which is responsible for data reading.

2.2 RTI DDS

Network data distribution services NDDS is a data distribution middleware product of RTI, compliant with the OMG's DDS standard completely. The NDDS middleware of RTI has been integrated with DDS API, all of data supply and collection program can still transfer data through a fixed API interface even after the system's communication devices upgraded or extended. For instance, a GPS sensor is publishing location information through DDS, RTI-DDS can offer an estimation of location information as an alternative when sensor paused, and information subscriber could not feel any change about it. The characteristic about transparent of data transmission is obtained by the standard API of decoupled data transmission and data application, which offered by RTI-DDS. Application can focus on solving the problem of the application layer with regardless of the data pass pattern specifically. RTI-DDS is a good choice for developers who need to implement data-centric published order communication network, particularly when these developers need the network to have the properties of high efficiency, ease of implementation, platform-independent and language-independent.

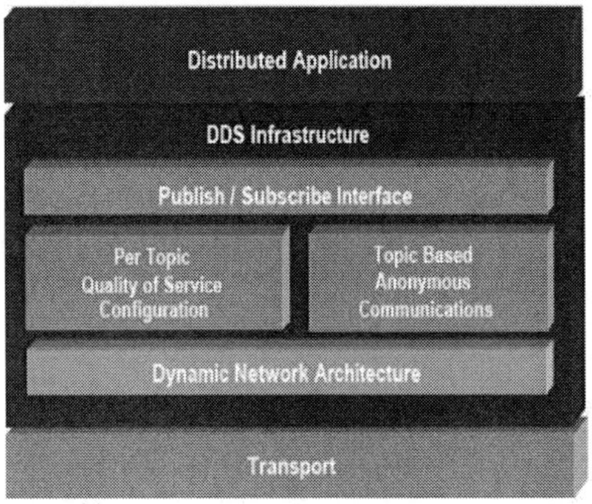

Figure 2 Transmission Architecture of Rti-Dds

3 Design of Communication Middleware

The communication middleware of the yacht supervision management system (YSM) which based on the DDS is the communication management software of the yacht supervision center. In supervision center, this software complete functions including information sending, receiving and recording, replaying, transferring in different means of communication and trafficking statistics between supervision center and ships. The software also offers timing services and the management function of various communication devices for yacht supervision center and the ship monitoring system.

3.1 System Workflow

System workflow is designed based on system requirements analysis. The main workflow of communication middleware is showed by Figure 3. As the figure shows, the system needs functional configuration before the software starts, and produces software functional configuration files after the software being functional configured. Software functional configuration is mainly a selection to system function. It helps improve the actual runtime efficiency of the system when we proceed functional configuration to software. We need configure the communication parameters and information forward relationship of communication equipment and produce configuration files of parameters and information forward relationship before the software starts. After starting the software, the system will start the related communication and location devices according to the configuration files, initialize communication interface, and establish information forward relation. As for information recording, traffic statistics, information playbacking, and communication channel, you can use the default settings or set up separately.

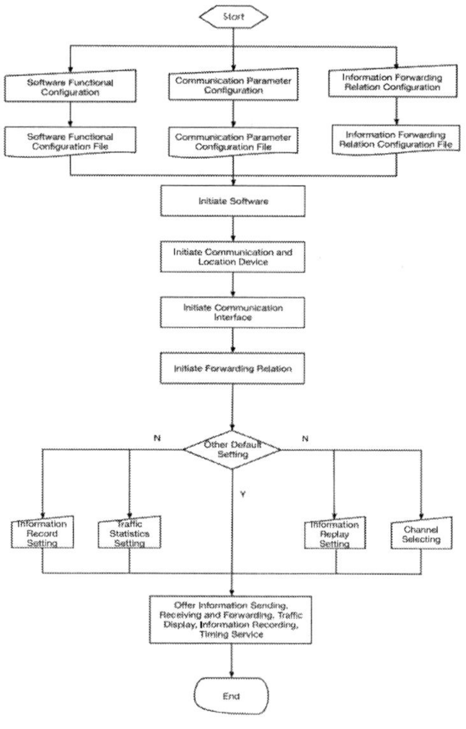

Figure 3 Workflow Diagram of Communication Middleware

3.2 Design of System Architecture

The basic architecture of the communication middleware of the yacht supervision management system based on DDS reflect the fundamental common properties of the software and offer an extension point which reflect changeable and updateable of the software. The common properties of the software can be showed by the fundamental architecture level and public components in Figure 4, the extension point mainly refers to software's update and the flexible extend of component. The basic architecture of this software is based on components. The lowest layer of architecture is composed of DDS communication component, Ethernet communication component, serial communication component and communication management component. Concrete business function layer is composed of information record, traffic statistics and function component of wireless communication devices. The top layer is an interface which offers all kinds of communication services to external user. In the software design process, we design component as a module, we will give a specific design in later.

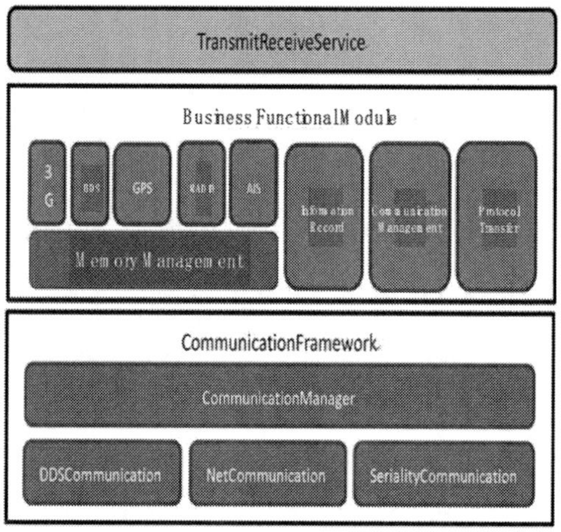

Figure 4 System Architecture of Communication Middleware

3.3 Design of System Transfer Link

Since the use of DDS in the communication middleware of the yacht supervision management system based on DDS, we must analyze the flow in the transfer software of data. We define the link which information enter the yacht supervision center system and the ship monitoring system through wireless communication devices as Information Input Link, the contrary information link is Output Link.

Information input link is showed in Figure 6. In this link, data is received by the receiving equipment of BDS (BeiDou Navigation Satellite System), GPS and radio, and pass into the system through the serial port, confirm the receiving information's internal system (the yacht supervision center system which deployed on different seats

DOI: 10.1051/itmconf/20160701003

and the ship monitoring system) through data process and receive-send mapping, and then transform the information into DDS information format and send it to the internal network. The data received by external network and 3G receiving equipment will be passed into system through Ethernet, after which the process is the same as above. Figure 6 shows the information output link, the information flow is at opposite direction with the process above, the detailed process has been shown clearly in Figure.

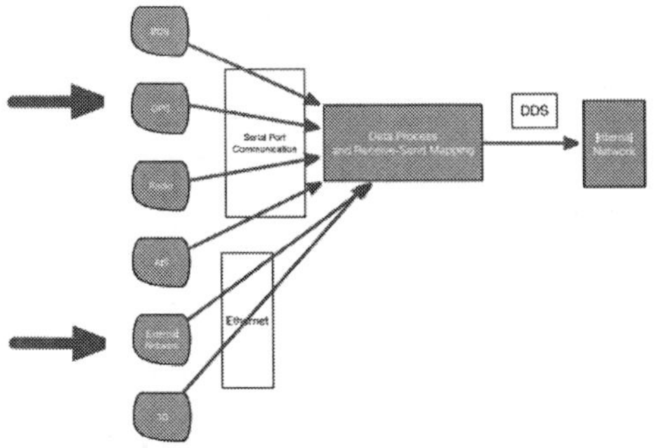

Figure 5 Information Input Link

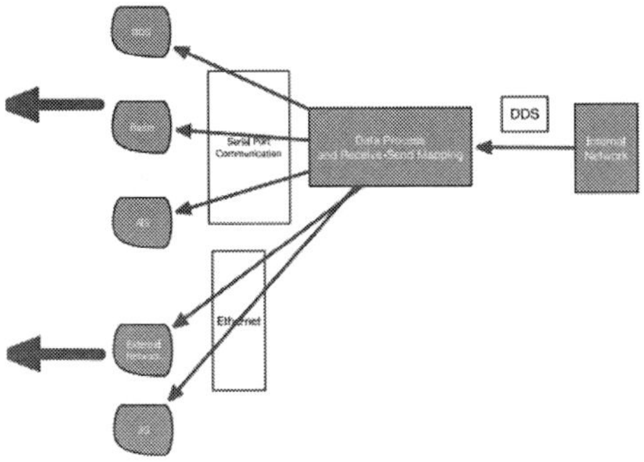

Figure 6 Information Output Link

The design of communication link above can make a communication device serves several business systems, laid the foundation to develop a distribution's internal system of supervision center or a larger yacht.

Since the communication middleware of the yacht supervision management system based on DDS also offered management function to all types of communication devices for the yacht supervision center system and the ship monitoring system, so we need to analyse and design the device control link. The ship monitoring system can control and manage the communication devices of this ship according to the requirements, also, supervision center can get some basic control to the communication device when ship system can't control the devices or require supervision center to control the communication device. The control information link is showed in Figure 7.

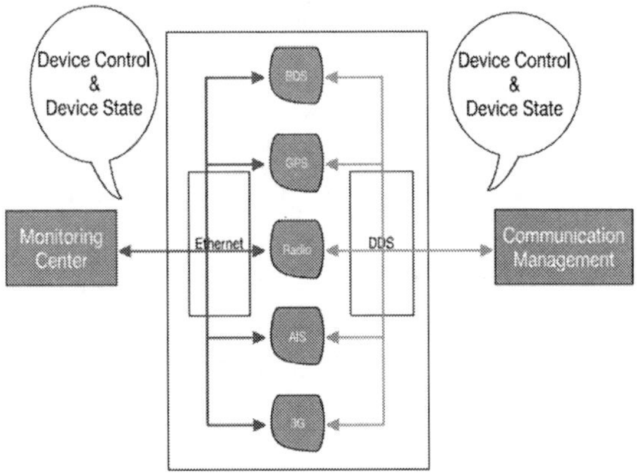

Figure 7 Device Control Link

4. Implementation and Test

4.1 Implementation of Communication Middleware

The communication middleware of the yacht supervision management system based on DDS is an underlying communication management software, so it has higher demand for running efficiency and stability. At present, the language for developing this software are C++, C#, JAVA and so on, the development conditions are also various.

Currently, the communication middleware of the yacht supervision management system based on DDS which implemented in this paper has been test running at a sea experimental base. During the test run, the scene was set to have a supervision management center and five yachts, there were four monitoring seats set around the monitoring center and configured related supervision management system, each yacht equipped a yacht supervision management software, monitoring center configured with a communication middleware, and each yacht configured with a communication middleware respectively.

What showed in Figure 8 is the practical running state of yacht supervision management center when it monitoring the four yachts. The upper part of this software is traffic statistics and display interface, the yellow curve shows the traffic of input information, the orange one shows the traffic of output information. At the lower right corner of the software interface shows the detail information, including information type, receiving and sending time and so on. The lower part of the software shows the detail information coming from different wireless communication device.

DOI: 10.1051/itmconf/20160701003

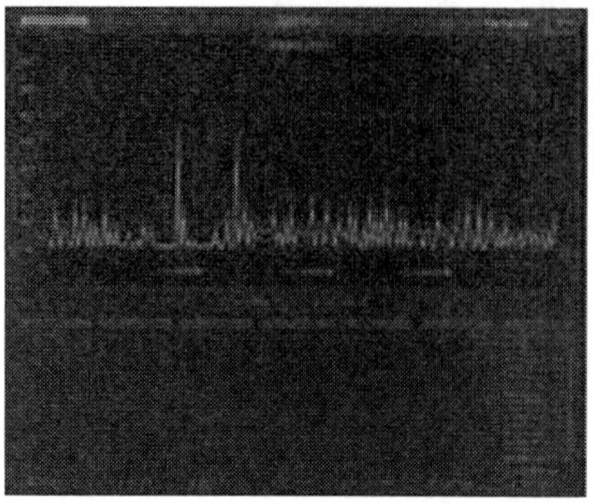

Figure 8 Running Diagram of Communication Middleware

4.2 Test of Communication Middleware

During the test process, we did unit test on transfer software first. During the test, the key functions were tested. Ultimately, 81% of the test cases passed test, 19% of the test cases failed. After a regression test, all the cases that didn't pass before had passed.

Then we took configuration item test on transfer software. The test types of configuration item include document review, functional test, static analysis, performance test, interface test, boundary test, intensity test, security test, recovery test and installation test.

After unit test and configuration item test, the software implemented in this paper achieve the following technical criterion: the throughput of the communication middleware of the monitoring center: ≥ 2Gbps; the simultaneously sessions of the communication middleware of the monitoring center: ≥ 1000; the throughput of the ship communication middleware: ≥ 100Mbps; the simultaneously sessions of the ship communication middleware: ≥ 100; the maximum connection number of roll call mechanism of each ratio modem: 50; the new establish connection number of naming mechanism of each ratio modem per second: ≥10; time of software initiate: <= 2s; time of each sub-interface switching at normal running state:<=2s; time from receive some data correctly to forward the data through DDS successfully at normal running state:<=1ms; time from receive some data correctly to forward the data through UDP successfully at normal running state:<=1ms; time from receive some data correctly to forward the data through a wireless communication device successfully at normal running state:<=60ms; response time of primary channel switching:<=200ms; time interval of device checking:1s; time from equipment error occurred to error confirmed:<=1500ms; time from equipment error confirmed to initiate redundant equipment:<=200ms; roll call time slice when ratio modem as the communication equipment:<=200ms; roll call cycle when ratio modem as the communication equipment:<=10s.

The technical criterion that this software achieved satisfy the software design requirements at the test process above, offering basis for software quality evaluation, and also offering technical criterion for software practical application.

5 Summary and Outlook

The communication equipment that yacht supervision management system(YSM)used is a multimode communication model with high reliability and efficiency, which consist of 3G, 4G, satellite, radio, ship automatic identification system(AIS). On the basis of in-depth analysis to multiple products of DDS, in order to guarantee the stability, security and efficiency of the software installed in the yacht supervision management system, we choose RTI-DDS as the communication middleware to implement the software in this paper, and design and implement a more flexible and more reliable communication management interface for RTI-DDS communication architecture. This paper achieves the preliminary design, detailed design, system implementation, system test of the communication middleware of the yacht supervision management system based on DDS and introduce the actual running situation. According to the test running situation, the communication middleware of the yacht supervision management system based on DDS which this paper design and implemented achieves the design goal and satisfies requirements.

Yacht supervision management is a complicated and could to be improved and updated information system according to market requirement, so the communication middleware of the yacht supervision management system based on DDS which this paper implemented need to be improved with respect of the update and upgrade of the YSM system. Currently, the software achieves the designed requirement, but adopt 3G communication forward interface while communication with 4G, and did not test the 4G communication particularly. In summary, we will continue to update and upgrade the communication middleware, and perfect the 4G communication forward interface in our future work.

References

Zhang Cong. Research on the Development Strategy of Marine Eco-tourism Resources. Ocean University of China, 2009.

Ma Yuting. Construction of Chinese marine strategy in the new era. ZheJiang University, 2013.

Tim Harrison, Irfan Pyarali. An Object Behavioral Pattern for Demultiplexing and Dispatching Handlers for Asynchronous Events[C]. 4th Pattern Languages of Programming conference in Allerton Park, Illinois, September 2-5, 1997.

Kyoungho An, Aniruddha Gokhale. A Cloud-enabled Coordination Service for Internet-scale OMG DDS applications[C]. Proceedings of the 8th ACM International

DOI: 10.1051/itmconf/20160701003

Conference on Distributed Event-Based Systems, New York, 2014.

1. P. Hunt, M. Konar, F. P. Junqueira, and B. Reed. Zookeeper: wait-free coordination for internet-scale systems [C]. In Proceedings of the 2010 USENIX conference on USENIX annual technical conference, volume 8, 2010, 11-11.
2. M. Li, F. Ye, M. Kim, H. Chen, and H. Lei. A scalable and elastic publish/subscribe service [C]. In Parallel &Distributed Processing Symposium (IPDPS), 2011IEEE International, 2011, 1254-1265.
3. Mei Hong, Shen Jun-Rong, Progress of Research on Software Architecture. Institute of Software.
4. National institute of Standards and Technology. Recommended Security Controls for Federal Information Systems and Organizations[EB/OL]. https://www.researchgate.net/publication/238776571_Recommended_Security_Controls_for_Federal_Information_Systems_and_Organizations, 2009-09-14.
5. Real-Time Innovations. RTI Connext: Comprehensive SummaryofQoS Policies[EB/OL]. http://community.rti.com/documentation, 2013.
6. Real-Time Innovations. RTI Connext DDS: Core Libraries and Utilities User's Manual[EB/OL]. http://community.rti.com/documentation, 2013.

ITM Web of Conferences 7, 01004 (2016) DOI: 10.1051/itmconf/20160701004
ITA 2016

Design and Development of Fire Gridding Platform Based on Internet of Things

San-Xi WEI[1, a], Jin-Chao XIAO[1,2]and Ji-Hai LIU[1]

[1]*Shenyang Institute of Automation, Guangzhou, Chinese Academy of Sciences, Guangzhou, China, 511458*
[2]*Shenyang Institute of Automation, Chinese Academy of Sciences, Shenyang, China, 110016*
[a]*San-Xi WEI: weisanxi@gz.sia.cn*

Abstract. This article describes the construction background about fire gridding platform, reviews the research and progress in fire Internet of Things and fire gridding. The platform includes perception / execution layer, field control layer, network layer, center platform layer and application layer, which provide a good bonding about site control and remote monitoring. This article supplies a detail design for the main functions of application and task flow of fire hazard investigation. At the same time, a digital management platform was developed.

1 Introduction

In recent years, Chinese economic development rapidly, industrialization, urbanization and modernization are all in a rapid progress. The explosion of various types of Industrial and commercial units in rural towns and communities increasing the pressure of fire prevention and control. The number of deaths in rural towns and communities related to fire was accounted for over 70% of the nation. In response to the severe fire safety situation, the State Council issued the "The opinions of state council on strengthening and improving the fire control work" in 2011 year. Opinions point out "the township people's governments and sub district offices must establish fire safety organization, confirm a person responsible for the fire service, push fire gridding management, enhance fire safety infrastructure, to promote the level of rural and community's fire-fighting work." In 2012, the Central Comprehensive Management of Public Security, Ministry of Public Security, the State Administration for Industry and Commerce, Ministry of Civil Affairs and the State Administration issued the "guidance about implement fire safety gridding management on villages and towns". Guidance clearly stipulate through full use of all kinds of technical protection facilities, Internet of Things (IOT) technologies and fire safety video surveillance, to achieve real-time monitoring and dynamic management for fire safety.

At present, there have same studies about fire Internet of Things and fire safety management. Wei Wang[1]explored the foundation of application of IOT in social fire safety management, presented the unsolved problems of application of IOT in social fire safety management, including the key technology of fire Internet of Things, the special technical standard, construction and operation and so on. Qi-Yao YANG, Quan-BoGE [2]analyzed the shortcoming of city firefighting system. Based on the 3-tier structure of IOT, they proposed a smart wireless firefighting system and introduced the functions and connections within every part of the smart fire, including fire information perception, fire equipment management and the key technology. Hui-Ping HANG[3] employed complex events processing engine integrating with My Eclipse to develop a prototype system. As a result, the entire process in the system including data stream processing from IOT, events and rules modeling and on-line discrimination of false fire reporting.

Now, most studies on fire Internet of Things and grid-based of fire safety are still in the prototype stage of exploration or theoretical exploration, a small number of studies applied to practice. Zhen-Kun WU[4] designs fire safety grid-based management system framework, which is composed of base layer, sense layer, network layer, platform layer and application layer. The fire safety grid-based management realized normalized running in Anhui. At the same time, city fire control facing the difficulties such as large range of fire hazards, high environmental complexity, big fire risk, high growth disaster factor and so on. Fire control work not only collect and process large amounts of information, but also put forward higher requirements for real-time detection and real-time processing. The platform starting from small area's fire information collection, through fire real-time detection[5], fire local handling and large areas of grid-based management, to achieve networked and intelligent for fire prevention and control.

2 Platform Architecture

Platform architecture proceed from IOT's three-tier architecture: perception layer, network layer and application layer, combined with real-time fire detection [6], real-time field control technical support and various basic services. Platform architecture include the perception/Execution Layer, control hierarchy layer, network layer, center platform layer and application layer, as shown in the Figure 1.

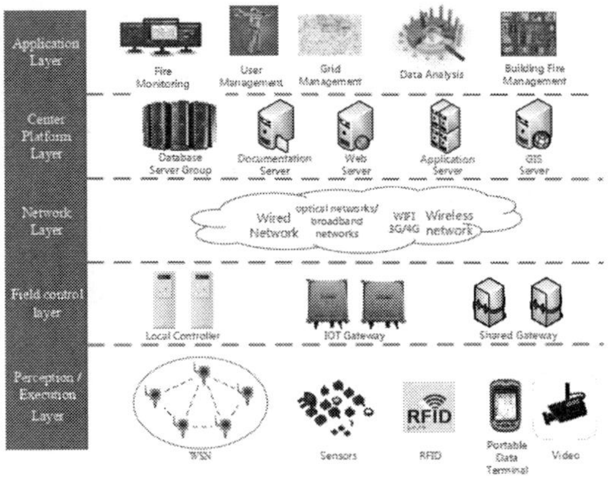

Figure 1. Platform Architecture

2.1 Perception / Execution layer

Perception / Execution layer including wireless sensor networks (WSN), fire sensors, video capture devices, mobile collection devices and various types of fire equipment.

Perception / Execution layer both as fire data gather agency, and as executive agency for commands from upon layers. Fire data includes the data gathered by collection equipment and person. The video surveillance equipment, temperature sensors, pressure sensors and other online perception devices constitute the main part of device data acquisition. Device data first centralized tolocal gateway and transmitted to the fire intelligence controller in field or network core of platform. Platform achieve real-time remote status monitoring of key unit's fire data by online device data acquisition. Data acquisition by personnel is complementary approaches for data acquisition, through grid inspector import the fire information by handheld devices, to achieve full coverage information collection. At the same time, the unit grid have the responsibility for perform the task of fire investigation and emergency reporting work. After the discovery of fire hazard or fire, the unit grid inspector reporting timely by handheld terminal. Control command including the commands form local fire intelligent controller and the platform. Firefighting equipment as the execution terminal for control command, realize the remote control.

2.2 Field control layer

Field control layer is mainly composed of fire intelligent controller and integrated gateways.

This layer plays a connecting role in the platform, including underlying devices connection and information exchange with cloud platform. Gateway collect fire equipment and fire status information to platform. Field fire intelligent controller automatically determine whether the disaster occurred and the severity of fire, make the corresponding treatment measure.

Field fire intelligent controller monitor fire alarm controller from different manufacturers and the real-time fire data; perform data frame analytical and send the monitoring information to fire control center. Controller also includes intelligence analysis function for monitoring information. Through the fire detection technology, realize real-time diagnosis for fire information. When the fire broke out, controller timely report the fire situation and location information, perform on-site emergency treatment, to promote platform field processing capacity. Controller also have the function that receive and execute commands from fire monitoring center.

Intelligent Integrated gateway contains network communication and intelligent management features. The gateway have flexible protocol processing module to support the processing of different communication protocols. Data interface section have the analytical capabilities of different application data and unified data description to support information interoperability among various network equipment. The gateway have wireless and wireline emergency switching function.

2.3 Network layer

Network layer composed by wireless and wired communication networks. Kinds of wired and wireless sensing devices, gateway devices, mobile terminals, grid nodes in perception layer tightly connect to platform center through network layer, achieve real-time interoperability and bidirectional flow of information. Mobile devices access platform communication center through 3G / 4G / GPRS wireless communication network. Office nodes of small grid, medium grid and large grid access platform communication center through wired network. For ensure information security, there have firewall between public network and system communication center, at the same time, the corresponding data connection in a encrypted way. Server rooms of fire brigade and fire detachments place the communication center and database of platform. High-speed LAN connect all the point. Platform set the communication center as a pivot, through information exchange and messaging mechanism to achieve real-time and reliable flow of information between internal departments, external devices and nodes.

2.4 Central platform layer

Center platform layer mainly composed by database server cluster, application servers and web servers and so on.

For large size, wide source, complex structure and heterogeneous fire data, using cluster application and distributed file systems technology to implement the cloud storage. The cloud resource management is the core of the cloud platform management .Through using performance prediction model and load forecasting model for dynamic and optimal design of resources, to achieve the smooth layer server management, storage management and network management. Resources include storage resources, computing resources and network resources.

For massive data mining of the cloud platform services layer, using distributed parallel data mining algorithms to forming high-value data such as fire management, fire prevention and control of data, emergency response data, security assessment data, etc.

2.5 Application Layer

Application layer mainly composed by the application functions oriented to various types of users, who associated with the fire grid management.

Application layer functions including statistical analysis, work instructions, process hazards, fire prevention, fire protection plans, risk review, task supervision, fire inspection, information collection, event handling and user management. Through the fire grid management and GIS map applications, users can view, manage, review and evaluation the fire safety unit area of jurisdiction, buildings and other hazard information. Platform establish the association a link between fire data, such the basis information of fire safety units, inspection records, hazard rectification records, fire attribute information (indoor fire facilities, floor plans, fire exits, etc.), as platform basis business data to achieve the fire safety supervision and management purpose.

3 Design of System Function

3.1 Data Collection and Management

Platform's data objects including fire safety basic data and real-time data [7].Fire safety basic data contains the GIS data, grid data and unit security data. GIS data include spatial data of different levels of the grid and spatial information of firefighting facilities within the grid.Grid cell data including attribute data of each grid, the task information and daily inspection data, etc.Unit security data including unit's basic information and fire safety information corresponding to grid cell. Fire safety real time data including real-time data collected by smoke sensors, gas sensors, temperature sensors and video surveillance. Based on "fire cloud" and cloud technology –like virtualization, distributed computing and storage, platform provide statistics, analysis and intelligent decision cloud computing support for a variety of fire data.

3.2 Gridding and Management

Based on existing urban geographic information systems, using spatial information gridding method, according to combining the principle of geographical division, functional division and administrative division, platform divides urban space into large, medium and small grid. Large grid corresponding to municipal districts. Medium grid corresponding to villages, towns and street community.Small grid corresponding to the administrative villages. Small grid refined into grid cell, the grid cell corresponding to village, residential, commercial area, District factories, mines and other basic spatial units.

Platform's grid management functions include grid information management, grid responsibilities management and fire unit relationships topology management. Grid management functions through the information entry, space dividing, relationships topology map and other functions to manage the information of grid and fire unit. Platform build topological relationship between large, medium and small grids, as well as topological relationship between grids with police station, fire brigade and other functional departments. The topological relations take a foundation for processes accurate, fast and efficient transfer of fire management task.

3.3 User and Permission Management

Platform uses topology rules between grids to achieve user management, namely achieve the differentiation and communication between large, medium, small grid and grid cell through the rule. After ensure the differentiation and communication between grids, grid users unique within the platform can to be sure. Platform provides search, interact, license, access control and other functions for users, achieves the interaction between a large number of grid users, users and services as well as users and resources. Platform achieves permission management by giving different users different functions conferred authority.

3.4 Fire Hazard Investigation Task Management

Platform sets module for fire hazard investigation. According to fire inspection laws, such as quarterly for large grid, monthly for medium grid, weekly for small grid, platform automatically generates inspection tasks for different grid users and design the different check table styles. Large grid and medium grid members release temporary and specific inspection tasks. Platform designs upload module for unit grid members, function of module including quickly and easily information entering, real-time pictures and voice notes sending, log automatically saving and uploading in real time.

DOI: 10.1051/itmconf/20160701004

3.5 Fire Awareness Training and Plans Management

According to requirement of fire prevention, platform sets fire awareness training and plans management modules. The first module used to manage the fire publicity training in large, medium and small grids, including generating awareness training mission, carrying out fire lectures and organizing evacuation training, at the same time , save and upload training records. The second module according the actual situation, design various types of fire emergency plans to deal with all types of emergencies of fire, reduce casualties and property losses. Plans aim at specific equipment, facilities, location and environment, on the basis on safety evaluation, made scientific, effective plans and arrangements for emergency rescue agencies and person, emergency rescue equipment, facilities, conditions and environment, procedures and programs of action, methods and procedures of accident control.

4 Process Design of Fire Hazard Investigation Task

Fire hazard including the various potential unsafe factors for cause fire or increase the fire harm. Fire safety management is the main task of the fire gridding platform, which around the fire hazard. In addition to effective control of fire hazards, fire safety management handle the fire caused by unsafe factors that without timely and effective control. Platform considering all kinds of fire hazard, such as illegal building that fireproof rank is not up to standard, electricity using for lack of fire safety measures, fire safety spacing do not match the requirements, fire road occupied and fire equipment is not complete. Platform automatically generates inspection tasks or large grid member regularly publish special inspection tasks for fire hazard. Unit grid members execute the task. The task execution flow as figure 2. In addition to receiving a task from large grid member, medium grid member also can publish regular fire inspection tasks to small grid member.

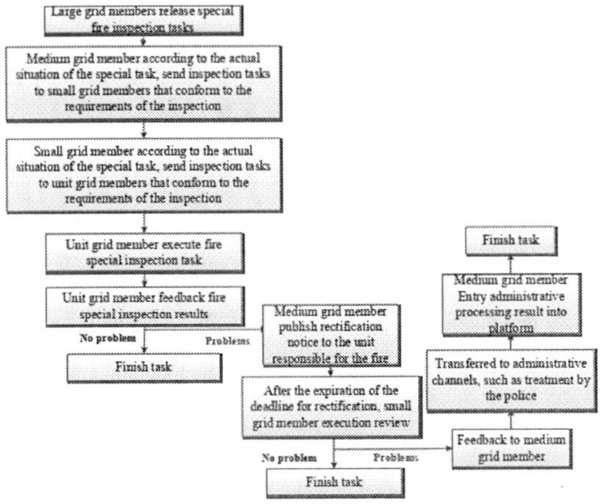

Figure 2. Task Execution Flow Diagram

5 Application Example

Platform uses SSH [8] software technology framework to building flexible, easily extensible and maintainable multi-tier Web applications. The SSH framework's persistence layer using Hibernate O / R mapping tools, containers using Spring Framework and the presentation layer uses Spring MVC framework. Platform's software technology architecture as Figure3,

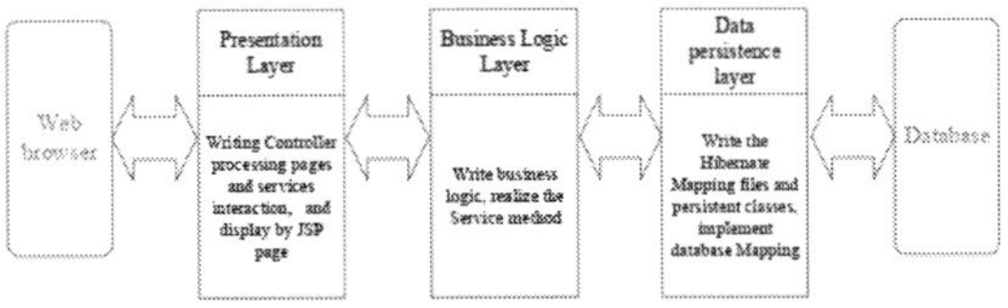

Figure 3. Software Technology Architecture

Platform management interface as figure 4,

Figure 4. Platform Management Interface

6 Summary

This paper proposes a fire gridding platform based on the Internet of Things. Platform constructed by perception / execution layer, field control layer, network layer, platform layer center and application layer. At the same time, there have detailed analysis on each layer. Platform realizes comprehensive information perception, the smallest unit of site control, multiple forms of network transmission, coverage for core service and application extensions for the actual needs. Platform provides a full coverage, visualization, intelligent grid management to fire authorities, effectively promote the improvement of the level of fire safety management.

Acknowledgement

Supported Project: National 863 plans projects (2014AA041801-1).

References

1. Wei WANG, Jing-Li NAN and Jian-Wei BO. Fire Science and Technology, 31, 864-866(2012).
2. Qi-Yao YANG, Quan-Bo GE. Fire Science and Technology, 33: 552-554(2014)
3. Hui-Ping HANG. Master's Thesis, Zhejiang University of Science and Technology, 2015.

DOI: 10.1051/itmconf/20160701004

4. Zhen-Kun WU, Hao HU, Tao WENG, Li-Wei PAN and Peng MEI. Fire Science and Technology, 34, 260-262(2015)
5. Jia WANG. Master's Thesis, Changchun University of Science and Technology. 2012.
6. Qing-Feng ZHOU, Xuan-Fang YANG and Xiang-Yi ZHAN. Fire Science and Technology, 34, 1641-1644(2015)
7. Yong-Xuan FANG, Bin-Bin LU, Li-Wei PAN and Peng MEI, China Public Security, Academy Edition, 35, 28-31(2014)
8. Xiu-Juan HUANG Computer Knowledge and Technology,11,63-65(2015).

Research on the Extraction Technology of Hot-words in Tibetan WebPages

Chang-Zhi WANG, Gui-Xian XU*and Hui WANG

Information Engineering College, Minzu University of China, Beijing, 100081, China
** Corresponding author, email: xuguixian2000@bit.edu.cn*

Abstract: The construction of Tibetan corpus is the field of Tibetan information processing of basic work. This paper uses the technology of web crawler and pretreatment and real-time acquisition of web sites to obtain a large number of Tibetan corpus in short time. The hot words reflected the hotspot of Tibetan people's attention in a certain period of time. The paper draws lessons from the TFIDF for Tibetan text information extraction and the words of different locations are given different weights to extract the hot words. It is really effective to realize the construction of the raw Tibetan corpus and the extraction of the hot-words by self-made software.

1 Introduction

With China's reform and opening up, Tibetan regions has witnessed a rapid development. China has strongly advocated the construction of information technology so that the Internet penetration rate in Tibetan areas is increasing year by year, the number of Tibetan Internet users is also growing exponentially, as information sites using Tibetan as the main language become more and more, Tibetan information generated daily on the Internet are beyond count. As a vocabulary phenomenon of the Internet age, hot words reflect hot topics and livelihood issues of a country and people of the region in a period .Hot words have the characteristics of the times, and this reflects immediately. How to extract the Tibetan information effectively and hot words is very hot topic of worthy study.

At present, both Chinese and English information researches techniques have achieved good results, but the researches on Chinese minority languages are in the primary state. For the past few years, Tibetan and other minority language website have witnessed a rapid increase, which provides the study of minority language with sufficient materials. The Tibetan corpus is important data resource of Tibetan information processing [1], we can summarize, analyze, generalize, extracted relevant knowledge and information from large-scale Tibetan corpus. Rapid identification and directional tracking for hot words [2], we can quickly understand the people feelings, know the social dynamics and development trends, faster and more comprehensive grasp the trend of public opinion, thereby performing the correct guidance of public opinion and propaganda.

2 Background

In the corpus construction [3] and hot words extraction, the traditional way of corpus construction is through a large number of experts and other human resources to collect, organize and process the data, and finally form the corpus. The original construction method of the corpus is generally not large, manual work is too much, the cost is too high, the cycle of construction is too long, so that it cannot be timely updated corpus. [4].As Web2.0 technology becomes more and more mature, everyone is content creator, and a large scale of language samples on the Internet can be used as the input of the basis corpus. Construction of large-scale corpus based on web can effectively build large-scale raw corpus in the short term, as the foundation of natural language processing research. Usually use the web crawler [5] to crawl on the Internet to grab data. Web pages are very blended got through the crawler, extracting effective information from the web page, mainly based on visual features [6], DOM tree [7], text features [8] and other methods of text extraction. As the acquired raw corpus, we use structured XML to preserve. In the specific operation, the majority of researchers use DOM4J and JSOUP to preprocess the web page.

Usually, the extraction of hot words is based on statistical strategy. This strategy is flexible and portable, but it still needs to train a large-scale corpus, and it will generate a lot of useless string affecting accuracy. The whole process needs to split words, filter stop words, count frequency of words and do other processing steps. Researchers assessing hot words are mostly based on the frequency of the hot words and historical frequency fluctuation. Some scholars put forward different weights according to the position of word, which is one of the schemes for extracting hot words.

This paper will introduce how to use web crawler to excavate Tibetan related sites, structured process the acquired resources, and store as raw Tibetan corpus. And then carry on Tibetan text pretreatment on the structure of the raw corpus, and go on research of hot words extraction, hot topic tracking based on the corpus of features including the time, the source and the author and others

3 The proposed method

3.1 Information Gathering

Information collection is the first part of the whole project. Hot words extraction needs enough material, while the way of manual acquisition cannot meet the needs of research obviously. Therefore, it needs to get a lot of Tibetan corpus by web crawler. Here we use the Crawler4j open source crawler to obtain the data. Crawler adopts the Breadth-First strategy, and the idea is that the initial URL is highly relevant with the theme of web page in a certain range, and is highly fresh.

3.2 Preprocessing

The set of acquired original web pages may contain a large amount of information that is not related to the content of the text, such as the HTML markup language of web pages. These interference information is called noise. Removing web noise is very important for the work of the system. After denoising, the system can improve the reliability of the results, and simplify the structure's complexity of web tab and reduce the page size significantly, thereby reduce the spending on the time and space in the subsequent processing. In recent years, the technology of web page pretreatment becomes more mature. The web pretreatment technology mainly includes: the page deduplication and denoising

About deduplication technology of the web page, Border proposed shingling algorithm and Charikar proposed random mapping method based on the word [9].These are the two current mainstream algorithms:the complexity of the method shingle time is lower, while the accuracy of the algorithm based on random mapping is higher. About page denoising technology, there are three methods, one is based on the structure of the page, other one is based on template and the last one based on visual information.

To improve the pretreatment's efficiency and resource's utilization rate, it requires special analysis of each website page structure and then set a specific extraction rules program due to different Tibetan website page structure varies.

3.3 Word segmentation and Remove stop word

Mainly based on dictionary, semantic and statistic, Chinese lexical analysis has matured and every technique has its merits and demerits[10]. With the deeper research of Tibetan information processing, after decades of research, Tibetan text automatic words segmentation technology also made good achievements, some scholars have realized an automatic Tibetan segmentation scheme based on case-auxiliary words and continuous features [11].

About the Tibetan removing stop words [12], in order to enhance the effectiveness of the extraction of the hot words, for modal particle, adverbs, prepositions, conjunctions, itself has no clear meaning, only to put it in a complete sentence have a certain effect, such as the common "of" and "in". We screened the high frequency of the Tibetan vocabulary then these Tibetan words were sorted into stop word list.

3.4 Hot words Extraction

After word segmentation and removing stop words, count multi-frequency data, which means that it not only needs to count frequency of a word using in different locations in an article, but also needs to count the total frequency of collected corpus appearing in a certain time period?

Hot words extraction algorithm draws feature extraction of TFIDF [13], and then give word strings different weights according to different locations in the article,and give double weight to the word strings that appears in the title .

Obtained data adopts UTF-8 Unicode. After segmenting the data of one day and removing stop words, it forms a large table named P, in which each word C points to corresponding weight value: weight(c).

The statistical algorithm of string frequency and weight about strings of the length N is as follows:

Input: L preprocessed articles.

Output: P table

1. Extract strings in L articles. Filter stop words, generate table P containing N strings, at this moment, the weight is initialized to 0.
2. Generate title table ,which total frequency is T1 ,and content table, which total frequency is T2(total frequency contains repetitive word count),in which each word C is corresponding with frequency value, such as title _tf (C), content _tf (C)
3. Generate article table recording the number of articles that the word C appeared, in which each word corresponds with a value of DF (Document Frequency) such as article_ df (C).
4. for i=1 to N
5. if title()!=null then
6. output title_ tf ( )
7. else
8. output 0
9. end
10. if content()!=null then
11. output content_ tf ( )
12. else
13. output 0
14. end
15. output article_ df ( )
16. weight()

DOI: 10.1051/itmconf/20160701005

17. end
18. output P table

The final weight calculation formula is as follows:

weight () =log ()*log ()(1)

In fact, it adopts natural logarithmic function. After calculate the heat weight of above the hot words, sort hot words on the foundation of the weights in table and then extract hot word according to the set number.

4 Experiment

We set the range of hot words for a day or a week, data originates from mainstream websites of Tibetan information. As it is rare to find Tibetan forum information websites, there isn't information acquisition involving this aspect.

We collect all valid text page from the six sites in recent years. Here sets crawling range in several popular Tibetan websites. For example: China Tibet Net (http://www.tibet.cn/), Tibet Xinhua channel (http://tibet.news.cn/), people's net Tibet channel (http://tibet.people.com.cn/) and Chinese Tibetans Netcom network (http://ti.tibet3.com)and so on. Then preprocess and organize into 38,768 XML file raw corpus, and then extract hot words from the XML files, after pretreatment, save an article as shown in figure 1:

Figure 1. Format of Corpus Text Saving After Preprocess

Then we selected the Tibetan information website news published on December 4, 2015 toextract hot words, totally grab 96 valid text files in this day. Thedistribution of the 96 pages is shown in figure 2:

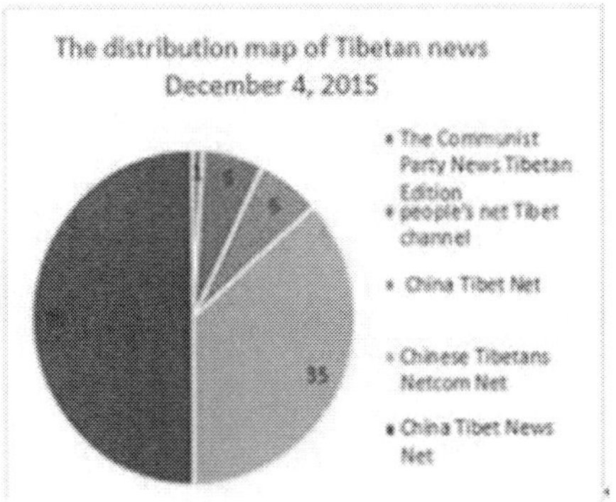

Figure 2: Distribution Map Of Tibetan News Text

The main program is shown in figure 3:

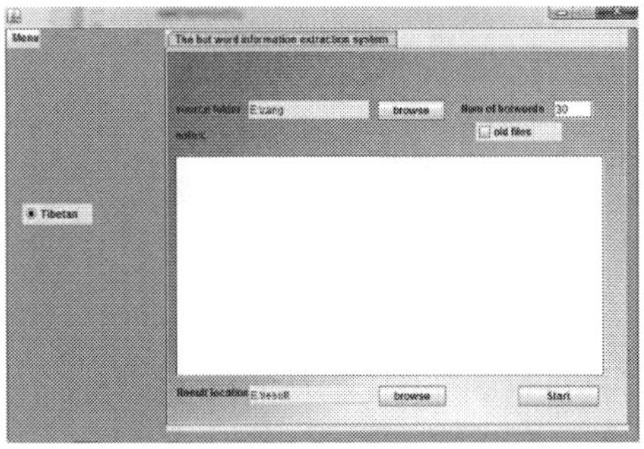

Figure 3: The Main Interfaceof Program

The results of the processing are shown in figure 4.

Experiments show that: applying the web crawler can effectively obtain all the corpus of news from Tibetan website, capture in real time, and analysis. Algorithm mentioned in this paper is effective to obtain the Tibetan hot words. As obtaining Tibetan websites almostbelong to the official website, the hot words distribute in multiple fields of politics, economy, culture, health care and other, and it reflects the main direction of publicity of Tibetan official website.

DOI: 10.1051/itmconf/20160701005

Hot-wd	TF	weight	DF	English
[illegible]	121	0.01268027	23	China
[illegible]	114	0.01024214	24	nation
[illegible]	131	0.01007369	31	country
[illegible]	68	0.00969097	7	Africa
[illegible]	68	0.00951198	8	Poverty alleviation
[illegible]	92	0.0092944	17	cooperation
[illegible]	141	0.00925053	40	The masses
[illegible]	57	0.00917713	6	The Panchen Lama
[illegible]	126	0.00855953	42	city
[illegible]	87	0.00833878	21	Culture
[illegible]	71	0.00828941	14	medical care
[illegible]	66	0.00826284	12	unite
[illegible]	44	0.00769701	5	Tibet
[illegible]	38	0.00694586	3	operation
[illegible]	44	0.0064345	8	Changdu
[illegible]	34	0.006398	3	event
[illegible]	64	0.00636982	21	activity
[illegible]	93	0.00604528	41	Sociology
[illegible]	59	0.00593786	17	propaganda
[illegible]	38	0.00590301	7	Xi Jinping
[illegible]	27	0.00590148	2	petroleum
[illegible]	38	0.00576261	7	Religion
[illegible]	26	0.00569813	2	transfer
[illegible]	61	0.00532392	23	Economics
[illegible]	35	0.00518429	6	hospital
[illegible]	35	0.00506051	7	Tourism
[illegible]	36	0.00500864	9	education
[illegible]	40	0.00499437	11	buddhism
[illegible]	70	0.00481832	36	the people
[illegible]	19	0.00478526	1	Yak

Figure. 4: Results of Hot Words Extraction

5 Conclusion

In this paper, software constantly obtains relevant Tibetan corpus by crawl on the multiple mainstream Tibetan websites. It grasps the main news material stored as structured Tibetan corpus through the relevant web information acquisition technology. After processing corpus segmentation and elimination of stop words, the final weight can be calculated by means of giving different weight to different words according to their places, as well as the word DF value, and hot words ranking can be drawn by ordering. The hot words are extracted by this method, which is simple and fast. Because of the lack of unified evaluation criteria for the extraction of network hot words, the accuracy of hot word recognition cannot be evaluated. The experimental results show that the method has higher accuracy. This paper provides a corpus of Tibetan information processing technology in this way. The classification of the hot words does not contain the parts of speech and recognition of some Tibetan names, Tibetan place names. There is no consideration of the historical frequency fluctuation of words, so the follow-up study needs to take it into consideration.

Acknowledgment

This work was supported by the National Key Technology Research and Development Program of the Ministry of Science and Technology of China(No. 2014BAK10B03), the Beijing Social Science Foundation (No. 14WYB040), and the National Natural Science Foundation of China (No. 61309012, No. 61331013).

References

1. DG Gao, B Guan. Retrospect on the Development of Tibetan Information Processing Technology [J]. Journal of Tibet University (2009)24(3):18-27.
2. YQ Li, LH Sun. Hot-Word Detection for Internet Public Sentiment [J]. Journal of Chinese Information Processing (2011)25 (1): 48-53+59.
3. DGGao, Tashigyal, DCZhao. Data Analyses of Large Basic Tibetan Corpus [J].Journal of Northwest University for Nationalities (Natural Science) (2013)34(92):46-51.
4. PFLi, QMZhu, PDQian. Construction Approach of Large-scale Corpus Based on Web [J]. Computer Engineering,(2008)34(7):41-46.
5. DZYang, GZhao, TWang. Application of WebCrawler in information search and data mining [J]. Computer Engineering and Design, (2009)30(24):5658-5662.
6. QWu, XYang, ZXZhao. Web information extraction based on visual characteristics [C], Symposium of the Sixth China Conference on Information Retrieval (2010).
7. RXZhang, MQSong, YLGong. Parsing DOM Tree Reversely and Extracting Web Main Page Information [J]. Computer Science. (2011)38(4):213-215.
8. JD Hu. Research on Web News Extraction and Duplicates Elimination [D].ZHEJIANG UNIVERSITY (2011).
9. CQMa, XGMao. Research on Near-duplicate Detection Algorithm Shingling and Simhash [J]. Computer & Digital Engineering(2009)39(1):15-17
10. JW Mo,Y Zheng, ZY Shou, SL Zhang.Improved Chinese word segmentation method based on dictionary[J].Computer Engineering and Design.(2013)34(5):1802-1807
11. YZChen, BLLi, SWYu, CJLan.An Automatic Tibetan Segmentation Scheme Based on Case-Auxiliary Words and Continuous Features [J]. Applied Linguistics(2003) (1):75-82
12. JZhu, TRLi.Research on Tibetan Stop Words Selection and Automatic Processing Method [J] Journal of Chinese Information Processing(2015)29 (2):125-132
13. CYShi, CJXu, XJYang. Study of TFIDF algorithm [J]. Journal of Computer Applications (2009)26:167-170.

 DOI: 10.1051/itmconf/20160701006

An Empirical Study for the Mobile Food Trace ability: Private Trace ability System for the White Gourd in Tianjin, China.

Yu-Chuan LIU [1, a] and Hong-Mei GAO [2]

[1] *Associate Professor, Department of Information Management, Tainan University of Technology, 71002 Tainan, Taiwan*
[2] *Professor, Department of Economic Management, Tianjin Agricultural University, 300384 Tianjin, PRC*
[a] Corresponding author: t00258@mail.tut.edu.tw

Abstract. As the food supply chain globalization became inevitable, transparency in the way agriculture was grown and handled throughout the supply chain process resulted in an important issue of 'traceability' in global food trade and safety for health management. Traceability in agriculture is faced with the technological challenges including food product label and identification, activity/process characterization, information systems for data capture, analysis, storage, and the integration of the overall traceable data for the supply chain, i.e., from farm to table. While some field data can be automatically acquired and transmitted by sensor networking, most agricultural activity information was recorded by manual handwriting for the traceability information systems. System architecture, operation scenarios, and the implementation examples for the mobile farming data collection system to automatically record the agricultural activities information for famers were proposed in this research. The farming information for farming activities is coded in two-dimensional labels of quick response (QR) codes. By scanning the proper operation labels, the corresponding farming data can be captured and uploaded simultaneously to the back-end web server. A collaborative research project for the traceability of white gourd planting in Tianjin was performed. The system can be implemented for public traceability system data collection and importing, as well as playing the roles of a private traceability system. The consumers' confidence for healthy food choices with clear food traceability can be improved.

1 What is Food Traceability

Issues for food safety, agro-processing, and the environmental and ecological impact of agriculture had been exacerbated by the incidences such as the human form of bovine spongiform encephalitis (BSE, mad cow disease), genetically engineered foods, and contamination of fresh and processed agriculture. The heightened awareness of food-related safety issues among food consumers drives the demand for more information about the vertical food supply chain about the origin and handling of the basic commodities and food products generated and consumed throughout the world. The term of traceability can be defined as, from International Organization for Standardization (ISO), the ability to trace the history, application or location of an entity, by means of recorded identifications. Traceability is an essential subsystem of quality management, and must be managed by setting up a traceability system, which keeps the data tracking of product routes and of selected attributes. A traceability system can consist two elements, the routes of the product, path along which products can be identified throughout the manufacturing, distribution and retail procedures, and the extent of traceability wanted [1]. Food traceability system is aimed to provide information visibility through the farming, production, packing, distribution, transportation, and sales process, and receiving enthusiastic research interests due to the food supply chain globalization. Accuracy and transparency of products and activities in the way food was grown and handled throughout the supply chain is becoming an important quality index in food and agribusiness [2]. Food traceability requires that all stakeholders within the food supply chain, including agriculture and feed producers, food manufacturers, retailers, etc., must be able to identify the source of all raw materials and ingredients and also to whom the products have been sold. The food companies must apply identification systems and data handling procedures and these must be integrated into their quality management system. The sector encompassing information technology (IT) centers ought to find a reasonable compromise between the simple, step by step passing of traceable unit IDs for the neighboring actors, and the accumulated enormously huge databases of the actors. The traceability system is to provide services for the supply chain actors on cooperative basis of the mutual interests [3]. In addition, the IT centers have to support the supply chain and value chain management, as well as the work of the authorities, that are responsible for the human health..

 DOI: 10.1051/itmconf/20160701006

Opera [4] reviewed the concepts of supply chain management and traceability in agriculture and highlighted the technological challenges, including food product label and identification, activity/process characterization, information systems for data capture, analysis, storage and communication, and the integration of the overall traceable supply chain in implementing traceable agricultural supply chains. Wang et al. [5] addressed that the values on traceability can be integrated with the supply chain management processes to manage the business process and improve its performance. Golan et al. [6] summarized that there were three motives for food suppliers to establish product tracing systems: to improve the supply (production) management, to differentiate and market foods with subtle or undetectable quality attributes, and to facilitate trace-back for food safety and/or quality. The aim of a traceability system is to collect the product related information along the supply chain. This information is essential when facing food safety crisis, and provides efficient management for the corresponding product recall action. Although a recall action could be absolutely critical for a company, both in terms of incurred costs and of media impact, at present most companies do not posses reliable methods to precisely estimate the amount of product that would be discarded in the case of recall. Considering the food traceability system as part of the logistics management, Boson a and Gebresenbet [7] summarized the literature review on the food traceability issues. The definition, driving forces, barriers, benefits, traceability technologies, improvements, and performances of food traceability system had been discussed. It was pointed out that the development of full chain food traceability system is quite complex in nature, and a deeper understanding of real processes from different perspectives such as economic, legal, technological, and social issues are essential. Consequently, studies on the integration of traceability activities with food logistics activities, the linkage between traceability system and food manufacturer, standardization of data capturing and communication protocol for different drivers, and performance evaluation frameworks for food traceability system need to be focused.

2 Information Technology Applications For agro-Food Industry

Developments of agro-food industries are facing global challenges that can only be supported by information technologies. The major IT development lines, the support potential of their integration, organizational requirements for the utilization, and possible consequences for the future organization of the agro-food sector were reviewed [8]. A new model and prototype of a new Farm Information Management System, which meets the changing requirements for advising managers with formal instructions, recommended guidelines and documentation requirements for various decision making processes, was developed [9]. As achieving end-to-end traceability across the supply chain is quite a challenge from a technical, a co-ordination and a cost perspective, Kelepouris et al. [10] suggested a radio frequency identification (RFID) technology and outlined both information data model and system architecture that made traceability feasible and easily deployable across a supply chain. Based on an integration of alphanumerical codes and RFID technology, the traceability system for Parmigiano Reggiano (the famous Italian cheese) was developed [11]. Manthou et al. [12] provided empirical insights regarding the use of Internet-based applications in the agri-food supply chain by focusing on the Greek fruit canning sector. The companies' perceptions regarding perceived benefits, constrained factors and motivation factors towards the use of Internet-based applications were studied. A PDA-based Record-keeping and Decision-support System for traceability in cucumber production was developed on Windows Mobile platform invoking a Geographic Information System (GIS) control [13]. Two agricultural production enterprises were chosen as case study to evaluate the system and the results show that the efficiency of production record-keeping and decision-support is improved by the simple and friendly system. The state-of-the-art review in the recent advancements of food processing and packaging industry in the fields of smart packaging and materials, automation and control technology, standards, and their application scenarios, and production management principles and their improvements was proposed [14].

The purpose of this research is to develop a mobile farming information system to collect the farming data by the daily used cell phone instead of handwriting and input to the traceability system. System architecture of the proposed mobile traceability system is shown in Fig. 1. The farming data are collected by the mobile devices that can provide data communication anytime and anywhere through the mobile 3G (4G) or Wi-Fi network. The data to be collected for traceability including the farming activities messages such as seeding, weeding, fertilizing, disease prevention, harvest and shipping, are designed to be stored in QR codes. By scamming the QR code with mobile device, the data stored in the QR code can be decoded and enabling a transaction with the application services to be uploaded to the traceability database.

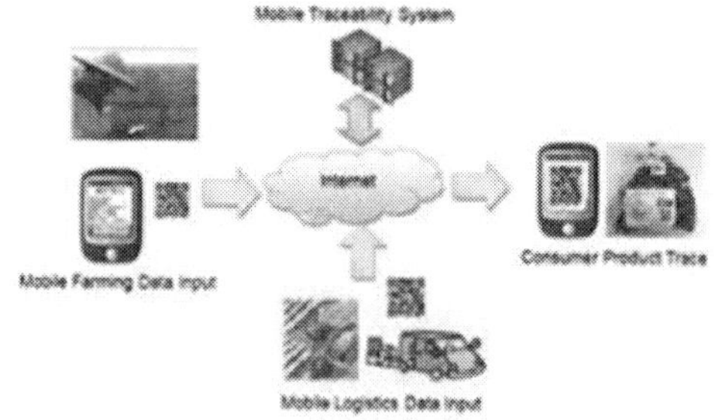

Figure 1. System Architecture of The Proposed Mobile Traceability System.

Operation scenarios for farming activity message collection are analyzed in Fig. 2. The farming information collection is started by scanning the corresponding QR code label. The mobile device will

DOI: 10.1051/itmconf/20160701006

decode and link to the application server and enabling the farmer authentication transaction performed by the application program (AP). The farmer should input the proper username and password and the mobile system will verify the validation. As the verification process completed, the AP will show the decoded farming operation message and start the confirm request transaction. The farmer needs to confirm the operation messages are identical with the one he performed. The operation messages will be uploaded to the database after the confirm signal is entered. For the case that more detail attributes are required to be recorded, the detail activity messages request transaction will be enabled after finishing the authentication. The messages required include the amount used, unit, and dilute ratio of fertilizer (or pesticide). Detailed operation scenario for the pesticide usage recording process can be found in [15]. This system is suitable for the traceability management of sub-contract supply farmers. Minimized interactive operations with the mobile devices are considered for the system. The farmer only need to scanning the QR code, input the amount used, and press the confirm button to finish the traceability data record and upload simultaneously.

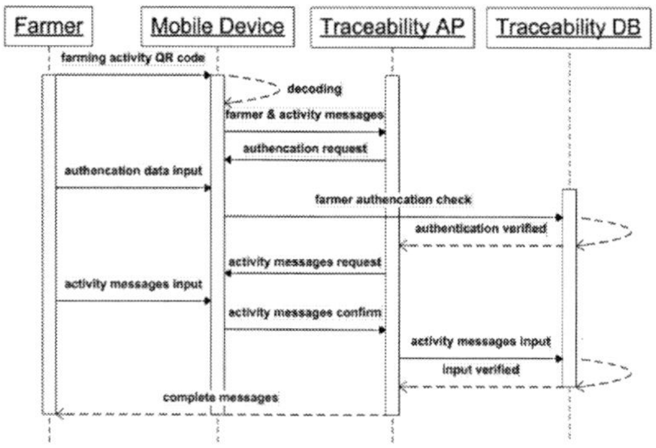

Figure 2. Sequential Diagram for the Farming Operations with Detail Ecords.

By properly encoding the farming messages to the QR codes, the messages can be read by the mobile devices and uploaded simultaneously to the application server of the mobile farming system. The farming activity information can be captured by simply scanning the QR code labels and uploaded in real time, instead of manual handwriting and input by batch to the traceability system. The miscellaneous traceability data construction can be significantly reduced. The mobile farming system can work for both traceability system of the public and private sectors. Data collected by the mobile farming information system is stored by the database system and can be output to the required file format for any electrical data exchange. The application example for the private traceability systems will be shown in the next section.

3 Private Traceability Systems for White Gourd in Tianjin

Traceability system in China is attracting more and more research and industrial interests. The food safety and traceability related projects and researches were one of the focus issues in the 12th 5-year national development plan started since 2012 by the China government. The academic cooperation between Tainan University of Technology (TUT) and Tianjin University of Agriculture (TUA) has been started since 2012. Researches about the food and agro-product traceability in TUA have got the financial support from the Spark Program 2013 of the Ministry of Science and Technology of PRC, and science and technology developing program form Tianjin Municipal Science and Technology Commission. The Tianjin Shunzi Vegetable Cooperative (TSVC) is one of the famous farms in Tianjin whose white gourd has won the 2012 "One Village One Product" paradigm of ministry of agriculture in China and became one of the distinguished agro-products in Tianjin. They joined the TUA project in 2014 to implement the mobile farming information system to build their own traceability system for the white gourd. The aim of the traceability system is not only to improve the safety traceability but also to promote the value of the brand "Qinmei" for TSVC.

The implementation of mobile farming data collection of the pilot project can be summarized as following.

3.1 Kickoff meeting

The pilot project began by the kickoff meeting hold by TSVC farmers, government employees, and the technical team form Tainan University of Technology and Tianjin University of Agriculture.

3.2 Farming data and QR code definition

The system analysis for the production activities and related information required for white gourd farming was firstly reviewed. The farming data definition, including farming activities, fertilizer, and pesticides, were applied for the pilot system. The QR code for every farming activities were encoded after the data definition decided.

3.3 Database and brief traceability system development

As analyzed in the previous section, all the function can be operated via the mobile devices. The normal farming activities, such as irrigation, weeding, branch trimming, etc., can be recorded by scanning and confirming the corresponding QR code label as shown in Fig. 3.

3.4 Mobile farming SOP and training

To provide effective training for the mobile farming information system, standard operation procedure was established including the brief operation instructions of the hardware device, the QR code scanning process, and the usual questions and answers for the usage.

3.5 Field testing and auditing

The field test for the mobile communication at the farmland is necessary to guarantee the effectiveness of the system. The field testing and auditing were performed at the site of farmland in Tianjin. The data communication through mobile 3G networking is worked effectively at the farmland.

Figure 3. Label Scanning Operation Scenario for the for the Pesticide Usage Recording Process, (1) Scanning The Qr Code For Cyhalothrin, (2) Username And Password Authentication, (3) The Message Input Transaction Enabled, (4) Input Usage Amount, Unit, And Dilute Ratio Of Cyhalothrin, (5) Confirm The Input, And (6) Message Uploaded Complete.

The home page for the back end server of the mobile platform is shown in Fig. 4. As a private traceability service platform, the home page of the service platform shows the organizations registered in this sector. After logged in to the system by the administrator of the organization, the production data of farm information, farmer, product, fertilizer, pesticides, harvesting, and packing information can all be maintained at the platform. The farm information (Fig. 4b) includes: name of the contact farmer, telephone and fax numbers, e-mail, address, facebook, and the multimedia video is also provided in accordance with the text information and pictures. The farming data uploaded can be queried and only the administrator can delete or edit the farming data to ensure the correctness and reliability (Fig. 4c).

Figure 4a. Mobile Server Platform User Interfaces, Home Page.

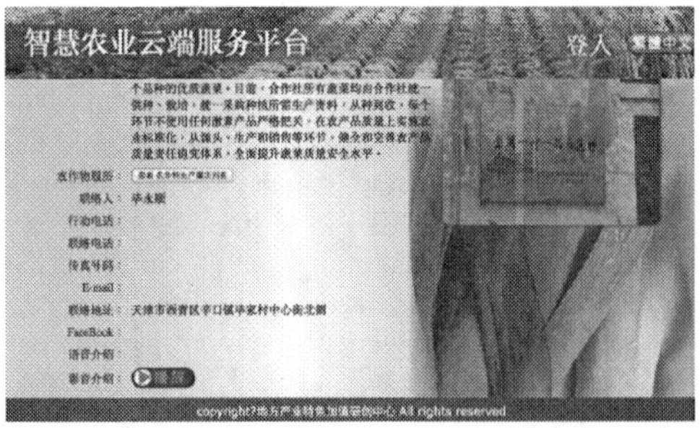

Figure 4b. Mobile Server Platform User Interfaces, Farmer Information.

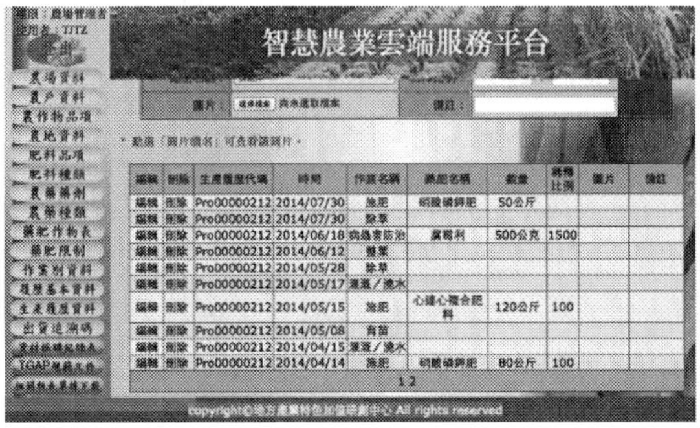

Figure 4c. Mobile Server Platform User Interfaces, Traceability Data.

By scanning the traceability label, the brief traceability information, including name of the organization and producer, traceability ID number, telephone number, and location of the farmland, is displayed on the mobile device (as shown in Fig. 5). The detail farm and traceability information can be obtained by further clicking the corresponding linkage. As the traceability system implemented, the white gourd of TSVC was becoming more and more famous and won the golden prize of the 2014 excellent agricultural products of Tianjin. The traceability system can improve not only the transparency of the farming procedure, but also the brand image of social responsibility.

Figure 4c. Traceability System User Interfaces, (1) First Page of Brief Traceability Information, (2) Farm Information, (3) Traceability Data, (4) the Farmland, (5) Traceability Label, (6)

~(7) Technical Team and the Farmers, and (8) the Golden Prize of 2014 Excellent Agricultural Products of Tianjin.

4 Summary and Conclusions

Implementation of traceability system for agriculture and food supply chains is necessary to enhance the competence of product. Traceability data involves miscellaneous records that mostly kept by manual handwriting. To reduce the minute and unreliable traceability data recording procedure, the mobile farming information system is developed to enhance the efficiency of e-traceability. The operation scenarios for the mobile traceability data construction and collection are studied, the architecture for the system and database are schemed, and the application examples are proposed in this research. By properly encoding the farming activity messages to the QR code labels, the farming data can be read by the mobile devices and uploaded simultaneously to the mobile platform server. The farming activity information can be captured by simply scanning the QR code labels and uploaded in real time. The miscellaneous traceability data collection can be significantly reduced. The mobile farming information proposed was implemented either as the mobile data collection tool for a private traceability system in Tianjin. The results showed that the mobile farming information can be successfully implemented. Food traceability can be more credible due to the farming data is collected more reliable.

Acknowledgements

This work was supported by 2013 Industrial Park Industry-Academia Cooperation Project from Ministry of Education of ROC (102B-26-006), the 2013 Spark Program of the Ministry of Science and Technology of PRC, and 2013 program of the Tianjin Municipal Science and Technology Commission (13ZLZLZF04400).

References

1. T. Moe, Trends Food Sci Tech. 9, 211 (1998)
2. L. U. Opera and F. Maraud, Outlook Agr. 30(4), 239 (2001)
3. M. Vargas and B. Csukas, Agr Infor. 1(1), 8 (2010)
4. L. U. Opera, J. of Food Agric. Environ. 1(1), 101 (2003)
5. X. Wang, D. Li, and L. Li, Int. J. of Serv. Oper. Informant. 4(3), 232 (2009)
6. E. Golan, B. Krissoff, F. Kuchler, K. Nelson, G. Price, and L. Calvin, Choices Magaz. of Food Farm and Res. Issues 2, 17 (2003)
7. T. Bosona and G. Gebresenbet, Food Control 33, 32 (2013)
8. G. Schiefer, Comput. And Electron. In Agr. 43(2), 163 (2004)
9. C. G. Sorensen, S. Fountasb, E. Nashf, L. Pesonend, D. Bochtisa, S. M. Pedersene, B. Bassoc, S. B. Blackmoreg, Comput. and Electron. in Agr. 72(1), 37 (2010)
10. T. Kelepouris, K. Pramatari, and G. Doukidis, Ind. Mana. Data Syst. 10 (2) , 183 (2007)
11. A. Regattieri, M. Gamberi, and R. Manzini, J. of Food Eng. 81(2), 347 (2007)
12. V. Manthou, A. Matopoulos, and M. Vlachopoulou, J. of Food Eng. 70(3), 447 (2005)
13. M. Li, J. P. Qian, X. T. Yang, C. H. Sun, and Z. T. Ji, Comput. and Electron. in Agr. 70(1), 69 (2010)
14. N. P. Mahalik and A. N. Nambiar, Trends Food Sci. Tech 21(3), 117 (2010)
15. Y. C. Liu and H. M. Gao, in Appl. Comput. Med. and Health 12, 244 (2015)

Design and Implementation of Henan Huinong Client System Based on iOS

Yan-Ling LI[a], Li ZHANG[b], Yu-Feng GUO[c], Lei XI[d], and Chang-Xia SUN*

Information and Management Science College of Henan Agricultural University, Zhengzhou, China
*[a]lyl_lingling@163.com, [b]zhangli200312@eyou.com, [c]gyfzhp@126.com, [d]hnaustu@126.com, *sunchang_xia@126.com*

Abstract. In order to meet the demands of customers related to agriculture who can obtain some Comprehensive agricultural information service of Henan Province through the intelligent mobile terminal, on the base of the Zhong yuan Rural Information Port integrated platform, employing IOS, Java, Eclipse, XML, SAX technology, we designed and developed Henan Huinong client systems based on ios mobile terminal. This system has achieved the multiple applications, such as agricultural information browsing, network consulting, expert online, crop rermote diagnosis and so on.

1 Introduction

The smart phone, as a means of media, with characteristics of high penetration and portability, provides a new information transmission tool for information mobile services in rural areas as well as strong support for the innovation of rural information service. With the continuous rapid increase of smart phone holding quantity in rural areas and the increase of recognition rate of farmers on mobile phone information spreading, the launch of relevant softwares and services based on mobile phones is relatively lagging. Therefore, it is particularly urgent to develop the corresponding application softwares and provide relevant mobile services.

Henan Province, located in the middle east of China, is a province with the largest population, a large agricultural province, strong grain-producing province and large animal husbandry province, which plays an important strategic role in the overall situation of reform and development in China. Accelerating the informatization is a key strategy to promote the construction of Central Plains Economic Zone, realize the rising of central China and promote leapfrog development of Henan Province. Improving the rural information service level and accelerating the rural informatization is the only way to realize agricultural modernization, and the effective method of realizing the"Sanhua" coordinated and scientific development of "Sanhua" in Central Plains Economic Zone. In February 2012, the pilot work of constructing national rural informatization demonstration province performed by Henan Province was approved by the Ministry of Science and Technology, the CPC's Organization Department and the Ministry of Industry and Information.

This paper, taking the implementation of provincial major special project "Development and Application of Key Technology of Henan Rural Information Integrated Service" as opportunity, based on the establishment of the Comprehensive Portal Platform of Central Plains Rural Information Port, and by means of the Huinong client software developed by Objective-C language and Xcode tool and suitable for smart phone of IOS platform, provides functions for smart phone users. These functions, based on the Comprehensive Portal Platform of Central Plains Rural Information Port, are about individual push of agricultural technology consultation, market directional push, agricultural information query as well as audio and video interaction.

2 Key Technologies

X Code is Apple's suite of development tools. It can be used to manage project, edit the code, structure the executable file, debug the source code level, manage the storage of source code, adjust the performance and so on. The core of the suite is XCode application itself, which is used to provide the development environment of source code. Key technologies that will be used in developing IOS software are as follows.

2.1 X code

X code is an integrated development environment, including processes from the establishment and management of the source file to chain programming of the

DOI: 10.1051/itmconf/20160701007

source code to executable file, and operating the code in equipments, or debugging all the tools required for the code on the iPhone simulator.

When the Xcode is used to program applications, it can be connected with the iPhone simulator or equipment. Simulator provides the local environment for application tests. It also can be used to test whether the application has the correct behavior. When the basic behavior of application meets the expected goals, connect it with the equipment with Xcode, then operate the application on the IOS device which has been connected to the computer. The operation of the application on the equipment is the final test environment. During the process of the test, Xcode allows you to bound the built-in debugger to the code operated on the equipment, and to debug it directly on the equipment.

2.2 Simulator

The iPhone Simulator is a useful tool in the iPhone SDK, which can be used to test the application without using the actual iPhone/iPod Touch. Usually there's no need to start the iPhone Simulator directly—it will start automatically when the application is operated (or debugged) by the Xcode. Xcode will automatically install the application on the iPhone Simulator.

During the process of creating applications with Xcode, developers have to choose the iPhone simulator as well as the equipment when compiling these applications. The iPhone simulator provides a local application test environment. After passing the test on the iPhone simulator, the application can be compiled by Xcode and operated on the iPhone which has been connected to the computer. Operating the application on the iPhone provides the most comprehensive test environment. Xcode can track the code by the built-in debugger during the period of equipment testing.

2.3 Interface Builder

Interface Builder is built into user's interface by WYSIWYG. Through Interface Builder, drag the standard system control to the application window, and finally assemble user interface of the application program. You can use inspector to configure component properties, and establish correct association between subjects and codes. When user's interface meets the requirement, save it and save the contents of the interface to the nib file (a customized resource file format).

After using Interface Builder, you will no longer need to write custom codes when creating, configuring, and placing interface objects, because it is a kind of visual editor, the interface you see when editing is what you get in running.

2.4 Instruments

To ensure that the software provides the best user experience, when the IOS application routine is running on the emulator or device, can use Instruments environment to analyze its performance. Instruments will collect data of the running programs, and show the data in a time line. The collectible application data including application memory usage, disk activity, network activity, and graphics performance.

3 The Overall Design and Huinong Mobile Phone Client

Huinong mobile client is the extension of the central plains rural information platform PC access terminal, according to the characteristics of the central plains rural information port service platform, the main functions mobile phone client needs to provide are convenient, clear user interface and data storage and fetch. Moreover, according to the characteristics of mobile communication, the client also needs to actively connect the server through background services within the corresponding time period to get information, while upload data to make it convenient for the server to analyze the users' using custom, and make adjustment. Huinong mobile client can realize agricultural technology consulting personalized push, market orientation push, agricultural information query, audio and video interaction and other functions, the client module diagram is as shown in Fig. 1.

 DOI: 10.1051/itmconf/20160701007

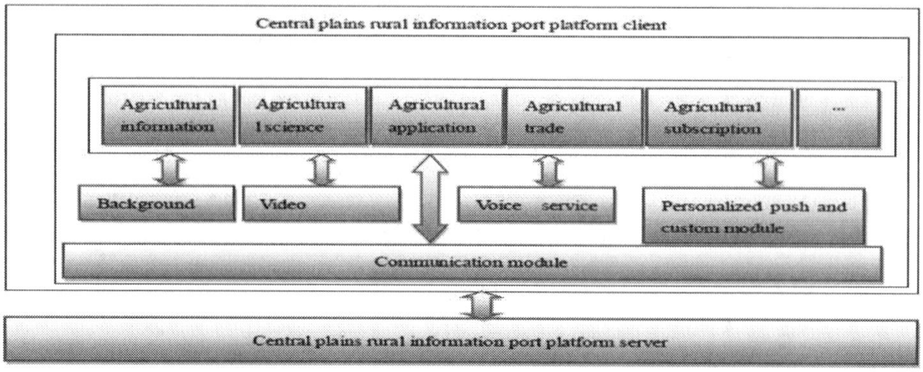

Figure1. Client Module Diagram

In Fig. 1, the business layer mainly provides agricultural policies and regulations information, agricultural market information (agricultural product supply and demand information, market prices, agricultural supplies, agricultural machinery prices, etc.) , agricultural foundational information (agricultural production knowledge: farming, forestry, animal husbandry and fishery), plant diseases and insect pests prevention and control knowledge, agricultural science knowledge (the common sense of science and technology, agriculture common sense, weather forecasting, etc.) and other agricultural information, these data all come from the background database of central plains rural information port platform. Through background service module, video diagnosis module, voice module and personalized push and custom module and other intelligent information processing platforms, the supporting layer can finally realize all kinds of agricultural information service, achieving agricultural information browsing, consulting, customization and push and other functions. Communication module realizes the communication between client and server, through wireless network on phones to make access to the servers on the Internet, through the communication module, the client calls WebService provided by the servers to get the data.

Huinong mobile client, based on central plains rural information port platform, provides a smart phone unified technology platform for agricultural information access and management for the majority of farmers, agricultural enterprises and agricultural experts. Through business interaction, business management, content management, statistical analysis and other functions with central plains rural information port platform, voice service system, video service system and other peripheral equipments, realized the service of browsing, consulting, customization of all kinds of agricultural information. The specific functions include: agricultural information, agricultural science and technology, agricultural application, agricultural trade, etc.

4 Detailed Design of Huinong Mobile Client

4.1 Interaction Method of Huinong Mobile Client and Server

The interaction of mobile client and server gets the data based on Http protocol, as shown in Fig. 2. Its working principle is to submit the client's request through a browser page to a Web application server, application server submits the received data to the server-side logic to process, then output the result to a Web page, the client program access website URL gets the data and makes analytical processing. According to client request, the server sends the corresponding data in the form of XML page to the browser. The client, after a visit to a web address, analyzes the obtained XML data and displays the results.

4.2 Data Interaction Method of Huinong Mobile Client

There are usually two methods for client data interaction: Json and XML. Json is a lightweight data interactive format, easy to read and write, also easy to parse and generate by machines at the same time, it is a subset based on JavaScript Programming Language Standard ECMA-262 3rd Edition-December 1999. Json uses a text format completely independent from language, but also uses custom similar to C language family. XML (extensible markup language) is a kind of language similar to HTML , it has no predefined tags, uses DTD (document type definition) document type definition to organize data, with unified format, cross-platform and cross-language, has become the industry recognized standards.

In this system, we designed to use XML files to solve the data format definition problem in network communication. XML (Extensible Markup Language) is a Standard released By W3C in February 1998, it beautifully integrated the rich functionality of SHML (Standard

 DOI: 10.1051/itmconf/20160701007

Generalized Markup Language) and the usability of HTML into Web applications, defined the data structure in an open and self description method. While describing the data content, it can also highlight the description of the structure, so as to reflect the relationship between the data, the data such organized are friendly and operational for both applications and users, because XML is described in text form, so it is suitable for data exchange of all kinds of platform environment, for the same reason, XML can also get over different platforms obstacle to make normal exchange.

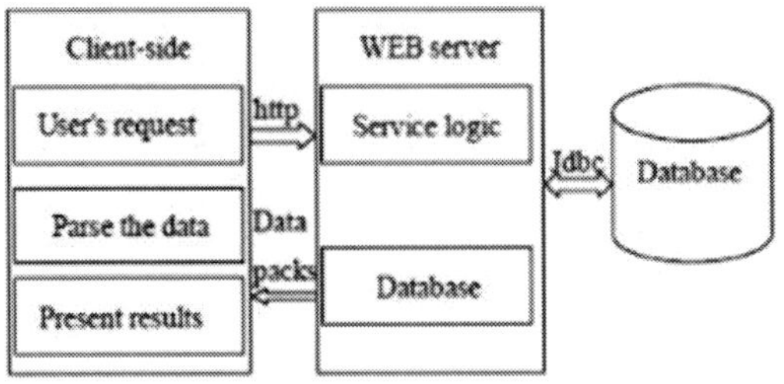

Figure 2. Working Principle of Interaction of the Client and Server

4.3 Interface Design of Huinong Mobile Client

According to the division of Huinong mobile client function modules, The bulk of the designed service interface is as shown in Table 1. In Table 1, [] means optional parameters, plate means the current node id, page means that the current displayed page, the size means how many items showed on one page, the default is 10, area is the id of information supply and demand zone, attr is the category name, character type of the supplied and demanded information.

4.4 Data Storage Design on Huinong Mobile Phone Client

Because the data of Huinong mobile phone client all comes from the background database of info port platform in rural area of central China, and the mobile phone client doesn't need to save much data, so instead of individual database in mobile phone client, it just needs effective buffer memory space. Therefore, this client uses the open source components application Android-Universal-Image-loader from the third party, which can provide a reusable device to load, cache and display asynchronous image, it is also one of the most common open source libraries as well as the mainstream application, timing buffer memory release can be carried out with its deletion strategy.

5 Huinong Mobile Phone Client System Implementation

Relevant interfaces of the client are as shown in Fig. 3 ~Fig. 6.

Table 1 Remarks Table of Service Interface

No.	Connection	Parameters	Remarks
1	phone/getnews.aspx	?type=zxtype	Obtain information of big categories
2		?type=zxstype&plate=X	Obtain information of small categories
3		?type=view&plate=X	Obtain detailed information of news
4		?type=img	Obtain 5 picture news by default on information home page
5	phone/getscience.aspx	?type=kjtype	Obtain agricultural technology of big categories
6		?type=kjstype&plate=X	Obtain agricultural technology of small categories
7		?type=kjlist&plate=X&page=X[&size=X]	Obtain agricultural technical news
8		?type=view&plate=X	Obtain detailed information of agricultural technology
9		?type=infolist&plate=X&page=X[&size=X][&area=X][&attr=X]	Obtain commodity list of supply and demand information
10	phone/getprice.aspx	?type=price&page=X[&size=X]	Obtain price information in application

Consultation column: to be divided into three parts: important news on three agricultures, working trends, policies and regulations.

Science and Technology Column: to be divided into animal husbandry and veterinary medicine, food crop, economic crop, landscape and horticulture, agriculture products processing, can be access to the following content classification information on agricultural science and technology.

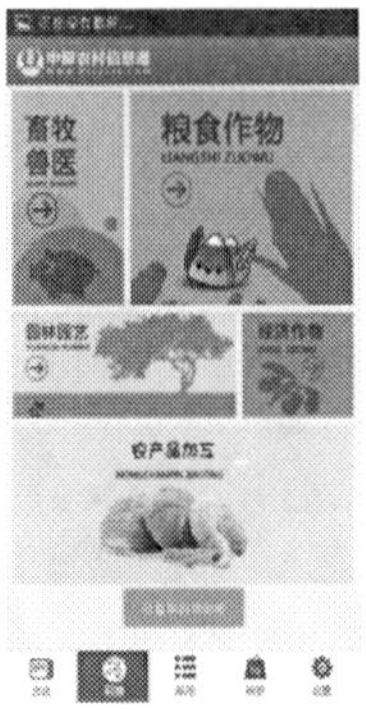

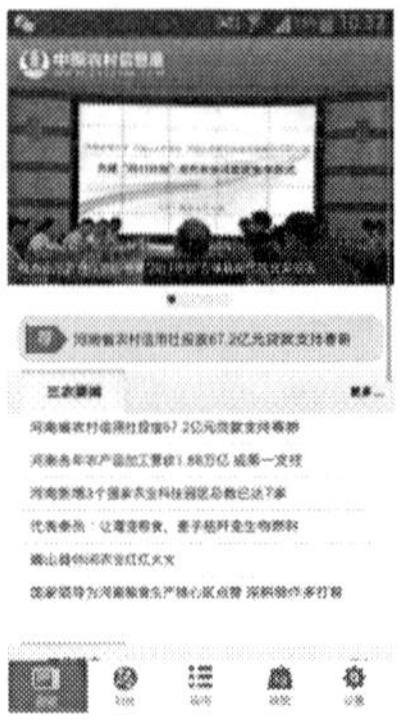

Figure 3. Information Column
Figure 4. Science and Technology Column

Application Column: to be divided into hotline(integration of the third-party system, the web page link is provided by the third party, clicking to call directly), remote diagnosis (invoking the software system of the third party), weather service, price information, it can realize agricultural condition guiding, livestock and poultry guiding, disaster warning and agricultural meteorology, etc.

Business Column: It can show the name of products, name of market, time of delivery and supply and demand information.

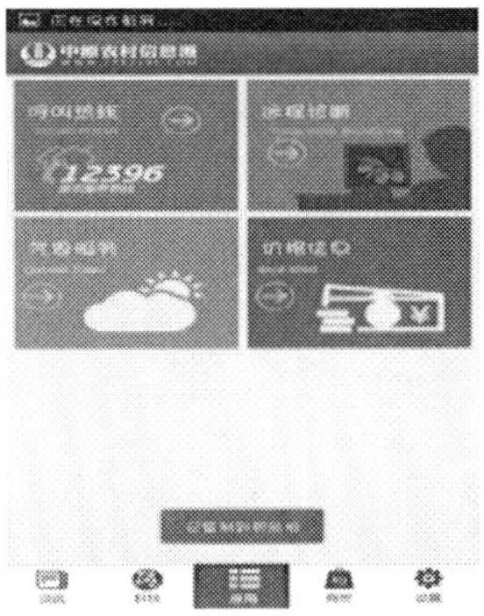

Figure 5. Application Column **Figure 6.** Business Column

Acknowledgement

This work was supported by two grants from the National "Twelfth Five-Year" Plan for Science & Technology Support Program(Grant No.2014BAD10B06) and Henan Province Key Project of Science and Technology (Grant No.131100110400).

References

[1] Chen Wei, Guo Shupu. Development situation and related issues of information technology in agriculture of China[J]. Transactions of the Chinese Society of Agricultural Engineering (CSAE), 29(22): 196-205, (2013)

[2] Wang Junhui, Cao Jing et al.. Rural Information Service Platform Based on Android Mobile Phone System[J]. Jiangsu Agricultural Sciences, 41(4): 370-371, 405, (2013)

[3] Ministry of Industry and Information Technology of the People's Republic of China. Mobile Has Become the New Growth Point of Mobile Internet Users Service [IR/OL]. (2011-6-25). http://www.cl 14.net, (2011)

[4] Yang Zhiwen. Google Android Application Design Guidelines [M]. Publishing House of Electronics Industry, (2009)

[5] Eckel(US.). JAVA Programming Basics[M]. China Machine Press, (2007)

[6] Zeng Hui. Design and Implementation of Tourism System Based on Android Platform[D]. Master's thesis of Jiangsu University, (2012)

[7] Wang Junmin. System and Implementation Based on XML Heterogeneous Data Conversion[D]. Master's thesis of Electronic and Science and Technology University, (2008)

[8] Du Wei. Intelligent Information Service Platform Server Design and Realization [D]. Master's degree thesis of Beijing University of Posts and Telecommunications, (2011)

[9] Deng Wen. BKBANK Client Design Based on Android System[D]. Master's degree thesis of Huazhong University of Science and Technology, (2012)

[10] Cui Dong. Development of 3G Server on the Agriculture Information Integrated Service Platform in Qingdao City[D]. Master's degree thesis of Shandong University, (2013)

[11] Yang Hua. Design on News Systems in Shanxi Agricultural University Based on Browsing on a Mobile Phone[J]. Journal of Shanxi Agricultural University (Natural Science Edition), 33(3): 271-273, (2013)

[12] Du Wei. Intelligent Information Service Platform Server Design and Realization [D]. Master's degree thesis of Beijing University of Posts and Telecommunications, (2011)

[13] Kunjie, Chen, Sun Weiwei, Zhu Liang, and Liu Weimo. An Adaptive Page-Replacement Strategy for Spatial Database Systems[J]. Journal of Computer Research and Development 10 (2011): 018.

DOI: 10.1051/itmconf/20160701008

A Method about the Propagation of Faults in Network

Yao-Nan LI[1,a] and Shi-Hai WANG[1,b]

[1] *Dept. Reliability and System Science, Beihang University, Beijing, China.*
Corresponding author: [a] *q2511757@126.com,* [b] *wangshihai@buaa.edu.cn*

Abstract. The study of network has been developed for several years. The research usually focuses on the attributes of the network, including the heterogeneity [1], the topology [2] [3]and the communities[4][5] of the network. About the propagation dynamics, reference [6][7] laid emphasis on the mathematical analysis of the propagation of networks. Although these researches are important, with the developing of computer, how to simulate the propagation weighs more and more. Abstraction of ways to propagate is limited to virus model. There are two virus propagation models. One is about bio-virus model. Although these 2 respects have been developed very well and there are lots of different attributes within, the faults propagation varies a lot from these two. For example, other forms of network like SOA and supply chain vary a lot in ways to propagate. This paper focuses on another useful way to simulate the propagation of faults within scale-free directed networks. Based on the fundamental analysis of propagation and the different situations of simulating complexity and amount of information, this paper gives different methods to simulate the propagation of faults in the whole network. This paper invents an ingenious way with pseudo-nodes to deal with nodes of small in-degree. This methods balance the performance of the simulation with the complexity of the simulation. Then this paper simply analyzes an example with two different methods to test their validation. Of course, there are several questions remaining in this method, like how to give the probability of propagation based on different exclusiveness. These are shown at the end of this paper.

1 Introduction

Not far from today, random graph theory dominated the research of complex network [8]. After reconnection of a few edges in regular network, Watts and Strogatz found the small world model, in which The Clustering Coefficient is relatively high, at the same time, the average path length is short.

After the attributes of small world in real world, Barabasi and Albert did deep research in World Wide Web [10]. Barabasi and Albert surprisingly found that, the distribution of World Wide Web was not like what random graph theory had forecasted, Poisson distribution. Instead, it conform the power law distribution, A.K.A. $P(k) = C \cdot k^{-\gamma}$ (C and γ is a constant number). From there on, the complex network has been widely studied.

Attributes of the network, including the heterogeneity [1], the topology [2][3]and the communities[4][5] of the network have been fully researched. About the propagation dynamics, reference [6][7] based on the mathematical analysis of the propagation of networks have the attention of lots of peers. Although these researches are important, with the developing of computer, simulating the propagation becomes very important, too. Also, the notion of propagation of virus developed, including not only the bio-virus but the computer virus.

Apparently there are more than 1 methods of propagation of failure, fault and virus in network. Actually, according to the different attributes of the network and the mechanism of propagation with virus, the methods should vary. Reference [11][9]give some hypotheses about the propagation mechanism including that "if there are more than one neighbors, the virus and fault can only choose one of them to propagate with probability" and "an infected node can't propagate its neighbors simultaneously " These are something apparently can be adapted to other kinds of networks. Noting that the way of infection between bio-virus and computer virus is different. The infection of bio-virus depends on the contact and the moving of the population. However, the computer virus propagates through the network directly. The bio-virus can lead to the death of the host, nevertheless the computer network will not loss a node in the network because of computer virus. The hosts of bio-virus vary a little. The key nodes like the server in the computer network weigh more than the PCs in the network. After the infection, the antibody plays a very important role in the next phases. Although the computer network can also be repaired, the whole process is of passiveness instead of activeness.

DOI: 10.1051/itmconf/20160701008

Building on the knowledge of virus propagation and the differences between propagating ways of bio-virus and computer virus, the propagation of fault is something special that we are interested. There are some the fundamental attributes within the faults propagation. To simplify the model, there are 2 aspects we are concerning here. One is the network where the faults may propagate is static. The other is the calling frequency is relevant to the node itself.

With the developing of the computer, the propagation simulation of faults can be done by the computer based on the mechanism of propagation and different amount of information people already have. According to aforementioned two points, studying the mechanism and the method of propagation in detail is not only prospective but necessary. This paper analyzes the fundamental things about propagation of failure in scale-free directed network and contributes an ingenious way to simulate the propagation under different amount of information.

2 Fundamental Analysis of Faults Propagation

In [9]the hypothesis that the virus can only choose one of those to propagate with probability can be easily overridden here. Suppose that node C is upper software, A, B is called at the same time by C. Similarly, node D calls node A and B when D is running (as shown in Figure 1). If node A failed, and if C and D run at the same time, node C and D definitely will fail. A naturally idea is come up with, which is to separate this graph into 2 simpler ones ideologically (as shown in Figure 2 Figure 3).

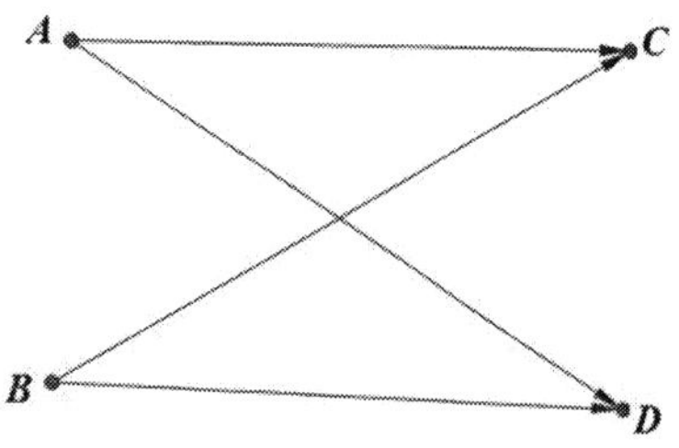

Figure 1.The Simlicity of Calling Structure

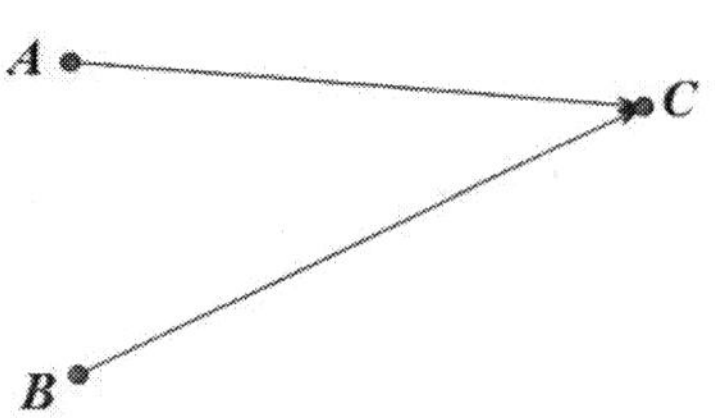

Figure 2.The Simlicity of Calling Structure (A)

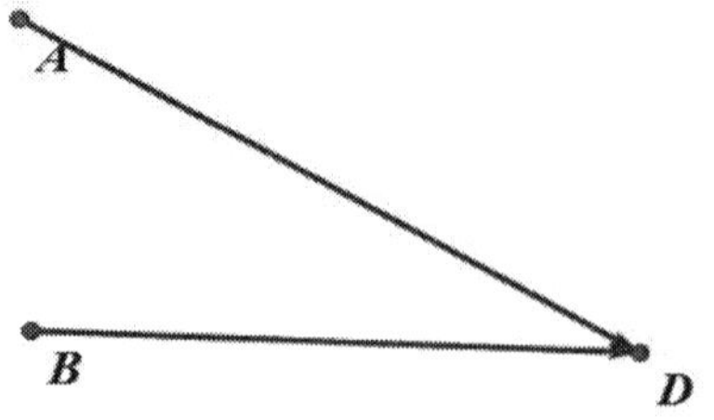

Figure 3.The Simlicity of Calling Structure (B)

Note that single propagation step can be separated and simplified with n front nodes $X_1, X_2 ... X_n$ and only one rear node O (As shown in Figure 4). The calling situation is that every member of subset of $\{X_1, X_2 ... X_n\}$ including empty set could be called at the same time. When all members in that subset are called at the same time, let's say the subset $\{X_{i_1} X_{i_2} ... X_{i_k}\}$ is called. The subset $\{X_{i_1} X_{i_2} ... X_{i_k}\}$ failed, when there is any member in that subset failed.

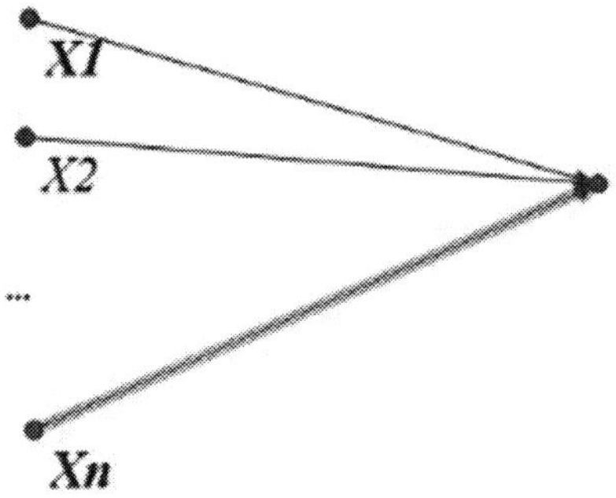

Figure 4.Details About Calling Structure

3 Different Amount of Information

The amount of information contributes to the complexity of the algorithm and simulation. As always, the more information you use, the more precise the answer is, the longer the time you spend. It is not usually necessary to use the whole information to get the precise situation ignoring the huge complexity and the time of simulation. This explains why we differentiate the methods when applying to different amount of information.

3.1. Full info situation

Full info means how often every subset is called has been known. In that way based on the frequency, the probability of every subset being called can be induced. Thus, suppose that $X_{i_1}, X_{i_2} \ldots X_{i_k}$ failed, by adding the probability of all subsets including $X_{i_1}, X_{i_2} \ldots X_{i_k}$, the probability of rear node O being failed is clear.

3.2 Little info situation

Albeit the situation of having full info is clear and easy to be accepted, the information usually won't be that much. Therefore, it is necessary to take a consideration of little information. Little information doesn't mean we know nothing but only the structure of the network. It means there are experts who can estimate the exclusiveness of the whole network. If the front nodes do not exclude others at all, it means for every calling, every front node has 50% chances to be called. If the nodes exclude others totally (It means there is only one front node can be called by the rear node O at a time), then the probability should be $\frac{1}{K}$ (K is the in-degree of rear node.) Building on exclusiveness from the experts, the probability should range from $\frac{1}{K}$ to 50%.

3.3 Situation with middle amount of info

Middle information situation is the most difficult one. The first problem is to what extent the amount of information you already have. Lots of situations should be considered. Only one special situation is going to be well developed.

The safety of scale-free network is different from evenly distributed network. Research has shown that scale-free network is robust to random attack and vulnerable to deliberate attack [12][13]. The phenomena aforementioned result from the existence of Hub nodes.

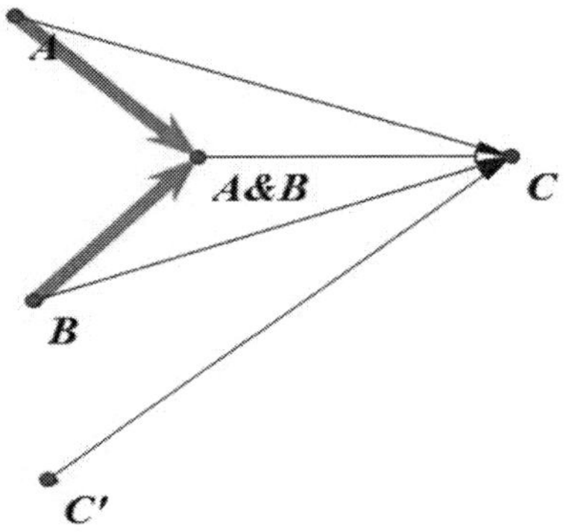

Figure 5. Pseudo-Nodes

A possible way to simulate the propagation situation is to add pseudo-nodes into the graph Figure 5. That node C calls node C' means node C calls itself. When node C calls A&B, it means node C calls A and B at the same time. In the graph, node C' and node A&B are called pseudo-nodes, but pseudo-nodes like A&B are alpha pseudo-nodes. Pseudo-nodes like C' are beta pseudo-nodes. When propagation starts, suppose node A is failed node, alpha pseudo-nodes get propagated firstly with a certain probability. Beta pseudo-nodes like C' act like normal nodes always have same state with their fathers.

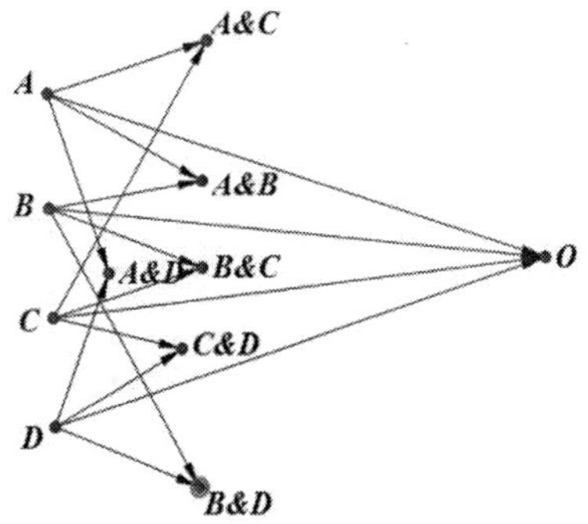

Figure 6. The Exploding Complexity With The Nodes

As can be seen in Figure 6, the more the front nodes are, the more complex the graph is. Apparently, this method can't be applied to all nodes in the graph. With the increasing of nodes, the complexity will go beyond our ability to handle. However, fortunately, in scale-free network what really matters is Hub nodes. When there are n front nodes to the Hub node and number n is big enough, the effect of a single front node will submerge to it of others. In addition, the complexity of pseudo-nodes method will increase with n dramatically. Therefore, using this method when n is big enough is not worthy Figure 6. It's better to apply this method only to Hub nodes with a few front nodes, while applying the low level information method to the rest nodes. By doing so, this method avoids big mistake with little increasing of complexity. Great balance between performance and complexity finally comes.

4 Examples and Analysis

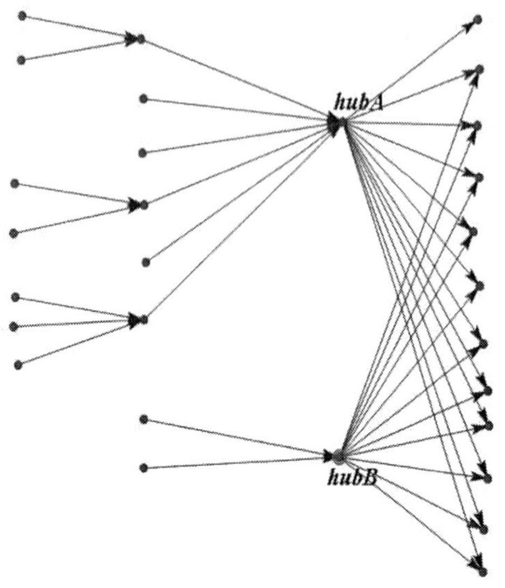

Figure 7.A Simple Example of Scale Free Network

We apply different methods to simulate and analyze faults propagation in Figure 7. The first method is computer virus propagation method. The computer virus propagates according to $\frac{1}{k}$ (k is the out degree of faulted node). The second method is the middle amount of info method mentioned in this paper. In detail, the propagation probability is given by these methods, and then the Monte Carlo simulation is used to test whether the methods are valid. Apparently, there are 2 hub nodes in the network, but the hubA is with too many front nodes. As a result, we only apply pseudo-nodes method to hub. On average, the $\frac{1}{k}$ propagating method has a probability of 23% to be exactly the same with the reality. However our method has a probability of 46 % to be exactly the same with the reality. The outcome is quite clear. The second method is much closer to the reality. The reason why this happened is the second method takes the calling frequency into consideration with the key nodes.

5 Questions Remaining

When there is little information to use, how to give the probability of propagation based on different exclusiveness is still unknown. The application of this method to free-scale network is meaningful. However, what is the complexity of this algorithm. Also, is it possible to apply this method to general network instead of Scale-free network? We are looking forward to the readers to give some clues of questions above.

Acknowledgement

Thanks to Feilong Wang, it is him who inspired me to do research about failure propagation in network. Also, during the cooperation with institute 716, we knew the application of propagation of failure in network. Without the application, we have no ways to know the flaws of the old model.

References

[1] Tan Yuejin, Wu jun. The entropy of network structure and its application in scale-free network. System engineering theory and application, 2004,24(6):1-3
[2] Faloutsos M, Faloutsos P, et al. On power-law relationships of the Internet topology.
[3] Chen Q, Chang H, et al. The origin of power-laws in internet topologies revisited. http://topology.eecs.umich.edu/data.html
[4] Newman M E J, Girvan M. Finding and evaluating community structure in networks. Phys. Rev.E, 2004, 69:026113
[5] Reichardt J, Bornholdt S. Detecting fuzzy community structures in complex networks with a Potts model. Phys. Rev. L, 2004,93(21):218701
[6] Pastor-Satorras R, Vespignani A. Epidemic dynamics and endemic states in complex networks. Phys. Rev. E, 2001, 63:066117
[7] Pastor-Satorras R, Vespignani A. Epidemic spreading in scale-free networks. Phys. Rev. Lett., 2001, 86: 3200-3203
[8] Albert R, Barabasi A L. statistical mechanics of complex networks. Reviews of modern physics 2002, 74(1): 47-97
[9] Wang Lin, Dai Guanzhong. The scale- free attributes in complex network, scale-free phenomena and its control. 2009 Science Press, 157
[10] [Barabasi A L, Albert R et al. Power-law distribution of the World Wide Web. Science, 2000, 287: 2115a]
[11] Chengxu, Wangyi, Zhu Huaihong. the probability model of computer network virus propagating. Microcomputer Developing, 14(12):204
[12] Albert R, Jeong H, et al. Eror and attack tolerance of complex networks. Nature, 2000,406:378-382
[13] Holme P, Kim B J, et al. Attack vulnerability of complex network. Phys. Rev. E, 2002, 65:056109/1-056109/5

DPDK-based Improvement of Packet Forwarding

Hao BI[1,a], Zhao-Hun WANG[2]
[1]*Postgraduate ,University of Science and Technology Beijing, Beijing P.R. ,China*
[2]*Professor,University of Science and Technology Beijing, Beijing P.R. ,China*
[a]Corresponding author: bihao@baidu.com

Abstract. Reel-time processing of packets occupies a significant position in the field of computer network security. With theexplosive growth of the backbone link rate,which is consistent with Gilder's law, many bottlenecks of server performance leave the real-time data stream unprocessed.Thus, we proposedto take use of DPDK(Data Plan Development Kit) framework to achieve an intelligent NIC packet forwarding system. During this research, we deeply analysis the forwarding process of packet in DPDK and improve its DMA mode.According to the results of experiment, the system greatly enhanced the performance of packet forwarding,and the throughput of forwarding 64-byet or random-length packets by 20Gbit NIC reaches13.3Gbps and 18.7Gbps(dual ports forwarding).

1 Introduction

High-speed network packet forwarding system plays a vital role in many fields, such as packet analysis, virus detection and traffic management. Universal NIC runs into a big bottleneck in many aspects, such as data buffering, packet copy and frequent interruptions which causes huge overhead. For the host, it causes excessive consumption of the computing, storage, I/O overhead which is too large to meet the requirements of line-speed data capture and handling on the Gigabit link.

In order to reduce the cost of data copies and complexity of kernel protocol stack process,Intel launched a data plane development kit (DPDK) of which the purpose is to provide programmers a simplee and complete fast packet processing framework[1].Useers can create prototypes or add their own protocol stack according to their requirements.DPDK achieves a zero-copy, large pages, lock-free buffer queue, DMA access mode, user-space drivers and other key technologies to enhance the packet processing capability. In the field of high-speed traffic processing, DPDK has a huge advantage: 1.High performance, the data provided by Intel shows that packet with random length forwarding can reach 10Gbit line-speed; 2.It supports almost all common Intel NIC; 3.For specific NIC, DPDK provides full support, users can take advantage of user-space drivers to build their own packet forwarding system, which greatly simplifies the development process [2].

In this paper, we analyze the key technologies of DPDK, and take advantage of DPDK framework to build a packet forwarding system. In the process of DMA transfer,DPDK needs to send descriptor separately, which wasted PCIe bandwidth, resulting in a performance bottleneck, therefore we propose a new method named Minimum Overhead DMA to solve this problem.

2 Key Technologies in DPDK

DPDK (Data Plane Development Kit) is an optimized data plane software solution developed by Intel for its multi-core processors. It includes high performance packet processing software formed by application processing, control processing, data plane processing, and signal processing tasks onto a single platform. It focuses on improving performance of packet processing.

2.1 Efficient Mmemory Mmanagement

In the DPDK initialization phase, it uses a large space to form a memory pool, which is an object allocator with fix size (storing packets entities require memory alignment to ensure that the object in memory allocated in different memory channels). In DPDK, the memory pool is identified by name, and uses a ring to manage free objects. In case of multiple consumers, you can use pipe-line mode to access the ring. To avoid competition, DPDK uses CAS (compare and swap) between multiple threads so that they can access the ring (lock-free queue) without using lock, which will greatly reducee the huge overhead of lock competition.

When large memory-intensive applications run on Linux platform of operating system, the usage of the default 4kb-size page will cause a lot of page faults and TLB misses, which greatly affect the performance of the application.DPDK uses huge page technology to solve this problem. The use of large pages can significantly reduce the frequency of TLB miss and page fault, reducing unnecessary consumption of memory access.

 DOI: 10.1051/itmconf/20160701009

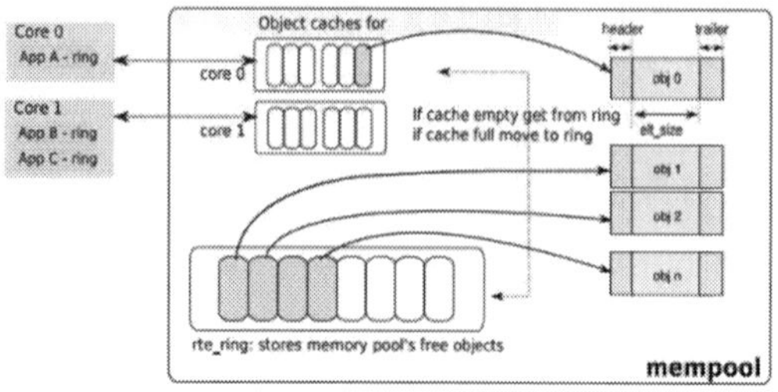

Figure 1. Efficient Memory Management

2.2 Implementation of Zero-copy

Through aanalysis of traditional packet capture mechanism, we can see how the data stream is flowing. When packets arrive, it will trigger an interrupt; packet is copied from the buffer in NIC to the kernel buffer queue, passes through the kernel then the packet copis from the kernel buffer to the user space, and finally processed the packet in user space. Date flow contains multiple copies of data, resulting in a significant reduction in performance. Since the two newly written data copy operations are inconsistent with localized features, it basically does not have cache hit; therefore the memory access efficiency is very low. Coupled with a large amount of data throughput, the overhead of copy is considerable. Depending on the packet length, a copy of one packet needs to consume about 259-8850 cpu cycles [2].

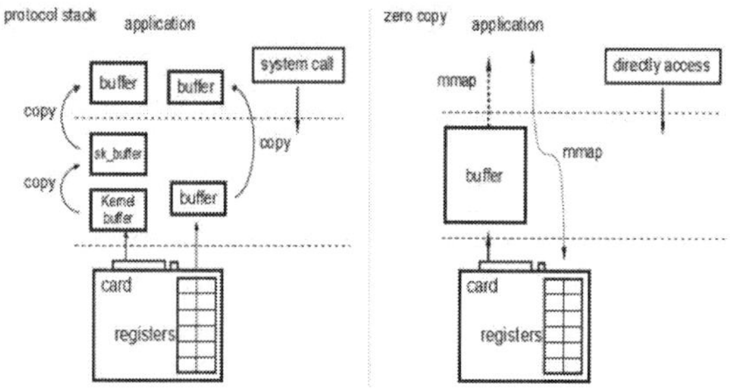

Figure 2. Comparison of Traditional Protocol Stack And Zero-Copy

Zero-copy maps kernel space to user space, the underlying driver transfer data directly to the user space through DMA, eliminating the copy from the kernel space to user space. Compared to the protocol stack process, zero-copy is an efficient and special communication technology; it avoids unnecessary data copying operation, and effectively improves the performance of packet processing.DPDK directly mapped buffer of packets in kernel space to user space, avoiding multiple copies of the data by using map.

Table1.CPU Writes Descriptor for Received Packet

	63 1	0
0	Packet Buffer Address[63:1]	AO
8	Packet Buffer Address[63:1]	DD

2.3 Pool-Mode driver in user space

Linux provides a kernel module named UIO, the user-space driver can be encoded using this module.DPDK uses module igb_uio to generate a file named uioX in the /dev directory, then the file is mapped to the user space by using map function. It will map the NIC register to user space,therefor users can directly access the NIC registers and that allows user-space driver .

Traditional packet capture requests constant switch between interrupt context and process contexts, In case of the arrival of high-speed packets, interrupt overhead will be enormous.DPDK disables the interrupt, using user-space polling mode driver (PMD), which allows the application access to NIC device without through Linux kernel, and it avoids abnormality of driver causing a risk of kernel crash, while greatly reduces the overhead of interruption [3, 4].

PMD is a direct interface upon DPDK specific NIC,different NICs achieve their own PMD which provides a unified interface to an upper layer application. Making specific card support DPDK, the main job is to write a corresponding PMD.

3 Aanalysis DMA Mode in DPDK

From the above description, DPDK manages the packet through by using rings. Each object in the ring is a packet descriptor which is associated with the packet buffer ,by reading the descriptor NIC can obtain the actual location of the packet in memory.PMD completes the interaction between the NIC and CPU by reading and writing the descriptor.

Take the Ixgbe 82599 as an example, we can analysis the process of receiving a packet in DPDK. It uses the ring buffer to manage the queue of packets received, and the ring buffer stores fixed length descriptors of incoming packet, rather than storing the actual packet. Descriptors of received packet are written by cpu into the circular queue.[5]When NIC receives the packets it will trigger a hardware interrupt, and make the CPU give up the control of the bus. Ixgbe NIC will receive descriptor of packet and place them into the FIFO buffer through the DMA read-engine. Then the NIC will sent the packet to the memory area where is specified by the descriptor through DMA write-engine, while updating content of the descriptor .Descriptor length is 16 bytes, using bit multiplexing. It has different meanings when the NIC read or write,it is used to indicate address of the packet or the value of the packet parsed via the NIC(Including identifier for the length of packet, which is used to determine whether release of the packet or not)[6].Take the descriptor for received packet as an example:

 DOI: 10.1051/itmconf/20160701009

Table 2.CPU Read Descriptor For Received Packet

	63 48	47 32	31	30 21	20 17	16 4	3 0
0	RSS Hash/Fragment Checksum		SPH	HDR_LEN	RSCCNT	Packet Type	RSS TYPE
8	VLAN Tag	PEK_LEN	Extended Error			Extended status	

DPDK uses descriptor controlling NIC to send and receive packets, a comparison made with using the entire buffer as a circular queue, which has both advantage and disadvantage [7].

Advantages: 1.Applications could maintain received packets until explicitly been freed. If the entire buffer is used as a circular queue, after reading the packet, the read pointer slides, the pointer to packet which application has stored before may have failed; 2.Buffer is shared by sending and receiving packet, therefore received packets can be sentt directly without copied.3.When CPU receives a packet it just needs to check descriptors instead of reading the NIC registers.

Disadvantage: While the NIC sendd or receive packets the descriptor must be written back to the ring, this increases DMA operation and causes excessive DMA overhead as well as a waste of PCIe bandwidth [8].

4 Implementation of Mminimum Over head DMA

Based on the above analysis, in the process of sending and receiving messages we need to write back to the descriptor, which resulted in excess DMA operation and caused unnecessary waste of bandwidth, so we proposed an alternative DMA approach, namely Minimum Overhead DMA [8, 9].

To reduce overhead, after receiving the or sending messages, we do not write back to the descriptor information.When NIC receives a packet, we put the additional information in front of the data packet and do not write the additional information back to the descriptor.When NIC send a packet, we do not write back any information to the host, and judge whether the corresponding data has been sent by the position of the pointer to descriptor.

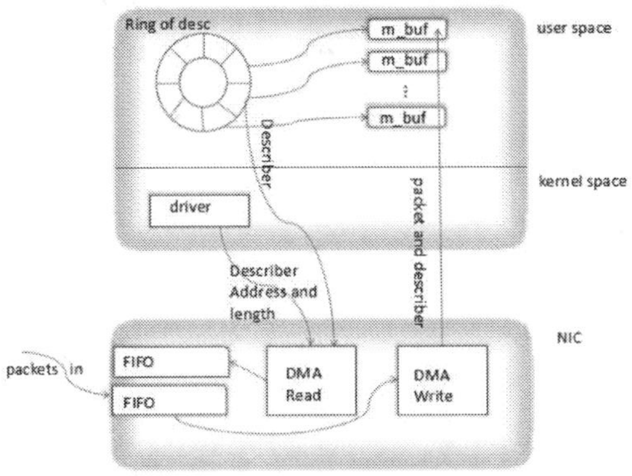

Figure 3. Process of Packets Uploading In Dpdk

Based on the analysis of PCIe bus protocol, we can get the PCIe bandwidth utilization before and after

Improvements. According to PCIe 2.0 specification, we can calculate two kinds of DMA modes PCIe theoretical bandwidth overhead. It need to be considered in the calculation include MAX_PAY_LOAD (single transfer maximum payload length, determined by the network card in consultation with the North-Bridge), as well as memory alignment strategy (transmission length is a multiple of cache line size), as well as TLP (transaction layer protocol of PCIe protocol) header overhead.

We assume that the MAX_PAY_LOAD is 256 bytes [10], using 64 byte alignment for transmission. In the process of a single descriptor DMA, descriptor 16 bytes plus the TLP header is less than 64, which needs to be aligned, thereforee the transmission length is 64 bytes in size. During receiving of packets before and after the improvements, it must firstly obtain descriptor, because this part uses the same mechanism so we do not contrast.We aanalyze the process of packet uploading, receiving 64 byte packets for example, each packet has to be encapsulated in the TLP, TLP header plus the 64-byte packet is less than 128 bytes but it needs to be filled to 128 bytes because of the alignment strategy, here for it costs 192 bytes to transmit one packet before improvement. After improvement, It costs 128 bytes to transmit one packet.Accordingly the bandwidth utilization improved by 33.3 percent. The following figure shows that along with the packet length increasing the bandwidth utilization rate after the improvement

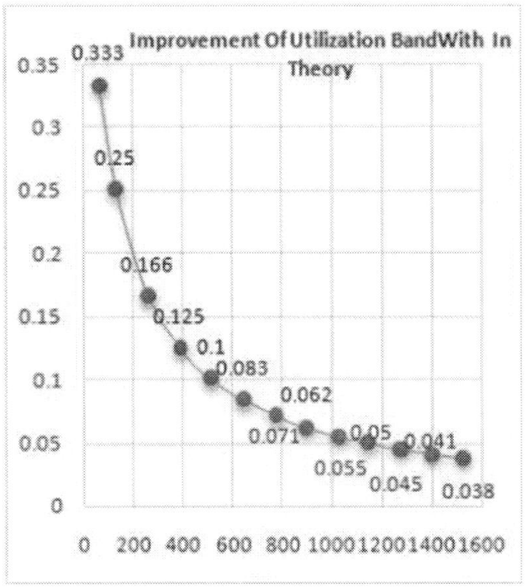

Figure 4. Improvement of The Bandwidth Utilization In Theory

4.1 Implementation of Packet Uuploading

1. When NIC receives data, it asks the host for descriptor;
2. Host transmit descriptors to NIC descriptor queue using DMA (bulk);
3. Packet and descriptor assembly into the corresponding format;
4. NIC transmits the data using DMA to the memory address (m_buf) where descriptor points to;
5. The CPU reads descriptor (head of the m_buf), and parse the head content;
6. According to the packet length which is parsed before, length> 0 means packet has transferred to memory, release corresponding descriptor;

4.2 Implementation of Packet Forwarding

1. When the host has data to sent, it puts the data in the corresponding position and puts descriptor in the ring buffer;
2. When PCIe module finds that a descriptor is valid, it asks the host for descriptor (bulk);
3. Host transmits descriptors to NIC descriptor queue using DMA;
4. The PCIe module requests data according to the information such as the address and size of memory described by the descriptor.
5. Host transmits the data to NIC,PCIe module cache the data to Fifo
6. NIC forwards packets through the port.

5. Evaluation

We tested and compared the packet forwarding performance of DPDK original DMA mode and Minimum Overhead DMA mode. It is based on a single Intel Xeon E5-2609 processor (8 logical cores) at 2.4 GHz, 64 GB of RAM. Operating system is Red Hat Enterprise 6.3, and kernel version is 2.6.32.we use a dedicated network tester (SPIRENT SPT-N11U) to transmit and receive packets. Network interface card is Intel 82599 (single-mode optical fibber; dual port Gigabit NIC).Each Ethernet port respectively accept 10Gbps, and forwards back to the network tester via the other port. The test results of the packet forwarding performance of before and after the improvement are shown in figure 5 and figure 6.

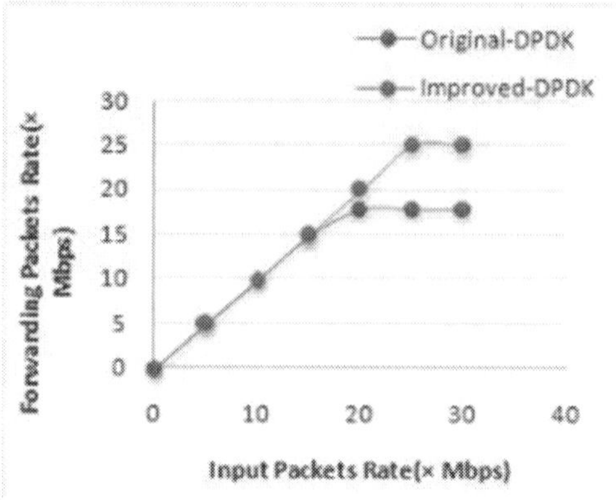

Figure 5. 64-Bytes Packets Forwarding

From figure 5we can see, the transfer system has a significant improvements. Especially in case of small packets of 64 bytes, the packet rate peaks at 13.3Gbps (25.3Mpps) after improvement, comparing with original DMA way it has been significantly improved.

We can learn that it also improves the performance of packet forwarding in the case of forwarding random length form figure6.The throughput increases with the length of packet, and it eventually stabledat 18.7Gbps.Conclusion confirms our previous analysis, packets of small bytes wasted a great deal of PCIe bandwidth before improvement, resulting in a performance bottleneck.

Testing shows that the improved DMA mode can effectively solve the waste of bandwidth because of packets transmitting separately with descriptors, and it enhanced performance of packet forwarding.

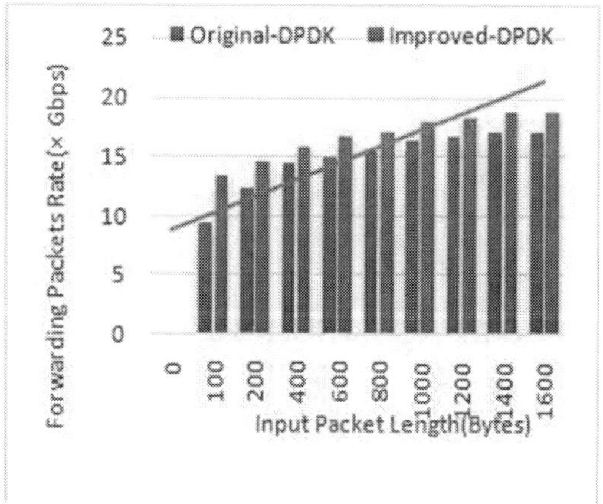

Figure 6. Random-Length Packets Forwarding

6. Conclusion

In the packet capture system, DPDK is being increasingly used. In this paper, we analyzed the DPDK bottlenecks in DMA mode, and proposed the Minimum Overhead DMA mode using descriptors and packets sending together to

DOI: 10.1051/itmconf/20160701009

improve the utilization of PCIe bandwidth. Experimental results show that MODMA can effectively solve the performance bottleneck of DPDK packet forwarding, make the system performance, especially in condition of the 64 byte packets improve significantly.

References

1. DPDKprogramer'sgiude .[Online]http://dpdk.org/doc /intel/dpdk-prog-giude-1.7.0.pdf
2. sample_app_ug-2.1.pdf.[Online].http://www.dpdk.or g/doc/pdf-guides/sample_app_ug-16.04.pdf(2014)
3. J.C Mogul and K.K.Ramakrishnan,Eliminating receive lovelock in an interrupt-driven kernel,USENIX Annual Technical Conference,99-112(1996).
4. .E.WANG,Q.ZHANG,B.SHEN,G.ZHANG,X.LU,Q. WU,and Y.Wang,Intel Math Kernel Library, High-Performance Computing on the Intel@Xeon Phi,pp.167-188(2014).
5. K. C. Claffy and T. Monk, What's next for Internet data analysis? Status and challenges facing the community, Proceedings of the IEEE,85, 10, (1997).
6. S.Yamagiwa,K.Aoki and K.Wada,Active Zero-copy: A performance study of non-deterministic messaging, Proceedings of the 4th International Symposium on Parallel and Distributed Computing ,325-332(2005).
7. TeleGeography Research,Overviews:Global bandwidth research products,TeleGeography Company Website(2012)
8. M. Necker, D. Contis, and D. Schimmel, TCP-stream reassembly and state tracking in hardware, IEEE Symposium on Field-Programmable Custom Computing Machines (FCCM), Napa, CA(2002).
9. K. C. Claffy and T. Monk, What's next for Internet data analysis? Status and challenges facing the community, Proceedings of the IEEE, 85, 10, (1997).
10. C Krueger, F Valeur, G Vigna, and R A Kemmerer, Stateful Intrusion Detection for High-Speed Networks, In Proceedings of the IEEE Symposium on Security and Privacy, 285-293(2002).

DOI: 10.1051/itmconf/20160701010

A New Method of Ambiguity Resolution for Triple-Frequency GPS PPP

Xiao-Feng LU[1,a], Sheng-Li ZHANG[1] and Ya-Chuan BAO[2]

[1]*State Key Laboratory of Integrated Service Networks, Xidian University, Xi'an China*
[2]*State Key Laboratory of Satellite Navigation System and Equiment Technology, Shijiazhuang, Hebei, 050081, China*

Abstract. At present, reliable ambiguity resolution in GPS precise point positioning (PPP) can be achieved through the traditional model called "EWL-WL-NL". In this paper, we proposed a new model of ambiguity resolution,"WL-WL-WL", where making use of linear independence of coefficient vector of wide-lane combination. Firstly, using the Melbourne-Wubbena combination observable on L2 and L5, we could resolve extra-wide-lane ambiguity instantaneously. Then, the resolved unambiguous extra-wide-lane carrier-phase assists wide-lane ambiguity resolution (AR). Three wide-lane combinations whose coefficient vectors are linearly independent are chosen to compose one full-rank matrix so that the three narrow-lane ambiguity resolution can be achieved. As a result, with the triple-frequency signals, the correctness rate of narrow-lane ambiguity resolution achieves 90% within 60s, in contrast to only 63% within 180s in dual-frequency PPP. Therefore, we demonstrate that triple-frequency PPP has the potential to achieve ambiguity-fixed solutions within a few minutes and the efficiency of ambiguity resolution in triple-frequency PPP is higher.

1 Introduction

To achieve an accuracy comparable to that of relative positioning, it is necessary to resolve integer-cycle carrier-phase ambiguities. This is straightforward in GPS relative positioning, which eliminates uncelebrated non-integer satellite and receiver carrier-phase hardware biases/delays (UPDs) through double differencing [1]. However, these biases will make it difficult to get integer ambiguities which make the integer ambiguity parameter loose integer property [2, 3]. One approach computing the FCBs for GPS PPP ambiguity resolution is to use undifferenced ambiguities estimate FCBs over a network of reference stations, and then the FCB estimates are provided for PPP clients to carry out ambiguity resolution at a single station [4-7].

Traditional Three-carrier ambiguity resolution (TCAR) and dual-carrier ambiguity resolution for PPP have been demonstrated that its positional accuracy will be improved substantially if its ambiguity is fixed [8-10]. However, at present, with dual-frequency global positioning system (GPS) measurements, the sufficiently precise narrow-lane ambiguity estimates can hardly be obtained using less than 15 min of measurements [11] because wide-lane ambiguity resolution requires around 20 min[8]. With the advent of triple-frequency signals, rapid re-convergences within 5 s to ambiguity-fixed solutions in real-time PPP are achieved at an over 95% success rate if we can precisely propagate ionospheric delay estimates [12].

During the last few years, it has been demonstrated that multi-frequency satellite signals from Global Navigation Satellite System (GNSS) will assist rapid TCAR/CIR (cascade integer resolution) in relative positioning [13]. While for multi-frequency PPP, there are only a limited number of studies. For example, Jianghui Geng formulates a series of ionosphere-free observables combination which are composed of both pseudorange and carrier-phase. With these combinations, it propose a new AR model, "extra-wide-lane, wide-lane, narrow-lane (EWL-WL-NL)",which achieve the decimeter-level positioning accuracy.

According to the studies above, we propose a new model of ambiguity resolution,"WL-WL-WL", where making use of linear independence of coefficient vector of wide-lane combination. This paper is organized as follows: firstly, introducing the method estimating FCBs; Secondly, formulating the combination observables; finally, showing the performance of triple-frequency PPP with ambiguity resolution.

2 Methodology

In this section, we briefly introduce the methods for GPS PPP to estimate FCBs, and then introduce the traditional model of ambiguity resolution and the new model, "WL-WL-WL", of ambiguity resolution proposed in this paper.

DOI: 10.1051/itmconf/20160701010

2.1 Estimation of Fractional-Cycle Biases

In this paper, we use the following equation to denote raw GPS measurements on frequency i(I = 1,2,5) from station r to satellite s. In this equation, some un-modeled errors are ignored such as multipath effects and some low influential factors are also ignored such as high-order ionospheric delay.

$$P_{ir}^{s} = \rho_{r}^{s} + \mu_{i} I_{1} + T + b_{ir} - b_{i}^{s} \tag{1}$$

$$L_{ir}^{s} = \rho_{r}^{s} - \mu_{i} I_{1} + T - \lambda_{i}\left(N_{ir}^{s} + B_{ir} - B_{i}^{s}\right) \tag{2}$$

where the subscripts r denotes the receiver; I = 1,2,5 denotes the L1, L2 and L5 frequencies, respectively. P_{ir}^{s} and L_{ir}^{s} are the un-differenced code and phase observation vector; ρ_{r}^{s} is the vector of geometric distances between satellites and a receiver; I_1 is the first-order ionospheric delay on frequency L_1 with $\mu_i = f_1^2 / f_i^2$; λ_i is the carrier phase wavelength; f is frequency; T is the Tropospheric Delays; N_{ir}^{s} is the integer ambiguity vector(cycle); b_{ir} is the receiver code biases and b_{i}^{s} is satellite code bias vector; B_{ir} is the receiver FCB and B_{i}^{s} is the satellite FCB vector;

In PPP, un-differenced float ambiguities can be formulated as the following equation.

$$B_{r}^{s} = N_{r}^{s} + \langle B_{r} \rangle - \langle B^{s} \rangle \tag{3}$$

where B_{r}^{s} is float un-differenced ambiguities; $\langle \cdot \rangle$ denotes the operation of estimating the fractional part; N_{r}^{s} is the integer ambiguity which contains the integer parts of receiver- and satellite-specific hardware biases.

According to Eq.(6) and Eq.(7) in [10], we can obtain the approximate extra-wide-lane FCBs and wide-lane FCBs for all receivers and satellites using a network of reference stations and then deliver the FCBs to PPP clients. Once PPP clients receive the extra-wide-lane and wide-lane FCBs, ambiguity resolution for triple-frequency PPP can be attempted.

2.2 Triple-Frequency PPP with Ambiguity Resolution

In the paper, we propose a new ambiguity resolution model called "WL-WL-WL", and the ambiguity resolution is divided into three steps.

Firstly, we can obtain extra-wide-lane ambiguity through traditional method of ambiguity resolution.

$$\begin{aligned} L_{ew,r}^{s} &= \frac{f_2 L_{2r}^{s} - f_5 L_{5r}^{s}}{f_2 - f_5} - \frac{f_2 P_{2r}^{s} + f_5 P_{5r}^{s}}{f_2 + f_5} \\ &= \lambda_{ew}\left(N_{ew,r}^{s} + \langle B_{ew,r} \rangle - \langle B_{ew}^{s} \rangle\right) \end{aligned} \tag{4}$$

where $L_{ew,r}^{s}$ is combination observable; λ_{ew} is extra-wide-lane wavelength; $N_{ew,r}^{s}$ is extra-wide-lane integer ambiguity; $B_{ew,r}$ and B_{ew}^{s} are the hardware biases within $L_{ew,r}^{s}$.

Secondly, with the assist of ambiguity-fixed extra-wide-lane carrier-phase observables, we can obtain wide-lane ambiguity. For wide-lane combination, three linearly independent vector are chosen as coefficient vector and they are (1,-1, 0), (1, 0,-1) and (-2, -4, 7), respectively. When the coefficient vector is (1,-1, 0), the wide-lane ambiguity can be obtained through traditional method.

$$\begin{cases} L_{mr}^{s} = \dfrac{f_1}{f_1 - f_2} L_{1r}^{s} - \dfrac{f_2}{f_1 - f_2} L_{2r}^{s} \\ L_{nr}^{s} = \dfrac{f_2}{f_2 - f_5} L_{2r}^{s} - \dfrac{f_5}{f_2 - f_5} L_{5r}^{s} - \lambda_{ew} N_{ew,r}^{s} \\ P_{3i}^{j} = \dfrac{f_1^2}{f_1^2 - f_2^2} P_{1r}^{s} - \dfrac{f_2^2}{f_1^2 - f_2^2} P_{2r}^{s} \\ L_{wr}^{s} = \dfrac{f_1}{f_1 - f_5} L_{mr}^{s} - \dfrac{f_5}{f_1 - f_5} L_{nr}^{s} \\ \quad = \rho_{r}^{s} + \lambda_{w} \dfrac{f_1}{f_1 - f_5}\left(N_{wr}^{s} + \langle B_{wr} \rangle - \langle B_{w}^{s} \rangle\right) \end{cases} \tag{5}$$

where L_{wr}^{s} is combination observable; λ_w is wide-lane wavelength; N_{wr}^{s} is extra-wide-lane integer ambiguity; B_{wr} and B_{w}^{s} are the hardware biases within L_{wr}^{s}.

When the coefficient vector is (1, 0,-1), the wide-lane ambiguity resolution can be carried out with the following equation, that is

$$P_{wr}^{s} = \frac{f_1^2}{f_1^2 - f_2^2} P_{1r}^{s} - \frac{f_2^2}{f_1^2 - f_2^2} P_{2r}^{s} \tag{6}$$

$$\begin{cases} L^s_{wa,r} = \dfrac{f_1}{f_1 - f_5} L^s_{1r} - \dfrac{f_5}{f_1 - f_5} L^s_{5r} \\ L^s_{wb,r} = \dfrac{f_2}{f_2 - f_5} L^s_{2r} - \dfrac{f_5}{f_2 - f_5} L^s_{5r} \\ L^s_{w1,r} = \dfrac{f_1}{f_1 - f_2} L^s_{wa,r} - \dfrac{f_2}{f_1 - f_2}\left(L^s_{wb,r} - \lambda_{ew} N^s_{ew,r}\right) \\ \quad = \rho^s_r + \lambda_{w1} \dfrac{f_1}{f_1 - f_2}\left(N^s_{w1,r} + \langle B_{w1,r}\rangle - \langle B^s_{w1}\rangle\right) \end{cases} \tag{7}$$

where

$$\lambda_{w1} = \frac{c}{f_1 - f_5}$$

$$\lambda_{ew} = \frac{c}{f_2 - f_5}$$

$$N^s_{w1,r} = N^s_{1r} - N^s_{5r} + \left[B_{w1,r}\right] + \left[B^s_{w1}\right]$$

$$N^s_{ew,r} = N^s_{2r} - N^s_{5r} + \left[B_{ew,r}\right] + \left[B^s_{ew}\right]$$

and P^s_{wr} is ionosphere-free pseudorange combination; $L^s_{w1,r}$ is wide-lane carrier phase measurements; $N^s_{w1,r}$ is the integer wide-lane ambiguity; $N^s_{ew,r}$ is the integer extra-wide-lane ambiguity; $B_{w1,r}$ and B^s_{w1} are the hardware biases within $L^s_{w1,r}$; $B_{ew,r}$ and B^s_{ew} are the hardware biases within extra-wide-lane combination observable; From the equation, we can easily find that the wide-lane wavelength is about 0.75m which is about 3.9 times to the wavelength on L1, which will facilitate rapid ambiguity resolution. Although its noise is amplified, the noise level is far less than its length, thereby showing that $N^s_{w1,r}$ can be rapidly, if not instantaneously, fixed to an integer.

When the coefficient vector is (-2,-4, 7), the wide-lane ambiguity resolution can be carried out with the following equation, that is

$$\begin{cases} L^s_{3r} = \dfrac{f_5^2}{f_1^2 - f_5^2} L^s_{5r} - \dfrac{f_1^2}{f_1^2 - f_5^2} L^s_{1r} \\ L^s_{w2,r} = L^s_{3r} - \dfrac{\lambda_1 f_1^2}{f_1^2 - f_5^2} N^s_{w1,r} - 2\lambda_{w1} N^s_{w1,r} - 4\lambda_{w1} N^s_{ew,r} \\ \quad = \rho^s_r - \lambda_{w1}\left(N^s_{w2r} + \langle B_{w2,r}\rangle - \langle B^s_{w2}\rangle\right) \end{cases} \tag{8}$$

where N^s_{w2r} is the integer wide-lane ambiguity; $B_{w2,r}$ and B^s_{w2} are the hardware biases within $L^s_{w2,r}$. In this equation, the wide-lane wavelength is about 1.72m, which is about 9 times to the wavelength on L1, which make it easily to fix ambiguity. The Eq.(6) is taken as pseudorange within the equation.

Thirdly, once wide-lane ambiguity resolution is completed, the fixed wide-lane ambiguity can be taken as known quantity to assist in narrow-lane ambiguity resolution. The equation of narrow-lane ambiguity resolution is as follows:

$$\begin{pmatrix} N_1 \\ N_2 \\ N_3 \end{pmatrix} = \begin{bmatrix} 1 & -1 & 0 \\ 1 & 0 & -1 \\ -2 & -4 & 7 \end{bmatrix}^{-1} \begin{pmatrix} N_{(1,-1,0)} \\ N_{(1,0,-1)} \\ N_{(-2,-4,7)} \end{pmatrix} \tag{9}$$

3 Results and Discussion

In this paper, the processing data resulting from IGS were used to estimate FCBs and fix ambiguity. Each epoch is 30s. There are five stations selected totally and they are 'jfng', 'wuh2', 'gmsd', 'mizu' and 'unb3', respectively. The station 'jfng' was selected as the reference station, and 'unb3' was selected as the PPP client. This paper presents the correctness rate of triple-frequency PPP ambiguity resolution proposed in this paper and comparing the performance of the method proposed in this paper with performance of dual-frequency PPP ambiguity resolution proposed in [12].

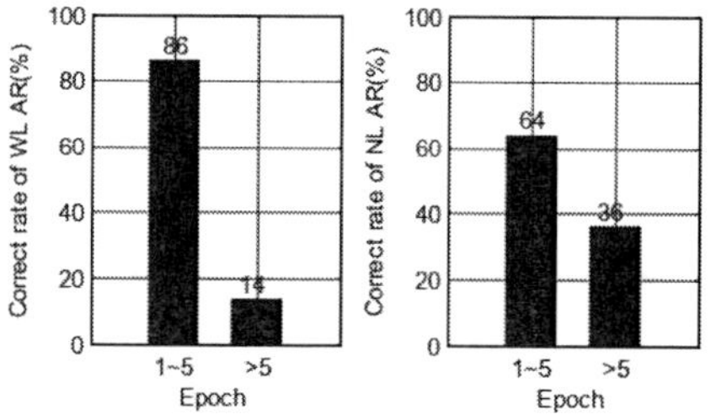

Fig. 1 Correct Rate of Wide-Lane(Wl) And Narrow-Lane(Nl) Ambiguity Resolution(Ar) In Dual-Freqnency Ppp.

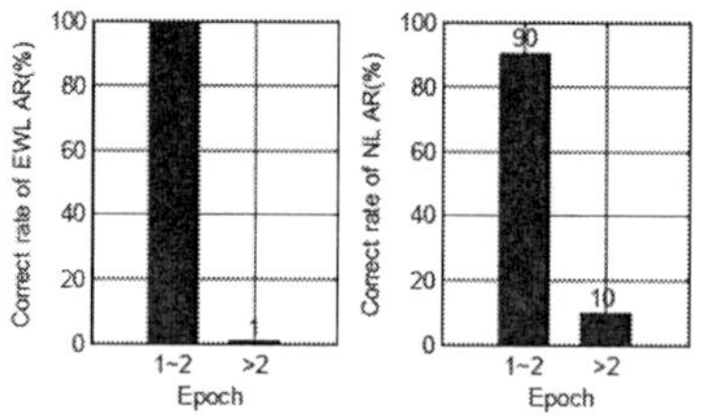

DOI: 10.1051/itmconf/20160701010

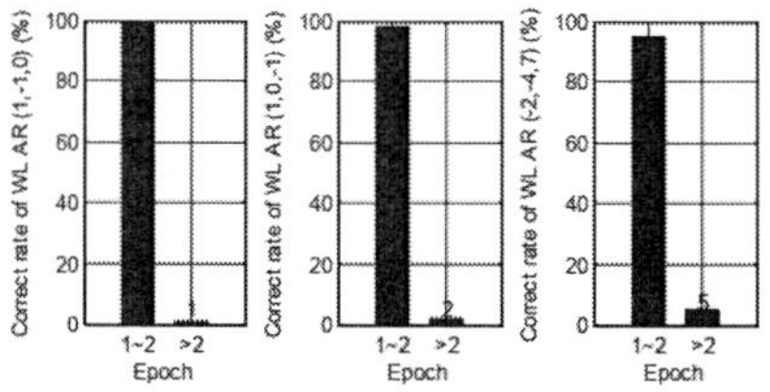

Fig.2 Correct Rate of Extra-Wide-Lane(Ewl), Three Wide-Lane(Wl) And Narrow-Lane(Nl) Ambiguity Resolution (Ar) In Triple-Frequency Ppp And Nl Frequency Is L1.

Figure 1 shows the correctness rate of dual-frequency PPP ambiguity resolution proposed in [12]. Figure 2 shows the correctness rate of triple-frequency PPP ambiguity resolution proposed in this paper including the extra-wide-lane, wide-lane and narrow-lane ambiguity. And for narrow-lane-ambiguity, we show the result on L1. According to figure 1, the correctness rates of narrow-lane ambiguity resolution of dual-frequency PPP can only reach 64% over 150-second observation periods. However, a 90% correctness rate can be achieved in triple-frequency PPP within 60s. It's obviously that the method proposed by this paper is superior to dual-frequency ambiguity resolution.

Compared with traditional ambiguity resolution, the method in this paper has two superiority. First, in the traditional method, it's necessary to estimate EWL, WL, NL FCBs. According to [2], we can find that NL FCBs are not stable and it has to be estimated every 15min at least, which need heavy computational effort at reference network and increasing network burden. However, it's unnecessary to estimate NL FCBs. Therefore, we can conclude that the ambiguity resolution proposed by this paper outperform the traditional triple-frequency ambiguity resolution within certain limits.

4 Conclusions

In this paper, we proposed a new method for triple-frequency GPS PPP in order to achieve rapid ambiguity resolution with a single receiver in real time. The key section of this method is to fix three linearly independent wide-lane combinations ambiguity with the assist of the ambiguity-fixed extra-wide-lane carrier-phase on L2 and L5. According to analysis, the correctness rate of narrow-lane ambiguity resolution in triple-frequency PPP can reach 90% within 60s, in contrast to 150s for 64% correctness rate in dual-frequency PPP. According to analysis, we can obtain two effective conclusions:(1) With the data of triple-frequency signal, the convergence rate of ambiguity solution accelerating obviously; (2) With appropriate extra-wide-lane and wide-lane combination, correctness rate of fixing narrow-lane ambiguity with triple-frequency signals is higher that with dual-frequency signals.

Finally, we can conclude that the ambiguity resolution efficiency in triple-frequency PPP is much higher than that in dual-frequency PPP. However, the wide-lane combinations in this paper may not be the optimal, which need to be researched deeply in future work.

Acknowledgement

This work was supported by National Natural Science Foundation of China (Grant No. 61371127, 61471361, 61401330, 61572389), EU FP7 Project CROWN (PIRSES-GA-2013-610524), National High-tech R&D Program of China (863 Program) (Grant No. 2015AA01A705), and 111 Project in Xidian University of China (Grant No.B08038).

References

1. Yanming Feng, Chris Rizos. GPS Solut 13 43-56 (2009)
2. Jianghui Geng, Chuang Shi, Maorong Ge, Alan H.Dodson, Yidong Lou, Qile Zhao, Jiangnan Liu. J Geod 86 579-589 (2012)
3. Jianghui Geng, Xiaolin Meng, Alan H. Dodson, Felix N. Teferle. J Geod 84 569-581 (2010)
4. Xingxing Li, Maorong Ge, Hongping Zhang,Jens Wichert. J Geod 87 405-416 (2013)
5. Shengfeng Gu, Yidong Lou, Chuang Shi, Jingnan Liu. J Geod 89 979-992 (2015)
6. Pan li, Xiaohong Zhang, Xiaodong Ren, Xiang Zuo, Yuming Pan. GPS Solut 2015
7. Jianghui Geng, Yehuda Rock. J Geod 90 379-396 (2016)
8. Jianghui Geng, F. N. Teferle, C. Shi, X. Meng, A. H. Dodson, J. Liu. GPS Solut 13 263-270 (2009)
9. M. Ge, G. Gendt, M. Rothacher, C. Shi, J. Liu. J Geod 82 389-399 (2008)
10. Yihe Li, Yang Gao, Junbo Shi. J Geod 90 437-450 (2016)
11. J. Geng, F.N. Teferle, X. Meng, A.H. Dodson. Adv. Space. Res 47 1664-1673 (2011)
12. Jianghui Geng, Yehuda Rock. J Geod 87 449-460 (2013)
13. Qile Zhao, Zhiqiang Dai, Zhigang Hu, Binzi Sun, Chuang Shi, Jiangnan Liu. GPS Solut 19 589-599 (2015)
14. Simon Banville. J Geod 90 487-496 (2016)

Vulnerability of Complex Networks under Approximate Longest Chain Attack Strategies

Yao-Hui HAO[1,2,a], Jia-Liang SONG[1], Yi LIN[1], Ji-Hong HAN[1]

[1]*ZhengZhou Institute of Information Science and technology, Zhengzhou 450001, China*
[2]*State Key Laboratory of Mathematical Engineering and Advanced Computing, Zhengzhou 450001, China*

Abstract. We proposed three approximate longest chain-attack strategies and studied the vulnerability of complex networks under these intentional attack strategies. Experimental results indicate that when random network and small-world network are under any one of the three chain-attacks, the larger the $<k>$ is, the smaller the iterative step T is. However, scale-free network shows different characteristics: the larger the $<k>$ is, the larger the T is. These findings supplement and extend the previous attack results on nodes and edges, and can thus help us better explain the vulnerability of different complex networks.

1 Introduction

Network vulnerability is one of the most important issues of complex networked systems. In recent decades, many researchers proposed many attack strategies and analyzed vulnerability of various complex network models and real world networks[1-4], ranging from biology to Internet [5,6], power to transportation[7-9].

However, when analyzing the vulnerability of the network structure, researchers generally adopted the attack strategy of randomly or intentionally removing a certain percentage of the network nodes or edges, according to selected centrality measurement indicators [13-15] (such as: initial or re-calculated degree and betweenness[10-12]). In addition, it is unnecessary for these removed nodes and edges to be adjacent. But, by analyzing kill chain attack mode [16,17], we find that nowadays attacks often follow two steps: to intrude nodes and to destroy nodes. In the first step, the attackers will invade a network node by implanting the virus program into it, but they won't immediately destroy the node after that. Instead, the attackers continue to invade one adjacent uninvaded node until the largest number of invaded nodes is met. Then, the attackers begin to enter the second phase, namely to destroy the nodes. Once it gets started, all nodes that are implanted with virus would be destroyed at the same time. That is to say, when attackers destroy nodes in the network, the destroyed nodes also present a chain structure way, instead of a discrete distribution way. This is distinctly different from the previous attack strategies.

As such, we proposed three types of approximate longest chain-attacks according to different node selection strategies, and investigated vulnerability of complex networks including three model networks: random network, scale-free network, small-world network and two real world networks. In this paper, the efficiency of chain-attacks is determined by the largest connected subgraph and the number of iterative steps. Note that, all the experiments and algorithms in this paper are based on the assumption that the networks are undirected and there is only one edge between two nodes.

2 Model of Chain Attack Strategies

2.1 Chain Structure of Invasion

The more nodes are invaded, the more nodes could be destroyed at a time. Thus, each invasion should better achieve the maximum length of the chain. According to the research results of network centrality, the nodes with max degree or max betweenness play an important role in network connectivity[18-20]. So, we propose three approximate longest chain-attack strategies based on these two centrality measures, which are suitable for large-scale attack implementation. The descriptions are as follows:

(1)RLC(random longest chain augmenting approach): First, RLC randomly selects a node in the network as the initial node. Second, RLC randomly chooses a neighboring node of the initial node as the second node of the chain, and then chooses a neighboring node of the second node as the

[a] Corresponding author: hao_yaohui@126.com

 DOI: 10.1051/itmconf/20160701011

third node of the chain, and so on [21]. No node should be invaded twice in the chain augmenting process and it continues until no appropriate node could be found.

(2)BLC(longest chain augmenting approach of max betweeness): First, BLC selects the max betweeness node in the network as the initial node, and then chooses the max betweeness node in initial node's neighboring nodes as the second node of the chain, and so on. No node should be invaded twice in the chain augmenting process and it continues until no appropriate node could be found. (If there is more than one max betweeness node, we randomly select a node from them.)

(3)DLC(longest chain augmenting approach of max degree): DLC adopts a similar method as (2), but the difference is DLC selects the nodes with the max degree.

In this paper, Degree of a node i is defined by

$$k_i = \sum_{j=1}^{N} a_{ij} = \sum_{j=1}^{N} a_{ji} ,$$

where aij is the element of the adjacency matrix A in the given network G, A=(aij)N×N.

Analogously, Betweenness of a node i is defined as the sum of proportions of the number of shortest paths between all pairs of destination nodes that go though node i:

$$B_i = \sum_{s \neq i \neq t} \frac{n_{st}^i}{g_{st}} ,$$

where gst is the total number of the shortest paths from node s to node t, and n_{st}^i is the number of those that pass through the node i. In a network, Betweenness counts the number of geodesic paths that pass through a node.

An example is given to explain the intrusion process of these three chains, as shown in figure 1.

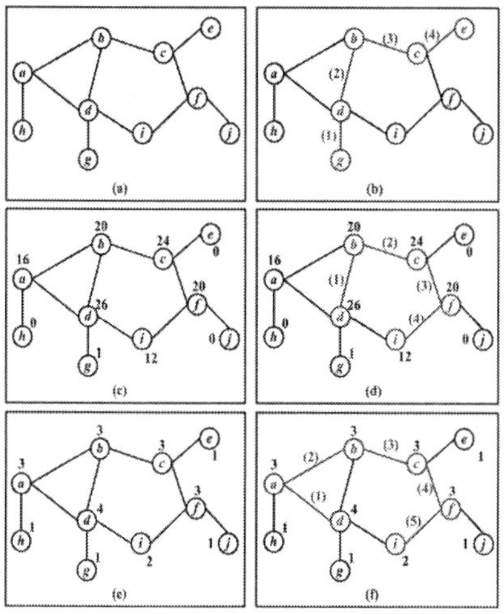

Fig.1. An Example for Intrusion Chain Structure

(a) Network topology; (b) Choose chain{g,d,b,c,e} by following RLC strategy; (c) Betweenness of each node in the network; (d) Choose chain{d,b,c,e,f,i} by following BLC strategy; (e) Degree of each node in the network; (f) Choose chain{d,a,b,c,e,f,i} by following DLC strategy (After the max degree node d is selected, the degrees of a and b are equal and we randomly select a or b node as the second node of the chain.)

2.2 Implement and Measure of Chain Attack

After successful invasion of the nodes, the attackers will implement nodes destruction. Provided that the invaded nodes are completely controlled by the attackers, it is clear that the attackers can easily destroy all the invaded chain nodes. In this paper, we show a node is destroyed by removing it. Obviously, each time the nodes removed is a chain. Furthermore, all edges incident with these removed nodes are also removed.

We use the number of nodes in the largest connected subgraph(S) to measure the vulnerability of different networks [11]. Here, N is the number of nodes in initial network, N' is the number of nodes in the largest connected subgraph after the attack, i.e. S = N'. To compare the initial networks with different number of nodes, we can execute a data reduction on the network size. The formula is as follows.

$$S' = \frac{S}{N} = \frac{N'}{N}$$

The size of S in a network reflects the communication capability of a network. This means that when the network is attacked, the larger the largest connected subgraph, the more robust the network. If S' ≈1, it means that the network is highly connected.

In this paper, the chain-attacks are implemented iteratively, i.e., each time the nodes of a chain are removed until all the nodes in the network are disconnected. The number of iterative steps (T) reflects the tolerance of a network [21]. The initial value of T is zero, and it increases by one each time with a chain-attack. The greater T is, the more iteration there is, and the more robust the network is. The specific implementation processes of the chain-attacks are shown in Fig. 2.

 DOI: 10.1051/itmconf/20160701011

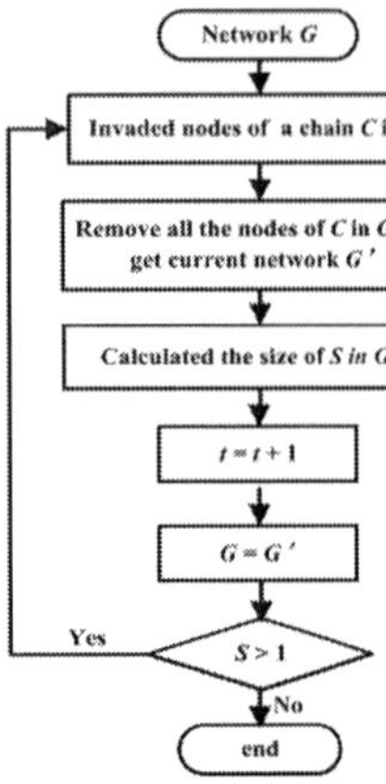

Fig. 2. The Flow Diagram of Chain Attacks

Each iteration indicates implementing a chain-attack, which includes two operations, invading nodes and removing nodes. When the size of the largest connected subgraph in the current network G is 1, which means all the nodes in G are isolated, the iteration will then be terminated.

3. Simulation and Analysis

In this part, we show the experimental results of three model networks under chain-attacks, including random network,scale-free network, small-world network.

Firstly, we study the change of the largest connected subgraph S for random, scale-free and small-world model networks, under three different chain-attacks. The change curves of S are shown in Figure 3.

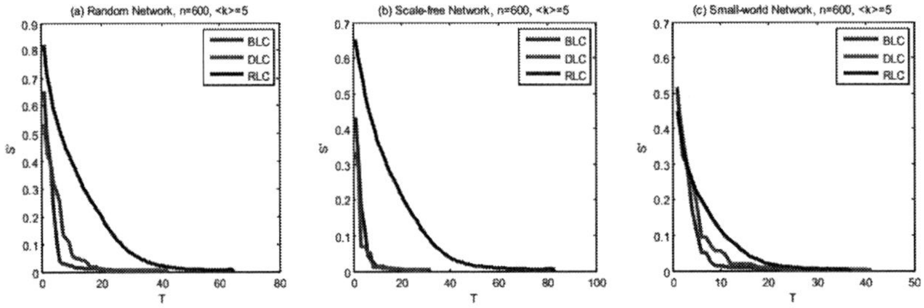

Fig. 3. The Variation of *s'* Under Three Chain-Attack Trategies.

(a) S' vs. T in Random Network; (b) S' vs. T in Scale-Free Network; (c) S' vs. T in Small-World Network

As shown in Fig.3(a)(b), in the whole iterative implementation of the chain-attacks for random and scale-free model networks, for a given t, S(t)RLC is larger than S(t)BLC and S(t)DLC. This indicates that the curve of S(t)RLC decreases significantly slower than S(t)BLC and S(t)DLC, namely, DLC and BLC chain-attack strategies are more destructive than RLC chain-attack strategy for three model networks.

Moreover, for random network, we can see two crosses (t=3, t=20) between DLC and BLC chain-attack strategies in Fig.3(a). When t≤3, BLC has similar destructive effect to DLC; while when 3 ≤ t ≤ 20, BLC can perform more destructive effect than DLC; as t≥20, BLC has the similar destructive effect to DLC again. And the max iterative steps are ranked as follows:

MAX(T)RLC>MAX(T)DLC>MAX(T)BLC.

As for scale-free network in Fig.3(b), the change curves of S are almost the same for BLC and DLC. Though, DLC has a more destructive effect at the beginning.

For small-world network (Fig.3(c)), there are two crosses (t=3, t=25) in three curves. While t≤3, the three chain-attack strategies have the similar destructive effect on the small-world network. However, when 3≤t≤25, BLC has the greatest destructive effect in these chain-attack strategies. In the latter fraction of the attacks, while t≥25, the changes of three curves are similar again, and the max iterative steps are ranked as follows: MAX(T)DLC > MAX(T)BLC > MAX(T)RLC. So, the efficiency of the chain-attack strategies is BLC>DLC>RLC for these three mode networks.

Secondly, we compare changes of the largest connected subgraphs S' of random, scale-free and small-world model networks under three chain-attacks, as shown in fig.4.

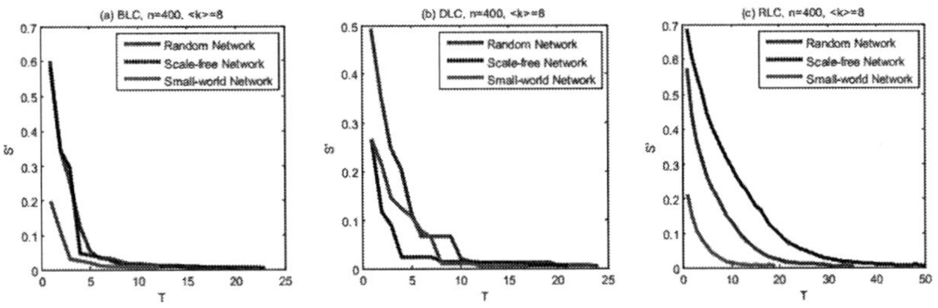

Fig. 4. S' vs. T (a) BLC; (b) DLC; (c) RLC

From Fig.4(a), we can see that the curves of random and scale-free networks are very similar under the BLC attack strategy, and for a given t, the S(t) of small-world is the lowest. The max iterative step of three model networks has the following relationship: MAX(T)SF > MAX(T)RN > MAX(T)SW, namely small-world network is most vulnerable under BLC chain-attack.

In Fig.4(b), under the DLC attack, the curve of Scale-free network has the fastest decline rate in the first fraction of three curves($t \leq 8$); while $t > 8$, for a given t, S has the following relationship: S(t)RN > S(t)SF > S(t)SW, and the max iterative step has the following relationship: MAX(T)RN > MAX(T)SF > MAX(T)SW. It means that scale-free network is the most vulnerable and random network is the most robust in the first fraction of DLC chain-attack. But, in the latter part, small-world network becomes the most vulnerable and random network is still the most robust. The vulnerability of scale-free network is between random and small-world network.

Fig.4 (c) shows that under the RLC attack, when the value of T is a given t, S(t)SF > S(t)RN > S(t)SW, and the max iterative step has the following relationship: MAX(T)SF > MAX(T)RN > MAX(T)SW. It shows that scale-free network has the best robustness, while small-world network has the weakest robustness, and the robustness of random network is in the middle.

And in Fig.4(a)(b)(c), for Random, scale-free and small-world model networks under three chain-attacks, all curves decrease rapidly in the first fraction and slowly in the latter part.

Lastly, we analyze change of the largest connected subgraph S of three modes networks, under these three chain-attacks with different network density. The analysis results are shown in fig.5.

Under the BLC, DLC and RLC chain-attacks, random network (Fig.5(a)(b)(c)) shows that the larger <k> is, the smaller MAX (T) is. In general, the larger <k> is, the faster S' declines. It indicates that the robustness of random network grows in inverse proportion to <k> under these three chain-attacks. scale-free network (Fig.5(d)(e)(f)) shows that the larger <k> is, the larger MAX (T) is. It means that the robustness of scale-free network is in proportion to <k> under chain-attacks. small-world network (Fig.5(g)(h)(i)) has shown a similar performance to the random network, that is, there is an inverse proportion between the robustness of small-world network and the size of <k> under chain-attacks.

In addition, we calculate the average distance of random, scale-free and small-world networks under different densities <k>. As can be seen from Table 1, for random network and small-world network, the greater the <k> is, the smaller the average distance is, but for the scale-free network, the opposite is the case. We also analyze the number of removed nodes at each iterative step of the chain-attacks, as shown in Fig. 6.

 DOI: 10.1051/itmconf/20160701011

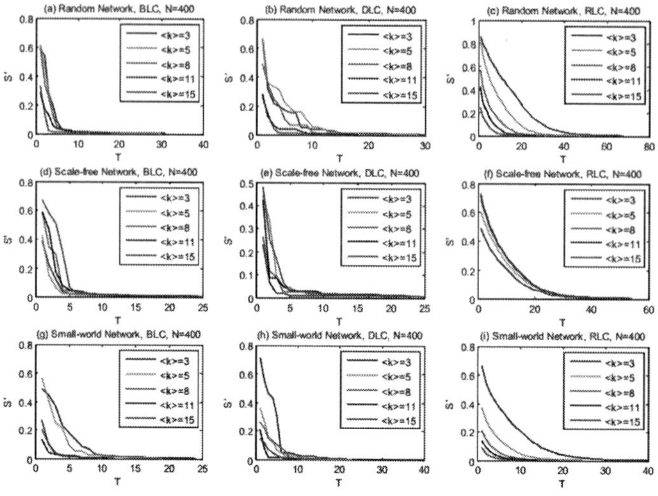

Fig.5. *S'* vs. *T*, *N*=400

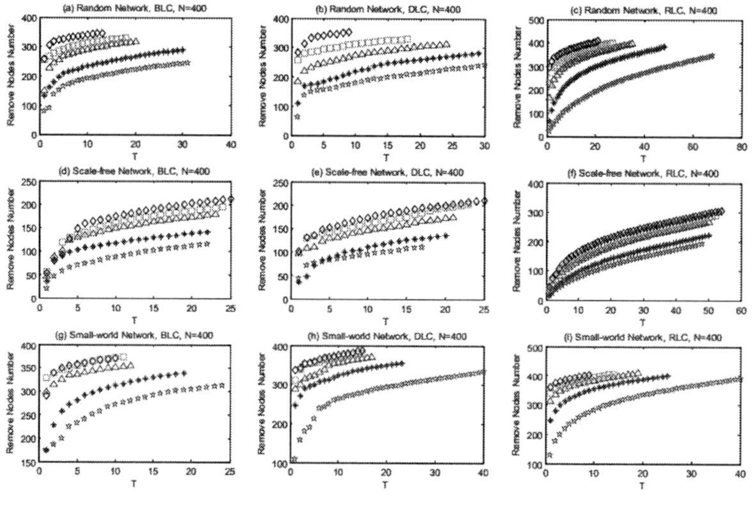

Fig. 6. *S'* vs. *T*, <*k*>=5; ☆<*k*>=3, *<*k*>=5, Δ<*k*>=8, □<*k*>=11, ◊ <*k*>=3

As can be seen from Fig. 6, for three model networks at the same iterative step t, the number of nodes removed increases accordingly as <k> increases. Combining the average distance of model networks under different <k> (Table 1), we can ascertain that the chain-attack is more efficient as the increasing <k> reduces the average distance among nodes in the random network and small-world network. So for the random network and small-world network under the chain-attacks, the larger the <k> is, the smaller the MAX(T) is.

Table 1. The Average Distance of Networks

	random	scale-free	small-world
<*k*>=3	4.6539	1.2662	3.6371

 DOI: 10.1051/itmconf/20160701011

<*k*>=5	3.9037	1.5523	2.9277
<*k*>=8	3.1518	2.1086	2.5215
<*k*>=11	2.7787	2.3257	2.2879
<k>=15	2.5149	2.4682	2.0719

4 Conclusions

In this study, we research on the vulnerability of complex network against new-type intentional attack strategies close to the real attack behavior. In sum, we analyze the vulnerability of some complex networks by iteratively implementing three different chain-attacks, RLC, BLC and DLC. We obtain that when random network and small-world network are under any one of the three chain-attacks, the larger the <*k*> is, the smaller the T is. However, scale-free network shows different characteristics: the larger the <*k*> is, the larger the T is. These findings supplement and extend the previous attack results and can thus help us to provide some insights into the design of more robust networks.

References

[1] M. Bellingeri, D. Cassi, S. Vincenzi, Phys. A 414, 174 (2014).
[2] A. Yehezkel, R. Cohen, PHYS. R. E 86 (2012).
[3] H. P. Ren, J. Song, R. Yang, M. S. Baptista, C. Grebogi, Phys. A 442, 239 (2016).
[4] B. P. Duan, J. Liu, M.X. Zhou, L. L. Ma, Phys. A 448, 144 (2016).
[5] R. Albert, H. Jeong, A. L. Barabasi, Nature 401, 307 (1999).
[6] S. N. Dorogovtsev, J. F. Mendes, *Evolution of Networks: From Biological Nets to the Internet and WWW* (Oxford University Press, 2013).
[7] R. Albert, I. Albert, G. L. Nakarado, Phys. Rev. E 69 (2004).
[8] M. Ouyang, L. J. Zhao, Z. Z. Pan, L. Hong, Phys. A 403, 45 (2014).
[9] H. Demirel, M. Kompil, F. Nemry, Trans. R. P. A 81, 62 (2015).
[10] R. Albert, H. Jeong, A. L. Barabasi, Nature 406, 387 (2000).
[11] P. Holme, B. J. Kim, C. N. Yoon, S. K. Han, Phys. Rev. E 65 (2002).
[12] T. Y. Nie, Z. Guo, K. Zhao, Z.M. Lu, Phys. A 424, 248 (2015).
[13] J. H. Zhang, L. Hong, S. L. Wang, IEEE International Conference on Service Operations, (2011).
[14] M. E. J. Newman, S. H. Strogatz, D. J. Watts, Phys. Rev. E. 64 (2001).
[15] W. J. Xiao, L. X. Lin, G. R. Chen, Phys. A 437, 437 (2015).
[16] A. K. Sood, R. J. Enbody, Proceedings of IEEE Security and Privacy Magazine 11, 54 (2013).
[17] F. Baiardi, F. Tonelli, A. D. R. D. Biase, 24th Euromicro International Conference on Parallel, Distributed, and Network-Based Processing (2016).
[18] J. W. Wang, L. L. Rong, Safety Science 47, 1331 (2009).
[19] J. Ugander, B. Karrer, L. Backstrom, C. Marlow, arXiv (2011).
[20] J. Hendler, N. Shadbolt, W. Hall, T. B. Lee, D. Weitzner, Communications of the ACM 51, 60 (2008).
[21] C. L. Pu, W. Cui, Phys. A 419, 622 (2015).

A Method for Detecting the Real Location of Agency Website Based On Search Engine

Xiao-Hui CHOU[a], Liang GAN[b], Ai-Ping LI, Zhong-He HE[c], Feng-Yu YANG

Department of Computer, National University of Defense Technology, Changsha
[a]cxh_nudt@126.com, [b]gl.nudt@gmail.com, [c]riterhe@outlook.com

Abstract. This paper provides a method to detect the real location of agency website based on search engine. We will analyze and process the target agency website to obtain the server routing information, extract critical feature information from web content, combine with search engine to acquire web data, and calculate word frequency. Through named entity recognition, web text matching calculation and syntactic analysis, we can infer real location of the target agency website in the real world. The experimental results show that our approach is reliable, correct and effective.

1 Introduction

The information of a large number of agency websites in the network is not complete, people can not directly know the real location of these agencies through the website information. Some reasons may lead to this phenomenon. Some agencies may hide the location information on their website deliberately for the purpose of illegal operation, or carelessly left this information during building their website. Thus, it's difficult to accurately judge the real location of the agency. Moreover, many institutions website with duplicate website names and same geographical name, such as *Phoenix Town*, there are 16 Phoenix towns with the same name in China, which are distributed in different provinces. So people can not identify the website refers to which town government agencies if only through the website title such as *The People's Government of Phoenix Town*. Location information is an important information for a website. The lack of the information brings great difficulties for the Internet management department to supervise network, and users can not determine the safety and authenticity of the website. If we can find out the real location of these agency websites in the real world, it will help users make risk assessments [1] and help network supervision departments rectify the network, gather intelligence, investigate agencies and do other routine inspections.

2 Related work

At present, the main method is to search the location of agency website through the Yellow Pages information service platform which is an artificial information collection platform. But many network information manually collected is missing or incomplete. Manual collection and collation of web information not only requires labor cost, but also consumes longer time. Real-time maintenance updating also be an problem. Besides, users need to pay a certain amount of service costs[2]. The other method is to get IP address by domain name resolution, and search the server address corresponding to the IP to obtain the location information. But the method of obtaining the geographic information of the website is not accurate[3]. There are many research results on IP localization method. Song Jian proposed a method to locate IP address based on network topology measurement[4]. The method will do network detection of trace route according to the detected target extracted from the existing IP address database. After that, the raw data will be preprocessed, statistics and clustering. And then analyzing and correcting IP address information on the basis of the topological relations between the IP addresses which are obtained by the network measurement. Zhu Bin proposed a method that through the research and implementation of a resemble SVD algorithm and efficient query algorithm about IP to make the positioning results more accurate and efficient[5]. Wang Ting et al proposed a IP localization method based on association rule mining(IPGEL)[6]. Jia Weiwei proposed a method of IP location optimization based on Routing[7]. But these methods are aimed at locating the server address, and only by virtue of the geographical location of the server can not determine the real location of the agency.

DOI: 10.1051/itmconf/20160701012

3 System framework

The system first analyzes the agency website URL and resolves the domain name into IP address. Then locate server address according to IP. The system will judge whether the IP address and the location of the server is the only corresponding relationship. If the relationship is exist, we will get the conclusion that the location of the server is the real location of the agency. If through the domain name resolution we get more than one server to provide the same service, thus we can not determine the real location through the server address. Therefore we need to be further analysis of the website content to determine the real location of the agency of the website. The System design flow is shown in Figure 1.

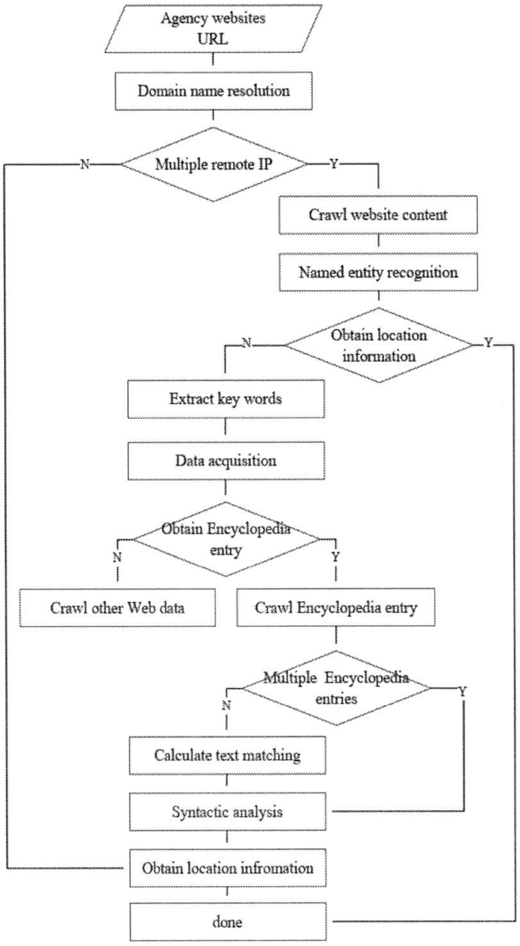

Figure 1. The system flow chart for detecting real location of agency website based on search engine.

Our method can be used to extract features from website content. The features will be used for reasoning about the organization's geographic information by analyzing the content of the target website. The main function module includes: server routing information analysis and processing, website structure and content crawling, data acquisition, named entity recognition computing, geographic information inference. The system structure is shown in Figure 2.

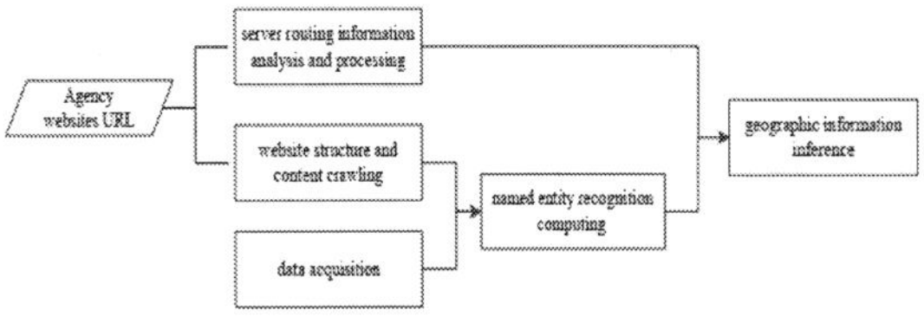

Figure 2. The system structure of real location of agency website detecting based on search engine.

4 Technologies

4.1. Data acquisition

The method uses search engine for data acquisition. Search engine is a system and a tool to return the relevant information according to the request of the user. Search engine includes three parts: information collection, information processing and user query. It collects information from the Internet or local database with a certain strategy and using a specific computer program. After organizing and arranging the information, search engine provides users with retrieval services, and will retrieve the relevant information to the user[8]. The combination of artificial intelligence, NLP, machine learning, big data and search engines has a great economic and academic value[9]. In our method, we acquire useful data returned by Baidu search engine, and analyze and process data in the next step.

4.2. Web crawling

The system uses the Jsoup framework to perform web crawling. Jsoup is a Java parser[10]. Through the target URL to crawl the corresponding web content and parse page. Jsoup can load the HTML document from string, the URL address, or local file, and generate a document object instance. It's very useful to crawl the information of website's record number or website structure according to the information provided by the website. Because record numbers are usually related to geographic location, so we may directly obtain the exact location of the agency.

4.3. Named entity recognition

Early named entity recognition work is mainly to identify the general proper nouns, including names, place names, organization names. Later research further subdivided the type of these nouns. More and more entity types are proposed. Current research methods are using supervised learning, automatic construction rules or sequence tagging. Hidden Markov model is a statistical model which is widely used in the field of Natural Language Processing. It takes context information into account and describes a Markov process with hidden location parameters[11]. Cascaded hidden Markov model (cascaded HMM) is an improved version of the hidden Markov model. Its aim is to merge the named entity recognition, such as the name recognition, the place name recognition and the organization name recognition, into a relatively uniform theoretical model[12]. We extract the key words such as the geographic information and the characters from the web content by named entity recognition.

4.4. Syntactic analysis

Dependency Parsing (DP) reveals the syntactic structure by analyzing the dependence relation among the components in the language unit. Compared with the syntactic analysis of phrase structure, the dependency structure syntax analysis describes the syntactic structure which is the dependency between words and words[13]. Dependency parsing can be decomposed into two sub tasks: identification and classification, and can be represented by a dependency tree[14]. For example, The people's Government of Bohai town is located in the town of Bohai Street revitalization. Its dependency tree is show in figure 3.

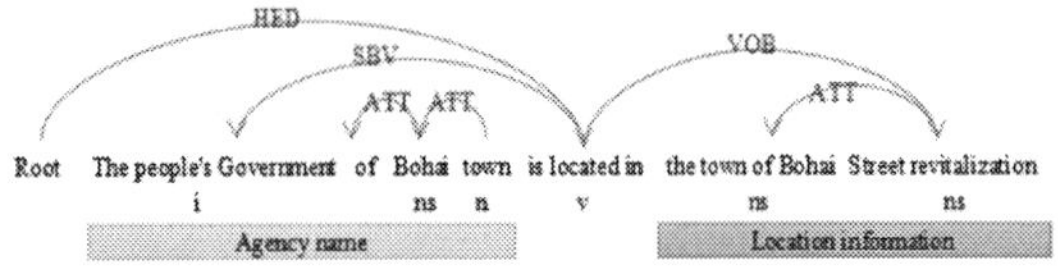

Figure 3. An example of dependency tree.

5 Experiment

The experiment uses Baidu as a search platform (http://www.baidu.com). In experiment, the initial query condition is submitted to the search engine. In the results page returned by Baidu, we select the top 30 results for analysis.

We selected three types of agency website including: government agencies, educational institutions, private enterprises. The number of test URL of each one is 100 and the result of experiment is show in figure 4.

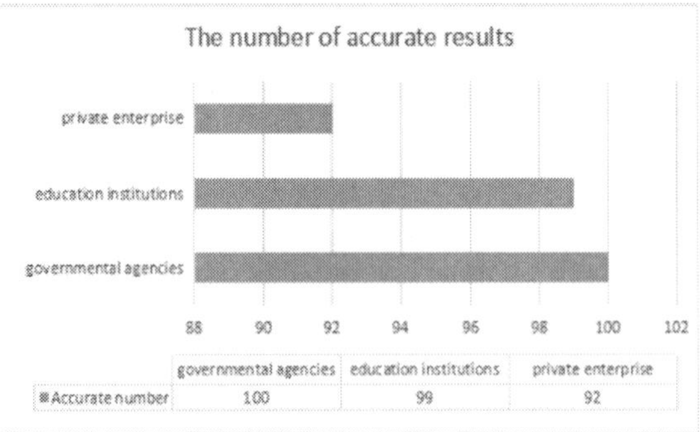

Figure 4. The number of accurate results.

The experimental results shows that the correct rate of the three types of agency websites were more than 90%. The output of detecting results are show in table 1.

Table 1. The Sample of recognition results

No.	Results		
	URL	**Agency**	**Location**
1	http://bhz.jingning.gov.cn/	The government of Bohai town	Heilongjiang province, Ningan city, Bohai Town, street revitalization
2	http://www.fenghuang.gov.cn/	The government of Phoenix town	Linzi District, Zibo City, Shandong Province
3	http://www.pku.edu.cn/	Beijing university	No. 5 the Summer Palace Road, Beijing, Haidian District
4	http://www.gdton.com/	Everbright Group	Guangdong Province, Dongguan City Dongcheng Jinghu blue County South four ring road

6 Conclusions

This paper provides a method based on the search engine to crawl and process the web data in real time. The system with multiple data acquisition analysis and processing module, can intelligently detect the real location of the website of agency. Compared with the manual sorting method, the method belongs to the automatic detection method and saves the time for manual judgment and processing. It has high chronergy because of collect and process data in real time and enhance the effectiveness of data. It covers a wider range of inquiries and has a better detection effect. But our method is mainly to deal with the type of agency websites. In the future, it can be extended to other types of websites. In the next work, we will pay more attention to improving algorithms to improve the detection rate.

Acknowledgment

The work is supported by National Basic Research and Development Program (No.2013CB329601, 2013CB329604) and National Natural Science Foundation of China (No.61502517, No.61472433, No.61372191, No.61572492).

References

1. Deng Haiping. To avoid the risk of lost contact with the private equity institutions [J]. Public financial advisor, 1 (2016)
2. The directory of national enterprises [EB/OL]. http://ml.fosang.com/post/1.html
3. Pan Xiaonan. Research and analysis of IP positioning technology [J]. Applied energy technology, 6: 47-49 (2015)
4. Song Jian. Design and implementation of IP address location system based on network topology measurement [D]. Beijing University of Posts and Telecommunications (2015)
5. Zhu Bin. Research and implementation of IP address based network entity geographic location technology [D]. Beijing University of Posts and Telecommunications (2015)
6. Wang Ting, Song Junde, Song Meina et al. A IP localization method based on association rules mining [J]. Journal of Southeast University (NATURAL SCIENCE EDITION), **45** 4: 657-662 (2015)
7. Jia Weiwei. IP positioning optimization based on routing tracking [D]. Zhengzhou University (2013)
8. Croft Donald, Metzler Trevor, Strohman. W.Bruce. Search Engine: information retrieval practice [M]. Beijing: Mechanical Industry Press (2009)
9. Liu Chao. Lightweight search engine based on Text Mining [D]. Southwestern University (2015)
10. Jsoup [EB/OL]. https://jsoup.org/
11. Chen Ji. A review of named entity recognition [J]. modern computer, 3: 24-26 (2016)
12. Yu Hongkui, Zhang Huaping, Liu Qun et al. Chinese Named Entity Recognition Based on cascading hidden Markov model [J]. Journal of communication, **27** 2: 87-94 (2006)
13. Wei Yong, Hu Danlu, Li Xiang, et al. Chinese place name recognition method considering syntactic features [J]. Journal of Surveying and Mapping Science and technology, 1 (2016)
14. Xiao Xin, Fan Shixi, Wang Xuan et al. Dependency parsing based on maximum entropy model [J]. Chinese Journal of information, **23** 2: 18-22 (2009)

The Irregularity Propagation Characteristics of Radio Signals For Wireless Sensor Network In Farmland

Hua-Ji ZHU[1,2,3], Hua-Rui WU[1,2,3,*], Li-Hong ZHANG[1,2,3] and Yi-Sheng MIAO[1,2,3]

[1]*National Engineering Research Center for Information Technology in Agriculture, Beijing 100097, PR China*
[2]*Beijing Research Center for Information Technology in Agriculture, Beijing Academy of Agriculture and Forestry Sciences, Beijing 100097, PR China*
[3]*Key Laboratory for Information Technologies in Agriculture, Ministry of Agriculture, Beijing 100097, PR China*
zhuhj@nercita.org.cn, wuhr@nercita.org.cn, zhanglh@nercita.org.cn, miaoys@nercita.org.cn
**Corresponding author: Hua-Rui WU*

Abstract. This work aims to investigate the irregular propagation characteristics of wireless sensor network (WSN) at frequency of 433 MHz. Through the analysis of the received signal strength indicator (RSSI), it is found that the variance in received signal strength is largely random, along with a continuous change with incremental changes in direction. For the transceiver distance is 20 m, the packet loss rate (PLR) in all directions is relatively small except for the east direction, indicating that the signal is still strong in all directions. While for the transceiver distance is 40 m, it can be found that there is about 90% packet loss in the east direction. That is, the received signal strength in the east direction is lower than that in the other directions. Moreover, the communication range varies with the degree of receiver direction ranging from 0 to 359. Through the regression analysis in Matlab, we find that the optimal fitting models in different directions are different. The optimal fitting model in east and west direction is the modified exponential decay, and in south and north direction is the linear logarithmic model. The values of R^2 vary from 0.935 to 0.961, and the values of RMSE range from 1.75 to 2.31.

1 Introduction

Wireless sensor network (WSN) is a recent novel technology and it has been increasingly used in agriculture [1]. WSN is composed of a number of sensor nodes which are capable of sensing, processing, and transmitting environmental information [2]. The sensor nodes are communicate with each other through wireless radio signals [3, 4].

In recent years, many studies have been performed to study the characteristics of wireless radio propagation through measuring the antenna height, vegetation depth, and the propagation frequency. Suwalak et al. [5] studied the propagation characteristics of a single vegetation type, such as durian and plum. Moreover, Azevedo et al. [6] researched the propagation characteristics of wireless radio in some complex agricultural environments such as forests with dozens of tree species. Ndzi et al. [7] conducted the wireless sensor network coverage measurements in a mixed crop farmland, and proposed a log-linear model. The existing empirical model regard the propagation environment as isotropic homogeneous. Unfortunately, radio irregularity is a common and non-negligible phenomenon in wireless sensor networks [8].

In order to characterize irregular propagation for WSN in agricultural fields like wheat filed, RF signal propagation experiments at different directions are done at frequency of 433 MHz. In this study, we investigate the impact of transceiver distance and degree of receiver direction on the propagation of RF signal. First, we study the received signal strength indicator (RSSI) and packet loss rate (PLR) at various transceiver distances at different directions. Then, we obtain the communication range at different directions. Finally, we focus on the regression analysis of path loss at various directions.

2 Related work

The radio irregularity can result in irregularity in radio range and variations in packet loss in different directions [9]. Ganesan et al. [10] found that the radio range varies significantly in different directions. The radio irregularity is mainly due to the variance of the signal path loss. Shankar et al. [11] proposed that the wireless radio signal may be reflected, diffracted, and scattered for propagating within a

 DOI: 10.1051/itmconf/20160701013

medium. Generally, the medium is different in different directions. Hence, radio propagation presents anisotropic in most environments.

3 Experimental method

As a major food crops in Northern China, winter wheat is taken as the research object in this paper. The impact of plant on RF signal propagation characteristic in different growing stages is different. Here, we choose the elongation stage for testing, and the average plant height is 0.40 m. We carry out the experiment at the wheat-field in xiaotangshan national precision agriculture research demonstration base. The 1100 SE RF wireless sensor node is selected, and the devices are equipped with the frequency of 433 MHz. The transmitted power and the Omni-directional antenna gain are 0 dBm, and 4dB, respectively. To avoid unnecessary loss caused by antenna polarity, transmitter and receiver are at the same height and kept in the same direction. The receiver sensitivity is -110 dBm. The RSSI and PLR are obtained for antenna heights of transmitter and receiver are 0 m.

4 Experimental results

4.1 Anisotropic RSSI

In this study, it is supposed that the antenna height of transmitter (h_t) and receiver (h_r) are the same, i.e., $h_t = h_r = h$ [12]. As shown in Figure 1, the RSSI at 433 MHz is plotted as a function of the number of measurement at different directions. It is found that received signal strength in each direction is relatively stable, and the small variance can be attributed to the fading effect [11]. Despite the same distance between transceiver, the received signal strength in the south is much higher than that in the east. Moreover, we study the relation between the signal strength and the degree of angular direction for the transceiver distance is 20 m and 40 m, respectively. As shown in Figure 2, the received signal strength varies continuously with the change of direction. That is to say, the incremental changes in direction lead to the incremental variation for RSSI, which is agreement with previous works [13].

4.2 Anisotropic PLR

The relationship between PLR and the degree in directions for the transceiver distance of 20 m and 40 m is presented in Figure 3. As shown in Figure 3, the PLR for the transceiver distance of 20 m is relatively small in all directions, except for in the east direction. In other words, the signal is still strong in other three directions. While for the transceiver distance is 20 m, it can be seen that there is about 90% packet loss in the east direction. The phenomenon demonstrates that the received signal strength in the east direction is lower than that in the other directions, which is consistent with the results in Figure 1. Interestingly, the PLR in north direction is relatively small in two transceiver distance in comparison with the other three directions.

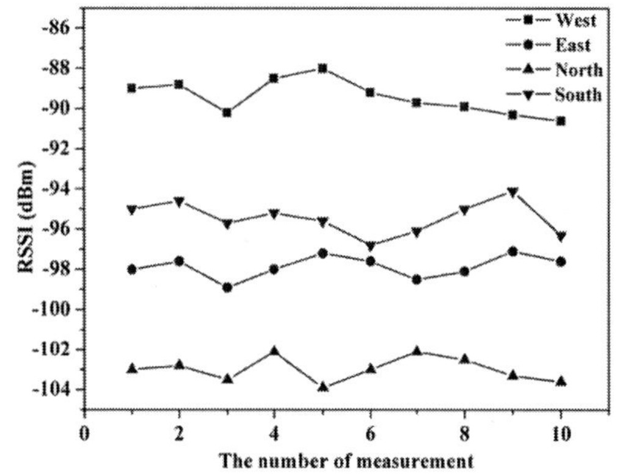

Figure 1. The Rssi of Various Number Of Measurement In Four Directions.

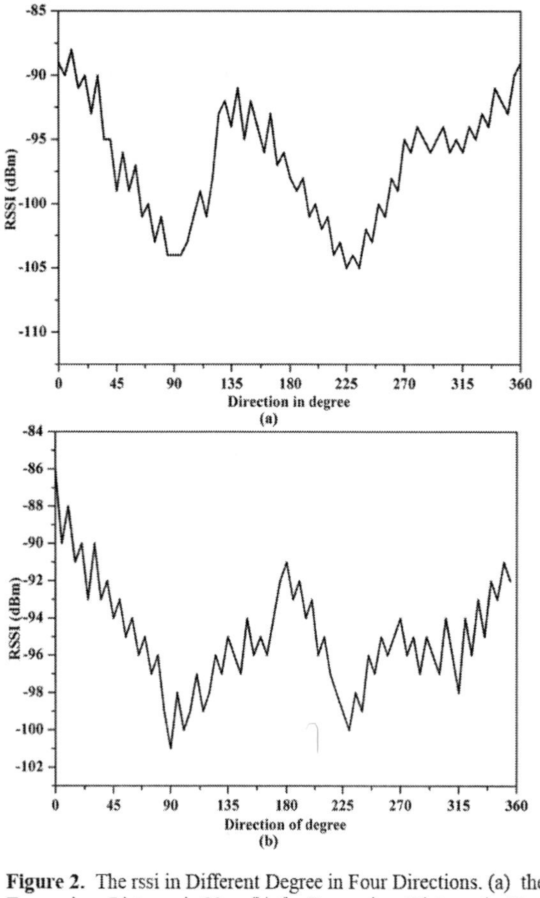

Figure 2. The rssi in Different Degree in Four Directions. (a) the Transceiver Distance is 20 m (b) the Transceiver Distance is 40 m.

 DOI: 10.1051/itmconf/20160701013

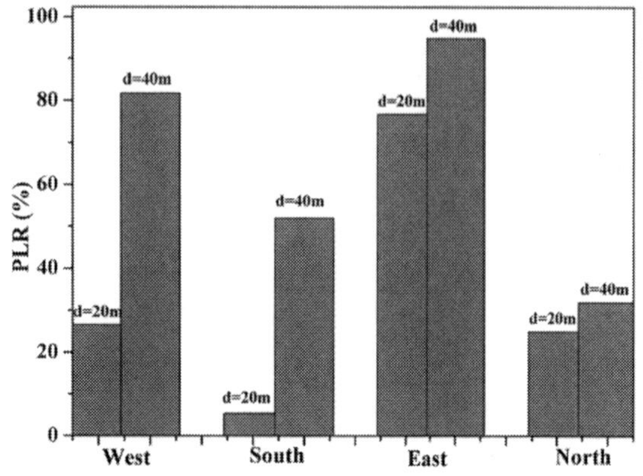

Figure 3. The Plr for Transceiver Distance is 20 m and 40 m in Four Directions.

4.3 Anisotropic communication range

To further demonstrate the irregularity, we research the communication range in all directions. In the experiment, the receiver sensitivity is -110 dBm. Then with such thresholds, the communications in different directions are measured. As shown in Figure 4, the communication range varies with the degree of receiver direction ranging from 0 to 359. In other words, the communication range is not uniform in all directions. The range map may be another illustrations for radio irregularity in a wireless medium.

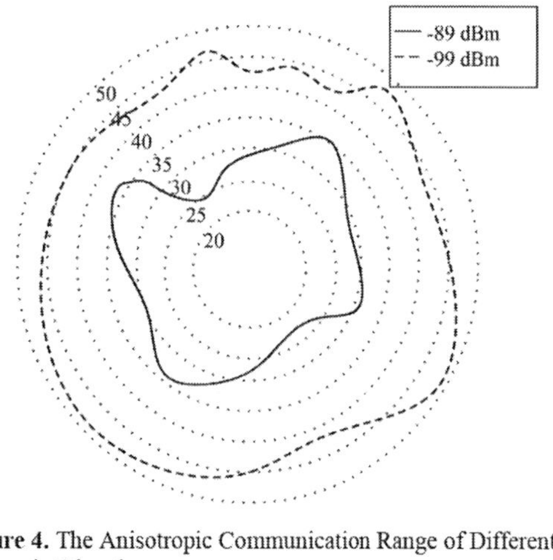

Figure 4. The Anisotropic Communication Range of Different Degree in Direction.

4.4 The regression analysis for path loss

For wireless signal propagate between transmitter and receiver, radio waves interact with environment, causing path loss [14]. Path loss (PL) is defined as the difference between the transmitted and the received power. It can be expressed by:

$$PL = P_t + G_t + G_r - P_r(d) \tag{1}$$

Where P_t is the transmitted power, G_t is the antenna gain of transmitter, G_r is the antenna gain of receiver, and $P_r(d)$ is the received power. In a transmission medium, the received power can be expressed by:

$$P_r = P_t G_t G_r \left(\lambda / 4\pi d\right)^n \tag{2}$$

Where λ and d are the wavelength of the wireless signal, and the distance between the transmitter and receiver, respectively. n is the transmission factor which value depends on the environment of propagation. For wireless signal propagation in free space, we assume that the wireless signal travels in a homogeneous medium. Under this circumstance, the rate of attenuation is constant, i.e., n is equal to 2 [15]. Generally speaking, the power attenuation can be defined as follows:

$$PL = 10\log_{10}(P_t / P_r) \tag{3}$$

Furthermore, the path loss in free space can be simplified as:

$$PL_{Freespace} = 20\log_{10}(f) + 20\log_{10}(d) - 27.56 \tag{4}$$

Where f is the frequency of RF signal. Through the logarithm processing, the equation (3) can be converted into the equation as follows:

$$PL = A - 10 * n * \log_{10}(d) \tag{5}$$

According to the previous studies [15, 16], there are many vegetation attenuation models, such as Non-zero Gradient model and Modified Exponential Decay (MED) model. From a propagation mechanisms perspective, at very shallow vegetation depths, signal propagation is dominated by coherent components which decrease rapidly with distance [15]. Beyond this point, propagation is mainly due to forward scattering and the signal is dominated by diffuse components [15]. However, because of the small transmitted power from wireless sensor nodes, most scattered or diffused components are very weak. Nonetheless, their presence is illustrated by the reduction in the signal decay gradient at distances further from the transmitter [16]. The generalized form of the MED vegetation attenuation models is given by:

$$P_r = Xf^Y d^Z \tag{6}$$

Where f and d are the frequency in megahertz (MHz) and the vegetation depth in meters. Moreover, X, Y, and Z are model parameters.

Based on the above models, we make regression analysis for path loss at different directions in Matlab. As

 DOI: 10.1051/itmconf/20160701013

we know, the important indicator in curve fitting is R^2 which reflect the correlation between theoretical calculation values and measured values. Generally speaking, R^2 is more closer to one, the correlation between theoretical calculation values and measured values is greater. To evaluate the reliability of models application, Root Mean Square Error (RMSE) between the models and the measured data are further calculated. The RMSE is a frequently used measure of the difference between values predicted by a model and the values actually measured from the environment [17]. RMSE is a good measure for accuracy of the models, and can be expressed by:

$$RMSE = \sqrt{\frac{\sum_{i=1}^{n}\left(X_{obs,i} - X_{mod,i}\right)}{n}} \tag{7}$$

Where X_{obs}, X_{mod}, and n are the measured values, the modeled values, and the number of samples, respectively. The fitting curves of path loss in four directions for the frequency of 433 MHz are presented in Figure 5. It can be observed that the differences of path loss in different directions are obvious. At frequency of 433 MHz, the path loss in east direction can be expressed by:

$$PL = 0.627 * f^{0.712} * d^{0.098} \tag{8}$$

While for the west direction, the path loss can be expressed by:

$$PL = 0.084 * f^{0.816} * d^{0.331} \tag{9}$$

In the south direction, the path loss model can be presented by:

$$PL = 41.83 + 25.8 * \log_{10}(d) \tag{10}$$

In the north direction, the path loss model can be expressed by:

$$PL = 38.54 + 36.4 * \log_{10}(d) \tag{11}$$

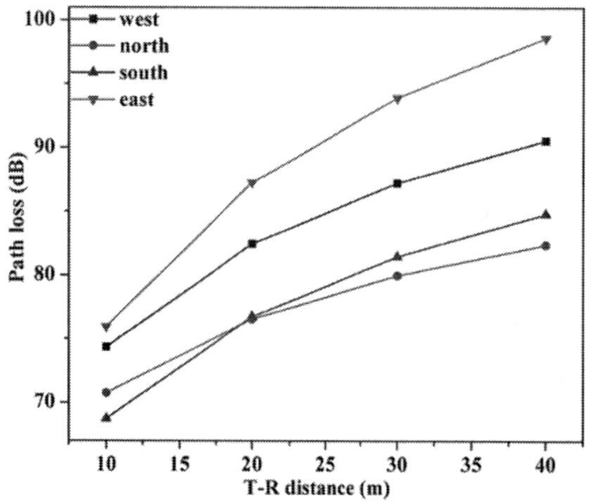

Figure 5. The Measured and the Fitting Path Loss in Four Different Directions.

5 Conclusions

This work aim to study the irregular propagation characteristics of wireless sensor network at frequency of 433 MHz. The radio irregularity depend on the direction of propagation, and can be caused by multiple factors, such as variance in RF sending power and different path losses. Through the analysis of the received signal strength indicator, it can be found that the variance in received signal strength is largely random, along with a continuous change with incremental changes in direction. For the transceiver distance is 20 m, the packet loss rate in all directions is relatively small except for the east direction, indicating that the signal is still strong in all directions. While for the distance is 40 m, it can be found that there is about 90% packet loss in the east direction. That is, the received signal strength in the east direction is lower than that in the other directions. Moreover, the communication range varies with the degree of receiver direction ranging from 0 to 359. Through the regression analysis in Matlab, we find that the optimal fitting models in different directions are different. The optimal fitting model in east and west direction is the modified exponential decay, and in south and north direction is the linear logarithmic model. The values of R^2 vary from 0.935 to 0.961, and the values of RMSE range from 1.75 to 2.31 at frequency of 433 MHz.

Acknowledgments

This work is supported by Natural Science Foundation of China (61571051, 61471067, 61271257).

References

1. Kone C. T., Hafid A, Boushaba M, IEEE. Sens. J, 15, 10 (2015)
2. An W, Ci S, Luo HY, Wu DL, Adamchuk V, Sharif H, Wang XY, Tang H, Wireless Communications and Mobile Computing, 15, 12 (2015)
3. Liu WM, Rahman M. F, Thirumuruganathan S, Nan Z, Das G, Proceedings of the VLDB Endowment, 8, 12 (2015)
4. Mao DD, Sun WW, Chen CN, Wu JJ, Liu WM, Jing YN, Journal of Chinese Computer Systems, 32, 6 (2011)
5. Vougioukas S, Anastassiu H. T, Regen C, Zude M, Biosyst Eng, 114, 4 (2013)
6. Azevedo J. A. R, Santos F. E. S, IEEE T Anten Propag, 59, 6 (2011)
7. Ndzi D. L, Harun A, Ramli F. M, Kamarudin M. L, Zakaria A, Shakaff A. Y. M, Jaafar M. N, Zhou Shikun, Farook R. S, Comput Electron Agr, 105 (2014)
8. Guo XM, Zhao CJ, Int J. Agr. Biol. Eng, 7, 6 (2014)
9. Cerpa A, Busek N, Estrin D, Center for Embedded Network Sensing, (2003)
10. Ganesan D, Krishnamachari B, Woo A, Culler D, Wicker S, Technical Report UCLA/CSD-TR 02, (2002)
11. Hamid M. A, Abdullah-Al-Wadud M, Chong I, The International Conference on Information Networking 2011 (ICOIN2011). IEEE, (2011)
12. Sai S, Niwa E, Mase K, Nishibori M, Inoue J, Obuchi M, Kizu M, IEEE Commun Mag, 47, 11 (2009)
13. Zhou G, He T, Krishnamurthy S, Stankovic J. A, ACM T Sensor Network, 2, 2 (2006)
14. Harun A, Shakaff A. Y. M, Zakaria A, Kamarudin L. M, Jaafar M. N., Ndzi D. L., 2011 Third International Conference on Computational Intelligence, Modelling & Simulation. IEEE, (2011)
15. Zhou, G., He, T., Krishnamurthy, S., Stankovic, J. A, In Proceedings of the 2nd international conference on Mobile systems, applications, and services, (2004)
16. Meng Y S, Lee Y H, Investigations of foliage effect on modern wireless communication systems: A review[J]. Prog Electromagn Res, 105 (2010)
17. Ndzi D. L., Kamarudin L. M., Muhammad Ezanuddin A. A., Zakaria A, Ahmad R. B., Malek M. F. B. A., Jafaar M. N, Prog Electromagn Res B, 36 (2012)

An Efficient Lattice-based Distributed IBE

Lu YIN, Quan ZHANG,and Rui-Lin LI

School of Electronic Science and Engineering, National University of Defense Technology, NUDT, Changsha , China

ruruyin@163.com,quanzhang@nudt.edu.cn, securitylrl@163.com

Abstract—This paper improves the lattice-based secret sharing method presented by Bansarkhani and Meziani and combines the method with the IBE based on the standard LWE problem constructing an efficient lattice-based distributed decryption IBE. Our construction avoids the weakness in the traditional method like Lagrange interpolation, Blakley's space geometry method or Chinese remainder theorem method. Through theoretical analysis, compared with the bilinear pairing based distributed IBE, our scheme refrains from the complex pairing operation and has less calculation cost. A proof of security holds in the standard model.

1 Introduction

In 1984, Shamir proposed the concept of Identity-Based Cryptography(IBC)[1]. The characteristic of IBC is that a user's public key can be calculated by an open algorithm according to some public information like the user's name, e-mail address or phone number, etc. The property simplifies public key distribution. In this aspect, the IBC has an advantage over traditional public key cryptosystem. Since the user's private key must be created by a trusted third party PKG, it results in the inherent key escrow problem and restricts the adoption of IBC.

In 2003, Boneh and Franklin designed the first practical Identity-Based Encryption scheme (IBE)[2] using bilinear maps on elliptic curves and proposed an approach to mitigate the key escrow problem. In this approach, the IBE system's master key is distributed to multiple PKGs using technique of Shamir (t, n) threshold secret sharing[3]. The BasicIdent scheme is briefly described below:

Let G_1 be an additive cyclic group of order p andG_T be a multiplicative group of order p, P is a generator ofG_1, $\hat{e}: G_1 \times G_1 \to G_T$ is a bilinear map.

Let H_1 and H_2 be two cryptographic hashfunctions $H_1: \{0,1\}^* \to G_1$, $H_2: G_T \to \{0,1\}^{lm}$, where l_m represents the bit length of the message.

1) Setup. The master PKG chooses a random master key $s \in \mathbf{Z}_p^*$ and sets $P_{pub} = sP$. $Q_{id} = H_1(id)$ is derived from the user's public key id. The master PKG then distributes sto nPKGs in a Shamir (t, n) threshold secret sharing fashion, each PKG_i gets one $shares_i$.

2) Encrypt. The sender picks a random $r \in \mathbf{Z}_p^*$ and encrypts the plaintext under the public key id, setting the ciphertext to be

$$C = (U,V) = (rP, m \oplus H_2(\hat{e}(Q_{id}, rP_{pub}))) \cdot$$

3) Decrypt. After receiving the ciphertext C, userid sends decryption request $R = (id, U)$ to PKG_i. When responding to the request more than t (t is the threshold value) PKG_i send $\hat{e}(s_i Q_{id}, U)$. Useridcan then construct plaintext m via $m = V \oplus H_2(\prod_{i=1}^{t} \hat{e}(\lambda_i s_i Q_{id}, U)) = V \oplus H_2(\hat{e}(sQ_{id}, U))$ where the λ_i's are the Lagrange coefficients.

In this scheme, each distributed PKG can either generate the decryption share $\hat{e}(s_i Q_{id}, U)$ online or provide the partial private key sQ_{id} for the user. Of course, the complete private key can be obtained when the collusion of more than t PKGs happens. Thus the honesty of these entities required in the application is comparable to PKG, which is the essential reason for these entities to be PKGs. Distributed PKGs required to be involved in the decryption online all the time, it violates the basic requirement of IBE, PKG can be offline after generating the private keys for the users in its domain, that Shamir proposed[1].

To solve this problem, in PKC 2004, Baek and Zheng Yuliang [4] gave a better approach to share a private key associated with an identity among n entities which appointed by user rather than sharing a master key. So these n entities are downgraded to pure decryption servers without the function of PKG. Because these servers have users' trust and the online/offline state controlled by the user, the problem of distributed PKGs online all the time in the decryption period can be solved.

However, due to the distributed decryption IBE in [4] is based on bilinear pairing and Shamir threshold secret sharing, considering the complex computation of pairing operation, it affects the overall efficiency of the protocol. In addition, from the point of view of security, their scheme is hard to resist quantum attacks.

In recent years, constructing IBE from some hard problems in lattice attracts much attention. In 2008, under the random oracle model Gentry, Peikert and Vaikuntanathan[5] constructed the first IBE based on the LWE problem in the lattice. Subsequently, Cash, Hofheinz and Kiltz[6], Agarwal, Boneh and Boyen[7] proposed lattice based IBE in the standard model. Since the operation on the lattice is mostly linear and the calculation speed is fast, so we combine the idea of distributed decryption presented by Baek and Zheng Yuliang[3] with efficient lattice IBE[7] to construct an efficient lattice-based distributed IBE.

If our construction follows the Lagrange polynomial interpolation used in Baek and Zheng Yuliang's scheme to distribute a secret n-dimensional vector, the communication cost will increase because the order of each vector component has to be recorded to recover the n-dimensional vector. Therefore, our construction uses the secret sharing approach presented by R. Bansarkhani and M. Meziani[8] to distribute the user's private key which is an n-dimensional vector in the lattice based IBE. However we argue that there is a scalability problem in the secret sharing construction of R. Bansarkhani and M. Meziani. We propose to employ a variable number of columns of a matrix to distribute the n-dimensional vector so that the number of decryption servers is available within a certain range.

The advantages of our lattice based distributed IBE are listed as follows:

-In the distribution and decryption share construction/reconstruction stage, the new secret sharing technique based on the variable matrix mitigates the scalability problem and avoids the weakness of recording the order of each vector component while recovering the whole n-dimensional vector using traditional methods like Lagrange polynomial interpolation[2], Blakley's geometry of space scheme[9] or Chinese remainder theorem method[10], etc.

-The secret shares and the reconstructed private key can be verified by a lattice-based hash function.

-The user makes a decryption request to each decryption server after receiving the ciphertext, then the decryption servers calculate decryption shares associated with the ciphertext and secret shares they possess. Through a secure channel, the corresponding decryption shares are delivered to the user. The whole encryption and decryption process including secret shares distribution, the generation of decryption shares or recovering the plaintext uses simple matrix operations. Through the theoretical analysis, compared with the distributed bilinear pairing-based IBE, our construction can not only resist quantum attacks, and also reduce the cost of calculation.

2 Preliminaries

2.1 Notation

The set of real numbers is defined as $\mathbf{R}$ and the integers as $\mathbf{Z}$. We denote a vector x and the i_{th} component of x is written as $x^{(i)}$.

Let S be a set of vectors $S=\{s_1,..,s_k\}$, where $s_1,...,s_k \in \mathbf{R}^m$. We define the L_2 length of the longest vector in S as $\|S\|$, namely $\|S\|:=\max_{1\le i\le k}\|s_i\|$. We let $\tilde{S}:=\{\tilde{s}_1,...,\tilde{s}_k\}$ denote the Gram-Schmidt orthogonalization of the vectors $s_1,...,s_k$ and $\|\tilde{S}\|$ denote the Gram-Schmidt norm of S.

The statistical distance between two distributions X and Y over a finite set Ω is defined as:

$$\Delta(X;Y):=\frac{1}{2}\sum_{s\in\Omega}|\Pr[X=s]-\Pr[Y=s]| \ . \quad (1)$$

Two distributions are statistically close if $\Delta(X;Y)$ is negligible. Let U_Ω be a uniform distribution over Ω. If $\Delta(X;U_\Omega)\le\delta$, we say X is δ-uniform over Ω.

2.2 Integer Lattices

An integer lattice is a discrete subgroup of $\mathbf{Z}^m$. Our article will use the q-ary integer lattices to construct the lattice-based IBE. The q-ary integer lattices contain $q\mathbf{Z}^m$ as a sublattice where q is some integer. Let q be a prime, $A\in\mathbf{Z}_q^{n\times m}$ be arbitrary, $u\in\mathbf{Z}_q^n$, define the full-rank q-ary lattice:

$$\Lambda_q^{\perp}(A):=\{e\in\mathbf{Z}^m \mid Ae=0\,(\bmod q)\} \ . \quad (2)$$

The coset or shifted lattice is defined to be:

$\Lambda_q^u(\mathrm{A}) := \{\mathrm{e} \in \mathbf{Z}^m \mid \mathrm{Ae} = u(\mathrm{mod\,q})\}$. (3)

For $t \in \Lambda_q^u(\mathrm{A})$, $\Lambda_q^u(\mathrm{A}) = \Lambda_q^{\perp}(\mathrm{A}) + t$.

2.3 Discrete Gaussians

For any $c \in \mathbf{R}^m$, real $\sigma > 0$, the m-dimensional Gaussian function $\rho_{\sigma,c}(x)$ is defined by:

$$\forall x \in \mathbf{R}^m, \rho_{\sigma,c}(x) = \exp(-\pi \frac{\|x-c\|^2}{\sigma^2}). \quad (4)$$

For any lattice $\Lambda \subset \mathbf{R}^m$, $\rho_{\sigma,c}(\Lambda) = \sum_{x\in\Lambda} \rho_{\sigma,c}(\mathrm{x})$. We define the probability mass function of the discrete Gaussian distribution $\mathrm{D}_{\Lambda,\sigma,c}$:

$$\forall x \in \Lambda, \mathrm{D}_{\Lambda,\sigma,c}(\mathrm{x}) = \frac{\rho_{\sigma,c}(\mathrm{x})}{\rho_{\sigma,c}(\Lambda)}. \quad (5)$$

Gentry etc.[5] proposed the Gaussian sampling algorithm that, given a basis of an arbitrary lattice, samples lattice points from a discrete Gaussian distribution.

2.4 Learning with Errors

For an integer q, a positive integern and a distribution χ on $\mathbf{Z}_q$, learning with errors problem $\mathrm{LWE}_{q,\chi}$ aims to distinguish between the distribution $\mathrm{A}_{s,\chi}$ ($s \in \mathbf{Z}_q^n$ is some uniform secret value) and the uniform distribution on $\mathbf{Z}_q^n \times \mathbf{Z}_q$. The instance of LWE problem[7] contains access to an unspecified oracle O (O_s or $\mathrm{O}_\$$). O_s denotes a noisy pseudo-random sampler, it outputs samples $(u_i, v_i) = (u_i, u_i^T s + x_i) \in \mathbf{Z}_q^n \times \mathbf{Z}_q$, where $x_i \in \mathbf{Z}_q$ taken freshly from χ and u_i is uniform in $\mathbf{Z}_q^n$. $\mathrm{O}_\$$ represents a truly random sampler whose output is some truly uniform random samples from $\mathbf{Z}_q^n \times \mathbf{Z}_q$.

We say A algorithm can decide the LWE problem, if $LWE-adv[\mathsf{A}] := \left|\Pr[\mathsf{A}^{\mathrm{O}_s}=1] - \Pr[\mathsf{A}^{\mathrm{O}_\$}=1]\right|$ is non-negligiblefor a random $s \in \mathbf{Z}_q^n$.

Regev[11] proved that for certain Gaussian noise distributions χ (denoted $\bar{\Psi}_\alpha$) on $\mathbf{Z}_q$, $\mathrm{LWE}_{q,\bar{\Psi}_\alpha}$ is as hard as using a quantum algorithm to solve the worst-case SIVP and GapSVP.

2.5 Trapdoor Generation Algorithm

In our construction, we use the TrapGen algorithm proposed by Alwen and Peikert[12] to generate a uniform matrix A, together with a good trapdoor basis T of $\Lambda_q^{\perp}(\mathrm{A})$.

Theorem 1.[12] Let odd $q \geq 3$, $m \geq \lceil 6n \log q \rceil$, $\delta = 1/3$. There is a probabilistic polynomial time algorithm TrapGen(q, n) outputs $(\mathrm{A} \in \mathbf{Z}_q^{n\times m}, T_A \in \mathbf{Z}^{m\times m})$ such that A is statistically close to a uniform matrix, T_A is a basis of $\Lambda_q^{\perp}(\mathrm{A})$ satisfying $\|\tilde{T}_A\| = O(\sqrt{n \log q})$, $\|T_A\| \leq O(n \log q)$.

2.6 SampleLeft and SampleRight Algorithm

Let matrixes $\mathrm{A}, B \in \mathbf{Z}_q^{n\times m}$ and R be a matrix in $\{-1,1\}^{m\times m}$, matrix $F = (\mathrm{A} \mid \mathrm{AR} + B) \in \mathbf{Z}_q^{n\times 2m}$. In our construction, we have to sample short vectors in $\Lambda_q^u(\mathrm{A})$ for $u \in \mathbf{Z}_q^n$ as the user's private key using SampleLeft algorithm or SampleRight algorithm for security game.

SampleLeft($A, \mathrm{M}_1, T_A, \mathrm{u}, \sigma$)[7]: Input a rank n matrix $A \in \mathbf{Z}_q^{n\times m}$, $\mathrm{M}_1 \in \mathbf{Z}_q^{n\times m_1}$, a short basis T_A of $\Lambda_q^{\perp}(\mathrm{A})$, a Gaussian parameter $\sigma > \|\tilde{T}_A\| \cdot \omega(\sqrt{\log(m+m_1)})$ and a vector $u \in \mathbf{Z}_q^n$, let $F_1 = (\mathrm{A} \mid \mathrm{M}_1)$. This algorithm outputs a vector $e \in \mathbf{Z}^{m+m_1}$ satisfying $F_1 \cdot e = u(\mathrm{modq})$, e is sampled from a distribution statistically close to $\mathrm{D}_{\Lambda_q^u(\mathrm{F}_1),\sigma}$.

SampleRight(A, B, R, T_B, u, σ)[7]: Input $A \in \mathbf{Z}_q^{n\times k}$ and a rank n matrix $B \in \mathbf{Z}_q^{n\times m}$, a matrix $R \in \mathbf{Z}^{k\times m}$ (Let $s_R := \|R\| = \sup_{\|x\|=1} \|Rx\|$), T_B is a basis of $\Lambda_q^{\perp}(\mathrm{B})$ and $u \in \mathbf{Z}_q^n$, the Gaussian parameter $\sigma > \|\tilde{T}_B\| \cdot s_R \omega(\sqrt{\log m})$. This algorithm outputs a vector $e \in \mathbf{Z}^{m+k}$, let F2be $(\mathrm{A} \mid \mathrm{AR} + B)$, e is sampled from a distribution statistically close to $\mathrm{D}_{\Lambda_q^u(\mathrm{F}_2),\sigma}$.

2.7 Lattice-based Hash function

Definition [13] For security parameter λ, we choose a random matrix $M \in \mathbf{Z}_q^{\lambda\times m}$, M_i denotes the i_{th} column ofM, for the input $x = (x_1, x_2, \ldots, x_m) \in \mathbf{Z}^m$, $h_M : \mathbf{Z}^m \to \mathbf{Z}_q^{\lambda}$ is defined as

$$H_M(x) = \mathrm{M}x \bmod q = \sum_{i=1}^{m} x_i \mathrm{M}_i \bmod q. \quad (6)$$

Let μ be polynomial in λ, denoted as $\mu = poly(\lambda)$, q be a λ -bits modulo, $m = 2\lambda^2$. When the input $x \in \{0,1,...,\mu\}^m$, the LBH is collision-free and its security can be reduced to $GAPSVP_{14\pi\sqrt{\lambda}\beta}$.

2.8 Full-rank Differences Function

In our construction, we first use a collision resistant hash to convert the identity in $\{0,1\}^*$ to elements in $\mathbf{Z}_q^n$. Then use the full-rank difference function encoding the $id = (d_1, d_2, \cdots, d_{n-1}) \in \mathbf{Z}_q^n$ to a matrix in $\mathbf{Z}_q^{n\times n}$. Let the polynomial $g_d(X)$ be $g_d(X) = \sum_{i=0}^{n-1} d_i x^i \in \mathbf{Z}_q[X]$, coeffs(g_d) means the n-dimensional vector of coefficients of g_d , $f \in \mathbf{Z}_q[X]$ be some polynomial of degree n, the Full-Rank Differences function (FRD) $H(\text{id})$ as the definition in [7],

$$H(\text{id}) = \begin{bmatrix} \text{coeffs}(g_d) \\ \text{coeffs}(X \cdot g_d \bmod f) \\ \text{coeffs}(X^2 \cdot g_d \bmod f) \\ \cdots \\ \text{coeffs}(X^{n-1} \cdot g_d \bmod f) \end{bmatrix} \in \mathbf{Z}^{n\times n} . \quad (7)$$

3 The Main Construction

3.1 Description of Generic Distributed IBE

The standard IBE includes four algorithms: Setup, Extract, Encrypt and Decrypt. Our construction introduces three new algorithms Distribution, Construct Dec and VerS.

The PKG runs the algorithm Setup to generate the master key, public key and all the public parameters.

The PKG runs the Extract algorithm after it receives the user's private key extraction request to generate the private key related with the user's identity.

In the application, the user can choose the number of decryption servers. Then the PKG or other authorized party that possesses the private key from PKG can run the Distribution algorithm to distribute the private key into k decryption servers Γ_i for $1 \le i \le k$ ($k \le 2m$ in our distributed IBE). The k decryption servers use a broadcast channel in common, each secret share is kept secretly by the decryption server. In the Distribution algorithm, an improved secret sharing method will be applied to generate shares of the private key and verify the validity of shares.

Thei_{th} server Γ_i receives its secret share and runs the algorithm VerS to verify the validity of the secret share.

Any user who wants to send message to otherscan run the algorithm Encrypt after obtaining the public parameter and the receiver's identity. The legal receiver gets the ciphertext and sends a decryption request to the decryption servers. Then the decryption server Γ_i implements the ConstructDec algorithm to generate corresponding decryption share and sends the decryption share to the user. The user can run the Decrypt algorithm combining the received valid decryption shares to recover the plaintext.

3.2 Our Distributed IBE

-Setup(n): On input n as a security parameter, set parameter, set q, m, σ, α (parameters set will be specified in the next section). Fist, this algorithm runs TrapGen(q,n) generating a uniformly random matrix $A_0 \in \mathbf{Z}_q^{n\times m}$ altogether with a short basis $T_{A_0} \in \mathbf{Z}^{m\times m}$ for $\Lambda_q^{\perp}(A_0)$. T_{A_0} is the master key. Then it chooses two uniformly random matrixes $A_1, B \in \mathbf{Z}_q^{n\times m}$ and a uniformly random vector $u \stackrel{R}{\leftarrow} \mathbf{Z}_q^n$. Finally, it returns the public parameters $PP = (A_0, A_1, B, u)$ while keeping the master key $MK = (T_{A_0})$ secretly.

-Extract(id, MK, PP): Given an identity $id \in \mathbf{Z}_q^n$, a mater key MK and public parameters PP, this algorithm uses $SampleLeft(A_0, A_1 + H(id)B, T_{A_0}, u, \sigma)$ to sample a vector $e \in \mathbf{Z}^{2m}$ as the private key SK_{id}. H is a full-rank differences map. Let $F_{id} := (A_0 \mid A_1 + H(id)B)$, clearly the private key satisfies $F_{id} \cdot e = u(\text{mod} q)$

-Distribution(SK_{id},k,q,2m): Given a private key SK_{id} and the number of decryption servers k, this algorithm first uses function TrapGen by choosing n', q and $2m \ge \lceil 6n' \log q \rceil$ as input to obtain a basis $T \in \mathbb{Z}^{2m\times 2m}$. Then it selects arbitrary k linearly independent column-vectors of T forming a matrix $Q := \{q_1, \dots, q_k\} \in \mathbb{Z}^{2m\times k}$ satisfying $\text{Rank}(Q) = \text{Rank}([Q\ SK_{id}])$. Then, it computes a vector v from $SK_{id} = Q \cdot v$ and selects k linearly independent vectors $\eta_i \stackrel{\$}{\leftarrow} \{0,1\}^k$ composing $\eta := \{\eta_1, \dots, \eta_k\}$ (the Hamming weight of η_i satisfying $1 < wt(\eta_i) < \lfloor k/2 \rfloor$).

It then computes each decryption server's secret share $d_i = Q \cdot \eta_i \in \mathbb{Z}^{2m}$. Subsequently, it confidentially sends the secret share d_i to decryption server Γ_i. By selecting a random matrix $M \in \mathbb{Z}_q^{k\times 2m}$ to pick a hash function $h_M: \mathbb{Z}^{2m} \to \mathbb{Z}_{q'}^{\lambda}$, it computes $h_M(q_i)$ ($1 \le i \le k$) and $h_M(SK_{id})$. The distributer makes common parameter $cp = (v, \eta, h_M, h_M(q_i), h_M(SK_{id}))$ public and keeps Q and SK_{id} secretly.

-VerS($h_M(d_i), \eta, h_M(q_j)$): This algorithm computes $h_M(d_i)$ and checks if $h_M(d_i) = \sum_{j=1}^{k} \eta_{ij} \cdot h_M(q_j)$, then accepts the secret share d_i and returns an acknowledgement, otherwise outputs "Invalid shares".

-Encrypt(PP, id, b): On input a message $b \in \{0,1\}$, an identity id, public parameters PP, this algorithm picks a uniformly random $s \stackrel{R}{\leftarrow} \mathbb{Z}_q^n$, a uniformly random matrix

$R \xleftarrow{R} \{-1,1\}^{m\times m}$ and noise vectors $x \xleftarrow{\bar{\Psi}_\alpha} \mathbb{Z}_q$, $y \xleftarrow{\bar{\Psi}_\alpha^m} \mathbb{Z}_q^m$, let $z = R^T y$, and subsequently computes $c_0 \longleftarrow u^T s + x + b\lfloor q/2 \rfloor \in \mathbb{Z}_q$, $c_1 \longleftarrow F_{id}^T s + \begin{bmatrix} y \\ z \end{bmatrix} \in \mathbb{Z}_q^{2m}$ and returns a ciphertext $C = (c_0, c_1)$.

-ConstructDec(η, v, c_1, d_j): On input η, v, c_1, this algorithm computes $E = [\eta_1, \dots, \eta_k] \cdot {A_2}^T$(E denotes $k \times k$ unit matrix) to obtain the matrix $A_2 = [a_1, \dots, a_k]$. The decryption server Γ_j computes decryption share W_j, $W_j = [(\sum_{i=1}^{k} v_i \cdot a_j^{(i)}) \cdot d_j^{(1)}, \dots, (\sum_{i=1}^{k} v_i \cdot a_j^{(i)}) \cdot d_j^{(2m)}]$. Then it computes $h_M(W_j^T)$ and outputs ζ_{j,c_1}, $\zeta_{j,c_1} = (W_j \cdot c_1, h_M(W_j^T))$.

-Decrypt(ζ_{j,c_1},PP,C): Given ζ_{j,c_1}, PP, $C = (c_0, c_1)$, it computes $\sum_{j=1}^{k} h_M(W_j^T)$ and checks if $\sum_{j=1}^{k} h_M(W_j^T) = h_M(SK_{id})$. If the test holds, accept the decryption shares and do as follows: compute $\omega \longleftarrow c_0 - \sum_{j=1}^{k}(W_j \cdot c_1) \in \mathbb{Z}_q$ and compare ω and $\lfloor q/2 \rfloor$, if $|\omega - \lfloor q/2 \rfloor| < \lfloor q/4 \rfloor$, output 1, otherwise output 0.

3.3 Correctness

Due to $\sum_{j=1}^{k}(W_j \cdot c_1) = (\sum_{j=1}^{k} W_j) \cdot c_1$, we can obtain $\sum_{j=1}^{k} W_j = (Q \cdot v)^T$ from the deduction for $\sum_{j=1}^{k} W_j$, as follows:

$$\sum_{j=1}^{k} W_j = \begin{bmatrix} (\sum_{i=1}^{k} v_i \cdot a_1^{(i)}) \cdot d_1^{(1)} + (\sum_{i=1}^{k} v_i \cdot a_2^{(i)}) \cdot d_2^{(1)} + \cdots + (\sum_{i=1}^{k} v_i \cdot a_k^{(i)}) \cdot d_k^{(1)} \\ (\sum_{i=1}^{k} v_i \cdot a_1^{(i)}) \cdot d_1^{(2)} + (\sum_{i=1}^{k} v_i \cdot a_2^{(i)}) \cdot d_2^{(2)} + \cdots + (\sum_{i=1}^{k} v_i \cdot a_k^{(i)}) \cdot d_k^{(2)} \\ \vdots \\ (\sum_{i=1}^{k} v_i \cdot a_1^{(i)}) \cdot d_1^{(2m)} + (\sum_{i=1}^{k} v_i \cdot a_2^{(i)}) \cdot d_2^{(2m)} + \cdots + (\sum_{i=1}^{k} v_i \cdot a_k^{(i)}) \cdot d_k^{(2m)} \end{bmatrix}^T$$

$$= \left[(\sum_{i=1}^{k} v_i \cdot a_1^{(i)}), (\sum_{i=1}^{k} v_i \cdot a_2^{(i)}), \cdots, (\sum_{i=1}^{k} v_i \cdot a_k^{(i)}) \right] \cdot [d_1, d_2, \cdots, d_k]^T$$

$$= v^T \cdot [a_1, a_2, \cdots, a_k] \cdot [d_1, d_2, \cdots, d_k]^T$$

$$= ([d_1, d_2, \cdots, d_k] \cdot [a_1, a_2, \cdots, a_k]^T \cdot v)^T$$

$$= ([q_1, q_2, \cdots, q_k] \cdot [\eta_1, \eta_2, \cdots, \eta_k] \cdot [a_1, a_2, \cdots, a_k]^T \cdot v)^T$$

$$= ([q_1, q_2, \cdots, q_k] \cdot E \cdot v)^T$$

$$= (Q \cdot v)^T.$$

When $\sum_{j=1}^{k} W_j = (Q \cdot v)^T = (SK_{id})^T$ is easily gotten,we have ω as follows:

$$\omega = c_0 - (SK_{id})^T c_1$$

$$= u^T s + x + b\lfloor q/2 \rfloor - SK_{id}^T (F_{id}^T s + \begin{bmatrix} y \\ z \end{bmatrix})$$

$$= b\lfloor q/2 \rfloor + x - SK_{id}^T \begin{bmatrix} y \\ z \end{bmatrix}.$$

Setting $(x - e_{id}^T \begin{bmatrix} y \\ z \end{bmatrix})$ as the error term, the decryption operates successfully when the error term is less than q/ 5with high probability. By Lemma 22 in [8], the norm of error term is bounded by $q\sigma m\alpha\omega(\sqrt{\log m} + O(\sigma m^{3/2}))$.

3.4 Parameters

To make the system work correctly, following conditions have to be satisfied:

1) Let $m > 6n\log q$, so the function TrapGen can operate.

2) Set the Gaussian parameter $\sigma > m\omega(\sqrt{\log m})$, so SampleLeft and SampleRight can operate.

3) Let $q > 2\sqrt{n}/\alpha$, so Regev's reduction holds.

4) Set $\alpha < [\sigma m\omega(\sqrt{\log m})]^{-1}$ and $q = \Omega(\sigma m^{\frac{3}{2}})$ for the error term is less than $q/5$.

5) Let $\mu = O(n\log q)$ and $\mu > m\omega(\sqrt{\log m})$, $\lambda^2 = m$ to satisfy that the input for lattice-based hash function is collision-free.

We assume that $n^\delta > \lceil \log q \rceil = O(\log n)$, n is the security parameter, we set the parameters $(m, q, \sigma, \alpha, \mu, \lambda)$ as follows:

$$m = 6n^{1+\delta}, q = m^{2.5} \cdot \omega(\sqrt{\log n}), \sigma = m \cdot \omega(\sqrt{\log n})$$

$$\alpha = [m^2 \cdot \omega(\sqrt{\log n})]^{-1}, \mu = mO(\log n), \lambda = \sqrt{m}\ .$$

We set λ and m to the nearest larger integer, q to the nearest larger prime.

4 Security Reduction

We define the security notion for our distributed IBE. INDr-sIDD-CPA is the notion of indistinguish ability of ciphertext under a selective identity chosen plaintext attack for the distributed IBE. INDr denotes indistinguishable from random, that means the challenge ciphertext is indistinguishable from random elements in the ciphertext space.

Definition. Let $\mathcal{A}$ be an INDr-sIDD-CPA PPT adversary. Consider the following Game 0 in which the adversary $\mathcal{A}$ interacts with the Chanllenger.

Initial: The adversary $\mathcal{A}$ outputs a target identity id^*.

Setup: Then Challenger runs algorithm Setup(n), n is a security parameter , and sends the resulting public system parameters $PP = (A_0, A_1, B, u)$ to $\mathcal{A}$. However, it keeps the master key MK secretly.

Phase 1: $\mathcal{A}$ corrupts $k - 1$ decryption servers.

Phase 2: The Challenger runs the Extract algorithm to obtain a private key d_{id^*} corresponding to the target identity id^*. Subsequently, the Challenger runs the Distribution algorithm on d_{id^*} with the input parameter k. It then obtains a set of secret shares $\{d_i | 1 \le i \le k\}$ and sends the $k - 1$ secret shares of corrupted decryption servers with the corresponding $h_M(d_i)$ to $\mathcal{A}$. Besides, the secret share of the uncorrupted server is kept secretly.

Phase 3: $\mathcal{A}$ issues adaptive private key extraction queries $q_1, \dots, q_m$, where q_i denotes the ith query on

$id_i(id_i \neq id^*)$. Then the Challenger runs Extract algorithm on id_i to obtain a corresponding private key e_i to respond the query q_i. It sends e_i to $\mathcal{A}$.

Challenge: After $\mathcal{A}$ finishes the Phase 3, it outputs a plaintext $\mathcal{M}$ to be challenged. The Challenger chooses a random bit $r \in \{0,1\}$ and a random ciphertext $\mathcal{C} \in \mathbb{Z}_q \times \mathbb{Z}_q^{2m}$. If $r = 0$ it gives the challenge ciphertext $\mathcal{C}^* = \mathrm{Encrypt}(PP, id^*, \mathcal{M})$ to $\mathcal{A}$. If $r = 1$, it sends the random ciphertext $\mathcal{C}^* = \mathcal{C}$ to $\mathcal{A}$.

Phase 4: $\mathcal{A}$ issues arbitrary adaptive private key extraction queries $q_{m+1}, \dots, q_n$, where q_i denotes the ith query on $id_i(id_i \neq id^*)$. The Challenger responds as in Phase 3.

Guess: $\mathcal{A}$ outputs a guess $r' \in \{0,1\}$. If $r = r'$, it wins the game.

We define the advantage of an INDr-sIDD-CPA adversary $\mathcal{A}$ in attacking the distributed IBE $\mathcal{E}$ as $Adv_{\mathcal{E},\mathcal{A}}(n) = |\Pr[r = r'] - 1/2|$.

Theorem 2. In the standard model, our distributed IBE with parameters setting as in Section*parameters* is INDr-sIDD-CPA secure if the $(\mathbb{Z}_q, n, \overline{\Psi}_\alpha) - \mathrm{LWE}$ assumption holds.

Proof.

Game 0. It is the original INDr-sIDD-CPA game as previously mentioned.

Game 1. In Game 1, we change slightly the way to generate A_1 which is one of public parameters in PP. Let the Challenger in Game 1 select a random matrix $R^* \in \{-1,1\}^{m \times m}$ at the Setup phase, id^* is the target identity that $\mathcal{A}$ wants to attack. A_1 is constructed as $A_1 = A_0R^* - H(id^*)B$. The Challenger use SampleRight algorithm to generate e_{id} to respond to a private key extraction query. The rest of the game is the same as Game 0.

By Lemma 13 in [7], Game 1 and Game 0 is statistically indistinguishable.

Game 2. We change the way to generate A_0 and B in PP. The Challenger chooses a random matrix in $\mathbb{Z}_q^{n \times m}$ as A_0 and runs the TrapGen(q,n) to generate a uniformly random matrix $B \in \mathbb{Z}_q^{n \times m}$ altogether with a trapdoor T_B. The construction of A_1 is the same as Game 1.

The Challenger runs $\mathrm{SampleRight}(A_0, (H(id) - H(id^*)B, R^*, T_B, u, \sigma)$ to sample a vector $e \in \mathbb{Z}_q^{2m}$ and sends $SK_{id} = e$ to $\mathcal{A}$ to respond to the private key query.

Let $F_{id} = (A_0|A_0R^* + (H(id) - H(id^*)) \cdot B)$, according to Theorem 19 in [7], when $\sigma > \|\widetilde{T}_B\| s_R \omega(\sqrt{\log m})$, the generated e is distributed statistically close to $D_{\Lambda_q^u(F_{id}),\sigma}$, as in Game 1.

So Game 2 and Game 1 is statistically indistinguishable.

Game 3. In Game 3, the challenge ciphertext $\mathcal{C}^* = (c_0^*, c_1^*)$ is selected by random independent elements in $\mathbb{Z}_q \times \mathbb{Z}_q^{2m}$. The rest of Game 3 is the same as Game 2. The advantage of $\mathcal{A}$ in this game is zero.

We can refer to the reduction from the LWE problem in [7] to show Game 2 and Game 3 are indistinguishable for $\mathcal{A}$.

The reduction from the LWE problem shows as follows:

We assume that $\mathcal{A}$'s advantage in distinguishing Game 2 and Game 3 is non-negligible and construct an LWE algorithm $\mathcal{B}$ using $\mathcal{A}$. $\mathcal{B}$ receives LWE samples $(u_i, v_i) \in \mathbb{Z}_q^n \times \mathbb{Z}_q$, $i = 0, \dots, m$ from an oracle $\mathcal{O}$ as mentioned in Section 2.4.

Initial: The adversary $\mathcal{A}$ outputs a target identity id^* to $\mathcal{B}$.

Setup: $\mathcal{B}$ constructs public parameters $PP = (A_0, A_1, B, u_0, R^*)$, where $A_0 = [u_1, u_2, \cdots, u_m] \in \mathbb{Z}_q^{n \times m}$, the construction of A_1andB is the same as in Game 2, u_0 is the 0th LWE sample, $R^* \in \{-1,1\}^{m \times m}$.

Queries: $\mathcal{B}$ responds to the private key extraction queries as in Game 2.

Challenge: $\mathcal{A}$ outputs a plaintext $b^* \in \{0,1\}$, then $\mathcal{B}$ sends a challenge ciphertext $\mathcal{C}^* = (c_0^*, c_1^*)$ for the target id^* to $\mathcal{A}$. We set $v^* = \begin{bmatrix} v_1 \\ \cdot \\ \cdot \\ \cdot \\ v_m \end{bmatrix} \in \mathbb{Z}_q^m$, $c_0^* = v_0 + b^* \lfloor q/2 \rfloor \in \mathbb{Z}_q$ and $c_1^* = \begin{bmatrix} v^* \\ (R^*)^T v^* \end{bmatrix} \in \mathbb{Z}_q^{2m}$.

When the LWE oracle $\mathcal{O} = \mathcal{O}_s$ (which is a pseudorandom sampler), then $\mathcal{C}^*$ is distributed the same as the challenge ciphertext in Game 2. When $\mathcal{O} = \mathcal{O}_\$$, the challenge ciphertext is the same as in Game 3.

Guess: $\mathcal{A}$ guesses if it interacts with a Game 2 Challenger or Game 3 Challenger after issuing arbitrary adaptive private key extraction queries $q_{m+1}, \dots, q_n$. then $\mathcal{B}$ outputs the guess of $\mathcal{A}$ to answer the LWE challenge.

The advantage of $\mathcal{B}$ to solve LWE problem is the same as the advantage of $\mathcal{A}$ to distinguish Game 2 and Game 3.

5 Efficiency Analysis

We show the comparison of our lattice-based distributed IBE and Baek and Zheng Yulliang's pairing-based distributed IBE in calculation cost.

Table1: Comparison of Our Scheme And Bz Scheme

comparison

	Baek's scheme	*Our scheme*
	Calculation cost	Calculation cost
Private key distribution	kM_1	(k+1)Mul
Secret share generation	tP	$Mul + 2m(kM + (k-1)A)$
Verification of secret share	$(n + 4t + 4)P + (t + 2)H$	(2k+1)H
Combination	$tL + tM_1 + (t - 1)M_T$	kMul

Table2: Notation Illustration

Notation	*Operation*	*Notation*	*Operation*
L	Lagrange interpolation operation	H	Hash operation
P	pairing	Mul	matrix

	operation		multiplication
M_1	the point multiplication in G_1	M	multiplication operation in $\mathbb{Z}$
M_T	multiplication in G_T	A	addition operation in $\mathbb{Z}$

The k represents the number of decryption servers, t represents the threshold.

Table II explains the meaning of the notations in Table I. For example, it shows that at private key distribution phase, Baek's scheme costs kM_1 (k times point multiplication in G_1) and it costs (k+1) times matrix multiplication. The advantages in our scheme appears in secret share generation and verification of secret share phase. As we know, the pairing operation is much more complicate than simple matrix multiplication and addition. Our distributed IBE avoids the complex pairing operation, so our scheme reduces the calculation cost and improves the efficiency.

Conclusion

In this paper, we improve the lattice-based secret sharing method and propose a lattice-based distributed IBE provably secure against selective identity chosen-plaintext attack. Through theoretical analysis, compared with the Baek and Zheng Yuliang's scheme, our scheme reduces calculation cost.

Acknowledgement

I would like to express my gratitude to all those who helped me for finishing this paper, especially to Professor Zhang Quan, my supervisor, for his encouragement and guidance.

References

[1] Shamir A. Identity-based cryptosystems and signature schemes[C]//Advances in cryptology. Springer Berlin Heidelberg, 1984: 47-53.

[2] Boneh D, Franklin M. Identity-based encryption from the Weil pairing[C]//Advances inCryptology-CRYPTO 2001. Springer Berlin Heidelberg, 2001: 213-229.

[3] Shamir A. How to share a secret[J]. Communications of the ACM, 1979, 22(11): 612-613.

[4] Baek J, Zheng Y. Identity-based threshold decryption[M]//Public Key Cryptography–PKC 2004. Springer Berlin Heidelberg, 2004: 262-276.

[5] Gentry C, Peikert C, Vaikuntanathan V. Trapdoors for hard lattices and new cryptographic constructions[C]//Proceedings of the fortieth annual ACM symposium on Theory of computing. ACM, 2008: 197-206.

[6] Cash D, Hofheinz D, Kiltz E, et al. Bonsai trees, or how to delegate a lattice basis[J]. Journal of cryptology, 2012, 25(4): 601-639.

[7] Agrawal S, Boneh D, Boyen X. Efficient lattice (H) IBE in the standard model[M]//Advances in Cryptology–EUROCRYPT 2010. Springer Berlin Heidelberg, 2010: 553-572.

[8] El Bansarkhani R, Meziani M. An efficient lattice-based secret sharing construction[M]//Information Security Theory and Practice. Security, Privacy and Trust in Computing Systems and Ambient Intelligent Ecosystems. Springer Berlin Heidelberg, 2012: 160-168.

[9] Blakely G R. Safeguarding cryptographic keys[C]//Proc. AFIPS. 1979, 48: 313-317.

[10] Asmuth C, Bloom J. A modular approach to key safeguarding[J]. IEEE transactions on information theory, 1983, 30(2): 208-210.

[11] Regev O. On lattices, learning with errors, random linear codes, and cryptography[J]. Journal of the ACM (JACM), 2009, 56(6): 34.

[12] Alwen J, Peikert C. Generating shorter bases for hard random lattices[J]. Theory of Computing Systems, 2011, 48(3): 535-553.

[13] Zhou F. Lattice theory and crypotography [M]. Science Press, 2013

Face Recognition under Varying Illumination Using Green's Function-based Bidimensional Empirical Mode Decomposition and Gradientfaces

Zhi-Jun Yang, Xue He, Wen-Yi Xiong, Xiang-Fei Nie

School of electronics and information engineering, Chongqing Three Gorges University,404000,wanzhou,Chongqing, China.

Abstract. A novel face recognition approach under varying illumination condition based on Green's function in tension-based bid imensional empirical mode decomposition (GiT-BEMD) and gradient faces (GBEMDGF) is present. Firstly, face image was illumination normalization by discrete cosine transform that an appropriate number of DCT coefficients are truncated in logarithm domain. And then, two intrinsic mode functions (IMFs) that relevant of intrinsic physical significances of face images are produced by Gi T-BEMD. At the same time, gradient faces is used to improve the high frequency component of face images and to extract illumination insensitive facial feature. The facial feature of discriminately are fused using IMFs and illumination insensitive feature. Secondly, the principal component analysis is adopted to reduce the dimension of face image. The nearest neighbourhood classifier based on cosine distance is implemented for face classification. Experimental results on Yale B database and CUM PIE face database demonstrate that the present technique is robust to varying lighting resource.

1 Introduction

It is a well-known fact that variation under illumination condition could seriously affect the performance of face recognition system [1 2]. The changes of same face image under different illumination condition are bigger compared with the change of different face image under same illumination condition. Within the past decade, many researchers were focused on illumination problem and many algorithms that deal with lighting under vary condition were proposed. In general, those algorithms are divided into three categories [3]. The first category is illumination pre-processing and illumination normalization. Histogram equalization (HE) [4], Gamma correction and Logarithm transform [5] are widely used for illumination normalization. However, those algorithms are consideration the global characteristic of face image rather than the local detail feature that is important to face recognition. Thus those algorithms cannot obtain ideal face recognition result. The second category attempts to extract the illumination invariant features. In [6], the author proposes a method to extract illumination insensitive facial feature under varying lighting condition called Gradientfaces in gradient domain. However, the data of face image was not reduced, so the calculation is complication .In [7], the author uses the gradient angle as the input feature. It generates the gradient vectors in different form, and then computes the gradient angle. The third category, which handle the illumination problem by construct the face model. In [8], the author present a method that a set of images in fixed pose, but under different lighting condition, can form light convex cone, which can generate different face images with different light direction. Nevertheless, this method needs a variety of train samples or face images under different lighting resource, which is not an ideal method for real time environment.

In this paper, we present a novel face illumination processing technique based on bidimensional empirical mode decomposition and gradient faces. Discrete cosine transform is adopted to normal face image. The high frequency intrinsic mode functions (IMFs) of face image are produced by GiT-BEMD. Gradient faces is adopted to enhance the high frequency detail of face image and to extract the Gradient faces, which is illumination insensitive facial feature. Two kinds of features are fused to improve the performance of image recognition. The BEMD can achieve intrinsic mode functions, which is physical feature relating to face image. Gradient faces extract illumination invariant feature. Two kinds of feature are fusion to as discriminative facial feature. The PCA is applied to reduce the dimension of face image and the nearest neighbourhood classifier based on cosine distance is utilized for face classification. Experiment results in this paper demonstrate that our method is robust to light change with different direction. The flowchart of this paper is shown in figure1.

The rest of this correspondence is organized as follows. In section 2, logarithm transform, green's function-based bidimensional empirical mode decomposition and gradient faces are present in detail. Many experimental results are described in section 3. Finally, the conclusion is given in section 4.

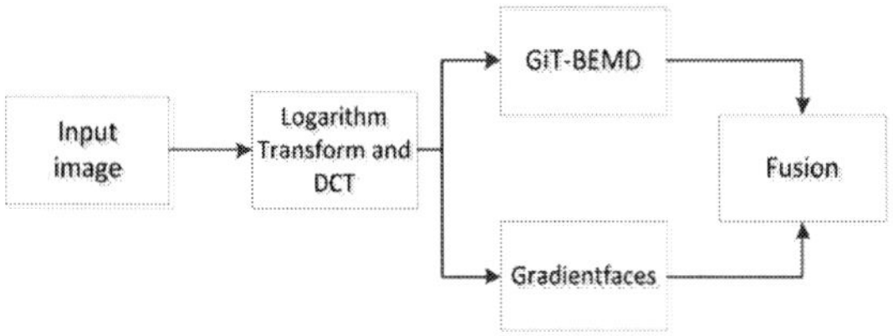

Fig.1 The Flowchart of Our Method

2 Methodologies

2.1 Logarithm transform

The reflectance model [9] can be expressed as follows:

$$I(x,y)=R(x,y)\times L(x,y) \qquad (1)$$

Where $I(x,y)$ is arbitrary image pixel value, $R(x,y)$ is the reflectance which is fast change part of the image and $L(x,y)$ is the illuminance which is slow change part of the image. The logarithmic operation is used to eq. (1).

$$\ln[I(x,y)]=\ln[R(x,y)]+\ln[L(x,y)] \qquad (2)$$

The reflectance component $R(x,y)$ is multiplied by the lighting component $L(x,y)$ in time domain. However, it is adding when the image was transformed into logarithm domain. Thus, the lighting component is subtracted from face images to eliminate the illumination effective in logarithm domain, which is similar to high-pass filter..

2.2 GiT-BEMD

Bidimensional empirical mode decomposition decomposes face image into a series of intrinsic mode functions (IMFs) which is high frequency and low frequency component of the face image and a residue. In this paper, the GiT-BEMD [10] is present here based on a representation of upper and lower surface envelopes via suitable Green's functions for spline interpolation including surface tension. The difference between canonical BEEMD and GiT-BEMD are the process of estimating the upper and lower surfaces and limiting the number of iterations per BIEMD to a few iterations only. In this method, a data point/pixel is considered as a local maximum (minimum), if its value is strictly higher (lower) than all of its neighbors. Let $P=\{p_i \mid i=1,2\cdots N\}$ be a set of local minima (maxima) of an $x\times y$ -dimensional data matrix such that it exists a small (large) neighbourhood around any such local optimal point p_i on which the pixel value is never larger (small) than $f(x_i,y_i)$ at p_i .Local extrema occur only at critical points. Let $D(x,y)=f_{xx}f_{yy}-(f_{xy})^2$. If $D>0$ at a critical point, then the critical p_i is a local extremum. The signs of f_{xx} and f_{yy} determine whether the point is a maximum or a minimum. If $D\le 0$ at a critical point, then the point p_i is a saddle point.

In BEMD, spline interpolation is basically used to find the smoothest surface passing through a grid of irregularly spaced extrema, either maxima or minima. In this word, it is proposed to employ Green's functions, deduced from proper data constraints, to expand the interpolating surface under tension. Interpolation with Green's functions implies that the points of the interpolating envelope surface can be expressed as

$$s(x_u)=\sum_{n=1}^{N} w_n\Phi(x_u,x_n) \qquad (3)$$

Where x_u denotes any point where the surface is unknown, x_n represents the nth data constraint, $\Phi(x_u,x_n)$ is the Green's function and w_n is the respective weight in the envelope representation.

2.3 Gradientfaces

The Gradientfaces [6] can be defined as follows:

For face image $I(x,y)$, the relationship between neighboring point (x,y) and $(x+\Delta x,y)$ defined as follows.

$$I(x+\Delta x,y)=R(x+\Delta x,y)\times L(x+\Delta x,y) \qquad (4)$$

According to the common assumption that L is approximately smooth and changing slowly:

$$\begin{aligned} &I(x+\Delta x,y)-I(x,y)\\ &=R(x+\Delta x,y)\times L(x+\Delta x,y)-R(x,y)L(x,y) \qquad (5)\\ &\approx(R(x+\Delta x,y)-R(x,y))L(x,y)\end{aligned}$$

Considering the limitation of the above equality (11), we have:

$$\frac{\partial I(x,y)}{\partial x}\approx L(x,y)\frac{\partial R(x,y)}{\partial x} \qquad (6)$$

Similarly, we have:

$$\frac{\partial I(x,y)}{\partial y}\approx L(x,y)\frac{\partial R(x,y)}{\partial y} \qquad (7)$$

Dividing (6) by (7), we have:

$$\frac{I_y}{I_x} \approx \frac{R_y}{R_x} \quad (8)$$

Where $I_x = \frac{\partial I(x,y)}{\partial x}$ and $I_y = \frac{\partial I(x,y)}{\partial y}$ is the gradient of face image under x and y direction, respectively. $R_x = \frac{\partial R(x,y)}{\partial x}$ and $R_y = \frac{\partial R(x,y)}{\partial y}$ are the gradient of reflectance component under x and y direction, respectively.

Considering the common assumption that R can be considered as an illumination insensitive component, so as to the radio of I_y and I_x.

Therefore the gradient faces is defined as follows:

$$G = \arctan(\frac{I_y}{I_x}), G \in [-\pi, \pi] \quad (9)$$

In order to compute gradient faces, we need to calculate the gradient of face image in x and y direction. We are smoothing face images by convolving Gaussian kernel function firstly. The Gaussian kernel function is expressed as following:

$$G(x,y,\sigma) = \frac{1}{2\pi\sigma^2}\exp(-\frac{x^2+y^2}{2\sigma^2}) \quad (10)$$

Where σ is standard deviation.

2.4 The fusion of facial feature

In this paper, the Green's Function - based Bidimensional Empirical Mode Decomposition is wielded to generate two IMFs and the illumination insensitive feature is extracted. Two kinds of features are combined to come up with distinguished facial feature. The algorithmic view of the proposed method is summarized as follows:

Input: Original face image I .

Output: The GBEMDGF of I'.

1. Logarithmic transform using eq. (2).
2. Apply Discrete Cosine Transform to discard low-frequency DCT coefficient on I to gain normalization face image f .
3. Apply GiT-BEMD on f to achieve IMF g . $g(i,j) = g_1(i,j) + g_2(i,j); i = 1,2 \cdots M; j = 1,2 \cdots N.$ Where M and N are the size of face image.
4. Apply Gradientfaces on f to extract illumination insensitive feature $q(i,j)$ using eq. (9).
5. Feature fusion by $I' = \begin{bmatrix} g(i,j) \\ q(i,j) \end{bmatrix}$ to attain lighting insensitive facial feature.

3 Experiments

3.1 Face Database

Our experiments are conducted on the Yale B face database and CUM PIE face database. The Yale B face database contains images of ten individuals with nine pose and 64 illuminations per pose. The frontal face images of all subjects, each with 64 different illuminations are used to evaluate the algorithm. In our experiment, all face images are cropped and resized to 128×128 and divided into five subsets based on the angle of lighting direction. Subset 1 (0o-12o), subset 2 (13o-25o), subset 3 (26o-50o), subset 4 (51o-77o) and subset 5 (above 78o) has 70,120,120,140,190 images, respectively. CUM PIE database contains 68 subjects with 41368 face images in total. We use illumination subset (C27) to as the experiment samples. In our experiment, we use 68 subjects with 1428 face images, each with 21 different illuminations for testing. All images are cropped and resized to 68×68.

3.2 Experiment results on Yale B

Fig.2 shows five images for one individual from different subsets and corresponding face images processed with our method.

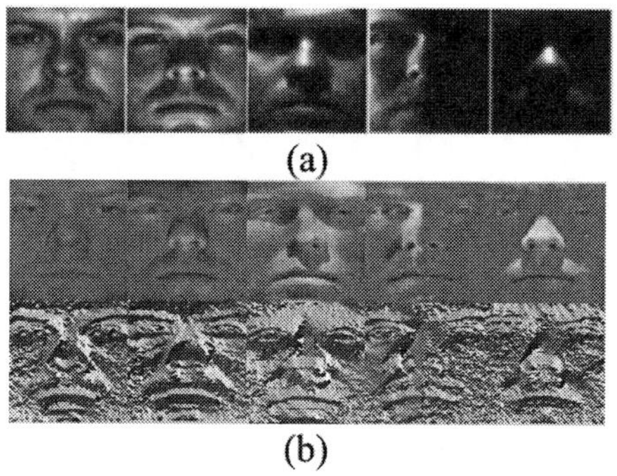

Figure2 (a) Original Face Images and (B) Face Image Processed with Our Method.

In order to compare with the results from important literature, the first experiment is devised to subset one as reference subset and other images from subset 2 to subset 5 as query subsets. Comparison results are shown in Table I. Bidimensional empirical mode decomposition (BEMD) and our method has the same experiment condition.

Table I Performance Comparison on Yale B Database

Method	Face Recognition(%)				
	Subset 2	Subset3	Subset4	Subset5	Average
BEMD	98.33	98.33	89.29	43.68	77.89

GF[6]	100	100	98.75	98.95	99.3
QI[11]	99.3	61.9	34.1	23.3	54.65
LBP[12]	100	97.6	65.2	44.4	76.8
Our method	100	100	100	100	100

The second experiment is devised to use every subset on Yale B database as train subset and other subset from subset 1 to subset 5 expect for train subset as test subset to indicate the effectiveness of our method. When subset 1 as train set, the average recognition of subset 2, subset 3, subset 4 and subset 5 are 100% . When subset 2 as train set, the average recognition of subset 1, subset 3, subset 4 and subset 5 are 100% . When subset 3 as train set, the average recognition of subset 1, subset 2, subset 4 and subset 5 are 100% . When subset 4 as train set, the average recognition of subset 1, subset 2, subset 3 and subset 5 are 100% . When subset 5 as train set, the average recognition of subset 1, subset 2, subset 3 and subset 4 are 100% .

3.3 Experiment results on CUM PIE

Some face image from CUM PIE database are shown in Fig.3.

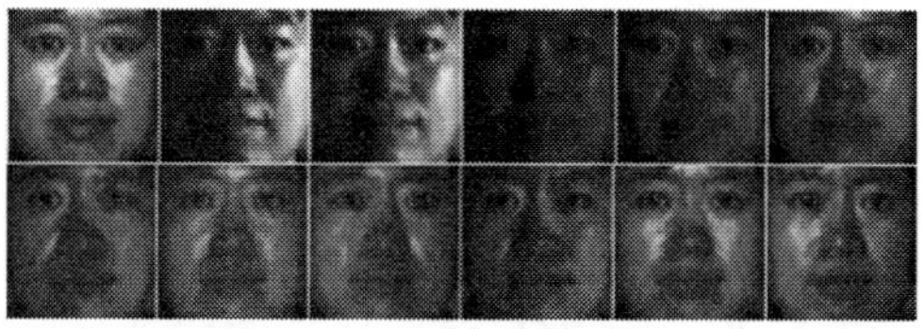

(c)

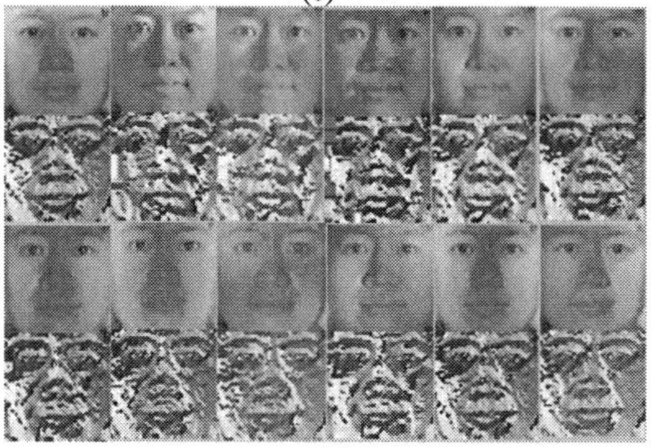

(d)

Figure3 (c) Original Images and (D) Face Images Processed With Our Method

We conduct one experiment on this face database. In this experiment, we chose one person in every subject as train image and others as test samples. Thus we have 68 reference images and 1360 query images. The experiment results are shown in Table II. BEMD, GF and our method have same experiment condition. The experiment results of SQI and MSR are from [6]. The recognition rate of BEMD, GF, SQI, MSR and our method are 90.22%, 95.07%, 77.94%, 62.07% and 100%. Thus our method can achieve ideal face recognition rate compared with BEMD, GF, SQI and MSR.

Table II Experiment Result Comparison with Different Methods on Cum Pie Database

	Methods				
	BEMD	GF	SQI[6]	MSR[6]	Our Methods
Rate (%)	90.22	95.07	77.94	62.07	100

4 Conclusions

In this correspondence, we propose a method based on the bidimensional empirical mode decomposition. And the gradient faces algorithm to process face image under varying lighting. The two IMFs of face image was decomposed in logarithm domain. And then, the gradient faces was adopted to enhance the high frequency component of face images after reconstruction. The PCA is used to extract facial feature and the nearest neighborhood classifier based on cosine distance is used to classify. Experimental results on Yale B database and CUM PIE database demonstrate that the method in our paper is robust algorithm for face recognition under varying illumination. We will test the effectiveness of this technique in bigger face database in the future.

Acknowledgment

This research was financially supported by the Project Foundation of Chongqing Municipal Education Committee (KJ121114).

References

1. Han H, Shan S, Chen X, et al. A comparative study on illumination preprocessing in face recognition [J]. Pattern Recognition, 2013, 46(6):1691-1699.
2. Ochoa-Villegas M A, Nolazco-Flores J A, Barron-Cano O, et al. Addressing the illumination challenge in two-dimensional face recognition: a survey [J]. Iet Computer Vision, 2015, 9(6):978-992.
3. Baradarani A, Wu Q M J, Ahmadi M. An efficient illumination invariant face recognition framework via illumination enhancement and DD-DTCCWT filtering[J]. Pattern Recognition,2013,46(1) :57-72.
4. Shan S, Gao B, et al. Illumination normalization for robust face recognition against varying lighting conditions[C]//IEEE International Workshop on Analysis and Modelling of Faces and Gestures. IEEE Computer Society, 2003:157-157.
5. Savvides M, Kumar B V K V.Illumination normalization using logarithm transforms for face authentication[C]// International Conference on Audio-and Video-Based Biometric Person Authentication. Springer-Verlag,2003 :549-556.

6. T Zhang, Y Y Tang, B Fang . et al, Face recognition under varying illumination using gradientfaces, IEEE Transactions on image processing, 2009, 18(11): 2599-2606.
7. An G, Wu J, Ruan Q. Improved Gradientface used in face recognition under varying illumination[C]// IEEE, International Conference on Signal Processing. IEEE, 2010:670-673.
8. A. S. Georghiades, P. N. Belhumeur, and D. J. Kriegman. From few to many: Illumination cone models for face recognition under variable lighting and pose. IEEE Trans. Pattern Anal. Mach. Intell, 23(6):643–660, 2001.
9. Shahamat H, Pouyan A A. Face recognition under large illumination variations using homomorphic filtering in spatial domain[J]. Journal of Visual Communication & Image Representation, 2014, 25(5):970-977.
10. Al-Baddai S, Al-Subari K, Tomé A M, et al. A green's function-based Bi-dimensional empirical mode decomposition[J]. Information Sciences, 2016, 348:305-321.
11. Shashua A, Riklin-Raviv T. The Quotient Image: Class-Based Re-Rendering and Recognition with Varying Illuminations [J]. Pattern Analysis & Machine Intelligence IEEE Transactions on, 2001, 23(2):129-139.
12. Ahonen T, Hadid A, Pietikainen M. Face Description with Local Binary Patterns: Application to Face Recognition[J]. IEEE Transactions on Pattern Analysis & Machine Intelligence, 2006, 28(12):2037-2041.

DOI: 10.1051/itmconf/20160701016

Research on the Solution Space of 2-SAT and Max-2-SAT

Bai-Feng Li[1,a], Wei -Wei[2] and Chao-Qun Liu[3]

[1] *Beihang University, Beijing, China*

Abstract. We study the properties of 2-SAT and Max-2-SAT problems by analyzing the node adding process on the factor graph. Two important structures, backbones and mutual-determinations are investigated, and the reduced solution graph for the expression of solution space of 2-SAT and Max-2-SAT is defined. For 2-SAT problem, a complete evolution process for the reduced graph is discussed and corresponding algorithm is obtained. For the Max-2-SAT problem, the analysis shows it's backbone number can evolve in a much harder way by which it can increase or decrease. The research in this paper provide a new view point for understanding the solution space of 2-SAT and Max-2-SAT, which will be benefit for recognizing the complexity nature of the NP-hard problems.

1 Introduction

As the first NPC problem (Cook, 1971), K-SAT is concerned by mathematicians, physicists and computer scientists [1]. It has a wide variety of applications such as consistency in expert systems knowledge bases ([2], [3]), integrity constraints in databases ([4], [5]).

A K-SAT formula contains N Boolean variables and M clauses, each of which is disjunction of K literals (variables or its negation). An assignment (to the N variables) forms by fixation of each Boolean variable. If there is at least one assignment that makes all clauses be true, the K-SAT formula is satisfiable (SAT); otherwise it's unsatisfiable (UNSAT) [6].

For the UNSAT instances, a natural question, of great practical importance, arises, i.e., how close can one get to satisfiability? Making that question precise leads to the Maximum Satisfiability problem ([7], [15]). This problem can also be expressed as an optimization problem Max-K-SAT and then takes the form: given a formula of M clauses involving N logical variables x1, x2, ... , xn, determine an assignment for the formula that satisfies the maximum number of clauses.

In the literature of computational complexity [13], Max-2-SAT is NP-hard [8] and even hard to approximate [9], which makes a strong contrast with 2-SAT which can be solvable in linear time [10]. At present, there are some methods to detect the structure of solution space. Like spin glass approach, cavity method, phase transition ([11], [12], [14]). In [17], a new method is proposed to detect the whole solution space of the minimum vertex cover problem, and we want to generalize the corresponding analysis to 2-SAT and Max-2-SAT problem.

Following [17], in this paper, we focus on the solution space of Max-2-SAT. Backbones and mutual determination are discussed to understand the structure of solution space of 2-SAT and Max-2-sat problems. By the reduced solution graph, we provide a complete analysis of the solution space evolution for the 2-SAT problem and a corresponding algorithm is given, by which we can detect the correlation of the nodes in the solution space and a clear prospect of the solution organization. Furthermore, some analysis is provided for the Max-2-SAT instances, which shows the complicated evolution of it's solution space and results from the NP-hard intricacy. The analysis in this paper illustrates that the solution space for 2-SAT can be expressed by a simple graph (the reduced solution graph) and it may not be the case for the Max-2-SAT problem.

2 Model Description

In this paper, we mainly use the technique of the nodes-states evolution on the factor graph of the satisfiability problem [12].

2.1 Factor graph

We investigate the solution space of Max-2-SAT problem by constructing a factor graph: each variable node xi represents a Boolean variable, and each pair of linked nodes represents a clause (constraint) [12]. On the graph, there are three types of connection — dashed to dashed, dashed to dotted, dotted to dotted: dashed lines mean that variables appear as their negations in the corresponding clauses, and dotted lines mean themselves in clauses, like that in Figure 1.

[a] libaifeng@buaa.edu.cn

DOI: 10.1051/itmconf/20160701016

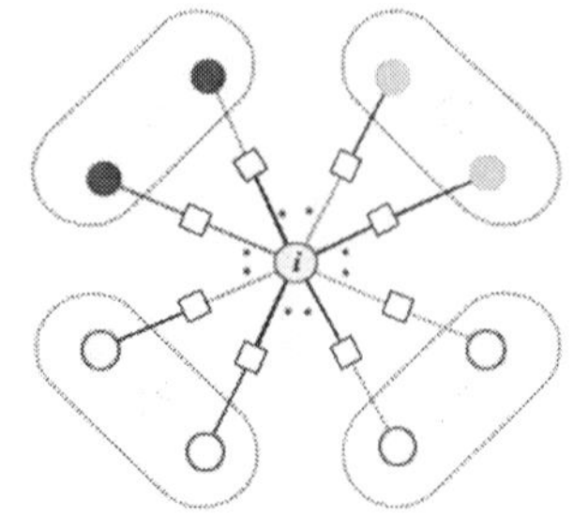

Figure 1. Circle Node Means Variable and Square node Means clause. Dash Line Means that Variables Appears in Its Connected Clause as A Negation and Dotted Line Means Itself.

2.2 Two basic structures

For each node's states of Max-2-SAT on its solution space, there are three types of possible values: x=1 backbones, x=0 backbones or free nodes, which always take value of x=1, x=0 or can take any one in the solution space. Similar as the analysis in the minimum vertex-Cover problem, we mainly concern with two structures on the solution space: backbones and mutual-determinations [17].

For $(x \vee y) \wedge (\neg x \vee y)=1$, to get the solution of this formula, we need to solve $(x \vee y)=1$ and $(\neg x \vee y)=1$ respectively. $(x \vee y)=1$ can be expressed by the form of $(\neg x \rightarrow y)$ that means $\neg x=1$ required y=1 and $(\neg y \rightarrow x)$. $(\neg x \vee y)=1$ can be expressed by the form of $(x \rightarrow y)$ that means x=1, y=1 and $(y \rightarrow x)$. Then, if $(x \rightarrow y)$ and $(y \rightarrow z)$, we can have $(x \rightarrow z)$ and this process is named as logical deduction.

Backbones: In 2-SAT problem, backbones are a set of variables which occupy fixation in every satisfying truth assignment, i.e., if one variable x and its negation $\neg x$ are both connected to another variable y by the logical deduction, we have $(\neg x \rightarrow y)$ and $(x \rightarrow y) \Rightarrow$ y is backbone; especially, $(\neg x \rightarrow x)$ and $(x \rightarrow x) \Rightarrow$ x is backbone [16].

Proof: In $(\neg x \rightarrow y)$, if $x=0 \Rightarrow y=1$; in $(x \rightarrow y)$, if $x=1 \Rightarrow y=1$, so no matter what x values, y is fixed. In a similar way, $(\neg x \rightarrow x)$ and $(x \rightarrow x) \Rightarrow$ x is fixed. These fixed variables are backbones.

For the instance in Figure 2, x1 =x2=x3=x4=1, and x1 =x2=x3=0, x4=1 are two solutions. According to the definition of backbones, x4 is a backbone.

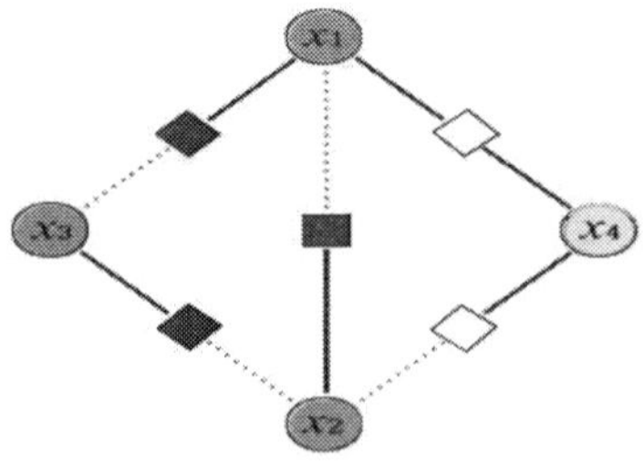

Figure 2. The Instance of Backbones

Mutual-determination: In 2-SAT problem, we named mutual-determination as an interactive relation of unfrozen variables in strong component in the viewpoint of logical deduction, i.e., a group of nodes are in a mutual-determination if and only if one node in them taking any value can force the others to be frozen in the solution space [7].

Proof: If the nodes form a mutual-determination, the fixation of anyone will result in the fixation of the others in strong component. Indeed, it is a special relation implied by the constraints that unfrozen variables can be mutually determined by the others. If some unfrozen variables $x \rightarrow y \rightarrow z \rightarrow x$ form a strong component, $x \rightarrow y \rightarrow z \rightarrow x \Rightarrow (\neg x \vee y), (\neg y \vee z)$ and $(\neg z \vee x)$, if $x=1 \Rightarrow y=1, z=1$.

Conversely, for $\neg x \leftarrow \neg y \leftarrow \neg z \leftarrow \neg x$, if $x=0 \Rightarrow z=0$, y=0. So we call x, y, z mutually determined.

For the instance in Figure 2, x1, x2, x3 are mutually determined.

2.3 Reduced solution graph for Max-2-SAT

Similar as the organization of solution space of Vertex-cover [17], we define the reduced solution graph of Max-2-SAT, which is mainly based on the two important structures backbones and mutual-determination and the evolution of them. The reduced graph is based on the factor graph with the x=1 backbones yellow circles, x=0 backbones red circles, free nodes blue circles and the mutual-determination red squares.

In order to detect the structure of solution space, directly applying the analysis of [12] and [17], we add one new node (called i) to previous N-1 system (N-1 nodes), new node connects to other k nodes x1, x2, … , xk. We suppose k1 nodes free, k2 nodes frozen to 1, k3 nodes frozen to 0 in previous system, by which k1 + k2 +k3=k.

When xi =1, all the clauses connected to xi with dotted lines are already satisfied and the variables connected to it are free. All the clauses connected to it with dashed lines must be satisfied by the variable connected to it to keep the minimum energy.

When xi =0, it is similar to the above case: all the clauses connected to xi with dashed lines are already satisfied and the variables connected to it are free. All the clauses connected to it with dotted lines must be satisfied by the variable connected to it to keep the minimum energy.

3 Solution Space Expression On 2-Sat

In this section, we will provide a complete process to obtain the reduced solution graph of 2-SAT problem, i.e., the whole solution space can be expressed by a graph. Considering an N-1 system and adding a new node i, we detect the solution space of new system. According to the types of nodes that connected to i, we have three cases below (here we only consider the instances in the satisfiable phase):

Case 1: If the nodes connected to i are only free in the N-1 system, no matter how i values, the whole system is satisfied. Now we want to detect the relationship between node i and the free nodes.

Subcase 1: If the nodes connected to i are free and no free neighbor can influence other free neighbors, no matter what value the node i takes, the new added clauses can be satisfied by its free neighbors. Then, in this case node i is also free in new system. Here, influence means that one free neighbor taking some value forces some other free neighbors to be fixed, and the mutual-determination relation is not included.

Subcase 2: If the nodes connected to i are free and some free neighbors can influence other free neighbors (no mutual-determination), the relationship of new node and the former free nodes may be backbone, mutual-determination or free.

Eg.1

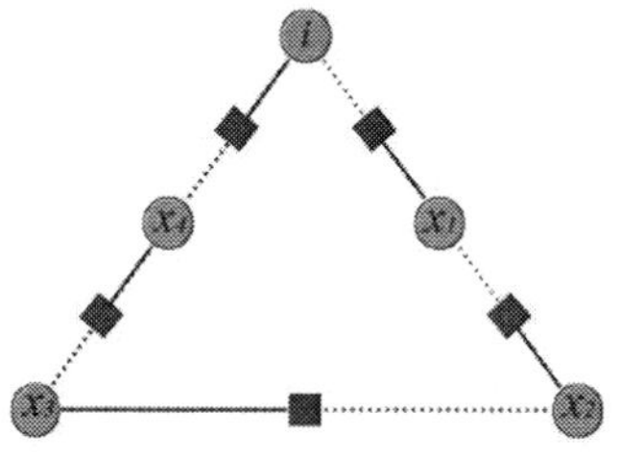

Figure 3. Eg.1

Analysis: In Eg.1, the former problem without node i have four free nodes, (x1 free, x2=x3=x4=1) and (x1 =x2=x3=0, x4 free) are all solutions of the problem. Some of them are influence others, but they are not mutual-determination. When add node i, we find the new node i and former free nodes form mutual-determination. Node i is free node in new problem.x1=x2=x3=x4=i=1 and x1 =x2=x3=x4=i=0 are all solutions.

Subcase 3: If the nodes connected to i are free and there are mutual-determinations in the neighborhood, as they can influence each other, the new node i may be backbone, mutual-determination or free in new system.

Eg.2

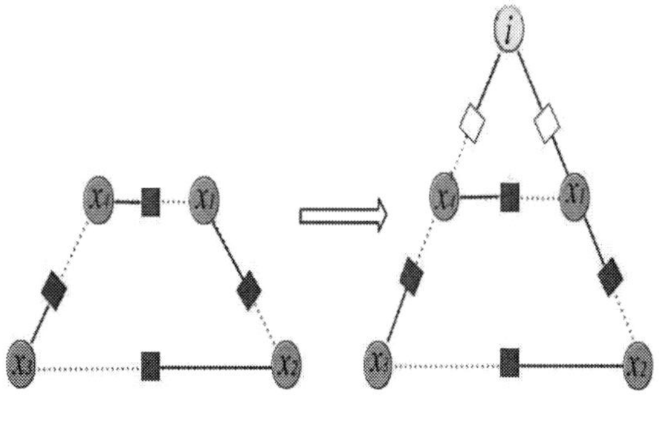

Figure 4. Eg.2

Analysis: In Eg.2, the former problem have four free nodes, x1 =x2=x3=x4=1 and x1 =x2=x3=x4=0 are all solutions of the problem. They are already mutual-determination. When add node i, we find that free nodes x1 and x4 can't satisfy the clauses they connected. So node i must be backbone valued 1 to satisfy the clauses.

Case 2: If the nodes connected to i are only backbones in N-1 system and the backbones have already satisfy the new clauses, the new added node i should be free node.

Case 3: If the nodes connected to i are only backbones in N-1 system and there exists backbones which don't satisfy the new clauses, the new added node i should be backbone to satisfy the new added clauses.

Eg.3

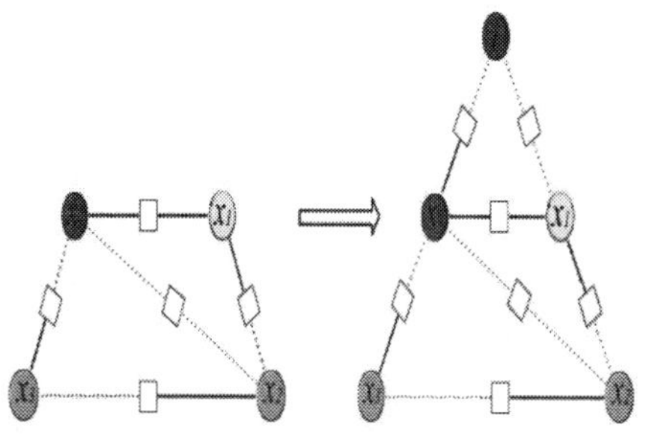

Figure 5. Eg.3

Analysis: In Eg.3, the former problem is satisfied with x1 =1 is backbone, x4=0 is backbone, x2 and x3 are all free. When add node i, we find that backbones nodes x1 and x4 are can't satisfy the clauses they connected. So node i must be backbone valued 0 to satisfy the clauses.

In a node adding process, all the above environment can be met with and the comprehensive analysis can be done using the above results. The new added node can be one backbone only when it faces Subcase 1-2, 1-3 and Case 3; the new added node can belong to some mutual-determination only when it faces Subcase 1-2, 1-3; and in the rest cases, the new added node should be a free node. In the following, the whole process for determining the reduced solution graph of 2-SAT is stated as an algorithm:

The Solution Space Expression Algorithm for 2-SAT

INPUT: Satisfiable 2-SAT Factor Graph *G*

 DOI: 10.1051/itmconf/20160701016

OUTPUT: The Reduced Solution Graph $S(G)$ of 2-SAT

```
Freezing (S(G), j)
begin
  for free neighbors l of j
    if state of j doesn't satisfy the clause (l, j)
        S(G)=Freezing (S(G), l)
    end
  end
 return(S(G))
end
main ( )
begin
initial S(G)=Ø
for i=1: N
  add node i with the edges to S(G)
  use analysis in Case 1-3 to determine state of i
  Nb ={neighbors of i change from free to backbones}
  for j ∈Nb
    S(G)=Freezing (S(G), j)
  end
end
end
```

4 Solution Space Expression On MAX-2-Sat

In this section, we will provide some simple discussion on the Max-2-SAT problem (NP hard field), we can get the solution space change with the increase of variables and the corresponding algorithm, but the details will be quite complicated and will be discussed in our future work.

By the analysis in the above section, the solution space can be exactly expressed when there is no energy increase, so we only concern on the energy increase cases as the increase of variables.

In the 2-SAT problem, the number of backbones is monotonic increasing during the node-adding process and the number of free variables is monotone decreasing, but free variables are not always mutual-determination, which is quite different with that of minimum vertex cover problem. In the Max-2-SAT problem, it is not the case and the backbones' number can increase or decrease during the node-adding process, evenly the solution space can't be expressed by one reduced solution graph and evolution of the solution space will be rather unpredictable and intricate.

Eg.4

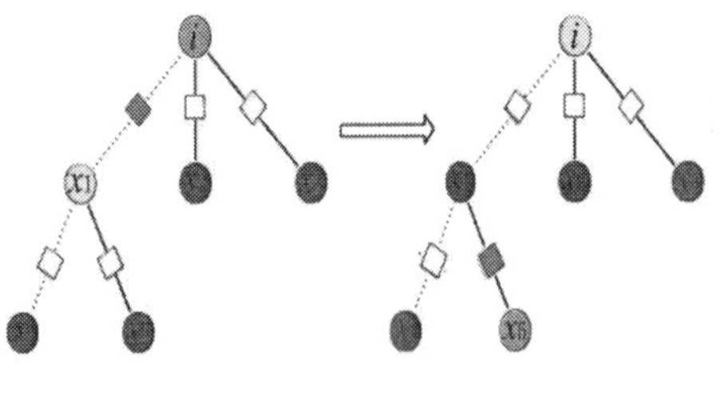

Figure 6. Unsatisfiable Situation

Analysis: In Eg.4, x1=1 and x2=x3=x4=x5=0 are backbones in the original problem, when we add a new node i, an unsatisfiable clause occurs. This causes energy increase, so node i should be xi=1 backbone and the clause of (i, 1) is unsatisfied. In order to satisfy the clauses added by node i, we can alternatively change the state of x1 to be x1=0, and the clause (i, 1) is satisfied but the clause (1, 5) is not.

5 Conclusion

Given a 2-sat formula, the objective is to judge whether it is satisfiable or not, and if it is, to find a satisfying solution. However, not all suitable results can be found for 2-sat formulas. For this case, we find the truth assignment that satisfies the maximum possible number of its clauses as solution [5]. We call it Max-2-sat problems.

Based on the long range frustration of nodes in Max-2-sat problem, backbones and mutual determination are proposed to study the solution space. Backbones are the fixed nodes in graph. It is the basic framework of the solution. Mutual determination shows how the nodes influence each other.

To study the correlation among the nodes, we add a new node to the former graph. By changing the state of some nodes to see the variation of solution, we find that when we change the state of some nodes, if the energy increase of the system less than the number of changed nodes, we take the new assignment for solution.

When add new node to the previous system, we know that may lead to unsatisfied of all system. At this moment, the energy of all system is increase.

References

[1] S. A. Cook, "The complexity of theorem-proving procedures," Proc. Third Annual ACM Sympos. Theory of Computing (1971), pp. 151–158.
[2] Kleer J D. Building expert systems: F. Hayes-Roth, D. A. Waterman and D. B. Lenat (Addison-Wesley Reading, MA, 1983); 444 pages, $32.50[J]. Artificial Intelligence, 1985, 25(1):105-107.
[3] Nguyen T A, Perkins W A, Laffey T J, et al. Checking an Expert Systems Knowledge Base for Consistency and Completeness.[C]// International Joint Conference on Artificial Intelligence. 1985:375-378.
[4] Asirelli P, Santis M D, Martelli M. Integrity constraints in logic databases[J]. Journal of Logic Programming, 1985, 2(3):221-232.
[5] Gallaire H, Minker J, Nicolas J M. Logic and Databases: A Deductive Approach[J]. Readings in Artificial Intelligence & Databases, 1989, 16(2):231-247.
[6] Scott Kirkpatrick, Bart Selman, Critical Behavior in the Satisfiability of Random Boolean Expressions, Science, Vol. 264, p. 1297-1301 (1994)
[7] Karp, R. M., Reducibility among combinatorial problems, in Complexity of Computer Computations,

DOI: 10.1051/itmconf/20160701016

R. E. Miller and J. W. Thatcher (eds.), Plenum Press, New York, 1972, 85-104.

[8] M.R. Garey, D.S. Johnson, L. Stockmeyer, Some simplified NP complete graph problems, Theoret. Comput. Sci. 1 (3) (1976) 237–267.

[9] J. Håstad, Some optimal inapproximability results, J. ACM 48 (4) (2001) 798–859.

[10] B. Aspvall, M.F. Plass, R.E. Tarjan, A linear-time algorithm for testing the truth of certain quantified Boolean formulas, Inform. Process. Lett. 8 (3) (1979) 121–123.

[11] Zecchina R. Analytic and Algorithmic Solution of Random Satisfiability Problem [J]. 2002.

[12] Zhou H. Long Range Frustration in Finite--Connectivity Spin Glasses: Application to the random K-satisfiability problem [J]. 2004.

[13] Rémi Monasson, Riccardo Zecchina, Scott Kirkpatrick, Bart Selman& Lidror Troyansky, Determining computational complexity from characteristic 'phase transitions',Nature,Vol.400,p.133-137(1999)

[14] William Wells Adams, Philippe Loustaunau, An Introduction to GrÄobner Bases. [M], Amer.Math.Society (1994).

[15] Coppersmith D, Gamarnik D, Hajiaghayi M and Sorkin G B 2004 Random MAX SAT, random MAX CUT, and their phase transitions Random. Struct. Algor. 24 4 502-545.

[16] Kilby P, Slaney J, Thiébaux S, et al. Backbones and Backdoors in Satisfiability.[C]// Conference on. 2005:1368-1373.

[17] Wei W, Zhang R, Guo B, et al. Detecting the solution space of vertex cover by mutual determinations and backbones. [J]. Physical Review E Statistical Physics Plasmas Fluids & Related Interdisciplinary Topics, 2012, 86(2):1-22.

ITM Web of Conferences 7, 02001 (2016) DOI: 10.1051/itmconf/20160702001
ITA 2016

Malware Classification Based on the Behavior Analysis and Back Propagation Neural Network

Zhi-Peng PAN[1, a], Chao FENG[1] and Chao-Jing TANG[1]

[1]*College of Electronic Science and Engineering, National University of Defense Technology, 410073 Changsha, China*
[a]Corresponding author: climbspider@hotmail.com

Abstract. With the development of the Internet, malwares have also been expanded on the network systems rapidly. In order to deal with the diversity and amount of the variants, a number of automated behavior analysis tools have emerged as the time requires. Yet these tools produce detailed behavior reports of the malwares, it still needs to specify its category and judge its criticality manually. In this paper, we propose an automated malware classification approach based on the behavior analysis. We firstly perform dynamic analyses to obtain the detailed behavior profiles of the malwares, which are then used to abstract the main features of the malwares and serve as the inputs of the Back Propagation (BP) Neural Network model.The experimental results demonstrate that our classification technique is able to classify the malware variants effectively and detect malware accurately.

1 Introduction

Malicious software (Malware), usually in forms of virus, Trojans, worms, botnets, rootkits, and some other potentially unwanted applications, has been the major threat to the internet security. Malware developers use the hiding techniques such as polymorphism and obfuscation [1] to against signature-based on detection and static malware analysis methods easily and effectively [2]. In contrast to static analysis, dynamic analysis of malware based on monitoring its behavior during the run-time, which renders the malware more difficult to conceal [3, 4], and it does become the mainstream method of malicious behavior mining.

Yet these dynamic technologies for the malware detection are not sufficient just by forming detailed behavior profiles [5]. What we need is the ability to automatically categorize of the malware and detect the malware by its behavior.

The main contributions of this paper are as follows:

1)Unlike many previous algorithms that monitor the malware behaviors directly on low-level data such as API call monitoring [6], we implement an automatic dynamic analysis framework by taking the advantages of the present behavior analysis systems. We get the detailed behaviors of the malware including process behaviors, registry behaviors, file behaviors, net behaviors, and other behaviors.

2)We extract the major features of the malware behavior profiles into the behavior vectors by counting the quantity of the every behavior.

3)We proposed a Back Propagation (BP) Neural Network model [7] for learning the behavior patterns of the same categories of the malwares and classifying the malwares. The experimental section verified the correctness and precision of our algorithm finally.

2 Related Work

There are three major methods for classification of the malicious softwares, traditional pattern matching, static analysis, and dynamic analysis. Although static analysis can improve accuracy than the methods of the traditional pattern matching, it can also have the difficulty to handle obfuscated and self-modifying codes.

In dynamic analysis, Konrad Rieck [8] et al. proposed a method using the CWSandbox to analysis the behaviors of the malwares and then using the Support Vector Machines (SVM) for learning and classification. Forrest [6] proposed fixed-length sequence of N-gram recognition model based on system call. Syed Zainudeen Mohd Shaid [9] proposed a behavior-based technique to visualize malware behavior in the form of images. This method uses the different color to indicate the different API calls. By using the behavior images, it can be possible to visually identify malware variants of the same family. Guanghui Liang [10] et al. capture malware behaviors based on the Temu platform and proposed a weighted Jaccard similarity matching algorithm to classify the malware variants.

In summary, when dealing with the malware variants classification, behavior analysis is the most effective method. In this paper, we use the present effective

 DOI: 10.1051/itmconf/20160702001

behavior analysis system to help analyse of the malware in contrast to just monitoring the API calls or the traces of the APIs as above.

3 Methodology

Classification of malware variants has been concerned by analysts in a long period [11-14]. Evolving malware generates a lot of variants and brings great challenges to analytical work. Although these variants change in the file format and appearance, there are still the same behavior patterns. For example, all variants of the Allaple worm acquire and lock of particular mutexes on infected systems [8]. Aiming to exploit these behavior patterns using machine learning techniques and propose a method which can classify the malware variants automatically based on their behaviors. An outline of our approach is given by the following basic steps:

1) Malware Data Acquisition. A corpus of malware binaries are obtained by collecting the upload suspicious files on the *Kafan Forum*. A Multi-Engine Online Virus Scan system *VirSCAN* is applied to identify the known malware instances.

2)Behavior Monitoring. Malware binaries are executed and monitored by the *HABO* behavior analysis system, which can generate detailed behavior reports.

3)Feature Extraction. Features reflect the behavior patterns, such as process created, foreign memory regions read, mutexes created, or registry key modified, are extracted from the analysis reports and used to map the malware behavior into a high-dimensional vector space.

4)Learning and classification. Back Propagation neural network model is applied to learning and training for the classification of the malwares.

3.1 Malware data acquisition

We have obtained up to 13600 unique samples, which are uploaded by the extensive users of the Kafan Forum, using for learning and subsequent classification. After obtaining the samples, we applied the online virus scan system VirSCAN to partition the malwares into common families, such as Adware, Potential Unwanted Application (PUA), Trojan/Downloader. Note that we chose the VirSCAN instead of one Unti-virus product, like Avira, Karpasky, to label the malware as the VirSCAN is multi-engine and we can chose the most of the result to label our sample. We selected 9 most common malware categories and one Non-Malware category on our samples. These families listed in Table 1 represent a broad range of malware categories such as Adware, PUA, and Trojans, and the Non-Malware category can be extend for malware detection directly in the future.

Table 1 Malware Families Labeled by The *Virscan* System

1. Adware(4352)	6. TR/Droppper(986)
2. PUA(1232)	7. TR/Spy(864)
3. Trojan(569)	8. Worm(562)
4. Tr/downloader(2524)	9. Win32(694)
5. Tr/Crypt(1023)	10. Non-Malware(794)

3.2 Behavior Monitoring and Feature Extraction

In this section, we use the online behavior analysis system, which called *HABO*, to monitor the samples' behavior. Like most of the other online behavior analysis systems, it can analyse the upload binaries and give you a detail behavior report about the malware. Note that our methodology is not bound to the *HABO* system; it can also be adapted to other behavior analysis systems.

Figure 1 shows a part of behavior report of one malware sample. It contains *five main aspects, process behaviours, file behaviours, register behaviours, net behaviours,* and *other behaviours*. Furthermore, these 5 main aspects contain 73 sub-behaviors which describe the behavior of the malware in detail.

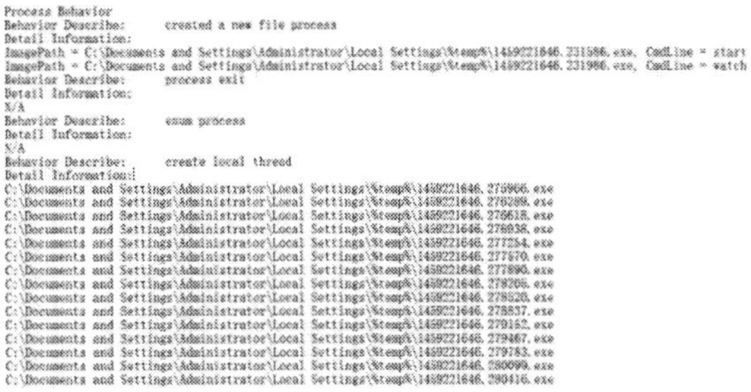
```
Process Behavior
Behavior Describe:      created a new file process
Detail Information:
ImagePath = C:\Documents and Settings\Administrator\Local Settings\%temp%\1459221646.231586.exe, CmdLine = start
ImagePath = C:\Documents and Settings\Administrator\Local Settings\%temp%\1459221646.231986.exe, CmdLine = watch
Behavior Describe:      process exit
Detail Information:
N/A
Behavior Describe:      enum process
Detail Information:
N/A
Behavior Describe:      create local thread
Detail Information:
C:\Documents and Settings\Administrator\Local Settings\%temp%\1459221646.275966.exe
C:\Documents and Settings\Administrator\Local Settings\%temp%\1459221646.276288.exe
C:\Documents and Settings\Administrator\Local Settings\%temp%\1459221646.276618.exe
C:\Documents and Settings\Administrator\Local Settings\%temp%\1459221646.276936.exe
C:\Documents and Settings\Administrator\Local Settings\%temp%\1459221646.277254.exe
C:\Documents and Settings\Administrator\Local Settings\%temp%\1459221646.277570.exe
C:\Documents and Settings\Administrator\Local Settings\%temp%\1459221646.277890.exe
C:\Documents and Settings\Administrator\Local Settings\%temp%\1459221646.278206.exe
C:\Documents and Settings\Administrator\Local Settings\%temp%\1459221646.278520.exe
C:\Documents and Settings\Administrator\Local Settings\%temp%\1459221646.278837.exe
C:\Documents and Settings\Administrator\Local Settings\%temp%\1459221646.279162.exe
C:\Documents and Settings\Administrator\Local Settings\%temp%\1459221646.279467.exe
C:\Documents and Settings\Administrator\Local Settings\%temp%\1459221646.279783.exe
C:\Documents and Settings\Administrator\Local Settings\%temp%\1459221646.280099.exe
C:\Documents and Settings\Administrator\Local Settings\%temp%\1459221646.280416.exe
```

Figure 1. Behavior Report of The Malware Sample

Although the reports show the detail information of the behavior of the malware, it can't be used for the BP neutral network model directly, which needs the vectorial data as the input. Hence we should extract the main features of the malwares' behavior from the reports firstly. The method used here is called frequency statistics method. The main steps are showed as follows:

1) Given all the sub-behaviors, we represent them at a particular sequence, such as, create local thread, enumerate process, create a new file process, and so on.

2) We made a count on the all sub-behaviors of the malware respectively. For example, the behavior showed in Figure 1, we can use [2, 1, 1, and 15,] to represent.

The figure 2 shows a detail behavior vector of one malware, and the number zero means that this malware doesn't have the behavior correspondingly.

```
11 2  0  2  2  2  0  0  0  0  16 12 0  16 13
16 7  5  2  3  6  0  0  0  0  2  3  2  4  2
4  3  3  0  0  3  3  2  13 3  2  0  0  0  0
0  0  2  4  15 0  3  2  0  12 12 4  16 2  0
0  0  0  0  0  0  0  0  0  0  0  0  0
```

Figure 2. A Detail Behavior Vector of One Malware

3.3 Learning and classification

3.3.1 Establish the Model

According to the previous description, the norm of our behavior vector is 73. And we can use the vector, r = [r1, r2, r3,..., r10] ri = 0 or 1, to represent the output result. Each element value of the output vector is 0 or 1, 0 represents the malware does not belong to the corresponding category while 1 represents the malware belong to the corresponding category.

Given the input vector and the output vector, we established a Back Propagation (BP) Neural Network, which includes one input layer, one hidden layer and one output layer. The input layer and the hidden layer both have 73 neurons and the output layer has 10 neurons. Additionally, the hidden and output neurons include adjustment factor a and b respectively. The connection weight between input layer and hidden layer, hidden layer and output layer is noted by $W_{ij}(1 \le i \le 73, 1 \le j \le 73)$ and $V_{jl}(1 \le j \le 73, 1 \le l \le 10)$. The network is showed in Figure 3.

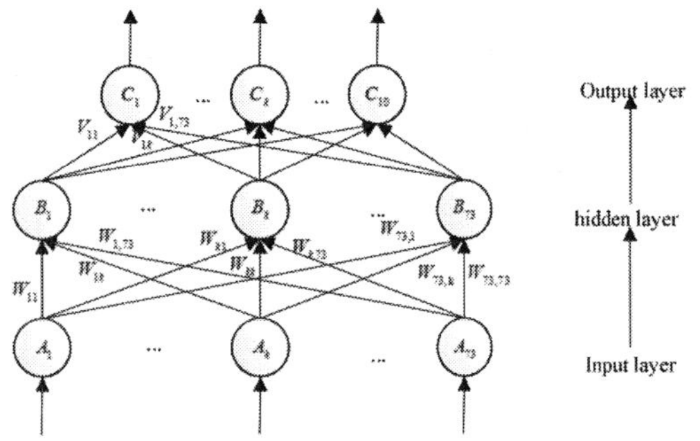

Figure 3. The Bp Neural Network

3.3.2 Identify the Parameter

We use the logistic function $f(x)=\frac{1}{1-e^{-x}}$ as the activation function of the hidden layer, and for convenience, the input of the network, hidden neuron h_j and output neuron O_l is denoted by $x_i(1 \le i \le 73)$, $net(h_j)(1 \le j \le 73)$ and $net(O_l)(1 \le l \le 10)$ respectively. The output of the hidden neuron h_j and output neuron O_l is $out(h_j)$ and $out(O_l)$. We define the error signals of the output layer and the hidden layer as δ_{oh} and δ_{hi} respectively. Additional, $E = \frac{1}{2}\sum_{k=1}^{l}(\text{target}(O_l) - \text{out}(O_l))^2$ is defined as output error. So according to the Back Propagation Neural Networks algorithm, we can derive the expression of the connection weight:

$$V_{jl}^{+} = V_{jl} + \eta\delta_{oh}\frac{\partial net(O_l)}{\partial V_{jl}}$$

* MERGEFORMAT (1)

$$W_{ij}^{+} = W_{ij} + \eta\delta_{hi}\frac{\partial net(h_j)}{\partial W_{ij}}$$

* MERGEFORMAT (2)

where $\delta_{oh} = -\frac{\partial E}{\partial out(O_l)} \cdot out'(O_l)$, $\delta_{hi} = -\frac{\partial E}{\partial out(h_j)} \cdot out'(h_j)$

and the symbol η means the learning rate of the network.

In this paper, the transform factor between the output layer and the hidden layer is denoted by a , and b means the transform factor between the hidden layer and the output layer.

1) The identification of the output function

Due to there is no experienced output function, we can only get the function by experiments. For the same samples, when trained 10000 times, we can get the results as shown in Table 2. And from the table, we finally choose the linear function $f(x) = 1.0 + x/5000$.

Table 2. Output Function and Some Results

Funtion	Convergence error	Whether fall into local minimum region
$f(x)=1/(1+\exp(-x))$	5.69	Yes
$f(x)=0.8+x/5000$	0.78	No
$f(x)=1.0+x/5000$	0.12	No
$f(x)=1.2+x/5000$	2.34	No
$f(x)=1.0+x/4000$	1.56	No
$f(x)=1.0+x/6000$	0.87	Yes

2) The identification of the Adjustment factors

Due to the value of the adjustment factors a and b has the important influence on the speed of the convergence. Figure 4 and Figure 5 show us the relationships between the adjustment factors and the convergence time, when the total error is set to be 0.64.

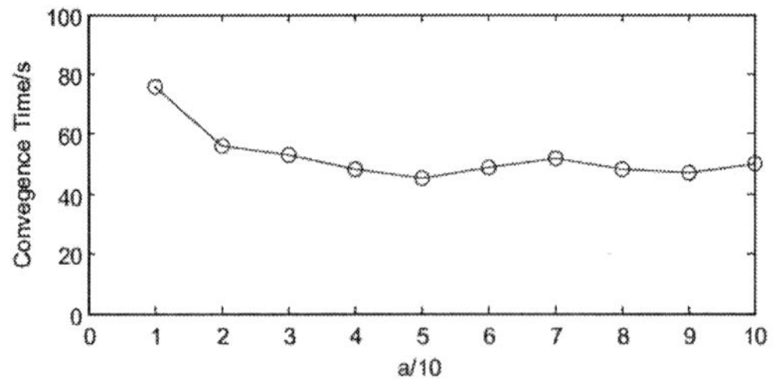

Figure 4. A and Convegence Time

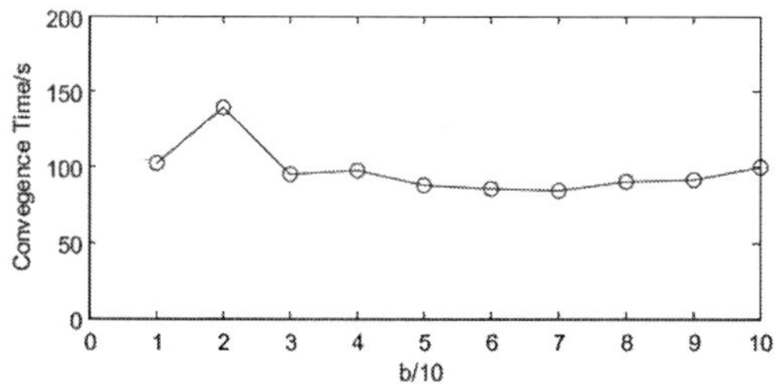

Figure 5. B and Convegence Time

4 Experiment and Evaluation

In order to evaluate the performance of our methodology, we firstly divided the malware corpus randomly into training and testing two partitions, and the samples sizes are 10000 and 3600 respectively. We used the training partition to train the BP neutral network, and used the testing partition to measure the overall performance of our methodology. Besides, the procedure showed above is repeated over five independent experimental runs and we use the average values as our final results.

The per-category accuracy for this experiment is shown in Figure 6, and the error bars indicate the variance measured during the experiment runs. From the figure, we can find our average accuracy is up to 86%. And in particular, we can find the last category, which we defined it as the non-malware, whose predict accuracy is up to 99%. In other words, if we used this model to detect the binary in our corpus is whether the malware or not, we have the correct probability approximate to 99%. This result shows that our methodology can be easily extend for malware detection. And more deeply, due to the boundaries of categories 3,4,5,6 and 9 are less obvious, which labelled as Trojan, Tr/downloader, Tr/Crypt, Tr/dropper amd Win32, we find that the variance of these categories are higher than other categories.

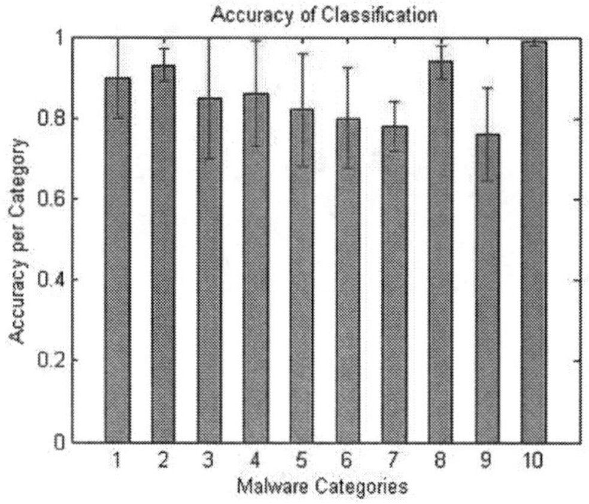

Figure 6. Accuracy per category

Figure 7 shows the confusion matrix for classification. If the color of the category is deeper, it means that this category is less error probability be classified into other categories. From the figure, we can find that the categories between 3 and 7 are easily be confused each other, and the category Win32 is most likely to be considered into other categories, which are consistent with our actual situation.

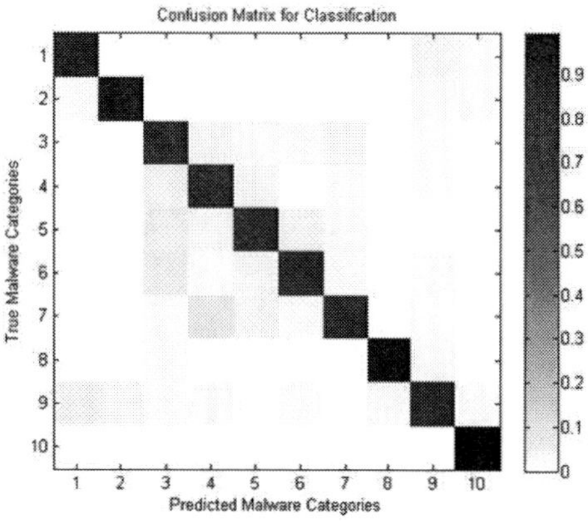

Figure 7. Confusion of Categories

5 Conclusion

In this paper, the behavior of the malware is captured by the online behavior analyze system. After that, we extracted the main feature of the malware in forms of vector and serve it as the input of out Back Propagation Neural Network model. Finally, by training the BP Neural Network, we can use it to classify the malware and detect the malware. Experimental results show that our methodology can classify the malware variants effectively and detect the malware accurately.

In the future work, we will focus on how to extracted malware feature that can represent the malware more accurately from the behavior analysis reports.

References

1. Rad B B, Masrom M, Ibrahim S. Camouflage in malware: from encryption to metamorphism[J]. International Journal of Computer Science and Network Security, 2012, 12(8): 74-83.
2. Moser A, Kruegel C, Kirda E. Limits of static analysis for malware detection[C]//Computer security applications conference, 2007. ACSAC 2007. Twenty-third annual. IEEE, 2007: 421-430.
3. Willems C, Holz T, Freiling F. Toward automated dynamic malware analysis using cwsandbox[J]. IEEE Security & Privacy, 2007 (2): 32-39.
4. Egele M, Scholte T, Kirda E, et al. A survey on automated dynamic malware-analysis techniques and tools[J]. ACM Computing Surveys (CSUR), 2012, 44(2): 6.
5. Bayer U, Comparetti P M, Hlauschek C, et al. Scalable, Behavior-Based Malware Clustering[C]//NDSS. 2009, 9: 8-11.
6. Forrest S, Hofmeyr S, Somayaji A. The evolution of system-call monitoring[C]//Computer Security

DOI: 10.1051/itmconf/20160702001

Applications Conference, 2008. ACSAC 2008. Annual. IEEE, 2008: 418-430.

7. Irwin G W, Warwick K, Hunt K J. Neural network applications in control[M]. Iet, 1995.
8. Rieck K, Holz T, Willems C, et al. Learning and classification of malware behavior[M]//Detection of Intrusions and Malware, and Vulnerability Assessment. Springer Berlin Heidelberg, 2008: 108-125.
9. Shaid M, Zainudeen S, Maarof M A. Malware behavior image for malware variant identification[C]//Biometrics and Security Technologies (ISBAST), 2014 International Symposium on. IEEE, 2014: 238-243.
10. Liang G, Pang J, Dai C. A Behavior-Based Malware Variant Classification Technique[J]. International Journal of Information and Education Technology, 2016, 6(4): 291.
11. Park Y, Reeves D, Mulukutla V, et al. Fast malware classification by automated behavioral graph matching[C]//Proceedings of the Sixth Annual Workshop on Cyber Security and Information Intelligence Research. ACM, 2010: 45.
12. Cesare S, Xiang Y. Classification of malware using structured control flow[C]//Proceedings of the Eighth Australasian Symposium on Parallel and Distributed Computing-Volume 107. Australian Computer Society, Inc., 2010: 61-70.
13. Tian R, Batten L M, Versteeg S C. Function length as a tool for malware classification[C]//Malicious and Unwanted Software, 2008. MALWARE 2008. 3rd International Conference on. IEEE, 2008: 69-76.
14. Islam R, Tian R, Batten L, et al. Classification of malware based on string and function feature selection[C]//Cybercrime and Trustworthy Computing Workshop (CTC), 2010 Second. IEEE, 2010: 9-17.

Fractal Signature Feature Analysis of MODIS NDVI Time Series Data

Shi-Wei Dong, Hong Li and Wei-Wei Zhang

Beijing Academy of Agriculture and Forestry Sciences, Beijing Research and Development Center for Grass and Environment, 100097 Beijing, China

Abstract. Fractal signature feature of MODIS Normalized Difference Vegetation Index (NDVI) time series data is proposed in this study in order to further mine its inherent information. Savitzky-Golay filter is adopted to reconstruct MODIS NDVI time series curves of Beijing in China. The blanket method used for computing fractal dimension of surface is modified and then transferred to compute upper and lower fractal signature of each pixel in NDVI time series images. The fractal signature and their corresponding scale are analyzed, and the results show that fractal signature curves and fractal signature images can clearly reflect different targets of land use and land cover at certain scales. This study also provides a new secondary characteristic parameter for related studies.

1 Introduction

Normalized Difference Vegetation Index (NDVI) time series data acquired by the satellite sensors can accurately reflect the dynamic state and seasonal variation characteristics of the vegetation [1]. It plays an important role in the range of global, continental and regional vegetation cover mapping, land cover monitoring, ecosystem dynamic monitoring and simulation, crop growth monitoring, crop yield estimation and other aspects.

Fractal theory is a very efficient method to depict chaotic, erratic, and natural phenomena [2]. After Mandelbrot [3] introduced the notion of fractals in the 1970s, fractal theory was applied to numerous domains like image segmentation [4, 5] and texture analysis [6]. Many articles have discussed the issue of fractal-based processing and interpretation of remote sensing image [7, 8]. When fractal signatures are applied in image analysis, fractal dimension is first chose to calculate. Mary methods exist to compute fractal dimension and are grouped into three classes: (1) box-counting methods, e.g. the differential box-counting method [9], (2) fractional Brownian motion methods, e.g. the power spectrum [10], and (3) area measurement methods, e.g. the blanket method [11].

The scale is greatly significant in NDVI time series images processing and there is an optimum observed scale for each land use and land cover type. The same ground target may be exhibited differently in remote sensing image under different scales [12]. In MODIS images, each pixel has a NDVI time series curve whose shape depends on specific target. Different target in land use and land cover must have different fractal dimension. Therefore, the objectives of this study are to try to introduce and analyze fractal signature feature of MODIS NDVI time series data in order to obtain optimum observed scales of different targets from fractal signature curves and fractal signature images. It is playing a very important role in image processing, feature extraction and pattern recognition.

The remainder of this paper is organized as follows. Study area is introduced in the next section. In section 3, experimental data are acquired and processed, and detailed method for fractal signature calculation is briefly presented. MODIS NDVI time series data are processed by fractal computer programs and fractal features are specifically analyzed in section 4. Finally, discussion and conclusions of this study are extracted in section 5 and 6, respectively.

2 Study Area

Beijing is located in the northwest of the North China Plain between longitude 115°25'-117°30' E and latitude 39°28'-41°05' N (Figure 1), and has an estimated area of 16,410 km^2. Hills and mountains in the northwest account for 62% of the entire area while plains in the southeast cover the remaining 38%, and the average elevation of Beijing is 43.5 m. The area belongs to the warm temperate semi-humid continental monsoon climate with an average annual temperature is 12.5°C, and the average precipitation is 566.1 mm. Beijing's population rose to 20.69 million in 2012.

The primary land use and land cover types in the area are divided into five general categories, including cropland, construction, forest, water and orchard. Additionally, agricultural cropping patterns in Beijing are dominated by double cropping and single cropping. The overwhelming majority of crops with double cropping are

 DOI: 10.1051/itmconf/20160702002

winter wheat-summer corn. Crops with single cropping are primarily spring corn or winter wheat.

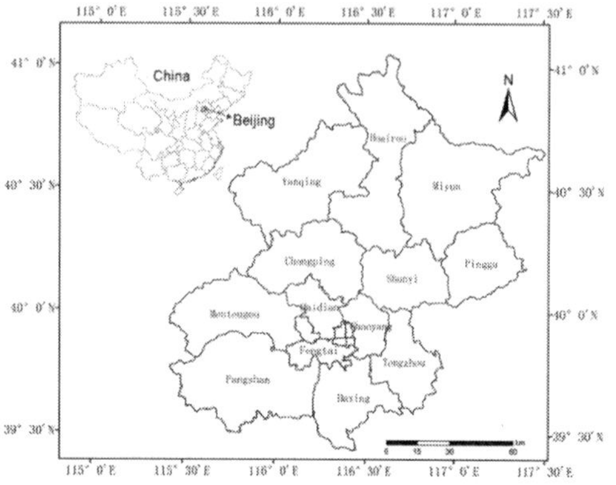

Figure 1. Study Area.

3 Data and Method

3.1 Data Acquisition and Processing

In this study, MOD09 MODIS product consisted of eight days of composite surface reflectance images are primarily employed, and they are freely available from the MODIS data product website (http://modis.gsfc.nasa.gov). A set of 46 time-phase images of Beijing (h26v04 and h26v05) can cover a full year observation period from Jan.1, 2007 to Jan.3, 2008. File formatting conversion and projection conversion are implemented by MODIS Reprojection Tool.

The NDVI produced at 250 m resolution from MODIS is normalized difference measure comparing the near infrared (846-885 nm) and visible red (600-680 nm) bands. Some noise derived from clouds and the atmosphere are detrimental to the trends analysis and information extraction, so the Savitzky-Golay filter [13] is used to obtain high-quality NDVI time series in this study, and the reconstructed NDVI time series can much more clearly reflect the trends and regularity in vegetation activity.

3.2 Method

Peleg et al [11] defined fractal signature as the change in measured area with changing scale and proposed blanket method to computer spatial fractal dimension of remote sensing image. The principle of this method is that a remote sensing image is treated as a 3-D topography, and the gray of each pixel as height. The terrain surface is then enveloped by two blankets on the each side with a distance of ε, the fractal dimension of the image can be computed by the relation between the area of the blankets and the volume of the space enveloped by the two blankets. 2-D curve can be considered as a special kind of 3-D ground surface, and the length of the 2-D curve as the 3-D terrain surface while the area enclosed by 2-D curve as the volume of the space enveloped by 3-D topography. Thus, this method is modified and then transferred to compute fractal dimension of MODIS NDVI time series curve.

4 Results and Analysis

4.1 Fractal Processing

Fractal computer programs are developed using the visualization interactive data language ENVI/IDL programming. MODIS NDVI time series data of Beijing are processed by this programming to obtain upper and lower fractal profiles. Different fractal signal images can be obtained after fractal processing with different values of measure scale. Pixel signal value in each fractal image reflects the complexity of the variation of the NDVI time series curve at certain scale. When the pixel signal value in fractal signature image is much higher, the NDVI time series curve has much more complex variation. Scale with the highest signal value and most obvious distinguish with other targets in fractal image is defined as fractal feature scale of this target.

4.2 Fractal Feature Analysis

4.2.1 Fractal Signature Curves

Figure 2-7 are the fractal signature curves with scale ε from 2 to 30 for upper and lower profiles of MODIS NDVI time series data in Beijing. We can find that typical targets can be clearly reflected at different fractal scale of upper and lower fractal profiles. Fractal feature scale of single cropping cropland is located in the upper fractal profiles at ε=23, Figure 2. Fractal feature scales of double cropping cropland are located in the upper fractal profiles at ε=12 and the lower fractal profiles at ε=5, Figure 3. Fractal feature scales of construction are located in the upper fractal profiles at ε=14 and the lower fractal profiles at ε=16, Figure 4. Fractal feature scales of forest are located in the upper fractal profiles at ε=15 and the lower fractal profiles at ε=11, Figure 5. Fractal feature scale of water is located in the upper fractal profiles at ε=22, Figure 6. Fractal feature scales of orchard are located in the upper fractal profiles at ε=23 and the lower fractal profiles at ε=12, Figure 7.

 DOI: 10.1051/itmconf/20160702002

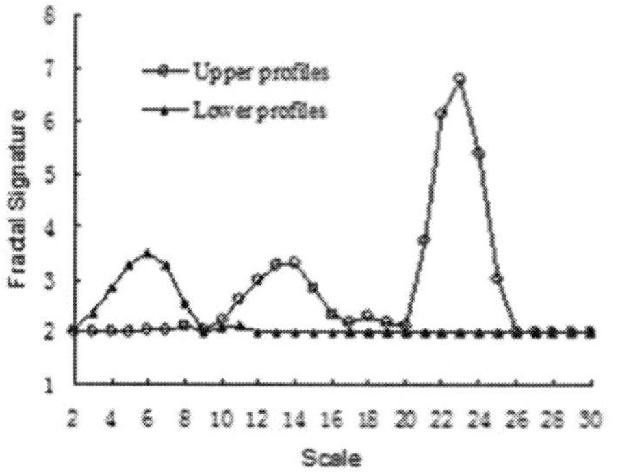

Figure 2. Fractal Signature Curves of Single Cropping Cropland.

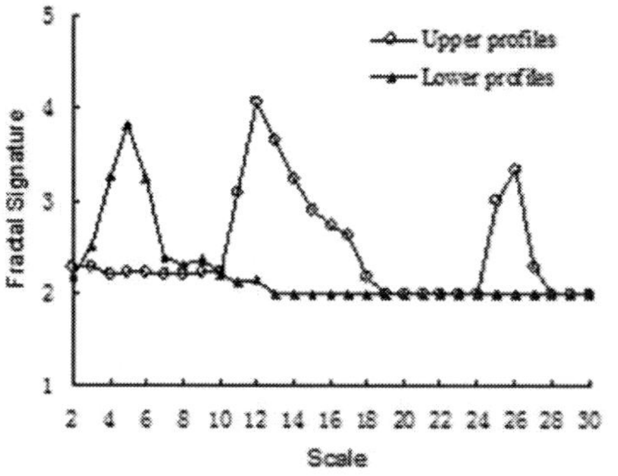

Figure 3. Fractal Signature Curves of Double Cropping Cropland.

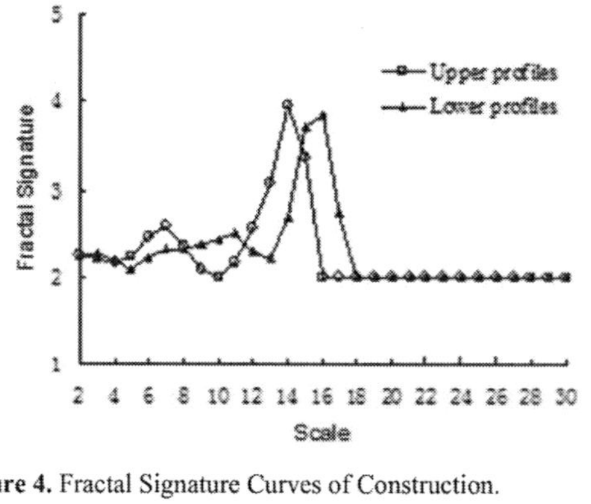

Figure 4. Fractal Signature Curves of Construction.

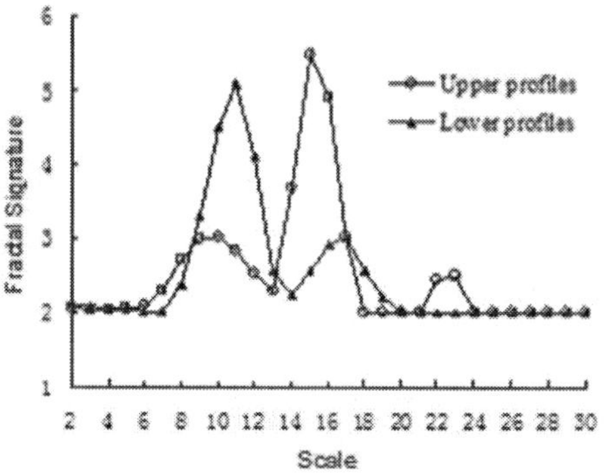

Figure 5. Fractal Signature Curves of Forest.

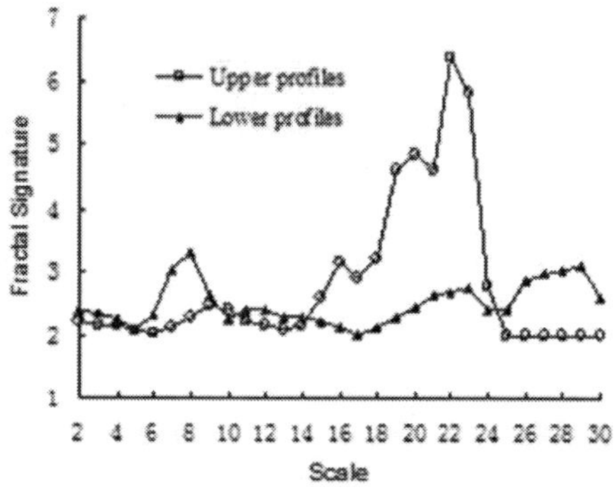

Figure 6. Fractal Signature Curves of Water.

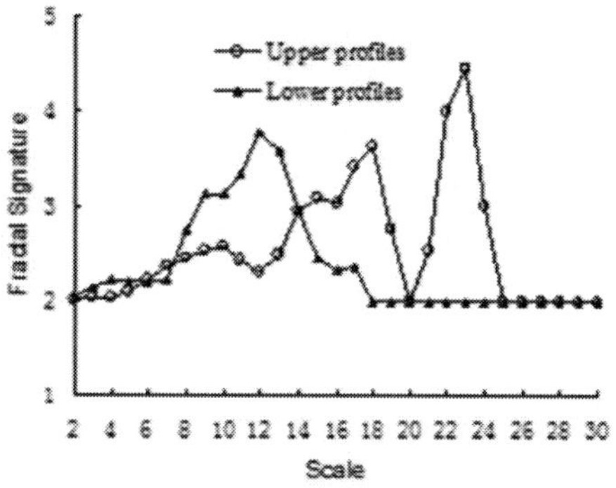

Figure 7. Fractal Signature Curves of Orchard.

In a word, different targets exhibit different fractal feature, and fractal signature can distinguish targets more effectively than the original data.

4.2.2 Fractal Signature Images

Figure 8-11 are fractal signature images obtained from upper fractal at $\varepsilon=4$ and $\varepsilon=23$, lower fractal at $\varepsilon=5$ and $\varepsilon=11$. Brightness in the image is on behalf of the value of fractal signal strength, and when the pixel is much brighter, the value of fractal signal strength is much higher. Preliminary analyses indicate that the fractal signature images can also reflect the land use and land cover types. Construction and water have relatively brighter tones in Figure 8. Single cropping cropland and orchard are reflected in Figure 9, which are in accord with the results from fractal signature curves in Figure 2 and Figure 7, respectively. Double cropping cropland is revealed in Figure 10, corresponding to the results from fractal signature curves in Figure 3. Correspondingly, forest is exhibited in Figure 11, which also conforms to the results from fractal signature curves in Figure 5.

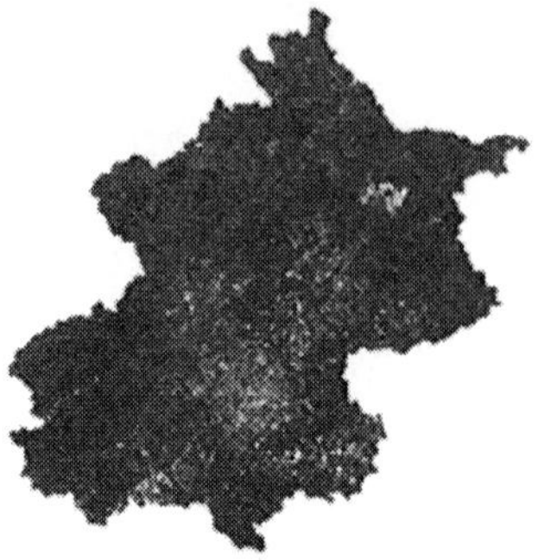

Figure 8. Upper Fractal Image of ε=4.

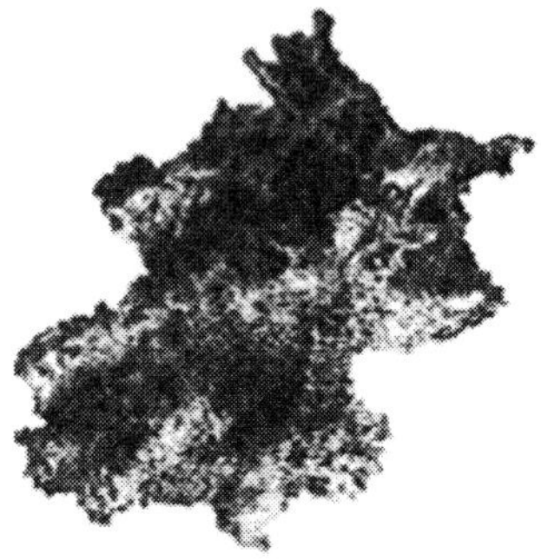

Figure 9. Upper Fractal Image of E=23.

Figure 10. Lower Fractal Image of ε=5.

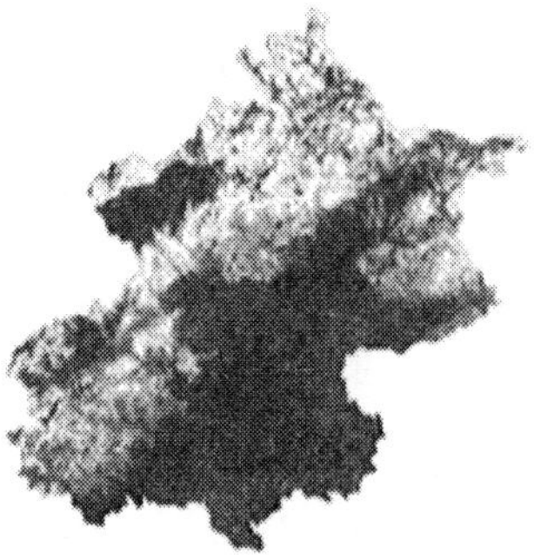

Figure 11. Lower Fractal Image of ε=11.

5 Discussion

Fractal signature feature of MODIS NDVI time series can reveal obvious differences in land use and land cover types at certain scales. This results are consistent with previous studies in recent years. Different targets can be characterized by fractal feature scale in reference [12]. Higher precision of classification may be expected based on fractal feature. The result shows that the overall accuracy with fractal-based textures increased 5.31% in reference [14].

6 Conclusions

This study provided a new secondary characteristic parameter of MODIS NDVI time series namely fractal signature, which was great benefit to image classification, pattern recognition, texture analysis and image segmentation, especially for low spatial resolution remote sensing images. The results showed that fractal signature feature of MODIS NDVI time series can reveal obvious differences in land use and land cover types at certain scales. Fractal feature scales of different targets were proposed based on analysing from fractal signature curves and fractal signature images.

In addition, the relation between fractal signature value and target types were not clear in this study. The fractal signature used for quantitative interpretation of remote sensing data was discussed in further research.

Acknowledgments

This work was supported by the Beijing Excellent Talent Support program (No. 2015000020060G136) and Beijing Science and Technology Programs.

References

1. M. Rees, R. Condit, M. Crawley, S. Pacala and D. Tilman, Science 293, 5530 (2001)
2. M. G. Hu, J. F. Wang and Y. Ge, Sensors 9, 11 (2009)
3. B. B. Mandelbrot and M. Aizenman, Phys. Today 32, 65 (1979)
4. Y. Xia, D. Feng and R. Zhao, IEEE Trans. Image Process. 15, 3 (2006)
5. Q. Guo, J. Shao, F. Guo and V. Ruiz, Int. J. Comput. Ass. Rad. 2 (2007)
6. M. P. Bishop, J. F. Shroder Jr, B. L. Hickman and L. Copland, Geomorphology 21, 3 (1998)
7. W. Sun, G. Xu, P. Gong and S. Liang, Int. J. Remote. Sens. 27, 22 (2006)
8. R. Lopes and N. Betrouni, Med. Image Anal. 13, 4 (2009)
9. B. B. Chaudhuri and N. Sarkar, IEEE T. Pattern Anal. 17, 1 (1995)
10. A. P. Pentland, IEEE T. Pattern Anal. 6 (1984)
11. S. Peleg, J. Naor, R. Hartley and D. Avnir, IEEE T. Pattern Anal. 4 (1984)
12. Z. Zhou and Q. Bu, Yaogan Xuebao- J. Remote Sens. 15, 1 (2011)

13. A. Savitzky and M. J. E. Golay, Anal. Chem. 36, 8 (1964)
14. S.Zheng, J. Zheng, M. Shi, et al, Yaogan Xuebao- J. Remote Sens. 18, 4 (2014)

Two Dimensional Harmonics Retrieval in Zero-Mean Independent Multiplicative and Additive Noises

Zheng- Wei ZHANG[1,a], Zhong CHEN[1], Li-Hui WANG[2]

[1] *The 28th Research Institute, China Electronics Technology Group Corporation, Nanjing, China*
[2] *Southeast University, School of instrument science and engineering, Key laboratory of micro-inertial instrument and advanced navigation technology, Ministry of education, Nanjing, China*

Abstract. For some theoretical problems and computational inefficiency, the problem of estimating the frequencies of two dimensional harmonics in zero-mean independent multiplicative and additive noises is not resolved completely. Existing methods based on cyclic statistics assume that the noise is non-Gaussian, and that the shape of the noise's distribution is not symmetrical. A novel approach which imposes no constraints on the distribution or the color of noises is developed. It relies on fourth-order special cumulant or moment slices. The fourth-order moment spectrum is shown to have computational advantages over existing method. As a byproduct, the variance of the noises can also be estimated directly from the spectrum. Finally we give as an illustrative example a complete experiment to corroborate the theoretical results. The results of this experiment do show preliminarily that the new method is valid and efficient for the problem of harmonics retrieval in zero-mean independent multiplicative and additive noises.

1 Introduction

Estimating harmonics with multiplicative noises using higher order spectra or cyclic statistics has been drawing a great deal of attention. Dwyer [1] estimated the frequencies of one-dimensional harmonic in the presence of Gaussian multiplicative and additive noises based on the spectrum of a special fourth-order cumulant. Zhou [2] developed a discrete time-averaged moment framework for retrieval of one dimensional harmonics with multiplicative noise using the notion of Fourier series moment polyspectra. And in contrast to what assumed in [1], both the additive and the multiplicative noises need not be Gaussian, as long as they are mutually independent with absolutely summable cumulants. Giannakis [3] studied the retrieval problem of one dimensional harmonics using cyclic statistics, and proved that as far as frequency estimation is concerned, cyclic and higher order statistics based approaches are equivalent. Kareem [4] provided a measure of the multiplicative nonlinear interactions of frequency components and offers physical insight into the nature and characteristics of nonlinear fluctuations Baars [5] reduced essentially to spectral Linear Stochastic Estimation when only first-order terms are considered, and is therefore presented in the context of stochastic estimation as spectral Higher-Order Stochastic Estimation. All these methods assume different noise background. For details, please refer these references and therein.

Frequencies estimation of two dimensional harmonics is the main problem [6-7] at present. Some methods above and others assume that the phase of harmonics is a uniformly distributed or Gaussian process, and that the mean of the noises is nonzero. However, the phase is always deterministic, as a single record of data is often available in practice, and the means of noises are not necessarily nonzero. Actually, correlativity between noises is also not guaranteed. Here, a novel method to estimate harmonics in zero-mean independent multiplicative and additive noises is developed based on higher order spectra using only a single record of data. This method only requires that the noises are mixing and stationary, and imposes no constraints on the distribution or color of the noises.

2 Base Problem Statements

The complex two dimensional harmonics model studied widely takes in discrete time the form

$$x(m,n)=\sum_{l=1}^{L}s_l(m,n)e^{-j(m\omega_{l1}+n\omega_{l2}+\phi_l)}+\eta(m,n)\,, \tag{1}$$

[a] Corresponding author: ytzzw126@126.com

where $m = 0,1,\cdots T_1 - 1$, $n = 0,1,\cdots T_2 - 1$, L represents the number of signal, $(\omega_{l1}, \omega_{l2})$ denotes the l th frequency pair, both ω_{l1} 's and ω_{l2} 's are distinct and nonzero mod (2π), ϕ_l represents the l th phase, $s_l(m,n)$ represents the l th multiplicative noise, $\eta(m,n)$ represents the additive noise.

Definition 1 Let the $(u+v)$ th order moment of the complex harmonic $x(m,n)$ with u unconjugated and v conjugated entries be

$$m_{uvx}(m,n,\tau,\xi) \triangleq E\{x(m,n)x(m+\tau_1,n+\xi_1)\cdots x(m+\tau_{u-1},n+\xi_{u-1}) \times x^*(m+\tau_u,n+\xi_u)\cdots x^*(m+\tau_{u+v-1},n+\xi_{u+v-1})\}, \quad (2)$$

where $\tau = \{\tau_1,\cdots,\tau_{u+v-1}\}$, $\xi = \{\xi_1,\cdots,\xi_{u+v-1}\}$, the symbol '*' denotes conjugate operator.

Similar notational convention will be adopted for the $(u+v)$ th order cumulant $c_{uvx}(m,n;\tau,\xi)$. Generally speaking, absolute cumulant summability does not imply absolute moment summability unless $x(m,n)$ is zero-mean and $u+v=1,2,3$, in which case cumulant coincide with moments. For zero-mean Gaussian process, the odd order moments equal 0, but not for even order. However, all the cumulants with third-order or higher equal 0. So higher order statistics is often applied to suppress additive Gaussian noises.

In general, all the noises in Eq. (1) are assumed to satisfy the mixing condition [8] as follows, $\forall u,v \ge 0, u+v = 1,\cdots,8$

$$\sum_{\tau_1\cdots\tau_{u+v-1}=-\infty}^{\infty} \sum_{\xi_1\cdots\xi_{u+v-1}=-\infty}^{\infty} \left|c_{uvs}(\tau,\xi)\right| < \infty, \quad (3)$$

The mixing condition holds similarly for $\eta(m,n)$ and $x(m,n)$.

If ϕ_l 's in Eq. (1) are uniformly i.i.d. random variables in $(-\pi,\pi]$ and independent of $s_l(m,n)$ as well as $\eta(m,n)$, and $s_l(m,n)$ and $\eta(m,n)$ are stationary, we can easily prove that $x(m,n)$ is stationary but not always mixing. We assert that under the deterministic ϕ_l assumption, $x(m,n)$ is nonstationary but mixing [9]. Now we give the assumptions in Eq. (1)

AS1. $s_l(m,n)$'s and $\eta(m,n)$ are zero-mean, stationary, mixing, real and mutually independent.

AS2. The ϕ_l 's are deterministic.

The uniform phase randomization assumption prevents $x(m,n)$ from being Gaussian, which otherwise would render Dwyer's fourth-order cumulant statistics method [1] useless for frequency estimation. However, for a single record of data, ϕ_l is always deterministic, so $x(m,n)$ is Gaussian under the assumption in Dwyer's method that $s_l(m,n)$ and $\eta(m,n)$ are both Gaussian and mutually independent. It is necessary to define special cumulant in order to prevent frequency information contained in the cumulant from losing. Dou's method [6] fails since it assumes that the noises are mutually correlative. Wang's method [7] fails for its constrain imposed on the distribution of the noises.

For the assumptions above, A novel time averaged moment approach is established in the next section, where noises $s_l(m,n)$'s and $\eta(m,n)$ are allowed to be non-Gaussian, provided that they satisfy the mixing condition, Eq. (3), which can be met in practical setups.

3 Harmonics Retrieval Algorithm

Let us rewrite Eq. (1) as

$$x(m,n) = \sum_{l=1}^{L+1} S_l(m,n) e^{-j(m\omega_{l1}+n\omega_{l2})}, \quad (4)$$

where $S_l(m,n) = s_l(m,n)e^{j\phi_l}$, $S_{L+1}(m,n) \triangleq \eta(m,n)$, $(\omega_{(L+1)1}, \omega_{(L+1)2}) \triangleq (0,0)$, $\phi_{L+1} \triangleq 0$. Thus we consider additive disturbance as a special multiplicative noise.

Let $\tau = (0,\tau,\tau)$, $\xi = (0,\xi,\xi)$, we get the special fourth-order moment of $x(m,n)$ according to Eq. (2) as follows

$$m_{22x}(m,n,\tau,\xi) \triangleq E\{x(m,n)x(m,n)x^*(m+\tau,n+\xi)x^*(m+\tau,n+\xi)\}$$

(5)

Since $x(m,n)$ is a zero-mean stationary process, we get its special fourth-order cumulant according to the M-C formula

$$c_{22x}(m,n,\tau,\xi) = m_{22x}(m,n,\tau,\xi) - 2m_{11x}{}^2(m,n,\tau,\xi) - m_{20x}{}^2(m,n,0,0) \quad (6)$$

Definition 2 Define the special $(2+2)$ th order time averaged moment of $x(m,n)$ be

$$\bar{m}_{22x}(\tau,\xi) \triangleq \lim_{T_1\to\infty} \lim_{T_2\to\infty} \frac{1}{T_1 T_2} \sum_{m=0}^{T_1-1} \sum_{n=0}^{T_2-1} m_{22x}(m,n,\tau,\xi), \quad (7)$$

where $m_{22x}(m,n,\tau,\xi)$ is given by Eq. (5).

Definition **3** The special $(2+2)$ th order time averaged moment spectrum of $x(m,n)$ corresponding to **Definition 2** is

$$\begin{aligned}\bar{M}_{22x}(\alpha,\beta) &\triangleq \lim_{T_1\to\infty}\lim_{T_2\to\infty}\frac{1}{T_1T_2}\sum_{\tau=0}^{T_1-1}\sum_{\xi=0}^{T_2-1}\bar{m}_{22x}(\tau,\xi)e^{-j\alpha\tau}e^{-j\beta\xi} \\ &= \lim_{T_1\to\infty}\lim_{T_2\to\infty}\frac{1}{T_1^2T_2^2}\sum_{\tau=0}^{T_1-1}\sum_{\xi=0}^{T_2-1}\sum_{m=0}^{T_1-1}\sum_{n=0}^{T_2-1}E\{x^2(m,n)(x^*(m+\tau,n+\xi))^2\} \\ &\quad * e^{-j\alpha\tau}e^{-j\beta\xi}\end{aligned} \tag{8}$$

An important identity used in below derivation is

$$\lim_{T\to\infty}\frac{1}{T}\sum_{t=0}^{T-1}e^{j\omega t}=\delta(\omega) \triangleq \begin{cases}1 & \alpha=0 \bmod(2\pi)\\ 0 & \alpha=others\end{cases} \tag{9}$$

Now we derive the fourth-order time averaged moment approach. Let

$$\begin{aligned}x^2(m,n) &= \sum_{l=1}^{L+1}S_l^2(m,n)e^{-2j(m\omega_{l1}+n\omega_{l2})} \\ &+ 2\sum_{\substack{l_1=1,l_2=1\\(l_1\neq l_2)}}^{L+1}S_{l_1}(m,n)S_{l_2}(m,n)e^{-jm(\omega_{l_1 1}+\omega_{l_2 1})}e^{-jn(\omega_{l_1 2}+\omega_{l_2 2})}\end{aligned} \tag{10}$$

$$\begin{aligned}(x^*(m+\tau,n+\xi))^2 &= \sum_{l=1}^{L+1}(S_l^*(m+\tau,n+\xi))^2e^{2j((m+\tau)\omega_{l1}+(n+\xi)\omega_{l2})} \\ &+ 2\sum_{\substack{l_1=1,l_2=1\\(l_1\neq l_2)}}^{L+1}S_{l_1}^*(m+\tau,n+\xi)S_{l_2}^*(m+\tau,n+\xi)e^{j(m+\tau)(\omega_{l_1 1}+\omega_{l_2 1})} \\ &* e^{j(n+\xi)(\omega_{l_1 2}+\omega_{l_2 2})}\end{aligned} \tag{11}$$

Substituting Eq. (9) and (10) into Eq. (7), we obtain

$$\bar{M}_{22x}(\alpha,\beta)=\sum_{l=1}^{L}\left|m_{20S_l}(0,0)\right|^2\delta(a-2\omega_{l1})\delta(\beta-2\omega_{l2})+\left|m_{20\eta}(0,0)\right|^2\delta(0)\delta(0). \tag{12}$$

From Eq. (12), we know that $\bar{M}_{22x}(\alpha,\beta)$ peaks at $(2\omega_{11},2\omega_{12})$, $\cdots$, $(2\omega_{(L+1)1},2\omega_{(L+1)2})$, which prompts the following harmonics retrieval expression

$$\{(\omega_{l1},\omega_{l2})\}_{l=1}^{L+1}=\frac{1}{2}\underset{(\alpha_1,\beta_1),\cdots,(\alpha_{L+1},\beta_{L+1})}{\arg\max}\sum_{l=1}^{L+1}\left|\hat{M}_{22x}(\alpha_l,\beta_l)\right|^2 \tag{13}$$

Actually, we also estimate the variance of the noises, since

$$\begin{aligned}\left|m_{20s}(0,0)\right|^2 &= \left|E_s\{(x(m,n)x(m,n)\}\right|^2 \\ &= \left|D_s(x(m,n))+E_s^2(x(m,n))\right|^2=\left|D_s(x(m,n))\right|^2=\sigma_s^4\end{aligned} \tag{14}$$

4 Performance Analysis

Before introducing the sample estimator, we wish to show an interesting equivalence

$$\begin{aligned}\bar{M}_{22x}(\alpha,\beta) &\triangleq \lim_{T_1\to\infty}\lim_{T_2\to\infty}\frac{1}{T_1^2T_2^2}\sum_{\tau=0}^{T_1-1}\sum_{\xi=0}^{T_2-1}\sum_{m=0}^{T_1-1}\sum_{n=0}^{T_2-1}E\{x^2(m,n)(x^*(m+\tau,n+\xi))^2\}e^{-j\alpha\tau}e^{-j\beta\xi} \\ &= \lim_{T_1\to\infty}\lim_{T_2\to\infty}\frac{1}{T_1^2T_2^2}E\{(\sum_{m=0}^{T_1-1}\sum_{n=0}^{T_2-1}x^2(m,n)e^{j\alpha m}e^{j\beta n}) \\ &\qquad \times\sum_{\tau=0}^{T_1-1}\sum_{\xi=0}^{T_2-1}(x^*(m+\tau,n+\xi))^2e^{-j\alpha(m+\tau)}e^{-j\beta(n+\xi)})\} \\ &= \lim_{T_1\to\infty}\lim_{T_2\to\infty}\frac{1}{T_1^2T_2^2}E\{\left|\sum_{m=0}^{T_1-1}\sum_{n=0}^{T_2-1}(x^*(m,n))^2e^{-j\alpha m}e^{-j\beta n}\right|^2\} \\ &= \lim_{T_1\to\infty}\lim_{T_2\to\infty}\frac{1}{T_1^2T_2^2}E\{\left|DFT((x^*(m,n))^2)\right|^2\}\end{aligned} \tag{15}$$

From Eq. (15), the natural estimator for $\bar{M}_{22x}(\alpha,\beta)$ is

$$\hat{\bar{M}}_{22x}(\alpha,\beta)=\frac{1}{T_1^2T_2^2}\left|DFT((x^*(m,n))^2)\right|^2 \tag{16}$$

Comparing Eq. (15) with Eq. (14), we know that $\hat{\bar{M}}_{22x}(\alpha,\beta)$ is asymptotically unbiased and can be computed efficiently by using FFT.

For similar consistency proof, we refer readers to the literature [2, 10] and therein. In literature [2] we also see that the variance of the estimator has a fast converging rate of $O(T^{-3})$.

5 Simulation Results

Since noises in Eq. (1) satisfy **AS1** and **AS2** different from that in literature [6], the methods there are apparently invalid. The method in literature [7] is also designed specially for harmonics retrieval problem in zero-mean independent noises, whereas it requires the multiplicative noises in Eq. (1) are nonsymmetrical or non-Gaussian. Here we only give an example to show our method is valid for the special conditions, despite that our method does not need to impose any constrains on the distribution or color of all the noises in Eq. (1).

Suppose there are three components in model (1) with parameters $(\omega_{11},\omega_{12})=(0.50,0.75)$, $(\omega_{21},\omega_{22})=(1.15,2.25)$, $(\omega_{31},\omega_{32})=(2.50,1.50)$, $\phi_1=0.2$, $\phi_2=0.1$, $\phi_3=0.4$, respectively. The noises are produced by second order MA model driven by different Gaussian white random process as follows

$$\begin{aligned}s_1(m,n)&=e_1(m,n)-0.5e_1(m-1,n)-0.3e_1(m-2,n)\\ s_2(m,n)&=e_2(m,n)-0.3e_2(m-1,n)-0.7e_2(m-2,n)\\ s_3(m,n)&=e_3(m,n)-0.35e_3(m-1,n)-0.65e_4(m-2,n)\\ \eta(m,n)&=e_4(m,n)-0.4e_4(m-1,n)-0.6e_4(m-2,n)\end{aligned} \tag{17}$$

where $e_1(m,n)$, $e_2(m,n)$, $e_3(m,n)$, and $e_4(m,n)$ are Gaussian random processes with mean zero and variance 1. The data length is 1024×1024.

Figure 1 and Figure 2 show the estimation results for $\hat{\bar{M}}_{22x}(\alpha,\beta)$ using the method proposed in literature [6] and [7], respectively. Figure 3 and Figure 4 are the results by the method in this paper, where $\bar{M}_{22x}(\alpha,\beta)$ precisely peaks at $(\omega_{11},\omega_{12})=(1.00,1.50)$, $(\omega_{21},\omega_{22})=(2.30,4.50)$ and $(\omega_{31},\omega_{32})=(5.00,3.00)$

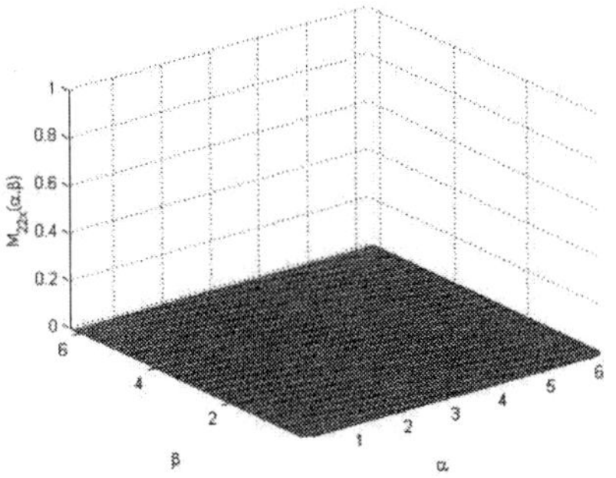

Figure 1. Results by Method in Ref. [6]

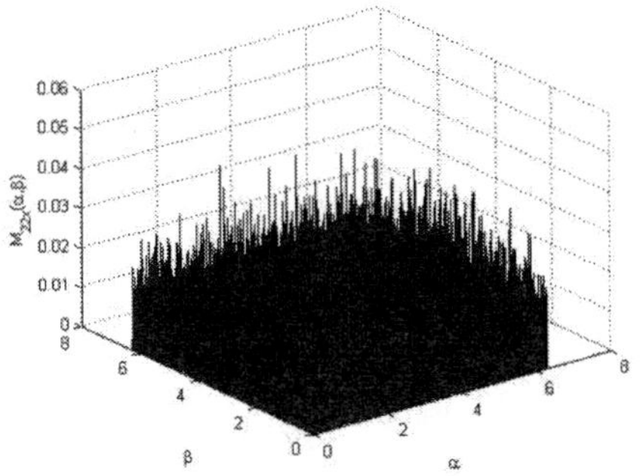

Figure 2. Results by Method in Ref. [7]

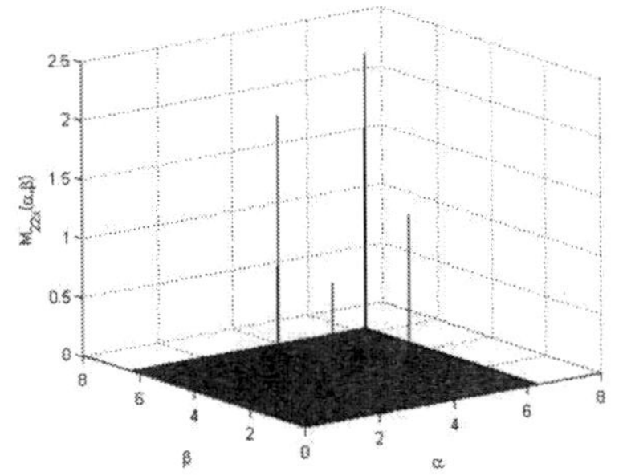

Figure 3. Results by Method in This Paper

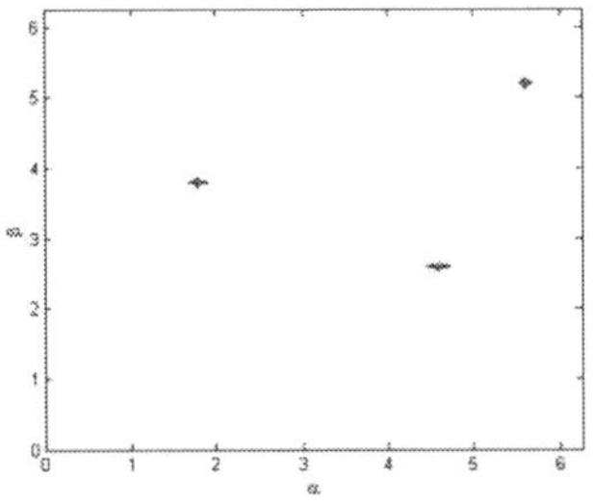

Figure 4. The Contour of $\hat{\bar{M}}_{22x}(\alpha,\beta)$

As analyzed above, the spectrum peak at $(2\pi,2\pi)$ in Fig. 3 is caused by the additive noise. The frequencies and the variances of the noises estimated from Eq. (21) and (22) are shown in Table 1. Increasing the data length, we can get more precise estimation, since the estimator is asymptotically unbiased.

Table 1. Estimation Results

l	ω_{l1}	ω_{l2}	δ_{sl}^2
1	0.5000	0.7485	0.8736
2	1.1504	2.2488	1.2032
3	2.5003	1.5002	1.6230
4	0	0	2.1012

6 Conclusions

We proposed a harmonics retrieval method based on a special time averaged moment and cumulant for the situations where the multiplicative and additive noises are zero-mean independent stationary processes. Here we consider the deterministic phases since we always obtain a single record data in practice, and only require the noises are mixing. The method in this paper does not need to impose any constraints on the distribution and color of the noises, and the estimator can be computed efficiently by using FFT. As a by product, the variances of the noises which appear as the amplitudes of the harmonics peaks of the special time averaged moment spectrum slice can also be estimated easily. Experiments confirm to the correctness and validity of the method.

But as mentioned in literature [2], the phenomenon that the frequency pairs are restricted to $(0,\pi]$ in order to avoid aliasing also happened in this paper. To develop a method without these limits will be the further research direction.

References

1. R. R. Dwyer., J. Acoust. Soc. Amer., 90, 918(1991)

2. G. T. Zhou, G. B. Giannakis., IEEE. J. Oceanic Eng., 19, 529(1994)
3. G. B. Giannakis, G. T. Zhou., IEEE Trans. Signal Processing, 43, 2217(1995)
4. A Kareem, Y Li. *Probabilistic Methods in Civil Engineering*, 384(2015)
5. WJ Baars, CE Tinney., Physics of Fluids, 8, 2182(2014)
6. H. J. Dou, S. X. Wang, F. Wang., Acta Electronica Sinica, 32, 83(2004)
7. F. Wang, S. X. Wang, H. J. Dou., Acta Electronica Sinica, 31, 1522 (2003)
8. G.T. Zhou, *Random amplitude and polynomial phase modeling of nonstationary process using higher order and cyclic statistics*., Canada Charlottesville, University of Virginia, VA 22903-2442
9. Z.W. Zhang, Y.Y. Fan, Z. Li., Journal of Information and Computational Science, 4, 387(2007)
10. H.W. Li, Q.S. Cheng, B. Z., *Signal processing proceedings*, Fourth ICSP'98, 43(1998)

 DOI: 10.1051/itmconf/20160702004

Robust Face Recognition Via Gabor Feature and Sparse Representation

Yu-Juan HAO[1,a], Li-Quan ZHANG[1]

[1] *College of Electrical and Information Engineering,Beijing University of Civil Engineering and Architecture, Beijing, China*
[a] *Corresponding author Yu-juan HAO.E-mail address:1243476593@qq.com*

Abstract. Sparse representation based on compressed sensing theory has been widely used in the field of face recognition, and has achieved good recognition results. but the face feature extraction based on sparse representation is too simple, and the sparse coefficient is not sparse. In this paper, we improve the classification algorithm based on the fusion of sparse representation and Gabor feature, and then improved algorithm for Gabor feature which overcomes the problem of large dimension of the vector dimension, reduces the computation and storage cost, and enhances the robustness of the algorithm to the changes of the environment.The classification efficiency of sparse representation is determined by the collaborative representation,we simplify the sparse constraint based on L1 norm to the least square constraint, which makes the sparse coefficients both positive and reduce the complexity of the algorithm. Experimental results show that the proposed method is robust to illumination, facial expression and pose variations of face recognition, and the recognition rate of the algorithm is improved.

1 Introduction

Face recognition has the advantage of convenience and safety, easy to accept, not easy to counterfeit, which are widely used in the identification, video retrieval, safety monitoring and other fields.It is a hot research topic in the field of pattern recognition and artificial intelligence. In recent years ,with development of compressed sensing theory and the L1 norm optimization technology , sparse representation has received the attention of many scholars at home and abroad .

In sparse representation, a signal can be represented as the most sparse linear combination of a given dictionary atom.Therefore, sparse representation has been widely used in image denoising and recovery, sparse representation has been widely used in pattern recognition and face recognition. In 2009, Wright John applied sparse representation to the field of face recognition, and achieved good recognition results in the face image under the condition of noise pollution or partial occlusion[1].The principle of sparse representation is to use the dictionary to process the signal processing[2], The signal represents a linear combination of a small number of atoms. Many scholars have done researches and improvement based the sparse representation algorithm.

Yang discuss the rationality of L1 norm solution of SRC and the validity of the classification method[3]. [6] believe that collaborative representation is more important than the L1 norm in the effective face recognition, and proposed a collaborative representation classification method (CRC), which is more efficient in computing. However, CRC does not provide a method to remove the image noise, so there is still a lack of recognition. Based on kernel principal component analysis (KPCA) and Fisher linear discriminant analysis (LDA), a complete kernel Fisher discriminant analysis (CKFD) algorithm is proposed by Yang [4]. Cevikalp propose kernel discriminant common vector method. The local tangent space alignment algorithm (LTSA) is proposed by [9], Zhang [10] propose an adaptive manifold learning based on LTSA. Lai[11] put up a sparse 2D local discriminant projection (S2DLDP) algorithm. [7][8] raise discriminant analysis of robust feature extraction of principal component analysis based on non parametric maximum entropy principle. Yang proposed GSRC (based SRC Gabor-feature) method,which uses Gabor features significantly reduce the size of the block dictionary and improve the rate of face recognition[12].

Huang [16] propose a neighborhood preserving embedding algorithm, the proposed algorithms not only solve the weakness of traditional linear methods such as PCA, which are difficult to maintain the nonlinear flow of the original data, but also solve the shortcomings of the nonlinear method which are hard to obtain the low dimensional projection of the new sample points. Chen [17] present a local discriminant embedding (LDE) method for popular learning and pattern classification.Yan [18] propose a graph embedding framework to develop a new dimension reduction algorithm.Cai [19] propose a subspace method of spatial smoothing for face recognition and orthogonal Laplacianfaces face recognition[21].Fan [20] raise an improved LDA framework (LLDA) that can effectively capture the local structure of the samples.

Based on the current level of technology development, L1 norm sparsity determines SRC method whether it can be successfully applied to the problem of face recognition. And for this issue , [13] analysis and experiment the basic principle of SRC, and propose that SRC is more important than L1 norm sparsity in the classification methods based SRC, Zhang proposed a classification method based on sparse representation and rule of least squares SRC-RLS [14] [15]. Compared with the CRC method [6], (SRC-RLS) the results of the recognition is not only much better, but also can reduce the complexity of calculating. However, the SRC-RLS method directly uses the gray characteristics of the image recognition, so when the situation changes of light, posture and facial expressions ,the accuracy of this recognition method will not be very high.

In the second part ,we introduced Gabor feature extraction principle and our improved method.We lists the data of the method,in the third part, we introduce the sparse representation theory and its shortcomings, and point out that the sparse coefficients contain negative values which affect the result of the experiment, and introduces the collaborative representation.Finally, we validate the effectiveness of our method on a database which can improve the robustness of face recognition.

This paper proposes a new face recognition algorithm based on a improved Gabor feature and sparse representation (GSRC), and the least square method is used to replace the L1 solution. After the feature extraction of face recognition image, we fully constitute a complete dictionary of facial features, and then fuse the sparse representation algorithm, which will improve the recognition rate.

2 Gabor Feature Extraction

2.1 Gabor Filter Principle

First, Gabor function is obtained through the Fourier transform, the spectrum feature of Fourier transform is only in the infinite time domain which is difficult to fit for the local signal frequency analysis . A part of the time domain signal is multiplied with the Gauss window function and the Fourier transform is performed,we can get Gabor transformation. It was first proposed by Gabor Dennis, in 1946. The Gabor transform will be defined as:

$$G_f(\omega,b)=\int_{-\infty}^{\infty} e^{-i\omega t} g_a(t-b) f(t)dt \tag{1}$$

The function of Gabor filter in the image processing is to achieve the input signal wavelet transform [17], so as to obtain the image of the local texture characteristics:

$$\begin{gathered} I_{mlpq}=\iint f(x,y)\varphi_{ml}(x-p\Delta x, y-q\Delta y)dxdy \\ (m=0,\cdots,M-1,\ l=0,\cdots,L-1) \end{gathered} \tag{2}$$

M represents directions, L represents the scales; p represents the x -coordinate of the image pixels, q represents the ordinate of the image pixels; Δx and Δy are spatial sampling interval,usually set $\Delta x=\Delta y=1$, $\varphi_{ml}(x,y)$ is the parent wave:

$$\varphi_{ml}(x,y)=a^{-m}\varphi(\tilde{x},\tilde{y}) \tag{3}$$

In Eq.(3),

$$\tilde{x}=a^{-m}(x\cos\theta+y\sin\theta), \tilde{y}=a^{-m}(-x\sin\theta+y\cos\theta)$$

Direction change is defined as

$$\begin{gathered} \theta=l\Delta\theta \\ \Delta\theta=2\pi/L \end{gathered} \tag{4}$$

θ can choose different angles with the same spacing in 2π, thus making the filter in different directions have the same size of energy.

$$g(x,y)=\left(\frac{1}{2\pi\delta_x\delta_y}\right)\exp\left[-\frac{1}{2}\left(\frac{x^2}{\delta_x^2}+\frac{y^2}{\delta_y^2}\right)+2\pi jW_x\right] \tag{5}$$

W represents frequency bandwidth.When $W=0.5$, the filter can match the visual system. The frequency characteristic of Gabor wavelet can be realized in the space of u axis and v axis:

$$\begin{aligned} \psi(u,v) &= \exp[-2\pi^2(\delta_x^2u^2+\delta_y^2v^2)]*\delta(u-W) \\ &= \exp\left(-2\pi^2\left(\delta_x^2(u-W)^2+\delta_y^2v^2\right)\right) \\ &= \exp\left(-\frac{1}{2}\left(\frac{(u-W)^2}{\delta_u^2}+\frac{v^2}{\delta_v^2}\right)\right) \end{aligned} \tag{6}$$

Frequency variance $\delta_u = \dfrac{1}{2\pi\delta_x}, \delta_v = \dfrac{1}{2\pi\delta_y}$

However, the output of Gabor filter in high frequency state is relatively small, and it is necessary to change the basis function calculation method.

For people's facial features, there is also a unique characteristics of unity. In order to separate people, it should make full use of the unique characteristics of these key features, including the texture distribution of facial organs, geometric distance and the crowd, which is also the main theoretical basis for face recognition. We use the "three vertical and five horizontal" law,face detection in the vertical direction is divided into three parts. In the horizontal direction ,the face is divided into five equal parts, each is equal to the width of a eyes.

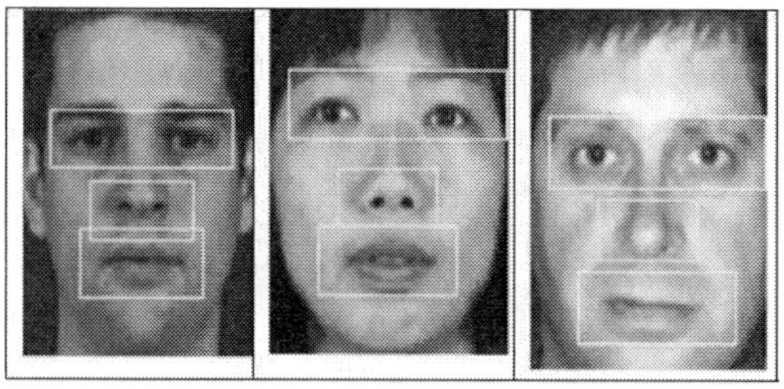

Figure1. Facial Organ Location .Figure 1 Shows the Location of the Eyes, Nose and Mouth.

We chose 40 filters to filter the image which contains 8 directions and 5 scales . The characteristics described by each filter is different. In order to be more intuitive to identify these differences, we intercepted a few filtered images were analyzed.

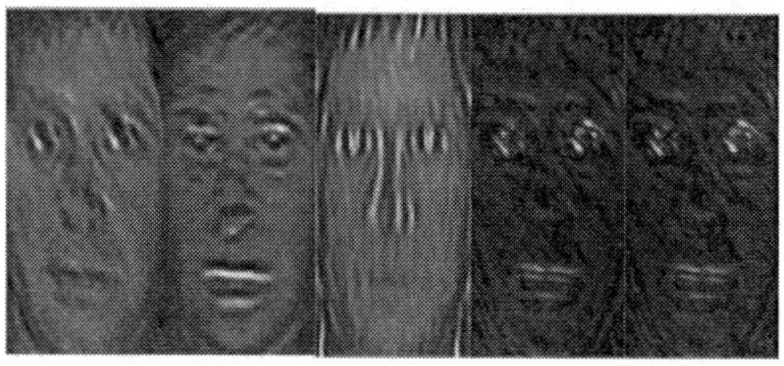

Figure2. Filtered Image It Shows The Characteristics Of Different Features After Filtering

In the face images,we need extract the key feature points ,we choose the distance between each feature points as the feature vector of the face.Such as Fig.3.

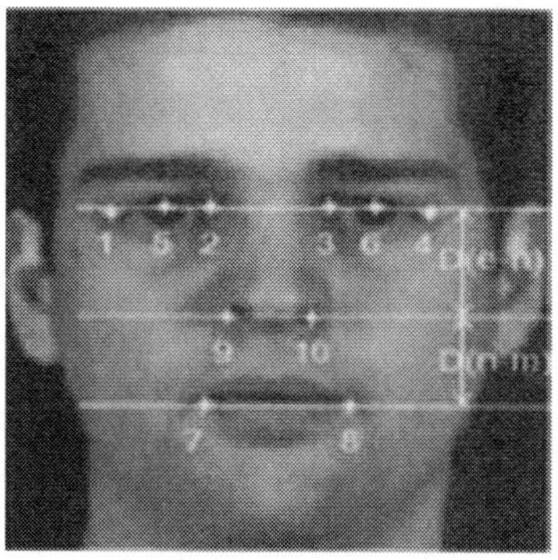

Figure3. Feature Map of Geometric Distance

In figure 3,we show the process of the feature extraction.Eye feature points : in the Cb image ,the eye section shows a high pixel value, in Cr image, the eye section shows a low pixel value. Considering the character and select the appropriate threshold which can separate the eyes into a black area (the eye) and two white areas . Finally, we can get 6 feature points of the eyes: it is easy to get the feature points of the mouth,Because the size of the pixel values in the Cr component has a great relationship with red.The red lips make it more in the pixel in the Cr component, then the sobel filter can be used to extract its contour. According to this inherent attribute ,we can roughly determined in the image of the nose area.For the extraction of the feature points of the nose, it also can be expressed by the Sobel filter, and then extract the points on both sides of the nose root as a feature point.

In the research of the face recognition system,we need use the key features of the human face organs , and the feature points are used to represent the human face organs.

2.2 Improved Gabor feature extraction method

Based on the Gabor function ,principle and design theory of filter, we have made some changes in the selection of Gabor kernel function, so as to be conducive to the implementation of the program. The two-dimensional Gabor kernel function we choose are shown in [18][19].

$$\begin{cases} W(x,y,\theta,\lambda,\phi,\sigma)=\exp\left(-\dfrac{x'^2+y'^2}{2\sigma^2}\right)\cos\left(2\pi\dfrac{x'}{\lambda}+\phi\right) \\ x'=x\cos(\theta)+y\sin(\theta) \\ y'=-x\sin(\theta)+y\cos(\theta) \end{cases} \tag{7}$$

(x, y) represent a pixel coordinates inthe diagram

$\theta, \lambda, \phi, \sigma$ The parameters of $\theta, \lambda, \phi, \sigma$ are shown in Table 1.

Table 1. Data of $\theta, \lambda, \phi, \sigma$

parameters	Symbol	Set value
direction	θ	$\left\{0, \frac{\pi}{8}, \frac{2\pi}{8}, \frac{3\pi}{8}, \frac{4\pi}{8}, \frac{5\pi}{8}, \frac{6\pi}{8}, \frac{7\pi}{8}\right\}$
wavelength	λ	$\{4, 4\sqrt{2}, 8, 8\sqrt{2}, 16\}$
phase	ϕ	$\left\{0, \frac{\pi}{2}\right\}$
Gauss radius	σ	$\sigma=\lambda$

Direction θ : Represent the direction of parallel stripes in the Gabor function. Wavelength λ : In image processing, it is said that the unit is a pixel, there is a certain range of needs less than the size of the image 1/5, the minimum is 2.Phase ϕ : In the range of -180 degrees to 180 degrees, Gauss radius σ : Represent the standard deviation of Gauss factor in the Gauss's function used in Gabor transform, $\sigma=\lambda$.

A set of filters consists of 5 different spatial frequencies and 8 different directions, which make up 40 different filters, as shown in Figure 4.

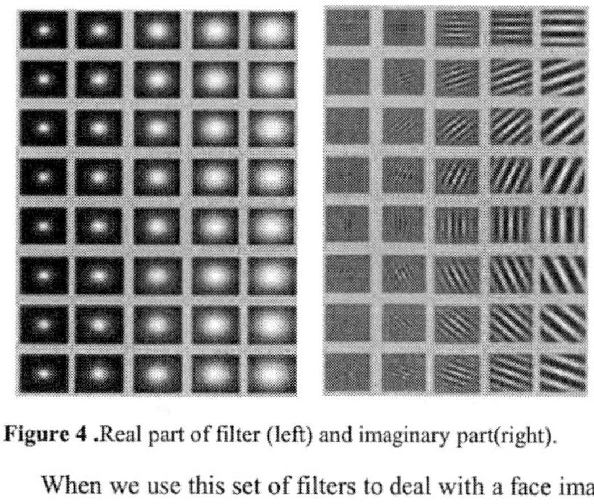

Figure 4 .Real part of filter (left) and imaginary part(right).

When we use this set of filters to deal with a face image, the number of processed images is equal to the number offilters. If these filters are applied to each pixel in the image, the filtered vector dimension is very large (proportional to the size of the image). So, this will lead to a huge amount of computing and storage costs, which will consume a lot of time to classify and identify. Our method is only applied to the filter to extract the ten benchmark points, to obtain the filter response. If the number of filters is M, then the vector dimension of the filter response is 10 * M. The number of filters corresponding to different values of is shown in Table 2.

Table 2 Numbers of Filter and the Values of θ

Numbers of filter	Values of different directions (θ)
5	$\{0\}$
10	$\left\{0, \frac{4\pi}{8}\right\}$
20	$\left\{0, \frac{2\pi}{8}, \frac{4\pi}{8}, \frac{6\pi}{8}\right\}$
30	$\left\{0, \frac{\pi}{8}, \frac{2\pi}{8}, \frac{4\pi}{8}, \frac{5\pi}{8}, \frac{6\pi}{8}\right\}$
40	$\left\{0, \frac{\pi}{8}, \frac{2\pi}{8}, \frac{3\pi}{8}, \frac{4\pi}{8}, \frac{5\pi}{8}, \frac{6\pi}{8}, \frac{7\pi}{8}\right\}$

3 Sparse Representation Robust Recognition

3.1. Sparse Representation Theory

The essence of sparse representation is the decomposition of signals under the constraint of sparse regularization. The basic model that natural signal can be expressed as a linear combination of atomic signal predefined, and the combination coefficients is sparse, i.e. most of the coefficients is zero or close to zero.

In the face recognition technology based on sparse representation,each image size is $w \times h$,which can be regarded as a point of m dimensional space, $m = w \times h$,The information of different brightness, expression and occlusion of the same face are expressed in the low dimensional linear subspace. We define n_i pictures., n_i training samples of i subject form a matrix, $A_i = [v_{i,1}, v_{i,2}, \cdots, v_{i,n}] \in R^{m \times n_i}$ .Any of the test samples ($y \in R^m$) of the class are similar to the linear subspace in which the columns are formed by the A_i .

$$y = a_{i,1}v_{i,1} + a_{i,2}v_{i,2} + \cdots + a_{i,n_i}v_{i,n_i} \quad (8)$$

$a_{i,j} \in R$ is combination coefficient, $j = 1, 2, \cdots n_i$.
Because the class of the test sample can not be predicted in advance, a matrix A is defined for the whole training sample set, it is regarded as a series of k classes of training samples.All n_i are added together: $n = n_1 + n_2 + \cdots + n_k$,

we regard n columns as vector A : $A=[A_1,A_2,\cdots,A_k]=[v_{1,1},v_{1,2},\cdots,v_{k,n_k}]$,

y can be expressed as a linear combination of the training sample set:

$$y = Ax_0 \in R^m \tag{9}$$

$x_0=[0,\cdots,a_{i,1},a_{i,2},\cdots,a_{i,n_i},0,\cdots,0]^T \in R^n$, x_0 is coefficient vector, Non - zero items of x_0 should be corresponding to the class i of the training set. At this time the problem is transformed into solving equations $y = Ax$. Under normal circumstances, the equation set is not under determined, and its solution is not unique, but it can be solved by the following optimal problem: (l^0):

$$\hat{x}_0 = \arg\min \|x\|_0 \, subjecttoAx = y \tag{10}$$

Symbol $\|x\|_0$ express the number of nonzero elements in vector x .We can prove that for an arbitrary set of equations, when the number of nonzero elements of one of the solutions x is less than $m/2$, x is the most sparse solution $\hat{x}_0 = x$ .However, the problem of finding the sparsest solution of an under determined system of linear equations is NP-hard, we need alternative ways to solve.By sparse representation and compression sensing theory, if the solution of X_0 is sparse enough, then the problem of l^0 norm can be replaced by the minimum l^1 norm: $(l^1)\,\hat{x}_1 = x\arg\min\|x\|_1$ subject to $Ax = y$ (11)

Due to the impact of noise or inadequate training samples and other reasons ,the linear constraint in the optimization problem is not always established, the actual model can be modified as: $y = Ax_0 + z$, $z \in R^m$ represent noise, $\|z\|_2 < \varepsilon$. At the same time, sparse solution X_0 can still be achieved by solving the problem of l^1 _ norm:

$$\hat{x}_1 = x\arg\min\|x\|_1 \text{ subject to } \|Ax - y\|_2 \le \varepsilon \tag{12}$$

We choose the ORL face database to illustrate the shortcomings of sparse representation.We select an image of subject 8,which have glasses occlusion from the test images to detect , whose mouth posture changes, the recognition result is not correct caused by linear conversion errors,the results as shown in figure 5 (a). From the figure 5 (b) and (c) show that the maximum coefficient does not belongs to the correct subject by the classical SRC method.The error of training images detected although sparse coefficient is the largest, but it also has a negative correlation coefficient absolute value maximum, other values are mostly negative. So the effect is not obvious.

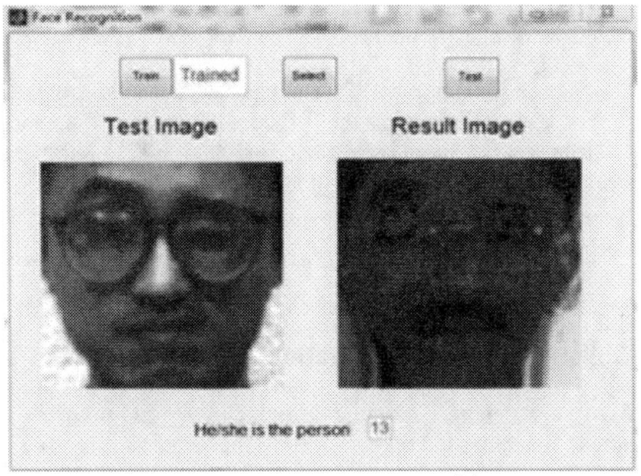

(a)

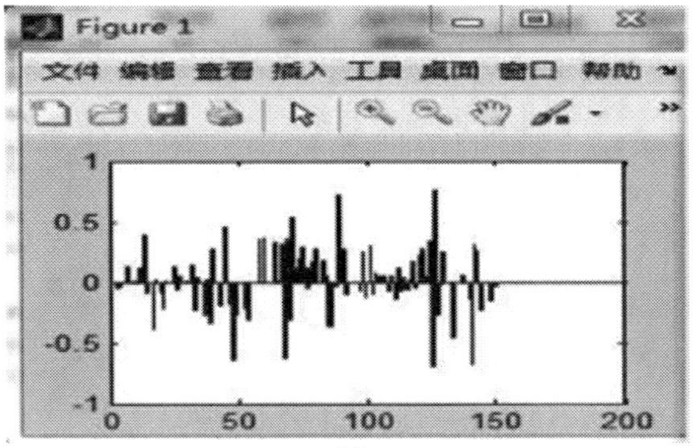

(b)

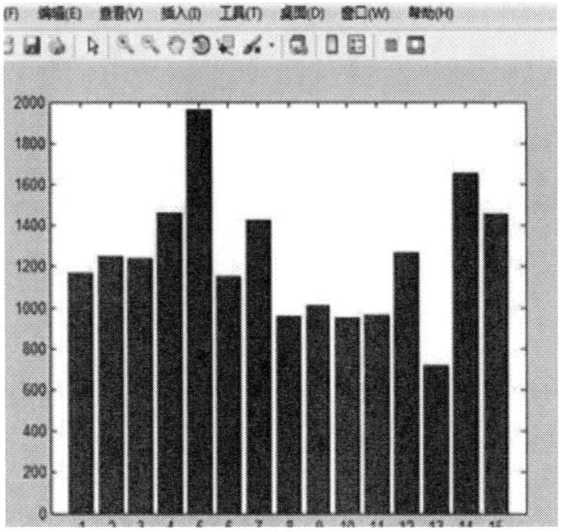

(c)

Figure 5. Classical Sparse Representation. We Choose the Orl face Database Which Contains 40 People,Each Person Has

11images.We Select 15 People , Every Has 10 Train Images,One as the Test Image.the Images are Dealt with 12*8 by Down Sample. (a)the Recognition Result,Test Image Belongs to Subject 8,the Result Shows It Belongs to Subject 13. (b)the Sparse Coefficients.(c)the Residuals of 15 People.

Feature obtained by the down sampling is not obvious, it also can not express the face feature. And the sparse coefficients of the traditional sparse said method are negative, which has great interference in the category judgment,if the coefficient is positive, this problem can be optimized.

3.2 Face Recognition Algorithm Based on Collaborative Representation

Many documents have highlighted the importance of sparse for classification, and have not studied the role of various training samples in the collaborative representation of test samples. Improve the accuracy of face recognition, a collaborative representation based classification (CRC) method is proposed in the literature [6].In a practical face recognition system, in order to ensure the high recognition rate, feature dimension usually cannot be set too low. Therefore, there is no need for us to l^1 - norm. Taking into account the dictionary X may be under determined, we use l^2 -norm regularization. in order to use x to express the test sample y we propose the following collaborative representation of the regularized least squares method:

$$\hat{a} = \arg\min_{a} \left\{ \|y - xa\|_2^2 + \lambda \|a\|_2^2 \right\} \quad (13)$$

λ is regularization parameter,The function of l^2-norm regularization $\|a\|_2$ is twofold. First of all, it makes the least squares solution stable, especially when x is less regular; secondly, it introduces a certain number of sparse to $\hat{a}$. However, this degree of sparsity is weaker than the l^1-norm.we can get this:

$$\hat{a} = \left(x^T x + \lambda I\right)^{-1} x^T y \quad (14)$$

Order $P = \left(x^T x + \lambda I\right)^{-1} x^T$ Obviously, P is independent relative to y , We can calculate P as a projection matrix. Once the test sample y arrival, we will simply pass the P to the Py , which makes the calculation speed of the collaborative representation is very fast.Depending on the classification of $\hat{a}$ in the CRC and the classification of the $\hat{a}$ depending on the SRC are similar. In addition to using the specified class of $\|y - X_j \hat{a}_j\|_2$ to classify the reconstructed residuals Where $\hat{a}_j$ is corresponding to the class of coding coefficient vector, l^2 - norm sparse term can also bring some discriminant information.Therefore, we propose to use both of them in classification, so that the classification accuracy can be improved by the use of $\|y - X_j \hat{a}_j\|_2$.

3.3 Combination of Improved Gabor Features and Sparse Representation

When the images exist illumination, expression and pose variation, the recognition rate of traditional sparse representation will be decreased. In order to further improve the algorithm accuracy and robustness, We will combine feature extraction method which characterize the facial feature vectors including the Gabor filter in response to the 10 x M value and 8 geometric distance parameters of the feature extraction method with sparse representation algorithm, and the least square method is used to solve the norm, and the condition of the sparse coefficient is positive.

According to the proposed extension of the Gabor feature definition, extracting all the Gabor features of the training sample set image,the corresponding Gabor feature set is extracted from the eyes, nose and lips,and set up the corresponding feature set. $X_i = [x_{i,1}, x_{i,2}, \ldots, x_{i,n_i}]$ .The Gabor feature set for all classes of training samples is $X = [X_1, X_2, \ldots, X_K]$,All the training samples are set to represent the test samples.That is to simplify the SRC algorithm based on norm of sparse constraints to the rule of least squares method,

$$(\hat{p}) = \arg\min_{p} \left\{ \|y - Xp\|_2^2 + \lambda \|p\|_2^2 \right\} \quad (15)$$

P is coefficient vector, λ is expressed rule parameter,Regularization term $\lambda \|p\|_2^2$ it makes the least squares solution stable, especially when X is less regular; secondly, it introduces a certain number of sparse to $\hat{p}$. P is independent relative to y , We can calculate P as a projection matrix.

Improved algorithm flow:

1. Extract the Gabor features of the three parts of the training sample set and the test sample, then respectively get X and Y;
2. The test sample feature vector y is based on the training sample set X collaborative representation coding $\hat{p} = Py$,The projection matrix is $P = \left(x^T x + \lambda I\right)^{-1} x^T$;

3. calculate regular residual $r_i = \|y - X_i\hat{p}_i\|_2 / \|\hat{p}_i\|_2$, $\hat{p}_i$ is the encoding coefficient vectors for class i ;
4. Output: $identity(y) = \arg\min_i \{r_i\}$

4 Simulation and Results

In order to verify the effectiveness of the algorithm, we conduct a simulation experiment, we select two standard face recognition databases , that is, the performance comparison test of the proposed algorithm is carried out on Extended Yale B database and AR database. In this paper, we use the support vector machine classification algorithm (SVM) and the classical SRC algorithm to compare with the improved algorithm.Compare with the Fig.5,we see the improved result.

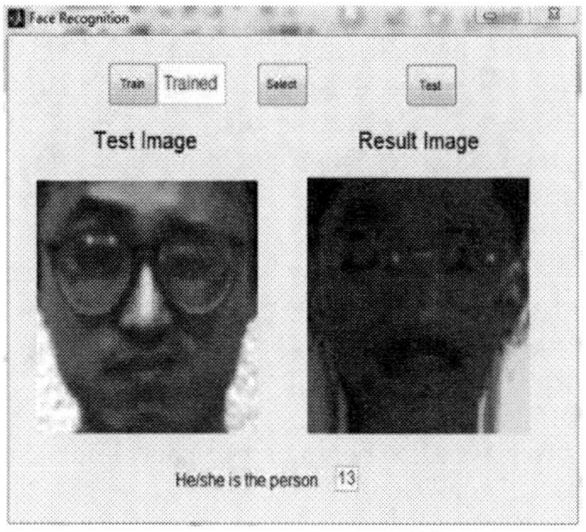

(a)

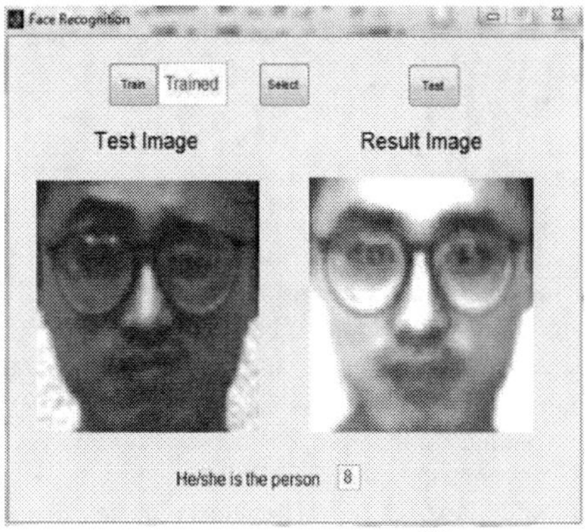

(b)

Figure6. Compare the Improved Result and the Src, the Progress is the Same as fig.5.(a) Represent the Result of Fig.5,(b)Shows the Correct Result by Our Method.

4.1 Face Experiment on Extended Yale B

The Extended Yale B face database contains 38 individual frontal face image, each in different illumination conditions have 64 pictures, the size of each photo is 192 168 . We randomly selected 32 samples as training samples, and the rest as the test samples. Like the classical sparse representation, we select the feature space dimension is 30,54,130,300, Fig.8 Recognition rate of three kinds of classifiers in four kinds of feature dimension.

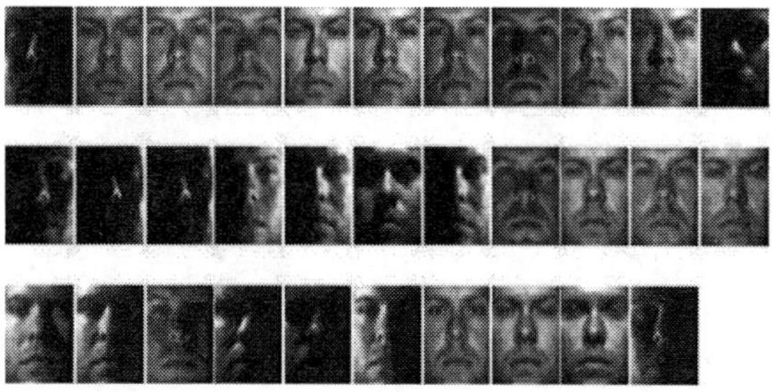

(a)

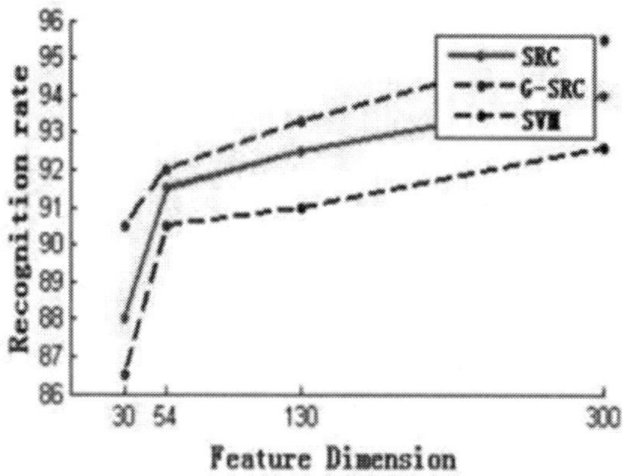

(b)

Figure 7. Recognition Rate on Extended Yale b Database, (a)Test Sample Images.(b)Recognition Rate of Three Kinds of Classification Methods.

We can see that the improved method has greatly improved the recognition rate compared with the original method. The feature space dimension is300,our method can achieve 95.3%,the SRC is 94.1% .

4.2 Face Experiment on AR Database

AR face database contains a total of 4000 images collected from 126 volunteers, including the changes in light, angle, facial expression and occlusion. We select 50 classes, each class of 26 samples, the image size is 165 120 .We choose 14 images per class as a training sample, and the others are used as test samples.The

 DOI: 10.1051/itmconf/20160702004

feature space dimension is30,54,130,300. Fig.9 The experimental results obtained by the three algorithms with the change of dimension.

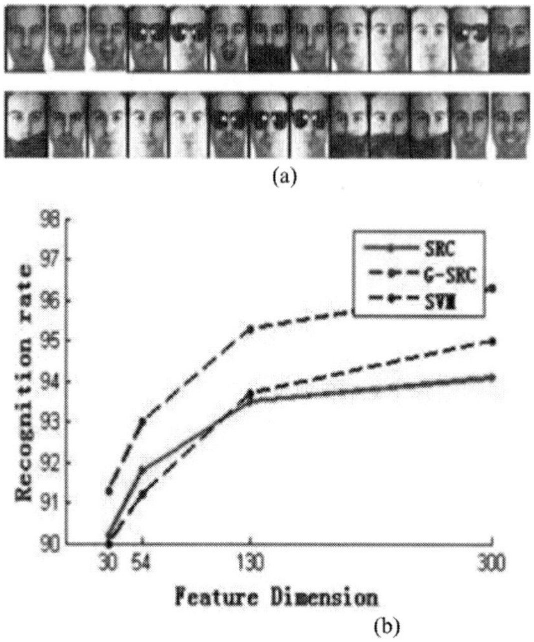

Figure8. Recognition Rate on Ar Database. (a) Sample of Someone. (b) the Recognition Rate of Three Kinds of Classification Methods.

We can see that the improved method has greatly improved the recognition rate compared with the original method.The feature space dimension is300,our method can achieve 96.3%,the SRC is 94.1% .

Acknowledgments

In the research of image recognition, feature extraction can be described as an essential step. The advantage of feature extraction determines the accuracy of the recognition. We propose an improved Gabor feature extraction algorithm to obtain the accurate position of the eyes and mouth and extract features; Using Sobel edge detection technology determines the position of the nose and extract the feature points.

We calibrate the facial feature points ,then apply Gabor filter at each characteristic point respectively, The purpose of this process is to extract the local details of the facial organs.

The Gabor feature extracted by this method is not only low in dimension, but also has good robustness. Then the least square method is used to solve the solution, which ensures the non-negativity of the coefficients. The experimental results show that the new method is robust to illumination, occlusion and other changes.

References

1. J. Wright, A Y.Yang, A. Ganesh , S. S. Sastry, Y.Ma . Robust face recognition via sparse representation. IEEE Transactions on Pattern Analysis and Machine Intelligence, 31 210-227(2009)
2. J .Z. Huang, X. L. Huang, D. Metaxas Simultaneous image transformation and sparse representation recovery. In: Proceedings of the 26th IEEE Conference on Computer Vision and Image Recognition. Anchorage United States. 1-8(2008)
3. J. Yang, L. Zhang, Y. Xu, and J.Y. Yang, Beyond sparsity: The role of L1-optimizer in pattern classification, Pattern Recognit,45 1104–1118(2012)
4. J. Yang, A. F. Frang, J.-Y. Yang, D. Zhang, and Z. Jin, KPCA plus LDA: A complete kernel fisher discriminant framework for feature extraction and recognition, IEEE Trans. Pattern Anal. Mach. Intell.27(2) 230–244(2005)
5. H. Cevikalp, M. Neamtu, and M. Wilkes, Discriminative common vector method with kernels, IEEE Trans. Neural Netw,17(6) 1550–1565(2006)
6. L. Zhang, M. Yang and X. C. Feng, Sparse representation or collaborative representation: Which helps face recognition? In Proc. IEEE Int. Conf. Comput.Vis., Nov. 3 7(2011)
7. R. He, W.-S. Zheng and B.G. Hu, Maximum Correntropy criterion for robust face recognition, IEEE Trans. Pattern Anal. Mach. Intell.33, 1561–1576(2011)
8. R. He, B.-G. Hu, and X. T. Yuan, Robust discriminant analysis based on non-parametric maximum entropy, In Proc. Asian Conf. Mach. Learn, 120–134(2009)
9. Z. Zhang, H. Zha. Principal manifolds and nonlinear dimensionality reduction via tangent space alignment. SIAM J. Scientific Computing,26 313–338(2004)
10. Z. Y. Zhang, J. Wang, H. Y. Zha. Adaptive manifold learning IEEE. Trans. Pattern .Anal. Mach. Int. 32 253–265(2012)
11. Z. Lai, M. Wan, Z. Jin, and J. Yang, Sparse two-dimensional local discriminant projections for feature extraction, Neuro.Computing,4 629–637,(2011)
12. M. Yang, L. Zhang ,Gabor feature based spare representation for face recognition with Gabor occlusion dictionary, In ECCV,448-461 (2010)
13. N. Zhang, J. K Yang. Nearest neighbor based local sparse representation classifier, In: Proceedings of the 2010 Chinese Conference on Pattern Recognition. Chongqing, China: CCPR,400-404 (2010)
14. R. Tibshiraniomput, Regression shrinkage and selection via the lasso: a retrospective. Journal of the Royal Statistical Society: Series B, 73(3) 273-282(2011)
15. J, Zhang, R. Jin, Y. M. Yang, Y. M. Hauptmann, A. G .Modified, Logistic regression: an approximation to SVM and its applications in large-scale text

categorization, In: Proceedings of the 20th International Conference on Machine Learning. Washington, United states: ICML, 888-895(2003)
16. Y.FU, T.S. Huang. Graph embedded analysis for head pose estimation, IEEE International Conf. on Automatic Face and Gesture Recognition. (2006)
17. H .T. Chen, H. W. Chang, and T. L. Liu, Local discriminant embedding and its variants, Proc. Conf. Comput.Vis. Pattern Recognit. 846–853(2005)
18. S. Yan, D. Xu, B. Zhang, H. Zhang, Q. Yang, and S. Lin, Graph embedding and extension: A general framework for dimensionality reduction, IEEE Trans. Pattern Anal. Mach. Intell. 29, 40–51(2007)
19. D.Cai, X. He, Y. Hu, J. Han and T. Huang, Learning a spatially smooth subspace for face recognition, Proc. Comput.Soc. Conf. Comput.Vis. Pattern Recognit.,1–7 (2007)
20. Z. Fan, Y. X u, and D. Zhang, Local linear discriminant analysis framework using sample neighbors, IEEE Trans. Neural Netw,22,1119–1132(2011)

A signal selection method for heterogeneous positioning sources

Lu YIN[a], Zhong-Liang DENG, Di ZHU and En-Wen HU

Beijing University of Posts and Telecommunications, School of Electronic Engineering, 100876, China
[a] Corresponding author: inlu_mail@bupt.edu.cn

Abstract. It can receive different signals in multi-system positioning. There might be dozens, even hundreds of signal sources. It is a great computation burden of hardware to process so many signals. On the other hands, the positioning accuracy of different signal systems is different; the worse signal may affect the positioning accuracy if there are too many signal sources. So it is necessary to select the better signal sources for positioning. This paper proposed a signal selection method for heterogeneous positioning sources. It combines the factors which affect the positioning accuracy to a function. Then assess the quality of the signals and select the best source set. The simulation results showed the efficiency of the algorithm.

1. Introduction

There are more than one signal systems in the multi-source heterogeneous positioning system [1]. Each of the signal system has different measurement and positioning accuracy [2]. It should consider the effect of the signal system when select the signal sources in heterogeneous positioning system. Meanwhile, there might be great amount of signal sources which may be up to dozens even hundreds. If there are some bad quality signals in positioning, the measurement error may be very large which lead to a low accuracy positioning [3]. On the other hand, huge amount of the signal sources leads to a huge computation which is a great burden of the hardware [4]. So it is necessary to assess the quality of the signals, and then select the best signal source set for a best positioning accuracy.

GDOP (Geometric Dilution of Precision) is often used for signal source selection of TOA (Time of Arrival) positioning system [5]. But it only considered the geometric relations between the signal sources and the receiver. It doesn't reflect the effect of the signal system and the environment factors which will greatly affect the positioning accuracy [6]. For this reason, we proposed a new signal selection method for heterogeneous sources. It considered the signal system, the positioning algorithm, the receiver parameter, the environment factors and the geometric relation between the signal sources and receiver to assess the quality of each signal sources. And then select the best signal sources set for positioning.

2. The factors that affect the positioning accuracy

The positioning error $\boldsymbol{\varepsilon}_x$ of TOA positioning system is:

$$\boldsymbol{\varepsilon}_{\mathbf{x}} = (\mathbf{G}^{\mathrm{T}}\mathbf{G})^{-1}\mathbf{G}^{\mathrm{T}}\boldsymbol{\varepsilon}_{\rho} \tag{1}$$

Where $\boldsymbol{\varepsilon}_{\rho}$ the pseudorange measurement error of each signal source, G is is the geometric matrix, and:

$$\begin{cases} \mathbf{G} = \begin{bmatrix} -\mathbf{l}_{x,1} & -\mathbf{l}_{y,1} & -\mathbf{l}_{z,1} & 1 \\ -\mathbf{l}_{x,2} & -\mathbf{l}_{y,2} & -\mathbf{l}_{z,2} & 1 \\ \cdots & \cdots & \cdots & \cdots \\ -\mathbf{l}_{x,N} & -\mathbf{l}_{y,N} & -\mathbf{l}_{z,N} & 1 \end{bmatrix} \\ \mathbf{l}_{X,i} = \dfrac{x_i - \hat{x}_u}{\hat{r}_i} \end{cases} \tag{2}$$

Where $\mathbf{l}_{X,i}$ is the measurement vector of each observation direction The positioning error is related to the geometric matrix and the pseudo range measurement errors as Equation (1) shows. Assuming that the pseudorange measurement errors of each source have the same statistic features for easy. If the pseudorange measurement errors accord with normal distribution which mean is 0 and variance is σ_{ρ}^2, and each of them is incoherent. We have:

$$\mathrm{Cov}(\boldsymbol{\varepsilon}_{\mathbf{x}}) = (\mathbf{G}^{\mathrm{T}}\mathbf{G})^{-1}\sigma_{\rho}^2 \tag{3}$$

Where Cov(•) is the covariance of a matrix enote that:

$$\mathbf{H}=(\mathbf{G}^{\mathrm{T}}\mathbf{G})^{-1} \qquad (4)$$

According to Equation (3) and (4), we can see that the positioning accuray is only related to the matrix **H** and the variance of the pseudo rang error σ_{ρ}^{2}. Because **H** is related to the relative position of the signal sources and the receiver, we can define the following equation:

$$\sigma_{p}^{2}=\mathbf{H}\sigma_{m}^{2} \qquad (5)$$

Where σ_{p}^{2} the variance of the positioning error is, σ_{m}^{2} is the measurement error of each signal. The positioning error is:

$$\varepsilon_{p}=\sqrt{\mathrm{trace}(\mathbf{H})}\varepsilon_{m}=GDOP\cdot\varepsilon_{m} \qquad (6)$$

Where ε_{p} is the positioning error, ε_{m} is the measurement error, *GDOP* is called the Geometric Dilution of Precision.

Equation (6) can also be used in non-TDOA positioning systems. For example, the matrix **H** is related to the number of APs and their position in the fingerprint positioning system [7]. So we summarized that the positioning error is related to the matrix **H** which is due to the position of the signal sources and the measurement errors $\boldsymbol{\varepsilon}_{m}$.

3. Signal selection method for heterogeneous sources

We assumed each measurement error is the same according to the analysis above. But when there are more than one positioning systems or the signal condition of each signal sources is different, the hypothesis will not be true. So only GDOP itself can't assess the positioning accuracy perfectly.

When each measurement error is not the same, the Equation (3) becomes:

$$\begin{aligned}\mathrm{Cov}(\boldsymbol{\varepsilon}_{x})&=\mathrm{E}[\boldsymbol{\varepsilon}_{x}\boldsymbol{\varepsilon}_{x}^{\mathrm{T}}]\\&=(\mathbf{G}^{\mathrm{T}}\mathbf{G})^{-1}\mathbf{G}^{\mathrm{T}}E[\boldsymbol{\varepsilon}_{m}\boldsymbol{\varepsilon}_{m}^{\mathrm{T}}]\mathbf{G}(\mathbf{G}^{\mathrm{T}}\mathbf{G})^{-1}\end{aligned} \qquad (7)$$

$\boldsymbol{\varepsilon}_{m}$ Includes all the factors that affect the measurement errors, such as the CN0 (Carrier to noise ratio), multipath, interference of the people streams, etc. It is the features of the building's environment, the interference of the people streams, etc., that can equivalent to the CN0 of the signal. Namely they affect the CN0s first, and then CN0s affect the positioning accuracy. And they are time-variant. While the signal features, measurement circus parameters, etc. are related to the signal itself and the design of the receiver. And they usually are non-time-variant.

In the real circumstances, the factors that affect the time-variant and non-time-variant errors are usually correlative. For example, the variance of the code loop noise in GPS (Global Positioning System) is:

$$\sigma_{tDLL}\approx\begin{cases}\sqrt{\dfrac{B_n}{2C/N_0}D\left[1+\dfrac{2}{TC/N_0(2-D)}\right]}, & D\geq\dfrac{\pi}{B_{fe}T_c}\\ \sqrt{\dfrac{B_n}{2C/N_0}\left[\dfrac{1}{B_{fe}T_c}+\dfrac{B_{fe}T_c}{\pi-1}\left(D-\dfrac{1}{B_{fe}T_c}\right)^2\right]\cdot\left[1+\dfrac{2}{TC/N_0(2-D)}\right]}, & \dfrac{1}{B_{fe}T_c}\leq D<\dfrac{\pi}{B_{fe}T_c}\\ \sqrt{\dfrac{B_n}{2C/N_0}\dfrac{1}{B_{fe}T_c}\left[1+\dfrac{2}{TC/N_0(2-D)}\right]}, & D\leq\dfrac{1}{B_{fe}T_c}\end{cases} \qquad (8)$$

where T is the redetection integration time, T_c is the code length, B_{fe} is the front-to-end bandwidth, B_n is the loop bandwidth, and D is the earl-to-late correlator spacing. They are all related to the signal system or the receiver's parameters. So they are non-time-variant. While the CN0 is related to the environment which is time-variant. So we must decouple them firstly:

$$\sigma(a_1a_2\cdots a_k)\approx\sigma_1(a_1)\sigma_2(a_2)\cdots\sigma_k(a_k) \qquad (9)$$

For Equation (8), it becomes:

$$\tilde{\iota}\_\_\_ \qquad \dot{}(C/N_0) \qquad (10)$$

Where

$$\alpha=\begin{cases}\sqrt{\dfrac{B_n}{2}D}, & D\geq\dfrac{\pi}{B_{fe}T_c}\\ \sqrt{\dfrac{B_n}{2}\left[\dfrac{1}{B_{fe}T_c}+\dfrac{B_{fe}T_c}{\pi-1}\left(D-\dfrac{1}{B_{fe}T_c}\right)^2\right]}, & \dfrac{1}{B_{fe}T_c}\leq D<\dfrac{\pi}{B_{fe}T_c}\\ \sqrt{\dfrac{B_n}{2B_{fe}T_c}}, & D\leq\dfrac{1}{B_{fe}T_c}\end{cases} \qquad (11)$$

$$f(C/N_0)=\frac{\sqrt{C/N_0+\eta}}{C/N_0} \qquad (12)$$

Where

$$\eta=\frac{2}{T(2-D)} \qquad (13)$$

The $1_{\sigma tDLL}$ results when B_{fe}=2.046MHz, T_c=1.023MHz, B_n=2Hz, D=1chip and T=1ms or 10ms respectively using Equation (8) and (10) are as Figure (1) and (2) shows. And we can see that the curves before and after decoupled are very similar.

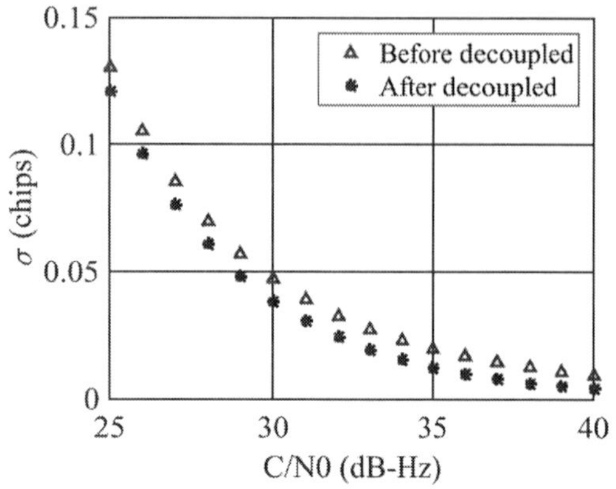

Figure 1. Comparison between the before and after decoupled $1\sigma_{tDLL}$ curves of GPS signal (T=1ms).

$$E\left[\boldsymbol{\varepsilon}_m\boldsymbol{\varepsilon}_m^{\mathrm{T}}\right]\approx\begin{pmatrix}\left[\sigma_{1,1}(a_1)\sigma_{2,1}(a_2)\cdots\sigma_{k,3}(a_k)\right]^2 & 0 & \cdots & 0\\ 0 & \left[\sigma_{1,2}(a_1)\sigma_{2,2}(a_2)\cdots\sigma_{k,2}(a_k)\right]^2 & \cdots & 0\\ \vdots & \vdots & \ddots & \vdots\\ 0 & 0 & \cdots & \left[\ldots(a_1)\sigma_{2,N}(a_2)\cdots\sigma_{k,N}(a_k)\right]^2\end{pmatrix} \tag{14}$$
$$=\boldsymbol{\sigma}_1^2\boldsymbol{\sigma}_2^2\cdots\boldsymbol{\sigma}_k^2$$

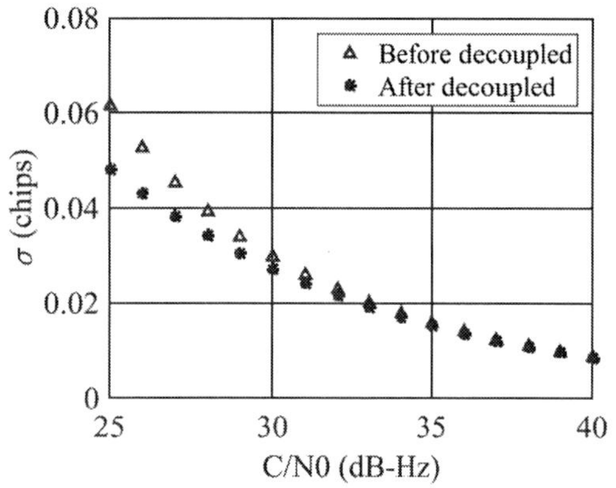

Figure 2. Comparison between the Before and after Decoupled $1\sigma_{tdll}$ Curves of gps Signal (t=10ms).

We assume that the measurement errors of each signal from each source are incoherent. We can get Equation (14). Where

$$\boldsymbol{\sigma}_k=\begin{pmatrix}\sigma_{k,1}(a_k) & 0 & \cdots & \\ 0 & \sigma_{k,2}(a_k) & \cdots & \\ \vdots & \vdots & \ddots & \vdots\\ 0 & 0 & \cdots & \ldots a_k)\end{pmatrix} \tag{15}$$

If $\boldsymbol{\sigma}_{1\sim i}$ is non-time-variant noise and $\boldsymbol{\sigma}_{i\sim k}$ is time-variant noise, then define:

$$E\left[\boldsymbol{\varepsilon}_m\boldsymbol{\varepsilon}_m^{\mathrm{T}}\right]\approx\boldsymbol{\sigma}_1^2\boldsymbol{\sigma}_2^2\cdots\boldsymbol{\sigma}_k^2=\boldsymbol{\alpha}^2\boldsymbol{\gamma}^2 \tag{16}$$

Where $\boldsymbol{\gamma}$ is related to the CN0 and the external factors. It is time-variant affected by the environment around. While $\boldsymbol{\alpha}$ is only related to the signal characteristics and the receiver parameters which are usually fixed or known in the receiver. So we can easily get $\boldsymbol{\alpha}$ via the signal systems because the same signal system usually has the same parameters in a receiver.

Then we can define the Measurement Error Coefficient Rate (MECR) as

$$\chi_{\mathrm{sig}k}=\frac{\alpha_{\mathrm{sig}k}}{\alpha_{\mathrm{sigRef}}} \tag{17}$$

Where the subscript sig$k$ represents the kth signal system, sigRef represents the reference signal system. MECR is only related to the signal characteristics and the receiver parameters. It can clearly reflect the inherent measurement errors of different signal systems with the same CN0. It depends on the signal characteristics itself, such as the signal system type, signal frequency, etc. Another, it also depends on the receiver's performance, such as the front-to-end bandwidth, the noise bandwidth, etc. MECR is usually fixed after the design of the receiver. On the other hand, the MECR also normalized the $\boldsymbol{\alpha}$. using the MECR, Equation (16) becomes:

$$E\left[\boldsymbol{\varepsilon}_m\boldsymbol{\varepsilon}_m^{\mathrm{T}}\right]\approx\boldsymbol{\chi}^2\boldsymbol{\gamma}^2\alpha_{\mathrm{sigRef}} \tag{18}$$

Put Equation (18) to Equation (7) we can get:

$$\begin{aligned}\mathrm{Cov}(\boldsymbol{\varepsilon}_x)&=(\mathbf{G}^{\mathrm{T}}\mathbf{G})^{-1}\mathbf{G}^{\mathrm{T}}\boldsymbol{\chi}^2\boldsymbol{\gamma}^2\mathbf{G}(\mathbf{G}^{\mathrm{T}}\mathbf{G})^{-1}\alpha_{\mathrm{sigRef}}\\&=\left(\mathbf{G}^{\mathrm{T}}\boldsymbol{\chi}^{-2}\boldsymbol{\gamma}^{-2}\mathbf{G}\right)^{-1}\alpha_{\mathrm{sigRef}}\end{aligned} \tag{19}$$

 DOI: 10.1051/itmconf/20160702005

Similar to GDOP, we can define Multivariate Dilution of Precision (MDOP) as:

$$MDOP = \sqrt{\text{trace}\left(\mathbf{G}^{\mathrm{T}}\chi^{-2}\gamma^{-2}\mathbf{G}\right)^{-1}} \quad (20)$$

MDOP reflects the range of the positioning error. The smallest MDOP means the best accuracy. And the largest MDOP means the worst one. So we can use MDOP to assess the quality of the signal source. And then select the best source set.

4. Simulation analysis

There were 2 kinds of positioning signal sources in simulation. And each of them had 10 notes. Their distribution is as Figure (3) shows. We assumed that the MECR=1:0.6, σ of the time-variant was inversely proportional to CN0. The CN0s of each note were 35dBHz except the one of A2# (the second not of the Source A) was 25dBHz. The standard deviation of measurement error of source A was 5m at 35dBHz.

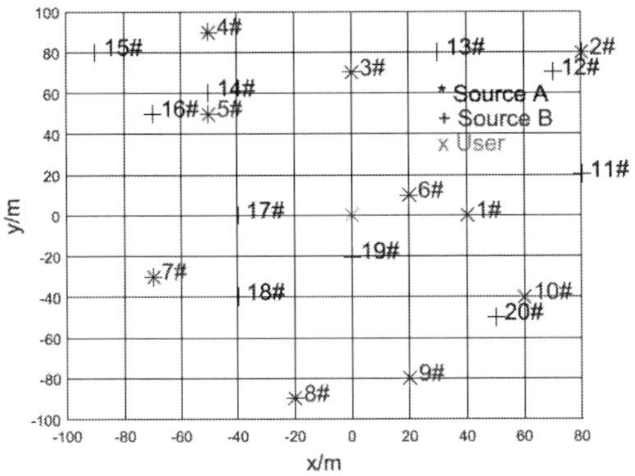

Figure 3. Distribution of All Signal Sources.

We selected 4 sources from 20 sources. And calculated CEP50s by 1000 times solution. Then acquired $C_{20}^{4} = 4845$ GDOPs, MDOPs and CEP50s. Figure (4) shows the relationships between MDOP and CEP50 while Figure (5) shows the relationships between GDOP and CEP50. The MDOPs were multiplied by 100 for clearly comparison. We can see from the figures that the CEP50 increases with the increasing of MDOP, while not that trend between CEP50 and GDOP. This means the GDOP don't acquire the best source set while the MDOP can.

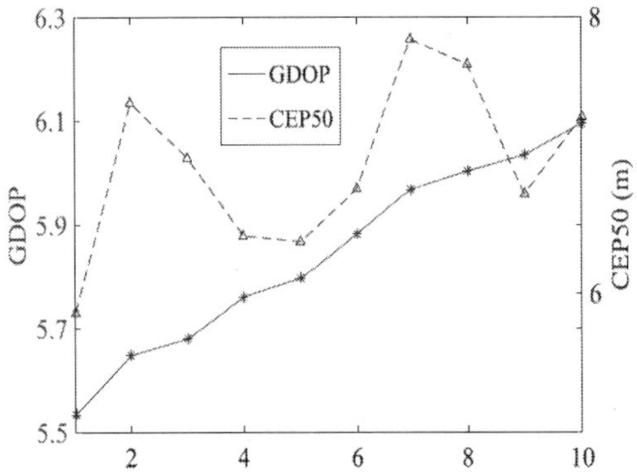

Figure 4. Relationship between CEP50 and GDOP.

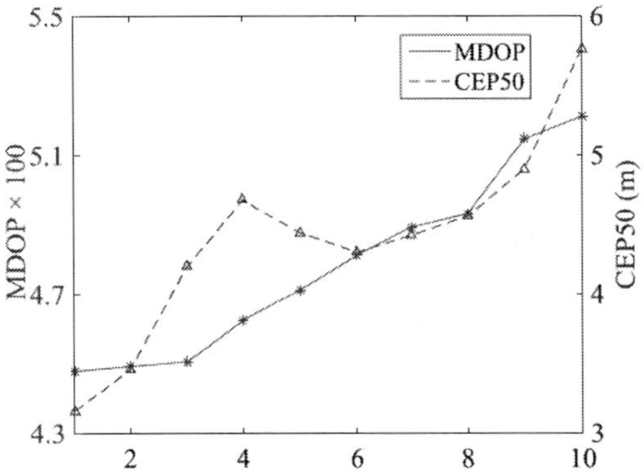

Figure 5. Relationship between CEP50 and MDOP.

Table 1 shows the source sets of the 5 smallest GDOP and MDOP. A2# is appeared in the GDOP column because of its good position. But it is not appeared in the MDOP column because of its bad CN0. So the MDOP eliminates the effect of the bad signal sources.

Table 1. The Source Sets of the 5 Smallest Gdops and Mdops

No.	Source sets of the 5 smallest GDOP	Source sets of the 5 smallest MDOP
1	A2, A6, A8, B5	A1, A5, A9, B2
2	A2, A6, A9, B5	A1, B5, B9, B10
3	A2, A4, A6, A8	A1, A4, A9, B2
4	A2, A6, A8, B6	A1, A4, A8, B1
5	A2, A8, B5, B9	A1, A7, A9, B2

5. Conclusion

With the development of the indoor/outdoor seamless positioning technology, there are more and more different positioning systems appeared. We can't have high positioning accuracy with any one single system. We must use multi positioning system for good accuracy. So the multi-source heterogeneous positioning system becomes more important. But in this kind of positioning, quality of the signal sources takes great effect to the positioning accuracy, how to assess the source quality and then select the best source set becomes very

DOI: 10.1051/itmconf/20160702005

important. In this paper, we proposed a signal selection method for heterogeneous positioning sources. It combines the factors which affect the positioning accuracy to a function. Then assess the quality of the signal sources and select the best source set. The simulation results showed the efficiency of the algorithm.

Acknowledge

This paper is supported by "the Fundamental Research Funds for the Central Universities".

References

1. M. Glocker, H. Landau, R Leandro, et.al. 6th ESA Workshop on Satellite Navigation Technologies and European Workshop on GNSS Signals and Signal. 1-8 (2012)
2. H. K. Su, Z. X. Liao, C. H. Lin, et.al. A hybrid indoor-position mechanism based on bluetooth and WiFi communications for smart mobile devices. International Symposium on Bioelectronics and Bioinformatics. 188-191 (2015)
3. B. Bernhard, S. Felix and B. Jan. GPS-equipped wireless sensor network node for high-accuracy positioning applications. 9th European Conference on Wireless Sensor Networks. 179-195 (2012)
4. J. Roth, M. Tummala, and J. McEachen. A computationally efficient approach for hidden-Markov model-augmented fingerprint-based positioning. INTERNATIONAL JOURNAL OF SYSTEMS SCIENCE. 47, 12, 2847-2858 (2016)
5. Y.L. Teng, J.L. Wang, Q. Huang. Mathematical minimum of Geometric Dilution of Precision (GDOP) for dual-GNSS constellations. ADVANCES IN SPACE RESEARCH. 57, 1, 183-188 (2016)
6. J. Liu. Research on Satellite Selection Algorithm in Complex Environment. Radio Engineering of China. 41, 7, 39-41 (2011)
7. J. G. Hwang, K. E. Lee, and J. G. Park. An AP Selection Criteria for Enhanced Indoor Positioning using IEEE 802.11 RSSI Measurements and AP Configuration Information. J Electr Eng Technol. 11, 2, 537-542 (2016)

DOI: 10.1051/itmconf/20160702006

Comparison research on iot oriented image classification algorithms

Ke Du[1] and Kai-Yu Cai[2]

[1]*College of Computer, National University of Defense Technology, 410073ChangSha,Hunan,P.R.China*
[2]*College of Computer, National University of Defense Technology, 410073ChangSha,Hunan,P.R.China*

Abstract. Image classificationbelongs to the machine learning and computer visionfields,it aims to recognize and classify objects in the image contents. How to applyimage classification algorithms to large-scale data in the IoT framework is the focus of current research. Based on Anaconda, this article implementsk-NN,SVM, Softmax and Neural Networkalgorithms by Python, performs data normalization, random search, HOG andcolour histogram feature extractionto enhance the algorithms, experiments on them in CIFAR-10 datasets, then conducts comparison from three aspects of training time, test timeand classification accuracy.The experimental results show that: the vectorizedimplementation of the algorithms ismore efficient than the loopimplementation;Thetraining time of k-NN is the shortest,SVM andSoftmaxspend more time, and the training time ofNeural Network is the longest;The test time of SVM, Softmax and Neural Network are much shorter than of k-NN;Neural Network gets the highest classification accuracy, SVM and Softmaxget lower and approximateaccuracies, andk-NN gets the lowest accuracy. The effects of three algorithmimprovement methods are obvious.

1 Introduction

With the fast development ofIoT and mobile Internet,the volumes of image data from different fields such as social networks and sensor networks are growing exponentially. How to process the large-scale image data and recognize objects from the image contents has became an important issue.Image classification is the way to handle this problem. In general, image classification algorith msaredata-driven approaches. They usually get global descriptions of the imagesbymanualfeaturing or learning methods, use the learned classifiers to determine whether there is a certain object in the image or not.Image classification algorithms have been applied to many fields, such as face recognition, car number recognition, image searching and so on.

Anaconda is an open source scientific computation and analysis platformreleased by Continuum Company.It installedmany scientific computation libraries, such as NumPy,SciPy andMatplotlib.It also provides an interactive toolIPython Notebook, whichcombines experiment and document writing.Based on Anaconda, researchers and developerscould usePython to implementand analysis different algorithms, and write document by markdown.

Image classification andobject detection are active research areasin the computer visionfield. AfterAlexNet[1]was proposed in 2012, those areas are developingrapidly.In ILSVRC 2015, ResNet[2]wonbyits 3.57% top5 error. In the same year, YOLO[3]provides a real-time object detection with a mAP of 63.4 and a FPS of 45.Based on Anaconda, this paperimplements k-NN,SVM, Softmax and Neural Networkalgorithms and data normalization, random search, HOG and colour histogram feature extractionalgorithmimprovement methods, and conducts comparison on them by the training time, test timeand classification accuracy.Results show that the performance of the different algorithms vary a lot,improvement methodsimprovethe classification accuracy.Algorithms should be deployed in the different parts of the IoTframework according to theirperformance.

2 Comparison on algorithms

2.1. k-NN algorithm

k-NN is short for k-Nearest Neighbour.Instead of finding the single closest image in the training set as Nearest Neighbor algorithm, k-NN finds the top k closest images, and makes them vote on the label of the test image. In particular, when $k = 1$, it recover to the Nearest Neighbor algorithm. Intuitively, higher values of k have a smoothing effect that makes the classifier more resistant to outliersit is improved.

k-NNtreats image as vector, using L2 distance, which has the geometric interpretation of computing the euclidean distance between two vectors, to compare the difference between two images. The distance formula takes the form:

 DOI: 10.1051/itmconf/20160702006

$$d_2(I_1, I_2) = \sqrt{\Sigma_p (I_1^p - I_2^p)^2} \quad (1)$$

The training process of k-NN is to store all training images in the memory, then the test process is to compare test image with stored images by L2 norm, finds the top k closest images,and makes them vote on the label of the test image.

2.2. SVM algorithm

Support Vector Machine algorithm uses score function:

$$f(x_i, W, b) = Wx_i + b(2)$$

tocomputetheclass scores of imagefor different classes, then uses loss function:

$$L_i = \Sigma_{j \neq y_i} \max(0, w_j^T x_i - w_{y_i}^T x_i + \Delta)(3)$$

Tocompute the loss value.SVM loss function is often called the hinge loss.Itmeasures how consistent the predictions on training data are with the ground truth labels. The loss value of entire dataset is composed of data loss and regularizationloss:

$$L = \frac{1}{N}\sum_i \sum_{j \neq y_i} [\max(0, f(x_i; W)_j - f(x_i; W)_{y_i} + \Delta)] + \lambda \sum_k \sum_l W_{kl}^2 \quad (4)$$

In the training process, SVMuses gradient descent method to find the optimal weights and biases, which make the loss value minimum,since making good predictions on the training set is equivalent to minimizing the loss.In the test process, algorithmusesthe optimal weights and biasesto classify test images.

2.3. Softmax algorithm

The score function ofSoftmax algorithm is the same with the SVM algorithm. However, it replaces the hinge loss with cross-entropy loss for its loss function:

$$L_i = -\log\left(\frac{e^{f_{y_i}}}{\Sigma_j e^{f_j}}\right)(5)$$

The training and test processes of Softmax are similar with SVM. However, the core idea of Softmax is different.Unlike SVM, it is never fully happy with the scores it produces: the correct class could always have a higher probability and the incorrect classes always a lower probability and the loss would always get better.

2.4. Neural network algorithm

Neural Network models are often organized into distinct layers of neurons. For regular neural networks, the most common layer type is the fully-connected layer in which neurons between two adjacent layers are fully pairwise connected, but neurons within a single layer share no connections. With an appropriate loss function on the neuron's output, it can turn a single neuron into a linear classifier.

The training process consists of two parts: the forward pass and back propagation. In forward pass, itperforms matrix multiplication and activation function to obtain image classification scoreby the current weights and biases.Take the two-layer neuralnetworkmodel in our experimentfor example, the forward pass formula is:

$$s = W_2 max(0, W_1 x)(6)$$

andare the matrix combined weightand biases , is the class score.

The backpropagationis a process of computing gradients of expressions through recursive application of chain rule in networks.Algorithm then uses gradient signalto perform parameters update, till the value of loss function get small enough. In the test process, algorithm obtainsclass score by forward pass. It have been proved that Neural Network algorithm can approximate any continuousfunction[4].

3 Algorithm improvement methods

3.1. Mean subtraction and normalization

Mean subtraction and normalization are both data preprocessing methods.Mean subtraction involves subtracting the mean across every individual feature in the data: .It has the geometric interpretation of centering the cloud of data around the origin along every dimension.

Data normalization refers to normalize the data dimensions: , so that they are of approximately the same scale.isthe average for all data samples, the is the standard deviation of all the sample data.

Since in image processing, the relative scales of pixels are already approximately equal (in range from 0 to 255), so it is not strictly necessary to perform this normalization step.

3.2 Random search

Random search is a hyperparameter optimizationmethod. Since hyperparameter tuning canbegenerally described as :

$$\lambda^{(*)} = \underset{\lambda \in \Lambda}{\mathrm{argmin}}\ \mathbb{E}_{x \sim \mathcal{G}_x}\left[\mathcal{L}\left(x; \mathcal{A}_\lambda(\mathcal{X}^{(\mathrm{train})})\right)\right](7)$$

represents hyperparameters, is a learning algorithm base on hyperparameter , is the loss function,samples are from a natural (grand truth) distribution , is the training set, a finite set of samples from.What we really need in practice is a way to choose so as to minimize generalization error. It has been proved that randomly chosen trials are more efficient for hyper-parameter optimization than trials on gridsearch[5].

3.3 HOG and colour histogram

HOG is short for Histogram of Oriented Gradients, this feature extraction method was proposed in 2005 by Dalai for pedestriandetection[6]. In our experiments, for each

DOI: 10.1051/itmconf/20160702006

image we will compute HOG as well as a colour histogram using the hue channel in HSV colour space. We form our final feature vector for each image by concatenating the HOG and colour histogram feature vectors.

HOG captures the texture of the image while ignoring colour information, and the colour histogram captures the colour of the input image while ignoring texture. As a result, we expect that using both together ought to work better than using either alone.

4 Experiments

4.1. Environments, datasets and measurements

The hardware environments are as follow: the CPU is Intel Core i5 2.8GHz, the capacity of memory is 8GB, and the capacity of disk is 500GB.The software environments are as follow: the operating system is OSX EI Capitan,we use Python2.7.11 and installed Anaconda 2.5.0 for Python 2.7 version.Additionally, since Anaconda installedmany thirdparty libraries by default, we list some main libraries and their versions:numpy1.10.4,scipy0.17.0, matplotlib 1.5.1,pandas 0.17.1, ipython 4.0.3, ipythonnotebook4.0.4.

We choose CIFAR-10 as our experimental dataset.CIFAR-10 is a subset of Tiny Images database, which contains 10categories.It contains 60000 images, 50000 for training, 10000 for test. Its image size is 32 x32 pixels.Although the image size is small, the amount of images for each category is large, so it is very suitable for training complex models such as deep learning model.Moreover, small image size means the request for computationalcapacity is not too high, which ease the pressure on our machine.

In experiments, algorithms are compared by three evaluation standards: classification accuracy， training time and test time.

The classification accuracy is defined as:

$$accuracy = N_{y_i=y_j}/M_{y_{test}} \quad (8)$$

Itevaluatesthe classification performance of the algorithms.Theis the amount of category labels corresponding to test set. Afteralgorithms finished classifying the test images, the number of prediction label which are consistent with real category is .

Use training time and test timeto measure the computational efficiency of the algorithms. isused to measure how long it takes algorithm to learn optimal parameters in the training process.isusedto measure how long it takes algorithm to classify the test image data in the test process.

4.2 Results

Since all algorithms need hyperparameter optimization, we divide CIFAR-10 dataset into three splits: the training set, validation set and test set. The training set contains 49000 images, the validation set and test set both contain 1000 images. k-NN algorithm divides training set into 5 subsets equally, uses cross validation to performhyperparameter optimization.Other algorithms perform hyperparameter optimizationon the validation set, and theirinitial hyper parameter tuning policy is grid search. Theiteration numbers of SVM, Softmaxand Neural Network algorithmsare set to 1500.Otherhyperparameters of algorithms are obtained in the tuning process.

4.2.1 Comparison on two kinds of implementations

Numpy library provides APIs that include efficient matrix computational operations and broadcasting mechanism, it can make algorithms implemented invectorizedcomputation.Comparedwith implementationbymultiple loops, vectorizedimplementationimproved the computation efficiency. The L2 distance computations in k-NN algorithm, and the loss functionsin SVM, Softmax and Neural Network algorithms can all be implemented in loops and vectorizedcomputations.Inexperiment, we use training timeand test time tocompareoperation efficiency of the twokinds ofimplementation.We count the time in seconds. Details are in the following table:

Table 1. T_{train} and T_{test} in Two Kinds of Implementation.

	Loops	Vectorize	Loops	Vectoriz e
k-NN	0.000066	0.000066	4288.6	9.1
SVM	65.5	6.6	0.47	0.044
Softmax	67.1	4.7	0.63	0.059
NN	687.3	66.3	0.60	0.065

Since the training process of k-NN algorithmsimply stores the training data into memory with no matrix computationaloperation,it is not strange that k-NN takes so little time to finish it training process.However,mostcomputational operationsofk-NN algorithm are in its test process.Unlike k-NN, Most computational operationsofthe SVM, Softmax and Neural Network algorithmsare in their training process for loss values and gradientscalculation, and in their test process, the computational cost is low.

According to the table, the loop implementation form of k-NN algorithm costs nearly 420 times than the vectorizedimplementation in . Moreover,the loop implementation forms ofthe SVM, Softmax and Neural Network algorithms cost about 10 times than the loop implementation forms in .

Therefore, it is obvious that theNumpyAPIcan greatly improve the efficiency of algorithm.Inthe follow experiments, the algorithms are implemented in vectorizedforms by default.

 DOI: 10.1051/itmconf/20160702006

4.2.2 Comparison on algorithms

The computational efficiency and classification accuracy of the four algorithms are compared in the following table:

Table 2. Algorithms Comparison.

k-NN	0.000066	9.1	32.7%
SVM	5.4	0.0044	31.8%
Softmax	4.8	0.0059	31.8%
NN	59.6	0.065	35.5%

The of k-NN algorithm is much short than its .On the contrary, the of SVM, Softmax and Neural Network algorithmsare much short than their . Note that the ofNeural Network algorithm is about 10 times than of SVM and Softmax algorithms.

For now, the classification accuraciesoffour algorithms are on the same level, and the performance of Neural Network algorithm is slightly better. However, there was no significant difference amongthem.The reasonisthat the SVM, Softmax and Neural Network algorithmsdid not perform data preprocessing, feature extraction and hyperparameter tuning, so the potential capacities of these algorithms have not been further explored.

4.2.3 Data preprocessing method

In the experiment, input image data normalization wasperformed.Theaccuracy improvementsoffouralgorithms are in the following table:

Table 3. Effect of Data Normalization.

k-NN	0.000066	9.1	32.7%
SVM	6.5	0.0045	33.6%
Softmax	4.7	0.0058	34.5%
NN	66.3	0.065	52.3%

From the table above, After performing datanormalization, the performance of k-NN algorithm does not improve. This is because k-NN is essentially comparing the differenceforpixel. On the contrary, the classification accuracies of SVM, Softmax and Neural Network algorithmsareimproved.The accuracy of SVM improved by 1.8%, the accuracy ofSoftmax improved by 2.7%, and the accuracyofNeural Network algorithm improved by16.8%, which is much higher than the otheralgorithms.Therefore, the presentation capacity of deep learningmodelsuch as Neural Network algorithm has been proved.

4.2.4 Hyperparameter optimization method

The 32.7% classification accuracy of k-NN algorithm is obtained by cross validation optimization method, so in this experiment, we list k-NN just for comparison convenience, it dose not use random search method, though cross validation, the hyperparameter k of k-NN algorithm is set to be 5. But the SVM, Softmax and Neural Network algorithms all take random search to get better hyperparameters.

Table 4. Accuracy ofSearch Methods.

	Gird Search	Random Search
k-NN	32.7%	32.7%
SVM	33.6%	33.2%
Softmax	34.5%	35.3%
NN	52.3%	53.3%

Through random search, the accuracy of Softmaximproved by 0.8%, and the accuracy of Neural Network algorithm improved by1%.It shows that the random searchdid find better parameters in the parameter space.However, the classification accuracy of SVM algorithmdescends by 0.4%. It can be explain that in the grid search, theparameters are already close to the optimal parameters.

Corresponding to the accuracies, the hyperparameters of the algorithms are as follow: the learning rate of SVM is 5.0e-05, regularization strength is 9.0e+04, itsiterations are 1500. The learning rate of Softmax is 4.866548e-07, regularization strength is 2.393255e+04, its iterations are 1500. The learning rate of Neural Network is 8.944667e-04, regularization strength is 9.493759e-01, its iterations are 1500, the number of layers are 2, and the number of neurons in the hidden layer are 360.

In general, the random search method is simple to implementand more efficient than grid search in hyperparameter optimization process.

4.2.5 Feature extraction method

We form our final feature vector for each image by concatenating the HOG and colour histogram feature vectors. Since k-NN algorithm simply compares the raw pixels, we did not perform the feature extraction process on it.ForSVM, Softmax and Neural Network algorithms, take the feature vectorsas the input data.The results showsaccuracy improvements in the following table:

Table 5. Effect of Feature Extraction.

	Raw pixel	Features
SVM	33.2%	42.4%
Softmax	35.3%	41.8%
NN	53.3%	59.4%

Using feature vector as input data, the classification accuracy of SVM, Softmaxand Neural Networkare all improved. The accuracy of SVM improvedby 9.2%, the accuracy ofSoftmaximprovedby 6.5%, the accuracy of Neural Network algorithm improved by 6.1%. The capacity of our combined feature extraction method has been proved.

4.3. Conclusion

Based on Anaconda, this paper implemented k-NN, SVM, Softmax and Neural Network four classical algorithms by Python, thencompared and analysed theperformance of thealgorithms from two respects: the image classification accuracy and the computational resource cost.According to the experimental results we can get the following conclusion:

• Thevectorizedimplementations of algorithms are much more efficient than the loop implementations.

• Based on vectorizedimplementation, the training time length of k-NN algorithm is the shorter than that of any other algorithms. The training time length of Neural Network algorithm is the longest. The training time lengths of SVM and Softmax are approximately the same. However, the test time lengths of SVM, Softmax and Neural Network algorithms are much shorter than that of k-NN algorithm, which means the algorithms are suitable for the practical applications in the IoT framework except k-NN algorithm.

• Theclassification accuracy of Neural Network algorithm is the highest of all, which means it should be deployed to handle the most complex classification task. The classification accuracies of SVM and Softmax are lower and approximately the same, which means they should be deployed to handle some simple but real-time required classification tasks. And the classification accuracy of k-NN algorithm is the lowest.

• Thedata normalization, random search and feature extraction are all improvement tricks of the algorithm. After applying these tricks, the classification accuracy of algorithms have been improved by different levels. The random search gives a little improvement,the effect of data normalization is better, and the effect of HOG and colour histogram feature extraction is the best of all three tricks. All the tricks should be applied to algorithms in practical application.

• k-NN algorithm is not suitable for any practical applications in the IoT framework, since its low classification accuracy and high computational cost. The performances of SVM and Softmax algorithms are approximately the same, both on their classification accuracy and computational cost. They can be deployed to some real-time required tasks to handle some specific objects classification. The classification accuracy of Neural Network algorithm is the highest of all the four algorithms, which means it can handle some complex classification tasks. However, the computational cost of the Neural Network algorithm is huge, therefore, it should be deployed to the server and provide classification API to the remote devices.

In the future, we will implement the algorithms by using the TensorFlow framework, which is provided by Google, and deploy algorithms to different parts of the IoT system, measure the performance of the whole system and the algorithms respectively.

References

1. Krizhevsky A, Sutskever I, Hinton G E. Imagenet classification with deep convolutional neural networks[C]//Advances in neural information processing systems. 2012: 1097-1105.
2. He K, Zhang X, Ren S, et al. Deep residual learning for image recognition[J]. arXiv preprint arXiv:1512.03385, 2015.
3. Redmon J, Divvala S, Girshick R, et al. You only look once: Unified, real-time object detection[J]. arXiv preprint arXiv:1506.02640, 2015.
4. Cybenko G. Approximation by superpositions of a sigmoidal function[J]. Mathematics of control, signals and systems, 1989, 2(4): 303-314.
5. Bergstra J, Bengio Y. Random search for hyper-parameter optimization[J]. Journal of Machine Learning Research, 2012, 13(Feb): 281-305.
6. Dalal N, Triggs B. Histograms of oriented gradients for human detection[C]//2005 IEEE Computer Society Conference on Computer Vision and Pattern Recognition (CVPR'05). IEEE, 2005, 1: 886-893.

DOI: 10.1051/itmconf/20160702007

A Hyper spectral Images Classification Method Based on Maximum Scatter Discriminant Analysis

Huo-Yuan LI [1] and Yong-Feng QI [2]

[1] *College of Physics and Electronic Engineering, Northwest Normal University,Lanzhou,730070,China*
[2] *College of Computer Science & Engineering, Northwest Normal University,Lanzhou,730070,China*

Abstract. To overcome "small sample size problem" problem faced by some hyper spectral classification methods, the Maximum Scatter Discriminant criterion is used to analyzed hyperspectral data. Maximum Scatter Discriminant analysis searches for the project axes by maximizing the difference of between-class scatter and within-class scatter matrices, which avoid to calculate the inverse of matrices. Experiment results on Indian Pines HSI data set show that the proposed method outperforms the other methods in terms of recognition accuracy. The proposed method is an effective and feasible method for hyper pectral data classification.

1 Introduction

With the constant development of imaging spectroscopy, Hyper spectral Images (HSI) collected by imaging spectrometers provides detailed spectral information about objects in hundreds of spectral bands in the electromagnetic, which increases the possibility of more accurately discriminating materials of interest[1]. However, the information content in a hyper spectral image is highly correlated with neighboring bands and suffers from the curse of dimensionality[2]. Dimensionality reduction is a common pre-processing step in the classification of hyper spectral images for various applications such as land cover mapping, and any spectral feature in the sample space can be represented in a lower-dimensional subspace without losing a significant amount of information. Principal Component Analysis (PCA)[3] and Linear Discriminant Analysis (LDA)[4] is two popular technique for finding such a lower dimensional subspace. PCA performs dimensionality reduction by projecting the original data onto a low dimensional linear subspace which is spanned by the leading eigenvectors of the covariance matrix of all the sample points. PCA projections are optimal for reconstruction from a low dimensional basis, but they may not be optimal from a discrimination standpoint due to not taking the class information of the input data into account. LDA is a supervised learning algorithm, which preserves discriminant information by maximizing the ratio of between-class scatter and within-class scatter. However, LDA often suffers from the so-called "small sample size problem" since the number of samples is generally smaller than the dimension of the sample space in face recognition task. To overcome the"small sample size problem", Song et al. [5] proposed a method, which adopts the difference of both between-class scatter and within-class scatter as discriminant criterion, was named as Maximum Scatter Discriminant (MSD) analysis. The goal of MSD is to search for the project axes by maximizing the difference of between-class scatter and within-class scatter matrices rather than the ratio of between-class against within-class scatter matrices.

The rest of the paper is organized as follows: the maximum scatter difference criterion is introduced in Section 2. In Section 3, a series of experiments and results are described. Finally, conclusions are summarized in Section 4.publisher.

2 Maximum Scatter Difference (MSD) Criterion

Suppose there are c known pattern classes. P is the total number of training samples, and N_i is the number of training samples in class i. In class i, the jth training sample, which is an n-dimension vector, is denoted by x_i^j. The

 DOI: 10.1051/itmconf/20160702007

within-class scatter matrix S_w^x and between-class scatter matrix S_w^b can be denoted as:

$$S_w^x = \frac{1}{P}\sum_{i=1}^{c}\sum_{j=1}^{N_i}(x_i^j - m_i)(x_i^j - m_i)^T \quad (1)$$

$$S_b^x = \frac{1}{P}\sum_{i=1}^{c} N_i(m_i - m_0)(m_i - m_0)^T \quad (2)$$

Where m_i is the mean of ith class samples, and m_0 is the mean of all training samples.

Unlike classical LDA, which search for the project axes on which the ratio of the between-class and the within-class scatter matrices of the projected samples reaches its maximum, the goal of maximum scatter difference criterion is find the project axes on which the difference of the between-class and the within-class scatter matrices is maximized. The criterion can be written as following:

$$J(a) = \max_{w} \arg\ A^T(S_b^x - S_w^x)A \quad (3)$$

Obviously, the projection axes are the eigenvectors $a_1, a_2, \cdots$ corresponding to the first k largest eigenvalues λ1, λ2, . . . , λk of $(S_b^x - S_w^x)$,where $\lambda_1 \geq \lambda_2 \geq \cdots$.

In fact, in hyper spectral images recognition task, the dimension of hyper spectral data is very high, which will consume much memory and time. To overcome this problem, we first project the hyper spectral data set to a PCA subspace to reduce the dimension, while using PCA as preprocessing can reduce the noise. Thus, a detailed description of the proposed method is stated as follows:

1. PCA projection: the training samples are projected into a PCA subspace which retains a certain level energy by throwing away the smallest principle components. The transformation matrix of PCA is denoted by A_{PCA}.
2. Constructing the within-class scatter matrix S_w^x and between-class scatter matrix S_w^b.
3. MSD projection: The optimal projection matrix A^* is acquired by maximizing (3)
4. OUT transformation matrix: $A = A_{PCA}A^*$

3 Feature Extraction and Classification

Supposed projection matrix A has been obtained, projecting a given spectral vector x onto A, yielding an n-dimensional column vector c:

$$c = A^T x \quad (4)$$

We called this vector **c** as the feature vector of x. For hyper spectral data recognition, projecting each training vector $x_1, x_2, \cdots$ onto A, we obtain the corresponding feature vectors $c_1, c_2, \cdots$. Given a test vector x, first use Eq. (4) to get its feature vector c, then a nearest neighbor classifier is used for classification. Here the distance between c and c_i is defined by

$$d(c, c_i) = \|c - c_i\| = \sqrt{\sum_{j=1}^{n}(c(j) - c_i(j))^2} \quad (5)$$

Where $c(j)$ denotes the j-th element of vector c

4. Experiments

In this section, we conduct a set of experiments on Indian Pines HSI data set[6] to further evaluate the effectiveness of the proposed method and the proposed method is also compare with PCA and LDA. The Indian Pines HSI data set is a scene of the Northwest Indiana gathered by the AVIRIS sensor in 1992.It consists of 145×145 pixels and 220 spectral bands within the range of 375–2500 nm. Several spectral bands with noise and water absorption phenomena are removed from the data set, leaving a total of 200 radiance channels to be used in the experiments. This HSI is available at https://engineering.purdue.edu/~biehl/. Sixteen ground truth classes of interest are considered in the data set. The HSI in false color and its corresponding ground truth are shown in Figure 1(a) and (b) respectively.

(a)

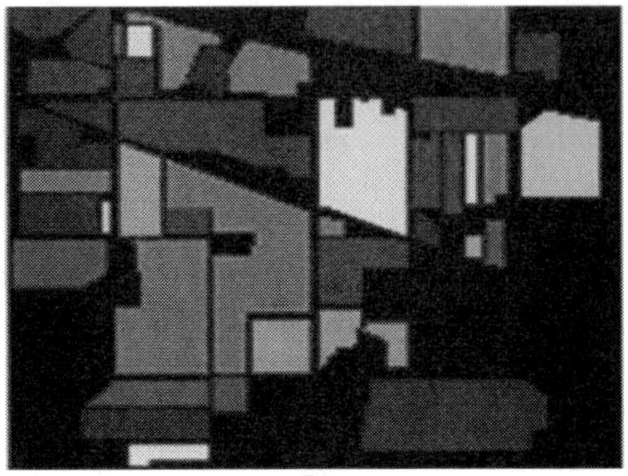

(b)

Figure 1. The Indian Pines Hsi Data Set. (a) the Hsi in False Color. (b) Corresponding Ground Truth.

10% pixels are randomly selected from each class to construct the training data set, the remaining images being used as the test images. Every algorithm is repeated 10 times, the recognition accuracies are plotted for the proposed method, PCA and LDA with varying dimension of feature vectors in Fig.2. It can be observed from Fig.2 that the proposed approach has better recognition rate and is more robust. Compared with LDA, the proposed method avoid to calculate the inverse of scatter matrices, which reduces the algorithm complexity

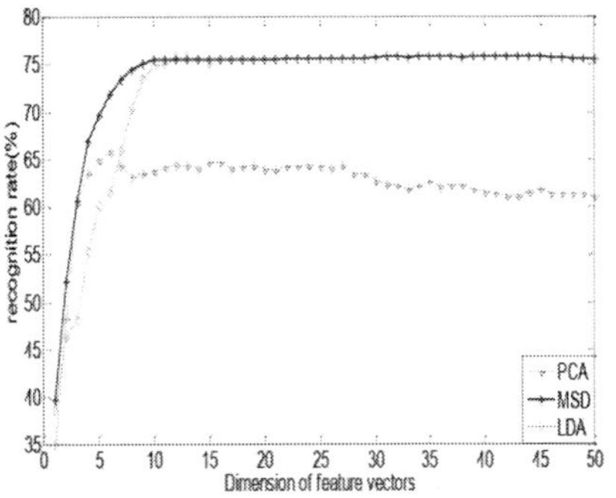

Figure 2. Performance Comparison of Recognition Rates Using LDA, MSD and PCA with Varying Dimension on Indian Pines HSI Data Set.

5. Conclusions

In this paper, an efficient hyper spectral images classification method which adopts maximum scatter discriminant analysis, the major advantage of the proposed is to overcome the "small sample size problem" faced by LDA. Experimental results on Indian Pines HSI data set reveal that the proposed method has better recognition accuracy and is more robust.

Acknowledgements

This article is partly supported by Program for Gansu Province Natural Science Fund (145RJZA183)

References

1. H. Huang, F.Luo, J. Liu and Y. Yang. Dimensionality reduction of hyperspectral images based on sparse discriminant manifold embedding. ISPRS Journal of Photogrammetry and Remote Sensing,2015,106:42-54
2. L.O. Jimenez, D.A. Landgrebe. Supervised classification in highdimensional space: geometrical, statistical, and asymptotical properties of multivariate data. IEEE Transactions on Systems Man & Cybernetics Part C,1998, 28(1):39–54.
3. N. D. Le Hanh, M. S Kim, and D. H.Kim. Comparison of Singular Value Decomposition and Principal Component Analysis applied to Hyper spectral Imaging of biofilm. IEEE Photonics Conference, 2012:6 - 7.
4. T. Bandos, L. Bruzzone and G. Camps-Valls. Classification of Hyper spectral Images With Regularized Linear Discriminant Analysis. IEEE Transactions on Geoscience & Remote Sensing, 2009, 47(3):862-873.
5. F. X. Song, K. Cheng, J.Y. Yang, et al., Maximum scatter difference, large margin linear projection and support vector machines, Acta Automat. Sin. 2004,30 (6):890-896. (in Chinese).
6. W. Sun, A. Halevy, J. J. Benedetto, et al. UL_isomap based nonlinear dimensionality reduction for hyperspectral imagery classification. Isprs Journal of Photogrammetry & Remote Sensing, 2014,89(2):25–36.

DOI: 10.1051/itmconf/20160702008

Ship Targets Discrimination Algorithm in SAR Images Based on Hu Moment Feature and Texture Feature

Lei LIU*, Yang ZHANG, Hai-Bo ZHANG, Qi FENG, Ting-Jun LI

Naval Aeronautical and Astronautical University, Yantai 264001, China
**e-mail: ythyliulei@sina.com*

Abstract—To discriminate the ship targets in SAR images, this paper proposed the method based on combination of Hu moment feature and texture feature. Firstly,7 Hu moment features should be extracted, while gray level co-occurrence matrix is then used to extract the features of mean, variance, uniformity, energy, entropy, inertia moment, correlation and differences. Finally the k-neighbour classifier was used to analysis the 15 dimensional feature vectors. The experimental results show that the method of this paper has a good effect.

1 Introduction

Marine environmental monitoring has become the common concern for all countries in the world [1].Ships are the main tools to develop Marine, so how to effectively get the ship information is becoming a hot spot of current research. Automatic target recognition (ATR) system can extract information of ship targets in SAR image, mainly includes three phases: detection, discrimination and classification [2]. The detection phase can remove the region that can't be the target area, while discrimination phase can remove natural clutter and artificial clutter false alarm, the classification phase is to classify ship target recognition. Target discrimination is the intermediate link of the ATR system and the basis of ship target classification [3].

Feature extraction is the foundation of SAR images of ship target identification [4,5]. In the late 1980s, Burl and Novak firstly put forward by using texture feature for SAR image target discrimination in Lincoln laboratory, in the next 30 years, scholars from all over the world had made many achievements in the discrimination of feature extraction [6]. Hu invariant moments features can reflect the global features of the image because of rotation, scaling and translation invariance, but it can't descript the details of the image effectively, and the recognition rate was be influenced. Gray level co-occurrence matrix describes the image gray level of the internal texture structure through the study of spatial correlation characteristics, which has strong adaptability and robustness [7]. Combining with 7 Hu invariant moments features and 8 texture feature extraction to form the feature vector 15d, and k-neighbor classifier are classified, and separately adopt the Hu invariant moment features and texture features of the classification results are compared, the results show that this algorithm can effectively improve the accuracy of classification [8,9].

2 Feature Extraction of Discrimination

2.1 Hu Moment Feature Extraction

Geometric moment was put forward by M.K.Hu in 1962, it provided theory basis for the choice of target torque characteristics of images because of translation, rotation and scaling invariance [10].

For the gray level distribution of 1 $f(x,y)$, the $(p+q)$ moment is defined as:

$$m_{pq} = \iint x^p y^q f(x,y)dxdy \quad p,q = 0,1,2,\cdots \tag{1}$$

$(p+q)$ central moment is defined as:

$$\mu_{pq} = \iint (x-x_0)^p (y-y_0)^q f(x,y)dxdy \tag{2}$$

The centroid (x_0, y_0) is:

$$x_0 = \frac{m_{10}}{m_{00}}, \quad y_0 = \frac{m_{01}}{m_{00}} \tag{3}$$

In the discrete state, the $(p+q)$ ordinary moment and central moment of $f(x,y)$ is as follows:

$$m_{pq} = \sum_{x=1}^{M}\sum_{y=1}^{N} x^p y^q f(x,y) \tag{4}$$

$$\mu_{pq}=\sum_{x=1}^{M}\sum_{y=1}^{N}(x-x_0)^p(y-y_0)^q f(x,y)\quad p,q=0,1,2,\cdots \tag{5}$$

As the image changes, m^{pq} also changes and μ^{pq} has translational invariance.

The normalized central moment is:

$$y_{pq}=\frac{\mu_{pq}}{\mu_{00}{}^{r}},r=\frac{p+q+2}{2},\quad p+q=2,3,\cdots \tag{6}$$

Hu constructed seven moment invariants by using the second order and third order central moments, they can keep unchanged translation, scaling and rotation under the condition of the continuous image, the definitions are:

$$I_1=y_{20}+y_{02} \tag{7}$$

$$I_2=(y_{20}-y_{02})^2+4y_{11}^2 \tag{8}$$

$$I_3=(y_{30}-3y_{12})^2+(3y_{21}-y_{03})^2 \tag{9}$$

$$I_4=(y_{30}+y_{12})^2+(y_{21}+y_{03})^2 \tag{10}$$

$$\begin{aligned}I_5&=(y_{30}-3y_{21})(y_{21}+y_{03})[(y_{30}+y_{21})^2-3(y_{21}+y_{03})^2]\\&+(3y_{21}-y_{03})(y_{21}+y_{03})[3(y_{30}+y_{12})^2-(y_{21}+y_{03})^2]\end{aligned} \tag{11}$$

$$\begin{aligned}I_6&=(y_{20}-y_{02})[(y_{30}+y_{12})^2-(y_{21}+y_{03})^2]\\&+4y_{11}(y_{30}+y_{12})(y_{21}+y_{03})\end{aligned} \tag{12}$$

$$\begin{aligned}I_7&=(3y_{21}-3y_{03})(y_{30}+y_{12})[(y_{30}+y_{12})^2-3(y_{21}+y_{03})^2]\\&+(y_{30}-3y_{12})(y_{21}+y_{03})[3(y_{30}+y_{12})^2-(y_{21}+y_{03})^2]\end{aligned} \tag{13}$$

So the target subspace is $V=[I_1,I_2,I_3,I_4,I_5,I_6,I_7,]$.

2.2 Texture Feature Extraction based on Gray Level Co-occurrence Matrix

SAR image contains abundant texture information. Texture feature extraction method based on gray level co-occurrence matrix is a classic method which can describe the randomness and texture details well and it has the characteristics of strong adaptability [11].

As shown in figure 1, gray level co-occurrence matrix calculated the probability of pixel (i,j) at a distance of d on the direction of θ:

$$p=p_{ijd\theta}\ (i,j=0,1,2,\cdots,l-1) \tag{14}$$

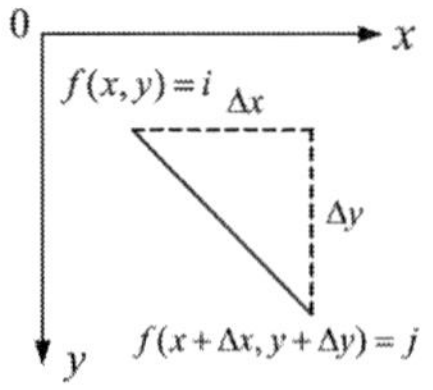

Figure 1 Gray Level Co-Occurrence Matrix Principle Diagram

$p_{ijd\theta}$ is the number of pixels to appear which gray is i and j ata distance of d on the direction of θ; l is the image gray-scale series.

The angle θ can do the following provisions:

$$\theta=\begin{cases}0^0,\Delta x=\pm1,\Delta y=0\\45^0,\Delta x=1,\Delta y=\pm1\\90^0,\Delta x=0,\Delta y=\pm1\\135^0,\Delta x=-1,\Delta y=\pm1\end{cases} \tag{15}$$

Although gray level co-occurrence matrix can reveal the texture rule of images, but it cannot directly be a digital feature of image classification. Therefore it is necessary to define some obvious physical meaning statistics based on gray level co-occurrence matrix that can describe the thickness and direction of the texture. This paper extracted eight texture characteristics that are mean, variance, uniformity, energy, entropy, inertia moment, correlation and differences [12].

(1) Mean

$$M=1\Big/mn\sum_{i=0}^{m}\sum_{j=0}^{n}p_{ijd\theta} \tag{16}$$

m,n are rows and columns of the gray level co-occurrence matrix

(2)Variance

$$V=\sum_{i=0}^{m}\sum_{j=0}^{n}(i-\mu)^2p^{*}_{ijd\theta} \tag{17}$$

$\mu=\sum_{i=0}^{m}\sum_{j=0}^{n}ip^{2}_{ijd\theta}$, $p^{*}_{ijd\theta}$ is the normalized value of $p_{ijd\theta}$.

(3) Uniformity

$$H=\sum_{i=0}^{m}\sum_{j=0}^{n}\frac{p^{*}_{ijd\theta}}{1+(i-j)^2} \tag{18}$$

Uniformity can measure local homogeneity, if the local uniform, the value is larger; otherwise, the value is smaller.

(4) Energy

$$A_{SM}=\sum_{i=0}^{m}\sum_{j=0}^{n}p^{2}_{ijd\theta} \tag{19}$$

Energy also calls the angular second moment, it reflects the image grayscale distribution uniformity.

 DOI: 10.1051/itmconf/20160702008

When angular second moment is large and texture is rough, energy is large; conversely, texture is thin, energy is small.

(5) Entropy

$$E=-\sum_{i=0}^{m}\sum_{j=0}^{n}p^{*}(i,j)\lg p^{*}_{ijd\theta} \qquad (20)$$

Entropy is associated with the density of texture. If the image is full of fine texture, the entropy is largest; if the texture is less, the entropy is smaller.

(6) Inertia moment

$$C_1=\sum_{i=0}^{m}\sum_{j=0}^{n}(i-j)^2 p^{*}_{ijd\theta} \qquad (21)$$

This parameter represents the distance of the larger elements from the extent of the principal diagonal, if texture is rough, the inertia moment is small, and otherwise, the inertia moment is large.

(7) Correlation

$$C_2=\sum_{i=0}^{m}\sum_{j=0}^{n}\frac{(i-\mu)(j-\mu)p^{*}_{ijd\theta}}{\sigma^2} \qquad (22)$$

with $\sigma^2=\sum_{i=0}^{m}\sum_{j=0}^{n}(i-\mu)^2 p_{ijd\theta}$

Correlation is used to measure the similarity degree of gray level co-occurrence matrix elements on the row or column direction. When the matrix element values are equal, the value is big; On the contrary, the value is small.

(8) Differences

$$D=\sum_{i=0}^{m}\sum_{j=0}^{n}|i-j|p^{*}_{ijd\theta} \qquad (23)$$

Differences can describe the difference of gray scale image pixels, the greater the difference, the easier to identify.

3 Classification Method

Classification algorithm flow chart is shown in figure 2.

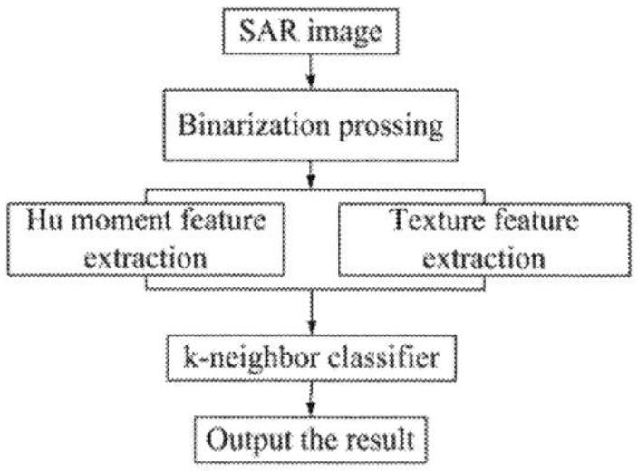

Figure 2 Algorithm Process

K-neighbor classifier is a mature method in theory. The idea of the method is: to a sample in the space, if most of the sample in the k most similar sample belongs to a category, then the sample also belongs to this category.

First the sample of the SAR image should be preprocessed, while the binary images would be got. Then we extract the seven invariant moment feature and eight texture features and get a set of 15 dimensional feature vectors. Therefore every image can be represented by the feature vector of the 15 d and we would get an n×15 dimensional feature vector database. Lastly we will put the database into k-neighbor classifier and calculate the classification accuracy.

4 Result of the Experiment and Analysis

The experimental data is taken from the C band RADARSAT-2 satellite. The resolution of image is 3m. Ship target and clutter images are cut into 60 samples of 100×100 pixel size, Put the image samples into morphology filter and get the binary image.

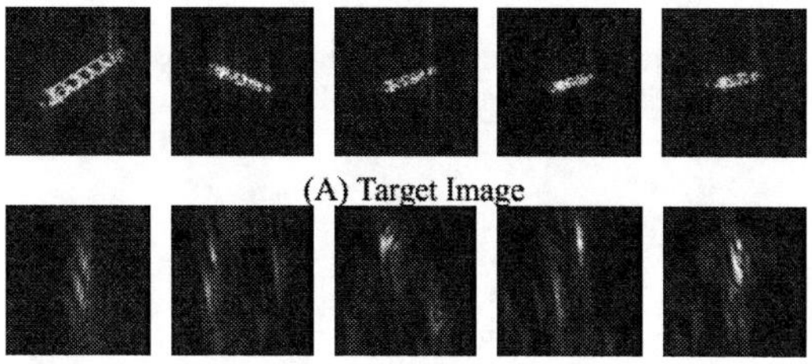

(B) Clutter Image

Figure 3 Image Samples of Thesar Image

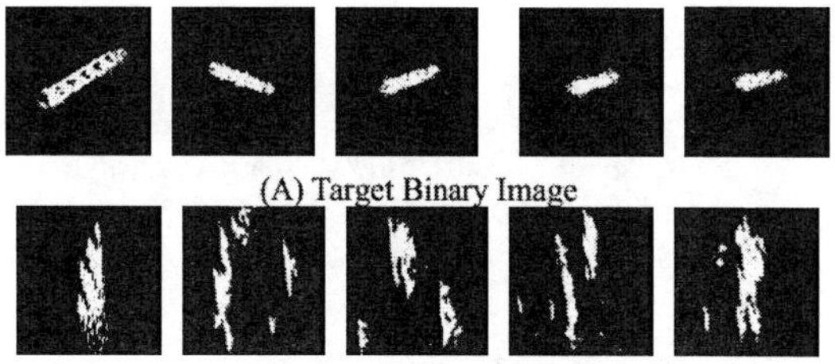

(B) Clutter Binary Image

Figure 4 Target And Clutter Binary Image

This section selected 60 target samples and 60 clutter samples. 50% of the samples are as the training sample and 50% as the test samples. According to the Hu invariant moment features and gray level co-occurrence we get the 60×15dtarget sample data and 60×15d clutter sample data. Put the data into k-neighbor classifier for training and testing to get the identification results, and then separate with the results of the Hu invariant moment features and texture features. In this paper, we set k=3.

Table 1 Classification Results

classification / feature	Hu moment feature	Texture feature	Feature of this paper
True number of target classification	26	29	30
False number of target classification	4	1	0
True number of clutter classification	25	28	29
False number of clutter classification	5	2	1
True number of clutter classification	51	57	59
False number of clutter classification	9	3	1
Accuracy	85%	95%	98.3%

By comparing test results above, we can get that the classification accuracy of using Hu moment feature alone to discriminate is 85%, because although Hu moment can reflect the global features of the image, it cannot describe the detail of the image well. So that caused the image description is not complete and classification accuracy is relatively low. Gray level co-occurrence matrix was used to extract texture structure, which has strong adaptability and robustness. Its classification effect is better; Combining Hu moment features and texture features can describe the image completely and the classification effect is remarkable.

5 Conclusion

This paper proposed a ship targets discrimination algorithm in SAR images based on Hu moment feature and texture feature. Hu moment feature reflects the shape information of the image and texture reflects all sorts of objective information of the image. Combining the Hu invariant moment features and the texture features extracted by gray level co-occurrence matrix, then put the data into k-neighbor classifier to discriminate. The experimental results show that this algorithm can effectively improve the classification accuracy and classification effect.

References

Here are some examples:

1. M. Liao, C. Wang, Y. Wang, and L. Jiang, "Using SAR images to detect ships from sea clutter," IEEE Geosci. Remote Sens. Lett., vol. 5, no. 2,pp. 194–198, Apr. 2008
2. M. C. Burl, G. J. Owirka, and L. M. Novak, "Texture discrimination in synthetic aperture radar imagery," in Proc. 23rd Asilomar Conf. Signals, Syst., Compute., 1989, pp. 399–404.
3. G. Gao, "An improved scheme for target discrimination in high-resolution SAR images," IEEE Trans. Geosci. Remote Sens., vol. 49, no. 1, pp. 277–294, Jan. 2011
4. O. Tuzel, F. Porikli, and P. Meer, "Region covariance: A fast descriptor for detection and classification," in Proc. ECCV, 2006, pp. 589–600
5. D. E. Kreithen, S. D. Halversen, and G. J. Owirka, "Discriminating targets from clutter," Lincoln Lab. J., vol. 6, no. 1, pp. 25–52, 1993
6. C. Zhu, H. Zhou, R. Wang, and J. Guo, "A novel hierarchical method of ship detection from space borne optical image based on shape and texture features," IEEE Trans. Geosci. Remote Sens., vol. 48, no. 9, pp. 3446–3456, Sep. 2010
7. D. Pastina, F. Fico, and P. Lombardo, "Detection of ship targets in COSMO-Sky Med SAR images," in Proc. IEEE RADAR, 2011,pp. 928–933
8. S. Brusch, S. Lehner, T. Fritz, M. Soccorsi, A. Soloviev, and B. van Schie,"Ship surveillance with Terra SAR-X," IEEE Trans. Geosci. Remote Sens., vol. 49, no. 3, pp. 1092–1103, Mar. 2011.
9. J. Chai, "Study of rejection algorithm and feature extraction technique on radar HRRP target recognition," Ph.D. Thesis, Xidian Univ., Xi'an, China,2010
10. S. I. Hwang and K. Ouchi, "On a novel approach using MLCC and CFAR for the improvement of ship detection by synthetic aperture radar," IEEE Geosci. Remote Sens. Lett., vol. 7, no. 2, pp. 391–395, Apr. 2010.
11. M. Liao, C. Wang, Y. Wang, and L. Jiang, "Using SAR images to detect ships from sea clutter," IEEE Geosci. Remote Sens. Lett., vol. 5, no. 2,pp. 194–198, Apr. 2008.
12. D. J. Crisp, The State-of-the-Art in Ship Detection in Synthetic Aperture Radar Imagery. Australia: DSTO Inf. Sci. Lab., 2004.

ITM Web of Conferences 7, 02009 (2016) DOI: 10.1051/itmconf/20160702009
ITA 2016

On The Lash Bar Count Algorithm Based on Image Recognition

Pan-Pan Chen[1,a], Wei-Dang Zhang[2,b] and Zhong-Rui Li[3,c]

[1]*School of Information Engineering, Zhengzhou University, Zhengzhou, HeNan ,China*
[2]*Zhengzhou University, Zhengzhou, HenNan, China*
[3]*School of Information Engineering, Zhengzhou University, Zhongzhou, HeNan, China*
[a]*1127556755@qq.com*, [b]*iewdzhang@zzu.com*, [c]*779398208@qq.com*

Abstract. This paper solved the problem that lash bars were difficult to be quickly and accurately counted,and proposed a kind of lash bar count algorithm based on image recognition through observation and study of the morphology of lash bars, namely the algorithm that combines cross type algorithm and flexible T type algorithm. Firstly,the color image is processed by graying and threshold method binarization. Secondly,the cross type discriminance is used in the middle section of the binary image. Thirdly,the flexible T type discriminance is used to detect on the boundary. Experimental analysis indicates that the detection algorithm saves time, which can be identified and gives the number of bars in a time less than 3s. The accuracy of bar count is as high as 98%. After joining the artificial modification, it can reach 100%.

1 Introduction

Bar as a common material products can be seen everywhere in all areas of production and life. With the development of Chinese society, the demands of all kinds of bar are more and more big, meanwhile, china is also a large bar production country. However, one of the big problems that bar production companies face is bar count.Therefore, how to efficiently and accurately solve the problem of bar count appears very important.

The artificial mean was commonly used in traditional bar count, which not only wasted manpower and time, but also was vulnerable to the impact of subjective judgment and large work intensity to cause misjudgment and omission. With the development of science and technology, currently, bar count mainly includes mechanical and electrical method, image method, RF Tag method. Mechanical and electrical method applys photoelectric sensor to collect bar information. And the serious overlapping situation easily leads to misjudgment and omission, lash bar does not use this method. RF Tag method is to post RF tag on the corresponding bar, through reading the label information to get the number of bars. Although it is not easy for misjudgment and omission, the cost is higher than the others. so this method is not generally used. Image method is to use the camera to shoot the images of the end surfaces of bars, which is transmitted to the processing end for processing and analysis to obtain the number of bars. Relatively speaking, the image method that has the least cost and the highest accuracy is the most popular method in the research field of bar count.

This paper proposes a lash bar count algorithm based on image recognition. The algorithm is by using cross type discriminance in the middle of the image and the flexible T type discriminance on the boundary for testing. The algorithm improves the shortcomings of traditional algorithm that has the large amount of computation and imperfect processing on the border area.

2 Algorithm design

According to the obtained images and the final effects, the algorithm framework is divided into four parts, namely image acquisition, image preprocessing, image processing and display results. Figure 1 shows Algorithm frame.

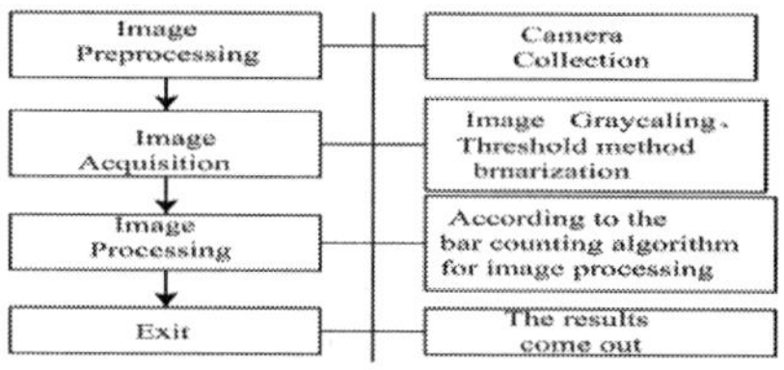

Figure 1. Algorithm Frame Diagram

2.1 Image acquisition

Image acquisition is based on the specific situation of hardware design to choose different focal length and resolution of the camera. In this paper, the collected images are saved in *RGB* mode.

RGB mode is one of the most important mode in

digital images, and R, G, B respectively show a pixel of red, green and blue sub- RGB in color images. R, G, B modes are additive models, and the three color synthesis becomes white when the R, G, B value is maximum. RGB mode is a 24-bit color depth. It consists of three channels and each channel has a depth of 8 bits. Three channels synthesizing together can generate 16.77 million kinds of colors, which are also called a "true color".

2.2 Image preprocessing

Image preprocessing includes the process of image graying and image binaryzation.

2.2.1 Image graying

There are many kinds of ways of image graying, the specific process is to convert color image RGB information into information that contain only brightness. Common conversion formula is as follows:

$$Gray = 0.229R + 0.587G + 0.114B \tag{1}$$

In formula (1), the R, G, B, respectively show a pixel of red, green, blue component in the color image. After the formula (1) conversion, color images can be converted to the image containing only brightness information.

2.2.2 Image binarization

Because there is a difference between bar and background in image, this article can use the method of image binarization to distinguish bar and background.

Threshold value method binarization is a method that separates the bar and the background. Through the figure 2 ,we can observe that the histogram of graying image presents the phenomenon of two peaks and one valley phenomenon. So global threshold can be gotten by using the method of automatic threshold selection. Then the image is segmented with the global threshold to obtain the desired binary image.

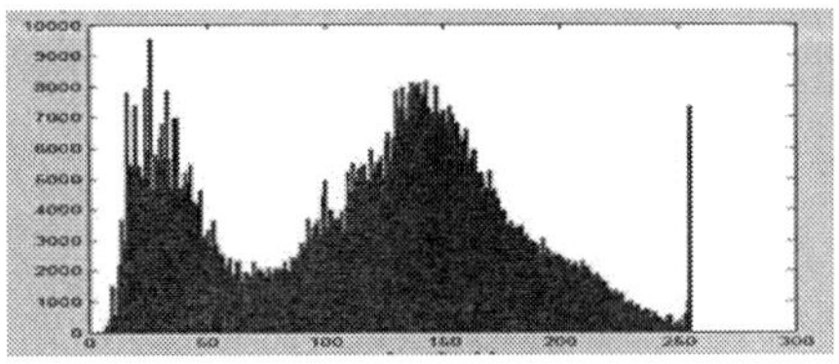

Figure 2. Histogram Graying Images (Abscissa Represents Gray Values And Ordinate Represents Proportion)

2.2.3 Bar count algorithm

Through observing and analyzing the form of lash bar, the morphological characteristics of lash bar can be summarized as three points:

1. The morphological characteristics of cross-section of each bar is similar, and similar to the circle that its diameter is R.
2. In lash bar, each bar around has about 2~6 roots bars inside lash bar. Each bar around has about 2~3 roots bars on the boundary of lash bar.
3. The center distance of each bar and the center distance of its surrounding bars are about the morphological diameter R.

According to the three morphological characteristics of lash bar, the algorithm that combines cross type algorithm and flexible T type algorithm is proposed. According to the current bar position detected, the corresponding cross or flexible T type algorithm is adopted. Specific operations are as follows:

When the center bar is judged to be in the interior of the image, the center bar is defined as the position of the initial bar, and the search of the cross type is carried out by the position of the initial bar. Cross type algorithm model is as follows:

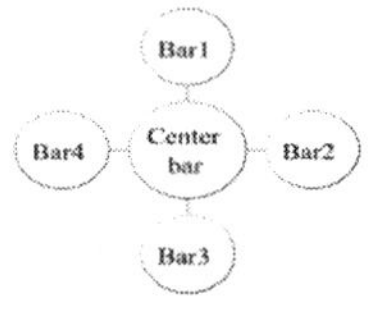

Figure 3. Cross Type Algorithm Model

As shown in Figure 3, the center bar is defined as the position of the initial bar, and the search for the cross type is carried out by the position of the initial bar. If the morphological diameter is R, we will start to search in the up and down, left and right four locations of the center bar. Center coordinate of the center bar is set (x_0, y_0). Structuring the matrix of the cross type algorithm is as follows:

$$Gradf1 = \begin{bmatrix} -1 & 0 \\ 1 & 0 \\ 0 & 1 \\ 0 & -1 \end{bmatrix} * R \tag{2}$$

In Figure 3, the coordinates of the center position of the bar 1~4 are

$$Grad\,(i) = (x_0 + Gradf\,1(i,1), y_0 + Gradf\,1(i,2)) \tag{3}$$

Formula (3) represents the label of the bar 1~4. $Grad(i)$ represents the center coordinates of the bar i. $Gradf1(i,1)$ represents the first elements of the i-th row of the matrix $Gradf1$. $Gradf1(i,2)$ represents the second element of the i-th row of the matrix $Gradf1$.

As shown in Figure 4, when judge out that the bar is located in the boundary of four image, the central bar is defined as the position of the initial bar as well, and according to the flexible T type algorithm to search near the bar. Flexible T type model is as follows:

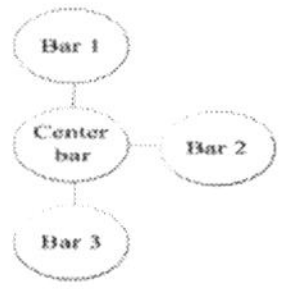

Figure 4-1. Model 1

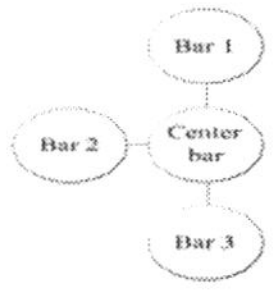

Figure 4-2 . Model 2

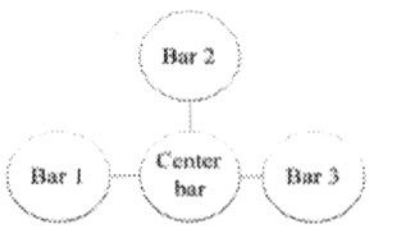

Figure 4-3. Model 3

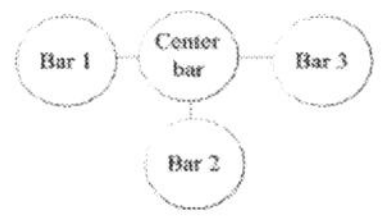

figure 4-4. Model 4

Figure 4. Flexible t Type Algorithm Model

As shown in Figure 4-1, it is detected that the current bar is located in the left boundary of the image. The center bar is defined as the position of the initial bar, In the T type algorithm model 1 shown in Figure 4-1 is applied to searching bar. If morphological diameter of the bar is R,the center coordinates of the center bar is (x_0, y_0) .Flexible T type algorithm matrix can be constructed

$$Gradf2 = \begin{bmatrix} 0 & -1 \\ 1 & 0 \\ 0 & 1 \end{bmatrix} * R \tag{4}$$

Formula (4) represents T type algorithm of bar corresponding to figure 4-1.The coordinate of center

position of the bar 1~3 is

$$Grad(i) = (x_0 + Gradf2(i,1), y_0 + Gradf2(i,2)) \tag{5}$$

Formula (5) indicates the label of the bar1~3. $Gradf(i)$ represents the center coordinates of the bar i . $Gradf2(i,1)$ represents the first elements of the i-th row of the matrix $Gradf2$. $Gradf2(i,2)$ represents the thesecond element of the i-th row of the matri $Gradf2$.

As shown in Figure 4-2, it is detected that the current bar is located in the right boundary of the image. The center bar is defined as the position of the initial bar, In the T type algorithm model 2 shown in Figure 4-2 is applied to searching bar. If morphological diameter of the bar is R,the center coordinates of the center bar is (x_0, y_0) . Flexible T type algorithm matrix can be constructed

$$Gradf3 = \begin{bmatrix} 0 & -1 \\ -1 & 0 \\ 0 & 1 \end{bmatrix} \tag{6}$$

Formula (6) corresponding to T type algorithm of bar in figure 4-2.The coordinate of center position of the bar 1~3 is as follows

$$Grad(i) = (x_0 + Gradf3(i,1), y_0 + Gradf3(i,2)) \tag{7}$$

Formula (7) indicates the label of the bar 1~3. $Grad(i)$ represents the center coordinates of the bar i . $Gradf3(i,1)$ represents the first elements of the i-th row of the matrix $Gradf2$. $Gradf3(i,2)$ represents the second element of the i-th row of the matrix $Gradf3$.

As shown in figure 4-3, it is detected that the current bar is located in the low boundary of the image. The center bar is defined as the position of the initial bar, In the T type algorithm model 3 shown in Figure 4-3 is applied to searching bar. If morphological diameter of the bar is R, the center coordinates of the center bar is (x_0, y_0) . Flexible T type algorithm matrix can be constructed

$$Gradf4 = \begin{bmatrix} -1 & 0 \\ 0 & 1 \\ 1 & 0 \end{bmatrix} * R \tag{8}$$

Formula (8) represents T type algorithm of bar corresponding to figure 4-3. The coordinate of center position of the bar 1~3 is

$$Grad(i) = (x_0 + Gradf4(i,1), y_0 + Gradf4(i,2)) \tag{9}$$

Formula (9) is indicated the label of the bar 1~3. $Grad(i)$ represents the center coordinates of the bar i . $Gradf4(i,1)$ represents the first elements of the i-th row of the matrix $Gradf4$. $Gradf4(i,2)$ represents the second element of the i-th row of the matrix $Gradf4$.

As shown in figure 4-4, it is detected that the current bar is located in the upper boundary of the image. The center bar is defined as the position of the initial bar, In the T type algorithm model 4 shown in figure 4-4 is applied to bar search. If morphological diameter of the bar is R, the center coordinates of the center bar is (x_0, y_0) . Flexible T type algorithm matrix can be constructed

$$Gradf5 = \begin{bmatrix} -1 & 0 \\ 0 & -1 \\ 1 & 0 \end{bmatrix} * R \tag{10}$$

Formula (10) represents T type algorithm of bar corresponding to figure 4-4. The coordinate of center position of the bar 1~3 is

$$Grad(i) = (x_0 + Gradf5(i,1), y_0 + Gradf5(i,2)) \tag{11}$$

Formula (11) is indicated the label of the bar 1~3. $Grad(i)$ represents the center coordinates of the bar i . $Gradf5(i,1)$ represents the first elements of the i-th row of the matrix $Gradf5$. $Gradf5(i,2)$ represents the second element of the i-th row of the matrix $Gradf5$.

3 Algorithm realization and analysis

The first step of the algorithm in this paper is to preprocess pictures by using grayscaling and threshold method binarization,then the binarization image is processed with cross and flexible T type algorithm to get the total number of bars. The specific flow chart of the algorithm is as follows:

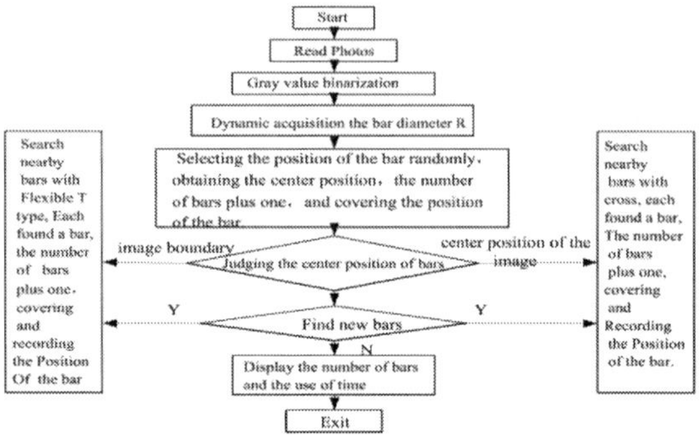

Figure 5. Specific Flow Chart of Algorithm

3.1 Realization of image graycaling

After the conversion of formula (1), the color image can be converted to the image that only contains brightness information, and realize the process of image grayscaling.

Figure 6. Original Image **Figure 7.** Grayscaling Image

Compared with figure 6, the figure 7 can be observed that the image after the grayscaling does not contain color pixels, contain only brightness information.

3.2 Realization of image binarization

Through figure 2 can be observed, the histogram of the grayscaling image shows the phenomenon of two peak and one valley. Therefore, the global threshold can be obtained by the method of automatic threshold selection, and then the image can be segmented by the global threshold to get required binary image.

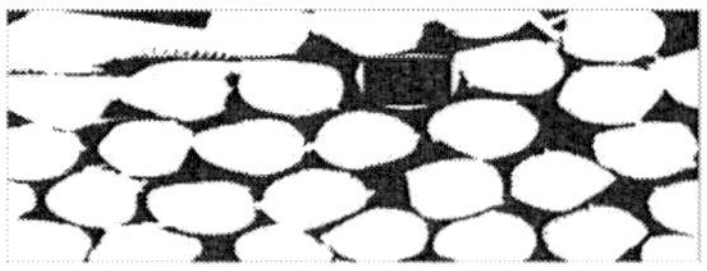

Figure 8. Binary Image

Through the figure 8 can be clearly observed: the image after binarization containes gray value of pixels only two 0 and two 255. In this paper, 0 represents the gray value of the background pixel, and 255 represents the gray value of bar pixel. By judging the gray value of any pixel points,you can judge out that the pixel is a background or a bar.

3.3 The realization of bar count

In this paper,we adopt the algorithm of bars that combines cross type and flexible T type. There Algorithm Step (6) can be seen. When a bar is searched, bar count plus one, calculating and judging out the center position of the bar at the same time. When the center position of the bar as shown in figure 14 is located in the image, cross type algorithm is adopted to search the center position of the bar. Search results are shown in figure 15:

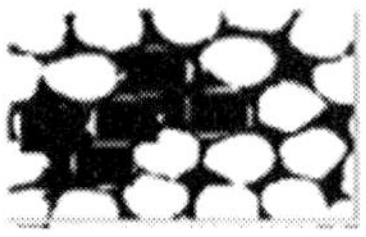

Figure 9-1 **Figure 9-2**

Figure 9. Simulation Results of Cross Type Algorithm(Figure 9-1 Center Bar of Cross Type Algorithm, Figure 9-2 Effect Diagram of Cross Type Algorithm)

According to effect picture can be observed: the bars are found by figure 9-1 as the center bar. We can see that the center bar is located in the interior of the image.

Therefore, we select cross type algorithm to search bar nearby, and the effect picture shown in figure 9-2 can be gotten. When bars have been searched in the up and down, left and right, the position of the bar is just covered, and bar count plus one, and the bar is put as a new centre bar, and the appropriate algorithm to continue their search is selected in the vicinity of the new center bar. When the center position of the bar as shown in Figure 10-1 is located in the image, flexible T type model 3 algorithm is adopted to search the central position of bars. Search results are shown in figure 10-2:

Figure 10-1 **Figure 10-2**

Figure 10. Simulation Results of Flexible T Type Algorithm

(Figure 10-1. The Center Bar of Flexible T Type Algorithm, Figure 10-2. Effect Diagram of Flexible T Type Algorithm)

According to the effect picture can be observed: the bars are found by figure 10-1 as the center bar. We can see that the center bar is located in the boundary of the image. The location of the bar belongs to the types of figure 4-3. Therefore,we adopt flexible T type model 3 algorithm as shown in figure 4-3 to search bars nearby. The effect picture shown in figure 10-2 can be gotten. When bars have been searched in the up and down, left and right, the position of the bar is just covered, and bar count plus one, and the bar is put as a new centre bar, and the appropriate algorithm to continue their search is selected in the vicinity of the new center bar.

3.4 Experimental result and performance analysis of bar counting

Through *MATLAB* simulation, the experimental result of the algorithm in this paper is as follows:

Figure 11. Simulation Result of the Algorithm in This Paper

According to the contrast of figure 2 and figure 11, we can directly observe that the number of bars in the original image are 23,and the results obtained from the *MATLAB* simulation experiment are 23. By processed image you can visually see which bars are not processed. Therefore, adding the artificial correction, the accuracy of bar counting can reach 100%.

In order to verify the effect of the algorithm in this paper,the paper under the 64 bit windows system uses *MATLAB* for statistics, getting counting results of various types of binding types. The experimental results are shown in table 1:

Table 1. Analysis of the Test Results and Performance of Lash Bar.

Bar Type (mm)	The actual number of bars	Detecting the number of bars	The time used	Algorithm accuracy rate
15	23	23	1.2173s	100%
17	68	68	1.4468s	100%
20	178	177	1.7822s	99.4%
25	249	246	2.0106s	98.7%
27	108	108	1.9015s	100%
30	135	135	1.5237s	100%

According to the data in table 1, this article take the bar counting algorithm that combines cross type and flexible T type, and the accuracy of the bar count is as high as 98%. For those bars whose diameter are in 15 ~ 30 *mm* can get better detection. And the accuracy can achieve 100% under adding the condition of artificial correction.

4 Conclusion

In this paper, according to number distribution of lash bar around , the cross type algorithm is proposed. At the same time, a flexible T type algorithm is proposed aiming at the boundary,by combining the cross type algorithm and the flexible T type algorithm as the whole bar detection algorithm. The algorithm does not need to consider the boundary problem, while adding artificial correction function on the result of the processing to achieve better 100% counting aiming at 5~30 *mm* bars. Through the above test results and performance analysis, summarizing the advantages of the algorithm in this paper are as follows:

(1) In this paper, the flexible T type algorithm is used to detect the bars around, and the detection effect is better.

(2) Because the number of surrounding bars in the vicinity of bars are basically 3~6 roots, the whole search volume of the algorithm is much less, saving the search time, while the whole calculation is also less.

(3) According to the processed image, you can visually see the detection results, Therefore, the bar count rate can reach 100% with the addition of artificial correction.

References

1. Hailong Huang, Liang Zhang. J. Machinery Design & Manufacture, 6 176-179 (2015)
2. Yanbing Xue. D. Shangdong: School of mechanical engineering, Shandong, University (2014)
3. Xiaoyu Liu, Bing Wu, Zhiqi Su, JiaGuo, Kangling Fang.J.Control engineering, 20 2 286-289 (2013)
4. Ling Huang, Baoqian Qi, Bo.J. Industry and Mine Automation,38 5 77-79 (2012)
5. Hong Wang, Fan Guo.J. Journal of Northeastern University:Natural Science, 32 2 281-284 (2011)
6. Abdulkadir Sengur, Guo Yan-hui.J.Computer Vision and Image Understanding,115 8 1134-1144 (2011)
7. Jiuquan Zhang, Youzhong Jin. J.Manufacturing Automation. 33 1 127-128 (2011)
8. Wenhuan Zhou, Lixin Zheng.J.Microcomputer & Its Applications. 30 18 38-41 (2011)
9. Zhang Hui, Iason EFritts,Sally. J.Computer Vision and Image Understanding, 110 2 260-280 (2008)
10. Gonzalez.R.C, Qiuqi Ruan. *Digital Image Processing(MATLAB Edition)* Beijing: electronic industry press.M. (2015)

 DOI: 10.1051/itmconf/20160702010

Double HEVC Compression Detection with the Same QPs Based on the PU Numbers

Rui-Shi JIA, Zhao-Hong LI ,[a]Zhen-Zhen ZHANG and Dong-Dong LI
school of Electronic and Information Engineering, Beijing Jiao tong University, Beijing, 100044
{15120012, zhhli2, 11111053, 14120011}@bjtu.edu.cn
[a] *Corresponding author: Zhaohong Li, zhhli2@bjtu.edu.cn*

Abstract. Double HEVC compression detection is of great importance in video forensics. However, effective detection algorithm based on the same Qps is rarely reported. In this paper, a novel method based on the same Qps is applied in dealing with double HEVC compression detection. Firstly, the numbers of PU blocks with the size of 4×4 in each I frame is extracted during the codec procedures when the video is compressed with the same Qps. Then, calculate the standard deviation of 4×4 PU blocks difference (SDoPU) before and after the compression. Finally, select the appropriate threshold for compression testing classification according to the SDoPU statistical feature. By performing numerical experiments, We prove that the proposed algorithm is of high classification accuracy for detecting double HEVC compression.

1. Introduction

Nowadays, with the advent of the era of network and multimedia information, digital video has become an indispensable part of our life. However, as the high-speed development of the video editing software such as Adobe Premiere, the authenticity and integrity of videos suffered severe damage. Therefore, video tampering forensics becomes a necessary link to ensure the authenticity of copyright problem and surveillance videos. Double compression detection as an important detection means of video forensics technology and therefore has become a hot spot in the field of information security.

So far, existing methods are effective for double compression detection. Su and Xu detect double compression by studying the distribution of quantized DCT coefficients for MPEG video in [1,2]. By judging whether the probability distribution of the first digits of the non-zero MPEG quantized AC coefficients will be disturbed, Chen in [3] distinguish the occurrence of the double compression. Jiang in [4] use Markov statistics to classify double compression. Huang detect double MPEG compression according to the change of the numbers of DCT coefficients for the primary and secondary compression. While, above algorithms are all for the compressed video before the coding standard HEVC. References [5,6] proposed the methods based on the co-occurrence of DCT coefficients, [7] use the odd-even feature of the DCT coefficients, and references [5,6,7] are based on the latest coding standard.

There is a lack of effective algorithm dealing with double compression detection based on the same Qps, Double HEVC compression detection with the same Qps is less. Nevertheless, as the latest coding standard, HEVC video coding standard will play an increasingly important role in Hd and High-definition video in the future. Therefore, double HEVC compression detection with the same Qps is of particular practical significance. In this paper, a novel method based on the same Qps for double HEVC compression detection is proposed. The main structure of this paper is divided into four parts, Section 2 introduces PU division pattern of HEVC video coding standard, Section 3 gives a description of the specific algorithm, while the part of video database and the experimental results is given in Section 4, we conclude this paper in Section 5 and list some promising directions for future work.

2. Materials and Methods

2.1 The Introduction of PU Types

As the latest generation of video coding standard, HEVC adopts much more flexible coding block structure, introduces residual coding and the quadtree partitioning structure. CU for coding unit, its size set to 8×8, 16×16, 32×32 and 64×64, of course, CU can be divided into smaller CU unit. Figure 1 shows the CU partitions and its quadtree structure. As shown in Figure1 (a), HEVC traverses the CU in the way of Z scanning when coding it and the number in the diagram block shows the coding sequence. Figure 1(b) shows the corresponding quad tree structure of CU, among them the "solid black spots"on

 DOI: 10.1051/itmconf/20160702010

behalf of the nodes can be broken down while the hollow ones can't, and there is no need to continue to break down when the size of CU is 8×8.

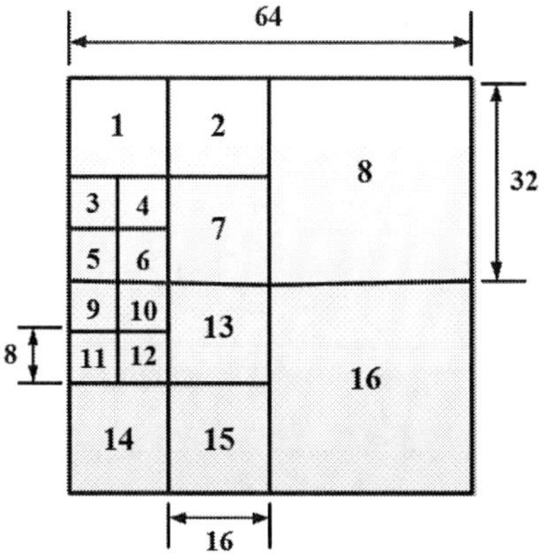

(a) CU Partitions.

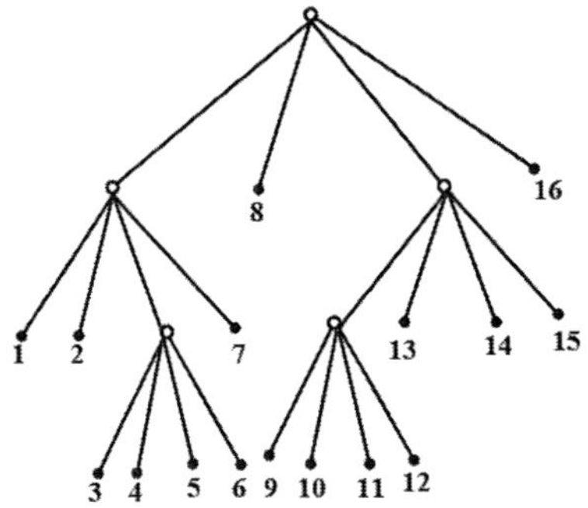

(b) Quadtree Structure

Figure 1. CU Partitions and Its Quadtree Structure.

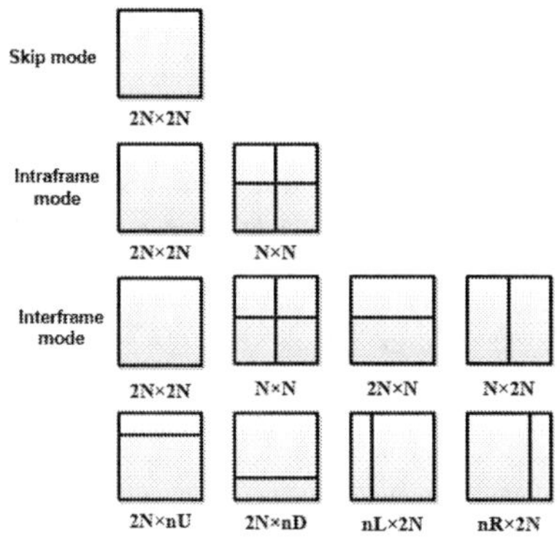

Figure 2. PU Types Under Different Prediction Mode.

PU is the basic unit of the frame and interframe prediction, each internal structure of CU can be divided into one or more PU, so can look CU as the outermost layer of the framework and the size of the PU can't larger than CU, its size can be 4×4, 8×8, 16×16, 32×32 and 64×64. Assuming that the size of the coding unit CU is 2N×2N, the CU can be divided into multiple prediction units PU depending on the prediction mode. HEVC provides eight kinds of PU division structure as shown in Figure 2. The size of the PU only can be 2N×2N when the forecast model is Skip, about the frame prediction, the PU size can be 2N×2N and N×N, While 8 types of classification are all available at the interframe prediction, 2N×nU, 2N×nD, and nR×2N is asymmetric mode, as optional mode, can control its open or close in encoding configuration file.

2.2 Feature Extraction

Our algorithm is based on the statistics features of the numbers of 4×4 PU numbers. Therefore, first of all we should extract the PU types of each video.

(a) Pu Types In Qp22

(b)Pu Types In Qp22_22

Figure 3. Pu Types for the First i Frame of the Compressed Video Part1_Coastguard in QP22 and QP22_22.

Figure 3 shows the PU types for the first I frame of the compressed video part1_coastguard in Qp22 and Qp22_22, Figure 3(a) shows the PU types for the first I frame of part1_coastguard in Qp22 and Figure 3(b) in Qp22_22, Among them, the boundary of the thick solid lines show the maximum size (64×64) of CU, And so on, the dotted line said the smallest size(4×4) for PU blocks.

Figure 4 shows the numbers of 4×4, 8×8 and 16×16 PU blocks for this two PU types. the curves with the triangle represent the numbers of 16×16 PU blocks for the under test video and it's one compressed ones, and

 DOI: 10.1051/itmconf/20160702010

the curves with the circle on behalf of the 8×8 PU blocks, we can clearly see that they are almost consistent. While the two curves with stars have certain gap, it shows that the numbers of the 4×4 PU blocks is different. So we can choose the change of 4×4 PU blocks numbers as the method to detect the double compression videos. Figure 5 is the standard deviation of 4×4 PU blocks difference (SDoPU) before and after the compression for single and Double compressed videos.

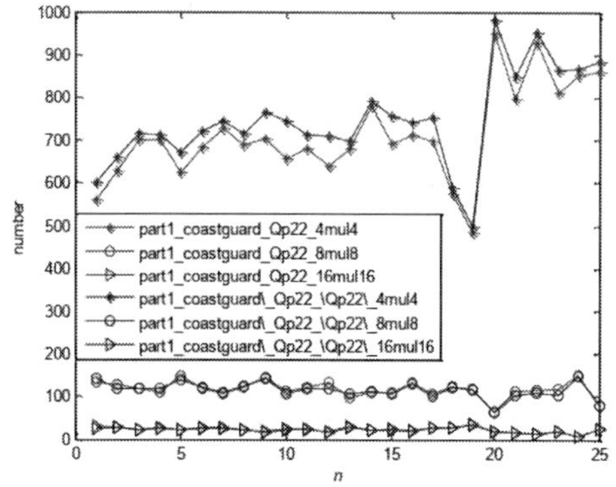

Figure 4. The Numbers of 4×4, 8×8 and 16×16 Pu Blocks for The Video Part1_Coastguard Based on QP22 and QP22_22

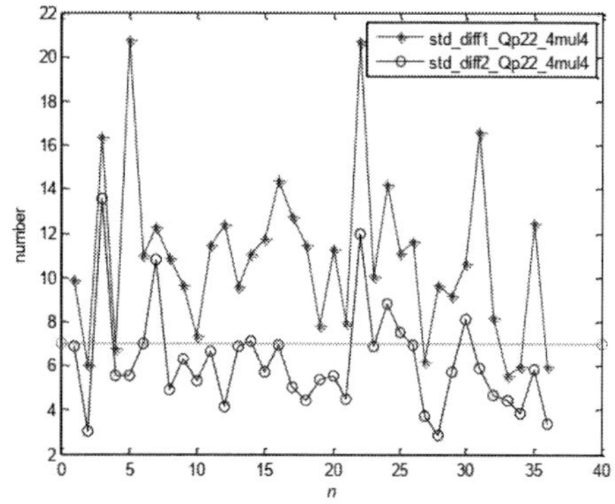

Figure 5. The Standard Deviation of 4×4 PU Blocks Difference (SDoPU) before and after the Compression for Single and Double Compressed Videos.

In Figure 5, we can see there are three different curves. The curve with the stars represents the values of SDoPU for single compressed videos based on Qp22, and the curve with the circle on behalf of the double compressed videos based on Qp22_22, Qp22_22 means a single compressed video is compressed twice with the same Qp22. Apparently, the two curves have big difference in values. We decide a appropriate threshold to classify them according to their statistics features as the green line shows.

2.3 Proposed Detection Scheme

For a given video under test, obviously we can't know whether it's a single or double compression ones. But we can draw the curves of the numbers for the 4×4 PU blocks, and distinguish the double compression according to the statistics features. The main process of the algorithm is as follows: First of all, decompress the under test video and extract the quantization parameter Qp. Secondly, compress the video with the same Qps extracted from the under test video. Thirdly, check the PU types of each I frame for the primary and secondary compressed videos using the code stream analysis software GtiHEVCAnalyzer [8] of the open source HEVC and draw the curve of the numbers for the 4×4 PU blocks for them. Then, calculate the standard deviation of 4×4 PU blocks difference (SDoPU) before and after the compression. Finally, select the appropriate threshold for compression testing classification according to the SDoPU statistical feature, namely, according to the two different curves, we select a general range of the threshold value, then select a straight line that the most of points on the two curves distribute on both sides of this line. Figure 6 is the flow chart of the algorithm.

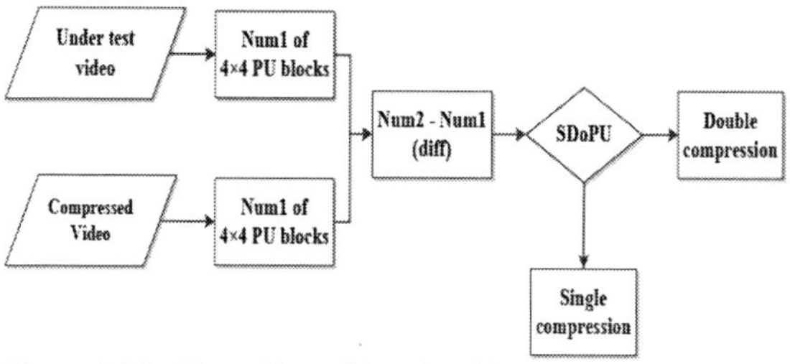

Figure 6. The Flow Chart of the Algorithm.

3. Results and Discussions

3.1 Video Database

In our experiments, with the resolution of 176×144 pixels, 36 original YUV sequences of QCIF format available at [9] were used, It's frame rate is 30 f/s and these videos have various kinds of content, such as people, scene, news, etc. Using the basic HM10.0 class [10], the experiment realizes the HEVC standard codec process, and the GOP structure is IPPP. To ensure the quality of these videos and the experiment better,we set the Qp as 22, 24, 26, 28 and 32.

3.2 The Test Standard and Experiment Result

In this paper, *AR* (accuracy) is adopted as the evolution standard for detection rate, as shown in formula (1):

$$AR = (PR+TNR)\ 2 \tag{1}$$

Where $TPR=TP\ /\ (TP+FN)$ and $TNR=TN\ /\ (TN+FP)$,*TN* (true negative) represents a single compressed video was found as single compressed, *TP*(true positive) for double compressed video was convicted as single compressed, *FN*(false negative) for double compressed video was classified as single compressed video, and *FP*(false positive) for a single compressed video was detected as double compressed video. Table 1 shows the detection rate of double HEVC compression.

Table 1. Detection Rate of double HEVC Compression .

Detection rate	Qp22	Qp24	Qp26	Qp28	Qp32
TNR (SDoPU)	0.8472	0.7778	0.8333	0.8333	0.8056
TRP (SDoPU)	0.8611	0.8056	0.7222	0.8611	0.8889
AR	0.8472	0.7917	0.7778	0.8472	0.8473

As shown in Table1, we set five quantization parameters Qps to compressed videos. When the quantization parameter is Qp32, the AR of the proposed method is 0.8473 for classifying firstly-compressed and doubly-compressed videos; this parameter achieves the best detection results. As the latest coding standard, there are few effective methods for HEVC video detection, The result demonstrates our algorithm is promising.

4. Conclusions

With the development of the advanced video editor, the authenticity and integrity of the videos can't be guaranteed anymore. In this paper, we conduct a research to detect double HEVC compression and proposed a novel method based on the same Qps. We extract the PU types of the under test videos and it's primary and secondary compressed ones, By calculating the SDoPU of 4×4 PU blocks, a set of statistics features have been extracted to classify double HEVC compression videos. Since there are few effective algorithms focusing on the detection for double HEVC compression, the performance of our proposed algorithm is promising, and we will further research to improve our algorithm in the future.

Acknowledgment

We would like to thank Xian Yang and Yawei Yuan for their help and kindly suggestions. This work was supported in part by the Fundamental Research Funds for the Central Universities (W15JB00280), in part by SRF for ROCS, SEM (W15C300020), in part by A Project Funded by the Priority Academic Program Development of Jiangsu Higer Education Institutions (PAPD), and in part by Jiangsu Collaborative Innovation Center on Atmospheric Environment and Equipment Technology (CICAEET).

References

[1] Tanfeng Sun, wan wang, and Xinghao Jiang, "Exposing video forgeries by detecting MPEG double compression," in Acoustics, Speech and signal Processing (ICASSP),2012 IEEE international Conference on IEEE, 2012, pp. 1389-1392.

[2] JUNYU XU, YUTING SU,QINGAHONG LIU. Detection of double MPEG-2 compression based on distribution of DCT coefficients [J]. International Journal of Pattern Recognition & Artificial Intelligence, 2013, 27(1):155-167.

[3] Wen Chen and Yun Q shi, "Detection of double MPEG compression based on first digit statistics," in Digital Watermarking, pp. 16-30. Springer,2009.

[4] Jiang, X, Wang, W, Sun, T, et al. Detection of Double compression in MPEG-4 Videos Based on Markov Statistics, Singal Procession Letters, 2003, 20, (5), pp. 447-450.

[5] Huang M, Wang R, Xu J, et al. Detection of Double Compression for HEVC Videos Based on the Co-occurrence Matrix of DCT Coefficients[M]// Digital-Forensics and Watermarking. Springer International Publishing, 2015.

[6] Jieyuan Chen, Xinghao Jiang, tangfeng Sun, Peisong He, Shilin Wang. DETECTING DOUBLE MPEG COMPRESSION WITH THE SAME QUANTISER SCALE BASED ON MBM FEATURE. Conference paper. ICASSP.2016.7472040.

[7] Huang M L, Wang R D, Xu J, et al. Detection of double compression in HEVC videos based on the statistical characteristic of DCT coefficients[J]. Guangdianzi Jiguang/journal of optoelectronics laser, 2015, 26(4):733-739..

[8] SourceForge.net,"GtilHEVCAnalyzer", https://sourceforge.net/projects/gtilhevcanalyzer/.

[9] 'YUV video sequences', http://trace.eas.asu.edu/yuv/index.html, accessed 2 August 2015.

[10] JVT-VC Reference Software version HM-10.0 Available on http://download.csdn.net/detail/amymayadi/7903385

Wireless Network Penetration Testing and Security Auditing

Shao-Long WANG, Jian WANG, Chao FENG and Zhi-Peng PAN

College of Electronic Science and Engineering, National University of Defense Technology Changsha, China
wangshaolong002@126.com,climbspider@hotmail.com

Abstract—IEEE802.11 wireless wireless networks have security issues that are vulnerable to a variety of attacks. Due to using radio to transport data, attackers can bypass firewalls, sniff sensitive information, intercept packets and send malicious packets. Security auditing and penetration testing is expected to ensure wireless networks security. The contributions of this work are analyzed the vulnerability and types of attacks pertaining to IEEE 802.11 WLAN, performed well known attacks in a laboratory environment to conduct penetration tests to confirm whether our wireless network is hackable or not. WAIDPS is configured as auditing tool to view wireless attacks, such as WEP/WPA/WPA2 cracking, rouge access points, denial of service attack. WAIDPS is designed to detect wireless intrusion with additional features. Penetration testing and auditing will mitigate the risk and threatening to protect WALN.

1 Introduction

WLAN uses radio frequencies as the medium to transport data. This exposes layer 1 and layer 2 in the range of the wireless network. WLANs typically operate within two frequency ranges—2.4 GHz and 5.0 GHz at the standard 802.11a/b/g/n. In each of band, there are multiple channels. Everyone can sniff the entire airspace by putting the card into monitor mode in the same channel. WALN communication happens over frames. There are three different types of 802.11 MAC frames, data, control, and management [1]. The majority of wireless attacks target management frames, because they are responsible for authentication, association, disassociation, beacons, and probe request/response [2]. Wireless attacks like denial of service attacks, man-in-the-middle attacks are implemented within the 802.11 frames and can't be detected at layer three past the access point [3]. Unlike traditional intrusion detection systems in a wired network, detecting attacks in a wireless network is at layer two. Penetration testing will help find and plug insecurities which could be exploited by attackers. Measures must be taken on a wireless network in order to have proper vision to view wireless attacks. We expect for a way to be used as a reference for practitioners to protect their WLAN from wireless attacks.

2 Security measures and Attacks Based on the Flaws of IEEE 802.11 WLAN

2.1 SSID Hiding and Packet Sniffing

Packet sniffer can give plentiful information about ESSID, BSSID, channels, encryption protocol, power etc. This allows attacker to gather information about a Wi-Fi access point. In general, access point will send out its SSID in the Beacon frames. Default SSID comes with its username and password. This brings potential security vulnerability. There are some common default username-passwords: "admin-admin"/TP-LINK, "adsl-adsl1234"/ASUS, "cisco-cisco"/CISCO etc.

Though SSID can be hidden, whenever a legitimate client tries to connect to the access point, they exchange Probe Request and Probe Response packets. These management contains SSID. So hidden SSIDs is a security feature which is relatively simple to beat.

2.2 MAC filter and spoofing

Once MAC filtering is enabled, only the authorized MAC address can be able to successfully authenticate to the access point. However there are various available tools we can utilize to change the wireless card's MAC address of the client like: "mac-changer" under LINUX and "MAC address changer" under Windows. It is possible to find authorized

 DOI: 10.1051/itmconf/20160703001

MAC address from unencrypted packets through packets sniffing. Consequently MAC address filters do not provide any security.

2.3 Denial of Service

For a high level security environment, there are a variety of ways attacker can still exploit. WPA2-AES is still regarded as a robust encryption standard, it only applies to data frames and not currently to the management frames. Attacker tries to inject forged management frame into the network to conduct a DOS attack [4]. Currently main wireless DOS attacks are the following: Access Point Overloaded attack, Authentication Flood Attack, De-authentication Attack, Association Flood Attack, Disassociation Attack [5]. These attacks will lead to a wireless access point overloaded, service interruption, packets loss rate increasing, even need to restart the suspended AP.

2.4 Cracking Encryption

In order to prevent unauthorized users from eavesdropping or invasive wireless network, Wired Equivalent Privacy (WEP), an IEEE standard security algorithm was proposed in 1999, But cryptanalyst has identified several weaknesses in WEP, so IEEE 802.11 standard was developed in 2003 called Wi-Fi Protected Access (WPA), and was replaced by the IEEE 802.11i standard (WPA2) in 2004 [6]. The WEP protocol has been known to be flawed since 2000, but surprisingly it is still continuing to be used and most access points are still equipped with WEP capabilities.

WPA/WPA2 is stronger than WPE, but still vulnerable to dictionary and brute force attacks [7]. An attacker who eavesdrops the entire conversation will get five key parameters: SSID of Network, Authenticator Nonce (ANONCE), Supplicant Nonce (SNONCE), Authenticator MAC address (Access Point MAC), and Suppliant MAC address (Wi-Fi Client MAC) [8], which are essential for a force attack. The only thing needed is the Pre-Shared Key.

A dictionary attack used in WPA/WPA2 PSK, would use a large dictionary of possible passphrases. Firstly it derives each of 256-bit Pre-Shared Key from the dictionary and use it with the other parameters to create the PTK showed in Fig.1. Then the PTK will be used to verify the Message Integrity Check (MIC) in the second handshake packets [9]. If it matches, the passphrase guessed from the dictionary is correct

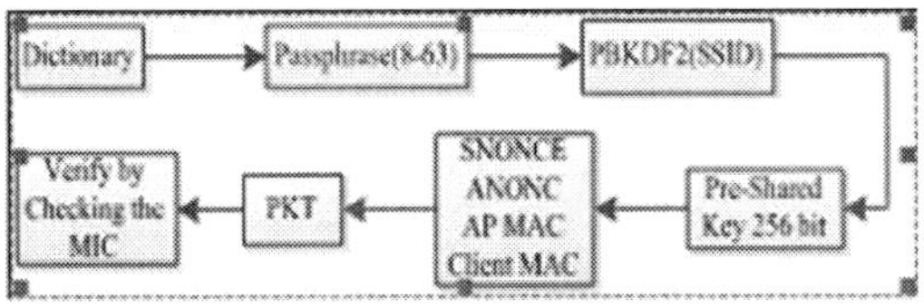

Figure 1. Steps of Dictionary Attack.

2.5 Man-in-the-Middle (MITM) Attack

MITM attacks are probably one of most potent attacks on a WLAN system by setting a rouge access point. Attacker prepare two interfaces, one creates the rouge access point and the other interface is connected to the authorized access point. Both these interfaces are bridged. These points broadcast an SSID similar to a local hotspot in vicinity. Users may accidently get connected to this rouge access point or can be forced to using the higher signal strength.

In MITM, victim's traffic is routed through the attacker's computer. Thus the attacker can eavesdrop on all the traffic sent to and from the victim's machine. It is often used with phishing sites. If the user's access to the bank's home page is redirected to the attacker's phishing sites, bank password will be defrauded. A rouge access point may even compromises the security of a WPA-Enterprise network running PEAP or EAP-TTLS [10].

3 Wireless Network Penetration Testing

Based on the vulnerabilities listed above, relevant attacks are executed in a wireless lab to conduct penetration testing. To setup the wireless local area network for performing the various attacks and monitoring or detecting them, the following hardware were used to set up the wireless lab: a wireless router, a Desktop machine, 2 laptops and 2 USB wireless adapters.

3.1 Wireless Sniffing and Bypass MAC Filters

In order to gain particular information about the local wireless network, an attacker would start running a packet sniffer. After discovering the brand of Wi-Fi router being used and authenticated clients, the attacker can try conducting more attacks. Airodump-ng is an excellent wireless network sniffer that can get plentiful information about local wireless network, including SSID, MAC address, channel, encryption protocol e.t, by setting the USB adapter into monitor mode. TABLE Ⅰ is the information gathered about Testing Lab, including its MAC address (BSSID), SSID (ESSID), encryption protocol (ENC), channel (CH), power (PWR), and packets transformed through the whole network.

Table 1 Information Gathered about Target Ap

BSSID	PWR	Beacons	#Data	#/ s	CH
80:89:17:A3:F8:96	-31	10	WEP	WEP	10
MB	ENC	CIPHER	AUTH	ESSID	
54e	WEP	WEP	Y	Testing Lab	

At the same time, connected to target AP can be seen in TABLE Ⅱ. It is easy to bypass MAC filters using authorized MAC address with command:

macchanger –m wlan0. 28:C2:DD:9F:B8:95

Table 2 Authorized Clients Connected to Target Ap

BSSID	STATION	PWR	Rate
80:89:17:A3:F8:96	BE:53:E5:A4:6F:20	-27	54e-54e
80:89:17:A3:F8:96	28:C2:DD:9F:B8:95	-27	54e-54e
Lost	Frames	Probe	
8	846	Testing Lab	
0	582	Testing Lab	

3.2 WEP Cracking

WEP is a really old encryption technique and can be easily cracked. Many attack examples show that using known initialization vector IV and the first byte of the key stream, and combined with the characteristics of RC4 stream key algorithm, can calculate the WEP key. Firstly using airodump-ng to capture all packets sending in Testing Lab, with the command:

airodump-ng --bssid 80:89:17:A3:F8:96 -c 10 --write WEPcracking wlan0

In WEP cracking, we exploit weaknesses in the protocol which is data packets encrypted with the same IV. The only requirement is a great number of data packets. We need to force the network to produce more data packets through replay attack by capturing ARP packets and injecting them back to the network using tool aireplay-ng. Once enough data packets have been captured, Aircrack-ng will be used to crack WEP key. If data packets captured in the file are not sufficient, aircrack-ng will pause. Fig.2 indicates that enough IVs is collected and key was successfully found.

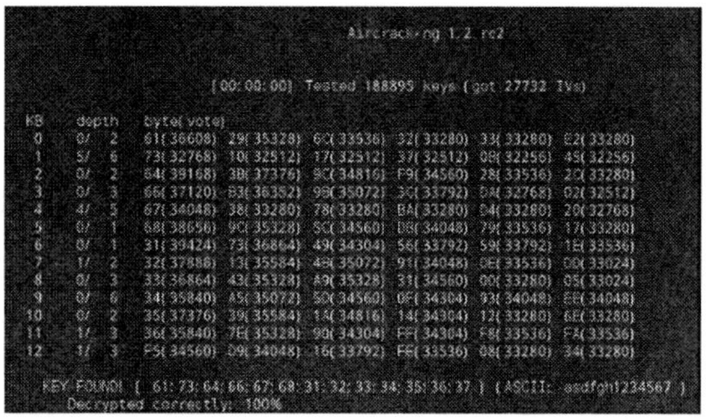

Figure 2. Successfully Cracking WEP.

3.3 WPA/WPA2-PSK Cracking

WPA/WPA2 PSK is vulnerable to a dictionary attack. The inputs required for this attack is the four-way WPA handshake between client and access point, and a wordlist containing common passphrases. In the same way, airodump-ng is used to capture the packets. The different is that we send broadcast de-authentication packets to force clients to reconnect, to speed up capturing the four-way WPA handshake packets using aireplay-ng.

The next is starting the dictionary key cracking. The prerequisite of a dictionary attack is that the passphrase must be present in the dictionary file. If the passphrase is not present, the attack will fail. Choosing dictionary is important, when going out for a penetration test. Passwords that people used depend on which country the users belong to, common names and phrases in that region, interests, range of birthday and security awareness of the users. We can execute the dictionary attack by aircrack-ng. WPACrackingDic.lst is the name of the default password file.

Aircrack-ng -w WPACrackingDic.lst WPAcracking-01.cap

In order to speed up cracking, another software uses dictionary to crack WPA and WPA2 password is Elcomsoft. Elcomsoft Wireless Security Auditor Professional (EWSA) is published by the Russian security firm Elcomsoft. The ability of this software is using the powerful graphics card parallel processing capability to crack wireless Wi-Fi network password. By offloading most runtime computation to NVIDIA/AMD GPU, overall hash cracking performance can be improved further. The cracking speed can be increased up to a hundred times compared to CPU. Fig.3 indicates that the key was successfully found.

Figure 3. Speed up Cracking WPA.

3.4 Man-in-the-Middle Attack with Rouge AP

MITM attack is one of the most damaged attacks in WLAN. There are many configurations could conducted a MITM attack. In WLAN the common method is setting up a rouge AP. Firstly, airbase-ng is used to create a soft access point. Then we create a bridge to consist the wired (eth0) and wireless (waln0) interface, and turn on IP Forwarding in the kernel. Traffic of clients will be forwarded through the attacker's host. Following command will set up a soft AP With the same name of Testing Lab. Then we send broadcast de-authentication packets. If clients miss-connect to rouge AP, we can eavesdrop on all the traffic sent to and from the clients using sniffer like Wireshark.

airbase-ng -a 3C:76:FB:5F:E3:81 --essid Testing Lab -c 1 wlan0

brctl addbr mitm-bridge

brctl addif mitm-bridge eth0

brctl addif mitm-bridge at0

ifconfig eth0 0.0.0.0 up

ifconfig at0 0.0.0.0 up

echo 1 >/proc/sys/net/ipv4/ip_forwar

The characteristics of wireless attacks are summarized. In the WEP active cracking, The ARP request is captured and replayed into the network for thousands of times. Each replayed packet gets a response from AP encrypted with WEP. And during WPA/WPA2 cracking, a mounts of de-authentication packets are not normal. An attacker implement a MITM attacker by configuring a rouge AP which is similar to legal AP, such as SSID and MAC address. To force clients to connect to rouge AP, DOS attack will be performed, and rouge AP usually providing a stronger signal than legal one. Association or authentication flooding indicates a DOS attack. We conduct security auditing based those characteristics.

4.Wireless Security Auditing Based on WAIDPS

WAIDPS is an open source wireless Swiss-knife written in Python and work on Linux environment. This is a multipurpose tools designed for audit (penetration testing) networks, detect wireless intrusion (WEP/WPA/WPS attacks).

Additional features are added to current script where previous WIDS does not have.

automatically save the attack packets into a file.

interactive mode where users are allow to perform many functions.

allow user to analyse captured packets.

load previously saved pcap file or any other pcap file to be examine.

customizing filters.

customize detection threshold (sensitivity of IDS in detection).

Fig.4 is the structure of the network in the lab. WAIDPS is installed on Host C, and Host C is the attacker, Host A is the target.

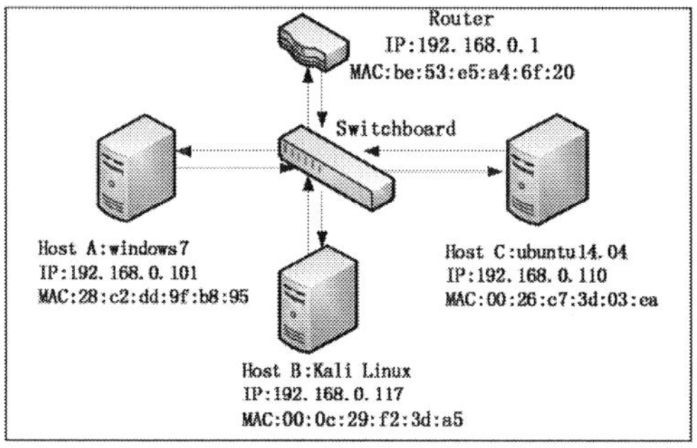

Figure 4. The Structure of the Network in the Lab.

Once wireless detect is found, WAIDPS will capture and analyze wireless packets, and detect and display suspicious data/activities, and display on screen and also log to file on the attack. Below is the alert log file during conducting the penetration testing. When we try to cracking WEP, we get an alert. In WEP cracking, the requirement is a great number of data packets, ARP Replay Requests will force the network to produce more data packets. This alert successfully detected WEP cracking attack, and actually the MAC of 00:0c:29:f2:3d:a5 is attacker's.

Possible Attack : [WEP . ARP . Replay Request] Detected !!!

:[00:0c:29:f2:3d:a5] is attacking Access Point [28:c2:dd:9f:b8:95]

When we send broadcast de-authentication packets in WPA/WPA2 cracking, DOS attack and MITM attack, the packets with frame type of de-authentication are high light show in TABLE III. And the command of deauth filter can be used to check those packets to locate attacker. De-authentication packets is used to force clients to reconnect and speed up capturing the four-way WPA handshake packets. If a mass of packets of frame type of Deauthentication is detected, it indicates that WPA/WPA2 cracking, DOS attack or MITM attack occurred. The source MAC 00:0c:29:f2:3d:a5 is attacker's.

Table3. Deauthentication Packets Captured

Rate	Source MAC	Destination MAC	LEN	Procotol	Frame Type
1 Mb/s	00:0c:29:f2:3d:a5	FF:FF:FF:FF:FF:FF	48	802.11	Deauthentication
1 Mb/s	00:0c:29:f2:3d:a5	FF:FF:FF:FF:FF:FF	48	802.11	Deauthentication

When we set up a soft AP to conduct a MITM attack, we get two alerts. Client with MAC address 00:0c:29:f2:3d:a5 is found to be both an access point and wireless client. That indicates it could be a MITM attacker. The alerts accurately allocate the MITM attacker's MAC is 00:0c:29:f2:3d:a5.

Sililar SSID Names Detected !!!

SSID Name [Testing Lab]

Sililar SSID Names Detected !!!

Dual Device Type Detected !!!

Device MAC [00:0c:29:f2:3d:a5] is found to be both an Access Point & Wireless Client.

Commercial IDS is available for 802.11 like AirDefense, Cisco, that needs not a few cost. Open source project Snort Wireless appeared to be defunct. Another WIDS Kismet involves using something like a WRT54G Linux based wireless access point. WAIDPS is an effective tool for auditing wireless networks, detecting wireless intrusion (WEP/WPA/WPS attacks). The most important is that the only hardware needed is one USB wireless adapter. It is could be a convenient and effective reference for auditing.

Conclusion

Wireless LAN is pervasive but still vulnerable. We try to minimize wireless threats through penetration testing and intrusion detection. According to the penetration testing of WLAN, it is better to avoid setting the security mode to WEP. WPA/WPA2 is reliable, but the premise is an enough complex passphrase compounding of a number of numbers, letters and symbols. In the WLAN security auditing, WAIDPS could successfully detect and alert attack behaviors and display on screen and also log to file on the attack. It is a valuable reference for practitioners to protect their WLAN. It is always a challenge to protect WLAN and ensure the security of our networks. Penetration testing and security auditing make it possible to mitigate threatening and risks for a better security situation.

References

[1] Abdallah C T, Jordan R. Wireless Communications Networking: and An Overview[J]. 2002.

[2] Sheldon F T, Weber J M, Yoo S M, et al. The insecurity of wireless networks[J]. Security & Privacy, IEEE, 2012, 10(4): 54-61.

[3] Wang L, Srinivasan B, Bhattacharjee N. Security analysis and improvements on WLANs[J]. Journal of Networks, 2011, 6(3): 470-481.

[4] Dacosta I, Chakradeo S, Ahamad M, et al. One-time cookies: Preventing session hijacking attacks with stateless authentication tokens[J]. ACM Transactions on Internet Technology (TOIT), 2012, 12(1): 1.

[5] Waliullah M, Moniruzzaman A B M, Rahman M S. An Experimental Study Analysis of Security Attacks at IEEE 802.11 Wireless Local Area Network[J]. International Journal of Future Generation Communication and Networking, 2015, 8(1): 9-18.

[6] Bernaschi M, Ferreri F, Valcamonici L. Access points vulnerabilities to DoS attacks in 802.11 networks[J]. Wireless Networks, 2008, 14(2): 159-169.

[7] Hwang H, Jung G, Sohn K, et al. A study on MITM (Man in the Middle) vulnerability in wireless network using 802.1 X and EAP[C]//Information Science and Security, 2008. ICISS. International Conference on. IEEE, 2008: 164-170.

[8] Mathews M, Hunt R. Evolution of wireless LAN security architecture to IEEE 802.11 i (WPA2)[C]//Proceedings of the fourth IASTED Asian Conference on Communication Systems and Networks. 2007.

[9] Parhi S. Attacks Due to Flaw of Protocols Used In Network Access Control (NAC), Their Solutions and Issues: A Survey[J]. International Journal of Computer Network and Information Security, 2012, 4(3): 31.

[10] Li J, Garuba M. Encryption as an Effective Tool in Reducing Wireless LAN Vulnerabilities[C]//Information Technology: New Generations, 2008. ITNG 2008. Fifth International Conference on. IEEE, 2008: 557-562.

DOI: 10.1051/itmconf/20160703002

On Strategies of Personal Information Protection in the Personalized Information Service in Big Data Times

Li-Ping ZHANG

Library of Shanghai Dianji University, Shanghai, China 201306
E-mail: zlp660112@163.com

Abstract: Obtaining personalized information service of library must inevitably involve the readers' personal information. In the Big Data times, the readers' personal information is often leaked out, which will directly influence the readers' satisfaction and trust for the personalized information service of the library. This article aims to discuss the sorts of potential security risks by using the descriptive method and the analytical method, and list the effective strategies for the defense of readers' personal information. The outcome is that only by working out effective strategies of protection can we strengthen the protection of readers' personal information, and eliminate the possible potential safety risks, and ensure the smooth development of personalized information service of the library.

1. Introduction

In Big Data times, library is facing the choice to tackle the Big Data challenge, such as the collecting, integrating and researching of the structural and nonstructural data, which is explicated and implicated in readers' behavior. Under this situation, in the process of the personalized information service of the library, the collecting, handling and sharing of the readers' data will tend to be opened and exposed to the outside world and it is obviously increasing that the readers' privacy be threatened and invaded. Thus, protecting the readers' privacy is an inevitably important project to solve in the personalized information service of the library in Big Data times. Therefore, only by working out effective strategies for protection can we strengthen the defense of readers' personal information, eliminate the possible potential safety risks, and ensure the smooth development of personalized information service of the library (PISL).

2. The meaning of the personal information in PISL

On the meaning of the personal information in PISL, it has not come to an agreement. The academia consistently holds that the personal information should have an important feature: recognition. There exists a certain objectively determined relevance between the recognized information and information subject, through which information subject can be "recognized" directly or indirectly by personal information. [1] Therefore, personal information can be regarded as a summary of all the information of the direct/ indirect identification of individual information of a natural person.

PISL refers to the individual needs based on specific readers, which is characterized by using a variety of technical means to track and analyze readers' habit of behavior and interest of using information, and it is also a kind of service that provides readers with specific informative content and systematic functions, such as the customized information service, the information push service and the reference service. In the process of PISL, to maximally meet the individual needs, the library must collect as much personal information of the readers as possible to identify personal characteristics, and infer the potential individual demand.

PISL includes the following personal information: the active information that readers provide directly, the automatic information that records readers' information behaviors and the interactive information in the process of reference services. The active information refers to the personal data and demand when they apply for PISL, among which lots of contents that can directly recognize the readers' identity and features are involved; automatic information is the personalized service system automatically captures and records all kinds of activities of personal log files every time they enter the website, apply for the service and transfer information, etc. Such personal information can be automatically preserved by the server in a long-term and successive way and it is a basis for PISL; interactive information refers to the response-answer information when readers get involved in it, and usually it is carried out in forms of using virtual chat software or e-mails to put forward the question that they want to consult and get the information of corresponding answer. Such information is usually related to the field of scientific research, and has certain creativity, advancement and potential economic value.

DOI: 10.1051/itmconf/20160703002

3. The Potential Security Risks Of Personal Information In Pisl

3.1 Security risks of personal information in Reference Service

Reference Service is a kind of academic, knowledge-based information service that the librarian of reference puts the mutual exchange of the shared information with the readers by aid of network interactive tools, which can have a discussion on a specific issue, and help readers with the answers or solutions to the problem, or making decisions. The security risks of personal information also exist in the process of reference service: (1) in *the real time reference consulting*, the virtual chat software is generally used for the text or the video communication. If the tracking device is artificially installed, then, the recorded information may be exposed to the third party without readers' awareness. Typically, the conversational record will be reserved in the system for a period of time. The longer it is kept in the system, the more dangerous it is. (2) *E-mailing reference service* involves the personal email addresses. If the consultant discloses personal e-mail address without permission, it may cause the network space of readers to be filled with a large number of spam emails or theft embezzlement. (3) *web form reference* may have readers chose whether or not to disclose personal information in the network discussing forum. If the reader lacks of the awareness of self-protection or the improper operation of the librarian, it may cause the reader's personal information to be disclosed to the public. (4) From the contents of reference, we can see that in the services of *Selective Dissemination of Information* (SDI) and *Novelty Retrieval of Sci Tech*, readers' research direction and research progress are involved. In order to ensure the originality, uniqueness and advancement of the research, readers are reluctant to disclose related information in advance. If librarian takes the information to be discussed in the public platform as common problems, it will cause certain damage to the readers, because of the lack of the protective awareness of personal information, (5) in *the reference service*, there are some items for fees and it requires readers to provide a bank account. If stolen, it may cause the readers certain economic losses.

3.2 Potential security risks in the personal information in Customized Information Service

Customized information service is a kind of service of specific systematic function, in which readers customize information resource and their service forms, in accordance with their wishes and needs. It usually includes ordering readers' interface, readers' navigation interface, readers' retrieval function, the system resources, and specific service functions, etc. Among personal information, basic personal information, the service demand and received content of customized information are included. [2]

In the service process, the main security potential risks include the following: (1) the readers' database directly gets malicious attacks and intrusion, resulting in personal information being illegally read, tampered, downloaded, and spread. (2) Because of the imperfect network technology, readers' personal information will be illegally downloaded in the automatic transmit of system and sharing with other websites.(3) As readers input user's name and password, they are tracked and stolen by illegal software, resulting in the leakage of the readers' individual information. (4) When customers are ready to utilize the customized service functions, readers' personal or customized information may be seen by others because they do not exit their personal information interface in time, or enter a search term but do not clear it in time. (5) The leak of personal information may be caused by the analysis and research from the library, such as improper storage of the information, unawareness of the importance for keeping individual information, disclosing personal information without any permission.

3.3 Security risks of the personal information in Information Push Service

Information Push Service is the informative behavior that the librarian analyzes the readers through personal log software, such as types of resources, access mode, access frequency, access length of time that readers regularly visit, the selective latest information through the matching algorithm for readers, and the regular taking the initiative to send to readers using a certain push technique and push mode.

Most of the readers' individual information and interests are involved in the personal logs, in which individual information in the process of the Information Push Service may exist some security risks: (1) because of the use of Cookie tech, many varieties of information that the readers input is allowed to be remained, and stored in a unified way in readers' PC hard drive for the next recognition of the reader, including registering information, the credit card number, etc. If the reader's computer card number is used by others, the information in the Cookie may be seen by others. This will cause the leakage of personal information. (2) If the server with the record of personal log files is illegally invaded by the third party (such as hackers), the readers' search habits, research field, demand tendency and other important information may be deduced after the received data. This will put readers' individual information to be in the risk of the infringement. (3) Without the permission of the readers, the information in readers' log is processed, transmitted, stored, computed, and reutilized by the librarian.

4. Strategy for removing the security risks

From the status quo of the present literature review, the research of the protection of personal information has

 DOI: 10.1051/itmconf/20160703002

been done separately on a single perspective, such as legal protection, industrial policy, technology innovation etc. Therefore, a systematic theory framework for guidance is needed. The author is attempting to set up a scientific system for the protection of the personal information, using the principles of the framework, to make an overall protection of personal information and to let the readers enjoy the PISL without fear.

4.1 Legal system as fundamental guarantee

4.1.1 Establishment of the right of personal information

At present, when we say "the protection of personal information", we often refer to the equivalence to the protection of the right of reputation in scope of the traditional right of privacy and personal right. However, due to the development of the times, the scope of personal information continues to expand, the contents continue to increase, and forms continue to update. Private contents have been unable to fully cover the privacy of personal information. The protection of personal information is not just the same privacy protection, which is a passive removal of the use by others, but, in most cases, it is a right for an autonomous control of information and for appropriate communication. In addition, the Right of Reputation in human right can not reflect the full respect for the personal control of the information. [3] So, each individual must be given the right to control its own information, that is, the right of personal information.

4.1.2 Speeding up the process of legislation for laws of personal information protection

The importance of the protection for personal information has been recognized by every country and many have issued special laws for the protection of personal information. At present, more than 50 countries or regions have formulated the laws for personal information protection.[4] In China, the legislation of personal information protection started late until in 2008 did the draft of *Law of Personal Information Protection* submit to the State Council, but when to put it into practice has not decided yet. Therefore, China should learn from the successful experience of the foreign relevant legislation, and speed up the formulation of *Law of Personal Information Protection* so as to protect personal information effectively from a legal point of view.

4.1.3 Speeding up the legislative process of Library Law

A sound legal protection system needs not only a unified *Law of Personal Information Protection* but some relevant laws for specific industries. Obviously, in the domain of the library, *Library Law* has to seriously take the historical responsibility to protect the readers' personal information. So, the relevant departments should speed up the legislative work of the *Library Law*, determine the rights and obligations for both library and readers in the process of PISL, restraint, limit or ban the use of information technology with a higher rational standard of value judgment, and clearly define the scope of its application and responsibility. [5]

4.2 Industrial self-discipline as a basic guarantee

4.2.1 Perfecting rules and regulations, and formulating industrial service guide

The violation of the right of readers' personal information by the library is related to the lack of perfect system and effective implementation of the industrial guide. Aiming at the problem of protecting readers' personal information, the library should formulate the specific rules and regulations to regulate the behaviors when each department of the library and the librarians deal with readers' personal information, and clearly define the responsibilities and obligations of the librarians in the aspect of protecting readers' personal information, so as to eliminate the problems of invading personal information through the internal management mechanism when the library deals with readers' information.

4.2.2 Declaration and conformation of protection statement of personal information

Because of the imperfect aspects of the laws, libraries with different systems have their own rules and regulations. This will make it difficult for readers to understand all the rules and regulations and the details for the protection of personal information in each library. If the library really wants to protect readers' personal information in the PISL and let readers have a sense of security, the declaration system of personal information protection must be established. The declaration bulletin board of personal information protection should be placed in a conspicuous place, with clear and detailed contents.

4.2.3 Improving the quality of Librarians

Now, many countries over the world have regulated the occupational moral principles of the library practitioners, which focus on the protection of the security of readers' personal information. *China's Librarians' Occupational Moral Maxims* issued in 2003 writes that the librarians should maintain the readers' rights and interests and protect readers' secrets.

In order to accomplish this mission, all kinds of libraries must take various measures to improve the quality of librarians: First, it should strengthen the education of librarians' legal sense and strengthen the study of related legal knowledge; Second, it should strengthen the construction of librarian's professional ethics, make the librarians respect the readers' personal information, and make the librarians protect personal information for readers; Third, it should strengthen the training of librarians for their information security technology, and make librarians have a good master of relevant skills for the protection of personal information; Fourth, regular evaluation takes the ability for protecting personal information as one of the evaluation contents for the librarians. Fifth, a full-time supervision post should be set up for the personal information safety. This will require that librarians grasp in time the new trend of the threat to personal information security. It should often assess the potential safety risks of PISL system and should improve the ability of individual information protection, using various technical means.

4.3 The self-protection as the inner motivation

The national legislation and the industrial self-discipline are a public protection device or a system to protect readers' personal information with the aid of outside forces. The readers' own protective consciousness cannot be ignored. As what Charles Fried pointed out, the protection of personal information does not seem to be limited to not let others get our personal information, but should be extended to that we ourselves control the use and flow of personal information.[6]

Librarians also put forward certain demands to readers on their information quality, which is usually stressed in the PISL statement that if because of the readers' own reasons for the leakage of personal information, resulting in personal loss, the library will not bear the legal responsibility. This requires that the readers must have the ability of self-protection. The improvement of the competence of readers' self-protection can be carried out from the following three aspects: (1) to enhance readers' awareness of self-protection through the education and the study of relevant laws and regulations; (2) to improve self-protection skills, and to build up a Trinity---an overall system of self-protection, which includes self-control, self-selection, and self-defense;[7] (3) the library should take the task to educate readers' ability of self-protection, and it will be incorporated into the readers' education content.

4.4 Safety Technology as the main tool

4.4.1 Maintaining the security of internet environment

Network moral loss and the temptation of economic interests can make some companies or some bad behaviorists stall a certain specific network program to technologically "stalk" in the library's website in order to copy, record the readers' personal data. Therefore, we must use a variety of new and high technology of network security measures to prevent the personal information security risks because of loopholes or defect in the system.

4.4.2 Developing simple and easy-to-operate technology for the protection of the personal information protection

Library readers are from all walks of life, with different ages, different educational levels. It is obviously too harsh to ask every reader to skillfully master the computer tech and it is also not realistic. So, our country should support and encourage the information tech industries to develop some simple and easy-to-operate soft ware for protection, which may allow readers to self-protect their own personal information by using this software technology.

4.4.3 Different technology projects of personal information protection for readers

Because every reader has different degrees of sensitivity to the personal information, the degree of the selection of service protection and the degree for their personalized information service are different. Therefore, the appropriate protective scheme for personal information should be well dynamically formulated for each reader. Because no unified policies and regulations for information protection is to be promulgated, P3P platform can be used to help readers identify the policy and regulation items for personal information protection to let the readers make the decision automatically or semi-automatically whether or not to accept them.[8]

5. Conclusion

At present, one of the main causes of the less quality of PISL is that the users have their worries in the use of PISL, that is, they are not willing to fill out in details or truthfully their personal information, and thus it will cause the deviation to the analysis of users' needs. Therefore, only dramatic protective strategies are worked out can the protection of readers' personal information be strengthened, and can the hidden safety risks be eliminated, can we have the chance to ensure the smooth development of PISL.

References

1. LIU Qing, Yuan-yuan, HUANG. 2007. Effects and Solutions of the *Law of Personal Information Protection* to Information Service of Library [J]. Journal of Academic Libraries. (3): 86-92.
2. Jing-cheng LI, Chang-ping WENG. 2012. On the protection of users' privacy in the personalized information service of the library [J]. Journal of Academic Library and Information Science, (3):67-70.
3. Li-ming WANG. 2012. Individual Information Right: an Independent Right [N]. Beijing Daily, July 9, 18.
4. XIE Jun. 2011. Obligations of Personal Information Protection and Completion of Legislation of the Library [J]. Library Construction, (8): 1-5.
5. Song-lin JIA. 2010. Comparison and Consideration

DOI: 10.1051/itmconf/20160703002

on the Privacy Protection Policy of Library in China and in Foreign Countries [J]. Library Tribune, (3): 156-158.
6. Shoeman, F. D. 1984. Philosophical Dimensions of Privacy: An Anthology [M]. New York: Cambridge University Press.
7. Faison, D. 2000. Privacy in the Internet Age [J]. Commercial Law Bulletin, (6): 8-12.
8. LIU Ying. 2007. on Personal Privacy Protection in the Personalized Information Service [J]. Information Science, (12): 1794 -1798.

Staticly Detect Stack Overflow Vulnerabilities with Taint Analysis

Zhang XING[1] , Zhang BIN[1] ,Feng CHAO[1] and Zhang QUAN[1]

[1]*School of Electronic Science and Engineering , National University of Defense Technology, ChangSha, China*

Abstract. Nowadays binary static analysis uses dangerous system library function to detect stack overflow vulnerary in program and there is no effective way to dig out the function which can cause stack overflow issue. List necessarily characteristics of the function which may cause stack overflow vulnerary and define stack overflow dangerous function(SODF). Then introduce static taint analysis to detect SODF include taint introduction, taint propagation and taint checking stragety. Next describe the particular process of detecting SODF in the program with static taint analysis. Finally choose 4 runtime library and 2 binary software, and detect whether the chosen software has SODF and locate the name of SODF with static taint analysis. Testing result shows that the algorithm can detect and locate plenty of SODF in test program which means the algorithm can work efficiently.

1 Introduction

Stack overflow is a well-known security issue, which can be used to execute unauthorized instructions and illegal operations. The study of stack overflow vulnerability detection is of great significance.

Current method of detecting stack overflow vulnerabilities can be divided into dynamic and static analysis. Dynamic analysis, mainly through checking data-integrity of an array of borders and return pointer, whose typical tools include StackGuard [1] and RAD [2]. Overall, stack overflow is often detected when the stack has been crashed.

Source code analysis and binary analysis provide effective performance in static analysis. Source code analysis detects possible vulnerabilities by comparison with known vulnerabilities after lexical analysis. Wherein, Flawfinder[3] and RATS[4] are typical analysis tools. Binary analysis aims at checking if there is boundary detection when calling library functions to determine whether exists stack overflow vulnerability.

Static analysis can efficiently locate the stack overflow vulnerability. And dynamic analysis can be more effective with the prior knowledge provided by the static analysis. However, it is very difficult to access most of the program's source code. And there is no good way to locate the function which has stack overflow risk and defined by the program itself.

Most static method to detect binary software's stack overflow vulnerability is based on analyzing known vulnerable library functions. However many programs have stack overflow vulnerability because of bad boundary condition of self-defined function. IKEView.exe has stack overflow vulnerability because of a self-define function with R60 version.

In this paper, we establish a model for stack overflow dangerous function, and propose an algorithm to detect stack overflow vulnerabilities. We have implemented our method and applied it to test several binary software. The results show that static taint analysis can achieve higher accuracy.

2 Basic Definitions

Despite the formats of executable files on different operation system are different, but the basic formulation methods are consistent.

Executable file contains import and export tables, global variables and functions. Function consists of basic blocks, which are made up of basic instructions. Here we give out some basic definitions in binary software.

2.1 Some Definitions

Instruction: Instruction is instructing a computer to perform a certain operation command, abbreviate as I , and it is the smallest unit of computer-implemented. It consists of a string of binary number, usually including opcode and operands. Opcodes represents the operation which the instruction is going to operate. Operands represent particular data which is operated by the instruction.

DOI: 10.1051/itmconf/20160703003

Basic Block: Basic Block is an execution sequence of instructions, abbreviate as *B* ,which has only one entrance and one exit. The entrance is the first instruction of the basic block while the exit is the last. Therefore, as long as the first instruction is executed in time, then all other instructions within a basic block will be executed once the order.

Basic Block Set: Basic Block Set is composed of several basic blocks that can access to each other, abbreviate as *BB* .

Function: Function is a basic unit of an executable module, and a combination of basic blocks that accomplish a specific function together, abbreviate as F.

2.2 Intermediate Languages

It is very difficult to analysis disassembled assembly code directly due to the wide range of assembly instructions. Normally we lift the disassembled assembly code into intermediate language.

Intermediate language abstracts form native assembly code and therefore makes it easier to develop analysis tools and algorithms.

In this paper, we use the REIL(Reverse Engineering Intermediate Language), a platform-independent intermediate language to represent disassembled assembly code.

3 Stack Overflow Dangerous Function Model

So far, most static code analysis methods decide whether a program has stack overflow vulnerability by looking for known dangerous functions such as *strcpy* and *memcpy*. However, the source of stack overflow is not the function name itself, but their approach to the data. For example, the dangerous function copies the source data into the destination buffer without correctly checking the size of the destination buffer.

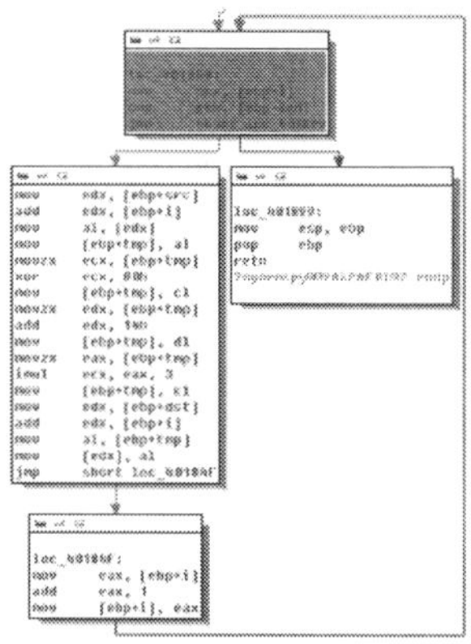

Figure 1 The Disassembly Code of the Function

Parameter *src* is the address of source buffer and parameter *dst* is the address of destination buffer of the function. And data transfer from the source buffer to the destination buffer through local variable *tmp* in the loop. The loop control variable *i* is independent on the destination buffer. So *mymemcpy* function is a SODF. The function is an unknown SODF, and many static analysis methods often ignore it.

3.1. Characteristic of SODF

Always, data transfer between source buffer and destination buffer in a loop, and the control condition of the loop depends on the source buffer. There are many self-defined functions that have the above characteristics, and they are likely to become internal factors for stack overflow.

Through the analysis of a large number of stack overflow vulnerabilities, we summarize the characteristics of Stack Overflow Dangerous Function as follow:

(1) Contains a loop

(2) Data transfer from the source buffer to the destination buffer in the loop

(3) The source buffer address is the parameter of the function

(4) The destination buffer is the parameter or a local variable of the function

(5) The loop control variable is not dependent on the destination buffer..

Next, we propose our static taint analysis method to locate that kind of function.

4 Detecting Stack Overflow Dangerous Function with Static Taint Analysis

4.1. Over View

In this section, we leverage static taint analysis to locate stack overflow dangerous function (SODF). And introduce an algorithm based on static taint analysis to analyze program.

The algorithm is divided into two phases: cyclic basic block set's filter and static taint analysis. The cyclic basic block set's filter (step one to step three) aims at locating the possible dangerous function address. Static taint analysis (step four to step five) checks whether data transfers from buffer to buffer in the loop and determines whether the function is a dangerous one.

General idea of the algorithm is as follows:

Step one, get the function fwith_args which introduces the parameter in the program.

Step two, locate loop basic block set BBwith_cycle which contains cycle relationship in fwith_args.

Step three, remove the jump instruction Jcc in every BBwith_cycle and form new basic block Bneed_analysis.

Step four, introduce taint for each basic block Bneed_analysis. If the basic block invokes the parameter of the function, then we mark the parameter as taint and on to the next step.

Step five, we translate the $B_{need\_analysis}$ into intermediate language basic block and start the taint propagation. If the destination buffer is tainted, then we can say the function is a stack overflow dangerous function.

4.2. Suspicious Basic Block

Suspicious basic block is a basic block set. It is a set of all possible basic blocks between loop start and loop end in the loop basic block set. We set the begin of a loop basic block set is the lowest address of the set and the end of a loop basic block set is the highest address of the set.

We adopt a conservative analysis strategy in static taint analysis. So we analysis all possible paths from loop starts to loop ends, and can effectively improve the accuracy of the algorithm through this method.

The mymemcpy function corresponding to that shown in Figure 1, its Suspicious BB is {0x401858, 0x401860, 0x40184F}.

4.3. Static Taint Analysis

4.3.1 Static Taint State

Static taint analysis does not real execute target program, there is no runtime information. We propose static taint state to introduce taint and taint propagation.

Every operand has two static taint state, the operand state $T: t \rightarrow Bool$ and memory state $M: t \rightarrow Bool$. State T and state M each has two states : tainted state and untainted state.

Before the propagation starts, all operands' static taint state are set to untainted.

4.3.2 Taint Analysis Strategy

Taint analysis strategy includes taint introduction, taint propagation and taint checking. It mainly checks whether to-be-analysis-basic-block-set transfers parameter of the function as the source buffer to destination buffer.

(1) Taint Introduction

Taint introduction here mainly concerns about the parameters of the function. According to the stack structure, parameters of the function get indexed by EBP/RBP register. When instruction introduce the parameter in the memory, then we mark the operand of the instruction as taint source, and set the operand state and memory state tainted.

(2) Taint Propagation

$T[t]$ indicates that intermediate instruction's operand t 's taint state. $M[t]$ indicates that intermediate the memory's taint state pointed to instruction's operand t . $a \mapsto$ indicates that operand a 's taint state updates for operand b 's taint state. $TM[a \mapsto$ indicates that operand a 's operand and memory state updates for operand b 's operand and memory state.

To express taint propagation process, Table 1 shows the intermediate instructions' operational semantics, where P_{xxx} represents the taint propagation strategy. And taint propagation strategy is shown in Table 2.

Table 1 Taint Operation Semantics

Instruction	Taint operation semantics
ADD t1,t2,y	$TM[y \mapsto \quad],T[t_2])]$
$SUB\,t_1,t_2,y$	$TM[y \mapsto \quad t_1],T[t_2])]$
$MUL\,t_1,t_2,y$	$TM[y \mapsto \quad],T[t_2])]$
$DIV\,t_1,t_2,y$	$TM[y \mapsto \quad],T[t_2])]$
$MOD\,t_1,t_2,y$	$TM[y \mapsto \quad],T[t_2])]$
$SHL\,t_1,t_2,y$	$TM[y \mapsto \quad],T[t_2])]$
$AND\,t_1,t_2,y$	$TM[y \mapsto \quad],T[t_2])]$
$OR\,t_1,t_2,y$	$TM[y \mapsto \quad],T[t_2])]$
$XOR\,t_1,t_2,y$	$TM[y \mapsto \quad t_1],T[t_2])]$
$LDM\,t_1,e,y$	$T[y \mapsto \quad [t_1])]$
$STR\,t_1,e,y$	$TM[y \mapsto \quad t_1])]$
$BISZ\,t_1,e,y$	Undefined
$JCC\,t_1,e,y$	Undefined
$UNDEF\,e,e,e$	Undefined
$NOP\,e,e,e$	Undefined
$UNKN\,e,e,e$	Undefined

Table 2 Taint Propagation Strategy

Propagation Strategy	Detail
$P_{or}(T[t1],T[t2])$	Returns tainted state if t_1 or t_2 is tainted.

DOI: 10.1051/itmconf/20160703003

$P_{xor}(T[t1],T[t2])$	Returns untainted state if t_1 and t_2 are the same, otherwise strategy is same as $P_{or}(T[t_1],T[t_2])$.
$P_{m2r}(M[t1])$	Returns t_1's memory taint state, and the destination operand must be operand taint state.
$P_{r2r}(T[t1])$	Returns t_1's operand taint state, and the destination operand must be operand taint state.

(3) Taint Checking Strategy

When instruction *STM* is executed, taint checking begins. Algorithm checks source operand's operand state and memory state. The function is stack overflow dangerous function if the operand's memory state is tainted.

The loop basic block set is extracted from the program in section III. Then it transformed to *Suspicious BB*. And the *Suspicious BB* is translated to the REIL basic block. The specific static taint analysis progress with the REIL basic block is shown below.

We can know from the Code II that the REIL basic block read data from memory pointed by parameter of function, and transfer the data to destination buffer. Thus, *mymemory* is an SODF.

The algorithm adopts conservative strategy, so it will costs a lot of time to analyze functions which has high cyclomatic complexity. State explosion problem will happen when cyclomatic complexity is higher than 50. We ignore those functions when practical analyzing program.

5 Testing

5.1. Experiment Design

This chapter chooses 4 runtime libraries and 2 software, which is shown in **Table** 3. And the detection of SODF is a new technique nowadays ,so no comparison with other techniques.

Static taint analysis algorithm is based on plugin of IDA pro. The plugin runs on Windows 7 SP1 x32 system, processor is i5 2510m@2.5GHz, and memory is 3GB.

Table 3 Specific Information of Library and Software

Name	Version	description
npFoxitReaderPlugin.dll	2.2.5.107	A dll of foxit reader,it is used to load plugin
Wpsio.dll	9.1.0.5041	A dll of WPS,it is used to process vsd/vsdx file
ffmpeg.dll	3.11.4.16	A dll which is used to handling multimedia data, and it is widely used
msvcrt.dll	16385	The Microsoft Visual C Run-Time Library for Visual C++ version 4.2 to 6.0
VulnApp.exe	-	A program which contains a self-defined stack overflow dangerous function
IKEView.exe	R60	A program which can

		diagnosis VPN's fault

5.2. Result

The result of the algorithm is shown in **Table** 4. Nk represents the known number of stack overflow dangerous function[NVD, CVE]. Nr represents the real number of stack overflow dangerous function. Ni represents the number of functions that algorithm ignore to analysis due to high cyclomatic complexity. Nc represents the number of repetitions that known SODF and detected SODF. Time represents the time that the algorithm performs one time costs.

Table 4 Analysis Result

Target Program	Nk	Nr	Ni	Nc	Time (min)
npFoxitReaderPlugin.dll	0	18	14	0	26
Wpsio.dll	0	23	5	0	35
ffmpeg.dll	0	20	71	0	87
msvcrt.dll	14	24	56	14	125
VulnApp	1	2	0	1	2
IKEView.exe	1	2	1	1	13

Figure 2 shows that the SODF that the algorithm detected. We can see that data stored in the address that pointed by arg_0 transfers to the address pointed by arg_4 in the cycle structure. And loop variable arg_8 is independent with destination buffer. So we can say the function is a SODF. And in practical the function is the cause of stack overflow vulnerability in IKEView.exe.

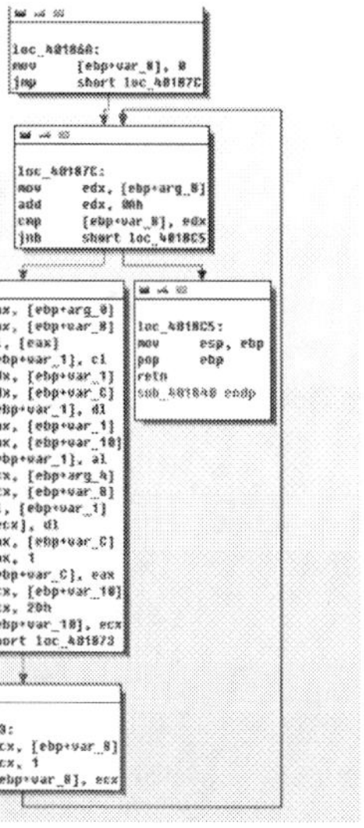

Figure 3 Disassembly Code in Ikeview.Exe

It will take quite long time to analysis the function that has high cyclomatic complexity, so the algorithm ignore those functions. However, the static taint analysis algorithm can accurately locate the SODF as shown in the result.

DOI: 10.1051/itmconf/20160703003

6. Conclusions

We proposed static taint analysis algorithm based on stack overflow vulnerabilities' behavior. Experimental result shows that algorithm can effectively locate self-defined SODF in program. However, algorithm will cost lots of time when analyzing functions with high cyclomatic complexity. Next, we will continue optimize the efficiency of the algorithm. Further static taint analysis algorithm can be used on other vulnerabilities' pattern.
The algorithm can be combined with dynamic analysis. By providing a possible position of SODF, making dynamic analysis more effectively to monitoring program.

References

1. Cowan C, Pu C, Maier D, et al. StackGuard: Automatic Adaptive Detection and Prevention of Buffer-Overflow Attacks[C]//Usenix Security. 1998, 98: 63-78.
2. Tzi-Cker Chiueh,Fu-Hau Hsu.RAD:a complie-time solution to buffer overflow attacks.Distributed Computing Systems,2001.21st International Conference on 08-12Jan.2006,pages 1-7
3. Ferschke O, Gurevych I, Rittberger M. FlawFinder: A Modular System for Predicting Quality Flaws in Wikipedia[C]//CLEF (Online Working Notes/Labs/Workshop). 2012.pages 1-10.
4. RATS. http://www.forifysoftware.com/security-resources/rats.jsp.
5. Lattner C,et al. The LLVM compiler infrastructure [J].The LLVM compiler infrastructure 2010.pages 1-8.
6. Nethercote N,Seward J.Valgrind: a framework for heavyweight dynamic binary instrumentation [C].In ACM Sigplan Notices.2007:89-100.
7. Song D,Brumley D,Yin H,et al. BitBlaze:A new approach to computer security via binary analysis[M].Information systems security.Spring,2008:2008:1-25.pages 2-5.
8. Brumley D,Jager I,Avgerinos T,et al.BAP:A binary analysis platform[C].In Computer Aided Verification.2011:463-469
9. Lattner C, Adve V. LLVM: A compilation framework for lifelong program analysis & transformation[C]//Code Generation and Optimization, 2004. CGO 2004. International Symposium on. IEEE, 2004: 75-86.
10. Dullien T, Porst S. REIL: A platform-independent intermediate representation of disassembled code for static code analysis[J]. Proceeding of CanSecWest, 2009.

ITM Web of Conferences 7, 03004 (2016) DOI: 10.1051/itmconf/20160703004
ITA 2016

Memory Vulnerability Diagnosis for Binary Program

Feng-Yi TANG, Chao FENG and Chao-Jing TANG

College of Electronic Science and Engineering, National University of Defense Technology, Changsha, China

Abstract. Vulnerability diagnosis is important for program security analysis. It is a further step to understand the vulnerability after it is detected, as well as a preparatory step for vulnerability repair or exploitation. This paper mainly analyses the inner theories of major memory vulnerabilities and the threats of them. And then suggests some methods to diagnose several types of memory vulnerabilities for the binary programs, which is a difficult task due to the lack of source code. The diagnosis methods target at buffer overflow, use after free (UAF) and format string vulnerabilities. We carried out some tests on the Linux platform to validate the effectiveness of the diagnosis methods. It is proved that the methods can judge the type of the vulnerability given a binary program.

1 Introduction

Memory vulnerabilities are difficult to detect and diagnose especially for those do not crash the program. Due to its importance, vulnerability diagnosis problem has been intensively studied. Researchers have proposed different techniques to diagnose memory vulnerabilities.

Jun Xu proposed a technique that uses the crash as a trigger to initiate an automatic diagnosis algorithm[1]. Moreover, the diagnosis process also generates a signature of the attack using data/address values embedded in the malicious input message, and is used to block future attacks. However, this technique needs an input that can trigger the program to crash and the validity of the generated signature cannot be verified.

Jiang Zheng combined both of the dynamic analysis techniques and static analysis techniques to solve automatic buffer overflow vulnerability diagnosis (BOVD) problem for commodity software[2]. However, the solution only targets at buffer overflow vulnerability and needs an effective exploit as input to finish the diagnosis process.

In this paper, we mainly focus on the memory vulnerabilities that might not lead to program corruption. Because of lack of source code, vulnerability analysis for binary programs have been a puzzle and the most popular solution may be fuzz test. But it is fair well known that the reported bugs are not always vulnerabilities. Therefore our work of vulnerability diagnosis is valuable for vulnerability fixing or exploitation and deserves attention.

2 Buffer Overflow Vulnerability Diagnosis

Buffer overflow vulnerabilities include heap overflow and stack overflow. Their theories are similar but the diagnosis methods to them are quite different.

2.1 Heap Overflow Diagnosis

A heap overflow condition is a buffer overflow, where the buffer that can be overwritten is allocated in the heap portion of memory, generally meaning that the buffer was allocated using a routine such as the malloc() call[3].

Heap overflows are usually just as dangerous as stack overflows. Besides important user data, heap overflows can be used to overwrite function pointers that may be living in memory, pointing it to the attacker's code.

It is comparatively easy to detect an overflow in the heap at runtime. When allocate an area in the heap, generally the memory allocator sets headers before or after (or both) the memory area. These headers can contain some information like size, used or not, and etc.

Therefore, we can monitor the allocator so as to determine the base address and the size of the allocation areas. Then, check all STORE and LOAD accesses in memory to see which one is outside the allocated area.

In the diagnosis process, we supervise all calls to the malloc function and save the base address and the size of our buffer in a std::list. Then, when a STORE or LOAD occurs, we just need to check if the destination address is in our list. If it is outside our area, there probably is heap overflow.

2.2 Stack Overflow Diagnosis

A stack overflow condition is another buffer overflow condition, where the buffer being overwritten is allocated on the stack (i.e., is a local variable or, rarely, a parameter to a function) [4].

It is much more complicated to diagnose stack overflow than heap overflow though their theories are nearly the same. First, we should be aware that there are not one but several variables in the same stack frame. The main problem is to detect the overflow between these variables, which will probably not crash the program, that's why it's possible to miss this type of vulnerabilities without a binary analysis. So, it is quite difficult to detect the overflow between the variables at runtime without changing the code execution

There are four main steps to diagnose the stack overflow vulnerability: First, isolate the functions. Then, determine how many variables are instantiated in the stack frame. We use a std::list of stack frame which contains a unique ID and another std::list which contains all variables instantiated in this stack frame. Next, detect the loops which contain a STORE instruction to our stack frame. Generally a loop ends with a conditional jump. Finally, analyze this STORE to detect a potential overflow. If a STORE instruction occurs, we check where the value is stored. If the value destination is in our stack frame, we monitor that for each STORE the value is stored in the same area.

3 UAF Vulnerability Diagnosis

Use after free errors occur when a program continues to use a pointer after it has been freed [5]. Like double free errors and memory leaks, use after free errors have two common and sometimes overlapping causes:

- Error conditions and other exceptional circumstances;
- Confusion over which part of the program is responsible for freeing the memory.

The use of previously freed memory can have any number of adverse consequences - ranging from the corruption of valid data to the execution of arbitrary code, depending on the instantiation and timing of the flaw. The use of previously freed memory can result in a write-what-where or buffer overflow (especially heap overflow) in several ways.

Use after free errors sometimes have no effect and other times cause a program to crash. While it is technically feasible for the freed memory to be re-allocated and for an attacker to use this reallocation to launch a buffer overflow attack, we are unaware of any exploits based on this type of attack.

In order to diagnose the UAF vulnerability, we maintain a free table (TF) and an allocation table (TA) which represent the states of pointers allocated or freed during the execution. When a LOAD or STORE instruction occurs, the tool checks if the memory access is referenced into TA or TF. If the memory access is in TF, then we regard it as a use after free vulnerability and may lead to memory leak.

4 Format String Vulnerability Diagnosis

The Format Function is an ANSI C conversion function, like printf, fprintf, which converts a primitive variable of the programming language into a human-readable string representation. The Format String is the argument of the Format Function and is an ASCII Z string which contains text and format parameters, like: printf ("The magic number is: %d\n", 1911). The Format String Parameter, like %x %s defines the type of conversion of the format function.

The Format String exploit occurs when the submitted data of an input string is evaluated as a command by the application. The attack could be executed when the application doesn't properly validate the submitted input. In this case, if a Format String parameter, like %x, is inserted into the posted data, the string is parsed by the Format Function, and the conversion specified in the parameters is executed. However, the Format Function is expecting more arguments as input, and if these arguments are not supplied, the function could read or write the stack.

In this way, the attacker could execute code, read the stack, or cause a segmentation fault in the running application, causing new behaviours that could compromise the security or the stability of the system[6].

We apply dynamic taint analysis to help diagnose the format string vulnerability. First, taint all arguments (*argv[]). And then check when a printf occurs if there are some tainted bytes in its first argument (generally stored in RDI register in x86_64). If RDI points on a memory area which contains tainted bytes, that means there is a potential vulnerability.

5 Experiment Results

Our memory vulnerability diagnosis tools for binary programs are built on Pin. Pin is a dynamic binary instrumentation framework for the IA-32 and x86-64 instruction-set architectures that enables the creation of dynamic program analysis tools. These tools called Pintools, can be used to perform program analysis on user space applications in Linux and Windows. We carried out the experiments on Ubuntu 12.04 64bits. As a dynamic binary instrumentation tool, instrumentation is performed at run time on the compiled binary files. Thus, it requires no recompiling of source code and can support instrumenting programs that dynamically generate code.

5.1. UAF Diagnosis Result

UAF vulnerability tends to lead to memory leak. As is described in Figure 1, we record the states of pointers allocated or freed during the execution to maintain a free table (TF) and an allocation table (TA). When a LOAD or STORE instruction occurs, the tool checks if the memory access is referenced into TA or TF. If the memory access is in TF, TF <- (0x19c2010, 0x20), then we regard it as a use after free vulnerability. And we check the free table, found that (0x19c2040, 0x20) would lead to 32 bytes memory leak.

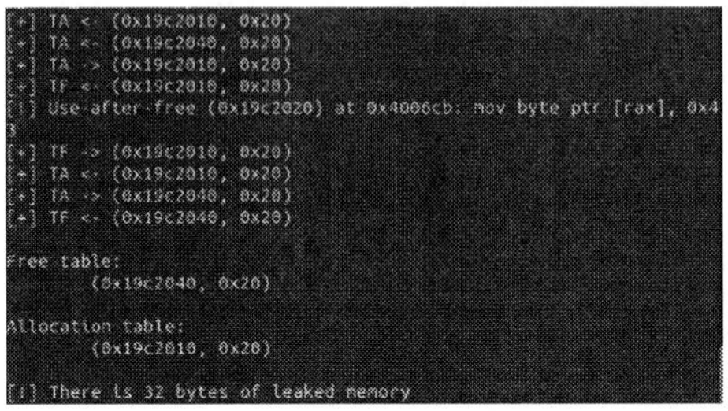

Figure 1. UAF Diagnosis Result.

5.2 Format String Diagnosis Result

As you can see in Figure 2, we first taint all arguments (*argv[]). And then check when a printf occurs if there are some tainted bytes in its first argument stored in RDI. If RDI points on a memory area which contains tainted bytes, that means there is a potential vulnerability. We can trace the execution related to the tainted data thanks to dynamic taint analysis.

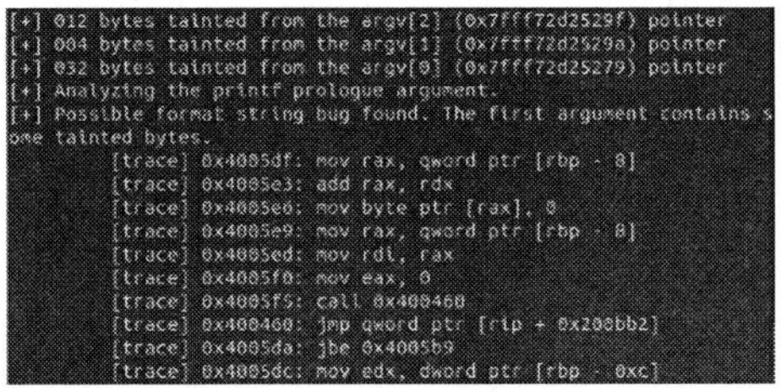

Figure 2. Format String Diagnosis Result.

5.3 Buffer Overflow Diagnosis Results

As is depicted in Figure 3, we supervise all calls to the malloc function and save the base address and the size of our buffer in a std::list. Then, when a STORE or LOAD occurs, we just need to check if the destination address is in our list. If it is outside our area, there probably is heap overflow.

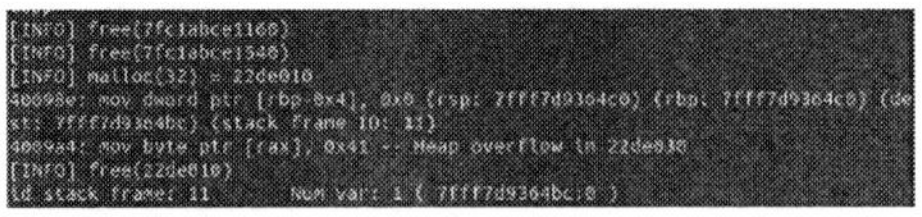

Figure 3. Heap Overflow Diagnosis Result.

As is shown in Figure 4, we use a std::list of stack frame which contains a unique ID and another std::list which contains all variables instantiated in this stack frame. And analyze this STORE to detect a potential overflow. If a STORE instruction occurs, we check where the value is stored. If the value destination is in our stack frame, we monitor that for each STORE the value is stored in the same area. When the continuous write operation counts to 4, then we regard it as 4 bytes overflow.

DOI: 10.1051/itmconf/20160703004

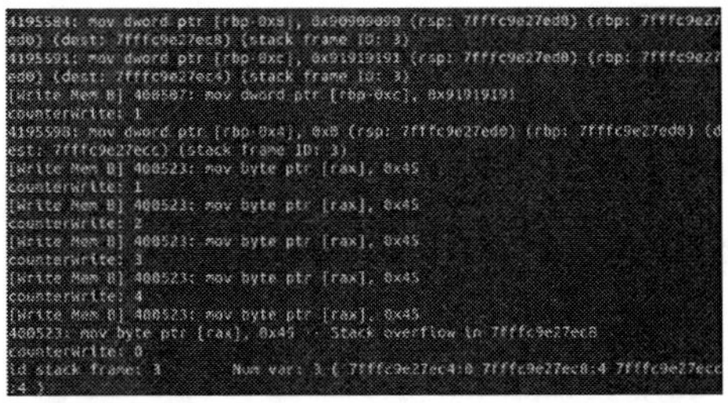

Figure 4. Stack Overflow Diagnosis Result.

6 Conclusion

This paper mainly analyses the inner theories of major memory vulnerabilities and the threats of them. And then suggests some methods to diagnose the several types of memory vulnerabilities for the binary programs, which is a difficult task due to the lack of source code. The diagnosis methods target at buffer overflow, use after free (UAF) and format string vulnerabilities. We carried out some tests on the Linux platform to validate the effectiveness of the diagnosis methods. It is proved that the methods can judge the type of the vulnerability given a binary program.

References

1. J. Xu, P. Ning, C. Kil, Y. Zhai, and C. Bookholt, "Automatic Diagnosis and Response to Memory Corruption Vulnerabilities," 2005.
2. "BUFFER OVERFLOW VULNERABILITY by Jiang Zheng M . S ., Northeastern University , Boston , USA , 2001 Submitted to the Graduate Faculty of the Department of Computer Science in partial fulfillment of the requirements for the degree of Doctor of Philosophy U," 2008.
3. https://www.owasp.org/index.php/Heap_overflow
4. https://www.owasp.org/index.php/Stack_overflow
5. https://www.owasp.org/index.php/Using_freed_memory
6. https://www.owasp.org/index.php/Format_string_attack
7. M. Zhang, A. Prakash, X. Li, Z. Liang, and H. Yin, "Identifying and Analyzing Pointer Misuses for Sophisticated Memory-corruption Exploit Diagnosis."
8. M. Zhang, A. Prakash, X. Li, Z. Liang, and H. Yin, "Identifying and Analyzing Pointer Misuses for Sophisticated Memory-corruption Exploit Diagnosis."
9. G. Chen, H. Jin, D. Zou, B. B. Zhou, Z. Liang, W. Zheng, and X. Shi, "SafeStack: Automatically Patching Stack-based Buffer Overflow Vulnerabilities," pp. 1–14, 2013.
10. D. Brumley, J. Newsome, D. Song, H. Wang, and S. Jha, "Towards Automatic Generation of Vulnerability-Based Signatures."
11. http://triton.quarkslab.com

ITM Web of Conferences 7, 03005 (2016)
ITA 2016
DOI: 10.1051/itmconf/20160703005

Design on Security Alarming System of Vehicle terminal equipment

Tong-Liang FAN [1,a], Wen Ye[1]

[1]*Department of Electronic Technology, China Maritime Police Academy, Ningbo 315801, China*
[a] *Corresponding author:libufan432@163.com*

Abstract. With the application and extension of the technology of networked vehicles, its security has already become a research focus in recent years. However, the security risk of the vehicle terminal is rarely considered. In this paper, we designed a security alarming system of vehicle terminal equipment. In this system, a variety of sensors are chosen to collect information. The network transmission module TC35i is used to sent a short message to the owner, so as to achieve the monitoring of vehicle security. This system is not only simple in structure, but also easy to adjust and use.

1 Introduction

With the popularity of vehicles and the development of mobile ad hoc network, The Vehicular Ad Hoc Networks which is regarded as one important realization approach of internet of vehicles has attracted great development. A vehicle in VANET is mainly considered as a node to form an inter-vehicle communication network. Usually, dynamic vehicular mobile communication systems include inner-vehicle communication systems, such as Vehicle to Sensor, and communication with other entities, such Vehicle to Infrastructure, Vehicle to Human and Vehicle to Internet [1-3]. Recently, The IoV will play an important role in the clean traffic environment, with increasing number of system technologies and system intelligence designs. What's more, security has already become a research focus in recent years [4].The primary goal for the internet of vehicles is to ensure that the sensor node for collecting traffic information can provide perceives data accurately, and timely. In order to guarantee the authenticity and reliability of the result in data fusion [5, 6], which described the involved technologies of vehicle Internet information terminal such as on-board diagnosis (OBD), GPRS communication, GPS positioning and speech synthesis.

The development and application of vehicular network is an important technical means of intelligent transportation system. The existing active safety equipment is developed independently by manufactures. However, the vehicle terminal security issues are often neglected. For example, the children was left in the can, and lead to death. In aspect of vehicle safety, we have desired a safety hazard reminder of vehicle terminal based on STC12 microcontroller, and TC35i as the network transmission module, OBD- II as the vehicle state monitoring module. In addition, it adopts multiple sensors to monitor the security of vehicles, and the RFID module to realize intelligent interaction, which achieves the remote constant supervision inside the vehicles. The result of the system test has mainly met the command of the design and gives alarms to the hazard.

2 System Composition and Function

2.1 System structure

The system mainly consists the acquistion terminal and control terminal. The system structure is illustrated in figure1. The system adoption mold piece turns a design, each function designs into an independent mold piece.

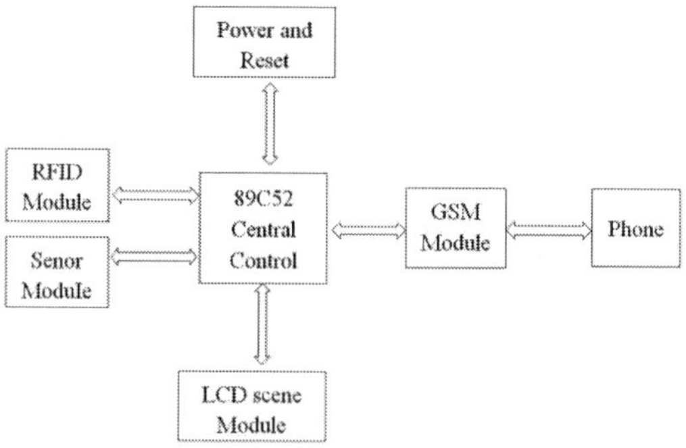

Figure 1. System Architecture

The circuit of system is shown figure 2. The hardware design of nodes needs to ensure the

DOI: 10.1051/itmconf/20160703005

following aspects: low consumption of power, good performance of the radio frequency, miniaturization, low cost, compatibility, etc. The main control module uses 89C52 single chip, which control the operation of system. The wireless communication module use TC35i, which sent a short message to the owner. The module of OBD- Ⅱ is used to examination the vehicle driving situation. The HC-SR501 is an auto control module based on infrared technology. Temperature/humidity sensor takes DHT11 digital temperature/humidity sensor, whose digital signal output has been calibrated. The product is of high reliability and excellent long-term stability. Gas leakage alarm MQ-2 is highly sensitive to liquid gas, propane and hydrogen. The RFID module is used to find vehicles.

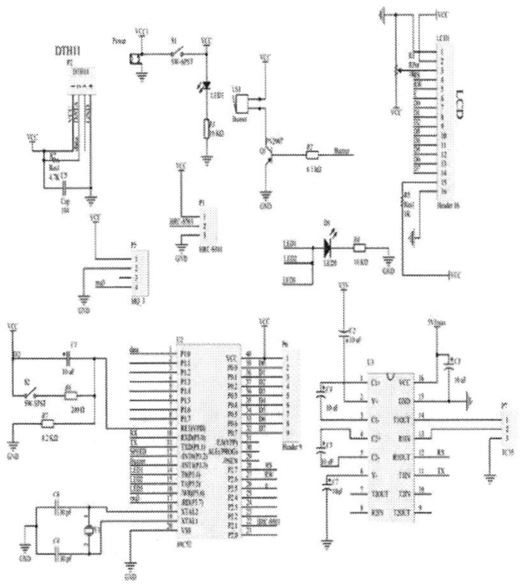

Figure 2. The Circuit of System Hardware

2.2 The system function

The main function is automatically vehicle safety alarm. Use OBD- Ⅱ the condition of mold piece monitor vehicle, and analyze it to circulate present condition and safe circumstance inside the car. When the vehicle is placed in to launch status, the system use alcohol sensor and combustible air sensor to collect a dangerous air information, when explore dangerous air send out an alert and send out a message to the cellular phone, remind that the driver drives after drinking. Judge if there are other combustible gas or not, for example the perfume vaporizes gas, prevent from the occurrence of a fire. When the vehicle motor closes for more than five minutes, moving temperature and humidity sensor and infrared sensor collect an information, whether the examination environment inside the car is comfortable, in order to prevent occurrence someone suffocated while going to bed in the car. Judge inside the car if someone for example leaves behind a child, and sends out a different hint information according to the enactment condition. This system can also sent out a message to open an air condition or seeks the car function like this in the so big parking lot. Mainly make use of a RFID module, when the car owner walks to vehicle side, briefing on device can respond a car owner according to the ID information and automatically open a car door.

3 The System Hardware Design

The whole systemis composed of the following.

3.1 Control module

The micro controller 89c52 as the central device and “heart” of the whole system, receives the alarm signal, controls and coordinates the proper functioning of functional modules. The machine is more opposite than general of 8051 micro controller. It has two ports which can be better realization mostly function generally, and its capacity of resisting disturbance also particularly is strong. So it can shield the external disturbance. Don't need an appropriative editor, programming in application directly is a superiority .Programming can better match is at the control of electrical engineering.

3.2 Wirelss transmission module

TC35i has an achievement in three things. Firstly, it consumes low and the physical volume of it is small. Secondly the weight is light. It is responsible for message and GPRS data to hand over with each other. The integration level of it is highly. Taking radio frequency electric circuit and radicle the system connecting together. Siemens Company also provided an AT order for customer to program easily. It adopts PDU mode and TXET mode in receiving and dispatching message, so it is easy to operation instruction better.

3.3 LCD module

Display module adopts LCD-1602 to show pictures. It has already saved 160 different character list sketch. In this design, display module which be used for displaying the environment in the car. When sensing the owner of the car, showing a number ID for the RFID module identifying in the screen.

3.4 RFID module

The RFID module is divided into two basic parts. One is interrogator, and the other is electronics label. The module has two kinds of work methods. There are read-only and write-only. Because of in this system, we only need to identify the owner of cars, choosing the style of read-only. The blast-off frequency of RFID mold piece is 13.56 MHz at the same time. Theoretically maximum transmission is 40 meters.

3.5 Acuistition module

The alcohol senor MQ-2 spreads a feeling machine to have very high and intelligent degree to distinguish alcohol, and the effective signal is low electricity, so it can be used for this design directly.

HC-SR501 is according to infrared ray technical of auto control module. It adopts German original package importing the LHI778 stretch forward a design, intelligent degree highly and the credibility is strong. It works on the super low electric. It adopts a full-automatic work method for responding.

DHT11 is composite sensor to monitor temperature and humidity of the car. It has small physical volume, the lowest achievement consumes, and 4 needle list the row lead a feet to pack for welding easily.

4 Software Design

The main procedure use C language of system writes, and compiled by Keil C is guided to the microcomputer. The adoption modularization of programming, after compiling the program for each module, combine some functions to carry out the function of each mold piece, be finally carry on overall debugging .Software flow chart such as Fig.3 show, among them network module the function is more complicated, and is the whole system to carry on the center that the information exchanges, and emphasize stress to carry on program to the network function.

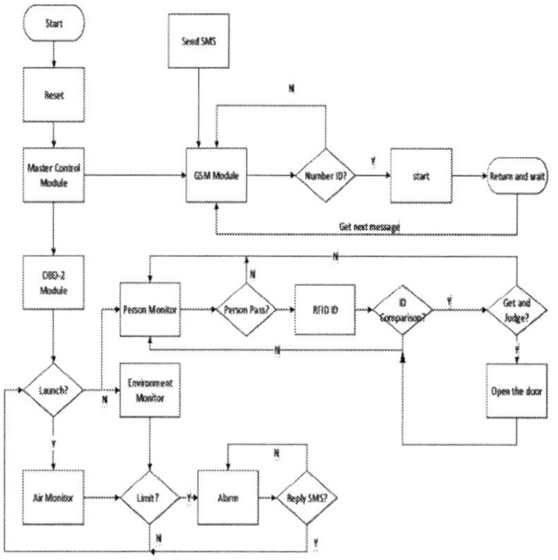

Figure 3. The Flow Chart of System

The system first to examination of OBD-II module, look into whether vehicle's professional drives status, if not vehicle's professional drive status ,and then open the temperature and humidity sensor module and infrared sensor module carries on a monitor to the environment inside the car, the monitor is the time of someone in the car, environment whether under the normal status. If the professional drives status and then carries on a monitor to the air, monitor whether drive after drinking and inside the car whether have combustible air, once reaching the threshold carry on reporting to the police. At the same time, when the car is not in the state of travel, the RFID module also automatically opens, be someone pass by of time, judge if it is a car owner. Sending out a message for GSM module under all circumstances, the GSM module delivers the information to the center processing module, pass an order, open a car window with the electrical engineering, turn on lamp or open the air condition in the car, carry out the function of auto control.

5 System Testing and Analysis

Next, we put the design through a preliminary test such as the figure 4. Testing process is divided into two parts. One is single module testing, the other one is the whole design testing.

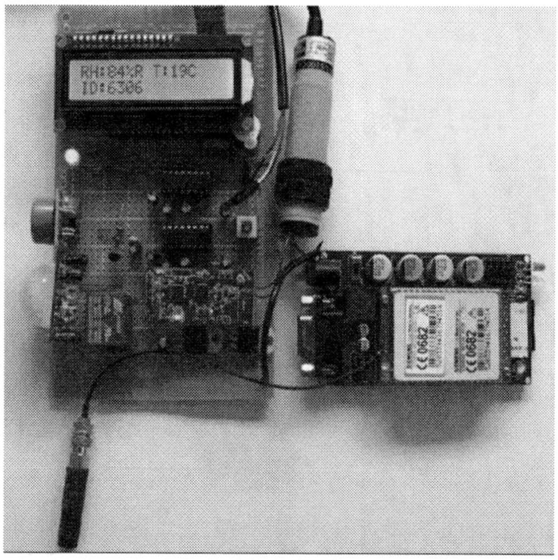

Figure 4. The Design Of Connected Vehicles Hazard Prompter

5.1 Temperature and humidity sensor module test

Firstly, we tested the module of temperature and humidity. At different times of the day, we get temperature and humidity test in different periods in the car, because the module is more sensitive to temperature and humidity. The result of test such as table 1 shows.

Table 1. Table of Temperature Result

Time	7:00	11:00	15:00	19:00	23:00
Temperature	12℃	23℃	19℃	16℃	11℃
humidity	79	72	71%	76%	73%

 DOI: 10.1051/itmconf/20160703005

	%	%			

The test environment is placed in the end of November deep autumn of rather wave. It can reflect whether the car environment is comfortable.

5.2 Automatic door control

Secondly, we tested the module of Automatic door control. Under the different scene, imitating whether the car door will open. At test of time, pass light putting on or putting out to mean the door open or close. The result of test such as table 2 shows.

Table 2 Experimental Door Control Result Table

Number	People Pass	Distance(meter)	light
1	Yes	53	NO
2	Yes	30	Yes
3	Yes	21(Wall)	NO
4	No	5	NO
5	NO(object)	2	YES

From test the result we can know, RFID module responded to once be apart from too far and not too match an actual circumstance and needed to be improved for adjusting the induction distance of module. Making its control is in the suitable distance inside. And the car door open after 5 automatic close, matching an actual application circumstance. Next, we will improve to the design.

5.3 Alcohol test

Thirdly, we tested the function of the alcohol senor MQ-3. Carrying on experimenting inside the car. And the design responded with the buzzer whether existence alcohol. When discovering in the car to have the circumstance of alcohol wet, the buzzer alarm.

Next, we tested the infrared sensors in the car inner part. When the light is green showing responding the person. At the same time, the light become red showing responding no person. The result of test such as table 3 shows.

Table 3 Experimental Human Result Table

Number	body length	color
1	170cm	Green
2	No person	Red
3	60cm	Green
4	No person inside	Red

5.4 Vehicle identification

The final commissioning is the open air conditioning function and yard function automatically find the car, to open air conditioning simulation scene, test, motor is used to replace the air conditioning in the operation, the actual process is will the reminder and the car connected to a computer. When the mobile phone sends the message: 'kongtiao (Air conditioner)', the simulation of the motor automatically rotates the air conditioner. According to the program, send the command "T21", when the indoor temperature reached 21 degrees, automatically stop the operation of the air. Mobile phone to send message 'xunche (Search cars)', the prompt device on the color light flashes always change color cue position.

6 Conclusion

Vehicular network is one of the important research directions in intelligent transportation field. A Security Alarming System for vehicular network was developed. The design takes 89C52 as the core module of data acquisition terminal. It can give an alarm by mounting temperature humidity sensor, gas sensor and the infrared induction device.This system has strong practical value and broad market development prospects with features of simple structure, strong stability and low cost. It can be easily used in the practical applications.

References

1. Wan, J.; Zou, C.; Zhou, K.; Lu, R.; Li, D. IoT Sensing Framework with Inter-cloud Computing Capability in Vehicular Networking. Electron. Commer. Res. 2014, 14, 389–416. [CrossRef]
2. Liu, N. Internet of Vehicles: Your Next Connection. Available online: http://www.huawei.com/es/static/ HW-110848.pdf (accessed on 20 December 2015).
3. Chen, M.; Mau, D.; Zhang, Y.; Taleb, T.; Leung, V. VENDNET: Vehicular Named Data Network. Veh. Commun. 2014, 1, 208–213. [CrossRef]
4. Wu Chuankun.A Preliminary Investigation on the Security Architecture of the Internet of things[J].Bulletin of ChineseAcademy of Sciences, 2010(4):411-419.
5. Huang C-L, Fallah YP, Sengupta R, Krishnan H. Adaptive intervehicle communication control for cooperative safety systems[J]. Network, 2010, 24(1): 6-13.
6. R Anbazhagan, S Vanangamudi, C Thamotharan. Design of Intelligent Car Security System. Middle East Journal of Scientific Research, 2014, 20(10):1229-1233.

ITM Web of Conferences 7, 03006 (2016) DOI: 10.1051/itmconf/20160703006
ITA 2016

Hardware-Assisted System for Program Execution Security of SOC

Xiang WANG, Shu-Song PANG, Wei- Ke WANG, Zong- Min ZHAO, Cheng ZHOU, Zhan-Hong HE, Xiao-CUI ANG and Yang XU

School of Electronic and Information Engineering, Beihang University, Beijing 100191, China
[a] Corresponding author: author@e-mail.org

Abstract. With the rapid development of embedded systems, the systems' security has become more and more important. Most embedded systems are at the risk of series of software attacks, such as buffer overflow attack, Trojan virus. In addition, with the rapid growth in the number of embedded systems and wide application, followed embedded hardware attacks are also increasing. This paper presents a new hardware assisted security mechanism to protect the program's code and data, monitoring its normal execution. The mechanism mainly monitors three types of information: the start/end address of the program of basic blocks; the lightweight hash value in basic blocks and address of the next basic block. These parameters are extracted through additional tools running on PC. The information will be stored in the security module. During normal program execution, the security module is designed to compare the real-time state of program with the information in the security module. If abnormal, it will trigger the appropriate security response, suspend the program and jump to the specified location. The module has been tested and validated on the SOPC with OR1200 processor. The experimental analysis shows that the proposed mechanism can defence a wide range of common software and physical attacks with low performance penalties and minimal overheads.

1. Introduction

The Embedded systems have rapidly evolved over the last years, which are being widely applied to military affairs, economy and other areas of society. Its related products can be found everywhere in our daily life, including smart cards, mobile, sensors, wearable devices, vehicles, ET, al. Thus the security design has become the most significant issues in embedded systems.

Due to the wide number of embedded devices as well as the great progress of the network technology, the embedded systems can be easily attacked. When the operating system is running on the embedded system, the virus has the potential to attack embedded systems. Then control and tamper embedded devices. At the same time embedded system performance has been greatly improved, but due to its own resource constraints and environmental needs, making the software of PC and cannot be ported to embedded systems.

Attacks for embedded system generally have two ways: software attack and hardware attack. The software attack mainly contains buffer overflow, logic bombs, Trojan viruses and worms. The buffer overflow attack is considered most destructive. Its attacks include stack overflows, heap overflows, dangling pointer references, format string vulnerabilities and integer errors. Hardware attack usually includes irreversible attacks like die shear, chemical attacks and reversible attacks like error signal injection, voltage temperature variation. At this stage, software attacks are more common, and the hardware attack need the attacker have more expertise.

So far, software protection has been mainly adopted to defend against most attacks. For example, safe programming language source code or security analysis is often used to fix the vulnerability. However, software protection requires a lot of rewriting the code, which leads to significant performance loss. And security is also very limited. In this paper, we propose a hardware-assisted solution to ensure the safety of program execution by compiler offline extraction program control flow, static data and static code. During program execution, the security module monitors the control flow and verifies data and code integrity.

2. Related Work

The security protection methods of system on chip (SOC) have been rapidly increased over the past years. The software-based and hardware-based protections are showed as below.

Richard et al [1] proposed a code rewrite and in-lining system (REINS) method to protect the code from malicious software attacks of untrusted sources. It's a software-based approach to detect attacks. Recently Schuster et al [2] came up with a new type of attack, called counterfeit object-oriented programming (COOP).

It abuses the C++ virtual dispatch mechanism to reuses whole functions. Stephen [3] presented a software way which improve and simplify the COOP attack and use table randomization to resist Code-reuse attacks. Abadi et al [4] proposed a new method to monitor the control flow of program. It derives the program execution process by static analysis and then check with CFG in the runtime.

In recent years, hardware-based approaches became prevalent. Jean-Luc et al [5] adopted a simple hardware solution to check good execution of one program by checking that each basic block is correctly executed and that the Control Flow Graph (CFG) is respected. But their solution has some shortage in overhead and grain. Lucas [6] tackled these limitations and presented a security hardware mechanism to deal with fine-grained CFI checks. Arora [7] also presented a hardware assisted mechanism to check control flow and integrity of code. Bu [8] is similar to Arora's design which protects the code and data integrity, but no concern about control flow protection. Zhao [9] presents a code security mechanism, which can accurately positioning error type. Guo [10] proposed hardware-based intrusion detection way called Control-flow Verification System (CONVERSE), which guaranteed control-flow integrity by checking the destination of control-flow branches at runtime.

3. Security Architecture

This section describes the working principle and process of hardware assisted monitoring model.

3.1. Overview

Fig. 1 depicts the relationship between the monitoring model and CPU.

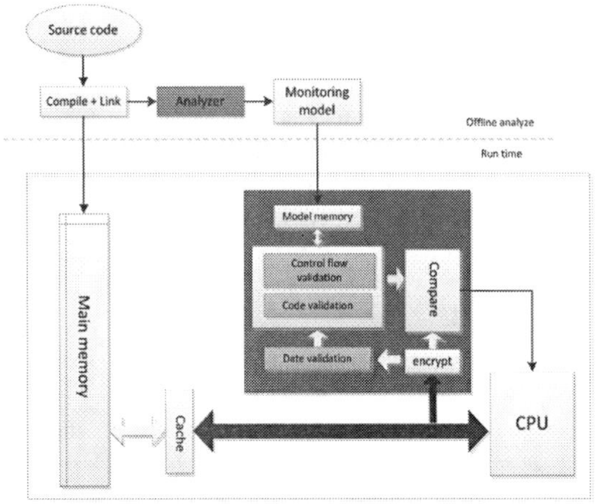

Figure1. The Monitoring Model Design Flow

3.2. The analyzer design

The main function of the analyzer is to analyze and extract static information from the object file. These include control flow information and code integrity information. The analyzer is written a script program running on PC. Here is a new definition of the concept of a basic block. Basic block refers to a code fragment which only contains the instructions executed sequentially. That is to say, there is no branching instruction in a basic block. The analyzer is marked by a jump instruction to divide the basic block, which means the starting and ending address of the basic block is the destination address of the jump instruction and the address of the next jump instruction. The designation of the analyzer is based on the basic block unit to extract and divide the program. The final result is used to initialize the security module.

Specific of extraction process are shown below:

Procedure1: Extraction process

P1: Variable initialization and some other settings, initialization operations. Enter the object file name. In addition, we also need to fill in some of the address information, such as address of boot code.

P2, P3: Executable file header contains a lot of information. The analyzer check the header files a) the file is a valid 32-bit executable ELF file or not. b) The platform this file run on is platform-specific or not. c) Extracting executable segment offset address.

P4: Call objdump tool to disassemble the object file.

P5: Functions of Interrupt table are end of jump instruction. But generally no program will call them directly. Therefore it cannot be inferred start address of basic block based on the jump instruction. So we want to add the start address based on specific documents.

P6: his is the most important step. After disassemble the executable file, actually obtained a text file of the disassembly format. By regular expressions, one can directly find the jump instruction and extract the address information based on the instruction format.

P7: Although P6 found the start and end addresses of all the basic blocks, but have not found the correspondence between the start and end address. This step would sort all addresses.

P8: After calculating the information of all the basic blocks, put each basic block instructions as input of lightweight hashing (L_Hash) algorithm and output a 16-bit result. It represents the completeness of code.

P9: Adding above information to the monitor model and use it to initialize Ram inside the security module.

3.3. The Code Integrity

This section describes the integrity protection program code, as well as the basic structure of the security model. Structure of monitoring model is shown in Table 1.

Table1. Monitoring Model of Code Integrity

Info	Wides	Address range
Current block start address	16bits	[59 :64]
Current block end address	16bits	[63:48]
L_Hash value between them	16bits	[47:32]
Successive basic block index S0	*16bits*	*[31:16]*

Info	Wides	Address range
Successive basic block index S1	*16bits*	*[15: 0]*

Current block start address:

The correct start address of basic block in currently executing program.

Current block end address:

The correct end address of basic block in currently executing program.

L Hash value between them:

The hash value of the currently executing program.

Next basic block start address:

The start address of next basic block.

After the security module is initialized, security module can start monitoring the execution of the program. At this time, the program counter of the CPU (PC) and instruction of decoding (ID) stage signal are connected to the security module. When the program starts running, the security module will monitor the execution of program. When the security module detects the start address of the program, L_Hash module becomes enabled. The current and subsequent instructions act as input of L_Hash function, until the end address of this basic block is detected by security module.

The next step is to calculate this basic block L_Hash value and compared with the L_Hash value stored in the security model. If not equal, the system must be attacked. Security model will output exception messages and freeze the CPU as well. If it do not detect a start or end address of basic block, it can be also concluded attack occurred and output the exception messages.

Procedure 2 describes how the security module protects the safety of the code.

Procedure 2 code integrity check flow

1: Inputs: PC(program counter) , Instruction

2: Output: abnormal_signal

3: B_S ← set of all basic blocks start address bb_si, 1 ≤ i ≤ the number of basic block

4: B_E ← set of all basic blocks end address bb_ei

5: I ← set of instructions of basic block i insnij, 1≤ j ≤ the number of instruction in a basic block

6: if pci = bb_si : bb_si ⊆ B_S then

7: L_Hashi = L_Hash(insni1,insni2......insnij)

8: if pci = bb_ei : bb_ei ⊆ B_E then

9: if L_Hashi = monitoring model_i[16:31] then

10: abnormal_signal = 000 /*no error*/

11: else abnormal_signal = 001 /*l_hash value error*/

12: else abnormal_signal = 010 /*end address error*/

13: else abnormal_signal = 100 /*start address error*/

3.4.The Control Flow Validation

This section describes the procedures for integrity verification of the control flow. The control flow attack occurs mainly through tampering return address of function or changing the condition of jump. The attacks occur around the jump instruction. So the security module monitor addresses of jump instruction. For direct jump instruction, the jump address which can predict where an unconditional jump instruction has only one and conditional jump address had a maximum of two. For indirect jump instruction, since the jump address in a register or memory, address of jump destination cannot be predict offline, and therefore should be special treatment. The architectural to protect control flow use two 16-bit memories S0 and S1 to store target addresses as the shown in Table2. Generation of transition table is shown in Procedure 3.

Table2. Monitoring Model of Control Flow

Info	Wides	Address range
Current block start address	16bits	[59 :64]
Current block end address	16bits	[63:48]
L_Hash value between them	16bits	[47:32]
Successive basic block index S0	16bits	[31:16]
Successive basic block index S1	16bits	[15: 0]

Procedure 3 Transition Table generation

1: input: B E

2: B← set of all basic blocks bi, 1 ≤ i ≤ the number of basic block

3: E← set of direct edge eij ⊆ E ⇔ bj is a successor of bi

4:output:T={row0,row1,...,rown} where rowi is a tuple(index,s0,s1)

5: for all bi ⊆ B do

6: rowi.index = i

7: if bi end with indirect jump then

8: Targets ← bj : eij ⊆ E

9: $row_i.s_0$ = special code

10: rowi.s1 = ||Targets||

11: rowi.s0 = j : bj is the branch-not-taken target

12: rowi.s1 = k : bk is the branch-taken target

13: else

14: rowi.s0 = k

15: rowi.s1 = 0

3.5.The Data Integrity

Both data and code are necessary for the execution of program. Attack for data may not change the control flow or destroy the integrity of the instruction code in the execution of the program. Protecting data is more difficult than code. Code information can be known after compile and it would not change in the execution time. But data information is highly dynamic. When the program is running, only a small fraction of the data is fixed and most of the data is uninitialized or unallocated. The data integrity validation architecture is shown as Fig. 2.

For the static data which can be determined after compiled, it is extracted offline and stored in the static data monitoring model. For the dynamic data, the module starts to calculate the memory access address when checking the stored instruction. Then data pre-processing model calculates the L_Hash value of current data and stores in the Dynamic data monitoring model.

Similarly, the module will compare the data in the data monitor model of current address with the L_Hash value of data on the bus when checking the load instruction of external memory. If not equal, it will output an interrupt signal to ensure that data is not modified in the external transfer process.

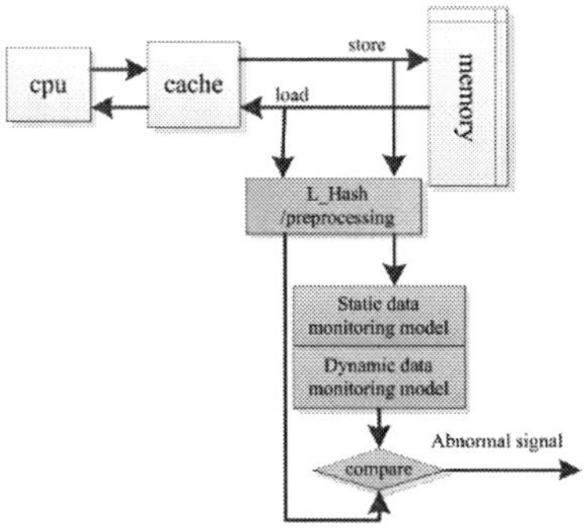

Figure2. The Data Integrity Validation Architecture

4. Analysis of Security

The design can defence many kinds of attacks. It's so difficult to do completely security analysis. So we divide attacks into the following categories.

4.1. Tampering Program Code

The design can defence most kinds of code attacks. The typical attack code as shown in the figure3.

```
C code of promgram:
int out=x+y; (normal)
int out=x-y; (tampered)

The disassembly code changes are as follows:
2118: e0 64 18 00    l.add r3,r4,r3 (normal)
2118: e0 64 18 02    l.sub r3,r4,r3  (tampered)
```

Figure3. The Tamper on Code

But there are two situations requiring attention. a) It cannot detect attacks immediately. The granularity of monitoring module is not every instruction but it was monitored using basic block as a unit. So it can detect the integrity of the code after a basic block executed in the program. This will decrease the detection efficiency of code attacks. But it can save the storage resource overhead and reduce the impact on the CPU's running speed. b) Collision attacks of checksum. L_Hash algorithm is applied in this design. It supports 80, 96, and 128 bits of three sizes of summary length and provides 64 bits to 120 bits between the original image of safety, 40 or 60 of the second preimage and collision resistance. Use serialization to achieve L_Hash, respectively, only 817 and 1028 gates. By adjusting the parameters, L_Hash can be a compromise among security, speed, energy consumption and the realization of the price and other indicators. At the same time, L_Hash has good performance in software implementation.

4.2.Tampering Control Flow

The detection of control flow is to monitor jump instructions. Common attacks are shown in Fig. 4. For direct jump which can be predicted its jump address offline, the design can be directly detect illegal jump address. But for the indirect jump instruction, the address of jump destination cannot be known before running the program. So directly detection of control flow is not available. However, considering the attack on the indirect jump instruction is either a direct attack on the code or the transfer of the conditions (data) of the attack. So it's also indirectly protected the control flow by protecting code and data.

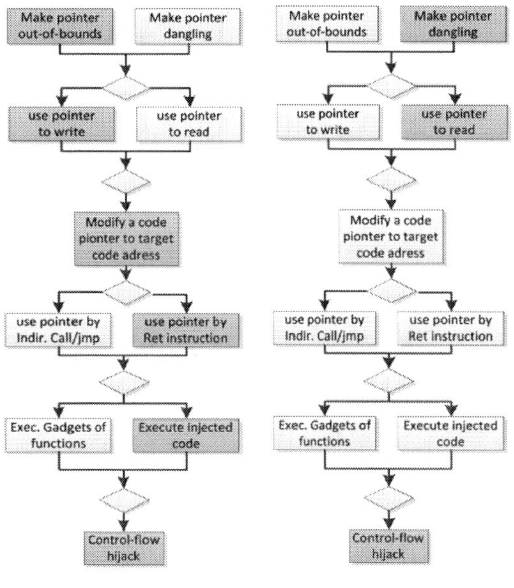

Figure4. The Tamper on Control Flow

4.3.Tampering Program Data

The attack of the data is mainly on the static data and dynamic data. Static data always exists in memory. The method of attack on that is to tamper memory content directly or attack in data transmission process. Dynamic data exists in external memory or cache. The attack can occur in cache and the above two kinds of attack in static data. Due to the memory off chip, the data attacks are likely to occur in the process of data transmission. This design is mainly aimed at that type of attack. As shown in the Figure5.

The following special circumstances need to be explained. a) During the execution of program, data may not be accessed through the external data bus. The data may be in the cache. If the data in the cache is attacked, the security module will not detect it. b) If you directly change the data in the memory, then the attack can be detected, but it cannot be restored.

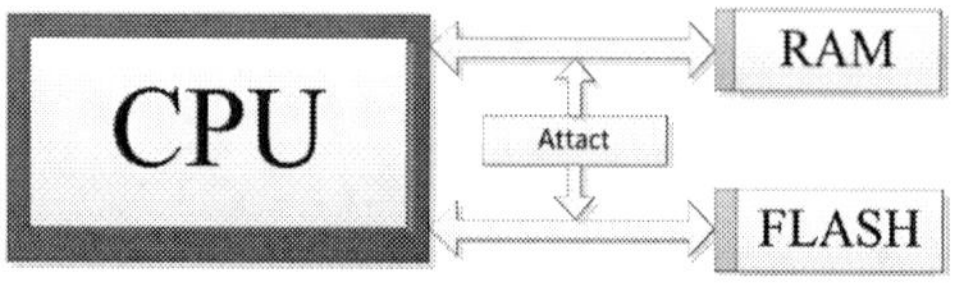

Figure5. The Tamper on Control Data

5. Experiment Result

In terms of platform building, OR1200 processor is adopted which is a 32-bit scalar RISC with Harvard micro architecture, 5 stage integer pipeline. The system on chip (SOC) platform is verified on a Xilinx virtex5 FPGA. Hardware resource consumption is shown in Table 3. The total used proportion of Slice Registers is about 25% and the Security module used used 3%. We can see this module has low resource consumption.

Table3. Platform Resource Consumption

Slice Logic Utilization	Used	Security module used	Available
Slice Registers	7,022	1,024	28,800
Slice LUTs	12,039	1,322	28,800
occupied Slices	4,716	585	7,200
LUT Flip Flop pairs used	14,185	1,672	
bonded IOBs	179	122	480
BlockRAM/FIFO	56	30	60
BUFG/BUFGCTRLs	8	2	32
Average Fanout of Non-Clock Nets	4.20	4.16	

6. Conclusion

This paper presents a hardware assisted for program secure execution mechanism. The proposed method relies on the compiler to generate the monitoring model at compile time; and the hardware monitor verifies the execution trace at runtime. The experimental result shows that the design can defend against code attack, data attack, and control flow attack effectivly. The structural design has run on an actual FPGA platform. Implementation of Implementation of security model has low resources consumption. And under normal circumstances, it meet the trade-offs between overhead and security.

Acknowledgment

This research is supported by the National Science Foundation of China (Grant No. 60973106, 81571142), the Key Project of National Science Foundation of China (Grant No. 61232009), National High-tech R&D Project of China (863 Grant No. 2011AA010404), and Fundamental Research Funds for the Central Universities, Astronautic Support Fund (Grant No.377054).

References

1. Wartell R, Mohan V, Hamlen K W, et al. Securing untrusted code via compiler-agnostic binary rewriting, Computer Security Applications Conference. 299-308 (2012)
2. Schuster F, Tendyck T, Liebchen C, et al. Counterfeit object-oriented programming: On the difficulty of preventing code reuse attacks in C++ applications, Security and Privacy (SP), 2015 IEEE Symposium on. IEEE, 745-762 (2015)
3. Crane S J, Volckaert S, Schuster F, et al. It's a TRaP: Table Randomization and Protection against Function-Reuse Attacks, Proceedings of the 22nd ACM SIGSAC Conference on Computer and Communications Security. ACM, 243-255 (2015)
4. Abadi, M.Budiu, U.Erlingsson, J.Ligatti. Control-Flow Integrity Principles, Implementations, and Applications, In ACM Conference on Computer and Communication Security (CCS) (Alexandria, VA), 340-353 (2005)
5. Danger J L, Guilley S, Porteboeuf T, et al. HCODE: Hardware-Enhanced Real-Time CFI, Proceedings of the 4th Program Protection and Reverse Engineering Workshop. ACM, **6** (2014)
6. Davi L, Koeberl P, Sadeghi A R. Hardware-assisted fine-grained control-flow integrity: Towards efficient protection of embedded systems against software exploitation, Proceedings of the 51st Annual Design Automation Conference. ACM, 2014: 1-6.
7. Arora Divya, Ravi Srivaths, Raghunathan Anand; Jha Niraj K, December 2006, Hardware-assisted runtime monitoring for secure program execution on embedded processors, IEEE Transactions on Very Large Scale Integration (VLSI) Systems, **14**, 12 (2014)
8. Bu C, Wang X, Zhang C, et al. Compiler/hardware assisted application code and data security in embedded systems, Digital Avionics Systems Conference, 2009. DASC'09. IEEE/AIAA 28th. IEEE, **7**. E. 2-1-7. E. 2-8 (2009)
9. Wang X, Zhao Z, et al. A Design of Security Module to Protect Program Execution in Embedded System, Green Computing and Communications (GreenCom),

IEEE and Internet of Things (iThings/CPSCom), IEEE International Conference on and IEEE Cyber, Physical and Social Computing. IEEE, 1750-1755 (2013)

10. Guo Z, Bhakta R, Harris I G. Control-flow checking for intrusion detection via a real-time debug interface, Smart Computing Workshops (SMARTCOMP Workshops), 2014 International Conference on. IEEE, 87-92 (2014)

ITM Web of Conferences 7, 03007 (2016) DOI: 10.1051/itmconf/20160703007
ITA 2016

Research on Improved DV-HOP Algorithm against Wormhole Attacks in WSN

Xue-Wen WANG[1,a],Feng HU[1],Chun-Xue ZHAI[1],Yuan ZHANG[1],Xing-Xing SU[1], Yan LI[1], Zhao-Ke WU[1], Ting-Ting LI[1] and Zhou-Hu DENG[1]

[1]*School of Information Science and Technology, Northwest University, Xi'an 710127, P. R. China*
Contacting e-mail: 815156932@qq.com
Corresponding author. Xue-Wen WANG Tel: 13488466766

Abstract. The secure location of node is significant in the WSN (Wireless Sensor Networks) of the troop frontier defence system. The wormhole attack is a big threat in the secure location. The credibility of the beacon node was used to determine the malicious nodes produced by wormhole attack in the WSN. The estimated method of multi-beacon nodes was adopted to improve DV-HOP algorithm after excluding the malicious nodes.In this paper,we compared the basic DV-HOP algorithm and the improved DV-HOP algorithm in the coverage percentage and the error of network localization by simulating. The simulation results indicate that the improved DV-HOP algorithm makes the localization coverage percentage can reach 90% on a certain scale of the network,andit makes the error percentage lower when the number of beacons is different.

1 Introduction

WSN (Wireless Sensor Networks) is a compound technology of the combination of sensor technology, wireless communication technology, embedded computer technology, network technology and so on.WSN has very significant application prospect in the troop frontier defence system. Because sensor nodes of WSN in the troop frontier defence system generally have high concealment and the advantages of high safety and reliability and its mobility, node localization is a key technology in sensor network architecture. The DV-HOPalgorithm is also the central issue of positioning technology in WSN localization technology. A series of positioning algorithm was put forward, like Centroid Algorithm, Amorphous Algorithm [1],[2] and so on. However, it cannot be applied to the complex environment of the troop frontier defence system, and it is based on the positioning technology of measuring the distance. So studying in range-free scheme against algorithms which has taken advantage of Network Connectivity or Topology Structures is considerably significant [3]. Since the DV-HOP [4],[5] (Distance Vector-Hop) algorithm has a low cost and high precision, it is a kind of algorithm in WSN which has the moderate node density and topology rules which are easy to achieve. The wormhole attack is one of the most common ways of attacks of the security problem of securing localization. This way of attack has great influence on the positioning precision, and wormhole attack even will endanger the hop counts of positioning DV–HOP algorithm and may cause data packets eavesdropping or denial of service [5], [6].So, compared with the security protocol of wireless sensor network and ultra-low power consumption routing, the research of unmanned border post information platform[7]and DV-Hop algorithm is increasingly important [8]. In this paper, in terms of theestimationof the distance between the unknown node and beacon nodes, we put forward the method to determine the wormhole attack of malicious nodes in WSN and improve the DV-HOP algorithm after the exclusion of malicious nodes.The improved algorithm enhances the precision of positioning and security after comparing the simulation results.

2 WSN in the Troop Frontier Defence System and Wormhole Attack

The WSN of the troop frontier defence system consists of sensor nodes, convergent nodes and terminals[8],[9].When the sensor nodes monitor the change of environment to the frontier, the data is transmitted by wireless transmission along the other nodes. Sensor nodes which are detected could use either single hop or multi-hop mode of communication to send their data to sink node though routing protocol for receiving and processing in the process. Data is transmitted to the terminal through the backbone network based on certain protocol configuration and management.

The wormhole attack, as atypical external attack, can be easily launched by two colluding attackers. One attacker sniffs packets of one point of the network,

DOI: 10.1051/itmconf/20160703007

tunnels them via the wormhole link to the other attacker which locates at the other point of the network. The wormhole attack affects sensor nodes from the calculation of the beacon nodes hop, forcing the packet of the path of the closer one hop (dotted line) transmission, then accuracy of fixed position can be reduced[13]. So, in the first phase, a sensor may obtain smaller hop counts to beacons. In the second phase, a beacon may calculate an incorrect hop size, which will be flooded with other nodes in the network.

Finally, each sensor may use incorrect hop counts and hop size to estimate the distances to the beacons, based on which the self-localization will be inaccurate. This paper presents an optimized algorithm whichmarked credibility of the beacon node based on DV-HOP localization algorithm.

3 DV-HOP Algorithms andimprovements

3.1 DV-HOP Algorithms

DV-HOP algorithm is a distance independent localization algorithm which is put forward on the basis of distance vectors routing principles. The basic principle is to represent the distance with the product of the average hop distance and the number of hops between the unknown nodes and beacon nodes instead of the distance between them. Then, calculate the unknown nodes coordinate using trilateration method or the method of Maximum Likelihood [10], [11]. The specific process is:

3.1.1 Calculating the Minimum Hops of the Unknown Node and Beacon Node

The beacon node sends information packets to position the nodes around, and the receiving node records the minimum number of hops from itself to each beacon node and forwards itself to its neighbors,adding 1. Thus, all nodes in the network will be able to know the minimum number of hops of each beacon node.

3.1.2 Calculating the Average Hop Distance between the Unknown Nodes and Beacon Nodes

Calculate the average hop distance between the unknown nodes and beacon nodes to broadcast it to the network when the node obtains hops beacon node by formula (1) to calculate the average of each beacon node hop distance, according to the hops of the beacon nodes to themselves and the received average jump distance, we can calculate the distance from each jump to abeacon node.

$$hopSize_i = \frac{\sum_{j \neq i} \sqrt{(x_i - x_j)^2 + (y_i - y_j)^2}}{\sum_{j \neq i} h_i} \quad (1)$$

[Where(x_i,y_i), (x_j,y_j)are thebeacon node i,j coordinates, h_i is the number of hops between i and j($j \neq i$)].

3.1.3 Calculating the Coordinates of Nodes

We can get the jump distance from the second step to each anchor node, and then calculate its own coordinates bytrilateration or maximum likelihood estimation method.

DV-HOP algorithm can position with theinformation of the multi-hop beacon nodes. We cannot consider the attack of malicious nodes on the network during positioning,resulting in positioning errors.

3.2 DV-HOP Algorithm Improvements

Based on the problems, we use the estimation of multi-beacon nodes to improve the accuracy of DV-HOP algorithm. The basic principle of the multi-beacon nodes estimation method is shown in Figure 1. Assuming that the distance of unknown node A away from the nearest beacon node is B, and the node A now can estimate the unknown distance to another beacon node C, d_{AC}. Node A, B and C constitute a triangle. The distance between nodes B and Care known is as a certain value. We can get d_{AC}, the distance from A to C, from the average number of hops of beacon node B and the product of hops.

$$d_{AB} = HopSize_C \times H_1 \, (2)$$

$$d_{AC} \approx \sqrt{d_{AB}^2 + d_{BC}^2 - \frac{H_1^2 + H_2^2 - H_3^2}{H_1 \times H_2} \times d_{AB} \times d_{BC}} \quad (3)$$

In these formulas above, $HopSize_C$is the average hop distance from the beacon node3.H_1 is the hop count from beacon node B to unknown node. H_2 is the hop count from beacon node B to C, and$H_3$is the hop count from beacon node C to unknown node A.

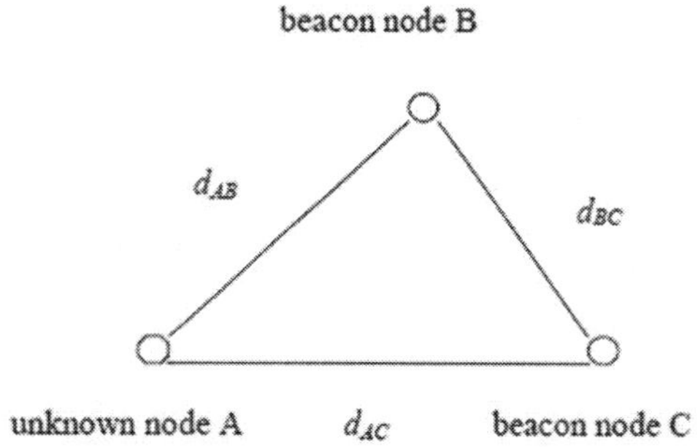

Figure 1. The Estimated Method of Multi-Beacon Nodes.

DOI: 10.1051/itmconf/20160703007

To make it meet the actual situations better, we used a method of multi-beacon nodes which based on DV-HOP algorithm[12],and corrected thefinal result with the certain valued_{BC}.

3.3 The Technology to Find Out Malicious Nodes by Using Credibility of the Beacon Node

To prevent wormhole attacks, this algorithm measured the reliability of beacon nodes when the unknown nodes located, using thecredibility of the beacon node[13],[14].If the number of nodes in sensor networks is X, there are(X-1) average hop distance (*H*opsize$_{ij}$, (j=1,2,3,X))between beacon node *i* and other (X-1) nodes. After the result, which normalized the average hop distance of one single path and node *i*, is the credibility of node j relative to node *i*. The formula for calculation is as follows:

$$w_{ij}=\begin{cases}\arctan\left(\dfrac{Hopsize_i}{Hopsize_i-Hopsize_{ij}}\right)\times\dfrac{2}{\pi}, & Hopsize_i\neq Hopsize_{ij}\\ 1, & Hopsize_i=Hopsize_{ij}\end{cases} \quad (4)$$

In formula (4), $Hopsize_i$ is the average hop distance from beacon node *i*. Hopsize$_{ij}$is the hop count away from beacon node *i*to *j*. The formula is as follows:

$$Hopsize_{ij}=\frac{\sqrt{\left(x_i-x_j\right)^2+\left(y_i-y_j\right)^2}}{h_{ij}} \quad (5)$$

W_{ij}will become smallerWhen the difference between $Hopsize_i$ and $Hopsize_{ij}$ becomes larger, which shows that there are some abnormal in the path form node*i*to node *j*, compared with other paths.Therefore, the average hop distance deviation in sensor networks was raised. In this case, we consider that compared with beacon node *i*, the credibility in node *j* is not enough. When the difference between $Hopsize_i$ and $Hopsize_{ij}$ becomes smaller,W_{ij}will tend towards 1, which means that the credibility is higher this time. After locating malicious nodes and excluding them, we use other nodes to locate unknown nodes.

4 Simulation and Results

4.1 Sensor Network Model Parameters Settings

In order to focus on the research of localization algorithm and simplify the simulation model, we make MATLAB as a simulation and data processing software, which only simulates the upper positioning module. The parameters of experiment are set as follows: there are 100 sensor nodes in a100 m * 100 msregion and make them uniform distribution randomly. Each sensor node has the same communication radius R. It adjusts the average network connectivity by adjusting the node communication radius [15]. The experiment data is the average ofmany simulationexperiments. In the simulation test, we measure the performance of the localization algorithm with the following parameters and the beacon nodes density: it means the ratio of beacon nodes and all number of nodes in a network.Beacon node coordinates are known, and there is no error of the location information. The average positioning error: the pending node distance between the actual position byestimating and the real value of node location indicates the error of each node positioning. The defined positioning error of the algorithm is as follows:

$$error=\frac{\sqrt{(\hat{x_i}-x_i)^2+(\hat{y_i}-y_i)^2}}{R}\times 100\% \quad (6)$$

Where (x_i, y_i) is the actual coordinate of a pending node, and itis the calculated coordinate of the pending node, R is the radius of a communication node. The node localization error of the node localization, compared with the simulation experiment, is the average positioning error after it runs 10 times. The fraction of coverage:we can get the ratio of the number of nodes to be located and the number of all nodes to be located.

4.2 Sensor Network Simulation Process

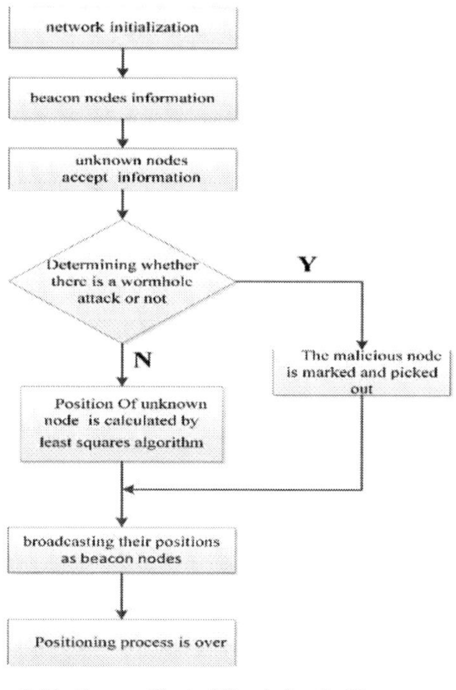

Figure2. The Process Chart of Simulation for Wsn

After the initialization of network, each beacon node will broadcast its own information on the network. When B, one of the positioned nodes, receives the broadcast information about beacon no descent by A, it will check the information if there is a wormhole attack.If there is an exsit of wormhole attack whenit broadcast information sent by the beacon node, the network will use the trust degree of beacon nodes to make sure the wormhole attack of malicious nodes and make the beacon node as a malicious beacon node, which is excluded from the network. If there is no existence of the wormhole attack, we use the least squares method to calculate the position of the positioned node B,which makes the node B become a beacon node to continue to broadcast their own location and proceed to localise the next time.

4.3 The Analysis of Experimental Simulation Results

First of all, we compare the positioning coverage of the DV-HOP algorithm and the improved DV-HOP algorithm. If the number of the beacon node is 14,the simulation experiment performed by changing the node communication radius. The results are as follows in Figure 3, Figure 4 and Figure 5.

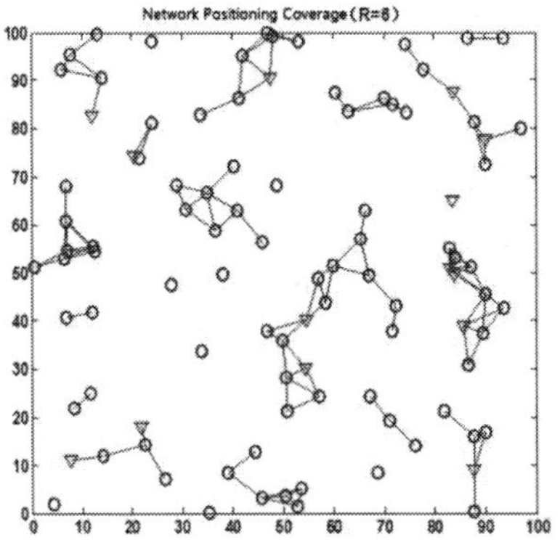

Figure 3. The Network Location Overlays Under 6-Meterradius of The Node Communication

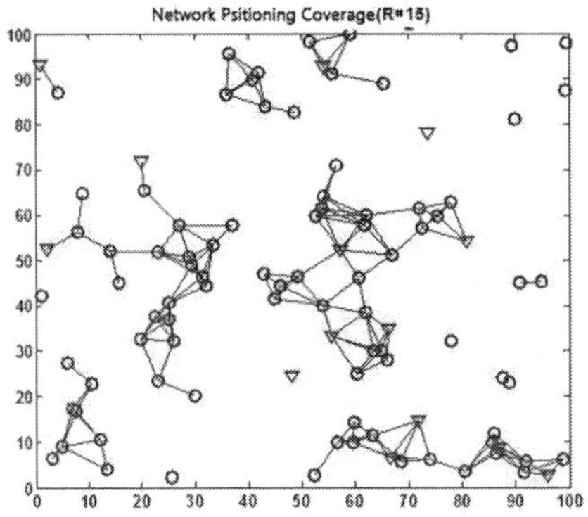

Figure 4. The Networklocation Overlays Under 15-Meter Radius of The Node Communication

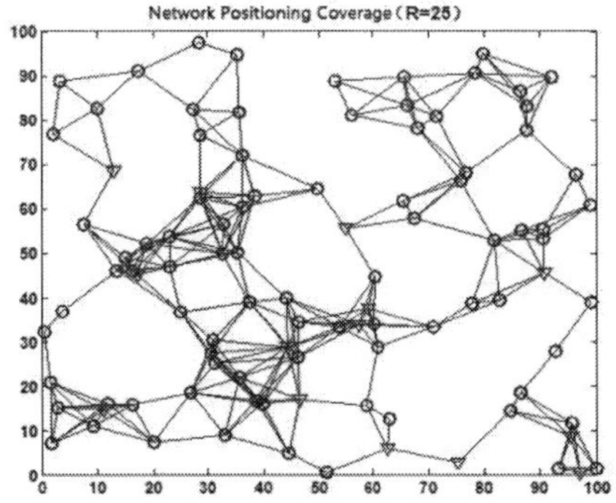

Figure 5. The Network Location Overlays Under 25-Meterradius Of The Node Communication

Figure 3, Figure 4 and Figure 5 give us the network coverage figure of the improved DV-HOP algorithm and the node communication radius of themareR=6,R=15, R=25 respectively.The red triangle represents the beacon nodes, blue circle represents the location undetermined nodes, a wired node that represents this part of the node is positioned.

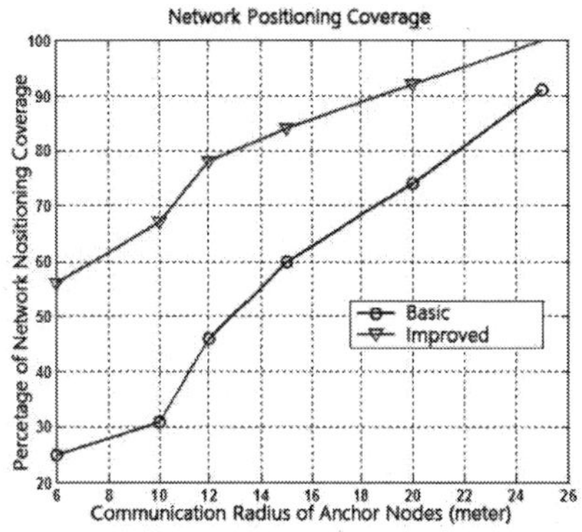

Figure 6.The Comparison Of The Positioning Coverage About The Improved Dv-Hop Algorithm And The Basic Dv-Hop Algorithm

Figure 6 shows that after the positioning coverage difference between the improved and unimproved DV-HOP algorithm under the same node communication radius, we can conclude that from the same beacon nodes, the improved algorithm is better than the basic DV-HOP algorithm in the network coverage. When the beacon node communication radius is small, the algorithm Coverage Percentage improved is nearly twice bigger than the Coverage Percentage of basic DV-HOP algorithm, and with the increase of the beacon node communication radius, the improved algorithm can quickly cover the whole network while the basic DV-HOP algorithm cannot. From the DV-HOP algorithm principle, we can know that the positioning accuracy of the algorithm is closely related to the beacon node density.

DOI: 10.1051/itmconf/20160703007

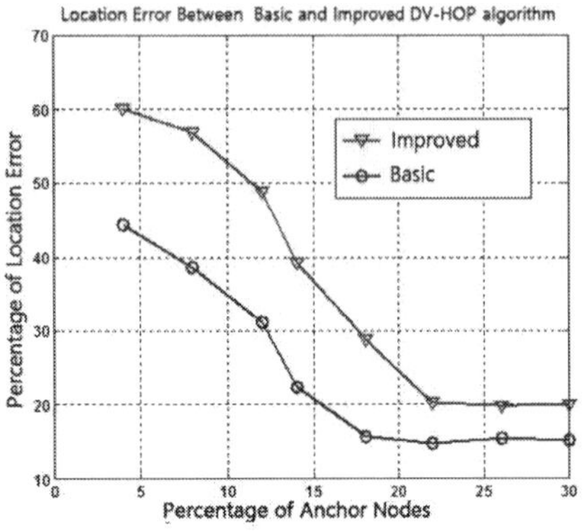

Figure 7. The Comparison About Positioning Error Of The Improved Dv-Hop Algorithm And The Basic Dv-Hop Algorithm

Figure 7 shows the relationship between the positioning error of DV-HOP algorithm and the beacon node proportion. The picture shows that when the beacon node number is 4, the average position error percentage of the DV-HOP algorithm is 60%, while the average position error percentage of the improved algorithm is 43%. As we increase the number of beacon nodes, the positioning accuracy is higher and higher. However, when the number of the beacon nodes is 22 or more, the positioning error percentageof two algorithms is kept in a relatively balanced state, the error percentage is maintained at about 20%. Since the localization process of the undetermined location node is determined by several key beacon nodes location information on its communication range which belongs to the public areas of the multi-coordinate system. It is not necessary to use the position information on all beacon nodes in its communication range. Therefore, after the beacon node density reaching a certain extent, positioning error is basically unchanged. We can conclude that the positioning accuracy of the improved algorithm will not rely too much on the number of beacon nodes, so in the condition that the beacon nodes is less, this algorithm can greatly improve the location accuracy than the former algorithm.

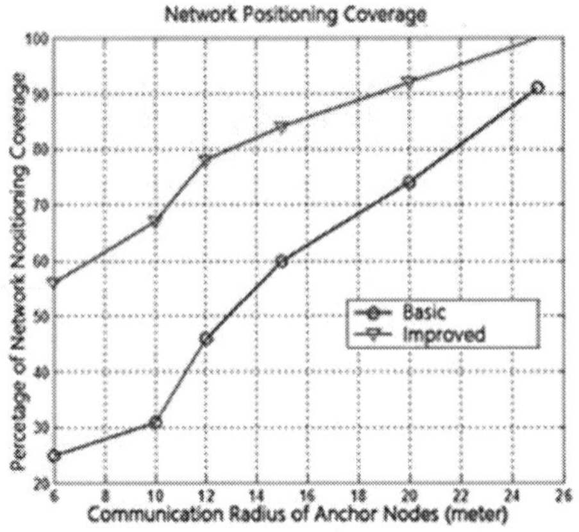

Figure 8. The Comparison About Affection Of The Beacon Nodes Ratio Attacking To The Positioning Node Proportion

In this figure, the ratio of the locatable nodes for basic DV-HOP algorithm and the improved DV-HOP algorithm are reduced when improvement for the percentage of attacked beacon nodes.The percentage of the located node improved is higher than the basic DV-HOP algorithm in the same case where the percentage of attacked beacon nodes is same.More proportion of malicious beacon node increase around the Node,unknown location,as augment for proportion of the attacked node.Position coordinates information produce large error in the process of node localization.Malicious nodes are eliminated by credibility of the beacon node through the improved DV-HOP algorithm. Therefore,the ratios of the referred beacon nodes and located node are descended.However, the accuracy of node being unknown location is stable.At last, under the condition of the mobile beacon nodes, the situation will become more complex, therefore algorithms need to be further improved[16].

Acknowledgments

This work was supported by the National Natural Science Foundation of China (No. 61405159), the National Natural Science Foundation ofChina (No. 61076002) and the Natural Science Foundation of Education Commission of Shaanxi Province (Grant No. 2012JK848).

5 Conclusions

To prevent the main network attacks of DV-HOP algorithm which named wormhole attack, this paper proposed a new technology to pick out malicious nodes by using the credibility of the beacon node. Furthermore, this paper has improved the original scheme after ruling some malicious peers.In terms of estimating the distance form an unknown node to a beacon node, this technology improved method by calculating more than one node. After all of this, we build a simulation platform in MATLAB to compare the difference between this improved DV-HOP algorithm and the basic DV-HOP

DOI: 10.1051/itmconf/20160703007

algorithm in network positioning coverage and location error. The simulation results show that under certain network size, network positioning coverage percentage can reach 90% using this new DV-HOP algorithm. When the number of beacon nodes is different, the improved DV-HOP algorithm is always better than the basic one in location error. In a word, the improved algorithm improved the safety and accuracy of location.

References

[1] Kirci, P.; Chaouchi, H., Recursive and ad hoc routing based localization in wireless sensor networks. Computer Standards & Interfaces (2016), 44, 258-263.

[2] FuBao, W.; Long, S.; Fengyuan, R. Self-Localization Syste`ms and Algorithms for Wireless Sensor Networks Self-localization systems and algorithms for wireless sensor networks. Journal of Software 2005, 16 (5), 857-868.

[3] Shi, X.; Ran, Q.; Fan, M.; Yu, H.; Wang, L.; University, C., Dynamic weighted DV-Distance algorithm for wireless sensor networks. Chinese Journal of Scientific Instrument (2013), 34 (9), 1975-1981.

[4] Gui, L.; Val, T.; Wei, A.; Dalce, R., Improvement of range-free localization technology by a novel DV-hop protocol in wireless sensor networks. Ad Hoc Networks(2014), 24, 55-73.

[5] Zhang, A.; Ye, X.; Hu, H.; Ding, X., Improved DV-HOP positioning algorithm based on one-hop subdivision and average hopping distance modification. Yi Qi Yi Biao Xue Bao/chinese Journal of Scientific Instrument (2012), 33 (11), 2552-2559.

[6] Zonghai, L. I.; Liu, S.; Wang, Y., Defending against wormhole attacks in wireless sensor networks. Computer Engineering & Applications (2012), 48 (27), 94-98.

[7] Yang, J.; Zhong, Y., The Research on unmanned border outposts Information Platform based on Wireless multimedia sensor networks. Network Security Technology & Application (2013).

[8] Huang, C. Z.; Li, X. U.; A-Yong, Y. E.; Zhong, J. F., Secure DV-Hop Algorithm Against Malicious Beacon Nodes. Computer Systems & Applications (2011).

[9] Sun, Y.; Shen, M.; Zhou, L.; Xiong, Y.; Lin, X., Simulation and realization of farmland wireless sensor networks nodes deployment. Transactions of the Chinese Society of Agricultural Engineering (2010), volume 26 (8), 211-215(5).

[10] Liu, X. S.; Chen, J. X.; Liu, Z. H.; Gai-Yan, L. I., Security localization based on DV-Hop in wireless sensor network. Journal of Computer Applications (2012), 32 (1),107-98.

[11] Hui, L. I.; Xiong, S.; Duan, P., An Improvement of DV-Hop Localization Algorithm for Wireless Sensor Network. Chinese Journal of Sensors & Actuators(2011).

[12] Liu, H.; Cui, J., Multivariate Classification-Based Malicious Node Detection for Wireless Sensor Network. Chinese Journal of Sensors &With the change of parameter r Actuators(2011), 24 (5), 771-777.

[13] Chen, H.; Lou, W.; Wang, Z.; Wu, J.; Wang, Z.; Xia, A., Securing DV-Hop localization against wormhole attacks in wireless sensor networks. Pervasive & Mobile Computing (2014), 16, 22–35.

[14] Labraoui, N.; Gueroui, M.; Aliouat, M., Secure DV-Hop localization scheme against wormhole attacks in wireless sensor networks. Springer Berlin Heidelberg: (2012); p 303–316.

[15] Amish, P.; Vaghela, V. B., Detection and Prevention of Wormhole Attack in Wireless Sensor Network using AOMDV Protocol. Procedia Computer Science(2016),79, 700-707.

[16] Han, G.; Chao, J.; Zhang, C.; Shu, L.; Li, Q., The impacts of mobility models on DV-hop based localization in Mobile Wireless Sensor Networks. Journal of Network & Computer Applications (2014), 42 (6), 70-79.

SecMAS: Security Enhanced Monitoring and Analysis Systems for Wireless Sensor Networks

Chao DING[1], Li-Jun YANG[2] and Meng WU[3,a]

[1]*College of Computer, Nanjing University of Posts and Telecommunications, 210003 Nanjing, China*
[2]*College of Internet of Things, Nanjing University of Posts and Telecommunications, 210003 Nanjing, China.*
[3]*College of Telecommunications & Information Engineering, Nanjing University of Posts and Telecommunications, 210003 Nanjing, China*

Abstract. The monitoring, control, and security guarantee for the communication in the wireless sensor networks (WSNs) are currently treated as three independent issues and addressed separately through specialized tools. However, most cases of WSNs applications requires the network administrator change the network configuration in a very short time to response to the change of observed phenomenon with security guarantee. To meet this requirement, we propose a security enhanced monitoring and control platform named SecMAS for WSNs, which provides the real-time visualization about network states and online reconfiguration of the network properties and behaviours in a resource-efficient way. Besides, basic cryptographic primitives and part of the anomaly detection functionalities are implemented in SecMAS to enabling the secure communication in WSNs. Furthermore, we conduct experiments to evaluate the performance of SecMAS in terms of the latency, throughput, communication overhead, and the security capacity. The experimental results demonstrate that the SecMAS system achieves stable, efficient and secure data collection with lightweight quick-response network control.

1 Introduction

Compared with traditional wired and wireless networks, low-power wireless sensor networks (WSNs) can be rapidly deployed in a large geographical area in a self-configured manner. This makes them particular suitable for real-time, large-scale information collection and event monitoring for mission-critical application in hostile environment. In most scenarios, WSNs are thought to be highly coupled with the physical environment. For instance, an event occurred in the observed region may cause dramatic changes of the traffic pattern, and the network should immediately reconfigure its parameters and control its sensors' behaviours to adapt these changes.

To meet this requirement, other than tracking the network state information such as network health and diagnosis data which are usually involved in the conventional network monitoring applications, the WSNs application needs to collect the detailed runtime state data of each sensor node in the network, and reconfigure the node behaviour strategies according to alteration of the physical environments. Furthermore, the network state information is usually security-sensitive in mission-critical applications, security guarantee should be included in WSNs data collection applications. Hence, a novel data collection and analysis framework which integrates the secure communication, real-time state query and network behaviour manipulation is essential for WSNs.

There are three main challenges existing in the research and development of WSNs monitoring: (1) real-time state tracing becomes more difficult when the network scale becomes larger due to the limited on-board resource of sensor node. (2) the dependence on the air reprogram widely existing in the current WSNs network management technologies constrain the efficiency and flexibility of the network reconfiguration. (3) the lack of security functionalities makes the sensory data and network configuration information operated without any secure guarantee in most WSNs monitoring applications.

To address these challenges, a variety of research efforts are made in the field of WSNs monitoring, most of which focus on data collection and remote code dissemination. Philips et. al propose the first data collection solution Surge [1] which works on a typical hierarchical network topology and support various types of sensory data (temperature, humidity, etc.). But this solution only support the TinyOS based Mint [2] route protocol. Mviz [3] is then developed based on Surge to strengthen the protocol compatibility. On

[a] Corresponding author: wum@njupt.edu.cn

the other hand, many schemes are proposed to enhance the performance of code dissemination such as the multihop over-the-air programing (MOAP) [4] and its improved version multihop network reprogramming (MNP) [5]. Besides, another state-of-art Deluge [2] is proposed to enable administrator to update the runtime code of remote sensor nodes. In this scheme each node which receives runtime code image broadcasts advertisement in the neighbourhood and on demand forwards the code image to the neighbour nodes. But the scheme is vulnerable to the malicious code injection attack. SLUICE [6] is then proposed to add the security guarantee Deluge. The code dissemination techniques enable management systems to flexibly update the remote sensor node configuration. However this type of techniques brings frequently code image transmission over the entire network, leading to high communication overhead.

To address the challenges and the limitation of existing WSNs monitoring schemes, we propose a security enhanced monitoring and control platform named SecMAS for WSNs, which provides the real-time visualization about network states and online reconfiguration of the network properties and behaviours in a resource-efficient way. Besides, basic cryptographic primitives and part of the anomaly detection functionalities are implemented in SecMAS to enabling the secure communication in WSNs.

2 System Design

2.1 Design Overview

To adapt the tight coupling of WSNs with the deployed environment, the proposed scheme is designed to satisfy the following system requirements:

Portability and scalability: The functionality of data visualization and network configuration of SecMAS is designed to work independent of the lower-layer communication protocols such as CTP [7] and ZigBee .

Hybrid network configuration: we adopt the centralized configuration strategy in basestation-end to ensure the control accuracy from a global perceptive. Meanwhile we adopt decentralized control strategy in sensornode-end to fasten the response to the change of observed target.

Integration of cryptographic and cryptography-free security guarantee: The proposed scheme introduce lightweight public key cryptographic technologies to mitigate the computation burden on the sensor nodes. Whereas it also adopt anomaly detection based techniques to resist the inside attacks launched by compromised nodes.

2.2 Software Architecture of SecMAS System

In the overall software design phase, we divide the functionalities of the proposed SecMAS system into three different components: RemoteMote, GatewayMote and Server, as illustrated in Figure 1.

The RemoteMote module takes the responsibility of the data collection, signalling transmission and local node configuration on the sensor nodes. In SecMAS, we provide two different versions of WSNs protocol (e.g. Trickle [1], Zigbee , etc.) implementation based on TI Z-stack and TinyOS [8] libraries.

The GatewayMote module takes responsibility of the protocol transform between network communication protocols and serial communication protocols, as well as the additional services such as data cache and resource allocation. In this work, we implement a message format generator (MFG) and network parameter generator (NPG) to shield the low-layer implementation difference, and generate a unified packet and parameter format.

The Server module takes responsibility of the data intelligent analysis, geographic visualization, historical data store and GUI interface. In this work, we implement the Server module on Java 2 standard edition (J2SE) and handle the data interaction between Server and local serial port using Java native interface (JNI) technique.

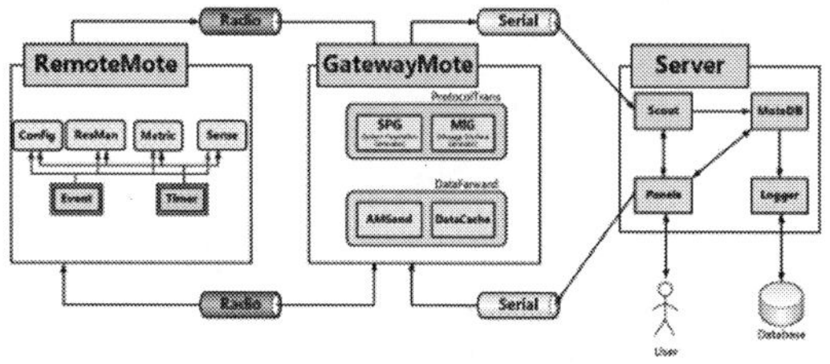

Figure 1. Software Architecture of the Proposed SecMAS

2.3 Definition of Unified Message Format

Unlike the existing WSNs monitoring schemes such as Surge and Mviz, the proposed SecMAS adopt a specific application layer message structure independent of lower-layer communication protocols. In the default case, SecMAS adopts Zigbee for information collection and Trickle for signalling dissemination. Accordingly SecMAS provides two categories of message formats: signalling message and data message format.

As illustrated in Figure 2(a), the signalling message includes a 16-bit targetID field which accounts for target node ID, a 8-bit request field which is used for specifying the signalling type, and 16-bit parameter field which stores the parameter that BS node intends to notify the target nodes. Note that regarding the length of request field, SecMAS support up to 256 types of signalling. For now the SecMAS has 15 types of signalling.

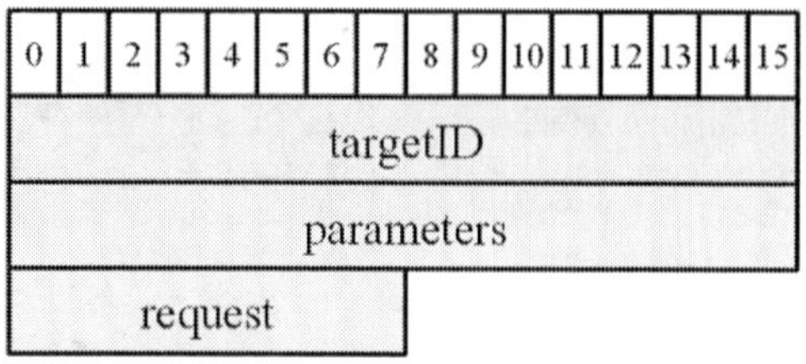

(a) Signalling Message Format

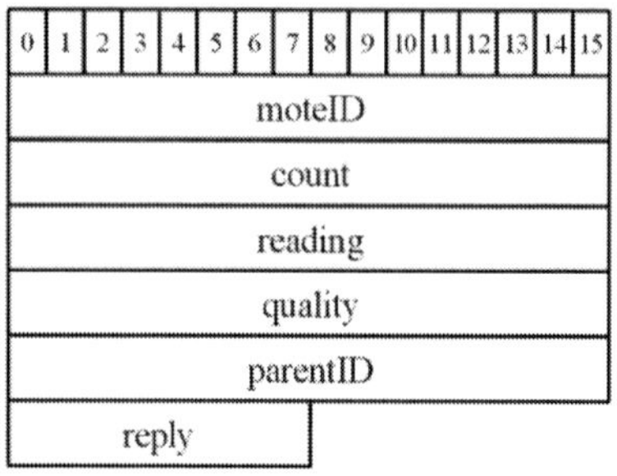

(b) Data Message Format

Figure 2. Definition of Unified Message Format

As shown in Figure 2(b), the data message includes five 16-bit fields, namely moteID, count, reading, quality, parentID and one 8-bit field reply. The field moteID represents the ID of the node which collects the data whereas the field parentID is active to represent the parent node of the source node in a hierarchical topology. The field quality account for the link quality between the source and parent nodes. The field reply represents the type of data message. In SecMAS, there are three different types of data message: reading, state info and signalling response. The field reading represent the data payload of the data message. Note that unlike other fields, parentID and quality are lower-layer protocol dependent since the quality field requires that the link layer protocol provides the link quality evaluation approach while the parentID field requires that the route protocol support the inquiry of parentID.

3 Prototype Implementation

3.1 RemoteMote Module Implementation

RemoteMote module which works on the ordinary sensor nodes, takes charge of the routine tasks of sensor nodes. A typical RemoteMote module is constructed of three different functionality components Timer, Event and Core, where Timer component calibrates the nodes' local clock, Event component handle both the hardware and software interruption requests. With the help of Timer and Event, RemoteMote is able to manipulate the rate of data collection and transmission.

In contrast, the Core component is much more complex. Its functionalities can be further divided into three subcomponents: Sense, ResMan and Config. The Sense subcomponent defines the interface of data collections, specifies the data collection mode, and generates the final data collection results. The ResMan subcomponent leverages the node into some sleep level or wake up the node on demand according to the user's specification, and report the remaining energy to BS. The Config subcomponent update local configuration and adjust the sensor node's behaviours based on the signalling message from BS.

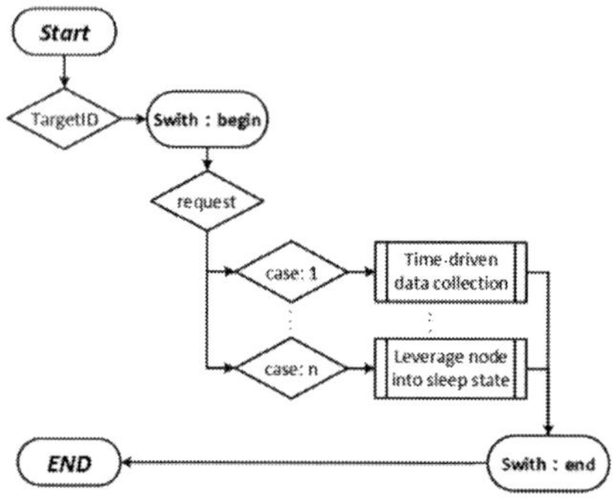

Figure 3. Workflow of the Processrequest Function

Additionally, Core component has a multiple selection function processRequest so as to invoke related functionality components such as Core, ResMan, and Config. The workflow of the function processRequest is illustrated in Figure 3.

3.2 Gateway Module Implementation

Gateway module which plays the role of the bridge between RemoteMote and Server modules, takes responsibility of reception the data from RemoteMote module, encapsulation of the received data, and transmission of the encapsulated objects.

Gateway module is constructed of two functionality components: DataForward and ProtocolTrans, where the DataForward component takes charge of data forwarding, caching, and data rate adjustment between different protocols. Whereas the ProtocolTrans component takes charge of protocol transformation.

3.3 Server Module Implementation

Server module which works on the BS node in the sensor networks, take responsibilities of the recording and storage of the readings and node state information, signalling dissemination and real-time data visualization. In this work, we implement the Server module using J2SE following the classic Model-View-Controller (MVC) design pattern, where *Model* handles the storage of events, readings and state information in the RAM and NAND Memory. *Controller* takes charge of data interaction including the interaction with Gateway module, interaction with database, interaction with graphic user interface (GUI). *View* represents the user request and feedback from GUI, and the dynamic data visualization.

Based on the adopted MVC design pattern, the functionalities of Server module is divided into several related classes with least coupling, as shown in Figure 4.

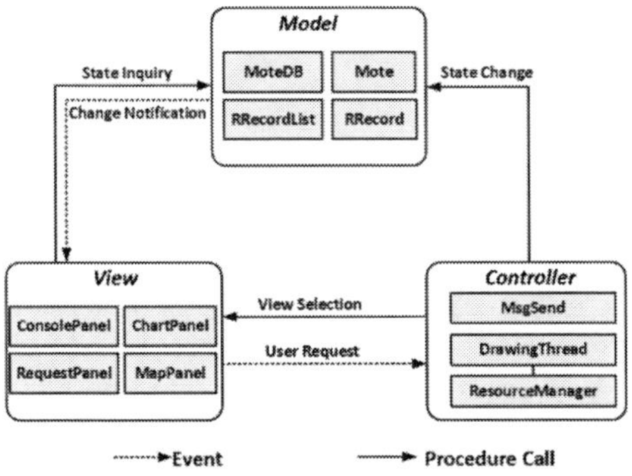

Figure 4. The MVC Design Pattern and Functionality Division Of **Server** Module.

3.4 Implementation of Security Guarantee

3.4.1 *Cryptography-Based Security Guarantee*

To achieve cryptographic security guarantee for WSNs, we develop a resource efficient cryptography library named LWCrypt based on Lynn's Pair Based Cryptography (PBC) library for SecMAS. We rewrite part of application program interface (API) in Lynn's library to eliminate the dependency with the Linux standard library such as GMP and OpenSSH, enabling the usage of LWCrypt on resource-constrained sensor network hardware.

We found that the basic cryptography operations large integer modular (LIMR), large integer multiplication (LIMS), elliptic curve scalar multiplication (ECSM) and bilinear pairing (BP) consume more than 70% computation resource in more than 90% cases during the runtime of LWCrypt. Thus it is important to reduce the computation complexity of LIMR, LIMS, ECSM, and BP.

To minimize the computation overhead of LIMR in the prime field, we adopt Berrett Reduction [9] algorithm instead of basic division operation to transform the LIMR to twice LIMS and 2^n modular operation which is much more lightweight in prime field.

To reduce the complexity of LIMS, Instead of storing the base and order in the RAM which is common in the conventional protocols like IEEE754, we adopt the Hybrid Multiplication algorithm [10] to enhance the efficiency by optimizing the usage of microprocessor registers, which significantly reduce the frequency of the interoperation between registers and RAM, leading to accelerate the cryptographic operations.

Since scalar multiplication on elliptic curves in the affine coordinate system requires resource-consuming *modular inverse* operation, we transfer modular inverse to several resource-efficient *modular multiplication* in the projection coordination system, and further adopt the Mix Point Addition and Repeated Doubling algorithms to enhance the performance of ECSM.

For BP, we choose appropriate elliptic curves to achieve best computation speed and memory allocation. In this work, we select the super singular elliptic curve $y^2 + y = x + x^3$ in the $\mathbf{F}_{2^{273}}$ binary field.

3.4.2 *Anomaly Detection Based Security Guarantee*

To defender the attacks from inside compromised nodes, we develop an anomaly detection based security algorithm library (ADSAL) for SecMAS. As illustrated in Figure 5, the architecture of ADSAL is constructed of four functionality components: DataFeatureExtractor, LocalDetector, ReportHandler and GlobalDetector.

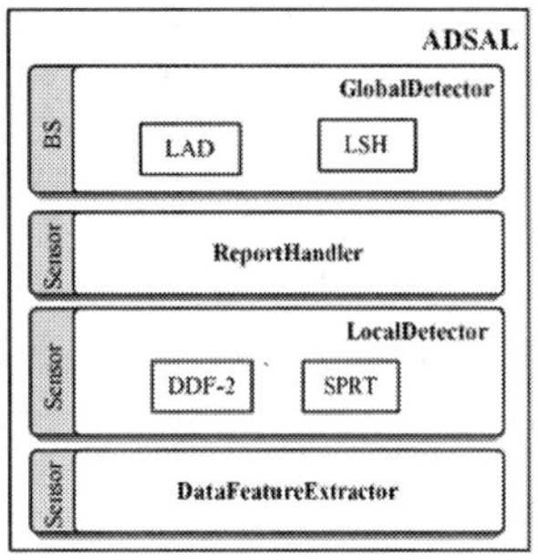

Figure 5. The **MVC** Design Pattern and Functionality Division Of Server Module.

The DataFeatureExtractor component provides the functionalities of data feature extraction and redundancy compression. This component parses the feature information for the further analysis of LocalDetector and GlobalDetector. The LocalDetector provides the functionalities of decentralized anomaly detection running on the local sensor nodes. In current version of SecMAS, we have implemented the the second-order divided difference filtering (DDF-2) [11] state estimation algorithm, the sequential probability ratio testing (SPRT) [12] based decision strategy. The GlobalDetector provides the functionalities of centralized anomaly detection. The implemented components in current version include the deployment knowledge based local anomaly detection (LAD) algorithm and locality sensitive hash (LSH) [13] algorithm.

4 Performance Evaluation

4.1 Experiment Setup and Methodology

We evaluate the performance of the proposed scheme in terms of data collection and network configuration. In order to establish a experimental network, we deploy 5 telosb motes of which one works as BS, and 28 MicaZ motes in a $10\times 6\ m^2$ area. Since SecMAS is able to remotely force the active nodes into sleep and wake up sleeping nodes, we can control the network scale by limit the number of active nodes.

We conduct two group of experiments, the first group evaluates impact of the node sampling frequency on the packet delivery rate, the second group evaluates the impact of duty cycle on the packet delivery rate.

4.2 Results and Discussion

We firstly study the varying sampling period and network scale on the packet delivery rate while fixing the duty cycle at 100%. We present the tendency of delivery rate while the sampling period varying from 1 second to 11 seconds whereas the number of sensor nodes varying from 10 to 32 in Figure 6. We notice that the delivery rate becomes higher when the sampling period becomes lower, which indicates that the congestion and collision happen much more easily when the behaviour of sampling is performed more frequently.

When the number of sensor nodes is fixed at 10, the delivery rate always keeps at approximately 100% while the sampling period varying from 1 to 11. However, the delivery rate is much lower while the sampling period varying from 1 to 6 when the number of sensor nodes is 32 compared with that when the number of sensor nodes is 10. This is because that channel contention in the neighbourhood becomes more frequently when network scale becomes larger.

Then we study the impact of duty cycle on the delivery rate while fixing the number of sensor nodes at 32. We present the tendency of delivery rate while the duty cycle varying from 1% to 100%, in Figure 7. We notice that the delivery rate increases with the rise of duty cycle. That is because when the value of duty cycle becomes higher, the sleep time becomes shorter, the sensor node has more efficient time to receive and forwards packets, leading the decrease of probability that the packets are dropped during the transmission. For example, the delivery rate is only 77% when the cycle duty is 1%, that is because the transceiver of each sensor node is at sleep in the 99% cases.

When the value of duty cycle ranges from 10% to 20%, the delivery rate increase linearly, and comes to 78.5% and 80.7%. However when the value of duty cycle further increases and exceeds 50%, the growth rate of delivery rate dramatically decreases. When the value of duty cycle ranges from 60%-100%, the delivery rate reaches a local peak at 70% with high variance among the experiment results. This means that the transceiver receives large amount of forwarding requests from the neighbour nodes, which causes severe congestion, leading to an increase of the data delivery rate. Furthermore, we infer that the high variance of packet delivery rate at certain values of duty cycle comes from some sensitivity of MAC and routing mechanisms in the protocols adopted by SecMAS.

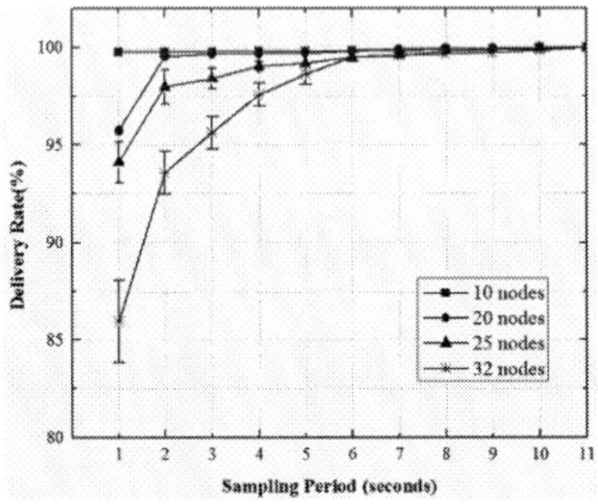

Figure 6. Impact of Sampling Period and Network Scale on The Packet Delivery Rate.

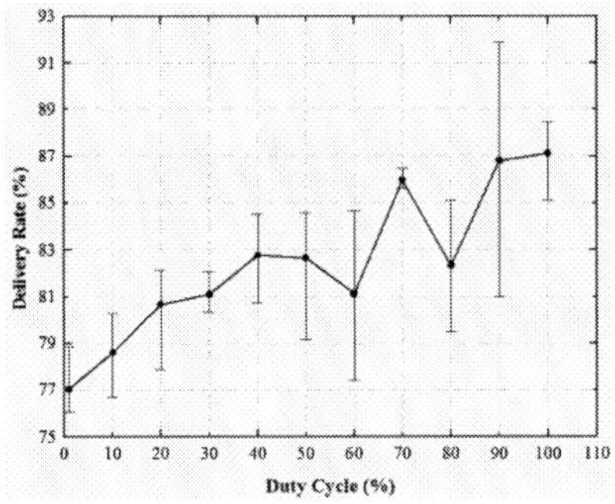

Figure 7. Impact of Duty Cycle On The Packet Delivery Rate.

5 Conclusions

In this work, we propose a security enhanced monitoring and analysis system SecMAS for WSNs to address the limitations including real-time monitoring and manipulation of the single node, inflexibility of network reconfiguration, and absence of security guarantees in the existing schemes. We present the design goals and software architecture, and further describe the implementation details of the key functionality components. Additionally, we evaluate the performance of the propose scheme through the experiments. The results demonstrate that SecMAS provide flexible strategies of network reconfiguration, and achieves promising network connectivity through appropriate network configuration.

Acknowledgment

This work is supported by National Basic Research Program of China (973 Program) under Grants 2011CB302903, the Natural Science Foundation of Jiangsu Province (Grant NO. BK20151507), the Natural Science Foundation of Jiangsu Province for Youth (Grant No. BK20160916), , the Key Program of Natural Science for Universities of Jiangsu Province (Grant No.10KJA510035).

References

1. L. Philips, Patel N., and Culer D., Trickle: a self-regulating algorithm for code propagation and maintenance in wireless sensor networks, Proc. NSDI'04, (2004).
2. J. Hui. TinyOS Network Programming [Online]. Available: http://www.cs.berkeley.edu/jwhui/deluge/
3. Mviz [Online]. Available: http://www.tinyos.net/tinyos-2.x/apps/Mviz
4. T. Stathopoulos, T. McHenry, J. Heidemann, and D. Estrin, Remote code update mechanism for wireless sensor networks, CENS Technical Report #30, (2003).
5. S. Kulkarni and L. Wang, MNP: multihop network programming for sensor networks, Proc. ICDCS'05 (2005).
6. P. Lanigan, R. Gandhi, and P. Narasimhan, Sluice: secure dissemination of code update in sensor netowrks, Proc. ICDCS'06, (2006).
7. P. Levis, N. Lee, M. Welsh, and D. Culler, TOSSIM: accurate and scalable simulation of entire TinyOS applications, Proc. Sensys'03, (2003).
8. L. Philips, M. S, and D. Gay, The emergence of networking abstractions and techniques in TinyOS, Proc. NSDI'04, (2004).
9. P. Barrett, Implementing the Rivest Shamir and Adleman Public Key Encryption Algorithm on a Standard Digital Signal Processor, CRYPTO'86, 311-323, (1986).
10. L. An and N. Peng, TinyECC: A Configurable Library for Elliptic Curve Cryptography in Wireless Sensor Networks, Proc. IPSN'08, 245-256, (2008).
11. M. Nørgaard, N. K. Poulsen, and O. Ravn, New developments in state estimation for nonlinear systems, Automatica, 1627-1638, 36(2000).
12. A. Wald, Sequential Tests of Statistical Hypothesis," The Annals of Mathematical Statistics, 117-186, (1945).
13. M. Charikar, Similarity estimation techniques from rounding algorithms, Proc.STC, 380-388, (2010).

Estimating Ads' Click through Rate with Recurrent Neural Network

Qiao-Hong Chen[1,a], Shi-Min Yu[1], Zi-Xuan Guo[1] and Yu-Bo Jia[1]

[1]School of Information, Zhejiang Sci-Tech University, Hangzhou, Zhejiang Province, China

Abstract. With the development of the Internet, online advertising spreads across every corner of the world, the ads' click through rate (CTR) estimation is an important method to improve the online advertising revenue. Compared with the linear model, the nonlinear models can study much more complex relationships between a large number of nonlinear characteristics, so as to improve the accuracy of the estimation of the ads' CTR. The recurrent neural network (RNN) based on Long-Short Term Memory (LSTM) is an improved model of the feedback neural network with ring structure. The model overcomes the problem of the gradient of the general RNN. Experiments show that the RNN based on LSTM exceeds the linear models, and it can effectively improve the estimation effect of the ads' click through rate.

1 Introduction

In 2014, online advertising has overshadowed television advertising for the first time in terms of market size, reaching the sum of 154 billion yuan in China with a 40% increase year-on-year. Compared with 77.3 billion yuan in 2012, the market size of online advertising almost doubles in 2014, and in 2015 it is more than 200 billion yuan.

As an important research area in the field of computational advertising, ads' click through-rate estimation is one important way to increase the online advertising revenue. Based on rich historical data, the ads' click through-rate estimation model makes full use of the complex relation among a large number of nonlinear characteristics of historical data as much as possible for the sake of the estimation accuracy.

In combination with the advertising position, ad auction mechanism and other factors, the increasing ads' click-through rate estimation accuracy could make online advertising be put more accurately, so as to improve the real advertisement click-through rate. According to the online advertising payment mechanisms, most companies are using "click pay cost per click" (CPC), namely, the more the ads are clicked, the more profit it makes[2].

Ads' click-through rate estimation process can be divided into four steps: feature extraction, model building, model training, and model estimation. There are many tries to estimate ads' click through rate. Joachims[3] came up with online Bayesian probability regression(OBPR), but it was based on the specific characteristics of advertisement, which made it difficult to achieve personalized recommendation accurately. Chapelle et al.[5] proposed the dynamic Bayesian network model. Dave et al.[6] adopted gradient boosting decision tree (GBDT) as a regression model to extract the similar characteristics. Richardson[7]used logistic regression (LR) model,which is used in the nonlinear characteristics of learning, but it doesn't fully reflect the relationship among many features and with the increasing of the number of iterations and learning time, it could easily cause the over fitting problems. Agrawal et al.[8] presented spatio-temporal predicting models in 2009. Agarwal et al.[9] proposed to use sparse data pre-existing hierarchy to solve the sparse event and sparse data rate estimation problem. Zhang et al.[10] put forward the COEC (clicks over expected clicks) model, which set an expected figure in advance. Cheng et al.[11] matched the user's search terms and the content of the advertisement. Zhang et al.[12] proposed the use of RNN to predict search advertising click through rate, adopting back-propagation through time (BPTT) for model training.

According to experimental results, it is more accurate compared with the LR models and NN models. However, there would be problems of gradient disappearance or gradient outbreak when using gradient falling algorithm for the RNN algorithm. In order to solve this problem, this paper adopts RNN based on LSTM, and uses LSTM special structure to avoid problems of gradient disappearance or gradient outbreak and to improve the model's accuracy.

Advertisement data in this paper is from Avazu Company. The implicit features are extracted according to the dominant features and hidden features such as users' attribute characteristics. The hidden layer of our model adopts three layers of connection structure, which makes the model to be trained adequately. The experimental results show that our model is more accurate than the LR model, BP neural network (NN) model and RNN model.

[a] Corresponding author: chen_lisa@zstu.edu.cn

The main contributions of this paper are in three folds:

First we analyze large number of advertising data features and extract hidden users' attributes with mosaic characters. Mosaic characters are hashed to new characters, so the original different types of characteristic values are turned into the same type of characteristic values. In accordance with the NN model, the characteristic values are mapped to [0,1] by using the normalization process.

The improved RNN model based on LSTM has three layers of hidden layer, each layer possessing 256 nodes. This model is used to simulate the users' click behavior and to estimate the ads' click through rate.

We use a large number of training data and test data to verify the validity of the model. The experimental results show that the model is better than the LR model and the general RNN model.

The first section of this paper gives the introduction of the researches for Ads' CTR prediction. In the second section, we propose the definition of the RNN model based on LSTM, including the training process and evaluation function of the model. After that, we analyze the advertising data and introduce experiments and results of each model in section four. Section five presents the conclusions and prospects for the future work.

2 Recurrent Neural Network Model Based on Lstm

2.1 Model Definition

Recurrent neural network based on LSTM , which uses LSTM structure to replace the hidden layer nodes of the general recurrent neural network, and the LSTM structure increases the input gates, output gates, forget gates and an internal unit (Cell).

The input gate indicates whether the input layer is allowed to enter the hidden layer node. The door is opened to allow the input layer of the output signal to enter, the door is closed to refuse to enter the signal ,input gate is denoted as ι . The output gate indicates whether the output value of the current node is output to the next layer. The door is opened to allow the hidden layer node of the signal output, the door is closed to refuse to signal output, output gate is denoted as ω . The forget gate decides whether to retain the current hidden layer node storage of historical information. The door is opened to keep the history information of the node of the hidden layer, and the door shut does not keep the history information of the node of the hidden layer,forget gate is denoted as ϕ . s_c^t represents the value of the information stored at the t time. And the input and output layers of the model are consistent with the RNN model , as shown in figure1:

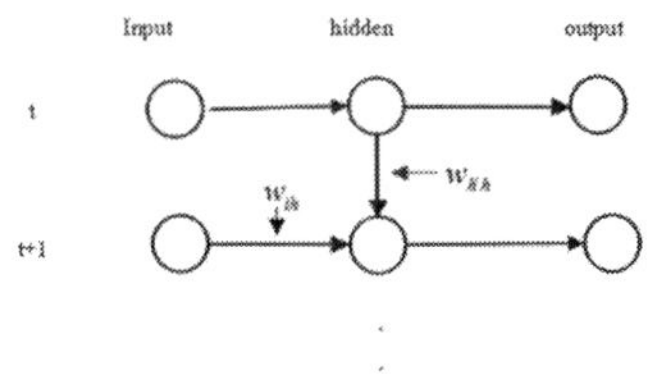

Figure 1. Recurrent Neural Network Structure

Where $w_{h\tau}$ is expressed as the weights between the hidden layer and the input gate unit.In the following part of this paper,the different subscript of w indicates the weights of different nodes.

The hidden layer nodes are replaced as shown in figure 2:

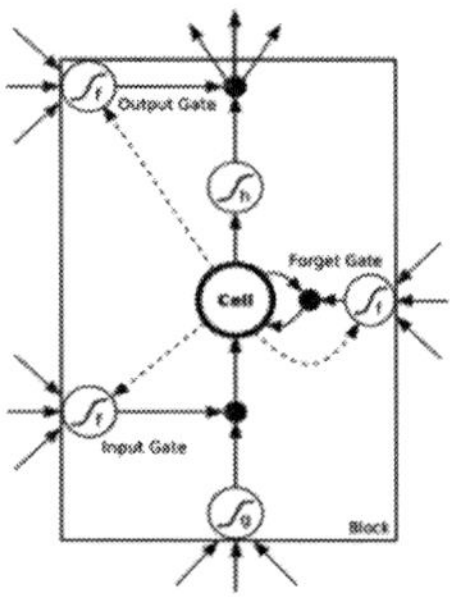

Figure 2. Long-Short Term Memory Structure

So, the structure of the recurrent neural network model based on LSTM is shown in figure 3.

2.2 Model Training

With the general recurrent neural network of the two values of the source as the input is different, The input of the input gate consists of three values. Including the input layer node of the output vector x_i^t , the first hidden layer of the cell's output vector b_h^{t-1} , the previous time cell of the retention of information s_c^{t-1} , the input vector of input gate at time t a_τ^t is as follows:

$$a_\iota^t = \sum_{i=1}^{I} w_{i\iota} x_i^t + \sum_{h=1}^{H} w_{h\iota} b_h^{t-1} + \sum_{c=1}^{C} w_{c\iota} s_c^{t-1} \tag{1}$$

Through the activation function f of the input gate, the output vector at t time b_τ^t is as follows:

$$b_\iota^t = f(a_\iota^t) \tag{2}$$

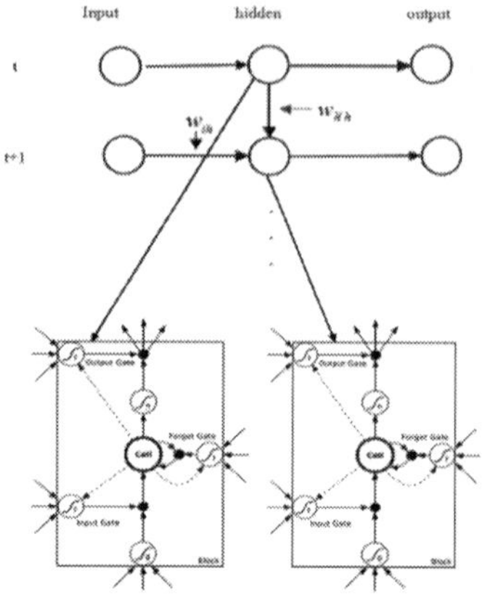

Figure 3. Recurrent neural network base on LSTM

The input of the forget gate is also made up of three input vectors, which is the same as the source of the input gate.the input vector of the forget gate at time t a_ϕ^t is as follows:

$$a_\phi^t = \sum_{i=1}^{I} w_{i\phi} x_i^t + \sum_{h=1}^{H} w_{h\phi} b_h^{t-1} + \sum_{c=1}^{C} w_{c\phi} s_c^{t-1} \quad (3)$$

Through the activation function f of the forget gate, the output vector formula of the gate is obtained at time t b_ϕ^t is as follows:

$$b_\phi^t = f(a_\phi^t) \quad (4)$$

Cells unit from the figure2, it can be known that its input is composed of two parts, one is the input vector of the input layer x_i^t, one is the output of the first hidden layer of the output gate b_h^t, the input vector of cell unit at time t a_c^t is as follows:

$$a_c^t = \sum_{i=1}^{I} w_{ic} x_i^t + \sum_{h=1}^{H} w_{hc} b_h^{t-1} \quad (5)$$

According to the Forget door to determine whether to retain the information value s_c^t of the past. s_c^t is as follows:

$$s_c^t = b_\phi^t s_c^{t-1} + b_i^t g(a_c^t) \quad (6)$$

The input of output gate is composed of three parts, the output vector of the input layer, a hidden the output vector of the layer of the cell and the cell retention of information, the input vector formula of the output gate at time t a_ω^t is as follows:

$$a_\omega^t = \sum_{i=1}^{I} w_{i\omega} x_i^t + \sum_{h=1}^{H} w_{h\omega} b_h^{t-1} + \sum_{c=1}^{C} w_{c\omega} s_c^t \quad (7)$$

The output vector b_ω^t of the output gate is obtained by using the activation function of the output gate unit at time t:

$$b_\omega^t = f(a_\omega^t) \quad (8)$$

The output vector of the Cell unit b_c^t is as follows:

$$b_c^t = b_\omega^t h(s_c^t) \quad (9)$$

The output vector a_k^t of cell unit, that is, the hidden layer of the output vector, as the input vector of the output layer, the formula is as follows:

$$a_k^t = \sum_{c=1}^{H} w_{ck} b_c^t \quad (10)$$

The resulting vector b_k^t of output from the output layer is as follows:

$$b_k^t = f(a_k^t) \quad (11)$$

The weights w_{ij} between the i node and the j node are updated as:

$$w_{ij} = w_{ij} - \eta \nabla L(w_{ij}) \quad (12)$$

Where η is expressed as Learning step, $\nabla L(w_{ij})$ is expressed as follows:

$$\nabla L(w_{ij}) = \frac{\partial L}{\partial w_{ij}} = \frac{\partial L}{\partial a_j^t} \frac{\partial a_j^t}{\partial w_{ij}} = \delta_j^t b_j^t \quad (13)$$

Where δ_j^t is expressed as residual error of the j node, b_j^t is expressed as output vector of the j node.So ,the formula 12 can be simplified using formula 13:

$$w_{ij} = w_{ij} - \eta \delta_j^t b_j^t \quad (14)$$

2.3 Loss Function and Evaluation Function

We need a criterion to judge whether the model is good or bad. Area Under roc Curve (AUC) is a common criterion. However, AUC focuses on the sorting of the CTR estimation, and logloss focuses on the accuracy of th e CTR estimation.When the click through rate all increase s in a certain proportion, it will not cause change in AUC. However, it will cause a change in logloss. Logloss is a r eflection of differences between the estimated click rate t hrough the model and the true click rate. The logloss is s

DOI: 10.1051/itmconf/20160704001

maller, the estimation results of the ads' CTR is more acc urate. This paper uses logloss in the scikit-learn, and loglo ss is defined as follows:

$$\log loss = -\frac{1}{N}\sum_{i=1}^{N}(y_i \log(p_i) + (1-y_i)\log(1-p_i)) \quad (15)$$

Where y_i is expressed as the i-th click true value, p_i is expressed as the i-th click value estimated by the model.

3 Experimental Result

3.1 Data Analysis

In this paper we use avazu company's advertising data (on ly the training set)to validate the model we proposed can enhance the CTR accuracy. The training set samples are made of 40428967 records. Each record consists of 24 fea tures , including 15 explicit features and 9 hidden encrypt ion features.We divide the training set samples into four p arts, the three parts as the training data, one part for the test data. As shown in the table 1, the click rate of test data set and the real hit rate of the training data set is similar, so the data will not affect the model's prediction.

Table 1. Data Set.

Data	Expression	Click	Click rate
Train	30000000	5102362	17%
Test	10428967	1762704	16.9%

3.2 Feature Processing

The analysis of the characteristics of advertising data indi cates that in 24 features there are most two sets of the feat ures beginning with "device_ip" or "device_id", and the value of the features beginning with "device_ip" or "devi ce_id" are too much small numbers, so that advertising da ta has a lot of the long tail of the characteristics. The anal ysis results are shown in table 2:

Table 2. The Feature Sets Of Device_Ip and Device_Id.

Feature	Sets
device_ip	2686408
device_id	6729486

In order to make the model more stable to learn, so we filter out some of the long tail characteristic values. In th e characteristics of samples, we filter the device_ip freque ncy less than 10 times and device_id frequency less than 10 times. Thus the size of training samples are reduced to 23548762 records.

We merge the characteristics of device_ip, device_id, device_ model and C14 into mosaic characters. Then mos aic characters are hashed to new characters, from which t he first 8 characters are denoted as the user_id. We merge feature C15 and feature C16 into a new feature, which is denoted as banner_size. Banner_size also is hashed. Rem ove the C15 and C16 features, add the features of banner_ size and user_id, the number of features is still 24.
The obtained features are normalized, and the characterist ic values are mapped to [0,1].

3.3 Result

Most machine learning models are adapted to find a line, plane or higher dimensional space to reach the trend of infinite approximation of data character.

Table 3 shows the logloss values of each model under different iteration times. As shown in the table3, the logloss value of LR reaches the minimum value 0.388364 in the fortieth iteration, and then the value begins to increase, which indicates that the model has been fully studied. The logloss value of BP reaches the minimum value 0.461315 in the fiftieth iteration. BP neural network model is essentially a gradient descent algorithm, so there are local minimum problems, which will lead to early termination. Compared with the LR model and the BP neural network model, the logloss value of RNN reaches the minimum value 0.386299 in the sixth iteration. Therefore, RNN has a better ads' click-through rate estimation.

In comparison with BP, RNN model has the input of the hidden layer nodes not only from the output of the input layer nodes, but also from last moment output of Hidden layer nodes, so our model can learn the relationships among the more complex characteristics.

Although the RNN can remember the historical infor mation, yet with the increasing of the depth of learning, RNN results in problems of vanishing gradient. We us e LSTM instead of the normal neuron, so that improved RNN model Based on LSTM can memorize history information as much as possible to prevent the disappeara nce of the gradient. The experimental results show that th e minimum logloss value of improved RNN mode based on LSTM is 0.383213, thus the model is better than other models in the estimation of ads 'click-through rate. The rectangular chart in Figure 4 is more intuitive to draw the logloss values of each model.

Table 3. Experimental Result.

	10	20	30	40	50	60
LR	0.396 062	0.391 579	0.38 970 2	0.388 364	0.389 496	0.39 1109
BP	0.467 845	0.464 784	0.46 284 7	0.461 937	0.461 315	0.46 167 4
RNN	0.410 213	0.408 456	0.40 221 5	0.394 515	0.390 126	0.38 626 6

DOI: 10.1051/itmconf/20160704001

LSTM	0.401 235	0.395 651	0.38 526 3	0.383 213	0.383 756	0.38 345 6

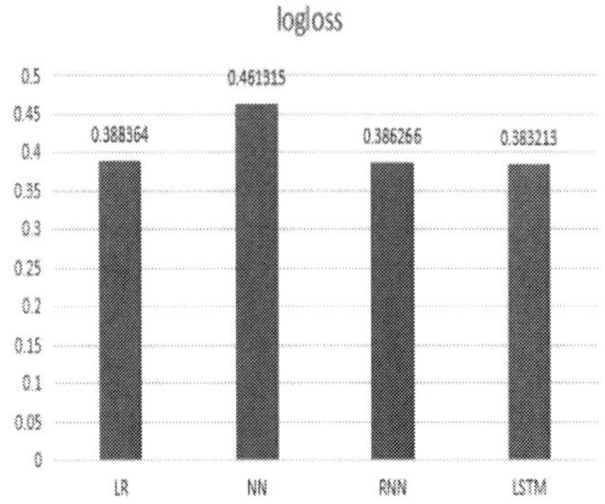

Figure 4. Experimental Result.

4. Conclusions and Prospects For Future Work

The problem of online advertising CTR estimation is one of the most popular fields of computational advertising, which has been drawing more and more attention. This paper is based on improved LSTM recurrent neural network model for the estimation of the advertising history data. The experimental results show that our model is better than the contrast models in accuracy concerning estimated advertising CTR. It turns out that the work done in this paper is effective.

The experimental data are from Kaggle data, provided by Avazu. The data has been encrypted and sampling processed. In the light of the data analysis, sampling data click rate is 17%, which is significantly higher than that in real life. Actually advertisement data is distributed extremely unevenly, so we are still committed to finding true advertisement data for training and evaluation of each model.

Gradually we begin to use deep learning neural network model for ad CTR, such as convolutional neural network and deep network learning model. This paper adopts improved RNN model based on LSTM for estimation of ads' click-through rate. In view of the experimental results, it is better than LR model and general NN model. The NN model is more sensitive to the input feature, and high dimensional features affect the model training, even result in its failure. So it would become a hot research prospect in the future to work more effectively among the sea quantity data for feature extraction, feature selection and feature reduction,

There are a lot of neural network optimization algorithm and the objective function. The optimization algorithm used in RNN in this paper is SGD algorithm. The new optimization algorithms have been constantly appearing, such as adaptive algorithm Adadelta[14], Adagrad[15] algorithm. Objective function in this paper is cross entropy function, and common objective function also includes MSE (mean squared error), MAE (mean absolute error) and categorical cross entropy as well. Optimization algorithm and objective function are also problems worthy of research in the future.

References

1. Iresearch. Analysis of the overall development of China's online advertising market[EB/OL], http://www.iyunying.org/seo/sjfx/12636.html
2. Zhou A Y, Zhou M Q, Gong X Q. Computational advertising: A data-centric comprehensive web application[J]. Jisuanji Xuebao(Chinese Journal of Computers), 2011, 34(10):pp.1805-1819.
3. Joachims T. Optimizing search engines using click through data[C]//Proceedings of the eighth ACM SIGKDD international conference on Knowledge discovery and data mining. ACM, 2002: pp.133-142.
4. Graepel T, Candela J Q, Borchert T, et al. Web-scale bayesian click-through rate estimation for sponsored search advertising in microsoft's bing search engine[C]//Proceedings of the 27th International Conference on Machine Learning (ICML-10). 2010: pp.13-20.
5. Chapelle O, Zhang Y. A dynamic bayesian network click model for web search ranking[C]//Proceedings of the 18th international conference on World wide web. ACM, 2009: pp.1-10.
6. Dave K, Varma V. Predicting the Click-Through Rate for Rare/New Ads[R]. Center for Search and Information Extraction Lab International Institute of Information Technology Hyderabad, INDIA, April 2010.
7. Richardson M, Dominowska E, Ragno R. Predicting clicks: estimation the click-through rate for new ads[C]//Proceedings of the 16th international conference on World Wide Web. ACM, 2007: pp.521-530.
8. Agarwal D, Broder A Z, Chakrabarti D, et al. estimation rates of rare events at multiple resolutions[C]//Proceedings of the 13th ACM SIGKDD international conference on Knowledge discovery and data mining. ACM, 2007: pp.16-25.
9. Agarwal D, Agrawal R, Khanna R, et al. estimation rates of rare events with multiple hierarchies through scalable log-linear models[C]//Proceedings of the 16th ACM SIGKDD international conference on Knowledge discovery and data mining. ACM, 2010:pp. 213-222.
10. Zhang W V, Jones R. Comparing click logs and editorial labels for training query rewriting[C]// WWW 2007 Workshop on Query Log Analysis: Social And Technological Challenges. 2007.
11. Cheng H, Cantu-Paz E. Personalized click estimation in sponsored search.[C]// Proceedings of the third ACM international conference on Web search and data mining. ACM, 2010:pp.351-360.
12. Zhang Y, Dai H, Xu C, et al. Sequential Click estimation for Sponsored Search with Recurrent Neural Networks[C]. AAAI 2014:pp.1369-1375.
13. LogarithmicLoss[EB/OL].https://www.kaggle.com/wiki/LogarithmicLoss.

14. Zeiler M D. ADADELTA: An adaptive learning rate method[J]. arXiv preprint arXiv:1212.5701, 2012.
15. Wager S, Wang S, Liang P. Dropout Training as Adaptive Regularization[J]. Advances in Neural Information Processing Systems, 2013:pp.351-359.

Traffic Distribution of IM Services

Rui-Bing Li [1,2,a],Fang-Fang Sun[1,2]

[1]*State Key Lab. of Networking and Switching Technology,*
[2]*Key Lab. of Network System Architecture and Convergence, Beijing University of Posts and Telecommunications, Beijing, P.R.China*
[a]*muzi2014@bupt.edu.cn* , [b]*cuihy@bupt.edu.cn*

Abstract—With the proposition of new opinion that the distribution of many human activities follows heavy-tailed distribution rather than Poisson distribution, the research on human behaviors has received widely attention. As the rapidly development of Immediate Message (IM) services in China, it could exactly reflect the characters of user online behaviors. QQ and We Chat are two of the most popular IM services in China. In the paper, we analyze the records of all QQ and We Chat users in City-A. We find the distribution of traffic records produced by IM service users follows heavy-tailed distribution, but it can't be fitted by existing functions properly. Then we present a new distribution --Lognormal Exponent (LNE) distribution to approximate the tail of the statistics. Our research will benefit for the research on human dynamics and the traffic engineering.

1 Introduction

In recent years, researchers have found that traditional Poisson distribution fail to describe the statistical time properties of human activities by analyzing records in massive database. Since Bara bási [1] found that interval time distribution of human behavior showed non-Poisson statistics, many researchers have tried to establish models to character the properties of human activity, including travels [2,3], task executions [4], physical contacts [5]and financial activities [6] etc. Recently, analyzing the multi-scale properties of Internet has drawn significant attention of researchers [7]. Papers prefer various models to explain the heavy-tailed properties of the Internet. In [8], the author use Zipf laws with a shape parameter less than one to fit the popularity curves of YouTube files. In [9], the distribution of the number of conversations of a user in a month is approximated by Lognormal. Distribution of time intervals between two consecutive messages of Cyworld is described by three sections of power-law distribution [10]. Also power-law distribution is applied to model the patterns of inter-event time between conversations in [11]. In [12] authors review power-law distribution and explore implications of power-law in computer networks.

According to Cisco [13], IP traffic will grow at a rate of 34% and the global IP traffic will reach 64EB per month till 2014. More than 97.5% share of Internet traffic will be content-related. ABI Research denotes that the mobile traffic has reached 13412 PB in 2012 with 69% growth every year. 3G data usage accounted for 46% of the total amount with 130% growth. Operator Verizon Wireless expects 50% of data usage is from 4G LTE network. Strategy Analytics [14] also points out that with the growing popularity of smart phones, the traffic of mobile data will grow three times by 2017. Smart phones and tablets PCs gradually replace the PCs becoming the main computing devices of consumers. So analysis on mobile service traffic is not only useful for operator to improve resource scheduling, solve traffic unbalanced and areas of congestion but also useful for the study of human behavior.

Mobile QQ and We Chat have the function of sending messages, voicing or videoing chat with friends, writing logs, and so on. Due to the convenience of the two applications, they have become two of the most popular IM services in China. There are tens of millions records produced by IM users one day in a developed city in China. Therefor in the paper we mainly analyze on the traffic distribution of QQ and We Chat.

2 Data Set and data processing

We use a data set which includes 940,000 IM users in City-A, 315511510 mobile users records from 00:00:00 17th November 2012 to 00:00:00 23th November 2013. The data set consists of various indexes like phone number of users, total traffic produced by users when they use services, traffic type, and so on. In the paper, we study the typical IM applications: QQ and WeChat.

For QQ and WeChat, there are many records with large size of traffic, so we group records by every 105 bytes. After grouping, we count the number of records in every group. Then we calculate the ration of the number of records belonging to any group and the number of total records to get the result of traffic distribution.

3 Lognormal Exponential Distribution

3.1 The Presentation of LNE Distribution

Studying the properties of the Internet has aroused the attention of many researchers with significant breakthroughs. Papers prefer to character the Internet by various distributions at different levels. Heavy-tailed distribution including Pareto and Lognormal is widely used in analyzing human behavior.

The probability density function of Pareto is

$$f(x) = ak^a x^{-a-1} \quad (1)$$

where k is the scale parameter and the tail index α is the shape parameter. Its cumulative distribution function is a straight line with a slope of $-\alpha$ in log-log plot.

The probability density function of standard Lognormal distribution is

$$f(x) = \frac{e^{-((\ln x)^2/2\sigma^2)}}{x\sigma\sqrt{2\pi}} \quad x > 0; \sigma > 0 \quad (2)$$

where the standard deviation σ is the scale parameter. A variable X is Lognormal distributed if $Y = \ln(X)$ is normally.

We find that the Lognormal and Pareto distribution can't well character the tail of the distribution of traffic from previous studies. Pareto tends to powerless when faced with nonlinear tail although it is widely used to research the character of Internet. While Lognormal fits well for nonlinear characteristics at the beginning, it decays faster or slower than the tail than the true distribution. So we present a new distribution - LNE to describe the temporal character of mobile Internet. The probability density function of LNE is

$$f(x) = \frac{1}{x}\exp(\frac{1}{\sqrt{2\pi\sigma^2}}\exp(-\frac{(\ln x - \mu)^2}{2\sigma^2})) \quad x > 0 \quad (3)$$

where mean μ and standard deviation σ are location parameter and the scale parameter respectively. We make the following transformations, assuming $m = \ln x$, $n = \ln(f(x))$

then

$$n = g(m) = \frac{1}{\sqrt{2\pi\sigma^2}}\exp(-\frac{(m-\mu)^2}{2\sigma^2}) \quad (4)$$

Variable m follows normally distribution with mean μ and variance σ^2. For a better fitter, in the paper we use the following function to character the distribution of m.

$$g(m) = a_1 e^{\frac{(m-b_1)^2}{c_1}} + a_2 e^{\frac{(m-b_2)^2}{c_2}} \quad (5)$$

In log-log plot, the curve of LNE approximates normal distribution. We can derive the parameters of LNE by coordinate transformations from $g(m)$ to simplify calculation. In the next section, we would compare the LNE, Lognormal and Pareto in detail by the real data.

3.2 Distribution of Traffic

We use Pareto, Lognormal and LNE three types of distribution to fit the traffic distribution of the IM.

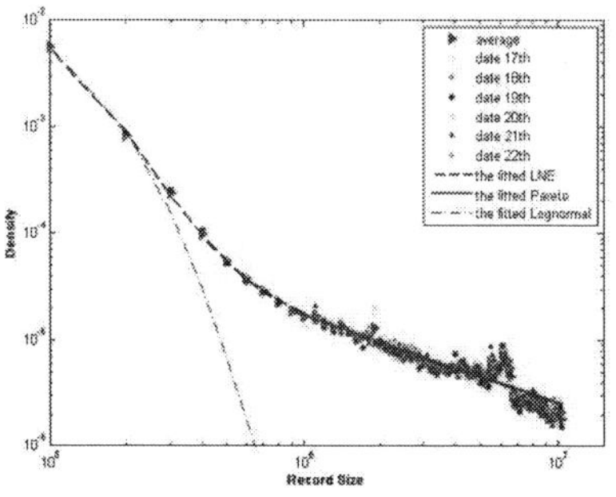

(a)Distribution of Traffic of QQ

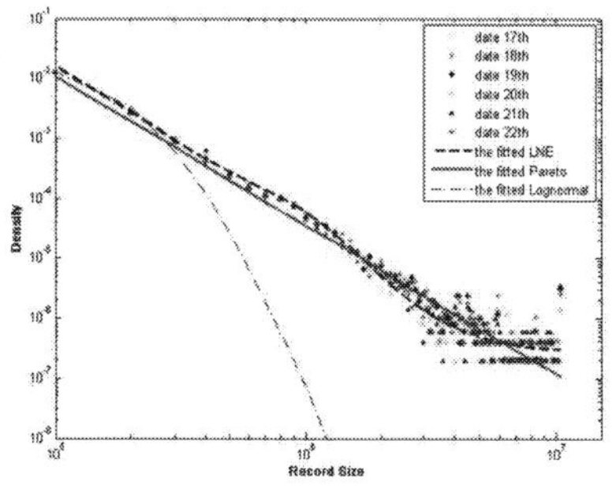

(b)Distribution of Traffic of WeChat

Fig.1. Comparison the goodness of fit of three kinds of distribution. The x coordinate represents the size of traffic records (bytes), y coordinate is the probability density corresponding to a certain size of traffic. We use different types of points to describe different dates. Red full curve, blue dotted curve, and black broken curve respectively represent the pareto, lognormal and lne distribution.

Table 1 Goodness of Fitting

Function / R^2 / App	Pareto	Lognormal	LNE
QQ	0.7674	0.8307	0.8587
WeChat	0.9329	0.9576	0.9651

From Fig.1 and Table I we can see that the probability density of IM decrease with the traffic size increasing in log-log coordinates. Classical Pareto distribution only describes part features of the distribution of QQ. The LNE distribution fits better than Pareto distribution on We Chat application. In log-log coordinates, the rate of decay in LNE distribution slow down even to 0 with the increase of traffic size which is consistent with the real value. The rate of decay in Pareto distribution is constant. However, the rate of decay in Lognormal distribution increases with the increase of traffic size, and it only can fit well for nonlinear characteristics at the beginning of traffic distribution.

By analyzing the distribution of the size of traffic records, we find the heavy tail characters of the internet traffic. Only a small number of traffic records is considerable. For example, the number of records whose size is smaller than 105 bytes in QQ application is 41,744,916, accounting 99.23% of total records. Only 77 records whose size between 102*105 bytes and 103*105 bytes. More than 98% of total records fall in 105 bytes in We Chat. Less than 2% of records fall in (105, 104*105) bytes.

Conclusion

In the paper, we mainly analyzed the traffic distribution of two IM services in City-A, a developed city in China. As a result of poor fitting effect of existing heavy-tailed function, we present a new distribution based on the properties of real traffic data. LNE combines the advantages of Pareto distribution and Lognormal distribution.

In log-log coordinate LNE can fit the distribution quite properly. With proper parameter LNE can fit nearly parallel tail which is impossible for Pareto and Lognormal distribution.

Acknowledgement

This work was supported by the National Natural Science Foundation of China (61201153), the National 973 Program of China under Grant (2012CB315805), Prospective Research Project on Future Networks in Jiangsu Future Networks Innovation Institute (BY2013095-2-16), the National Basic Research Program 973 of China (2012CB315801), and the Fundamental Research Funds of China for the Central Universities (2013RC0113).

References

[1] BARABÁSI A L. The origin of bursts and heavy tails in human dynamics[J]. Nature, 2005,435(7039): 207-211
[2] Brockmann Dirk, Lars Hufnagel, Theo Geisel. The scaling laws of human travel[J]. Nature,2006,439(7075): 462-465.
[3] Lu Xin, Linus Bengtsson, Petter Holme. Predictability of population displacement after the 2010 Haiti earthquake [J]. Proceedings of the National Academy of Sciences,2012,109(29): 11576-11581.
[4] Pickard, Galen, et al. "Time-critical social mobilization." Science, 2011, 334(6055):509-512.
[5] Zhao Kun, Juliette Stehlé, Ginestra Bianconi, Alain Barrat. Social network dynamics of face-to-face interactions [J]. Physical Review E,2011,83: 056109.
[6] Sun-Chong Wang, Jie-Jun Tseng, Chung-Ching Tai, Ke-Hung Lai, Wei-Shao Wu, Shu-Heng Chen. Network topology of an experimental futures exchange [J]. The European Physical Journal B, 2008, 62(1): 105-111.
[7] Vespignani, Alessandro. Predicting the behavior of techno-social systems [J].Science, 2009, 325(5939): 425-428.
[8] Guillemin, Fabrice, Thierry Houdoin, Stephanie Moteau. Volatility of YouTube content in Orange networks and consequences [C]. In Communications (ICC), 2013 IEEE International Conference on, pp. 2381-2385. IEEE, 2013.
[9] Leskovec, Jure, Eric Horvitz. Planetary-scale views on a large instant-messaging network [C]. In Proceedings of the 17th international conference on World Wide Web, pp. 915-924. ACM, 2008.
[10] Chun, Hyunwoo, Haewoon Kwak, Young-Ho Eom, Yong-Yeol Ahn, Sue Moon, Hawoong Jeong. Comparison of online social relations in volume vs interaction: a case study of cyworld [C]. In Proceedings of the 8th ACM SIGCOMM conference on Internet measurement, pp. 57-70. ACM, 2008.
[11] Wei HONG, HAN Xiao-Pu, ZHOU Tao, WANG Bing-Hong. Heavy-tailed statistics in short-message communication[J]. Chinese Physics Letters,2009,2009(2):297-299.
[12] Mahanti. A, Carlsson. N, Arlitt. M, Williamson. C. A tale of the tails: Power-laws in Internet measurements [J]. Network, 2013,27(1): 59-64.
[13] Forecast C V N I. Cisco Visual Networking Index: Global Mobile data Traffic Forecast Update 2009-2014[J]. Cisco Public Information, February, 2010, 9.
[14] Ingrid Lunden. Mobile Data Traffic To Grow 300% Globally By 2017 Led By Video, Web Use, Says Strategy Analytics.
http://techcrunch.com/2013/07/03/mobile-data-use-to-grow-300-globally-by-2017-led-by-video-web-traffic-says-strategy-analytics/

Parameters Identification of Photovoltaic Cells Based on Differential Evolution Algorithm

Liao Hui[1,2], Qiao-Dongkai [1], Huang-Chong lin[1], Li–Shi dong[1]

[1] *Guangdong University of Petrochemical Technology, Maoming, Guangdong, 525000*
[2] *Development center of technology for fruit & vegetables storage and processing engineering, Maoming, Guangdong, 525000*

Abstract. For the complex nonlinear model of photovoltaic cells, traditional evolution strategy is easy to fall into the local optimal and its identification time is too long when taking parameters identification, then the difference algorithm is proposed in this study, which is to solve the problems of parameter identification in photovoltaic cell model, where it is very difficult to achieve with other identification algorithms. In this method, the random data is selected as the initial generation; the successful evolution to the next generation is done through a certain strategy of difference algorithm, which can achieve the effective identification of control parameters. It is proved that the method has a good global optimization and the fast convergence ability, and the simulation results are shown that the differential evolution has high identification ability and it is an effective method to identify the parameters of photovoltaic cells, where the photovoltaic cells can be widely used in other places with these parameters.

1 Introduction

Photoelectric system is to convert solar energy into electrical energy by means of PV components, due to the reasons of battery materials and preparation technology, the conversion efficiency is low at present. In order to improve the conversion efficiency of solar energy, the characteristics of photovoltaic cells were in-depth study by people [1-5]. When people studied the characteristics of PV cell, they mainly focused on the volt-ampere characteristics of the solar cells output, which can be applied to the control of the maximum power output of battery, these parameters of the battery model including current Iph, reverse saturation current I0, diode quality sub, a series resistance (RS) and the shunt resistance Rsh, through the analysis on battery power input parameters we can control of photovoltaic energy conversion efficiency and battery fault situation in real-time, and then adjust the power to ensure the production smoothly has the very important significance [6-7].

Parameters of the photovoltaic battery can be measured in the experiment under standard conditions, however, these parameters will change also along with its test condition, so it is necessary to identify the parameters of the photovoltaic cell by use of the I-V relationship, the energy efficiency of the photovoltaic battery can be improved when these parameters taken into the experiment usage[8-10], therefore, the parameters identification of photovoltaic cells are very important, however, the mathematical model of photovoltaic cells is a Lambert W function, which has a high degree of nonlinear [11]. In recent years, people have tried to describe the optoelectronic system by the derivative method, these data are from the experimental I-V curve [12, 13], under the standard conditions, the parameter values of photovoltaic battery model can be measured through the battery characteristic equation, such as the short-circuit current (ISC), open circuit voltage UOC, the maximum power point of current IM and voltage um and the maximum power value Pm [14]. Due to the effect of the environment working on the parameters of photovoltaic cells, the reference [15] taked into account of the use of conditions when taking identification, and analyzed its impacts on the parameters of the case. it reflects the relationship between the parameters in the steady state of photovoltaic cells and the transient state, the literature [16] have done much research on the case, and then the accuracy of the parameter estimation method were proposed. However, due to the complexity of the nonlinear process of the photovoltaic cell model, when the parameters of this kind of problems are identified, most of the optimization algorithms are easy to fall into the local optimum or the optimization time is too long [17].

 DOI: 10.1051/itmconf/20160704003

Through the cooperation and competition among individuals within the group, the differential evolution algorithm (DE) is produced by swarm intelligence to guide the optimization search, retaining the population with global search strategy, which is taking the real coding, a simple mutation operation and the competition strategies, reducing the genetic manipulation of complexity, it has function of memory and dynamic tracking search, which has a strong global convergence ability and robustness by adjusting the searching strategy,, the main advantage is that it is not easy to fall into the local optimum, and it has the fast convergence rate [18].

For the above reasons, DE algorithm is proposed in this paper, through the method of selection, crossover and mutation operation, it randomly selected individual, and then evaluating to the better next generation, it can avoid into local optimal in the process of evolution, which ensures the high global optimization success rate, and improving the convergence speed.

2 De Algorithm

Assumed to the solved optimization problems has a n-dimensional vector, the problem to be solved is composed of the individual $xi=(x_{i1},x_{i2},\cdots,x_{in})$, a single individual with a random space is a random number of $(x_{1\min},x_{2\min},\cdots x_{i\min})$ and $(x_{1\max},x_{2\max},\cdots x_{i\max})$, its the solution space is [xmin, xmax], on the basis of a population, in the process of solving, each individual has an evolutionary vector target value.

DE will differ between a generation of individual component vectors evolution crossover and mutation operation, so as to generate a new individual, according to a certain code selection mechanism, decides in the offspring and parent retains, and has been in this selection mechanism evolution until meets the solution conditions setting by the termination.

Differential evolution algorithm is based on the real coded evolutionary algorithm; the overall structure is similar to other evolutionary algorithms, including 3 basic operations of mutation, crossover and selection. Standard differential evolution algorithm mainly includes the following 4 steps.

2.1 Generating Initial Population

Assuming that all individuals are in an n-dimensional data set, the data distribution is random, and the randomly generated numbers are expressed as a chromosome.

$$x_{ij}(0)=radn_{ij}(0,1)(x_{ij}^{U}-x_{ij}^{L})+x_{ij}^{L}$$

Where $radn_{ij}(0,1)$ is one of randomly generated numbers, whose scope is [0,1], the upper and lower bounds of the first j chromosome are x_{ij}^{U} and x_{ij}^{L} respectively.

2.2 Mutation Operation

The three individuals of x_{p1}, x_{p2} and x_{p3} are randomly selected, the individuals are not the same as each other. That is $i\neq p1\neq p2\neq p3$, the basic mutation operator is

$$h_{ij}(t+1)=x_{p1j}(t)+F(x_{p2j}(t)-x_{p3j}(t))$$

If there is no local optimization problem, the variation operation can be written as

$$h_{ij}(t+1)=x_{bj}(t)+F(x_{p2j}(t)-x_{p3j}(t))$$

where, $x_{p2j}(t)-x_{p3j}(t)$ is the difference of trace, this differential operation is the key of differential evolution algorithm, and F is the scale variation factor of difference vector. $p1,p2,p3$ are the random integer that represent the number of individuals in the population; $x_{bj}(t)$ is the best individual in the current generation. The first vector on the right side of the equation is called the base vector, which is called the differential vector with F factor, according to the need to select the appropriate difference vector factor, through the differential evolution algorithm, the evolution population has the best individual information of the current population in the mutation operation, which can improve the convergence rate.

2.3 Cross Operation

Crossover operation is to increase the diversity of the population, which can avoid the local optimization in the process of optimization, the algorithm increases the crossover operation, and generates the test vector, and the specific operations are as follows:

$$v_{ij}(t+1)=\begin{cases}h_{ij}(t+1), rand\ l_{ij}\leq CR\\ x_{ij}(t), rand\ l_{ij}>CR\end{cases}$$

Where, $rand\ l_{ij}$ is a random function in [0, 1], this selection can ensure that the test vectors are different from their corresponding target vectors; CR is the crossover probability, $CR\in[0,1]$.

2.4 Select Operation

In the setting of search space, the algorithm will be the mutation and crossover operations on the basis of the generation of the initial population, in the corresponding search space, the algorithm will judge the test vector of each generation whether beyond its upper generation or not, which will be the initialization with a uniform random number when it beyond the searching space of the corresponding dimension, and the greedy selection method of operation will avoid the premature convergence in certain procedures, and then it will get better in the next generation of individuals.

In order to determine whether $x_i(t)$ is a member of the next generation, the test vector $v_{ij}(t+1)$ and the target vector $v_{ij}(t)$ are compared to the evaluation function:

$$x_i(t+1)\begin{cases} v_i(t+1), f(v_{i1}(t+1),\cdots,v_{in}(t+1)) < f(v_{i1}(t),\cdots,v_{in}(t)) \\ x_{ij}(t), f(v_{i1}(t+1),\cdots,v_{in}(t+1)) \geq f(v_{i1}(t),\cdots,v_{in}(t)) \end{cases}$$

Repeat steps (2) to step (4), the final generation will be the best generation until the maximum number of iterations to reach G.

3 Identification of Photovoltaic Cells Model Parameters

The photovoltaic cell is a circuit that converts light energy into electric energy by photovoltaic panels, which can be equivalent to the circuit shown in Fig.1. The expression of the current and voltage characteristics in the circuit can be expressed as Rp model.

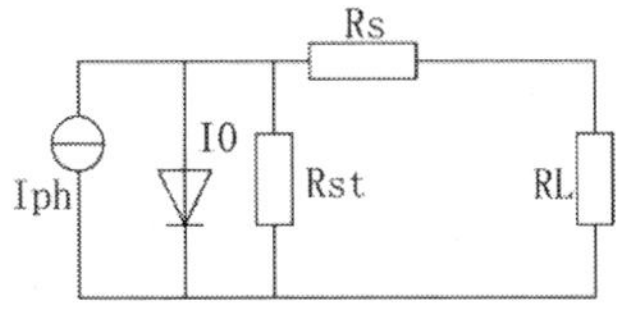

Fig. 1 Equivalent Circuit of Photovoltaic Cell

$$I = I_{ph} - I_0\{\exp\frac{q(V+IR_s)}{KAT} - 1\} - \frac{V+IR_s}{R_{sh}}$$

Where :
V - load voltage at both ends;
I - by load current;
Iph - photo induced current;
I0 - diode reverse saturation current;
A - diode quality factor;
Rs - battery series resistance;
Rsh - battery parallel resistance;
T - absolute temperature of the battery;
K - Pohl Seidman constant (1.380e-23 J/K);
Q - electron charge (1.608e-19 DEG C).

3.1 Establishment of Parameter Identification Model

Photovoltaic cell model is a highly nonlinear equation; differential evolution algorithm will establish the fitness function by the use of the explicit expression of the current, and then converting the PV model into an explicit expression. According to the characteristics of photovoltaic cells, it can be transformed to the transcendental function of Y(x)=XeX. Lambert W function which can be used to solve the current voltage equation, the solution of the form is W(Y(x)), the differential evolution algorithm can be used to identify the parameters of the photovoltaic cell model.
Depending on the upper type, the current and voltage of the photovoltaic cell are converted to an explicit equation that can be obtained.

$$I = \frac{R_{sh}(I_{ph}+I_0)-V}{R_{sh}+R_s} - \frac{AV_{th}}{R_s}W\left(\frac{R_{sh}R_sI_0}{(R_{sh}+R_s)AV_{th}}\exp\left(\frac{R_{sh}V+R_{sh}R_s(I_{ph}+I_0)}{AV_{th}(R_{sh}+R_s)}\right)\right)$$

Tab.1 shows the parameters under standard conditions (25℃ 1000W/m2,) of SFM50-18 photovoltaic cell panel. Fig.2 is the I-V curves under different illumination conditions.

Tab.1 Parameters of Photovoltaic Cell Panel

Parameter	parameter value	Parameter	parameter value
Imp	2.9A	Voc	21.5V
Vmp	17.3 V	Pmax,e	50W
Isc	3.18 A	Ns	36

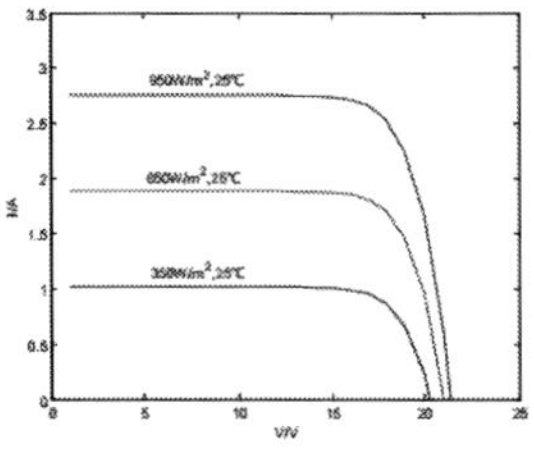

Fig.2 The Change Of Current-Voltage Under Different Light Intensity

3.2 Parameter Identification

After the conversion of the explicit expression of the photovoltaic cell model, the 5 parameters of the photovoltaic cell current-voltage model are identified by using DE. Objective function value change reflects the algorithm to identify the effect of the model; fig.2 shows the parameters of the DE algorithm to identify the value of the objective function. It can be seen from the figure that the parameter identification can be fast and stable in a numerical value, for the PV cell voltage model parameters identification, DE algorithm has a better stability.

 DOI: 10.1051/itmconf/20160704003

For different size of the population, the speed of the algorithm is not consistent, the smaller the size of the population received faster. Fig.3 is the comparison of the size of the 3 different populations, From which it can be calculated, in fact, when improving the identification of convergence rate, the smaller the size of the population is suitable, however, the small size of the population will induce accuracy of parameter identification. Table 3 is a comparison of the results of the identification of 3 different species.

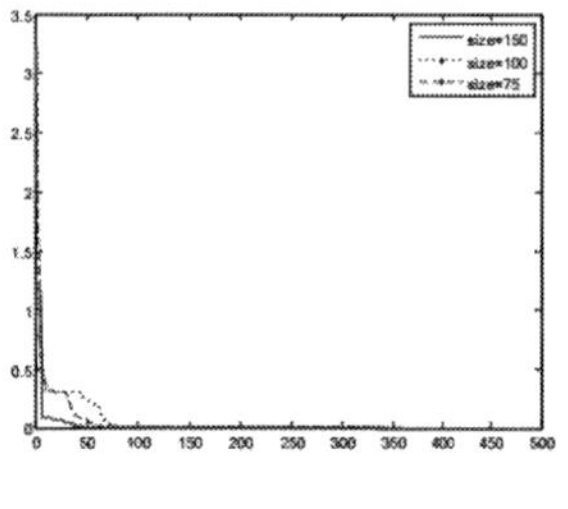

Fig.3 Convergence of Parameter Identification under Different Population

When the condition is changed, the parameter values of the photovoltaic cell will be changed. Therefore, changing the intensity of the light will be identified, the parameter identification results are shown in Tab.2 under different light intensity conditions, the results show that, the identification parameters were changed along with the test conditions.

Tab.2 Parameters of the Battery Model for De Identification When the Light Intensity Changes

light intensity (W/m2)	*I*ph	*Io*/A	*A*	*Rs*/Ω	*Rsh*/Ω
700	2.836	8.201	1.420	0.027	203.36
600	2.421	8.182	1.428	0.029	214.66
500	2.105	8.168	1.536	0.031	249.50
400	1.666	8.147	1.471	0.034	289.71
300	1.258	8.126	1.513	0.036	311.65
200	0.978	8.106	1.505	0.039	379.89
100	0.685	8.085	1.498	0.041	440.89

The data of identification and the actual data were applied in the volt-ampere circuit test, fig.4 was the results of simulation experiments, both capitals of error is very small that the parameter identification results can be applied to the actual current-voltage in the model.

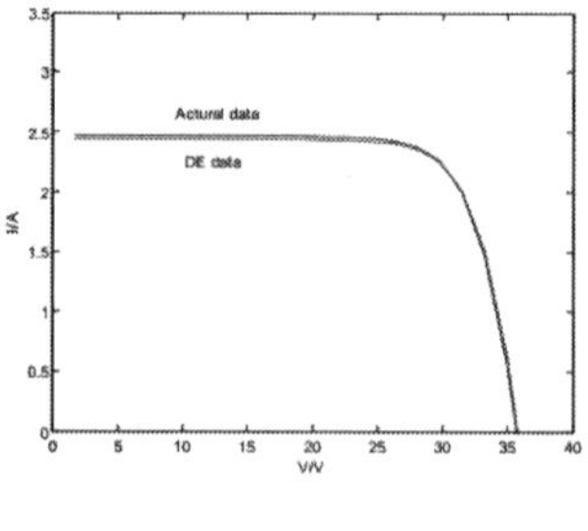

Fig.4 Identification results and Measured Conditions, the I-V Curve of Photovoltaic Cells

4 Conclusions

In view of the problems is difficult to determine the parameters of the photovoltaic battery, this paper presents a differential evolution algorithm, and the corresponding research is carried out, for example, the parameters of differential evolution algorithm will quickly and accurately identify the parameters of the photovoltaic cell when it set reasonably, such as population size, the identification results showed that, after a certain time of calculation, the DE algorithm can take identification for photovoltaic battery model parameters accurately, which were close to the actual value of the optimal solution, and proved that the algorithm has higher stability and precision of identification; at the same time, for different population sizes, the algorithm also have global optimization and rapid convergence ability, and in fact, the speed and accuracy of identification process have a certain impact on the convergence, as to how to choose a reasonable initial value, which can reach a higher accuracy under the random initial value, and the system fault can be online identification is the key direction of the next step work.

Acknowledgement

This paper is supported by the science and technology project of Guangdong province (2014A010106033); the natural science foundation of Guangdong Province, the startup project of Guangdong province (2014A030310376);The project of young innovative talents in Colleges and universities of Guangdong province (631051)

References

1. Fayrouz Dkhichi; Benyounes Oukarfi; Youssef El Kouari; David Ouoba; Abderrahim Fakkar. Neural network based integration of MPPT and diagnosis of degradation for photovoltaic module[J]. Optical and Quantum Electronics, 2016,48(2)
2. SACHIN VRAJLAL RAJANI; VIVEK J PANDYA. Simulation and comparison of perturb and observe and

DOI: 10.1051/itmconf/20160704003

incremental conductance MPPT algorithms for solar energy system connected to grid[J]. Sadhana, 2015, Vol.40 (1):139-153.

3. Mahdi Rajabi Vincheh; Abbas Kargar; Gholamreza Arab Markadeh. Arabian A Hybrid Control Method for Maximum Power Point Tracking (MPPT) in Photovoltaic Systems[J].Journal for Science and Engineering. Section A: Sciences. 2014,39(6):4715-4725.
4. Hua Zhu; Zhang-lu Xu; Zi-juan Cao. Experimental research on charging characteristics of a solar photovoltaic system by the pressure-control method[J]. Journal of Zhejiang University. Science, 2011,12(6):470-474.
5. Ismail Nakir;Ali Durusu;Hakan Akca;Ali Ajder;Ramazan Ayaz;Enes Ugur;Mugdesem Tanrioven. A New MPPT Algorithm for Vehicle Integrated Solar Energy System[J]. Journal of Energy Resources Technology, 2015,138(2):1034-1038.
6. Nezihe Yildirana; Emin Tacerb. Identification of photovoltaic cell single diode discrete model parameters based on datasheet values[J]. Solar Energy, 2016,(127):175-183.
7. Dani Rusirawana; István Farkasb. Identification of Model Parameters of the Photovoltaic Solar Cells[J]. Energy Procedia, 2014 (57): 39-46.
8. LIU Fangrui, DUAN Shanxu, LIU Fei, et al. A variable step size INC MPPT method for PV systems[J]. IEEE Transactions on Industrial Electronics, 2008, 55(7): 2622-2628.
9. PATEL H, AGARWAL V. Maximum power point tracking scheme for PV systems operating under partially shaded condition[J]. IEEE Transactions on Industrial Electronics, 2008, 55(4):1689-1698.
10. KOTTAS T L, BOUTALIS Y S, KARLIS A D. New maximum power point tracker for PV arrays using fuzzy controller in close cooperation with fuzzy cognitive networks[J].. IEEE Transactions on Energy Conversion, 2006, 21(3): 793-803.
11. Ghani, F.;Duke, M.;Carson, J. Numerical calculation of series and shunt resistance of a photovoltaic cell using theLambert W-function: Experimental evaluation[J]. Solar Energy, 2013(87):246-253.
12. Yadir S, Benhmida M, Sidki M, et al. New method for extracting the model physical parameters of solar cells using explicit analytic solutions of current-voltage equation[C]. International Conference on icroelectronics(ICM), 2009: 390-393.
13. Lyden S, Haque M E, Gargoom A. et al. Modelling and parameter estimation of photovoltaic cell[C]. Universities Power Engineering Conference (AUPEC), 2012: 1-6.
14. Zhou Jianliang, Wang Bing, Zhang Yiming. Parameter identification and output power prediction of photovoltaic array based on the measured data[J]. Renewable Energy Resources, 2012, 30(7): 1-4.
15. Lyden S, Haque M E, Gargoom A. et al. Modelling and parameter estimation of photovoltaic cell[C]. Universities Power Engineering Conference (AUPEC), 2012: 1-6.
16. Neukom M T, Zufle S, Ruhstaller B. Reliable extraction of organic solar cell parameters by combining steady-state and transient techniques[J]. Organic Electronics, 2012, 13(12): 2910-2916.
17. Cheng Ze Dong Mengnan Yang Tiankai Han Lijie. Extraction of Solar Cell Model Parameters Based on Self-Adaptive Chaos Particle Swarm Optimization Algorithm[J]. TRANSACTIONS OF CHINA ELECTROTECHNICAL SOCIETY, 2014, 29(9): 245-252.
18. JIAN Xian-zhong, YAN Jun, FAN Jian-pen, HOU Yi-xin1, GUO Qiang. MPPT Control Method of Photovoltaic Array Based on Differential Evolution Algorithm[J]. Control Engineering of China, 2014, 21(4):559-556.

ITM Web of Conferences 7, 04004 (2016) DOI: 10.1051/itmconf/20160704004
ITA 2016

DEVS Models of Palletized Ground Stacking in Storeyed Grain Warehouse

Shu-Yi HOU[1,a], Yu-Kun LIU[1] and Xiao-Guang ZHOU[1]

[1]*Logistics engineering, School of Automation, Beijing University of Posts and Telecommunications, China*

Abstract. Processed grain stored in storeyed warehouse is generally stacked on the ground without pallets. However, in order to improve the storing way, we developed a new stacking method, palletized ground stacking. Simulation should be used to present this new storing way. DEVS provides a formalized way to describe the system model. In this paper, DEVS models of palletized ground stacking in storeyed grain warehouse are given and a simulation model is developed by AutoMod.

1 Introduction

Mostly grain is stored by stack on the ground without pallets in the warehouse. However, this way of storing has many disadvantages: (1) Mechanization degree is low. A lot of workers are needed to do loading, unloading and stacking operations when the grain is being moved into or out of the warehouse. If an emergency happens, high-intensive manual operation would decrease efficiency and lead to the delay of relief. (2) This way of storing would damage the grain because loading and unloading manual operations must be done. (3) Frequently walking into and out of the storing room would pollute the storing environment.

In order to improve the storing way of grain, we develop a new stacking method, palletized ground stacking. It not only can increase the mechanization level, but decrease the cost and the probability of damaging grain as well. The system of storeyed grain warehouse is always complicated and has many random factors, so analyzing it using traditional mathematical tools is difficult. Simulation is a useful tool than can be used to analyze this new storing way better. In most cases, we abstract the target system in the real world into system model before designing simulation model. DEVS is short for discrete event system specification. It provides a formalized method to describe system model based on system theory. It is a mechanism to modularize, hierarchize and formalize system modeling and simulation. DEVS has been proved that it is a general formalized mechanism to describe every subclass of discrete event system. DEVS can make developers share their achievement at modeling and simulation at most. So we use DEVS to build the system model of palletized ground stacking in storeyed grain warehouse.

2 The DEVS Formalism

DEVS model can describe the system by two levels, namely, atomic DEVS and coupled DEVS. Atomic DEVS models describe autonomous behaviors of a system including transitions of system state, responses to external inputs, system outputs and so on. Several atomic DEVS models can be connected into a coupled DEVS model, generating a hierarchical construction. A coupled DEVS model is comprised of many components which can be either atomic DEVS or coupled DEVS.

An atomic DEVS model can be written as follows.

$$\textit{Atomic DEVS}{=}{<}X, S, Y, \delta_{int}, \delta_{ext}, \lambda, ta{>} \quad (1)$$

X is external input event set. Y is output set. S is system state set. ta is time advance function. ta(s) denotes the time that the system state remains at s without any external events. ta(s)=+∞ means that when there are no external events arrive, the system state will be s forever. ta(s)=0 indicates the simulation clock will not be advanced as long as the system state remains s.ext is external state transition function. int is internal state transition function. If there are no external events arrive, state s will transit to int(s) after the time ta(s). At the same time, e will be reset to 0. is output function.

A coupled DEVS model can be written as follows.

$$\textit{Coupled DEVS}{=}{<}X_{self}, Y_{self}, D, \{M_i\}, \{I_i\}, \{Z_{i,j}\}, select{>} \quad (2)$$

self is coupled DEVS self. Xself is external input event set. Yself is output event set. D is unique component names set (self∉ D). {Mi} is coupled DEVS component set. {Mi|i∈ D} and every Mi is an atomic DEVS. {Ii} is a

[a] houshuyi2928@163.com

set of influences of a component. {Zi,j} is the transition of component i's output into component j's input. The input and output transition set is {Zi,j|i∈ D∪{self}, j∈ Ii}. {Zi,j} denotes the coupled construction. select is select function. When several components transform their states, select function is used to choose one of these state transitions as coupled model state transition.

3 DEVS Models of Palletized Ground Stacking in Storeyed Grain Warehouse

The model of delivering grain into warehouse is similar to the model of delivering grain out of warehouse. Hence, there are only given the DEVS models of delivering grain out of warehouse. The grain is palletized stacked on the ground. The entities in this system include forklifts, control center (core), trucks, elevators, slideways, reciprocating lifts and every single room in the warehouse. Forklifts move the grain out of every single storage room. The grain on the first floor is delivered out of warehouse to trucks by forklift. The grain on the higher floor is delivered to the first floor by elevator, slideway or reciprocating lift and then be taken into trucks by forklift. In this paper, coupled DEVS is built first to illustrate the relationship of every entity and then each entity is described as atomic DEVS.

3.1. Coupled DEVS Models

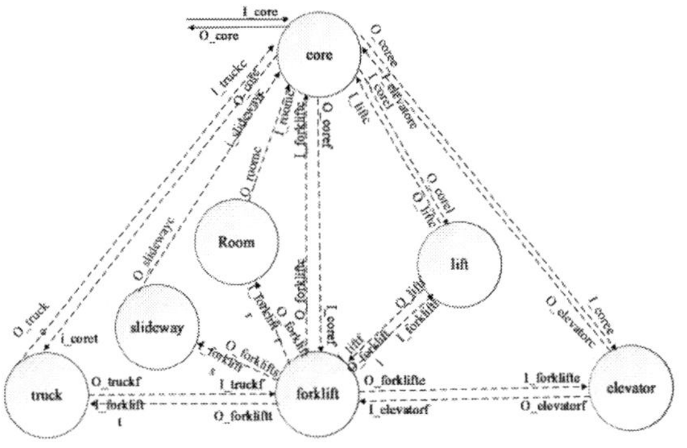

Figure 1. Coupled DEVS of Palletized Ground Stacking In Storeyed Warehouse.

The circles in Fig.1 stand for components in coupled DEVS including every atomic DEVS model, namely, truck, forklift, room, slideway, reciprocating lift, elevator, core and room. Arrows stand for the relationship between external world and coupled DEVS and the relationship between input and output of every atomic DEVS. The words on the arrow stand for the input and output port of atomic DEVS. For example, i_truckf stands for the input port of forklift which can receive information from truck. i stands for input port and f is short for forklift. O_elevatorc stands for the output port of elevator which can send information to core. o stands for output port and c is short for core. It is the same expressing way as other input and output ports. Coupled DEVS inputs external events by i_core (the information about the grain in the warehouse) and outputs statistical information such as grain quantity, departure time and machine utility through o_core.

3.2 Atomic DEVS Models

The atomic DEVS model of reciprocating lift is described in detail by Fig. 2 and equation 3-10. The atomic DEVS model of elevator is described in detail by Fig. 3 and equation 11-18. The atomic DEVS model of truck is described in detail by Fig. 4 and equation 19-26. The atomic DEVS model of forklift is described in detail by Fig. 5 and equation 27-34.

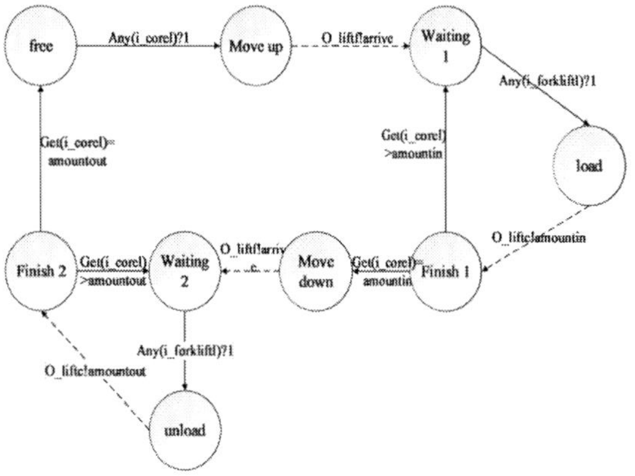

Figure 2. Reciprocating Lift Atomic DEVS

Any(i_corel)?1: receive outbound task from core
O_liftf!arrive: inform forklift that it has already been arrived
Any(i_forkliftl)?1: loading and unloading request from forklift
O_liftc!amountin: the accumulated quantity of grain that is loading into the lift
Get(i_forkliftl)>amountin: the outbound task has not been finished
Get(i_corel)=amountin: finish outbound task
O_liftc!amountout: the accumulated quantity of grain that is unloading out of the lift
Get(i_corel)=amountout: finish loading and unloading task

$$Lift=\langle X, S, Y, \delta_{int}, \delta_{ext}, \lambda, ta\rangle \quad (3)$$

$$X=\{i\_corel, i\_forkliftl\} \quad (4)$$

$$Y=\{O\_liftc, O\_liftf\} \quad (5)$$

 DOI: 10.1051/itmconf/20160704004

$$s = \begin{Bmatrix} free \\ move\ up \\ waiting1 \\ load \\ finish1 \\ move\ down \\ waiting2 \\ unload \\ finish2 \end{Bmatrix} \quad (6)$$

$$\delta_{int} = \begin{Bmatrix} \delta_{int}(move\ up) = waiting1 \\ \delta_{int}(load) = finish1 \\ \delta_{int}(move\ down) = waiting2 \\ \delta_{int}(unload) = finish2 \end{Bmatrix} \quad (7)$$

$$\delta_{out} = \begin{Bmatrix} \delta_{out}(waiting1, i\_forkliftl) = load \\ \delta_{out}(free, i\_corel) = move\ up \\ \delta_{out}(finish1, i\_corel) = move\ down \\ \delta_{out}(finish1, i\_corel) = waiting1 \\ \delta_{out}(waiting2, i\_corel) = finish2 \\ \delta_{out}(finish2, i\_corel) = free \\ \delta_{out}(waiting2, i\_forkliftl) = unload \end{Bmatrix} \quad (8)$$

$$\lambda = \begin{Bmatrix} \lambda(move\ up) = O\_liftf \\ \lambda(load) = O\_liftc \\ \lambda(move\ down) = O\_liftf \\ \lambda(unload) = O\_liftc \end{Bmatrix} \quad (9)$$

$$ta = \begin{cases} ta(free) = ta(waiting1) = ta(waiting2) = ta(finish1) = ta(finish2) = +\infty \\ ta(move\ up) = move\ up - time \\ ta(move\ down) = move\ down - time \\ ta(load) = load - time \\ ta(unload) = unload - time \end{cases} \quad (10)$$

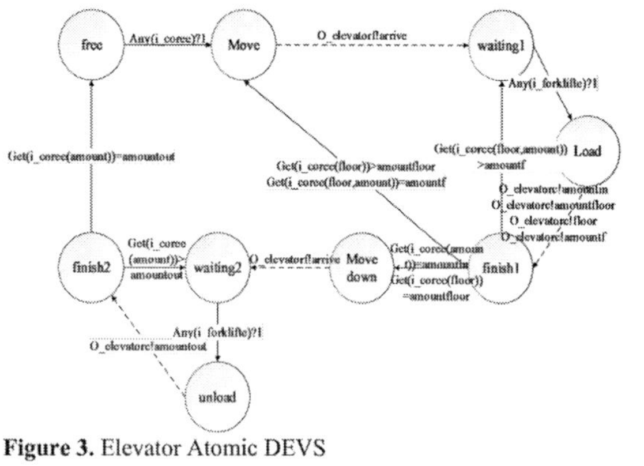

Figure 3. Elevator Atomic DEVS

Any(i_coree)?1: receive outbound task from core
O_elevatorf!arrive: inform forklift that it has already been arrived

Any(i_forklifte)?1: loading and unloading request from forklift
O_elevatorc!amountin: the accumulated quantity of grain that is loading into the elevator
O_elevatorc!amountfloor: the accumulated floor quantity that elevator stops
O_elevatorc!floor: the floor number that elevator is stopping at
O_elevatorc!amountf: the loading quantity from the floor that elevator is stopping at
Get(i_coree(floor,amount))>amountf: the task of loading into the elevator at the current floor has not been finished
Get(i_coree(floor,amount))=amountf: finish the task of loading into the elevator at the current floor
Get(i_coree(floor))>amountfloor: the amount of total floor that elevator should stop has not been reached
Get(i_coree(floor))=amountfloor: reach the amount of total floor that elevator should stop
Get(i_coree(amount))=amountin: finish loading task
O_elevatorc!amountout: the accumulated quantity of grain that is unloading out of the elevator
Get(i_corec(amount))>amountout: the task of unloading from elevator has not been finished
Get(i_corec(amount))=amountout: finish loading and unloading task

$$Elevator = <X, S, Y, \delta_{int}, \delta_{ext}, \lambda, ta> \quad (11)$$

$$X = \{i\_coree, i\_forklifte, i\_corec\} \quad (12)$$

$$Y = \{O\_elevatorf, O\_elevatorc\} \quad (13)$$

$$s = \begin{Bmatrix} free \\ move \\ waiting1 \\ load \\ finish1 \\ move\ down \\ waiting2 \\ unload \\ finish2 \end{Bmatrix} \quad (14)$$

$$\delta_{int} = \begin{Bmatrix} \delta_{int}(move) = waiting1 \\ \delta_{int}(load) = finish1 \\ \delta_{int}(move\ down) = waiting2 \\ \delta_{int}(unload) = finish2 \end{Bmatrix} \quad (15)$$

$$\delta_{out} = \begin{Bmatrix} \delta_{out}(waiting1, i\_forklifte) = load \\ \delta_{out}(free, i\_coree) = move \\ \delta_{out}(finish1, i\_coree) = move\ down \\ \delta_{out}(finish1, i\_coree) = waiting1 \\ \delta_{out}(waiting2, i\_coree) = finish2 \\ \delta_{out}(finish2, i\_coree) = free \\ \delta_{out}(finish1, i\_coree) = waiting1 \\ \delta_{out}(finish1, i\_coree) = move \\ \delta_{out}(waiting2, i\_forklifte) = unload \end{Bmatrix} \quad (16)$$

$$\lambda = \begin{Bmatrix} \lambda(move) = O\_elevatorf \\ \lambda(load) = O\_elevatorc \\ \lambda(move\ down) = O\_elevatorf \\ \lambda(unload) = O\_elevatorc \end{Bmatrix} \quad (17)$$

$$ta = \begin{cases} ta(free) = ta(waiting1) = ta(waiting2) = ta(finish1) = ta(finish2) = +\infty \\ ta(move) = move - time \\ ta(move\ down) = move\ down - time \\ ta(load) = load - time \\ ta(unload) = unload - time \end{cases} \quad (18)$$

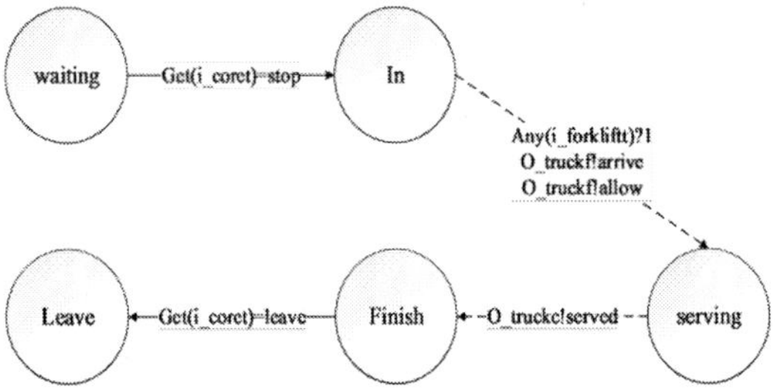

Figure 4. Truck Atomic DEVS

Get(i_coret)=stop: receive stopping information from core

Any(i_forkliftt)?1: loading and unloading request from forklift

O_truckf!arrive: truck has already been stopped

O_truckf!allow: truck can be loaded and unloaded

O_truckc!served: finish loading and unloading task

Get(i_coret)=leave: receive leaving information from core

$$Truck=<X, S, Y, \delta_{int}, \delta_{ext}, \lambda, ta> \quad (19)$$

$$X=\{i\_coret, i\_forkliftt\} \quad (20)$$

$$Y=\{O\_truckf, O\_truckc\} \quad (21)$$

$$s = \begin{Bmatrix} waiting \\ in \\ serving \\ finish \\ leave \end{Bmatrix} \quad (22)$$

$$\delta_{int} = \begin{Bmatrix} \delta_{int}(in) = serving \\ \delta_{int}(serving) = finish \end{Bmatrix} \quad (23)$$

$$\delta_{out} = \begin{Bmatrix} \delta_{out}(in, i\_forkliftt) = serving \\ \delta_{out}(waiting, i\_coret) = in \\ \delta_{out}(finish, i\_coret) = leave \end{Bmatrix} \quad (24)$$

$$\lambda = \begin{Bmatrix} \lambda(in) = O\_truckf \\ \lambda(serving) = O\_truckc \end{Bmatrix} \quad (25)$$

$$ta = \begin{cases} ta(waiting) = ta(leave) = ta(finish) + \infty \\ ta(in) = in - time \\ ta(serving) = serving - time \end{cases} \quad (26)$$

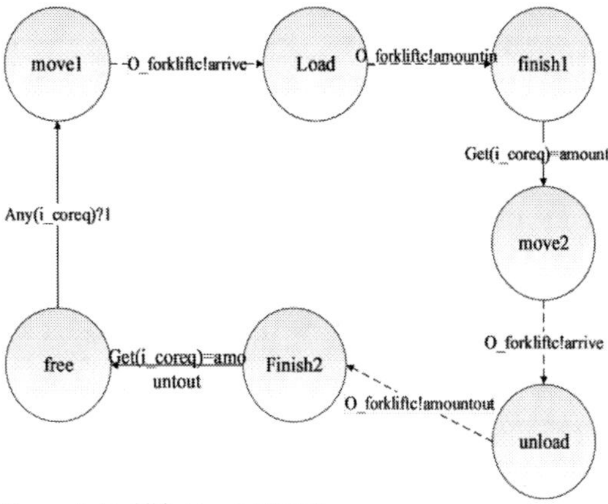

Figure 5. Forklift Atomic DEVS

Any(i_coref)?1: receive outbound task from core

O_forkliftc!arrive: arrive at the destination

O_forkliftc!amountin: the quantity of grain that the forklift picks up

Get(i_coref)=amountin: finish the task of picking up a pallet of grain

O_forkliftc!amountout: the accumulated unloading quantity

Get(i_coref)=amountout: finish outbound task

$$Forklift=<X, S, Y, \delta_{int}, \delta_{ext}, \lambda, ta> \quad (27)$$

$$X=\{i\_coref\} \quad (28)$$

$$Y=\{O\_forkliftc\} \quad (29)$$

 DOI: 10.1051/itmconf/20160704004

$$s = \begin{Bmatrix} move1 \\ load \\ finish1 \\ move2 \\ unload \\ finish2 \\ free \end{Bmatrix} \quad (30)$$

$$\delta_{int} = \begin{Bmatrix} \delta_{int}(move1) = load \\ \delta_{int}(load) = finish1 \\ \delta_{int}(move2) = unload \\ \delta_{int}(unload) = finish2 \end{Bmatrix} \quad (31)$$

$$\delta_{out} = \begin{Bmatrix} \delta_{out}(finish1, i\_coref) = move2 \\ \delta_{out}(finish2, i\_coref) = free \\ \delta_{out}(free, i\_coref) = move1 \end{Bmatrix} \quad (32)$$

$$\lambda = \begin{Bmatrix} \lambda(move1) = O\_forkliftc \\ \lambda(load) = O\_forkliftc \\ \lambda(move2) = O\_forkliftc \\ \lambda(unload) = O\_forkliftc \end{Bmatrix} \quad (33)$$

$$ta = \begin{cases} ta(waiting1) = ta(waiting2) = ta(finish1) = ta(finish2) = +\infty \\ ta(move1) = move1 - time \\ ta(move2) = move2 - time \\ ta(load) = load - time \\ ta(unload) = unload - time \end{cases} \quad (34)$$

4 Simulation Experiment

We use the DEVS models above as the system model and then develop a simulation model to present this new storing way, palletized ground stacking, by AutoMod.

4.1. Transformation Process

The following steps indicate the process that transforming DEVS models into simulation model.

4.1.1 Model initialization

Information about the grain in the storeyed warehouse is input into control center through i_core. Trucks, forklifts, elevators and reciprocating lifts inform their current states to control center through o_truckc, o_forkliftc, o_elevatorc, o_liftc. We use variables and load attributes in AutoMod to replace input and output ports in DEVS models. Every atomic DEVS model is transformed into sub models in AutoMod.

4.1.2 Model implementation

(1) According to the outbound task information sent by core, forklifts send information of arriving and the amount of loading and unloading to input port i_truckc through output port o_truckc.

(2) After trucks arrive, trucks send information of arriving and loading amount to i_truckf through o_truckf. If the loading task has already been finished, trucks send information of finishing to input port i_truckc through o_truckc. Then core orders truck to leave through input port i_coret.

(3) According to the outbound task information sent by core, reciprocating lifts send information of arriving to input port i_liftf through output port o_liftf. Then reciprocating lifts send information of loading and unloading amount to input port i_liftc through output port o_liftc.

(4) According to the outbound task information sent by core, elevators send information of arriving to input port i_elevatorf through output port o_elevatorf. Then elevators send information of loading and unloading amount to input port i_elevatorc through output port o_elevatorc.

4.2. A Simulation Example

A storeyed grain warehouse has five floors. The first floor is 7.2 meters high and there are five single rooms to store processed grain. The second floor is 7.2 meters high and there are six rooms. Other floors are all six meters high and there are four rooms on every floor. The storing way is palletized ground stacking. 40 bags of grain can be stacked on one pallet and one bag of grain weighs 25 kilograms. One reciprocating lift, two elevators and two slideways can be used to deliver grain from higher floors to the first floor. The reciprocating lift can be only used by the grain on the second floor. The capacity of elevators is 4 pallets of grain. The grain can be delivered by either elevator or slideway. When the grain on two different floors need to use one and the same elevator, this elevator can be used to deliver grain on both floors but the grain on higher floor has the priority to be delivered first. The storeyed grain warehouse has 9 platforms for trucks. We developed a simulation model of this storeyed grain warehouse in AutoMod and the simulation panorama is shown in Fig. 6.

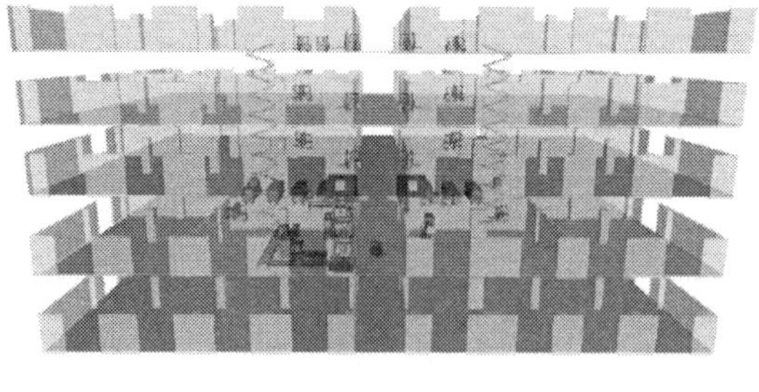

Figure 6. Simulation Panorama

DOI: 10.1051/itmconf/20160704004

5 Summary

To improve the way of storing grain in storeyed warehouse, a new storing way, palletized ground stacking, is developed. Furthermore, to better present this new storing way, we build DEVS models as the system model before developing simulation model. Finally, we develop a simulation model according to the DEVS models.

Acknowledgements

This work is supported by Natural Public Industry (Food) Special Funds for Scientific Research (No. 201313009-06).

References

1. W. Bin, Communication and network 12, 128-130, (2008)
2. K.H. Kim, Y.R. Seong, T.G. Kim, and K.H. Park, Transactions of the Society for Computer Simulation International, 13, 135-154,(1996)
3. S. Robinson, R.E. Nance, R.J. Paul, M. Pidd, and S.J.E. Taylor, Simulation modeling practice and theory, 12, 479-494, (2004)
4. H. Rui, Z. Guo-chun, and L. Shao-jun, Journal of system simulation, 23, 30-33, (2001)
5. M. Spiegel, P.F. Reynolds, and D.C. Brogan, Proceedings of the 2005 winter simulation conference, 437-444, (2005)
6. H. Vangheluwe, CS522 Fall Term 2001, (2001)
7. Q. Xiao-gang, and D. Wei, Journal of system simulation, 21, 6697-6709, (2009)
8. C. Yun, Q. Yue, and Z. Yu, Technology and Method, 33, 253-256, (2013)

DOI: 10.1051/itmconf/20160704005

Design of Tropical Flowers Environmental Parameters Wireless Monitoring System Based on MSP430

Jian-Qing HUANG[a] , Qi YUAN[b,*] ,Wan-Ping LI[a] , and Jia-Bao GAO[a]

1College of Applied Science and Technology, Hainan University, Danzhou, China
2College of Mechanical & Electrical Engineering, Hainan University, Haikou, China
[a]hjqoffice@163.com, [a]165078707@qq.com, [a] 568101889@qq.com
*hainuyq @163.com

Abstract. Considering the importance of real-time monitoring tropical flower environment parameters, the paper designs a wireless monitoring system based on MSP430F149 for tropical flower growing parameters. The proposed system uses sensor nodes to obtain data of temperature, humidity and light intensity, sink node to collect data from sensor nodes through wireless sensor network, and monitoring center to process data downloaded from the sink node through RS232 serial port. The node hardware platform is composed of a MSP430F149 processor, AM2306 and NHZD10AI sensors used to adopt temperature, humidity and light intensity data, and an nRF905 RF chip used to receive and send data. The node software, operated in IAR Embedded Workbench, adopts C Language to do node data collection and process, wireless transmission and serial port communication. The software of monitoring center develops in VB6.0, which can provide vivid and explicit real-time monitoring platform for flower farmers.

1 Introduction

Tropical flowers are fine ornamental plants, with broad leaves and colorful flowers, often as the exquisite gift among people. But the growth of tropical flowers requires strict environmental parameters, such as temperature, humidity and light intensity. Without sound environment, the growth and ornamental effect of tropical flowers would be negatively affected. Like anthurium, it favors warm and humid climate, intolerable of dry wind, burning sun as well as low and high temperature. And the ideal growth temperature is between 18°C-30°C. The relevant humidity should maintain between 75%-85% [1], better with light intensity in the range of 8, 000lx-18, 000lx. The lack of light can result in plants overgrowth, bud abortion and soft stem. Too much light can lead to color fading of leaves and bracts, even worse, burning and withering [2]. Hence in the growth of tropical flowers, environmental parameters, including temperature, humidity and light intensity should be constantly monitored. In this way, specific and efficient measures can be taken to guarantee the growth of tropical flowers under the most favorable conditions.

Data collecting in traditional flower greenhouse adopts the way of instruments and manual work, with high cost, intensive labor and long period of data collecting, which can not guarantee its real-time validity. Using serial bus and fieldbus to collect data requires to lay massive electric cable, difficult in construction. Let alone the fact that the electric cables are easily eroded and broken down, with high cost in maintenance and limitations in data collecting scale[3-4]. The wireless sensor unit is new technology to collect and process data, with wider monitoring scale, smaller size, lower cost and self-network [5-6]. The wireless sensor nodes are deployed in the greenhouse to collect data can cut down the cost in laying electric cables and maintenance, alleviate labor intensity and coordinate data perception, monitoring and collection. This can help technicians better know the conditions in the greenhouse and make wise decision. In light of this, this paper designs a wireless monitoring system to collect data on environmental parameters in the greenhouse of tropical flowers. The wireless monitoring system can collect, process and report the environmental parameters, including temperature, humidity and light intensity in real-time. This can help technicians instantly know the growth condition of tropical flowers, which is significant in its effort to ensure safety production, lighten labor intensity and improve efficiency.

2 System Structure

DOI: 10.1051/itmconf/20160704005

The whole system is formed by sensor node, route node, sink node, local monitoring center and distant monitoring center, as presented in Figure 1. The sensor nodes and route nodes are deployed in the greenhouse and its surrounding, constituted by self-organizing network. The sensor nodes can collect data on temperature, humidity and light intensity. And these data can be sent to the sink node in the way of multi-hop. Then the local monitoring center will analyze, proceed, store, visualize and report data sent from sink node by serial port RS232. The sink node can also be connected into Internet, thereof sending data to distant monitoring center.

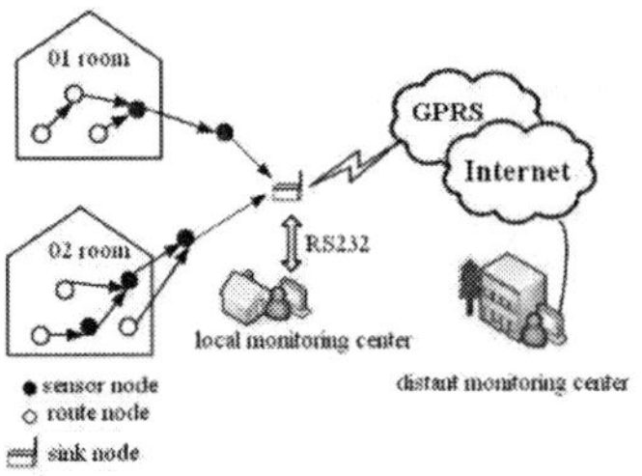

Figure 1. Network Structure of the Monitoring System

3 Hardware Design

The wireless sensor network nodes include sensor node, route node and sink node. The routing node can be substituted by sensor node. The sink node is connected with computers in monitoring center. As for hardware structure, it only needs to reduce sensor modules and increase serial communication ports modules. The design of rest parts are almost the same with the sensor nodes.

3.1 Hardware Structure

The sensor nodes include sensor module, processor module, wireless communication module and battery module. The sensor module is formed by temperature and humidity sensor, light sensor and peripheral circuit, responsible for collecting and transforming data on temperature, humidity and light intensity in the greenhouse. The processor adopts SCM MSP430F149, with low voltage and low power consumption, to collect data, configure parameters of each module and control data sending and receiving. The wireless communication module adopts nRF905, with low power consumption and adjustable transmitting power, to send local data among modules. The battery module provides electric power to maintain the normal function of each module.

3.2 Sensor Module Design

To guarantee the range and accuracy of data collected in the greenhouse, the temperature and humidity measuring device adopts the sensor, AM2306, developed by Guangzhou Lexiang Co. Ltd. AM2306, which contains calibrated digital signal output, is a compound sensor to measure temperature and humidity. The sensor includes one capacitive humidity sensor and one high-precision temperature sensor, connected with 8-bit SCM (Single Chip Microcomputer). And its advantages mainly reflect in quick response, anti-interference and high cost performance. Its precision of temperature measuring is within ±1°C and humidity measuring within ±2%RH. The 1-wire pin DATA of AM2306 connects with 5.1kΩ pull-up resistor and SCM port P2.0, as presented in Figure 2.

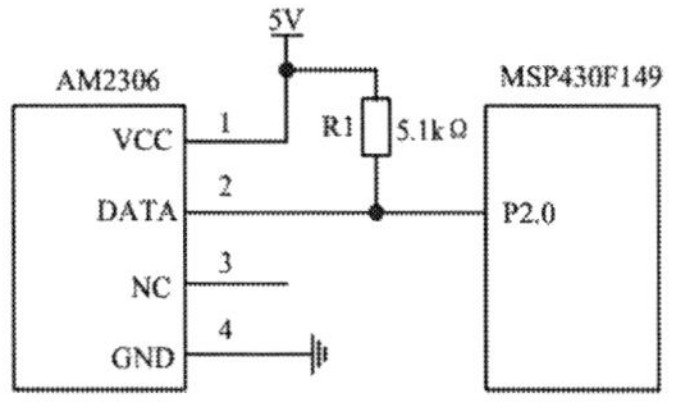

Figure 2. Interface between AM2306 and MSP430F149

The light intensity sensor adopts NHZD10AI, developed by Wuhan Zhongke Nenghui Technology Development Co., Ltd. The NHZD10AI adopts imported luminance as its core, with output electric current 4-20mA and precision of ±5% rdg. NHZD10AI is connected into inside A/D converter P6.0 port after its output electricity current has been transformed into voltage through resistor R2, as presented in Figure 3.

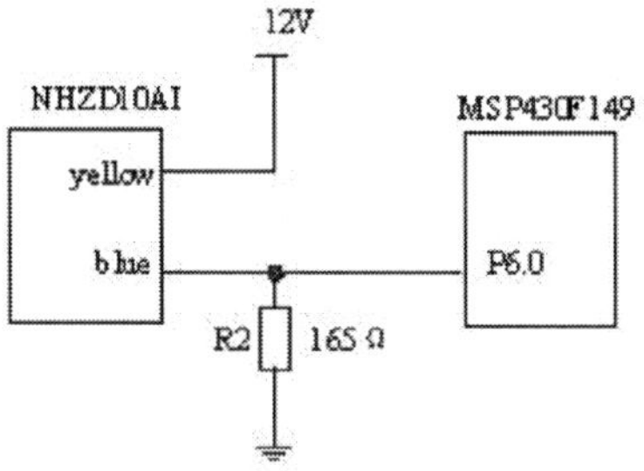

Figure 3. Interface between NHZD10AI and MSP430F149

3.3 Processor Module and Wireless Communication Module Design

The processor module adopts SCM MSP430F149. Its main advantages reflect in low voltage, low power consumption and support 1.8V-3.6V electric power supply, with only 280μA electric current in its full swing and 0.1μA in dormant state. It provides 5 low power modes, especially suitable for working condition of low power consumption.[7,8]. The wireless communication module adopts nRF905, with low power and adjustable transmitting power. Its supply voltage is 1.9V-3.6V, with only 11mA under output power of -10dBm, 12.5mA in working mode and 2.5μA in shutdown mode. The idle mode and shutdown are set inside to save energy[9].

The nRF905 has 3 sets of interface, including SPI transmission interface, state output interface and mode control interface. The SPI transmission interface is used to transform and exchange data with SCM, including 4 pins, CSN, SCK, MISO and MOSI, which respectively connects the port P1.0, P1.2, P1.6 and P1.4 of SCM MSP430F149. The state output interface is used to monitor data nRF905, including 3 pins, CD, AM and DR, which respectively connects the port P2.4, P2.2 and P2.0 of SCM MSP430F149. The mode control interface decides working mode of nRF905, including 3 pins, RX_CE, TX_EN, PWR_UP, which respectively connects with the port P3.0, P3.2 and P2.6 of SCM MSP430F149. The connection of nRF905 and SCM MSP430F149 is presented in Figure 4.

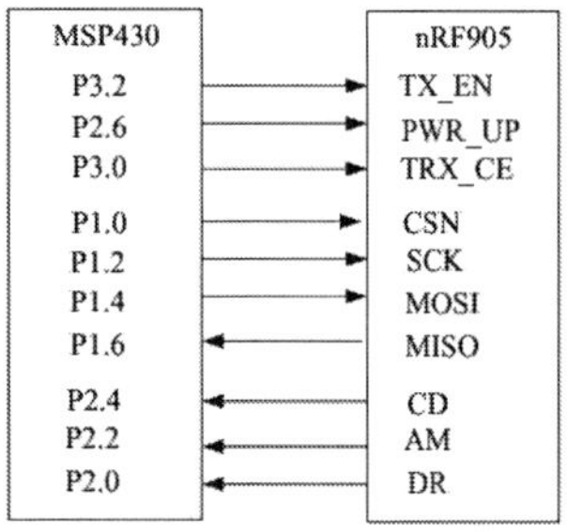

Figure 4. Interface between NRF905 and MSP430F149

3.4 Battery Module Design

Considering the requirements for outside monitoring, the battery module adopts 1200mAh and 3.2V lithium-ion ferrous phosphate battery to provide electricity. The voltage of two pcs of Li-battery is transformed into 5V after series connection through LT1129-5, and then 3.3V through LT1129-3.3, to provide electricity for the wireless communication module. Besides, the 5V voltage will be transformed into 12V voltage through LT1930, to provide electricity for sensor modules.

4 Software Design

4.1 Node Software Design

The embedded node software, based on IAR Embedded Workbench, is developed by SCM C Language in hardware and modular programming in software, which include modules of major programmes, data collection, data receiving and sending, serial port communication.

4.1.1 Main Program

The node first initializes the hardware, including system clock, I/O port, timer and nRF905. Then the wireless communication module begins to synchronize information, adjust system time and send data based on time-to-be-received. Later the node starts to periodically collect, send and receive data. Time intervals of data collection are set in 30 minutes. Every time data collection finished, the sensor will automatically power off to save electricity. Meanwhile, another timer is set up to mark the time of sending local data. During the period, the node can receive and send data from other nodes. When sending time is up, the node will send local collected data. If synchronized information received from sink node, the sensor will accordingly adjust system time and then stay in dormant state. Till the next time of data collection, a new cycle will begin, as presented in Figure 5.

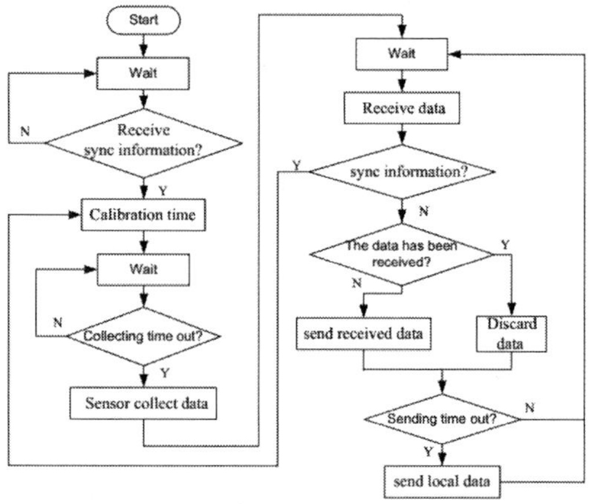

Figure 5. Main program flow chart of sensor node

4.1.2 Temperature and humidity measurement

The AM2306 adopts 1-wire to communicate with SCM MSP430F149. Firstly, SCM MSP430F149 pulls down DATA bus through port P4.0 and maintain above 500μs as starting signal, then pulls up 20~40μs of DATA, waiting responding signal of AM2306. When AM2306 monitor the starting signal, it transmits 80 μs low current through DATA pin as responding signal, then pulls up DATA to send data. The time and sequence are presented in Figure 6.

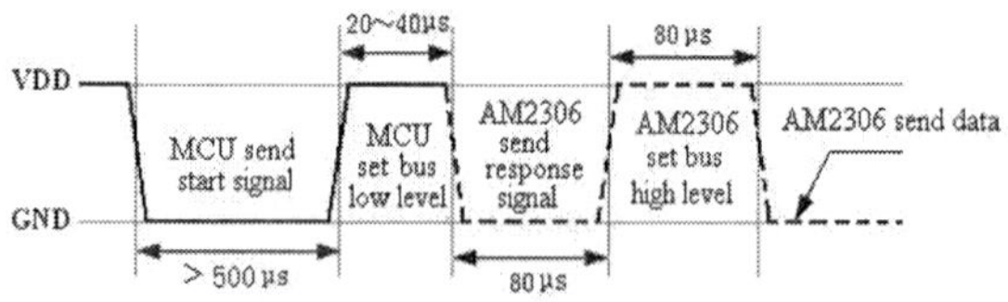

Figure 6. AM2306 Waveform

 DOI: 10.1051/itmconf/20160704005

The AM2306 once transmits 40-bit data, from high to low. The data format: 8 bit humidity integer data + 8 bit humidity decimal data + 8 bit temperature integer data + 8 bit temperature decimal data + 8 bit check code. The check code is the total amount of the former four bytes. For example, the AM2306 sends 40 bit data: 0000 0010 1001 0010 0000 0001 0000 1101 1010 0010; Humidity: 0000 0010 1001 0010 =0292H=65.8%; Temperature: 0000 0001 0000 1101=10DH=26.9°C; Check code: 1010 0010=62H. The check code of SCM: 0000 0010+1001 0010 +0000 0001+0000 1101= 1010 0010=62H. As is calculated, the check code is same, which shows the data is received correctly, or it will abandon data receiving. The process of measuring humidity and temperature is presented in Figure 7.

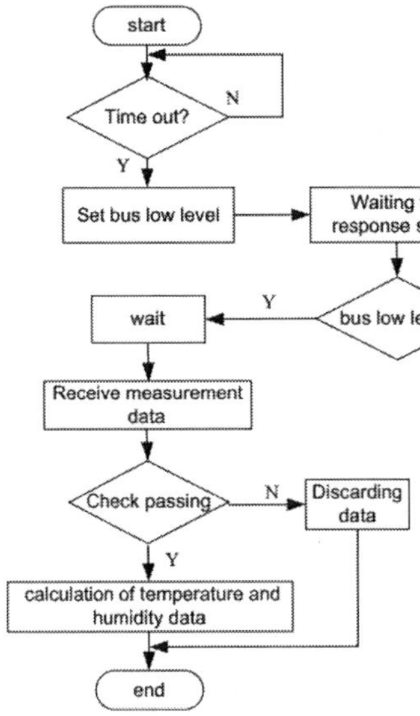

Figure 7. Flow Chart of Software for Temperature and Humidity Measurement

4.1.3 Light Intensity Measurement

When the output electricity current of NHZD10AI is transformed into voltage through resistor R2, the 12-bit A/D converter inside SCM will transform that into digital quantity. Then the processor will calculate output electricity of NHZD10AI according to {[(1)]} and calculate light intensity according to {[(2)]}.

$$I_{out} = \frac{3.3N_{ADC}}{4095R_2} \quad (1)$$

In Formula, N_{ADC} is digital quantity transformed by A/D converter. Iout is output electricity current of NHZD10AI, mA.

$$LG = \frac{I_{out} - 4}{16} \times LG_{max} \quad (2)$$

In Formula, *LG* light intensity, Lx. LG_{max} is maximum value for light intensity, up to 2000 Lx.

4.2 Monitoring Center Software Design

The software in monitoring center can make it possible for technicians to look up real-time data. The software, developed by VB6.0, mainly conducts efficient serial communication with sink node through the control MSComm. Once the sink node begins to send data to serial port, the incident OnComm of MSComm will be triggered. The computer can collect data in OnComm incident, then adopts embedding function of external programmes to save and manage data in EXCEL. The software mainly achieves real-time monitoring of environmental parameters, real-time curve plotting, historical curve plotting, and historical data search and collection, warning and parameters set. The operating surface of real-time monitoring on environmental parameters is presented in Figure 8.

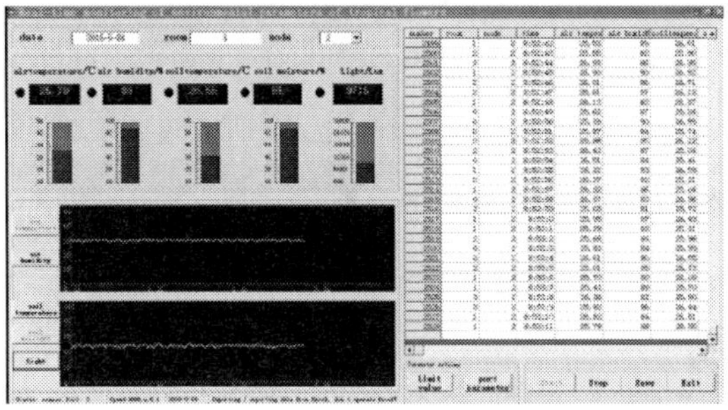

Figure 8. Real-time Monitoring Interface

5 Results

The measurement data of sensor node in flowers greenhouses was compared with HTC-1 temperature and humidity meter. HTC-1 temperature measurement accuracy is ± 1% °C, and its humidity measurement accuracy ± 5% RH. It is shown that the maximum relative errors of temperature and humidity are 5.78% and 1.37% in Table1 and Table2. The results demonstrate that the system can implement real-time monitoring of parameters in the greenhouse of tropical flowers.

Table 1. Temperature Measurement Data

time	Sensor node(°C)	HTC-1(°C)	relative error(%)
9:00	21.3	22.4	4.91
9:10	21.2	22.4	5.35
9:20	21.2	22.5	5.78
9:30	21.8	22.6	3.53

9:40	21.8	22.6	3.53
9:50	21.8	22.5	3.11
10:00	21.7	22.5	3.56
10:10	21.8	22.6	3.53
10:20	21.8	22.5	3.11
10:30	21.9	22.6	3.09

Table 2. Humidity Measurement Data

time	Sensor node(%)	HTC-1(%)	relative error(%)
9:00	78.5	79	0.63
9:10	78.9	79	0.13
9:20	78.7	78	0.89
9:30	78.9	78	1.15
9:40	78.9	79	0.12
9:50	79.3	79	0.38
10:00	79.2	79	0.25
10:10	78.9	80	1.37
10:20	78.9	80	1.37
10:30	79	80	1.25

6 Conclusions

The paper designs a wireless monitoring system for environmental parameters of tropical flowers. The sensor node is controlled by SCM MSP430F149, to collect data on temperature, humidity and light intensity by AM2306 and NHZD10AI, and to send and receive data through nRF905. The sensor node sends the data to sink node in the way of multi-hop. Then the sink node sends the processed data to local monitoring center through serial port RS232. This has achieved the wireless collection and monitoring of environmental parameters in the greenhouse of tropical flowers. The system has practical and realistic significance in safety production, alleviating labor intensity and improving efficiency in tropical flowers industry.

References

1. J.L.Han, "Ordinary plant diseases and insect pests and methods of prevention and cure in Anthurium andraeanum planting Greenhouse", Forest By-Product and Speciality in China, vol.3, pp.56-59,2010.
2. Y.M. Sun, "Control Measures of facilities environment for pot anthurium andraeanum in Xinjiang", Forestry of Xinjiang, vol.3, pp.25-26,2013.
3. C. F. Wan, S. F. Du, and L. Zhao, "Aquaculture Field Environmental Monitoring System Based on WSN", Journal of agricultural mechanization research, vol.32, pp.170-173, 2010.
4. H. H. Hao, "Data acquisition system for greenhouse based on wireless sensor network", Electronic design engineering, vol.20, pp.70-73, 2012.
5. A.Willig, "Wireless Sensor Networks:concept,Challenges and Approaches", Elektrotechnik & informationstechnik, vol.6, pp.224-231, 2006.
6. W.C.Guo, H. J. Cheng, and R. M. Li, "Greenhouse Monitoring System Based on Wireless Sensor Networks", Transactions of the Chinese Society for Agricultural Machinery, vol.41, pp.181-185, 2010.
7. W.X.Wang, X.W.Luo, and D.Z.Sun, "Design of wireless sensor network node for data transmission in tea plantations", Transaction of the CSAE, vol.27, pp.169-173, 2010.
8. C.Q. Liu, Y.N.Zhang, and K.T.Feng, "Wireless and real-time monitoring system for temperature and humidity based on MSP430F149", Microcontrollers & Embedded Systems, vol.5, pp.61-64, 2015.
9. M.D. Xue, "Low power Temperature and Humidity Measurement System Based on nRF905", Modern electronics technique, vol.33, pp.135-138, 2010.

DOI: 10.1051/itmconf/20160704006

A Testable Design Method for Memories by Boundary Scan Technique

Guo-Hui QIAO[1], Zhong-Liang DENG[1], Ke HAN[1], Dong-Yang YAO[1] and Zhi-Heng YUE[1]

[1] *School of Electronic Engineering, Beijing University of Posts and Telecommunications, Beijing 100876, China*

Abstract: This paper presents a design for test the embedded flash in an object System-on-a-chip (SoC). The feature of the Flash TAP (Test Access Port) complies with the IEEE std.1149.1, and it can select different scan chains and other control registers for other test. By the trade-off between the test time and the circuit area, an IST (In System Test) circuit is designed in the SoC. Experiment results on the embedded memory have shown that the proposed method costs small testing timing by the use of IST.

1 Introduction

The increasingly complex design of SoC (System On a Chip) causes not only the chip area increases, and the testability of circuit and system also declines sharply[1]. The test time account for a bigger and bigger proportion of the whole SoC design time, the regular testing methods is facing serious test difficulty. With the design and test cycle shortens, combine the test and design to complete the DFT (Design for Testability) has become an inevitable trend[2]. As a kind of important technique of testable design, boundary scan technique can not only test the test function of entire SoC or PCB, it can also test the connection between each module.

In 1990, IEEE and JTAG (Joint Test Action Group) worked out the boundary scan standard of JTAG[3]. namely IEEE1149.1 standard. This specification provides a complete and standardized method of testable design[4], so it gets the support of the world's most integrated circuit manufacturers and test contractor, such as ARM Company's ARM7TDMI processor[5], Xilinx company's series of FPGA above XC3000.

In this paper, we discussed a testable design method based JTAG boundary scan technique to complete the test of SoC's Flash module. Using this method, it'll be convenient to test the storage control circuit and the quantity of external testing interface will be reduced. The standard test port makes the testing mechanism standardized, thus to improve test efficiency, reduce product development cycle and test cost.

2 Analysis of Common test Structures

In order to test IP (Intellectual Property) core, the common test structure design is shown in Fig. 1, and normally is composed of Source, Sink, TAM (Test Access Mechanism), Wrapper. Source and Sink, which are responsible for generating test stimulus and receive test response respectively, can be designed as required to be internal or external parts of SoC. TAM is a set of methods designed for the delivery of test data between exterior and SoC's internal IP ports. As shown in Fig. 1, test data is delivered from Source to IP ports and from IP ports to Sink through TAM. Wrapper is the interface between IP ports and TAM. There are two main functions of Wrapper: offering appropriate test access to load stimulus and capture response; insulating the pending IP cores and the non-tested IP cores from the testing IP cores.

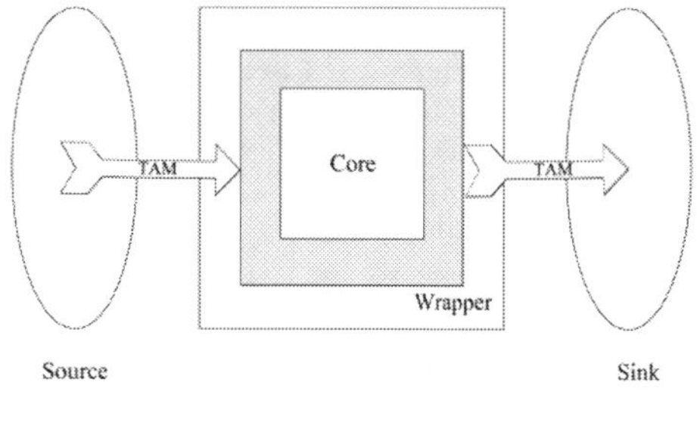

Fig. 1. IP Core Test Structure.

As for the TAM, the wider bandwidth, the faster test vectors' interaction, and the higher efficiency. The bandwidth is restricted by the design of SoC, such as the

DOI: 10.1051/itmconf/20160704006

bus width, the extra area and time of the testable design, and the number of top ports. TAM normally includes direct access mechanism, IP core transparency access mechanism, boundary scan mechanism and bus based access mechanism.

2.1 The Test Structure Design of the Direct Access Mechanism

The simplest way to test SoC internal IP models is using pin mux to access the internal IP's test ports after choosing external test mode[6].

This method under normal working mode also needs to configure different test modes for the completion of different IP tests. There are three working modes in this direct accessing strategy for each IP model: user mode is the normal working mode; inactive test mode indicates this IP model is being insulated while another IP model is under testing. The output driven is configured as inactive state, and the bidirectional port is set as input state. Active test mode indicates this IP model's ports are linked to exterior directly for external test and observation while other IP models are inactive and cannot be tested.

Although the test structure of the direct access mechanism is simple, its shortcomings cannot be ignored. First, this mechanism is not suitable for the external testing interface with huge number of ports. Besides, the interconnect test between IP models is not supported. In other words, testing a single IP model through this mechanism is available while checking the performance between models is not. Thus, this mechanism cannot meet the requirement for all IP models test. And as the design of SoC is becoming more and more complicated, SoC will contain more and more IP cores. If every IP core is required to be tested, then the cost of area has to be increased.

2.2 The Test Structure Design of the IP Core Transparency Access Mechanism

In this test access mechanism, the non-tested IP cores are transparent, which means the test vectors will not be changed when they pass through these non-tested IP cores. It is inevitable for some test vectors to pass through non-tested IP cores when transmited from exterior to testing IP cores or from testing IP cores to chip's output pins.

This test access mechanism is proposed by F. Bouwman in 1992[7]. F. Bouwman proposed a testable design method to test the macro models on a chip. This method bases on boundary scan technology and uses models' function information to simplify the test of circuits.

The simplest design of transparency strategy is shown in Fig. 2. The solution is placing a mutiplexer between IP core's input port and output port, which is a direct method to block the influence of inner logic on test vector, implementing the transparency.

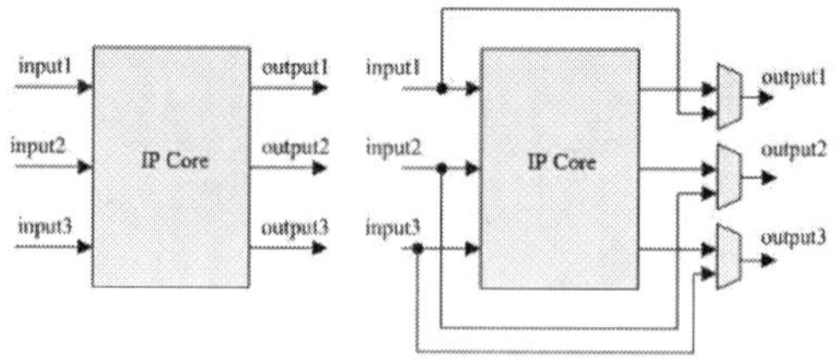

Fig. 2. Transparent IP Core with Multiplexer.

The design of this method is simple but still not available when facing with SoC's complex internal structure. The number of IP core's interface is too large to afford because too many mutiplexers are needed. Besides, the cabling between input and output is also very complicated.

In 1996, I. Ghosh proposed a structurized IP core transparency TAM strategy which is improved afterwards. Altough similar with hierarchical bounary scan technology, H-SCAN (High Level Alternative to Full-Scan) technology is outstanding in low-cost of area and short-time of test vectors' carryout. This method is triggerd by SoC's existing mutiplexers and triggers. Scanning path is constructed by combining these two components. Through the choice of the mutiplexer, non-texted IP cores enter into tranparency state, and the pending IP core starts testing.

In Fig. 3, there are two modes, user mode and H-SCAN mode, in a transparent core. The mode is selected by TEST. REG A and REG B both are 16-bit registers, and there is a 16-bit mutiplexer between them. The REG A, REG B and mutiplexer compose a parallel scan path. One port of mutiplexer is used as the channel for test data. In the user mode, two registers are isolated. In the H-SCAN mode, the scan path is constructed.

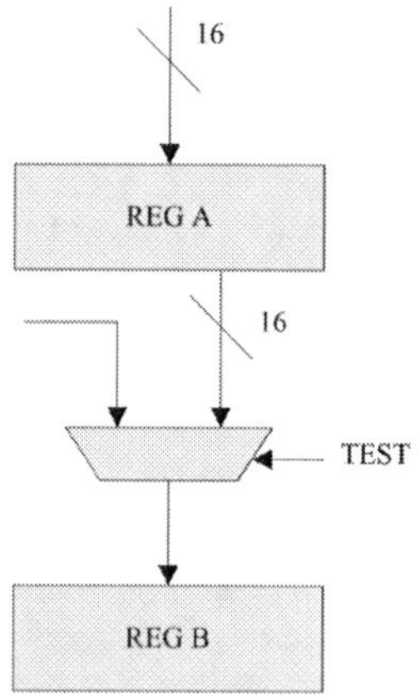

Fig. 3. The Structure of H-SCAN.

Since reusing the mutiplexers on the chip, H-SCAN can reduce the cost of area. In the meantime, the test efficiency is increased due to muti-scanning path. However, this structure relies on the SoC's test logic structure. If there is no mutiplexer in the test logic structure, it is necessary to add.

The test access mechanisms above have kinds of limitations. However, the most widely used method is the JTAG testable design. Because of its early relevant standards, this method has great value in reusability.

3 System Structure of JTAG Testable Design

The boundary scan standard of JTAG defines a kind of standard boundary scan structure and testing interface, the basic idea is to insert a shift register unit between external I/O port and internal logic circuit[8]. These shift register units distribute in the boundary of the chip, so called boundary scan register (Boundary-Scan Register Cell). The boundary scan registers can link up to each other, forming a boundary scan chain around the chip[9] (Boundary-Scan Chain). General chip provides several independent scan chains, setting the external JTAG interface to access boundary scan registers then to observe and control chip's I/O terminal, to complete the test in chip level, board level and system level[10].

There are five testing interfaces in the standard JTAG, which are used to control the whole test process. It has four inputs and one output, which are defined as follows:

TDI——test data input terminal, to serial input control data or instruction;

TDO——test data output terminal, can read serial data or instruction of the last status;

TMS——test status selection input terminal, used to control the status transition of TAP, control the status of TAP;

TCK——clock input of the test, sampling the input along the rise;

nTRST——test reset input terminal, used to reset TAP controller.

Specific design of boundary scan mainly consists of the TAP control circuit, instruction register and decoding circuit, data register:

(1) Instruction register (IR) and decoding circuit. Instruction register is used for meeting the different control needs of boundary scan unit. The decoding circuits can decode different instruction; give the corresponding control signal to meet the different needs of the test.

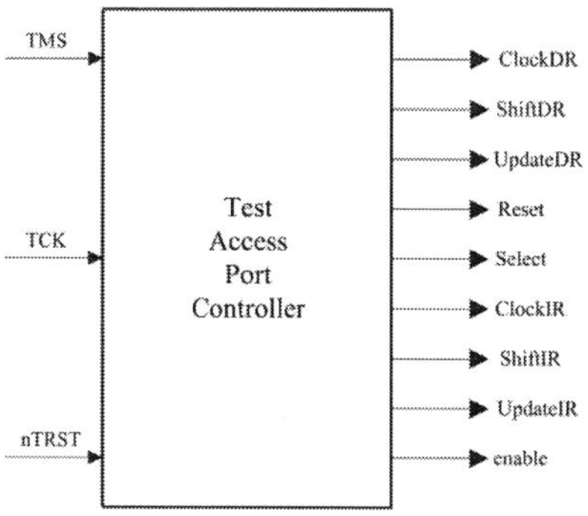

Fig. 4. Structure of TAP Controller.

(2) The design of data register (DR), which is used to store the data for testing or the result. Boundary scan chain is one of them. The boundary scan chain inserts around the logic for test, cooperates with access to instruction register to test internal logic and the external connection of the chip conveniently. Besides that, data register also includes bypass register, product identity register, which are used for different test requirements.

(3) TAP controller, as shown in Fig. 4, its main function is to generate control signal that is used to access instruction register and data register.

Where ClockIR, UpdateIR, ShiftIR are used for access to instruction register and ClockDR, UpdateDR, ShiftDR are used for access to data register.

IEEE1149.4 defines TAP controller status machine, as shown in Fig. 5. All of the internal control signals are realized by decoding statuses.TAP controller will be automatically initialized to test logic reset status when power on (Test-Logic Reset), it'll also enter test logic reset status through the nTRST or TMS keep high for five clock periods. If it turns into instruction register operate status (Select-IR-Scan), TDI and TDO will be connected by instruction register. Then we can input the needed instruction sequence through the TDI, and the decoding circuit will automatically decode and generate the corresponding execution of the control signals. When it turns into data register operate status (Select-DR-Scan), TDI and TDO will be automatically connected by data register. Then we can serial input the data for testing through the TDI, put the test vector into the memory port, at the same time, the test results will be serial output from the TDO.

 DOI: 10.1051/itmconf/20160704006

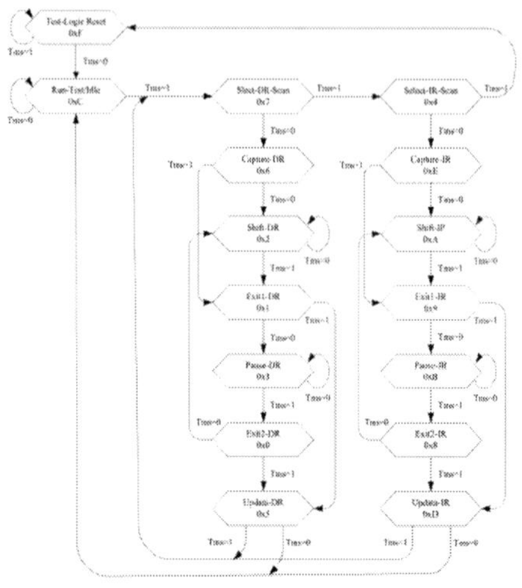

Fig. 5. Status Transition of TAP Controller.

4 The JTAG Test Implementation of Flash

As shown in Fig. 6, what used in our SoC design is Flash with 128kx8 of TSMC, whose control ports include X address line, Y address line, erase control signal, write gating signal, data input and output lines, etc. In order to facilitate testing Flash, in addition to the definition of the bypass register instruction register, ID register which comply with the std.1149.1, according to the characteristic of Flash, we design two boundary scan chains (Scan Chain). The two scan chains all belong to data register. Each one is made by several JTAG scanning units. Each of the scanning units can be configured to input unit that can obtain external signal or output unit. Relying on the shift register, the data can be output to every JTAG scanning unit through the TDI signal of JTAG, the data of each scanning unit can also be read from TDO signal line.

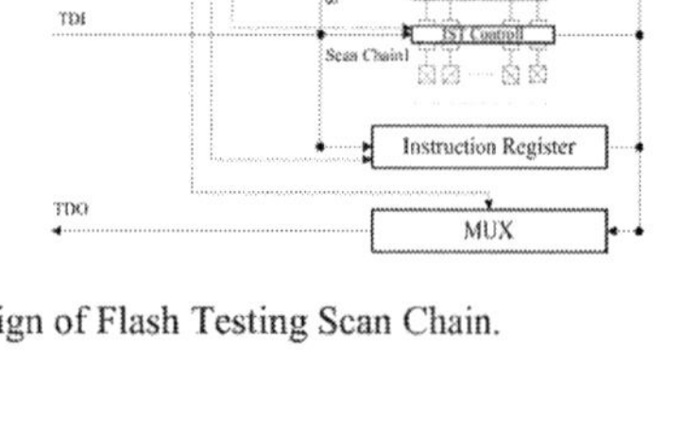

Fig. 6. Design of Flash Testing Scan Chain.

Through the TAP controller we can control which instruction register to access, and then choose different scan chain to complete the corresponding test. Scan chain0 directly connects each port of Flash, it controls through the shift register. According to the timing sequence of Flash, the test can be completed by sending each test vector ordinarily. Scan chain0 have 41 scanning units, the definition of scan chain registers are shown in Table 1.

Table 1. Setting Word's Margins.

Scan chain register	*Control signal*
BSR[0]	NVSTR
BSR[1]	PROG
BSR[2]	MAS1
BSR[3]	ERASE
BSR[4]	OE
BSR[5]	SE
BSR[6]	YE
BSR[7]	XE
BSR[8]	IFREN
BSR[13:9]	YADR[4:0]
BSR[24:14]	XADR[10:0]
BSR[32:25]	DIN[7:0]
BSR[40:33]	DOUT[7:0]

The Table 1 shows, this scan chain includes all I/O of Flash, through this scan chain we can directly control Flash to test.

If we solely depend on external direct access to test Flash, more test vectors would be used and the test time would be longer, considering that, we add the design of IST (In System Program) module to our design, as shown in Fig. 7. Scan chain1 is inserted into the port of IST. Through the IST control circuit, we only need to input simple control word to finish the test of Flash module, we can read and write full chip, write tessellated or diagonally to complete the BIST (Build in Self Test) of Flash.

There are seven scanning units in scan chain1, mainly used to access IST control circuit. The control order of this scan chain is: IST control signal R/W, used to control the read-write of register. Control instructions 3 to 0 (Command [3-0]) are used to control IST to execute different operations. Data line 7 to 0 (Data [7:0]) are used to input data for writing when write full chip, or input data for comparing when read full chip. Finish signal of the operation, used to learn whether the IST finished. Marking signal of the F/S, use for marking the success of Flash operations. Therefore, through this scan chain we can control IST, thus we can finish operating Flash by inputting simple control word and it can simplify the process, save the cost more than accelerate the test time.

DOI: 10.1051/itmconf/20160704006

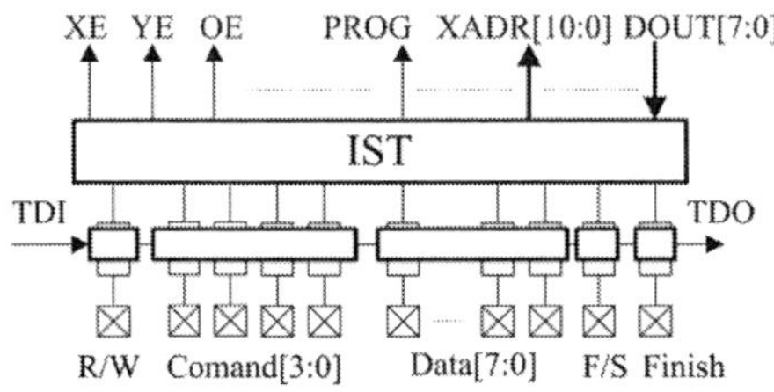

Fig. 7. Detail Drawing of The Scan Chain of Ist Circuit.

5 Simulations and Result

We use the EDA development tool of Synopsys Company to simulate and the entire verification environment is programmed by System Verilog language. We write test vector according to the read-write timing sequence of Flash then output the simulation model through the JTAG control signal written by System Verilog and then input through the boundary scan interface of Flash to complete the test of Flash. Fig. 8 shows the process of writing test data through the JTAG testing interface. The process is to write the data A5 to the place whose address XADR is 0x009, YADR is 0x00 in C2.

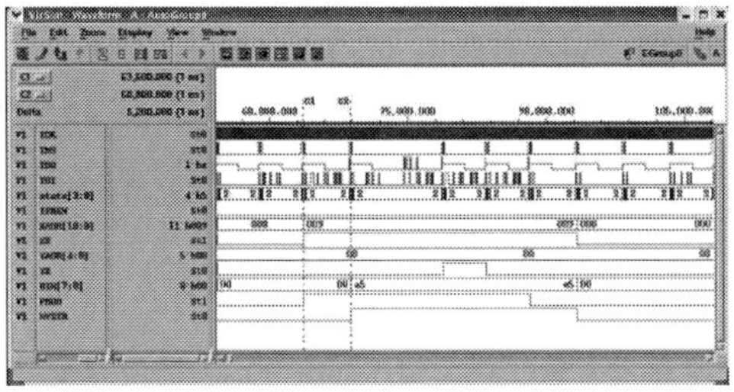

Fig. 8. Write Data Simulation Waveform with Flash.

The process of reading the data A5 from the place whose address XADR is 0x009, YADR is 0x00 is shown in Fig. 9. The data will be removed from TDO and the JTAG simulation test host will cache the data after receiving it and then distinguish whether it is A5. BSR [40:33] insert in DOUT and we can see the TDO output from the Fig. 9.

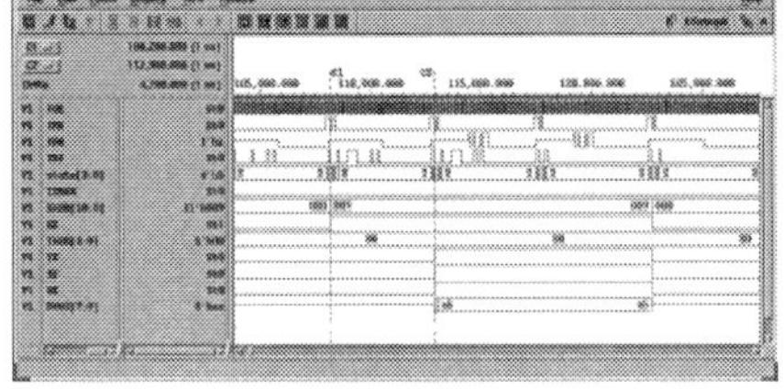

Fig. 9. Write data simulation waveform with Flash.

From what have been discussed we know that controlling the read-write of Flash directly through the scan chain0 will make the writing of test vector complicated,because the test vector for each signal have to be modified when the signal changes with time.

But using the scan chain1 can decrease the test control input, operating Flash through the IST will save a lot of testing time. Take full chip writing for example, if the operating frequency of TCK is 5MHz, the input of each a set of test vector probably need 8200 ns (42 cycles), the time of realize full chip writing through scan chain0 is about 7.5 s and if the operating frequency of TCK is 10MHz, the time is 4.5s. But using the scan chain1 can save input time of each test vector, the time to realize full chip writing is shorten to 2.5 s. But the weakness of IST is complexity of the error locating. Considering comprehensively, we can combine the two test plans, which is that the most of the test can be completed by scanning chain1, including the test of checkerboard and diagonal, and scanning chain0 can be used for test positioning and the analysis of specific problem when we found problems.

6 Conclusions

This paper proposed a testable design method of Flash based on the detailed analysis of the boundary scan technique. This testing method of Flash has been applied to the high-capacity storage card that is designed by our lab, the simulation result and actual chip test are indicate that this method can effectively save the test time and cost. This paper just applies the scheme to the test of Flash, how to use the combination of boundary scan technique and built-in test to realize DFT design of the entire chip should be studied in further research.

Acknowledgment

This work is supported by the National High Technology Research Development Program ("863" Program) of China (NO. 2015AA016501).

References

1. Van Der Wolf, Pieter (Synopsys, Eindhoven, Netherlands), Geuzebroek, Jeroen, "SoC infrastructures for predictable system integration" Proceedings - Design, Automation and Test in Europe, DATE, p 857-861, 2011, Proceedings - Design, Automation and Test in Europe Conference and Exhibition, DATE 2011.
2. Guo, Jian-Min (Department of Automation, Xiamen University, Xiamen, 361005, China); Luo, De-Lin, "A functional enhancement methodology to JTAG controller in complex SOC" Proceedings of 2009 4th International Conference on Computer Science and Education, ICCSE 2009, p 1128-1131, 2009,

 DOI: 10.1051/itmconf/20160704006

Proceedings of 2009 4th International Conference on Computer Science and Education, ICCSE 2009.
3. Zhang, Pin(School of Electronic Engineering, Tianjin University of Technology and Education, Tianjin, 300222, China); Xing, Zuocheng, "Design of structure of debugging software in CPU based on JTAG" Applied Mechanics and Materials, v 58-60, p 1866-1870, 2011, Information Technology for Manufacturing Systems II.
4. Balasubramanian, Lakshmanan (Texas Instruments India Private Limited, Bangalore, India), Sabbarwal, Puneet, Mittal, Rajesh Kumar, Narayanan, Prakash, Dash, Ranjit Kumar, Kudari, Anand Devendra, Manian, Srikanth, Polarouthu, Sudhir; Parthasarathy, Harikrishna, Vijayaraghavan, Ravi C., Turkewadikar, Sachin, "Circuit and DFT techniques for robust and low cost qualification of a mixed-signal SoC with integrated power management system" Proceedings - Design, Automation and Test in Europe, DATE, p 551-554, 2011, Proceedings - Design, Automation and Test in Europe Conference and Exhibition.
5. K. S. Kushal, S. Chetan and Shivaputra, "Design and Implementation of a Smart Automated OUT-ward (SAT OUT) System Using ARM Processor for Aircrafts," Computational Intelligence and Communication Networks (CICN), 2012 Fourth International Conference on, Mathura, pp. 463-467, 2012.
6. S. Chen and L. Xu, "A boundary-scan test bus controller design for mixed-signal test," Wireless Communications, Networking and Information Security (WCNIS), 2010 IEEE International Conference on, Beijing, China, pp. 22-25, 2010.
7. F. Bouwman, S. Oostdijk, R. Stans, B. Pouya. Macro Testability: The Results of Production Device Application. Test Conference, 1992. Proceedings., International. P.232-241.
8. Melo, Rodrigo A., David M. Caruso, and Salvador E. Tropea. "Memory-mapped I/O over dual port BRAM on FPGA." Programmable Logic (SPL), 2012 VIII Southern Conference on. IEEE, 2012.
9. T. Borroz, "Flexible high performance architecture for boundary scan execution hardware," IEEE AUTOTESTCON, 2015, National Harbor, MD, pp. 232-235, 2015.
10. Mandal, Debashis (Department of Electronics and Electrical Communication Engineering, Indian Institute of Technology Kharagpur, Kharagpur-721302, India), Bhattacharyya, T.K., "Implementation of CMOS low-power integer-N frequency synthesizer for SOC design" Journal of Computers, v 3, n 4, p 31-38, April 2008.

Water vapor transport in the Pearl River basin and its influence on NDVI

Yin-Xia WANG, Ji-Sheng ZENG, Ling TANG and Duo ZHUANG

South China Sea Institute of Planning and Environmental Research, State Oceanic Administration, Guangzhou, China

Abstract. Using NECP/NCAR monthly average data and 216 months average monthly precipitation data of the University of Delaware during 1982-1999. Analyzed the precipitation vapour transport process affects precipitation in the Pearl River Basin in different seasons. On this basis, the seasonal differences NDVI changes in climate-driven factors in the Pearl River Basin.

1 Introduction

Pearl River basin is one of the seasonal rains; scientists pay lots of attention on flood season in South China and early summer precipitation. In the 1980s the South China have been systematically studied during the test in South China rainstorms. Water vapor transport process is important in the process of influence of precipitation. Furthermore lots of people made a detailed analysis in the impact of precipitation vapor transport process (Zhou Xiaoxia et 2008). This article focuses on the water vapor transport process influenced precipitation of the Pearl River basin in different season. Climate change is considered to be caused by changes in vegetation cover of one of the main reasons, surface NDVI(Normalized Difference Vegetation Index) certain extent represent the land cover changes, precipitation is one of the important climate factors, this paper analyzes the changes in precipitation driving influence of NDVI in the Pearl River basin.

2. Data and Methods

Using NECP / NCAR monthly mean data in 1982-1999, including eight standard pressure values from 300Pa to 1000Pa layer wind data (u, v components), specific humidity q and the corresponding surface pressure data ps data with horizontal grid of 2.5 ° × 2.5 °. Precipitation data used in this paper is the University of Delaware 1982--1999 total of 216 monthly average rainfall gridded data[1], with a resolution of 0.5 ° × 0.5 °. NDVI data is provided by GIMMS during 1982-1999, with a resolution of 0.25 ° × 0.25 °.

In this paper, the water vapor transmission intensity is defined as the vertical integral water vapor flux from the ground to 300 pa. Monthly average data is used to calculate the water vapor transport of constant weight. According to tian-jun zhou (1999), such as constant component is one order of magnitude larger than the transient components, is to determine the main part of the water vapor transport, especially in the land, so the calculation is reasonable.

The water vapor flux calculation formula is:

Zonal water vapor flux:

$$Q_\lambda = \frac{1}{g}\int_{300}^{p_s}(uq)dp \qquad (1)$$

Vertical water vapor flux:

$$Q_\varphi = \frac{1}{g}\int_{300}^{p_s}(vq)dp \qquad (2)$$

3. The Moisture Balance And Precipitation In The Pearl River Basin

It is a multi-year average moisture balance of payments and the Pearl River Basin precipitation inFigure 1. As it can be seen from the figure moisture change and precipitation changes are substantially synchronized. beginning from January vapor and precipitation are fast rising after April, the Pearl River Basin in the South China flood season, also in April after an increase of precipitation rapid acceleration, moisture balance to maintain a strong rise in the state, to June reached the maximum water vapor and precipitation simultaneously, from June to August, began a slow decline, water vapor and precipitation after a sharp decline in September, especially in November and eleven February moisture balance is negative, namely the Pearl River Basin as a source of water vapor and outward transport of water vapor, so especially in the winter and less precipitation. Pearl River Valley in the monsoon zone, therefore its monsoon rainfall and the water vapor has a significant impact on the transformation and strong monsoon cause a corresponding change in the transport of water vapor, which in turn cause changes in water vapor transport in the Pearl River Basin, which have an impact on precipitation.

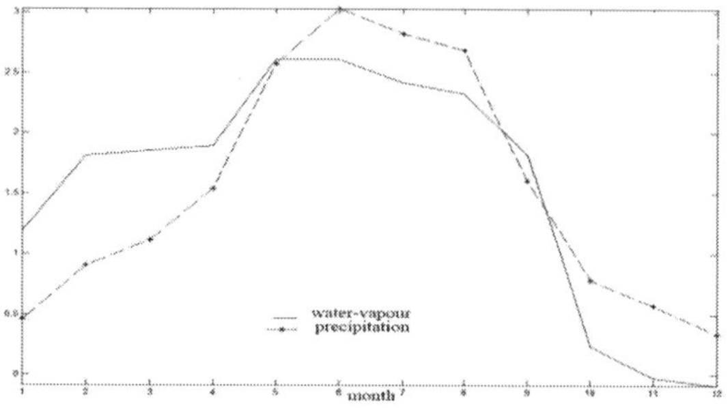

Figure 1. Annual Average Seasonal Changes in Precipitation And Water Vapor Transport (Standardized Data)

4. Water Vapor Transport Process In Each Season

Figure 2 is multi-year average of whole layer moisture flux for each season during 1982 to 1999. In winter you can see the water vapor in mainland China mainly through input westerly water vapor across the Bay of Bengal, Myanmar and Thailand entered into the Chinese mainland South, and the South China Sea due to the winter wind control, water vapor cannot enter from the South China Sea to the Chinese mainland, while the West Pacific Chinese mainland as a vapor outflow area. In the spring westerly belt is still an important input in mainland China with moisture, since the beginning of the monsoon establishment of water vapor transport in the Bay of Bengal to the southeast into the east dominated by the winter to transport, the South China Sea has become an important source of water vapor in the south, the channel is still the Pacific outlet channel. In summer, the monsoon has grown strong and prosperous, in the Bay of Bengal was strong meridional transport, between 18 ° N to 30 ° N in the Bay of Bengal westerly interruption, but remained at high latitudes transport moisture to the Chinese mainland, the South China Sea was southwest monsoon controlled by one of the main sources of water vapor southeastern China. In the fall, the low-latitude westerlies still break out in the Bay of Bengal, entered the Bay of Bengal to the mainland vapor began to show obvious bias of the East, the South China Sea began to control the northeast monsoon, the Chinese mainland has become a regional output moisture. You can see into the Chinese water vapor mainly from the South China Sea, the Bay of Bengal, westerly and Pacific region China mainland vapor output, this paper selected four channels, analyze it and the Pearl River Basin Precipitation: South China Sea channel: (20 ° N, 110 ° E-117.5 ° E); Bay of Bengal passage: (20 ° N, 85 ° E-100 ° E); Pacific channel: (25 ° N-30 ° N, 120 ° E); westerly passage: (20 ° N-27.5 ° N, 82.5 ° E).

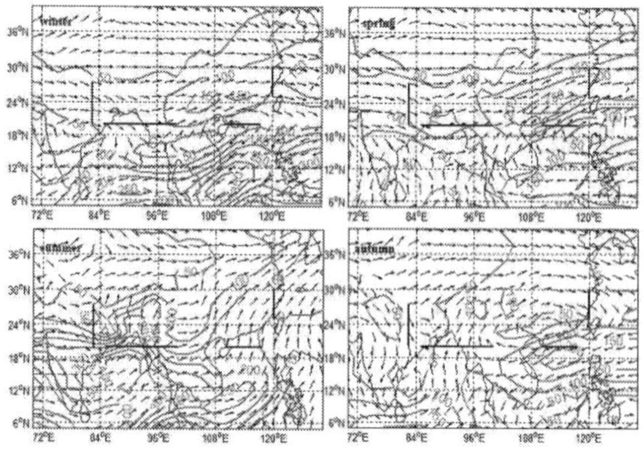

Figure 2. Annual Average Water Vapor Transport (the Arrows Indicate The Direction of The Contour of the Water Vapor Transport Size.)

Table 1 shows the mean and standard deviation, and correlation coefficient of water vapor channel in four seasons with the Pearl River Basin precipitation. Table 1a indicates in descending order of intensity of winter moisture passage to the Pacific, westerlies, the South China Sea and the Bay of Bengal. Pearl River Basin is closely related to the degree of precipitation followed by the South China Sea, the Bay of Bengal, the Pacific and the westerlies, the South China Sea where the channel significantly by 99% confidence. Table 1b can be seen, in descending order of spring water vapor channel strength for the Pacific channel, the westerlies, the South China Sea and the Bay of Bengal, and spring precipitation and the closeness of the Pearl River Basin were westerly, Bay of Bengal, the South China Sea and the Pacific Ocean. And westerly passage significantly by 95% confidence, the Bay of Bengal by a significant 90% confidence. Table 1c is the information of each channel in summer, you can see the strength of each channel in descending order of the Bay of Bengal, the South China Sea, the Pacific and the westerlies, and the Pearl River Basin and the closeness of summer rainfall in the order of the South China Sea, the Bay of Bengal, the Pacific and the westerlies, and significant South China Sea passage through the 99% confidence, however, and significant obvious other channels, it may be the South China Sea summer southwest monsoon is controlled, its water vapor transport is the main source of the Pearl River Basin water vapor, while the other channel very small compared to the impact. In the autumn (Table 1d) vapor passage strength decreasing order, the South China Sea, the Bay of Bengal, the Pacific and the westerlies, and each passage of water vapor and the closeness of the Pearl River Basin autumn rainfall in the order of the South China Sea, the Pacific Ocean, the Bay of Bengal and the westerlies, westerlies and relationship between the Bay of Bengal and autumn precipitation Pearl River Basin is not obvious, the South China Sea and the relevant channel significantly by 99% confidence, significant correlation between the Pacific Ocean through the passage 90% confidence.

 DOI: 10.1051/itmconf/20160704007

Table 1a. The Mean and Standard Deviation of Water Vapor Channel, And Correlation Coefficient Between It and Precipitation (Winter)

Water vapor channel	mean	Standard deviation	correlation coefficient
South China Sea Channel	-60.6	22.8	0.65*
Channel Bay of Bengal	-9.7	8.6	-0.32
Pacific channel	110.0	22.8	0.31
Westerly passage	87.7	32.7	0.27

Table 1b. The Mean And Standard Deviation Of Water Vapor Channel, And Correlation Coefficient Between It And Precipitation (Spring)

Water vapor channel	mean	Standard deviation	correlation coefficient
South China Sea Channel	81.4	26.3	0.35
Channel Bay of Bengal	21.5	12.7	-0.38□
Pacific channel	214.5	29.9	-0.32
Westerly passage	169.9	23.8	0.47△

Table 1c. The Mean and Standard Deviation of Water Vapor Channel, and Correlation Coefficient Between It and Precipitation (Summer)

Water vapor channel	mean	Standard deviation	correlation coefficient
South China Sea Channel	157.4	36.9	0.64*
Channel Bay of Bengal	157.6	15.6	0.14
Pacific channel	123.5	63.3	-0.1
Westerly passage	86.0	47.0	0.034

Table 1d. The mean and Standard Deviation of Water Vapor Channel, and Correlation Coefficient between It and Precipitation (autumn)

Water vapor channel	mean	Standard deviation	correlation coefficient
South China Sea Channel	-63.6	26.1	0.58*
Channel Bay of Bengal	53.7	15.4	0.015
Pacific channel	38.9	29.4	0.40□
Westerly passage	29.9	39.9	0.14

Note: * indicates significant by 99% confidence; △ indicates significant by 95% confidence; □ indicates significant by 90% confidence.

5. Seasonal and Interannual Svd Analysis Between Precipitation And Ndvi In Pearl River Basin

First, the Pearl River Basin precipitation and NDVI years SVD(Singular Value Decomposition) were analyzed and discussed in both years coupled modes. Figure 3 shows the first mode and the spatial distribution of both the time coefficients, and the first mode and explained reached 97.17%, i.e., the first mode explains the relationship between the main coupling. First look abnormal distribution of precipitation, with significant precipitation change in the consistency of the direction of the entire Pearl River Basin, but things change in strength but has differences, changes in precipitation in the eastern part of the year is less than the west, and generally to 110 ° E is bounded to the west differences oriented east-west and north-south difference is based on the east side of the main. NDVI and rainfall during the year abnormal distribution similarities in NDVI change the direction of the entire Pearl River Basin is also consistent, the same as the east and west high. This configuration instructions when abnormal changes in precipitation, NDVI also have a similar change. From both the time coefficient can see NDVI significantly lag behind changes in precipitation from January to April rainfall anomalies and negative precipitation gradually increased, but the NDVI and lag 2-3 months began to increase in precipitation June reached the maximum, but you want to reach the maximum NDVI in August. From the spatial distribution and temporal change, the increase or decrease of changes in precipitation on NDVI has a hysteresis effect is the same but the direction of change.

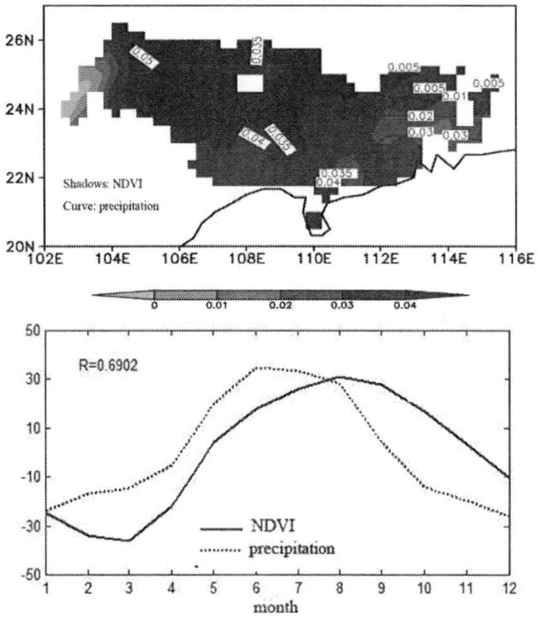

Figure 3. NDVI and Precipitation Season Svd First Mode Field Space and Time Field

DOI: 10.1051/itmconf/20160704007

Figure 4 is a scale SVD annual precipitation and NDVI seasonal analysis. The first mode of explained variance rate of four seasons from winter to autumn as follows: 86.38%, 58.39%, 78.29% and 58.58%, showing the first mode of the two variance possession major contribution.

In winter, the spatial distribution of precipitation anomalies and the same number from west to east, but NDVI in the distribution space is not the same number in the western presence of two positive centers, others are negative. Overall, the distribution of precipitation anomalies and distribution of NDVI anomalies of opposite sign in the space. See the first two modes winter time coefficient, correlation coefficient of 0.5, more than 95% confidence level. And both the time coefficient is substantially the same number, indicating that in addition to the east of 110 ° E in both the positive change in the intensity distribution at two centers in other regions NDVI change direction and precipitation are consistent, and basically consistent.

In spring, abnormal distribution of precipitation still has the same number of spaces, and in the center of the Pearl River Basin strongest change, decreasing to four weeks. But NDVI spatial anomalies apparent something different, east due west negative. Both the first mode of the time factor, the correlation coefficient reaches 0.73, more than 99.9% confidence level, and substantially the same sign. Description in the east, the Pearl River Basin precipitation and NDVI reverse change, while in the West, compared to the same changes.

In summer, the spatial distribution of precipitation anomalies in the basin are still the same number, NDVI and precipitation versa but different numbers. Instead of both the strength and the distribution center. Correlation coefficients between 0.57 time, more than 95% confidence level, and substantially the same sign. This configuration instructions space and time, in the opposite direction of change in summer precipitation and NDVI.

In autumn, precipitation anomaly field is still the same number throughout the region, the central small and large sides. NDVI throughout the region is substantially the same number, but the number and distribution of inverse precipitation anomalies, strong northwest southeast weaker. Both time correlation coefficient reached 0.49, more than 95% confidence level, and still is with the main positive and negative. Such configuration instructions in the autumn precipitation and NDVI change is in the opposite direction.

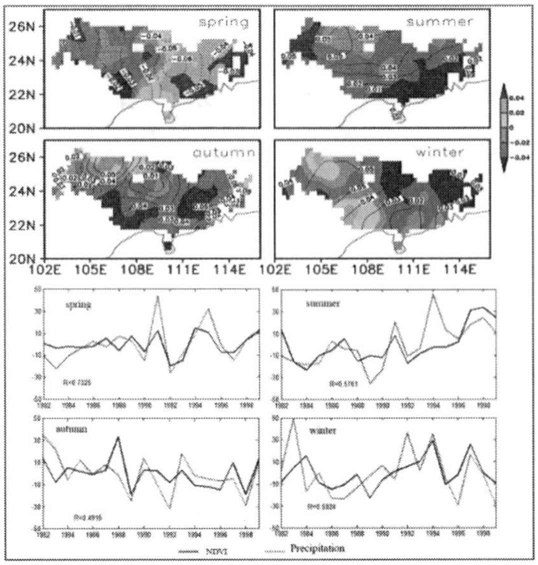

Figure 4. NDVI and Precipitation in Four Seasons on the Occasion of the First Svd Mode (Shadows: Ndvi, Curve: Precipitation)

6. Conclusion

Through the above analysis we can get the following conclusions:

(1) Pearl River Basin precipitation and the water vapor has a significant change in sync, it began to rise in January, reaching the maximum in June, after the rapid decline starting in August.

(2) the impact of the main sources of water vapor in the Pearl River Basin of South China Sea, the Bay of Bengal, the westerlies, the Pacific region is predominantly a Chinese output moisture. Vary in different seasons affect the Pearl River Basin precipitation mainly water vapor channel differences, major winter the South China Sea channel followed by the Bay of Bengal; the close relationship between the spring followed by westerlies, the Bay of Bengal, South China Sea and the Pacific channel; in the summer the South China Sea passage and the Pearl River Basin Precipitation most closely, the other channel is not obvious; the South China Sea and the main autumn passage and their closely related to the Bay of Bengal.

(3) years of precipitation and NDVI SVD analysis showed increased or decreased precipitation changes in NDVI has a lag effect, but the direction of change is the same; in different seasons of the SVD precipitation and NDVI analysis shows that in the winter in most parts of the Pearl River Basin NDVI change direction and the direction of change precipitation consistency and east of 110 ° E between changes in the intensity distribution are basically the same; east, rainfall and NDVI reverse changes in the Pearl River Basin in the spring, and in the west compared to the same change; in precipitation and NDVI opposite direction of change; changes in

precipitation and NDVI autumn is in the opposite direction.

References

[1]http://apdrc.soest.hawaii.edu:80/dods/public_data/Interpolated_precipitation/UDel_prec_airT.
[2] Jis-han Xue. Rainstorm research in South China In the summer of 1994[M]. Beijing, China Meteorological Press, 1999: 185.
[3] Xiao-xia Zhou, Yi-hui Ding, Pan-xing WANG. Water vapor transport summer Asian monsoon region and its impact on precipitation in China [J]. Meteorological Science. 2008.9,28: 193-203.
[4] Yun-hao Chen, Xiao-bing Li, Pei-jun Shi .1983 ~ Chinese land NDVI changing climatic factor driving the 1992 analysis [J] Chinese Journal of Plant Ecology, 2001,25 (6): 716-720.
[5] Ben-gang LI, Song Tao, R.W.Dawson. Relations between AVHRR NDVI and ecoclimatic parameters in China[J]. Remote Sensing,2002,23(5):989–999.
[6] Willmott C.J, Robeson S.M. Climatologically aided interpolation (CAI) of terrestrial air temperature[J]. International Journal of Climatology, 1995, 15(2):221–229.
[7] Krishnamurti T N.Numerical Simulation of Somali Jet[J].Journal of Atmaspheric Sciences,1976,33:2350-2362.
[8] Shi-yan Tao, Yi-hui Ding. Observational Evidence of the Influence of the Qinghai-Xizang (Tibet) Plateau on the Occurrence of Heavy Rain and Severe Convective Storms in China[J].Bulletin of the American Meteorological Society,1981,62(1):23-30.
[9] Tian-jun Zhou,Xue-hong Zhang, Shao-wu Wang. Marine component of global water cycle research [J]. Journal of meteorological, 1999, 57 (3) : 264-282.

The Analysis of Engineering Data Information System Based on Knowledge Management and Internet plus Technology

Nian Lv[1,a], Xuan Zhang[2]

[1]*Shandong electric power T&T engineering company, road No. 1000, Huaiyin District, Ji'nan City, Shandong Province, China*
[2]*Shandong province training center of construction technology development*
[a]*570227019@qq.com*

Abstract—Adopted information classification and coding technology, the author try to write the WBS code of electric power transformation project and study on the content and form of engineering data. Taking advantage of Internet plus technology, the management information system which conform to the reality of electric power transformation can be developed. Adopted knowledge management theory, we could make use of knowledge to direct movement through the change from information into knowledge.

1 Introduction

Currently, power net construction has become the main direction of the power construction in China. However, the archive management to the construction data of electric power transformation does not have a unified standard. The requirements of different clients vary. And the project units are lack of instructive document to the classification, arrangement and encode of electric power transformation, which lead to the disorder and non-standard of construction data filling. Then, there are lots of problem appeared when the project be checked and accepted. Therefore, the management of the data of electric power transformation and the collection, classification, storage, transformation and usage of data are an essential problem for electric power engineering enterprises. The research and study on the contruation data management of electric power transformation would have good influence on the enhancement of management level of electric power transformation projects.

Shandong electric power Transformation Company adopted information classification and encoding technology and encode the WBS code of electric power transformation. Based on WBS code, they studied on the content, form and filling instruction. Through conclusion, classification and encoding, they created code content and wrote down filling indication and example of every forms. Then, with the direction of the theory of management information system, taking advantage of information and Internet technology, the computer management information system which conform to the reality of electric power transformation been developed.

It is different from general computer management information system of construction data. First of all, it is a management information system based on the classification and arrangement of construction data, which makes its functions become more suitable for the reality of the management of electric power transformation and more useful. Secondly, the system connect construction teams, project department, branch companies with head quarter closely, which eliminated isolation and made communication and exchange freely. Finally, it adopted knowledge management and Internet plus technology, which make this system become more advanced and reasonable. From information to knowledge which could direct decision making and movement, and from movement to profit, it improved the technology of this system.

2 Specific Method

2.1 Adopted line classification to classify and encode construction data

Information classification and encoding refer to the scientific classification of information and then encode data. This method could gather information with same features and tell the information different. And it could encode data with symbol system which could be recognized and dealt with by people or computer

2.2 The application of WBS structure could decompose the project and make the project scientific

WBS can decompose the program via its structural features and is convenient to manage the complicated engineer in scale, as well makes it easy to assess and make a conclusion. Compiling the WBS code of it is an important task when managing and studying the execution materials. Due to the existing differences amid engineering decomposition in the construction between computing part and program department, it can go on with the study based on the classified methods in respect of program (tech, quality branches), which is aimed at the real situation of Power transmission industry as well as the study of engineering material management. Using the information coding tech, a classic power line of an engineer WBS codes is as below:

A preparation

B retesting and locating

C basic program

C/01 classified pits C/02 basic pits to be dug c/03 transmission of materials c/04 basic cushions C/05 basic module C/06 basic casting C/07basic backfill

D Tower engineering

D/01 basic leveling D/02 counting material in division D/03 decomposing the tower D/04 bolt-on

E ground connection program

E/01 digging and connecting ditches E/02 laying ground connector E/03 installing downlead E/04 welding ground connector E/05ground backfill E/06 ground resistance wave measurement

F stringing work

F/01 preparation F/02 ground connector transportation F/03 setting up crossing structure F/04 laying leading rope F/05laying ground connectors F/06 Anchor Line F/07tight string F/08 accessory installation F/08.01spacing bars F/08.02 cable clamp installation F/08.03 Spark gap adjustment F/08.04 Shock hammer F/08.05heavy hammer

G Optical Cable Engineering

G/01 Fiber optic cable full plate test G/02 laying leading rope G/03 laying the optical cable G/04 accessory installation G/05 optical fiber cable jointing H Maintenance and repair

2.3 Combining various material resources, completing material sorting and studying task

According to WBS codes, in the course of processing, it collects the useful data inside and outside our province, the necessary tables which must be filled up by the State Grid Corporation, and the Supervision of tabular involving the construction. Besides, the integrated management system, recording and forms of Shandong power transmission Engineering Corporation are also concluded. Consequently, though those forms and recording are used by the enterprise itself, they are a valuable record for the management of the project department.

2.4 Constructing knowledge management system of transmission and distribution project in Shandong Province with the use of knowledge management theory

Knowledge management is the new stage of the development of information management, and it is also the extension and development of information management. Knowledge management is a series of question and answer sequence that is the collection of solutions to search for and recognize the key information related to questions, and draw the information to form the specialized knowledge to one question as the basis of decision. In the society of information and knowledge, information, knowledge and some special skills are the tools to gain profits. Knowledge management transform information to knowledge, and guide decisions into practice via knowledge, thus translate acts to profits.

2.5 Conducting data mining with engineering data management system, thus providing basis for decision.

The transmission and distribution project in Shandong Province is a temporary project, new knowledge created by the project members only exists in the minds of certain people or project members, few of the knowledge can be stored in the organization. When the task is completed, the knowledge will be distributed among the various departments, and once the individuals or groups who master the key knowledge leave the enterprises, the knowledge chain of the enterprises will be interrupted. Therefore, it is not suitable for the project department to use and spread the knowledge during the transmission and distribution continuously and extensively, which is not conducive to the accumulation of corporate knowledge. Therefore, we need to use the engineering data management system to integrate and mine all the engineering data of project department. Data Mining refers to the process of automatic analysis and extraction of the implicit and previously unknown knowledge that people are interested in and potentially useful for policy makers from a large database or data warehouse. Data mining is the key supporting technology of knowledge management, it is an inevitable process in which data rises to knowledge. Knowledge management system owns the ability to manage and collaborate the knowledge base, and knowledge management processes can also be seen as the mining and use of knowledge. After the combination with data mining techniques, the value of the entire knowledge management system is reflected by the knowledge discovery and learning. Through data mining, by using the engineering data of every project, the red flag and high-quality engineering data can be formed and updated. And we can mine the quality, safety and other data through engineering data to provide a base for the project management of transmission and distribution project in Shandong Province.

2.6 Building database of the transmission and distribution project in Shandong Province to realize big data of engineering materials

Establishing database of transmission and distribution project in Shandong Province, and realizing replication capacity of projects gradually. The accumulation of many projects benefits the extraction of files of the same type, when facing with the similar project, new project can be created via information platform to make replication capacity to be possible; At the same time, the accumulation of many projects can help new or inexperienced employees find their positions in engineering data management system quickly, and work according to standards of work flow is beneficial to the cultivation of talents.

3 Application Achievements

3.1 Engineering data system cut down the cost of data management

Engineering data system change the situation of personnel on-site inspection and management, which can cut down large amount of labor costs, vehicle costs and unnecessary food costs, and improve working efficiency greatly, reducing rework cost of materials as well. The cost of every inspection of each project need RMB3000-4000 at least just from the points of food, live, transport and labour. The cost of data organization, rework of every project needs 5000-10000. In one enterprise, there are 80 transmission and distribution projects annually, and inspects projects every quarter, more than 1.5 million direct benefits can be saved annually...

3.2 Engineering data management system improves the level of projects management

The system connects construction materials of corporation headquarters, division headquarters, projects, construction team via internet, thus related leaders, managers can see the real materials to know the schedule, quality, safety situation in time, which will also improve management efficiency. The management of construction materials in the past was at will and false, and memoirs were made usually, which can be changed. The update of materials should be synchronize with construction, so the confidence of construction materials can be improved. The precontrol before construction, the supervision during construction, the retrospect after construction can make engineering data reveal the level of project management actually.

The application of engineering data management platform reveals the improvement of the management of engineering data, and strengthen the security, quality, schedule of projects at a deeper level. This system adapts the trend of the industry of transmission and distribution, and realizes the information management construction materials, thus make sure the standardized and complete of engineering data management, and improve the efficiency and quality to meet the demand of the development of project management. The system improve the depth, vigor, and speed of the project management of transmission and distribution, so greater management benefits and social benefits can be realized.

3.3 Use the engineering data management system to strengthen knowledge transfer and sharing

A mature enterprise must be convenient for the employees to inspire and communicate with each other in transformation and sharing of knowledge. The engineering data management system of transmission and distribution project in Shandong Province is beneficial to internal members to learn from each other, communication with and share knowledge with each other; to the knowledge communication between enterprise and the external organizations; to the horizontal exchange of knowledge among all sectors of the knowledge transformation; to the knowledge integration in various areas. The communication not only happens between internal employees, departments, but also should take place among the enterprise, the owner and the supervisor.

3.4 Use the engineering data management system is in favor of the depth of the knowledge updating

Setting this system enables all the projects and departments of transmission and distribution project in Shandong Province to exchange their knowledge so that the latest knowledge of the outside world is able to quickly enter the enterprise and be aware of the employees, and the knowledge owned by enterprises and employees can be deepen and updated in the internal and external communication and cooperation.

3.5 The engineering data management system improves the enterprise's ability to adapt to the environment.s in favor of the depth of the knowledge updating

The engineering data management system enables the electricity transmission and transformation in Shandong

DOI: 10.1051/itmconf/20160704008

Province to keep its vibrant during the "Adapt to the correct rehabilitation" process, and keep high organizational efficiency to respond swiftly to the external uncertainties and dynamic nature.

3.6 The engineering data management system improves the teamwork spirits of the employees

Since the engineering data management system need to involve a variety of people and activities, we must rely on the cooperation between the employees leading to the successful completion of engineering data management. Companies, branches, all levels of the project department need to participate in the process of engineering data management altogether to improve the team spirit of employees and enhance the competitiveness of enterprises.

3.7 Lay solid foundation for the creation of good projects

In the national high quality awards on-site review, experts speak highly of DaiZong 500kv transformer substation with engineering data management and South HaMi-Zhengzhou±800kv high-tension line. DaiZong 500kv transformer substation wins 2014-2015 national high quality award, South HaMi-Zhengzhou±800kv high-tension line wins 2014-2015 national high quality gold award.

References

1. Maryam Alavi; Dorothy E.Leidner; Deng wen quan, Knowledge management and knowledge management systems: conceptual foundations and research topics, Management World, 2012-05-15.
2. Dai bibo, Research on performance evaluation of knowledge management in enterprise ERP, Journal of Harbin Engineering University, 2012-04-01.
3. Yan haibin, Chen caiyin, Preparation and optimization management of engineering data, Architecture Technology, 2010-06-15
4. Liu jinxing, Application of improved WBS method in engineering project management, Construction Economy, 2011-06-05
5. Xu zhibin, Design and implementation of engineering data management subsystem, Journal of Jilin University, 2011-05-01.
6. WANG Dong ying, Application of Digital Archives in Engineering Management, Electric Power Constructionty, 2001-01
7. Xu zong wei, Gai su xia, Research on the key success factors and management strategies of knowledge management in Chinese Enterprises, Management World, 2012-03.

Research on application mode of monitoring the illegal constructions for sale based on multi-source data and 3S technology—a case study in Shenzhen, China

Rui LIU [1, 2], Yun-Fan LI [3]

[1]*Harbin Institute of Technology Shenzhen Graduate School, Shenzhen, 518055, China*
[2]*Center for Assessment and Development of Real Estate, Shenzhen, 518040, China*
[3]*Yangze River Scientific Research Institute, Wuhan 430010, China*

Abstract. Although there are lots of researches on illegal constructions monitoring and some cities in China have been carried out operational monitoring, there are few researches on monitoring ones for sale. It is hard to monitoring the illegal constructions for sale through the traditional ways from one kind of data, multi-source data are used in the research, including remote sensing data, aerial images, street map data, media and network monitoring data and regular field data. Application mode is done by combining 3S technology, and monitoring standards and processes are defined in the paper. The principles of using 3S technology for illegal constructions for sale is obtained location information in large area through RS, get exact coordinates from field survey using GPS and combining link the two and other data into various query and analysis to complete the monitoring process In monitoring the illegal constructions for sale in Shenzhen, the proposed method has made some achievements and it will provide valuable experience for other district in monitoring the illegal constructions

1 Introduction

A large number of illegal constructions are existed in China, especially in the first class cities, and the transactions in private are already a matter of face. Due to the limit of policy and traditional technical methods, the underground market of the illegal causes not only the severe constructions obstruction in scientific decision-making of urban social and economic development, but also restricted the planning of urban real estate construction, the regulation of the market, the services of the resident population management.

The traditional ways of monitoring the illegal constructions mainly rely on the public report and regular surveys which is time cost and low efficiency. With urban development, illegal constructions are more and more difficult to find, the traditional ways are hard to meet the monitoring need. In recent years, 3S technology is widely used in urban planning, especially in monitoring the illegal constructions, such as Beijing, Hangzhou, Wuhan [1-4].

According to statistics, the area of Shenzhen construction land is 917 square kilometres, of which the area of illegal constructions accounting for up to 42%. The number of the illegal construction is large, the distribution is wide and the impact of the social and economic is deep. Both the purpose and the means of monitoring share the similarities and differences with other cities.

Unlike previous studies for all kinds of illegal constructions, we focused on the particular class—the illegal constructions which are on sale. In the paper, application mode of monitoring is explored with multi-sources data and 3S technology, and some achievement is made. Research on the model and relative experiences will not only promote the researches on social and economic impact in Shenzhen, but also have good reference to other cities monitoring works.

2 Introduction of 3S technology and multi-source data

2.1 3S technology

3S is an abbreviation for geographic information system (GIS), remote sensing (RS) and global positioning system (GPS). These three technologies are both independent and closely related.

2.1.1 Geographic information system (GIS)

Geographic information system (GIS) is a system designed to capture, store, manipulate, analyse, manage, and present all types of spatial or geographical data. In a general sense, the term describes any information system that integrates, stores, edits, analyses, shares, and displays geographic information. GIS applications are tools that allow users to create interactive queries (user-created searches), analyse spatial information, edit data in maps, and present the results of all these operations.

In illegal constructions monitoring, GIS can be used for spatial analysis, data storage and thematic mapping.

2.1.2 Remote sensing (RS)

Remote sensing is the acquisition of information about an object or phenomenon without making physical contact with the object and thus in contrast to on site observation. Various sensors can be used to detect reflected radiation of the object. After transform, image enhancement and recognition, features of large area can be extracted from remote sensing data

Remote sensing data provide base map during the investigation and through multi-temporal data change information about illegal buildings can be found easily.

2.1.3 Global positioning system (GPS)

The Global Positioning System (GPS) is a space-based navigation system that provides location and time information in all weather conditions, anywhere on or near the Earth where there is an unobstructed line of sight to four or more GPS satellites.

The GPS data provide the location information of the illegal buildings.

3S technology is the support technology in monitoring illegal constructions, but there are some disadvantages while using these three technologies alone. Geographic information about illegal constructions can be obtained rapidly through remote sensing, but detail information cannot be obtained. GPS can provide the exact coordinates, but is unable to provide geographical attributes. GIS has abilities to space retrieval and analysis capabilities, but data acquisition becomes the bottleneck [5].

The principles of using 3S technology for illegal constructions for sale is obtained location information in large area through RS, get exact coordinates from field survey using GPS and combining link the two and other data into various query and analysis to complete the monitoring process.

2.2 Multi-source data

Compared to legal real estate sale market, the data of illegal constructions are hard to obtain. Relying on one single data collection way cannot get reliable, comprehensive and authenticable data. So besides using traditional survey data and remote sensing data and GIS data, a variety of new and readily available data sources, such as Internet communication soft wares, website information, web map, street view data are introduced into the monitoring process.

There are disadvantages in using survey data, remote sensing media etc. Using survey data lack of valid evidence to support the need of verification work, which is low efficiency. Although it is wide coverage and high efficiency using remote sensing data, the identification ability in high dense building area is poor and is easy to find error in field survey.

The main sources of data used in the paper and their usage are shown in the following table:

Table 1. Multi-Source Data and Their Usages.

No	Data name	Usages
1	Multi-temporal remote sensing data	In order to obtain illegal constructions information such as location and status, new illegal constructions can be found and existing ones can be seen by comparing multi-temporal remote sensing images.
2	Routine survey data	Routine patrol routes are planned by the government in order to find the new illegal constructions on sale.
3	Media and network data	Due to the large number and long history of illegal constructions, a variety of sale channels are used on Internet besides traditional publicity leaflets, such as QQ, WeChat, blog and etc. Some sale information can be obtained by this way.
4	Street view data	Street view data are introduced into the monitoring process in order to improve the efficiency of the sale market investigation of illegal constructions.
5	Investigation data	To suspected polygons or missing property polygons, it is inevitable to do some field work to obtain detail information about structure, price, etc.
6	Aerial images	Aerial data are used to get information about building appearance and surrounding environment when field survey cannot easily enter.

3 Application mode of monitoring the illegal constructions for sale

Although there are lots of researches on illegal constructions monitoring and some cities in China have been carried out operational monitoring, there are few researches on monitoring ones for sale. Multi-source data and 3S technology are used in the process of monitoring in the paper in order to get the location information and transaction information. The application mode provides solid foundation on data of social and economic impact.

DOI: 10.1051/itmconf/20160704009

3.1. Monitoring standards

Firstly, all aspects of monitoring using multi-source data and 3S technology are discussed in-depth, and the monitoring standard is established which is divided into three parts-elements, requirements and results. It is showed in Figure 1.

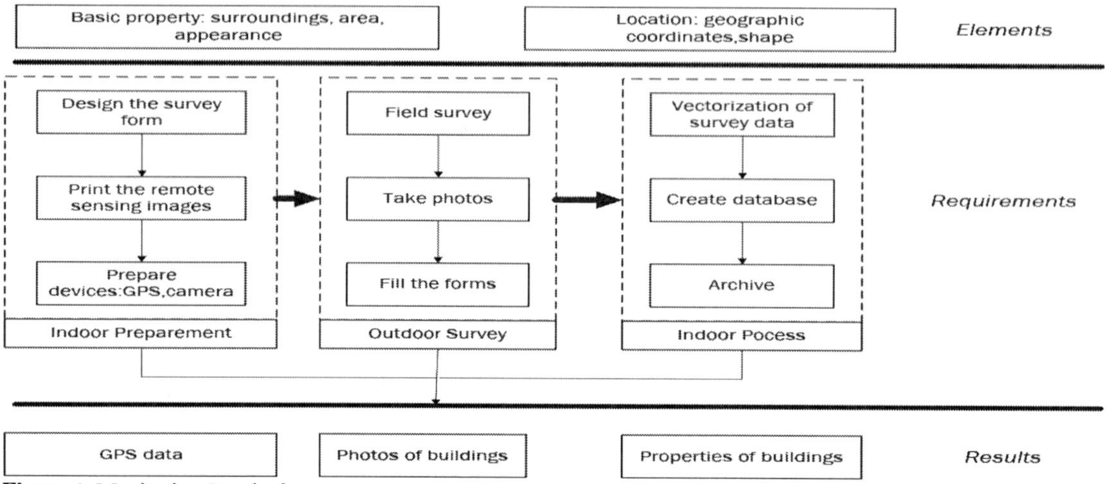

Figure 1. Monitoring Standards

Monitoring elements are provided in the standard, including basic properties and location information such as area, appearance, surrounding environment.

Secondly, monitoring requirements are provided in the standard. They are divided into three sections: indoor preparation, outdoor survey, indoor process and the operational standards in each section are provided too. In the first section, the survey objects are determined by multi-source data, survey forms are designed and printed out with other relative documents. In this section, street view data are introduced into the process which is different from relying on field investigators' photos and is greatly reducing the workload of investigators. In the second section, it is mainly relying on field survey to fill in the form. When it is hard to enter the field to survey, aerial data are used. In the last section, after vectorising the investigate data, database of the illegal constructions is built to manager their properties, shapefiles and photos.

Finally, the results of the monitoring are provided including GPS location, photos of the buildings and the investigation forms.

3.2 Monitoring process

The monitoring process is divided into six steps, shown in Figure 2:

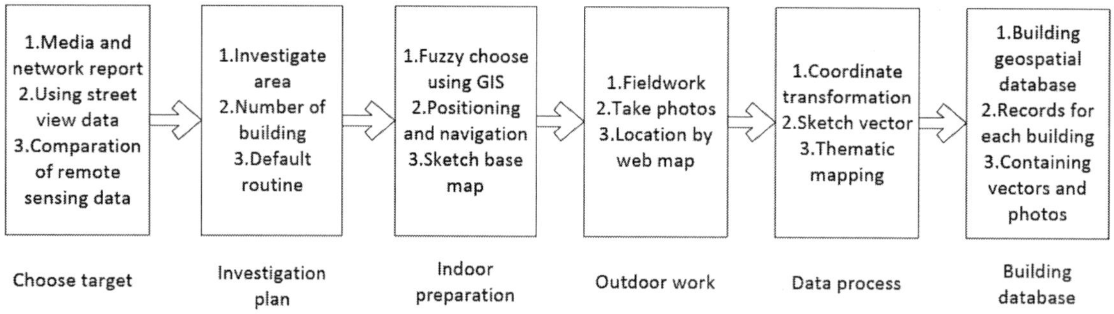

Figure 2. Workflow of Monitoring Process

3.2.1 Choose target

The illegal constructions are divided into two categories: the stock ones and the new ones. For the stock ones, routine inspection, media and network data and street view are used to collect relative information. Addresses are matched with existing data to locate the final ones that are needed to do field survey. For the new ones, multi-temporal remote sensing data are used to discover the location of them and judge the building type with other data.

DOI: 10.1051/itmconf/20160704009

3.2.2 Investigation plan

First the approximate locations of the illegal constructions for sale are found. survey schedule, personnel tasks and investigation contents are arranged in order to ensure the tasks are completed on time.

3.2.3 Indoor preparation

Indoor workers choose areas where the illegal buildings lays using GIS technology, make identification on the base map and develop the best survey lines according to the areas, distributions of the buildings and the road conditions.

3.2.4 Outdoor work

(1) Fieldwork
According to the existing images to locate the illegal building for sale, building names, shape, floor number, usage and construction time are verified. Identifications are made in the images and the latitudes and longitudes are record by the handheld GPS device. Property information is confirmed by the actual situation and the outdoor survey forms are filled, such as addresses and number of floors, etc.

(2) Take photos

Building architectural, entrance doors, building number and surrounding environment must be record fully and clearly. If the investigators were unable to enter the area, unmanned aerial vehicles are used to get photos.

(3) Location by web map

During the investigation process, location information on the web map is confirmed and record for the subsequent process.

3.2.5 Data process

(1) Coordinate transformation

Using the ArcGIS software, data of GPS device are exported and converted from latitude and longitude coordinate system into Shenzhen local coordinate system.

(2) Sketch vector

Taking buildings as basic unit, vectors of the illegal constructions for sale are sketched by using the results of previous outdoor work and comparison of multi-temporal remote sensing images.

(3) Thematic mapping

Thematic maps are made using GIS overlay technology with geological disaster layer, road red line layer, basic farmland layer, etc.

3.2.6 Building database

Geospatial database is built to store all the data which can contain both vectors and raster data. Each building has a record in the database which contains a vector that has all the properties obtained from investigation forms and photos of survey forms and buildings.

3.3 Monitoring application

At present, the monitoring process based on multi-source data and 3S technology has been put into practice to form routine business. In the first quarter of 2014 in Shenzhen, 87 illegal buildings for sale are found amount which 40 of them are the stock ones, the rest are the new ones that are distributed in six administrative regions. The sale area, price, and other building information are obtained.

Using remote sensing data and other data, the distribution thematic map of the 1st quarter of 2014 are made. It can be found that the spatial distribution clearly shows that an obvious spatial aggregation is existed.

While collecting 12 leaflets, removing duplicates and already surveyed ones, there are 5 buildings confirmed by the fieldwork. All the leaflets of the 5 buildings can be used as an evidence for the further law enforcement.

These monitoring results can provide powerful support to the governments to understand the sale market of illegal constructions and to make better decisions on treatment of them.

4 Conclusions

In the paper, an application mode of monitoring illegal constructions based on multi-source data and 3S technology is studied. For the specific type of illegal constructions which are for sale, not only the traditional routine data and field survey data but also the network data are introduced into the monitoring process. To target objects, media and network monitoring data, web map and street view data are also used to improve the efficiency of monitoring. In field survey stage, aerial images are used to obtain the target photos. Meanwhile, 3S technology is widely used in every section of the monitoring which has played a great role in the monitoring. According to the results of the application mode in Shenzhen, it shows that the mode achieved certain results and can provide valuable experience for monitoring illegal constructions for sale.

References

1. Fen Wenbing, Applocation of 3S Technique to the City Planning and Building. Anhui Architecture, **13**,16-17(2006).(In Chinese)
2. Yuan Jinqiu, The Utilization of 3S Technology in National Territory Resources Law Enforcement Supervision. Urban Geotechnical Investigation & Surveying, **2**, 117-119(2012). (In Chinese)
3. Li Deren, Wang Mi, Hu Fen, Monitoring Beijing Illegal Constructions Using Chinese High Resolution Satellite Images, Chinese Science Bulletin, 03, 305-311(2009). (In Chinese)
4. Chen Shihong, Wang Lei, Chen Qinghua, etc, Establishment of 3S Technologies –Baesd System for Digital City Planning Supervision, Geomatics & Spatial Information, 01, 95-100(2011). (In Chinese)
5. Sun Yan, Li Lijun, Wang Chen, etc, Frame and Technology for Monitoring and Management of Illegal Buildings Based on 3S Technologies, Computer Technology and Development, 10, 172-176(2006). (In Chinese)

ITM Web of Conferences 7, 04010 (2016) DOI: 10.1051/itmconf/20160704010
ITA 2016

Construct Primary Education Semantic Ontology Library Based Mind Mapping

Dong-Hong Hu[1] and Xue-Jun YU[2]

[1] *the Information Center of Civil Aviation Administration of China, Beijing 100710, China*
[2] *School of Software Engineering, Beijing University of Technology, Beijing 100124, China*

Abstract. Researches conducted for Mind mapping application in primary education semantic ontology, while considering unique characteristics of primary education, found there were rare widely used ontology libraries and few connections between ontology libraries for information sharing and reuse. In addition, primary semantic ontology library lack precise definitions of the semantics. This paper proposed a solution based on cluster structure derived from mind mapping by providing logical description of the ontologies to precisely define semantics; Meanwhile, tags were adapted to associate different ontologies to form ontology library.

1 Introduction

Mind mapping is a thinking tool that presents a thought process, its application can be roughly summarized in the three aspects which are teaching, business management and personal knowledge management. Tony Buzan who is Britain's memories of father defined mind mapping as this: mind mapping is an expression of radioactive thinking, and therefore it is the natural functions of the human mind. It is a very useful graphics technology, is the master key to open the brain potential. Mind mapping can be used in various aspects of life, learning ability and clear thinking improved by mind mapping will improve people's behavior.[1]

The thinking process presents by mind map is a key of information organization and sharing.[2] The introduction of the mind map aided design in teaching, not only to give full play to the role of the students left and right brain, improve students' learning efficiency, but also can develop students' thinking ability, and form their own way of thinking.

Different from the traditional mind map creation mode, automatically generate mind map through semantic links is a new creation, this approach needs to be realized by means of semantic ontology library. Meanwhile, the mind map by showing a clear relationship can be used as a reference and basis of semantic ontology structure.

The ontology of educational resources can construct a clear knowledge architecture of learning content to conveniently organize and manage learning resources, can provide a guarantee for learning resources sharing and collaborative, provide the basis for learning activities and optimize the process, greatly improve the reuse rate of educational resources. Although the application of education resource ontology has become a research hot spot, receives the widespread attention of scholars, and some achievements have been obtained, but its development especially in the primary school education still not mature enough, mainly in the following aspects: first, there were rare widely used ontology libraries; second, sharing and reuse of ontology model is not enough, and ontologies that constructed by many developers are according to theirs' subjective experience; third, the related technology of ontology that automatically acquired and expanded is still immature, domain ontology acquisition, organization, processing mainly in manual way; fourth, there is no unified standardized ontology modeling method, and lack corresponding standards of ontology evaluation.

Thus, the research goal is to define primary education domain ontology, including the analysis and design of ontology, to explore the method of creating primary education ontology and expanding primary education ontology library.

The rest of the paper is organized as follows. In Section 2, paper presents requirement analysis of ontology. Section 3 describes the construction ideas and creation method of primary education ontology. Section 4 contains the conclusions and future work.

2 Requirement Analysis of Primary Education Semantic Ontology

From the basic pattern of mind map view, its hierarchical structure can be regarded as a tree structure that divergent from the center to the periphery. There is a central node, surrounded by the divergence of the child node. The central node and child node is the inheritance relation, inclusion relation, whole and part relation or attribute relation. The relationship between sub nodes is paratactic. This tree structure basically satisfy the ontology definition of original hierarchical structure. This paper defined for primary education ontology is based on the hierarchical structure of mind mapping. Meanwhile, tags were adapted to associate different ontologies to form ontology library.

2.1 Requirement Analysis of Ontology

Primary education followed the gradual rules, old knowledge set the stage for learning new knowledge. There is a hyponymy or cross relation between knowledge points. A knowledge point usually includes the concept, the nature of concept, the relationship of concepts, the general rule of concepts, and so on. Therefore, the research of primary education ontology needs to explicitly establish links among concepts which according to generic relationship of concepts, and also needs to clearly define the attribute of the concept, value restriction of the attribute, process, relationship etc. Through the study to confirm the essential relation and subjection rapport between the concepts, to establish the complete structure of primary education field, which is conducive to obtain, analyze and use the knowledge.

In this paper, we defined primary education ontology as a five tuple {N,F,A,R,T}, where N is name of education ontology, F is parent ontology name of N, A is attributes set of ontology, R is ontology network, composed by basic relationship between ontologies, T is a set of tag that attached to the ontology.

2.2 Requirement Elicitation of Ontology

Based on the construction of primary education ontology, this paper use the classification system of education theme for reference, design ontology structure from the primary education ontology itself needs. The goal is to be able to describe knowledge structure of primary education field by providing primary education ontology, provide knowledge expression and reasoning support for primary education informatization.

Based on the above understanding, at the same time, considering the knowledge characteristics of primary education field, this paper divided primary education ontology into three major categories which are education activities, education subject, education architecture, then, divided the class into two level. For example, education activities can be divided into the education management activities, teaching activities; education subject can be divided into some branches, such as Chinese, Mathematics, English; education architecture is divided into various types of education and all levels of education. The rest can be done in the same manner, concept can be subdivided step by step, thus forming the concept hierarchy of primary education ontology. Concept hierarchy of primary education ontology is shown in Figure 1.

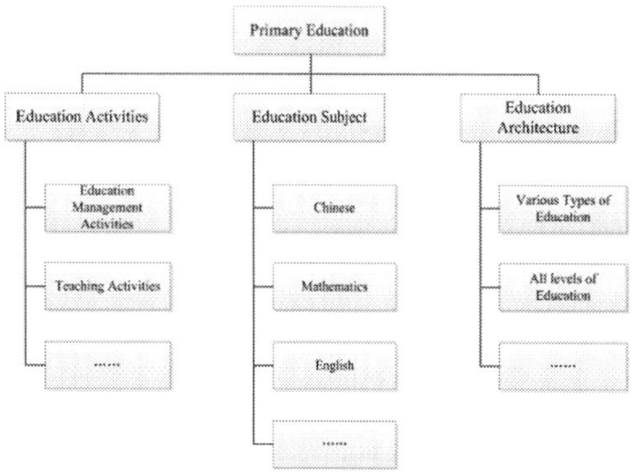

Figure.1 Structure of Primary Education Ontology

2.2.1 Name of Ontology and Father Ontology

Through the above analysis and the test of practical application, concept that appeared in the hierarchy of primary education ontology become the name of ontology and father ontology.

2.2.2 Attribute Sets

In this paper, attribute is relative to the relation of ontology. As shown in Figure 1, sub ontology can be seen as one of parent ontology properties. The attribute definition of primary education ontology not only fully express the relationship and characteristics of the education concept, but also should not be too complicated. Although the complex attribute definition has strong expressiveness, it also bring difficulty to knowledge sharing, and knowledge sharing is the original intention of the construction of primary education ontology. Considering the meaning of the concept and the simple relationship, more specific concept needs to choose as the attribute.

2.2.3 Ontology Network

At the beginning of this section mentioned that there are four relations between central nodes and sub nodes of mind mapping. They are inheritance, inclusion, part and whole, attribute. To a certain extent, there are some similarity between the relationship of ontology and mind mapping. Ontology has four basic relationship, they are kindOf, partOf, instanceOf and attributeOf. KindOf express the relation of category and predictability between ontologies,

DOI: 10.1051/itmconf/20160704010

the equivalent of inheritance in object-oriented, as defined in ontology: if X is a subclass of Y, each instance of X at the same time is the instance of Y, such as the education management activities is the lower class of the education activities. KindOf relation is transitive, if X is a subclass of Y, Y is a subclass of Z, then X is a subclass of Z. PartOf express the relation of part and whole between ontologies, part and whole relation is also transitive. InstanceOf express the relation between instance and ontology, similar to relationship with an instance of a class in object-oriented[3], such as the specific subject is the instance of curriculum. AttributeOf express the attribute of ontology, it can express attribute relationship between ontologies, such as age and name are the attributes of student. Based on the four basic relations, we can carry on the expansion and deletion. There will be a cross between these relations, and then forming ontology network.

2.2.4Tag Sets

Usually, there are some phrases or sentences between the nodes of mind mapping, their role is to describe the relationship between two nodes or is to make sign for sub node. Tag is the key word that marked product target and classification or content. Tags can classify the ontology, usually mark multiple category to different ontologies, point out affiliation between different ontologies. In addition, tag describes the key attribute of ontology, more importantly, social attribute of tag consistent with original intention that constructed the primary education semantic ontology library to realize knowledge sharing. In this paper, the tag is based on attribute significance of ontology.

3 Construction of Primary Education Ontology Library

Ontology learning is the way that obtain domain knowledge from existing information sources, and automatically construct or extend ontology.[4] Now, there is no mature scheme for ontology learning, manual method of ontology construction is time-consuming, therefore, the way of construction by automated means, using semi manual mode to realize primary education ontology library is an effective compromise.

Machine learning and statistical techniques are the main automation means of ontology learning, for the processing of structured, semi-structured or unstructured data through these methods, domain knowledge is acquired from the data. Structured data mainly come from the database, and the XML file; the main source of semi-structured and unstructured data is HTML Webpage, plain text files, electronic documents, etc. The main method of processing structured data is mapping model to the ontology structure, for example, mapping the relation model of relational database to ontology structure[5]; for semi-structured or unstructured data, using machine learning and natural language analysis to obtain the implicit domain knowledge.

For the construction of primary education semantic ontology, a more convenient way is to make use of education thesaurus, education dictionary and corpus set of primary education field for machine learning, to get the knowledge for constructing ontology, and then manually construct primary education ontology. The specific constructing process is shown in Figure 2.

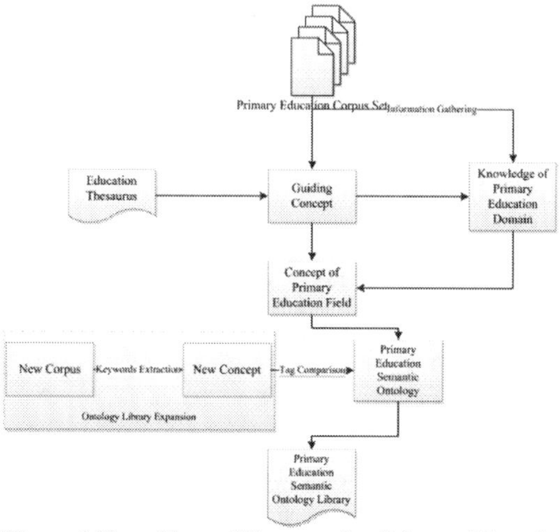

Figure.2 Flow Chart of Constructing Primary Education Semantic Ontology

3.1 Collection and Acquisition of Primary Education Domain Knowledge

Primary education domain knowledge is easy to understand, but it is rich and wide in content. It is important to collect the relevant knowledge of primary education domain before construct primary education ontology. Part concept of education thesaurus and faceted classification relationship of word are some basis for this research; basic knowledge of primary education is an important supplement; tacit knowledge of authoritative expert in primary education domain is key to select concepts of primary education ontology and to delineate the relationship. In addition, the relevant documents for constructing domain knowledge otology, the existing rules, the primary education major literature in network and the books of primary school are object of primary education domain knowledge for collection and acquisition.

3.2 Concept Selection

The main task of this step is to choose the basic vocabulary of terms for primary education domain, to accurately define concept of vocabulary. The core concept that extended from top to bottom form reasonable and complete concept

 DOI: 10.1051/itmconf/20160704010

hierarchy. The choice of primary education vocabulary and the definition of hierarchy usually needs to draw on existing thesaurus, professional dictionary, dictionary, primary education professional books and terminology. In addition, original concept can be got through the Chinese word segmentation. For example, a definition of the parallelogram which means is "The four sides of the diagonal are parallel to each other. " could get the following string by word segmentation: "diagonal / mutual divide /the/ quadrilateral // parallelogram ". "the " and "is " is stop word that need to be give up. "diagonal", "mutual divide ", "quadrilateral ", "parallelogram " these four phrases, namely original concept, need to be retain.

3.3 Establishing Attribute Relationship

The Attributes and relationships are the foundation of constructing primary education ontology.[6] In this step, the selected concept vocabulary need to be standardly defined according to the basic relationship that mentioned above section. These logical relationships arranged in a crisscross pattern, so as to form a stereo and intuitive semantic net. For example, the relationship among "diagonal line ", "Divide equally between each other ", "Quadrilateral", "Parallel quadrilateral " these four concepts is shown in table 1.

Table.1 Example of the relationship between the concepts

Concept	Relationship
diagonal line	attribute Of
Divide equally between each other	attribute Of
Quadrilateral	—
Parallel quadrilateral	kind Of

These relationships can simply construct part ontology of parallelogram.

3.4 Adjunction of Semantic Tags

In this paper, tag that has rich semantic information is used to represent the similarity between ontologies. These information form a tag similarity calculation method that based on hierarchical structure of ontology. In the following, we collectively named the labels that generated by upper ontology as tag in the absence of ambiguous cases. For example, in Figure 3, f is the upper ontology of a, a is the lower ontology of f, so f make a mark to a.

Figure 3 take solid shape for instance to show hierarchical structure of ontology and tag.

Because of hierarchy of tag and multi-tag of ontology, in using the tag hierarchy to measure the similarity between two ontologies should also satisfy some properties, in this paper, we use sim to represent the similarity.

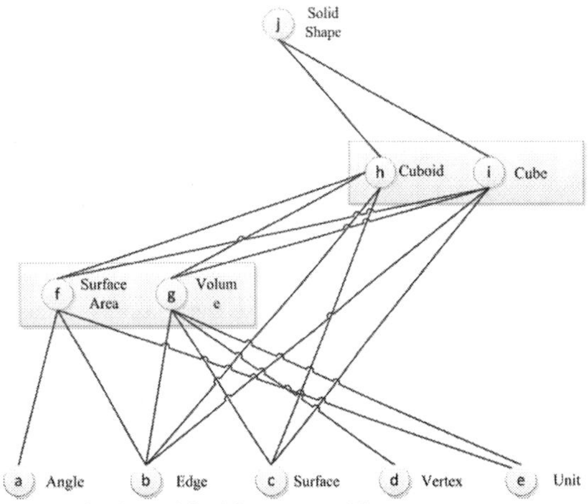

Figure.3 Hierarchical Structure of Tags

Character 1: expansion. If the two ontologies only share a tag, then the tag marked more ontologies, the similarity of these two ontologies is lower. For example, in Figure 3, a and b only share tag f, b and e only share tag g, of which three ontologies have been annotated with f, but there are four ontologies have been marked the tag g, so you can have this conclusion: sim (a, b) >sim (b, e).

Character 2: distance. If common tag of two ontologies close to them, then the similarity of the two ontologies is more than the similarity of the two ontologies which public tag far from them. As shown in Figure 3, the common tag f of ontology a and b is the sub node of tag h which is public tag of ontology b and c, so sim (a, b) >sim (b, c).

Character 3: binding. If the two ontologies have a plurality of public tags, then the similarity of these two ontologies is more than the similarity of these two ontologies which have a single common tag, is smaller than the summation of each tag similarity. As shown in Figure 3, b and c have a common ontology tag g and h, so max $sim(b,c|T) \leq sim(b,c) \leq \sum T sim(b,c|T)$, where T refers to the common tag set {g, h}. Tag can be regarded as brief description of some attribute of ontology, two ontologies have public tag means they have same attributes. More public tags they have, more similarity of attributes they have. However, the attributes of each tag may be repeated, the actual similarity is smaller than calculation of each tag.

3.5 Extension Methods of Ontology Library

During or after the construction of ontology library, there will be a larger space to supply and improve. Quickly increasing vocabulary, the development of semantic technology and subdivision of primary education domain ontology type ask us to construct semantic ontology with considering to extend the ontology library.

3.5.1 Keywords Extraction

There are many words to constitute new corpus. Vector dimension of text is very large if see all words as keywords without distinguishing. This will not only have an impact on the operational efficiency, but also make the key features are submerged in the non-key words. Therefore, keywords of categories can be accessed by machine learning, and to reach the purpose of increasing the discrimination and reducing dimensions.

Keyword extraction can use the word frequency statistics to complete.[7] First, select the text that matches theme features as the corpus, randomly select a part of corpus as training sample, the rest is test sample; then use Chinese segmentation to divide training sample, and make frequency statistics of the training samples. Vast majority of text are likely to appear stop word, it will produce "noise " effect on the automatic text categorization. Therefore, stop word need to be filtered in the preprocessing stage. After making word frequency statistics and removing stop words, vocabulary weight can be calculated by using the TF.IDF method. Finally, word frequency is sorted according to the calculation results of TF.IDF. Part of vocabulary with high weight value are selected as keywords. The number of keywords need to be set initial value, then test it by using test samples, select the best value according to the repeated experimental results.

3.5.2 Tag Comparison

After knowledge collection, concept selection, establishing attribute relationship and adjunction of semantic tags, the corpus that formed by extracting keywords become a new ontology. Then, to add the ontology into ontology library needs to use the way of tag comparison.

The way that presented in reference[8] can almost meet the three properties which are proposed in section 3.4. This method is concept similarity calculating method based on ontology.[9] The formula of this method is as follows, assuming that the node p is the parent node of node c in ontology, the distance between node c and node p is calculated for:

$$wt(c,p)=(\beta+(1-\beta)\frac{E}{E(p)})(\frac{d(p)+1}{d(p)})\alpha[IC(c)-IC(p)]T(c,p) \quad (1)$$

d(p) means the hierarchy depth of node p, E(p) means the connection number of the child nodes, E represents the number of average child link nodes in the whole hierarchy, T(c,p) represents a connection type, α and β control the effects that made by depth and local density of the node on edge weight value. The information entropy of each node is calculated as IC(c)=-logP(c), where P(c) refers to the occurrence probability of node c and all its child nodes.

Reference[8] said that using shortest distance reciprocal of public tags to represent the similarity of ontology c1 and c2, i.e. sim(c1,c2)=1/minpdt(c1,p,c2). The range of similarity between [0,1].

In this paper, tag comparison is finished by similarity computation of tag. If similarity of the two tags is greater than 0.7, we believe that these two tags are similar, then the ontology of these two tags are similar. In reality, a ontology comprises a plurality of tags, so we need to calculate the similarity of all tags, and then determine the similarity by variance calculations of the value.

4 Conclusions and Future Work

To construct and improve the ontology is an iterative process, a method that easy to model and expand can guide the construction of ontology library. This paper propose a method to construct primary education semantic ontology library based on analysis of primary education domain knowledge, which take hierarchical structure of mind mapping for model, depend on and reference to the existing method of ontology construction with some concept relationship of education thesaurus. This method can show up knowledge concept and relationship of primary education domain in the form of ontology library. Of course, any one of ontology that successfully constructed will have a larger space to supplement and improve. In a word, the construction of primary education library is a huge and tedious task, effective construction method and extended rules need to be further research and improve.

References

[1] Tony. Buzan. Mind Mapping[M].LISi, translate. Beijing: Writers Publishing House, 1999, (3):56.

[2] Anonymous. Maricl, Inc.; Cutting-Edge Social Mind Mapping Web Site Marici.com Launches[J]. China Weekly News, 2008(1):121-122.

[3] LIU Chun-lei. Study on Methodology for Subject Knowledge Modeling Based on ontology[D]. Chongqing: Chongqing University, 2008.

[4] LIU Bai-song. A Study on Web-Based Domain Independent Ontology Learning [D]. Zhejiang: Zhejiang Universtiy, 2007.

[5] CHA Song-li, MA Zong-ming, JIAO Xiao-long. Survey on methodology for constructing ontology based on structured information source[J]. Application Research of Computers, 2012, 29(7):2407.

[6] HAN Ren, HUANG Yong-zhong, LIU Zhen-lin,et al. Research on OWL ontology building method[J]. Computer Engineering and Desing, 2008,29(6):1398.

[7] YANG Yin, DAI Bin. Chinese Keyword Extraction Method Based on Multi-Features[J]. Computer Application and Software, 2014,31(11):110.

[8] Sun Yuan-shuai. Recommendation Algorithms in the Big Data Era[D]. Fujian:Xiamen University, 2014.

[9] Jiang J, Conrath D. Semantic Similarity Based on Corpus Statistics and Lexical Taxonomy[C]. In Proceedings of ROCLING'1997. New York: ACM Press, 1997:19-33.

Analysis and Research about Characteristics of Online Learning Behaviours of SPOC Learners

Qiang-Ping SONG[1], Hai-Guang FANG[1,a], Ying TENG[2] and Bao-Cong JIAO[1]

[1] *Capital Normal University, Department of Educational Technology, Beijing, China*
[2] *Capital Normal Universities, Department of Education, Beijing, China*
[a] Corresponding author: fanghg2013@163.com

Abstract. SPOC (small private online course) has recently evolved into a typical representative in post-MOOC (massive open online courses) times. Current researches about SPOC mainly focus on blended learning mode, teaching process, and teaching mode etc., paying less attention to online behaviors of learners. Based on online platforms of the general knowledge course *Game Theory*, this paper analyzes and researches online behaviors of SPOC learners. In addition, this paper summarizes differences of SPOC and MOOC in online learning behaviors by collecting online learning behavioral data of 145 learners and investigating their online behavioral characteristics during their learning process. The research reveals, learners are fond of video media in terms of the communication form, tend to answer questions instead of coming up with their own questions in terms of interactions, and focus on quizzes and homework due to pressures of credits.

1. Introduction

SPOC (small private online course) emerges as a new concept which was forward after MOOC (massive open online courses) of the Harvard University [1]. In essence, SPOC and MOOC can be classified into the same category [2]. SPOC aims to realize organic combination of MOOC and class teaching [3]. Current researches only focus on blended learning mode [4], teaching process [5], and teaching mode [6]. Analysis about online learning behaviours of learnings mainly relies on the MOOC online research. At present, there are international comparative researches [7] about MOOC online behaviors and influence factors of MOOC learning behaviors etc. [8]. Different from thousands of learners in MOOC, SPOC limits the number of learners to dozens or several hundred at maximum. With regard to SPOC, its learning activities appear more flexible and efficient and its quizzes seem more rigorous [9]. Online learning behaviors of SPOC learners are different from those of MOOC. While drawing experience from current analysis about MOOC learning behaviors, this paper tries to carry out explanation and quantitative analysis about the general knowledge course *Game Theory* on basis of SPOC mode. This paper compared similarities and differences between online behaviors of SPOC and those of MOOC by analyzing and categorizing characteristics. At last, this paper predicts academic performance learners and summarizes characteristics of online learning behaviors.

2. SPOC online learning behaviours

2.1 Brief Introduction to the Game Theory

As a general knowledge course of a university, the *Game Theory* is available for learners who have completed mathematics program of a senior high school. The *Game Theory* on basis of SPOC combines online learning with offline face-to-face teaching. The course and its first lecture were put on "MOOC Platform of Chines Universities" in September, 2015. This course is updated every other week later on for 9 lectures. The offline face-to-face teaching lasts for 9 times in every other week. Details of the course are shown as the Table 1.

Table 1. Basic information of the SPOC course *Game Theory*

Faculty	Teaching Assistant	Credit	Attendant
8 Persons	9 Persons	2	145 Attendants

2.2 Categorization of SPOC online learning behaviors

The SPOC blended learning mode combines online learning with offline class and thus changes traditional class teaching mode of the *Game Theory*, bringing different learning experience to learners. The SPOC blended learning mode applied to *Game Theory* is shown in Figure 1. This paper discusses online links from perspectives of independent learning preparation, feedback and evaluation, as well as discussion and communication.

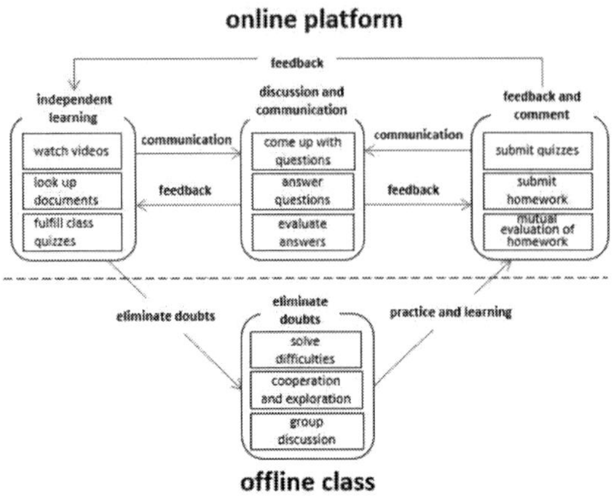

Figure 1. SPOC Blended Learning Mode of the Game Theory

According to implementation of SPOC of the *Game Theory*, this paper summarizes behavioral natures of online and office learning behaviors just as shown in Table 2. Independent learning refers to a process in which learners complete independent learning by using courseware resources offered by the platform. As an indispensable important link in learning. The feedback and comment mean the platform checks and recognizes the learning achievements and learning process through quizzes offered by it. The feedback and comment mainly include submission of homework, submission of quizzes, and mutual evaluation of homework. Discussion and communication refers to an exchange process between teachers and students on basis of the platform. Such interactions mainly include posting, replying, and commenting. Online discussion offers bases for preparation of offline face-to-face teaching.

Table 2. Learning mode, learning behaviors and natures of SPOC learners

Learning Mode	Learning Behaviors	Behavioral Natures
Independent Learning	Watching Videos	Video status (read or not read), watching times, playback times, watching time
	Look up Documents	Document status (review or not review), looking-up times, review times, looking-up time
	Fulfill class quizzes	Homework status (submitted, not submitted)
Feedback and Comment	Submit quizzes	Submission time, quiz status (submitted, not submitted), score, times
	Submit homework	Submission time, homework status (submitted, not submitted), score, times
	Evaluate each other's homework	Time of mutual evaluation, scores of mutual evaluation, contents of mutual evaluation, and times of mutual evaluation
Discussion and Evaluation	Come up with questions	Questions, frequency, times of coming up with questions
	Answer questions	Answers, frequency, times of giving right answers, times of giving wrong answers
	Comments on answers	Contents, frequency, commenting times, posts with thumbs-up.

3. Analysis about online learning behaviors of SPOC learners

3.1 Analysis about online learning behaviors

3.1.1 Independent Learning

SPOC courseware resources for independent learning of the *Game Theory* consist of videos, documents (graphs and texts), and class quizzes. This paper collects statistical data about person-times of learning of 45 videos and 83 documents. Figure 2 shows the statistical distribution of person-times of video watching. The persons-times register 245 at maximum and pumps to 45 at minimum. Figure 3 shows the statistical distribution of person-times of document review. The person-times of document reviews posts 155 at peak and falls to 50 at bottom. The person-times of video watching and document review fluctuate to decline, which indicates learners' passions for independent learning decrease with progress of learning. As shown in Figure 2, this paper video watching prevails over document review in terms of times. This reflects learners expect knowledge can be displayed in form of videos.

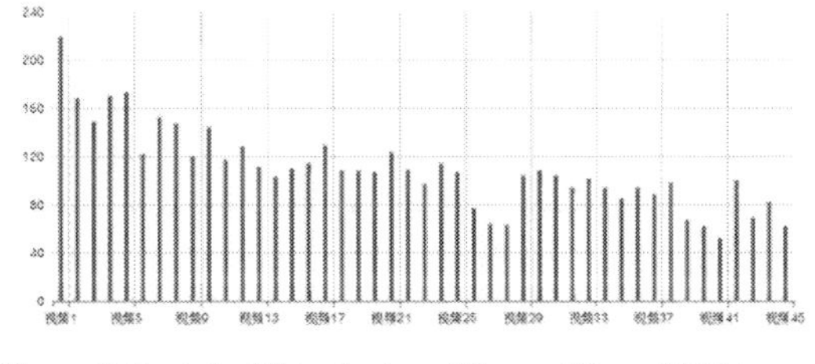

Figure 2. Statistical Distribution of Person-Times Of Video Watching

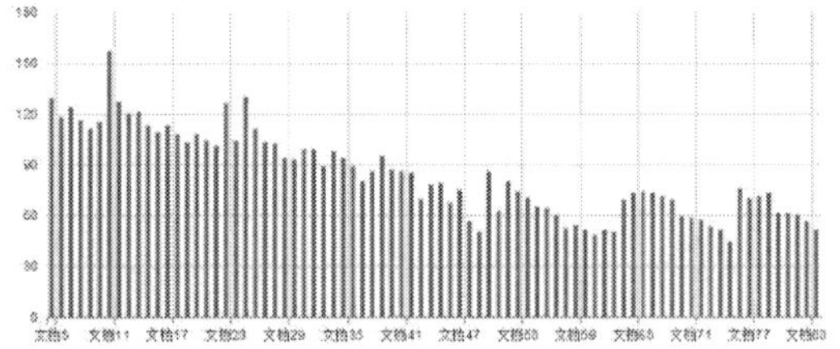

Figure 3. Document review statistical distribution of person-times

3.1.2 Feedback and Comment

The feedback and comment are mainly displayed in quizzes. Quizzes after every lecture consist of objective part and subjective part. The quizzes adopt automatic scoring system and the homework implements mutual evaluation mechanism. This paper counts attendants and average scores of quizzes and homework of these 9 lectures, just as shown in Figure 4. Except homework 3 and homework 9, attendants of other homework register 90% of all the students with an average score ranging from 75 to 85. The data indicates attendance rate of quizzes and homework of every lecture is relatively high. Learners pay much attention to the feedback and comment, because such evaluation will influence their final score. According to the line chart, it can be found attendants decline in the third lecture and come to the bottom in the fourth lecture. This indicates learners require external supervision and intervention.

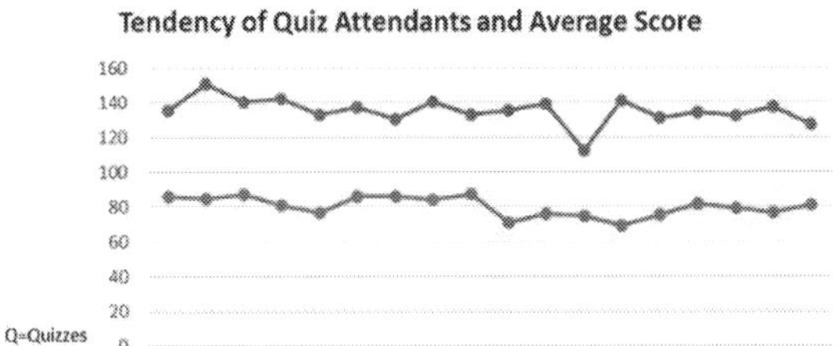

Q=Quizzes H=Homework	Q1	Q2	Q3	Q4	Q1	Q2	Q3	Q4	Q1	H1	H2	H3	H4	H5	H6	H7	H8	H9
Attendants	135	151	140	142	133	137	130	140	133	135	139	112	141	131	134	132	137	127
Average	85.7	85	87.3	81.2	76.5	86.1	85.8	83.9	87	71.1	76	74.7	69	75.2	81.9	79.4	76.4	80.9

Figure 4.Tendency of Quiz Attendants and Average Scores

3.1.3 Discussion and Communication

This platform establishes several discussion sections for teachers and students to solve problems and exchange their ideas by posting, replaying, commenting and clicking thumbs-up. Every interaction can win thumbs-up of others. The background system can export the number of themes, replies, comments, posts, and thumbs-up of learners. The statistical data are shown in the following Table 3.

Table 3. Descriptive Statistical Data about Discussion and Communication

	N	Min	Max	Mean	SD
Themes	145	0	34	2.37	4.633
Replies	145	0	100	13.69	13.505
Comments	145	0	27	1.59	4.294
Posts	145	0	144	17.65	19.084
Thumbs-up	145	0	118	6.67	13.298
Effective N	145				

Posting times per capital in theme discussions is 2.37 with a maximum value of 34 and a minimum value of 0. The mean value of total replies is 13.69. Students are highly involved in replies to theme discussions. The total number of comments refers to the times of commenting on replies of classmates. The mean value of total number of comments is 1.59, lower than that of replies. Students tend to comment on theme discussions instead of posts of classmates. The mean value of the total number of posts is 17.65 and the mean value of posts in every lecture is 1.96. Involvement of students in the forum still needs to be improved. The mean value of thumbs-up is 6.67 and the thumb-up rate is 37.78%. This reflects posts of some students are recognized by other classmates.

3.2 Behavioral characteristics of online learners

This paper summarizes four major characteristics of SPOC online learners by investigating details of practice and analyzing online behaviors of learners. These characteristics are respectively, easy start and difficulties in persistence, emphasis on videos instead of graphs, focus on quizzes instead of process, as well as stress on replies instead of comments

3.2.1 Easy start and difficulties in persistence

Learners are interested in SPOC online learning within first two weeks of the class. With further progress, learners reduce their times of watching videos and reviewing documents. During the implementation process, it takes us more time to sustain enthusiasm of learners and lower possibilities of stopping leaning instead of attract these learners just at the very beginning.

3.2.2 Emphasis on videos instead of documents

During the independent leaning process, learners pay much more time in watching videos than that in reviewing documents. Learners prefer videos during the process of explaining knowledge, because videos are characterized by rich contents, various sounds, and images of teachers. These elements can be easily received by learners. It is suggested to use videos as core elements and adopt documents as supplementary elements during the process of preparing independent learning courseware resources.

3.2.3 Focus on quizzes instead of process

Videos, discussions and videos aims to help student's master knowledge and gain better performance. However, these elements only occupy a small portion in final score. Students show less involvement in comparison with quizzes which take up a large portion in scores of learners. Quizzes show higher completion rate and involvement rate. It is advised to establish multiple and reasonable evaluation mechanisms during the SPOC practice process, so as to evaluate final learning achievements of students in a comprehensive way.

3.2.4 Stress on replies instead of comments

Learners tend to reply to posts during discussion and communication. It is obvious learners only replay to corresponding posts according to teaching instructions, failing to offer in-depth and positive comments on replies. This frustrates the mutual discussion and learning atmosphere. Teachers are supposed to guide students to come up with questions through independent thinking and comment on replies through sharing and communication mechanism.

4. Relevance analyses

4.1 Analysis about the relevance of online learning behaviors

Relationships between research behaviors can eliminate isolated views about occurrence of online leaning behaviors of SPOC learners. This paper uses Pearson relevance analysis method to explore the relevant of different behaviors, just as shown in Table 4.

Table 4. The Relevance of Various Elements of Online Learning Behaviors

	Videos	Watch-ing	Themes	Replies	Com-ments	Thumbs-up	Quizzes
Watching	.732**						
Themes	.185*	.276**					
Replies	.181*	.180*	.609**				
Comments	.048	.207*	.523**	.395**			
Thumbs-up	.137	.169	.692**	.789**	.519**		
Quizzes	.488**	.613**	.164	.309**	.120	.199*	
Homework	.345**	.648**	.239**	.347**	.173	.257**	.798**

Notes:: ①**. significate relevant on both sides of 0.01 level.
②*. significant relevant on both sides of 0.05 level.

It can be found from this chart, the number of videos and the time of watching videos exceed 0.6. This illustrates online learning behaviors of independent learning have significant relevance. With regard to discussion and communication, the total number of themes, replies, and comments also shows significant relevance. In addition, the relevance between the total number of thumbs-up and that of replies registers 0.789 (significant relevance). The relevance between the total number of thumbs-up and that of comments posts 0.519 (medium relevance), also indicating relevance between replies and thumbs-up. For the feedback and comment, the relevance between quizzes and homework achieves 0.789 (significant relevant), reflecting the consistency of quiz scores and homework.

For independent learning, discussion and communication, the time of watching videos is less related to the total number of themes. In addition, it has no relevance with the total number of replies, comments and thumbs-up. Feedbacks and communication of learners share significant relevant with multiple behaviors. This indicates feedbacks and communication are closed related to online learning behaviors. This can be found through the significant relevance (0.613) between quiz scores and the time of watching videos. The relevance between homework and the time of watching videos is 0.648 (significant relevance) and the relevance between homework score and the total number of posts is 5.42 (medium relevance).

4.2 Regression analysis about online quiz scores

This paper uses regression analysis method to conduct stepwise linear regression analysis about influence factors of SPOC online quiz scores. This analysis takes online quiz scores as independent variables and considers the number of videos, the time of watching videos, as well as the total number of themes, replies, comments, thumbs-up and other online learning behaviors as dependent variables (predictive variables), just as shown in Table 5.

Table 5. Abstract of Stepwise Diversified Regression Analysis about Online Quiz Scores

Model	R	R Square	Adjusted R Square	B	Beta
(Constant)				55.958	
1. Videos	.615	.378	.378	1.010	.615
2. Replies	.714	.509	.131	.900	.548

Table 5 is the abstract of the regression analysis. Failing to achieve the standard of significant independent variables, the regression coefficient is excluded from the regression model. Only the number of videos and the total number of replies can be taken as significant variables of the regression model. The multiple relevance coefficients are 0.714 and the unified explanation variance of the two factors R Square is 0.509. In other words, the two factors can be united to predict 50.9% of variables of scores. The explanation variance of the number of videos (Adjusted R Square) is 0.378, namely 37.8%. In addition, the explanation variance of the total number of replies (Adjusted R Square) is 0.131, namely 13.1%. Therefore, the number of videos is a major influence factor for quiz scores and the total number of replies is a minor one.

5. Discussion and summary

5.1 Comparison of SPOC and MOOC online learning behaviors

SPOC and MOOC show big differences in openness, student number, learning mode, evaluation form and learning cost [10] etc. These differences also lead to differences in online learning behaviors of learners. Based on previous researches about MOOC online learning behaviors, this paper compares differences of online behaviors of SPOC and MOOC learners.

5.1.1 High involvement rate of SPOC learners in online learning activities

For involvement rate, the data indicates the involvement rate of MOOC learners is 20% and the course completion rate of them is 4%. 60% of above learners watch videos and 40% of above learners submit quizzes [11]. SPOC learners show higher involvement rate. Their forum involvement rate is 98% and the mean value of replies is 13.69. The course completion rate of SPOC learners can register 95% and their video completion rate is 71%. Quiz submission rate of every lecture is sustained above 85% and their average scores range from 75 to 85.

5.1.2 Online learning behaviors of SPOC learners are restrictive

The research indicates, the more course MOOC learners take, the high possibility MOOC learners show to complete courses [12]. Due to pressures of credits, SPOC learners need to attend online learning independently. In addition, teachers can supervise and guide online learning behaviors of learners, which restrict their online learning behaviors.

5.2 Suggestions for implementation of SPOC

Through research about online learning behaviors of SPOC learners in the course *Game Theory*, this paper comes up with suggestions for construction and implementation of SPOC.

(1) Learners prefer to take videos as the manifestation form of learning contents. They are less involved in document review. During the development of SPOC, it is suggested to explain knowledge points by taking videos as major method and documents as a supplementary method.

(2) Learners tend to answer questions put forward by their classmates instead of themselves. During the implementation process, teachers should stimulate the ability of students to find questions and come up with questions by establishing a reward mechanism for coming up with questions.

(3) Due to pressures of credits, SPOC learners pay much attention to quizzes and homework contents. Other modules of SPOC courses are easily ignored. It is suggested to introduce diversified evaluation mechanisms for online score evaluation.

Research about online learning behaviors of SPOC learners can help us analyze contents and manifestation forms which attract attention of online learners. How to handle online learning and offline class will become a major topic for researches about SPOC.

References

1. S.Coughlan,(2013),http://www.bbc.com/news/business-24166247.
2. Z.T. Zhu, M.Z. Liu, Open Education Research 20, 36 (2014)
3. W. Xu, Y.Z. Jia, A. Fox, Modern Distance Education Research 27, 13 (2014)
4. R. Chen, Z.M. Liu, Distance Education In China 34, 42 (2015)
5. B. He, Y. Cao, China Educational Technology 36, 22 (2015)
6. J.J. lv, Journal Of Distance Education 33, 72 (2015)
7. Y.F. Xue, Z.Z. Huang, F. Shi, Open Education Research 21, 80 (2015)
8. X. Fang, Open Education Research 21, 46 (2015)
9. A. Fox, COMMUN ACM 56, 38 (2013)
10. F.YLiu,http://epaper.heeact.edu.tw/images/epaper_heeact_edu_tw/2014_0301_No48/P-40F1.png
11. Z.X. Jiang, Y. Zhang, X.M. Li, Comput Res Dev 58, 614 (2015)
12. M.L. LI, S.P. Xu, M.L. Sun, Open Education Research 21, 63 (2015)

ITM Web of Conferences 7, 04012 (2016) DOI: 10.1051/itmconf/20160704012
ITA 2016

A flexible approach for the hierarchical community detection

Guang-Cao LIU[1,a], Guang ZHAO[1,2], Jiao CHEN[1] and Yu-Lin ZHUANG[1,2]

[1]*Xiamen Great Power Geo Information Technology Co. Ltd., Xiamen, China*
[2]*State Grid Information & Telecommunication Group Co. Ltd., Beijing, China*

Abstract. The hierarchical community detection is able to demonstrate the intrinsic structure of the network, but a deficiency is that the final structure is invariable. In this study, a flexible extension of the hierarchical approach is proposed. The modularity increasement is substituted by a ratio that should be larger than a threshold. We are able to adjust the hierarchical structure by modifying the threshold. The experiments display that such a variation of hierarchical structure is sensible if the modularity metric Q does not change too much.

1 Introduction

The study of community structure detection is a hot topic in both computer science and statistical physics. It is closely related to graph partition, such as the METIS algorithm [1, 2]. Graph partition is able to precisely divide the network into a small number of parts, e. g. 8 parts, in order to facilitate parallel computation, but the results are not close related to the nature structure of the network. By contrast, community detection is able to find the nature community structure of the network, and probably dozens of or hundreds of communities are found. Since there are so many communities, a hierarchical structure is preferred to demonstrate the network, as shown on figure 1. However, the hierarchical community detection is not as flexible as the graph partition that can divide the network into any number. It would be ideal if we can slightly adjust the hierarchical results, especially the number of communities.

The modularity metric Q to evaluate the community structure has been proposed by Newman and Girvan, as shown in equation (1) [3, 4]. The range of Q is between 0 and 1. The large Q indicates an evident community structure. Normally, if Q is below 0.3, the partition of the community structure may not be reasonable.

$$Q = \frac{1}{2m}\sum_{ij}[A_{ij} - \frac{k_i k_j}{2m}]\delta(c_i, c_j) \qquad (1)$$

A_{ij} is the weight of the edge between vertex i and vertex j, $m = \frac{1}{2}\sum_{ij} A_{ij}$ is the sum of weights of all edges, $k_i = \sum_l A_{il}$ is the sum of the weights of the edges attached to vertex i, c_i is the community to which vertex i is assigned, and the $\delta(c_i, c_j)$ is 1 if vertex i and vertex j are assigned to the same community and 0 otherwise.

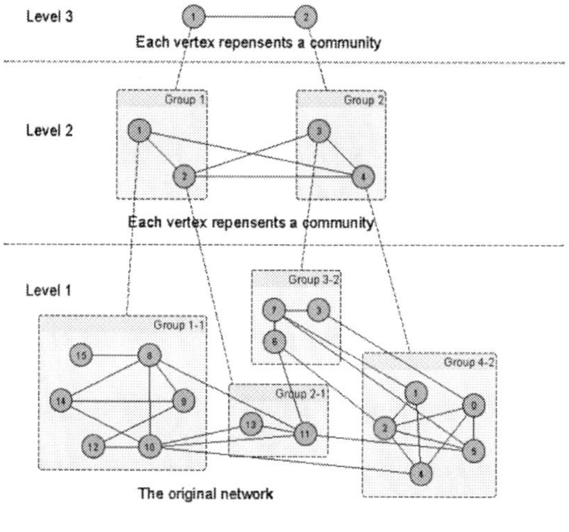

Figure 1. The Example of the Hierarchical Community Structure Detected By the Bgll Method.

There are many community detection methods which either base on or profit from the modularity metric Q [5-8]. Among these methods, a fast and hierarchical approach method has been proposed by Blondel, Guillaume, Lambiotte, and Lefebvre, namely the BGLL method [9]. This method contains two phases that are repeated iteratively. The first phase increases Q by the community adjustment, which tries to move each vertex from its original community and choose one of its neighbour vertex's community to join in so as to maximize Q. The second phase builds a new network which condenses communities found during the first

DOI: 10.1051/itmconf/20160704012

phase into new vertexes, and new edges are assigned with the sum of weights of previous edges between communities. The two phases are repeated until there is no more changes so that Q cannot be further increased.

2 Method

In the BGLL method, when vertex i is removed from its original community, it re-chooses a connecting community to join in. The increasement of Q, i.e. $\Delta Q_i(C_j)$, for moving vertex i into vertex j's community, is

$$\begin{aligned}\Delta Q_i(C_j) &= \tfrac{1}{2m}[(A_{i,C_j} + A_{C_j,i}) - \tfrac{k_i k_{C_j} + k_{C_j} k_i}{2m}] \\ &= \tfrac{1}{2m}[(A_{i,C_j} - \tfrac{k_i k_{C_j}}{2m}) \times 2]\end{aligned}, \quad (2)$$

where $A_{i,C_j} = A_{C_j,i} = \sum_{j \in C_j} A_{i,j}$ is the sum of weights of edges that connect vertex i with any vertex in community Cj, and $k_{C_j} = \sum_{j \in C_j} k_j$ is the sum of weights of all edges inside the community Cj.

In all vertexes connected to vertex i, vertex i will choose the maximum one $Max[\Delta Q_i(C_j)]$. If $Max[\Delta Q_i(C_j)] > 0$, vertex i joins into the maximum one community Cj, otherwise vertex i stay alone as a community.

In order to adjust the result of the BGLL method, we define a new judgement instead of $Max[\Delta Q_i(C_j)] > 0$. The new judgement is

$$\begin{cases} P_i(C_j) = \frac{2mA_{i,C_j}}{k_i k_{C_j}} \\ Max[P_i(C_j)] > P_{thres} \end{cases}, \quad (3)$$

where Pthres is a global threshold that control whether some vertexes can join to their neighbour's communities or stay alone otherwise. The following gives the meaning of this new judgement.

First, the new judgement is an extension of the original BGLL method. When Pthres=1, i.e. the maximum $\frac{2mA_{i,C_j}}{k_i k_{C_j}} > 1$, the partition result is the same as the BGLL method, since $\Delta Q_i(C_j) > 0$ is equal to $A_{i,C_j} - \frac{k_i k_{C_j}}{2m} > 0$ or $\frac{2mA_{i,C_j}}{k_i k_{C_j}} > 1$.

Second, $\frac{k_{C_j}}{2m}$ is the ratio of Cj's degrees of links (k_{C_j}) to the sum of degrees of all links (2m), hence $k_i \cdot \frac{k_{C_j}}{2m}$ gives the estimated links from vertex i to community Cj. A_{i,C_j} represents the real links between vertex i and community Cj. Therefore, $\frac{A_{i,C_j}}{k_i k_{C_j}/(2m)}$ is the ratio between the real links and the estimated links. Finally, $\frac{A_{i,C_j}}{k_i k_{C_j}/(2m)} > P_{thres}$ only allows the ratio above the threshold so as to join vertex i into community Cj.

The whole process is carried out as follows.

Step 1. Set the value of Pthres, which is often set to 1 initially.

Step 2. At the beginning of the first phase, assign every vertex a different community. There are as many communities as vertexes.

Step 3. Optimize the belonging community of each vertex.

Step 3.1. Visit all vertexes one by one. A random order is recommended.

Step 3.1.1. Each time pick a vertex out of its original communities, and renew the number of vertexes and edges in its original community.

Step 3.1.2. For the picked out vertex, find out all its adjacent communities, which contain at least one edge connecting to this vertex.

Step 3.1.3. Calculate $P_i(C_j) = \frac{2mA_{i,C_j}}{k_i k_{C_j}}$ for all the adjacent communities found in the above step, in which i denotes the picked out vertex and Cj is an adjacent community.

Step 3.1.4. Choose the maximum one among all of $P_i(C_j)$ obtained above. If the maximum one $Max[P_i(C_j)] > P_{thres}$, vertex i joins into the community Cj, and if community Cj is not i's last community before i is picked out, this is a change in the community structure. On the other hand, if $Max[P_i(C_j)] \le P_{thres}$, vertex i go back to its original community, in which i stay alone without any other vertex in its community. All the values of $Max[P_i(C_j)]$ are recorded as references for tuning Pthres.

Step 3.2. After all vertexes are optimized, if the community structure changes during Step 3.1.4, repeat from step 3.1 to optimize all vertexes again.

Step 4. In the second phase a new network is constructed as follows.

Step 4.1. If any community contains more than one vertex, it is replaced by a new vetex. Otherwise, there is no more than one vertex in every community, and jump to step 6 instead.

Step 4.2. In the new network, new edges are assigned the sum of weights of previous edges between communities. All previous edges inside a commuity generates self loops on the new vertex.

Step 5. Repeat from step 2 to detect communities on the new network.

Step 6. If the detected communities are not desired, adjust the value of Pthres according to recorded $Max[P_i(C_j)]$ in step 3.1.4, and repeat the two phases from step 2.

3 Experiments and results

The proposed method is applied in a Matlab program, which is a modification of the BGLL algorithm originally coded by Antoine Scherrer. Experiments are carried out on many different data sets.

As an example, a small network composed of 20 vertexes are tested. The results are plotted with the yEd graph editor shown on figure 2 to figure 7. For each Pthres, the corresponding modularity Q and the number of top level communities are listed on Table 1. The number of top level communities changes from 7 to 3, but the modularity Q only slightly varies from 0.3682 to 0.3462. Therefore, in such a case, slightly adjust Pthres to change the hierarchical structure is feasible. However, when the number of top level communities is further reduced to 2, the modularity suddenly goes down to Q=0.2949. Hence, it is not suitable to divide the network into only 2 communities due to the low Q value.

Table 1. Results for the Modified P_{thres}.

P_{thres}	Q	Top level communities
1.642	0.3682	7
1.334	0.384	6
1	0.3882	5
0.830	0.3755	4
0.799	0.3462	3
0.590	0.2949	2

Among these variations, some small communities never split in all figures, such as 1 2 3 vertexes, 5 7 9 vertexes, and etc. These invariant small communities validate this method.

The Pthres is modified according to the recorded $Max[P_i(C_j)]$ values in Step 3.1.4. During the community detection process with Pthres=1 on figure 2, all the recorded $Max[P_i(C_j)]$ are {..., 0.7033, 0.800, 0.831, 1.333, 1.641, 2.909, ...}. The closest values to Pthres=1 on both sides are 0.831 and 1.333. Based on the reference to 1.333, Pthres is revised to 1.334 in figure 3. As a result, the number of top level communities grows up to 6. Similarly, based on the reference to 0.831, Pthres is revised from 1 to 0.830 in figure 5, and the number of top level communities decreases to 4.

For each Pthres, the complexity is O[m*log(m)], in which m denotes the number of edges, and the complexity is the same as that of the BGLL method. We have tested the proposed method on networks containing tens of thousands of edges. The BGLL method has been tested on larger networks, such as a network of 1 million edges which could be processed in only 3 seconds [9].

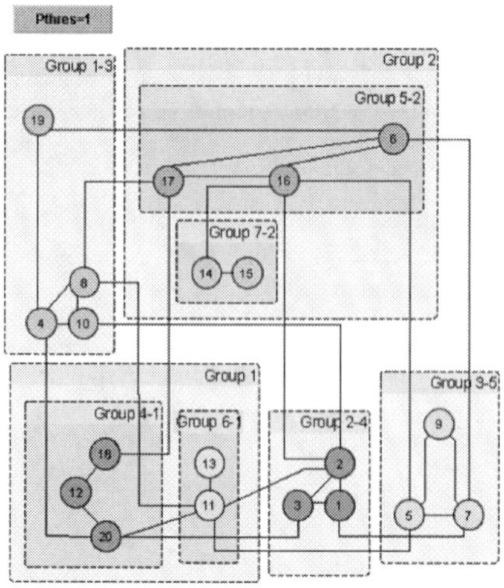

Figure 2. Start from Pthres=1, Q=0.3882, and the Network is Divided to 5 Communities on the Top Level.

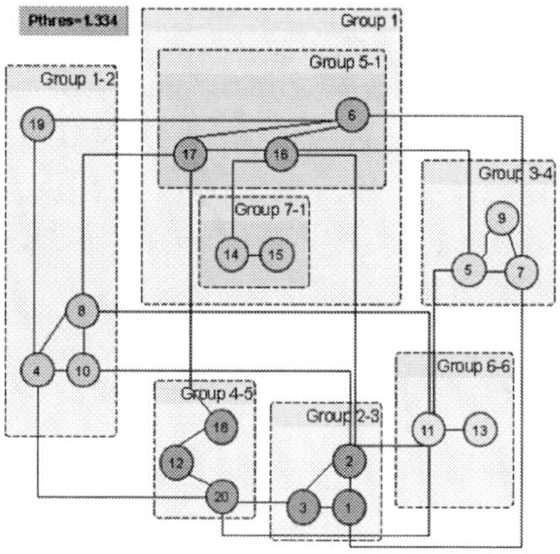

Figure 3. Turn Up the Pthres to 1.334, Q=0.3804. the Number of Communities Grows up to 6 on the Top Level.

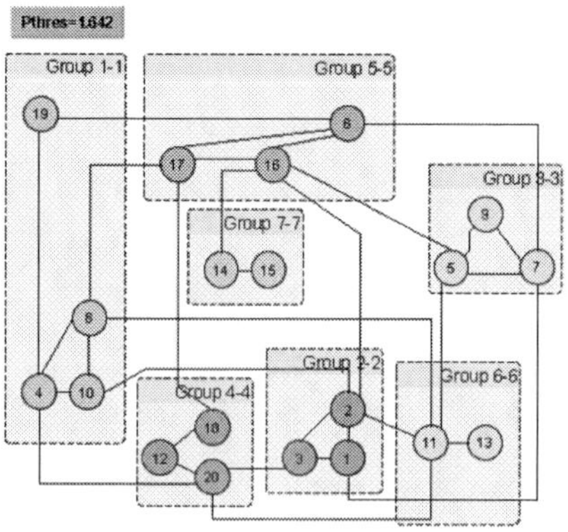

Figure 4. Turn Up the Pthres to 1.642, Q=0.3682. the Number of Communities Grows Up to 7 on the Top Level.

DOI: 10.1051/itmconf/20160704012

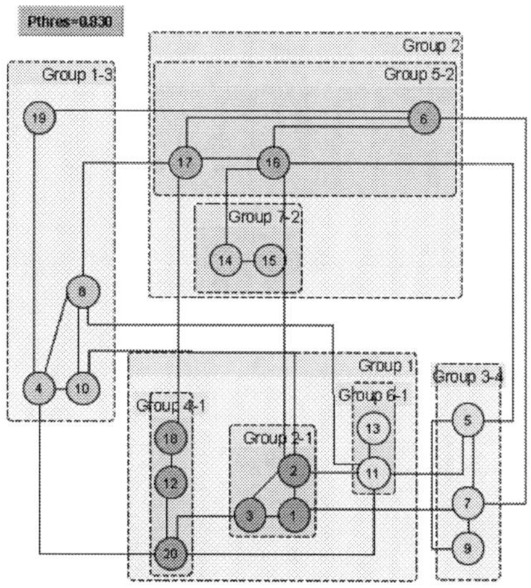

Figure 5. Turn Down the Pthres from 1 to 0.830, Q=0.3755. The Number Of Communities Decreases to 4 on the Top Level.

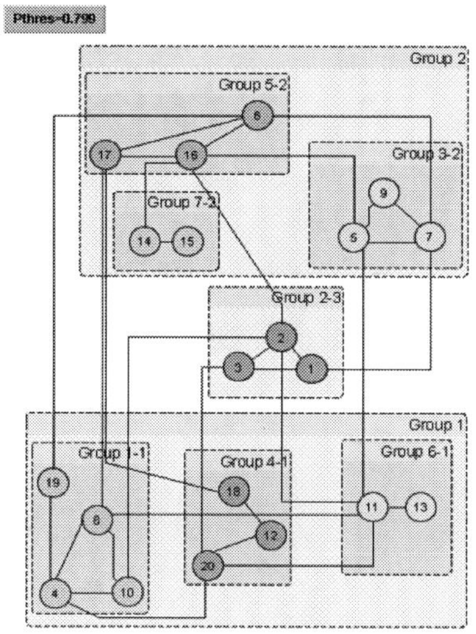

Figure 6. Turn Down the Pthres To 0.799, Q=0.3462. the Number of Communities Decreased to 3 on the Top Level.

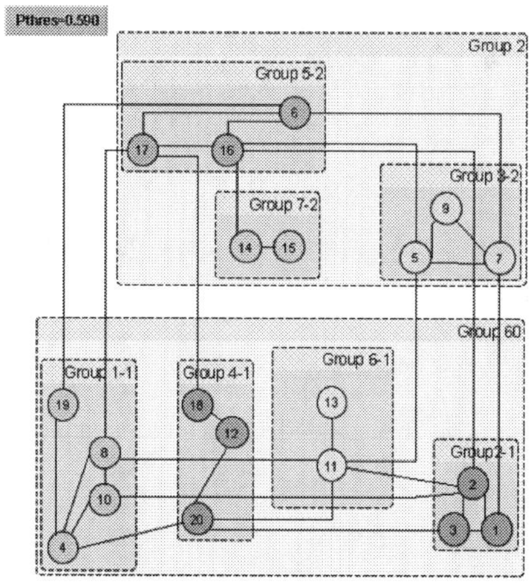

Figure 7. Turn Down the Pthres to 0.590, Q=0.2949. the Number of Communities Decreased to 2 On the Top Level.

4 Discussion

Sometimes setting the Pthres to the closest value according to the recorded $Max[P_i(C_j)]$ may not increase/decrease the number of top level communities, but make a change to the community structure. As an example, there are 3 top level communities on figure 6, and the closest recorded value below Pthres=0.799 is 0.646. If Pthres is set to 0.645, there are also 3 top level communities shown on figure 8, but the structure is different in comparison with figure 6.

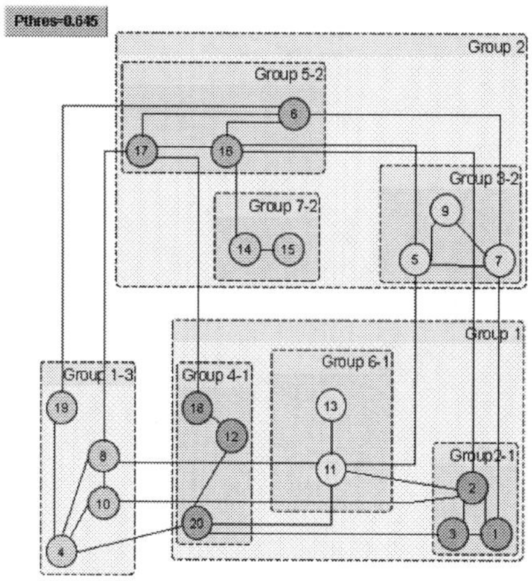

Figure 8. Turn Down the Pthres to 0.799. the Number of Communities Does Not Change on the Top Level in Comparison with Figure 6.

5 Conclusion

We introduce a flexible approach for the hierarchical community detection. The community detection process is an extension of the BGLL method. The flexibility is accomplished according to that $\frac{2mA_{i,C_j}}{k_i k_{C_j}}$ should be larger than a threshold. Experiments prove the availability of this approach.

Acknowledgement

This research is supported by Science and Technology Project of SGCC (Grant No. SGITG-KJ-JSKF[2015]0012).

References

1. G. Karypis, V. Kumar, J Parallel Distr. com. 48, 96 (1998)
2. G. Karypis, V. Kumar, SIAM J. Sci. Comput. 20, 359 (1998)
3. M.E.J. Newman, M. Girvan, Phys. Rev. E 69, 026113 (2004).
4. A. Clauset, M.E.J. Newman, C. Moore, Phys. Rev. E 70 (2004).
5. K. Wakita, T. Tsurumi, *Proceedings of the 16th international conference on world wide web*, 1275 (2007)
6. U.N. Raghavan, R. Albert, S. Kumara, Phys. Rev. E 76, 036106 (2007)
7. R. Ghosh, K. Lerman, Lect. Notes Comput. SC. 5498, 20 (2008)
8. L. Tang, X. Wang, H. Liu, L. Wang, *Workshop on Social Media Analytics*, 14 (2010)
9. V.D. Blondel, J.L. Guillaume, R. Lambiotte, E. Lefebvre, J. Stat. Mech. Theor. Exp. (2008)

DOI: 10.1051/itmconf/20160704013

A review of Technologies on Tracking Tibetan Public Opinion Topics

Bi-Rong CHEN[1], Gui-Xian XU[2,a]

School of Information Engineering,Minzu University of ChinaBeijing 100081,China
[1]913756830@qq.com,[2]xuguixian2000@bit.edu.cn

Abstract. The target of technologies on tracking Tibetan-based network public opinion topics is to track the development of some known topics. By tracking these topics could help people to grasp the trend of public opinion. This research area becomes more and more important on Natural Language Processing domain and how to apply these state-of-the-art computer science technologies on the study of national language has drawn lots of awareness to related researchers. This article will introduce some features about Tibetan language and its grammar. Some technologies about categorizing Tibetan text and tracking Tibetan-based network public opinion will also be talked about.

1 Introduction

With the rise of social media, more and more professional researchers pay attention to the public opinion generated from social applications, such as Weibo, Tieba. Public opinion indicates a reflection of individuals or communities' reaction on the social phenomenon which are related to their own concern or profit. During a period of time, public opinion could influence people's emotion and lead to conformity. So, it is very important to analysis public opinion and prevent some harmful public opinions from misleading people's emotion. In Tibet, with the booming of economy and support of central organization on development of science and technology, the number of netizens in Tibet grows significantly. Unverified information is exaggerated or distorted by the internet usually affects national unity and social stability. It is not reality to let humanbeings to filter public opinion, since we are in an information explosion age. That will cost lots of recourses and amount of time to handle that. So, applying start-of-the-art technologies on supervise public opinion of minority languages is a good approach and that will support the government on supervise public information.

2 The situation of tracking Tibetan-based network public opinion in China and abroad

2.1 Features of Tibetan language and grammar

[1]introduced Tibetan language belongs to phonetic system, it consists of consonants, vowels and punctuation symbols. There are thirty consonants.As shown in Figure 1.

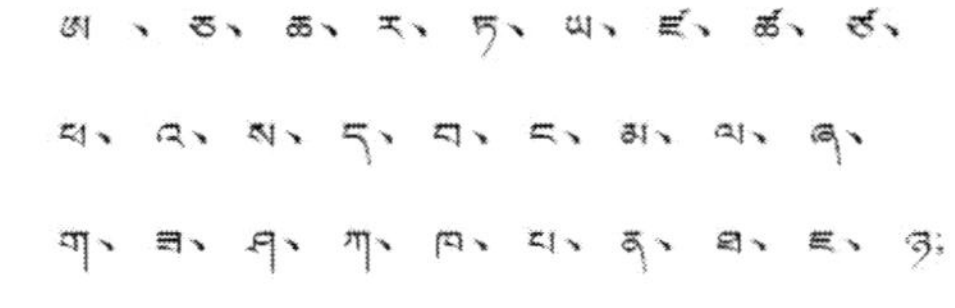

Figure 1. Thirty Consonants

There are four vowels, as shown in Figure 2.

Figure 2. Four Vowels

According to the different position of syllable, Tibetan character could be divided into six categories, which are "base-word", "adding before word", "adding after word", "adding top of word", "adding bottom of word" and "double adding after word". [2]introduced in the article named The specification of Tibetan character category based on information processing. Tibetan character has been categorized into 29 base cluster and 6 special clusters.

2.2 Situation in abroad

The research of public opinion in western counties start more earlier and develop very fast. For example, [3] started the research on public opinion since 1973.[4] introduced a basic cluster algorithm called Ant colony algorithm. [5]applied this algorithm on text analysis.[6]

invented a system called Opinion Finder, which could automatically find the sentence high related to the subject or the terms in a sentence which are relate to the subject.

2.3 Domestic situation

The research on public opinion tracking begins a bit late in China, and some technologies specific on Tibetan language are also not perfect. But with the development of the technology.[7]applied a distributed solution of Multi- Agent algorithm on Tibetan text clustering.[8]combined entropy and conditional random field models to recognize Tibetan names and get a good performance, the accuracy is above 93%.[9]combined emotion pattern and machine learning algorithm and introduce a new algorithm called PMML.

3The technique detail of tracking network public opinion

3.1 Text pre-processing

3.1.1 Remove noise of whole Tibetan web page

Web pages contains two kinds of information, one is subject related information and the other one is off-subject information, which contains pictures, videos etc. we call all of these off-subject information as "web noise". The appearance of web noise not only cause ambiguity of web subject but also influence the tracking of web subject information. So, before analysis the web page, all noises should be removed at first. A cleaner web text could significant increase the performance of categorization.

3.1.2 Tibetan text decode

[10]introduced Tibetan language belongs to phonetic system. The Tibetan National Standard formulated in 1997 has set some rules for Tibetan character encoding and a set of base Tibetan characters.Tibetan script in the memory of the computer requires a plurality of two-byte characters to represent the Tibetan script Ding.But Tibetan based on web coded in different ways, Have the same element code, Himalaya, basic set, spread code, Pandita,etc. [11]convert different coding Tibetan to Unicode format,in order to better analyze the Tibetan public opinion tracking and follow-up work.

3.1.3 Tibetan segmentation

Tibetan language is a phonetic language, which differs from English, no special symbol mark between the Tibetan word for segmentation.[12]The theme of representation and classification are based on good segmentation results,so merits of corpus participle will directly affect the accuracy of the Tibetan public opinion analysis.For general segmentation method has the following four: Mechanical word segmentation,Rule word segmentation,Statistics word segmentation,and Combine statistics and rules word segmentation.

3.1.4 Removing stop words

After the segmentation of the corpus, the corpus text will be a collection of words.Like many languages, Tibetan also has a lot of stop words.[13]believed that in addition to digital, daily life too common nouns, pronouns and verbs have no actual meaning can also be divided into within the stop word category.The general use of word list to remove the stop words.[14]introduced construct a stop word list procedure can be divided into two steps:first, the corpus of function words, pronouns, conjunctions, auxiliary and other stop words added into word list,then calculate the frequency of the word through the corpus, selected frequency is higher than a certain threshold, these words will also join in the word list.

3.2 Text representation

Text is often regarded as a string consisting of many characters, but this form is not conducive to the machine to do the classification and learning,So first we should translate the text to be processed into a format that is easy for machine learning and classification..Commonly used text representation methods include: vector space model (VSM), probability model, Boolean model, language model. For the main Tibetan network public opinion analysis model is vector space model and language model.

3.3 Text similarity comparison

[15]introduced text similarity is a statistic that used to measure the degree of similarity between two text, generally used to represent.

3.3.1.Inner product between vectors

The larger the value of the inner product obtained, the greater the similarity, the text D1, D2 vector inner product of similarity is calculated as follows:

$$Sim\ (D_1, D_2) = \sum_{k=1}^{n} W_{k1} \times W_{k2} \tag{1}$$

3.3.2 Cosine similarity

This method control the value of the similarity between -1 to 1, the cosine is calculated news text D1 and D2 similarity such as:

$$Sim\ (D_1, D_2) = \frac{\sum_{k=1}^{n} W_{1k} \times W_{2k}}{\sqrt{\left(\sum_{k=1}^{n} W_{1k}^2\right)\left(\sum_{k=1}^{n} W_{2k}^2\right)}} \tag{2}$$

 DOI: 10.1051/itmconf/20160704013

3.3.3 The maximum and minimum method

The maximum and minimum method, the calculation of this method is simple, also can through the mathematical calculation, remove maximum minimum brings difference in each category.

$$Sim(D_1, D_2) = \frac{\sum_{k=1}^{n} Min(W_{1k}, W_{2k})}{\sum_{k=1}^{n} Max(W_{1k}, W_{2k})} \quad (3)$$

3.4 Feature extraction and weight calculation

3.4.1 Feature extraction

After segmentation of the Tibetan text in the network, has a series of features set,Feature selection is to extract the effective feature set from the original feature set, remove the original feature set some weight over the small feature set, to achieve the purpose of dimension reduction,improved the efficiency of clustering , and the complexity of time and space is reduced.

Commonly used feature selection methods include: Document Frequency, Mutual Information, Information Gain, Estimation of, χ^2 etc.

3.4.2 Weight calculation

There are many methods to calculate the weight of feature items.Such as TF algorithm, IDF algorithm, tf*idf algorithm and mutual information algorithm, etc..[16]Among them, the tf*idf algorithm combined TF with the IDF algorithm is the most widely used algorithm.The formula used Tf*IDF algorithm calculate the weights of the feature item as shown in (4):

$$w_i = tf_i * idf_i * f_i(w) \quad (4)$$

Where tfi represents the frequency of a feature item i in the document,idfi represents inverted file,fi(w) indicates the weight given to the feature item of named entity or a in the title.

3.5 Public opinion tracking technology

[17]introduced topic tracking process is to detect new topics or follow-up related reports in the follow-up news.The basic process is , first to detect new news, and if it is not aware of the relevance of topics, it is considered a new topic, and if you can find it linked to the subject , it will be the news text classification among this topic.topics Tracking is different from the traditional classification algorithm, The traditional classification algorithms have identified the number of categories is the number of topics, but topics tracking technology is a dynamic classification techniques.Over time, constantly testing the new text,the number of topics will increase because detect the text does not belong to the pre-existing topics.

Tibetan network public opinion tracking technology in fact is equivalent to a mapping relationship .Mapped The hot topic which was later detected to the topic categories which were classified by the training data.Public opinion tracking technology includes two aspects, the first is the discovery of the topic, the second is the topic of tracking.

3.5.1 topic discovery technology

In this part , the main work includes:
a).Selection of feature items from training samples;
b).Representation the feature item we choose;
c).Through a number of classification algorithms to achieve our discovery result.

The choice of feature items and the representation of the feature items have been introduced respectively in3.2, 3.4, and the classification of the topic is the application of text classification technology.

The text classification of Technologies on Tracking Tibetan-Based Network Public Opinion Topics is an important branch of machine learning and data mining direction,so, many algorithms based on machine learning can be used for text classification.[18]introduced text classification algorithms can be roughly divided into two categories: rule-based algorithms and statistical-based methods,Rule-based algorithms include decision tree algorithm and Rough Set;the text classification based on Statistical algorithm can be divided into unsupervised learning, supervised learning and semi-supervised learning,including the k-nearest neighbor algorithm, least squares fitting,Neural Networks,Support Vector Machine, Rocchio and Naive Bayesian.At present, most classification algorithms are all supervised machine learning.It contains the training data and test data ,hrough a collection of training data is formed classifier,Then use the classification processing text to be analyzed,Therefore, use of which algorithm structure text categorization It is an important step in the ability to accurately track the Internet public opinion.

(1)Naive Bayesian

Theoretical Basis of Naive Bayesian is Bayes Theorem,In seeking the probability of an event provided another one occurred at a time

$$P(A \mid B) = \frac{P(B \mid A)P(B)}{P(B)} \quad (5)$$

[19]introduced use Bayesian probability algorithm applied to text categorization is:When a text appears, the probability of It belongs to each of Subject categories,Depending on the size of the calculated probability, can get the category the text belongs to.

[20]introduced the shortcomings of the naive Bayesian algorithm:

First, we use Bayesian formula for classification, assumption that the feature are independent of each other, each feature is not affected by other feature.But in real life, this assumption is difficult to set up.There is a mutual relationship between feature items, which indicates that the feature items may not be completely independent.

Second, using naive Bayesian algorithm to train the classification samples, we need a lot of training data to get the probability of each feature item appears in each category,It will cost a lot of energy and time.

(2)KNN algorithm

KNN algorithm, also known as K-nearest neighbor algorithm.In 1967, proposed by Cover Hart, It is an inert algorithm , based on the instance.The basic idea of KNN Algorithm is set traversal similarity comparison to the newly added text with training text.selected K text of most similarity,According to the text of subject categories to determine the categories of newly added text.[21]

K-NN algorithm is relatively simple, its classification effect is better, but also has its own shortcomings:

The first one is to compare the ergodic similarity between the new text and the text of the training set,So you need to store all the training set of text, Storage capacity is very large.

Second, the classification effect of KNN algorithm depends on the choice of K value, how to choose the appropriate K value is very critical, which has become an urgent task of the KNN algorithm to achieve.

(3)Support Vector Machine(SVM)

Support Vector Machine seeking the optimal categories on the case of linear separable ,Wherein the optimal classification refers to the ability to conduct two classes of error-free division,and to ensure that the maximum interval between these two classes.Core content of SVM made by Vapnik between 1992 with 1995,this algorithm based on Structural Risk Minimization Theory and Statistical Learning VC Theory .

[22]introduced the basic idea of SVM classification algorithm is: First, the training text is represented by a vector space model,then solving quadratic programming problems,get optimal classification function(optimal hyperplane),finally,generate vector of the text to be classified into the model for category function ,according to the value we calculated to determine the category of the text.If the training set could be correct linear segmentation by a hyperplane ,And the distance between the nearest vectors with hyperplane are maximum,then this hyperplane as the best hyperplane.

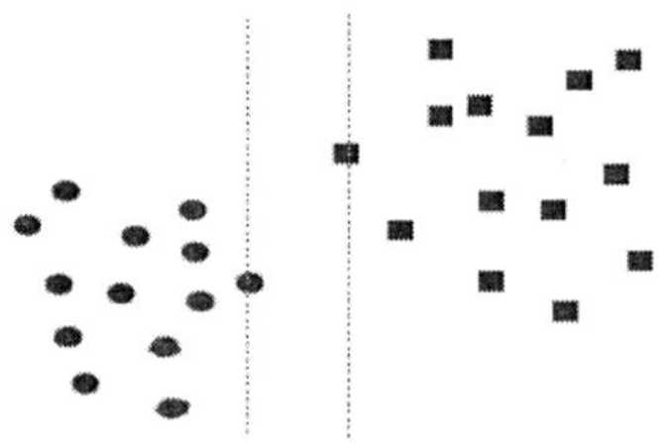

Figure 3. Non-Optimal Decision

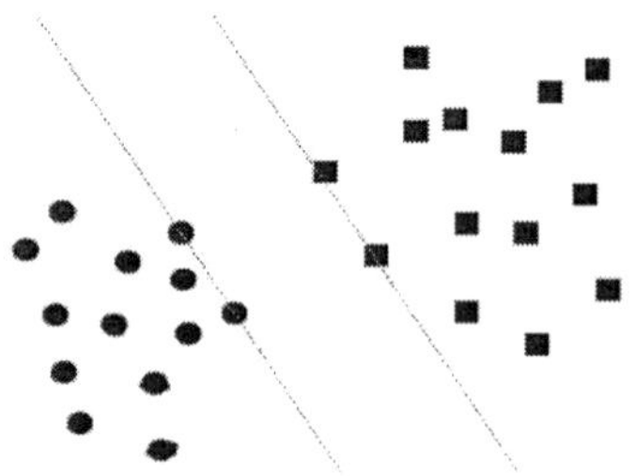

Figure 4. Optimal Decision

3.5.2 Topic Tracking Technology

Topic tracking is when a new web text appears,first,preprocessing the network text ,Compare it with the different categories that we calculated from discovered the topic .the main work includes.

a).After the emergence of the new text, preprocessing the text,Selection of feature items, weight calculation and so on ;

b).Compare the similarity between the new text and the previous classification model, Within a certain threshold, Division of text.If not set the threshold range,set the text to a new topic

c).Form a new text classification model.

For the text preprocessing, similarity search, feature selection, weight calculation, have been introduced in 3.3, 3.1, 3.4.

4 Conclusions

With the rise of social media, the number of netizens in Tibet grows significantly, more and more professional researchers pay attention to the public opinion generated from social applications.This article summarizes the process and the difficulties of network public opinion analysis techniques by consult the large number of documents,explain technologies on tracking Tibetan-Based network public opinion topics by features of Tibetan language and grammar,the situation of tracking Tibetan-based network public opinion in China and abroad,text pre-processing,text representation,text similarity calculation,text eigenvalues selection,calculate eigenvalues weights,classical text classification algorithm.Technologies on tracking Tibetan-Based network public opinion topics is still in the development stage,in the future also need to continually improve the classification model,more precisely on the track and public opinion research.

Acknowledgment

This work was supported by the National Key Technolog y Research and Development Program of the Ministry of Science and Technology of China (No. 2014BAK10B03), the Beijing Social Science Foundation (No. 14WYB040), and the National Natural Science Foundation of China (No. 61309012, No. 61331013).

References

[1]MENG Xiang-he, *Key Technology Research on* Tibetan Websites Topic Detection and Tracking[D]. Gansu:Northwest University For Nationalities.5-6,April (2013).

[2]WAN De-wen,Study on Tibetan Information Retrieval&Search Result Clustering and System Implementation[D]. Sichuan: Southwest Jiao Tong University, 7,(2013).

[3]LI Ai-lin ,The Research of Tibetan Text Classification Algorithms for the Analysis of Network Public Opinion[D].Gansu: Northwest University For Nationalities, 6,(2014).

[4]E.Bonabeau,M.Dorigo,and G. Theraulaz. Swarm Intelligence:From Natural to Artificial Systems[M].New York,Oxford University Press,(1999)

[5]D.J.L.,Goss5,FrallksN,etal. The Dyamies of CoLIeetiveSorting:Robot-Like ALLt and Ant-like Robot.Proceedings First Confereneeon Simulation of Adaptive Behavior;From Animals to Animates[C]. Cambridge,MA:MITPress,(1991)

[6] WU Yu,Research and Implementation of Key Technologies in Network Public Opinion Analysis[D].Sichuan: University of Electronic Science and technology,4,(2011)

[7] KANG Jian,Research on Multi-Agent and Swarm Intelligence Tibetan Network Public Opinion Management[D].Sichuan:Southwest Jiao Tong University, 3,(2015)

[8]JIA Yang-ji,LI Ya-chao,ZONG Cheng-qing,YU Hong-zhi A Hybrid Approach to Tibetan Person Name Identification by Maximum Entropy Model and Conditional Random Fields[J]. Journal of Chinese Information Processing,8,1,108-110,(2014)

[9] WAN Yuan Research on Mining of Internet Public Opinion Based on Semantic and Statistic Analysis[D].Hubei: Wuhan University of Technology, II ,(2012)

[10] HAN Xiao-bin Design of Hot Event Detection System in Tibetan Web[D].Gansu: Northwest University For Nationalities, 10-11,(2012)

[11] JIANG Tao Study on Hot Topic Detection Based on the Analysis of Tibetan Public Opinion[D].Gansu: Northwest University For Nationalities, 13-15,(2010)

[12] LI Ai-lin The Research of Tibetan text classification algorithms for the Analysis of Network Public Opinion[D].Gansu: Northwest University For Nationalities,23, (2014)

[13] LUO Jie,CHEN Li,XIA De-lin,Research on Fast Text Classifier Based on New Key Words Extraction Method[J].computer application,04,32-34(2006)

[14] LI Ai-lin The Research of Tibetan text classification algorithms for the Analysis of Network Public Opinion[D].Gansu: Northwest University For Nationalities,24, (2014)

[15]KANG Jian Research on Multi-agent and Swarm Intelligence Tibetan Network Public Opinion Management[D].Sichuan:Southwest Jiao Tong University, 6,(2015)

[16] JIANG Tao Study on Hot Topic Detection Based on the Analysis of Tibetan Public Opinion [D].Gansu: Northwest University For Nationalities, 20-21,(2010)

[17]MENG Xiang-he Key Technology Research on Tibetan Websites Topic Detection and Tracking[D]. Gansu: Northwest University For Nationalities, 10-11,(2013)

[18]LI Xiao-di Research and Application on the Technology of Web Text Mining[D].Beijing: Beijing Jiaotong University, 16-17,(2015)

[19] LI Dan The Study of Chinese Text Categorization Based on Naive Bayes[D].Hebei: Hebei University, 17-18,(2011)

[20] LI Xiang-dong,XU Peng,HUANG Li,SHEN Xiang-xing,Research of Journals Manuscript Categorization Based on KNN Algorithm[J]. The Library and Information Knowledge ,71-75,04,(2010)

[21]Chen, Chunan, Weiwei Sun, Baihua Zheng, Dingding Mao, and Weimo Liu. "An incremental approach to closest pair queries in spatial networks using best-first search." In International Conference on Database and Expert Systems Applications, pp. 136-143. Springer Berlin Heidelberg, (2011).

[22] CUI Jian-ming,LIU Jian-ming,LIAO Zhou-yu Research of Text Categorization Based on Support Vector Machine[J].computer simulation,299-302,30(2013)

A Dynamic and Interactive Monitoring System of Data Center Resources

Ling-Fei YU[1,a], and Sheng-Er ZHOU[2]

[1] *Hangzhou College of Commerce, Zhejiang GongShang University, Hangzhou, P.R. China*
[2] *School of Computer Science and Engineering, University of Electronic Science and Technology of China, Chengdu, P.R. china*
[a] *Corresponding author: linphie@163.com*

Abstract. To maximize the utilization and effectiveness of resources, it is very necessary to have a well suited management system for modern data centers. Traditional approaches to resource provisioning and service requests have proven to be ill suited for virtualization and cloud computing. The manual handoffs between technology teams were also highly inefficient and poorly documented. In this paper, a dynamic and interactive monitoring system for data center resources, ResourceView, is presented. By consolidating all data center management functionality into a single interface, ResourceView shares a common view of the timeline metric status, while providing comprehensive, centralized monitoring of data center physical and virtual IT assets including power, cooling, physical space and VMs, so that to improve availability and efficiency. In addition, servers and VMs can be monitored from several viewpoints such as clusters, racks and projects, which is very convenient for users.

1 Introduction

Cloud Computing[1] can be classified as a new paradigm for the dynamic provisioning of computing services supported by state-of-the-art data centers that usually employ Virtual Machine (VM) technologies for consolidation and environment isolation purposes [2].A data center can be seen as a virtual supercomputer which integrates large sets of computer systems and associated components, such as telecommunications and storage systems, power supplies, environmental controls (e.g., air conditioning, fire suppression) and security devices. Increasing efficiencies, reducing costs and maintaining availability are top priorities for today's data center administrators. To maximize the utilization and effectiveness of resources, it is very necessary to have a well suited management system for modern data centers. Traditional approaches [3-5] to resource provisioning and service requests have proven to be ill suited for virtualization and cloud computing. The manual handoffs between technology teams were also highly inefficient and poorly documented.

The management system should centralize real-time monitoring and help for intelligent capacity planning, high-fidelity visualization of a data center's critical systems. It can help data center managers identify and eliminate sources of risk to increase availability of critical IT systems. A lot of the discussion in this area has focused on energy issues, but other metrics beyond the Power usage effectiveness (PUE)can give a more detailed picture of the data center operations[6]. These intrinsic risks have resulted in an increase in market demand for integrated monitoring and management solutions capable of "bridging the gap between IT and facilities" systems[7]. It leads to the development of "intelligent capacity planning" solutions that support synchronized monitoring and management of both physical and virtual infrastructures. More effective automation tools can also improve the number of servers or virtual machines that a single admin can handle.

Existing solutions in data center operating, however, has several problems. Firstly, while technologies such as cloud computing and software defined networking (SDN) [8] provide methods for dynamic management, data center runtime status data, on which dynamic management is based, usually received little attention. Secondly, a technology only focuses on a single domain, e.g., VM management in cloud computing and network management in SDN may not be able to offer an optimal solution. We argue that information collected in each domain should be shared and control methods enabled by individual technologies should be combined. And thirdly, existing solution such as Ganglia [9] is widely used, but it is mainly focused on host servers organized in clusters and grids. No runtime information about VMs, power supplies and cooling system is collected and managed. And its data storage and visualization is using RRD tool, which is difficult for function extension and user customization[9]. Another management system CloudStack mainly manages the network, storage, and computing nodes, and is more focused on configuration of a data center. Runtime metric status monitoring is not covered [10].

In this paper, we present ResourceView, a dynamic and interactive monitoring system for data center resources. By consolidating all data center management functionality into a single interface, we delivers the complete data center monitoring system for the 24/7 data center, shares a common view of the timeline metric status, provides comprehensive, centralized monitoring of data center physical and virtual IT assets including power, cooling, physical space and VMs to improve availability and efficiency, proactively monitors and maintains server health to support faster troubleshooting. So users can simply plan and manage your data center in a more intelligent way. In addition, servers and VMs can be monitored from several viewpoints such as clusters, racks and projects. It's very convenient for users. With animated transitions and well-crafted interfaces, ResourceView makes exploring data feel more like playing a game. Interactivity can also encourage engagement with the data in ways that static images cannot. It can help users see the world in a new way, revealing unexpected patterns and trends, making intelligent decisions.

The remainder of the paper is organized as follows. In section 2, we introduce background. Our system design and implementation are presented in section 3 and section 4, respectively. At last, we conclude our work in section 5.

2 Background

ResourceView is our intelligent capacity planning solution that deals with the monitoring, collection and analysis of real-time, continuous and accurate information from an intelligent data center infrastructure that allows for immediate action. It's designed to keep the data center in an optimal state of balance between availability, efficiency and capacity.

The basic of the whole solution is to gain and present an integrated real-time holistic view of the entire data center infrastructure. Real time data presented in an integrated view allows you to diagnose individual components without having to walk the floor. It can make intelligent assessments of your assets so you can address problems and proactively prevent issues happening. Consequently, you can make faster and smarter decisions that will align data center performance with your business goals.

ResourceView is a data center management system to collect sufficient information, providing user-friendly interfaces for visualization and control of the whole system, and provide an extensible platform to implement various system tuning strategies so as to better utilize a data center infrastructure.

We will provide five functions to build a generic data center management system:

1) Data Collection: This function focuses on collecting data center equipment status for monitoring, analysis, visualization, and management;

2) Data Storage: This function focuses on storing data efficiently and providing effective API for data visualization and data mining;

3) Data Mining: This function focuses on analyzing collected data and provide solutions to various applications, for example, green data center.

4) System Monitoring: This function visualizes the data in web pages and a 3D animation system.

5) System Management: This function mainly focuses on managing physical servers, VMs, applications and network devices, such as VM immigration.

A data center infrastructure can be roughly divided into several components, including PDUs for power supply, air conditioners for cooling, servers and networking devices for ICT service provisioning. Challenges arise to manage and optimize these devices as a whole system, since these devices provide inherently different methods for monitoring and control. Most devices provide command line interfaces (CLIs) and web user interfaces (WUIs) via computer network. To shield the differences among these various devices, Data Collection is responsible to provide a unified API to collect all the information of various devices and store into the database. Meanwhile, we must provide a unified comprehensive user interface for users to monitor and manage all the data center devices. As a solution for web based management, we present ResourceView system in this paper. Data Collection design is beyond the scope of the paper.

3 Design of ResourceView

3.1 High Level Design

To develop the dynamic, interactive data-driven web application ResourceView, we chose the popular stack which includes the Linux operating system, Apache web server, and scripting language PHP. There are so many candidates for database, like MySQL, MongoDB[11] and many others. Considering its maturity and open-source characteristics, MongoDB is our current choice of Data Collection Subsystem. As growth of data volume and rising of other constraints, for example, performance, the choice may evolve. Hence, database access interfaces should be designed to shield differences between different database options and provide a unified access interface ideally (or work with little code changes). Since data collecting and storing into the database is beyond the scope of this paper, ResourceView can be divided into the following layers.

3.1.1Database Access Layer

Database access layer encapsulates all the related interfaces for accessing database, such as acquiring the cloud hierarchy structure, acquiring the latest metric information of resources utilization and host server configuration information.PHP MongoDB Driver is used here to provide low-level interfaces for accessing our MongoDB database from the PHP code on the server side. Users can request to view the metric data of any time range freely, even the whole year. But in practice, we must sample the mass data. Otherwise, it may results in memory overflow or network congestion, since a huge amount of data is transferred between web server and database server.

3.1.2Data Communication Layer

Data Communication Layer is responsible to handle the data communication between the PHP pageson the server side and the JavaScript code on the client browser side. After getting data from the database on the server side, the data of information should be sent to the client to feed the graph engine and then the data can be displayed. Especially, the web application should be able to make quick, incremental updates to the related charts without reloading the entire browser page. This makes the application faster and more responsive to user actions.

The implementation of this layer will include two parts: the server side and the client side. In our design, JSON is the exchanging data format between the server and the client. When the web page loads, or the charts need automatically refresh, the client will start an Ajax request for the data. As response, the server will then acquire the related data from database, encode it into JSON format, and send back as the Ajax response to the client.

3.1.3Data Pre-processing Layer

The data from Ajax response actually may not directly be applied for the graph engine. So there is Data Pre-processing layer, to handle the data received from Ajax response. The functions may include data transforming, setting the label and color of each kind of data, setting axis formats and things like that. All these data pre-processing things usually depend on the data visualization techniques, or say the graph engine. So there comes Data Presentation Layer.

3.1.4Data Presentation Layer

Data Presentation layer is responsible for drawing data-driven attractive and perspicuous charts. The key of the layer is the graph engine. There are bundles of choices for this. Here we choose D3[12] and HighCharts[13] because of their good performance and attractive user experience.

3.2 Metric Data Parameters

The goal of our web system is to eliminate isolated island of information, to make data center administrators easily and efficiently get desired information. In the integrated user interface, administrators can get one or more types of data including CPU workload, CPU utilization, memory utilization, network utilization for physical servers and VMs, power and environment information. Parameter means our collected data from data center. Since we have collected a lot of data, and many of them may not be used in practice. We only display parts of them which users are most interested in. All of this information is modelled in a single data structure with an extremely high level of fidelity so any combination of devices (or even the data center as a whole) can be studied and actively managed using various planning scenarios.

4 System Implementation

We are running several data centers on a scale from dozens of servers to hundreds of servers. Now we have deployed this dynamic monitoring web system ResourceView for the data center infrastructures management.

4.1. Main User Interfaces

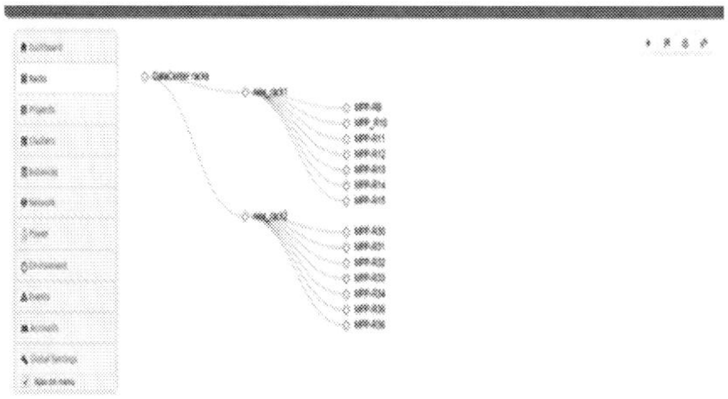

Figure 1. Tree View of Data Center

We provide three different views on our web pages: tree views, static views and dynamic views. In a data center, large sets of diverse geographically distributed servers can be seen from different viewpoints: Rackspace, Grid, and Project. So respectively, servers can be grouped into different racks, or into various grids, or in various projects. Our web system delivers the administrators all the three viewpoints to view the entire data center, and to locate any one of the servers and VMs. The tree view is used to see each hierarchy structures of a data center organized in the three viewpoints.

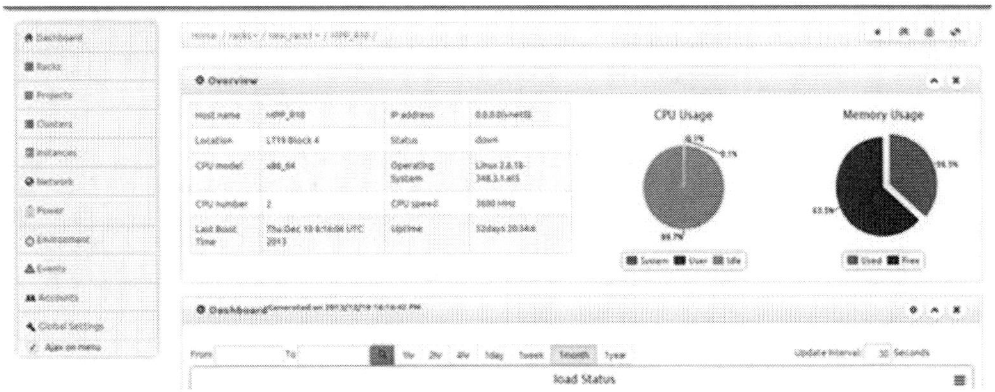

Figure 2. The Static View of A Node

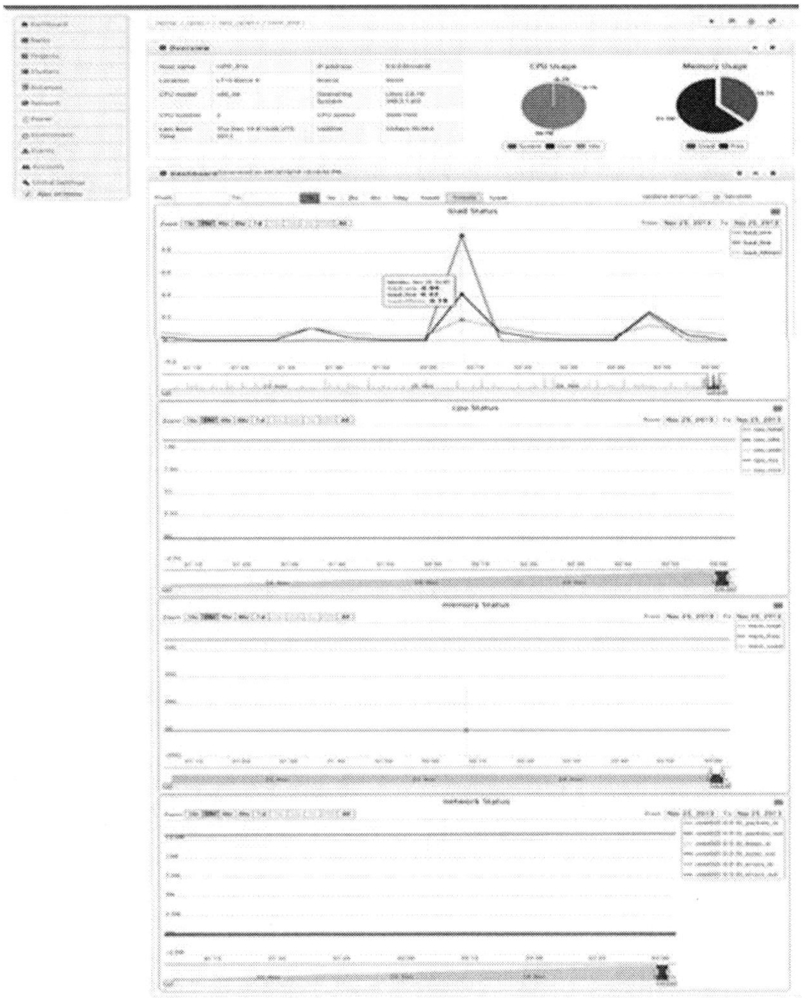

Figure 3. The Dynamic View of A Node

It's very convenient and important for users to get a clear whole image of a data center. Users can quickly find out the location relationship and relocate to the integrated monitoring page of a specific node. The tree is displayed in a dynamic collapsible layout. On the tree, users can click on a node dot to expand or collapse a subtree. More importantly, users can click on a node name to access the node's integrated monitoring page. For example, a tree of the data center racks is shown in Fig. 1.

Fig. 2 and Fig. 3 are the static view and dynamic view of a specific node. They provide homogeneous views of the underlying heterogeneous data. The static view simply displays the configuration or overall information of a server or VM in a well-organized table, including name, IP, location, status, CPU model , CPU number, CPU speed, operating system, last boot time, uptime, and things like that, as shown in Fig. 2.

The dynamic view shows pie charts of the latest CPU and memory usage, and also the animated charts of timeline metric parameters like CPU average workload, CPU usage, memory usage, network utilization. The charts can automatically refresh according to the update interval set by users. The time cycle can be different from the data collecting cycle. From the single page, users can easily know all about the specified node, and help users make intelligent decisions.

4.2 Main Features

The main features of ResourceView are as follows:

4.2.1 Quick search any one of the data center resources

A data center usually includes dozens, hundreds, or even thousands of servers. In this project, we provide several quick ways to find any one of the data center nodes and relocate to the node's monitoring page. One fast way is to use the search function in the top bar. Also, you can use three kinds of data center hierarchy trees to find a node.

4.2.2 Different query time range

We provide a group of quick query ways for viewing metric data, including the last 1 hour, 2 hours, 4 hours, 1 day, 1 week,1 month, 1 year and user customized query time range;

4.2.3 Auto Refresh time-series data charts

The metric status charts can automatically refresh according to the update interval set by users. The time cycle can be different from the data collecting cycle.

4.2.4 Enable/disable data series line in a chart

Users can directly disable or enable the display of a data series line in a chart by clicking on the label or line. It's very convenient for users to just compare part of the data parameters.

4.2.5 Tracking tooltip

On hovering a chart, it can display a tooltip text with information on each point and data series. The tooltip follows as the user moves the mouse over the graph, making it easy and intuitive to read out the values from the chart.

4.2.6 Navigating Range selector

While navigating a large dataset, perhaps hourly values over several years, it is important for the charting library to provide a quick way to view a certain time range. Highstock provides a range selector where the user can zoom in on preselected time ranges like 1m, 1y or YTD, or manually add date ranges.

4.2.7 Multiple Axes

Sometimes there may be several data series that are not the same scale, such as packets_in, packets_out, bytes_in, bytes_out may be in different unitsbut all of them are put in a network utilization chart. We may provide respective y axis for each series.

5 Conclusions

In this paper, we present an interactive dynamic monitoring system of a data center; provide users more friendly and perspicuous ways to monitor the runtime status of various resources in a data center. The paper describes the system architecture, design and implementation. We are planning to improve its functions and make a more intelligent system in the future, such as adding the trigger mechanism to connect user actions on the page and the low-level action engine system.

Acknowledgement

This work is supported in part by Zhejiang Provincial Natural Science Foundation of China under Grant No. LQ16F02001.

References

Here are some examples:

1. R Buyya, CS Yeo, S Venugopal, Cloud computing and emerging IT platforms: Vision, hype, and reality for delivering computing, Future Generation Computer Systems, 25(2009)
2. B Barham, S Fraser, A Harris, A.Warfield. Xen and the Artof Virtualization, Proc. Acm Symposium on Operating Systems Principles, 36 (2003).
3. K Chen, W Sun, L Zhu, et al. An Adaptive Page-Replacement Strategy for Spatial Database Systems. Journal of Computer Research and Development 10 (2011): 018
4. J Bi, H Yuan, W Tan, Application-Aware Dynamic Fine-Grained Resource Provisioning in a Virtualized Cloud Data Center, J. IEEE Transactions on Automation Science and Engineering, (2015).
5. W Song, Z Xiao, Q Chen, H Luo, Adaptive Resource Provisioning for the Cloud Using Online Bin Packing, 63 (2013)

6. DL Beaty, DL Beaty, Data center energy metric: Power Usage Effectiveness (PUE), J. Ashrae, 2013.
7. Data center infrastructure management , on http://en.wikipedia.org/wiki/Data_center_infrastructure_management
8. N Feamster, J Rexford, E Zegura, The road to SDN: an intellectual history of programmable networks, J. Acm Sigcomm Computer Communication Review, 44(2014)
9. Ganglia, on http://ganglia.sourceforge.net/
10. CloudStack, on http://cloudstack.apache.org/
11. MongoDB, on http://www.mongodb.org/
12. D3.js, on http://d3js.org/
13. Highcharts, on http://www.highcharts.com/

Large hoisting machinery local damage acoustic emission monitoring of optical information acquisition research

Shuai WAN, Qing LI,[a] and Xian-Jin WANG

College of Mechanical and Electrical Engineering, China Jiliang University, Hang Zhou, Zhe Jiang, China
[a] Corresponding author:Qing Li E-mail:lq13306532957@163.com

Abstract:AE technology,an advanced fault diagnosis technique,is impacted by environmental noise during monitoring equipment. The occurrence of interfere noise,the fashion of interfere and the effect to the system in the AE automatic online monitoring system is analyzed. At present, most of the acoustic emission signal transmission by cable, this way of transmission has a limited transmission distance, shortcomings and so on signal easily disturbed. Is proposed in this paper based on the optical fiber transmission technology, designed and developed a information collection system based on optical fiber acoustic emission monitoring.This way has the advantages of long distance transmission, strong anti-jamming capability.

1 Guideline

At present, the safety guarantee of the hoisting machinery in the operation process mainly depends on the checking and routine maintenance. And the fixed time interval of the inspection, and the conventional non-destructive testing technology only detecting some geometric and physical quantities of the lifting machine, and can not be detected under the condition of the lifting machine. Lack of hoisting machinery operating state for the related factors of safety monitoring, not of hoisting machinery health to achieve the real-time and comprehensive grasp, also do not track crane damage propagation and damage alarming. Lead to heavy machinery often pass the conventional test, but in the normal operating conditions are still likely to occur structural failure, crack growth and other damage caused by major accidents[1].Acoustic emission technique is the main method to detect large equipment active defects, such as crack propagation, but due to the complexity of the work site of the large equipment, harsh environment, traditional acoustic emission technology was influenced by the physical properties of cable transmission inherent, with transmission distance is limited, vulnerable to interference and other shortcomings, for traditional acoustic emission monitoring difficult.Therefore, this paper proposes to replace the traditional cable with optical fiber transmission signal, not only can achieve long-distance transmission and greatly reduce the external interference and signal attenuation.

2 Principle of acoustic emission detec -tion

Acoustic emission (AE), also known as stress wave emission is materials or components by external force deformation, fracture or internal stress exceeds the yield limit and enter the irreversible plastic deformation stage, the transient elastic wave in the form of the release of the strain energy of the phenomenon. Since acoustic emission testing, in the key part of the equipment, generally choose design stress value is larger or prone to corrosion, cracks or actual use of defects (such as cracks) parts of the arrangement of sensors had occurred in the process. During the normal operation of the hoisting machine, the source of corrosion and crack in the material will produce acoustic emission (stress wave) signal, which contains information of serious structural defects [2].Acoustic emission detection principle as shown in Fig.1, from the acoustic emission source to produce the wave reaching the material surface, causing the surface displacement, the sensor will mechanical vibration of materials conversion into electrical signals and are then amplified, processing and recording. Based on the observed acoustic emission signals, the mechanism of acoustic emission is analyzed and deduced.

DOI: 10.1051/itmconf/20160704015

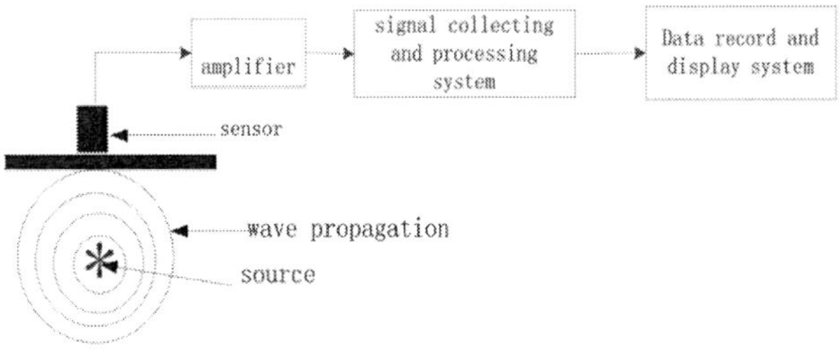

Fig .1 Principle of Acoustic Emission Detection

The frequency range of acoustic emission wave can be from a few Hz to several thousand MHz, which is related to the properties of the material, the microstructure of the sound source and the micro process of the release energy. The larger the size of the acoustic emission source, the faster the frequency, the wider the frequency range. Different acoustic emission mechanism of the spectrum is different, corresponding to the amplitude of various frequency components are also different [2].

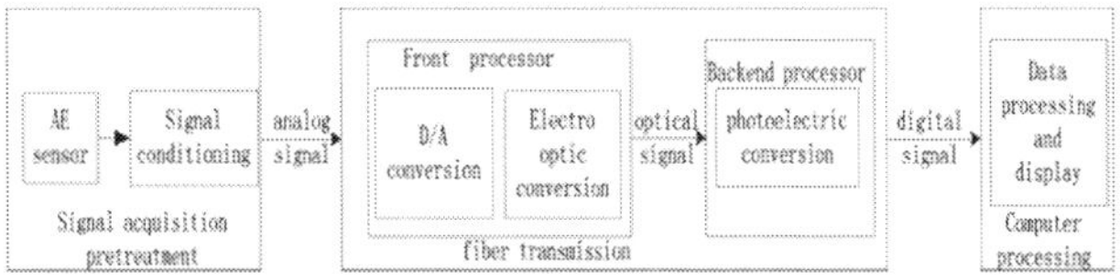

Fig.2 Acoustic Emission Optical Fiber Information Acquisition of System

3 Acoustic emission fiber information acquisition of system

As Fig.2,the acoustic emission optical fiber information acquisition of system is composed of four parts, which are acoustic emission sensor, data acquisition module, optical fiber transmission module and PC software system.

3.1 Signal acquisition pretreatment

Signal acquisition and preprocessing mainly by acoustic emission sensor and signal conditioning is composed of two parts, the acoustic emission sensors to collect acoustic emission signal, which is faint, require a signal conditioning of the conditioning.Because the signal received by the acoustic emission sensor is relatively weak, the first to be amplified, and then the analog signal conditioning for the A/D chip can receive the standard signal. Finally, the real-time acoustic emission is completed by the FPGA control, the feature extraction and acoustic emission waveform acquisition. As the output signal of the sensor is very weak, it is necessary to reduce the signal to noise ratio in the long distance transmission. Therefore, it is necessary in close proximity to the sensor placement of the front-end amplifier, according to a certain ratio of signal amplification to a level suitable for subsequent processing module processing,[3] then the output amplification analog signal by adjusting the transmission to the signal processing unit (capture card) for processing.Front end amplifier is an analog circuit and the working power supply of the power supply, signal collinear way transportation, working principle as shown in Fig .3.

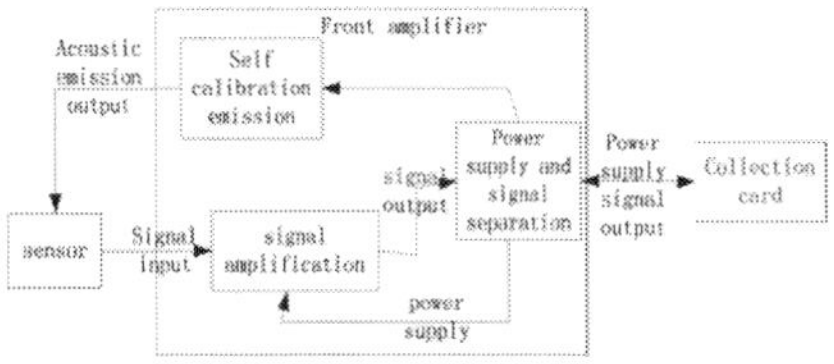

Fig.3 Working Principle Diagram

3.2 Fiber transmission module

The optical signal is transmitted by the optical fiber transmission system, so the analog signal transmitted by the acquisition card is converted into a digital signal, and the digital signal is modulated by the digital signal. In the optical fiber transmission system, the change of the electrical signal with the information is added to the optical carrier, which makes the optical carrier change according to the change of the information. This is the modulation of the optical wave [4].Speaking from the essence, the light carrier modulation and radio carrier modulation as, can carry the signal amplitude, intensity, frequency, phase and polarization parameters make light to carry information, with amplitude modulation (AM), intensity modulation, frequency modulation, phase modulation, the modulated offset multiple modulation. But in order to facilitate the demodulation, the intensity modulation mode is adopted in the optical frequency band.The back end of the optical fiber transmission needs to be photoelectric demodulation. The task of the photoelectric demodulation module is to recover the information carried by the optical fiber transmission and optical carrier with the minimum additional noise and distortion. The front end of the photoelectric demodulation module includes a photodiode and a preamplifier [5] under reverse bias.A photodiode receives an optical signal coupled to an optical fiber. In actual circuit analysis, the photodiode can be regarded as a current source in parallel with its junction capacitance C_d, equivalent circuit is shown in Fig.4, where R_L is the load resistance.

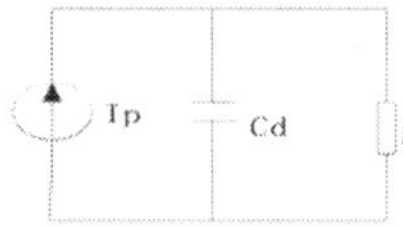

Fig.4 Photo Diode Equivalent Circuit Diagram

The design of the front end of the photoelectric demodulation module is shown in Fig. 5. Ci for the total input capacitance, which includes the junction capacitance of the photodiode and pre amplifier transistor induced capacitance.

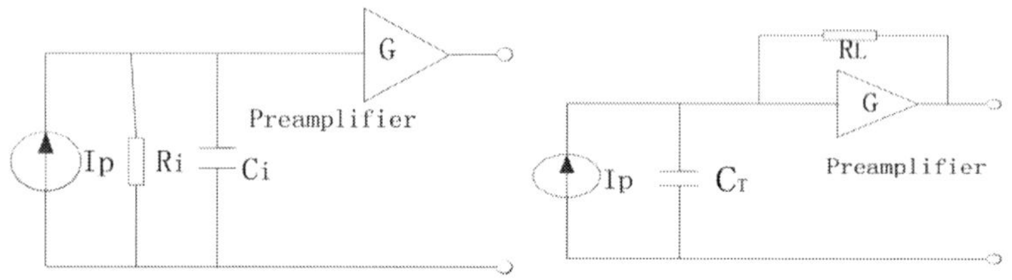

Fig.5 Photoelectric Demodulation Front-End Circuit

In the high impedance preamplifier, due to the input circuit of the total resistance R_i is larger, can increase the input voltage of the preamplifier, the larger R_i values can also reduce the thermal noise and increased receiver sensitivity, but the drawback is bandwidth delta f is narrow. The bandwidth of this circuit can be expressed as

$$\triangle f=(2\pi R_i C_i)^{-1} \quad . \qquad (1)$$

The total resistance of the input circuit R_i is connected in parallel with the input resistance R_b of the amplifier and the D_C load resistance R_L of the photodiode. Equivalent input resistance R_i is expressed as

$$Ri=Rb//RL. \qquad (2)$$

The thermal noise introduced by the input circuit is expressed as

$$E2Rn=4kTRi\triangle f. \qquad (3)$$

As can be seen, the greater the R_L, the smaller the bandwidth. The equalizer can be used to increase the bandwidth of the high frequency band,[6] and it can be used to reduce the R_i to increase the bandwidth when the receiver sensitivity is up to the requirement.

3.3 Software design and development

In view of the requirement of acoustic emission optical fiber information acquisition system, the acoustic emission information acquisition software is developed, which is used in visual studio2010 development environment, which provides a large number of controls to facilitate the development of the system.Acoustic emission optical fiber information acquisition system mainly consists of four parts, such as data acquisition module, parameter setting module, feature parameter extraction module, historical data query module and so on. The block diagram of the software system is shown in Fig .6.

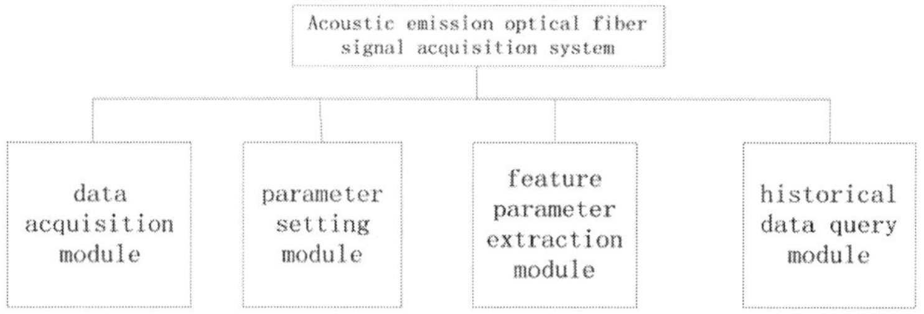

Fig.6 Block Diagram of the Software System

4.Data acquisition experiment

In order to validate the reliability of fiber acquisition system emission, in the process of tensile specimen design acoustic emission signal monitoring experiment, using acoustic emission (AE) fiber collection system and the traditional acoustic emission detection system to detect the sample at the same position, through comparative analysis to verify the acoustic emission (AE) optical fiber acquisition system whether to replace the acoustic emission signal transmission cable.

 DOI: 10.1051/itmconf/20160704015

4.1 Experimental apparatus and materials

The test equipment mainly includes: steel test specimens, tensile testing machine, acoustic emission fiber acquisition system, PC software and so on.

The sample is made of steel Q235-B, plate thickness is 4mm, and the standard specimen of long 340mm is shown in Fig.7.

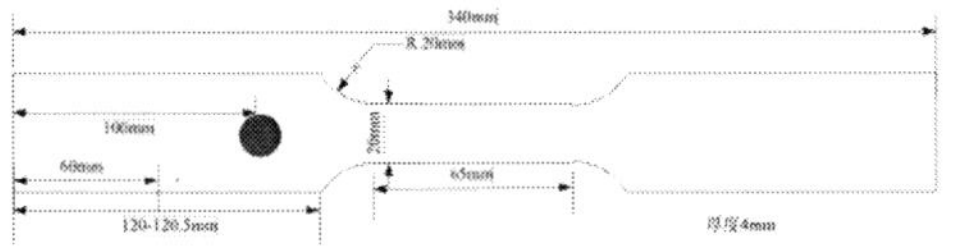

Fig.7 Schematic Diagram of The Sample (Round For The Sensor Installation Location)

4.2 Experimental procedure

Before the experiment, first of all, on the test machine electric clamping test pieces and to adjust the clamping distance of the test piece, set aside the location of the sensor installation. Connection monitoring equipment, monitoring system of optical fiber transmission distance of about 500m, through experimental lead, in the surface of the specimen broken lead core simulation of acoustic emission source, test the sensor amplitude of the two sets of system response and calibration of the sensor sensitivity.

First measurement of the field environmental noise, according to the measured noise value (40dB), the threshold value is set to 45dB, lower than the 45dB signal will be treated as noise filter out, the system sampling 10MSPS, length 2K. To start the tensile testing machine, the tensile testing machine is set up to 5 mm/min. After the start, the tension machine is loaded (5mm/min) according to the predetermined loading speed, until the specimen is stretched and broken. The acoustic emission monitoring system records the data of the whole process, and the test device is shown in Fig.8.

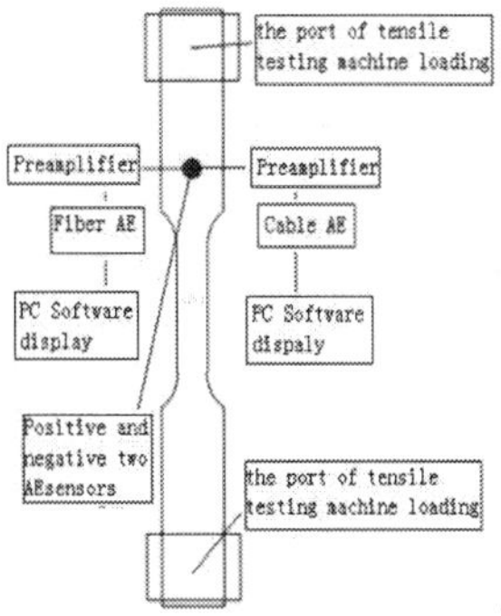

Fig.8 Test Equipment Diagram

4.3 Data comparison and analysis

When the tensile specimen after the cessation of monitoring, monitoring system records the tensile process of signal. The amplitude of the 2 samples is shown in Fig.9 of the time.The horizontal axis is time, the vertical axis is amplitude.Amplitude: the maximum amplitude of the event signal waveform, not affected by the threshold. Usually with dB (sensor output 1 V to 0 dB).

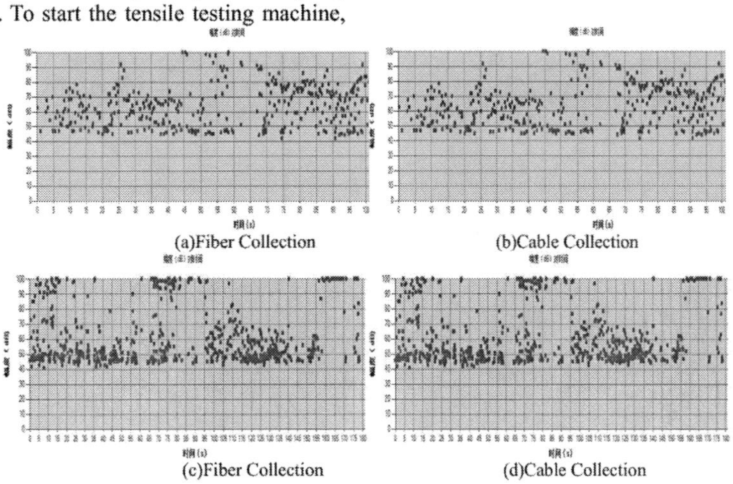

Fig.9 Amplitude to Time Scatter Plot Comparison Diagram

From the above comparison shows that acoustic emission fiber information acquisition system and traditional cable acquisition results are basically the same, predictably, acoustic emission fiber information acquisition system which can effectively extend the monitoring distance and strong anti-interference ability, can realize the long-distance monitoring of local damage.

5. Conclusion

Verified by experiment, the system can adapt to long distance acoustic emission monitoring tasks under the complex environment of long distance transmission of signals. Acoustic emission optical fiber acquisition technology provides a powerful technical means to carry

 DOI: 10.1051/itmconf/20160704015

out the monitoring of long distance structural defects, and has broad application prospects.

References

[1]. LiLi,Chen,Xiang-qian Zhao.Meiyun.Acoustic EmissionSignal Characteristics of Active Defects in Crane[J].Nondestructive Testing,2008,30（6）:334～337.

[2]. ShengGongtian,Dai Guang,Liu Shifeng.Development of Acoustic Emission Detection Technology in China[J].Nondestructive Testing,2003,25(6):302-307.

[3]. Liu Juan,Ding Keqing.Research Status and Prospect of Optical Fiber Acoustic Emission Sensor[J].Sensors and Micro Systems,,2010,29(9): 5-7.

[4]. Li Wei,Lun Chunhua,Yang Zhen.Bullet Velocity Measurement System Based on Photoelectric Signal Conversion Principle and Single Chip Microcomputer[J].Mechanical Management and Development,2008,23(6):29-30.

[5]. Zeng Qingjun,Liu Li,Huang Qiaoliang.Optical Fiber Transceiver with Remote Monitoring Function and Data Transmission Method[J].China:Jiangsu University of Science and Technology invention,, 200910234398,2009,11,24.

[6]. Ding Keqing.Research on The Application of Virtual Simulation and Dynamic Evaluation Method for The OperationState of Large Hoisting Machinery[R].Project supported by "11th Five-Year"(2006BAK02B04)Research Report.CSEI,2009.

Design of the reliable collection and control scheme of the relay node status of the train carborne control system

Wan-Ting Zhao[1,a], Gui-Ning Cao[1], Xiang-Xian Chen[1], Zhu-Jun Ling[2], Zhen-Peng Nie[2], Wen-Bin Tang[2], Guo-Dong Teng[2] and Lan-Qing Hu[2]

[1] *Department of Instrumentation Science and Engineering, Zhejiang University, Hangzhou, China*
[2] *Research and Development Canter, Zhejiang United Science and Technology Co. Ltd, Hangzhou, China*
[a]*wtzhao@zju.edu.cn*

Abstract. Train operation control system is the core of urban rail transit system, and the train carborne control system is an important part of the whole train operation control systems, and its reliability will directly affect the safety of the train. In this paper, two out of three closed-loop dynamic input detection technology and hardware dynamic two out of two voting output technology and time synchronization technology were used to design relay node status acquisition and control scheme of the train carborne control system respectively, and effectively guaranteed the reliability of relay node status acquisition and control of the train carborne control system and therefore ensure the safety of operation of the train.

1. Introduction

The basic task of urban rail transit is transporting passengers in a safety, punctuality, high efficiency and high density way. In recent years, with the rapid development of Chinese economy and the acceleration of urbanization, urban rail transit has entered a period of rapid development1. With the continuous progress of science and technology, the rail transit signal control system has experienced the development process from manual control to automatic control. Automatic Train Control (ATC) System has been applied and gradually become the future development trend of signal control system. CBTC System is currently the most advanced implement of ATC system.

Train carborne control system is one of the core of urban rail transit system, which plays an important role in improving the operational efficiency of rail transit and ensuring the safety of train operation [1, 2].The train carborne control system is the core of the train operation control system, and also the guarantee of the normal operation of the transportation system [3].It is connected with some equipment or system such as the train, traction, line and rail. It also realizes the functions of operation controlling, train operation safety, automatic operation and scheduling management [4, 5].And therefore, the reliability of the system greatly affects the safety of the whole transport control system. [6]

The train carborne control system of relay node state acquisition and control scheme can effectively guarantee the reliability of the system to the data acquisition and control of the external device relay node working state, and effectively ensure safe operation of train carborne control system.

2. Design of relay node state acquisition scheme

The working state of external equipment relay node in train carborne control system is divided into two kinds of state, closed and separated. The correct collection of the state data is an important measure of knowing the real running condition and ensuring the running safety of trains. The status of the relay node of the train carborne control system is shown in Figure 1.

As can be seen from figure 1, the collection of the status of the relay node in train carborne control system uses two out of three closed-loop dynamic input detection schemes. The scheme consists of three parts, Input Output Vital (VIO) board, Signal Acquisition Conditional (SAC) board and CPU board. The VIO board input dynamic pulses through the channel A, channel B and channel C respectively which are electrically separated from each other. And the dynamic pulse of the output format is 01010101, which controls the switch on each channel. When the external device nodes to relay is closed, three channels can collect dynamic pulses which are consistent with output pulses, when external equipment relay nodes is separated, three channels cannot get dynamic pulses which are consistent with output pulses. By the way, it can distinguish the two kinds of working states of the relay node for the external equipment effectively .Through three buses, the CAN1,

CAN2 and CAN3, VIO board is connected with SAC1, SAC2 and SAC3 board respectively, which can achieve the transmission of the working status collection of the relay node in the external equipment by the channel A, channel B and channel C. Three SAC boards are independent of each other, which are connected with CPU1, CPU2 and CPU3 through PCI1, PCI2 and PCI3 bus， and achieve the transmission of three channel state acquisition results of VIO board to three CPU boards. Through the point to point network communications, three CPU boards respectively exchange their respective received state acquisition results and take two to three votes. If the three CPU boards are collected the same dynamic pulse with three channel output pulses of VIO boards, the relay nodes of external equipment are considered to be closed, otherwise it is regarded that the relay nodes of external equipment are separated, which can realize the reliable acquisition to relay nodes of the train carborne control system.

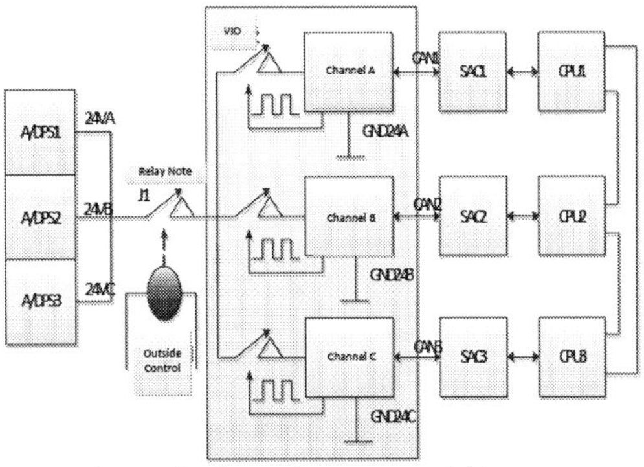

Fig.1 Scheme of Relay Node Status Acquisition

3. Design of Relay Driving Scheme

Reliable acquisition to the working state of the relay node is an effective guarantee to know about the train running state, and the reliable driving for relay nodes is an essential and important part of the correct control of train running state. The relay driver of the train carborne control system is shown in Figure 2.

As can be seen from Figure 2, the relay driver of the vehicle operation control system uses the hardware dynamic two take two voting output scheme. The output board is composed of channel A and channel B, which is controlled by CPU1 and CPU2 of two processing units respectively. The ground circuit of external relay is control by relay SR which is independent. When the relay nodes are separated, the output board can output. When the relay nodes are closed, output board cannot output, by this way, it can realize the purpose of main standby switching by changing the operating condition of the relay.

When the system is working normally, the channel A and channel B will simultaneously output the dynamic pulse, and the voting circuit will be successful, therefore, the successful output will drive the external relay. When the system work abnormally, channels A and B cannot output dynamic pulse at the same time and voting circuit cannot output because of inconsistency, therefore, the failure of external relay drive would finally steer a safe system .in this way, it can achieve the reliably drive of relay nodes of train carborne control system and ensure safe operation of the train.

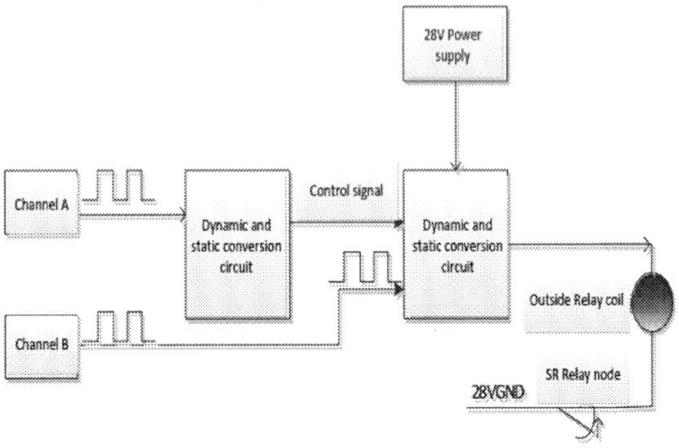

fig. 2 Relay Driving Scheme

4. Design of CPU Time Synchronization

In order to guarantee reliable data acquisition and control of working states of relay nodes in train carborne control system, we use the two out of three state acquisition schemes and two out of two relay driving scheme respectively. Both of these two schemes require reliable time synchronization between CPU.

In the time synchronization of the train carborne control system, a custom time synchronization protocol is adopted, which consists of four time stamps:

1) org(Origin Timestamp) : Client time, The time that the client issues a time synchronization request;

2) rec (Timestamp Receive): Server time, The time that the server receives the client time synchronization request;

3) xmt (Timestamp Transmit):Server time, The time that the server sends a time synchronization response;

4) dst (Destination Timestamp):Client time, The time that the client receives the server time synchronization response;

5) The process of completing the multiple CPU time synchronization of the train carborne control system is shown in Figure 3.

As can be seen from Figure 3, the time synchronization is divided into five steps, respectively as follows:

1. At time T1,the client sends a time synchronization request that contains the t1 value to server, and copies the t1 value to the local state variable T1;

2. At time T2,the server receives the time synchronization request which is sent by the client, and the t2 value and the org time stamps in time synchronization request were copied to the local state variables T2 and T1 respectively;

3. At time T3, the server sends the rec time stamp which contains a t2 value and time synchronization response of xmt time stamp which contains a t3 value to the client, and copy the t3 value to the local state variable T3;
4. At timeT4 ,the client receives the time synchronization response which is sent by the service, and the t4 value and the rec time stamp in time synchronization response , xmt time stamp were copied to the local state variables T4 and T2, T3 respectively;
5. After judging the legality of all data, by using formula (1) and formula (2), the client can calculate the time warp offset and round trip delay of the server with respect to the client, thus completing multiple CPU time synchronization of the vehicle operation control system.

Real offset should be in the range shown in the formula (3) because of the system time precision .The lambda in formula (3) is the synchronous distance, the value of which is shown in formula (4) The epsilon in the formula (4) is the dispersion, and its value varies with time, which is shown in the formula (5): The r.rho, s.rho and PHI In formula (6) respectively express time precision of the data packet, time precision of the system and the system frequency tolerance.

By using the above formulas, the range of the time variation offset of the server and the client can be calculated, and a plurality of different ranges of values can be obtained after the time synchronization. By using these different ranges of values, the interval of offset value which contains the highest confidence can be found through Marzullo's Algorithm. Therefore, it can guarantee the time synchronization between the multiple CPU mostly, and provide the guarantee for the reliable collection and control of the relay node status of the vehicle operation control system.

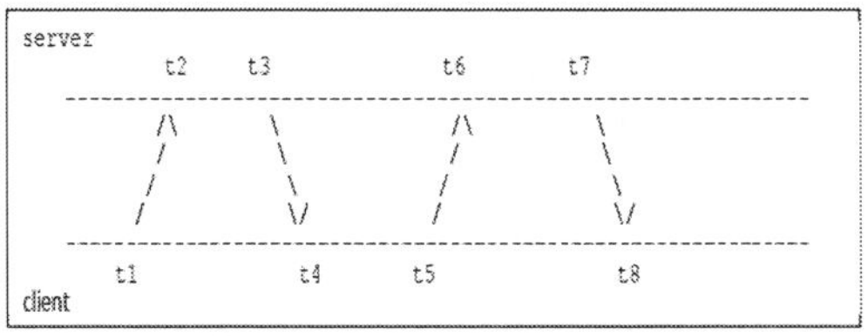

Fig. 3 Time Synchronization Process of Train Operation Control System

5. Summary

In this paper, two out of three closed-loop dynamic input detection technologies and hardware dynamic two out of two voting output technology were used to design relay node status acquisition and control scheme of the train carborne control system respectively. It can effectively guarantee the reliable collection and control of the working status of each relay node. And it also effectively ensures the reliability and safety of train carborne control system, and prevents the train from abnormal operation because of status acquisition or control error of the relay node in the train control system ,which can reduce the occurrence of railway traffic accidents.

Acknowledgment

This work is supported by the funding from the National Science and Technology Infrastructure Program of China under Grant 2015BAG19B03

References

1. Duan Hongwei. Research on Distributed Vehicle Operation Control System for Urban Mass Transit[D]. Beijing Jiaotong University, 2013.
2. Yan Fei. The Formal Modelling and Model Checking Research of Rail Transportation Train Control System[D]. Beijing Jiaotong University, 2006.
3. Zhang Yadong. Study on the Safety Risk Identification and Analysis of Train Control System of High-speed Railway[D]. Southwest Jiaotong University, 2013.
4. Song Yan. Design and Implementation of the Principle Prototype for Tuberail On-board Operation Control System[D]. Beijing Jiaotong University, 2009.
5. Yuan Zhibin. Development of Novel Vehicle Operation Control System Elementary Prototype for Modern Tram[D]. Beijing Jiaotong University, 2012.
6. Panfeng Liu, Xixi Qiu, Xiangxian Chen. Urban Rail Transit Train Automatic Protection Operation System Software Design[J].Computer Engineering.2012,38(19): 1-5
7. Rail Transit Vehicle Interface Standards Committee of the IEEE Vehicular Society.IEEE Standard for Communications— Based Train Control(CBTC) Performanceand Functional Requirements[M].New York :IEEE Publisher,1999 :5—8

Design and Implementation of the Omni Media Content Production and Service Platform

Shi-Min Liu[1,a], Ling-Jun Yang[1] and San-Xing Cao[2]

[1]*Information Engineering school, Communication University of China, Beijing, China*
[2] *New Media Institute, Communication University of China, Beijing, China*
[a] *Corresponding author:liushimin28@163.com*

Abstract. In the context of media convergence and screen integration, Omni media has become the trend of development in the field of information services, the demand of the high-quality omni media content is more and more intensive. In this paper, an omni media content production and service system is designed that can produce and manage omni media content quickly and efficiently, crop and merge and catalogue media materials conveniently. The platform accomplish those functions of cropping and merging and transcoding source materials by calling Ffmpeg

1 Introduction

As the general trend of information communication and service, omni media draws the attention of the public. In the period of integration of new media and traditional media, all kinds of communication institutions aim at enhancing their influence by implementing the omni media strategy [1]. Nowadays, the demand for Internet tends to fragmentation, which is the inevitable product of the development of new media. For new media, the process of program production, as a matter of fact, is the secondary processing on traditional media. Efficient and convenient operation mode is essential to current media market. A system that be able to operate media material database efficiently is extremely urgent and significant.

At present, the content production and service platform that traditional broadcast and TV system used bases on Client/Server, which connect client with server directly [2]. However, because of weak compatibility, the program bases on C/S development pattern require to override it entirely whenever operation environment changes, high cost and inefficiency are its disadvantages. Browser/Server overcomes those defects of C/S, and expands the business only by adding pages and server functions. In this paper, A system is designed base on B/S with Spring which helps build simple, portable, fast and flexible JVM-based systems and applications, and it integrates all functions about media content production and service into the system perfectly, and implement system functionality by calling FFmpeg, a complete, cross-platform solution to record, convert and stream audio and video. Besides, there is a real-time monitor system is designed to transcode product in materials library timely, in order to meet the multiple requirements in a variety of media terminals.

2 Design of the Omni Media Content Production and Service Platform

The omni media content production and service platform include four subsystems, which are content management system, cropping and merging system, video transcoding system and cataloging system, the workflow of the platform as follows. Content management system includes programs from program sources, store and operate them in material library. Cropping and merging system could crop and merge the videos in library as required and store in finished-parts storage, at the same time, transcoding system convert the data being stored just now to ready-for-use formats. To cataloging system, edit the finished product's details, it is the end of the flow, as shown in Figure 1.

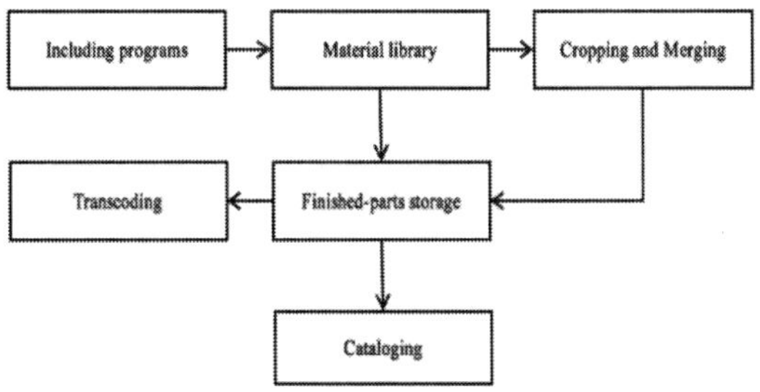

Figure 1. Flow of Omni Media Content Production and Service Platform.

In the technology architecture, an application development framework of Java EE Web be built through study in open source framework, such as Spring, Hibernate, FreeMarker, Ehcache, which includes Presentation Layer, Control Layer, Business Logic Layer and Persistence Layer . Presentation Layer and Control Layer implement by Spring MVC, combine with Spring Data IPA to manipulate Business Logic Layer and Persistence Layer. For business logic layer, Spring Data JPA is adopted to deal with business logic automatically.

3 Implement Frame work of the Omni Media Content Production and Service Platform

3.1 Spring MVC

The framework of omni media content production and service platform works with Spring MVC, it is a kind of lightweight Web framework, based on Java, requested driven about Web MVC , decoupled web layer according to different responsibilities. The front controller of Spring MVC is DispatcherServlet and Application Controller can be split into Handler Mapping and View Resolver, Handler Mapping is mainly to manage processors and View Resolver is to views. Page Controller and Action Handler implement by Controller API. Spring MVC support for theme resolution and file upload, and provide flexible data validation, formatting and data binding.

3.2 Configuration of Other Integrated Frameworks

Because of good compatibility of Spring with other frameworks, function conformity design by integrating different frameworks. In Persistence Layer, Spring Data JPA combines with Hibernate to form framework, then configure manager, entity Manager Factory defined and transaction Manger configure transaction manager.

To cache, omni media content production and service platform adopt Ehcache, an open source cache framework. Some parameters are supposed to configure, including max ElementsInMemory,eternal,timeToldleSeconds,timeToLive Seconds,diskSpoolBufferSizeMB,maxElementsOnDisk,me moryStoreEvictionPolicy diskExpiryThreadIntervalSeconds and so on.

Finally, call FreeMarker to deal with outputting text according to a template. Add freemarker.jar to the project, integrate them together, and the mainly progress is configurating file path of profile and defining load path of template and some common global variables. In order to present views by Freemarker, view resolver still need to be configured, and the resolver can resolve the views of .html and .jsp.

3.3 Configuration of Other Integrated Frameworks

The framework of omni media content production and service platform includes some common functions, such as user management, role management, and module management. The structure of common functions of system is shown as Figure 2.

In users management system, administrator can add new users, and set the value of the username and password and other details. Then the added user can login in omni media content production and service platform to do himself work according to its permission. Besides, administrator also can edit and delete users.

In roles management system, administrator can authorize different roles to different users, it mainly contains three kinds of roles: super administrator, administrator and normal user. Super administrator has highest permission, he can execute any operation in this system. There is only one super administrator, which has permission to manage and authorize administrators and normal users. The permission of administrator is lower than super administrator's, they can manage and authorize normal users in their permission scope. Generally, one administrator is responsible for a part of management, and several administrators accomplish daily system management together. Normal users are mainly users of this platform, they can operate the system to meet their demand after being audited and authorized by administrator. Because of the limit permission of normal user, they just have access to one module of the platform.

 DOI: 10.1051/itmconf/20160704017

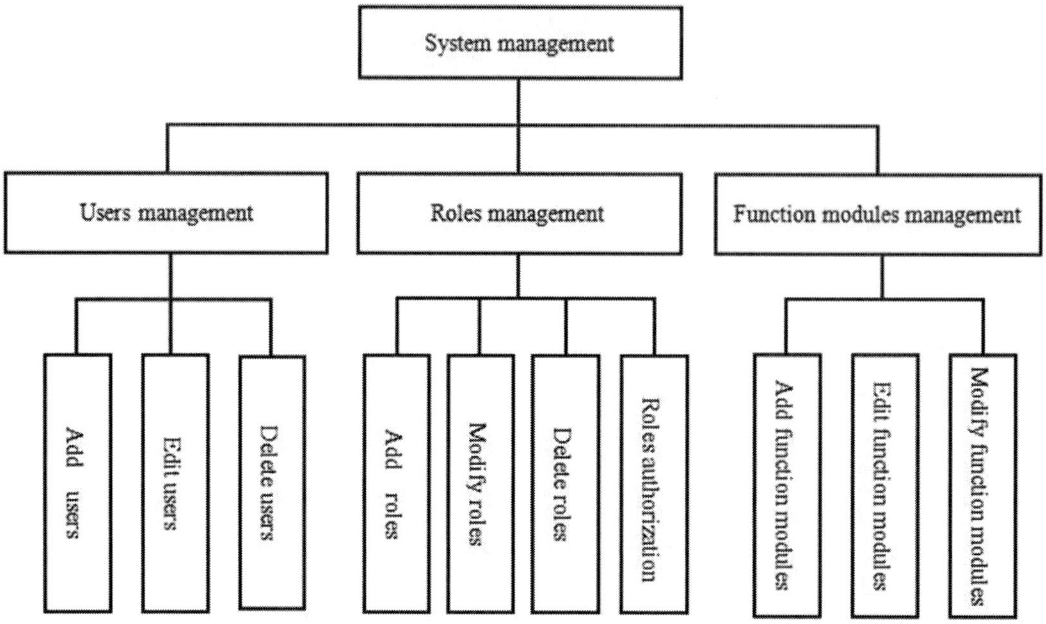

Figure 2. The Structure of Common Functions of System

Function modules management system is mainly targeted at subsequent each function module development of omni media content production and service platform. Before adding a new function module, developer are supposed to register this module's basic information in function modules management system including module name, relative path, display mode, and whether add to the menubar.

By implement above three common modules, the basic framework of the platform is erected. In order to simplified development in subsequent development, general system functions are compiled and generate a .jar file. In later development, this .jar file will be imported into project, thus can implement common module's function quickly.

4 Implement of the Omni Media Content Production and Service Platform

The platform implement functions in each module with compiling package of Java, mainly includes the following sections, Controller, Service, Po, Vo and Dao. Controller serves to process the user's request, and submit to Service implementation class for further processing. Service mainly defines methods that are called by delivering the requested of Controller, it's internal methods implement by implementation class in Service. impl, and Service.impl is concrete implementations of methods defined by Service interface layer. Po corresponds with table's fields by new JPA entity in the table. Vo's attribute values are in correspondence with Po's, and can extend extra attributes and methods as well to meet user's requirements in interactive perfectly. Dao can add, delete, check and change database by defining it's interface level [3].

4.1 Content Management System

Content management system is mainly to include materials, users can choose the channel from acceptable source list, set start time and end time, edit the material and save in the library. In this part Ajax be used to avoid names overlapping as named new material. Ajax, short for asynchronous JavaScript and Xml, is a web development technology which colligated a few of techniques to create interactive pages. Ajax only transmit indispensable date to server, users can compile the rest of date while waiting for a response, and browser partial refresh returned data dynamically, thus could improve program efficiency.The function of $.ajasx() in JQuery be called to implement Ajax. For program recording part, it achieved through Java call ffmpegforWindows.Runtime.getRuntime().exec(command Text) in Java be able to call CDM, so commands of CMD are supposed to compile to execute video recording function in FFmpeg. The flow of this part is shown as Figure 3.

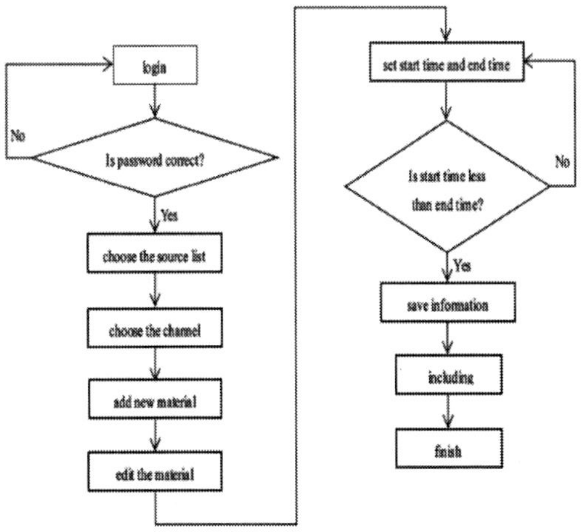

Figure 3. Flow of Content Management System

4.2 Cropping and Merging System

Cropping and merging system is mainly to process programmes further which have been included in library but often have some undesired fragments, such as advertisements. So in this part, the programme be cropped, the undesired parts be deleted, the valuable parts be saved and recoded as new material. In this paper, a cropping and merging software based on FFmpeg and SDL be used to implement the function. SDL library, used by video playback, short for Simple Direct Media Play, is an open source, cross-platform multimedia development library [4].

In order to clip video, point of cut and merge should be determined. The video decoded by FFmpeg is a serial of images constituted by frames, so the point must be a certain point of key frame. However, get the key frame only by human beings may not be accurate enough, video play in frame-by-frame be used in cropping system to get the start and end point. In interface of video player, a list of image is added to show the current frame, former two frames and later two frames, users can click the button of forward or backward to preview for videos, and pick up the key frame.

At present, radio and television systems use MPED-2 and H.246 as standard, videos in both of these standard are made up of three kind of frames, I-frame, P-frame and B-frame. I-frame is the key frame of video, P-frame is difference frame between current frame and previous ones. B-frame is bidirectionally and predictively coded frame, it is the result that contrast with previous I-frame and behind I-frame. I-frame, P-frame and B-frame formed a group of images in order, and a number of images formed a video. The type of frame is not sure about start and end point, clip directly may lead to data loss. To prevent that situation, the videos are supposed to recode before clipping, but it takes some time.

Accordingly, in this paper, a precise and efficient way be designed that just recode beginning and end section of the video, and reuse the middle part. Finally, merge necessary fragments into an integral video and save in finished-parts storage.

4.3 Video Transcoding System

Video transcoding system is mainly to convert the programme in finished-parts storage to MP4, Transport Stream and WebM, which are applicable to different devices. In this part, a monitoring system is designed to listen for finished-parts storage. When the new programmer is added to storage, the monitoring system generates command automatically to convert. There are several methods of listening for filesystem, thread polling and hook. When monitor a large number of files, thread polling takes a good deal of time with low efficiency. However hook take the way of event-driven, scan with no directory and is high efficiency. In this paper, monitoring files adopted the way of hook and call a open source library named JNotify, which support monitoring files and folders dynamically. The key part of JNotify is disposing of different type monitoring events, the class of JNotifyListener be supposed to programmed, and create fileCreated, fileRenamed and fileDeleted to implements the interface. The flow of video transcoding system is shown as Figure 4.

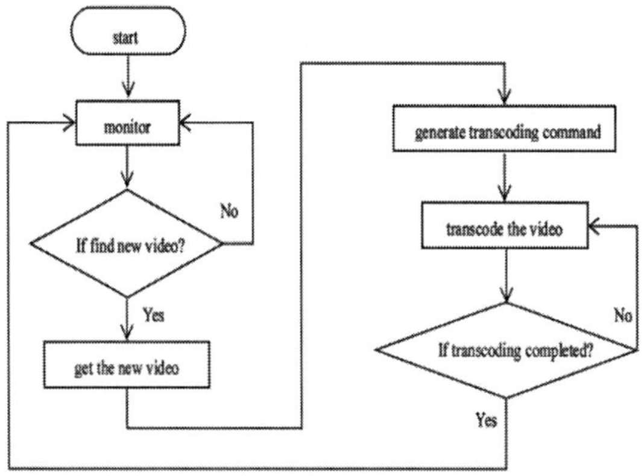

Figure 4. Flow of video Transcoding System

The function of video transcoding in this part still implement by calling FFmpeg. When find new video material in finished-parts storage, the monitor system trigger the function named fileCreated(int, wd, String rootPath, String name). As a result, a function is defined to generate transcoding command automatically and call the transcoding method named convert(String rootPath, String name, String type) in FFmpeg, and called after triggering fileCreated(). The parameter type of convert() is package format after transcoding and depend on requirements [5]. At present, there are three formats in this system, Transport Stream for Set-Top Box, MP4 for mobile and WebM for most of browsers.

DOI: 10.1051/itmconf/20160704017

4.4 Cataloging System

Cataloging system is mainly to edit video materials including information of title proper, series title, expiration time, production pipeline, column name, number of periods, number of years and editor. In order to ensure the content of video materials and catalog expediently, VLC player is used in previewing them to obtain information. Catalogued information template can be applied to improve efficiency in this system.

5 Conclusion

This paper analyses traditional media content production and service platform at present, establishes the development framework of omni media content production and service platform with Spring, and develops a integral omni media content production and service system base on the framework, which can step up omni media content production obviously. JQuery and JQuery EasyUI be used in the platform to implement user interface and event responsive logic well, application of Ajax to transmit date and save works dynamically. This work mainly focuses on the key technologies in omni media content production and service platform, and implement a series of functions the above mentioned.

In addition, cropping and merging system demands to further integration with the other systems, the current way of calling client still has its limits. These will be improved in the following study to make the platform more efficient and convenient.

References

1. CNNIC. Chinese mobile Internet research of 2013-2014[EB/OL].http://www.cnnic.cn/hlwfzyj/hlwxzbg/ydhlwbg/201408/t20140826_47880.htm, 2014-08-06.
2. Xuejun Cao. The construction of digital newspapers and media resource service platform[J]. Science & Technology for China's Mass Media, 2007, 11 : 60 - 61.
3. Johnson R. J2EE Development Frameworks[J]. Computer, 2005, 38(1):107-110.
4. SamLantinga.AboutSDL[EB/OL].https://www.libsdl.org/index.php.
5. QIN Yan.The Research of The Video Format Conversion Technology Base on The Project of FFMPEG[J]. Computer Knowledge and Technology,2011, 12 : 2912 - 2913.

 DOI: 10.1051/itmconf/20160704018

Modeling of Learners' Interest in Blended Learning: Insights from Emotional Cognition

Hai-Jian CHEN[1], Bi-Rong ZHAO[2], Yong-Hui DAI[3,a], and Guo-Wei LI[4]

[1]*Institute of science and technology, Shanghai Open University, Shanghai 200433, China*
[2]*School of Management, Fudan University, Shanghai 200433, China*
[3]*Management School, Shanghai University of International Business and Economics, Shanghai 201620, China*
[4]*School of Information Management and Engineering, Shanghai University of Finance and Economics, Shanghai 200433, China*
[a] *Corresponding author: Yong-Hui DAI, Email: dyh822@163.com*

Abstract. In blended learning, how to explore and evaluate the learner's interest is very important. In this paper, we study on modeling of learners' interest from the perspective of cognitive neuroscience. Emotional cognitive theory and brain cognitive process for situational learning interest were introduced. In addition, in order to solve the problem of quantitative assessment of interest, learner's online operation behaviour was summarized through data mining methods, and the learners' interest regression model was built. Experimental results show that the accuracy of the model is more than 91% and it has good applicability in blended learning.

1 Introduction

In recent years, profound changes have occurred in teaching methods with the development of information technology. In particular, E-learning method emerged the end of twentieth century, which makes it possible to learn at any time and at any place. Although E-learning method provides a lot of convenience in learning, but also it has some shortcomings. For example, it is lack of face-to-face communication between teacher and student, and depends on digital teaching too much, especially, it faces to high drop-out rate and low completion rate. It was reported that there are more than 50,000 registered students selected software engineering course of UC Berkley on Coursera platform, but only 7% of them passed the exam [1]. As another example, MOOCs has developed rapidly in recent years, but the data indicated that the number of learners who can finish MOOCs was only 6% in China [2]. Therefore, in order to improve the above situation, the blended teaching is put forward, which combines the advantages of traditional teaching and E-learning [3]. Because blended teaching includes the advantages of previous teaching method, then this kind of learning is deeply loved by the learners.

Because learner's interest seriously affects completion of his studies, the study of learner interest has been concerned by scholars, and there are a lot of research results. However, learners in blended teaching have different social experiences and educational background, which make research of learners' interest show a lot of complexity. Previous research methods are often ineffective, such as learning path analysis, web log mining. It is well known that online learning process often involves a large number of text, pictures, semi-structured and unstructured data, which is very closed related to learner's interest and difficult to analyse. Taking into account the above difficulties, we adopt cognitive neuroscience as theory basis to research above issue, which has proven to be successful in the study of emotions, advertising and marketing [4]-[6].

2 Theories and Methodology

2.1 Emotion classification theory

Emotion is a kind of attitude experience of people toward the objective matters [7]. Although emotions have long been known, however, the classifications and the descriptions of emotions have not reached consensus in scholars for a long time. Relatively speaking, the classification from the perspective of psychology is generally accepted by most of scholars. From psychological point of view, human emotions are divided into two categories, one is basic emotion, and the other is dimensional emotion [8].

2.1.1 The basic emotion theory

The basic emotion theory thought that human emotions are composed of body experience, physiological arousal and external expression. And typical classification of basic emotion is concluded by American scholar Orthony (1990), which is shown in Table 1 [9].

DOI: 10.1051/itmconf/20160704018

Table 1. Classifications of Emotions

Scholars	Classifications
Arnold	Anger, aversion, courage, desire, despair, hate, hope, love, etc.
Ekman, Friesen & Ellsworth	Anger, joy, sadness, surprise, etc.
Frijda	Desire, happiness, interest, surprise, wonder, sorrow
Gray	Rage and terror, anxiety, joy
Izard	Anger, disgust, distress, fear, interest, shame, surprise, etc.
James	Fear, grief, love, rage
McDougall	Anger, disgust, fear, subjection, wonder, etc.
Mowrer	Pain, pleasure
Oatley & Johnson-laird	Anger, disgust, anxiety, happiness, sadness
Panksepp	Expectancy, fear, rage, panic
Plutchik	Ecstacy, admiration, terror, amazement, grief, loathing, rage, vigilance
Tomkins	Anger, interest, disgust, fear, joy, shame, surprise, etc.
Watson	Fear, love, rage
Weiner & Graham	Happiness, sadness

2.1.2 The dimensional emotion theory

The dimensional theory thinks that all human emotions are composed of multiple dimensions, and every kind of emotion is not independent, it is continuous. On the method of dimensional division, wheel of emotions is proposed by Plutchik (1980). In Plutchik′s wheel of emotions, eight kinds of emotion were divided. That is, ecstacy, admiration, terror, amazement, grief, loathing, rage and vigilance. These emotions are in a round structure centred on the original point. All emotions can be obtained based on the above eight emotions. For example, contempt is composed of loathing and rage.

In addition, the three-dimensional theory of emotion was put forth by Wundt. And it was developed after that. Especially, PAD (Pleasure-Arousal-Dominance) three dimensional emotions model has great effect on related research, which was proposed by Mahrabian and Russell. Among their model, P dimension reflects individual positive emotion or negative emotion. A dimension means level of individual physiological activation. D dimension refers to individual control state for situation or other people [6].

2.2 Autonomous Learning Theory

In the concept of autonomous learning, different researchers give different opinions, for example, Holee think it is a kind of ability, Pintrich think it is a process of active construction of learning, Yu et al., think it is a way of learning [1]. No matter what kind of definition is, it is identical in essence, that is, learner autonomy determines learning style and learning behaviour in autonomous learning. From the perspective of research, the theory of autonomous learning can be divided into behavioural perspective [10] and Humanism perspective [11]. From behavioural perspective of view, it is considered that the nature of autonomous learning is a kind of learning behaviours of 'stimulus response', which is based on the response of reinforcement.

From humanism perspective of view, it emphasizes learners' autonomous learning ability, and it is believed that autonomous learning needs to play their own initiative and combine learning activities with their own requirement to carry out meaningful learning. The learning process of autonomous learning involves many aspects, such as mental, emotion, motivation, demand and so on. The process of autonomous learning is shown as Figure 1.

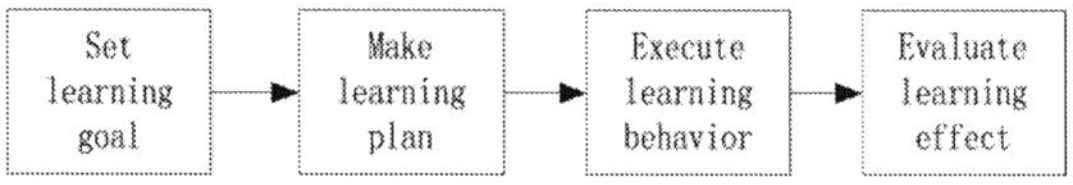

Figure 1. Process of Autonomous Learning

3 Brain cognitive mechanism for context learning interest

3.1 Brain cognitive activity for interest

Human emotion is produced by the interaction of three factors, that is, stimulation, physiology and cognition. Among them, cognitive factor is the key factor [12]. When learners logged on online learning platform, web page will firstly arouse their attention. Web information was delivered to learner's limbic system by selective attention mechanism and sensory pathway, and then produced first emotional information. Due to first emotion come from the superficial information of stimulus signal. Therefore, it is very important to how to design an attractive web course interface to arouse learners' first interest in online learning platform.

Based on the first emotional response, the content of stimulus signal will generate the second response, which comes from advanced cerebral cortex cognitive activities respond to semantic information. As a result, it is equally important to provide attractive course content for online learning platform. If online learning platform can provide attractive web pages and course, which is easy to arouse learner's selective attention, and make his brain produce first emotional response and second emotional response, and can arouse learner's independent learning interest and good learning behaviour.

Overall, brain cognitive process of context interest can be seen as three parts, context generation, cognitive neural activities and emotional experience. The brain cognitive process of context learning interest is shown as Figure 2.

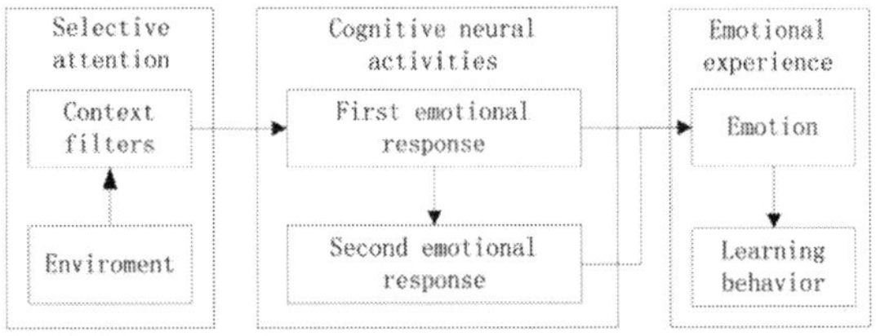

Figure 2. Brain Cognitive Process of Context Learning Interest

As we known, learners' brain constructs the emotional symbol system for the specific stimulus symbols under the action of memory based on the first and the second emotional experience. Once a familiar semantic symbol occurs, the learner will give selective attention according to emotional experience in memory, and adjust the distribution of cognitive time on visual and hearing sense. According to the above analysis, we know if pleasant learning experience was provided in blended learning, it will help learners to form their own learning habits and behaviours, and awaken their learning interest. At the same time, the memory stored in the brain will be more profound, and interest is also easy to be perceived.

3.2 EEG experiment for context interest

In recent years, EEG (Electroencephalography) method has been applied to much research [13], such as the research of marketing strategy and advertising effectiveness. In our study, EEG method was used in study of learners' interest.

3.2.1 Experimental subjects

Our experiment includes eighteen participants, and all of them come from learners of 'Shanghai study website'. Among them, eleven were male and seven were female, average age was 22.7 years old. All subjects were physically and mentally healthy, right hand in hand, normal vision or corrected visual acuity, and had signed the informed consent before testing.

3.2.2 Experimental design

In order to study on learners' interest in blended learning, we designed two test tasks, task 1 is material browsing, Task 2 is designed to test human cognition for symbolic information, and test material is composed of variety of content material, include animation, colour, voice, picture and text. Among them, text material preparation is as follows.

Firstly, we visit some teachers and collect one hundred related words. Then, fifty words were selected by field experts and were used in experiment. Each word is classified the degree of relevance of the level of judgment (0-5), among which, 0 refers to no relationship, 5 refers to the highest correlation. At the same time, fifty families living words were selected as neutral word materials. Finally, the above words consist of stimulus and neutral words.

3.2.3 Experimental procedure

The experiment of EEG is shown as Figure 3. It includes signal collection, signal processing and EEG analysis etc. Among them, the methods of signal processing include Support Vector Machine, Bayesian method, Back-Propagation neural network etc. In our study, Wavelet Transform were used.

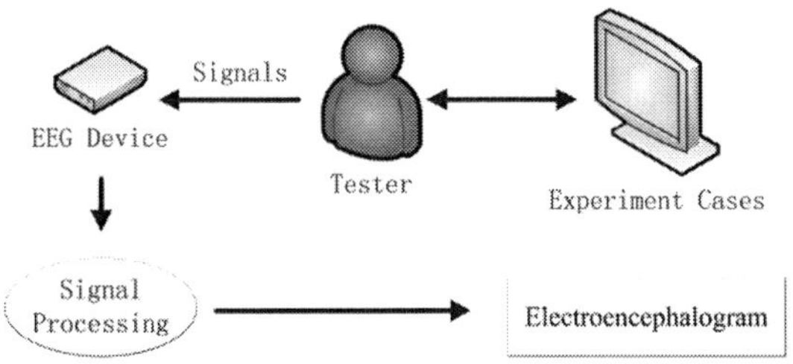

Figure 3. Process of EEG Experiment

3.2.4 Analysis of experiment

The data of four categories of brainwaves (α , β , δ , θ) is collected after subjects finished experiment. Previous studies have shown that when the human brain is thinking or excited, a large number of beta waves will appear [14]. Our experiment show that when the content of interest appears, learners often express more attention or mood-swings, and it is easy to cause beta rhythm. Then the relative energy of the beta rhythm wave is used to analyse the different cognitive load of the learner. The results of EEG experiment show that the relative energy ratio of beta rhythm wave is higher when executing the stimulus words. And Mann-Whitney U test shows P value below 0.05, which means the difference of relative energy are significant between stimulus and neutral words.

In the above of EEG experiment, we also found that human brain's cognitive time is different when it faces to different material. The human brain's cognitive time for text information is more than animation, which is very important for us to research interest.

4 Representation of online learning interests

4.1 Learning interest parameters

Learners' online operation behaviours reflect their mental state, which is an important representation of interest. After reference to previous studies, we divide online operation behaviours of learners' interests into six categories, and the following sets were used to represent online learning interest.

$$I = (T0, T1, T2, T3, T4, T5) \qquad (1)$$

In (1), *T0* means the type of displaying interest behaviour, *T1* is the type of marked interest behaviour,

 DOI: 10.1051/itmconf/20160704018

T2 is the type of interest behaviour of course link, *T3* is the type of learning time, *T4* is the type of rolling span of page, and *T5* is the type of text interest. Expand to say, *T0* is obtained through feedback of interest questions on the web page, which indicates learners' interest. *T1* is obtained by calculating the behaviours of all these online operations, such as add tag, add bookmark, save page etc. *T2* implies that more times the course resources are clicked and the more learners' interest is shown. Similarly, *T3* implies that the longer the accumulated learning time and the more learners' interests it shows. *T4* is also can be regarded as the longer the distance of rolling and the more learners' interest is shown. *T5* is obtained by calculating the learner's interest from his online text.

According to the results of previous EEG experiments, human brain's cognitive time is different. When learner studies on the Internet, his brain's cognitive time is closely related to the symbol information. If learner's operation time is significantly different from normal threshold, this operation will be filtered out.

5 Modeling of learners' interest

5.1 Selection of parameters

Due to learners' behaviour on online learning platform is closely related to their psychological activities. That's to say, learning behaviour is the external expression of mentality. If learner likes one course, then he will learn it seriously and give feedback on time. According to previous theoretical analysis, some behaviour can reflect the actual interest of learner toward this kind of resource, such as learning frequency, time, collection, questionnaire, information of focus, answering process, evaluation, etc. In our study reading and operation behaviours were selected as represent learners' interest.

5.1.1 Reading behaviour of learners' interest

In learning process, the main behaviour is reading, including browse text and watch video. Learning is accompanied by click operation (For example: drag the scroll bar, turn the page, and click back). According to our analysis, if learner often drags mouse which indicates he browse carefully. Forward and backward operation indicates that the learner is not very interested in this part of content or he thinks it too simple to learn.

5.1.2 Operation behaviour of learners' interest

In learning process, if interest content encounters, learner will do some operations, such as collect, copy, concern, save, print, add bookmarks, share, etc. These behaviours often represent learner's interest. For example, online star rating, if the evaluation is one star, which indicates learner isn't interested in this content. Conversely, if the evaluation is five stars means learners are very interested in the resources or knowledge.

5.2 Modeling

5.2.1 Sample data collection

In our study, sample data were collected from the registered learners of website (http://www.shlll.net), and the date from August 2013 to August 2015. The learning behaviours of 33 learners are selected as samples and the learner interest sample data after unification as shown in Table 2.

Table 2. Sample Data for Learners' Interest

Stu ID	Course	A_0	A_1	A_2	A_3	A_4	A_5
201301	08001	0.556	0.067	0.778	0.022	0.744	0.042
201302	08001	1.000	0.111	0.754	0.062	0.744	0.050
...	...	...	...	...	...	...	...

5.2.2 Modeling of course interest

According to collected data, regression equation was established and obtained regression coefficient as following. β_0=0.0844, β_1=0.4347, β_2=0.0938, β_3=0.1607, β_4=0.1772, β_5=0.0492. Therefore, regression equation of the course interest is as follows.

$$Y = 0.4347x_1 + 0.0938x_2 + 0.1607x_3 + 0.1772x_4 + 0.0492x_5 + 0.0844 \quad (2)$$

Among which, X_1 is the set of marked interest behaviour coefficient. X_2 is the set of course linked interest behaviour. X_3 is the set of learning time interest behaviour. X_4 is the set of moving span interest behaviour. X_5 is the set of text interest behaviour.

In (2), we can see the coefficients of X_1 and X_4 are great, which suggests that these two kinds of behaviours are important to leaners' interests. The coefficient of X_5 is less, and the explanation for this is most of online learners are not very much involved in text discussion. Then the effectiveness of this model is tested, and R^2=0.9132, which suggests the fitting effect is good. Besides, P value of every coefficient is below 0.05, means the regression coefficient is significant. Then this model is used to predict learner interest for other ten learners. The result is shown as Figure 4.

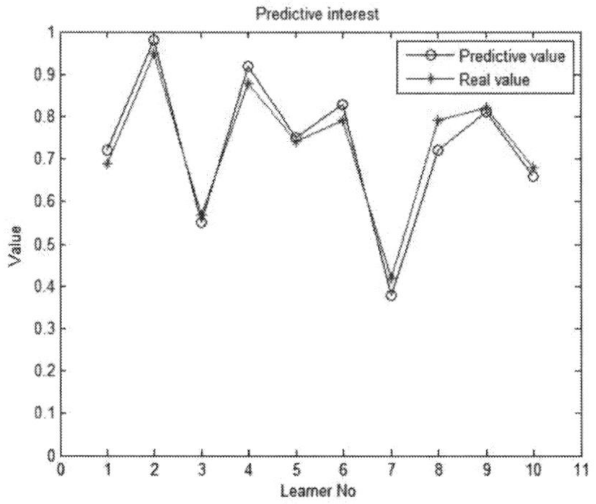

Figure 4. Compare Predictive Interest to Real Interest

It can be seen from Figure 4, the value of predicitive interest is close to the value of real interest. Calculation results show that the overall accuracy of ten learners is 91.04%, then it can be used to estimate interest.

6 Conclusions

Based on the characteristics of blended learning education, this paper studies the learners' interest modeling from the perspective of emotional cognition. We investigate the learning interests by observing the brain cognition experiment and data mining of learning behaviours. Our study contributes is to provide brain mechanism model for context learning interest, and put forward quantitative evaluation learning interest for six kinds of online operation behaviour. In addition, learners' interest regression model is established. The experiment suggests this model can represent effectively the learners' interests in blended learning.

In general, the future study can use eye tracker or other wearable devices and analyse the learning interest behaviour from the perspective of physiological features, which can improve the accuracy of our model.

Acknowledgment

This work was supported by Science and Technology Commission of Shanghai Municipality Research Project of China (13DZ2252200, KFKT1501).

References

1. Chen H J, *Study on learners' interest mining in MOOCs* [D], Shanghai: Shanghai University of Finance and Economics, 2015.
2. Breslow L, Pritchard D E, DeBoer J, et al., Studying learning in the worldwide classroom: Research into edX's first MOOC [J], Research & Practice in Assessment, **8(1)**: 13-25(2013).
3. Young K, Voci E, Blended learning working in a leadership development programme [J]. Industrial & Commercial Training, 33(5):157-161 (2001).
4. Huang S, Zhou X, Xue K., et al., Neural Cognition and Affective Computing on Cyber Language [J]. Computational Intelligence & Neuroscience, 2015(2):1-10 (2015).
5. Ma Q G, Feng Y D, Xu Q, et al., Brain potentials associated with the outcome processing in framing effects [J], Neuroscience letters, 528(2):110-113 (2012).
6. Dai W H, Han D M, Dai Y H, et al., Emotion recognition and affective computing on vocal social media [J], Information & Management, 52(7):777-788 (2015).
7. Lin C D, *Psychology Dictionary* [M]. (Shanghai Education Publishing, 2003).
8. Adomavicius G, Tuzhilin A, Using Data Mining Methods to Build Customer Profiles [J], Computer, 34(3):74-82 (2001).
9. Ortony A, Turner T J, What's basic about basic emotions? [J], Psychological Review, 97(3):315-331 (1990).
10. Stewart M, Autonomous Learning in Higher Education [J], Physiotherapy, 79(4):238-238(1993).
11. Rostami K, Khadjooi K, The implications of Behaviorism and Humanism theories in medical education [J]. Gastroenterology & Hepatology from Bed to Bench, (3):65-70(2010).
12. Schachter S, Singer J E, Cognitive, social, and physiological determinants of emotional state [J], Psychological Review, 69(5):379-399(1962).
13. Ko K E, Yang H C, Sim K B, Emotion recognition using EEG signals with relative power values and Bayesian network [J], International Journal of Control Automation & Systems, 7(5):865-870 (2009).
14. Han D M, Dai Y H, Dai X Y, et al., Explore Awareness of Information Security: Insights from Cognitive Neuromechanism [J], Computational Intelligence and Neuroscience, 2015(1):1-8(2015).

ITM Web of Conferences 7, 04019 (2016) DOI: 10.1051/itmconf/20160704019
ITA 2016

Design and Implementation of SMS Extraction and Analysis System

Yu-Yang WAN, Hui XU* ,and Rong-Rong FANG

College of computer science and technology, Nantong University, 226009,Nantong, China
** Corresponding Author: xu.h@ntu.edu.cn*

Abstract. With more and more applications of smart phone, more and more text messages in mobile phone, and then more and more information possibly contained in text messages. How to dig out useful information form SMS? This paper discusses techniques of the SMS extraction and analysis. Taking the bank SMS as example, key information is extracted to inform, is formatted to story in APP database, and then be analysed and statistic result shown in chart. The APP with the function is run well on Android phone and has Practical value. This technology helps to expand the application of SMS.

1 Introduction

"Intelligent" of smart phone greatly extends the functionality of the phone[1], the phone call is not just a call tool, it has become a good assistant and an indispensable tool in people work, live, entertainment, communication and transaction processing. Meanwhile, SMS(Short Message Service) is no longer a text communication tool. As one of the guarantees real-name system, SMS gradually become a tool of receiving verification information, accessing to the notification, and making transaction confirmation. With the development of fast payment such as online banking, Paypal, WeChat pay, etc., people are more inclined to quickly and easily done through mobile payment, during this process, SMS link in the whole play, timely notification, preserve transaction records and play an important role. So, it is cleared that SMS-based treatment processing, statistical analysis becomes significant and promising.

2 System Design

2.1 Business Process

Data is extracted automatically in the background. When the client first starts, SMS inbox is scanned automatically, key information is extracted from the corresponding text by regular expressions, including transaction time, transaction amount, transaction type, transaction banking, and etc., and automatically recorded in the APP database. When new message arrives, critical information also extracted by regular expressions [2], simplified refining and give a notification. Business process is shown in Figure 1.

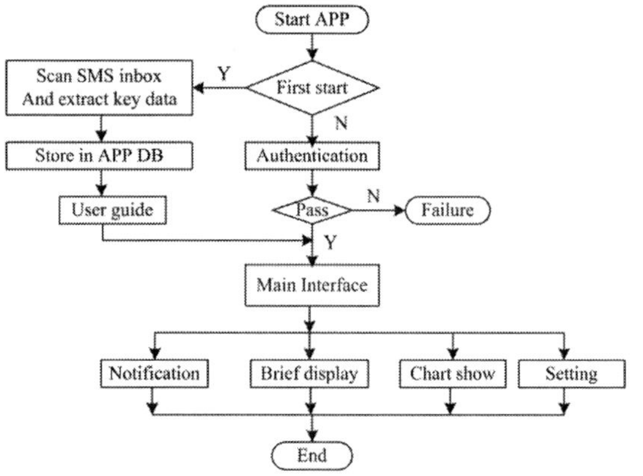

Figure 1. Business Process

2.2 System Function

This system based on Android platform[1], the system function module include: (1) User guide module;(2) Authentication module;(3) Data porcessing module; (4) Regex module; (5) SMS broadcast receiver module; (6) SMS summary module;(7) Chart module;(8) QR code scanning.

2.2.1 User Guide

The main function of this module is to show the main function and characteristics of the APP for the first use. This module is to be beautiful with elegant design and natural smooth transition animation. Leave a great impression to the users, meanwhile hiding the database processing module processing in the background.

2.2.2 Authentication

The main function of this module is to ensure the safety of personal privacy [3]. Because APP involves important information such as bank card, belong to the category of personal financial privacy, therefore, before entering the APP take two authentication mechanisms, including the Pin code and fingerprint recognize authentication.

Pin code validation:4 digit Pin code is used as the authentication information, and be set by the user.

Fingerprint authentication: fingerprintsis used as authentication schemes. a system level verification, access to key information in the TrustZone hardware, security is guaranteed.

2.2.3 Data Processing

Data extraction occurs at two moments: one is the first start of the application; another is the arrival of a new message after the starts. For the first case, the inbox database is scanned. In both case, data are acquired through match by regular expression, then are formatted and stored into APP database for analysis.

Database processing flow of the first case is shown in figure 1.

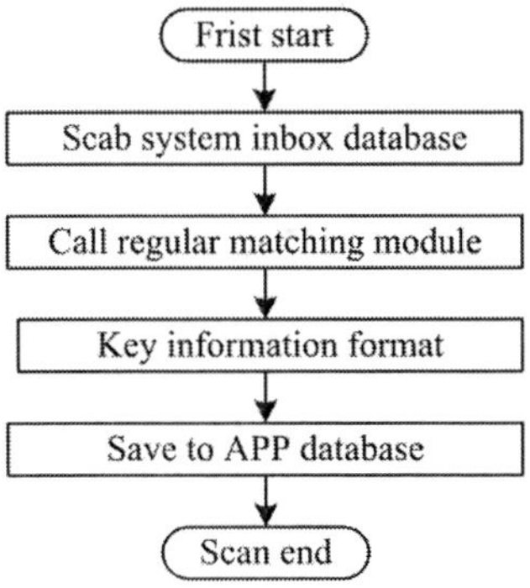

Figure 2. The Flow of Data Processing

2.2.4 Regular Expression

The main function of this module is to get key information using a regular expression. Regular Expression[4] (abbreviated as regex, regexp or RE), is syntax rules described by single string which is used to match a series of sentence. In many text editor, Regular expression are typically used to retrieve, replace the text that fits a pattern.

Different types of message take different regular expressions [5], Part of the regular expression, function and the matching results are shown in table 1. the key message is not the same, use Bank and Express message as examples.

Bank SMS: the bank name, bank card number and transaction amount, transaction time and transaction details information are necessary. Some information needs to format to show in charts.

Express SMS: Courier name, delivery time, delivery take the key information are necessary to ensure information notice.

Table 1. Example of Some Regular Expression

Function	Regex expression	Result
Extract Card	Suffix\w+	Suffix:6666
Extract Bank	(?<=[)[\u4e00-\u9fa5]+(? =])	the bank name
Extract Left Money	Balance\d+.\d+Yuan	Balance1000.00 Yuan

2.2.5 SMS Broadcast Receiver

The main function of this module is to get messages broadcast and analyze the message transmitting and text messages when phone received new messages, if the message is from bank or express , call the regular key information processing module to extract data, and call the information notification module of key information to make a notice, at the same time to write the key information into the database for storage. The business flow chart is shown in figure 3.

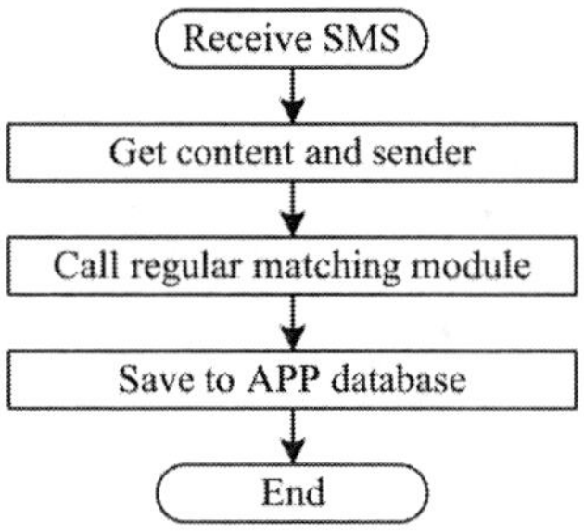

Figure 3. Receiving and Process of SMS

2.2.6 SMS Summary

The main function of this module is to show the information of the database. Using CardView and RecyclerView layout, only show the key information, Such as bank logo, bank card, transaction type, trade time, trade amount, etc. The key technologies including dynamic hidden and loading step by step.

dynamic hidden:Hide Toolbar when move up to show more data information.

loading step by step:Load 20 items while o the interface is initialized, cooperate with the drop-down refresh and tensile load, more data to be loaded when the action triggers, reduce page rendering time. While adding a refresh and load the animation, in line with the intuitive operation.

2.2.7 Statistic Chart

Charts display visually the user's income and expenditure. For data stored in the APP database give statistics daily expenses and income; illustrate result monthly time periods, illustrating statistical results for each month. Expenditure and revenue respectively below and above the horizontal axis, a head understand. The results of the monthly income and expenditure are given in text.

2.2.8 QR Code Scanning

The main function of this module is to read the Courier number, at the same time for the APP to join more extensions provide reliable interface.

3 System Implementation

3.1 Guide Interface

The interface uses a light background color with a flat Schematic diagram. It introduces APP features, while completing the database scan task in the background. The running effect as show in Figure 4.

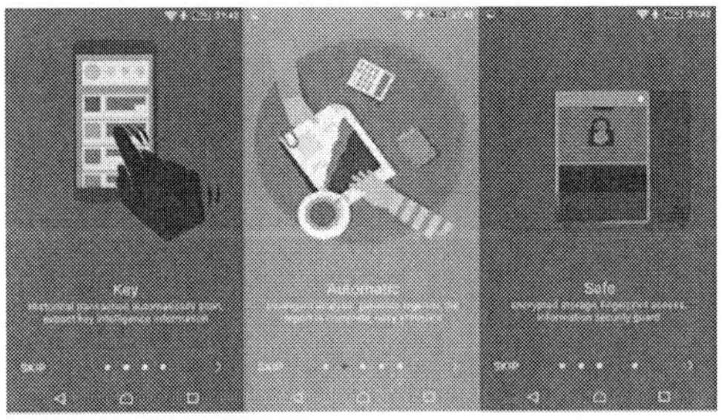

Figure 4 Guide Interface

3.2 Authentication Interface

The interface provides two authentication ways: fingerprint verification and password verification, shown in Figure 5.

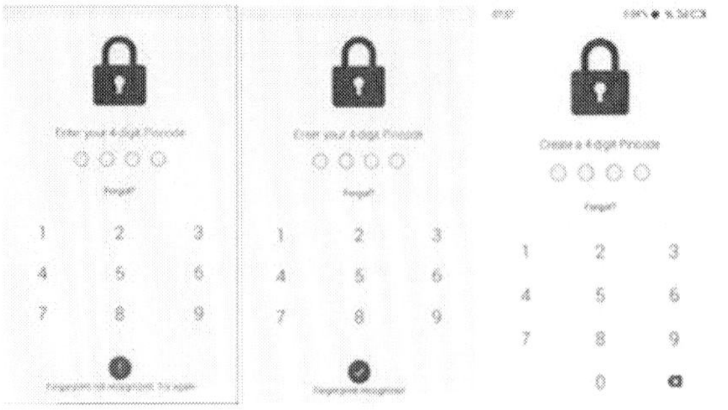

Figure **5**. Authentication Interface

In Fig. 5, the left one for fingerprint verification error, the center one for fingerprint authentication is successful interface, and the right one to enter the Pin code validation interface.

3.3 SMS Summary

Use the card layout, left for conventional interface, center for the drop-down refresh, on the right for tensile load and dynamic hide the ToolBar, shown in Figure 6.

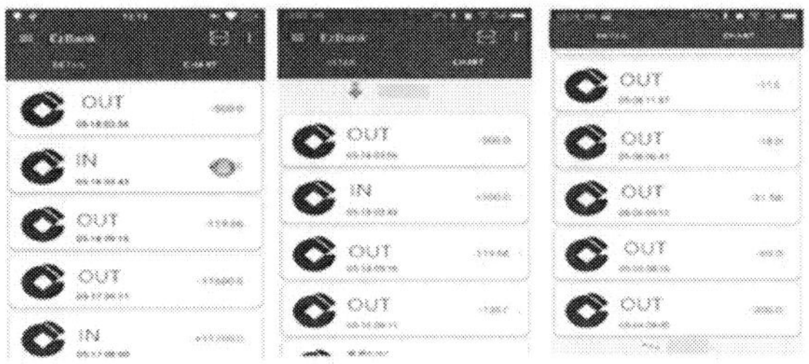

Figure 6. Infromation Display Interface

3.4 Chart Interface

Income and expenditure are labeled in different color and different position. Income for the direction of the green, red spending a negative direction. It supports two-finger zoom, zoom in to view details of the data. Statistics of the month shows below the table including the total revenue and total expenditure of current month with all auto-complete without manual settings. Graphics are made by google charts plugin.

Operation interface as shown in figure 7, support in switch, left with statistical figure of May and April respectively. Spending double refers to scaling, center and right are the same as for April, the width of the histogram.

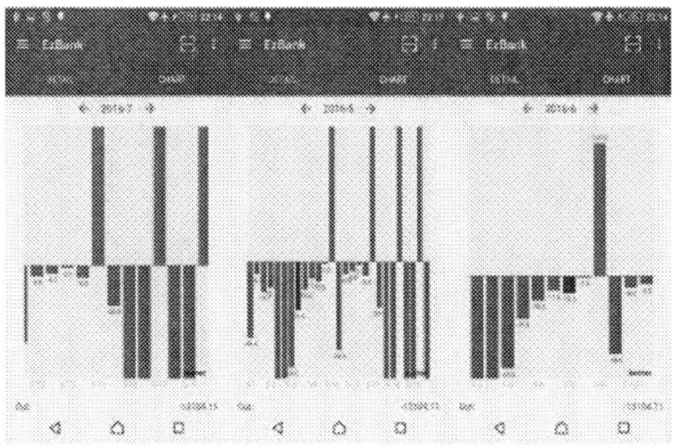

Figure 7. Chart Interface

The key code is as follow:

```
private void setDataFromDB(String sYear, String sMonth) {
    toShowData = DataSupport.where("year = ?", sYear).where("month = ?", sMonth).order("id
desc").find(BankCard.class);
    if (toShowData.size() > 0) {
        ......
        for (int m = 0; m < toShowData.size(); m++) {
            listFmoney = toShowData.get(m).getFmoney();
            if (listFmoney > 0) {
                in_sum = in_sum + listFmoney;
            } else {
                out_sum = out_sum + listFmoney;
            }
            all_sum = all_sum + listFmoney;
            listDate = toShowData.get(m).getMonth() + "-" + toShowData.get(m).getDay();
            dataToShow.add(new ChartData(m, listFmoney, listDate));
            }
        setData(dataToShow);
       ......
```

4 Conclusion

This system developed on the Android[6] platform with Java language and MVC [7] architecture. The system develop a complete text extraction, stored, ,analysis and gracphic display static result. System interface has the stytle of Google official Material Design style, with a good visual effect and interactive experience. Using a regular expression to extract text information, has high flexibility and extensibility.

References

[1] Research and trend analysis reports of 2016 China's smart phone market outlook Situation [EB/OL]. http://wenku.baidu.com/view/5076-968858fafab068dc024b,2016
[2] Q. Y. Qiu. Patented infromattion extration based on reqular expression 2007,18(19): 271-350
[3] S. Biswas, W. Haipeng, J. Rashid. Android Permissions Management at App Installing[J]. International Journal of Security and Its Applications, 2016,**10**(3):223-232
[4] J. E. Fried, S Yu. Mastering regular expressions [M]. Beijing: Electronic industry Press,2007
[5] M. C. Lian. POS endowed Corpus retrieval and that the regular expression [J]. Chinese Language Education, 2009, 2:65-73
[6] Android [EB/OL], https://zh.wikipedia.org/wiki/Android.
[7] MVC framework in Android mode of use, [EB / OL], http://blog.csdn.com/fxds/detail/324632.

Text Clustering Algorithm Based on Random Cluster Core

Long-Jun HUANG[1,a], Meng-Zhen CHENG[1] and Yao XIAO[2]

[1]*School of Software, Jiangxi Normal University, Jiangxi, 330022*
[2]*Baidu Time Network Technology (Beijing) Co., Ltd, Beijing, 100081*
[a] *huanglong98614@163.com*

Abstract. Nowadays clustering has become a popular text mining algorithm, but the huge data can put forward higher requirements for the accuracy and performance of text mining. In view of the performance bottleneck of traditional text clustering algorithm, this paper proposes a text clustering algorithm with random features. This is a kind of clustering algorithm based on text density, at the same time using the neighboring heuristic rules, the concept of random cluster is introduced, which effectively reduces the complexity of the distance calculation.

1 Introduction

Cluster analysis as an important means of text information mining, is widely used in log analysis, statistics of public opinion and other areas .In recent years, the means of text and word frequency word bag clustering emerge in endlessly, these algorithms extracted a lot of valuable information available from the vast amounts of data, creating a huge amount of wealth.However, with the rapid development of computer and Internet industry, many companies store data reaches TB or even PB level, such background puts forward higher requirements for data mining algorithms. Some traditional text clustering methods cannot adapt to the massive and high dimension data mining tasks, because of the bottleneck of performance, so it is necessary to design some efficient and agile clustering methods[1].

Experts at home and abroad, according to the characteristic of text mining, many classical clustering scheme applied to the text field, among them, the k-means algorithm proposed by Queen Mac provides an efficient random clustering, but the method of obtaining the center of mass in iteration makes the clustering result very vulnerable to outliers. And The DBSCAN algorithm proposed by Arlia Massimo and Domenica accurately describes the density of clustering objects, and excludes the interference of noise points, but its O() time complexity often makes it helpless in the face of massive data clustering task[2]. In this paper, we combine the advantages of these two clustering schemes, and use the concept of relative distance to effectively reduce the time complexity of the distance calculation[3]. At the same time, this paper introduces a heuristic rule, which greatly reduces the computation of the distance of the whole object. This algorithm can not only efficiently get the clustering result in a short time, but also can ensure the correctness of the conclusion. Under the conditions of meeting the user's requirements, minimizing the cost of distance computation and the effect of noise points[4].

2 Related Notion

2.1 Text distance calculation based on DWC structure

Structure for storing a document's word bag information. After completing the full text scanning, remove the duplicated words and get a "dictionary", which records the various words and numbers[5]. Referring to the dictionary, available for each document DWC structure [Doc:Word:Count] of the storage unit, the doc said document number, the word represents the number of a word in the dictionary, and the count said the number of times the term appears in the document. So a document can be seen as a collection of several DWC structures such as the above. Combined with the cosine similarity formula, the relative distance of the two documents can be easily obtained:

$$Directio\,(A,B) = CAiCBiCAj\ \ 2\times CBj\,2 \tag{1}$$

Max cluster radius R: If the cluster space as a sphere, which means that the user can accept the biggest difference between the same object is 2R.

Minimum number of clusters N: If a cluster has fewer than N objects, then ignore this clustering result, and this cluster core is labeled as "illegal cluster core".

2.2 Random cluster core heuristic rule

In the clustering process, a heuristic rule is used to simplify the whole clustering process:

Transitivity of adjacent properties, that is, for the same cluster core A, If B and C all are close neighbors with A, then B and C are also neighbors (i.e., In the case of not calculating the distance between B and C, the B and C fall into the same class), this clustering algorithm is very efficient, when the cost of computation of distance between objects is very heavy.

3 Clustering Algorithm Based on Random Cluster Core

3.1. Characteristics of K-means and DBSCAN clustering algorithms

Among the numerous clustering algorithms, K-MEANS and DBSCAN are commonly used. In the process of repeated iteration, K-MEANS is constantly assigned each point to the nearest neighbor cluster core, and then through the average position of all the objects in a cluster to update the location of the cluster core, and finally get the clustering results. After scanning the all of the distance between the objects, the DBSCAN method excludes the interference of outliers, starting from the density of clusters, the high density of objects cluster into a class[6].

3.2 Clustering algorithm based on random cluster core

The method used in this paper is based on the two classical algorithms, which can ensure the clustering results to meet the requirements, as far as possible to retain the advantages of these two classic algorithms:

1) Requires the user to specify the two input parameters:

a.Max cluster radius R.

b.Minimum number of clusters N.

By using the random cluster core heuristic rule, we can know that the distance between any two objects and another object in the R can be considered as a class of the three objects.

2) Accept the user's input data, select a certain object as the first cluster core of cluster:

Like K-means this object can be specified by the user, can also be randomly selected[7].

3) Then imitate the DBSCAN based on the cluster core density algorithm,all objects are scanned once,and if any one of the distance between the target and the cluster core in R, it can be argued that the objects belonging to this cluster.

4) After the scan is complete, the cluster core is checked once, if the number of objects larger than N, it is confirmed that the formation of new clusters, if less than N ,it will be labeled as "illegal".

5) Then select an object that has not been labeled as a new cluster core, and repeat step (2) -(4) to generate a new cluster. When all objects are attributed to a cluster or labeled as "illegal", the algorithm ends.

In addition, you need to consider a situation: when the new cluster core scan an object, and the distance between this object and the current cluster core is less than R, it is found that this object has been classified as a certain cluster[8]. At this point to the precise classification, the object is assigned to a more recent cluster core. This makes the clustering results more accurate, the entire algorithm pseudo-code is described as follows:

```
  Random Cluster Core Algorithm:
function randomCluster(List obj_list, int K,int R){
  While  There are no labeled objects {
     If  Random object not assigned{
          Generate new clusters and the object as the
                                          cluster core
         While  New objects are found at random and
                calculate the  distance to the cluster core.
              If  Within the distance K
                 If  The object has been assigned{
                      Assign the object to the nearest cluster
                 }else{
                      Assign the object to the current cluster
                      }
                }
             }
        }
}
```

Examples of iterative clustering results:

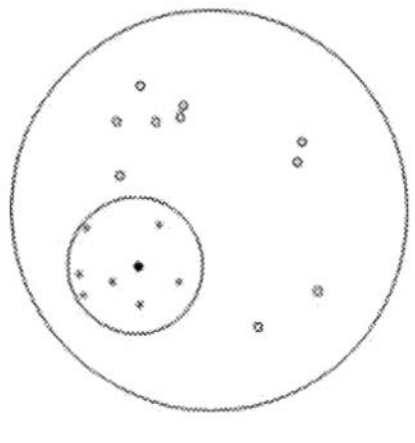

Figure 1. Clustering[A]

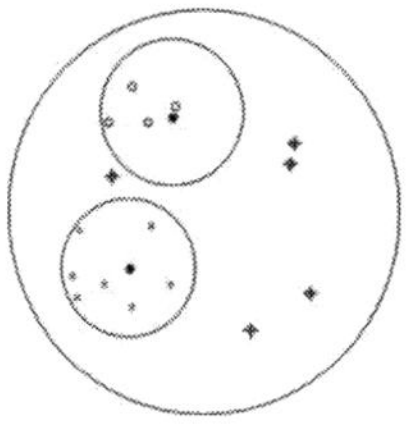

Figure 2. Clustering[B]

In the above two clustering figures, A figure shows the result of the once clustering iteration, and the B figure is the final clustering result. Clearly the object set is clustered into two classes, and the points outside the two classes are identified as "illegal cluster core" (N=3), which are not assigned to any of the classes. The clustering results meet two conditions: 1. the distance between any two objects in each class is less than 2R. 2. the number of objects in each class is not less than N.

4 Algorithm Analysis

4.1. Complexity analysis of algorithm

As mentioned above, the algorithm discussed in this paper has a certain randomness. So now the time complexity of the algorithm, in order to facilitate the description, the assumption that the computation space in a plane, all objects furthest distance of two objects as R'. The computation space can be described as $\pi R'^2$, in the first iteration, the range of the cluster core chosen is the whole computing space[9].

Before the first iteration, the space that the cluster core can be chosen is entire circular area: $\pi R'^2$. Assuming that the user specified radius of the class is R, after the completion of the first iteration, the second iteration can choose the range of the cluster center S is $\pi R'^2 - \pi R^2$, this reduces the problem area. The scope that the third iteration can choose have two cases:

1) The area of clusters formed in the previous two iterations is not overlap: $S_2 = \pi R'^2 - 2\pi R^2$ (2)

2) The overlap area of the previous two iterations is s':

$$S_2 = \pi R'^2 - 2\pi R^2 + s' \quad (3)$$

Based on the rule of selecting the cluster core, when the cluster core that the second iteration selected is on the edge of the first cluster, s' reached the maximum value: max $s' = 0.135\ \pi R'^2$. Comprehensive (2) (3) :

$$S_2 \le 1.135\ \pi R'^2 - 2\pi R^2 \quad (4)$$

3) As mentioned above, the conclusion can be drawn that each iteration can reduce the computation space by at least $0.32\ \pi R'^2$. In the iterative process of the algorithm, each iteration reduces the computation space. When the computation space is reduced to 0, the whole algorithm is over. Therefore, the number of iterations of the algorithm is up to $\pi R^2 / 0.32\ \pi R'^2$ times[10]. So from the above description, we can see that the complexity of the algorithm is related to the radius of the user's setting, the greater the radius of the user set, the less the number of iterations and the lower the complexity.

4.2. Advantages Compared to the Traditional Clustering Algorithm

As the same as K-means, the algorithm of this paper needs to set the random cluster core, and the clustering results are random[11]. But in K-means clustering, the clustering results are very easy to be disturbed by outliers. It lead to that K-means clustering to degree of standardization of data is very demanding[12]. The algorithm described in this paper is a good method to remove the outliers by the density characteristics of the cluster[13][14].

The same as the DBSCAN algorithm, the proposed algorithm is a kind of clustering algorithm based on density[15]. But on the performance of the proposed algorithm is better, because DBSCAN need to scan all the distance between two objects, which makes it a very large time cost of text clustering in the calculation of similarity. Text clustering algorithm based on random cluster core only calculate the distance from the object to the cluster core without calculating the similarity within the same cluster any two objects.

4.3. Agility of the algorithm

In addition, the clustering algorithm has the characteristics of agility, and the clustering results are not obtained after the whole algorithm is finished. Each cluster is produced one by one, so in the case of urgent need to get the clustering results may wish to get a part of the good class (these results are still reliable) for analysis.

4.4. Algorithm needs to be improved.

This algorithm also has some places to be improved, such as random cluster core selection may enable the clustering effect is not stable, the clustering radius R user can accept is difficult to grasp, all of these are need to be addressed in the following study.

5 Experimental Design And Evaluation

In this paper, the experimental data are taken from the Encyclopedia of Tourism's 35270 tourist attractions introduction. All the attractions of the tourist site and its attractions introduction are described as attractions entities, according to these entities set clustering experiment, to prove the point of view in this paper.

In the course of the experiment, more than 30000 tourism texts are divided into groups and do the clustering, first, use the Chinese Academy of Sciences of the open source algorithm on all the attractions of word segmentation to do the calculation of document similarity.

Clustering method is mainly used in this paper random cluster core algorithm, K-means algorithm and DBSCAN algorithm, and their execution time and the implementation of the results were analyzed and summarized. The execution time of the algorithm is used to evaluate the time efficiency, and the average distance from cluster core to each points is taken as the index to measure the accuracy of clustering after the completion of the cluster. In this paper, we introduce an effective clustering time index to evaluate the agility of the algorithm, and at the same time, we use the cosine angle to measure the distance between the text. Finally get the following results table:

Table 1. Comparison of Algorithms.

	execution time(hour)	average distance(cosine)	effective clustering time (hour)
Random cluster core	3.5	0.55432	1.4
K-MEANS	7.2	0.63221	7
DBSCAN	12	0.735	10

The experimental results show that these three kinds of clustering methods can achieve the classification of tourist attractions into the humanities, landscape, architecture, landscape and other clustering. The random cluster core algorithm is superior to the two classical algorithms in time efficiency, but in the clustering effect, random cluster algorithm has a lot to be improved. That is to say, the random cluster core clustering algorithm is a relatively fast, agile but rough clustering method.

According to the mentioned algorithm in time efficiency advantage. According to the mentioned algorithm in time efficiency advantage. Precise experiments under different number of test samples, samples were divided into 5000, 10000, 20000 document, measured their time, finally get the following coordinate figure:

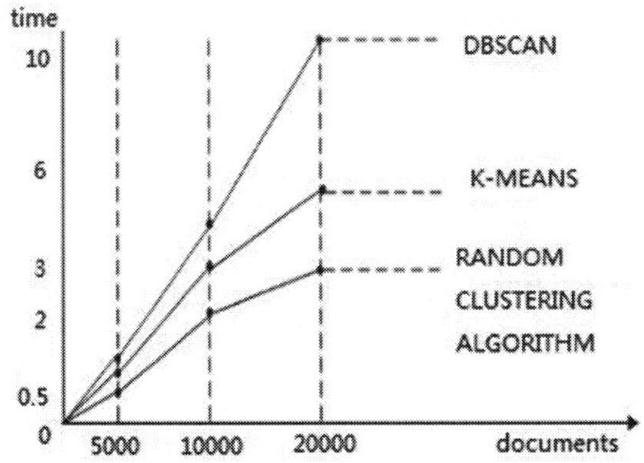

Figure 3. Sample Analysis Coordinate Chart

It can be seen that the time efficiency advantage of random cluster core algorithm is very obvious in the experiment of different number of documents. Of course, as with the K-means algorithm, random clustering algorithm also have the cluster core selection caused by unstable situation, the advantages of this algorithm compared with the traditional algorithm also needs to be defined in the future work.

6 Conclusion

This paper provides an effective solution for clustering tasks. In this paper, we analyze the two mature methods in clustering scheme: DBSCAN and K-means algorithm, and propose the improvement measures on the iterative scheme, and the outliers are discarded. From the experimental results, it is faster and more flexible. In the future research work, it is necessary to make further amendments to the clustering of the algorithm.

References

1. Guha S, Rastogi R, Shim K. CURE: An Efficient Clustering Algorithm for Large Databases[C] . Seattle: Proceedings of the ACM S IGMOD Conference, 1998. 73-84.
2. JA Hartigan, MA Wong. A k-means clustering algorithm, Applied statistics, 1979.
3. Pang-Ning Tan,Michael Steinbach ,Vipin Kumar. Data Mining:Introduction, 2005.
4. Jiawei Han,Micheline Kamber.Data Mining:Concepts and Techniques, 2006.
5. Gullo F, Domeniconi C, Tagarelli A. Enhancing single-objective projective clustering ensembles. Data Mining (ICDM), 2010 IEEE 10th International Conference on. IEEE, 2010, 833-838.
6. RONG Qiu-sheng, YAN Jun-biao, GUOGuo-qiang. Research and Implementation of Clustering Algorithm Based on DBSCAN. Computer Applications, 2004, 04.
7. YANG Li, ZUO Chun, WANG Yu-Guo. K-Nearest Neighbor Classification Based on Semantic Distance . Journal of Software, 2005, 12.
8. K Hattori, Y Torii. Effective algorithms for the nearest neighbor method in the clustering problem Pattern Recognition, 1993.
9. PAN Li-fang, YANG Bing-ru. Study on KNN arithmetic based on cluster. Computer Engineering and Des, 2009, 18.
10. MENG Yujian, MA Jianghong. An improved K algorithm for the initial cluster core. Statistics & Decision, 2014,12.
11. WANG Yongcheng. Chinese information processing technology and its foundation[M]. Shanghai: Shanghai Jiao Tong University press, 1990.
12. CHU Yue-zhong, XU Bo. Research on optimization of dynamic nearest neighbor clustering algorithm, Computer Engineering and Design, 2011, 05.
13. WANG Qiong. An Improved K-means Optimization Approach for Text Clustering. Computer and Modernization, 2015, 03.
14. R en Lifang. SPEEDING K-NN CLASSIFICATION METHOD BASED ON CLUSTE R ING. Computer Applications and Software, 2015, 10.
15. LI Shuangqing, MU Shengdi. Improved DBSCAN algorithm and its application. Computer Engineering and Applications, 2014, 50(8) :72-76.

Review on Application of Control Algorithms to Power Regulations of Reactor Cores

Gang LI [1,2,3,4,5], Xue-qian WANG[1,2,3,4,5,a], Bin LIANG[1,2,3,4,5], Xiu LI[1,2,3,4,5] and Rong-jian LIANG[1,2,3,4,5]

[1]*National Laboratory for Information Science and Technology, Tsinghua University, 100084 Beijing, China*
[2]*Graduate School at Shenzhen, Tsinghua University, 518055 Shenzhen, China*
[3]*Department of Automation, Tsinghua University, 100084 Beijing, China*
[4]*Shenzhen Key Lab of Space Robotic Technology and Telescience, 518055 Shenzhen, China*
[5]*Shenzhen Engineering Lab of Precision Geometry Measurement Technology, 518055 Shenzhen, China*
[a] Corresponding author: wychug@163.com

Abstract. This research is to solve the stability analysis issue of nonlinear pressurized water reactor cores. On the basis of modeling a nonlinear pressurized water reactor core using the lumped parameter method, its linearized model is achieved via the small perturbation linearization way. Linearized models of the nonlinear core at six power levels are selected as local models of this core. The T-S fuzzy idea for the core is exploited to construct the T-S fuzzy model of the nonlinear core based on the local models and the triangle membership function, which approximates the nonlinear core model within the entire range of power level. This fuzzy model as a bridge is to cater to the stability analysis of the nonlinear core after defining its stability. One stability theorem is deduced to define the nonlinear core is globally asymptotically stable in the global range of power level. Finally, the simulation work and stability analyses are separately completed. Numerical simulations show that the fuzzy model can substitute the nonlinear core model; stability analyses verify the nonlinear core is globally asymptotically stable in the global range of power level.

1 Introduction

Nuclear power plants (NPPs) have underwent the sixty-year development process of generating electricity since 1950s. Though nuclear accidents such as Three Mile Island, Chernobyl and Fukushima invoked society fears of NPPs in different extent, nuclear energy as a clear energy makes the nuclear power industry be able to obtain sustainable development guaranteeing that NPPs operate safely and effectively. In terms of the nuclear power planning [1], the four-generation technologies of NPPs will be applied in 2030s. Hence, developing technologies of NPPs is an inevitable trend.

Of NPP technologies, the power regulation technology of reactor cores is a key one. Improving power regulation technology of cores by the introduction of control algorithms is an important measure for safety and availability of NPPs. Over the decades, many control algorithms have been exploited and applied by researchers to core power regulations, which are the state- or output-feedback control with a state observer [2-17], the optimal control [18,19], the neural network or fuzzy intelligent control [20-25], the model predictive control [26-28], the H_∞ robust control [29-31], the sliding model control [32-35], the fractional order control [36-41] and other control algorithms [42-50].

In the paper, a review on these control algorithms for core power regulations is proposed. This review can contribute to understand the past research work with separate merits, and exploit novel research directions about core control schemes in the light of this work. Eventually, conclusions are drawn.

The remainder of this paper is organized as follows. The review on the state- or output-feedback control with a state observer of cores is presented in Section 2. Section 3 shows the review on the optimal control of cores. The review on the neural network or fuzzy intelligent control of cores is provided in Section 4. Section 5 shows the review on the model predictive control of cores. The review on the H_∞ robust control of cores is provided in Section 6. Section 7 shows the review on the sliding model control of cores. The review on the fractional order control of cores is provided in Section 8. Section 9 shows other control algorithms of cores. This paper ends with Section 10 of making conclusions and references separately.

2 Feedback Control with State Observer

Edwards et al. [2,3] proposed the state-feedback assisted classical control (SFAC) for regulating the power of reactor cores which retains a classical output-feedback control part and uses state-feedback to modify reference load signals so that desired reference inputs can be obtained. Simulations showed that SFAC is competent to perform power regulations. The flexibility idea, the multi-model modeling, and the state- or output-feedback control with full-state Kalman filters in which LQG, LQG/LTR, the robust or Ackermann pole placement method were applied were proposed by Li et al. [4-7] to design pressurized water reactor (PWR) core control systems for power regulations in the whole range of power level. Ben-Abdennour et al. [8] used the LQG/LTR control to contrive a PWR core robust control system in order to improve dynamics of the fuel temperature and coolant temperature during core power regulations. The improved PWR core power LQG/LTR control system was achieved by Arab-Alibeik et al. [9] based on SFAC, where there are an inner loop to regulate reference load signals and a outer loop to control model outputs. Dong et al. [10-14] presented a physically-based feedback control approach with observers such as a dissipative high gain filter to devise reactor core power-level control systems. A multi-model feedback control with a state observer was proposed by Wu et al. [15] to carry out power regulations of a PWR core. Sharma et al. [16] developed the state-feedback based controller to control the power of a large PWR core through the introduction of an output sampling technique and a LMI formulation. A state-feedback controller is contrived by Xia et al. [17] to obtain desired power distributions of a CANDU reactor core based on the linear quadratic regulator control.

3 Optimal Controls

Park et al. [18] proposed the control method including coarse and fine regulation stages under the optimal control theory framework in order to design a core power control system. The partial-state-feedback was adopted by Zhao et al. [19] into the optimal transfer control method so that a core power optimal control system was achieved with optimal dynamic performance.

4 Neural Networks or Fuzzy Intelligent Control

Ku et al. [20] devised the core coolant temperature control system using the diagonal recurrent neural network control which contains a neuro-controller and a neuro-identifier so that core power regulations can be achieved well. The core power neural network control system was presented by Khajavi et al. [21] in which a robust optimal self-tuning regulator response is utilized as a reference trajectory to determine the feedback, feedforward and observer gains of this neural network controller. Khorramabadi et al. [22] designed the emotional learning based intelligent controller for regulating the core power which includes a neuro-fuzzy system with power error and its derivative as inputs. The novel fuzzy intelligent control system for core power regulations was provided by Rojas-Ramírez et al. [23] tuning fuzzy system parameters through the use of a program based on a Lyapunov theory. Coban et al. [24] employed the multi-feedback layer neural network with a optimal process of using the particle swarm optimization to devise a core power control system. Simulations showed that the system has remarkable performance on the power level control for tracking step reference trajectories. The fuzzy intelligent control system to regulate the power of a reactor core was achieved by Coban et al. [25] exploiting genetic algorithms to optimize membership functions and weights.

5 Model predictive control

Etchepareborda et al. [26] applied a constrained output-feedback nonlinear receding horizon control to design a research core power controller with excellent performance for power regulation and known disturbances rejection. The robust model predictive control was utilized by Eliasi et al. [27] to devise a core power control system considering the limited input and output of this controlled core. Tai et al. [28] proposed the multi-model predictive control method to deal with the global power control issue for a PWR core within the whole range of power level.

6 H-infinity Robust Control

The H_∞ control was introduced by Suzuki et al. [29] to contrive a core power control system. Simulation results of the H_∞ control system were compared with that of the LQG control system, and comparisons showed the H_∞ control system has stronger robustness for stability and disturbances rejection. Chi et al. [30] adopted the H_∞ optimal control to control xenon oscillations in a core, and the designed H_∞ control system has desired stability robustness and performance robustness. Emara et al. [31] presented the combination of the H_∞ state-feedback control with LMI solution and the Schur model reduction approach to contrive a nonlinear reactor core power robust control system with satisfied dynamics.

7 Sliding model control

Shtessel [32] designed a sliding model control system for core power regulations so that robustness of the power control and tracking accuracy of the controlled power are enhanced. Simulation work showed that this system has good control performance. The combination of a sliding mode control method and a sliding mode observer was exploited by Ansarifar et al. [33] to devise a reactor core power control system, and stability analysis of this control system was also accomplished using the Lyapunov theory. Reddy et al. [34] contrived a PWR core spatial power control system by the use of the sliding mode control and a core state observer. The spatial power distribution control system of an advanced heavy water reactor core was achieved by Munje et al. [35] based on the sliding mode control.

8 Fractional Order Control

Linear reactor core models corresponding to five core power levels were solved and obtained by Das et al. [36] proposing innovative applications of the fractional order PID control with the genetic algorithm for optimizations of control parameters to these models, and simulations showed that this core power regulations can be carried out well. Saha et al. [37-39] devised a fractional order PID controller of the identification model and reduced order model for a CANDU type pressurized heavy water reactor with practical test data in order to regulate this reactor power. The combination of the fractional order PID control and the new neural network algorithm to optimize controller parameters was effectively exploited by Zhao et al. [40] to develop a PWR core power control system. Bhase et al. [41] contrived a fractional order PI power control system for a pressurized heavy water reactor using the locus algorithm considering stability boundaries and step-back condition.

9 Other control

Torabi et al. [42] researched the PWR core power control issue for large operating ranges using the quantitative feedback control theory, and study conclusions show robust control performance of such control approach. The feedback dissipation and backstepping, or the physically-based control approach was applied by Dong et al. [43-45] to study core power nonlinear control systems for a modular high temperature gas-cooled nuclear reactor or PWR core. Dasgupta et al. [46] accomplished stability analysis of a networked discrete PID control system of a large pressurized heavy water reactor with incomplete data and varying delay developing a switching system solution. The fuzzy-like PD control system for spatial power regulations of an advanced heavy water reactor was achieved by Londhe et al. [47] introducing a robust rule base. Banerjee et al. [48] contrived a reactor power PID robust control system through the adoption of an interval approach for shift of reactor parameters based on a model of pressurized heavy water reactor. Sun et al. [49] tackled the power control issue for movable operation conditions modeling a multivariable model of a supercritical water-cooled reactor and developing a decoupling control system of this model according to the feedback control with gain scheduling. The feedback linearization robust control system of a research reactor core was proposed by Eom et al. [50], which possesses the ability of observing states and limiting the core power change rate.

10 Discussions

Obviously, the design of control systems for regulating the reactor core power can be achieved applying control algorithms aforementioned to linearized or nonlinear core models at the full power or the core multi-model at varying operation conditions. Generally speaking, linear core power control systems possess desired control ability in the ±10%FP range of power level, whereas nonlinear or intelligent core power control systems have suitable control performance in larger ranges of power level; multi-model core power control systems show global control capability for nonlinear plants such as reactor cores.

11 Conclusions

Using nuclear energy to produce electricity will be an inevitable trend in the future. Continuous improvement for NPP technologies is required. Obviously, it is meaningful to research and develop high-performance control techniques for reactor cores. Great community efforts have been continuously made to propose advanced power control approaches of cores. The review on these core power control algorithms is necessary from the theoretical research or practical application level.

In this paper, this reviewing work is achieved, which involves the state- or output-feedback control with a state observer, the optimal control, the neural network or fuzzy intelligent control, the model predictive control, the H∞ robust control, the sliding model control, the fractional order control and other control algorithms. The review provides a new viewpoint to understand the past work with respective advantages and exploit novel research fields on core power control.

Acknowledgment

The authors would like to thank anonymous reviewers for their valuable comments. The work is funded by National High Technology Research and Development Program of China (863 Program) (No.2015AAXX46611, No.2015AAXX46201), China Postdoctoral Science Foundation (No.20159200078, No.2016T90102), Natural Science Foundation of Guangdong Province (No.2015A030313881) and Research Foundation of Shenzhen (JCYJ20140509172959962).

References

1. G. Li, X.Q. Wang, B. Liang, X. Li, B. Zhang, Y. Zou, Renew. Sustain. Energy Rev., 60, 116-128 (2016)
2. R.M. Edwards, *Robust optimal control of nuclear reactors* (Pennsylvania State University, 1991)
3. R.M. Edwards, K.Y. Lee, M.A. Schultz, Nucl. Technol., 92, 167-185 (1990)
4. G. Li, *Research on dynamic characteristics and control systems for pressurized water reactor cores* (Xi'an Jiaotong University, 2014)
5. G. Li, F.Y. Zhao, Prog. Nucl. Energy, 66, 80-89 (2013)
6. G. Li, F.Y. Zhao, Ann. Nucl. Energy, 56, 179-188 (2013)
7. G. Li, F.Y. Zhao, Ann. Nucl. Energy, 63, 696-710 (2014)
8. A. Ben-Abdennour, R.M. Edwards, K.Y. Lee, IEEE Trans. Nucl. Sci., 39, 2286-2294 (1992)
9. H. Arab-Alibeik, S. Setayeshi, IEEE Trans. Nucl. Sci., 50, 211-218 (2003)

10. Z. Dong, X.J. Huang, L.J. Zhang, Nucl. Eng. Des., 241, 4783-4793 (2011)
11. Z. Dong, Prog. Nucl. Energy, 68, 223-234 (2013)
12. Z. Dong, Prog. Nucl. Energy, 78, 216-230 (2015)
13. Z. Dong, IEEE Trans. Nucl. Sci., 58, 241-257 (2011)
14. Z. Dong, IEEE Trans. Nucl. Sci., 60, 1332-1345 (2013)
15. Y.Z. Wu, S.H. Chen, G. Li, F.Y. Zhao, Nucl. Power Eng., 34, 104-107 (2013)
16. G.L. Sharma, B. Bandyopadhyay, A.P. Tiwari, IEEE Trans. Nucl. Sci., 50, 1740-1751 (2003)
17. L.Z. Xia, J. Jiang, J.C. Luxat, Nucl. Eng. Des., 278, 323-332 (2014)
18. M.G. Park, N.Z. Cho, IEEE Trans. Nucl. Sci., 40, 266-270 (1993)
19. F. Zhao, K.C. Cheung, R.M.K. Yeung, Nucl. Eng. Des., 219, 247-252 (2002)
20. C.C. Ku, K.Y. Lee, R.M. Edwards, IEEE Trans. Nucl. Sci., 39, 2298-2308 (1992)
21. M.N. Khajavi, M.B. Menhaj, A.A. Suratgar, Ann. Nucl. Energy, 29, 751-760 (2002)
22. S.S. Khorramabadi, M. Boroushaki, C. Lucas, Ann. Nucl. Energy, 35, 2051-2058 (2008)
23. E. Rojas-Ramírez, J.S. Benítez-Read, A.S. Ríos, Ann. Nucl. Energy, 58, 238-245 (2013)
24. R. Coban, Ann. Nucl. Energy, 69, 260-266 (2014)
25. R. Coban, B. Can, Energy Convers. Manage., 51, 587-593 (2010)
26. A. Etchepareborda, J. Lolich, Nucl. Eng. Des., 237, 268-276 (2007)
27. H. Eliasi, M.B. Menhaj, H. Davilu, Prog. Nucl. Energy, 54, 177-185 (2012)
28. Y. Tai, S.X. Hou, C. Li, F.Y. Zhao, Nucl. Eng. Des., 240, 3582-3585 (2010)
29. K. Suzuki, J. Shimazaki, Y. Shinohara, Nucl. Sci. Eng., 115, 142-151 (1993)
30. S.G. Chi, N.Z. Cho, Nucl. Technol., 137, 127-138 (2002)
31. H.M. Emara, A.A. Hanafy, M.M.Z. Abdelaal, S. Elaraby, Nucl. Sci. Eng., 174, 87-95 (2013)
32. Y.B. Shtessel, IEEE Trans. Aerosp. Electron. Syst., 34, 579-589 (1998)
33. G.R. Ansarifar, H.R. Akhavan, Ann. Nucl. Energy, 75, 611-619 (2015)
34. G.D. Reddy, B. Bandyopadhyay, A.P. Tiwari, T. Fernando, *Proc. of 10th International Conference on Control, Automation, Robotics and Vision*, 2142-2147 (2008)
35. R.K. Munje, B.M. Patre, S.R. Shimjith, A.P. Tiwari, IEEE Trans. Nucl. Sci., 60, 3040-3050 (2013)
36. S. Das, I. Pan, S. Das, Energy Convers. Manage., 68, 200-218 (2013)
37. S. Saha, S. Das, R. Ghosh, B. Goswami, R. Balasubramanian, A.K. Chandra, S. Das, A. Gupta, IEEE Trans. Nucl. Sci., 57, 1602-1612 (2010)
38. S. Das, S. Das, A. Gupta, IEEE Trans Nucl. Sci., 58, 2431-2441 (2011)
39. S. Das, S. Mukherjee, S. Das, I. Pan, A. Gupta, Nucl. Eng. Des., 257, 109-127 (2013)
40. Y.X. Zhao, X. Du, G.L. Xia, Math. Probl. Eng., 1-13 (2014)
41. S.S. Bhase, B.M. Patre, Nucl. Eng. Des., 274, 20-29 (2014)
42. K. Torabi, O. Safarzadeh, A. Rahimi-Moghaddam, IEEE Trans. Nucl. Sci., 58, 258-266 (2011)
43. Z. Dong, J.T. Feng, X.J. Huang, L.J. Zhang, IEEE Trans. Nucl. Sci., 57, 1577-1588 (2010)
44. Z. Dong, IEEE Trans. Nucl. Sci., 59, 2531-2549 (2012)
45. Z. Dong, IEEE Trans. Nucl. Sci., 60, 3889-3898 (2013)
46. S. Dasgupta, A. Routh, S. Banerjee, K. Agilageswari, R. Balasubramanian, S.G. Bhandarkar, S. Chattopadhyay, M. Kumar, IEEE Trans. Nucl. Sci., 60, 3879-3888 (2013)
47. P.S. Londhe, B.M. Patre, A.P. Tiwari, Nucl. Eng. Des., 274, 77-89 (2014)
48. S. Banerjee, K. Halder, S. Dasgupta, S. Mukhopadhyay, K. Ghosh, A. Gupta, IEEE Trans. Nucl. Sci., 62, 281-292 (2015)
49. P.W. Sun, B.S. Wang, J.M. Zhang, G.H. Su, Ann. Nucl. Energy, 81, 6-17 (2015)
50. M. Eom, D.K. Chwa, D. Baang, IEEE Trans. Nucl. Sci., 62, 1301-1312 (2015)

DOI: 10.1051/itmconf/20160705003

An Improved Particle Swarm Optimization Algorithm and Its Application in the Community Division

Hao JIANG[1, a], Liu-Yi ZHANG [2, b]

School of Computer Science and Engineering, Southeast University, Nanjing, 211189, China
[a]email: hjiang@seu.edu.cn, [b]email:dtzly888@163.com

Abstract. With the deepening of the research on complex networks, the method of detecting and classifying social network is springing up. In this essay, the basic particle swarm algorithm is improved based on the GN algorithm. Modularity is taken as a measure of community division [1]. In view of the dynamic network community division, scrolling calculation method is put forward. Experiments show that using the improved particle swarm optimization algorithm can improve the accuracy of the community division and can also get higher value of the modularity in the dynamic community

Among the classic community division algorithms, GN algorithm and Newman algorithm are the most representative. The GN algorithm is to delete the highest weight of the network edge each time. It stops when each node is degenerated into a community. The GN algorithm is based on the greedy strategy. The advantage of this algorithm is the low space complexity, meanwhile, the defect of the algorithm lies in the fact that the termination of the community division is unknown when the result of division is uncertain. The Newman fast algorithm is improved based on the GN algorithm which has a good performance in the static network. However, social networks is interactive and dynamic as the relationship in the network changes over time. In order to solve the problems above, this essay refers to the concepts of modularity and designs the objective function based on particle swarm optimization algorithm. By using the penalty function method and other constraints strategy, the particles which do not meet the requirements will be timely eliminated. Through the mutation strategy and the optimization of convergence factor, the convergence of the algorithm is improved. This essay also adopts a scrolling calculation method to update the dynamic network of community structure.

1 An Improved Particle Swarm Optimization Algorithm

1.1 Description of particle swarm optimization

Particle swarm optimization algorithm is proposed by Kennedy and Eberhart in 1995[2]. This is a kind of evolutionary computation technique based on the swarm intelligence which is inspired by the behavior of the birds. This algorithm eventually converges to the global optimal particle through the cooperation between the particles. These particles adjust their speed and position in order to find the local optimal and global optimal particles. The process is described as follows. First of all, the value of each particle variable is assigned including the position vector and velocity vector of the searching space. Then the iterative calculation is started. The particles renew themselves through the two "extreme values" at each time of iterations. One "extreme value" is the optimal solution called pbest which is found by each particle itself and the other is found by the whole particles called gbest. Then, the particles update their speed and position vector according to the following formula.

$$\left.\begin{aligned} v_{id} &= wv_{id} + c_1 r_1(pbest - x_{id}) + c_2 r_2(gbest - x_{id}) \\ x_{id} &= x_{id} + v_{id} \end{aligned}\right\} \quad (1)$$

In formula (1), the learning factor c_1 and c_2 are the nonnegative constants, r_1 and r_2 are the random numbers in the interval (0,1), inertial factor w is often set no greater than 0.

The basic particle swarm optimization algorithm finds the best target by the cooperation between particles. However, it is easy to fall into the local optimum in the real problem. So we often need to make some improvements on it.

1.2 Improvements on particle swarm optimization

1.2.1 Optimization based on the parameter

In formula 1, the parameter which affects the search ability of the algorithm is the inertia weight w. The parameters which affect the convergence rate of the algorithm is the accelerate weights c_1 and c_2. How to set parameters has no unified standard which just depends on experiences. Reference [3] points out that the greater w is, the weaker the global search ability is and the smaller the w is and the stronger global search ability is. So we need to set up a proper inertia weight to balance the global search and local search ability. Meanwhile, the convergence speed of the PSO algorithm is determined by acceleration weight c_1 and c_2. This essay assigns the value to c_1 and c_2 respectively because this is advantageous for speeding the convergence. Formula is as follows:

$$\left.\begin{aligned} & w = a - e^{(-(iteration/IT_{\max})^{\wedge}0.2)}; \\ & c_1 = b - \Upsilon/(iteration/IT_{\max})^{\wedge}0.2 \\ & c_2 = b + \Upsilon/(iteration/IT_{\max})^{\wedge}0.2 \end{aligned}\right\} \quad (2)$$

In formula 2, the inertia weights c_1 and c_2 are becoming smaller as the time of iterations increases, $IT_{\max}$ is the largest time of iterations and $iteration$ is the current time of iterations, $iteration / IT_{\max}$ is in the interval (0, 1]. As the time of iterations increases, c_1 is reduced and c_2 is increased gradually. a, b and Υ are the constants which are set between 1 and 2.

1.2.2 Optimization based on particle diversity

As the iteration times are increased, the similarity between the particles will get higher in the PSO algorithm. If the optimal solution is unable to be further optimized, this algorithm is very easy to fall into the local optimum. For this kind of situation, the diversity of the particles should be optimized. This optimization is mainly revealed in two aspects. One is to take random variation for each particle variable. Each particle variable contains the increase or decrease of the community ID which is represented in 1 or -1. During the process that each particle finds the optimal solution, those two integer variables are taken complementary mutation. This will be further elaborated in the part of community division. The other aspect is to take the random search for the current global optimum, gbest. As the particles converge towards the global optimal particle eventually, if gbest is the local optimal particle, the algorithm can't search for another space. Reference [4] puts forward a formula which is described as follows:

$$\text{if } (rand() < c) \text{ then } x_{id} = random(l_d, u_d) \quad (3)$$

In formula (3), the value c is the noise factor which is set in the interval [0,1], $random(l_d,u_d)$ is a random number which is between l_d and u_d ,the value l_d and u_d are the part of position vector.

In this essay, combined with the conditions in social networks, the formula is designed as follows:

$$\text{if } (rand() < c) \text{ then } x_{id} = 1 - x_{id} \quad (4)$$

Using the formula 4, the value gbest is randomly chosen a bit inversion and assigned to the position vector after being calculated. Experiments prove that this kind of random mutation can maintain the diversity of particles.

2 Community division

2.1 Particle fitness function

In order to add the termination conditions, this essay makes reference to the concept of modularity. Assuming that the network is divided into k communities, a k*k matrix E= (e_{ij}) is defined. In this matrix, e_{ij} represents the proportion of the edges connect two community nodes i and j in all edges. The sum of the elements on the diagonal of the matrix Trace（E)= $\sum_i e_{ii}$ is defined. In this matrix, the sum of the elements in each row is $a_i = \sum_j e_{ij}$. It represents the proportion of the edges linked to the i th community of all edges. On this basis, the fitness function is:

$$Q = \sum_i (e_{ii} - a_i^2) = Trace(E) - \| e^2 \| \quad (5)$$

In formula 5, Q represents the proportion of the inside edges minus the expectations of the edges which connect both arbitrary sides. If the proportion of the edge inside is no greater than expected for any connection, Q = 0. The upper limit of Q is 1. The closer Q gets to the value 1, the more obvious the community structure is.

2.2 Particle coding

Reference [5] puts forward that each particle variable stores the ID number of the current community. Because the number of the divided community is unknown, the initialized ID number of the community is set randomly from 1 to the total number of the nodes. If the community division is reasonable, the convergence of the algorithm can be accelerated. So this essay proposes a new particle coding scheme. Each particle variable stores the current ID number of the community and the increase or decrease of the community ID. The increase or decrease of the community ID is represented by 1 and -1. -1 represents that the current community ID minus 1 and 1 represents that the current community ID plus 1. At each period of time, the modularity is decided by both of them. These two variables are coded into the coding chains. For an example, if there are eight nodes, each particle on the search space at each time is represented as follows:

87287425-11-11-111-1

In this coding chain, 87287425 is the distribution of the ID numbers in eight communities , 11-11-111-1is the increase or decrease of the community ID direction.

2.3 Penalty function strategy

During the community division, the decision variables are affected by various constraints such as community ID, modularity and so on. Under these constraints, if the algorithm runs beyond the scope of constraint a little bit, the optimal solution will not be reached. By using the penalty function strategy, the problem is transformed into no constraint problems.

2.3.1 Penalty function

In the community division, if the modularity does not meet the prescribed requirements, some isolated points are generated. Isolated points are dissimilar to the majority of the nodes and their appearance is as a result of improper community convergence direction. In this essay, isolated points are avoided by adjusting the penalty factor. The core idea is to increase the weight coefficient as the error between the modularity and the expected modularity is increased. When the error meets the maximum limit, the punishment will be infinite in order to timely eliminate those particles.

Its mathematical formula is as follows:

$$\left.\begin{aligned} &s=1000 \\ &\delta(X)=Q_0-Q \\ &f=s*\delta(X)=1000*(Q_0-Q) \end{aligned}\right\} \qquad (6)$$

In formula 6, Q_0 represents expected modularity, Q represents the actual modularity, s represents penalty factor of the isolated points.

2.3.2 Integer Penalty function

In the improved PSO algorithm, the projection of the random solution found by particles should be 1 or -1. If the increase or decrease of the community ID direction during the random solution is not 1 or -1, integer penalty function is designed in order to eliminate the particles which do not meet the requirements. The formula is as follows:

$$con = Kch*|(y+1)*(y-1))| \qquad (7)$$

In formula 7, con represents the integer penalty function, Kch represents integer penalty coefficient, $|(y+1)*(y-1))|$ represents the situation when y is not -1 or 1.

Taking the two custom penalty functions into consideration, the extended objective function is improved as follows:

$$F = Q + f + con \qquad (8)$$

In formula 8, F represents the extended target function, Q represents the current modularity, con represents integer penalty function, f represents the penalty function.

2.4 Mutation strategy

In the process of finding the optimal solutions, taking random mutations for the particles can enhance the search efficiency. This paper puts forward mutation strategy for the increase or decrease of the community ID. For example, the increase or decrease of the community ID is 1 1 1 1 -1 -1 -1 -1, this series of the integer number is -1 -1 -1 -1 1 1 1 1 after taking the bit-inversion mutation. In this paper, when taking the particle mutation is determined by fitness change rate delta. Fitness change rate is the rate of best position found by particles in the history and the mathematical expression is as follows:

$$Delta = \frac{F_{Pbest(t)} - F_{Pbest(t-M)}}{F_{Pbest(t)}} \quad (t>M) \qquad (9)$$

When the Delta is less than a certain threshold, the mutation strategy is taken. This strategy can save the cost of time and space because of the continuous iterations.

2.5 Scrolling calculation for the Dynamic community

Traditional community divisions are mostly applied in the static social network which is an analysis of the static network. However, the interaction among the members changes over time in real social networks. Static network is usually a snapshot of the social network but the structure of real social networks often changes and connection between the nodes is dynamic. The newest community structure can no longer achieved. For this kind of situation, this essay proposes a daily scrolling calculation which is applied to analyze the evolution of the network according to the separate community structure in the discrete time.

According to the current social network structure, the nodes in the community are monitored and current value of modularity is calculated. In **Fig.1**, operation 1 is monitoring current nodes && calculating current modularity and operation i is monitoring nodes && calculating modularity.

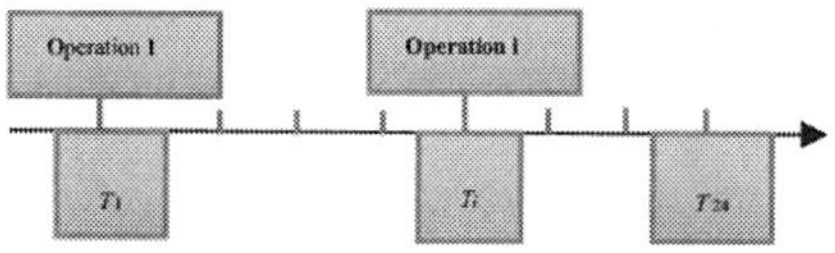

Fig.1 Scrolling Calculation For The Dynamic Community

Algorithm is described as follows:

Step 1 **(Initializing the community):** Traversing the network and assigning the community ID to each node. Coding the particle and initializing the population size m and the number of iterations (generally 3 to 4 times of population size).

Step 2 **(Finding the optimal solution):** Duplicating the particle's current location to the historical location and

 DOI: 10.1051/itmconf/20160705003

calculating the fitness degree of the current position. Finding the particles which have the highest fitness degree and making their position vector as the global optimal position.

Step 3 **(Iterative evolution):** In every update of the iteration, the particles update themselves according to the two "extreme values". One is the optimal solution that the particle finds by itself. The other is the global optimal position.

Step 4 **(The terminating conditions):** If the current number of iterations is no less than the maximum number of iterations which is set from the start or meets requirements of minimum error, the iteration is terminated. Otherwise, the algorithm goes into step (3) to continue the iteration.

3 Experiments and Result Analysis

In order to verify the effectiveness of the community division, this paper adopts two commonly used data sets including Zachary data set and arXiv data set. Zachary data set reflects the true relationship in a karate club. This network contains 34 nodes and 78 edges.

Zachary data set is a commonly used dataset in the community division, so the correctness of its community classification can be measured. This paper uses the following formula to measure the correctness:

$$\gamma = \frac{w_s - w_0}{w_s} \times 100\% \qquad (10)$$

In formula 10, w_s represents the number of nodes in the correct division, w_0 represents the total number of the nodes. This paper will make comparisons among the three algorithms below. Reference [6] mentioned that Fast - Newman algorithm is the quick Newman algorithm based on the modularity.

Table1. The Accuracy Compared with Three Algorithms

Algorithm	Accuracy	Q	Number of the divided community
Basic PSO	0.94	0.390	2
Fast-Newman	0.96	0.371	3
Improved PSO	0.97	0.470	2

As can be seen from the table1, the best result comes from the improved PSO. In its results, the correct divided nodes accounted for 97% and the value Q meets 0.47 closed to the maximum.

Then, we set Zachary data as the input data and run the algorithms. The tendency of the modularity is recorded in Fig.2.

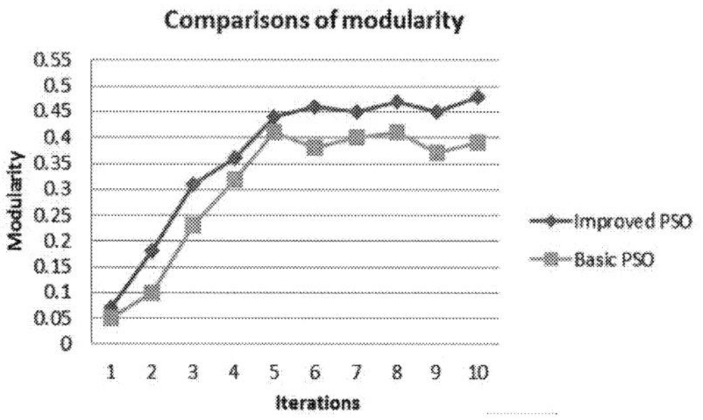

Fig.2 Comparisons of Modularity in the Static Community

As can be seen from the Fig.2, the value of modularity is increased during the iteration. The modularity is steady at the end of the iteration. The improved PSO this paper proposed has a higher value of the modularity at each time of iterations.

Zachary data set is a static community but the real community is dynamic. This paper uses the airXiv data set as the initial data set and adds the behavior of network changes in the community. We gather 24 time in a day and start the community division. The CNM algorithm is used as the comparison. Reference [7] mentions that CNM algorithm is developed based on Newman fast algorithm.

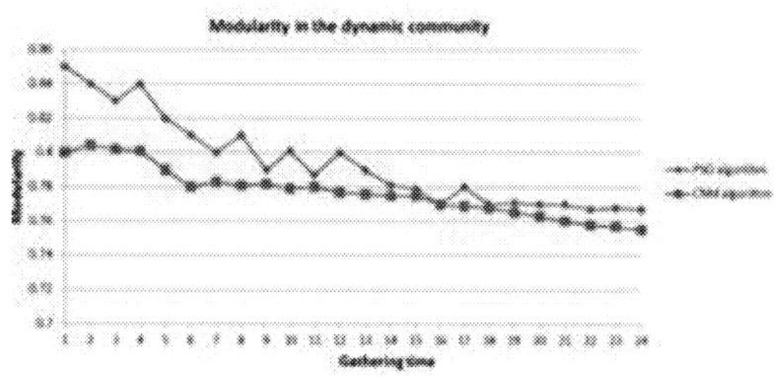

Fig.3 Comparisons of Modularity In The Dynamic Community

As the Fig.3 can be seen, this algorithm can obtain a better value of the modularity according to the latest community structure. When calculating modularity at each point of the time, the result of the improved PSO is higher than CNM algorithm does.

4. Conclusion and prospect

In this paper, the particle variables are designed and coded creatively on the basis of the basic particle swarm optimization algorithm and other community division algorithms. The fitness function of the particle swarm is established by referring to the concept of modularity. We also put forward the strategy of the penalty function to eliminate the particles which do not meet the requirements. Furthermore, we adopt the mutation strategy to improve the efficiency of the algorithm. In order to extend the scope of the application of this algorithm to the dynamic community, scrolling calculation method is put forward which is to monitor the nodes of the current network and calculate the value of the modularity. But due to the limitation of the theoretical level, there are still many aspects to be improved such as the simple particle fitness function and the value of the modularity can be calculated by every hour and so on.

Acknowledgement

This work was supported by Collaborative Innovation Center of Wireless Communications Technology and the National Natural Science Foundation of China (Grant No.6157060279) us

References

[1] M.E.J. Newman, Proceedings of the national academy of sciences,23, 8577-8582, (2006)
[2] J.Kennedy, Encyclopedia of machine learning. Springer US, 760-766,(2011)
[3] M.E.J. Newman, Physical review E, 69,6(2004)
[4] XF.Xie, WJ.Zhang, ZL.Yang, arXiv preprint cs,(2005)
[5] U.N.Raghavan,R.Albert, S.Kumara,Physical Review E,76,3,(2007)
[6] M.Tasgin, A.Herdagdelen, H.Bingol, arXiv preprint arXiv,(2007)
[7] K.Wakita, T.Tsurumi, Proceedings of the 16th international conference on World Wide Web. ACM, 1275-1276 ,(2007)
[8] K.Wakita, T.Tsurumi, Proceedings of the 16th international conference on World Wide Web. ACM, 1275-1276 ,(2007)

ITM Web of Conferences 7, 05004 (2016) DOI: 10.1051/itmconf/20160705004
ITA 2016

An Aerial Video Stabilization Method Based on SURF Feature

Hao WU [1] and Shao-Yang HE [1]

[1]*School of Information and Electronics, Beijing Institute of Technology*

Abstract: The video captured by Micro Aerial Vehicle is often degraded due to unexpected random trembling and jitter caused by wind and the shake of the aerial platform. An approach for stabilizing the aerial video based on SURF feature and Kalman filter is proposed. SURF feature points are extracted in each frame, and the feature points between adjacent frames are matched using Fast Library for Approximate Nearest Neighbors search method. Then Random Sampling Consensus matching algorithm and Least Squares Method are used to remove mismatching points pairs, and estimate the transformation between the adjacent images. Finally, Kalman filter is applied to smooth the motion parameters and separate Intentional Motion from Unwanted Motion to stabilize the aerial video. Experiments results show that the approach can stabilize aerial video efficiently with high accuracy, and it is robust to the translation, rotation and zooming motion of camera.

1 Introduction

Videos of specified target area can be acquired flexibly and efficiently by Micro Aerial Vehicle (MAV) which is wildly used in military and civilian fields. Because of its small size, lightweight and poor stability, MAV jitters easily because of wind blows and mechanical vibration, which results in the unstability of image sequence captured by MAV camera. This unstability of image sequence is harmful to the subsequent image processing. Therefore it's necessary to stabilize the image sequence in order to reduce the influence of random trembling of the image system on MAV. Compared to Mechanical Stabilization and Optical Stabilization, Electronic Stabilization has the advantage of high accuracy, low-power consumption, small volume and low-cost, and Electronic Stabilization has become the most important video stabilization technique.

Electronic Stabilization consists of two processes: Global Motion Estimation and Motion Compensation. Global motion estimation estimates the global motion vector between frames, and removes the interference of local motion at the same time. Motion compensation separates the intentional motion from random jitter in the global motion obtained by global motion estimation, acquires compensation vector, and moves the frame in the opposite direction of the compensation vector equivalently to obtain stabilized video.

Global motion estimation acquires transformation relation between frames by using gray information or feature points. The methods using gray information directly include Block Matching Algorithm[1], Bit Plane Algorithm[2] and Gray Projection Algorithm. These methods have the advantages of fast computation speed and accurate estimation for translation motion. But they are sensitive to illumination change, and could not estimate rotation and zooming motion. The methods based on feature points mainly use the results of feature points matching to obtain the transformation relation between frames, and the feature points generally include edge points, Harris corner points and SIFT feature points[3]. These methods have robustness, and can estimate motion parameters well. In these methods, the performance of SIFT algorithm is outstanding, and SURF algorithm which derives from SIFT is enhanced in the computation speed. Therefore, SURF algorithm is applicable for the real-time requirements of MAV video stabilization.

Motion compensation is mainly used to adjust the global motion parameters, and keep the intentional motion of camera. The motion compensation methods include mean filtering[4], curve fitting, Gaussian Mixture filtering[5] and Kalman filtering[6]. Kalman filtering which smooths the motion parameters by low-pass filtering the motion vectors is outstanding in video stabilization.

According to the advantages of SURF algorithm and Kalman filter, in this paper SURF is used to estimate the motion vector between frames, and Kalman filter is adopted to adjust the similar transformation array to estimate the intentional motion in order to stabilize video.

2 SURF Feature Extraction and Matching

SURF Feature is a rapid local feature points detection algorithm which is proposed by Bay based on SIFT feature[7]. SURF speeds up by using integral image and Boxlets filtering to approximate the Gauss-Laplace second-order differential response of image in order to simplify the process of different size convolution to several additions and subtractions. The contrast experiments which were done by Bauer indicated that the speed of SURF is enhanced three times compare to SIFT, and the key performances such as repeatability and resolving ability are equivalent[8].

SURF feature has rotational invariance by assigning main orientation for each feature point. First, select a certain number of sample points in the neighbourhood of the feature point, do statistic of their Harr wavelet filtering response components along x-axis and y-axis, named d_x and d_y, and map to a point (d_x, d_y) in response coordinates, as shown in Figure 1. Then, rotate the fan-shaped window whose opening angle is 60°around the origin with fixed step size as 15°. The accumulation of all the response values in the fan-shaped window is regarded as the centering direction response value of the window. Assign the max response value of all directions as the main orientation of the SURF feature point.

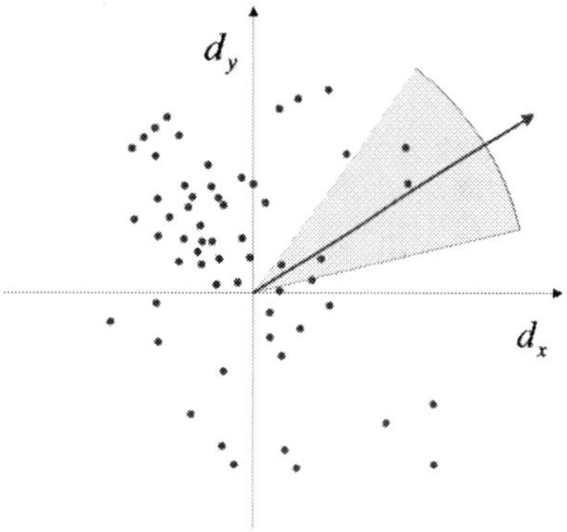

Figure 1.Orientation Assignment

SURF descriptor is constructed by doing statistics to the distribution of the sample points Haar wavelet effect. First, construct a 4×4 square mesh region in the neighbourhood of the feature point. Then, rotate the region to the main orientation. Next, select 5×5 sample points in each grid, and apply Haar wavelet filtering to every sample point to calculate their response d_x and d_y along x-axis and y-axis. As a result, a four-dimensional description vector is constructed in each grid, that is

$$v=(\sum d_x, \sum d_y, \sum |d_x|, \sum |d_y|) \quad (1)$$

Combine these 16 description vectors to a 64-dimensional SURF descriptor of the feature point, as shown in Figure 2.

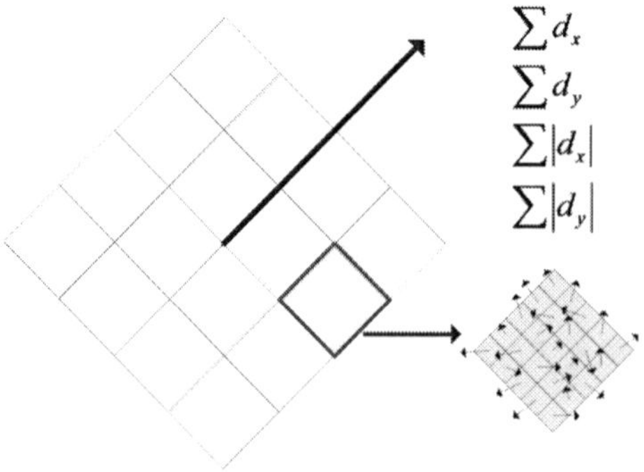

Figure 2.Build SURF Descriptor

3 Global Motion Estimation

According to the interframe feature points matching relations acquired by Fast Library for Approximate Nearest Neighbors searching algorithm, the following motion model is used to describe the translation, rotation and zooming motion of image sequence.

$$\begin{bmatrix} x_i \\ y_i \\ 1 \end{bmatrix} = M \begin{bmatrix} x_j \\ y_j \\ 1 \end{bmatrix} \quad (2)$$

$$M = \begin{bmatrix} s\cos\theta & -s\sin\theta & \Delta x \\ s\sin\theta & s\cos\theta & \Delta y \\ 0 & 0 & 1 \end{bmatrix} \quad (3)$$

Where (x_i,y_i) and (x_j,y_j) are the matching points coordinates of t_i and t_j frames, M is the similar transformation matrix, ($\triangle x$, $\triangle y$) is the translation motion vector between frames, θ is the rotation angle between frames, and s is the zoom coefficient of camera.

In the process of SURF feature point extraction and matching, some outliers are produced due to mismatching and local motion. If this original feature points set which contains outliers is used directly to estimate the translation, rotation and zooming motion parameters, the consequence is completely wrong or has greater error.

In order to eliminate the influence of these outliers, RANSAC (RANdom SAmple Consensus) algorithm is used to modify the matching points pairs set[9], and then Least Square Method is used to estimate model parameter. RANSAC uses minimum data set to estimate model parameter repeatedly for seeking the data set supported by most estimated model to obtain inlier set. The steps are as follows

Step 1 Sample n times repeatedly, randomly pick up two matching point pairs to form a sample set P each time, calculate similarity transformation matrix M, then calculate the error of matching points pair in complementary set Q based on M, select points whose error less than certain threshold t to form inlier set.

 DOI: 10.1051/itmconf/20160705004

Step 2 Select a inlier set which contains greatest number of matching points pairs as the modified matching points pairs set.

Step 3 Use Least Square Method to calculate similarity transformation matrix parameters based on the modified matching points pairs set.

This method eliminates the influence of mismatching and moving foregrounds by removing the outliers that do not meet the criteria, and obtains precise translation, rotation and zooming motion parameters.

4 Motion Compensation

According to the processing sequence of observations, Kalman filtering can be divided into Fixed Point Filtering, Fixed Delay Filtering and Recursive Filtering. Considering the calculation speed requirement, this paper adopts Recursive Filtering algorithm to modify the estimated global motion in order to remove random jitter and reserve the intentional motion.

Variable θ and s respectively describe the rotation and zooming motion of aerial camera. For most aerial video, the stability of θ and s is commonly influenced by Gaussian white noise. Therefore, the dynamic model is set as follows,

$$\theta^{k+1} = \theta^k + N(0,\sigma_\theta) \tag{4}$$

$$s^{k+1} = s^k + N(0,\sigma_s) \tag{5}$$

Where $N(0, \sigma_\theta)$ and $N(0, \sigma_s)$ are Gaussian white noise.

Variables $\triangle x$ and $\triangle y$ describe the translation motion of camera. For most aerial video, $\triangle x$ and $\triangle y$ reflect the intentional motion of the camera, and the variation of speed follows certain random distribution. Therefore, the dynamic model is as follows

$$\begin{bmatrix} \Delta x \\ v_x \end{bmatrix}^{k+1} = \begin{bmatrix} 1 & 1 \\ 0 & 1 \end{bmatrix} \begin{bmatrix} \Delta x \\ v_x \end{bmatrix}^k + \begin{bmatrix} 0 \\ N(0,\sigma_x) \end{bmatrix} \tag{6}$$

$$\begin{bmatrix} \Delta y \\ v_y \end{bmatrix}^{k+1} = \begin{bmatrix} 1 & 1 \\ 0 & 1 \end{bmatrix} \begin{bmatrix} \Delta y \\ v_y \end{bmatrix}^k + \begin{bmatrix} 0 \\ N(0,\sigma_y) \end{bmatrix} \tag{7}$$

Where vx is the variation of horizontal movement $\triangle$x, vy is the variation of vertical movement $\triangle$y, N(0,σx) and N(0,σy) are Gaussian white noise.

In conclusion, the Kalman state space model of camera is

$$\begin{bmatrix} \theta \\ s \\ \Delta x \\ v_x \\ \Delta y \\ v_y \end{bmatrix}^{k+1} = \begin{bmatrix} 1 & 0 & 0 & 0 & 0 & 0 \\ 0 & 1 & 0 & 0 & 0 & 0 \\ 0 & 0 & 1 & 1 & 0 & 0 \\ 0 & 0 & 0 & 1 & 0 & 0 \\ 0 & 0 & 0 & 0 & 1 & 1 \\ 0 & 0 & 0 & 0 & 0 & 1 \end{bmatrix} \begin{bmatrix} \theta \\ s \\ \Delta x \\ v_x \\ \Delta y \\ v_y \end{bmatrix}^{k} + \begin{bmatrix} N(0,\sigma_\theta) \\ N(0,\sigma_s) \\ 0 \\ N(0,\sigma_x) \\ 0 \\ N(0,\sigma_y) \end{bmatrix} \tag{8}$$

Where σθ, σs, σx and σy are mutually independent and decided by the smoothness of the camera intentional motion. The greater the variance of the observation noise, the greater the variability of state variables is, which results in the stronger the randomness of intentional motion and the less stability of the compensated image sequence. Otherwise, if the variance is 0, the state variable is immutable, and it can be compensated completely.

For the translation, rotation and zooming motion, the observation equation of state space is

$$\begin{bmatrix} \theta \\ s \\ \Delta x \\ \Delta y \end{bmatrix}^{k+1} = \begin{bmatrix} \theta \\ s \\ \Delta x \\ \Delta y \end{bmatrix}^{k} + \begin{bmatrix} N(0,\sigma_{obs,\theta}) \\ N(0,\sigma_{obs,s}) \\ N(0,\sigma_{obs,x}) \\ N(0,\sigma_{obs,y}) \end{bmatrix} \tag{9}$$

Where N(0, σobs,θ), N(0, σobs,s), N(0, σobs,x) and N(0, σ obs,y) are observation Gaussian white noise. σ obs, θ , σ obs,s, σ obs,x and σ obs,y are mutually independent, and describe the variability of the interframe unintentional motion. Their influences are opposite to the process noise, the greater the variance of the observation noise, the greater the unintentional movement variability is, and the more stable the compensated image is. Otherwise, if the variance is 0, the observation variable varies randomly, and the image is uncompensated completely.

5 Experiments and Analysis

To verify the accuracy and usefulness of the method which is proposed in this paper, we made a set of air-to-ground video whose resolution is 640×480.

Extract SURF feature points separately from the reference frame and the current frame, and get the matching relations between feature points by using FLANN searching algorithm, then eliminate outliers by RANSAC. The consequence is shown in Figure 3, which indicates SURF feature has better recognition capability, and can get satisfying matching results.

 DOI: 10.1051/itmconf/20160705004

Figure 3.SURF feature detection and matching

After getting the translation, rotation and zooming motion parameters of every frame relative to the reference frame, the parameters are smoothed by Kalman filter to separate the intentional motion and random jitter. Figure 4 and Figure 5 are the movement curves of horizontal motion and vertical motion after Kalman filtering, in which the dotted line is the original estimated parameters curve and solid line is the motion parameters curve after Kalman filtering. The experiment results show that the original data varied intensely, and the differences between frames are obvious. But the movement curves become smoother after Kalman filtering, and keep the original movement tendency, which indicates the stabilization performances are very good.

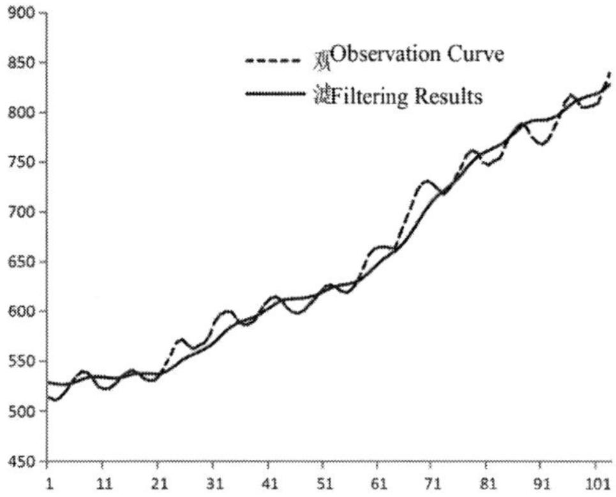

Figure 4. Measured Curve and Filtered Result for △x

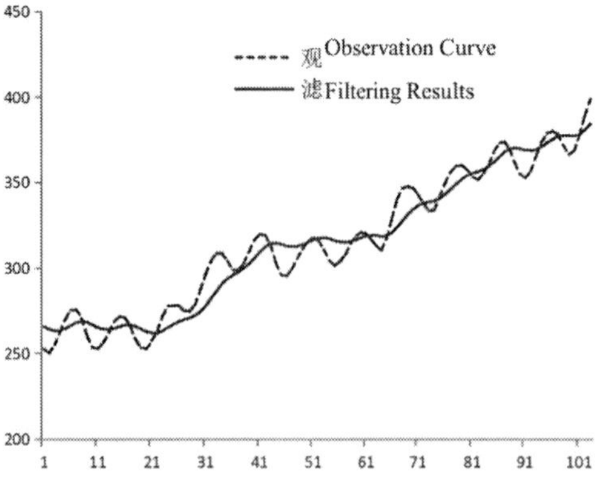

Figure 5. Measured Curve and Filtered Result For △y

Based on the consequences of Kalman filtering, transform the coordinate of each image in the video to acquire stabilized aerial video, as shown in Figure 6. For the sake of observing easily, select one frame in every five frames. The (a) to (d) are the original video frames, and the (e) to (h) are the stabilized video frames, from which we can see that the Horizontal and Vertical motions are all stabilized well.

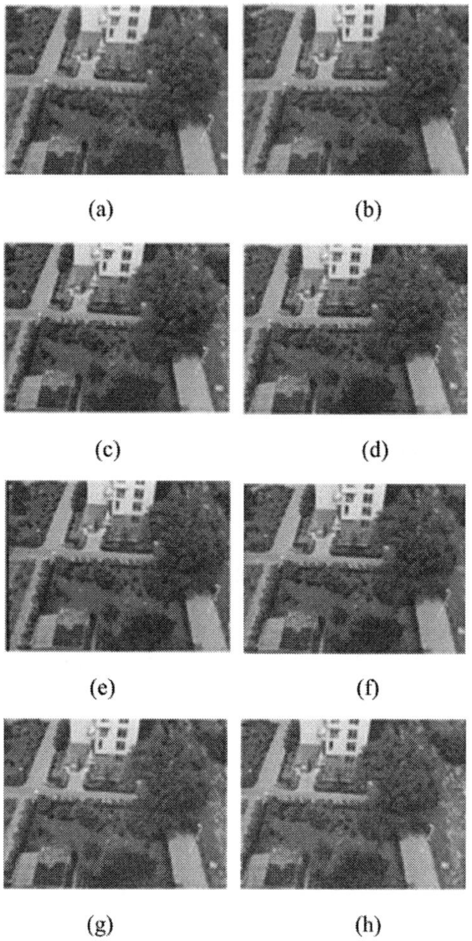

Figure 6. Experimental Results of Aerial Video Stabilization

6 Conclusion

According to the movement feature of the aerial camera on MAV, this paper proposed a method based on SURF feature and Kalman filter to acquire stabilized aerial video. SURF algorithm is used to extract and match feature points, then RANSAC and Least Square method are used to get the similar transformation matrix between frames, which can eliminate the influence of the mismatching points pair and local movements to acquire high-accuracy translation, rotation and zooming motion parameters. On this basis, Kalman filter is used to smooth the motion parameters, and separate the intentional motion and random jitter to stabilize the aerial video.

DOI: 10.1051/itmconf/20160705004

Experiments results show that the method has high calculation accuracy and can satisfy most requirements of aerial video stabilization.

The deficiency of this paper is that three-dimensional information of the scene is not considered, which lead to the limitations of motion model setting and computational accuracy. The follow-up work will be the intensive study of stabilization method based on three-dimensional information.

References

1. X. Li-dong, L. Xing-gang. Digital image stabilization based on circular block matching. IEEE Transactions on Consumer Electronics, **52**, 566(2006)
2. S. Ko, Sung-Hee, K. Lee. Digital image stabilizing algorithms based on bit-plane matching. IEEE Transactions on Consumer Electronics, **44**, 617 (1998)
3. D. G. Lowe. Distinctive Image Features from Scale-Invariant Keypoints. International Journal of Computer Vision, **60**, 91(2004)
4. Z. Yu-wen, W. Jun, J. Yun-de. A Feature Tracking Based Method for Image Stabilization. Transactions of Beijing Institute of Technology, **23**, 596(2003)
5. Z. Min, Z. Meng, J. Yun-de, Wang Jun. Image Stabilization Based on Adaptive Gaussian Mixture Model. Transactions of Beijing Institute of Technology, **24**, 897(2004)
6. S. Erturk. Image sequence stabilization based on Kalman filtering of frame positions. Electronics Letters, **37**, 1217(2001)
7. H. Bay, T. Tuytelaars, L. Van Gool. SURF: Speeded Up Robust Features. in Proc. of European Conference on Computer Vision, 404(2006)
8. J. Bauer, N. Sunderhauf, P. Protzel. Comparing several implementations of two recently published feature detectors. Proceedings of Proc. of the International Conference on Intelligent and Autonomous Systems(2007)
9. Y. Shen, P. Guturu, T. Damarla Buckles, B. Namuduri K. Video stabilization using principal component analysis and scale invariant feature transform in particle filter framework [J]. IEEE Transactions on Consumer Electronics, **55**, 1714(2009)

ITM Web of Conferences 7, 05005 (2016) DOI: 10.1051/itmconf/20160705005
ITA 2016

Research on Calculation Method of Semantic Correlation of Chinese Text

Yan-Fang Li[1] , Shu-Tao SUN[2], Shuang FENG[3] AND Qi WANG[4]

[1,, 2, 3, 4] *Communication University of China, Dingfuzhuang NO. 1, Chaoyang District, Beijing, China*

Abstract. The semantic correlation is a very important research direction in Natural Language Processing, and the semantic relatedness is different from the semantic similarity . At present, the semantic correlation algorithm, which is based on the similarity of the semantic meaning, and it can't achieve the desired results in a certain extent. In this paper, byusing the large-scale corpus and How Net words' concepts to dig out the hidden semantic relations between the words, finally, according to the semantic relations of the words in the text, the text correlation algorithm is proposed . Experimental results show that the use of How Net calculation of the text relevance which use less time than the use of large-scale corpus and Tongyici Cilin calculation of the text relevance, and in terms of accuracy of the calculation results also have to upgrade.

1 Introduction

With the popularity of the Internet, there are a variety of resources to grow in an explosive way every day, and their share of the degree is also getting higher and higher. The information is convenient for people's life, but how to deal with and use it, which is the top priority. According to reliable statistics, 70. 2% of the information is in the form of text, and how to present the specific field of text information to the user, which is the problem that needs to be solved currently.

At present the theory and technology of existing natural language processing are mostly in English as the research object, because English is hypotaxis (merplotactic) language and sentence structure requirements of word form which change in accordance with the rules, and pay attention to the syntactic level. But Chinese pronunciation, shape, word formation, word forms and semantic aspects are quite different, these significant differences let western the current relatively mature theory and technology can't be directly in Chinese information processing.

At present, there are two methods for calculation the words similarity, which are based on the semantic dictionary and statistical method. In this paper, the word similarity algorithm is improved to calculate the correlation of the words, and then calculate the correlation of the text.

2 Basic Knowledge

In this chapter, some preprocessing are required before calculating the correlation of the Chinese text. In this experiment, it is very important to calculate the correlation of the words, because this result can directly affect the calculation results of the correlation of the text. Therefore, the first step is to text segmentation, and then is the data pre processing. This chapter is the introduction of these technologies.

2.1 HowNet

How Netuse concepts to describe object, the concept isin Chinese and English. HowNetis the basic content of commonsense knowledge, which reveals the relationship between concepts and the concept of attribute [1]. It uses Knowledge Dictionary Mark-up Language KDML, which is a special knowledge dictionary. The word is expressed as a number of "concepts", the use of "concept" to describe the semantic meaning of the words [2]. So before calculation the correlation of the words, the first is to read glossary. dat, because the file stores the words and its concept. To "安慰"(comfort), there are three concepts, as follows:

安慰: V AtEase|安心

安慰: N emotion|情感, AtEase|安心

安慰: V soothe|安慰

There are comma in word's concept, and the function of the comma is used to separate word's concepts. The words is included in the HowNet which can be divided into the

DOI: 10.1051/itmconf/20160705005

content words and the function words. In this paper, when we use HowNet to calculate the semantic relatedness, we will always use the content words. And the HowNet primitive can be divided into the first primitive, other primitive, relational primitive, relational symbol primitive. In this paper, we mainly focus on the relationship between the words to compute the semantic relatedness of the words.

2. 2 Tongyici Cilin

In this experiment, the use of the dictionary is the Harbin Institute of Technology Information Retrieval Lab TongyiciCilin extended edition [3]. It is edited by Harbin Industrial University Information Retrieval Laboratory which use many words related resources, and put a lot of manpower and material resources to complete the Chinese words table. However, at present, the full version of the thesaurus does not share, only the dictionary file can be used, and the dictionary file records some of the words. Such as: computer Bo01A27=, computer Bo01A27=, microcomputer Bo01A27=, microcomputer Bo01A27=. The thesaurus dictionary mainly use a collection of some characters to represent the meaning of the words. If the meaning of the two words is the same, the two words will have a set of the same character set. If the words is an ambivalent word, there will be many groups of character set to represent the different meanings of the words.

2. 3 The Data Preprocessing

The first step is the data preprocessing when we calculate the correlation of the text. The data preprocessing includes word segmentation, feature extraction and de - stop word. The purpose of feature extraction is to reduce the dimension of data and remove noise. In this experiment, we use the feature extraction and that is TFIDF. TF-IDF(term frequency–inverse document frequency) is a commonly used weighting technique, which is mainly used for data mining and information retrieval. TF-IDF is a statistical method that uses to assess the importance of a word [4]. The importance of the words is proportional to the presentation times in the document, but it is inversely proportional to the frequency of the word in corpus. In this experiment, we need to use a large number of text sets to calculate the TFIDF of all words in a text, the formula of TFIDF is:

$$TFIDF_{i,j}=\frac{n_{i,j}}{\sum_k n_{k,j}}*\log\frac{|D|}{\{j:t_i\in d_i\}} \quad (1)$$

The $n_{i,j}$ expresses the number of times that a word appears in the text, the$\sum_k n_{k,i}$ expresses the total number of the words in the text, |D| expresses the total number of text in corpus. $\{j: t_i \in d_i\}$ expresses the number of text that appears in the text of a certain word. The formula shows the high frequency of the word in a particular file, and the low file frequency in the entire document collection, can produce a high weight of TF-IDF. Therefore, TF-IDF tends to filter out the common words and keep the important words.

The data preprocessing also includes word segmentation. in this experiment, the word segmentation method is ICTCLAS(Institute of Computing Technology, Chinese Lexical Analysis System) Chinese word segmentation system, and it is a Chinese word segmentation system which is developed by a number of researchers in the Institute of computing technology of the Chinese Academy of Sciences after years of research. Its main functions include Chinese word segmentation, part of speech tagging, microblogging word, word recognition, named entity recognition, keyword extraction. At the same time it also supports the user dictionary, support traditional Chinese, supports GB2312, GBK, UTF8 and other coding formats. ICTCLAS can be widely used, because it has a good segmentation effect, and the word segmentation accuracy is up to 98. 45%.

3The Calculation Method of Word Correlation Based On HowNet

Using HowNet calculates the correlation of the two words, mostly according to the relationship between the word similarity and word correlation. The semantic similarity of the words is that the words can be replaced by each other in different texts, which means the words' meaning is the same [5]. In this paper, we should compute word correlation, which is to calculate the word similarity and the semantic relationship according the relationship of the words, and then the two data are weighted average as the final result.

According to HowNet word, similarity calculation formula is as follows [6]:

$$sim(p_1,p_2)=\begin{cases}\frac{\delta}{(\delta+d)}, if(pos=1)\\ 1, if(pos\neq 1, p_1=p_2)\\ 0, if(pos\neq 1, p_1\neq p_2)\end{cases} \quad (2)$$

p_1 and p_2 represent the word concept, d represents the path length of p_1 and p_2 in the original hierarchy, δis a regulating parameter, pos represents the position of concept in the concept description, pos=1 represents the word concept is the first primitive. In HowNet the words' concepts are primarily divided into three types, respectively the first primitive, other primitive, the relational primitive and the relational symbol primitive as a type. In the calculation of the similarity of the words, the formula will get a lot of results, then make the maximum value as the final result. In this experiment, we mainly compute the correlation of the words based on HowNet concept relation, and table 1 is a summary of the symbol about the relational symbol primitives.

Table 1. Summary of the symbol.

Symbol	Defination
#	This symbol represents the related concept.
%	This symbol represents the overall concept.
$	This symbol represents the object.
*	This symbol represents the main body of action.
&	This symbol represents the host.
@	This symbol represents the time or place.
?	This symbol represents the material.

Symbol in Table 1 describes the symbol's meaning in relational symbol primitives. In this experiment, the researchers finds that there are eight relations in the word concepts, namely: universal correlation, Finished product - the whole-property of the host relationship, original meaning/ Finished goods/ host-first primitive, original meaning/ Finished goods/ host-dynamic role object, Agent-object-time/ place relationship, Agent/object/time-first primitive, Agent/object/time-dynamic role object, First primitive-dynamic role object. And universal correlation can be divided into eight kinds, namely: two words have the same related concept; a word's related concept is other word's first primitive; a word's related concept is other word's other primitive; a word's related concept is other word's overall concept; a word's r related concept is other word's dynamic role object; a word's related concept is other word's Finished goods; a word's related concept is other word's event semantics; a word's related concept is other word's host. According to these eight relationships, the weight of each relationship is r_i, and $\sum_{i=1}^{8} r_i = 1$, then the formula for calculating the correlation of the word is as follows:

$$asso(p_1, p_2) = \begin{cases} 1, if(p_1 = p_2) \\ 0, if(p_1 \neq p_2) \end{cases} \quad (3)$$

p_1 and p_2 represent the word concept, The calculation method for the correlation of Chinese words is as follows:

$$asso(s_1, s_2) = \sum_{i=1}^{8} r_i \times asso(p_1, p_2) \quad (4)$$

The higher the similarity of the two words, the higher they are related. So when we calculate the correlation degree of the words, we should also take into account the similarity of the words. According to the similarity of the words and the correlation of the words, the formula of calculating the correlation of the words is obtained, as follows:

$$Sim(s_1, s_2) = \alpha_1 \times sim(s_1, s_2) + \alpha_2 \times asso(s_1, s_2) \quad (5)$$

And $\alpha_1 + \alpha_2 = 1$, α_1 and α_2 is adjustable parameters, which are obtained by a lot of experiments and experience to assign. In this experiment, α_1 is 0. 4, and α_2 is 0. 6.

4The Calculation Method of Word Correlation Based On Cilin and Corpus

In this paper, we use the Cilin, which is mainly used to calculate the synonyms. In this chapter, the understanding of the relevance of words, that is, the probability of statistics of two words is in an article. Therefore, we need to crawl to get a large of texts, of course, as the text is marked by a specific area. For this experiment, the use of the corpus is a type of sports news text. However, in this experiment, we exclude the ambiguous words, when a word has a number of meanings, we will not calculate their synonyms which appearing in the text. But in this experiment, when a word has a number of synonyms, we calculate thesynonym which appearing in the text in corpus. Mainly because a word if there are a number of different meanings, on behalf of the different contexts in which the meaning will be different, so if you get rid of such words which can increase the accuracy of the calculation.

The calculation formula is as follows:

$$wordCount = AB/(A+B-AB) \quad (6)$$

According to the following figure, you can clearly understand that the use of corpus to calculate the relevance of words.

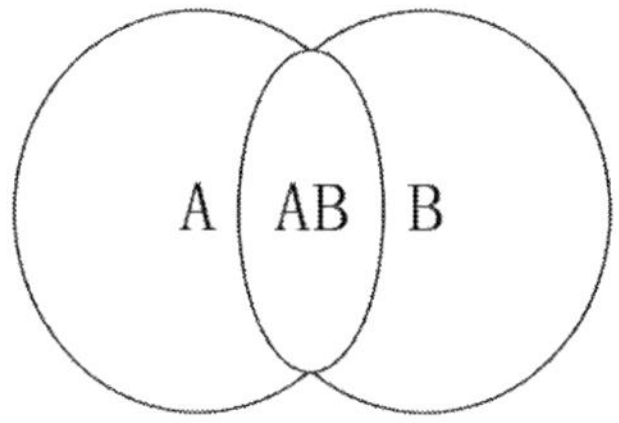

Figure 1. Algorithm principle of this chapter.

The AB represents the number of these two words and their synonyms appear at the same time in the text in corpus, A represents the number of A and its synonymsappear in corpus, and B represents the number of B and its synonyms appear in a corpus. But in statistical terms, the number of text, if the words or any of its synonyms has appeared once, don't repeat counting.

5 Method for Calculating Text Correlation Based On Word Correlation

Above the use of HowNet, Cilin and corpus compute the word correlation, and this chapter is according to the word correlation calculation the textual relevance. Because Chinese sentence pattern structure is complex and each person has different ways, and according to the relationship

DOI: 10.1051/itmconf/20160705005

between sentences to compute the text relevance which is very complex and that can be very difficult nowadays. In this experiment, we only calculate the relevance of the words in the text, and then calculate the correlation of the text.

After the data preprocessing, the remaining words of permutation and combination, calculate the correlation of each group of the words and the calculation results are stored in a matrix, which the rows of the matrix is the words of a text, and the columns is the words of other text. Then traverse the matrix, find the maximum value, and the value stores in an array, then remove all the values of the row and column of the value, and then continue to traverse until the matrix is empty. Finally, the maximum value is found by the statistics of the array. Then the weighted average of these values is obtained, and the result represents the correlation of the two texts, and the value is obtained by the relationship between the words of the two texts.

6 Comparison of Experimental Results

The purpose of this experiment that it is to use the method mentioned in this paper to calculate text correlation, then compare the two methods which has the high accuracy, and it also needs to consider the efficiency of running the program, such as the use of corpus, the time of reading the text. The figure 2 is the use of the two methods to calculate the results screenshot.

Figure 2. Algorithm Principle of This Chapter.

From the experimental result, it can be inferred, the result which is obtained by using of HowNet, which is often greater than the resultthat is obtained by using ofCilin and corpus. Textual relevance principle by using of HowNet mainly takes into account the relationship between the words' concepts, it weakness iswithout taking into account the context of the text, and some words have no relationship, but they are fixed collocation. The Cilin and corpus, whichare the relationship between the words and expressions, are found through extensive texts. So using HowNet, is according the word itself meaning to calculate text correlation, and the use of Cilin and corpus is through inductive statistical method to get the relationship between the words, and then calculate the text correlation. But if we use HowNet to calculate the text relevance, there will be a defect, such as: For the two meaning of the text is completely different, if the words of the two text is very similar, then it can get a high correlation between them.

Acknowledgement

The paper is supported by the National key Science & Technology Pillar Program of China (2015BAK05B03).

References

1. Dong Z, Dong Q. HowNet – a hybrid language and knowledge resource[C]. International Conference on Natural Language Processing and Knowledge Engineering, 2003. Proceedings. 2003:820-824.
2. Guan Y, Wang X L, Kong X Y, et al. Quantifying semantic similarity of Chinese words from HowNet[C]. International Conference on Machine Learning and Cybernetics, 2002. Proceedings. 2002 :234-239 vol. 1.
3. LLiang C, Shao Y, Zhao J. Construction of a Chinese Semantic Dictionary by Integrating Two Heterogeneous Dictionaries: TongYiCi Cilin and HowNet[C]. Ieee/wic/acm International Joint Conferences on Web Intelligence. IEEE Computer Society, 2013:203-207.
4. Zhang W, Yoshida T, Tang X. TFIDF, LSI and multi-word in information retrieval and text categorization[C]. IEEE International Conference on Systems. IEEE, 2008:108-113.
5. Li T, Yang X, Hong Q, et al. A hybrid method for syntactic and semantic structure disambiguation for Chinese[J]. 2001, 2:847-852 vol. 2.
6. Dai L, Liu B, Xia Y, et al. Measuring Semantic Similarity between Words Using HowNet[C]. International Conference on Computer Science and Information Technology. 2008:601-605.

The Random Walk Model Based on Bipartite Network

Man- Dun Zhang[1,2], Shun-Shun Chang[1,2], Jia-Wei Zhao[1,2] and Jian-Hong Ma[1,2]

[1]*School of computer science and engineering, Hebei University of Technology*

[2]*Hebei province key laboratory of big data calculation, China*

Corresponding Author: Jianhong Ma, majianhong@scse.hebut.edu.cn

E-mail: [a]zhangmandun@scse.hebut.edu.cn, [b]846176284@qq.com, [c]zhaoJwvsMike@outlook.com

Abstract. With the continuing development of the electronic commerce and growth of network information, there is a growing possibility for citizens to be confused by the information. Though the traditional technology of information retrieval have the ability to relieve the overload of information in some extent, it can not offer a targeted personality service based on user's interests and activities. In this context, the recommendation algorithm arose. In this paper, on the basis of conventional recommendation, we studied the scheme of random walk based on bipartite network and the application of it. We put forward a similarity measurement based on implicit feedback. In this method, a uneven character vector is imported(the weight of item in the system). We put forward a improved random walk pattern which make use of partial or incomplete neighbor information to create recommendation information. In the end, there is an experiment in the real data set, the recommendation accuracy and practicality are improved. We promise the reality of the result of the experiment

1. Introduction

Unlike the technology of information retrieval, the information filtering technology, in some extent, can alleviate the information overload, and the personalized recommendation technology is one of the most successful application of it. The core of a recommendation system is the recommendation algorithm. These algorithms or models have many functions: simulating users' behavior, predicting users' interests and recommending items that users may buy or interests in. In the existing recommendation algorithms, the collaborative filtering is the most widely used and effective algorithm. It can predict users' preference of a new product by their neighbors' historical behavior. Under normal circumstances, the collaborate filtering consists of three parts: 1.A measurement method calculating the similarity between user-user and product-product;2.Intergrating the similarity measurement method to create the recommended list.3.Getting the best performance patterns by adjusting the data trace.

Collaborative filtering is generally applied in recreational products like films and music. Yet when it comes to a system consists of products that can be bought repetitively, the collaborative filtering is not widely used. In addition, many existing recommendation algorithms are based on matrix of products' score grated by users. Generally speaking, these scores are classified obviously, and they represent the users' interest from lowest to highest level clearly by discrete values. However, the items generally transfer implicit motion data, so the expression of specifically fixed values is unreasonable..

2 Correlation Technique

2.1 Similarity

The key to recommendation algorithm is similarity technique. For example, the literature[1] proposed a similarity measure method based on information entropy. Literature[2] provided a method of clustering to find similar users in order to produce recommendations. They both achieved some effect. In general, in a recommendation system, there is a set consists of user u and products i, and some scores of products purchased by user u. The aim of recommendation system is to predict some other products' scores grated by users, and recommend the product set i users u might like. In the following part, we take cosine similarity as an example to introduce similarity algorithm. Cosine similar degree, also known as cosine similarity, is a assessment of

 DOI: 10.1051/itmconf/20160705006

similarity by calculation the angle between two cosine vectors.

$$\mathrm{sim}(i,j) = \frac{R_{*,i} \cdot R_{*,j}}{|R_{*,i}||R_{*,j}|} \quad (1)$$

In this formula, the vector R represents the item v's score matrix grated by user u. And is the expression of the line i score vector of R.

2.2 The model of random walk

The model of random walk originate from google'spagerank algorithm. This algorithm is firstly used to calculate the importance of web pages. The importance of web pages expressed in formula is as follows:

$$R^n = d \cdot P \cdot R^{n-1} + (1-d) \cdot U \quad (2)$$

3 The random walk model based on Bipartite network

In order to solve existing problems by using the method presented previously, we put forward a improved random walk model. In the algorithm this paper proposed, similarity is defined as the transition probability of bipartite network. The relationship between the items is simulated by the random walk model.

3.1 The first-order transition probability

Shopping data can be described as a node of a bipartite network: customer and product. In the network, every edge represents customer's purchase frequency of corresponding product. The user set can be described as U = , and the item set is described as V = . The customer's purchase frequency of products can be expressed as F={f(1,1),f(1,2),......f(u,v)}.

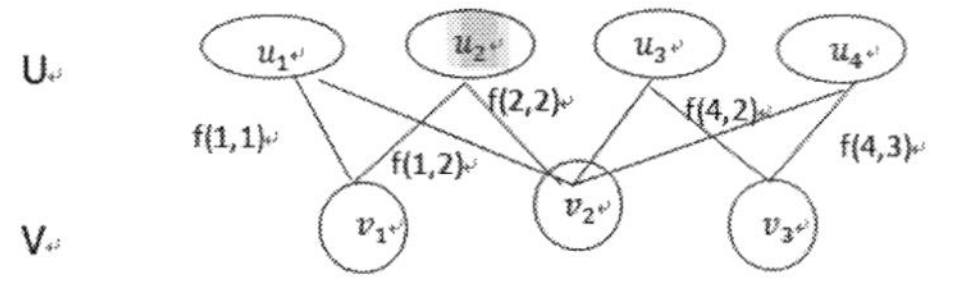

Figure 1. User-Item Bipartite Network

From the point of view of random walk, the conditional probability of under , P(|), can be expressed as the probability of random walk from to , and the formula of it is

$$P(v_j|v_i)=\sum_{k=1}^{|U|} P(v_j|u_k)\,P(u_k|v_i) \quad (3)$$

In this formula, the represents the probability of random walk from the product node to the user node . denotes the probability of random walk from the customer node to product node . P(|) refers to the sum of all the marginal probability. Generally speaking, P(|) is called the popularity of products among users who purchased .

Literature[1] regards P(|) as the first-order similarity between users and products. The definition of similarity based on the condition that users have bought both of the products. But the truth is two items can be similar even if they are not bought together. It is obvious when the data is sparse. And we will discuss it in the following research. In this paper, is estimated as the quotient between the time buy and purchase history. The formula is:

$$P(v_j|u_k)=\frac{f(u_k,v_j)}{(\sum f(u_k,*))^{\alpha_1}} \quad (4)$$

In the same way:

$$P(u_k|v_i)=\frac{f(u_k,v_i)}{(\sum f(*,v_i))^{\alpha_2}} \quad (5)$$

∈[0,1] are used to adjust the effects brought by data sparse and data redundancy

3.2 the random walk based on bipartite network

Now we apply the first-order similarity to the whole bipartite network, and we can infer that:

$$P^* = \sum_{n=1}^{\infty} \frac{(dP)^n}{|(dP)^n|} \quad (6)$$

In formula(6), P is calculated by the formula(4), d∈[0,1] is called damping coefficient. Obviously we can conclude that: when n tends to infinity, converges to .

P is directly got by the user's purchase behavior. In order to get the recommendation set R, we improved the model by adjusting and biasing. A heterogeneous personality vector called U is imported in every random walk model iteration. The formula is:

$$R = d \cdot P \cdot R + (1-d) \cdot U \quad (7)$$

In the formula(7), R represents the set of vital parameters in the recommendation order. When the item number is i, =1/m, m is called the purchase frequency of the users in figure 1. In other conditions,

Then we will do further calculation and derivation of formula(8). To reduce the response time, we import a fast approaching method:

Then we call the recommended item's major parameter. m denotes the product's purchase frequency in the purchase history. Compared with $\widehat{R}$, R improves the accuracy of the recommendation list, and we call this model the Random Walk model based on Bipartite Network(BNRW)

$$\widehat{R} = \sum R_i \quad (8)$$

$$R_i = d \cdot P \cdot R_i + (1-d) \cdot U_i \quad (9)$$

$$R = \frac{1-d}{1-d \cdot p} U = \frac{1-d}{1-d \cdot p} \sum \frac{U_i}{m} = \frac{1}{m} \sum R_i \quad (10)$$

4. Experiment

4.1 Judgement Criteria

With the development of the recommendation system, there are many judgement criteria of recommendation precision. There are three other judgements in the field of information retrieval and personality recommendation: precision, recall and F-measure. In this paper, we use the method of literature(3) called Weighted Hit Rates as the judgement. The formula is:

$$\text{wHR} = \frac{\sum_i (1-p(x_i)) * HIT(x_i)}{\sum_i (1-p(x_i))} \quad (11)$$

represents item i, p() denotes prior probability. When it is hit , HIT()=1 and on the contrary HIT()=0.

4.2 Data Set

In this paper, all the data comes from the purchase history of a market in China, and it can be described as follows:

Table 1 data set description

	customer	product	behavior
training set	88000	846321	78625165
testing set	12000	45789	236548

4.3 Result

We regard every customer as a single carrier, so the purchase frequency is a vital property

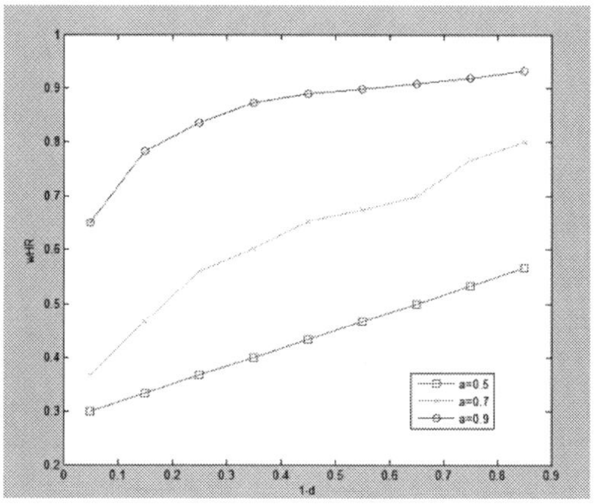

Figure 2 parameter analysis

Now we find appropriate by continuing fitting data.

In figure 2, the x coordinate denotes 1-d, and y ordinate represents hit rate(wHR). The three lines represents the results of respectively. We can infer from the figure 2 that when, the result of the experiment reaches a peak. Then there's a compare between the conventional algorithms of cosine, content-base CF and project-based. And the result is in the following figure:

Table 2 compare of data set between algorithms of BNRW

	Precision	Recall	Fmeasure	wHR
BNRW	0.6573	0.5864	0.5168	0.7653
CBCF	0.5372	0.5126	0.5053	0.6010
PBCF	0.5139	0.4986	0.5042	0.5886
Cosine	0.4568	0.4856	0.4986	0.6046

In the figure 3 below, there is the wHr distribution situation of part of users:

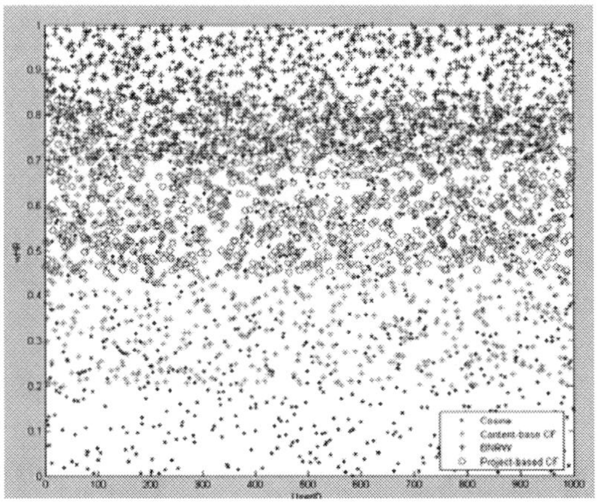

Figure 3 Whr distribution figure of part of users

5.Conclusions

This paper put forward an improved random walk model based on bipartite network. The item's weight in system is imported, with the parameter, we can find the area close to user and create the recommendation. The experiment traced the data in a real data set, compared the difference between other two algorithms, the hit race improved obviously. However, the recommendation algorithm is always easy to learn and hard to master, and our future goal is to make recommendation results perform better in diversity and precision.

References

1. XiaPeiyong, Ding Xiangqian, Research on Collaborative Filtering Algorithm of Personalized Recommendation Technology[d], Ocean University of China, 2011.
2. Jin Di, Yang Bo, Liu Jie, Liu Dayou, He Dongxiao. Ant Colony Optimization Based on Random Walk for Community Detection in Complex Networks[J]. Journal of Software. 2012
3. Malcolm Benjamin Dias, Jan Jarman, Grocery shopping recommendations based on basket-sensitive random walk,2016.4.
4. He Jianjun, Li Renfa. Modified nodes ranking methods using random walk model. Computer Engineering and Applications,2011,47(12):87-89
5. Guo Lei, Ma jun, Chen Zhumin, Jiang Haoran. Incorporating Item Relations for Social Recommendation[J]. 2014, 37(1):219-226.
6. Ma H, King I,L Yum, Learning to recommend with social trust ensemble//Proceeding of the 32nd Internationnal ACM SIGIR Conference on Reserch and Develoment in Information Retrieval.Boston,USA,2009:203-210
7. Xiang Liang. Recommendation in Practice. Beijing: Postd & Telecom Press,2012(in Chinese).
8. Gleiser PM, Danon L. Community structure in jazz. Advances in Complex Systems, 2003,6(4):565 573. [doi: 10.1142/ S0219525 903001067].
9. Zachary WW. An information flow model for conflict and fission in small groups. Journal of Anthropological Research, 1977, 33(4):452 473.
10. Fortunato S, Barthélemy M. Resolution limit in community detection. Proceedings of National Academy of Science, 2007,104(1): 36 41. [doi: 10.1073/pnas.0605965104]
11. Chen Dengke. Hybrid Lantent Vector Model-and Item-based Collaborative Filtering Recommendation[D], Zhejiang University.2010
12. Chen T,TangL, Combining factorization model and additive forest for collaborative followee recommendation[J].KDD CUP,2012 hed)

ITM Web of Conferences 7, 05007 (2016) DOI: 10.1051/itmconf/20160705007
ITA 2016

An Overlapping Communities Detection Algorithm via Maxing Modularity in Opportunistic Networks

Zhi-Peng GAO[1],Jing-Jing ZHANG[1,a] and Kun NIU[2]

[1]*State Key Laboratory of Networking and Switching Technology, Beijing University of Posts and Telecommunications, Beijing, China*
[2]*School of Software Engineering, Beijing University of Posts and Telecommunications, Beijing, China*

[a] Corresponding author: jingjing_zhang1992@163.com

Abstract. Community detection in opportunistic networks has been a significant and hot issue, which is used to understand characteristics of networks through analyzing structure of it. Community is used to represent a group of nodes in a network where nodes inside the community have more internal connections than external connections. However, most of the existing community detection algorithms focus on binary networks or disjoint community detection. In this paper, we propose a novel algorithm via maxing modularity of communities (MMC)to find overlapping community structure in opportunistic networks. It utilizes contact history of nodes to calculate the relation intensity between nodes. It finds nodes with high relation intensity as the initial community and extend the community with nodes of higher belong degree. The algorithm achieves a rapid and efficient overlapping community detection method by maxing the modularity of community continuously. The experiments prove that MMC is effective for uncovering overlapping communities and it achieves better performance than COPRA and Conductance.

1 Introduction

Opportunistic networks[1] are special networks in which nodes contact each other opportunistically to forward information. Due to unpredictable node mobility and without any fixed infrastructures, there is not an end-to-end path in most situations. Different from the store-and-forward manner in traditional networks, information are forwarded in a store-carry-and-forward manner, so applications need to tolerant long period of time delay in opportunistic networks. For example, people can use portable intelligent devices with short-range wireless communication capability (e.g. Bluetooth, WiFi) or some computing power to store and forward information, it can forward information more conveniently and easily without network infrastructure.

Community detection in opportunistic networks has become a significant and hot issue, which is used to understand characteristics of network through analyzing structure of it. Community is used to represent a group of nodes in opportunistic networks where internal connections of nodes inside the community are denser than external connections. Community detection can help us to uncover and understand local community structure in both offline mobile trace analysis and online applications, and it is helpful in decreasing forwarding time as well as the storage capacity of nodes. Since the relationships between nodes usually seem to be stable and less volatile than node mobility, forwarding schemes based on community [2-6]outperform traditional approaches [7, 8]. Overlapping community detection, one of the most interesting research of community detection, is the primary focus of this paper. Overlapping community means that a node may participate in more than one community in the network. Furthermore, most of real-world networks exhibit the feature of overlapping communities, such as social networks, information networks and biological networks. For example, we divide communities according to people's interests. A man may belong to multiple communities. People who like sports may have interests in music and others may still have interests in cooking.

The rest of this paper is organized as follows. Section 2 introduces related work in community detection. Section 3 presents our community detection algorithm for opportunistic networks. Then, we evaluates the performance of our proposed algorithms with COPRA and Conductancein Section 4. Section 5 concludes the paper and states the future of the field.

2 Related Work

Several community detection algorithms have been proposed for opportunistic networks. In this section, we divide the community detection algorithms into three categories: modularity-based, label propagation-based and attribute-based.

In modularity-based detection algorithms, early scheme is GN algorithm [9].Girvan and Newman proposed edge betweenness which means the number of shortest paths in which the given edge is included. In this method, the edges with high edge betweenness score will be removed in every step. However, the method needs to recalculate the score of edge betweenness for all edges every time after each removements. It is computationally intensive and suffers with scalability problem. Additionally, Newman et al. [10] proposed a bottom-up hierarchical approach that optimizes the modularity score in a greedy manner. Initially, every node is a community. Communities are merged iteratively based on optimal modularity score until there is no increasement in modularity score. In [4], Pan Hui et al. proposed a detection algorithm based on cliques and modularity. In addition, CPM is proposed in [11], which is based on the assumption that a community consists of all k-cliques that can be reached from each other through a series of adjacent k-cliques. A k-clique is a fully connected subgraph and two k-cliques are said to be adjacent if they share k-1 nodes. However, it doesn't consider all the characteristics of links, such as connection time or connection frequency. The value of k is also hard to be determined and the method is more suitable for networks with dense connected parts.

In label propagation-based detection algorithms, the typical algorithm is the Label Propagation Algorithm (LPA) [12], researchers present an algorithm that assigns k labels to each node in the network and updates its label according to the most frequent label in its neighborhood. This method is faster than others but produces different results each time based on initial configuration. So one need to run the algorithm several times to build the consensus. It consumes time. SLPA[13] is an extension of LPA, in this method each node has a memory and considers information that has been observed in the past to make current decision. COPRA[14] can achieve good performance in some cases, but it limits the number of communities for each node which decreases the accuracy whenever*v*is too big or too small. In[15] , authors propose a balanced multi-label propagation algorithm(BMLPA) for overlapping community detection. Compared to COPRA, the advantage of the strategy is that it allows nodes to belong to any number of communities without a global limit*v*.

In [16], researchers present an Interest Community Routing(ICR) algorithm which is founded on social network theory. Authors define an interest metric and a message header to represent individual interests and data types in the networks. By comparing the similarity between the message header and the interest metric of node, the node will be put into corresponding interest community. However, the interest is not stable and one may have many kinds of interests in reality, so it's not applicable.

These methods only detect disjoint communities, or are applied in networks where nodes are in frequent contacts, or need to run many times to achieve stable status. Those are not sufficient to process opportunistic networks with overlapping communities effectively.

In this paper, we first calculate relation intensity between nodes in opportunistic networks, it can solve the problem which community structure is fuzzy in binary networks. In binary networks, multiple contacts and single contact are considered the same as having contacts. We consider nodes with higher relation intensity as initial community. Finally, we extend the community with nodes of higher belong degree so that the modularity of community can be increased continuously while solve the problem of overlapped community detection.

3 MMC Algorithm

We aggregate node mobility traces into weighted contact graphs. The vertices of the graphs are nodes, the edges are relationships, and the weight of edge is computed based on the times of contacts and the duration of each contact between two nodes. Like social networks, the more often they contact, the more familiar they are. And the more time they spend together, the closer they are. For simplicity, we use $G=(V,E)$ to represent weighted contact graphs, where V is the set of nodes and $E\{(v,w)\}$ is the set of edges. We use the adjacency matrix A to represent the edge in E and A_{vw} to denote the weight of the edge between two nodes $v,w\in V$.

3.1 Definitions

3.1.1 Relation Intensity

In order to help us present the contact information between two nodes and make it easier for further processing, we simplify the presentation of contact record in[19]. We use a three tuples $g_v^s=\{id,t_s,t_e\}$ to simply represent a contact between two nodes in opportunistic networks. g_v^s is the *sth* contact record of node*v*, *id* is the node which *v* have contact with, t_s represents the time that contact starts and t_e represents the time that contact ends. Thus, node *v* can get n contact records after a short time which we can show like $G_v=\{g_v^1,g_v^2,g_v^3,\dots,g_v^n\}$,where G_v is the contact history of node *v*. So we can get the following equations to calculate the relation intensity between node *v* and any other node *w*.

$$fre_v^w=\frac{|G_v^w|}{|G_v|} \tag{1}$$

$$int_v^w=\frac{\sum_{g_v^s\in G_v^w}(t_e-t_s)}{\sum_{g_v^s\in G_v}(t_e-t_s)} \tag{2}$$

Where $G_v^w = \{g \mid g_v^s \in G_v, id = w\}$. fre_v^w is the contact frequency, int_v^w is the fraction of time that node v spend with node w over the time that node v spend with all nodes.

The relation intensity between node v and node w is shown in Eqs(3):

$$A_{vw} = \left[\left(\alpha fre_v^w \right)^2 + \left(\beta int_v^w \right)^2 \right]^{\frac{1}{2}} \tag{3}$$

$$s.t.\alpha \in [0,1], \beta \in [0,1], \alpha + \beta \le 1$$

Where α and β are the weighting factors. Values of α and β as the case may be can be changed considering the proportion between the number of contacts and the duration of each contact.

3.1.2 Modularity

In this paper, we use Newman's weighted modularity proposed in [4] as a measurement of the quality of the community structure it detects. One can get the corresponding fitness value with the following definition of modularity (Q):

$$Q = \sum_{vw} \left[\frac{A_{vw}}{2m} - \frac{k_v k_w}{(2m)^2} \right] \delta(c_v, c_w) \tag{4}$$

$$m = \frac{1}{2} \sum_{vw} A_{vw} \tag{5}$$

$$\delta(c_v, c_w) = \begin{cases} 1, c_v = c_w \\ 0, c_v \ne c_w \end{cases} \tag{6}$$

where A_{vw} is the relation intensity between node v and w, if such an edge exist, and 0 otherwise; k_v is the degree of v defined as the total weight of edges connected with v, thus $k_v = \sum_v A_{vw}$; m is the sum weight of all edges in the network; and c_v denotes the community which node v belong to. The network community structure is represented by $C = \{C_1, C_2, C_3, \ldots\}$, where $C_v \in C$ .We do not require $C_v \cap C_w = \varnothing$, as we detect overlapping community here.

From the formula (4), Q is defined as this fraction minus the fraction of the edges that would be expected to fall within the communities if the edges were assigned randomly while we keep the degrees of the vertices unchanged. Generally, if Q is greater, community structure is clearer; on the contrary, if Q is smaller, community structure is more ambiguous.

3.1.3 Belonging Degree

During the detection of community structure, the belonging degree proposed in [17] between a node v and a community C is defined as:

$$B(v, C) = \frac{\sum_{w \in C} A_{vw}}{k_v} \tag{7}$$

If all neighbors of a node v are included in community C, $B(v, C) = 1$.

3.2 The Community Detection Algorithm

Our detection algorithm works as follows:

Step 1: After a period of warm time t, each node begin to calculate the relation intensity between itself and other nodes according to the contact history. We get a weighted contact graph.

Step 2: Sort edges of contact graph by size. Then choose two nodes with highest relation intensity as a new community C and calculate its modularity according to Eqs.(4).

Step 3: Expand C, put neighbors of nodes in C into N_C and sort them by belonging degree. Choose the node with the highest degree to C' to form a new community C', calculate Q of C'. Then there are two situations need to be handled:

If Q increases, repeat from Step 3 and the expanding process is continued for community C';

Otherwise, the expanding process of C is finished. Meanwhile, the edges within community C are removed from the edge set E.

Step 4: Repeat from Step 2 to Step 3 until E is empty. For completeness, the pseudo code of the detecting algorithm is shown as follows.

```
Input: traces of nodes and nodes set V
Output: Community of node
G = (V, E) ← compute relation intensity
between nodes ofV;
sort edge e ∈ E ;
foreach edge e ∈ E
    e.visited = false;
end foreach
foreach edge e ∈ E
    if e.visited = false;
        C ← v, w ;
        N_C ← Neighbours(v) ∪ Neighbours(w) ;
        foreach node u ∈ N_C
            compute belongDegree(u);
        end foreach
        sort u ∈ N_C ;
        foreach node u ∈ N_C
        if ∇Q > 0
            C ← u ;
```

DOI: 10.1051/itmconf/20160705007

```
            N_C ← Neighbours(u) ∪ N_C ;
            goto (10);
        else
            complete detection of C;
    end for each
    foreach edge e between nodes in C
        e. visited = true;
  end if
end foreach
return Community of node;
```

According to formula (4), if Q increase, node u is involved in community C, we have:

$$\nabla Q = \frac{1}{2m}\left(\sum\nolimits_{v\in(C\cap N_u)} A_{uv} - \frac{k_u \sum\nolimits_{v\in(C\cap N_u)} k_v}{2m}\right) > 0 \quad (8)$$

From formula (7), we have:

$$B(v,C) > \frac{\sum\nolimits_{v\in(C\cap N_u)} k_v}{2m} \quad (9)$$

Node *u* will be added into Community *C* when (9) is founded.

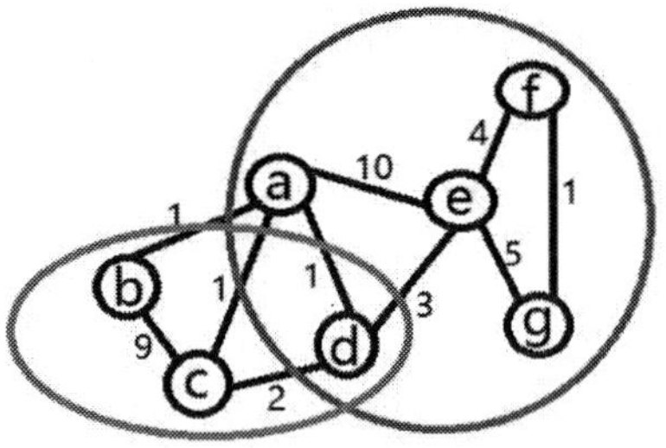

Figure 1. An example for community detection.

We use an example to illustrate the expanding process. Fig.1 shows an example of overlapping community detection using our detection algorithm. Two communities are detected and shown in different circles. As shown in Fig.1, we consider $C=\{a,e\}$ as initial community, neighbors of nodes in C is $N_C=\{b,c,d,f,g\}$. The belonging degree of nodes in N_C is $\{1/10, 1/12, 2/3, 4/5, 5/6\}$. We put node *g* with the highest value into *C* and we get $C^{'}=\{a,e,g\}$. Because $\nabla Q > 0$, the expanding process is continued for newly formed *C*, and now $N_C=\{b,c,d,f\}$. The belong degree is $\{1/10, 1/12, 2/3, 1\}$. Thus, node *f* is added into*C*directly. Repeat the expanding process until we get $C^{'}=\{a,e,g,f,d\}$. Now $N_C=\{b,c\}$, and the belonging degree is $\{1/10, 1/4\}$. We try to put node *c*into the community and compute ∇Q. Since $\nabla Q < 0$, the expanding process of current community is finished. We remove edges in this community from*E*. Then we choose $C=\{b,c\}$ as the new community. The expanding process is continued for new community. Finally, we get another community $C=\{b,c,d\}$. Remove the edges in new community, and the algorithm is ended because*E*is empty. We get two communities: $\{a,e,g,f,d\}$ and $\{b,c,d\}$. The overlapping node is $\{d\}$.

4 Experiments

In this section, we present some representative numerical results to validate the effectiveness of MMC comparing with two other schemes: Conductance [17] and COPRA [14], both of which can detect overlapping communities.

We use LFR benchmark [18] proposed by Lancichinetti et al. to test overlapping community detection algorithms. LFR is a well-known benchmark which can generate synthetic unweighted or weighted networks. It provides power-law distributions of node degree and community size, allows overlaps between communities. We can set many parameters to control the generated network, such as the fraction of nodes that belong to more than one community over all nodes and the number of communities that a node belongs to simultaneously. And the settings of parameters we set are shown in Table 1.

Table 1. Parameter Settings in LFR.

Parameter	Value	Parameter	Value
N	1000, 4000	γ	0~0.5
mut	0.1, 0.3	muw	0.1, 0.3
ε	1.5	k	20, 40
k_{max}	50, 100	τ_1	2
τ_2	2	o_m	2

The meanings of all these parameters are as follows:

N is the number of all nodes while γ is the fraction of overlapping nodes over all nodes. *mut* and *muw* denote mixing parameter for topology and mixing parameter for edge weights respectively. The exponent for weight distribution is ε. *k*and k_{max}represent the average of node degree and the maximum of node degree respectively.

 DOI: 10.1051/itmconf/20160705007

τ_1 is minus exponent for degree sequence while τ_2 is minus exponent for community size distribution. In addition, the number of communities that overlapping nodes belong to is denoted by o_m.

We use above metrics and different parameter settings: *mut* = *muw* = 0.1,*mut* = *muw* = 0.3, *N*=1000,4000. And the overlapping fraction γ is changed from 0 to 0.5 for each setting to evaluate the performance of these algorithms. Fig. 2 to Fig.5 show the experimental results of three algorithms: COPRA, Conductance, and MMC.

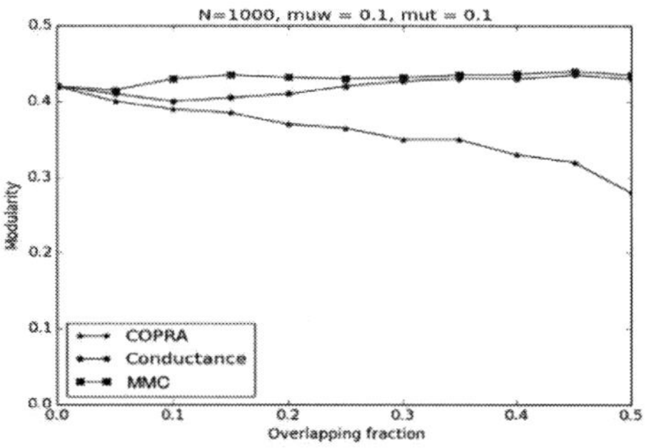

Figure 2. Modularity of the community structure detected by COPRA, Conductance and MMC while *N*=1000 and *muw*=*mut*=0.1.

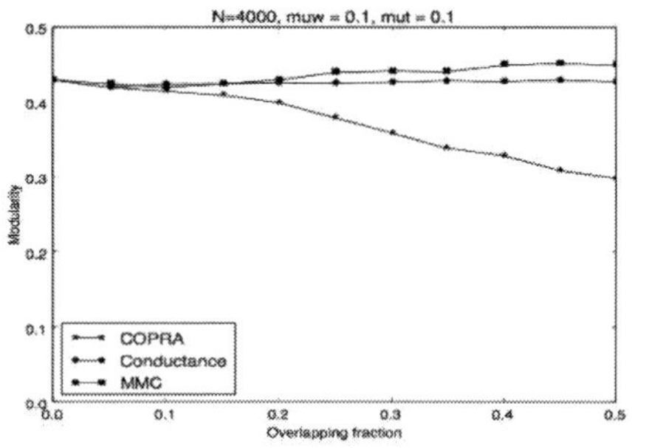

Figure 3. Modularity of the community structure detected by COPRA, Conductance and MMC while *N*=4000 and *muw*=*mut*=0.1.

Fig.2 and Fig.3 show modularity of the community structure detected by three algorithms while *mut*=*muw*=0.1 and number of nodes is different. As is shown, the modularity of all algorithms is higher. This may be because network structure is not very complex. For both COPRA and Conductance, the modularity is lower than MMC. In addition, the modularity of COPRA dramatically decreases while the overlapping fraction increases in all settings.

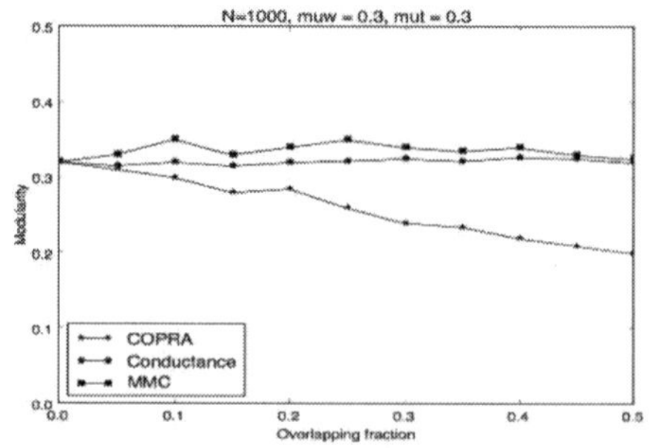

Figure 4. Modularity of the community structure detected by COPRA, Conductance and MMC while *N*=1000 and *muw*=*mut*=0.3.

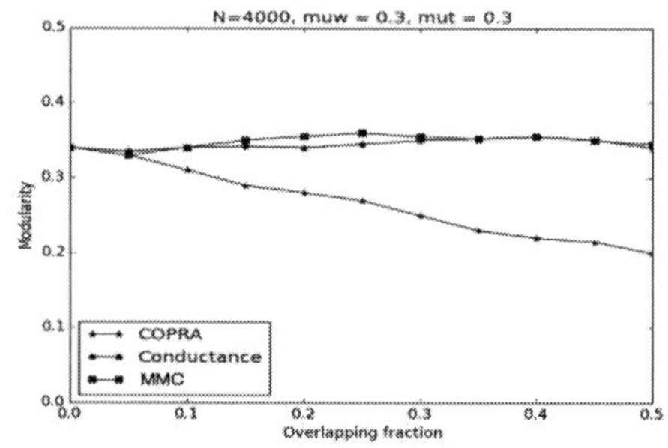

Figure 5. Modularity of the community structure detected by COPRA, Conductance and MMC while *N*=4000 and *muw*=*mut*=0.3.

Fig.4 and Fig.5 show modularity of the community structure detected by three algorithms for while *mut*=*muw*=0.3 and number of nodes is different. When *mut* and *muw* is higher, and the number of nodes do not change, the modularity of all algorithms is lower. The performance of COPRA is still worse while γ increases. In real situation, it's hard to determine a global limit v which has a great influence on performance for COPRA. However, MMC is stable with the increase of the overlapping fraction γ . Thus, we can conclude that MMC has the ability to detect overlapping communities.

5 Conclusions

In this paper, we propose an overlapping community detection algorithm for opportunistic networks. First, we introduce relation intensity to measure relationships among nodes. Then we design a new detection algorithm based on maxing modularity of communities. Simulation results on synthetic networks show that our community detection algorithm is much better than other algorithms in terms of modularity. In future, we will do more work on the validations in different environments. We will evaluate this algorithm on large scale networks coming from real networks.

 DOI: 10.1051/itmconf/20160705007

Acknowledgment

This work was supported by the National Natural Science Foundation of China (Grant no. 61272515, 61372108, 61401033), and National Science & Technology Pillar Program (Grant no. 2015BAH03F02).

References

1. Huang, C. M., Lan, K. C., & Tsai, C. Z. *A survey of opportunistic networks.* In Advanced Information Networking and Applications-Workshops. 22nd International Conference onIEEE(pp.1672-1677)(2008).
2. Daly, E. M., & Haahr, M. *Social network analysis for routing in disconnected delay-tolerant manets.* In Proceedings of the 8th ACM international symposium on Mobile ad hoc networking and computing (pp. 32-40) (2007).
3. Hossmann, T., Spyropoulos, T., & Legendre, F. *Know thy neighbor: Towards optimal mapping of contacts to social graphs for dtn routing.* In INFOCOM, 2010 Proceedings IEEE (pp. 1-9)(2010).
4. Hui, P., Crowcroft, J., & Yoneki, E. *Bubble rap: Social-based forwarding in delay-tolerant networks.* IEEE Transactions on Mobile Computing, **10**(11), 1576-1589(2011).
5. Gao, W., Li, Q., Zhao, B., & Cao, G. *Social-aware multicast in disruption-tolerant networks.* IEEE/ACM Transactions on Networking (TON), **20**(5), 1553-1566(2012).
6. Gao, W., et al., *On Exploiting Transient Social Contact Patterns for Data Forwarding in Delay-Tolerant Networks.* IEEE Transactions on Mobile Computing, **12**(1): p. 151-165(2013).
7. Becker, V. D. *Epidemic routing for partially connected ad hoc networks.* Proceedings of Technique Report, Department of Computer Science, Duke University, Durham, UK (2000).
8. Yuan, Q., Cardei, I., & Wu, J. *Predict and relay: an efficient routing in disruption-tolerant networks.* In Proceedings of the tenth ACM international symposium on Mobile ad hoc networking and computing (pp. 95-104)(2009).
9. Girvan, M. and M. Newman, *Community structure in social and biological networks.*Proceedings of the national academy of sciences,**99**(12): p. 7821-7826(2002).
10. Newman, M.E. and M. Girvan, *Finding and evaluating community structure in networks.* Phys Rev E Stat Nonlin Soft Matter Phys, **69**(2 Pt 2): p. 026113(2004).
11. Palla, G., et al., *Uncovering the overlapping community structure of complex networks in nature and society.* NATURE, 435(7043): p. 814-818(2005).
12. Raghavan, U.N., R. Albert and S. Kumara, *Near linear time algorithm to detect community structures in large-scale networks.* Phys Rev E Stat Nonlin Soft Matter Phys, **76**(3 Pt 2): p. 036106(2007).
13. Xie J, S.B.K.L., *SLPA: Uncovering Overlapping Communities in Social Networks via a Speaker-Listener Interaction Dynamic Process.* (2011).
14. Gregory, S., *Finding overlapping communities in networks by label propagation.* NEW JOURNAL OF PHYSICS, **12**(103018)(2010).
15. Wu, Z., et al., *Balanced Multi-Label Propagation for Overlapping Community Detection in Social Networks.* Journal of Computer Science and Technology, **27**(3): p. 468-479(2012).
16. Liu, Q., et al., *An Interest Community Routing Scheme for Opportunistic Networks,* in IEEE Global Telecommunications Conference (Globecom). p. 4366-4371(2013).
17. Lu Z, Sun X, Wen Y, et al. *Algorithms and applications for community detection in weighted networks[J].* Parallel and Distributed Systems, IEEE Transactions on, **26**(11): 2916-2926(2015).
18. Lancichinetti A, Fortunato S. *Benchmarks for testing community detection algorithms on directed and weighted graphs with overlapping communities[J].* Physical Review E, **80**(1): 016118(2009).
19. Ma, X. and X. Bai, *A Community-Based Routing Algorithm for Opportunistic Networks,* in International Conference on Ubiquitous and Future Networks. p. 701-706(2013).

Improved Collaborative Filtering Algorithm using Topic Model

Na LIU[1, a], Ying LU[1], Xiao-Jun TANG[1], Hai-Wen WANG[1], Peng XIAO[1], Ming-Xia LI[1]

[1] *School of Information Science & Engineering, Dalian Polytechnic University, China*
[a] *Corresponding author: liuna@dlpu.edu.cn*

Abstract. Collaborative filtering algorithms make use of interactions rates between users and items for generating recommendations. Similarity among users or items is calculated based on rating mostly, without considering explicit properties of users or items involved. In this paper, we proposed collaborative filtering algorithm using topic model. We describe user-item matrix as document-word matrix and user are represented as random mixtures over item, each item is characterized by a distribution over users. The experiments showed that the proposed algorithm achieved better performance compared the other state-of-the-art algorithms on Movie Lens data sets.

1 Introduction

With the emergence of Internet, there is more and more information disseminating all over this channel. The abundant amount of information, however, causes difficulty for users to locate desired information, which is referred to as the information overload problem due to our limited processing ability. Therefore, recommender systems arise to assist users to acquire useful information based on their past preferences or collaborative preferences from other sources.

Most recommendation algorithms start by finding a set of customers whose purchased and rated items overlap the user's purchased and rated items. The algorithm aggregates items from these similar customers, eliminates items the user has already purchased or rated, and recommends the remaining items to the user.

Recommender systems are often based on Collaborative Filtering (CF), which relies only on past user behavior—for example, their previous transactions or product ratings—and does not require the creation of explicit profiles[1]. Notably, CF techniques do not require domain knowledge and avoid the need for extensive data collection. In addition, relying directly on user behavior allows uncovering complex and unexpected patterns that would be difficult or impossible to profile using known data attributes. As a consequence, CF attracted much of attention in the past decade, resulting in significant progress and being adopted by some successful commercial systems[2][3]. Herlocker et al. estimated a user's preference for those items by ratings, these rating is given by similar people on an items[4]. Sarwar et al. exploited similarity of items with other items that the user has already rated to predict the user's preference on items[5]. Koren et al. made use of Singular Value Decomposition (SVD) to factorize user-item rating matrix to determine latent properties of users and items[6]. Chen, Chunan et al. addresses the problem of k Closest Pairs (kCP) query in spatial network databases[7]. Chang et al. proposed an LDA based document recommendation system which utilized an Item Based CF algorithm with document similarity calculation based on latent topic distribution of documents[8]. Liu, Qi, et al proposed a latent factor model based on LDA to model evolution of user interests based on personalized ranking[9]. Ortega et al. pointed out that there were four stages in the CF process where the users' data could be aggregated into the data of the group. According to their finding, the system performance would be significantly improved if the aggregation was done at an earlier stage of the process[10]. Wang Z et al. present Friendbook, a novel semantic-based friend recommendation system for social networks, which recommends friends to users based on their life styles instead of social graphs[11].

Our approach utilizes topic model to infer latent properties of items and then calculates user's preferences on historical ratings. We compute a hybrid user similarity score, which make use of user similarity in the topic model along with user similarity based on cosine. This way, our approach differs from the above references to improve quality of recommendations.

The paper is organized as follows. Section 2 describes Collaborative Filtering Algorithms. Section 3 defines the proposed algorithm, and Section 4 presents the results of applying this algorithm to MovieLens datasets. We conclude and discuss further research directions in Section 5.

2 Collaborative Filtering Algorithms

A traditional collaborative filtering algorithm is usually represented as an m×n customer-product matrix, R, such that $r_{i,j}$ is one if the ith customer has purchased the jth product, where $U=\{u_1,u_2...u_m\}$ is the set of customers, $I=\{i_1,i_2...i_n\}$ is the set of product. It is shown as Figure 1. We term this m×n representation of the input data set as original representation.

$$\begin{array}{c} \\ u_1 \\ u_2 \\ \vdots \\ u_m \end{array} \begin{array}{c} \begin{array}{cccc} i_1 & i_2 & \cdots & i_n \end{array} \\ \begin{bmatrix} r_{11} & r_{12} & \cdots & r_{1n} \\ r_{21} & r_{22} & \cdots & r_{2n} \\ \vdots & \vdots & \vdots & \vdots \\ r_{m1} & r_{m2} & \cdots & r_{mn} \end{bmatrix} \end{array}$$

Figure 1. User-item rating matrix

The most important step in collaborative filtering algorithm is that of computing the similarity between customers as it is used to form a proximity-based neighborhood between a target customer and a number of like-minded customers. The main goal of neighborhood of formation is to find, for each customer u, an ordered list of l customers $N=\{n_1,n_2...n_l\}$ such that $sim(u,N_1)$ is maximum, $sim(u,N_2)$ is the next maximum and so on. The proximity between two customers is usually measured by

Cosine:

$$sim^c_{i,j} = \frac{\sum_{u\in U} r_{u,i} \cdot r_{u,j}}{\sqrt{\sum_{u\in U} r_{u,i}^2 \cdot \sum_{u\in U} r_{u,j}^2}} \quad (1)$$

Pearson Correlation:

$$sim^p_{i,j} = \frac{\sum_{u\in U} (r_{u,i} - \bar{r}_i)(r_{u,j} - \bar{r}_j)}{\sqrt{\sum_{u\in U} (r_{u,i} - \bar{r}_i)^2 \sum_{u\in U} (r_{u,j} - \bar{r}_j)^2}} \quad (2)$$

Adjusted Cosine:

$$sim^{ac}_{i,j} = \frac{\sum_{u\in U} (r_{u,i} - \bar{r}_u)(r_{u,j} - \bar{r}_u)}{\sqrt{\sum_{u\in U} (r_{u,i} - \bar{r}_u)^2 \sum_{u\in U} (r_{u,j} - \bar{r}_u)^2}} \quad (3)$$

where $\bar{r}_i$ is the average of r_i.

The final step of collaborative filtering algorithm is to derive the top-N recommendations from the neighborhood of customers.

3 Collaborative Filtering Recommenders Using Topic Model

The main step of collaborative filtering algorithm is to rank each item according to how many similar customers purchased it. Either cosine or correlation is bags of words. They cannot find the relation between words deeply. Topic model is another good choice.

3.1 LDA Model

LDA is a generative probabilistic model of a corpus. The basic idea of LDA is that documents are represented as random mixtures over latent topics, each topic is characterized by a distribution over words.

The LDA model is represented as a probabilistic graphical model in Figure 1. The boxes are "plates" representing replicates. The outer plate represents documents, while the inner plate represents the repeated choice of topics and words within a document. As the figure makes clear, there are three levels to the LDA representation. The parameters α and β are corpus level parameters, assumed to be sampled once in the process of generating a corpus. The variables θ_d are document-level variables, sampled once per document. Finally, the variables z_{dn} and w_{dn} are word-level variables and are sampled once for each word in each document.

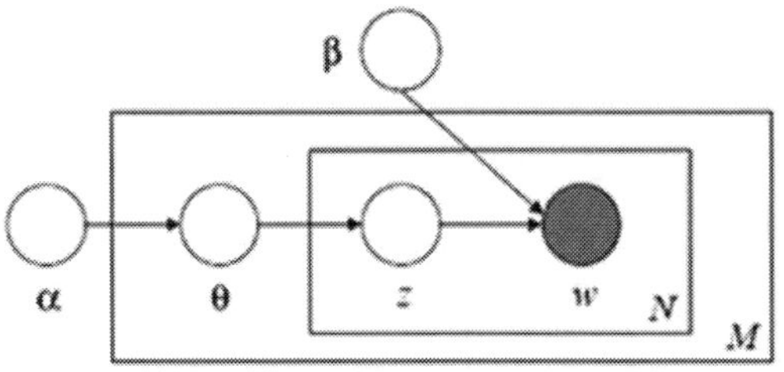

Figure 2. Graphical model representation of LDA.

A k-dimensional Dirichlet random variable θ can take values in the $(k-1)$-simplex, and has the following probability density on this simplex:

$$p(\theta|\alpha) = \frac{\Gamma(\sum_{i=1}^{k}\alpha_i)}{\prod_{i=1}^{k}\Gamma(\alpha_i)}\theta_1^{\alpha_1-1}\cdots\theta_k^{\alpha_k-1} \quad (4)$$

where the parameter α is a k-vector with components α_i >0, and where $\Gamma(x)$ is the Gamma function. The Dirichlet is a convenient distribution on the simplex, has finite dimensional sufficient statistics, and is conjugate to the multinomial distribution. Given the parameters α and β, the joint distribution of a topic mixture , a set of θ topics **z**, and a set of N words **w** is given by:

$$p(\theta,z,w|\alpha,\beta) = p(\theta|\alpha)\prod_{n=1}^{N} p(z_n|\theta)p(w_n|z_n,\beta) \quad (5)$$

where $p(z_n|\theta)$ is simply θ_i for the unique i. Integrating over θ and summing over z, we obtain the marginal distribution of a document:

$$p(w|\alpha,\beta) = \int p(\theta|\alpha)(\prod_{n=1}^{N}\sum_{z_n} p(z_n|\theta)p(w_n|z_n,\beta))d\theta \quad (6)$$

Finally, taking the product of the marginal probabilities of single documents, we obtain the probability of a corpus:

$$p(D \mid \alpha,\beta)=\prod_{d=1}^{M}\int p(\theta_d \mid \alpha)\left(\prod_{n=1}^{N_d}\sum_{z_{dn}} p(z_{dn} \mid \theta_d)p(w_{dn} \mid z_{dn},\beta)\right)d\theta_d \quad (7)$$

3.2 Collaborative Filtering Recommenders using Topic Model

In collaborative filtering algorithm, the input data is m×n matrix as shown in Table1. The matrix is the input of topic model. The matrix is computed as Figure 3 using LDA, where θ_{ij} is distribution of user *i* over item *j*.

$$\begin{array}{c} \\ u_1 \\ u_2 \\ \vdots \\ u_m \end{array}\begin{array}{c} \begin{array}{cccc} i_1 & i_2 & \cdots & i_n \end{array} \\ \begin{bmatrix} \theta_{11} & \theta_{12} & \cdots & \theta_{1n} \\ \theta_{21} & \theta_{22} & \cdots & \theta_{2n} \\ \vdots & \vdots & \vdots & \vdots \\ \theta_{m1} & \theta_{m2} & \cdots & \theta_{mn} \end{bmatrix} \end{array}$$

Figure 3. user-item distribution matrix

By LDA, the count of user purchase item in matrix is denoted as distribution. The similarity of users is calculated as:

$$\begin{aligned} sim_{i,j}^{\text{LDA}} &= \exp^{-KL(u_i,u_j)} = \exp^{-\left(KL(u_i\|u_j)+KL(u_j\|u_i)\right)} \\ &= \exp^{-\left(\sum_{k\in m}\ln\left(\frac{\theta_i}{\theta_k}\right)\theta_i+\sum_{k\in m}\ln\left(\frac{\theta_j}{\theta_k}\right)\theta_j\right)} \end{aligned} \quad (8)$$

3.3 Proposed Algorithm

Collaborative filtering recommenders using topic model is described as follows:

Input: user-item rate matrix
Output: Top-N *recommender*
(*a*)Compute similarity $sim_{i,j} = sim_{i,j}^{c} + sim_{i,j}^{\text{LDA}}$
(*b*)Find neighbor according to similarity and the number of the nearest
(*c*)Predict users as Equation (9)where M is set of neighbor.

$$\hat{r}_{u,i} = \frac{\sum_{j\in M_i} sim_{i,j}\cdot r_{u,j}}{\sum_{j\in M_i}\left|sim_{i,j}\right|} \quad (9)$$

(*d*)Recommender the Top-N users.

---

4 Experiments

We evaluated our algorithms on the MovieLens data sets. This data set consists of 100,000 ratings (1-5) from 943 users on 1682 movies. In order to evaluate our algorithm, we use Mean Absolute Error(MAE) as measure. MAE is a common measure in recommender system. It is an average of the absolute errors between predictions of target user and eventual outcomes. MAE is given by

$$MAE(u_i) = \frac{\sum_{u\in U}\left|r_{u,i} - \hat{r}_{u,i}\right|}{n} \quad (10)$$

where $\hat{r}_{u,i}$ is predict value of product *i* which is calculated as Equation (9).

Collaborative Filtering algorithm includes user-based and item-based. In order to identify our proposed algorithm, we take experiments on these two side.

4.1 User-based LDA Collaborative Filtering

In this part of experiments, we first identify the validation of our proposed algorithm. we set cluster is 5, 10, 20, 30, 40, 50 respectively and neighbor size is 5, 10, 20, 30, 40, 50, 60, 80, 100, 130, 160, 200 respectively. The number of topic is 20. The experiment result is shown in Figure 4. The x-axis of Figure 4 is neighbour size, y-axis is MAE calculated by Equation (10). There are 5 curve in Figure 4,which reprents MAE of different cluster.

To compare with baseline, we also run the user-based collaborative filtering algorithm with cosine, pearson correlation and adjusted cosine when cluster is 5. The compared result is shown in Figure 5. The neighbour size is the same as Figure 4. There are 4 curves in Figure5,which reprents MAE of different method.

4.2 Item-based LDA Collaborative Filtering

We also take experiments with item-based. The experiment results are shown in Figure 6 and Figure 7. The experiments parameter is the same as section 4.1.

From experiment results we can see that

(1) Figure 4 and Figure 6 are results of our proposed method under different clusters and different neighbour size. The results are evaluated by MAE, which is an average of the absolute errors between predictions of target. It is obvious that the lower,the better. Neither user-based or item-based, the cluster is lager, the MAE is lower.

(2)The contribution of our proposed algothrim is using topic model to compute similarity between users. To identify the effectiveness, we also compare our algorithm with others. The baseline is cosine, pearson correlation and adjusted cosine. Figure 5 and Figure 7 are compared results with user-based and item-based. It is clear that MAE of our proposed method is lower than baseline. It indicates the precision of recommender is higher.

DOI: 10.1051/itmconf/20160705008

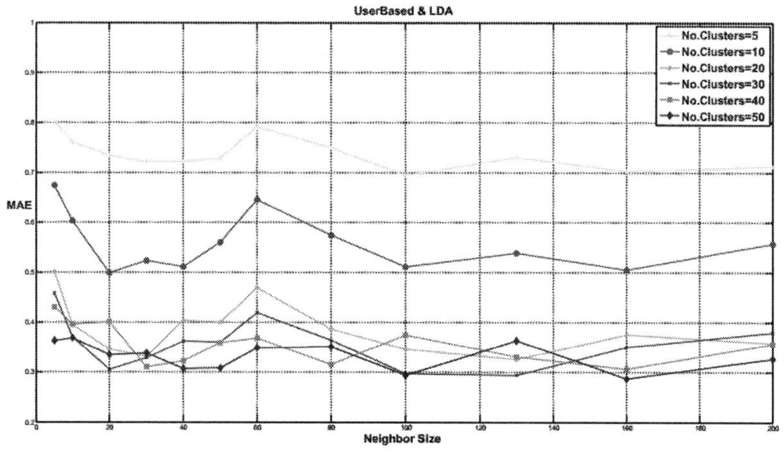

Figure 4. User-based LDA Collaborative Filtering algorithm

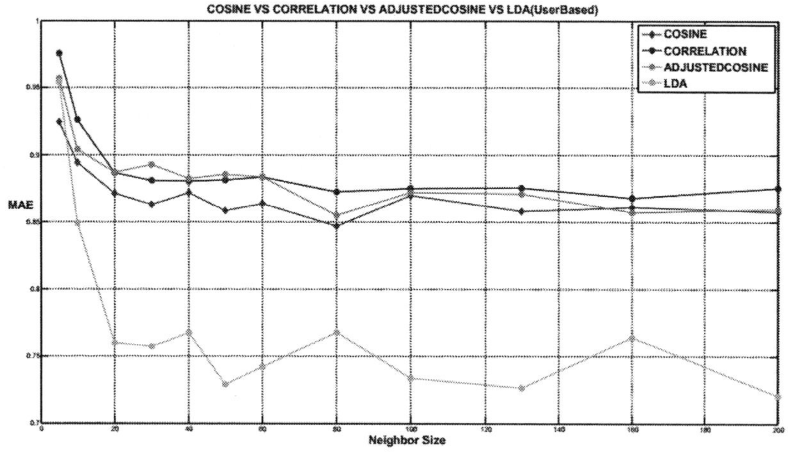

Figure 5. Results of four user-based Collaborative Filtering algorithm

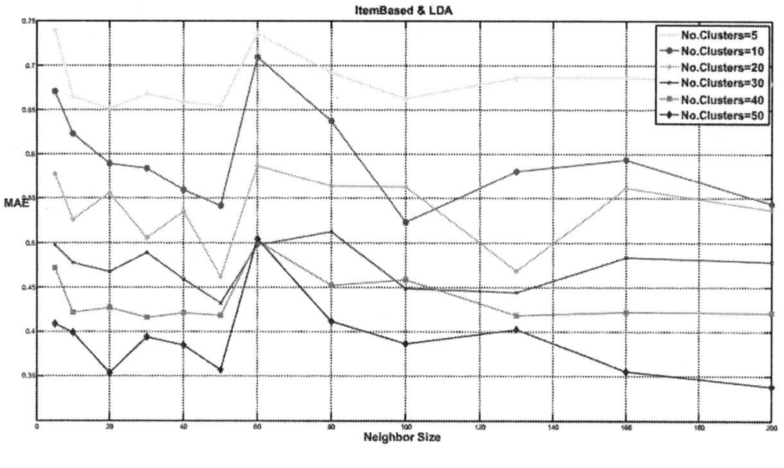

Figure 6. Item-based LDA Collaborative Filtering algorithm

DOI: 10.1051/itmconf/20160705008

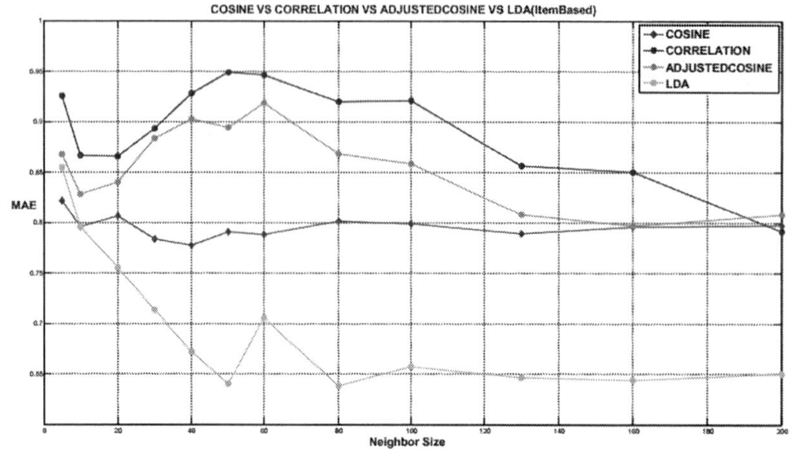

Figure 7. Results of four item-based Collaborative Filtering algorithm

5 Conclusions

Collaborative Filtering algorithms make use of interactions between users and items in the form of implicit or explicit ratings alone for generating recommendations. Similarity among users or items is calculated purely based on rating overlap in this case, without considering explicit properties of users or items involved, limiting their applicability in domains with very sparse rating spaces. In this paper, we proposed collaborative filtering algorithms using topic model, which can improved the similarity between users and items.

Acknowledgment

This work was supported by National Natural Science Foundation of China (NO. 61402069, NO.61272369, NO.61175053), General project of Liaoning Provincial Department of Education (NO.L2015047).

References

1. GOLDBERG, D., NICHOLS, D., OKI, B. M., AND TERRY, D. 1992. Using collaborative filtering to weave an information tapestry. Comm. ACM 35, 12, 61–70.
2. LINDEN, G., SMITH, B., AND YORK, J. 2003. Amazon.com recommendations: Item-to-item collaborative filtering. IEEE Internet Comput. 7, 1, 76–80.
3. ALI, K. AND VAN STAM, W. Tivo: making show recommendations using a distributed collaborative filtering architecture. In Proceedings of the 10th ACM SIGKDD International Conference on Knowledge Discovery and Data Mining. ACM, New York, NY, 2004, 394–401.
4. Herlocker, Jonathan L., Joseph A. Konstan, Al Borchers, and John Riedl. "An algorithmic framework for performing collaborative filtering." In Proceedings of the 22nd annual international ACM SIGIR conference on Research and development in information retrieval, pp. 230-237. ACM, 1999.
5. Sarwar, Badrul, George Karypis, Joseph Konstan, and John Riedl. "Item-based collaborative filtering recommendation algorithms." In Proceedings of the 10th international conference on World Wide Web, ACM, 2001, 285-295
6. Koren, Yehuda. "Factorization meets the neighborhood: a multifaceted collaborative filtering model." In Proceedings of the 14th ACM SIGKDD international conference on Knowledge discovery and data mining, ACM, 2008 ,426-434.
7. Chen, Chunan, Weiwei Sun, Baihua Zheng, Dingding Mao, and Weimo Liu. "An incremental approach to closest pair queries in spatial networks using best-first search." In International Conference on Database and Expert Systems Applications, pp. 136-143. Springer Berlin Heidelberg, 2011.
8. Chang, Te-Min, and Wen-Feng Hsiao. "LDA-based Personalized Document Recommendation." , 2013.
9. Liu, Qi, et al. "Enhancing collaborative filtering by user interest expansion via personalized ranking." Systems, Man, and Cybernetics, Part B: Cybernetics, IEEE Transactions on 42.1 ,2012,218-233.
10. Ortega, F., Bobadilla, J., Hernando, A., and Guti'errez, A. Incorporating group recommendations to recommender systems: Alternatives and performance. Information Processing & Management, 2013, 49(4): 895–901.
11. Wang Z, Liao J, Cao Q, et al. Friendbook: A Semantic-Based Friend Recommendation System for Social Networks[J]. IEEE Transactions on Mobile Computing, 2015, 14(3):538-551.

ITM Web of Conferences 7, 05009 (2016) DOI: 10.1051/itmconf/20160705009
ITA 2016

An Improved Convolutional Neural Network on CrowdDensity Estimation

Shao-Yun PAN [1,a], Jie GUO[1] and Zheng HUANG [1]

[1]*School of Information Security, Shanghai Jiao Tong university, China*

Abstract. In this paper, a new method is proposed for crowd density estimation. An improved convolutional neural network is combined with traditional texture feature. The data calculated by the convolutional layer can be treated as a new kind of features.So more useful information of images can be extracted by different features.In the meantime, the size of image has little effect on the result of convolutional neural network. Experimental results indicate that our scheme has adequate performance to allow for its use in real world applications.

1 Introduction

Stampede may happen while people are too overcrowding, which always results in casualties. In 2016, for example, the New Year's day in Shanghai, there are too many people gathered in the bund. It results in casualties due to no effective evacuation. In order to prevent such incidents, the crowd density detection in video detection system is important. We always expect the system to inform us when people's density reaches a certain range we gave. In this way, people can be evacuated in time, avoiding an accident.

In the past decades, many efforts have been made in the respect. It is proposed a method based on detection individuals [1]. But the severe crowd occlusion makes the approach not up to our expectations [2]. In general, texture feature and a classifier are used to estimate the crowd density. It introduced the grey level co-occurrence matrix(GLCM) of an image [3, 4]. Then the support vector machine (SVM)is used to analyse crowd density [4]. The feature is effect when the crowd is very dense. But when the light changed seriously, the accuracy is not high [2]. A new feature is introduced named Local Binary Patterns(LBP) feature [5, 6]. It can have little change when the light condition changes thus it has advantages over GLCM. A new approach is discussed [7]. It is based on optical flow and hierarchical clustering. However, the method is not very good when the pedestrians are long period static.

In recent years, deep learning is very popular. It has been more and more widely applied. The paper proposes a method based on the convolutional neural network(CNN) to analyse the crowd density [8]. However, the network is too low that it is not always good in all areas. In this paper, we combined LBP texture feature and convolutional neural network. The features learned by convolutional layer tend to be partial. It can be more global with deeper layers. So we add one more convolutional layer and fully connection layer which can get more deep features. The LBP features extract other information which enhances the resolution of images. It can improve the overall recognition of images, controlling the error in a smaller range.

The rest of this paper is organized as follows: in Section 2, we will present our model briefly. And then we will discuss the basic concepts of LBP texture feature and CNN used in our model. In Section3, we discuss the result of our experiment. A brief summary showed in section 4.

2 Model

In this section, we propose an approach which is how to combine Local Binary Patterns (LBP) and convolutional neural network in our model. It can improve the accuracy in the experiment. We then discuss basic knowledge of LBP and convolutional neural network used in our experiment.

The overview of our method is shown in Fig. 1. In this paper, we design the model that has three convolutional layers and pooling layers. Each convolutional layer follows a pooling layer in order to decrease parameters' numbers. It can reduce computation complexity. C1 contains three filters and we design 32 feature maps to output in first stage. In the second stage, 32 feature maps change to 64 that each feature map generates two in the convolutional layer. The pooling layer just changes the size of maps. It has no effect for numbers. After the last stage, 90 feature maps obtain to output. In order to get better results, the convolutional neural network contains two full connections. The features of local binary patterns input the first full connection with feature maps together. The classifier is trained until 200 optimizations and selects parameters of the lowest error one.

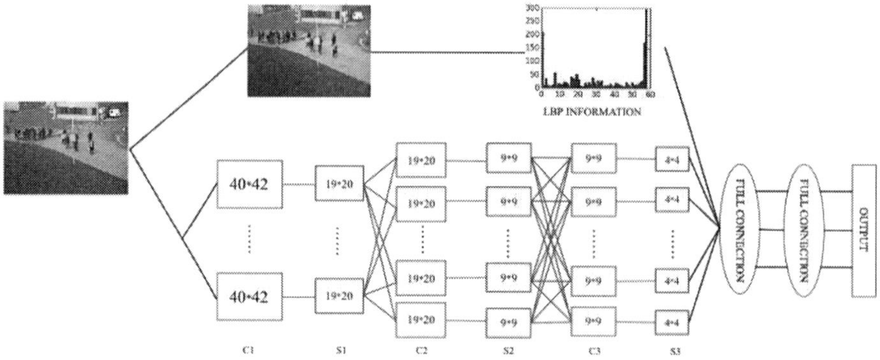

Figure 1. The structure of our model concludingthreeconvolutionallayers

2.1 Local Binary Patterns

Local Binary Patterns is a very common operator used to describe the image local texture features in the field of machine vision. LBP has some significant advantages, such as grey scale invariance and rotation invariance. It was firstly proposed by T. Ojala, M. Pietikäinen, and D. Harwood in 1994 [9]. LBP is very powerful in classification field when using features of images, so that it is widely used in image classification. Due to strong discrimination and simple to calculate, the operator of local binary patterns has been applied in many different scenarios.

On the side of texture analysis, image texture feature of a pixel refers to the relationship among this point and the surrounding pixels in most cases. In other words, it means the relationship of a point and its neighbourhoods. It will form different types of features after extracting feature from different angles. LBP constructs a measure of the relationship among a pixel and its surrounding pixels. LBP is a simple but very effective texture feature operator. Firstly, selecta pixel as centre. And then its neighbouring pixels will be compared to the central pixel. If the grey-level value of neighbouring pixel is larger, then the location is marked as 1, else marked as 0. Then every pixel will get a string of binary values. This is a process of converting the original image to LBP image. Finally, figure out its histogram.

LBP has a very good features. When the light of an image changes, the LBP feature extracted from an image changes little. So it has good robustness to illumination. This is the reason that it is more popular that other texture features

In this paper, we do not use the basic method because the binary modes are too many. Ojala proposed a uniform LBP [10]. With such improvement, even though the types of binary modes are greatly reduced, the information is not lost. Patternsare reduced as P*(P-1)+2 from the origin, where P represents the neighbourhood points. Figure 2 shows the procedure of extracting the feature. It can reduce the effect of high frequency noise, for dimensions of the feature vector are decreased.

2.2 Convolutional Neural Network

Convolutional neural network is a kind of artificial neural networks. It has become a hot topic in speech analytics and image recognition field. The weight sharing makes it more similar to the biological neural network. It reduces the complexity of network models and numbers of weight values [11]. This performance will be more obvious when dealing with multi-dimensional images. Images can input directly to the network, to avoid the complex feature extraction and data reconstruction in traditional recognition algorithm. Convolutional network is specially designed as a multi-layer perceptron to identify two-dimensional shape.

CNNs as a deep learning framework is proposed in order to minimize data in the preprocessing stage. Local receptive field is the input data in the lowest level of CNN structure[12]. Then the information is in turn transmitted to different layers. Each layer will obtain the most significant features through a digital filter. Local receptive field of an image can access to the most basic features by neurons and processing units.

Thereare two important parts in convolutional neural network. One is named alternating convolutional layer, and another one is pooling layer [13]. Generally, C layer is a layer of feature extraction. The input of each neuron is connected to the local receptive field of preceding layer, and extracting the local feature [14]. Once the local features are extracted, the positional relationship among it and other characteristics are also subsequently finalized. Computing convolution of theimage is actually a filtering process. Eq. (1) shows the process of convolutions.

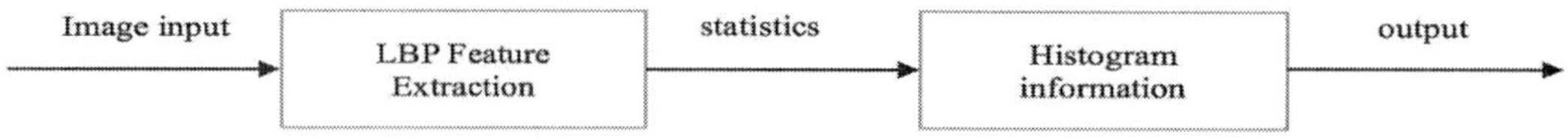

Figure 2. The procedure of LBP feature extraction

$$Y=sigmoïde(\sum x*w+b) \qquad (1)$$

 DOI: 10.1051/itmconf/20160705009

Each feature map is calculated by a convolution kernel, and plus a bias. Finally, it calculates the sigmoid function. Eq. (2) defines the sigmoid function.

$$S(x)=1/(1+e^{-x}) \quad (2)$$

S layer is a feature mapping layer. Each layer is composed of multiple feature maps. Each of them is a flat, and weights of all neurons in the plane are equal. The layer is designed to reduce the feature map. Generally, to sum every four neighborhood pixels. The sum is weighted by w, and plus a bias b, and then activated by a function.

Due to sharing weights of all neurons in a same plane, the number of free parameters and the complexity of network parameters selection are reduced. In Convolutional neural network, each feature extraction layer is followed by a calculation layer used for local average and secondary extraction. It makes the network have a higher tolerance for distortion when identifying the input samples.

3 Experiment

In our paper, the Pets2009 dataset is used for experiment [15]. Table 1 shows the number of each class including training data and testing data.

Table 1. The number of images of each class.

Number	Very low	Low	Medium	High	Very high
training	120	141	137	97	217
testing	40	71	83	60	120

The dataset has three different crowd scenarios [16]. We use dataset S1 for density estimation. The dataset is not available directly. Firstly, according to the number of people in each image, images are divided into five categories. The range of number of people of each class refer to [8].

Table 2. Result of PETS_2009 by cascade optimized CNN and CNN combined LBP.

result	Very low	Low	Medium	High	Very high
CNN	100	88	87	78	90
LBP+CNN	100	91	92	88	92

Table 2 shows the result of our experiment. Our method getsbetter performance comparing with the method in Literature [8], especially for the low, medium and high class. The very low and very high class is almost the same. The main reason may be our approach takes advantage of both convolutional neural network and traditional features. Both of them have own advantage alone. Each of them play a role, forming complementarily in our model.

Table 3. Result of PETS_2009 by LBP and common CNN.

Result (%)	Very low	Low	Medium	High	Very high
LBP1	95	83	69	72	94
LBP2	85	79	56	28	96
CNN1	91	88	90	83	97
CNN2	87	87	92	81	95

Table 3 shows the result of experiment with images of different scales. LBP1 represents the result of images in large size, and LBP2 is for the small images. Others also are the case. The image size has a great impact on our result to the LBP feature. Almost the accuracy of all categories have decreased, especially for the kind of high. To the CNN method, the performance has a little change. Of course, we use three convolutional layers similarly, since the result is better than two.

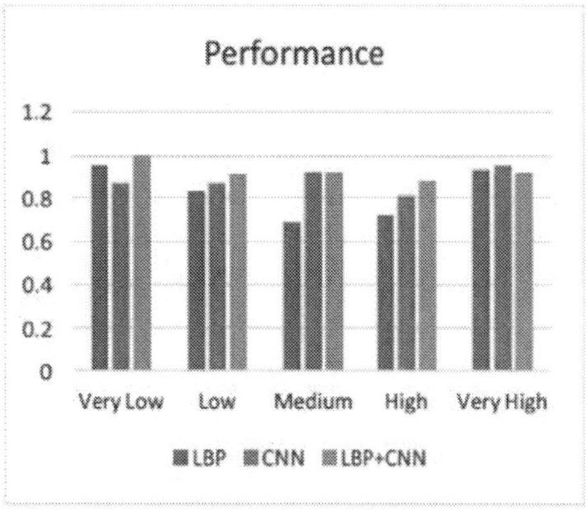

Figure3. Crowd density estimation performance of different methods Crowd density estimation performance of different methods.

Itis clearly shown in Fig.3 that our method has the better result. The performance is always stable. The LBP feature does work as well as the CNN. But when the size of images is very small, the feature of LBP is very bad. In other words, it depends on high quality images.The model is very useful when the crowd density is high. This information is important in reality.

4 Conclusion

Video surveillance has become an integral part in people's daily life. It's more and more widely used, because it can significantly relieve labor. The crowd density estimation which is an important component of abnormal behavior monitoring, can effectively prevent the loss caused by the crowd out of control. For the estimation of the crowd density problem, the most common method is texture analysis. The first step is to extract texture feature of the

DOI: 10.1051/itmconf/20160705009

image, and then select some appropriate classifier for training. Nowadays, deep learning has been greatly developed and applied to the crowd density estimation. It has been proved that the deep learning algorithm is more effective than the ordinary methods.

There are different approaches to estimate crowd density, but all of the methods have its own problems. The paper introduces some LBP information and convolutional neural network knowledge. Inspired by the idea of boosting algorithm, we present a new approach based on LBP and CNN in the paper.The resultcan be better when the two are combined, since the model extracts more features from images. These two kinds of information have little relationship. It gets stronger since combining two different features.

References

1. Rittscher Jens, Tu Peter H., Krahnstoever Nils, Simultaneous estimation of segmentation and shape, Proceedings of the IEEE Computer Society Conference on Computer Vision and Pattern Recognition, **2**, 486-493(2005)
2. Saleh S.A.M, Suandi S.A, Ibrahim H., Recent survey on crowd density estimation and counting for visual surveillance[J]. Engineering Applications of Artificial Intelligence, **41**,103-114(2015)
3. Wu Xinyu,Liang Guoyuan, Lee K.K, Xu Yangsheng, Crowd density estimation using texture analysis and learning, 2006 IEEE International Conference on Robotics and Biomimetics, ROBIO, 214-219 (2006)
4. Wang B, Bao H, Yang S, et al. Crowd Density Estimation Based on Texture Feature Extraction[J]. Journal of Multimedia, **8(4)**: 331-337 (2013)
5. Wang Zhe, Liu Hong, Qian Yueliang, Xu Tao, Crowd density estimation based on local binary pattern co-occurrence matrix, Proceedings of the 2012 IEEE International Conference on Multimedia and Expo Workshops,ICMEW, 372-377 (2012)
6. Yang H, Su H, Zheng S, et al. The large-scale crowd density estimation based on sparse spatiotemporal local binary pattern[C]//2011 IEEE International Conference on Multimedia and Expo. IEEE, 1-6 (2011)
7. Rao Aravinda S, GubbiJayavardhana, MarusicSlaven, Stanley Paul, PalaniswamiMarimuthu, Crowddensity estimation based on optical flow and hierarchicalclustering, Proceedings of the 2013 International Conference on Advances in Computing, Communications and Informatics, ICACCI, 494-499 (2013)
8. Fu Min, Xu Pei, Li Xudong, Liu Qihe, Ye Mao, Zhu Ce, Fast crowd density estimation with convolutional neural networks, Engineering Applications of Artificial Intelligence, **43**, 81-88, August 1 (2015)
9. Ojala T., Pietikainen M., Harwood D., Performance evaluation of texture measures with classification based on Kullback discrimination of distributions[C]//Pattern Recognition, 1994. Vol. 1-Conference A: Computer Vision & Image Processing., Proceedings of the 12th IAPR International Conference on. IEEE, **1**: 582-585 (1994)
10. OjalaTimo, PietikäinenMatti, MäenpääTopi, Multiresolution gray-scale and rotation invariant texture classification with local binary patterns, IEEE Transactions on Pattern Analysis and Machine Intelligence, **24**, n 7, 971-987, July (2002)
11. MrazováIveta, Kukacka, Marek, Hybrid convolutional neural networks, IEEE International Conference on Industrial Informatics (INDIN), 469-474 (2008)
12. LeCun Y, Kavukcuoglu K, Farabet C. Convolutional networks and applications in vision[C]//ISCAS, 253-256 (2010)
13. Sermanet Pierre, ChintalaSoumith, Lecun Yann, Convolutional Neural Networks Applied to House Numbers Digit Classification, Proceedings - International Conference on Pattern Recognition, 3288-3291 (2012)
14. Scherer D, Müller A, Behnke S. Evaluation of pooling operations in convolutional architectures for object recognition[C]//International Conference on Artificial Neural Networks, 92-101 (2010)
15. http://ftp.pets.rdg.ac.uk/pub/PETS2009/Crowd_PETS09_dataset/a_data/a.html
16. Saleh Sami Abdulla Mohsen, SuandiShahrelAzmin, Ibrahim Haidi, Recent survey on crowd density estimation and counting for visual surveillance, Engineering Applications of Artificial Intelligence, **41**, 103-114, May 1 (2015)

ITM Web of Conferences 7, 05010 (2016) DOI: 10.1051/itmconf/20160705010
ITA 2016

Ontology Update in the Cognitive Model of Ontology Learning

De-Hai ZHANG, Nai-Yao WANG, Bin WANG, Zhong-Hao YANG and Hang ZHAO

Software College, Yunnan University, Kunming, China

Abstract. Ontology has been used in many hot-spot fields, but most ontology construction methods are semiautomatic, and the construction process of ontology is still a tedious and painstaking task. In this paper, a kind of cognitive models is presented for ontology learning which can simulate human being's learning from world. In this model, the cognitive strategies are applied with the constrained axioms. Ontology update is a key step when the new knowledge adds into the existing ontology and conflict with old knowledge in the process of ontology learning. This proposal designs and validates the method of ontology update based on the axiomatic cognitive model, which include the ontology update postulates, axioms and operations of the learning model. It is proved that these operators subject to the established axiom system.

1. Introduction

Ontology as an effective semantic modelling method has been widely used not only in the Semantic Web[1-2], Knowledge Base[3], E-commerce[4], Information Retrieval[5] and Digital Library[6], but also in many reasoning-based fields such as bio information and medicine information analysis[7-8] fields.

A kind of cognitive models is presented for ontology learning which can simulate human being's learning from world. In this model, we adopt the axiomatic methodology to represent the five cognitive strategies: ontology extension, ontology reduction, ontology induction, ontology revision and ontology update. In this paper, an ontology update strategy is proposed to maintain the coordination of the ontology when it changed with time.

In the cognitive modelof ontology learning, when learner agent acquiring a new assertion from the outside world Wand the assertion is conflict with the original knowledge of the learner agent, it need to change the existing knowledge if it is due to the outside world changing. In this case, the agent should update the corresponding knowledge in the ontology by updating strategy.

The update strategy includes ontology update postulates and ontology update axiom to show the update strategy that is possible to appear in the process of ontology learning. For using the update strategy in practice, the update operators that are corresponding to the axiom for the specific operating of ontology update is defined and it is easy to translate into algorithms in computer.

When the learner agent has obtained a new statement θ about the outside world, it would add θ into its knowledge base that represented by assertion, then the learner agent checks the ontology consistency and whether the assertion has time constrains, if the new assertion meets both of the update conditions, we take update operations.

2. Related Works

Ontology as a formal representation of a domain knowledge has played an important role in many fields, and the updating of ontology receives researcher's widespread attention recently. A Flahive, D Taniar, W Rahayu and BO Apduhan particularly focus on formalizing and validating the process of ontology update, whereby sections of one ontology are replaced by a subset extracted from another ontology [9]. J Sangers, F Hogenboom and F Frasincar propose an event-driven automated ontology updating approach. They propose different execution models, providing flexibility with respect to the update process [10]. A Hamilton, EJ González, L Acosta, Arnay and J Espelosín present a semantic approach for route determination and support for several vehicles sharing the same environment. In their paper, a real-time ontology update procedure is also proposed to face unforeseen circumstances [11]. According to one embodiment, L Wang, Murayama and A Hosokawa present an ontology updating apparatus that includes a generation unit, an updating unit, a detection unit and a notification unit [12]. An ontology update scheme keeps the document annotation available even if changes in the original data would remove the corresponding portions of the ontology [13].Kim, Jeong and Baik's paper is focus on the quantitative experiment on the performance of XPOS model, Sesame, and the XML file system-based storage (XFSS) model regarding query processing and ontology update for comparative evaluation [14]. C Chen, Sun, Zheng, Mao and W Liu address the problem of k Closest Pairs (kCP) query in spatial network databases and propose a Best-First search approach namely BFCP (Best-First Closest Pair) [15].

3. Ontology Update Postulates

The update strategy is worked under the following postulates:

P0: The result of the ontology after the update operation after ontology remains ontology.

P1: Update operations satisfy the success principles, coordination principles and minimum change principles.

P2: The form of updating assertion is the slot value assertions with facet constrains about class and individuals and the negative form, that is $c[s \leftarrow v; \mathrm{F}\ ]$,, $\neg g[s \leftarrow v; \mathrm{F}\ ]$.For the convenient of representation, when $\theta = c[s \leftarrow v; T = t]$ or $\theta = g[s \leftarrow v; T = t]$, it is represented as $\theta(t)$, that is the assertion when the time facet value is t.

P3: Update operations update only the ontology itself, rather than updating the Logical Closures of ontology.

P4: The form of assertion that is updated can be either with facet constraints or to be without facet constraints. Slot value assertions with facet constraints can update that without facet constraints assertion, but not vice versa. If the individual is a slot value assertion, when you cannot determine the time that is in its class and it has the facet constraints which in the same slot values, then only update the individual slot value without updating their slot value of their class.

P5:In the time facet constraints, the assertion updated by the time value has a higher priority than the older assertions of the time value.

P6: Updating assertion θ doesn't belong to $Th(O)$

4. Ontology Update Axiom

According to the ontology updatingpostulates, the axioms of ontology updatingstrategy are defined as follows.

A1: $O \diamond \theta$ is ontology; (structural maintain principle)

A2: If $t < t'$, $\theta(t') \notin Th(O)$, then $\theta(t) \in O \diamond \theta(t)$; (conditional principles of success)

A3: If $\neg\theta \notin Th(O)$, then $\neg\theta \notin Th(O \diamond \theta)$; (principle of coordination)

A4: If the facet time value $t < t'$, then $(O \diamond \theta(t)) \diamond \theta(t') = O \diamond \theta(t')$;

What the axiom A1mean is: The updated ontology remains ontology;

What the axiom A2mean is: If the original ontology don't exist assertion newer than θ, then use θ to update the ontology, θ is contained in the updated ontology.

What the axiom A3mean is: If the ontology before the update does not include negation of θ, then the ontology updated by θ does not contain θ negation;

What the axiom A4mean is: For the slot value assertion on the same slot, if $\theta(t')$ is an assertion newer than $\theta(t)$, we use $\theta(t)$ to update ontology first, then we use $\theta(t')$ to update ontology, the result is equivalent to the direct use of $\theta(t')$ to update the ontology.

5. Ontology Update Operators

Here, we combine the specific form of assertions, given ontology updating operator.

The definition of ontology updating operator is as follows:

Definition1: Ontology updating operator '$\diamond$'is the function that satisfies axioms A1-A4 and ontology update postulates P0-P6, and for the specific form of the following assertions, give the operations for updating ontology O (C, S, E, Γ, Φ, Ω) as follows:

U1: If $\theta = \neg c[s \leftarrow v; \mathrm{F}\ ]$, among them, facet expression $T = t \in \mathrm{F}$

U1.1: $\varphi = c[s \leftarrow v'; \mathrm{F}\ '] \in O$, $T = t' \in \mathrm{F}\ '$

U1.1.1If $t < t'$, then $O \diamond \theta = O$

U1.1.2If $t \geq t'$, then $O \diamond \theta = O - \varphi$; $Hst = Hst \cup \{\varphi\}$

U1.2: $\varphi = c[s \leftarrow v'; \mathrm{F}\ '] \in Th(O)$, $T = t' \in \mathrm{F}\ '$, there exist $c' \in C$, satisfying $c \subset c'$ or $c \subset {}^*c'$, and $\mu = c'[s \leftarrow v'; \mathrm{F}\ '] \in O$

U1.2.1If $t < t'$, then $O \diamond \theta = O$

U1.2.2If $t \geq t'$, there does not exist $c'' \in C$, satisfying $c'' \subset c'$, then $O \diamond \theta = O - \mu$; $Hst = Hst \cup \{\mu\}$

U1.2.3If $t \geq t'$, there exists $c'' \in C$, satisfying $c'' \subset c'$, then $O \diamond \theta = O - \mu$ + { $c''[s \leftarrow v'; \mathrm{F}\ ']$ | $c'' \subset c'$ }; $Hst = Hst \cup \{\mu\}$

U2: If $\theta = c[s \leftarrow v; \mathrm{F}\ ]$, among them, facet expression $T = t \in \mathrm{F}$

U2.1: $\varphi = c[s \leftarrow v'; \mathrm{F}\ '] \in O$, $T = t' \in \mathrm{F}\ '$

U2.1.1 If $t < t'$, then $O \diamond \theta = O$; $Hst = Hst \cup \{\theta\}$

U2.1.2If $t \geq t'$, then $O \diamond \theta = O + \theta - \varphi$; $Hst = Hst \cup \{\varphi\}$

U2.2:If $\varphi = c[s \leftarrow v'; \mathrm{F}\ '] \in Th(O)$, $T = t'$ $\in \mathrm{F}\ '$, there exists $c' \in C$, satisfying $c \subset c'$ or $c \subset {}^*c'$ and $\mu = c'[s \leftarrow v'; \mathrm{F}\ '] \in O$

U2.2.1If $t < t'$, then $O \diamond \theta = O$; $Hst = Hst \cup \{\theta\}$

U2.2.2If $t \geq t'$, there does not exist $c'' \in C$, satisfying $c'' \subset c'$, then $O \diamond \theta = O + \theta - \mu$; $Hst = Hst \cup \{\mu\}$

U2.2.3If $t \geq t'$, there exists $c'' \in C$, satisfying $c'' \subset c'$, then $O \diamond \theta = O + \theta - \mu$ + { $c''[s \leftarrow v'; \mathrm{F}\ ']$ | $c'' \subset c'$ }; $Hst = Hst \cup \{\mu\}$

U2.3: $\varphi = c'[s \leftarrow v';F'] \in O$, $T = t' \in F'$, and $c' \subset c$ or $c' \subset *c$

U2.3.1If $t < t'$, then $O \Diamond \theta = O + \theta$; $Hst = Hst \cup \{\theta\}$

U2.3.2If $t = t'$, but $F \neq F'$, then $O \Diamond \theta = O + \theta$

U2.3.3If $t = t'$, and $F = F'$, and $v = v'$, then $O \Diamond \theta = O + \theta - \varphi$; $Hst = Hst \cup \{\varphi\}$

U2.3.4If $t = t'$, and $F = F'$, but $v \neq v'$, then $O \Diamond \theta = O \circ \theta$

*U2.3.5*If $t > t'$, then $O \Diamond \theta = O + \theta - \varphi$; $Hst = Hst \cup \{\varphi\}$

U2.4: $\varphi = g[s \leftarrow v';F'] \in O$, $T = t' \in F'$, and $g :: c$ or $g :: *c$

U2.4.1If $t < t'$, then $O \Diamond \theta = O + \theta$; $Hst = Hst \cup \{\theta\}$

U2.4.2If $t = t'$, but $F \neq F'$, then $O \Diamond \theta = O + \theta$

U2.4.3If $t = t'$, and $F = F'$, $v = v'$, then $O \Diamond \theta = O + \theta - \varphi$; $Hst = Hst \cup \{\varphi\}$

U2.4.4If $t = t'$, and $F = F'$, but $v \neq v'$, then $O \Diamond \theta = O \circ \theta$

U2.4.5If $t > t'$, then $O \Diamond \theta = O + \theta - \varphi$; $Hst = Hst \cup \{\varphi\}$;

U3: If $\theta = \neg g[s \leftarrow v;F]$, among them, facet expression $T = t \in F$

U3.1: $\varphi = g[s \leftarrow v';F'] \in O$, $T = t' \in F'$

U3.1.1If $t < t'$, then $O \Diamond \theta = O$

U3.1.2If $t \geq t'$, then $O \Diamond \theta = O - \varphi$; $Hst = Hst \cup \{\varphi\}$;

U3.2: $\varphi = c[s \leftarrow v';F'] \in O$, $T = t' \in F'$ and satisfying $g :: c$ or $g :: *c$

*U3.2.1*If $t < t'$, then $O \Diamond \theta = O$

U3.2.2If $t \geq t'$, there does not exist $c' \in C$, satisfying $c' \subset c$, then $O \Diamond \theta = O - \varphi$; $Hst = Hst \cup \{\varphi\}$

U3.2.3If $t \geq t'$, there exists $c' \in C$, satisfying $c' \subset c$, then $O \Diamond \theta = O - \varphi + \{c'[s \leftarrow v';F'] \mid c' \subset c\}$; $Hst = Hst \cup \{\varphi\}$.

U4: If $\theta = g[s \leftarrow v;F]$, among them, facet expression $T = t \in F$

U4.1: $\varphi = g[s \leftarrow v';F'] \in O$, $T = t' \in F'$

U4.1.1 If $t < t'$, then $O \Diamond \theta = O$; $Hst = Hst \cup \{\theta\}$

U4.1.2If $t \geq t'$, then $O \Diamond \theta = O + \theta - \varphi$; $Hst = Hst \cup \{\varphi\}$.

U4.2: $\varphi = g[s \leftarrow v';F'] \in Th(O)$, $T = t' \in F'$, there exists $c \in C$, satisfying $g :: c$ or $g :: *c$ and $\mu = c[s \leftarrow v';F'] \in O$

U4.2.1If $t < t'$, then $O \Diamond \theta = O$; $Hst = Hst \cup \{\theta\}$

U4.2.2If $t \geq t'$, there does not exist $c' \in C$, satisfying $c' \subset c$, and there does not exist $g' \in E$, satisfying $g' :: c$, then $O \Diamond \theta = O + \theta - \mu$; $Hst = Hst \cup \{\mu\}$;

U4.2.3If $t \geq t'$, there does not exist $c' \in C$, satisfying $c' \subset c$, but there exists $g' \in E$, satisfying $g' :: c$, then $O \Diamond \theta = O + \theta - \mu + \{g'[s \leftarrow v';F'] \mid g' :: c\}$; $Hst = Hst \cup \{\mu\}$

U4.2.4If $t \geq t'$, there exists $c' \in C$, satisfying $c' \subset c$, then $O \Diamond \theta = O + \theta - \mu + \{c'[s \leftarrow v';F'] \mid c' \subset c\}$; $Hst = Hst \cup \{\mu\}$

Here, we show that ontology updating operator satisfies axiom A1-A4.

Theorem 1: Ontology updating operators' $\Diamond$ ' of definition 1 satisfy axiom A1-A4.

Proof:

According to ontology updating rules, the used operations can guarantee that $O \Diamond \theta$ is ontology, satisfying axiom ***A1***.

In U1-U4, if the assertion in ontology is newer than the updating assertion, then don't update it, otherwise update it to the new assertion, satisfying axiom A2.

In ***U2*** and ***U4***, no introduction of $\neg\theta$ due to updating operation. So the updated ontology should be coordinated' satisfying axiom ***A3***.

In updating rules U1-U4, all the assertions that are older than the updating assertions are deleted from ontology, and are put into the history assertion set HST. So ontology always keeps the newest assertions, satisfying axiom A4.

6. Illustrations

According to the update postulates***P0-P6***, update axiom ***A1-A4*** and the update operators***U1-U4***, we can get the process diagram of induction strategy showed in Figure 1, and give a simple illustration.

DOI: 10.1051/itmconf/20160705010

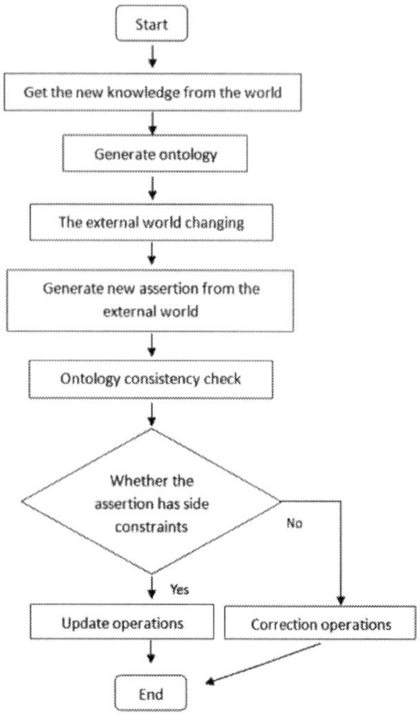

Figure 1.System function structure diagram

We first get the new knowledge from the world and generate the ontology as Figure 2.

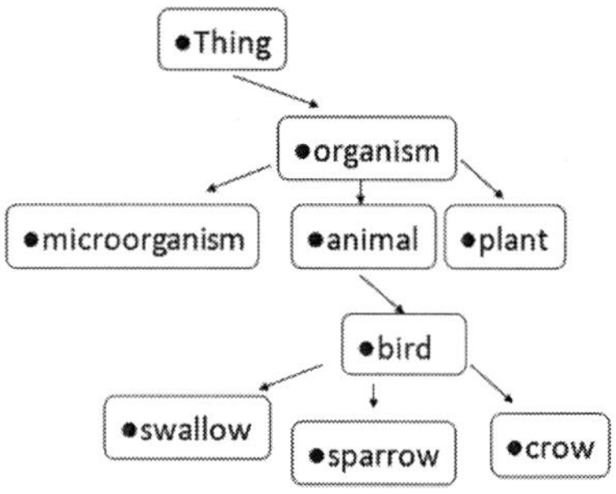

Figure 2. Ontology

As the external world changes, we generate the new assertion from the world as Figure 3..

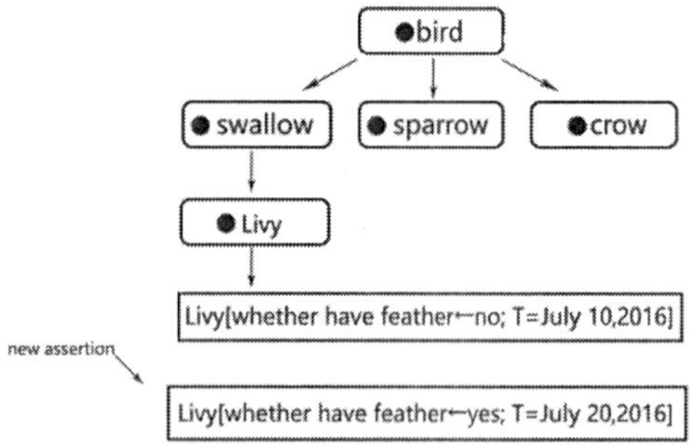

Figure 3. New assertion and ontology

Then we check the ontology consistency and whether the assertion has facet constrains, if the new assertion meets both of the conditions, we take update operations as Figure 4.

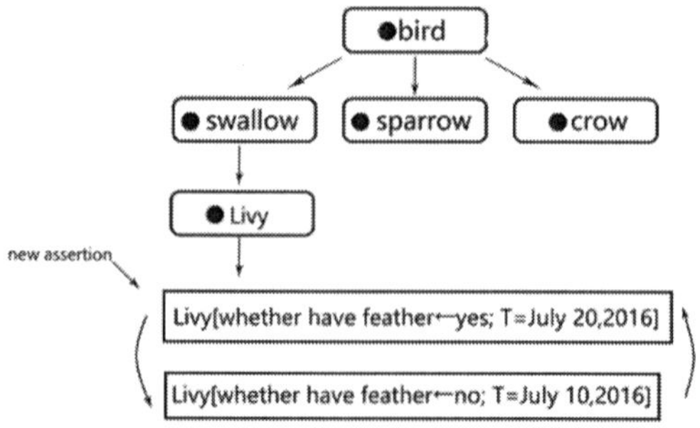

Figure 4. Update operations

7. Conclusions

This paper presented an approach for ontology update based on the axiomatic cognitive model of ontology learning, which reduces the cost of ontology construction. Corresponding axioms are created for the ontology update strategy of the model. The specific operators of the operation are given to do the specific operating of ontology update. It is proved that these operators satisfy the established system. And we give an illustration to show how to implement our approach step by step.

In the near future, we plan to develop a prototype implementation of the proposed model and test it on existing ontologies, and to show characterization results to prove theoretically the practical relevance and the tractability of the proposed model.

Acknowledgment

This work is supported by the National Natural Science Foundation of China (Grant No.61263043).

References

1. Berners-Lee T, Hendler J, Lassila O, et al. The Semantic Web", Scientific American[J]. Lecture Notes in Computer Science, 2001, 284(October):34--43.
2. Yuan H. The Knowledge Base Based on Ontology Semantic WEB Expanded Search Method[J]. Electronic Test, 2013.J. Clerk Maxwell, A Treatise on Electricity and Magnetism, 3rd ed., vol. 2. Oxford: Clarendon, 1892, pp.68–73.
3. Craven M, Dan D P, Freitag D, et al. Learning to construct knowledge bases from the World Wide Web [J]. Artificial Intelligence, 2000, 118(1–2):69-113.
4. Malucelli A, Palzer D, Oliveira E. Ontology-based Services to help solving the heterogeneity problem in e-commerce negotiations ☆[J]. Electronic

Commerce Research & Applications, 2006, 5(1):29-43.
5. Qing-Mao L I, Yang X J, Zhou X B. Research on topic maps-based ontology information retrieval model [J]. Journal of Computer Applications, 2010, 30(1):240-242.
6. Shum S B, Motta E, Domingue J. ScholOnto: an ontology-based digital library server for research documents and discourse[J]. International Journal on Digital Libraries, 2000, 3(3):237-248.
7. Ashburner M, Ball C A, Blake J A, et al. Gene ontology: tool for the unification of biology. The Gene Ontology Consortium.[J]. Nature Genetics, 2000, 25(1):25-29.
8. Stevens R, Goble C A, Bechhofer S. Ontology-based knowledge representation for bioinformatics.[J]. Briefings in Bioinformatics, 2000, 1(4):398-414.
9. Flahive A, Taniar D, Rahayu W, et al. A methodology for ontology update in the semantic grid environment[J]. Concurrency & Computation Practice & Experience, 2015, 27(4):782-808.
10. Sangers J, Hogenboom F, Frasincar F. Event-Driven Ontology Updating[C]// International Conference on Web Information Systems Engineering. Springer-Verlag, 2012:44-57.
11. Hamilton A, González E J, Acosta L, et al. Semantic-based approach for route determination and ontology updating[J]. Engineering Applications of Artificial Intelligence, 2013, 26(26):1174–1184.
12. Wang L, Murayama H, Hosokawa A. Ontology updating apparatus, method and system[J]. 2014.
13. Oberle D, Scheidl S. Updating Ontology while Maintaining Document Annotations: US, US20110078215[P]. 2011.
14. Kim J, Jeong D, Baik D K. Performance Evaluation of XPath Form-Based Ontology Storage Model Regarding Query Processing and Ontology Update[C]// International Conference on Convergence and Hybrid Information Technology. IEEE, 2008:1067-1074.
15. Chen C, Sun W, Zheng B, et al. An Incremental Approach to Closest Pair Queries in Spatial Networks Using Best-First Search[C]// Database and Expert Systems Applications -, International Conference, DEXA 2011, Toulouse, France, August 29 - September 2, 2011, Proceedings. 2011:136-143.

 DOI: 10.1051/itmconf/20160705011

An Optimized Ant System For Clustering With Elitist Ant And Local Search

Ming-Pan LI[a], Min YAO[b]

[1] Department of Computer Science ZheJiang University HangZhou 310000, China
[2] Department of Computer Science ZheJiang University, HangZhou 310000, China

[a]kinglmp@163.com [b]myao@zju.edu.cn

Abstract: Clustering analysis is an important field in data mining, and also one of the current research hotspots in computer science. This paper focus on some classical data clustering algorithms and swarm intelligence, especially ant colony optimization, trying to combine these two kinds of algorithms and improve the efficiency and accuracy of data clustering. This paper proposes a new ant colony optimization data clustering algorithm, named ant colony clustering algorithm with elitist ant and local search (ACC-EAL). This algorithm adopts a new pheromone incremental calculation method, making the distances among the clusters tend to increase, and the clusters get denser. Meanwhile local search provides the ants more opportunity to find optimal solution and the elite ant strategy makes the ants with optimal solutions contribute more to the pheromone increment.

1.Introduction

Ant system (AS) algorithm is a kind of heuristic bionic evolutionary system based on swarm intelligence, and is proposed by Italian scholar M.Dorigo first to solve the TSP problem[1-4]. The experimental results prove that ant algorithm is very robust and has the ability to find the optimal solution, but on the other hand it has the defect of low convergence speed and the tendency to stagnate. Later L.M. Gambardella and M. Dorigo put forward an improved ant algorithm, that is, Ant-Q, which replace the stochastic proportional choice rule of AS by pseudo random proportional state transition rule in Ant-Q, making the algorithm get better balance between knowledge exploration and knowledge exploitation. And based on Ant-Q M.Dorigo proposed the ant colony system (ACS)[5,6] . M.Dorigo and other scholars further develop ant algorithms into a general used optimization technique, named ant colony optimization (ACO), and all the algorithms that match the ACO framework is called ant optimization algorithm. At the moment ant colony optimization algorithm has been used in solving combination optimal problem, function optimization problem, robot path planning, data mining, network routing, and has achieved good results. At present some well-studied ant system includes ant optimization algorithm, the Rank-based Version of Ant System proposed by Bullnhemier[7] , the ant nest and ant eggs classification model raised by Deneubourg, and the MAX-MIN Ant System (MMAS) by T.Stützle and H.Hoos[8-9], and the Best-Worst Ant System (BWAS) by O.Cordón[10], etc.

Overall, the present study of ant colony algorithm is still in its infancy, many ideas are still budding, the theoretical system has not been well established, and the convergence has not yet been rigorously proven, but there is no doubt that the algorithm has a great advantage and a bright outlook in solving complex optimization problems, especially discrete optimization.

Data mining aims to extract knowledge from data, and data mining is an interdisciplinary research field, the goal of data mining is to discover knowledge that is accurate and more important, is comprehensible for the users. There are several different aspects of data mining, that is, classification, regression, dependence modeling and clustering, etc. Clustering aims to discover some groups or organizations of data samples in a given dataset, often by quantifying the similarities and dissimilarities between two different objects. And the samples in a cluster are similar with the samples in the same cluster while are dissimilar with the samples not in the different cluster. There are many cluster algorithms are based on swarm intelligence, such algorithms are often distributed, and well self-organized, robust and scalable. Currently most swarm intelligence based clustering algorithms are ant clustering algorithms and particle clustering algorithms. Ant based clustering models include

DOI: 10.1051/itmconf/20160705011

the ant nest and ant eggs classification model raised by Deneubourg, and the ants task assignment models put forward by Bonabeau, and the ant nests classification model by Lumer and Faieta. There are many other models such as models based on information entropy, fuzzy neural network. All these models and algorithms, although have made great progress, is still flawed, for example, some models need to set a lot of parameters. Another type of clustering algorithms attempts to combine classical clustering algorithm and ant optimization algorithm, such as combining fuzzy c-means clusters and ACO [11], also achieved remarkable results.

In this paper we proposed an ant colony optimization (ACO) algorithm for the cluster task of data mining. In this task, the goal is to assign each case to one cluster, based on the similarity of the case with others. The rest of this paper is organized as follows. In section II we present a brief overview of ant colony optimization, we will introduce the characteristic and basic framework of ACO algorithms. In section III we will introduce our new cluster algorithm based on ant colony. And in Section IV we will introduce some experiments and show the performance of our algorithm compared with some classical cluster algorithm. Finally, section V concludes this paper and points directions of the future research.

2. Ant Colony Optimization

2.1 An overview of ACO

ACO algorithms are stochastic search procedures. Their central component is the pheromone model, which is used to probabilistically sample the search space [12]. An ACO algorithm is a system based on agents which simulate the natural behavior of real ants, such as foraging, nest, and task assignment, etc. This kind of system as a new metaheuristic was proposed to solve combinatorial optimization problem, and is proven robust, scalable and versatile. In ACO, each path followed by an ant is associated with a candidate solution for a given problem. And how much pheromone an ant deposited on a path is proportional to the quality of the candidate solution for the problem correspond to the path; Another idea behind ACO is that when an ant need to make a choice between more than two paths, the path with larger amount of pheromone is more likely to be chosen.

In general, the ACO approach attempts to solve an optimization problem by repeating the following two steps [11]:

1) Candidate solutions are constructed using a pheromone model, that is, a parametrized probability distribution over the solution space;

2) The candidate solutions are used to modify the pheromone values in a way that is deemed to bias future sampling toward high quality solutions.

2.2 The framework of basic ACO algorithms

We have to know that ACO is a very general definition, which is a desirable feature making the algorithm robust but also makes the theoretical analysis about ACO complicated. Actually, we can capture the framework of basic ACO algorithm like follows. At first, the pheromone values are initiated to a constant positive value. Then, a series of constructive heuristic steps constructing and searching candidate solutions follow, in each iteration, each ant probabilistically constructs solutions for the optimization problem according to the present pheromone model, and then for every valid solution, a local search is optionally implemented to find a better solution around this candidate solution. And before the next iteration starts, the pheromone value must be updated according to the current valid solutions. When the iteration stop condition met, output the best-so-far solution. We summarize the process above in a clearer way as follows.

The framework of basic ACO algorithms:

Pheromone initiation. At the beginning of the algorithm, first initiate the pheromone values to a constant positive value.

Constructing solution. A main component of any ACO algorithms is heuristically and constructively construct the candidate solutions. And a solution construction starts from an empty solution space, and at each construction step, the solution space will be extended by adding new feasible component to it.

Local search. This step is optional. A local search step may be used by an ant to improve the solution it has got. This step may help improve the performance of the whole algorithm.

Apply pheromone update rule. The goal of updating the pheromone value is to deposit more pheromone on the path of higher quality.

If the iteration stop condition met, output the best-so-far solution, otherwise go back to *b.* to execute the iteration again,

2.3 Pheromone Update Rule

The pheromone update rule is one of the keys to obtain a satisfactory performance in ACO algorithms, and it helps search for the candidate solutions and influence the convergence speed. M.Dorigo once proposed three different methods of calculating the pheromone increment corresponding to three different algorithm models, that is, ant-cycle system, ant-density system, and ant quantity system [13]. In ant-cycle system, the pheromone update rule between sample i and sample j is

$$\Delta\tau_{ij}^{k} = Q \,/\, L_K \tag{1}$$

where Lk is the path length that ant k traveled during last

 DOI: 10.1051/itmconf/20160705011

iteration, so that the amount of pheromone will depend on the quality of the solution, and the amount of pheromone on the optimal path will increase gradually. While in ant-density system, the pheromone increment between sample i and sample j could be calculated by the following formula.

$$\Delta\tau_{ij} = Q / d_{ij} \tag{2}$$

where dij represent the distance between sample i and sample j, so that the short edge in the graph will be favorable. And in ant-quantity system, the pheromone increment is a constant value Q which is uncorrelated with the path.

Obviously the three models above are different from each other. Some scholars have used the three models to solve the TSP problem, and there are 20 cities and 20 ants in the problem, every experiment performs 3000 iterations. And finally the result shows that ant-cycle is obviously better than the other two [14]. The reason for the difference between the three models is the different feedback information, ant-cycle can get the global information and are more likely to find the shorter path, while the other two models just use local information, and their search process will not benefit from the optimal solution. In this paper, we will propose a new pheromone update rule, and will be discussed later.

3 An Improved Aco Cluster Algorithm

In our algorithm, we try to fuse the ACO algorithm and some classical cluster algorithm, and put some improvement proposal for the ACO algorithm. Our algorithm is somehow like k-means algorithm, the basic process is just like k-means. In k-means algorithm, a sample is assigned to a group depends on the distance from the sample to the cluster centers, while in our algorithm, which cluster a sample belongs to is decided by the pheromone model, and is probabilistically determined. And we also adopt the concept of *elitist ant*, make the ants that find optimal solution have a greater influence on the pheromone model. Moreover we also use a local search strategy, which make the ants more likely to find the optimal solution. And in our algorithm, we introduced a new pheromone update rule and a new method to calculate the heuristic function, which makes the clusters become denser and get far away from each other. Later we will explain the details about our ACO cluster algorithm based on elitist ant and local search.

The idea of our new pheromone update rule and the local search strategy are inspired by the work in [17] and [18].

3.1 New pheromone update rule

In our algorithm, we use elitist ants to update pheromone values, for every elitist ant, if sample x does not belong to cluster C_i, then $\Delta\tau^k_{xi} = 0$, otherwise,

$$\Delta\tau^k_{xi} = \frac{Q * minCenterDist(k)}{\frac{1}{\# C_i}\sum_{x\in C_i} Dist(x, C_i)} \tag{3}$$

where Q is a constant positive number, and $\#C_i$ represent the number of samples in cluster C_i, *minCenterDist(k)* represents the minimum distance between any two different clusters in the solution of ant k, $Dist(x,C_i)$ represents the distance between sample x and the cluster center of cluster C_i. We can easily inference from formula (3) that this definition of pheromone increment will make the clusters denser and get far away from each other, that the samples in a cluster will be more similar with the ones in the same cluster while distinct from the samples in the different clusters.

A. The pheromone volatile factor

It is common sense that the pheromone will evaporate, so in ACO algorithm, the pheromone update rule includes a factor that represent the pheromone evaporation speed. After each iteration the pheromone value is updated as follows.

$$\tau(t+1) = (1-\rho)\tau_{xi}(t) + \Delta\tau \tag{4}$$

And ρ is the volatile factor. The volatile factor influences the search capability and the convergence of the ACO algorithm, so carefully choose a reasonable volatile factor is very important. If the volatile value is too large and the problem is of large scale, some region unsearched will has a very low pheromone level and may even become zero, which will terribly reduce the search performance of the algorithm. While with a too small volatile factor will make the searched solution may be searched again, and slow down the convergence speed of the algorithm. Generally speaking, 0.3 or so will be reasonable for the volatile factor, in this paper we choose the volatile factor to be 0.2.

3.2 The heuristic function

In our ACO cluster algorithm, the probability of sample x to be assigned to cluster C_i will be [15]

$$P(x, C_i) = \frac{\tau^{\alpha}_{x,C_i}\eta^{\beta}_{x,C_i}}{\sum_{j=0}^{K}(\tau^{\alpha}_{x,Cj}\eta^{\beta}_{x,C_j})} \tag{5}$$

where K is the total number of clusters and

$$\eta_{x,C_i} = \frac{K}{Dist(x, C_i)} \tag{6}$$

In equation (5) and (6), η is the value of a problem-dependent function for sample x and cluster C_i, the higher is that value of η, the more likely x be assigned to cluster C_i. And κ is a constant to adjust the heuristic function, κ should be properly set according to the problem and initial pheromone level, in our experiment, κ is set to be 2000. We can see from equation (6) that a sample is more likely to be classified into the nearer clusters.

In equation (5), the pheromone heuristic factor α reflects the importance of the information (the pheromone) obtained by the ants in the search process, and the expectation heuristic factor β reflects the importance of the heuristic information for the search process. α and β balance the relative weight of the pheromone versus the heuristic information, they are relevant and contradictory. β reflects the strength of the local information, the bigger β is, the more likely the ant will choose the local shortest path, which will speed up the convergence, but will reduce the randomness of the search process and will be trapped into a local optimum. On the other hand, the heuristic factor α reflects the strength of the randomness factors influence the search process, the bigger α is, the more likely the ant will choose the path that has already be searched and also reduce the randomness of the search process and also will trap the algorithm into a local optimum. The appropriate value of α and β can be determined by simulation experiments. In this paper, we choose α =1.5, and β =4.5.

3.3 The Local Search Strategy

We have mentioned that local search will help the ACO algorithms to get better performance, in our algorithm, we also adopted the local search strategy, and our local search strategy is like follows.

For an ant a, if the solution a gets for the cluster task is $solution_a = [c_1, c_2, c_3 \ldots\ldots, c_N]$, and c_i is a number between 1 and K which indicate which cluster sample i belongs to. For every i from 1 to N, generate a random number r_i, and r_i is greater than 0 and less than 1, if r_i is greater than the local search threshold value P, then we need to assign a random number between 1 and K inclusive to c_i, and after all the samples is processed, we recalculate the cluster center. And if the new solution is better than the original one, then replace the original solution with the new solution.

3.4 The Ant System With Elitist Ant And Local Search

We introduced our new pheromone update rule and heuristic function above, in this section the details of the algorithm will be discussed.

Our algorithm complies with the framework of the basic ACO algorithms. At first, assume that the number of clusters is K, then for each ant, we need to randomly choose K cluster centers. After that we need to initiate the initial pheromone level from every sample to each cluster center, assume that the number of sample is N, then the data structure is a N by K matrix.

After the initiation process, then comes the main loop, for each ant, it need to assign each sample to different clusters, the ant use equation (5) to calculate the probability of each sample belong to the clusters, and every sample will be assigned to one cluster according to the following strategy: For each cluster sorted by the corresponding probability decreasingly, generate a random number r between 0 and 1, if r is smaller than the probability, then the sample is assigned to the corresponding cluster. If after the loop the sample is not assigned to any cluster, then assign the sample to the cluster with the largest probability.

After every sample is assigned to one of the clusters, the ant need to recalculate the cluster center for each cluster C_i, just in the follow method

$$\mu_i = \frac{\sum_{j=1}^{N} 1\{c_j == i\} x_j}{\sum_{j=1}^{N} 1\{c_j == i\}} \tag{7}$$

where *1{condition c}* return 1 if the condition is true and 0 otherwise. After the above step, we need to rank the ants according to the quality of their solution, the method to measure the quality of the solution is

$$f(X, C) = \sum_{i=1}^{N} (x_i - c_i)(x_i - c_i)^T \tag{8}$$

After ranking the ants, the next step is local search, after which we re-rank the ants according to their new solution, finally we use the elitist ants to update the pheromone level, the method is adding up the pheromone increment and the amount of volatile, just like follows.

$$\tau_{xi}(t+1) = (1-\rho)\tau_{xi}(t) + \sum_{k=1}^{m} \Delta\tau_{xi}^{k} \tag{9}$$

Then all the non-elitist ants need to update their cluster center again. The algorithm repeats the above process until the termination conditions is satisfied.

From what has been discussed above, our algorithm can be described and can be performed by the following steps:

Algorithm: *ant colony clustering algorithm with elitist ant and local search (ACC-EAL).*

Input: the dataset to be clustered and the number of clusters.

Output: the dataset marked with the cluster label.

Algorithm details:

Initiation. We need to initiate the pheromone level, the number of ants, the number of clusters, and for every ant, needs to initiate K cluster centers randomly.

DOI: 10.1051/itmconf/20160705011

Cluster the data. For every ant and every data sample, assign each data sample to one cluster according to $p(x,c_i)$, we should calculate $p(x,c_i)$ as equation (5).

Recalculate the new cluster centers, using equation (7).

Rank all the ants according to the qualities of their solutions, using equation (8) to measure the solutions.

Local search. For the top 10% elitist ants, perform local search, the strategy has been introduced above.

Pheromone update. Update the pheromone level using equation (3) and equation (9).

For the non-elitist ants, update the cluster centers randomly.

If the termination condition is satisfied, then output the so-far-best solution and exit, otherwise, go to step 3.

In our ACO cluster algorithm with elitist ants and local search strategy, we adopt the elitist ant strategy, making the optimal solutions contribute more to the pheromone increment, and the local search strategy helps the algorithm converge more quickly. And we create a new pheromone update rule, and intuitively we can figure out that the denser the clusters are and the further the clusters are away from each other, the more the pheromone level will be incremented.

4 Experimental Result and Discussion

We implemented our ACO based cluster algorithm on three datasets, the output of the algorithm is a vector that indicate which cluster the corresponding data sample belongs to. And we use the Hungarian algorithm to match the output cluster label with the real label and calculate the accuracy of our algorithm. The result shows that our algorithm performs much better than the classical k-means algorithm.

4.1 Dataset

We use 3 different kinds of datasets, and all the dataset are from UCI machine learning repository. The first dataset we use is *Iris*, which is perhaps the best known database to be found in the pattern recognition literature. The data set contains 3 classes of 50 instances each, where each class refers to a type of iris plant. One class is linearly separable from the other 2; the latter are NOT linearly separable from each other. *Iris* contains 3 kind of iris flowers, that is, *Setosa*, *Versicolour* and *Virginica*, and *Iris* consist of 150 data samples, and each sample include 4 features, that is, sepal length, sepal width, petal length and petal width. The second dataset is *Wine*, which is the result of a chemical analysis of wines grown in the same region in Italy but derived from three different cultivars. The analysis determined the quantities of 13 constituents found in each of the three types of wines. *Wine* consists of 179 samples, and each sample includes 13 attributes, such as the content level of alcohol and malic acid, flavonoid and the color intensity, etc. And all the features are continuous. The third dataset is *Vehicle silhouettes*, which is used to classify a given silhouette as one of four types of vehicle, using a set of features extracted from the silhouette. The vehicle may be viewed from one of many different angles. This dataset has 946 samples and each sample includes 18 features extracted from the silhouettes by the HIPS (Hierarchical Image Processing System) extension BINATTS, which extracts a combination of scale independent features utilizing both classical moments based measures such as scaled variance, skewness and kurtosis about the major/minor axes and heuristic measures such as hollows, circularity, rectangularity and compactness. [16]

4.2 Experimental Result

At first we mainly explore the relationship between the ant colony size and the clustering accuracy. Table I shows how the clustering accuracy change with the ant colony size.

TABLE I. Clustering Accuracy Of Different Ant Colony Size

Datase/ Ant colony size	3	5	8	10	15	20	25	30	40	50
Iris	88. 90	89. 40	89. 60	90. 03	90. 16	90. 60	89. 63	89. 93	90. 00	89. 56
Wine	69. 69	69. 75	70. 00	70. 47	70. 55	70. 64	70. 16	70. 19	70. 08	70. 16
Vehicle silhouettes	45. 00	45. 11	45. 24	45. 98	46. 09	45. 96	45. 98	45. 98	46. 09	45. 86

We also draw the curve to observe the relationship between the clustering accuracy and the and colony size more clearly.

We can see from Table I and Figure 1 that when the ant colony size is relatively small, the clustering accuracy will grow as the ant colony size get larger. But when the ant colony size is big enough, the grow of ant colony size helps little with increasing the clustering accuracy. We will explore the reason later.

We also compare our algorithm with the classical k-means algorithm, the following table shows that our algorithm is much better that the k-means.

TABLE II. Acc-Eal Vs K-Means

Dataset/ algorithm	ACC-EAL	k-means
Iris	90.60	81.61
Wine	70.64	64.04
Vehicle silhouettes	46.09	44.79

DOI: 10.1051/itmconf/20160705011

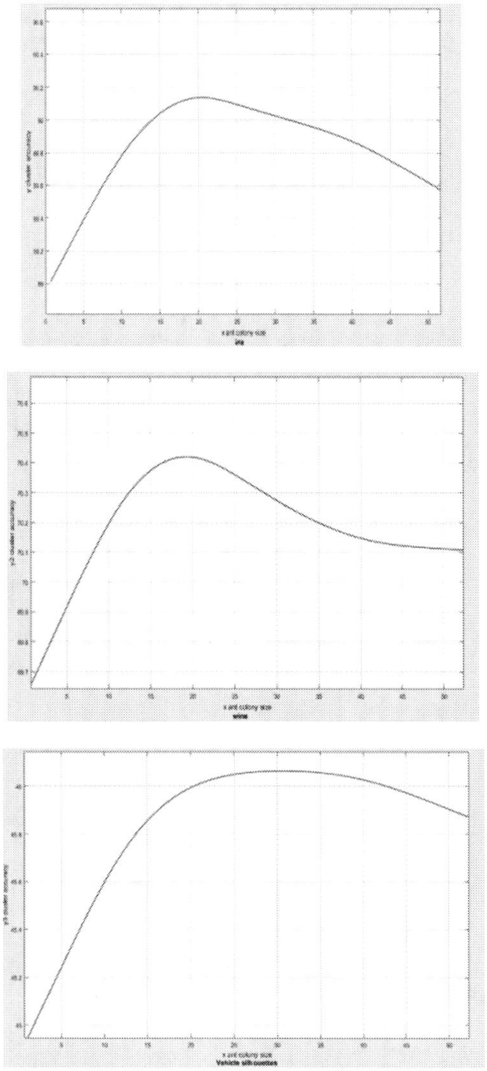

Figure1 The Figure Of Table 1

On the whole, we can see that compared with the k-means algorithm, our algorithm gets a higher clustering accuracy.

ACO algorithm is a kind of stochastic search algorithm, and just like other simulated evolvement algorithm, ACO algorithm finds the optimal solution from the solution space constituted by multiple feasible solutions. In this process, not only the adaptive ability of each individual, but also cooperation between individuals is needed. The ant colony can orderly converge toward the optimal solution in the complex search process, which benefit a lot from the exchange of information and cooperation between the individuals. When the ant colony is relatively large, many ants will get the similar solution, and it doesn't help to improve the cluster accuracy just by increasing the ant colony size.

Conclusion

This paper proposed a cluster algorithm called ACC-EAL based on ACO. The goal of ACC-EAL is to discover clusters in dataset. In ACC-EAL we introduced a new pheromone update rule and heuristic function, and we also adopted the local search and elitist ant strategy. All the improvements aim to make the cluster denser inside and the distance among clusters become further. And ACC-EAL is well suited for parallel and distributed implementation to improve the program efficiency, because the ants are non-interfering during the search process.

ACO proves to be an efficient tool to solve optimization problem, but it is not as mature as genetic algorithm and neural network, so I think further research is very urgent, such as further studying the behavior of real ants, and studying ACO mathematically, and optimizing ACO to speed up the convergence, etc.

Acknowledgment

This paper is the partial achievement of project 2014BAD10B02 supported by the National Support Program.

References

1. M. Dorigo, "Optimization learning and natural algorithms", PhD Thesis, Dipartimento Elettronica, Politecnico di Milano, Italy, 1992.
2. M. Dorigo, L. M. Gambardella, "Ant colony system: a cooperative learning approach to the traveling salesman problem", IEEE Transactions on Evolutionary Computation, Vol. 1, No. 1, pp.53-66, 1997.
3. M.Dorigo, L. M. Gambardella, "Ant colonies for the traveling salesman problem", BioSystems, Vol. 43, No. 1, 1997, pp. 73-81.
4. L. M. Gambardella, M. Dorigo, "Solving symmetric and asymmetric TSPs by ant colonies", Proceedings of the IEEE International Conference on Evolutionary Computation, IEEE Press, Piscataway, pp.622-627, 1996.
5. Luca M. Gambardella, M.Dorigo. "Ant-Q: A Reinforcement Learning approach to the traveling salesman problem", Proceedings of ML-95, Twelfth Intern. Conf. on Machine Learning, Morgan Kaufmann, 1995, 252–260.
6. Marco Dorigo, Luca Maria Gambardella. "A STUDY OF SOME PROPERTIES OF ANT-Q", Proceedings of PPSN IV–Fourth International Conference on Parallel Problem Solving From Nature, H.–M. Voigt, W. Ebeling, I. Rechenberg and H.–S. Schwefel (Eds.),

Springer-Verlag, Berlin, 656–665.

7. B.Bullnheimer,R.F.Hartl,and C.Strauss.A new rank-based version of the ant system:A computational study[J].Central Europe on Journal for Operations Research and Economics,7(1) :25-38,1999.
8. T.Stützle and H.Hoos.The MAX-MIN ant system and local search for
9. the traveling salesman problem[C].In T.Baeck,Z.Michal ewicz,and X.Yao,editors Proceedings of IEEE-ICEC-EPS' 97, IEEE International
10. Conference on Evolutionary Computation and Evolutio nary Programming Conference,pages 309-314.IEEE Press,1997.
11. T.Stützle and H.Hoos.Improvements on the ant system: Introducing MAX-MIN ant system[C]. In Proceedings of the International Conference on Artificial Neural Networks and Genetic Algorithms, pages 245-249.Springer Verlag,Wien,1997.
12. O.Cordón,I.Fernández de Viana,F.Herrera,and L.Moren o.A New ACO model intergrating evolutionary comput ation concepts:The best-worst ant system[C]. Proc of the 2nd International Workshop on Ant Algorithms, 2000: 22-29.
13. C.Immaculate Mary,Dr. S.V. Kasmir Raja, Dean. Improved Fuzzy C-Means Clusters With Ant Colony Optimization. International Journal of Computer Science & Emerging Technologies (E-ISSN: 2044-6004) 1Volume 1, Issue 4, December 2010
14. Marco Dorigo, Christian Blum. Ant colony optimization theory: A survey. Theoretical Computer Science 344 (2005) 243–278
15. HAN-CHEN HUANG. "THE APPLICATION OF ANT COLONY OPTIMIZATION ALGORITHM IN TOUR ROUTE PLANNING", Journal of Theoretical and Applied Information Technology, 2013
16. JIAN-FENG YANG. "The Ant Colony Algorithm And Its Application Research". CNKI, 2007:23-26
17. Mr.Pankaj K. Bharne, Mr.V. S. Gulhane, Miss. Shweta K. Yewale:" Data Clustering Algorithms B- ased On Swarm Intelligence".IEEE. 2011
18. http://archive.ics.uci.edu/ml
19. Sara Saatchi, Chih Cheng Hung. "Hybridization of the Ant Colony Optimization with the K-Means Algorithm for Clustering". SCIA 2005.
20. [18] P.S. Shelokar, V.K. Jayaraman, B.D. Kulkarni*. "An ant colony approach for clustering". Analytica Chimica Acta 2004.

DOI: 10.1051/itmconf/20160705012

A Data Flow Model to Solve the Data Distribution Changing Problem in Machine Learning

Bo-Wen SHANG[1,a], Ke WANG[1]

[1] *College of Computer Science, National University of Defense Technology Changsha, 410072, China*

Abstract. Continuous prediction is widely used in broad communities spreading from social to business and the machine learning method is an important method in this problem.When we use the machine learning method to predict a problem.We use the data in the training set to fit the model and estimate the distribution of data in the test set.But when we use machine learning to do the continuous prediction we get new data as time goes by and use the data to predict the future data,there may be a problem. As the size of the data set increasing over time, the distribution changes and there will be many garbage data in the training set.We should remove the garbage data as it reduces the accuracy of the prediction.The main contribution of this article is using the new data to detect the timeliness of historical data and remove the garbage data.We build a data flow model to describe how the data flow among the test set,training set ,validation set and the garbage set and improve the accuracy of prediction .As the change of the data set,the best machine learning model will change.We design a hybrid voting algorithm to fit the data set better that uses seven machine learning models predicting the same problem and uses the validation set putting different weights on the learning models to give better model more weights.Experimental results show that,when the distribution of the data set changes over time,our time flow model can remove most of the garbage data and get a better result than the traditional method that adds all the data to the data set;our hybrid voting algorithm has a better prediction result than the average accuracy of other predict models.

1 Introduction

Machine learning and deep learning are the most commonly used methods through training by large data set with high dimensions to predict the unknown target. As some data is continuous, in many cases, we use the training data set to predict the unknown test data set. Over a period of time, the test data set will be known and added to the training data set,Then the new training data set is used to predict the new unknown test data, as in [1]. So we need a predictive model that can evolve with the time.However, with the change of the data set, the best machine learning model and the best hyper parameters will change. The common method is to split the data set into three parts: training set(used for model fitting),validation set(used for model test and get the estimated score),and test set(used for final model assessment).This method needs to refit all the data set and try all the machine learning methods to find the best model,so it costs too much if the data set updates frequently. In [2],they propose a new methods bases on a new data splitting strategies, but this method needs a lot of data.

In some prediction problems, such as the trend prediction,the distribution of the data set changes as the time goes by, so we should remove the garbage data. In this paper, we propose a data flow predictive model based on the voting algorithm. We use different machine learning models to fit the data sets, and use a new validation set to give every model a score, then we use the history data to give each methods a weight for each method to vote the result. We use our new data to test the history data and let the data flow among different data sets to use data efficiently(e.g. [3]–[6]).

2 The Data Flow Model

The main research of the data flow model is to find the best training set through the way that let the garbage data flow out of the training set and let the useful data flow into the training set.

The process is like getting new knowledge every day that we use our experiments to checkout if the message is true or not.We will forget the error message that we think it's wrong and remember the message that we think it's true.The message that we think it's true will become our

[a] Corresponding author: 819089115@qq.com

DOI: 10.1051/itmconf/20160705012

knowledge. Then we use our knowledge to predict new message and to judge whether it is true or not.

When we use a machine learning model to continuous predict the unknown data set that updates with the time, we can use the data flow model. The process is using the training set to predict the unknown data in the test set ,over a period of time, the unknown data will be known,then we use the data to update our training set and adjustment with our machine learning model.

As time goes by,the unknown data set will be known and the distribution of the data set may change. When we use all the known data to train our machine learning model and predict the new unknown data, there may be the a problem: whether all the known data is useful to our prediction? Research shows that for some data with strong timeliness, the distribution of the data will change with the time, and the distribution of the new data is different from the old data, so some old data will not be useful to predict the new data. Then the training set should be updated following the coming of the new data.

Machine learning model fits to the training data set to get the distribution of the data, but some data in the training data set can't reflect the distribution of the data in the test set. For example, some error data in the data set and some data out of date. Here we call them garbage data and use db to express the garbage data set.

Let some of the data in the test set at time T flow into the training set at time T+1 as the target column in the test set is known at time T+1.In order to distinguish the data join the training set at different times, we give them a time label. For example, the test set at time T will have a time label T.To promptly clean up the garbage data, we use the data with the new time label to test the other data in the data set and find the garbage data.Then we remove the garbage data and use the training set to predict the test set.

In data flow model, there are two problems to solve. The first one is that finding the data that flow from the training set to the garbage data set as we want to drop the garbage data that may be harmful to the predict. The second one is that finding the data that flow from the test set to the training set as we can use the useful data to predict the future data.

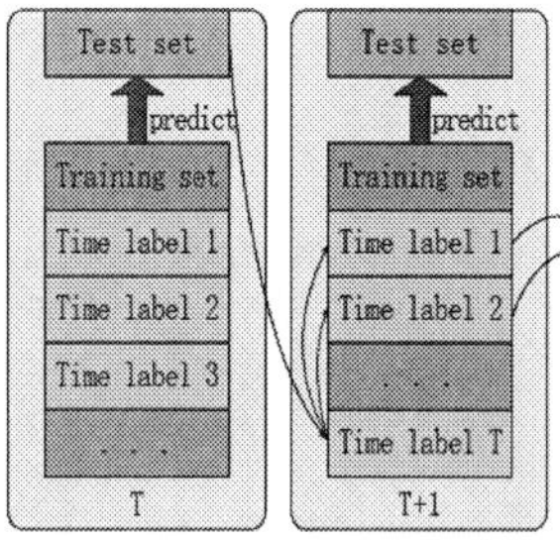

Figure 1. The date flow model

As time T+1,the target of the test set with time label T will be known.Then we can add some of the data to the training set. As the distribution of the data maybe change, the old data may have different distribution from the new data.At the same time,the distribution of the data will change.But only the test data with the same distribution with the training data that can be predict.It will cause a problem that the data in the training set has different distribution from the test data will reduce the accuracy of prediction.

In order to indicate the time that the data joins the training set,we give the data different time labels.For example,the data that joins the data set first will have the time label as t1,and the data set join the data set last have the time label tn.This time label is different from the time label T.As the distribution of the data changes over time,the oldest data may have the most different distribution from the new data.Here we define a difference function D to measure the difference between two data set's distribution:

$$D(t_1, t_n) \tag{1}$$

Firstly,we calculate the difference function between the data that have the same target with different time labels and use d(ti,tn) to express the result.Then we calculate the difference function between the data have the different target and use r(dp,dq,ti,tj) to express the value.If the value of D(ti,tn) is bigger than the biggest r(dp,dq,ti,tj), the data with the time label t flow is out.

But in practice,it's very hard to calculate the difference function as the distribution function of the data set is unknown.However,we can validates the history data with different targets and labels reversely. If there is enough new data,we use the new data as the training data and use all the history data as the test date.Then we divide the test error by the time label.If the test error of a data set is bigger than a threshold, the data with the label flow is out.

In the data flow model,we use the new data set as the training set and all the history data set with different time labels as the test set and use the predict result to decide the data flow.Before that we define a simple two classification machine learning model.The data set of the model have two kinds of data that with the target A and B,the distribution of class A is a and the distribution of class B is b.We use the confusion matrix of the predict result to present the test error.In the confusion matrix,each column of the matrix represents the instances in a predicted class while each row represents the instances in an actual class as in [5]. We build a confusion matrix for each data set with different time label.In the confusion matrix:

Table 1. The confusion matrix table

Predictive class A	**Predictive class B**	
True_class _A	False_class _A	Recall of class_A(RA)

DOI: 10.1051/itmconf/20160705012

False_class _B	True_class _B	Recall of class_B(RB)
Precision of class_A(PA)	Precision of class_B(PB)	Likelihood of class_A(LA) Likelihood of class_B(LB)

Recall of class_A:

$$\frac{\sum True\_class\_A}{\sum Class\_A} \tag{2}$$

Recall of class_B:

$$\frac{\sum True\_class\_B}{\sum Class\_B} \tag{3}$$

Accuracy:

$$\frac{\sum True\_class\_A + \sum True\_class\_B}{\sum Total\_population} \tag{4}$$

Precision of class_A:

$$\frac{\sum True\_class\_A}{\sum predictive\_class\_A} \tag{5}$$

Precision of class_B:

$$\frac{\sum True\_class\_B}{\sum predictive\_class\_B} \tag{6}$$

Likelihood of class_A:

$$\frac{RA}{RB} \tag{7}$$

Likelihood of class_B:

$$\frac{RB}{RA} \tag{8}$$

Through RA we can know the different between the new data set and the data set with the special time label. If RA is lower than the half of the maximum value, we can think that the data set with the time label is out of date.Some times,the LA or LB is very high,and one of the PA or PB is very low, then we should retain one kind of data and make the other kind flow out.

In the data flow model, we use the unknown data set as the test set and the history data set as the train when we predict the unknown target. After a period of time, the unknown target will be known and then the data set will be used as a part of the training set and we call it the new data set. Before using the new data set as the training set ,we use it to find which data set is out of date.After that ,the new data set and the history data set will be used to train the machine learning model.

3 Hybrid Voting Algorithm Based on History Data

In practice, the data set that we use to predict increases every day. Such as in some shopping website, users do different things every day. If we want to use the behavior data to predict their future behaviors, we should add them to our data set. However, in many cases ,the best machine learning method we use is based on experiment ,it will change follow the data set's change. To solve this problem, a method is to add the daily data to the data set and fit all the machine learning methods to find the best one. But this method is not only complex, but also lose a very important score for every method's accuracy rate in history. To solve this problem, we use a hybrid voting algorithm. In this method, we use different processes to run different machine learning models and use the new data to improve them in parallel. All the models will take part in the vote to decide the predict result, but the weights of them is different. Weight of models is decided by the score in the history. In the supervised machine models, the data set is divided into three parts: the training set d, the validation set v and the test set t. As we get the new data set n, the data in all data set will flow. The training data set d consists of n instances.

$$d = \{(x_i, y_i)\}_{i=1}^{n} \tag{9}$$

In the training data set,xi is a d-dimensional feature vector and yi is the corresponding known label.Our task is to find a function f:

$$f: X \to Y, x_i \in X, y_i \in Y \tag{10}$$

Then we want to get the f can perform better on an independent test data set.we define a loss function to measure the test errors(errors between target response y and the prediction f(x)):

$$L(y, \hat{f}(x)) \tag{11}$$

Because the training data set d is fixed,so the test error is refer to the special training data set d.So we define the test error when we use the training data set d :

$$E_d = T_{(x,y)}[L(y, \hat{f}(x)) \mid d] \tag{12}$$

In the formula above , T(x,y) is the test data set we randomly select.Assessment the Ed is a major method to measure the performance of the machine learning model and tune the parameters of the model.Our target is to chose the best machine model and tune the parameters to reduce

DOI: 10.1051/itmconf/20160705012

the test error. In the same time,the training error often be ignored.

$$E_t = \frac{1}{n}\sum_{i=1}^{n} L(y_i, \hat{f}_\theta(x_i)) \quad (13)$$

The training error Et is the average loss of the training data. We can drop the training error to zero if we improve the model. But the training error isn't a good measure of the test error and a zero training error is over-fit to the training data set.

We want to choose a machine learning model that can have less test error, but we should measure the model with the training error. The training error is decided by the training set.With the change of the training set, we must change our machine learning model to get a better result. If we change our machine learning model, we can't compare the results on different data sets and we don't know the prediction result when we use the other machine learning model.

So we use a hybrid voting algorithm to reduce the impact of the using of different models on the results of the experiment .In this method ,we split the behavior data into three parts: training set(used for model fit),validation set(used for model test and get the estimated score),and test set(for final model assessment) as in [4].We use different predictive models to fit the behavior features and use the validation set to get the estimated score of each models, at last, predict the test set through voting by all the models. The weight of each model in voting is based on the score that they get when they predict the validation set.

Training set	Validation set	Test set

Figure 2. The structure of data sets

For example,method A get score 24,35,13,24,32 in the last five days,so today method A's score is :

$$(1\times24+2\times35+3\times13+4\times24+5\times32)/15$$

In the same time ,the score is method's weight.Then we use all the method's results to predict a binary problem,all the methods' result and weight is:

Table 2. The methods' result and weight

method	A	B	C	D	E
weight	20	30	25	35	15
result	0	1	0	1	0

The result is that three methods votes 0,two methods votes 1.Add the weight of different methods ,the result 0's total weight is 60 and the total weight of 1 is 65,so we think 1 is the better result.

4 Case Study

We use a time varying data sets and contract two models. The data set contains two kinds of data with the target A and B. Each kind of data has 5 different time labels. Same kind of data with different time labels have the distribution changes continuously over time. Each item of the data has two features, a target and a time label.

We use the scikit-learn kit,the make_blobs function to generate data set.The centers of the class A with different time label is[[0,3],[1,2.8],[2,2.6],[3,2.4],[4,2.2],[5,2]]. The centers of the class B with different time label is[[5,2],[4,1.8],[3,1.6],[2,1.4],[1,1.2],[0,1]].The cluster is 0.5 and every time label will use 1000 samples.

In the traditional machine learning model,we use the history data as the training set and use the new data as the test set.As the time goes by,we have more and more new data,if we add the data to our data set without choose and not reduce the history data,our predict accuracy will drop.

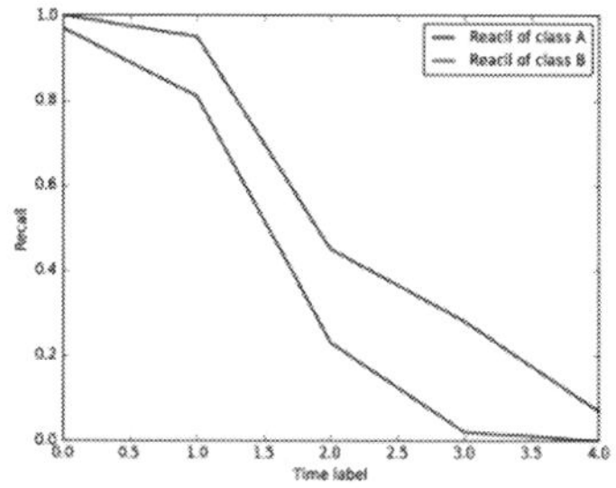

Figure 3. The recall of the traction methods

In this chart,we add the new data to the history data set,as the distribution of the data changes continuously over time,the recall of the data is dropping.

Why we have more data but the predict accuracy is down?That's because the distribution of the data set is changing with the time goes by,the new distribution of one kind of data may be more like that of a data set in the history,and some of the history data won't be useful or even harmful to our prediction result.Then we should find the useless data and remove them.

Here we design a method that use the new data set to test the history data set.We use the new data set as the training set and the history data set as the test set.

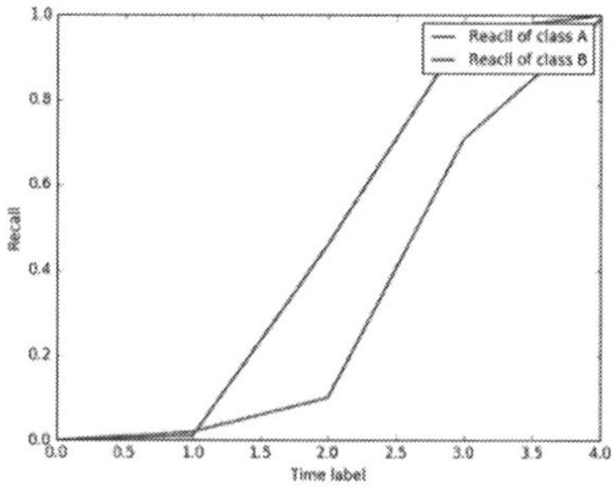

Figure 4. The recall of the data with different time label

DOI: 10.1051/itmconf/20160705012

We can see that the new data has higher test recall.The old data has low recall.We can use the threshold T=0.5,if the data set's average recall less than T,the data set with the time label can be remove.

When we use this methods,we can get a new result.

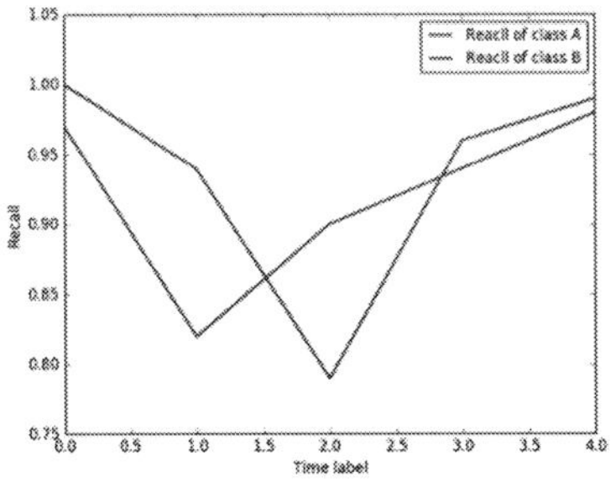

Figure 5. The recall of the predict result based on the data flow model

The recall of the prediction result is higher than the traditional method that we add all the data to the data set.

5 Conclusions

In this paper,we propose a data flow model that use the new data set to update the old data as the time goes by.In this way,we can add the new data to the history data set and remove the garbage data.At the same time ,the best machine learning model is changing as the update of the data set,we use the hybrid vote algorithm to get a better machine learning model. According to the experiment result,in the case of the distribution of the data set changes with time,we use the data flow model can get a better result than the traditional method that add all the data to the data set.

Acknowledgment

In this paper, the research was sponsored by the Nature Science Foundation of china (project number 61402511, project number 61572514)

References

1. L. Cao,T. Joachims, C. Wang, IEEE Intelligent Systems, **29**, 62-80 (2014)
2. V. Craykar,A. Saha, European Conference on Principles of Data Mining and Knowledge Discovery, (2015)
3. S. Valsan ,Backward Sequential Feature Elimination And Joining Algorithms In Machine Learning,(2014)
4. S.Chen,J. Lmoore,D. Turnbull,Knowledge Discovery and Data Mining,(2012)
5. M. David,Journal of Machine Learning Technologies,**2**, 37-63(2011).
6. Z.Abawab, G.Hmills,J.Crespo,,Knowledge Discovery and Data Mining, (2012)
7. B. Springer,S. Martin,Principal Component Analysis,**87**,41-64(2010)

Research on Monitoring Crowd Density Method Based on GIS and Mobile Location Data

Hao ZHAO[1,a,*],Yi-Fan QIU[2] and Wei DENG[3]

[1,2,3]*School of Resource and Environment Engineering, Wuhan University of Technology, Wuhan, China*

[a]zhaohao_wut@163.com
*Corresponding author: Hao ZHAO

Abstract: To effectively control and reduce the occurrence of accidents in public places, where crowds are easily gathered, is the problem of urban management. The paper proposes a method of monitoring population density which based on the combination of GIS and mobile location data. With the secondary-development which based on component GIS, this method can position the mobile location data in order to map the graph model and monitor the area, counting the number, area and crowddensity of monitoring area. We design and implement some system functions such as display warning messages and cartographic visualization to provide decision support for urban population management and control.

1 Introduction

In recent years, the safety accidents caused by gatherings are common, which have brought bad influence to the stability and development of the society. Therefore, it is particularly important to monitor the crowds, it is not only to estimate the movement of the crowds, but also more important to prevent the happening of the personnel casualty accidents.

At present, the monitoring of the crowd is mainly dependent on the analysis of video images or mobile phone positioning data. Compared to the results of other video estimation method, the improved hybrid Gauss model used by Shen Na et al is better1. Through the analysis of the characteristics of pixels and texture, Ren Qingyun3 and Yue Xiaojuan2 divided the crowd density into several degrees such as dense, denser and crowded to implement monitoring. But the scope of video surveillance is limited, high image resolution is required and it's difficult to recognize the dark image. Baidu uses mobile location data to generate the heat map 7 which divide the population density into several density degrees, but clients cannot get alert and the specific density from it. Martin Wirz et al get continuous positioning data by mobile app8, verify the relationship between walking speed and population density, but the method is only an analysis of the data, cannot display warnings.

In this paper, with the combination of the advantages of mobile location data-low cost, large sample size, wide coverage, strong real-time performance and so on6,11. Using powerful spatial analysis, data processing and other functions of GIS, we divide public space into several monitoring areas. It calculate the crowd density according to monitoring areas and the number of location data, and display warnings. The experiment results show that the system can display warning messages according to the threshold crowd density and highlight the crowded area. This will help the relevant departments grasp the aggregation of the population changes and trends in time, and provide data support for developing contingency plans and taking emergency measures to avoid the occurrence of such public safety incidents.

2 Crowd Density Estimation Method

Crowd density estimation method which based on GIS and mobile location data includes extracting monitoring areas, counting the number of people, determining the threshold crowd density and displaying warning messages.

DOI: 10.1051/itmconf/20160705013

2.1 Extracting Monitoring Areas

In the traditional methods, video images is divided into a number of sub areas to monitor which is according to the proportion of visual9. Another method is generating the monitoring areas based on kernel density analysis automatically. The first method needs a large number of video images to reflect the overall situation of crowd. The second method lacks the objectivity. This paper uses remote sensing image with resolution of 0.3m and *EPSG:3785*projection. After visual interpretation, we extracted monitoring areas.

2.2 Obtaining Mobile Location Data

With the development of technology, positioning terminal can be designed into chip size11.Each phone has a positioning function. In big data context, more than 90% of mobile phone users access the Internet every day. This laid the foundation to access mobile location data. Smart phone location data includes geo-tagged photos, location data and so on4. On the one hand, we can use data mining technique to select and process a large number of network data to obtain location data. On the other hand, mobile locating methods is based on cell phone towers and telephone network. We can negotiate with urban management departments or mobile operators to obtain anonymous location data10.

2.3 Determining the Threshold Crowd Density

When holdinglarge-scale events, the crowd density will grow rapidly in a limited space. And the probability of accident will increase. Hu Qingmei et al did a research on behavior characters of pedestrian and mechanism of stampede12. She got a conclusion that people prefer to own a 0.27m2-0.84m2 buffer area. The optimum density of crowd is 1.3m-2-1.8 m-2. Ran Lijun et al raised that the maximum crowd density of stampede accident is 9m-2 according to human physiological size of China5.

Martin Wirzet al evaluated the threshold crowd density of Fuin.J's research findings (Table 1)8. 5.5m^{-2} is an alarming value of crowd density. Dangerous crowd forces begin to develop potentially. The stampede accident is probably to occur when the crowd density is between 2m^{-2} and 5.5m^{-2}. 2m^{-2} is a safety value.

Table 1. Chart of crowd density

Density(m^{-2})	Explains
≤2	Safety value
2<<5.5	Danger value
≥5.5	Alarming value

2.4 Steps of Calculating Crowd Density

Mobile location data and monitoring areas are combined together based on overlay analysis. Then performing statistical analysis on number of people in every monitoring area.

Calculating the crowd density in every monitoring area. Hence, the density is given as

$$\rho = \frac{N}{S}, \qquad (1)$$

where N is the number of people in monitoring area and S is the area of monitoring area.

Monitoring areas are rendered in different colors according to their density. When reaching the alarming value, it offers warning messages.

3 Simulation Experiment

3.1 Experimental Environment

The experiment is for testing the method based on GIS and mobile locating data. The experiment used the development methods of GIS which based on C# language. In a new form, the grading state of crowd density is displayed.

3.1.1 Simulation of Mobile Location Data

Based on various researches, the accuracy of mobile phone positioning which based on base station is ±50m in the city. In the target zone, some location data are generate randomly. Then these data are superposed a positioning error of ±50m. The processed data are represented for crowd.

 DOI: 10.1051/itmconf/20160705013

3.2 Experiment Process

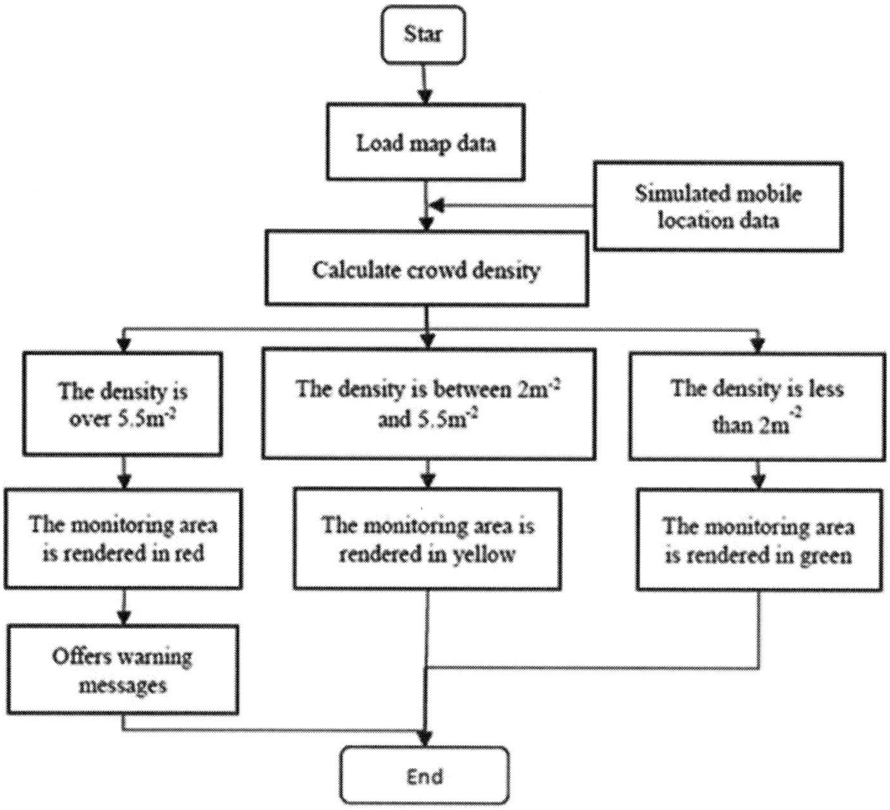

Figure1. Experiment process

3.3 Analysis of Results

The crowd density of monitoring area is represented in tabular (Fig 2). It showed the condition of every monitoring area intuitively. Compared to thermodynamic chart, the values of density have more reference value. We can master the degree of congestion from values. Warning messages are displayed in a new form (Fig 3). It can rapidly locate where need management and control.

DOI: 10.1051/itmconf/20160705013

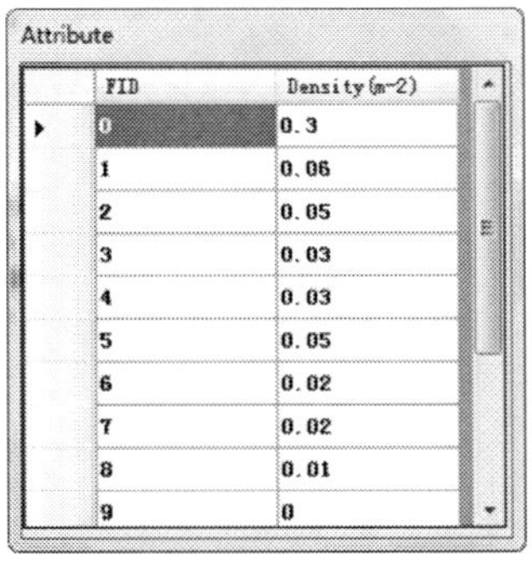

	FID	Density (m-2)
▶	0	0.3
	1	0.06
	2	0.05
	3	0.03
	4	0.03
	5	0.05
	6	0.02
	7	0.02
	8	0.01
	9	0

Figure 2.Table of monitoring areas' crowd density

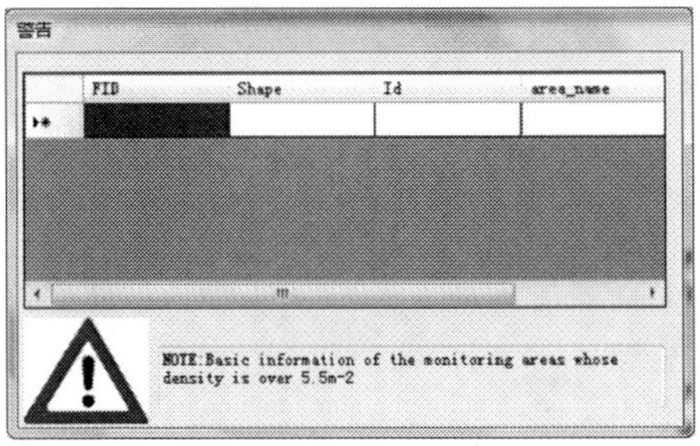

Figure 3.Warning messages

Thermodynamic diagram (Fig 4) showed the crowd distribution. But it was hard to recognize where needmanagement. Some location data were also omitted. Fig5 shows the situation of every monitoring area.

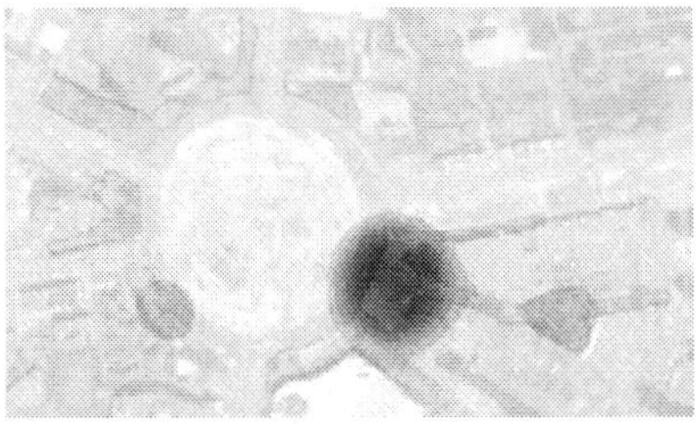

Figure 4.Thermodynamic diagram

Figure 5.The condition of monitoring areas

4 Summary

This paper presents a monitoring crowd density method based GIS and mobile location data. The experiment used simulated mobile location data. The result showed that the method can represent monitoring areas' crowd density. On the basis of monitoring, the system can display warning messages. The timely messages are useful for related stuffs. They can take prearranged plans to prevent the happening of the personnel casualty accidents immediately.

Besides, the mobile location data is applied to the system. So the accuracy of data affects the reliability of monitoring results. To improve the accuracy of monitoring results, how to improve the localization accuracy has become a further research project.

References

1. Shen Na, Li Ning, Chang Qinglong. Crowd Density Estimation Based on Improved Gaussian Mixture Model. Computer and Digital Engineering, 2012,(7):108-111
2. Yue Xiaojuan. The Algorithm of Crowd Density Detection in Intelligent Monitoring System. Harbin Institute of Technology:2012
3. Ren Qingyun. Crowd Density Estimation methods in Intelligent Video Surveillance.Hebei Normal University: 2011
4. Guo Can, Zhen Feng, Zhu Shoujia. Progress and Prospect of the Application of Smart Phone LBS Data in Urban Researches. Human Geography, 2014,(6):18-23
5. Ran Lijun, Liu Mao. Effects of crowded people density on crushing fatalities. Journal of Safety and Environment,2007,7(4):135-138
6. Lai Jianhui. Research on Data Mining and Analysis in Transportation Based on Mobile Communication Location. Beijing University of Technology:2014
7. Baidu Online Network Technology (Beijing) Co., Ltd.Statistical method and apparatus for passenger flow distribution :China,201010597583.2[P],2011
8. W. Martin, T. Franke, D. Roggen, et al. Probing crowd density through smartphones in city-scale mass gatherings .EPJ Data Science,2013,2:5
9. Zhang Yan, Li Ning, Liu Fumei. A Fast Crowd Density

 DOI: 10.1051/itmconf/20160705013

Estimation Based on Region Division. Computer and Digital Engineering,2011,(4):128-131

10. Qin Xiao, Zhen Feng, Xiong Lifang, et al. Methods in urban temporal and spatial behavior research in the Big Data Era. PROGRESS IN GEOGRAPHY, 2013, **32**(9):1352-1361
11. Chai Yanwei, Zhao Ying, Ma Xiujun, et al. Mobile Positioning Method for Spatial-temporal Behavioral Data Collection and Its Geographical Applications. AREAL RESEARCH AND DEVELOPMENT, 2010,**29**(6):1-7
12. Hu Qingmei. Review on Pedestrian Behavior Characteristics and Crowding Mechanism in Public Buildings. China Safety Science Journal, 2008,**8**(18):69-73

ITM Web of Conferences 7, 06001 (2016) DOI: 10.1051/itmconf/20160706001
ITA 2016

The Extension of Hypothesis in Propositional Logic

Qian Guo[1] and An-Sheng Deng[1]

[1]*Information Science and Technology College, Dalian Maritime University, 116026 Dalian, China*

Abstract. The belief non-revision method can achieve a consistent hypothesis extension by limiting the process of reasoning. In propositional logic, several valuable properties of the hypothesis extension have been proved. The hypothesis extension is an infinite set. It includes some clauses. For improving the efficiency of the non-revision method, this paper proposed an algorithm of hypothesis extension in propositional logic. Hypothesis extension is still a limited set of clauses according to this method. And it is logically equivalent with the existing hypothesis extension. The experimental results and theoretical results are consistent.

1 Introduction

Common sense reasoning is reasoning for the limited information. Non-monotonic logic [1] is an effective method to deal with the reasoning by default. Therefore, it is the most important logic tool in common sense reasoning.

At present, there are two main methods to deal with the problems of non-monotonic logic in common sense reasoning. One method is the default logic and the other method is the belief revision method. There are many important research results about the field of the common sense reasoning. For the first method, McCarthy proposed the restrictive reasoning method [2-3]. In addition, Sandewall [4] proposed the method that it put the operator UNLESS in the first method. Later, the research about the monotonicity is becoming increasingly important in many fields. And it also achieved a lot of research results. For example, Reiter proposed the default logic [5]. McDermott and Doyle proposed the non-monotonic logic [6] and the related theory based on the modal logic [7]. A few years later, the equivalence relation between the default logic and the auto-epistemic logic [8] have been proved by Konolige. Until the mid of 1980s, Alchourron, Gardenfors and Makinsond proposed the famous theory of belief revision [9], it can also be named as AGM [10].

The belief revision method has been widely studied in common sense reasoning. However, some useful information may be lost or the result is unexpected during the process of revision. Therefore, the belief non-revision method [11] has been proposed. It can achieves the consistent set by limiting the process of reasoning. This method dose not change the original database.

This paper proposed a hypothesis extension algorithm based on the belief non-revision method. It provides the definition of hypothesis extension in propositional logic. The method of primitive implication was adopted in the algorithm. We will show that each hypothesis has the only extension. The experimental results demonstrate the process of reasoning is correct.

The remainder of the paper is structured as follows. In section 2, the theoretical basis are reviewed. Section 3 introduces the extension of hypothesis in propositional logic in detail and the results of experiment. Section 4 concludes the paper with a short discussion of future work.

2 Theoretical basis

2.1 The definitions of the propositional logic

In this paper, the hypothesis is limited to the propositional logic. The hypothesis extension is defined with the general resolution principle.

Definition 1 Proposition is a statement. It can determine the relationship described by the statement is either true or false.

Proposition can be divided into the atomic proposition and the complex proposition.

The atomic proposition is indecomposable. And it does not contain the logical connector.

$$P, Q, R, \cdots, P_i, Q_i, R_i \left(i \geq 1\right) \tag{1}$$

The logical connector is shown as the follows:

$$\neg, \wedge, \vee, \rightarrow, \leftrightarrow \tag{2}$$

The complex proposition consist of some atomic propositions by connecting with the logical connector, e.g., $(P\vee Q)\to\neg R$.

Definition 2 If A is a formula, then A must satisfies one of the following criteria:

(1)'0' and '1' are formulas.

(2) A atomic proposition is a formula.

(3) If P,Q are formulas, then

$$(\neg P),(P\wedge Q),(P\vee Q),(P\to Q)and\ (P\leftrightarrow Q)$$

are formulas.

(4)The symbol string could be any limited combination of (1), (2)and (3). It is still a formula.

Definition 3 Literal is a atomic or a negation of atomic. A atomic and a negation of itself are collectively called a complementary pair.

Example 1 $P,\neg P,\neg T$ are literals, $P,\neg P$ are a complementary pair.

Definition 4 Clause is the disjunctive form of finite literals.

Example 2 $A=\neg P\vee Q\vee T\vee W\vee S$ is a clause.

2.2 The resolution principle

The resolution principle is inference rule. It means that a clause can be derived by two clauses.

Definition 5 For two clauses S_1 and S_2, there is a literal l_1 in the clause S_1, there is another literal l_2 in the clause S_2, if $l_1=\neg l_2$ then delete l_1,l_2 and connect the remaining part with the logical connector. The resolution of S_1,S_2 is denoted by $R(S_1,S_2)$.

Example 3 If A,B are two clauses, and C is the resolution of A,B, then $A\wedge B\to C$ is true. $R(A,B)$ is the result of resolution.

2.3 The primitive implication

In the 1950s, Quine [12] proposed a mechanized procedures. It can achieve the minimalist equivalent type of a formula. Actually, this is the original definition of the primitive implication. This problem is related to many fields of research. For example, the minimization of Boolean function [13], the update problem of logical database [14], finding the minimum support set in the truth maintenance system and so on.

Definition 6 Let C be a clause in propositional logic. A set of all literals of C is denoted by $literal(C)$. And $|literal(C)|$ is the cardinality of C.

Definition 7 C_i,C_j are two clauses. Both of them are not empty. If $literal(C_i)\subseteq literal(C_j)$, then the clause C_j subsume the clause C_i.

Definition 8 The primitive implication of a theory T is donoted by $\forall PI(\Gamma)$. If a disjunctive form C is the primitive implication of a theory T, then it must satisfies the following properties:

(1) C is not a tautology.

(2) $T\models C$.

(3) There is not exist a clause C' such that $T\models C'$ and $C'\subseteq C$.

Definition 9 If Γ is a consistent set of some clauses, then Γ and $\forall PI(\Gamma)$ are logically equivalent. (the process of proof can be seen in [15])

3 Hypothesis extension in propositional logic

3.1. The definition of hypothesis extension

This paper gives an algorithm of hypothesis extension in propositional logic. In this section, the relative definitions are introduced.

Definition 10 Let $\Gamma=\{C_1,\cdots,C_n\}$ be a set of clauses in propositional logic. $C_1,\cdots,C_n$ are clauses. Γ is a hypothesis and Γ may be inconsistent.

Definition 11 Let Γ be a hypothesis. C is a clause but it is not empty. There is $C\in Con(\Gamma)$. There is a finite sequence $C_1,\cdots,C_n$ satisfies the following properties:

(1)Let C_i be a clause in the sequence. The clause C_i satisfies the following conditions:

① $C_i\in\Gamma$.

② There are clauses $C_{i_1},\cdots,C_{i_k}$ in front of C_i in the sequence such that $C_{i_1}\wedge\cdots\wedge C_{i_k}\to C_i$ and $\{C_{i_1},\cdots,C_{i_k}\}$ is consistent.

(2)$C=C_i$.

According to the definition, the attribute set $Con(\Gamma)$ is a set of all results of reasoning.

Definition 12 Let Γ be a hypothesis. If a clause is empty, then $\Gamma=\square$. The set of reconstruction is denoted by $R(\Gamma)$. For $\forall C\in R(\Gamma)$ should satisfies the following properties:

(1)$C\in Con(\Gamma)$.

(2)$C\neq\square$.

(3)There is no clause $D\in Con(\Gamma)$ such that $|lliteral(R(C,D))|<|lliteral(C)|$.

Theorem 1 If Γ is a hypothesis, then the set of reconstruction $R(\Gamma)$ is consistent. (the details can be seen in [16])

Definition 13 Let Γ be the set of some consistent formulas. C_i is a formula in Γ. For $\forall PI(\Gamma)$, C_i should satisfies the following properties:

(1) C_i is not a tautology.

(2) $\Gamma \models C_i$.

(3) There is not exist a formula C_j and $C_i \subseteq C_j$ such that $\Gamma \models C_j$.

According to the above definitions, $PI(\Gamma)$ is the primitive implication of Γ.

Definition 14 If Γ is a hypothesis, then the hypothesis extension is $E(\Gamma) = PI(R(\Gamma))$.

Example 4 $\Gamma = \{p \vee q, \neg p \vee r, q \vee r \vee s, \neg r\}$ then $R(\Gamma) = (\neg p, \neg r, q \vee s, q)$ and

$$E(\Gamma) = PI((R(\Gamma)))$$
$$= PI(\neg p, \neg r, q \vee s, q)$$
$$= (\neg p, \neg r, q)$$

3.2 Hypothesis extension algorithm

Actually, if Γ is consistent, then $E(\Gamma) \Leftrightarrow PI(\Gamma)$. If Γ is inconsistent, then $PI(\Gamma)$ is empty according to the definition of the primitive implication. However, Γ may be inconsistent in this paper. Therefore, the process of hypothesis extension is divided into three steps. First, the attribute set $Con(\Gamma)$ can be achieved by using the resolution principle. Second, the set of reconstruction $R(\Gamma)$ can be achieved by deleting the conflicts in $Con(\Gamma)$. Finally, due to $R(\Gamma)$ is consistent, we can achieve the hypothesis extension $E(\Gamma) = PI(R(\Gamma))$ according to the definition 14.

$$\Gamma \rightarrow Con(\Gamma) \rightarrow R(\Gamma) \rightarrow E(\Gamma) \quad (3)$$

But in the process of the resolution, we found that some operations are redundant because the results of different resolutions may be the same.

Therefore, the method Tison [17] have been adopted. This method is initially used for structure the primitive implication . It can optimizes the process of the resolution. And it also can improves the efficiency of the resolution.

The method Tison can be understood through the following example:

Example 6 $\Gamma = \{A \vee B, \neg B \vee C, \neg C \vee D\}$

The ordinary resolution:

1. $A \vee B$
2. $\neg B \vee C$
3. $\neg C \vee D$
4. $A \vee C$ $\quad R(A \vee B, \neg B \vee C), B$
5. $\neg B \vee D$ $\quad R(\neg B \vee C, \neg C \vee D), C$
6. $A \vee D$ $\quad R(A \vee C, \neg C \vee D), C$
7. $A \vee D$ $\quad R(A \vee B, \neg B \vee D), B$

The method Tision puts forwards a point. If the process of the resolution is executed according to the order of the literals, then the resolution can avoids redundancy (let the order be A, B, D).

The method Tison :

1. $A \vee B$
2. $\neg B \vee C$
3. $\neg C \vee D$
4. $A \vee C$ $\quad R(A \vee B, \neg B \vee C), B$
5. $\neg B \vee D$ $\quad R(\neg B \vee C, \neg C \vee D), C$
6. $A \vee D$ $\quad R(A \vee C, \neg C \vee D), C$

Obviously, the steps of the method Tison is less than the steps of the ordinary resolution.

Algorithm As the following step shows:

The set of beliefs is denoted by Γ.

The literal set is denoted by $literal(\Gamma)$.

The attribute set is denoted by $Con(\Gamma)$.

The set of reconstruction $R(\Gamma)$.

The hypothesis extension is denoted by $E(\Gamma)$.

1. $\Gamma \leftarrow \{C_1, \ldots, C_n\}, E(\Gamma) = \varnothing, R(\Gamma) = \varnothing$
2. foreach C_x in Γ
3. if $"\vee" \in C_x$
4. $C_x = C_x - "\vee"; literal(\Gamma) \leftarrow C_x$
5. foreach $C_x \in literal(\Gamma); C_y \in literal(\Gamma)$
6. if $\neg C_x \cap C_y \neq \varnothing$
7. $literal(\Gamma) = literal(\Gamma) - \{\neg C_x, C_y\}$
8. $\Gamma \leftarrow C_x$, until $literal(\Gamma) = \varnothing$
9. foreach $C_x \in \Gamma; C_y \in \Gamma$
10. if $x \in y$, then $\Gamma = \Gamma - \{C_x\}$
11. else, then $R(C_x, C_y) \rightarrow C_z$
12. if $C_z \in \Gamma$
13. $\Gamma = \Gamma - \{C_z\}; Con(\Gamma) \leftarrow C_x, C_y$
14. else $Con(\Gamma) \leftarrow C_x, C_y, C_z$

15. until $\Gamma = \varnothing$
16. $R(\Gamma) \leftarrow Con(\Gamma)$
17. Let $\Gamma = R(\Gamma)$
18. repeat the step 2 to the step 8
19. $R(\Gamma) = \Gamma$
20. return $E(\Gamma) = PI(R(\Gamma))$

3.3 Experimental Case

The process of the experiment as the following:

(1)The hypothesis is consistent and there are no inclusion relation in it:

$\Gamma = \{A \vee B, \neg B \vee C \vee D, \neg C \vee D\}$

1. $A \vee B$
2. $\neg B \vee C \vee D$
3. $\neg C \vee D$
4. $A \vee C \vee D$ $R(A\vee B, \neg B\vee C\vee D), B$
5. $\neg B \vee D$ $R(\neg B\vee C\vee D, \neg C\vee D), C$
6. $A \vee D$ $R(A\vee B, \neg B\vee D), B$

$E(\Gamma) = \{A\vee B, \neg B\vee C\vee D, \neg C\vee D, A\vee C\vee D, \neg B\vee D, A\vee D\}$

(2)The hypothesis is inconsistent and there are no inclusion relation in it:

$\Gamma = \{A\vee B, \neg B\vee C\vee D, \neg C\vee D, E, \neg E\}$

1. $A \vee B$
2. $\neg B \vee C \vee D$
3. $\neg C \vee D$
4. $\neg E$
5. E
6. $A \vee C \vee D$ $R(A\vee B, \neg B\vee C\vee D), B$
7. $\neg B \vee D$ $R(\neg B\vee C\vee D, \neg C\vee D), C$
8. $A \vee D$ $R(A\vee B, \neg B\vee D), B$
9. $\square$ $R(\neg E, E), E$

$E(\Gamma) = \{A\vee B, \neg B\vee C\vee D, \neg C\vee D, A\vee C\vee D, \neg B\vee D, A\vee L$

(3) The hypothesis is consistent and the inclusion relation exist in it:

$\Gamma = \{A\vee B, \neg B\vee C\vee D, \neg C\vee D, C\vee D\}$

1. $A \vee B$
2. $\neg B \vee C \vee D$
3. $\neg C \vee D$
4. $C \vee D$
5. $A \vee C \vee D$ $R(A\vee B, \neg B\vee C\vee D), B$
6. $\neg B \vee D$ $R(\neg B\vee C\vee D, \neg C\vee D), C$
7. $A \vee D$ $R(A\vee B, \neg B\vee D), B$
8. D $R(\neg C\vee D, C\vee D), C$

$E(\Gamma) = \{A\vee B, D\}$

(4) The hypothesis is inconsistent and the inclusion relation exist in it:

$\Gamma = \{A\vee B, \neg B\vee C\vee D, \neg C\vee D, C, \neg C\}$

1. $A \vee B$
2. $\neg B \vee C \vee D$
3. $\neg C \vee D$
4. $\neg C$
5. C
6. $A \vee C \vee D$ $R(A\vee B, \neg B\vee C\vee D), B$
7. $\neg B \vee D$ $R(\neg B\vee C\vee D, \neg C\vee D), C$
8. $\neg B \vee D$ $R(\neg B\vee C\vee D, \neg C), C$
9. D $R(\neg C\vee D, C), C$
10. $A \vee D$ $R(A\vee B, \neg B\vee D), B$
11. $\square$ $R(\neg C, C), C$

$E(\Gamma) = \{A\vee B, D\}$

The experiment shows that the experimental result is consistent with the theoretical result. The algorithm obtains the good effect. It does not appear the situation that the important information is lost. In the process of experiment, we found that the working time will increases with the amount of data increases. However, this kind of situation is inevitable. In general, the algorithm is accurate and comprehensive.

4 Conclusions

The hypothesis extension has many good mathematical properties based on the non-revision method. The process of cognition is convergent in this paper. This nature shows that the non-revision method conforms to the process of cognition. And it is an effective solution to the non-monotonic reasoning in practice. In order to improve the application value of the non-revision method, this paper redefined the hypothesis extension based on the primitive implication. In the future, the research could be extended to the And/Or clause and the first-order logic.

References

1. Brewka, Gerhard, Non-monotonic reasoning: logical foundations of common sense, Cambridge University Press. (1991).
2. J. McCarthy, Circumscription a form of non-monotonic reasoning, Artificial Intelligence, 13: 27-39 (1980).
3. J. McCarthy, Applications of circumscription to formalize commonsense konwledge. Artificial Intellifence, 13: 7-39 (1986).
4. E. Sandewall, An approach to the frame Problem and its implementation. Machine Intelligence, 7: 195-204 (1972).
5. R. Reiter, A logic for default reasoning, Artificial Intelligence, 13: 81-132 (1980).
6. D. McDermott, J. Doyle, Non-monotonic logic. Artificial Intelligence, 13: 41-72 (1980).
7. C. Mihir, G. Suiata, Non-monotonic Logics and Algebras, Journal of Chongqing University of Posts and Telecommunications (Natural Science Edition), 20: 355-360 (2008).
8. D.M. Gabbay, Heoretical foundations for non-monotonic reasoning in expert systems. in: K. R. Apt

(Ed.), Proceedings NATO Advanced Study Institute on Logics and Models of Concurrent Systems, Springer, Berlin, 439-457 (1985).
9. C.E. Alchourrón, D. Makinson, On the logic of theory change: Safe contraction, Symbolic Logic, 405-422 (1985).
10. A. Darwiche, J. Pearl, On the logic of iterated belief revision, Artificial Intelligence, 1-29 (1997).
11. Y. Shang, A.S. Deng, X.D. Jiu, The Quantitative Correction Method of Inconsistent belief meet the AGM public discussion, Computer Engineering and Science, 26: 106-109 (2004).
12. W.V. Quine, The problem of simplifying truth functions. American Mathematical Monthly, 521-531 (1952).
13. P. Tison, Generalization of consensus theory and application to the minimization of boolean functions. Electronic Computers, IEEE.
14. J. Pais, P. Jackson, Partial monotonicity and a new version of the Ramsey test. Studia Logica, 51(1): 21-47 (1992).
15. M.A. Falappa, Explanations belief revision and defeasible reasoning. Artificial Intelligence, 141: 1-28 (2002).
16. J.X. Zhang, The research about inconsistent beliefs quantitative a modified hierarchical. Dalian, Dalian Maritime University (2013).
17. P. Tison, Generalization of consensus theory and application to the minimization of boolean functions. Electronic Computers, 4: 446-456 (1967).

Design of intelligent house system based on Yeelink

Zhi-Huang LIN [a], Kun LI [b], Zheng-Hao KE [c], and Shang-Yu XIE [d]

Tianjin University of Technology, School of Electronic Information Engineering, Tianjin, Tianjin
E-mail:13821094424@163.com, E-mail: likun_tjut@163.com, E-mail: kzh409380559@126.com, E-mail: 1370706872@qq.com

Abstract—In order to monitor the security situation of house in real time, an intelligent house remote monitoring system is designed based on Yeelink cloud services and ZigBee wireless communication technology. This system includes three parts, ZigBee wireless sensor networks, intelligent house gateway and Yeelink Cloud Services. Users can access Yeelink website or APP to get real time information in the house, receiving information including gas concentration, temperature. Also, remote commands can be sent from mobile devices to control the household appliances. The user who can monitor and control the house effectively through a simple and convenient user interface, will feel much more safe and comfortable.

1 Introduction

In the 21th century, the quality of people's life has been gradually improved, which leads to the promotion of living environment requirements and the aspiration of "lazy man" mode. In this situation, people are pursuing a more convenient and intelligent life in a higher technology way. Therefore, intelligent house system arises in consequence.

Intelligent house system can help household to perceive the environment of house with accuracy and control the domestic appliances with convenience. For instance, it could monitor the temperature and humidity in the house, and then control the running of conditioner to make the households feel comfortable. Actually, China had introduced intelligent house system in the 1990s, however it was a flash in the pan. Customers had a common complaint about its disadvantages, such as low intelligence, dense wiring, high cost and delayed service. In recent years, intelligent house system has greeted a bright spring again with the rise of the internet of things.

Because the ZigBee technology has been matured, some researchers use it to achieve the wireless of intelligent house. W. Shao etc. utilized the microprocessor (MSP430F169) and the ZigBee chip (CC2420) to control infrared node for realizing the control of some domestic appliances in the year of 2012[1]. In the year of 2015, T. Zhang etc. adopted Z-STACK protocol stack of TI company, in the developmental environment of IAR, to structure house wireless sensor network in the control of sensors by CC2530 chip as the core[2] .In the same year, Z. Z. Fang realized the intelligent control of curtain based on CC2530 and analyzed ZigBee network topology in depth[6].

With the spread of 3G network and WIFI network, some researchers applied these technologies to develop remotely accessible intelligent house system. In the year of 2015, H. X. Yu etc. sent monitor image and alarm information to mobile terminals timely by multimedia message and short message of 3G network, and then sent and received commands by mobile terminals to achieve the remote intelligent control of house[3]. L. G. Su etc. obtained working condition of various kinds of sensors on all nodes by intelligent house gateway, focus on controlling all kinds of appliances, and realized remote control by mobile phone terminal[4].

The spread of cloud services technology makes more and more researchers to study this aspect. This topic is to utilize the combination of ZigBee wireless sensor network and Yeelink, which makes users to check environmental data of house, control the running of appliances anytime and anywhere, and enquire data in cloud storage.

2 Solution To System

The integral block diagram of intelligent house system in this paper is shown as Figure 1. The top layer is "customer layer". Customers can use mobile phone, tablet PC such kinds of intelligent device to login in cloud

 DOI: 10.1051/itmconf/20160706002

platform, browse sensor information and send control commands. The middle layer is "family core network". And STM32 controller is the core part, which can read and send data to the ZigBee coordinator by UART. The bottom layer is "ZigBee wireless sensor networks". It mainly detects indoor condition using sensor, then sends collected data to ZigBee coordinator, and transmits controlling instruction to household appliances to the end of network.

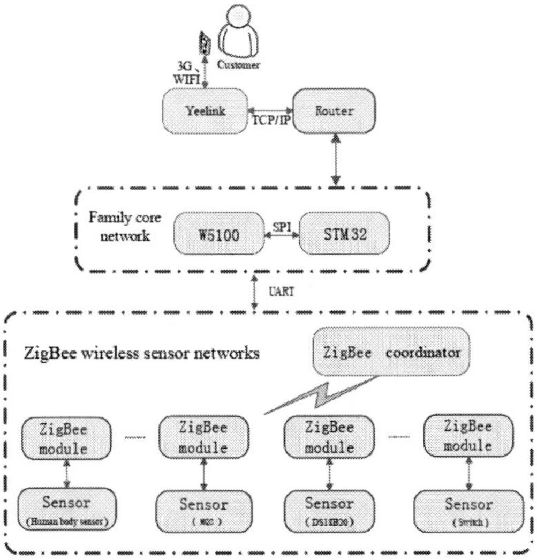

Figure 1 Block Diagram of Intelligent House System

3 Detailed Design of software and hardware

3.1 Related operations of cloud platform

Yeelink is a platform of "internet of things" which opens to all developing users, helping the user has his own "internet of things" quickly. This platform which has unique designed data server supporting many users to access and store their mass sensor data consequently. Furthermore, the massive sensor data is kept on internet in safety. Based on these advantages, this paper chooses Yeelink as the data platform of intelligent house system.

As shown in Figure 2, in terms of system settings, we register account on Yeelink website, then add STM32 as the device to this account, and add links to all kinds of sensors and household appliances. All the added devices and sensors have independent ID by which it could access and storage data in accurate way.

Figure 2 Device Management

3.2 Design of Family Core Network

In terms of hardware, we choose STM32F103 as the core processor. It is integrated inside of 128KB FLSH, four timers, 20KB RAM and plenty of I/O ports, which are qualified to the software and hardware resources needed in this intelligent house system. In the design of circuit, there is W5100 module linked to STM32 peripheral through SPI interface, thus externally expanding the Ethernet interface. In addition, this processor links ZigBee coordinator module in wireless sensor layer by UART interface.

The schematic of the hardware is shown in Fig. 3.

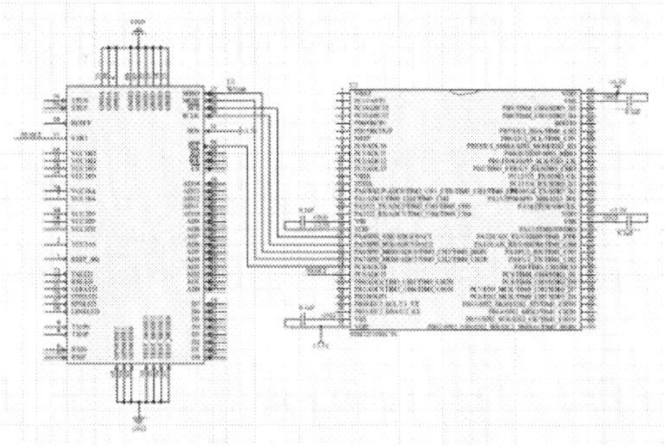

Figure 3 Hardware Design

The software design of family core network mainly focuses on STM32 programming with the following functions: peripheral hardware initialization, communication with W5100 via SPI port, communication with ZigBee coordinator via UART interface. The communication described above follows the frame format designed in this system.

W5100 is initialized to TCP client mode and the network parameter is set as required. And STM32 calls the "data sending function" to make the W5100 send one frame of data to Yeelink platform. Furthermore, STM32 will not send another frame until it receives the interrupt signal from W5100.

The main process is shown in Fig.4.

DOI: 10.1051/itmconf/20160706002

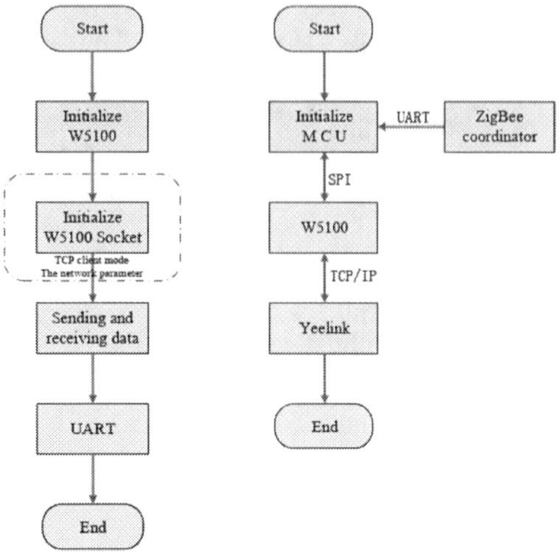

Figure 4 Software Process

3.3 Sensor Network Design

The hardware of sensor network design is constituted of ZigBee modules and sensors. The ZigBee modules is constructed mainly with chip CC2530. And there are kinds of sensors such as: MQ2(gas sensor), DS18B20 (temperature sensor), human body sensor, etc.

The software of this part has two main functions: on one hand, ZigBee router will automatically upload information from sensor to coordinator in a fixed period. On the other hand, router will send data to coordinator when receiving a data requisition from the coordinator.

We use IAR Embedded Workbench to develop software and read data from sensor that is linked to ZigBee modules. If the signal from sensor is a digital signal (such as DS18B20), it is only need to connect the output pin of the sensor to the I/O pin of CC2530. If the signal is an analog signal, then it needs an A/D converter to sample the signal.

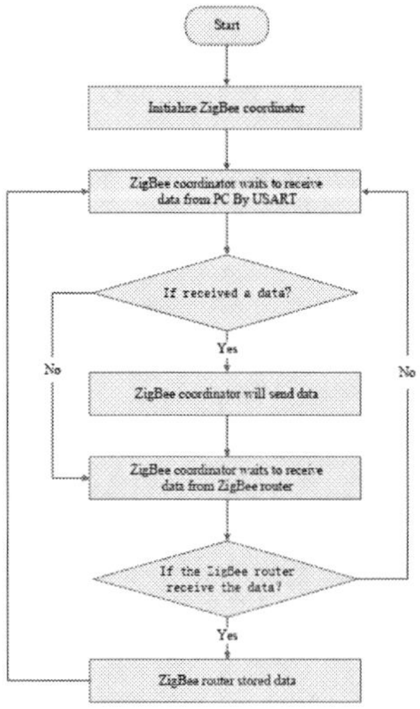

Figure 5 ZigBee Software Configure

Z-Stack which is provided by TI company is a ZigBee wireless communication protocol stack for CC2530 and CC2538. Z-Stack is embedded in a real real-time operating system OSAL which has operating mechanism of event flag, message queuing, time queuing and task scheduling mechanism with different priorities. The difficulty of designing a ZigBee software is much reduced since each part of ZigBee stack, such as MAC layer, NWK layer, APS layer and ZigBee Device Object(ZDO), is handhold as one task in OSAL (shown in Figure. 6) And user just need concern to develop their own applications.

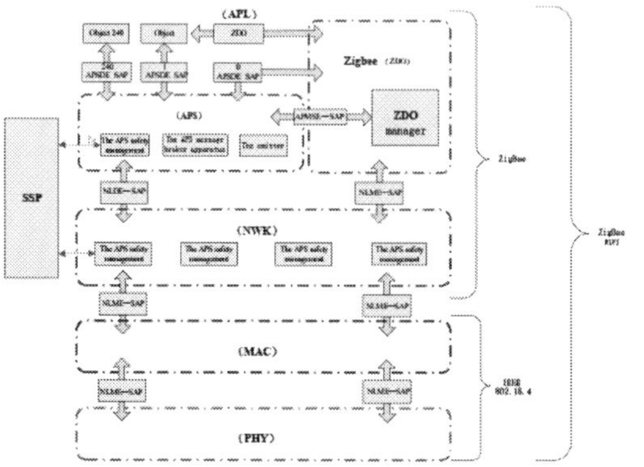

Figure 6 Block Diagram of Z-Stack

I. Results

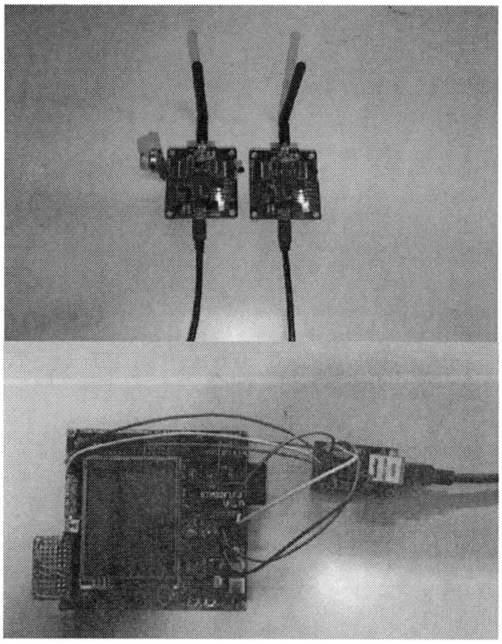

Figure 7 The photo of experiment boards

Fig.7 shows the photo of experiment boards. In this experiment, MQ2 gas sensor is applied to read carbon monoxide concentration which is sent to Yeelink cloud services by STM32 and W5100. Users can browse gas concentration data on Yeelink website or mobile terminal APP.

Fig.8 is screenshot of viewing data from Yeelink website and mobile terminal.

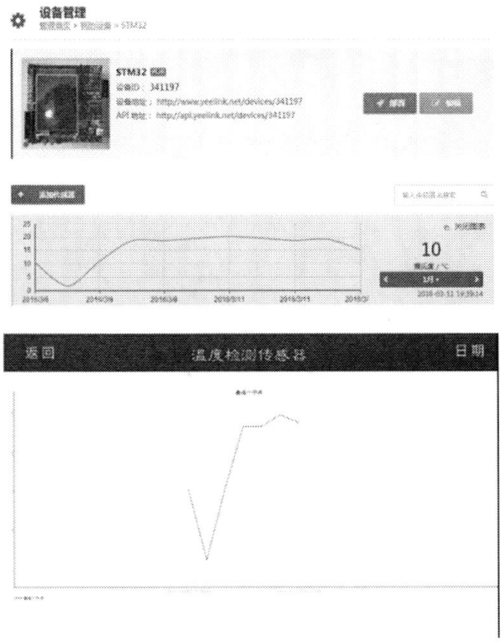

Figure 8 Experimental Data

4 Conclusion

A set of intelligent house remote monitoring system is designed and realized based on Yeelink cloud services and ZigBee wireless communication technology. The three layers of this design: ZigBee wireless sensor network, intelligent house gateway and Yeelink cloud services, are introduced in this paper. With this intelligent house system, the users can view the environmental information of house, receive alarming like gas concentrations exceeding in time, and even send remote commands to the household appliances through a simple and convenient user interface.

Acknowledgment

We really appreciate the comments and the suggestions from the editor and the

reviewers. This work is partially supported by College students innovation and Entrepreneurship Project (201410060030) and Natural Science Foundation of Tianjin under Grant (13JCQNJC01300).

References

1. W. Shao, "Design of intelligent house system based on ZigBee," China Computer & Communication. April 2012.
2. T. Zhang, and Z. Y. Wang., "Design of ZigBee Smart Home Base on CC2530," Industrial Control Computer, April 2015.
3. H. X. Yu, and, H. H. Zhang, "Design of intelligent house system based on ZigBee," Journal of Shenyang Normal University. April 2015.
4. L. G. Su, and Y. Zhu, "Smart Home System Based on ZigBee Wireless Sensor Network," Computer Systems & Applications. June 2015.
5. X. B. Zhang, "Intelligent home system based on embedded controller and RS485," Electronic Measurement Technology. vol. 35, Dec.2012. pp. 1002-7300.
6. Z. Z. Fang, "The design and implementation of smart home system based on ZigBee," Practical Electronics. 2014.
7. C. C. Li, "Wireless intelligent home control devices based on embedded," FOREIGN ELECTRONIC MEASUREMENT TECHNOLOGY. Vol. 28, Dec.2009.
8. W. Y. Yu, "Research on the Smart Home System Based on Internet of Things," Process Automation Instrumentation. vol.32, Dec. 2011. pp. 1000-0380.

 DOI: 10.1051/itmconf/20160706003

Application and Research on The Model of Distributed Intelligent Cooperative Decision Support System

Peng-Fei Peng, Hao-Tian Cui

Electronic Engineering College , Navy University of Engineering , WuHan,China

Abstract. Combined with distributed processing, traditional decision support and collaborative technology, an intelligent distributed collaborative decision support system model is proposed. The architecture, component and functions of the model is described in detail .Analyzed the problem solving process of distributed collaborative decision problem and intelligent collaborative decision-making model is proposed. Finally the intelligent agent model of the system and its application technology is given , which laid the foundation of this new model and its application in military decision making system.

1 Introduction

DSS (Decision Support System, DSS) is a problem of computer information systems faced by research in the field of advanced stage. With the development of networking, artificial intelligence, distributed processing, system integration, decision support system[1-3] has came into a new stage. Focusing on shortcomings of traditional decision support systems, the model of distributed intelligent collaborative decision support system has been presented. The model fully combined the conclusion of distributed processing[4-6], decision support methods and techniques[7] research, which can meet the multi-level and targeted of decision needed in real life, and multiple users of a variety of application types.

The main body of the model consists of multiple applications, intelligent cooperative decision-making and intelligent agent service nodes. Users can use the Web browser, Windows application client, video the user can be either individual users or workgroups user. System can simultaneously login multiple users of a variety of types, provide a collaborative working environment for the user in order to discuss the result of decisions ,also can make record for results of every decision- making for usage and inquiry in other time.

2 System Model

Intelligent distributed collaborative decision supported system is made up of several physically separate massage processing nodes of network collaborative computing environment[8], each node can include application processing, intelligent collaborative decision and intelligent decision agent one or more entities in a proxy service. The model is shown in Figure.1.

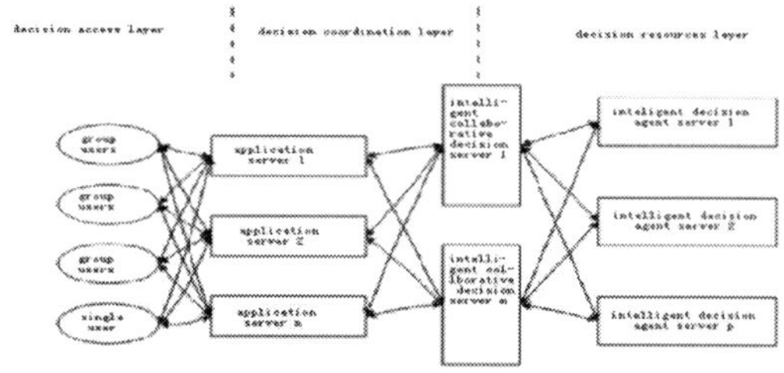

Figure 1 Model of System Architecture

Application server mainly provides users with a variety of human-computer interactive interface and service software, including Web pages, application forms, electronic notebook, E-mail, etc. The diversity of application server determines the users or groups of users will have more choice of ways to participate in decision-making.

Intelligent decision server mainly help to collaborate users on task decomposition of decision making, then look for intelligent decision agents for a problem, and help them to complete all of the decision-making process. Intelligent decision server can manage users to enter, quit, and add, delete of server, and send request information of collaborative decision server to users and output the result; receive and process the results of several intelligent agents' decision process; collaborative the work of each application server, responsible for the maintenance of communication functions such as paths, timing, logic of Information transmission.In addition, share real-time global information between intelligent collaborative decision servers of distributed system, collaborate and complete the mission distribution of intelligent decision agents together, and also integrate the results of decisions.

Intelligent decision proxy server accepts the distribute tasks of intelligent collaborative decision server ,activated their own ability of decision dealing, searching for the models, knowledge, data and other content of decision-making, complete the mission of decision-making , and return the results or intermediate results of decision-making to the intelligent decision server.

3 Intelligent Collaborative Decision Making Model

In distributed intelligent collaborative decision supported system, there can be more than one intelligent decision server, which distributed in several different nodes. Each intelligent decision server can finish a decision mission on its own, also can complete a decision-making tasks together according to the demand the way to use of users. Each intelligent decision server can connect with multiple application servers, allowed one or more users (teams) joint or independent implement a decision-making process.

As shown in Figure.2, intelligent decision server consists of four basic components: Intelligent user Manager, intelligent problem processor, intelligent decision creator, Communications manager. Intelligent collaborative decision-making independent of network operating systems, database management systems, knowledge database management systems, and the underlying multimedia management systems, adapted to networking distributed systems, workflow :users (groups)log on system through a variety of application servers , inquire the decision or historical decision record of problems with the guide of intelligent user manager. If make decision, systems can distribute the problem according to the specific information of intelligent problem processor, and can make interactive consultation and decomposition of problem and weights case with users(group). After the Atomic issue is reached, users(group), enter the relevant information, solve the atomic issues through each intelligent decision agent of communication manager, result returns to the intelligent collaborative decision server and integrate to build the final result back to the users. In particular, as for group users, sponsor or leader of decision has the final power of decision of input or modify, team members share the information, complete the discussions through the collaboration between intelligent collaborative decision servers or intelligent collaborative decision Server and application server.

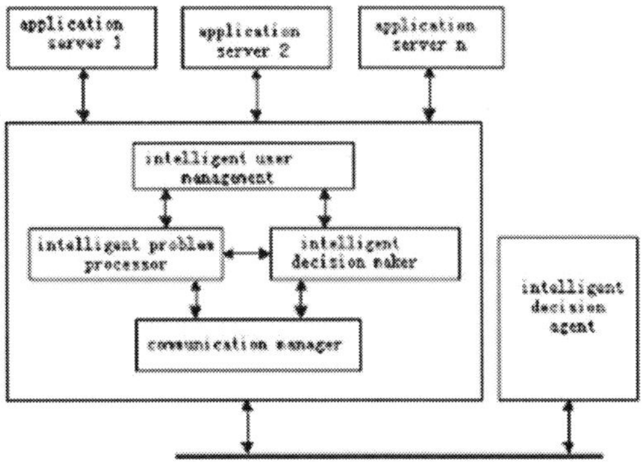

Figure 2 Architecture of Intelligent Cooperative Decision-Making

3.1 Intelligent user Management

The intelligent user manager monitor the decision request of users in real-time, responsible for explaining the application sent to intelligence problems processor and forwarding the end result of decision.

Intelligentt user management provide a global view for all users (including which users, which application servers, users are distributed on hich application servers, users' initial information and suggestions to the decision), makes it easy for users to make collaborative decisions. Application servers focusing on specific functions and services of applications provided themselves, and under a unified and collaborated management of Intelligent user manager, its application tools provide all kinds of user interfaces and clients for users to access different applications..

For group of users, sponsor of the decision problem is automatically set as a leader, the leader has the ultimate power with modifying the input information, team member only have the power of discussions and view.

3.2 Intelligent Problem Solving

Intelligent problem processor is a core part of intelligent collaborative decision-making service system, its main features are: ① manage intelligent decision making proxy information, including the position of agent, functions of agent, characteristics of agent and its performance monitoring, call control of agent. ② Analyzing, processing and managing the problem decomposition and the decomposition of knowledge base.Expert intervention factors of problem decomposition process is also managed by intelligent problem processor.

Architecture of intelligent problem handling is shown in Figure. 3. Through continuously modify and wealth of agent information, decomposition of file information and knowledge information of intelligent problem processing, which can make the whole system solve different problems. That is the process of intelligent problem solving.

Problem decomposition results are stored in archives, constitute a tree-like hierarchical graph according to the level of decomposition. The leaves of each tree node associated with the intelligent agent, which makes the process of intelligent agents can be processed in parallel. Intelligent problem processor will activate the appropriate intelligent decision agent to collaboratively complete the decisions according to the problem decomposition factor and user's intervention .

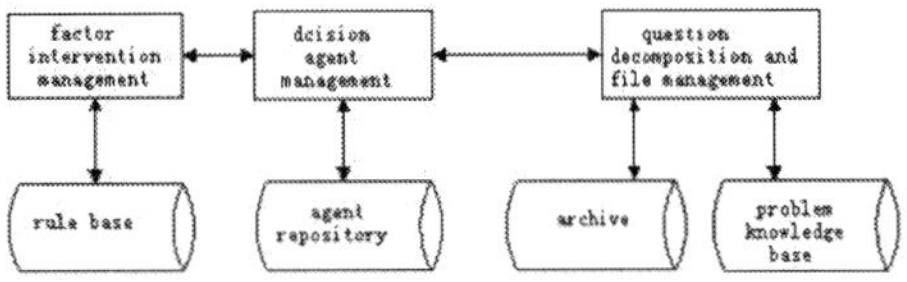

Figure 3 Architecture of Intelligent Agents

3.3 Intelligent Decision Generate

The intelligent decision generated part is mainly consists of decision agent result manager and decision generated controller. all decision results finished by intelligent decision agent complete the decomposition of overall mission through collaborative decision server. The result of decision can save as the form of document according to the category of problem decomposition, set the index of file and save in the archive in convenient of inquiry and usage. Besides the result of decision can be sent to the application server in different kinds of forms in order to be showed to users in different forms.

3.4 Communication Management

Communication management is mainly complete the communication information management between users and collaborative decision server, collaborative decision server and intelligent decision agent, collaborative decision servers. Communication management is the basic for system to achieve collaborative work, communication is separated to high level and low level. low level use the TCP/IP network communication protocol, the communication mechanism is achieved by agent languages(Java, C#,etc).The high level communication protocol is consisted of system dedicated orders, which achieved by programming of system developers.

4 Intelligent Decision Agent Model

Intelligent decision agent[9] is unified activated using by intelligent decision server, which can solve an atomic problem of decision problem. The features of intelligent decision agent is:①There is no relation between interpreted mode and system structure. ② Portability, which means intelligent decision agent can run in every computer system which equipped with interpreter and operating environment, that made intelligent decision agent can be in every nodes of distributed system.③ Dynamic. System can determine cited decision agent during system running, which can make sure that the revise and update of intelligent decision agent can be reflected in the process of decision-making. By the end of system decision-making, the intelligent decision agent of system will wither away automatically.

The structure of intelligent decision agent is shown as Figure. 4.

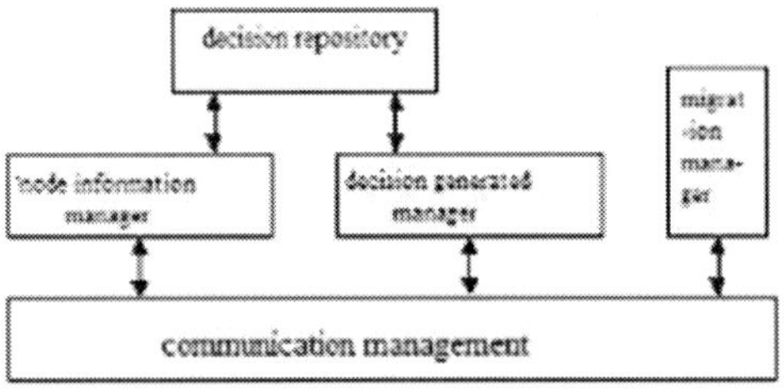

Figure 4 The Structure of Intelligent Decision Agent

The system function of intelligent decision agent is including: ① Communication management. Its function is similar to communication management in collaborative server, mainly achieve the news and information delivering of intelligent decision agent and collaborative decision service, intelligent decision agent. ② Migration management. When current decision agent complete its decision-making mission, it will do the decision-making process migration according to the scheduling instructions and related information of intelligent collaborative decision server. it will shut down the agent process, and sends all the information from the current node to the destination node under the instruction of intelligent collaboration server. When all the decision-making agent node complete their missions, the global decision results will be finished by the last intelligent agent server. ③ Decision result generated. All the intelligent decision agent of system will share the public cache provided by intelligent collaborative decision server to save their results, and then the results of decision solving will be achieved by intelligent decision generated agent and intelligent collaborative decision server together.

5 Achievement Technology of Model

The prototype of intelligent distributed collaborative decision support system is the Windows2007 operating system. Using C# language to developmenta certain type of warship combat simulation and decision support systems in NET environment. Intelligent collaborative decision server is a multi-threaded server established by thread mechanism. The application server of system can provide B/S or C/S access mode to users. Communication in collaborative processing set Socket based on node protocol by setting Windows service, achieve by using the trigger and recycle receiving of network messages .Information-sharing in collaboration achieved by setting blackboard information buffer in intelligent collaborative serves. Intelligent decision Agent uses Web Service distributed processing technology[10] to implement, by using software or model as the concept of service for intelligent collaborative decision server to dispatch. The treatment of atomic problem used the hybrid reasoning based on cases and rules in intelligent decision agent.

6 Conclusion

The distributed intelligent collaborative decision system support model is a new model which is completely different from traditional model of decision support system .Which combined the collaborative, distributed technology with traditional decision support technology, which greatly improved the reliability, portability, reusability, and invulnerability of decision support system. This system model, especially in military decision-making system ,has comprehensive and practical prospect in research and application.

References

1. Sun Yongyong.Research on Intelligent Decision Support System Based on Multi-Agent[J]. Value Engineering,2014(27):0223-0225.
2. Yu Weihong.Intelligent Support System for Maritime Search and Rescue Based on JADE[J].Computer Application and Software, 2011,28(8).
3. Yang Fei, Wang Qing, Wu Zhendong.Missile Target Assignment Intelligent Support System Based on GIS[J].Computer Engineering,2010,36(21).
4. Ma Yuxing, Cao Hui, Huang Xiahua.The Application of Multilayer Distributed Processing Technology to Main Engine Remote Control System[J].Ship Electricity Technlogy,2014,34(8).
5. Xue Junjie, Wang Ying, Zhu Jie, Xiao Jiyang, Li Hao.Research Stutus Summary of United States UAV Distributed Processing System[J].Flight Missile,2015.
6. Chen Zhangsheng, Lv Zhiping, Cui Yang, Wang Yupu.Implementation of Distributed Computing with Large-Scale GNSS Data[J].Geomatics and Information Science of Wuhan University,2015,40(3).
7. Li Weigang, Tang Chaosheng, Antonio C. de A. Junior, Liu Peng, Zhang Yaming.A Study on Collborative Decision Making in Air Transportation[J].Complex Systems And Complexity Science,2015,12(2).
8. Liu Yon, Guo Yinzhan, "Expression And Product Design Knowledge Sharing System In Web-Based Collaborative Design,"Jourmal Of Taiyuan University Of Science And Technology,2015,36(4).
9. Wen Bohua, Si Guangya, Hu Xiaofeng, Luo Pi.Research AndImplementation Of The Third Party Intelligent Agent'S Stretagy Decision-Making Behavior Model[J].Journal Of System Simulation,2005,17(11).
10. Zhu Hongkang, Yu Xueli.Distributed Web Service Mining Technology Based On P2P[J].Computer Engineering,2010,36(9).

 DOI: 10.1051/itmconf/20160706004

The Design and Realization of Household Intelligent Security System

Sheng-Bo HUANG [1], Tong-Liang FAN [1,a]

[1] *Department of Electronic Technology, China Maritime Police Academy, Ningbo 315801, China*
[a] *Corresponding author: libufan432@163.com*

Abstract. It is known that Smart home has brought great convenience to the lives of humans. However, we have attached quantities of interest in its security as the development of technology goes on. According to the security requirements at the moment, we introduce the scheme of smart home security system based on ZigBee, and design system hardware and software process. By applying a STC89C52 microcontroller, our system is able to accurately detect and give alarms automatically to house fire, harmful gases and thefts.

1 Introduction

With the rapid development of social progress and science and technology, people's demands on the quality of life are becoming higher and higher. They want it be more humane as well as intelligent, which makes smart home come into being. While human beings enjoy the convenience brought from smart home, some potential safety hazards should not be neglected, for example, fire caused by a short circuit due to the use of high power home appliances, gas poisoning and exploration and thefts, which new commands for home safety has been proposed[1].

At present, the majority of smart security systems in the market are wired connection, which has influenced the appearance and space utilization of the home wiring[7]. Here, we introduce a system taking STC89C52 chip as control core, with CC2530 coordinator, MQ-2 smoke sensor, DHT11 temperature and humidity sensor, HC-SR501 infrared sensor, 12864 LCD, alarm module and so on. It is of high reliability, small size, which is able to give alarms and process to a fire, combustible gas and illegal invasions.

2 Overall System Design

ZigBee is a low power protocol based on IEEE802.15.4 standard, which is a kind of short distance, low power wireless communication technology. It outperforms in low power consumption, high reliability, large network capacity, high network stability. In addition, it can also set several levels of security, facilitating the users according to their personal needs. Also embedded technology is another advantage of ZigBee over other wireless devices[2,5,6]. Consequently, it is adopted in our smart home security system.

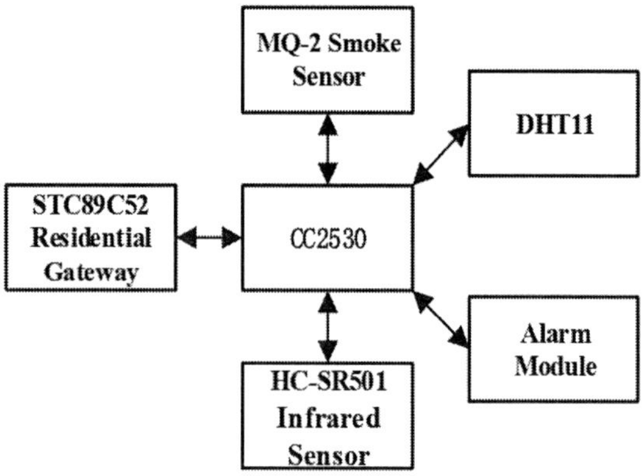

Figure 1 The Overall Structure Diagram of The System

Smart home security system is mainly composed of STC89C52 master chip, DHT11 temperature and humidity sensor, MQ-2 smoke sensor, HC-SR501 infrared sensor, CC2530 coordinator, 12864 LCD, alarm module and so on. The overall structure diagram of the system is shown in figures 1.

3 System Hardware Design

3.1 Master control module

The system uses STC89C52 as the master chip, which has 8K bytes of programmable Flash memory, 512 bytes of RAM and 32 bit I/O interface and other standard functions. As the main control module of the system, it is mainly responsible for the analysis and processing of the collected data. When the dangerous signal is detected, the buzzer gives alarm signals. And the information is passed to the users through the Internet network, assisting the circuits of other modules together.

3.2 Temperature and humidity sensor

DHT11 is a widely used digital temperature and humidity sensor, the working voltage is 3~5.5V, the measurement range is 20-90%RH, the temperature is 0~50 with high resolution.

DHT11DTH11 uses a single row 4 pins, pin 1 for power supply, pin 2 for data port, pin 3 is left vacant, pin 4 for ground, and it can be directly connected to the I/O CC2530 port. To get a more accurate result, a 4.7KΩ pull-up resister is connected between data terminal and power supply while the length of the connecting wire is less than20m[3]. Its circuit is shown in figures 2.

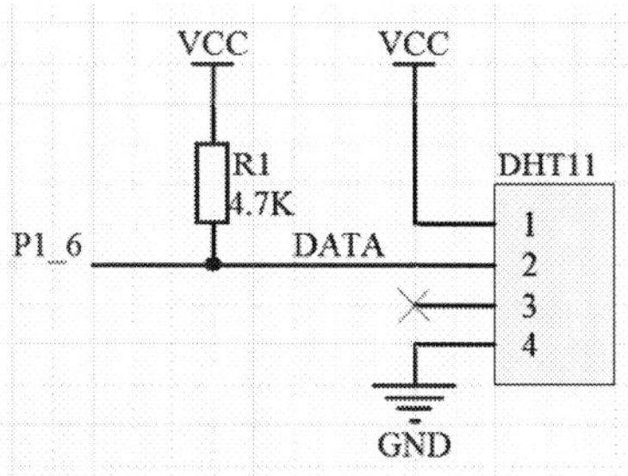

Figure 2 Temperature and Humidity Sensor

3.3 MQ-2 Smoke sensor

MQ-2 smoke sensor is designed following the characteristics that its electrical conductivity is sensitive to the combustible gas. The pin 4 of MQ-2 is connected to pin 2 of U1A, and the outputs a DC signal varying with the smoke concentration. U1A is a comparator, the threshold voltage of the comparator Rp can adjust the sensitivity of the alarms. When the smoke concentration is higher than the threshold voltage, U1A outputs low level (0V), and LED light alarms; otherwise, U1A outputs high (VCC), LED goes out. The circuit diagram of the module is shown in figures 3.

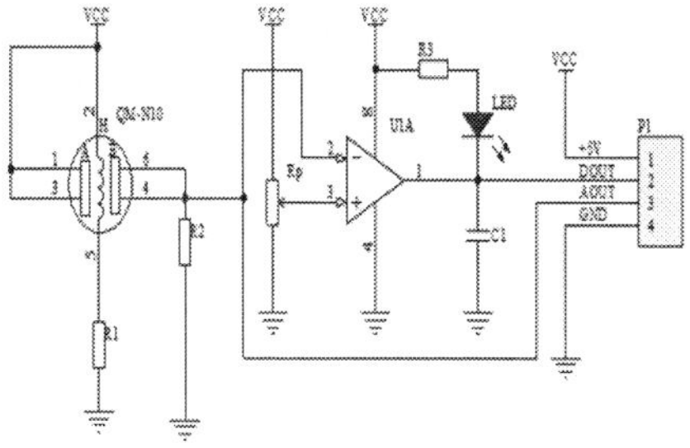

Figure 3 MQ-2 Smoke Sensor

3.4 HC-SR501 Infrared sensor

In our system, HC-SR501 human sensing module is applied as an infrared sensor, which has high sensitivity, reliability, at a working voltage in 4.5~20V. It is already known that the central wavelength of the radiation of the human body is about 10um. By adding a Finel lens on the probe, the wavelength passing through it is suitable for human detection range. The infrared rays released in human bodies produce weak signals via Finel lens. The weak signal is processed by the filter amplifier circuit, which is transmitted to the MCU. Its work flow is illustrated in figures 4.

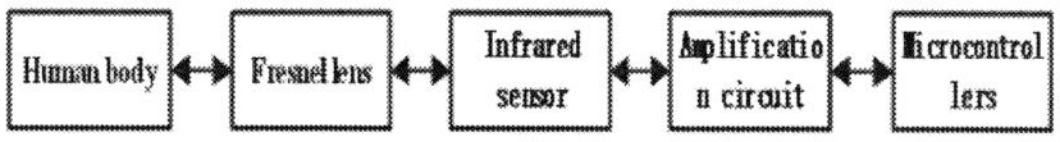

Figure 4 Work Flow of Infrared Sensor

3.5 CC2530 Coordinator

CC2530 is a system on chip (SoC) that can be used in ZigBee, building a strong network node at a low cost. It has low power consumption of the core, 32/64/128/256KB programmable flash memory, RAM 8KB and excellent RF transceiver. Besides, its radio frequency signal is transmitted by differential method, which can enhance the signal level, reduce the scattering of signal and reduce the noise. It can also be isolated from the power supply system of the circuit board, ensuring a stronger signal rate and anti-interference ability.

3.6 12864 LCD

The main function of the 12864 LCD module is displaying information of collected temperature and humidity on the screen, and users can readily understand the environments in the home, adjusting temperature and humidity in time to achieve a comfortable living environment.

3.7 The alarm module

In an alarm module, when the microcontroller transmits a low level signal, the buzzer will send an alarm signal after confirmation, informing the user of indoor smoke concentrations over normal concentrations or illegal invasion in order to prevent the occurrence of the accident in time.

4 Software Design

System software is mainly composed of three parts, respectively detection, control and alarm. When the system is initialized, sensors in the system begin to work, and the temperature and humidity in the home is detected constantly. When the detection value exceeds the normal setting, the system gives the following reactions, such as opening the fan, starting the heater, and the alarm. IF the infrared sensor detects an illegal invasion, an alarm will

 DOI: 10.1051/itmconf/20160706004

be sent to the user through a buzzer. The software flow chart of the system is shown in figures 5.

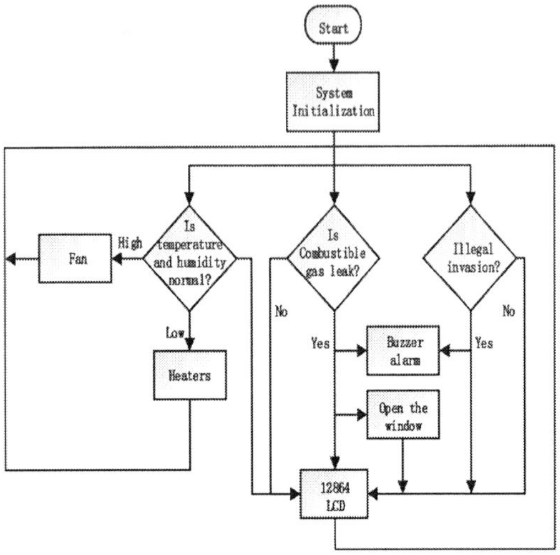

Figure 5 Software Flow Chart of The System

5 System Test

As shown in figures 6, The overall of the system is based on STC89C52 type microcomputer as the core control. The information collection module is composed of Infrared sensor, vibration sensor, combustible gas sensor, temperature and humidity sensor. While the wireless communication module mainly contains NRF24L01 module and GSM SMS module. The mainframe and vice machines achieve information exchange through wireless communication module. The GSM module is attached to the host machine, which forms an intelligent home security system, with functions of anti-theft, fire, indoor multi-point prevention and remote alarm. After the system boots, the indoor temperature and humidity collected by the sensors will be showed on the LCD1602 liquid crystal display. Meanwhile, the sensors detect flammable gases, fire and human illegal intrusion signals, if these values has been beyond the threshold, they will be transformed into electrical signals and transmitted to the single-chip for post-process, and the microcomputer give alarms according to different cases. The employment of single-chip makes the system has the advantages of simple operation, stable function, low cost, low power consumption, high practical value and wide application.

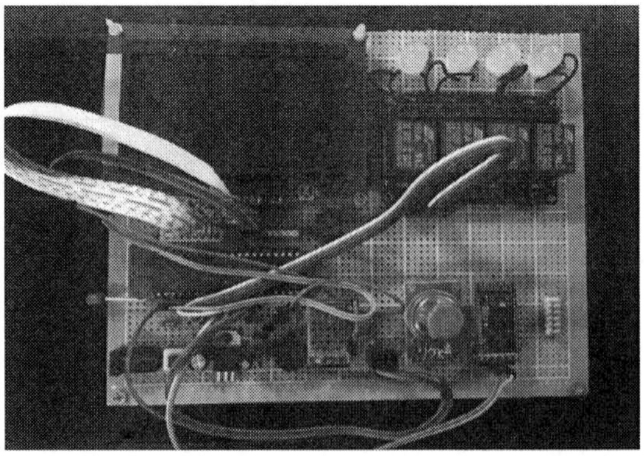

Figure 6 The Testing Design

5.1 Temperature and humidity sensor module test

The temperature measurement range of DHT11 sensor is 0~50. Under the experimental conditions, when the ambient temperature is 20, the temperature and humidity module is tested, the test results are 20 times, and the success probability is then calculated, the number of warning times of the alarm is reach 85%. While replaced with 40°C, the temperature and humidity module was tested, the test was 20 times, the success probability is figured out, and the number of warning times of the alarm now reach 100%.The test result is related to the setting temperature threshold.

Table 1. Test of temperature

	tempera ture is 10°C	tempera ture is 40°C	tempera ture is 30°C	tempera ture is 40°C
Testing times	20	20	20	20
Probabi lity of alarm	10%	85%	100%	100%

5.2 Smoke sensor module test

For the MQ-2 smoke sensor module, we use the burning paper method to detect the smoke sensor in the indoor environment. The test was carried out in four different distance, and then the statistical time was obtained by different data. Its sensitivity characteristics are shown in figures 7. From the figure 7, the MQ-2 smoke sensor module is sensitive to different gases. It can be used in gas leakage detecting equipment in family and industry.

DOI: 10.1051/itmconf/20160706004

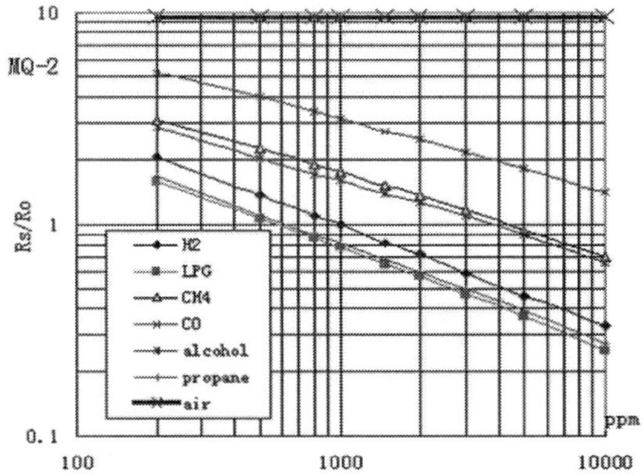

Figures 7 Sensitivity Characteristics of Mq-2

5.3 Infrared sensing module test

Under the experimental conditions, the maximum distance of infrared induction module of the human body is tested individually. In the interior, in the range of 2 meters, it can detect a person; in the 5 meter range from the right and left direction can be detected, from the front into the can not be detected.

Conclusion

In this paper, we have presented a low cost, low power smart home security system through the system design, hardware structure, software flow and other aspects. The system uses ZigBee as the transmission medium, and the security function is realized through the single chip microcomputer. With the continuous progress of science and technology and the diversification of smart home appliances, smart home security system development prospects will be more ideal.

References

1. G Ke. Research and Design of Smart Home System based on Single-chip Micro-computer[D]. Hefei University of Technology, 2010.
2. F Zhou. The Design of System Used for Smart Home Based on Zigbee[D]. Dalian University of Technology,2013.
3. X Zhang. ZigBee Circuit Design and its Application in Smart Home [D]. Nanjing University of Posts and Telecommunications, 2013.
4. W Hao. Design and Implementation of Temperature and Humidity Gathering Communication System Based on ZigBee Technology. Journal of Yancheng Institute of Technology, vol. 26, no. 1, pp. 64-68, 2013.
5. J Hou, Design of Office Intelligent Fire Monitoring System Based on ZigBee. Advanced Materials Research, 2012, 562-564:1903-1906.
6. W Li,K Dai. Design of Coal Mine Intelligent Monitoring System based on ZigBee Wireless Sensor Network. International Conference on Mechanics, 2016.
7. B Chang, XR Zhang, LH Li. Design on Monitoring System of Fire Disaster Based on Zigbee CC2530. Applied Mechanics & Materials, 2013, 397-400:1718-1722

 DOI: 10.1051/itmconf/20160707001

A Novel Fast Method for Point-sampled Model Simplification

Zhi CAO

School of Art and Design,Nanchang Hangkong University, Nanchang, china
e-mail: 517887498@qq.com

Abstract—A novel fast simplification method for point-sampled statue model is proposed. Simplifying method for 3d model reconstruction is a hot topic in the field of 3D surface construction. But it is difficult as point cloud of many 3d models is very large, so its running time becomes very long. In this paper, a two-stage simplifying method is proposed. Firstly, a feature-preserved non-uniform simplification method for cloud points is presented, which simplifies the data set to remove the redundancy while keeping down the features of the model. Secondly, an affinity clustering simplifying method is used to classify the point cloud into a sharp point or a simple point. The advantage of Affinity Propagation clustering is passing messages among data points and fast speed of processing. Together with the re-sampling, it can dramatically reduce the duration of the process while keep a lower memory cost. Both theoretical analysis and experimental results show that after the simplification, the performance of the proposed method is efficient as well as the details of the surface are preserved well.

1 Introduction

With the development of 3D scanning technologies, obtain complex point cloud is not difficult, and modeling and surface reconstructing complex objects from these samples become a significant recent trend in geometric modeling [1-2]. To address this problem, many surface reconstruction methods have been proposed[3-7]. But the production of such a large point data is due to the fact that scanning devices are not able to determine the required density of the point cloud in order to represent faithfully the real object. The material limitation causes the generation of data with big redundancy. Because modeling such large point cloud is cost so many time, the surface reconstruction is often followed by a step of simplification. Simplification will serve to eliminate the data redundancy, accelerate significantly the surface reconstruction process.

Recently, many point cloud simplifying techniques have been adopted to implement the simplification problem discussed above. Representative simplifying methods for point cloud can be summarized as clustering methods, coarse-to-fine methods and iterative methods. Among this simplifying methods, the clustering methods [8] is paid more and more attention. Clustering means to partition the point cloud into subsets and choose an exemplar in each subset. Most of clustering algorithms need to randomly select some cluster centers in original point sets but the initial choices will affect the resultant exemplars. Nowadays, a new clustering approach named Affinity Propagation clustering (AP) is devised to overcome the disadvantage. Its main idea is consider all data points as exemplars and passing messages among data points. However, it is not suitable for a large dense similarity matrix as most of other clustering algorithms, so can not handle large-scale point cloud as its high time complexity,.

In this paper, we propose a fast two-stage point cloud simplification method for statue data. Firstly, non-uniform simplification method is used to simplify the point data to a more coarse point cloud. Second, the affinity clustering methods is used to simplify the point cloud. Finally the surface is been reconstructed. Experiments show the surface is smooth and the method works effectively.

2 Non-uniformly Down Sampling

The number of samples for surface reconstruction usually is huge. So here we use a technology called non-uniformly down sampling to decrease the number of the points.

If S is an r-sample of F and p is a point on F, then the distance between p and its nearest sample point s is within r · LFS(p) . Since every sample is also a point on F, the distance between s and s1 is no more than r · LFS(s), where s1 is the nearest point of s in S.

As show in figure 1, s is a point in S, v is the negative pole of s, s1 is another point in S that d(s, s1) = rs · LFS(s). Let s be the center and rs · LFS(s) be the radius, we have the ball B1. Let v be the center, LFS(s) be the radius, we have another ball B2. In accordance with the definition of local feature size, s1 is outside ball B2. Passing through s we make a plane L tangent to F. Because of the assumption that the surface is smooth, s1 and B2 must be located the same side of L. From the above discussion, we can see that F must be in the shaded region of figure 1 if it is in B1.

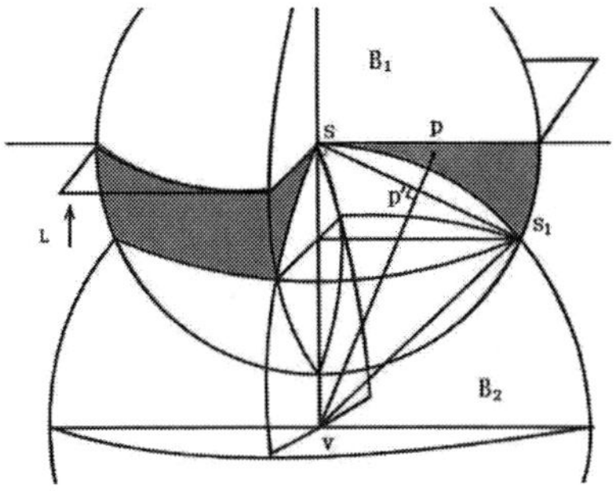

Figure 1. Down sampling

There are two factors influencing local feature size – the curvature and proximity of the other parts of the surface. However, the second factor can't affect the local feature size in a small region, so we need not take into account the factor in a local area. Let p be a point on the surface in the shaded region, and p' is the intersection of the line pv and B2. As we all known, the more flat the surface is, the lower the curvature is. It is apparent that the curvature of point p is smaller than that of point p'. Since point p' and s are both on the ball B2, their curvatures are the same. Thus, we have LFS(p) ≥ LFS(s) . In addition, on account of that p is in the shaded region, we have d(s, p) ≤ d(s, s1) . As a result, we get d(s, p) ≤rs · LFS(s). As S satisfies the requirement for r-sample, rs is less than r. So, we have d(s, p) ≤r · LFS(p) .

Then, we can make the following conclusion: if we can find another point s'∈S that satisfied equation d(s, s') ≤r · LFS(p), S is an r-sample of a surface F. Therefore, if we delete all the points in the shaded area excepting the farthest one and s itself, the down sampled point set S ' is still an r-sample of F, and an r-sample point set is sufficiently dense for correctly reconstruction if r is no more than 0.5[4]. Thus, r should be less than 0.5 here. In fact, we obtain the adoptive value of r through affinity propagation clustering algorithm, which will been discussed in the next section.

Down sampling:

```
Initial every point in S as unmarked
for(i=0;i<n;i++){
 if si is unmarked{
 dmax=0;m=0
   for(j=0;j<n;j++)
            if sj is unmarked{
   S
if d(si, sj) ≤ r· LFS(si){
   marked sj;
            if (d(si, sj)<dmax update dmax and m
  }}
  unmarked sm;
  select all the unmarked points as the down sampled point set
```

We first extract global symmetries from point set. We limit the symmetry transformation to reflection symmetry since it is the most dominant symmetry category in ancient architectures. We follow the basic idea in [4] and adapt it to point sets obtained from multi-view reconstruction method. We evenly sample 1000 to 2000 points in the original point set and each pair of sampling points is viewed as a pair of potential symmetric points. In 3D space, the plane of symmetry determined by this pair of points can be expressed as Ax+By+Cz+D =0. We represent the plane using a 4D vector (A, B,C,D) which defines the reflection transformation space, and each pair is associated with such a 4D vector. By looking at the original point set, we can deduce that all of the 4D vectors should be clustered around the 4D vector corresponding to the reflection transformation actually present in the object, since there are more pairs agree on the true reflection plane. In practice, the sampling point sets exhibits approximate symmetries instead of precise symmetries. Thus, we utilize affinity propagation clustring algorithm to explore the distribution of the 4D vectors and find clusters in the transformation space.

3 Affinity Propagation Clustering algorithm

AP has been proved to be useful for many domains such as in face images, gene expressions and text summarization [8-9]. The main idea of this algorithm is regarding each data point as a node in network and recursively transmits messages among nodes until a good subset appear. AP takes a collection of real-valued similarities among data points as input, denotes S(i, k) as similarity between point i and point k. Similarity S(i, k) indicates that how well the data point k is suited to be the exemplar for data point i. Generally speaking, each similarity is set to a negative squared error. In point cloud simplification, set

$$S(i,k) = -(\|x_i - x_k\|^2 + \|y_i - y_k\|^2 + \|z_i - z_k\|^2) \quad (1)$$

Where (x_i, y_i, z_i) is the coordinate of point i. Another parameter of input is S(k, k), it locates the diagonal of S, and shows probability of point k to be chosen as exemplar. Larger values of S(k, k) are more likely to be chosen as exemplars. Therefore S(k, k) are called 'preferences'. In this

DOI: 10.1051/itmconf/20160707001

sense the numbers of exemplars are influenced by the values of the S(k, k).

AP has two kinds of messages to exchange between data points, and each takes a different competition into account, i.e., 'responsibility' and 'availability'. The 'responsibility' R(i, k) sends from data i to candidate exemplar point k, and reflects the accumulated evidence for point k as the exemplar for point i. The 'availability' A (i, k) reflects the accumulated evidence for appropriate of point i to choose point k as its exemplar. R and A update and exchange messages between pairs of points with known similarities. After several iterations, some points are assigned to other exemplars, and availabilities of them will drop below zero by updated rules.

Table 1. Algorithm Ap

Algorithm AP:	
Input	*S*, *P* (similarities and preferences of point sets).
Output	*D* (exemplars for point sets)
Step1	initialize $A(i, k)$=0.
Step2	update *R*, $R(i,k) = S(i,k) - \{A(i,j) + S(i,j)\}$, $R(k,k) = S(i,k) - \{A(i,j) + S(i,j)\}$
Step3	update *A*, $A(i,k) = \min\{0, R(k,k) + \sum_{j\in\{i,k\}} \max(0, R(j,k)\}$, $A(k,k) = \sum_{j\in\{i,k\}} \max(0, R(j,k)\}$
Step4	iteratively update terminated after a fixed number of iterations or messages stay constantly.

From the setp2 of algorithm AP, equal mark both add A(i,k) to the left and right of $R(i,k) = S(i,k) - \{A(i,j) + S(i,j)\}$,we get

$$R(i,k) + A(i,k) = S(i,k) + A(i,k) - \{A(i,j) + S(i,j)\} \quad (2)$$

The value of R+A shows the effective of affinity points and decides the probability of point i as exemplar of point k. In iterations responsibilities and availabilities are both related to the input similarities, and they are combined to confirm exemplars. R(k, k) and A(k, k) are increasing along with the accretion of S(k, k), and then the probability of point k as exemplar is increasing. In order to void oscillations, the algorithm introduces damp factor, and generally set λ=0.5. In each iteratively update, the formulas are changed as follows.

$$R^{(t)}(i,k) = (1-\lambda)*\{S(i,k) - \max\{A(i,j) + R(i,j)\}\} + \lambda * R^{(t-1)}(i,k) \quad (3)$$

$$A^{(t)}(i,k) = (1-\lambda)*\{0, S(k,k) + \sum_{j\in\{i,k\}} \max\{0, R(j,k)\}\}\} + \lambda * A^{(t-1)}(i,k) \quad (4)$$

$$A^{(t)}(k,k) = (1-\lambda)*\{\sum_{j\notin k} \max\{0, R(j,k)\}\} + \lambda * A^{(t-1)}(k,k) \quad (5)$$

Points send messages like Fig 2.

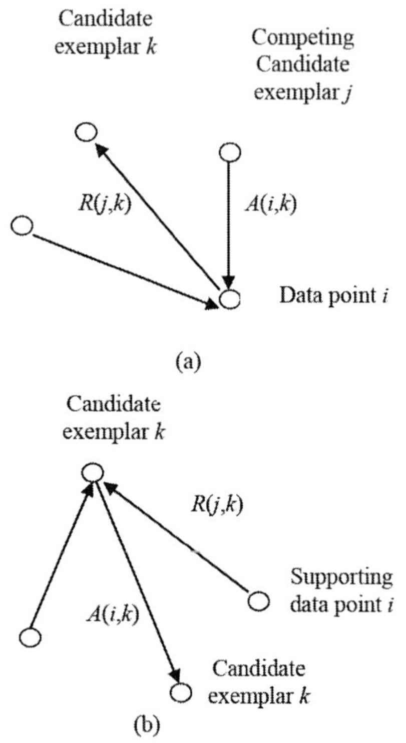

Figure 2. (a)Sending Responsibilities (b)Sending Availabilities

4 Simplification Algorithm

Our simplification algorithm is presented as follow:

Table 2. Simplification Algorithm

Simplification algorithm	
Input	Original statue point cloud *D*
Output	Final simplified statue point cloud *FSD*
Step1	Get a more simple statue point cloud *SD* after non-uniformly down sampling
Step2	Compute similarity matrix *T* of *SD*
Step3	Set the threshold value, run AP clustering with *T*
Step4	If the number of exemplar points output is less than threshold value, back to step1, reset the parameter *r* of the non-uniformly down sampling method
Step5	Output the point set exemplar points *ED* as *FSD*

DOI: 10.1051/itmconf/20160707001

5 Experimental Results and Analysis

We experiment with the point-sampled model Twirl and Squirrel. The models both download from the webset of Stanford University computer graphics laboratory. Fig.3 illustrated the results of our proposed method on Twirl and Fig.4illustrated the results of our proposed method on Squirrel.

From Fig.3, we can see, in the original data, large part of data is missing in the right side, our method still captures the symmetry accurately and completes the missing data successfully. Fig. 4 illustrates that the missing data in the ear, leg and feet of the Squirrel are completed.

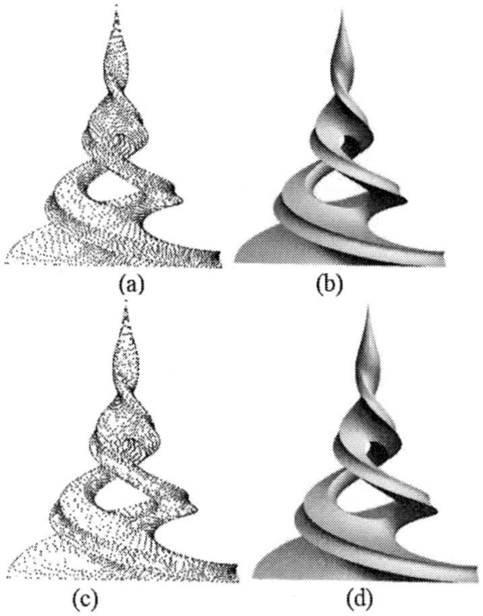

Figure 3. Simplification off Twirl and Squirrel model. (a)Original point clouds Twirl, the number of the point is 7000. (b)Original Twirl model surface. (c) Simplified by our methd, the number of the Twirl preserved is 3600. (d)The output of our algorithm running on the Twist model.

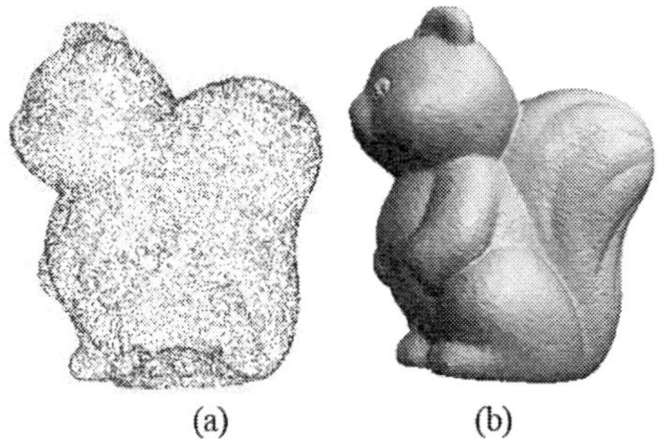

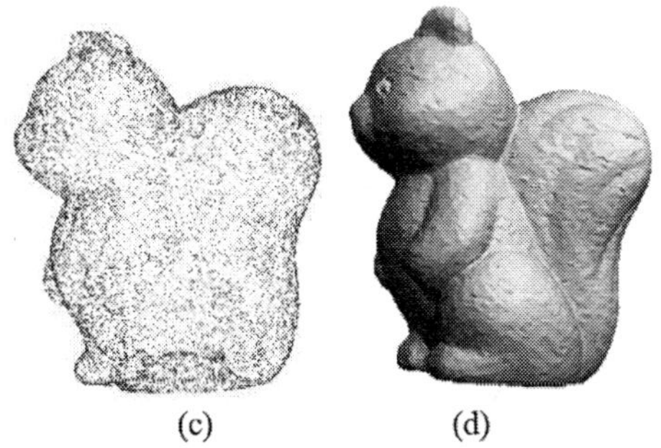

Figure 4. Simplification of Squirrel model. (a)Original point clouds Squirrel, the number of the point is 9000. (b)Original Squirrel model surface. (c) Simplified by our methd, the number of the Squirrel preserved is 4560. (d)The output of our algorithm running on theSquirrel model.

Just as our expectation, almost all the missing parts of point-sampled models are reconstructed and the density of final point cloud is varied according to the surface's detail. For example, the samples are still very dense in the region like the top of Twirl and the eyes of Squirrel.

6 Conclusion

We have presented a novel simplification method for point-sampled models using non-uniform down sampling and affinity propagation clustering. Guaranteeing the topological shape, we use non-uniform down sampling to generate a more simple point cloud. With the change of parameter r, the detail of the point cloud is change. So we use affinity propagation clustering to get an optimistic value of r. Experiments prove the efficiency of this algorithm.

References

1. Shengjun Liu, Charlie C.L. Wang. Orienting unorganized points for surface reconstruction. Computers & Graphics, 2010:34(3),209-218
2. Wei-Cheng Xie, Xiu-Fen Zou, Jian-Dong Yang, Jie-Bin Yang. Iteration and optimization scheme for the reconstruction of 3D surfaces based on non-uniform rational B-splines. Computer-Aided Design, 2012: 44(1),1127-1140
3. J. Stiller, "Point-normal interpolation schemes reproducing spheres cylinders and cones," Geometric Design, 2007, v24, n5, pp286-301.
4. Y.b.Wang, Y.h Sheng., G.n Lv., et al, "A Delaunay-based Surface Reconstrution Algrithm for Unorganized Sampling Points," Journal of Image and Graphics, 2007, v12, n9, pp1537-1543.
5. J.G. Li, D, Yang, X.H. Meng, Q.M. Chen, et al, "Conforming Voronoi Tessellation in 3D," Journal of

DOI: 10.1051/itmconf/20160707001

Computer-Aided Design&Computer Graphics, 2005, v17, n10, 2143-2151.
6. M. Berger, A. Tagliasacchi, L. Seversky, etc. State of the Art in Surface Reconstruction from Point Clouds, Eurographics 2014 - State of the Art Reports, Apr 2014, Strasbourg, France. 1 (1), pp.161-185, 2014
7. Y. Nagai, Y. Ohtake, H. Suzuki. Tomographic surface reconstruction from point cloud, Computers and Graphics, Volume 46 Issue C, February 2015, pp55-63
8. B.J.Frey and Delbert Dueck, "Clustering by Passing Messages Between Data Points", SCIENCE,vol.315, Feb 2007.
9. Ding-yin Xia, Fei WU, "Local and global approaches of affinity propagation clustering for large scale data", Jounal of Zhejiang University SCIENCE.: PP 1373-1381,Sep 2008.

DOI: 10.1051/itmconf/20160707002

Incomplete Surface Reconstruction for Statue Point Cloud based on Symmetry

Jie SHAO

School of Art and Design,Nanchang Hangkong University,Nanchang, china
e-mail: 2262570580@qq.com

Abstract—Advanced 3D scanning technologies enable us to obtain a great mound of point clouds for 3D objects. Among these point clouds, many of them are incomplete, so reconstruction from them is difficult. To address this problem, a novel method of reconstruction from incomplete statue point cloud is proposed. The proposed method complete the missing parts of statue models before reconstruction using the symmetry of statue model. Then the point cloud is reconstructed by Power Crust algorithm. Experiments show that our method can reconstruct the statue point cloud efficiently.

1. Introduction

With the development of 3D scanning technologies, we are now able to obtain a great mound of real objects' surface, and modeling complex objects from samples becomes a significant recent trend in geometric modeling [1][2][3]. But many of the samples acquired with 3D scanners is incomplete. Moreover, in the fields, such as archaeology, ancient architecture, almost all of the scanned models are incomplete. Therefore, it is crucial that we develop efficient algorithms for surface reconstruction from incomplete point cloud.

Symmetry is an essential and ubiquitous concept in nature, science, and art [4], and has been exploited in a variety of geometry processing applications, such as remshing [5], segmentation [6], shape matching [7] and shape retrieval [8]. Extracting symmetry from 3D model is essential for understanding and manipulating the geometric structure of 3D object. Lipman et al. [9] detect and quantify symmetry in point sets by analyzing symmetries in correspondence space with spectral analysis. The method is able to extract symmetries in point set containing noise and missing data. Ghosh et al. [10] solve for the optimal deformation that reconciles a set of local bilateral symmetries and apply it in the symmetrization of fossils. Jiang et at. [11] use symmetry to reconstruct 3D model of building from a single image. Ceylan et at. [12] propose a framework for image-based 3D reconstruction of urban buildings based on symmetry priors. They detect symmetric line arrangements from image-level edges.

In this paper, we propose to exploit symmetry features to address the data missing issues, and apply it in building 3D model from incomplete statue point cloud. As man-made objects, statue often exhibit strict symmetry features and we can use the symmetry to estimate the geometrical structure and appearance of missing area from existing data. Based on this observation, we first detect symmetry at global scale and adopt it to repair for the missing data. We then reconstruct the point cloud using Power Crust[13] algorithm. Experiments show that the proposed algorithm gives a good visual effect of the resulting reconstruction.

2. Extract Symmetry

We first extract global symmetries from point set. We limit the symmetry transformation to reflection symmetry since it is the most dominant symmetry category in ancient architectures. We follow the basic idea in [4] and adapt it to point sets obtained from multi-view reconstruction method. We evenly sample 1000 to 2000 points in the original point set and each pair of sampling points is viewed as a pair of potential symmetric points. In 3D space, the plane of symmetry determined by this pair of points can be expressed as $Ax+By+Cz+D=0$. We represent the plane using a 4D vector (A, B,C,D) which defines the reflection transformation space, and each pair is associated with such a 4D vector. By looking at the original point set, we can

 DOI: 10.1051/itmconf/20160707002

deduce that all of the 4D vectors should be clustered around the 4D vector corresponding to the reflection transformation actually present in the object, since there are more pairs agree on the true reflection plane. In practice, the sampling point sets exhibits approximate symmetries instead of precise symmetries. Thus, we utilize affinity propagation clustering algorithm to explore the distribution of the 4D vectors and find clusters in the transformation space.

3. Affinity Propagation Clustering Algorithm

AP has been proved to be useful for many domains such as in face images, gene expressions and text summarization [14-15]. The main idea of this algorithm is regarding each data point as a node in network and recursively transmits messages among nodes until a good subset appear. AP takes a collection of real-valued similarities among data points as input, denotes S(i, k) as similarity between point i and point k. Similarity S(i, k) indicates that how well the data point k is suited to be the exemplar for data point i. Generally speaking, each similarity is set to a negative squared error. In point cloud simplification, set

$$S(i,k) = -(\|x_i - x_k\|^2 + \|y_i - y_k\|^2 + \|z_i - z_k\|^2) \quad (1)$$

Where (x_i, y_i, z_i) is the coordinate of point i. Another parameter of input is S(k, k), it locates the diagonal of S, and shows probability of point k to be chosen as exemplar. Larger values of S(k, k) are more likely to be chosen as exemplars. Therefore S(k, k) are called 'preferences'. In this sense the numbers of exemplars are influenced by the values of the S(k, k).

AP has two kinds of messages to exchange between data points, and each takes a different competition into account, i.e., 'responsibility' and 'availability'. The 'responsibility' R(i, k) sends from data i to candidate exemplar point k, and reflects the accumulated evidence for point k as the exemplar for point i. The 'availability' A (i, k) reflects the accumulated evidence for appropriate of point i to choose point k as its exemplar. R and A update and exchange messages between pairs of points with known similarities. After several iterations, some points are assigned to other exemplars, and availabilities of them will drop below zero by updated rules.

TABLE I. ALGORITHM AP

Algorithm AP:	
Input	*S*, *P* (similarities and preferences of point sets).
Output	*D* (exemplars for point sets)
Step1	initialize *A*(*i*, *k*)=0.
Step2	update *R*, $R(i,k) = S(i,k) - \{A(i,j) + S(i,j)\}$, $R(k,k) = S(i,k) - \{A(i,j) + S(i,j)\}$
Step3	update *A*, $A(i,k) = \min\{0, R(k,k) + \sum_{j \in \{i,k\}} \max(0, R(j,k)\}$, $A(k,k) = \sum_{j \in \{i,k\}} \max(0, R(j,k)\}$
Step4	iteratively update terminated after a fixed number of iterations or messages stay constantly.

From the setp2 of algorithm AP, equal mark both add A(i,k) to the left and right of $R(i,k) = S(i,k) - \{A(i,j) + S(i,j)\}$,we get

$$R(i,k) + A(i,k) = S(i,k) + A(i,k) - \{A(i,j) + S(i,j)\} \quad (2)$$

The value of R+A shows the effectiveness of affinity points and decides the probability of point i as exemplar of point k. In iterations responsibilities and availabilities are both related to the input similarities, and they are combined to confirm exemplars. R(k, k) and A(k, k) are increasing along with the accretion of S(k, k), and then the probability of point k as exemplar is increasing. In order to void oscillations, the algorithm introduces damp factor, and generally set λ=0.5. In each iteratively update, the formulas are changed as follows.

$$R^{(t)}(i,k) = (1-\lambda) * \{S(i,k) - \max\{A(i,j) + R(i,j)\}\} + \lambda * R^{(t-1)}(i,k) \quad (3)$$

$$A^{(t)}(i,k) = (1-\lambda) * \{0, S(k,k) + \sum_{j \in \{i,k\}} \max\{0, R(j,k)\}\}\} + \lambda * A^{(t-1)}(i,k) \quad (4)$$

$$A^{(t)}(k,k) = (1-\lambda) * \{\sum_{j \notin k} \max\{0, R(j,k)\}\} + \lambda * A^{(t-1)}(k,k) \quad (5)$$

Points send messages like Fig. 1.

DOI: 10.1051/itmconf/20160707002

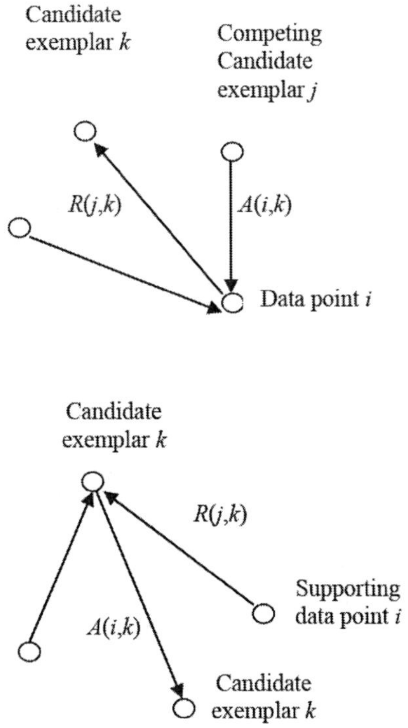

Figure 1. Sending Availabilities

4. Reconstruction Algorithm

Our simplification algorithm is presented as follow:

TABLE II. Reconstruction Algorithm

Reconstruction algorithm	
Input	Original incomplete statue point cloud *D*
Output	Final statue point cloud *FD*
Step1	Sampling the original point set, the percept is about 1/10
Step2	Use AP clustering algorithm to cluster in symmetry transformation space
Step3	Use Power Crust algorithm to construct the point cloud

5. Experimental Results and Analysis

We experiment with the point-sampled model Twirl and Squirrel. The models both download from the web set of Stanford University computer graphics laboratory. Fig.3 illustrates the results of our proposed method on Twirl and Fig.4illustrates the results of our proposed method on Squirrel.

From Fig.2, we can see, (a) is the original point clouds of Twirl, the number of the point is 7000. (b) is the original surface of Twirl model. In the original data, large part of data is missing in the right side, as shown in (c), the number of the remained points is 5235. (d) is the output of our algorithm running on the Twist model. Our method still captures the symmetry accurately and completes the missing data successfully.

From Fig.3, we can see, (a) is the original point clouds of Squirrel, the number of the point is 9000. (b) is the original surface of Squirrel model. In the original data, large part of data is missing in the right side, as shown in (c), the number of the remained points is 6711. (d) is the output of our algorithm running on the Squirrel model. Our method still captures the symmetry accurately and completes the missing data successfully. Fig. 3 illustrates that the missing data in the ear, leg and feet of the Squirrel are completed.

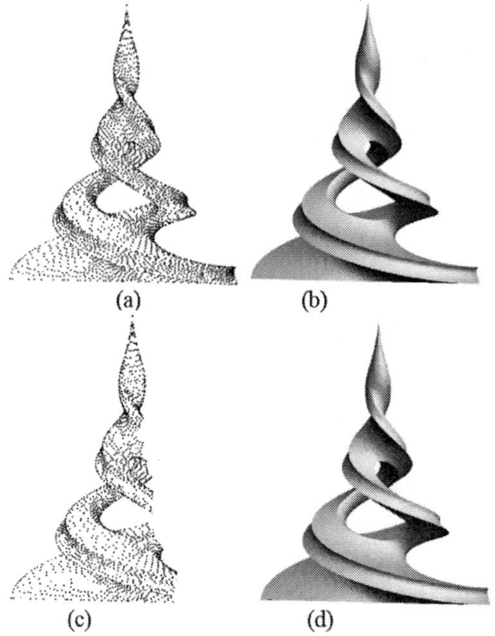

Figure 2. Simplification off Twirl and Squirrel model.

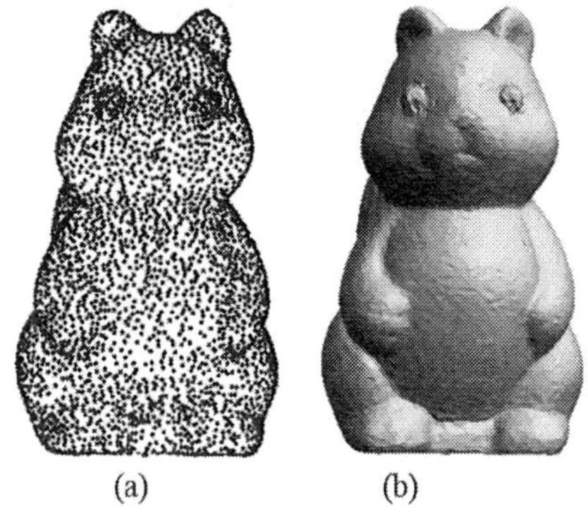

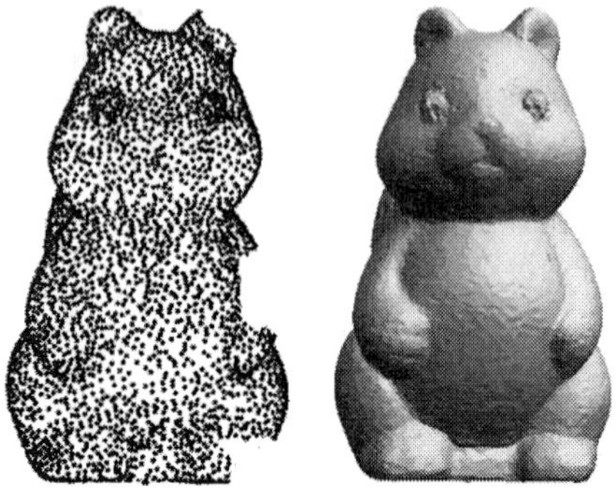

Figure 3. Simplification of Squirrel model.

Just as our expectation, almost all the missing parts of point-sampled models are reconstructed and the density of final point cloud is varied according to the surface's detail. For example, the samples are still very dense in the region like the top of Twirl and the eyes of Squirrel.

6. Conclusion

We have presented a novel reconstruction method for statue point-sampled models using symmetry. Our method first automatically extracts symmetries and completes the missing data using the extracted symmetry transformations. Next we use Power Crust algorithm to construct the statue point cloud. Experiments demonstrate the effectiveness of our method. However, for a surface without obvious symmetry plenty of textures, our method might incur visual artifacts. We plan to explore texture synthesize techniques to achieve more realistic results in the future.

References

1. Hyojoo Son, Changwan Kim, Kwangnam Ch. Rapid 3D object detection and modeling using range data from 3D range imaging camera for heavy equipment operation,Automation in Construction, 2010:19(7), 898-906 .
2. Shengjun Liu, Charlie C.L. Wang. Orienting unorganized points for surface reconstruction. Computers & Graphics, 2010:34(3),209-218.
3. Wei-Cheng Xie, Xiu-Fen Zou, Jian-Dong Yang, Jie-Bin Yang. Iteration and optimization scheme for the reconstruction of 3D surfaces based on non-uniform rational B-splines. Computer-Aided Design, 2012: 44(1),1127-1140.
4. N. J. Mitra, L. J. Guibas, and M. Pauly, "Partial and approximatesymmetry detection for 3d geometry," ACM Trans. Graph. , vol. 25,no. 3, pp. 560–568, 2006.
5. J. Podolak, A. Golovinskiy, and S. Rusinkiewicz, "Symmetry-enhanced remeshing of surfaces," in Proceedings of the fifth Eurographics sym-posium on Geometry processing, 2007, pp. 235–242.
6. T. Riklin-Raviv, N. Kiryati, and N. Sochen, "Segmentation by level sets and symmetry," in Proceedings of the 2006 IEEE Computer Society Conference on Computer Vision and Pattern Recognition - Volume 1,ser. CVPR '06, 2006, pp. 1015–1022.
7. R. Gal and D. Cohen-Or, "Salient geometric features for partial shapematching and similarity," ACM Trans. Graph., vol. 25, no. 1, pp. 130–150, 2006.
8. M. Kazhdan, T. Funkhouser, and S. Rusinkiewicz, "Symmetry descrip-tors and 3d shape matching," in Proceedings of the 2004 Eurograph-ics/ACM SIGGRAPH symposium on Geometry processing, 2004, pp.115–123
9. Y. Lipman, X. Chen, I. Daubechies, and T. Funkhouser, "Symmetry factored embedding and distance," ACM Trans. Graph., vol. 29, no. 4,pp. 103:1–103:12, 2010.
10. D. Ghosh, N. Amenta, and M. Kazhdan, "Closed-form blending of local symmetries," Computer Graphics Forum, vol. 29, no. 5, pp. 1681–1688, 2010.
11. N. Jiang, P. Tan, and L.-F. Cheong, "Symmetric architecture modeling with a single image," ACM Trans. Graph., vol. 28, no. 5, pp. 113:1–113:8, 2009.
12. D. Ceylan, N. J. Mitra, H. Li, T. Weise, and M. Pauly, "Factored facade acquisition using symmetric line arrangements," Computer Graphics Forum (EUROGRAPHICS), 2012.
13. N.Amenta, S.Choi, T.K.Dey and N.Leekha. A simple algorithm for homeomorphic surface reconstruction. Internat. J. Comput. Applications, 12, 2002, pp.125-141.
14. B.J.Frey and Delbert Dueck, "Clustering by Passing Messages Between Data Points", SCIENCE,vol.315, Feb 2007.
15. Ding-yin Xia, Fei WU, "Local and global approaches of affinity propagation clustering for large scale data", Jounal of Zhejiang University SCIENCE.: PP 1373-1381,Sep 2008.

ITM Web of Conferences 7, 07003 (2016)
ITA 2016
DOI: 10.1051/itmconf/20160707003

Some properties of *k*-gamma and *k*-beta functions

Wu-Sheng WANG

School of Mathematics and Statistics, Hechi University, Yizhou, Guangxi, 546300, P. R. China

Abstract: In this paper, firstly, we introduce the several definitions of classic gamma function and beta function, and the several definitions of k-gamma function and k-beta function. Secondly, we discuss the relations between the several definitions and properties of gamma function, beta function, k-gamma function and k-beta function. Finally, we prove these properties by mathematical induction and integral transformation method.

1 Definitions of Gamma and Beta Functions

The gamma function is an extension of the factorial function, with its argument shifted down by 1, to real and complex numbers. That is, if n is a positive integer,

$$\Gamma(n) = (n-1)!. \quad (1)$$

There are many forms on the definition of gamma function. Euler's integral form

$$\Gamma(x) = \int_0^{\infty} v^x e^{-v} dv , \quad (2)$$

or

$$\Gamma(x) = 2\int_0^{\infty} v^{x^2} e^{-2v-1} dv , \quad (3)$$

or

$$\Gamma(x) = \int_0^1 \left[\ln\frac{1}{v} \right]^{x-1} dv . \quad (4)$$

The problem of extending the factorial to non-integer arguments was apparently first considered by Daniel Bernoulli and Christian Goldbach in the 1720s, and was solved at the end of the same decade by Leonhard Euler (see [1-4]). Euler gave two different definitions: the first was not his integral but an infinite product,

$$n! = \prod_{k=1}^{\infty} \frac{\left(1+\frac{1}{k}\right)^n}{1+\frac{n}{k}} . \quad (5)$$

In the 19th century, Carl Friedrich Gauss rewrote Euler's product as (see [1])

$$\Gamma(x) = \lim_{x\to\infty} \frac{n^x (n-1)!}{x(x+1)...(x+n-1)} . \quad (6)$$

Karl Weierstrass further established the role of the gamma function in complex analysis, starting from yet another product representation. The gamma function can also be defined by an infinite product form (Weierstrass form) (Krantz 1999, p. 157; Havil 2003, p. 57) (see [3,4]).

$$\Gamma(z) = \frac{e^{-\gamma z}}{z} \prod_{n=1}^{\infty} \left(1+\frac{z}{n}\right)^{-1} e^{z/n} , \quad (7)$$

where $\gamma \approx$ =0.577216 is Euler's constant.
The Euler limit form is

$$-\ln\Gamma(z) = \ln z + \gamma z + \sum_{n=1}^{\infty} \left[\ln\left(1+\frac{z}{n}\right) - \frac{z}{n} \right] . \quad (8)$$

In 1933, Egan defined the gamma function as (see [5])

$$\ln\Gamma(x) = (x-\frac{1}{2})\ln x - x + c + \phi(x), \quad (9)$$

where

$$\phi(x) = \Delta(x) + \Delta(x+1) + \Delta(x+2) + ..., c = 1 - \phi(1),$$

and

$$\Delta(x) = \int_x^{x+1} \ln s ds - \frac{1}{2}\ln x - \frac{1}{2}\ln(x+1). \quad (10)$$

The Beta function is defined as

$$B(x,y) = \int_0^1 u^{x-1}(1-u)^{y-1} du. \quad (11)$$

Let $u = \frac{1}{1+v}$, then

$$B(x,y) = \int_0^\infty v^{y-1}(1+v)^{-x-y} dv. \quad (12)$$

The definitions of gamma function given by Euler, Carl Friedrich Gauss, Karl Weierstrass and Egan are equivalent to each other.

2 Properties of Gamma and Beta Functions

By the definitions of the gamma function and beta function, their properties can be derived as the following (see [5]):

$\ln\Gamma(x)$ is a convex function on $(0,\infty)$,

$$\Gamma(1) = 1, \quad (13)$$

$$x\Gamma(x) = \Gamma(x+1), \quad (14)$$

$$\lim_{y\to\infty} \frac{\Gamma(y+x)}{y^x\Gamma(y)} = 1, \quad (15)$$

$$\Gamma(x)\Gamma(1-x) = \frac{\pi}{\sin(\pi x)}, \quad (16)$$

$$B(x,y) = \frac{\Gamma(x)\Gamma(y)}{\Gamma(x+y)}, \quad (17)$$

$$\Gamma(x) = \lim_{y\to\infty}(y+a)^x B(y+b,x). \quad (18)$$

In (16), x is non integer complex number. The proof of these properties may be found in literatures [1-5] and the references cited therein.

3 Definitions of *k*-gamma and *k*-beta Functions

The motivation to introduce k-gamma function comes from the repeated appearance of expressions of the form

$$(x)_{n,k} = x(x+k)(x+2k)...(x+(n-1)k) \quad (19)$$

in a variety of contexts, such as the combination of creation and annihilation operators (see [6, 7]) and the perturbation computation of Feynman integrals(see [8]). The function of variable x given by formula (19) will be called the Pochhammer k-symbol. Setting $k = 1$ one obtains the usual Pochhammer symbol $(x)_n$, also known as the raising factorial (see [9, 10]).

Definition 1(see [11]) For k > 0, the k-gamma function is given by

$$\Gamma_k(x) = \lim_{n\to\infty} \frac{n!k^n(nk)^{\frac{x}{k}-1}}{(x)_{n,k}}, \quad (20)$$

where x is a complex number.

Definition 2(see [11]) For k > 0, the k-beta function is given by

$$B_k(x,y) = \frac{\Gamma_k(x)\Gamma_k(y)}{\Gamma_k(x+y)}. \quad (21)$$

4 Properties of *k*-gamma Function

Proposition 1(see [11]) For a positive real number k and a complex number x with *Re x*>0, the k-Gamma function is given by the integral

$$\Gamma_k(x) = \int_0^\infty t^{x-1}e^{-\frac{t^k}{k}}dt. \quad (22)$$

Proof: We observe that

$$\int_0^\infty t^{x-1}e^{-\frac{t^k}{k}}dt = \lim_{n\to\infty}\int_0^{(nk)^{1/k}} \left(1-\frac{t^k}{nk}\right)^n t^{x-1}dt. \quad (23)$$

Let $A_{n,i}(x), i = 0,1,2,...,n,$ be given by

$$A_{n,i}(x) = \int_0^{(nk)^{1/k}} \left(1-\frac{t^k}{nk}\right)^i t^{x-1}dt. \quad (24)$$

The following recursive formula is proven using integration by parts

$$A_{n,i}(x) = \int_0^{(nk)^{1/k}} \left(1-\frac{t^k}{nk}\right)^i t^{x-1}dt$$

$$= \frac{1}{x}\left(1-\frac{t^k}{nk}\right)^i t^x \Big|_0^{(nk)^{1/k}}$$

$$+\frac{i}{x}\int_0^{(nk)^{1/k}}\left(1-\frac{t^k}{nk}\right)^{i-1}\frac{t^{k-1}}{n}t^x dt$$

$$=\frac{i}{nx}\int_0^{(nk)^{1/k}}\left(1-\frac{t^k}{nk}\right)^{i-1}t^{x+k-1}dt$$

$$=\frac{i}{nx}A_{n,i-1}(x+k). \qquad (25)$$

When i=0, we have

$$A_{n,0}(x)=\int_0^{(nk)^{1/k}}t^{x-1}dt=\frac{(nk)^{x/k}}{x}. \qquad (26)$$

When *i=1,2,...,n,* we get

$$A_{n,1}(x)=\frac{1}{nx}A_{n,0}(x+k)=\frac{1}{nx}\frac{(nk)^{\frac{x+k}{k}}}{x+k}, \qquad (27)$$

$$A_{n,2}(x)=\frac{2}{nx}A_{n,1}(x+k)=\frac{1}{nx}\frac{2}{n(x+k)}\frac{(nk)^{\frac{x+2k}{k}}}{x+2k}, \qquad (28)$$

$$A_{n,n}(x)=\frac{n}{nx}A_{n,n-1}(x+k)$$

$$=\frac{1}{nx}\frac{2}{n(x+k)}\cdots\frac{n}{n(x+(n-1)k)}\frac{(nk)^{\frac{x+nk}{k}}}{x+nk}$$

$$=\frac{n!k^n(nk)^{\frac{x}{k}-1}}{(x)_{n,k}(1+\frac{x}{nk})}. \qquad (29)$$

By Definition 1, we have

$$\lim_{n\to\infty}A_{n,n}(x)=\lim_{n\to\infty}\frac{n!k^n(nk)^{\frac{x}{k}-1}}{(x)_{n,k}(1+\frac{x}{nk})}$$

$$=\lim_{n\to\infty}\frac{n!k^n(nk)^{\frac{x}{k}-1}}{(x)_{n,k}}=\Gamma_k(x). \qquad (30)$$

From (23), (24) and (30), we obtain

$$\Gamma_k(x)=\int_0^{\infty}t^{x-1}e^{-\frac{t^k}{k}}dt.$$

This completes the proof of **Proposition 1**.

Proposition 2(see [11]) For a complex number x and a positive real number k, the k-gamma function and the classical Gamma function have the relation

$$\Gamma_k(x)=k^{\frac{x}{k}-1}\Gamma\left(\frac{x}{k}\right). \qquad (31)$$

Proof: Let $s=t^k/k$, then $ds=t^{k-1}dt$ and

$$\Gamma_k(x)=\int_0^{\infty}t^{x-1}e^{-\frac{t^k}{k}}dt=\int_0^{\infty}t^{x-k}e^{-\frac{t^k}{k}}t^{k-1}dt$$

$$=\int_0^{\infty}(t^k)^{\frac{x}{k}-1}e^{-\frac{t^k}{k}}t^{k-1}dt=k^{\frac{x}{k}-1}\int_0^{\infty}(s)^{\frac{x}{k}-1}e^{-s}ds$$

$$=k^{\frac{x}{k}-1}\Gamma\left(\frac{x}{k}\right). \qquad (32)$$

The proof of **Proposition 2** is completed.

Proposition 3(see [11]) For a non-integer complex number x and positive real numbers k, s, the following identities hold

$$(x)_{n,s}=\left(\frac{s}{k}\right)^n\left(\frac{kx}{s}\right)_{n,k}, \qquad (33)$$

$$\Gamma_s(x)=\left(\frac{s}{k}\right)^{\frac{x}{s}-1}\Gamma_k\left(\frac{kx}{s}\right). \qquad (34)$$

Proof: By the definition of the Pochhammer k-symbol, we have

$$(x)_{n,s}=x(x+s)(x+2s)...(x+(n-1)s)$$

$$=\frac{s}{k}\frac{kx}{s}\left(\frac{s}{k}\frac{kx}{s}+s\right)\left(\frac{s}{k}\frac{kx}{s}+2s\right)...\left(\frac{s}{k}\frac{kx}{s}+(n-1)s\right)$$

$$=\left(\frac{s}{k}\right)^n\frac{kx}{s}\left(\frac{kx}{s}+k\right)\left(\frac{kx}{s}+2k\right)...\left(\frac{kx}{s}+(n-1)k\right)$$

$$=\left(\frac{s}{k}\right)^n\left(\frac{kx}{s}\right)_{n,k}. \qquad (35)$$

By Definition 1, we have

$$\Gamma_s(x)=\lim_{n\to\infty}\frac{n!s^n(ns)^{\frac{x}{s}-1}}{(x)_{n,s}}$$

$$= \lim_{n\to\infty} \frac{n!k^n \left(\frac{s}{k}\right)^n \left(\frac{s}{k}\right)^{\frac{x}{s}-1} (nk)^{(\frac{kx}{s})/k-1}}{\left(\frac{s}{k}\right)^n \left(\frac{kx}{s}\right)_{n,k}}$$

$$= \left(\frac{s}{k}\right)^{\frac{x}{s}-1} \Gamma_k\left(\frac{kx}{s}\right). \quad (36)$$

The proof of Proposition 3 is completed.

Proposition 4(see [11]) For a positive real number k, the k-gamma function satisfies the following properties

$$\Gamma_k(x+k) = x\Gamma_k(x); \quad (37)$$

$$(x)_{n,k} = \frac{\Gamma_k(x+nk)}{\Gamma_k(x)}; \quad (38)$$

$$\Gamma_k(k) = 1; \quad (39)$$

$$\frac{1}{\Gamma_k(x)} = xk^{-\frac{x}{k}} e^{\frac{x}{k}\gamma} \prod_{n=1}^{\infty}\left(\left(1+\tfrac{x}{nk}\right)e^{-\frac{x}{nk}}\right), \quad (40)$$

where

$$\gamma = \lim_{n\to\infty}(1+\frac{1}{2}+\ldots\frac{1}{n}-\ln(n)); \quad (41)$$

$$\Gamma_k(x) = a^{\frac{x}{k}} \int_0^\infty t^{x-1} e^{-\frac{t^k}{k}a} dt; \quad (42)$$

where a and x are real numbers;

$$\Gamma_k(x)\Gamma_k(k-x) = \frac{\pi}{k\sin(\frac{\pi x}{k})}. \quad (43)$$

where x is a non-integer complex number;

For a real number x, $\Gamma_k(x)$ is logarithmically convex.

Proof 1: From (31), we have

$$\Gamma_k(x+k) = k^{\frac{x+k}{k}-1}\Gamma\left(\frac{x+k}{k}\right) = k^{\frac{x}{k}} \frac{x}{k} \Gamma\left(\frac{x}{k}\right)$$

$$= xk^{\frac{x}{k}-1}\Gamma\left(\frac{x}{k}\right) = x\Gamma_k(x). \quad (44)$$

2. By **Definition 1** of the k-gamma function, we have

$$\Gamma_k(x+nk) = \lim_{n\to\infty} \frac{n!k^n (nk)^{\frac{x+nk}{k}-1}}{(x+nk)_{n,k}}$$

$$= \lim_{n\to\infty} \frac{n!k^n (nk)^{\frac{x}{k}-1}}{(x)_{n,k}} \frac{(x)_{n,k}(nk)^n}{(x+nk)_{n,k}}$$

$$= \Gamma_k(x) \lim_{n\to\infty} \frac{(x)_{n,k}(nk)^n}{(x+nk)_{n,k}} = \Gamma_k(x)(x)_{n,k}. \quad (45)$$

It implies that

$$(x)_{n,k} = \frac{\Gamma_k(x+nk)}{\Gamma_k(x)}. \quad (46)$$

3. By **Definition 1** of the k-gamma function, we have

$$\Gamma_k(k) = \lim_{n\to\infty} \frac{n!k^n (nk)^{\frac{k}{k}-1}}{(k)_{n,k}} = \lim_{n\to\infty} \frac{n!k^n}{(k)_{n,k}} = 1. \quad (47)$$

4. From (7) and (32), we obtain the required formula:

$$\frac{1}{\Gamma_k(x)} = \frac{1}{k^{\frac{x}{k}-1}\Gamma\left(\frac{x}{k}\right)} = xk^{-\frac{x}{k}} e^{\frac{x}{k}\gamma} \prod_{n=1}^{\infty}\left(\left(1+\frac{x}{nk}\right)e^{-\frac{x}{nk}}\right). \quad (48)$$

5. Let $t = a^{\frac{1}{k}}s$, from (22) we get

$$\Gamma_k(x) = \int_0^\infty t^{x-1} e^{-\frac{t^k}{k}} dt = a^{\frac{1}{k}} \int_0^\infty (a^{\frac{1}{k}}s)^{x-1} e^{-\frac{s^k}{k}a} ds$$

$$= a^{\frac{x}{k}} \int_0^\infty s^{x-1} e^{-\frac{s^k}{k}a} ds. \quad (49)$$

6. From (16) and (22), we obtain

$$\Gamma_k(x)\Gamma_k(k-x) = k^{\frac{x}{k}-1}\Gamma\left(\frac{x}{k}\right) k^{\frac{k-x}{k}-1}\Gamma\left(\frac{k-x}{k}\right)$$

$$= k^{-1}\Gamma\left(\frac{x}{k}\right)\Gamma\left(\frac{k-x}{k}\right) = \frac{\pi}{k\sin(\frac{\pi x}{k})}. \quad (50)$$

7. Let $\varphi(k,x) = \ln\Gamma_k(x)$. We obtain

$$\varphi(k,x) = -\ln x + \frac{x}{k}\ln(k) - \frac{x}{k}\gamma$$

$$-\sum_{n=1}^{\infty}\left(\ln\left(1+\frac{x}{nk}\right)-\frac{x}{nk}\right), \quad (51)$$

$$\frac{\partial\varphi(k,x)}{\partial x}=-\frac{1}{x}+\frac{\ln(k)-\gamma}{k}-\sum_{n=1}^{\infty}\left(\frac{1}{x+nk}-\frac{1}{nk}\right), \quad (52)$$

and

$$\frac{\partial^2\varphi(k,x)}{\partial x^2}=\sum_{n=0}^{\infty}\frac{1}{(x+nk)^2}. \quad (53)$$

It implies that $\Gamma_k(k)$ is logarithmically convex on $(0,\infty)$.

The proof of **Proposition 4** is completed.

5 Properties of *k*-beta Function

Proposition 5(see [11]) For a positive real number *k*, the *k*-beta function satisfies the following properties

$$B_k(x,y)=\frac{1}{k}B(\frac{x}{k},\frac{y}{k}). \quad (54)$$

$$B_k(x,y)=\int_0^{\infty}t^{x-1}(1+t^k)^{-\frac{x+y}{k}}dt. \quad (55)$$

$$B_k(x,y)=\frac{1}{k}\int_0^1 t^{\frac{x}{k}-1}(1-t)^{\frac{y}{k}-1}dt. \quad (56)$$

$$B_k(x,y)=\frac{x+y}{xy}\prod_{n=0}^{\infty}\frac{nk(nk+x+y)}{(nk+x)(nk+y)}. \quad (57)$$

Proof: From (21) and (31), we have

$$B_k(x,y)=\frac{\Gamma_k(x)\Gamma_k(y)}{\Gamma_k(x+y)}$$

$$=\frac{k^{\frac{x}{k}-1}\Gamma\left(\frac{x}{k}\right)k^{\frac{y}{k}-1}\Gamma\left(\frac{y}{k}\right)}{k^{\frac{x+y}{k}-1}\Gamma\left(\frac{x+y}{k}\right)}=\frac{1}{k}B\left(\frac{x}{k},\frac{y}{k}\right). \quad (58)$$

From (12) and (58), we get

$$B_k(x,y)=\frac{1}{k}B(\frac{x}{k},\frac{y}{k})=\frac{1}{k}\int_0^{\infty}(1+v)^{-\frac{x}{k}-\frac{y}{k}}v^{\frac{y}{k}-1}dv$$

$$=\int_0^{\infty}(1+t^k)^{-\frac{x+y}{k}}t^{x-1}dt. \quad (59)$$

From (11) and (58), we obtain

$$B_k(x,y)=\frac{1}{k}B(\frac{x}{k},\frac{y}{k})=\frac{1}{k}\int_0^1 t^{\frac{x}{k}-1}(1-t)^{\frac{y}{k}-1}dt. \quad (60)$$

From (21) and (40), we have

$$B_k(x,y)=\frac{\Gamma_k(x)\Gamma_k(y)}{\Gamma_k(x+y)}=\frac{x+y}{xy}\prod_{n=1}^{\infty}\frac{nk(nk+x+y)}{(nk+x)(nk+y)}. \quad (61)$$

The proof of **Proposition 5** is completed.

Summary

In this paper, firstly, we introduce the several definitions of classic gamma function and beta function, and discuss the relations between the several definitions and properties of gamma function and beta function by mathematical induction and integral transformation method. Secondly, we introduce the several definitions of *k*-gamma function and *k*-beta function, discuss the relations between *k*-gamma function, *k*-beta function, classic gamma function and beta function, and also discuss properties of *k*-gamma function and *k*-beta function by method of mathematical deduction. Finally, we prove these properties.

Acknowledgements

This research was supported by National Natural Science Foundation of China (Project No. 11161018, 11561019).

References

1. Eric W. Weisstein, Gamma Function, From MathWorld--A Wolfram Web Resource. http://mathworld.wolfram.com/GammaFunction.html.
2. W. N. Bailey, *Generalised Hypergeometric Series*(Cambridge, England: Cambridge University Press, 1935).
3. S. G. Krantz, *The Gamma and Beta Functions*(§13.1 in Handbook of Complex Variables. Boston, MA: Birkhäuser, pp. 155-158, 1999).
4. J. Havil, *The Gamma Function*(Ch. 6 in Gamma: Exploring Euler's Constant. Princeton, NJ: Princeton University Press, pp. 53-60, 2003).
5. M. F. Egan, On Stirling's Theorem as a definition of the gamma function, Math. Gazette, **17**(223): 114-121(1933).
6. R. Diaz and E. Pariguan, Quantum symmetric functions, Communications in Algebra, **6** (33): 1947-1978(2005).
7. R. Diaz and E. Pariguan, Symmetric quantum Weyl algebras, Annales Math. Blaise Pascal, **11**: 187-203(2004).

8. P. Deligne, P. Etingof, D. Freed, L. Jeffrey, D. Kazhdan, J. Morgan, D. Morrison and E. Witten, *Quantum fields and strings*(A course for mathematicians, American Mathematical Society, 1999).
9. S. A. Joni, G. C Rota and B. Sagan, From sets to functions: Three elementery examples, Discrete Mathematics, **37**:193-202(1981).
10. K. H. Wehrhahn, *Combinatorics. An introduction*(Carslaw Publications, 1990).
11. Diaz and E. Pariguan, On hyperge-ometric functions and Pochhammer k-symbol, Divulgaciones Matematicas, **15**(2): 179-192(2007).

Research of Dependent Tasks Scheduling Algorithm in Cloud Computing Environments

Qing-Yi CHEN[1], Zhi-Hong LIANG[2,*], Hong-Wei KANG[3], Yu-Ming MA[4] and Dong WANG

[1,2,3,4]*School of Software, Yunnan University, Kunming, Yunnan, 650091, China*
E-mail: zhliang@ynu.edu.cn

Abstract: With the dependent relationship of tasks submitted by the users in the model of Cloud computing resources scheduling become stronger and stronger, it is worthy of studying how to optimize the scheduling strategy and algorithm to meet the different demands of the users, and it is absolutely importance. In this article, the author analysed the factors that will affect the entire task-sets execution firstly. Then proposed a new tasks scheduling model based on the original priority calculation method and the idea of redundant duplication of tasks. In the phase of tasks scheduling in the model, the execution results of all parent tasks of the subtask that being executing are considered. The costs of communication between task-sets has reduced by the method of redundant duplication of tasks, so that the execution time of some subtasks share be advanced, and the entire execution efficiency of task-sets can be increased. At the end of this article, from the comparative results of the space-time complexity of contrast algorithms and the algorithm proposed by the author during the process of processing dependent tasks, we can find that subtasks execution time can be advanced and the complete time of the whole task-set can be cut down to a certain extent

1 Dependent Tasks and the Resource Node Modelling

The dependent tasks are the tasks that in the task-sets submitted by users exist a certain dependent relationship between each other, and the relationship shows up in that before the subtask be executed, the execution results of its parent tasks must be known. And we can use a directed acyclic graph G to represent the dependent tasks [1]. As is shown in the following figure:

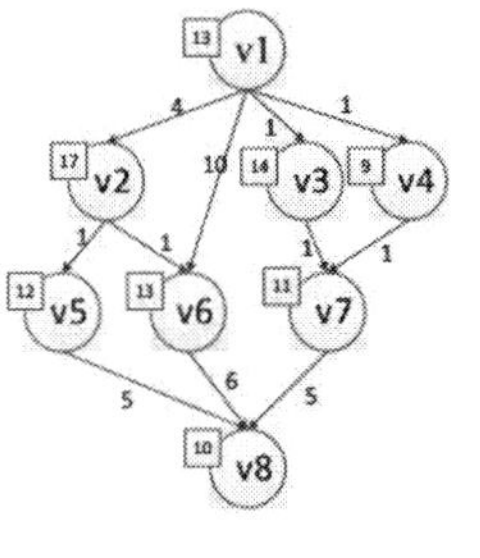

Figure 1. Sketch of Dependent Task

The figure is represented as a four-tuples: $G =< N,\ E,\ Q,\ W >$ in which $N = \{v_1, v_2, \dots,\ v_n\}$, $E = \{e_{ij} | i,j \in n,\ i \neq j\}$, $Q = \{q_1, q_2, \dots,\ q_m\}$ and $W = \{w_{ij} | i,j \in m,\ i \neq j\}$. The N represents the task node collection and the v_i represents a single task node. The E represents the collection of "edge", and the edge determines the dependent relationship between tasks. If tow task nodes are connected by the edge, then there is a dependency relationship between them, and the sub task is the task node that the arrow points to, another side points to the parent task. The Q represents the average calculation cost collection for each task node, and the average calculation cost here refers to the average value of the cost of the task node in all resource nodes. The W represents the collection of communication cost between the tasks. And the special note here is that if tow dependencies are distributed to the same computing node, there is no communication cost between them[2].

We can also make the following definition:

Definition 1: $\mathrm{pre}(v_i)$ represents the predecessor task node set (or parent task node set) of the single task node v_i, and $\mathrm{sub}(v_i)$ represents the subsequent task node set (or sub task set) of the single task node v_i.

Here we consider the computing node modelling next. Before that we need to do some declare first, the scheduling model of dependent tasks is consistent with the scheduling model of independent tasks, which has demonstrated in the previous chapter and I will not repeat again.

The resource layer is mainly responsible for the calculation of the tasks that based on some prioritization sorting and scheduling, and returns the results [3]. Due to the resource layer consists of large computer clusters and network devices, each computing node is connected by the hubs, gateways and routers. It will inevitably lead to the cost of communication in the course of the process of each computing node communicates with the others. And the cost of communication here just refers to the loss of time. In the heterogeneous computing node sets, the computing ability of each node is different, so we can also consider these nodes as an undirected graph G' as follows:

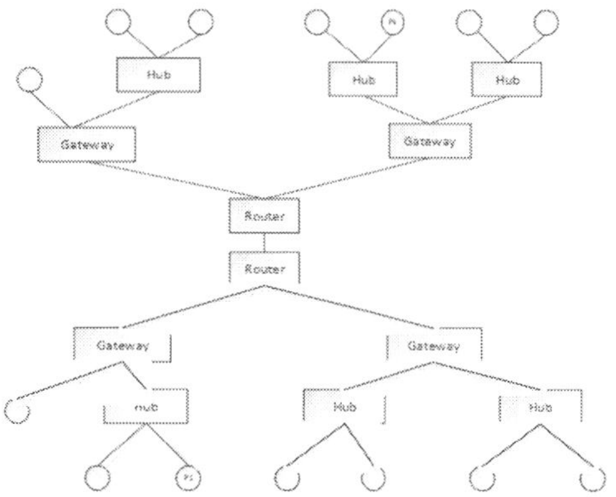

Figure 2. sketch map of computing nodes in resource layer

We use a tow-tuples to represent this figure as $G' =< P, L >$ in which the P represents a collection of computing nodes and it is expressed as $P = \{p_1, p_2, \ldots, p_m\}$, m is the total number of the computing nodes. The L represents a collection of edges between each tow computing nodes, it is expressed as $L = \{l_{ij} | i, j \in m,\ i \neq j\}$. In this article, we assume that each computing node can be interconnected with others. In other words, there is always an edge between each tow computing nodes.

In the process of task modelling, we have defined q_i as the average value of computing cost of each task in all resource nodes. However, in order to further analysis, we will make the cost of task computing in node p_i is $q(v_i, p_j)$. We assume that the total number of computing nodes in the resource layer is m, and the total number of tasks in the task-set is n, then we have the table as following:

Table 1. the cost of task computing in resource node p_i

$q(v_i, p_j)$	p_1	p_2	…	p_m
v_1	$q(v_1, p_1)$	$q(v_1, p_2)$	…	$q(v_1, p_m)$
v_2	$q(v_2, p_1)$	$q(v_2, p_2)$	…	$q(v_2, p_m)$
…	…	…	…	…
v_n	$q(v_n, p_1)$	$q(v_n, p_2)$	…	$q(v_n, p_m)$

From the table above, we can find that the costs of task computing in different nodes are inconsistent. In the process of quantitate the computing nodes, we can't judge the speed of calculation of computing nodes simply by the speed of the task processing (dominant frequency), but quantitate the execution time of the computing nodes by different task types. And thus, it is closer to the actual situation of the real life [4].

2 The Analysis of Tasks Execution

Before analysing the problem of scheduling, we should have a study of the execution conditions and time points of the dependent tasks firstly, and then schedule it according to the correspond scheduling strategy [5].

2.1 Definitions

We should make sure that the resource nodes are in the ready state first, and the execution results of all parent tasks must be known before a task be executed. If not, the task node can't be executed. Based on this feature, we make definitions of the concept of time as follows:

Definition 2: $ready(p_j)$ is the time of computing node p_j get ready. Otherwise the task node can be calculated on the computing node while the computing node gets in the point of time.

Definition 3: $finit(v_i, p_j)$ is the completion time of task v_i that be executed on the computing node p_j. In this article, if the start time is 0, then the $finit(v_i, p_j)$ is given by: $finit(v_i, p_j) = q(v_i, p_j)$.

Definition 4: $start(v_i, p_j)$ is the beginning time of task v_i, be executed on computing node p_j.

If the parent task-sets $pre(v_i)$ of task v_i are all on the same computing node p_j, the cost of communication $w_{ij} = 0$. That means $start(v_i, p_j) = finit(pre(v_i),\ p_j)$. But in general circumstances, different task nodes will be distributed to different computing nodes, thus we can give more complete definition to definition 3 and definition 4 as follows:

$$start(v_j, p_j) = max\{ready(p_j), max\{finit(v_j, p_k) + w_{kj}\}\},\ v_j \in pre(v_i) \quad (1)$$

From the equation above we can know that if we want to get the execution time of task node v_i, we shall calculate the ready time $ready(p_j)$ of the computing node p_j which task v_i will be executed on, and the maximum value of the sum of the complete time of task node v_j, the parent task node of v_i, and the cost of communication of them. Then the execution time is the larger one of the time above. Similarly, the complete time of task node v_i that will be executed on computing node p_j is the sum of the start execution time of task v_i and the cost of execution.

$$finit(v_j, p_k) = start(v_i, p_j) + q(v_i, p_j) \quad (2)$$

As we know that the start time of a task and the ready time of the computing node which the task will be executed on would not necessarily equal, so we can give a definition as follows:

Definition 5: $wait(v_j, p_k)$ is the time that the task node v_i has arrived the computing node p_j which has ready, but the result of parent task node of task v_i have not been transmitted over. We call this period as the waiting time for the task.

2.2 Correlation analysis

In this paper, the research of the algorithm focuses on that how to complete the task scheduling in the shortest time through a strategy. And to a certain extent, we can suppose that the unit energy consumption of the computing node is known, and cut down the execution time is helpful to reduce the energy consumption, so as to achieve the effect of energy-saving [6]. How to adjust the frequency of computing node in the resource layer to ensure that the tasks have been completed before deadlines will not be considered in this article.

At the same time, we need to make the following assumptions on the algorithm as below:

1. The real-time status between the computing nodes has known. Such as the energy consumption of computing nodes, the CPU performance, memory size, the bandwidth of network and the status of the computing nodes, and so on.
2. It is interconnected between each tow computing nodes, and the cost of communication is known.
3. Since the model map of the task nodes has been identified, so the dependent relationship between tasks has been clear.
4. Each task can be executed on different computing nodes, and there is no case can not be executed.

The algorithm is inspired by the table scheduling algorithm and task duplication algorithm in this paper. In the table scheduling algorithm, we should establish the priority of task-set first. And the priority is established by the sum of the maximum length of task node v_i to the end task node on the critical path and the maximum length of start task node to task node v_i on the critical path. In this way, the tasks node v_i on the critical path can be executed in advance. But on the whole, only the tasks on the critical path can be executed in this way, and the other tasks can not be. Due to there are lots of key factors that will affect the dependency of tasks, so we should consider more factors to adjust the algorithm to ensure the execution time of other tasks can be optimized.

In the table scheduling algorithm, the task queue formed according to the established priority, and then it will be distributed to the computing nodes. In process of choosing computing nodes, the nodes that can ensure the task v_i can be completed in the shortest time are needed. And thus, the cost of communication between the computing nodes or the cost of communication between tasks doesn't take into account. It would lead to the waiting time of task node v_i is too long while the results of the parent task nodes haven't been transmitted over under the circumstance that the task dependence degree is so strong, and it would delay the whole complete time of task-set further. After we were inspired by the thought of task duplication, we know that if the parent tasks are duplicated to the computing node which the task v_i will be executed, the costs of communication will be eliminated, then the task node v_i can be executed in advance [7]. In the HCPFD algorithm has proposed to cut down the cost of communication between tasks by duplicating the parent tasks that on the critical path, but it doesn't take the tasks on non-critical path into account on the whole. Based on the analysis above, we know, when we duplicate the parent tasks we should choose not only the tasks on the critical path but also the tasks on non-critical path to analysis, then pick the tasks by the priority that determined by a certain rule, only in this way can we cut down the execution time of the entire task-set on the whole [8]. Finally, the computing nodes that can guarantee the complete time of task node v_i shortest are the nodes we needed in the process we choose the optimized computing nodes.

3 Algorithm Analysis and design

Based on the analysis of previous chapters and sections, we know that there are two major research directions of the algorithm:

1. Make the tasks in descending order of priority. The first task has the highest priority in the task-set.
2. In the task distributing phase, before to distribute the tasks to the computing nodes, whether the task meets the conditions of task duplication or not should be taken into account first.

3.1 Task priority calculation

In the analysis of previous, we have mentioned that we should not just consider the tasks on the critical path while prioritizing the tasks, but all tasks shall be taken into account. As we know, there are dependences between tasks, a single task node possesses out-degree, in-degree, cost of task execution and cost of communication etc. In this article, our consideration will focus on the out-degree of task and the cost of communication between tasks, and prioritize the priority of task nodes based on this.

3.1.1 The out-degree of task node

We use $\mathrm{Out}(v_i)$ to represent the out-degree of tasks, and from the figure 1, we know that $\mathrm{Out}(v_1) = 4, \mathrm{Out}(v_2) = 2, \mathrm{Out}(v_8) = 0$, the out-degrees of other tasks are all 1. If the out-degree value of a task is larger, the impact to the subsequent task is greater. Because if the task is not done, the execution time of a larger number of subsequent tasks will be delayed. And if the task can be completed preferentially, the start time of the subsequent tasks will be brought forward, too.

3.1.2 The cost of communication between task nodes

In general, each tow dependence task nodes exist the cost of communication, unless the tow tasks are both on the same computing node and the cost of communication can be ignored. According to the definition of start time $\mathrm{start}(v_i, p_j)$ we can know that before task v_i be executed on computing node p_j, the results of parent tasks must be transmitted over to p_j, or else task v_i must wait. So the cost of communication on the out-degree of a task node should also be considered. But in order to reflect the integrity and the global view better, the algorithm proposed in this article take the costs of communication of all out-degrees of the task node into account. And we can get the equation as below:

$$SC(v_i) = \sum w_{ij} \quad (3)$$

w_{ij} is the cost of communication between the task node v_i and its sub task node v_j. We call the $SC(v_i)$ as the sum of cost of communication on out-degree of task node v_i. And the larger $SC(v_i)$ is, the greater impact to the start execution time of the subsequent tasks is. Conversely, the earlier the subsequent tasks will be executed.

Above all, this article gives the method of calculating the priority of each task as the equation below:

$$PL = (v_i) = q_i + max\{PL(v_j) + w_{ij}\},\ v_j \in sub(v_i) \quad (4)$$

We can find that from the equation above, the task nodes are traversed from bottom-up in the algorithm. If there is no subsequent task node following task v_i, the priority of v_i is the average cost of calculation. Or else, select a task node v_j from the subsequent task-set, which ensures the sum of the priority of v_j and the cost of communication between v_j and v_i is maximum. And due to the equation above just takes only one task node from the task-set into account unilaterally, but not all the subsequent nodes, so we can reform the equation based on the analysis above as below:

$$PL'(v_i) = Out(v_i) \times PL(v_i) + SC(v_i) \quad (5)$$

In this formula, the priority of each task node will be calculated by traversing in the way of bottom-up, and it can reflect the integrity of all tasks very well, what's more, all tasks will be taken into account but not just the tasks on the critical path in the process of priority calculating, and this idea is consistent with the original purpose of this paper [9].

3.2 Task Duplication

As we know, the cost of calculation of each task on the computing nodes is known, and if you want the tasks to be completed in the earliest time, tasks shall be executed as early as possible so that the total completion time of the task-set can be promoted.

And here the analysis of the factors that will affect the begin time of task execution is especially important. The begin time of task execution is determined by the time of the results of parent nodes transmitted over to the computing nodes and the time of computing node ready. So we give the factors that will affect the begin time of tasks as follows:

1. The computing node p_j which the task v_i will be executed on has ready.
2. The execution results of parent nodes of task v_i has transmitted over to the computing node p_j.

Both of factors above are necessary. If the results of parent have arrived but the computing node not yet ready, the task v_i can't be executed. If the computing node p_j has ready but the results of parent nodes haven't arrived, the task v_i can't be executed, and it must be wait. And we can give the equation as follows:

$$wait(v_i, p_j) = start(v_i, p_j) - ready(p_j) \quad (6)$$

So we can know that task waiting time is the difference between the start time of the task node and the ready time of the computing node. And take full advantage of the task waiting time $\mathrm{wait}(v_i, p_j)$ before the task v_i be executed will be an effective way to bring forward the complete time. Based on the elicitation of the task duplication, if the parent task nodes of task v_i are copied redundantly to the computing node p_j and the execution time of parent nodes are shorter than $\mathrm{wait}(v_i, p_j)$ can help to promote the overall completion time.

We can give the factors that will affect the parent task nodes duplication from the idea above as follows:

1. The parent task nodes execution time on the computing node p_j shouldn't longer than $wait(v_i, p_j)$.
2. The relationship of priority between task nodes can't be violated.

Furthermore, we can make some rules as below:

Rule1. If the execution time of task node v_i on the computing node p_j is $\mathrm{wait}(v_i, p_j)$, the execution time of parent task node of v_i on computing node p_j is $\mathrm{q}(v_j, p_j)$, while the equation below is true then the parent nodes of task v_i can be duplicated.

$$wait(v_i, p_j) \geq q(v_j, p_j) \& start(v_i, p_j) > finit(v_j, p_j),$$

$$v_j \in pre(v_i) \quad (7)$$

Maybe there are several parent task nodes that meet the equation above, so we should sort the parent tasks, and then select the parent task with longest of both completion time and transmission time to duplicate every time. And in order to describe the parent task node with longest time, we can make the definition to the optimal parent task node as follows:

Definition 5: the parent task node $mv\{v_i, p_j\}$ of task v_i should meet the following formula:

$$mv\{v_i, p_j\} = max\{finit(v_j, p_k) + w_{kj}\}, v_j \in pre(v_i) \quad (8)$$

For facilitating the following analysis, we stipulate the parent task that meets the rule of 1 and sorted in the second place in the task queue that based on the definition of 5 is the subordinate parent task, and record as $smv\{v_i, p_j\}$.

After that, we can get the following character and make a simple proof as below:

Character 1: when a task v_j exists on the computing node p_j, and if $mv\{v_i, p_j\}$ meets the rule of 1, then the $mv\{v_i, p_j\}$ can be copied to the computing node p_j, so as the start time $start(v_i, p_j)$ of task v_i can be brought forward.

And the proof steps are as follows:

1. It's unnecessary to consider duplication while task v_i have no parent task node.
2. The start time $start(v_i, p_j)$ can be brought forward as $finit(mv\{v_i, p_j\}, p_j)$ while there is only one parent task node of task v_i.
3. While task v_i has two or more parent nodes, and we shall discuss on two cases:

Case 1: The result of $finit(mv\{v_i, p_j\}, p_j) > smv\{v_i, p_k\}$ has arrived on the computing node p_j. In this case, $mv\{v_i, p_j\}$ has already on the computing node p_j, and the start time $start(v_i, p_j)$ of task v_i will be brought forward to $finit(mv\{v_i, p_j\}, p_j)$.

Case 2: The result of $finit(mv\{v_i, p_j\}, p_j) < smv\{v_i, p_k\}$ has arrived on the computing node p_j. In this case, the start time $start(v_i, p_j)$ of task v_i will be brought forward to $finit(smv\{v_i, p_j\}, p_j) + w_{kj}$.

In summary, the start execution time $start(v_i, p_j)$ of task v_i will always be brought forward in circumstances. And the proof end.

At this point, we can elaborate the strategy of task duplication as following:

1. Traverse through all task nodes and confirm the dependence relationship between task nodes.
2. For each task node v_i, find the parent task-set, and sort the parent task nodes in descending order according to the arrival time of execution results. And the first one is the optimal parent task node $mv\{v_i, p_j\}$.
3. Calculate the waiting time of task v_i. If the optimal parent task node meets the rule of 1, add the parent task into the waiting time of computing node which task v_i will be executed. Then delete this parent task node in the parent task-set. After that, the first one in the rest tasks becomes the optimal target.
4. Update the waiting time of the computing node.
5. Repeat the step 1to step 4.

If the rule of 1can be met, it's obviously that it would not bring forward the start time $start(v_i, p_j)$ of task v_i and even delay the time if parent tasks of v_i be duplicated redundantly to the computing node.

3.3 Algorithm

Based on the analysis above, the algorithm proposed in this article scheduling the dependent tasks in 3 steps. Firstly, traverse through all tasks and calculate the priority of each task, then sort the tasks in descending order. Secondly, calculate the execution time of task v_i on each computing node and confirm the waiting time of task v_i. Find all parent task nodes, and sort them. Copy the parent tasks that meet the rule of 1 to the waiting time and wait to be executed. Finally, calculate the complete time of the task and update the ready time of computing node [10].

A detailed description is as follows:

1. Calculate the out-degree of each task in the task-set, the cost of communication of out-degree, the average cost of calculation of tasks and the task priority PL.
2. Calculate each task priority $PL'(v_i)$ that in the task-set.
3. Sort the tasks in descending order according to the task priority, and form a task queue.
4. If the task set is not empty, do
5. Pick out the task with highest priority, find all the parent tasks of it.
6. Traverse through all the computing nodes.
7. For every computing node p_j, calculate the arrival time $finit(v_j, p_k) + w_{ki}$ of the results of the parent nodes of task v_j that will be executed on p_j. Sort the tasks according to the results and we can get the optimal parent task $mv\{v_i, p_j\}$.
8. Calculate the waiting time of tasks.
9. Judge whether the optimal parent task meets the rule of 1. If satisfied, copy it to the waiting time of task and update the waiting time, then repeat. Or else, turn to the step 10.
10. Calculate $finit(v_j, p_j)$.
11. End traverse of the computing node p_j.
12. Distribute the task to the corresponding computing node that can complete the task in shortest time.
13. Update the ready time of computing node.
14. Repeat step 5 to step 13 until the task queue is empty.

We assume that there are n tasks will be distributed to m computing nodes, then we can get the time complexity is $O(n)$ in phase of task sorting, and the time complexity is $O(mn^2)$ in phase of task duplicating and distributing. So we can get the time complexity of this algorithm is $O(mn^2)$.

DOI: 10.1051/itmconf/20160708001

Summary

We have analysed and modelled the dependent task nodes and the computing nodes in this paper, and taken the relationships between task-sets and the heterogeneous characteristics of computing nodes in resource layer in Cloud computing environment into account. Inspired by the table scheduling algorithm and the idea of task duplication, proposed a dependent task scheduling algorithm. And at last, we can find that it is possible to bring forward the execution time of the dependent tasks in the task-sets, so as to shorten the finish time to a certain extent.

Acknowledgement

This work is financially supported by Yunnan Provincial Department of Education Fund for Scientific Research of major special projects under Grant No. ZD2014001, and by the Open Foundation of Key Laboratory of Software Engineering of Yunnan Province under Grant No. 2015SE102, 2015SE204.

References

1. Jayaswal S, Agarwal P. Balancing U-shaped assembly lines with resource dependent task times: A Simulated Annealing approach[J]. Journal of Manufacturing Systems, 2014, 33(4): 522-534.
2. Munir E U, Mohsin S, Hussain A, et al. SDBATS: a novel algorithm for task scheduling in heterogeneous computing systems[C]//Parallel and Distributed Processing Symposium Workshops & PhD Forum (IPDPSW), 2013 IEEE 27th International. IEEE, 2013: 43-53.
3. Ye, Hong. "Research on Emergency Resource Scheduling in Smart City based on HPSO Algorithm." city 5 (2015): 6.
4. Mu R. Node Resource Optimization Algorithm Based on Wireless Network[J]. Journal of Software Engineering, 2015, 9(4): 702-720.
5. Wu Z, Liu X, Ni Z, et al. A market-oriented hierarchical scheduling strategy in cloud workflow systems[J]. The Journal of Supercomputing, 2013, 63(1): 256-293.
6. Xiong W, Wang Y, Mathiesen B V, et al. Heat roadmap China: New heat strategy to reduce energy consumption towards 2030[J]. Energy, 2015, 81: 274-285.
7. Arabnejad H, Barbosa J G. List scheduling algorithm for heterogeneous systems by an optimistic cost table[J]. Parallel and Distributed Systems, IEEE Transactions on, 2014, 25(3): 682-694.
8. Kaur R, Kaur R. Multiprocessor scheduling using task duplication based scheduling algorithms: A review paper[J]. International Journal of Application or Innovation in Engineering and Management, 2013, 2(4): 311-317.
9. Zhang S, Wang Y, Liu W, et al. A model for estimating the out-degree of nodes in associated semantic network from semantic feature view[J]. Concurrency and Computation: Practice and Experience, 2016.
10. Qian Z, Hong L, Jin S. A Scheduling Algorithm of Dependent Tasks on Virtual Computing Environment[C]//Computer Sciences and Applications (CSA), 2013 International Conference on. IEEE, 2013: 266-271.

Cotton Area and Yield Estimation at Zhanhua County of China Using HJ-1 EVI Time Series

Qing-Sheng LIU, Xin-Yang LI, Gao-Huan LIU, Chong HUANG and Yu-Shan GUO

Institute of Geographic Sciences and Natural Resources Research, Chinese Academy of Sciences, LREIS, 11A Datun Road, Chaoyang, Beijing, P.R. of China

Abstract. Cotton is a significant cash crop of China. Timely and accurate cotton area and yield estimation is useful for management decisions related to the cotton procurement and sales. This study is a first research on cotton area and yield estimation based on remote sensing at Zhanhua County which is one of the high-quality cotton production demonstration bases of China. After normalization of Enhanced Vegetation Index (EVI) time series derived from Huanjin 1 A/B satellite (HJ-1 A/B), decision tree classifier was used to identify the cotton, and then K-Means classifier was applied to estimate cotton yield. The results indicated an overall accuracy of 95% for the cotton area estimation and 91% for the cotton yield classification. With further validation, it suggests that this method can be used to timely achieve the cotton area and growth information of this region.

1 Introduction

Cotton is a significant cash crop of China which is mainly planted in Xinjiang, Henan, Shandong, Hebei Province and so on [1]. Timely and accurate cotton area and yield estimation is useful for management decisions related to the cotton procurement, sales, import and export program of a country [2, 3]. Remote sensing imagery can offer a repeated unbiased view of large areas, and has thus been widely used to estimate crop yields. Lots of studies have shown that cotton area and yield can be efficiently estimated by remote sensing [2-13]. National Oceanic and Atmospheric Administration (NOAA) Advanced Very High Resolution Radiometer (AVHRR) and Moderate Resolution Imaging Spectroradiometer (MODIS) data with the higher temporal resolution are usually used to assess early cotton production information and predict the cotton yields at national and regional levels [6, 7]. Landsat Thematic Mapper (Landsat TM), Indian Remote Sensing (IRS), China-Brazil Earth Resource Satellite (CBERS) and Huanjin (HJ-1 A/B) satellite with the higher spatial resolution are often used to estimate cotton yields at regional and field levels [2, 3, 8, 11-13]. Site-specific lint yields were estimated using field soil and multispectral images data [4, 5, 9, 10].

In both cotton area and yield estimation, the use of remote sensing multispectral data from the visible and near infrared range of the electromagnetic spectrum generally involves the use of the vegetation indices. By far, the most commonly used vegetation indices include the Normalized Difference Vegetation Index (NDVI) and the Enhanced Vegetation Index (EVI). The NDVI is chlorophyll sensitive, and the EVI is more responsive to canopy type, plant physiognomy and canopy architecture. Compared with NDVI, EVI was found to be more linearly correlated with green leaf area index in crop filed, less prone to saturation in the regions with the high vegetation fraction, and minimally sensitive to residual aerosol contamination from extensive fires [12, 14].

HJ-1 A/B satellites were launched at Taiyuan city of China on September 6, 2008. HJ-1 A/B were equipped with wide-coverage CCD scanner with the same design principle and observed in parallel to complete scanning and imaging for earth with swath width of 700 km, ground pixel resolution of 30 m with 4 spectrum bands and the revisit period of 2 days after two CCD cameras networking [15]. These high spatial and temporal resolution characteristics of HJ-1 A/B are very useful for crop acreage estimation and yield prediction, so it has been used to estimate winter wheat, rice, sugarcane and cotton area and yields in China [8, 16-19].

However, in China, most of the studies on cotton area and yield estimation were carried out in Xinjiang Province and site-specific applications. Zhanhua County of Shandong Province is one of the high-quality cotton production demonstration bases of China which recently was confirmed as one demonstration base for Cotton Integrated Pest Management by the United Nations and one important production base by Better Cotton Initiative [20, 21]. The aim of this research is to extract the spatially distributed cotton fields and estimate the cotton yields at Zhanhua County using HJ-1 A/B EVI time series.

DOI: 10.1051/itmconf/20160709001

2 Materials and Methods

2.1 Study Area

Zhanhua County (Fig. 1) lies in the north of Binzhou City of Shandong Province of China from 117° 43′ 45″ to 118° 21′ 52″ East longitude and 37° 33′ 28″ to 38° 9′ 59″ North latitude and covers a total geographical area of 221,500 ha. The district has the semi-arid East Asia monsoon climate in warm-temperate zone with four distinct seasons. The mean annual temperature is 12.5° C and the average annual precipitation is 543 mm. The main soil type in the region is calcaric fluvisols. Agriculture plays an important role in the economy of the Zhanhua County. Zhanhua County is well known for winter Jujube in China, which covered about 3,300 ha. The most import crop of Zhanhua County is cotton, which covered about 140,000 ha in 2012, while winter wheat, corn and other crops have a markedly smaller area share. In general, the cotton growing season in Zhanhua County extends from mid-April to the end of October.

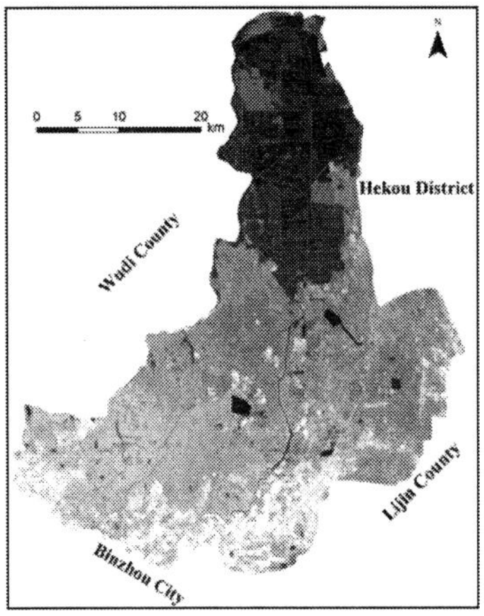

Figure 1. Zhanhua County-5 May, 2014 EVI image of HJ 1B.

2.2 Data

2.1.1 Ground Survey Data

In this study, for acreage estimation, ground data were collected at the 36 sampling sites in May, 2014, and for yield estimation, the data were collected from questionnaires on 19 farming households in November, 2014 (Fig. 2) and the cotton acreage and yield statistical data were collected on the county level.

2.1.2 HJ-1 A/B Data

In order to classify and identify the cotton acreage, imagery data comprised 24 acquisition dates from 21 March 2014 to 13 November 2014 which was provided in Table 1 below.

The raw digital numbers (DNs) of singe date satellite data were converted to at-satellite reflectance using the parameters from the header file of each image which was described by Satellite Environment Center, Ministry of Environmental Protection22 and the default values for HJ-1 A/B CCD which was described by China Centre for Resources Satellite Data and Application 23. Then, a relative radiometric normalization method using spectrally pseudo-invariant features (PIFs) was used to reduce atmospheric and other unexpected variations in the date of data acquired24. EVI was derived to generate a profile curve of the crop (Fig. 3) using the formula:

$$\text{EVI} = G \times \frac{(\rho_{nir} - \rho_{red})}{(\rho_{nir} + C_1\rho_{red} - C_2\rho_{blue} + L)} \quad (1)$$

where ρ_{nir}, ρ_{red} and ρ_{blue} are relative radiometric normalization at-satellite reflectance in near-infrared, red and blue bands respectively; G=2.5 is a gain factor, C1=6, C2=7.5 are the coefficients of the aerosol resistance term and L=1 is the soil adjustment factor.

- Table 1. Dates of Hj-1 A/B Used For Cotton Area And Yield Estimation

Satellite Sensor	Path/Row	Date
HJ-1 A CCD2	454/68	21 March 2014
HJ-1 B CCD2	455/68	23 March 2014
HJ-1 B CCD1	453/71	4 April 2014
HJ-1 A CCD1	453/68	6 April 2014
HJ-1 B CCD1	454/68	8 April 2014
HJ-1 A CCD1	455/68	14 April 2014
HJ-1B CCD2	455/68	23 April 2014
HJ-1A CCD2	455/68	29 April 2014
HJ-1B CCD2	456/68	1 May 2014
HJ-1A CCD2	456/68	3 May 2014
HJ-1B CCD2	457/68	5 May 2014
HJ-1B CCD2	454/71	28 May 2014
HJ-1B CCD2	455/70	5 June 2014
HJ-1B CCD2	455/68	14 July 2014
HJ-1A CCD2	456/68	20 July 2014
HJ-1B CCD2	457/68	26 July 2014
HJ-1A CCD2	453/68	20 Aug. 2014
HJ-1B CCD1	1/68	4 Sept. 2014
HJ-1A CCD1	455/68	3 Oct. 2014
HJ-1A CCD1	456/70	7 Oct. 2014
HJ-1A CCD1	457/70	15 Oct. 2014
HJ-1B CCD2	454/68	28 Oct. 2014
HJ-1B CCD2	455/68	9 Nov. 2014
HJ-1B CCD2	456/68	13 Nov. 2014

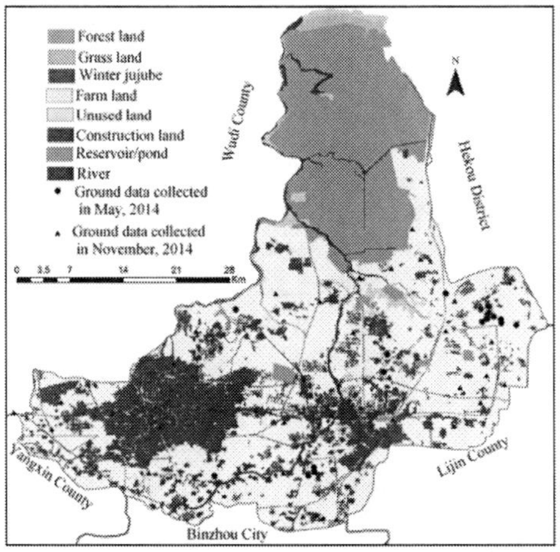

Figure 2. Land use map in 2010 and the location of ground survey data in 2014.

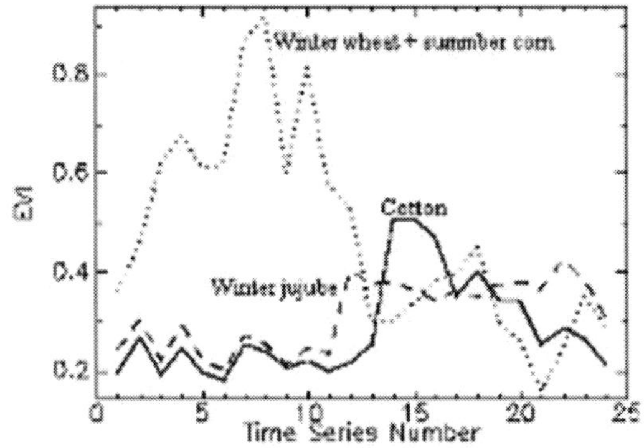

Figure 3. HJ-1 A/B EVI time series curve of winter wheat, winter jujube and cotton in 2014.

2.1.3 Acreage Classification

The area under cotton at Zhanhua County for the year 2014 was estimated using 24 EVI time series data which almost cover the cotton and other crops/vegetations development stage. County boundary overlaying and decision tree classifier was used for cotton crop identification and acreage estimation. For acreage estimation, the ground survey sites for cotton, winter wheat, winter jujube and other crops/vegetation were overlaid on the RBG false color image (R, G and B stand for EVI image acquired on 29 April, 14 July and 29 October 2014 respectively). Then, decision tree was created to extract cotton crop using machine learning techniques with a training subset (Fig. 4). The decision tree classifier performs multistage classifications by using a series of binary decisions to place pixels into classes. Each decision divides the pixels in a set of images into two classes based on an expression. You can divide each new class into two more classes based on another expression. In the initial decision tree, background, non-vegetation, winter wheat, winter jujube, cotton and other crops/vegetations were able to be separated using more than one band. The band or band combinations used to separate these classes were determined while performing the classification by visually checking their classification performance on the sites which the training samples were taken. Therefore, the final decision tree was determined while classifying the images. For example, winter wheat was observed to be easily separable using the maximum EVI > 0.5 of the images acquired from 6 April to 5 May and the EVI <0.35 of the images acquired on 5 June and 14 July. Winter Jujube was easily separable using the maximum of EVI of all images less than 0.5 and EVI >0.35 of the 28 May image. Cotton can be identified using the maximum EVI < 0.4 of the images acquired from 6 April to 5 May, EVI <0.35 of the 28 May image and EVI >0.35 of the 14 July image. After the decision tree classification, farm land mask derived from an existing land use map in 2010 was used to reduce some classification errors resulted from spectral similarity between cotton and natural vegetations. The total classification accuracy was calculated by confusion matrix and amounted to 90% with an accuracy of 95% regarding the classification of cotton compared to the county statistical data on cotton planting acreage.

2.1.4 Yield Estimation

The spectral profile is the temporal variation of spectral vegetation index of the cotton during the growth period. The area under a profile is related to the total photosynthesis over that period. Thus, it is related to above ground biomass and cotton yield. Through analysis on the profile curves of the different cotton fields (Fig. 5), it proved that there is a strong relationship between the profile and yield. K-Means unsupervised classifier was used to classify the cotton fields into low, medium and high yield lands (Fig. 6). K-Means unsupervised classification calculates initial class means evenly distributed in the data space then iteratively clusters the pixels into the nearest class using a minimum distance technique. Each iteration recalculates class means and reclassifies pixels with respect to the new means. All pixels are classified to the nearest class unless a standard deviation or distance threshold is specified, in which case some pixels may be unclassified if they do not meet the selected criteria. This process continues until the number of pixels in each class changes by less than the selected pixel change threshold or the maximum number of iterations is reached. The total classification accuracy was evaluated by the data collected from questionnaires on 19 farming households and the county statistical data, and amounted to 91%.

3 Results and Discussions

3.1 HJ-1 A/B EVI Time Series Images

Table 1shows the images data used in this research were from two satellites (HJ-1 A and HJ-1 B) with four CCD cameras (HJ-1 A CCD1, CCD2 and HJ-1 B CCD1 and CCD2). Therefore, it is easy to acquire the images of crop growing season and hence improve the cotton acreage and yield estimation accuracy. But it brings about some problems. Although a relative radiometric normalization was done, EVI time series data from the different sensors could be influenced and then cause cotton acreage and yield estimation errors. In addition, HJ-1 A/B equipped with wide-coverage CCD scanner could bring about the geometric distortion which is difficult to be corrected, it could cause the registration errors between the images and hence increasing the cotton acreage and yield estimation errors.

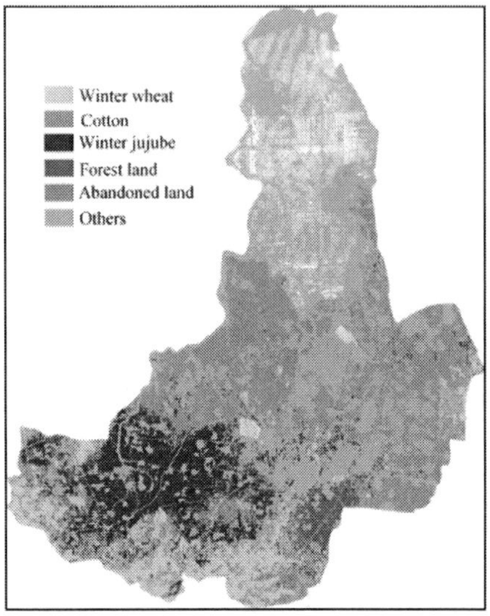

Figure 4. Cotton areas in Zhanhua County in 2014.

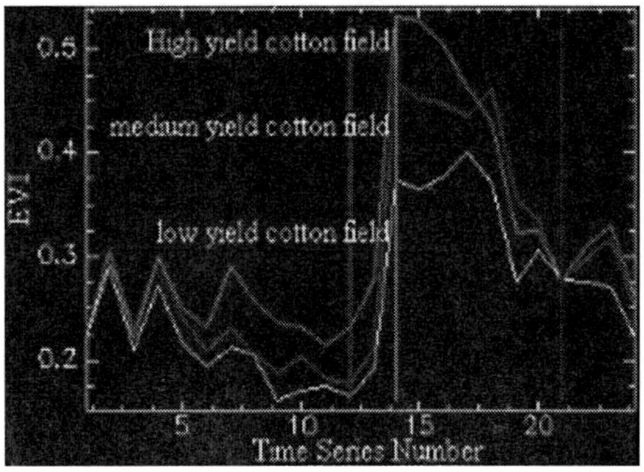

Figure 5. The profile curves of EVI time series of low, medium and high yield cotton fields.

3.2 Cotton Classification

An area 38,393.1 ha of cotton was estimated at Zhanhua County in 2014. Compared with 140,000 ha in 2012, cotton acreage has declined by 72.6 percent. Through analysis on the relative materials, it could be found that this was due to low income from cotton planting. It also indicated that cotton acreage estimation of this paper was reliable. Figure 4 shows the cotton area distribution at Zhanhua County in 2014. Some cotton fields were found around the winter jujube land. The majority of cotton fields were found in the more salinized northern and northeastern areas near the Bohai Sea.

Because the growing season of cotton often overlays those of spring corn, watermelon, sorghum and other crops/natural vegetations such as reed and endive, it led to cotton classification errors. Through an existing farmland map mask, this type of cotton classification errors could be partly reduced. Of course, the more cotton classification accuracy needs the more spatial and temporal resolution remote sensing data and field survey data.

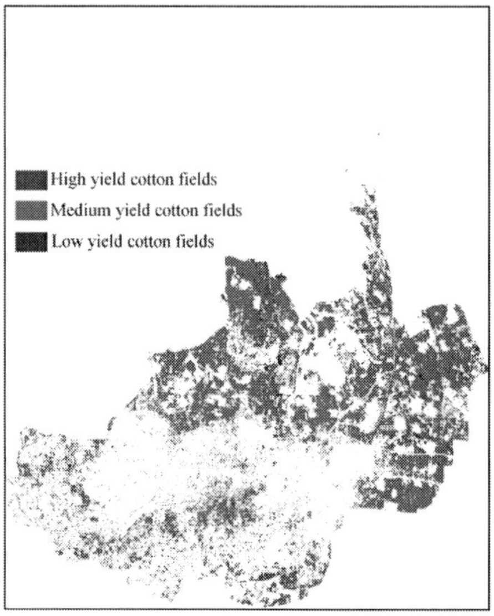

Figure 6. Low, medium and high yield cotton fields in Zhanhua County in 2014.

3.3 Spatial Cotton Yield Estimation

The results from the present research indicated that on the basis of the cotton acreage map, K-Means unsupervised classifier could be used to classify the cotton fields into low, medium and high yield lands using HJ-1 A/B EVI time series data. The high yield cotton fields covered about 8.5% of the total cotton area and sparsely distributed in the southern and southwestern areas, and the low yield cotton fields covered about 7.5% of the total cotton area and sparsely distributed in the northern and northeastern areas, and the medium yield cotton fields covered about 84.0% of the total cotton area.

Because the cotton yield data collected from questionnaires on 19 farming households were rough and the cotton yield statistical data were at county level, the quantitative yield estimation of raw cotton could not be done. In the future, the quantitative yield data of cotton field will be collected including more field-based spatially distributed information such as cotton types, agricultural practices that influence yields.

4 Conclusions

In this paper, HJ-1 A/B EVI time series data was applied to estimate cotton area and yield estimation based on at Zhanhua County. The results showed that decision tree classifier could be used to identify the cotton acreage and

K-Means unsupervised classifier could be used to classify the cotton fields into low, medium and high yield lands using HJ-1 A/B EVI time series data, and there is a strong relationship between the profile and yield of cotton. Thus, with further validation, it suggests that this method can be used to timely achieve the cotton area and yield information at county scale.

Acknowledgment

This research work was jointly financially supported by the National Science-Technology Support Plan Projects (Project No.2013BAD05B03), the Strategic Priority Research Program of CAS (Project No.XDA05050601), International Cooperation in Science and Technology Special Project (Project No.2012DFG22050, 2013DFA91700) and National Natural Science Foundation of China (Project No.41271407, 41023010).

References

1. X. B. Pan, Y. Y. Liu, *Proc. of the 2005 annual conference of the Chinese Meteorological Society,* 3424-3432 (2005). (In Chinese)
2. S. S. Ray, S. S. Pokharna, Ajai, International Journal of Remote Sensing, 15, 1085-1090 (1994).
3. S. S. Ray, S. S. Pokharna, Ajai, International Journal of Remote Sensing, 20, 2693-2702 (1999).
4. C. Richard, Photogrammetric Engineering & Remote Sensing, 66, 1219-1227 (2000).
5. K. R. Reddy, D. L. Zhao, V. G. Kakani, J. J. Read, K. Sailaja, *Proc. SPIE 5153*, doi:10.1117/12.515226 (2004).
6. C. Domenikiotis, M. Spiliotopoulos, E. Tsiros, N. R. Dalezios, International Journal of Remote Sensing, 25, 5373-5388 (2004)
7. B. Little, M. Schucking, B. Gartrell, B. Chen, K. Ross, R. Mckellip, *Proc. of IEEE International Conference on Data Mining Workshops*, 426-435 (2008)
8. M. Li, G. X. Zhao, Y. W. Qin, *Proc. of IEEE International Conference on Computer Distributed Control and Intelligent Environmental Monitoring,* 816-823 (2011)
9. J. Iqbal, J. J. Read, F. D. Whisler, Turkish Journal of Field Crops, 18, 158-165 (2013)
10. D. L. Zhao, K. R. Reddy, V. G. Kakani, J.J. Read, S. Koti, Europ. J. Agronomy, 26, 335-344 (2007)
11. G. R. Ruecker, Z. Shi, M. Mueller, C. Conrad, N. Ibragimov, J. P. A. Lamers, C. Martius, G. Strunz, S. W. Dech, *Proc. of ISPRS XXXVI-8/W48 workshop,* 123-128 (2006)
12. F. Ahmad, K. Shafique, S. R. Ahmad, S. U. Rehman, R. M. Ali Khan, A. Raoof, Global Journal of Human Social Science (B), 13, 21-42 (2013)
13. H. J. Liu, L. H. Meng, X. L. Zhang, U. Susan, D. H. Ning, S. Y. Sun, Transactions of the Chinese Society of Agricultural Engineering, 31, 215-220 (2015)
14. Z. Y. Jiang, A. R. Huete, K. Didan, T. Miura, Remote Sensing of Environment, 112, 3833-3845 (2008)
15. CBERS, http://cresda.com/EN/satellite/7117.shtml (3 November 2015)
16. J. S. Zhang, K. J. Shen, Y. Z. Pan, L. L. Li, D. Hou, Scientia Agricultura Sinica, 43, 3306-3315 (2010). (In Chinese with English Abstract)
17. X. C. Wei, X.S. Wang, H. Liu, J. Xu, Journal of Geo-Information Science, 14, 382-388 (2012). (In Chinese with English Abstract)
18. M. H. Ding, H. Li, Y. H. Yang, H. Q. Zhang, J.F. Mo, L. He, W. H. Mo, J. H. Wang, Chinese Journal of Agrometeorology, 33, 265-270 (2012). (In Chinese with English Abstract)
19. Q. Wang, K. R. Wang, S. K. Li, C. H. Xiao, J. G. Dai, L. F. Fang, Cotton Science, 24, 503-510 (2012). (In Chinese with English Abstract)
20. Z. Q. Lu, Q. C. Guo, http://binzhou.dzwww.com/bzhxw/201410/t20141010_11149988.htm (10 October 2014). (In Chinese)
21. X. Li, http://www.bzcm.net/news/2015-06/03/content_1772332.htm (3 June 2015). (In Chinese)
22. Satellite Environment Center, Ministry of Environmental Protection of China, http://www.secmep.cn/secPortal/portal/column/itemDetails.faces?itemid=297e855148f8b9360148f8ed0f4d0008 (10 October 2014). (In Chinese)
23. CBERS, http://www.cresda.com/n16/n1115/n1522/n2134/9677.html (29 December 2009). (In Chinese)
24. Y. L. Du, P. M. Teillet, J. Cihlar, Remote Sensing of Environment, 82, 123-134 (2002)

ITM Web of Conferences 7, 09002 (2016) DOI: 10.1051/itmconf/20160709002
ITA 2016

Research on the Optimization in the Continuous-fire Strategy of the HPM-Bomb

Hui WENG[1,a], Xu-Chang ZHOU[2] and Chao MAO[1,b]

[1]*Dept. of Management Eng., Naval Univ. of Engineering, Wuhan, China*
[2]*Dept. of Weaponry Eng., Naval Univ. of Engineering, Wuhan, China*
[a]*26458711@qq.com,* [b]*hjklyuiop@126.com*

Abstract—The electronic damage feasibility and the operational characteristics of the high power electromagnetic pulse bomb shot by shipboard gun are analyzed. As the destruction of the electronic components caused by the high power electromagnetic pulse is hard to evaluate, the spatial distribution of the anti-ship missiles is analyzed, and the strategic model for the continuous fire is built. Aimed at the maximum damage effectiveness, the crux of the lasted shift shooting tactics is a TSP problem. The genetic algorithm is applied in the TSP problem. Simulation experiments demonstrate that the model and the algorithm are effective.

1 Introduction

For the development of the microelectronics technology, the large scale integrated circuit and the computer control technology, these technologies have been widely applied in the weapon system. The high technology weapons such as the flights, missiles and etc. have made great progress in the smart, intelligent, etc. However, with a growing reliance of the survival and combat capability on precision electronic equipment, they are more likely damaged and interfered with by the electromagnetic power. The theoretical and experimental studies have shown that the more sophisticated and more complex electronic system, it is more easily interfered with and damaged by the high power microwave (HPM) [1]. So, the HPM weapons have become the focus of the development of the weapons system in the military powers [2].

HPM-Bomb uses the electromagnetic vulnerability of the military equipment to attack electronic targets. The HPM pulse radiation gets through the antennas and apertures into the interior of the target electronic system. The breakdown of electronic components could cause the electronic system not to work indefinitely and then reduce the operational efficiency of the target.

2.Features of the Operation

2.1 Feasibility Analysis

Conventional HPM warhead is mainly composed by the primary power (electric energy or chemical energy), the excitation power supply, the explosive magnetic flux compression generator, the pulse power modulation system, the high power microwave source, the antenna system and etc.

The HPM-Bomb is composed by three major components which were shown as the structure diagram.

2.1.1 Microwave Tube and Antenna

Microwave tube is the microwave source which generates the electromagnetic radiation. For the dimensional restraint, the microwave tube which is used at the HPM-Bomb is the virtual cathode oscillator (VCO). The electromagnetic pulse (EMP) power generated by the VCO is over 1GW. The microwave generated by microwave tube is transmitted by the antenna. For strengthen the radiation direction, the antenna of HPM-Bomb is the spiral antenna.

2.1.2 Magnetic Flux Compression Generator (MFCG)

This is composed by primary energy (battery and capacitor), magnetic field of a current-carrying solenoid (stator), explosives and the metal casing for explosive charge (armature).

2.1.3 *Pulse-forming Network*

There are three main functions of the pulse-forming network. Firstly, it is a impedance-matching element, which transforms the low impedance into high-impedance. Secondly, it is a voltage changer, which transforms the low voltage of the MFCG output into a high voltage output, and loads on microwave source. Thirdly, it is a waveform rectifier, which transforms the slow rise pulse leading edge into a fast rising leading edge of the pulse output.

As the development of the explosive MFCG, the energy density of the explosive MFCG could arrive at 30J/cm3~60J/cm3, the energy conversion efficiency of the explosives energy to the load energy is close to 4.8%[4]。And as the development of the virtual cathode oscillator which is smaller volume among the high power microwave sources, the electromagnetic conversion efficiency increases from 1%~3% to above 12% [5]. As the motion of the electron of the coaxial virtual cathode oscillator is radial, the radial dimension should be reduced effectively. For the strong constraint of the radial of the gun firing HPM-Bomb, the coaxial geometry of the virtual cathode oscillator should help improve the efficiency of system integration. These developments of the HPM technologies should help HPM-Bomb to meet the electromagnetic operational requirements.

2.2 Operation Characteristics

HPM-Bomb emits the high power electromagnetic pulse, and it enters the weapon system through the front-door (such as the antenna, connector, and etc of the target) or the back-door (as the apertures, connect cables, ports). The high power electromagnetic pulse produces induced currents and voltage at the metal surface or metallic wire. The induced current and voltage cause the heating of the semiconductor medium and lead to the abnormal state or decrease the device performance. The normal function of target system is destroyed and the objective of electromagnetic operation is achieved.

The electronic attack by the HPM-Bomb has the following characteristics:

(1)For the mostly military equipment is not completely shielding, the electromagnetic pulse should enter the target system through the front-door or back-door.

(2)The coverage is so large that could cover several targets, so the location and tracking accuracy is reduced.

(3)Compared with the other directed energy weapons (such as laser weapons, particle beam weapons), the HPM weapon has the advantage of easy to spread, and independent of weather (such as fog, rain and etc.).

(4)Compared with the HPM radar weapons, the demand of the destroyed maximum peak power is lower for the approaching radiation, and the HPM-Bomb is far away from the friendly platform of avoiding electromagnetic accidentally injury to maximum extent possible.

(5)Compared the normal electromagnetic countermeasure (ECM), the high power electromagnetic pulse could cause the physical damage.

(6)The ultra-wide-band high power microwave should cover the working frequency band of the modern military radio equipment, such as radar, communication, navigation and etc., it has broadband electronic warfare features.

But the electromagnetic weapon damage effect evaluation especially real-time evaluation is hardly. Signal interruption cannot completely represent that the attack is effective. The target which is attacked effectively seems to work properly. Such as the receiver or data processor of the anti-ship missile is destroyed by the HPM attack, the radar seeker still emits electromagnetic waves. So, when HPM-Bomb shoots at several targets, there is no need to continue shooting at one target.

3 Strategy Model of Continuing Shooting

3.1 Saptial Distribution Model of the Missile Saturation Attack

For the saturation attack by anti-ship missile, the azimuth angle and pitching angle space distribution characteristics of single shipboard gun within the effective firing range are mainly discussed to provide the basis for the establishment of the continuing shifting firepower strategy.

3.1.1 *ltitude angle (ε) Distribution of anti-ship Missile*

The distance between the anti-ship missile and target and the flying height is the main influencing factors of the altitude angle (ε) distribution of anti-ship missile. For the shipboard gun range constraint, the space distribution of anti-ship missile is bound to the vertical plane at the maximum shipboard gun range constraint. Based on the analysis of all kinds of anti-ship missile route characteristic, at the maximum effective shooting range of the large and medium caliber naval gun (maximum effective shooting range of AK-130 shipboard gun is 18km); the anti-ship missiles are cruising at a constant altitude. To achieve coordinated attack, the anti-ship missile trajectories are high-low collocations. Assumed that the height of the cruise missile flying at high-altitude is 400m and the height of the cruise missile flying at low-altitude is 10m. In order to make full use of the height space, assumed that the cruise height distribution is Gaussian distribution. With the firing table, the cruise height distribution is available.

3.1.2 Azimuth Angle(β) Distribution of the Anti-ship Missile

For strengthen the attacking effectiveness of the anti-ship missile, especially penetrating the multi-level defense surface warship formation, saturation attack is frequently used in anti-ship missile penetrating. At the same time or within a certain time range, the penetrating anti-ship missiles exceed the available fire channels of the anti-missiles; this is called as anti-ship missile saturation attack. When the saturation attack is applied, to increase the penetrating possibility of anti-ship missile, multi-direction attack is usually chosen. The multi-direction attack should force greater dispersion of the shipboard defense system firepower. When the saturation anti-ship missiles attack from two or more directions, the chosen attack directions have a direct impact on penetrating possibility. For increasing the penetrating possibility, on the precondition to satisfy route planning principle, the different directions should be chosen by anti-ship missile attacking.

Obviously, the different direction chosen strategies should lead to different attack effectiveness. According to the direction chosen strategy proposed by the reference [6], when the saturation attack is being forced by several anti-ship missiles, the directions should be 90° attack angle pairings. For one side of the surface ship, it is just generate the azimuth angle distribution between 0~90° of signal side. As the analysis of altitude angle distribution, the azimuth distribution is even-distributed. When the number of the attack directions is odd number, the attack angle which is closest to 90° relative bearing is not need to pair.

The above analysis is based on the direction chosen strategy of the anti-ship missile route planning, and it is suitable for the normal anti-ship missile saturation attack situation.

3.2 Strategy Model of the Continuing Shifting Firepower

The following assumptions are made for the progress of the continuing shifting firepower.

(1)When the shipboard gun weapon shifts firepower, the aiming rotation speeds are constant, and equal to the maximum aiming speed.

(2)The damage probability of HPM-Bomb is static; the shifting firepower influence on the damage probability is neglected.

(3)The shifting firepower time from the fire control system of firing data to the gun pointing to the target is neglected, its influence is not considered too.

(4)The targets risk ranking is neglected, the target space distribution is considered only.

The shifting firepower distance is the larger between the abs of azimuth angles and the abs of altitude angles. Then the distance of shifting firepower between the (T_i, T_j) could be expressed as:

$$\theta_{i,j} = \max\left(\left|\varepsilon_i - \varepsilon_j\right|, \left|\beta_i - \beta_j\right|\right) \qquad (1)$$

Based on the above analysis, the continuing shifting firepower strategy could be described as below.

The coordinates of n targets and the shifting firepower distance between them is given. The optimal objective is the shortest path which is a closed path and travels every target only once.

3.3 Basic Simulation Process

The basic simulation process is shown as follows.

(1)Input the anti-ship missile number.

(2)According the space distribution of the incident anti-ship missile, the coordinates of the targets which meet the distribution characteristics are generated in the spherical coordinate system.

(3)Confirm the GA control parameters [7], and computing the optimal shifting firepower path with the GA.

(4)Determine the optimal shooting strategy.

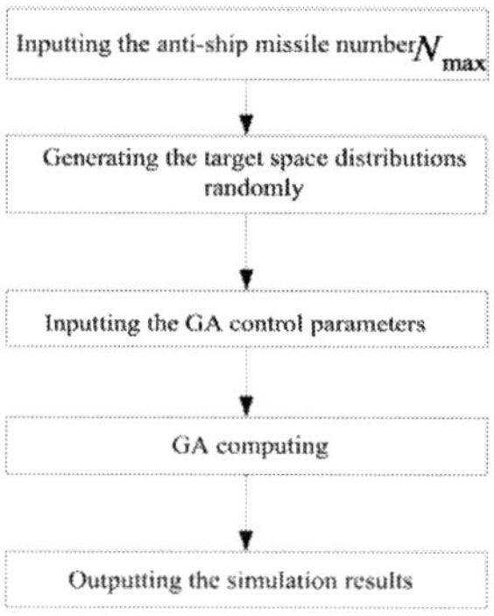

Figure 1. Simulation Flow Chart

The Genetic Algorithm control parameters are: using the tournament selection method, population size is 3, intensity of selection is 0.85, loss in the diversity is 0.385, and operation times of genetic algorithm are 500.

4 Simulation and Analysis

4.1 Initial Simulation Conditions Setting

Based on the spatial distribution model of the target, the target space position is generated randomly. The spatial position of 20 randomly selected targets is shown in the tab.1.

DOI: 10.1051/itmconf/20160709002

TABLE I. Spatial distribution of the target coordinates.

No.	ε (°)	β (°)	No.	ε (°)	β (°)
1	26.674	43.637	11	32.846	133.64
2	15.969	51.135	12	37.987	141.13
3	18.97	73.848	13	16.894	163.85
4	38.703	43.332	14	31.12	133.33
5	32.512	6.6634	15	24.712	96.663
6	17.659	37.317	16	29.171	127.32
7	22.892	62.232	17	31.13	152.23
8	20.795	53.43	18	38.352	143.43
9	33.679	82.451	19	29.45	172.45
10	39.351	14.106	20	19.307	104.11

4.2 Simulation Results and Analysis

The spatial angle distribution of the target can be obtained from the Tab.1 is shown as Fig.3. The strategy model of continuing shifting firepower is calculated by GA and the optimal shifting path is shown as Fig.4.

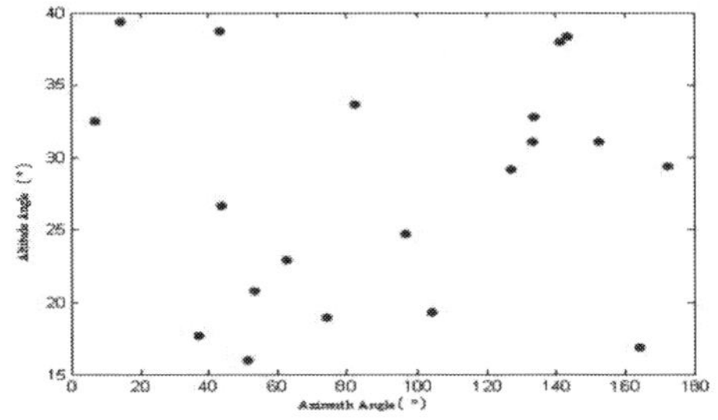

Figure 2. Target coordinates

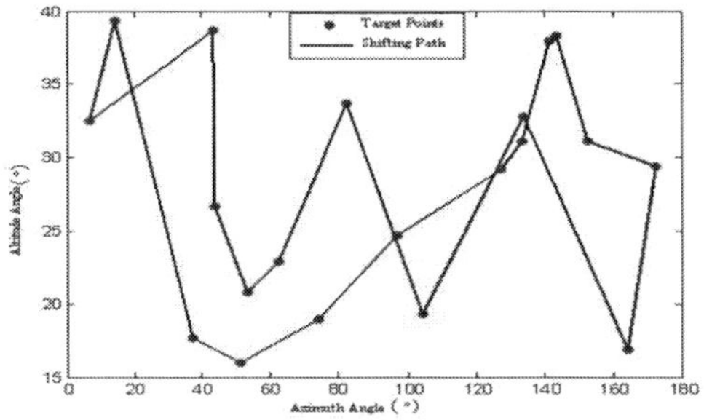

Figure 3. Optimal shifting firepower path

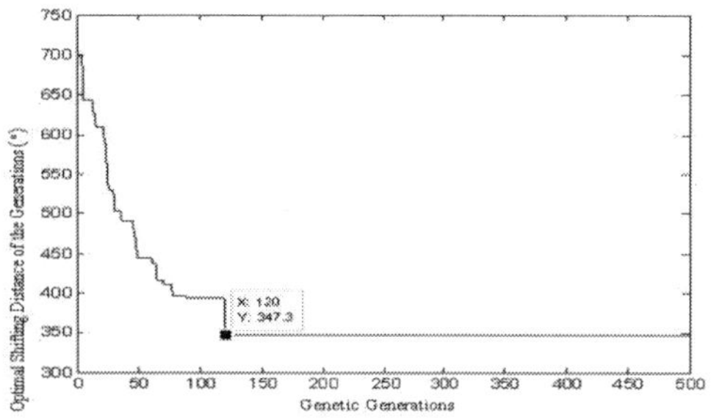

Figure 4. Optimal shifting distance

As Fig. 5 showed, the rotary angle of the unordered shifting firepower is about 700°. For the GA optimization, the GA convergence generations are 120, the rotary angle is 347.3°. Neglected the fire time influence and assume that the rotational speed of the shipboard gun 30°/s, the time of shifting firepower is reduced from 23.3s to 11.6s. From the simulation results, GA is feasible for the continuing shifting firepower model.

5 Conclusions

The large scale integrated circuit and the computer control technology are widely used in the modern military equipment. The electromagnetic vulnerability is exposed in combat with high power electromagnetic pulse. From the operational characteristic analysis of HPM-Bomb, the real-time damage evaluation of electromagnetic attack is very hardly. The continuing shifting firepower strategy is proposed in this paper. The continuing shifting firepower path is optimized by GA. The simulation result demonstrates that the GA is suitable for resolving the continuing shifting firepower path problem, and the shifting firing time is effectively reduced.

References

1. Clay W.High altitude electromagnetic pulse (HEMP) and high power microwave (HPM) devices: threat assessments[R].Washington, DC: Library of Congress,2006.
2. Xiao Jin-shi, Liu Wen-hua, Zhang Shi-ying, et al. Analysis and Simulation on Killing Ability of Cascaded Flux Compression Electromagnetic Pulse Bomb.Journal of Ballistics, 2009, 21(1):91-94.
3. Kopp C. The Electromagnetic Bomb – a Weapon of Electrical Mass Destruction. ADA332511. December 1997.
4. L. L. Altgilbers, M. D. J. Brown, I. Grishnaev, et al. Magnetocumulative Generators. New York: Springer-Verlag, 2000.

DOI: 10.1051/itmconf/20160709002

5. Liu Jing, Shu Ting, Li ZhiQiang. A novel configuration of vircator with coaxial waveguide. Acta Physica Sinica, 2010, 59(4): 2629-2633.
6. Zhou Lijun, Wang Changjin, Wang Jingheng.Analysis on selection tactic of attacking direction of anti-ship missile.Command Control&Simulation, 2008, 30(4): 44-47.
7. Wang Xiaoping,Cao Liming.Genetic algorithms-theory, application and software implementation.Xi'an: Xi'an Jiaotong University Press,2002.

ITM Web of Conferences 7, 09003 (2016) DOI: 10.1051/itmconf/20160709003
ITA 2016

Analysis and Forecast of Grain Supply and Demand in China's thirteen-five Period

Wei-Ya SHI, Tie-jun YANG and Yi-Tao LIANG

College of Information Science and Engineering, Henan University of Technology, Zhengzhou 450001, China

Abstract. In recent years, the demand and supply of grain has dramatically changed. The paper uses the intelligent information processing method to analyse grain supply and demand of China. The gray model and Back Propagation neural network are used to forecast the trend of grain supply and demand in the thirteen-five period. The result shows that both grain supply and demand will increase in long trend, but grain demand has more than grain supply. The forecasting grain supply growth ratio will be separately 0.88% and 0.79%, the grain demand will be increased 32.2% and 19.5% in 2020 using the grey model and BP, compared with the supply and demand in 2014. At last, the suggestions are given. In order to guarantee the grain safety, scientific method should be used to monitor and analysis the grain market.

1 Introduction

The grain is the main portion of people daily lives. The food security is the foundation for national stability. It is especially important for china who has about 1.4 billion population, but only has seven percent of world arable land.

The demand and supply of grain has dramatically changed at different times. Many scholars at home and abroad had done many qualitative and quantitative researches. Wang [1] had proposed to give responsible forecast in advance of food production by analyzing grain yields from 1978 to 2004 in China. Xie [2] had found that grain yield is closely related to the cultivating acreage, usage of chemical fertilizer, political factor using linear regression model. Sun [3] had built forecasting system to give prediction for grain demand and pointed out there had gap between demand and supply in future. Zhao [4] had used GARCH and ARMA model to forecast the future trend of grain and found the shortage will last for many years. Gu [5] also investigated many influential factors to analyze the demand and supply situation. There are also some researchers [6,7] who considered the relation between grain production and many other factors, such as climate, water resource. In Wu's dissertation, the GM(1,1) model are constructed to simulate the medium and long term trend of grain demand and supply. Zhang [9] used different grain variety to forecast the demand from 2007 to 2030 and found that the grain demand will have sustainable growth in China.

The problem of grain demand and supply has increasingly serious with the expansion of city scale, the increase of extreme weather, the growth of population and many other uncertainties. How to efficiently solve the imbalance between supply and demand of grain is directly related to national food security. However, it cannot adapt to the new conditions only using the traditional historical experience and some simple statistical computation. This paper uses the intelligent information processing method to investigate the problem of supply and demand of grain and gives the forecasting model. The model can provide service for government to adjust the grain market.

2 The History and Present Situation Analysis of China Grain Supply and Demand

Considering the historical situation, natural disaster and the Cultural Revolution in China, the paper only uses the data since 1978.

Figure 1(a) gives the trend of grain yield from 1978 to 2013. It can be found that the grain yield has a growth trend in general. Figure 1(b) is the clustering result using K-mean algorithm, which shows four stages denoted by '*', '.', '◇'and '□'.

 DOI: 10.1051/itmconf/20160709003

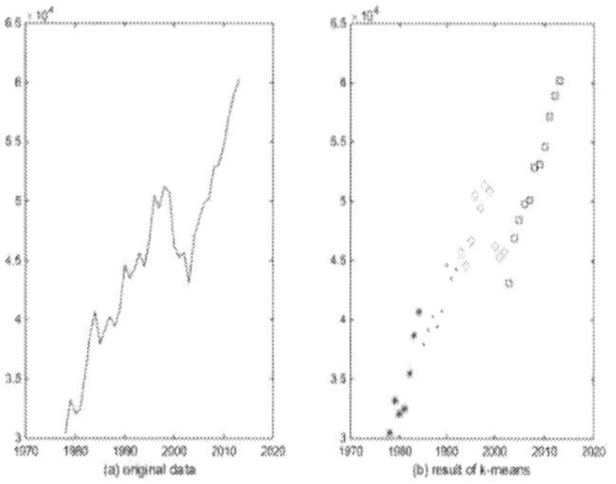

Figure 1. Historical trend of grain yield and clustering result using k-means

The description of four stages is given as follows:

- First stage: The grain yield has quickly increased from 1978 to 1984. The main reason is that grain yield per unit area has a fast growth. According to national statistical yearbook, although the national grain sown area has declined 6.4%, grain yield per unit area in 1984 increased about 42.8% compared to one in 1978.
- Second stage: The grain yield has also similarly increased from 1985 to 1992. But the growth rate has slightly declined. The main reason also comes from the grain yield per unit area.
- Third stage: The grain yield has declined from 1993 to 2003. It dues to that the national grain sown area has reduced in a large extend.
- Fourth stage: The grain yield has quickly increased from 2003 to 2013. The growth of grain sown area and grain yield per unit area can explain the fact.

Table 1 gives the mean of different stage.

Table 1. Clustering result of grain yield using K-means

period of time (year)	**Average grain yield (Ten thousand tons)**
1978--1984	34736
1985~1992	41423
1993--2002	47595
2003--2013	52296

The national grain demand generally consists of food consumption, feed consumption, seed consumption, industrial consumption and grain loss. With the improvement of people's living standard, the food consumption has been declining gradually in recent years. But the industrial consumption and feed consumption has a faster growth. For example, the food consumption, feed consumption and industrial consumption was respectively 25389, 14722 and 10130 ten thousand tons in 2012, which has a comparable growth of 6.9%, 23.1% and 123.8% in 2003.

3 Forecast of Grain Demand and Supply

The paper respectively uses back propagation neural network [11-13] and grey model [14-16] to give predication of grain demand and supply in China's thirteenth five-year development planning.

3.1. Basic Concepts of BP

BP (Back Propagation) neural network is one of neural network model which has been extensively used. It uses the algorithm of gradient descent and adjusts the weight value based on back propagation. Its goal is to find a mapping between inputs and its correct output. Figure 2 gives the structure of neural network, which is generally composed with input layer, hidden layer and output layer. Input layer is in charge of receiving the external information, hidden layer is responsible for the information processing, and the output layer gives the finally result.

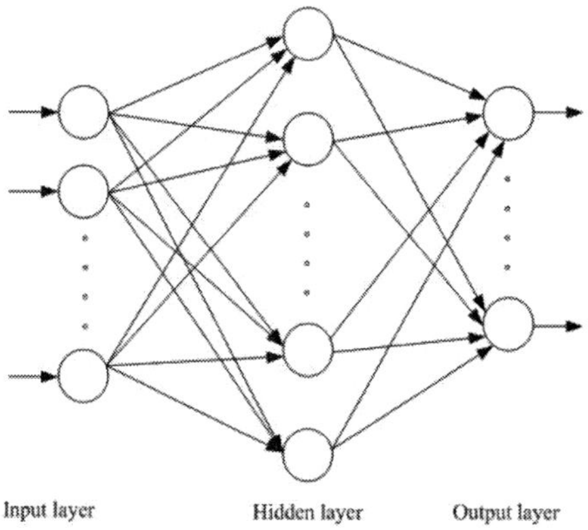

Figure 2. Structure of Neural Network

The BP algorithm can be outlined into two parts: forward and back propagation. In the part of forward propagation, the input information is transferred to output layer and given the output. When the output is inconsistent with correct result, error propagates to the forward neurons. In the whole learning process, the weights and bias values are continuously updated until error is less than predefined value. The learning parameters are weights and bias values.

3.2. Basic Concepts of Gray Model

The gray model is firstly proposed in 1982. After that, the gray theory has been rapidly developed and caught the attention of many scholars. It has been widely used in various fields.

In the gray theory, a system can be defined according to its color, which represents the different degree of information about that system. For example, a system is called white system if all information about it has been known. Similarly, if we has any idea about one system, we denoted it black system. If part information has been known, the system is the grey system. In real application, because each system has some uncertainties, it can be regarded as a grey system.

The gray forecasting model has many advantages, for example, it needs less information about the system, in addition, the gray model has the characteristic of convenient computation and high accuracy. The main goal of gray model is to extract realistic principles of the system using available data.

3.3. The Dataset

Selection of sample data: the sample data mainly comes from China Statistical Yearbook, State Statistics Bureau, and website of United Nations Food and Agriculture Organization (FAO). The grain yield data is selected from 1978 to 2013. We only consider the food consumer price index from 1995 to 2013 for the sake of statistical cause.

3.4. Trend Forecast of Grain Supply

In the experiment, the grey model uses all historical data to forecast next year grain yield. Autoregressive order is 10 in the neural model. The neuron of hidden layer is 10. The tan-sigmoid and purelin function are separately chosen as the transferring function for hidden and output layer of neural network. Seventy percent of raw data are used as training sample and the others are used as testing samples.

Table 2. Forecasting Result of Grain Yield Using Grey Model And Bp(*E+04).

year	Grey model	BP
2014	5.8086	6.3402
2015	5.8910	6.6468
2016	5.9745	6.7205
2017	6.0592	6.7621
2018	6.1451	6.8319
2019	6.2322	6.8458
2020	6.3206	6.8473

Table 2 and figure 3 give the result. The error of grey model and BP neural network is 5.22% and 4.96%, respectively. From the result, both of two methods predict that the grain yield will increase in short term. The forecast growth ratio will be separately 0.88% and 0.79% in 2020 using the grey model and BP, compared with the yield in 2014. But the BP give more smooth result than the grey model.

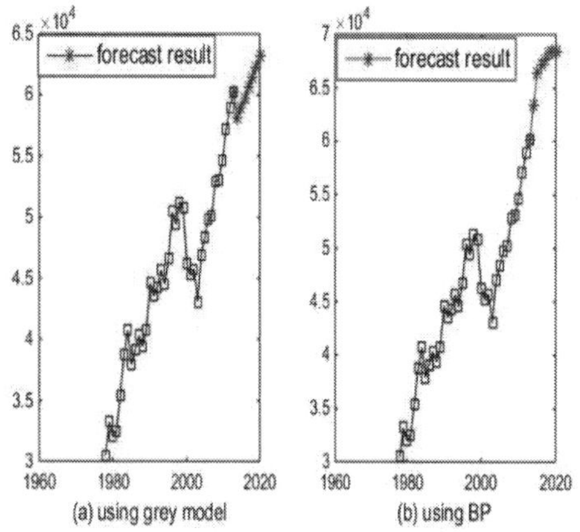

Figure 3. Forecasting Result of Grain Yield Using Grey Model and Bp

3.5 Trend Forecast of Grain Demand

Because there has not the exact statistical data for grain demand, the food consumer price index is considered as index to judge grain demand.

The similar parameters are used as the experiment of grain supply. Table 3 and figure4 give the final result. The error of grey model and BP neural network is 4.80% and 4.60%, respectively. The grain demand in 2020 will be increased 32.2% in 2020 that 2014 using the grey model. But the BP neural network gives a growth of 19.5%. In total, the two methods give similar result. From the view of long term, the food consumer price index will experience a sustainable growth.

Table 3. Forecasting result of food consumer price index using grey model and BP.

year	Grey model	BP
2014	173.5	183.4
2015	181.8	195.1
2016	190.5	204.6
2017	199.5	206.4
2018	209.0	205.1
2019	218.9	213.1
2020	229.4	219.2

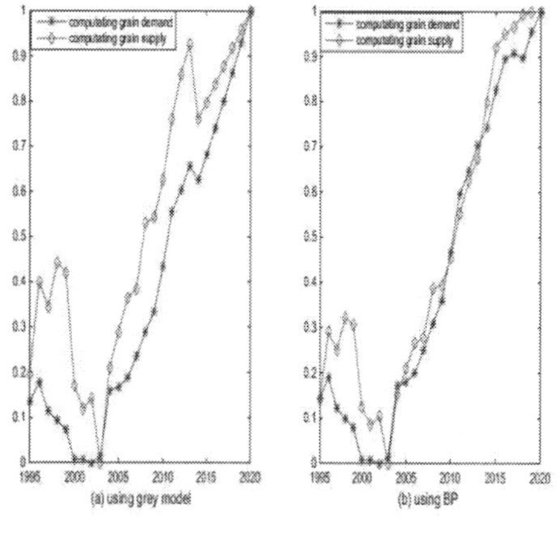

Figure 4. Forecasting Result of Food Consumer Price Index Using Grey Model and Bp

Figure 4 also gives the forecast result for grain yield. It can be found that the grain demand has larger growth than the grain yield. It shows the demand is greater than supply and the grain supply may be tension in China's thirteenth five-year.

4 Proposal for grain supply and demand

In this paper, we uses gray model and Back Propagation neural network to analyses and predict grain supply and demand of China in the thirteen-five period. The result shows that both grain supply and demand will increase in long trend, but grain demand has more than grain supply.

As mentioned above, there exists the imbalance between grain supply and demand. As a result, some methods should be adopted to guarantee the balance between grain supply and demand. It has been point out that government should build grain early warning and monitoring system and establish a sound and efficient grain control mechanism in the Long-term plan for China's food security (2008-2020).

In order to maintain the balance of grain supply and demand, the following methods can be implemented.

technology and steadily improve the comprehensive grain production capacity.

and build sound grain macro control system.

system and establish early warning model and index system of grain supply and demand balance.

policy to protect and enhance the enthusiasm of farmers.

reduce food waste.

though International grain market. Promote grain trade balance and macroeconomic regulation and control of grain prices

Acknowledgements

This work was supported in part by Special Fund for Agro-scientific Research in the Public Interest under contract 201413001, the National Natural Science Foundation of China under contract 31171775, Natural Science Foundation of Henan Educational Committee under contract 14B550002, and the key technologies R&D program of Henan science and technology committee under contract 112102210190.

References

grain yield in China, (2007)

2. Jie Xie, Study on the influencing factors of grain production in China, inquiry into economic issues, 36-40,9(2007)
3. Baomin Sun, Prediction index system and model design of grain supply and demand in China, economic issue, 39-43,3(2012)
4. Xuan Zhao, Yishan Shao, Analysis and prediction of grain supply and demand in China, Research of Agricultural Modernization, 277---280,3(2014)
5. Guoda Gu, Jinghua Yi, Analysis on the trend of global medium and long term grain supply and demand, Journal of Huazhong Agricultural University (Social Science Edition), 6-16,6(2014)
6. HUEY L L, The impact of climate change on global food supply and demand, food prices, and land use, Paddy Water Environ, 321-331,7(2009)
7. HANJRA M A, QURESHIM E, Global water crisis and future food security in an era of climate change, Food Policy, 365—377,10(2010)
8. Le Wu, Research on the long term trend of China's grain demand, Doctoral Dissertation of Huazhong Agricultural University, (2011)
9. Yumei Zhang, Yuqiang Li, Zhemin Li, Shiwei Xu, China Grains Demand Forecast Analysis Based on China Economywide Multimarket Model, Food and Nutrition in China, 40-45,2(2012)
10. Bishop, Christopher M, Pattern Recognition and Machine Learning, Springer (2010)
11. Simon Haykin, *Neural Networks and Learning Machines*, China Machine Press, (2011)
12. Alpaydın, Ethem, Introduction to machine learning (2nd ed. ed.), Cambridge, Mass.: MIT Press, 2010.
13. Rumelhart, David E., Hinton, Geoffrey E., Williams, Ronald J, Learning representations by back-propagating errors, Nature. 323 (6088) (1986) 533–536.
14. Julong Deng, *Grey theory foundation*, Huazhong University of Science and Technology Press, (2005)
15. Xiu Wang, Comparative study on grain yield prediction of grey forecasting model, journal of agricultural mechanization research, 78-80,9(2011)
16. Erdal Kayacan, Baris Ulutas, Okyay Kaynak, Grey system theory-based models in time series prediction, Expert Systems with Applications, 1784–1789,37(2010)

DOI: 10.1051/itmconf/20160709004

INSAR Flat-earth Phase Removal Approach Based on DEM to Settlement Area

Xing-Tong CHEN, Xiao-Feng ZHU, Xiao-Hong WANG, and Yang Cai

North China University of Science and Technology,Hebei,Tangshan,063009,China
1604464340@qq.com

Abstract. The difficulties of phase unwrapping was increased with the existence of flat-earth phase removal, at the same time ,it covered up the real topographical conditions .In order to solve this problem ,the paper presented a method of re-flattening. based on DEM to eliminate flat-earth phase, with the interferogram, and then chose some special control points to construct polynomial fitting, removed residual phase and noise. By analyzing the ALOS/PALSAR at the mine subsidence area, the contrast experiment was carried out. The results showed that the method can clearly reflect the earth's surface changes, reduce the surface deformation error, get a more accurate interferogram phase and improve the precision of the INSAR interferometry.

Synthetic Aperture Radar Interferometry (INSAR)measurement technique combined the synthetic aperture radar imaging theory and electromagnetic interference technology, using the observations of two or more SAR image complex data in the same area to process coherence to obtain more precise digital elevation model and more accurate millimeter surface deformation information[1]. However, Flat-earth phase removal had a very important effect on the entire INSAR data. Due to the using of synthetic aperture radar imaging with slant range way. Flat-earth phase removal appeared, so the distance was different when the radar echo signal propagated, and phase position changed which should remain unchanged at the same height in the interference figure, the phenomenon also showed that the interferogram presented periodically interference fringes.The presence of flat-earth phase removal obscured the change of interference fringes, so the interferogram can not reflect the real situation of geomorphology, and made fringes intensive, so the difficulty of phase unwrapping increased. There fore, before unwrapping the interferogram, the flat-earth phase must be removed. Approaching to common flat-earth phase removal were mainly the following methods[2-3]: (1) A method of flat-earth phase removal based on orbit parameters was to eliminate flat-earth phase that the reference ellipsoid caused by the position and orbital parameters of the imaging area. The principle of the method was simple and high precision theory but lowering efficiency, which depended on the accuracy of the orbit position.(2) Frequency shift method had a small amount of calculation and no other additional conditions merit. Tocalculate the flat phase by frequency interference fringes, eliminate the flat-earth phase. It was more effective for flat areas, But for the settlement of the surface area, the fringe frequency that some part of terrain changes was as same as peaceful fringes of the frequency, if it was removed. It was likely to cause an error, and can notaccurately eliminate the influence of the flat phase. (3) Flat-earth phase removal based on DEM method can achieve high elevation accuracy under the conditions of little parameter data. However, this method was influenced by abnormal phase and phase noise, made some difficult terrain of the interferogram which was still not clearly reflected. Based on DEM data to eliminate the flat-earth phase, This paper presented a method of re-flattening to improve accuracy.

1 Geometric principles of flat-earth phase removal

According to INSAR imaging techniques, as shown in figure 1, the figure had two points of the level terrain: P1and P2. the heights of points P1 and P2 are same. In the interference pattern the phase difference between P1and P2 was ΔΦ[4], as in

$$\Delta\Phi = \frac{4\pi B_{\perp}\Delta r_s}{\lambda r_0 \tan\theta} \tag{1}$$

Where $B_{\perp}$ was expressed as the vertical baseline; B was expressed as the distance between the antennas; Δr_s was expressed as the slope distance difference of P1 and P2 points; θ was expressed as the look-angle of radar; r0was expressed as the initial slope distance length.

As it can be seen from the equation (1) the ground surface without elevation variation also generated linear varied interference phase. so the specific geometry of

INSAR interferometer system leaded to the existence of the flat-earth phase. For the the different range positions and the exact same point, height of which was different from the interferogram phase. Not only the flat-earth phase existed in the range, but the satellite orbit was not perfectly parallel, the earth was irregular ellipsoid , there also existed in the azimuth direction. According to the equation (1),the common method of flat-earth phase removal calculated the relative change in the flat-earth phase of the scene to realize the purpose.

To eliminate the flat-earth phase of the range, multiplied the complex intensity of each pixel in the interference pattern with the complex exponential related slant distance phase. it was possible to correct the impact of flat-earth phase[5]:

$$\beta = \exp(-i\frac{4\pi B_{\perp}\Delta r_s}{\lambda r_0 \tan\theta}) \tag{2}$$

The interference phase difference became :

$$\Delta\Phi = \frac{4\pi B_{\perp}\Delta z}{\lambda r_0 \sin\theta} \tag{3}$$

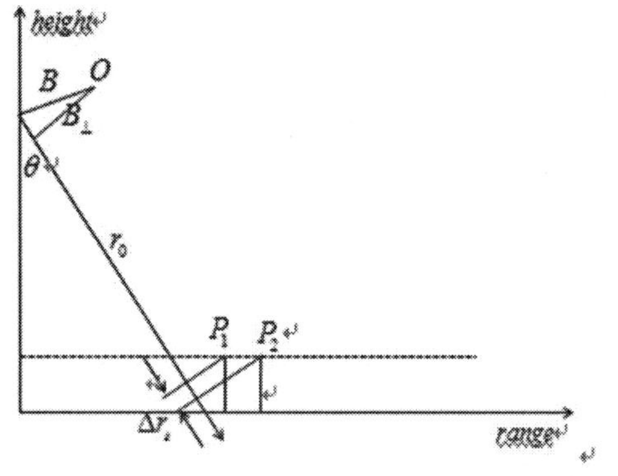

Figure 1.The Diagram of Interferogram Phase Changes With The Slant range geometry

Where Δz was the actual height difference of the terrain. As can be seen from the above equation, after phase compensation, the phase can directly reflect the topology of the terrain height.

2 Flat-earth Phase Removal Based on DEM Method

Flat-earth phase removal based on DEM, the first step was to get DEM data in the study area. This paper used a global DEM data to eliminate flat-earth phase, it can easily get DEM data in the study area, such as a resolution of about 90 m of the SRTM DEM, the reference coordinate system was WGS84 coordinate system. Specific methods using DEM data to eliminate flat-earth phase was as follows:

2.1 DEM Resampling

Read and calculate the interval of the midpoint between the DEM, while calculating intervals of the element points in the interference picture and their ratio. According to the ratio between the interference pattern and the DEM, proceeded resample for the DEM point, and bilinear interpolation method was used to obtain its pixel elevation value. The expression for the bilinear interpolation [6]:

$$f(i+u,j+v)=(1-u)(1-v)f(i,j)+(1-u)vf(i,j+1) \\ +u(1-v)f(i+1,j)+uvf(i+1,j+1) \tag{4}$$

Where f (*, *) denoted a pixel gray values, u and v were non-integers.

2.2 Flat-earth Phase Removal

According to the oblique projection equations of the Doppler equation, nonlinear equations and ellipsoid equation posed, by using of orbital parameters, the DEM data was converted to geocentric coordinate system. By orbit interpolation and bilinear interpolation, the DEM data was converted into phase values, and then subtracted reference value calculated DEM data from the interferogram fringe phase, it achieved the purpose of flat-earth phase removal.

2.3 Re-flattening

Since the interference patterns till existed abnormal phase and phase noise caused by orbit parameters, the phenomena madeflat-earth phase removal not completely, to further Refinement and Re-flattening. After the interferogram, selecting some correlation coefficient greater than 0.7 control points from figure 2, which facilitated extraction of elevation, and control point were selected relatively flat and stable place. The distribution of control points was not too scattered. The number of control points were less than 7, the error range was less than one pixel resolution. The selected control points data can see in table 1.

By using the selected point setting orbit correction parameters, recalculated the satellite position, and then calculated the points on the datum to the distance of the satellite, and then get the corresponding points of the flat phase. In the interferogram, by subtracting the datum from the interferogram fringe phase, it achieved the purpose of Re-flattening

DOI: 10.1051/itmconf/20160709004

Table 1. Control Point Statistics

Number	Correlation Coefficient
1	0.798
2	0.781
3	0.791
4	0.848
5	0.767
6	0.751
7	0.856
8	0.843
9	0.726

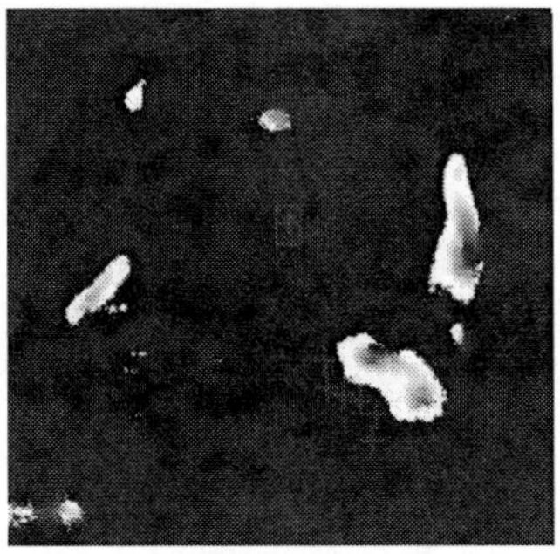

Figure 2. Control Points Distribution

The number of polynomial coefficients was used to remove residual phase, the degrees of polynomial was used to estimate the phase slope, If the number of coefficients was higher, the control points inputting will automatically decreased, The default value was 3, which indicated phase ramp in the range and azimuth direction which added a constant phase to correct, its polynomial expression was:

$$\begin{aligned} \phi = k_1 + k_2 x + k_3 y + k_4 x^2 + k_5 xy \\ + k_6 y^2 + k_7 x^3 + k_8 x^2 y + k_9 xy^2 + k_{10} y^3 \end{aligned} \quad (5)$$

3 Experimental analysis

3.1 Experimental Area and the Experimental data

The area of surface subsidence was as the experimental area. ALOS/PALSAR images were chosen to processed interference experiments. External DEM data was obtained by using the EV-INSAR.

Since the surface subsidence area was complex, the baseline data would be estimated before the experiment. the purpose was to determine whether data can be interference from time baseline and space baseline. The long spatial baseline was better in INSAR data processing, and it was best if it was less than 1/3 of the critical baseline. Time baseline of master and slave images was 90d in the experimental data area. space baseline was 661.798m,and critical baseline was between -6196.108m and 6196.108m, it conformed to interference condition for INSAR data.

3.2 Experimental Results and analysis

Two scene Spaceborne INSAR experimental data was get, by using the DEM data to remove flat-earth phase, selecting WGS84 model as a reference to remove flat-earth phase. Comparison of two methods of extracting DEM image was given. After the master and slave images make coregistration in the study area, the plurality of master and slave images corresponding pixels proceeds conjugate multiplier to obtain the interferogram, figure 3 was obtained interference phase. As can be seen from the figure 3,Regular interference fringes covered up the real terrain, fringes were displayed, because correlation coefficient was relatively poor. Interference fringe spacing expressed the altitude difference, by means of the baseline estimate, and its altitude difference was 93.048m. Interference phase ranges from -л to л. the interference fringe showed dense and diagonal. Its characteristics were not parallel to the fringe direction of the range and azimuth, the flat-earth phase existed mainly direction of the range.It was mainly due to the two parallel orbits. Therefore, the range and azimuth have to remove the flat-earth phase.

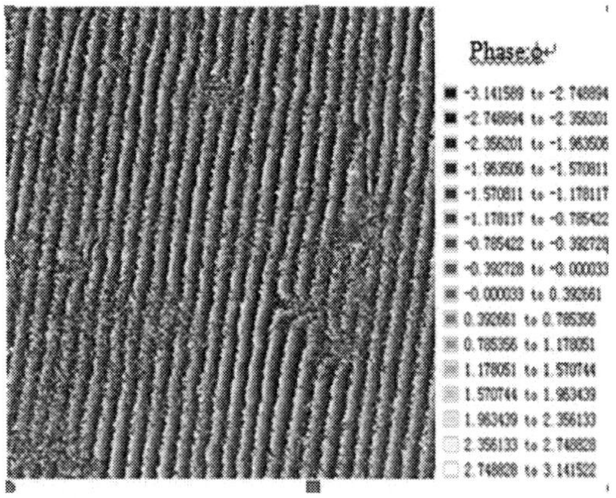

Figure 3.The Interference Phase Image

Figure 4 was the interference phase after removing flat-earth phase. It used the DEM data to remove the flat-earth phase. Interference fringe Substantially removed in the figure, it showed the flat-earth phase had been removed from the direction of range and azimuth. Interferogram can reflect changes in the terrain. However, due to the effects of noise and residual phase, Unwrapped phase do not correctly translate into deformation value. So it was necessary to re-flattening.

DOI: 10.1051/itmconf/20160709004

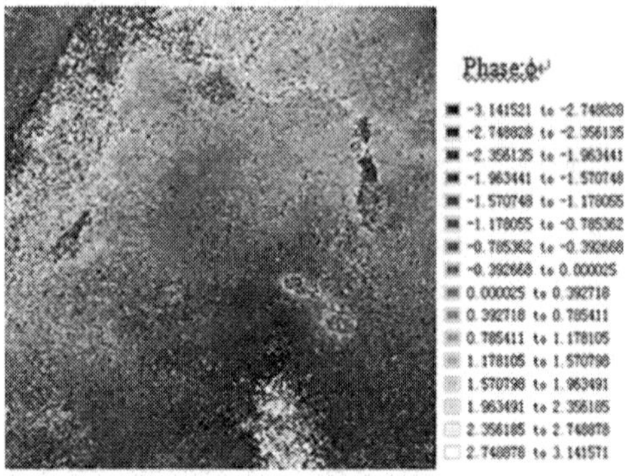

Figure 4. The Interference Image of Flat-earth phase Removal

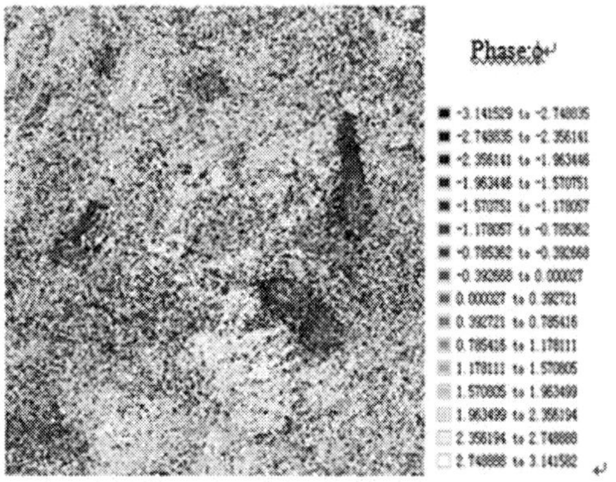

Figure 5.The Interference Phase Image of Re-flattening

Figure 5 was the interference phase after re-flattening. Compared withfigure4, figure 5 interferogram phase information was more obvious, the invisible levels became more clear before re-flattening. Interferogram can clearly see the terrain change information.

In order to demonstrate consistent visual and quantitative evaluation of the results of the evaluation results, this paper quantitatively analyzed from the surface deformation and phase standarddeviation. It more fully and objectively showed that the method was effective.

Figure 6 was the surface deformation image by flat-earth phaseremoval based on DEM method. Figure 7 was the surface deformation image by the method of re-flattening. Comparing figure 6 and figure 7,it can be seen, the surface deformation was generally lower in the same area, maximum deformation reached 0.666146m. By refinement and noise removal, the highly data error by this method slowly reduced Δz approaches terrain changed.

Comparing with flat-earth phase removal based on DEM method, re-flattening method removed better phase noise. According to the indicator of quantitative evaluation phase standard deviation, the size of the standard deviation reflected dynamic range of phase amplitude. As can be seen from Table 2, Phase standard deviation became1.2878 to 1.4638,increasedby0.176. It suggested that standard deviation of the phase changed small, the method maintained the dynamic range of phase amplitude.

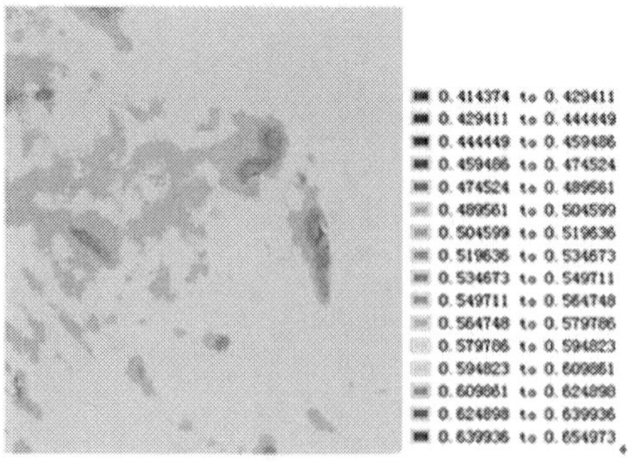

Figure 6.The Surface Deformation of Flat-earth Phase Removal Image(unit: m)

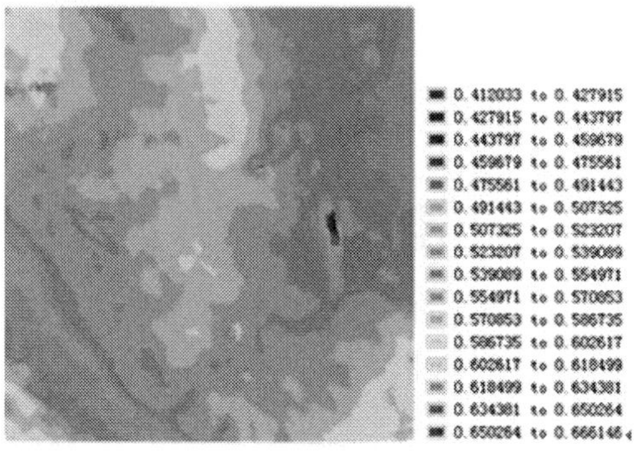

Figure 7.The Surface Deformation of Re-flattening(unit: m)

Table 2.Two Methods Have The Impact of Standard Deviation

methods	Standard deviation/rad
Flat-earth phase removal based on DEM method	1.2878
Re-flattening method	1.4638

Summary

By analyzing the ALOS/PALSAR actual experimental data and the original DEM data, it showed that the purpose of the removal re-flattening method can be achieved with DEM data. Constructing polynomial fitting can make DEM terrain's change more obvious, the accuracy of elevation improved effectively, and reduce the surface elevation error. Experimental results showed this method was very effective. It had important significance on improving the accuracy of DEM reconstruction and reducing the complexity level of the INSAR data processing. By using INSAR technology to extract DEM, it had all-weather, high accuracy of extracting DEM data, fast speed and other characteristics, it can solve very difficult problem that the conventional method while extracting DEM.INSAR technology provided more efficient, cost-effective new method for the subsidence monitoring, and had good application prospects.

DOI: 10.1051/itmconf/20160709004

References

1. Hanssen RF.Radar Interferometry Data Interpretation and Error Analysis[M].New York: Kluwer Academic Publishers(2002).
2. Hong-An W, Yi-Xian T, Hong Z, Chao W. Flat-Phase Removal for ALOS/PALSAR Interferometry Based on Orbit State Vectors[J]. Geomatics and Information Science of Wuhan University, **35(1)**:91-96(2010).
3. Zhi-Ming L, Xiao-Tao T. Baseline Estimation and Flat Earth Removal ofERS-l/2 Data Based on Orbital Parameter[J]. Geomatic Science and Engineering, **24(1)**:26-28(2004).
4. Fen-Fen H, Ji-Xian Z, Ke-Zhong D. Comparative Study on Several Methods of Removing the Flat-earth Effect in Airborne InSAR System[J]. Remote Sensing Information, **5**:57-61(2010).
5. Lei Y, Yong-Jun Z, Zhi-Gang W. Frequency Shifted-based Approach for InSAR Flat Earth Effect Removal[J]. Journal of Electronic Measurement and Instrument, **18(4)**:15-20.(2004).
6. Cai D. Research of Image Interpolation Algorithm. Ph D Thesis. Chongqing: Chongqing University(2011).

An Assessment Model of National Grants of University Based on Fuzzy Analytic Hierarchy Process

Yang XIA[1],Cheng-Gang JIANG[2]

[1]*Student Affairs Office, Suzhou University of Science and Technology, Suzhou 215009, P. R. China*
[2] *Youth League Committee, Suzhou University of Science and Technology, Suzhou 215009, P. R. China*

Abstract How to assess kinds of grants scientifically, effectively and regularly is an important topic for the funding workers to study. According to the national grants' basic conditions, an assessment model is established on the basis of fuzzy analytic hierarchy process. And Finally an example is given to illustrate the scientificalness and operability of this model.

1 Introduction

China has established a fairly perfect student financial assistance policy system, covering from preschool to graduate education, particularly in higher education which has national scholarships, student loans, tuition reimbursement compensatory loans, school scholarships, work-study subsidies, difficult subsidies, food subsidies, tuition waiver, "green channel" and other mixed funding systems. How to put these funding initiatives in place scientifically, effectively and normatively has become an important subject of workers who focus on funding in universities. Some domestic scholars use the AHP to make a study of the identification system of students from poor families [1] and the evaluation system of state grants [2]. Because it is difficult to test the consistency of judging matrix in the Analytic Hierarchy Process, consistency test of judging matrix is often achieved by the constant adjustments according to the subjective factors of the decision-makers during the specific implementation processes. The author has studied the identified evaluation about university students from poor families using the Fuzzy Analytic Hierarchy Process [3]. In order to further strengthen the research results, ensure that state stipend is given fairly and reasonably, and enhance the scientific and normative work of university funding, the author will use the fuzzy analytic hierarchy process to model the assessment of state stipend for colleges and universities, and provide quantitative and feasible approaches for the university funding workers.

2 The Current Problems of National Grants in Colleges and Universities

According to The tentative Management Method of National Grants in General Undergraduate Colleges and Higher Vocational Colleges (The finance and education[2007]NO.92), the basic application conditions of national grants are as follow: ① Deep love for socialist motherland and advocacy of Chinese Communist Party; ② Compliance with constitution, law and school regulations; ③ Honesty, trustworthiness, and good moral quality. ④Study diligently and be positive; ⑤Having economical difficulties with family. Based on this, the universities have also developed a corresponding assessment rules. But in view of the versatility of the basic conditions and evaluation work still confronts with some objective difficulties. For example, how to evaluate ④ and ⑤ in the basic condition? And how to stable the student who apply for the national student financial aid? It's obvious that the evaluation of the state grants is a multi-level, multi factor comprehensive evaluation problems. If the single factor is under evaluation, the fairness of education can't be ensured and many indicators cannot be analyzed by normal mathematical methods.

3 The Basic Principles of Fuzzy Analytic Hierarchy Process

Fuzzy Analytic Hierarchy Process [4] is a kind of idea and method, which is established by introducing fuzzy mathematics to the Analytic Hierarchy Process. It means to make improvements in Analytic Hierarchy Process because the judging matrix is much difficult to achieve and evaluate the matrix's consistency and the differences of decision making. And it is a useful and efficient decision making way that through setting up an optimized hierarchy structure model, constructing a prioritized matrix. All in all, the Fuzzy Analytic Hierarchy Process is a combination of Fuzzy Analytic Process and Analytic Hierarchy Process. In the sequel,

 DOI: 10.1051/itmconf/20160709005

we will introduce the basic principles and the basic steps of Fuzzy Analytic Hierarchy Process

3.1 The Basic Knowledge of Fuzzy Analytic Hierarchy Process

Definition **1** ([5]) If the matrix $\boldsymbol{R}=\left(r_{ij}\right)_{n\times n}$ satisfies $0\le r_{ij}\le 1,\ i,j=1,2,\cdots,n$, then $\boldsymbol{R}$ is called the analytic hierarchy process.

Definition **2** ([5]) If the matrix $\boldsymbol{R}=\left(r_{ij}\right)_{n\times n}$ satisfies $r_{ij}+r_{ji}=1,\ i,j=1,2,\cdots,n$, then $\boldsymbol{R}$ is called the fuzzy reciprocal matrix.

Definition **3** ([6]) If the fuzzy reciprocal matrix $\boldsymbol{R}=\left(r_{ij}\right)_{n\times n}$ satisfies $r_{ij}=r_{ik}-r_{jk}+0.5$ for any k, then $\boldsymbol{R}$ is called the fuzzy consistent matrix.

Theorem **1** ([7]) Let the fuzzy reciprocal matrix $\boldsymbol{R}=\left(r_{ij}\right)_{n\times n}$ sum up with lines, denoting as $f_i=\sum_{k=1}^{n} r_{ik}$, and use the transformation $f_{ij}=\dfrac{r_i-r_j}{2n}+0.5$, then we can get the fuzzy consistent matrix $\mathbf{F}=(f_{ij})_{n\times n}$.

3.2 The Basic Steps of Fuzzy Analytic Hierarchy Process

There are four steps to model with Analytic Hierarchy Process: setting up a hierarchy structure model, constructing a judging matrix, ordering in single hierarchy, and ranking in general hierarchy. Compared to Analytic Hierarchy Process, Fuzzy Analytic Hierarchy Process has made improvements in its consistency of judging matrix. Therefore, the steps of modeling of Fuzzy Analytic Hierarchy Process are similar to those of Analytic Hierarchy Process: setting up an optimized hierarchy structure model, constructing a prioritized matrix, creating an optimized relation hierarchy, building a fuzzy consistency hierarchy, and ranking both in single hierarchy and general hierarchy.

4 The Construction of the Assessment Model of National Grants of University Based on Fuzzy Analytic Hierarchy Process

Being multi-leveled and multi-factored, the assessment of national grants for financially disadvantaged university students turns out to be comprehensive. At the same time, the assessment has its root in both quantity analysis and quality analysis. Therefore, this section will follow the basic steps of fuzzy analytic hierarchy process to build up an assessment model of national grants of university.

4.1 Constructing A Prioritized Matrix

First of all, the complicated problem should be grouped into several multi-elements parts by the standard of essential requirements. Then, those elements need to be classified into smaller groups to form various hierarchies. As criteria, those elements not only have an influence on the next hierarchy, but also are affected by the former hierarchy. This top-down structure establishes a prioritized matrix.

Secondly, according to the essential requirements of the assessment of national grants of university, factor set A is created:

$A=\left\{A_1,A_2,A_3,A_4\right\}$ ={moral performance, academic record, family background, consumption level}.

And the subsets are:

$A_1=\left\{A_{11},A_{12}\right\}$ ={excellent, favorable}, the moral performance aims at evaluating the first three essential requirements;

$A_2=\left\{A_{21},A_{22},A_{23}\right\}$ ={excellent, favorable, qualified}, the academic record aims at evaluating the fourth essential requirement. Being excellent means the student ranks among the first third in the whole class; being favorable means the student ranks between the first third and the second third; being qualified means the student studies hard and never fails in any exam;

$A_3=\left\{A_{31},A_{32},A_{33}\right\}$ = {averagely disadvantaged, disadvantaged, and relatively disadvantaged};

$A_4=\left\{A_{41},A_{42},A_{43}\right\}$ = {up to the average level of consumption, slightly below the average level of consumption, far below the average level of consumption}.

All the sets of factors above use both quantity analysis and quality analysis to build up a system of the assessment factors of the national grants of university (see Table 1). In this way, the precision of the assessment can be improved

Table 1 The System of the Assessment Factors of the National Grants of University

Destination Layer A	Criterion Layer B	Criterion Layer C
The System of the Assessment Factors of the National Grants of University	Moral Performance	Excellent
		Favorable
	Academic Record	Excellent
		Favorable
		qualified
	Family Background	Averagely Disadvantaged
		Disadvantaged
		Relatively Disadvantaged
	Consumption Level	Up to the Average Level of Consumption
		Slightly Below the Average Level of Consumption
		Far Below the Average Level of Consumption

4.2 Setting up Prioritized Relation Matrix

After priority hierarchy has been established, subordinate relationship between each level (which can use $\leftarrow$ to show the relationship) is clear. The author divided the importance of evaluation standards with assistance of the Satty 9 degree scale [8] (shown in the table 2) and quantified the complicated evaluation of National grants which are influenced by multi-elements and multi-levels and combined with quality and quantity.

Table 2 The Definition of Satty 9 Degree Scale

scale	definition	explanation
0.5	Equally important	Comparing two factors, they are equally important
0.6	A little more important	Comparing two factors, one is a little more important than the other
0.7	Apparently more important	Comparing two factors, one is apparently more important than the other
0.8	Much more important	Comparing two factors, one is much more important than the other
0.9	extremely important	Comparing two factors, one is extremely important
0.1, 0.2, 0.3, 0.4	Comparison on the contrary	comparing a_i and a_j, judging b_{ji}, comparing a_j and a_i, then judging $b_{ji}=1-b_{ij}$

According to the method, the above-mentioned prioritized relation matrices are as follows.

$$\mathbf{A}\leftarrow\mathbf{A}_i=\begin{bmatrix}0.5&0.7&0.3&0.2\\0.3&0.5&0.4&0.3\\0.7&0.6&0.5&0.9\\0.8&0.7&0.1&0.5\end{bmatrix},\mathbf{A}_1\leftarrow\mathbf{A}_{1i}=\begin{bmatrix}0.5&0.8\\0.2&0.5\end{bmatrix},\mathbf{A}_2\leftarrow\mathbf{A}_{2i}=\begin{bmatrix}0.5&0.7&0.9\\0.3&0.5&0.7\\0.1&0.3&0.5\end{bmatrix}.$$

$$\mathbf{A}_3\leftarrow\mathbf{A}_{3i}=\begin{bmatrix}0.5&0.2&0.3\\0.8&0.5&0.1\\0.7&0.9&0.5\end{bmatrix},\mathbf{A}_4\leftarrow\mathbf{A}_{4i}=\begin{bmatrix}0.5&0.3&0.1\\0.7&0.5&0.3\\0.9&0.7&0.5\end{bmatrix}.$$

4.3 Setting up Fuzzy Consistent Matrix

According to Definition 1 and Definition 2, the above prioritized relation matrix are all fuzzy reciprocal matrix, and form the following fuzzy consistent matrix of Theorem 1.

$$\mathbf{F}\leftarrow\mathbf{F}_i=\begin{bmatrix}0.5&0.525&0.375&0.45\\0.475&0.5&0.35&0.425\\0.625&0.65&0.5&0.575\\0.55&0.575&0.425&0.5\end{bmatrix},\mathbf{F}_1\leftarrow\mathbf{F}_{1i}=\begin{bmatrix}0.5&0.575\\0.425&0.5\end{bmatrix},\mathbf{F}_2\leftarrow\mathbf{F}_{2i}=\begin{bmatrix}0.5&0.6&0.7\\0.4&0.5&0.6\\0.3&0.4&0.5\end{bmatrix},$$

$$\mathbf{F}_3\leftarrow\mathbf{F}_{3i}=\begin{bmatrix}0.5&0.433&0.317\\0.567&0.5&0.383\\0.683&0.617&0.5\end{bmatrix},\mathbf{F}_4\leftarrow\mathbf{F}_{4i}=\begin{bmatrix}0.5&0.4&0.3\\0.6&0.5&0.4\\0.7&0.6&0.5\end{bmatrix}.$$

According to Definition 3, it's easy to prove that these matrixes are fuzzy consistent matrix.

4.4 Ranking

4.4.1 Ranking in Single Hierarchy

Ranking in single hierarchy is to calculate the corresponding feature vectors according to the above fuzzy consistent matrix. And their corresponding weight values are as follows. (The computing method of the weight values could be seen in ref.3,the calculation process is omitted here.)

$\mathbf{w}=\{0.2310,0.2183,0.2943,0.2563\},\mathbf{w}_1=\{0.5377,0.4623\},\mathbf{w}_2=\{0.4019,0.333,0.2648\},$

$\mathbf{w}_3=\{0.2765,0.3219,0.4016\},\mathbf{w}_4=\{0.2648,0.333,0.4019\}.$

3.4.2 Ranking in General Hierarchy w_{ij} ($w_{ij}=A_{ij}\times A_i, i=1,2,3,4; j=1,2,3$)

Table 3 Comprehensive weight values

	A_1	A_2	A_3	A_4	w_{ij}
	0.2310	0.2183	0.2943	0.2563	
A_{11}	0.5377				0.1242
A_{12}	0.4623				0.1068
A_{21}		0.4019			0.0877
A_{22}		0.333			0.0727
A_{23}		0.2648			0.0578
A_{31}			0.2765		0.0814
A_{32}			0.3219		0.0947
A_{33}			0.4016		0.1182
A_{41}				0.2648	0.0679
A_{42}				0.333	0.0853
A_{43}				0.4019	0.1030

According to the table 3, it concludes that in the aspect of relative importance of each factors in $A=\{A_1,A_2,A_3,A_4\}$, family background, consumption level, the moral performance and the academic records in turn rank in the first-degree factors that influence evaluation of national grants, which indicates that students financial disadvantaged are major beneficiaries of national grants. It fits in with the intention of funds. Meanwhile, the grade two requires high standard in conduct, which also shows that the destination of the national grants is to educate people and matches the national financial aid policies. Surely, moral performance, consumption level and the academic records also make their corresponding difference in the grade two factors.

5 Example and conclusion

Take an example of four students, Zhang, Wang, Li,

Qian. According to available evaluation factors, people in charge of evaluation can effectively evaluate these four applicants. The result of evaluation is shown in table 4.

Table 4 The evaluation of four applicants

Destination Layer A	Criterion Layer B	Criterion Layer C	Zhang	Wang	Li	Qian
The System of the Assessment Factors of the National Grants of University	Moral Performance	excellent		√		√
		Favorable	√		√	
	Academic Record	excellent		√		
		Favorable	√			
		qualified			√	√
	Family Background	Averagely Disadvantaged	√			
		Disadvantaged		√		
		Relatively Disadvantaged			√	√
	consumption level	Up to the Average Level of Consumption				√
		Slightly Below the Average Level of Consumption	√			
		Far Below the Average Level of Consumption		√	√	

For the convenience of calculation, we assume that all marked checks are assigned the value 1 and the rest the value 0. In that case, a matrix **D** can be got as follows.

$$\mathbf{D} = \begin{bmatrix} 0 & 1 & 0 & 1 \\ 1 & 0 & 1 & 0 \\ 0 & 1 & 0 & 0 \\ 1 & 0 & 0 & 0 \\ 0 & 0 & 1 & 1 \\ 1 & 0 & 0 & 0 \\ 0 & 1 & 0 & 0 \\ 0 & 0 & 1 & 1 \\ 0 & 0 & 0 & 1 \\ 1 & 0 & 0 & 0 \\ 0 & 1 & 1 & 0 \end{bmatrix}_{11\times 4}$$

At the same time, having w_{ij} expanded a hundredfold, choosing their approximate numbers and taking calculation

$$[12\ \ 11\ \ 9\ \ 7\ \ 6\ \ 8\ \ 9\ \ 12\ \ 7\ \ 9\ \ 10] \begin{bmatrix} 0 & 1 & 0 & 1 \\ 1 & 0 & 1 & 0 \\ 0 & 1 & 0 & 0 \\ 1 & 0 & 0 & 0 \\ 0 & 0 & 1 & 1 \\ 1 & 0 & 0 & 0 \\ 0 & 1 & 0 & 0 \\ 0 & 0 & 1 & 1 \\ 0 & 0 & 0 & 1 \\ 1 & 0 & 0 & 0 \\ 0 & 1 & 1 & 0 \end{bmatrix} = [35\ \ 40\ \ 39\ \ 37]$$

Among them, the four numerical values [35 40 39 37] correspondingly refer to the comprehensive values of four students, Zhang, Wang, Li, Qian. Through analyzing the statistics, it is found that Wang is less financially disadvantaged than Li but Wang scores higher than Li, which is for the reason that the former moral performance and academic records are better than the latter ones. Comparing with Li and Qian, their family economies nearly reach the same level. However, their different consumption levels lead to their different scores. The scientific evaluation towards applicants can finally decide which level of the financial aids they can approved to gain. This above mentioned examples illustrates that the model has a strong operation and guiding significance regarding assessment of national grants.

The study, based on fuzzy analytic hierarchy, employs the qualitative and quantitative methods to set up an assessment model of national grants of university, comprehensive evaluation model, which consists of four first-degree factors and 12 secondary factors. And the list of appraisal factor weights helps workers who manage the funding system in the universities to better put the assessment of national grants into effect. However, the construction of a prioritized matrix in the paper still has some limitations and the study concerning the first-degree factors and secondary factors is not comprehensive. So other scholars and the author himself will dedicate to building up a more detailed and more integrated evaluation model. As the research on the fuzzy analytic hierarchy deepens gradually, it is believed that this will play a greater role in a wide range of fields.

Acknowledgement

This work is supported by the 2014 Fund Project for students in Jiangsu province (grant No.2014JSAIDB06). Besides, I'd like to express my heartful gratitude to Professor Jian-Rong Wu for his valuable suggestions.

References

1. H.Q. Liu, Grey Comprehensive Identification Method of Poor College Students Based on AHP Method. Journal of Chongqing Institute of Technology (social science), 28 (2014) . (in Chinese)
2. Y.Yu, X. Li,J.B.Lu,etal, Scholarship Evaluation Based on Gray System Theory. Journal of Shenyang University (social science), 14: 91-94 (2012) . (in Chinese)
3. Y. Xia, C.G. Jiang,A FAHP-based Assessment Model of Poverty-ridden College Students. Journal

DOI: 10.1051/itmconf/20160709005

of Suzhou University of Science and Technology (Natural Science), 32:11-13(2015). (in Chinese)
4. J.J. Wang, Group Fuzzy Analytical Hierarchy Process Based on the 0-1 Programming. Fuzzy Systems and Mathematics, 29: 117-125(2015). (in Chinese)
5. L.K. Jiang,The Fuzzy Consistent Matrix Applied in Analytic Hierarchy Process. Journal of Shanghai Maritime University, 19: 55-60(1998). (in Chinese)
6. M. Yao, S. Zhang,Fuzzy Consistent Matrix and Its Application in Decision making. Systems Engineering Theory& Practice, 5: 78-81(1998). (in Chinese)
7. X.Chen, Application of Fuzzy Analytic Hierarchy Process for Optimum Selection in Decision-making. Computer Engineering and Design, 25: 1847-1849(2004). (in Chinese)
8. J.J. Zhang, Fuzzy Analytical Hierarchy Process. Fuzzy Systems and Mathematics, 14: 80-88(2000). (in Chinese)

Gas Emission Prediction Model of Coal Mine Based on CSBP Algorithm

Yan XIONG, Jia-Tang CHENG*,and Zhi-Mei DUAN

The Engineering College of Honghe University, Yunnan Mengzi 661199, China

Abstract: In view of the nonlinear characteristics of gas emission in a coal working face, a prediction method is proposed based on cuckoo search algorithm optimized BP neural network (CSBP). In the CSBP algorithm, the cuckoo search is adopted to optimize weight and threshold parameters of BP network, and obtains the global optimal solutions. Furthermore, the twelve main affecting factors of the gas emission in the coal working face are taken as input vectors of CSBP algorithm, the gas emission is acted as output vector, and then the prediction model of BP neural network with optimal parameters is established. The results show that the CSBP algorithm has batter generalization ability and higher prediction accuracy, and can be utilized effectively in the prediction of coal mine gas emission.

1 Introduction

Gas is one of the major natural disasters of the coal mine safety production, the security problem caused by it account to more than 80% of the coal mine safety in production accidents [1]. Therefore, accurate prediction gas emission is important to ensure the safety of the mine production and has practical significance. In recent years, in view of the gas emission prediction research, a series of models and methods are put forward by related personnel. Fu Hua et al. [2] used ant colony algorithm (ACO) to optimize the weights and threshold of the Elman neural network, and established the dynamic prediction method of absolute gas emission. Shi liang et al. [3] established gas emission prediction model based on the empirical mode decomposition (EMD), support vector machine (SVM) combined with particle swarm optimization algorithm (PSO). Fan Baolong et al. [4] used the local mean decomposition (LMD) method to get the production function component (PF component) and SVM model, and constructed the prediction model of gas emission in a coal working face.

However, due to the gas emission in working face is influenced by natural factors combine with mining technology, such as coal seam gas content, coal seam buried depth, coal seam thickness, coal seam dip angle and length of working face, complex nonlinear characteristics lie in them, so that the accurate prediction is difficult. Although the artificial neural network has good nonlinear mapping ability, it is easy to fall into local minimum point. Moreover, the parameters of the SVM algorithm are difficult to determine and affect the prediction precision [5].

As heuristic optimization algorithm, swarm intelligence optimization algorithm has been proposed in recent years. According to the natural biological behavior, some bionic algorithms have emerged such as genetic algorithm (GA), particle swarm optimization algorithm, ant colony algorithm, and Cuckoo Search (CS), etc. However, the genetic algorithm need to reproduction, crossover and mutation operations, and is prone to premature convergence. Ant colony algorithm programming is relatively complex and has low generality and then limits the scope of its application. The implementation process of particle swarm algorithm is simple. However, it is difficult to search for the global optimal solution and has other defects. As a kind of global searching method of intelligent optimization, the Cuckoo Search has the advantages of easy to implement, less parameter setting and so on. Studies show that the CS algorithm is superior to the GA algorithm and PSO algorithm [6,7]. Therefore, Cuckoo Search algorithm is combined with BP neural network to build a CSBP prediction model of gas emission, and the experimental data are used to validate the accuracy of the prediction results.

2 Cuckoo Search Algorithm

As a heuristic algorithm, cuckoo search [8] is put forward by Xin-she Yang and Suash Deb in 2009, which is used to simulate the parasitic brood behavior on the part of the Cuckoo. In the CS algorithm, the bird's nests are used to represent the solutions, and each of the cuckoo egg represents a data processing. The bad solutions are replaced with the new potential solutions. During the iteration process, the eggs with the best fitness will be held until the next generation. In addition, when the host finds exotic birds' eggs in the nest, they will abandon the exotic birds' eggs or build another new nest. According to the

*Corresponding author: Jia-Tang CHENG, chjt@163.com

principle, the bird's nest is updated as follow:

$$x_i^{k+1} = x_i^k + \alpha \oplus L(\lambda) \quad (1)$$

Where, k is the current iteration number, α donates the step length; $\oplus$ is entry-wise multiplication, $L(\lambda)$ donates random search path, and a random step length is produced with Levy distribution.

$$L(\lambda) \sim u = t^{-\lambda}, \quad 1 < \lambda \le 3 \quad (2)$$

In addition, the parameter p_a is set to simulate the probability of host finds exotic birds' eggs. A random number is used to compare with the discovery probability p_a, so as to determine whether or not generate new individual. At this point, location update formula is given as:

$$x_i^{k+1} = x_i^k + \gamma \times H(p_a - \varepsilon) \oplus [x_m^k - x_n^k] \quad (3)$$

Where, ε and γ are the random numbers generated uniformly in the interval (0, 1), $H(p_a - \varepsilon)$ is Heaviside function.

In the CS algorithm, Levy flight consists in frequent short jumps and occasional long jump, and step length has randomness. In order to balance the global exploration and local development ability of the algorithm, the step length is adjusted dynamically, and given as:

$$\alpha = (\alpha_{\max} - \alpha_{\min})(k / k_{\max} - 1)^2 + \alpha_{\min} \quad (4)$$

Where, $k_{\max}$ is the maximum number of iterations, $\alpha_{\max}$ and $\alpha_{\min}$ are the step size values of maximum and minimum.

At the same time, in order to enhance the diversity of population, a reverse learning strategy is used to search for the optimal position as much as possible. The one dimensional position of a bird's nest is chosen randomly at first, and then the dimension vector reversely is obtained to get a new site of bird's nest. At last, optimization operation is carried out according to the size of the fitness value. Reverse learning formula is:

$$x_{ij}^*(k) = a_j(k) + b_j(k) - x_{ij}(k) \quad (5)$$

Where, $x_{ij}^*(k)$ and $x_{ij}(k)$ donate the reverse learning position and the current position of nest, respectively; $a_j(k)$ and $b_j(k)$ are the j dimension border of the search space, respectively.

3 CSBP Algorithm Implementation

In the CSBP algorithm, each egg of cuckoo represents the initial weights and threshold of BP neural network, and CS algorithm is used to optimize the parameters. Then, the optimal solutions are transferred to the BP neural network and obtain the final output results. Implementation steps [9] are given as follows:

1) Initialize parameters of CS algorithm.

2) Generate initial solution randomly, and take as the weight and threshold parameters of BP network.

3) Choose the best fitness and the best position of the bird's nests.

4) According to the formula (1), the position of new bird's nests is calculated, and according to the size of the fitness value to keep good position and fitness of bird's nest.

5) Using random number ε compare to discovery probability p_a, the part of the original individuals are abandoned by formula (3) .At the same time, the new nests are generated. Then the bad bird's nests are replaced, and the fitness is updated subsequently.

6) To judge whether meet the condition of algorithm to stop , if it meet the condition then turn into the next step, or transfer into step 4) to continue.

7) Output the optimal position of the bird's nests, and they are taken as the initial parameters of weight and threshold of BP network. Finally, the learning and training are complimented through the BP network.

4 Gas Emission Prediction

4.1 Parameters Selection

The influence factors of gas emission in coal working face are numerous, and seriously affected by the gas content in coal seam and its occurrence conditions. Therefore, how to correctly select these factors is the precondition to establishment the prediction model of gas emission. Research shows that the main influencing factors of gas emission Y(m^3/t)in working face are: coal seam gas content X_1(m^3/t), buried depth of coal seam X_2(m), coal seam thickness X_3(m), dip Angle of coal seam X_4(°), working face length X_5(m), propulsion speed X_6(m/min), extraction rate X_7, adjacent layer gas content X_8(m^3/t), adjacent layer thickness X_9(m), the distance between adjacent layers X_{10}(m), interlayer litho logy X_{11} and mining depth X_{12}(m). Despite the roof management mode has a great influence on the gas emission, the roof management style of mining working face is the equal value, so it is not considered. Specific data [10] is shown in Table 1.

 DOI: 10.1051/itmconf/20160709006

Table 1 The statistical data

No.	X_1	X_2	X_3	X_4	X_5	X_6	X_7	X_8	X_9	X_{10}	X_{11}	X_{12}	Y
1	1.92	408	2.0	155	155	4.42	0.960	2.02	1.50	20	5.03	1825	3.34
2	2.15	411	2.0	140	140	4.16	0.950	2.10	1.21	22	4.87	1527	2.97
3	2.14	420	1.8	175	175	4.13	0.950	2.64	1.62	19	4.75	1751	3.56
4	2.58	432	2.3	145	145	4.67	0.950	2.40	1.48	17	4.91	2078	3.62
5	2.40	456	2.2	160	160	4.51	0.940	2.55	1.75	20	4.63	2104	4.17
6	3.22	516	2.8	180	180	3.45	0.930	2.21	1.72	12	4.78	2242	4.60
7	2.80	527	2.5	180	180	3.28	0.940	2.81	1.81	11	4.51	1979	4.92
8	3.35	531	2.9	165	165	3.68	0.930	1.88	1.42	13	4.82	2288	4.78
9	3.61	550	2.9	155	155	4.02	0.920	2.12	1.60	14	4.83	2325	5.23
10	3.68	563	3.0	175	175	3.53	0.940	3.11	1.46	12	4.53	2410	5.56
11	4.21	590	5.9	170	170	2.85	0.795	3.40	1.50	18	4.77	3139	7.24
12	4.03	604	6.2	180	180	2.64	0.812	3.15	1.80	16	4.70	3354	7.80
13	4.34	607	6.1	165	165	2.77	0.785	3.02	1.74	17	4.62	3087	7.68
14	4.80	634	5.5	175	175	2.92	0.773	2.98	1.92	15	4.55	3620	8.51
15	4.67	640	6.3	175	175	2.75	0.802	2.56	1.75	15	4.60	3412	7.95
16	2.43	450	2.2	160	160	4.32	0.950	2.00	1.70	16	4.84	1996	4.06
17	3.16	544	2.7	165	165	3.81	0.930	2.30	1.80	13	4.90	2207	4.92
18	4.62	629	6.4	170	170	2.80	0.803	3.35	1.61	19	4.63	3456	8.04

4.2 Model Establishment

According to the actual data of coal mine gas emission in table 1, the first 14 groups as training samples are selected after the normalized processing, the last four groups are taken as the test data, and the prediction model of gas emission is establish based on CSBP algorithm. The main parameters are given as follows: the topology of the BP neural network is 12-15-1, learning rate 0.1, vector error convergence factor 10^{-5}, the initial population size 25, the maximum number of iterations $k_{max} = 100$, the initial step length $a_{max} = 1$, $a_{min} = 0.1$, limiting range of optimal parameters [-5, 5], the discovery probability $p_a = 0.25$. According to the training data, the curve of the fitness function of the CSBP algorithm is shown in Figure 1.

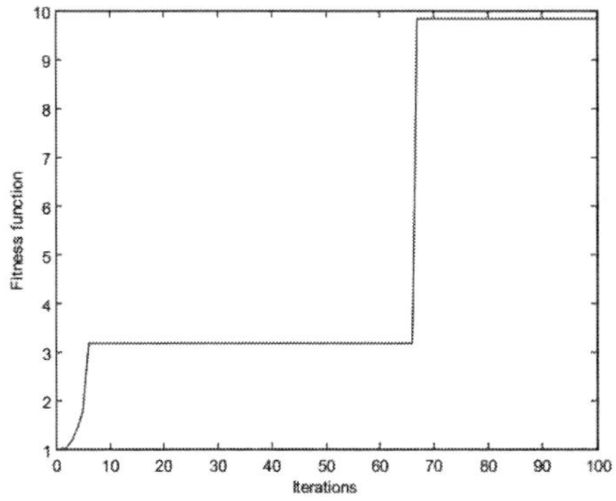

Figure 1 The curve of fitness function

It can be seen from Figure 1, the fitness value of CS algorithm is increased gradually from 0, the iteration number is about 7 times or so, the fitness function curve entries into a longer flat area, it is illustrated that the algorithm falls into local optimum. Due to Levy flight strategy in the CS algorithm consists of frequent short leap and occasional long jump, when iterative 67 times, the value of fitness function increases again, the algorithm has been jump out of the local optimal area, and search continually the optimal solution in the solution space, and the fitness value steady at 9.83 finally. Therefore, the CS algorithm has the good capability of local exploration, and can be applied effectively to the parameters optimization system of BP neural network.

4.3 Result Analysis

The last 4 groups' sample data is used to forecast the gas emission based on the CSBP algorithm, and the results are compared with BP neural network prediction outputs, the comparison is shown in Table 2. It is shown that maximum the relative error of CSBP algorithm is 4.78%, the average relative error (ARE) is 2.435%. And the maximum relative error of BP neural network is 10.34%, the average relative error is 7.49%. Obviously, comparing with BP neural network, the CSBP algorithm has higher prediction precision which can better meet the engineering needs of gas emission prediction.

Table 2 The prediction effects contrast and analysis

No.	The actual value	CSBP prediction		BP prediction	
		Predictive value	The relative error /%	Predictive value	The relative error /%
15	7.95	8.33	4.78	7.29	8.30
16	4.06	3.94	2.96	4.48	10.34
17	4.92	4.92	0	4.73	3.86
18	8.04	7.88	2.00	7.40	7.46
ARE /%			2.435		7.49

In addition, as a variable to measure the difference between actual value with predictive value, the generalization ability of neural network can be used the average relative variation (ARV). The smaller value is, the stronger generalization ability of the network obtains. The formula is given as:

$$ARV = \frac{\sum_{i=1}^{n}[Y(i) - \hat{Y}(i)]^2}{\sum_{i=1}^{n}[Y(i) - \overline{Y}(i)]^2} \tag{6}$$

Where, $Y(i)$, $\hat{Y}(i)$ and $\overline{Y}(i)$ are the actual, forecast and average value of gas emission, respectively.

By calculation, the AVR of the CSBP and BP neural network are 1.46% and 8.36%, respectively. Obviously, the CSBP algorithm enhances the generalization ability of neural network.

5 Summary

The influence factors of gas emission in a coal working face are numerous, so the prediction model of gas emission based on CSBP is proposed. The CS algorithm is used to optimist the weights and threshold parameters of BP neural network, and avoids the defect of the BP network is easy to fall into local minimum.

According to the test samples of gas emission, the results show that the average relative error based on CSBP algorithm is 2.435%, the average relative variation is 1.46%, which is less than the corresponding value of the BP neural network, and a new idea is provided for gas emission prediction in a coal mine working face.

References

1. LIU June, AN Fengping, LIN Dachao, et al, Prediction of gas emission from coalface by intrinsic mode SVM modeling, Systems Engineering-Theory & Practice, 33(2), 505-511 (2013)
2. FU Hua, XIE Sen, XU Yaosong, et al, Gas emission dynamic prediction model of coal mine based on ACC-ENN algorithm, Journal of China Coal Society, 39(7), 1296-1301 (2014)
3. SHI Shiliang, LI Runqiu, LUO Wenke, Method for predicting coal mine gas emission based on EMD-PSO-SVM and its application, China Safety Science Journal, 24(7), 43-49 (2014)
4. FAN Baolong, BAI Chunhua, LI Jianping, Forecasting model of coalface gas emission based on LMD-SVM method, Journal of Mining & Safety Engineering, 30(6), 946-952 (2013).
5. CHENG Jiatang, DUAN Zhimei, XIONG Yan, QAPSO-BP algorithm and its application in vibration fault diagnosis for a hydroelectric generating unit, JOURNAL OF VIBRATION AND SHOCK, 34(23), 177-181, 201 (2015)
6. VALIAN E, MOHANNA S, TAVAKOLI S, Improved cuckoo search algorithm for feedforward neural network training, Int J Artif Intell Appl, 2(3) , 36-43 (2011)
7. Sadollah A, Bahreininejad A, Eskandar H, Mine blast algorithm: A new population based algorithm for solving constrained engineering optimization problems, Applied Soft Computing, 13(5), 2592-2612 (2013)
8. Thang Trung Nguyen, Dieu Ngoc Vo, Bach Hoang Dinh, Cuckoo search algorithm for combined heat and power economic dispatch, Electrical Power and Energy Systems, (81), 204-214 (2016)
9. SHEN Mingke, HUANG Zhenyu, WANG Zhihua, et al, Prediction of coal ash deformation temperature based on Cuckoo Search and BP Neural Network, Journal of Fuel Chemistry and Technology, 42(12), 1423-1430 (2014)
10. Lü Fu, LIANG Bing, SUN Weiji, et al, Gas emission quantity prediction of working face based on principal component regression analysis method, Journal of China Coal Society, 37(1), 113-116 (2012)

The Production Measurement Model of Open Pit Mine Based on Truck Operation Diagram

Xiao-Yu SUN, Xiao KONG and Wei-Guo ZHANG

School of Resources & Civil Engineering, Northeastern University, Shenyang 110819, China

Abstract: Conventional production measurement of truck dispatching system in open pit mine has not been effectively expressed by a mathematical model, whichbrings a negative effect on the subsequent data mining and a compatibility issue to apply the production measurement with fixed assignment of truck. In this study, based on the proposed concept that truck is not only the carrier of transport material, but also act as the bridges and linkages between the loadingsites and the unloading sites, a new truck operation diagram was established, which was further developed to a basic data matrix and a production measurement model. The new model allowed to calculatethe production measurement of the transport, loading, unloading, material and etc, respectively, as well as with any calculation in combination of more than one factor as needed.It solved the compatibility issue between conventional production measurement and the production measurement of fixed assignment of truck with good practical results.

1 Introduction

The production process of an open pit mine is mainly completed by both mining and transporting equipment. With the continuous development of equipment size, mechanization, and automation [1], it is more and more important for the equipment to be automated in production measurement, scientific assessment and highly efficient in management[2].

Traditionally, manual production organization of open pit mine uses fixed assignment of truck, that is, each truck fixed on one loading site and one unloading site. Only can we know the production output of each truck, the production output of each loading and unloading site can be calculated. At the same time, the distance between the two sites is a fixed value, therefore, it is very easy to calculate the distance and the ton-kilometre. The production measurement mainly counts output and distance, which is for calculating contracted unit and drivers' payment.

However, automatic dispatching system assigns truck in an optimized and random way, the fixed relationship between truck loading site and unloading site is no longer existed. Therefore, a logic conventional measurement processing is developed as follows[3]:

(1) First of all, equipment status can be recognized according to the mining - transportation - unloading process, and the key information is to determine both loading and unloading sites of a truck;

(2)Also, with the determined loading and unloading sites, production and transportation distance data can be generated and stored under the categories of trucks, loading sites, unloading sites and materials, and ultimately the generated data forms the database by taking "shift" as the unit;

(3) Finally, based on the shift database, daily production, monthly production statistics can be further completed.

However, the main problems of this approach is:

(1) It is not compatible to the traditional fixed assignment of truck.

(2) The process is complex, and has not been effectively expressed by a mathematical model.

(3) Calculation results were independently stored by trucks, loading sites, unloading sites and materials with no indication of the relationship of mining - transportation - unloading, such information plays a significant role for the analysis of the production process and mining production potential[4-6]. For example, when problem occurs, the only way for back tracing of a measurement is to use the trajectory playback mode, such as indicated in Figure 1, which has poor visualization and time consuming.

2 General idea

The operation process of a single truck is a repeated process from first loading →first unloading→ second loading→ second unloading→...→n-th loading →n-th unloading. Although automatic dispatching system does not have the fixed loading and unloading sites as in the fixed assignment of truck, but for every delivery, the corresponding loading and unloading sites are still existing and unique. That is to say, for fixed assignment, every truck has the corresponding loading and unloading sites, and for automatic dispatching system, the production of each delivery have corresponding sites for loading and unloading. Therefore, in both cases, the logic that truck is the material carrier and the link to connect the two sites remains the same. Since fixed assignment can calculate the product of loading and unloading sites from the data of trucks' production, then the same rational should be also apply for the optimized and random assignment if the problem of measuring trucks can be solved. In addition, the solution can be used to deal with the mining, unloading, materials measurement problems.

So, this paper put forward the concept of truck operation diagram, which is shown in Figure 2,wherethe X axis represents time and the Y axis represents loading and unloading sites; and, the solid lines indicates that truck is heavy, and the dash lines indicates truck is empty. Also, different colours represent different materials as the condition may apply. Through the graph, it is very clear to see the number of deliveries have been made by a truck, and the type of material and the locations of load and unload of each time truck transportation.

From Figure 2, the corresponding data structure can be built, and the inter-conversion between the data structure and the diagram can be performed. And then, through the model, it can be easily used to calculate the production of loading sites, unloading sites, delivery trucks and conveyed materials. And, the model also provides the flexibility for combination calculations. However, it is noted that the model lacks the required information of distance to calculate mileage and ton-kilometre. Therefore, for the convenience of application, we use the approach of cumulating the loading and unloading site mileage.

3 Measurement Model

3.1 Basic Data Matrix

Suppose that the following 4 sets: loading site (shovel) set S, unloading sites set U, material set M, trucks set C.

For a single truck c in C, the number of completed truck is n_c. $n_c \times 8$ matrix is established as follows:

$$A_c = \begin{bmatrix} a^c_{1,1}, a^c_{1,2}, \dots, a^c_{1,8} \\ a^c_{2,1}, a^c_{2,2}, \dots, a^c_{2,8} \\ \dots \\ a^c_{n_c,1}, a^c_{n_c,2}, \dots, a^c_{n_c,8} \end{bmatrix} \quad (1)$$

1-3 column $a^c_{i,1}, a^c_{i,2}, a^c_{i,3}$: the i-th loading information of truck c, respectively is the loading site index, loading time and the truck accumulated running mileage. $a^c_{i,1} \in S(i = 1, \dots, n_c)$.

4-6 column $a^c_{i,4}, a^c_{i,5}, a^c_{i,6}$: the i-th time unloading information of truck c, respectively is unloading site index, unloading time, trucks accumulated running mileage, $a^c_{i,4} \in U(i = 1, \dots, n_c)$.

7 column $a^c_{i,7}$: The i-th transport materials of truck c.

8 column $a^c_{i,8}$: The i-th transport weight or volume of truck c.

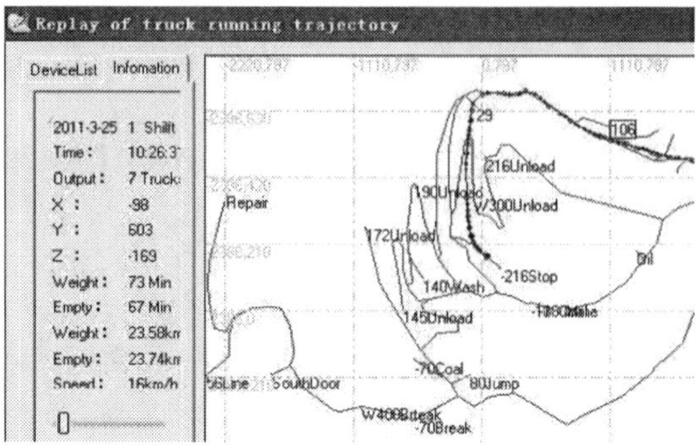

Figure1.Replay of truck running trajectory

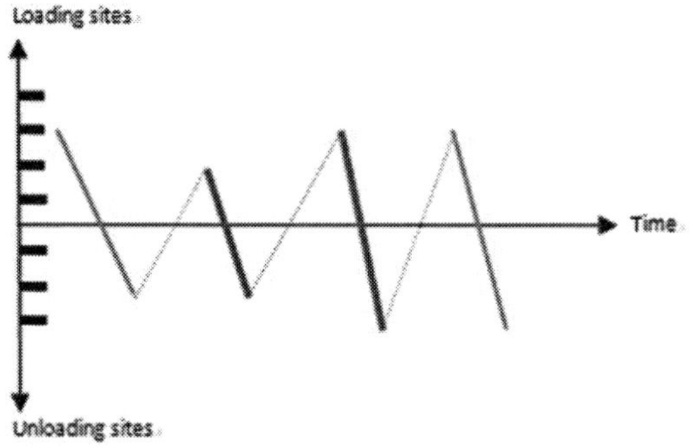

Figure2. Truck operation diagram

3.2 Calculation column vector

The matrix has recorded each truck's transport loading site, unloading site, transport material, loading time and unloading time, the cumulative running mileage of arriving at the loading site and unloading site. Based on it, through defining the following five different n_c dimensional column vector [7, 8], so that a variety of production calculation can be obtained.

(1) n_c dimensional column vector of truck c loading at shovel s:

$$\vec{V}_{c,s} = [v_i^{c,s}]_{n_c} \quad (2)$$

Its elements are as follows:

$$v_i^{c,s} = \begin{cases} 1, a^c_{i,1} = s \\ 0, others \end{cases}$$

(2) n_c dimensional column vector of truck c unloading at unload site u:

$$\vec{V}_{c,u} = [v_i^{c,u}]_{n_c} \quad (3)$$

Its elements are as follows:

 DOI: 10.1051/itmconf/20160709007

$$v_i^{c,u} = \begin{cases} 1, a_{i,4}^c = u \\ 0, others \end{cases}$$

(3) nc dimensional column vector of truck c transporting material m:

$$\vec{\mathbf{V}}_{c,m} = [v_i^{c,m}]_{n_c} \quad (4)$$

Its elements are as follows:

$$v_i^{c,m} = \begin{cases} 1, a_{i,7}^c = m \\ 0, others \end{cases}$$

(4) nc dimensional 1 column vector:

$$\vec{1} = \begin{bmatrix} 1 \\ \cdots \\ 1 \end{bmatrix}_{n_c} \quad (5)$$

This column vector is used to aggregate production and mileage.

(5) Ac matrix extract j-th column to be n_c dimensional column vector:

$$\vec{\mathrm{A}}_j^c = \begin{bmatrix} a_{1,j}^c \\ a_{2,j}^c \\ \cdots \\ a_{n_c,j}^c \end{bmatrix}, j=1,2,\ldots,8. \quad (6)$$

This column vector is used to extract 3-rd,6-th, 8-th,which can be used to calculate mileage, production, ton-kilometre.

3.3 Calculation Method

This paper includes transportnumber of truck, production (m^3 or t), and mileage (km), to prevent such ambiguity, defined as follows:

Definition 1: truck running ton kilometre= ∑truck single volume × heavy transport mileage.

Definition 2: average distance = truck heavy transport mileage ÷ heavy truck number, according to the truck, shovel, unloading site, the material alone or in combination calculation. Such as material m(mM) average distance is the average distance of all the transport material truck, similarly known the meaning of shovel and the unloading site.

3.3.1 General Calculation

The loading number of truck c in shovel s:

$$n_c^s = \vec{1}^{\mathrm{T}} \vec{\mathrm{V}}_{c,s} \quad (7)$$

The unloading number of truck c in unloads site u:

$$n_c^u = \vec{1}^{\mathrm{T}} \vec{\mathrm{V}}_{c,u} \quad (8)$$

The number of truck c transporting materiel m:

$$n_c^m = \vec{1}^{\mathrm{T}} \vec{\mathrm{V}}_{c,m} \quad (9)$$

The loading quantity of truck c in shovel s:

$$G_c^s = [\vec{\mathrm{A}}_8^c]^{\mathrm{T}} \vec{\mathrm{V}}_{c,s} \quad (10)$$

The unloading quantity of truck c in unloads site u:

$$G_c^u = [\vec{\mathrm{A}}_8^c]^{\mathrm{T}} \vec{\mathrm{V}}_{c,u} \quad (11)$$

The quantity of truck c transporting materiel m:

$$G_c^m = [\vec{\mathrm{A}}_8^c]^{\mathrm{T}} \vec{\mathrm{V}}_{c,m} \quad (12)$$

3.3.2 Truck Calculation

The transport number of truck c:n_c

The transport quantity of truck c:

$$G_c = \vec{1}^{\mathrm{T}} \vec{\mathrm{A}}_8^c \quad (13)$$

The transport ton kilometre of truck c:

$$W_c = [\vec{\mathrm{A}}_8^c]^{\mathrm{T}} (\vec{\mathrm{A}}_6^c - \vec{\mathrm{A}}_3^c) \quad (14)$$

Truck heavy transport mileage:

$$D_c^{full} = \vec{1}^{\mathrm{T}} (\vec{\mathrm{A}}_6^c - \vec{\mathrm{A}}_3^c) \quad (15)$$

The total transport mileage of truck:

$$D_c^{total} = A_{n_c,6} - A_{1,3} \quad (16)$$

The empty transport mileage:

$$D_c^{empty} = D_c^{total} - D_c^{full} \quad (17)$$

The average transport distance of truck c:

$$d_c = D_c^{full} / n_c \quad (18)$$

The reason that the total mileage was calculated first and then the empty mileage is that not only the total mileage is easy to calculate, but also in order to unify the calculation with matrix. In addition, it was to ensure that the model has a strong versatility, practicality and can be extension for future use. Otherwise, the empty mileage calculation requires an additional model and algorithm.

3.3.3 Shovel Calculation

According to type (7), (10) and definition 2, three types can be getting as follows:

The loading number of shovel s:

$$n_s = \sum_{c\in C} n_c^s = \sum_{c\in C} \vec{1}^T \vec{V}_{c,s} \tag{19}$$

The loading quantity of shovel s:

$$G_s = \sum_{c\in C} G_c^s = \sum_{c\in C} [\vec{A}_8^c]^T \vec{V}_{c,s} \tag{20}$$

The average transport distance of shovel s:

$$d_s = \frac{1}{n_s} \sum_{c\in C} (\vec{A}_6^c - \vec{A}_3^c)^T \vec{V}_{c,s} \tag{21}$$

3.3.4 Unloading Site Calculation

According to type (8), (11) and definition 2, three types can be get as follows:

The unloading number of unloading site u:

$$n_u = \sum_{c\in C} n_c^u = \sum_{c\in C} \vec{1}^T \vec{V}_{c,u} \tag{22}$$

The unloading quantity of unloading site u:

$$G_u = \sum_{c\in C} G_c^u = \sum_{c\in C} [\vec{A}_8^c]^T \vec{V}_{c,u} \tag{23}$$

The average transport distance of unloading site u:

$$d_u = \frac{1}{n_u} \sum_{c\in C} (\vec{A}_6^c - \vec{A}_3^c)^T \vec{V}_{c,u} \tag{24}$$

3.3.5 Material Calculation

According to type (9), (12) and definition 2, three types can be getting as follows:

The number of material m:

$$n_m = \sum_{c\in C} n_c^m = \sum_{c\in C} \vec{1}^T \vec{V}_{c,m} \tag{25}$$

The quantity of material m:

$$G_m = \sum_{c\in C} G_c^m = \sum_{c\in C} [\vec{A}_8^c]^T \vec{V}_{c,m} \tag{26}$$

The average transport distance of material m:

$$d_m = \frac{1}{n_m} \sum_{c\in C} (\vec{A}_6^c - \vec{A}_3^c)^T \vec{V}_{c,m} \tag{27}$$

3.3.6 Combination Calculation

Based on $\vec{V}_{c,s}$, $\vec{V}_{c,u}$, $\vec{V}_{c,m}$, we can derive other column vectors forconducting combination calculations in a flexible way, such as the average distance between loading and unloading sites, summary of different loading materials of loading sites and unloading sites,the details of material transportation between the loading and the unloading site and so on. For example, the calculation of loading and unloading transport distance as follow:

According to $\vec{V}_{c,s}$, $\vec{V}_{c,u}$,n_c dimensional vectors are defined as follows:

$$\vec{V}_{c,s,u} = [v_i^{c,s,u}]_{n_c} \tag{28}$$

Its elements are as follows:

$$v_i^{c,s,u} = v_i^{c,s} \times v_i^{c,u} \tag{29}$$

The average transport distance of loading s and unloading u

$$d_{s,u} = \frac{\sum_{c\in C} (\vec{A}_6^c - \vec{A}_3^c)^T \vec{V}_{c,s,u}}{\sum_{c\in C} \vec{1}^T \vec{V}_{c,s,u}} \tag{30}$$

4 Application and discussion

According to this model, the corresponding measurement procedure is programmed through VB embedded MatrixVB way [9, 10]. Some measurement results of the actual application in an open pit mine are shown in Figure 3 to figure 6.

Discussion as follows:

(1) The fixed assignment of truck is a special case of this method.For any truck c in C, the loading and unloading sites are fixed, so all $a_{i,1}^c$ (i = 1,2,..., n_c) in (1) are same, as well as $a_{i,4}^c$ (i = 1,2,..., n_c). Therefore, this method is fully compatible with the measurement method of fixed assignment of truck.

(2) Equations insection 2.3.2, 2.3.3, 2.3.4, 2.3.5 are derived for the calculations based on trucks, loading site, unloading site and material, which is the main component in conventional measurement method. Therefore, this method can easily export conventional econometric results. However, the conventional method cannot perform any combination calculation as indicated in section 2.3.6. Therefore, this method is fully compatible with conventional measurement methods of random assignment of truck.

(3) Usually, a load distance is represented by the distance between the loading and unloading site. In order to correspond to the base matrix data structure, the total running mileage of loading site and unloading site were used to represent load distance, that is $a_{i,3}^c$, $a_{i,6}^c$ in (1), in this paper. This approach has the following advantages:

- it can easily derive load distance between loading and unloading site;
- subtraction can be used for calculation distance of any period of time, without piecewise summation;
- it can be checked with the odometer by the driver;
- it can be used to trace the mileage for equipment maintenance purpose.

(4) Conventional methods storage measurement results of trucks, shovels, unload site, material independently, which does not reflect the relationships between each other. The matrix can be more effectively reflect the relationships between loading, transportation and unloading, and it is easy to derive independent measurement results.

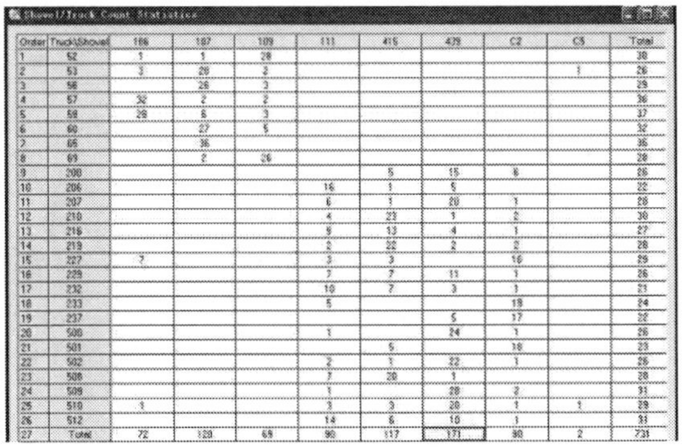

Order	Truck\Shovel	106	107	109	111	415	439	C2	C5	Total
1	52	1	1	28						30
2	53	3	20	2					1	26
3	56		26	3						29
4	57	32	2	2						36
5	58	28	6	3						37
6	60		27	5						32
7	65		36							36
8	69		2	26						28
9	200					5	15	6		26
10	206				16	1	5			22
11	207				6	1	20	1		28
12	210				4	23	1	2		30
13	216				9	13	4	1		27
14	219				2	22	2	2		28
15	227	7			3	3		16		29
16	229				7	7	11	1		26
17	232				10	7	3	1		21
18	233				5			19		24
19	237						5	17		22
20	500				1		24	1		26
21	501					5		18		23
22	502				2	1	22	1		26
23	508				7	20	1			28
24	509				1		28	2		31
25	510	1			3	3	20	1	1	29
26	512				14	6	10	1		31
27	Total	72	120	69	90	117	171	90	2	731

Figure 3.Comparison of Shovel-Truck loading results

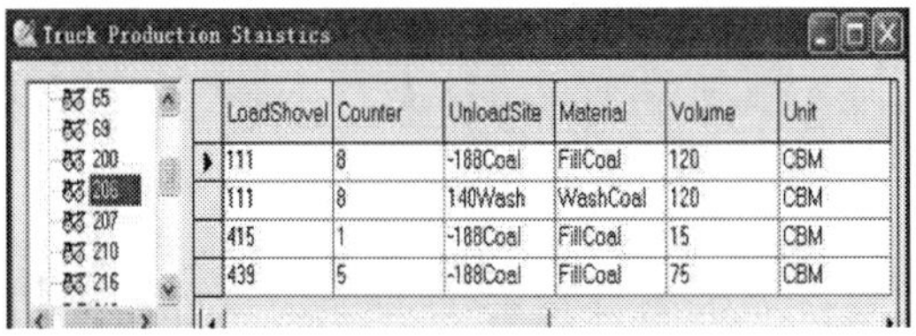

LoadShovel	Counter	UnloadSite	Material	Volume	Unit
111	8	-188Coal	FillCoal	120	CBM
111	8	140Wash	WashCoal	120	CBM
415	1	-188Coal	FillCoal	15	CBM
439	5	-188Coal	FillCoal	75	CBM

Figure4.Summary of No. 206 truck production output

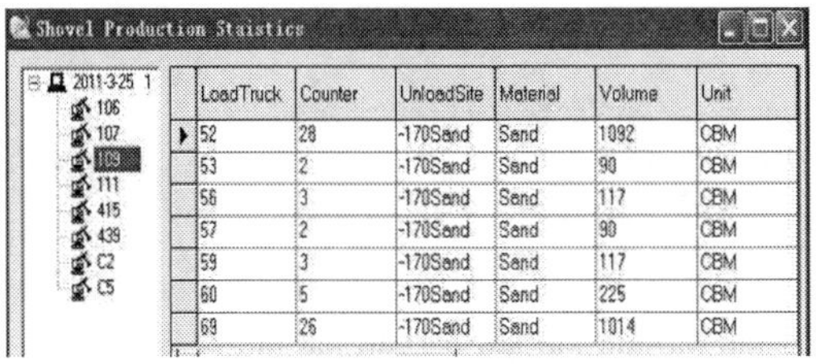

LoadTruck	Counter	UnloadSite	Material	Volume	Unit
52	28	-170Sand	Sand	1092	CBM
53	2	-170Sand	Sand	90	CBM
56	3	-170Sand	Sand	117	CBM
57	2	-170Sand	Sand	90	CBM
59	3	-170Sand	Sand	117	CBM
60	5	-170Sand	Sand	225	CBM
69	26	-170Sand	Sand	1014	CBM

Figure5.Summary of No. 109 shovel production output

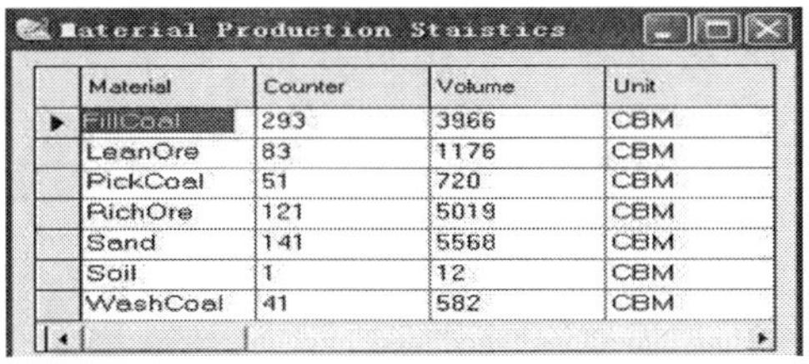

Material	Counter	Volume	Unit
FillCoal	293	3966	CBM
LeanOre	83	1176	CBM
PickCoal	51	720	CBM
RichOre	121	5019	CBM
Sand	141	5568	CBM
Soil	1	12	CBM
WashCoal	41	582	CBM

Figure6.Summary of material production

5 Conclusion

This paper developed a mathematical model and data structure based on the proposed the truck operation diagram in open pit mine. The model was proven compatible with production measurement methods for both fixed assignment and conventional random assignment of truck. The data structure was used to calculate production measurement of loading, transportation, unloading and materials, respectively and in combinations with more than one factor. The model also showed better versatility, practicality and potential for expansion, which is significant for analysing production process and mining production potential.

References

1. M. B. Khorzoughi, R. Hall, Int. J. Min. Reclam. Env, **29**, 380(2015)
2. D. K.Ahangaran, A B Yasrebi, A Wetherelt, P. Foste,Arch. Min. Sci, **57**, 39(2012)
3. X. M. Zheng, Y. F. Qiao, Metal Mine, **11**,103(2008).
4. Q. H. Gu, C. W. Lu, S. G. Jing,Journal of Mines, Metals and F, **63**, 126(2015)
5. S. Alarie, M. Gamache,Int J Surf Min Reclamat Enviro, **16**,59(2002)
6. X. Y. Sun, Y. T. Yu, X. T. Wang, Z. Y. Yang, C. Y. Chen,Mining Engineering, **3**,41(2005)
7. G.Strang,Linear algebra and its applications(Thomson Learning Inc, 2007)
8. L. F. Liu,Linear algebra(Northeastern University press, Shenyang, 2014)
9. Microsoft Corporation,Microsoft visual basic .Net language reference (Microsoft Press,2008)
10. Bradley, J. Case, Programming in visual basic, version 6.0(McGraw-Hill/Irwin, Boston, 2002)

Research on Structural Stress Optical Fiber Testing Technology Based on Brillouin Scattering

Xian-Jin WANG[a], Qing LI[b] and Shuai WAN

College of Mechanical and Electrical Engineering, China Jiliang University,HangZhou, ZheJiang, China
[a]wangxianjin028@126.com, [b]lq13306532957@163.com

Abstract. In this paper, the principle of distributed optical fiber measurement and measurement of axial stress is introduced by analyzing the principle of Brillouin scattering in an optical fiber with a certain power. Making the experimental device, measuring the individual strain model, analyzing the wave shape of the scattered wave, and preliminary understanding of the image characteristics of the stress in the optical fiber Brillouin scattering spectrum. The effect of stress on the different position of the fiber, and the difference between them and the scattering waveform obtained from the stress free action poetry are compared, and the effect of the light pulse on the optical fiber transmission is studied. The results show that the effect of the stress is different in the position of the action, and the effect of the propagation of the pulse light is mainly affected by the Stokes and anti Stokes light scattering. The research can provide reference for distributed optical fiber measurement, and it can promote the application of distributed optical fiber in measuring micro deformation. The innovative point of this study is to use the pulley method to solve the effect of the different position of the same stress in the distribution of optical fiber.

1 Guidelines

The propagation of optical fiber in the optical fiber, because the fiber is a non crystalline material, the uneven structure in the micro space, so there is a small amount of scattering phenomenon. Brillouin scattering is the scattering of light waves propagating in the optical fiber, which is generated by the interaction between the light wave and the sound wave.

Large hoisting equipment is very common in industrial equipment, with China's rapid urbanization, large heavy equipment in industrial production everywhere, heavy lifting equipments take heavy beams by stress and strain is not intuitive performance, so frequent over expression of construction will be to the naked eye is difficult to observe the damage created by force, local regions of relatively large deformation, causing potential safety hazard. These deformation can be observed through the strain of the small changes in the micro stress, so as to achieve the purpose of prevention. The distributed observation of the deformation stress can be realized by the Brillouin scattering effect of the optical fiber in the optical fiber.

2 Distributed Optical Fiber Sensing Technology Based on Brillouin Scattering

2.1 Distributed Optical Fiber Sensing Technology Based on Brillouin Optical Time Domain Reflection Analyzer

BOTDA technique is a kind of optical time domain analysis technique based on stimulated Brillouin scattering. Implantation certain frequency f of the optical pulse signal at one end of the single-mode fiber. At the other end of the injection frequency f is the center of the fluctuation f_B continuous probe, in the two beams of light to meet the position changes of stimulated Brillouin scattering, $f + f_B$ frequency continuous probe in this position will provide gain or attenuation, thus all the places in the entire length of the fiber optical power transformation can be detected in the time domain. So as to realize the measurement of environmental variables of distributed optical fiber. The basic principle is shown in Figure 1:

DOI: 10.1051/itmconf/20160709008

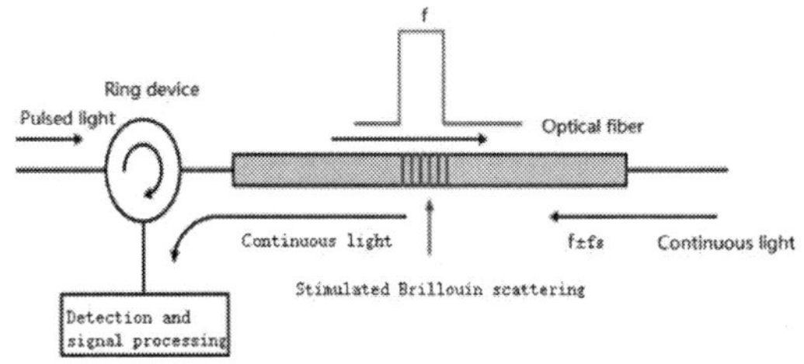

Figure 1. The technology principle of Brillouin optical time-domain analysis

2.2 The Relationship between the Frequency of Brillouin Scattering and Axial Strain

According to the optical signal of Brillouin frequency shift and linear relationship between the optical fiber temperature and axial strain, fiber optic strain variation in temperature compensation (or strain compensation) conditions (or temperature) by the formula (1) said:

$\Delta V_B = C_{vt}\Delta t + C_{v\varepsilon}\Delta\varepsilon$ (1)

Type, ΔV_B as the Brillouin frequency shift, the Cvt for Brillouin frequency shift temperature coefficient, Cvε as a Brillouin frequency shift to strain coefficient, Δt is the change of temperature, Δεis the change of strain variation. In this experiment we ignore the effect of temperature on the Brillouin frequency shift (assuming constant temperature), which is that temperature does not change or change range is very small, so the Brillouin frequency shift and stress there is a clear linear relationship.

3 Design and Construction of Experimental Platform

3.1 Design and Fabrication of Experimental Device

The experimental device is designed as a pipeline structure, which is distributed to a single mode optical fiber, and makes the stress distribution model. The frequency shift pattern of the Brillouin scattering wave is measured by the BOTDA equipment. Experimental pipeline section size is 0.6m external diameter is 0.7m, the length is 7m, at the bottom of the conjoined tripod overall to the in the distance from the center of the total length of 6m to prop up, and in the center of the device to add pipeline strain is applied on the part and support part can be fixed screw, when the strain at the middle, both ends of the free will not move. On one side of the pipe to take way of grinding to make it a smooth surface, easy laying optical fiber, after the completion of the layout, in order to make the strain effect reaches the maximum, here we put fiber on the applied strain device on the side, namely the whole fiber layout part in the cross section of the pipeline from the ground at the lowest point. In the pipeline, the distance between each part of the tag is put up to facilitate the analysis of the frequency shift between the distance and the Brillouin scattering. After the completion of the production of the overall device as shown in figure 2.

Figure 2. Integral device complete graph

3.2 Experimental Instruments and Related Parameters Setting

The instrument used in this experiment is a distributed optical fiber temperature and strain monitoring system DiTeST STA-R. The instrument is in the XP Windows system under the data acquisition and analysis instrument, after opening the instrument, in the parameter adjustment zone as shown in the following table 1 Parameters of the setting, after the completion of the setting can be started.

Table 1. Ditest Sta-R Device Parameter Setting

Instrument parameters	Set value
spatial resolution	0.5(m)
Sampling distance	0.1(m)
Start frequency	automatic detection
Sensing optical fiber length	automatic detection

3.3 Study on the influence of Brillouin scattering frequency shift

3.3.1 Effect of Different Axial Stresses on Frequency Shift

Because the bare fiber is easy to break, so in this experiment we take is with two movable pulley can move the optical fiber fixing way, as shown in Figure 3, 1, 4 lines coincide, and in the graph at the left end of the fixed 1, line 4, the right end of the dynamic fixed pulley, and the left end of the movable pulley moves to the right position, observe the Brillouin frequency shift and the free section (fixed in the pipeline not stress fiber), getting the frequency change as shown:

DOI: 10.1051/itmconf/20160709008

Figure 3. Bonding arrangement of fiber on steel pipe

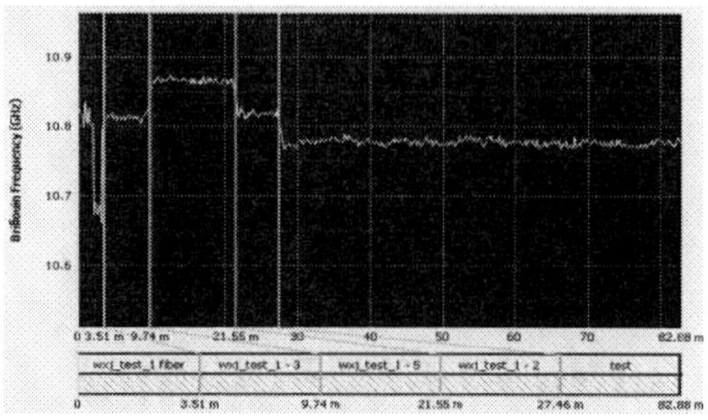

Figure 4. Map distance distribution of Brillouin frequency space

We can see from Figure 4 (27.46-82.88m) of the free end of the Brillouin frequency is 10.78GHz, relative to the free section can be seen in the section we applied axial stress (3.51-27.46m) have different degrees of freedom with respect to the frequency of the mobile terminal, wherein the 0-3.51m is pulse light emission opening to start jumper cable length between fixed ends of BOTDA instrument 3.51-9.74m, No. 1 fiber frequency fixed, 9.74-21.55m is 2, 3 fiber frequency state left movable sheave connected, 21.55-27.46 4 fiber frequency fixed state, we can see from Figure 2, 3, 1, 4, relative to the optical fiber optical fiber has a significantly different frequency mobile, this is because we have 1, 2 of the left and right pulley is fixed, when we move the left wheel, right around the fiber due to friction pulley existence, guide To the 1, 4 and 2, 3 optical fiber has significantly different frequency shift, in order to verify the conclusion, from the new design of a test pulley friction between the 1, 4, 2, 3, and the frequency difference between the fiber.

3.3.2 The Effect of Friction Force on the Experimental Results of Pulley

In the last experiment based, continue to shift left the pulley on the left, and the No. 2 fiber toward the direction of fiber 1 slightly manual marathon relaxed a little and let the free recovery, fiber optic frequency as shown in Figure 5 below:

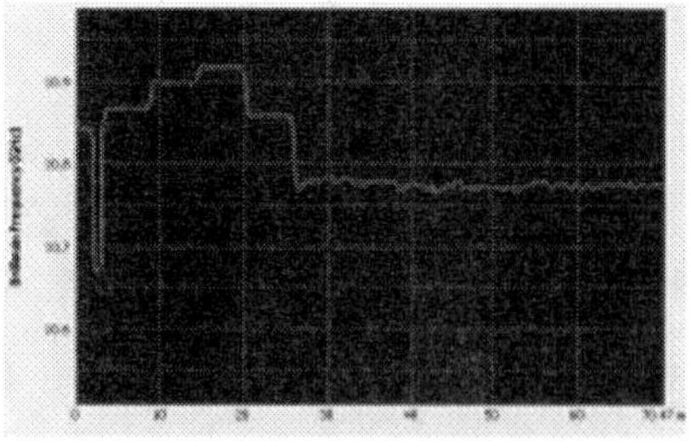

Figure 5. Effect of friction between the pulley of Brillouin frequency shift

As shown in the figure, the total length of the optical fiber to 70.47. This is because in the experimental process, fiber breaking a, from the new layout of the fiber, the length of the measurement of the fracture part for 12.2m, combined with optical fiber fusion intercepted length is about 0.2m and so reduce length is 12.4, combined with 82.88-70.47=12.41m. Therefore on Brillouin scattering measurement of fiber length accuracy is very high. Analysis diagram of intermediate frequency shift size we can see 3 optical frequency shift relative to the 1, 2, 4, theory on 1, 2, 3, 4 optical frequency shift should is the same, but due to the existence of the friction between the pulley around, resulting in stress on 1, 2, 3, 4 fiber on is force varies is the result of the above results.

3.3.3 Frequency Shift Effect of Different Stresses

Thereafter from the newly laid optical fiber, and constantly increase the stress at the center, the application of stress devices such as the following figure 6:

Figure 6. The middle of the pipeline booster

The different stress frequency shift images are obtained as shown in figure 7:

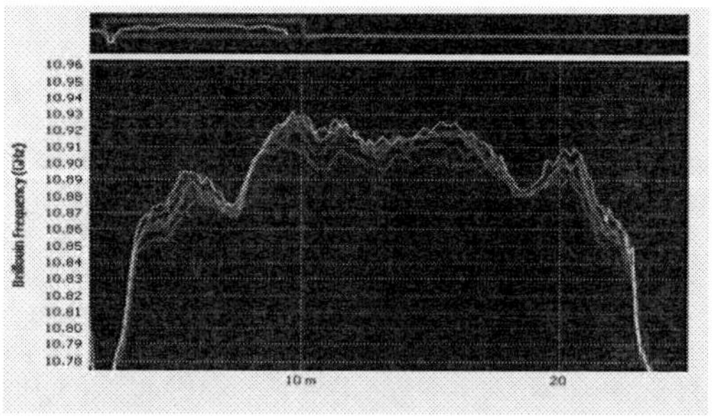

Figure 7. Different Brillouin frequency state corresponding to the stress gradient

Figure from brown to white frequency curve are never should be the initial state of the force to the maximum stress of 5 should be gradient force corresponding to the frequency, can be roughly seen with the increase of stress, the frequency corresponding move and by the graph we can see and 1, 4 optical fiber is directly connected on the right side of the pulley is basically no frequency shift of

 DOI: 10.1051/itmconf/20160709008

(figure around 8.5m and 18.5 m or so), but the pulley on the left junction has a frequency shift (12m), where speculation is different on both sides of the pulley friction, leading to the pulley on the left than the right side pulley frequency shift occurred.

The maximum frequency shift and non stress time frequency shift can be obtained frequency shift effect chart, as follows

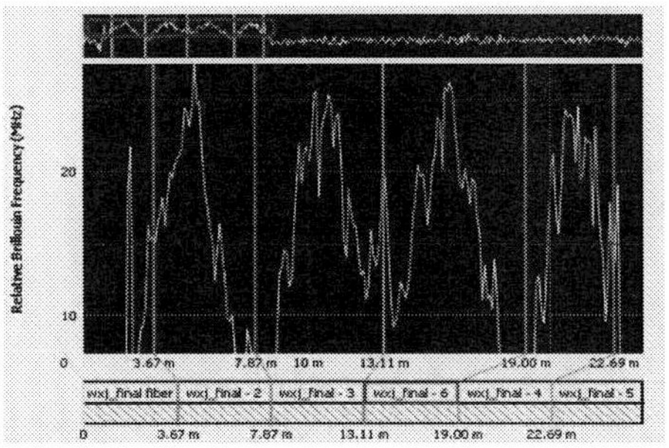

Figure 8. Comparison between different stress gradients

From the figure we can seen in our design of pulley fiber this experiment, 1, 2, 3, 4 fiber in the center position of the tube have taken place in the frequency shift, and in both sides of the maximum stress decreasing, size and frequency shift is basically the same, can draw Brillouin frequency shift depends on the initial state of the state of optical fiber has nothing to do, and by force is proportional to the and the maximum should force near presenting reduced state. The average length of fiber bonding is(22.69-3.67) /4=4.755m, combined with the frequency shift of the 4 sections of the state, you can see that the frequency of each section of the gradient of nearly 5 gradient, so that its spatial resolution is 4.755/5, nearly 1m.

4 Conclusion

Through the experiment to verify the distributed optical fiber measurement of axial stress of Brillouin scattering frequency shift effect, provides the theoretical support for the distributed optical fiber Chang'an Technology in engineering application, and take this as the basis for quantitative analysis of the frequency shift and should be the relationship between the force, and explore the distributed optical fiber sensing technology of maximum spatial resolution and sensing accuracy.Compared with the traditional optical fiber layout and pulley arrangement can intuitively find Brillouin frequency shift is obviously position, so as to achieve the best experimental results.

References

1. Zhang Chun shu, Bao Xiao yi, Ozkan Istemi F, et al. Prediction of thepipe buckling by using broadening factor with distributed Brillouin fiber sensors[J]. Optical Fiber Technology, 2008, 14(2): 109-113
2. Yi Liqi, Qian Caifu,Ding Keqin.A method for calculating deformation of long-distance pipleline based on strain. Advanced Materials Reasearch.(EI)2011,vols.291-294:3385-3390
3. Yi Liqi,Qian Caifu,Ding Keqin,Qiao Song.A method for detecting deformation of pipleline based on distributed fiber optic strain sensor. Advanced Materials Reasearch. (EI) 2011, vols. 301-303:1574-1577
4. Bao Xiao-yi, MERCHANT M De, BROWN A,et.al. Tensile and compressive strain measurement in the lab and field with the distributed Brillouin scattering sensor[J].Journal of Lightwave Technology, 2001, 19(11):1698-1704
5. Zhang C, Bao X, Ozkan I F, et al. Prediction of the pipe buckling by using broadening factor with distributed Brillouin fiber sensors[J]. Optical Fiber Technology, 2008, 14(2): 109-113

DOI: 10.1051/itmconf/20160709009

Research on Computer Integrated Manufacturing of Sheet Metal Parts for Lithium Battery

Wei-Min PAN[1, a], Guo-Hua LI[1, b] and Meng-Han LI[1]

[1]*College of Mechanical and electrical engineering, Henan University of Science & Technology, Henan province, China*
Email: [a]Wmpool1@163.com, [b]liguohua311@163.com

Abstract. Lithium battery has been widely used as the main driving force of the new energy vehicle in recent years. Sheet metal parts are formed by means of pressure forming techniques with the characteristics of light weight, small size and high structural strength. The sheet metal forming has higher productivity and material utilization than the mechanical cutting, therefore sheet metal parts are widely used in many fields, such as modern automotive industry, aviation, aerospace, machine tools, instruments and household appliances. In this paper, taking a complex lithium battery box as an example, the integrated manufacturing of sheet metal parts is studied, and the digital integrated design and manufacturing process system is proposed. The technology is studied such as sheet metal design, unfolding, sheet nesting and laser cutting, CNC turret punch stamping programming, CNC bending etc. The feasibility of the method is verified through the examples of products and the integrated manufacturing of sheet metal box is completed.

1 Introduction

With the rapid development of new energy vehicles and electric vehicles, lithium battery has been widely used as the main driving force in recent years. Sheet metal parts are formed by means of pressure forming techniques with the characteristics of light weight, small size and high structural strength. The sheet metal forming has higher productivity and material utilization than the mechanical cutting, therefore sheet metal parts are widely used in many fields, such as modern automotive industry, aviation, aerospace, machine tools, instruments and household appliances. Nowadays the digital integrated manufacturing technology and the computer-aided engineering software have been used to achieve the integration of design and manufacturing in the production of sheet metal parts [1].

In this paper, taking a complex lithium battery box as an example, using UG, Bysoft, and AP100 software, the integrated manufacturing of sheet metal parts is studied, and the digital integrated design and manufacturing process system is proposed. The technology is studied such as sheet metal design, unfolding, sheet nesting and laser cutting, CNC turret punch stamping programming, CNC bending etc. The feasibility of the method is verified through the examples of products.

2 Digital Integrated Manufacturing Process

In modern sheet metal industry, the computer aided design and manufacturing technology have been widely used. The computer-aided design software is used for 2D and 3D design of sheet metal parts. The sheet is machined by punching, molding and other processing methods. The product is finished through weld, renovation, painting and assembly [2].

In the manufacturing process, the computer-aided manufacturing software is utilized for unfolding, nesting, generating NC programs etc. The digital integrated manufacturing process is shown in Figure 1.

3 Sheet Metal Design

With the industrial development, the parametric design and CAD integration technology based on the constraint are paid more and more attention. The so-called parameterization is that the design requirement, principle, method and result are indicated with flexible parameters, the parameter can be changed based on the actual situation in the course of human-computer interaction. The CAD system is that the constraint is used to express the shape characteristics of the product model, the parameters are defined to control the design result, thus the design model can be modified by adjusting the

 DOI: 10.1051/itmconf/20160709009

parameters, and a series of design programs can be easily created similar in shape or feature [3].

In sheet metal design industry, the modelling method and sculpting method are main design method by using CAD. The sculpting method is the most widely used and CAD. The sculpting method is the most widely used and the model method is a traditional method of sheet metal design. The regular surface modeling is used for sheet metal parts with simple structure shape sheet. The surface modeling and solid modeling are used for sheet metal parts with complex structure such as scanning, pulling, spiral, cutting and other functions. In this paper, the sheet metal part is a lithium battery box, and the three-dimensional modeling is completed by using the sheet metal module of UG. The model is shown in Figure 2.

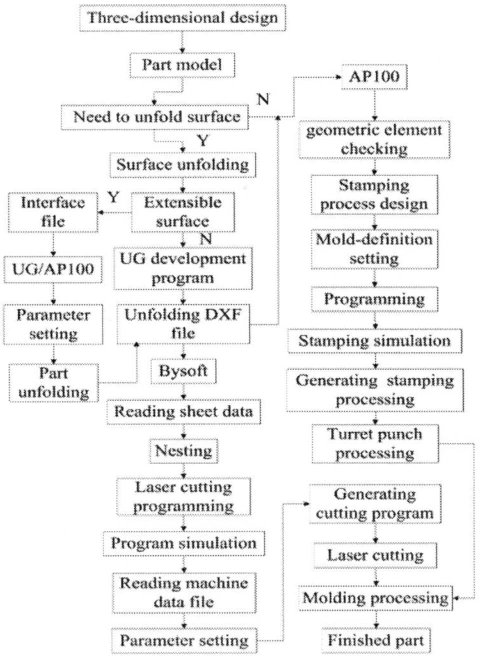

Figure 1. Digital integrated design and manufacturing process.

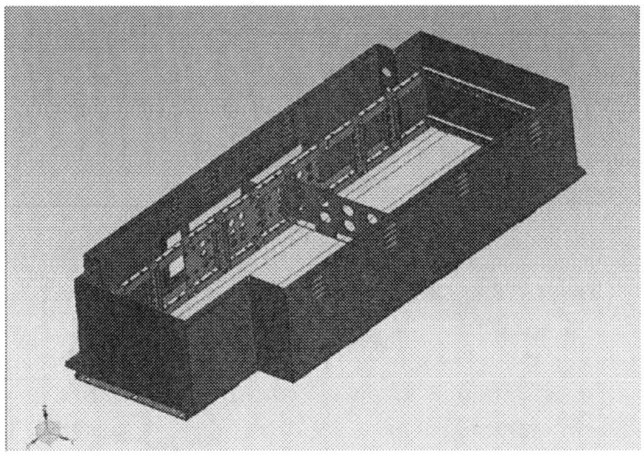

Figure 2. Box model.

4 Sheet Metal Unfolding

Compared with the general machinery part, the sheet metal part has its own characteristics in the structure, material and technology. In modern sheet metal processing, it is very important to design reasonably the basic parameter and manufacturing, and draw accurately the unfolding view [4].

The length of the neutral layer is usually considered as the developed length of sheet metal parts for the developable surface. The unfolded size of the plane is shown in Figure 3.

$$L = \frac{\pi \times (R + KT) \times \theta}{180} \tag{1}$$

Where, L is the developed length; R is the inner bending radius; θ is the bending angle; T is the thickness of the material; K is the factor of neutral layer, $K = t / T$; t is the distance between the inner surface and the neutral plane. It can be seen from Eq.1 that the developed length is determined mainly by the bend angle θ, the neutral layer coefficient K, the material thickness T. Notches or regional block processing are usually carried out at first in unfolding the surface with complex structure or the closed surface. The unfolding of the complex surface is transformed into the unfolding of one or a few relatively simple surfaces.

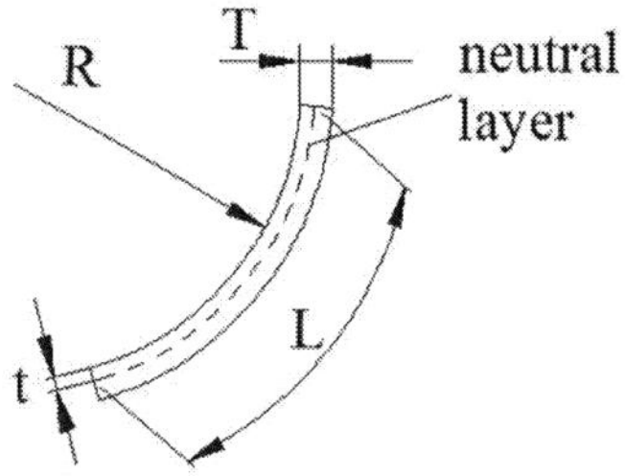

Figure 3. Expanded dimension calculation.

The approximate algorithm is used to unfold the non-developable surface. The surface is divided into many small quadrilateral mesh elements before the unfolding and the mesh elements are converted into the same plane. The developable size is got by adopting approximately numerical methods of equal area and developable algorithms of quadrilateral mesh elements. The file of the unfolded surface is obtained by reconstructing the model at last.

Part a and part b are selected from the box. The three-dimensional graphics and the developable view of part a and part b are shown in Figure 4 and Figure 5, they are unfolded by using the sheet metal module of UG or AP100 software. The maximum developable size of part a is 180.3 mm × 105.3 mm, and the thickness is 1.5 mm; the maximum developable size of part b is 570.1mm × 65.3 mm, and the thickness is1.5mm.

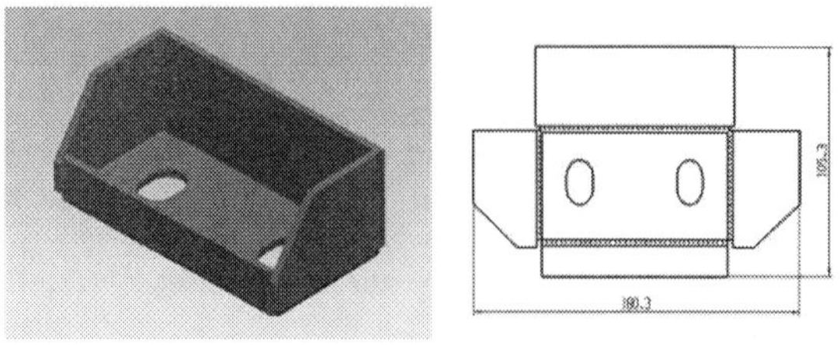

Figure 4. Three-dimensional and unfolded graphics of part a.

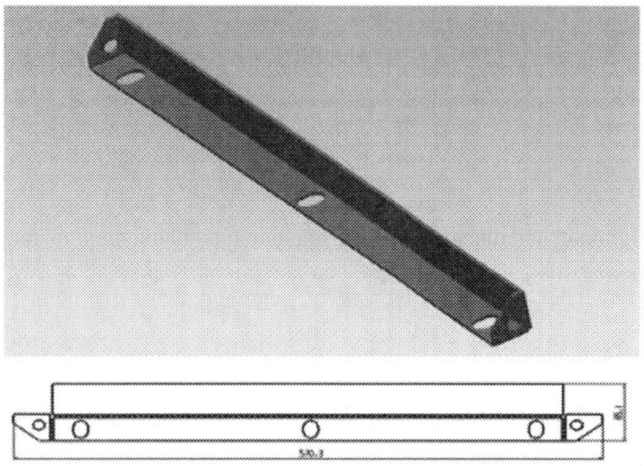

Figure 5. Three-dimensional and unfolded graphics of part b.

5 Sheet Nesting and Cutting

The more variety and less bulk are often required in the sheet metal production. In order to shorten the production cycle and improve the material utilization, the parts with the same material and thickness are generally arranged on the same sheet to machine in one clamping, therefore the problem of optimizing nesting must be solved. The nesting is generally divided into the non-constrained nesting and the constrained nesting. In terms of optimizing nesting, a computer is stronger than manual nesting. The nesting result is rapidly given by the sheet metal software according to the processing condition and the machine parameter in nesting. The user can make some changes on the automatic nesting to meet special production requirement [5].

In modern industrial manufacturing field, the cutting is one basic process with a large amount of application. The modern cutting technology is on the basis of modern computer technology. For different cutting equipments, the traditional cutting technology is improved to develop into the computer-aided cutting production and management software with the technology of nesting optimization, sheet metal unfolding and remaining material database management as the core. The software can be used to improve the comprehensive utilization of the steel and the cutting efficiency and cutting quality [6].

The Swiss Bystronic laser cutting machine is used. The Bysoft software is utilized for nesting and cutting to make full use of the material by using mixed nesting methods with the constraint. The overall dimension of the sheet is 2500mm × 1250 mm, and the thickness is 1.5 mm. Part a and part b will be cut on a plate, and the number of part a is 12, and the number of part b is 8. The angle is not limited in material fiber direction in the cutting, and the distance between the two parts is set independently. The automatical nesting result is shown in Figure 6.

6 CNC punching and bending

CNC punching techniques can be used to automatically punch the shape on the sheet, reduce die wear with a standard mold and get high production efficiency. It is necessary to accurately calculate the punching pressure when punching the plate with a greater thickness and a relatively large hole.

$$F = C \times T \times K \times \tau \times 0.345 \qquad (2)$$

Where, F is the press force, and the unit is *kN*; C is the circumference of the punched hole, and the unit is mm; T is the thickness of the material, and the unit is mm; K is the factor of the material; τ is the shear factor.

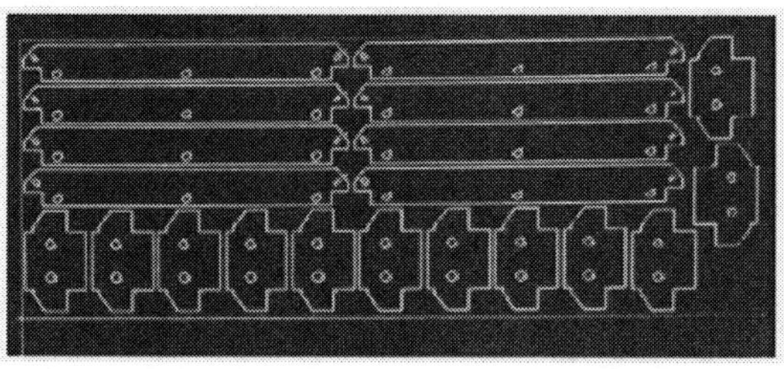

Figure 6. Nesting result.

For the large-diameter round or square holes, if F is greater than the punching pressure of the CNC turret punch, the holes can be completed in many stamping. The principle of procedure concentration should be followed in the stamping, namely the all processible holes and the profile of the part are possibly completed in one clamping to prevent positioning errors from repeating. If the positioning must be repeated, the hole with the position tolerance is completed in one stamping. The molds should be choose with a reasonable order to stamping according to some rules, and the rules are that the round hole is before the square hole, the small hole is before the big hole, the middle before the profile. When designing the stamping process, the rigidity of the work is improved by adding the micro connection between two parts on one sheet to avoid the interference between the part warpage and the movement of the turret and the die [7].

The CNC punching procedure is programmed with AP100 software. The analog processing method is used to check the reliability of the CNC program. In this paper, part a is unfolded to punch with the CNC turret punch and programmed with AP100 software. A part of CNC punching program of part a is shown in figure 7.

```
(PR/XIANG-19)
(MC/AC2510NT)
(MN/ 203)
(TR/AC2510NT)
(MA/SPC-3.0)
(PZ/  178.80X  103.80)
(WK/  3.00T 1200.00X 1000.00)
(CL/  200.00   800.00)
(CS/)
(BP/  15.00X  100.00)
(CM/)
(UT/T220GREXL  30.00YL 5.00 AN 0.00  DC 0.00RL 0.00P I 0)
(UT/T349ASQXL  5.00YL  5.00 AN 0.00  DC 0.00RL 0.00P I  )
(UT/T150BROXL  14.50YL 14.50 AN 0.00 DC 0.00RL 0.00P I  )
(TT/ H  M OS)
(CR/Y2016M 4D28)
G06A3.B0
G92X2500.Y1270.
G93X15.Y100.
G72X148.65Y12.4
G66I7.75J180.P5.T349
G72X140.9Y12.4
G66I12.4J270.P5.
G72X37.9Y0.
G66I12.4J90.P5.
G72X37.9Y12.4
G66I7.75J180.P5.
G72X66.65Y39.4
G69I6.J90.P14.5Q1.8T150
G72X126.65Y45.4
G69I6.J270.P-14.5Q1.8
X161.64Y18.21T220C34.22
X168.63Y22.96
X176.3Y46.9C90.
Y55.4
X164.8Y71.9C0.
X160.9
X143.4Y84.4C90.
```

Figure 7. CNC punching Programming.

The bending method is used most commonly to achieve a specific sheet metal structure. The CNC bending machine can be used to obtain specific sheet metal forming process and realize the bending process precisely and rapidly. The finished box is shown in Figure 8. The box has a relatively regular geometric structure. The internal ribs are used for strengthening the structure; the shutters in both sides are used for cooling; the external welding parts are conducive to moving and fixing. The box body is mainly used in the electric vehicle to install the lithium battery.

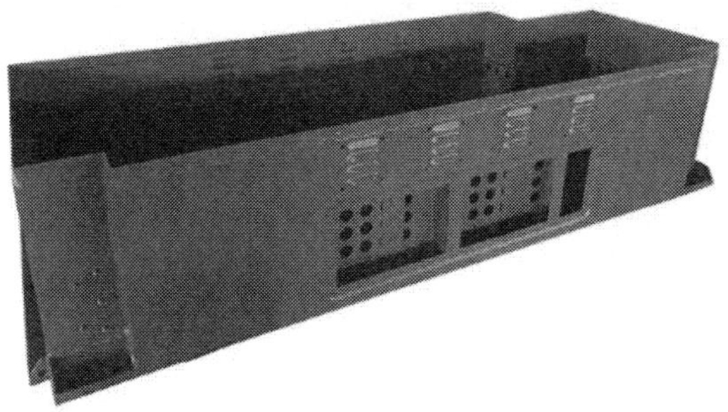

Figure 8. Finished product.

Conclusion

The CAD / CAM technology is used in the sheet metal design and processing. Based on the three-dimensional modeling of sheet metal parts of the lithium battery box, the data in unfolding, nesting, laser cutting, CNC punching and other aspects are shared and the integrated manufacturing is completed. The strong technical support is provided to accelerate the product development, improve the product quality and enhance the market competitiveness for enterprises.

References

1. J.S. Huang, A DFM Oriented Sheet Metal CAD and Its Development (Southeast University, China 2008)
2. J.Z. Xia, Practitioners of Sheet Metal (Mechanical Industry Press, China 2001)
3. X.X. Meng, Y.N. Xu, A Survey of the Research Works on Parametric Design, Journal of Computer-aided Design & Computer Graphics, **14,** 11 (2002)
4. J.Y. Liu, Research on Key Techniques of Unfolding and Optional Nesting System of Sheet Metal Parts (Xi'an Technological University, China 2011)
5. Z.X. Jia, State-of-the-art and Future Trends of Cutting and Packing Studies, Journal of Computer-aided Design & Computer Graphics, **16,** 7 (2004)
6. Y.W. Zhu, Research on modern incision technology and its application in enterprise, Technological Development of Enterprise, **24,** 8 (2005)
7. M.F. Wu, H. Jin, M. Chen, Technology Research for Numerical Control Machine of Rotate Punch Tower, Electro-Mechanical Engineering, **26,** 1 (2010)

Rapid Determination of Biochar Energy Quality Based on Visible and Near-infrared Spectroscopy (400-1000nm)

Hai-Qing YANG[1, a], Geng-Xin GUO[1] and Jian-Bing JI[2]

[1]*College of Information Engineering, Zhejiang University of Technology, 310023 Hangzhou, China*
[2]*Zhejiang Provincal Key Laboratory of Biofuel, Zhejiang University of Technology, 310014 Hangzhou, China*
[a] Corresponding author: yanghq@zjut.edu.cn

Abstract. Rapid determination of biochar energy quality is fundamental for the purpose of biomass efficient utilization. In this work, visible and near-infrared spectroscopy was used to measure ash, volatile matter, fixed carbon content and calorific value of biochar samples produced at different pyrolysis temperatures from agricultural biomass feedstocks. Biochar samples were detected by a USB4000 spectrometer with 400-1000nm reflectance spectra recorded for investigation. The spectra were transformed by Savitzky-Golay smoothing followed by baseline offset correction (BOC). The BOC-transformed spectra of calibration set were subjected to a partial least squares regression (PLSR) algorithm for obtaining a PLSR calibration model for each biochar property. Prediction result shows that the PLSR models developed for 400-1000nm spectra achieve good prediction performance with coefficient of determination (R^2) of 0.85, 0.86, 0.87 and residual prediction deviation (RPD) of 2.61, 2.64, 2.85 for ash, volatile matter and fixed carbon content, respectively. For the prediction of biochar calorific value, the PLSR model developed for 400-780nm spectra performs better with R^2 of 0.82 and RPD of 2.51 compared with the 400-1000nm spectra. It is suggested that biochar energy quality can be rapidly measured with acceptable accuracy based on a 400-1000nm spectrum which can be obtained by a low-cost spectrometer.

1 Introduction

Biochar is a product of thermal degradation of organic materials in the absence of air (pyrolysis). Except for being an excellent material for improving soil fertility as well as ecosystem services such as mitigating climate change by sequester carbon; biochar has also been utilized for energy purpose [1]. Conversion of agricultural wastes into biochar not only can save natural resource but also protect environment. Biochar energy quality is mainly influenced by its feedstock type as well as pyrolysis conditions. However, it is very cost- and time-consuming to determinate biochar energy quality, for example, to measure calorific value conventionally should be conducted by physic-chemical means in laboratory. Thus, it is necessary to develop an alternative for rapid determination of biochar energy quality cheaply and conveniently.

Recently, visible and near-infrared reflectance spectroscopy (vis-NIR) has received increasing attention because it is characteristic of rapid measurement, ease to use and absence of agents. This technology has been used for the analysis of biomass feedstock properties. Sanderson et al. used the technology to determine chemical compositions of several woody and herbaceous feedstocks', such as ethanol extractives, ash and lignin [2]. Based on an OSC-treated kernel PLSR method, Labbé et al. achieved highest coefficient of correlation and lowest root-mean square of error (RMSE) for the prediction of ash and char content of three types of woody biomass (red oak, yellow poplar, hickory) and three herbaceous biomasses (switch grass, corn Stover, sugarcane bagasse)[3]. Allison et al. measured several key compositional parameters (alkali index, nitrogen, carbon and ash contents) in two species of energy grass (switch grass and reed canary grass) by Fourier transform infrared spectroscopy [4]. Nkansah et al. used the spectroscopy as a process analysis tool for the rapid characterization of physical (bulk density) and chemical properties (insoluble and acid-soluble lignin, extractives, and ash) of yellow-poplar [5]. Fagan et al. predicted the moisture, calorific value, ash and carbon content of two dedicated bio-energy crops (Miscanthus and Short Rotational Coppice Willow)[6]. All the above-mentioned reports focused on the measurement of biomass feedstock properties. To our knowledge, however, there is no report on using the vis-NIR spectroscopy to predict biochar energy quality.

As known, weak overtones and combinations of the middle-infrared fundamental vibrations (2500-25000nm or 4000-400cm-1) due to the stretching and bending of N-H, O-H and C-H groups dominate the NIR (780~2500nm) and electronic transitions in the visible (350~780nm) portions of the electromagnetic (EM) spectrum[7]. It might be probable to use the vis-NIR spectroscopy for the characterization of biochar energy quality, although using middle-infrared wavelengths range may produce higher performance than vis-NIR range, as shown in other reports [7,8].

This study aims to explore the potential of using a vis-NIR spectrum of 400-1000nm to determinate biochar energy quality, namely, to measure ash, volatile matter, fixed-carbon content and calorific value of biochar samples produced at different pyrolysis temperatures from three selected types of agricultural biomass feed stocks. Calibration models were also developed for different wavelengths range with the purpose of model optimization.

2 Materials and Methods

2.1 Biochar Samples Preparation

Pine and cedar wood chips were collected from a local timber production factory. Cotton stalk was gathered from a local farmland. The biomass wastes were left outdoors for air-drying one month. The dried materials were broken by machine and further ground to pass through a 40-mesh screen. Biochar was produced via the pyrolysis of the raw biomass at various temperatures under oxygen-limited conditions, which allowed the materials to be charred rather than combusted. Briefly, the biomass was placed in a ceramic pot covered with a fitting lid, and underwent pyrolysis in a muffle furnace with peak temperatures of 300, 350, 400, 450, 500, 550 and 600°C for 2h. For each temperature, four biochar samples were prepared for cedar and pine wood and eight samples for cotton stalk. A total of 112 biochar samples were prepared with 28, 28 and 56 samples for cedar wood, pine wood and cotton stalk biomass, respectively.

From each sample, 4~5g was used for laboratory measurement of ash(wt.%), volatile matter(*VM*, wt.%) and calorific value(*CV*, MJ/kg). The ash and *VM* were measured according to the criteria of NY/T1881.4-2010(China) and the *CV* according to the standard of GB/T 213-2003(China). Measurements were conducted on the dry base. Fixed carbon content (*FC*, wt.%) was calculated by

$$FC\ (wt.\%)=1-Ash(wt.\%)-VM(wt.\%). \tag{1}$$

2.2 Spectral Data Acquisition

A subsample of about 5g was loaded into a static ring cup and measured with a USB4000 spectrometer (Ocean Optics, USA) equipped with an optic fiber for light transmission. The light source was a halogen bulb of 3000K. The spectrometer provided spectra with 3648 wavelengths from 345.61nm to 1047.63nm. Due to the noise at both ends, only the range of 400-1000nm was remained for further investigation. All spectra were recorded in diffuse reflectance mode. Before sample spectral scanning, ten reference scans were taken on a ceramic standard supplied with the spectrometer. Twenty photometric scans were conducted and averaged for each sample.

2.3 Spectral Data Processing Methods

The spectra were processed with the Unscramble X10.1 (CAMO, Oslo, Norway). The spectra were randomly divided into two separate set for calibration (2/3) and prediction (1/3). Several spectral pre-processing algorithms including Savitzky-Golay smoothing, multiplicative scatter correction, standard normal variate, de-trending and derivatives were investigated but were not useful for model improvement. The only beneficial spectrum transformation was baseline offset correction (BOC), conducted by

$$f(x) = x - \min(X) \tag{2}$$

where x is a variable and X denotes all selected variables. The value of the lowest point in a spectrum is subtracted from all the variables. BOC can eliminate light-path difference caused by rough sample surface.

The BOC-transformed spectra in the calibration set were subjected to a partial least squares regression (PLSR) to build a calibration model for each bio char property. All PLSR models were conducted with leave-one-out cross-validation and the number of latent variables (LVs) used in the PLSR models was determined by minimizing the predicted residual error sum of squares (*PRESS*). The performance of PLSR models was evaluated for the prediction set.

PLSR model performance was evaluated by the root mean squared error (*RMSE*) of calibration (*RMSEC*), cross-validation (*RMSECV*) and prediction (*RMSEP*). The formula of *RMSE* is

$$RMSE = \sqrt{\frac{\sum (X_m - X_p)^2}{N}} \tag{3}$$

where X_m is the reference value, X_p is the PLS-predicted value, and N is the number of samples used for calibration or prediction. PLSR models were also evaluated by the residual predictive deviation (*RPD*), which is the ratio of standard deviation of reference values of the prediction set to the *RMSEP*. The criteria adopted for *RPD* classification [8] was that an *RPD* of 1.5~2.0 indicates a possibility of distinguishing between large and small values, while a value of 2.0~2.5 makes approximate quantitative predictions possible. Prediction is classified as good if *RPD* of 2.5~3.0. We also evaluated the model performance by means of the coefficient of determination (R^2) for prediction. In fact, R^2 indicates the percentage of the variance in the Y variable that is accounted for by the X variable [9]. R^2 Of 0.66~0.81 indicates approximate quantitative prediction, whereas a value of 0.82~0.90 reveals good prediction. Generally, a good model prediction would have large values of R^2 and *RPD*, and small values of *RMSE*.

3 Results and Discussion

3.1 Characteristics of Biochar Reflectance spectra

Figure 1 shows the changes of BOC-transformed bio char reflectance with spectral wavelengths from 400nm to 1000nm. The spectra present low reflectance in visible range of 450-650nm, which corresponds to the black color of bio char. However, the reflectance became stronger and stronger in the near infrared range of above 780nm.

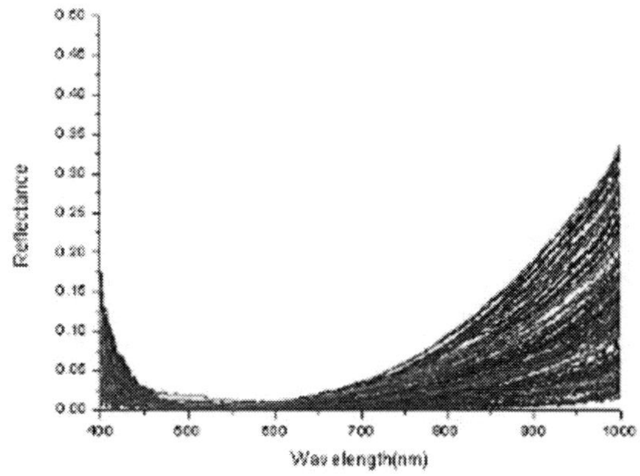

Figure 1. Reflectance spectra of all biochar samples

3.2 PLSR Determination of Biochar Energy Quality

In order to investigate the contribution of different range of wavelengths to the performance of PLSR models calibrated for biochar energy quality, the spectrometer-recorded vis-NIR spectra of 400-1000nm were divided into two ranges, visible range of 400-780nm and short-wave near-infrared range of 780-1000nm. Thus, three groups of PLSR models were established respectively for the vis-NIR range of 400-1000nm, the vis range of 400-780nm and the NIR range of 780-1000nm. The different groups of PLSR models were compared with each others in terms of the values of R^2 and RPD of calibration and prediction sets.

The PLSR models calibrating the wavelengths of 400-1000nm to biochar energy properties achieved good performance for calibration and prediction (Table 1). For example, the PLSR model for ash content produced R^2 of 0.93 and *RMSE* of 1.0% for calibration, and R^2 of 0.85, *RMSE* of 1.3%, and *RPD* of 2.61 for prediction. The PLSR models for volatile matter and fixed carbon contents were develop with 3 or 4 latent variables and achieved similar performance with R^2 of 0.89-0.91 for calibration, and R^2 of 0.86-0.87 for prediction. By comparison, the PLSR model for biochar calorific value produced middle-level accuracy with R^2 of 0.80 and *RMSE* of 0.56MJ/kg for calibration, and R^2 of 0.80, *RMSE* of 0.60MJ/kg, and *RPD* of 2.27 for prediction.

Table 1. Performance of PLSR models developed for 400-1000nm spectra

Biochar energy property	PLSR LVs	Calibration set		Prediction set		
		R^2	*RMSE*	R^2	*RMSE*	*RPD*
Ash (wt.%)	5	0.93	1.0	0.85	1.3	2.61
VM (wt.%)	3	0.89	2.1	0.86	2.5	2.64
FC (wt.%)	4	0.91	1.6	0.87	2.0	2.85
CV (MJ/kg)	4	0.80	0.56	0.80	0.60	2.27

By comparison, the PLSR models calibrating the visible range of 400-780nm to biochar energy properties present different performance(Table 2). For example, the PLSR model for ash content performs worse with R^2 of 0.76, *RMSE* of 1.7%, and *RPD* of 2.06 for prediction. The PLSR models for volatile matter and fixed carbon contents which were developed with more latent variables cannot produce good performance for calibration and prediction as well. The only improvement can be found in the performance of the PLSR model developed for biochar calorific value based on the visible range of 400-780nm. The PLSR model achieves R^2 of 0.84, *RMSE* of 0.52MJ/kg for calibration, and R^2 of 0.82, *RMSE* of 0.54MJ/kg, and *RPD* of 2.51 for prediction.

Table 2. Performance of PLSR models developed for 400-780nm spectra

Biochar energy property	PLSR LVs	Calibration set		Prediction set		
		R^2	*RMSE*	R^2	*RMSE*	*RPD*
Ash (wt.%)	5	0.88	1.2	0.76	1.7	2.06
VM (wt.%)	5	0.89	2.1	0.79	3.0	2.20
FC (wt. %)	4	0.88	1.8	0.85	2.1	2.71
CV (MJ/kg)	4	0.84	0.52	0.82	0.54	2.51

Similarly, the PLSR models calibrating the NIR range of 780-1000nm to biochar energy properties perform differently (Table 3). Although the PLSR model for ash content obtains slightly better performance with R^2 of 0.93, and *RMSE* of 0.9% for calibration, it does not improve prediction performance. The similar results can be found for fixed carbon content and calorific value. The only improvement was achieved for the PLSR model developed for biochar calorific value. It produces similar performance with R^2 of 0.88, *RMSE* of 2.3% for calibration, and R^2 of 0.85, *RMSE* of 2.6%, and *RPD* of 2.54 for prediction with only 2 latent variables for PLSR model.

 DOI: 10.1051/itmconf/20160709010

Table 3. Performance of PLSR models developed for 780-1000nm spectra

Biochar energy property	PLSR LVs	Calibration set		Prediction set		
		R^2	*RMSE*	R^2	*RMSE*	*RPD*
Ash (wt.%)	5	0.93	0.9	0.76	1.7	2.06
VM (wt.%)	2	0.88	2.3	0.85	2.6	2.54
FC (wt.%)	4	0.89	1.7	0.84	2.2	2.59
CV (MJ/kg)	4	0.80	0.56	0.68	0.75	1.81

3.3 Discussion

Although we did not exploit the issue of how different charring temperatures make influences on the molecular structures of biochar, published reports may support us some useful knowledge on it. For examples, Peng et al. revealed by scanning electron microscopy(SEM) that with increasing temperature, biochar particles became smaller and retained less original cell structure[10]. Besides, Fourier transform infrared spectra of biochar derived from rice straw, pitch pine and wood showed that charring temperature alters the functional group of biochar, indicating a weaker adsorption intensity of O, H and aliphatic C but stronger adsorption intensity of aromatic C with charring temperature[11,12]. Putun et al. reported that degradation of hemicelluloses and cellulose takes place at 200-300°C and 300-400°C, respectively, while lignin degradation takes place at 200-700°C[13]. Kim et al. found that formation of highly ordered aromatic structure of biochar begins at 400°C[11]. As the chemical, physical and morphological changes of biochar affected by charring temperature would result in spectral changes of molecular vibration, spectroscopic analysis should be a useful tool for biochar energy quality monitoring, although more efforts must be conducted for further investigation.

4 Conclusions

In the study, vis-NIR reflectance spectra with wavelengths from 400 to 1000nm were calibrated to the ash, volatile matter, fixed carbon content and calorific value of three types of biochar samples produced at different pyolysis temperatures.

Conclusions can be drawn as follows.

(1) Biochar energy quality can be predicted successfully by PLSR models developed or the 400-1000nm reflectance spectra. In our case, PLSR models developed for BOC-transformed spectra achieved good prediction accuracy with R^2 of 0.85-0.87 and *RPD* of 2.61-2.85 for ash, volatile matter and fixed carbon content, and R^2 of 0.80 and *RPD* of 2.27 for calorific value.

(2) The PLSR models calibrated for different wavelengths range present different prediction performance. In our case, the models developed for ash, volatile matter and fixed carbon content based on vis-NIR range of 400-1000nm achieve higher values of R^2 and *RPD* for prediction compared with those based on visible range of 400-780nm or NIR range of 780-1000nm. However, the PLSR model developed for biochar calorific value based on visible range of 400-780nm performs better than other two wavelength ranges. It may indicate that biochar natural colors have some relationship with biochar enengy quality.

(3) Biochar energy quality can be rapidly measured by a 400-1000nm spectrometer with acceptable prediction. Although a spectrometer with wider wavelengths range, for examples, of 350-2500nm, may produce better prediction result with higher accuracy, it is usually much more expensive. In our case, a USB4000 spectrometer could be fabricated as a low-cost tool for predicting biochar energy quality in practice.

Acknowledgement

This work was supported by research funds of China Postdoctoral Science Foundation (No.2013M540499), Zhejiang Provincial Postdoctoral Science Foundation of Year 2013, and Zhejiang Provincial Natural Science Foundation (No. LY13F010008).

References

1. J. Lehmann, Front. Ecol. Environ 5,7(2007)
2. M.A. Sanderson, F. Agblevor, M. Collins, D.K. Johnson, Biomass Bioenerg 11,6(1996)
3. N. Labbé, S.-H. Lee, H.-W. Cho, M.K. Jeong, N. André, Bioresour. Technol 99,8(2008)
4. G.G. Allison, C. Morris, E. Hodgson, J. Jones, M. Kubacki, T. Barraclough, N. Yates, I. Shield, A.V. Bridgwater, I.S. Donnison, Bioresour. Technol 100,6(2009)
5. K. Nkansah, B. Dawson-Andoh, J. Slahor, Bioresour. Technol 101,7(2010)
6. C.C. Fagan, C.D. Everard, K. McDonnell, Bioresour. Technol 102,7(2015)
7. H. Yang, B. Kuang, A.M. Mouazen, Eur. J. Soil Sci 63,11(2012)
8. H. Yang, A.M. Mouazen, *Infrared Spectroscopy-Life and Biomedical Sciences* (Intech Press 2012)
9. H. Yang, B. Kuang, A.M. Mouazen, Appl. Spectrosc 65,8(2011)
10. X. Peng, L.L. Ye, C.H. Wang, H. Zhou, B. Sun, Soil Tillage Res 112,8(2011)
11. K.H. Kim, J.-Y. Kim, T.-S. Cho, J.W. Choi, Bioresour. Technol 118,5(2012)
12. M. Keiluweit, P.S. Nico, M.G. Johnson, M. Kleber, Environ. Sci. Technol 44,7(2010)
13. E. Putun, B.B. Uzun, A.E. Putun, J. Anal. Appl. Pyrolysis 79,7(2007)

The Research on Chinese Idioms Educational Games in TCFL Based on Virtual Reality

Xiao-Qiang HU, Rui SU[a], and Ling HE

Jiangxi Science & Technology Normal University, 330038 Nanchang, China
[a] Corresponding author: suruigx1990@163.com

Abstract: In recent years, overseas set off a craze for learning Chinese. Chinese Idioms teaching is important but difficult for foreigners in Teaching Chinese as a Foreign Language (TCFL). The VR educational game should be a good choice to solve the problem with education, entertainment, and high immerse. In this study , 'Yu Gong moves the mountain' is designed as an example. Unity 3D is the main development tool, Leap Motion is interactive way, and also doing an interview with some findings and conclusions. Comparison of textbooks or teachers explaining, VR Chinese Idioms educational game can enhance most of the learners understanding with intense interest. However, the educational game should be integrated into more entertainment and it costs at least 10 minutes or more to adapt the operation of Leap Motion. In the further research, the VR Chinese Idioms educational games for the TCFL can be better gradually based on this research.

1 Introduction

In recent years, overseas set off a craze for learning Chinese. Development of TCFL is meaningful for promoting Chinese, spreading the excellent culture of the China and enhancing mutual understanding between the Chinese and abroad. What's more, it is significance to enhance China's influence in the world by TCFL. Chinese Idioms are formed in the long-term practice of Chinese people's life. They are usually made of fixed phrase and fixed structure with special cultural connotations. So that, foreign students whose mother language isn't Chinese often think that the vocabulary and emphases in Chinese idioms are real difficulties to get. In fact, most Chinese idioms are generated from the historical story. If new media and teaching theory could be used in Chinese Idioms teaching of TCFL, learners will understand the meaning of Chinese Idioms directly with more fun.

In 2015, VR is developing rapidly, both hardware and software. With rapid popularization of VR, it brings unprecedented convenience and entertainment to human's daily life. The applications of VR have been utilized into many research fields, such as medicine, entertainment, military, electronic commerce and so on. In recent years, with combination of education, VR becomes a widespread focus. The educational games based on VR technology are more entertainment and immersed than normal ones, especially natural human-computer interaction. That's the reason why the educational games are an effective to combine VR and education.

An educational game for Chinese Idioms in TCFL based on VR Technology is designed. After that, some foreign learners are invited to test it. The conclusion of the is shown at the end of this paper.

2 Related Work

2.1 The Related Work of Chinese Idioms Teaching in TCFL

Chinese Idioms teaching plays an important role in TCFL to foreign learners. No only expanding their vocabulary, but also improving their ability to express and reading. And it helps them understand Chinese traditional culture. Because of the bias form, semantics, grammar, and pragmatics, foreign learners usually think Chinese Idioms learning is a difficulty. In traditional TCFL, teaching structure method, correction method and translation method are often adopted. In those methods, students can't teach in accordance with their aptitude with lower efficiency and effect.

Bo HONG (2003) points out that foreign students who are learning Chinese Idioms can't accurately understand the Chinese Idioms meaning. It's not clear idiomatic collocation, is also not clear about the usefulness of Chinese Idioms. He also analyzes bias in TCFL and thinks that that the Chinese idioms teaching should be focused on three points: the meaning of the Chinese Idioms teaching; Chinese Idioms pragmatic and collocation of idiom teaching.

Lina SHEN (2007) affirms teaching Chinese to foreign research results of TCFL in the ten years and predicts that idiom teaching research in TCFL tends to be diversified.

According to the source, Juan FENG (2011) analyses the characteristics of Chinese Idioms and the necessity for learning. And he comes out eight teaching methods in TCFL: function method, contrastive method between

Chinese and English, animated graphics, performance realization method and so on.

Zhen XU (2013) proceed from the cultural introduction, put forward the necessity of reforming in Chinese idioms teaching method, improving its quality, and enhancing in TCFL.

2.2 The Related Work of VR Educational Games

In the game-based learning, learners have to learn by doing. Compared to traditional teaching, game-based learning is better with higher memory retention rate by 5%. After experiencing the retention rate can be increased to 75%. Watching, listening and doing at the same time, the retention rate of learners increases to 90% (Magennis & Farrell, 2005). Junjie SHANG (2015), school of education, Peking University, believes that the real society is constantly merging with the virtual society, and the method of the virtual system is the solution to the real problem in the future. Game-based learning can create the immersive situation so that learners are more interested in learning and have the deep learning and get a better effect.

At present, the researchers have made some achievements of educational games in the TCFL. Ni ZHANG, Zhang YI, Kuiyuan ZHANG (2008) design the game platform, content, scene and plot contents, standing on the basis of empirical research, combining with the characteristics of learners for TCFL.

Based on the effective learning environment and the theory of multiple intelligences , Li CAI and Fangyu LIU (2011) proposes TCFL education game design model, according to game-based learning environment, characteristic and detailed design steps. They think about how to combine education and game, by designing characteristics, model designing, content and curriculum and making the example of DONGYOUJI.

After analyzing characteristics of the network game, Yang YI (2012) does some researches about network educational game for TCFL. Combined with the specific situation of the game, the possibility and advantage of network games in a foreign language are analyzed. And he tries to design the scripting tasks of network educational game for TCFL.

About VR educational game, Jianrong MA and Jingsu ZHANG (2012) design and development a parenting education game based on the Kinect. Jiali LIU has used the Unity3D game engine to achieve a child safety education. VR educational games are more applied in the field of early childhood education. There is any example in TCFL.

In this study, according to a combination of education and entertainment, VR Chinese Idioms educational games are design and tested. It could be a new form of edutainment in TCFL and also as an auxiliary means of TCFL. Through the Internet and other media, it can be extended to Chinese education for overseas students and Confucius Institute overseas.

3 Methodology

3.1. Main Process

Methods in this study include the literature data method, interview, and observation method. The purpose is to designing and implication of VR Chinese Idioms educational games in TCFL. After designing the case, some learners are invited to test the VR Chinese Idioms educational game, interview contents they given will be analyzed, then coming to some conclusion. 20 learners who are non-Chinese speakers are selected to participate in the experiment. The flow chart of this research is as shown in Figure 1.

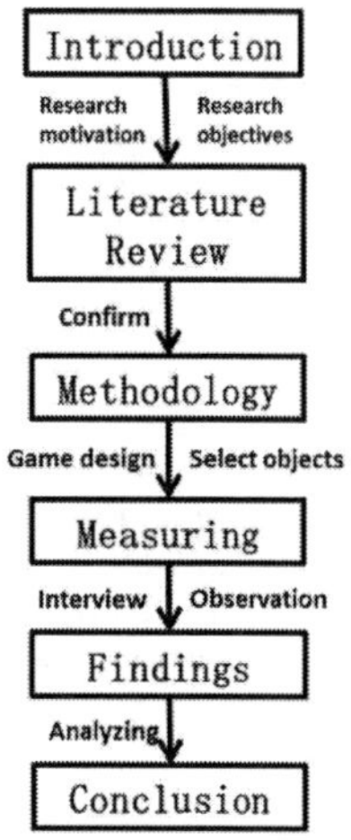

Figure 1. The flow chart in this research.

3.2 Objects Selection

There is an ancient Chinese fable 'The Foolish Old Man Who Removed the Mountains'. And it becomes an idiom that is named 'Yu Gong moves the mountain' reminds us that a person can never know what's possible unless he tries to make it happen. 'Yu Gong moves the mountains' is the case of the educational game based on VR for TCFL in this study.

Once upon a time, there is a very old man called Yu Gong. There are two mountains near his house. They are so high and big that it took a long time to walk to the other side. Yu Gong tells his family that they should all help him to move the mountains. And he said they could put the earth and stone into the sea because it's big enough to hold everything. So they start digging the next day. Yu Gong and his family began to move some of the earth and stone to the sea. One day, Zhi Sou see Yu Gong and his children when they are working on moving the mountains. He tells Yu Gong that he could never do it because he is old and weak. As soon as the Zhi Sou finished talking, Yu Gong said that his family could continue to move the mountains after his died. His family would live and grow, but the mountains could not get larger. So Yu Gong and his family keep on digging day after day and year after year. Finally,the god is so moved that he calls for two gods to move the mountains away.

 DOI: 10.1051/itmconf/20160709011

3.3 Game Design

Educational games design is not only to consider the education but also to consider the entertainment. Educational game designers have the plan to allow learners to complete some goals, and learners should achieve educational goals. The task design of educational games is shown in the following three tables.

Table 1. Previous tasks in educational game design.

	Content	Level	Time
Task 1	Have conversation with Yu Gong	Simple	2 mins
Learning objectives: Understanding the reason for moving mountain.			
Task describe: In a trip, you find that an old man is digging a mountain with tools, feeling very strange, and then stepped forward to ask the reason.			
	Content	**Level**	**Time**
Task 2	Have a look at surroundings	Simple	2 mins
Learning objectives: Analysing feasibility of 'Yu Gong moves the mountains'.			
Task describe: There are two mountains near his house. They are so high and big that it took a long time to walk to the other side. Yu Gong tells his family that they should all help him to move the mountain.			

Table 2. Middle tasks in educational game design.

	Content	Level	Time
Task 3	Cheer Yu Gong up	Medium	3 mins
Learning objectives: Understanding the spirit of 'Yu Gong moves the mountains'.			
Task describe: One day, Zhi Sou sees Yu Gong and his children when they are working on moving the mountains. He tells Yu Gong that he could never do it because he is old and weak. You should cheer Yu Gong up.			
	Content	**Level**	**Time**
Task 4	Help Yu Gong move mountain	Difficulty	5 mins
Learning objectives: Analysis feasibility of moving the mountain.			
Task describe: As soon as the Zhi Sou finished talking, Yu Gong said that his family could continue to move the mountains after he died. His family would live and grow, but the mountains could not get bigger.			

Table 3. Final tasks in educational game design.

	Content	Level	Time
Task 5	To have Conversation with Yu Gong	Difficulty	5 mins
Learning objectives: Summarize Yu Gong 's spirit and learn how to tells others.			
Task describe: To explain the great determination and courage of Yu Gong to god and ask for the help.			

3.4 Scene creating

The high immersive virtual learning environment can stimulate learners' interest, arise the enthusiasm of learners so that learners participate and immerse them actively. The modeling tool is Using 3D, a Chinese traditional scene for the educational game is created, as shown in Figure 2.

Figure 2. Scene creating of 'Yu Gong moves the mountain'.

Learners in the virtual environment when roaming through the rotation of the head of the action, to trigger the VR head wearing a display device in the mobile terminal of the gyroscope positioning function, learners will be able to observe the living environment of the ancients from 360 degrees different perspective.

3.5 The interactive way

The interactive way is a key part pf educational game design, including interface, NPC, controller and so on. Because VR belongs to the 3D media, it is not accurately by 2D. In the traditional desktop virtual reality system, users can only rely on the mouse to move and other ways to change the viewing angle.In this study, Motion Leap is the input of the educational game learner, as shown in Fig.3.

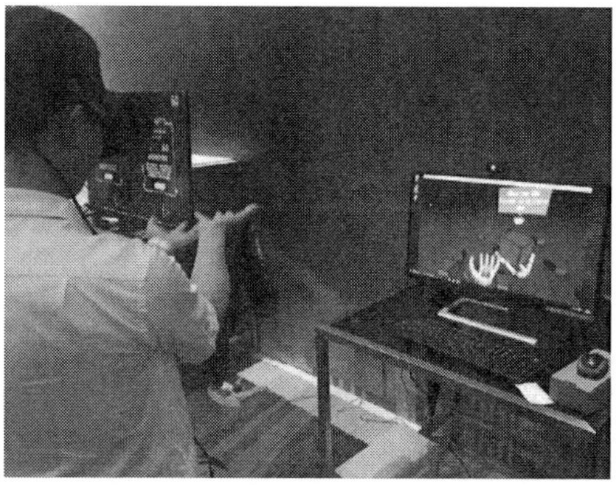

Figure 3. The interactive way of 'Yu Gong moves the mountains'.

The key part of code that makes combination with Unity 3D and Leap Motion is given:
public class FingerMatch

DOI: 10.1051/itmconf/20160709011

```
{
static readonly float FingerBendState_Radian =
Mathf.PI*4f / 18 ;
static readonly float FingerStrightState_Radian =
Mathf.PI/12;
public static bool StrightState(FingerData fingerData,
float adjustBorder=0f)
{bool isStright =false;
Vector disalDir = fingerData.m_Point.m_Direction;
if (!disalDir.Equals(Vector.Zero))
{Vector fingerDir = fingerData.m_Point.m_Position -
fingerData.m_Position;
float radian = fingerDir.AngleTo(disalDir);
if (radian < FingerStrightState_Radian + adjustBorder)
{isStright = true;}}
return isStright;}
public static bool BendState(FingerData fingerData, float
adjustBorder=0f)//,out float eulerAugle)
{bool isBend = false;
Vector disalDir = fingerData.m_Point.m_Direction;
if( !disalDir.Equals(Vector.Zero) )
{Vector fingerDir = fingerData.m_Point.m_Position -
fingerData.m_Position;
float radian = fingerDir.AngleTo(disalDir);
if (radian > FingerBendState_Radian + adjustBorder)
{isBend = true;}}
 return isBend;}
}
```

Motion Leap can recognize the meaning of the user's gestures, and learners control the educational game as a natural human-computer interaction. In the case of the "Yu Gong moves the mountains", "Hands parallel expansion" on the leap Motion refers to moving in the educational game. If learners want to talk with the NPC, they should make a fist on the Leap Motion around the NPC. Scratching gesture stands for that mountain is bored. Users are helping Yu Gong to move the mountain.

4 Conclusion

After the development of Chinese Idioms Educational Games in TCFL, there are some findings. Comparison of textbooks or teachers explaining, VR Chinese Idioms educational game can enhance most of the learners understanding with intense interest. However, some feedbacks are negative. The educational game should be integrated into more entertainment. It costs at least 10 minutes or more to adapt the operation of Leap Motion.

According to current researches (Chinese Idioms teaching in TCFL and educational games), an idiom educational game for the TCFL based on VR is feasibility planning. In this study, 'Yu Gong moves the mountain' as a case is design and tested. After the interview, it should be improved, such as education and entertainment of the educational game are needed to be balanced. In the further research, the VR Chinese Idioms educational games for the TCFL can be better gradually. It will be an effective solution for promoting development in the TCFL.

References

1. Bo HONG, "Study on Chinese Idioms teaching in teaching Chinese as a second language," SUN YATSEN UNIVERSITY FORUM. Guangzhou. China, vol.23, pp. 297-300, February 2003.
2. Lina SHEN, "Summary of Chinese Idioms teaching in teaching Chinese as a second language in the past ten years," Journal of Language and Literature Studies,. Nanjing. China, vol 7, pp. 159-160, February 2007.
3. Juan FENG, The Discussion On Meaning And Teaching Method In Teaching Chinese As A Foreign Language.Wuhan,China: Central China normal university,2011.
4. Zhen XU, A Study on the Culture Lead-in in TCFL Chinese Idiom Teaching.Hangzhou,China: Zhejiang university,2013.
5. Junjie SHANG, "What is the most important value of virtual reality?"China Information Technology Education. Beijing. China, vol.10, pp.,October 2015.
6. Jianrong Ma,Sujing Zhang, "Parent-child interactive game design and implementation of technology-based somatosensory"China Electronic Education. Beijing. China, vol.09, pp.85-88,September 2015.
7. Xiaoqiang HU ,The Foundation and Application of Virtual Reality Technology. Beijing: BEIJING UNIVERSITY OF POSTS AND TELECOMMUCATIONS PRESS,2009.

Research on Configurable Workflow Technology in PDM System

Kang CAO[a], Li LIU[b], and Zheng CHENG[c]

Institute of Computer Application, China Academy of Engineering Physics, Mianyang Sichuan ,621900,China
[a]ckhad@126.com, [b]liuli@caep.cn, [c]cghz2804@163.com
Corresponding author: Li LIU

Abstract: This paper analyzed the deficiency of the static process management in the traditional PDM workflow system, and proposed a new configurable workflow system model for the dynamic and multiple characteristics of the equipment product design business process. On the basis of PDM workflow engine, the model introduced the configurable workflow form and logic processing program, the total workflow template definition and customized workflow participant selection module, and put forward the key technology solutions. This model could solve the problem of the lack of flexibility in workflow design and maintenance. It had been successfully applied to the design management process for multiple equipment products, and improved the dynamic process management capability of PDM system.

1. Introduction

Workflow is presented in order to improve the work efficiency. By decomposing the work activities into well-defined tasks, roles, rules and processes, the execution and monitoring of the workflow is achieved, so as to improve the level of the production organization and the efficiency of the work. Workflow Management Coalition defines workflow as: The whole or part of the business process automation.In the process, documents, information or tasks flow according to certain rules of the process, to achieve the coordination among the organization members and the overall objectives of the business.[1]

Based on product structure, with production data as the core, product data management (PDM) system uses modern network communication technology and database technology, realizes the integration management of design tools, design data, design process and design resources. Through logically connecting each CAX information isolated island, PDM can manage the whole product design and development process, gradually establish a virtual product model, and finally form a complete product description, production process description and production process control data. It provides a fine management and control mechanism for enterprise product related information and process. [2]

PDM usually has functions of product structure management, document management, report management and other static data management. At the same time, it also provides the function of process management to manage the dynamic flow of product data.

2 Process Management in PDM System

For the fixed business processes of similar business object, PDM workflow management system usually uses graphical process designer to define process tasks and execute logic, and completes process automatic execution by workflow engine. There may be many differences in the process management system of different PDM products, but they generally provide the following three aspects support: construction time function, run-time control function, run-time interactive function.

Construction time function. It is responsible for defining and organizing the business process, each task of process, and task control relationship. Process management module in PDM system generally provides the function of process template. Through the definition of process start and end, process task, task executor, executive order, authority of related data, etc. , we can construct a fixed workflow template in PDM system.

Run-time control function. It is responsible for creating, executing and controlling the workflow template, activating the corresponding resources and applications, controlling the transformation of a task to another task, using system message to notify task executor, and so on.

Run-time interactive function. It mainly refers to the interactive function between the workflow management system and the users (the workflow executor and the system administrator) and the external application program. Such as online browsing files, comments, route selection, etc.

According to the requirements of equipment product configuration management, the design documents and reports generated in the process of product design need to be audited and changed control. Because of the different organizational structure and management requirements, the examining and changing procedure of the product design files are different. In the complex equipment product design process, configuration management procedures of different type design files are different, even the same type design files also have differences in the different lifecycle stage. Therefore, for each type of business object constructing and executing a fixed workflow template by traditional PDM workflow management system, it will greatly increase the workload of the workflow definition and maintenance. That is difficult to adapt to the diversity and dynamic changes of product design process.

3 Configurable Workflow System Model

According to the configuration management requirements of complex equipment product design process, this paper established a configurable workflow system model based on the traditional PDM workflow system, to solve the problem of lack of flexibility in the design and implementation of the existing PDM workflow. As shown in Figure 1, the model includes the execution control layer, the logic processing layer and the user interface layer.

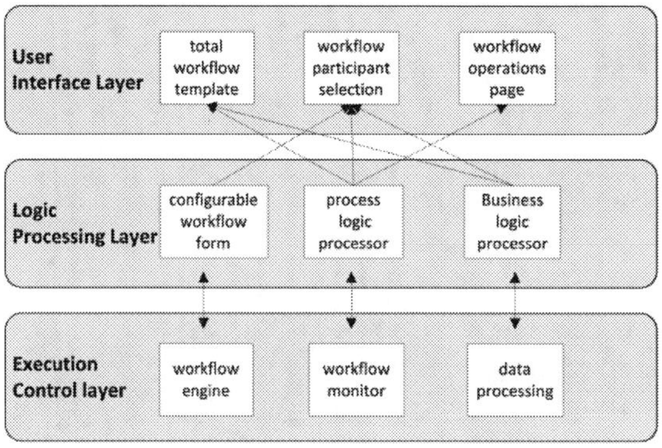

Figure 1. Configurable Workflow System Model

The execution control layer. It mainly realizes the execution of the workflow, the state monitoring and data processing. The workflow engine and interface API of PDM system are used to achieve the conversion, synchronization, asynchronous, cycle and other processing logic of the process node, to achieve process start, stop, recovery, monitoring and management of execution status and other operations. And it will complete data processing such as participant and organization structure storing in the database.

The logic processing layer. It provides business logic processing services for configurable workflow systems. According to the business requirements, configurable workflow form are designed. It can define the workflow of different business objects under different conditions; The total workflow of multi type business objects can be dynamically calculated by configurable workflow form which provides business logic support for the workflow participant selection; Combined with the workflow participant selection, the execution logic of the workflow node is dynamically determined through logic processing program. It support configurable workflow instance running.

The user interface layer. It provides graphical process definition and operation services for users. It uses the PDM workflow designer to define the total workflow template; For configuring the workflow runtime nodes, it inserts the workflow participant selection page into the workflow template, and associates the participant selection rules with the workflow configuration form by the business logic processing program; It uses PDM workflow system to realize the workflow task notification, workflow opinion recording and route selection, etc.

On the basis of traditional PDM workflow system , a configurable workflow system model is established by designing workflow configuration form and logic processing program, simplifying the method of workflow template definition and customizing workflow participant selection. In this model, configurable related content is mainly focused on the logic processing layer and user interface layer. The logic processing layer is the core of the configurable workflow, and the total workflow template definition and the workflow participant selection are the key of the configurable workflow implementation.

4 Configurable Workflow Key Technologies

4.1 Total Workflow Template Definition

On the basis of PDM workflow engine, the general total workflow template is defined according to the classification of business, rather than the traditional single workflow template for specific business. This workflow template is one of the largest sets of workflow nodes that may be involved in the process. It contains all the possible business conditions. Such as the design document approval process, the complete set of workflow template task node includes: proofread, audit, standardized examination, countersignature, technical approval and administrative approval. However, the design file does not need to countersignature, technical and administrative approval in the early stage of product design; Engineering drawings need countersignature by process department; Project report need countersignature by management department; Some files need countersignature by multiple departments. Thus, establishing a total workflow template for a class of business areas of enterprises and realizing the dynamic configuration of the process are conducive to the unified management and maintenance of business processes.

Workflow template uses a lot of workflow logical operations to organize and connect all the workflow task nodes. Such as conditional judgment branch, AND/OR connection, threshold value judgment, workflow wait and synchronization. It also uses the embedded code to call the executable program of the logic processing layer for complex logic processing, which will eventually build the complete workflow process.

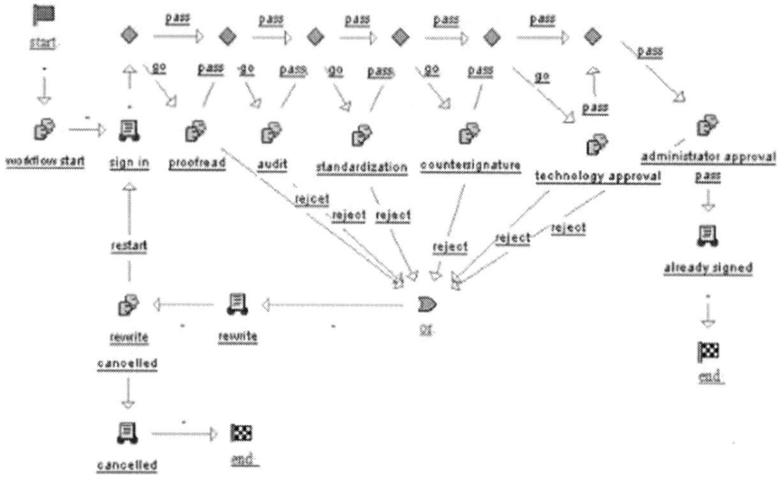

Figure 2. Example of Total Workflow Template

4.2 Workflow Configuration form and Logic Processing Program

On the basis of the total workflow template, in response to the specific requirements of product configuration management, the configurable workflow form is established. According to the business changes, business manager can dynamically adjust the workflow by this form. Workflow configuration form includes business objects, object attributes and process participants. It can realize the dynamic configuration of different business objects in different conditions. Configuration form can be applied to the full product design lifecycle of multiple products, single product, or product components. It works by a logic processing program when the workflow is running. Figure 3 is an example of document approval workflow configuration form. It defines the file types, process nodes, and design phases. It includes large, middle and small three kinds of document types, six document approval nodes, and five product design phases. It can configure process nodes of different file types in different design phases.For example, the assignment book in the document small class. It needs to proofread, audit, standardized examination, technical and administrative approval in all design phases, but countersignature only in the phase of G and D.

document large class	document middle class	document small class	proofread	audit	standardized examination	counter signature	technical approval	administrative approval
Design Documents	Writing class	assignment book	FCSGD	FCSGD	FCSGD	GD	FCSGD	FCSGD
		operating procedures	FCSGD	FCSGD	FCSGD	GD		GD
		specifications	FCSGD	FCSGD	FCSGD	GD		GD
		debugging instructions	FCSGD	FCSGD	FCSGD			GD
	Report class	project report	FCSGD	FCSGD	FCSGD	GD	FCSGD	FCSGD
		quality analysis report	FCSGD	FCSGD	FCSGD	GD		GD
		Research Report	FCSGD	FCSGD	FCSGD	GD		GD
		opening report	FCSGD	FCSGD	FCSGD			GD
		originalrecording	FCSGD	FCSGD	FCSGD			GD
		evaluation report	FCSGD	FCSGD	FCSGD	GD		GD
		test report	FCSGD	FCSGD	FCSGD	GD		GD
		process review report	FCSGD	FCSGD	FCSGD	GD		GD
		component inspection report	FCSGD	FCSGD	FCSGD	GD		GD
		product inspection report	FCSGD	FCSGD	FCSGD	GD	D	GD

Figure 3. Document Approval Process Configuration Form Example

The main processing logic of workflow configuration form is: When the process contains a single business object, according to the corresponding single record in the configuration form configure the workflow. When process contains more than one business object, reading more rows in the form through the corresponding object types, it will calculate the most complete workflow task nodes.

The core logic processing program code is as below:

if (obj instanceof WTDocument) {// If the workflow object is a single document

WTDocument doc = (WTDocument)obj;

String phase = IBAHelper.getIBAValue(doc, PartConstraints.IBA_YZJD);//get phase property value

rtn = getSignatureRoleDefine(qspz, TypedUtility.getTypeIdentifier(doc), phase);//get workflow nodes configuration for this file

}

else if (obj instanceof PromotionNotice) {// If the workflow object is a file package

QueryResult qr=MyPromotionHelpe.getPromotable((

PromotionNotice)obj);//access to all the objects in the

```
file package
    HashMap typeDef = sc.getAllDocumentTypeIdentifier();
    Sheet sheet = sc.getQspzSheet(qspz);//get the workflow configuration form
    HashMap roleMap = sc.getAllRoleMap(sheet);//get configuration information about all workflow nodes in the configuration form
    while (qr.hasMoreElements()) {//get each object of file package
    Persistable p=(Persistable)qr.nextElement();
    if(p instanceof WTDocument) {// If it is a document
    WTDocument doc = (WTDocument)p;
    String phase = IBAHelper.getIBAValue(doc, PartConstraints.IBA_YZJD); // get phase property value
    TypeIdentifier ti = TypedUtility.getTypeIdentifier(doc);
    ArrayList list = sc.getSignatureRoleDefine(ti, phase,typeDef,sheet,roleMap);//get the workflow node configuration of this document type
    rtn.addAll(list);//add to workflow nodes configuration information set
            }
        }
}
```

4.3 Main Processing Logic of Configurable Workflow Instantiation Runtime

The main processing logic of configurable workflow instantiation runtime is shown in figure 4. The first step is to select workflow participants. According to process the business object and the configuration form, logical processing program summary calculate the necessary workflow nodes. They are displayed in a custom workflow participant selection page on the first workflow node. Workflow originator need to select participants for these necessary workflow nodes. All workflow personnel information will be stored in the database through the interface program. Before entering each workflow task node, workflow need to judge the existence of node. If the node has participants, it need to be performed. Otherwise it will go to the next node.

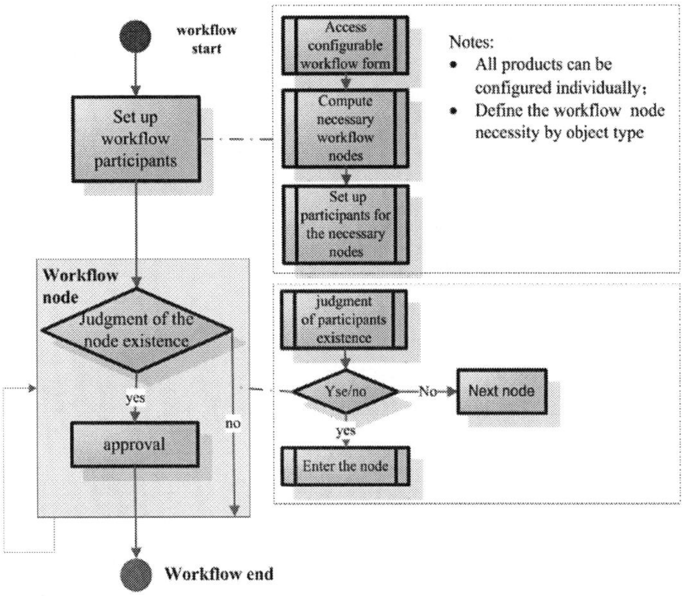

Figure 4. Main Processing Logic of the Configurable Workflow Runtime

The configurable workflow technology combines workflow task node selection and execution logic with workflow configuration form. Through summary calculation of the workflow task nodes, general workflow template is instantiated as a specific workflow that can satisfy the requirement of different configuration management. It implements the configurable workflow management in different products, different business objects and different conditions. The new workflow design pattern has been applied in the development and management of multiple equipment products. It reduced the workload of workflow template definition and process maintenance, simplified and facilitated the process redefinition and business adjustment for business manager.

Summary

In this paper, on the basis of analyzing the characteristics of the function of PDM workflow system and the requirements of equipment product configuration management, we proposed a configurable workflow system model, and realized total workflow template definition, workflow configuration form and logical processing program, the main processing logic of workflow template instantiation runtime, etc. It well solved the problem of the dynamics and diversity of

DOI: 10.1051/itmconf/20160709012

product design process, and effectively improved the capacity of the process management in PDM system.

References

1. Y.S. Fan, Beijing: tsinghua university press (2001)
2. W.H. Fan, T. Li, Beijing: Mechanical Industry Press, 20 (2004)
3. Workflow Management Coalition Specification:Term Glossary, Document Number WfMC-TC-1011 (1996)
4. Y.P. Liu, W. Zhao, X. Xiong, Journal of Mechanical Design and Manufacturing 1, 225 (2009)
5. Z.H. Xu, Y.J. Dai, Y.F. Wang, Journal of Design and Research 5, 13 (2007)
6. Y.B. Guo, Z.Y. Cai, Z.W. Lin, Y.P. Peng, Journal of Computer Engineering and Design 3, 35 (2014)
7. W. Chao, Z.Z. Nong, W. Xiong, Journal of Computer Research and Development Suppl., 46 (2009)

Novel UEP LT Coding Scheme with Feedback Based on Different Degree Distributions

Ya-Fang LI[1,a], Wei-Dang ZHANG[2]

[1,2]*School of Information Engineering, Zhengzhou University, Zhengzhou, Henan, China*
[1]*yafangzzu@foxmail.com*, [2]*iewdzhang@zzu.edu.cn*
[a]*Corresponding author: Ya-Fang LI*

Abstract. Traditional unequal error protection (UEP) schemes have some limitations and problems, such as the poor UEP performance of high priority data and the seriously sacrifice of low priority data in decoding property. Based on the reasonable applications of different degree distributions in LT codes, this paper puts forward a novel UEP LT coding scheme with a simple feedback to compile these data packets separately. Simulation results show that the proposed scheme can effectively protect high priority data, and improve the transmission efficiency of low priority data from 2.9% to 22.3%. Furthermore, it is fairly suitable to apply this novel scheme to multicast and broadcast environments since only a simple feedback introduced.

1 Introduction

With the prevalence of Intrenet, communication service combined with image and video is more and more familiar to people. Usually these data hold different levels of importance, such as Scalable Video Coding (SVC) [1,2], which needs to receive information with high priority level firstly, and then low priority level. The earliest concept of Unequal Error Protection (UEP) is proposed in [3]. It achieves the purpose of protecting more important data using different channel protection mechanism. LT codes are the first fountain codes in practice. The encoder produces a steady stream of encoded packets according to a degree distribution function. There are two sorts of distribution: one kind is single degree distribution, such as Binary Exponential Distribution (BED) [4] and Robust Soliton Distribution (RSD) [5], the other is joint degree distribution [6], called Switch Degree Distribution (SDD). The decoder only needs to receive enough encoded packets without considering which packet is obtained. It is named UEP LT codes by applying LT coding method to unequal error protection.

The early UEP LT coding structure is Weighted UEP (WUEP) and put forward in [7], which raises the selected probability of high priority data in encoding process by adding the weighting factor *km*. Expanding Window Fountain (EWF) codes are designed in [8] by choosing different window probability in LT coding. Duplication Window Fountain (DWF) codes are realized in [9] through setting different multiples of replicator.

The purpose of these traditional UEP LT coding scheme above is to protect high priority data under no feedback condition, but they have such a disadvantage: the improvement of high priority data in decoding performance is always at the sacrifice of low priority data [10]. Considering the heavy cost to recover low priority data, it is advisable to combine feedback with unequal error protection. The UEP LT coding method in [11] is proposed in 2013, which proves the decoding performance of low priority segment can improve dramatically with feedback. According to the thought of feedback in [12], UEP LT codes with multiple feedbacks is raised in [13]. By exploring the impact between recovered packets and decoding property, optimized UEP LT codes with single feedback is gained in [13], which reduces the number of feedback packet to 1, but it has a lower decoding performance than UEP LT codes with multiple feedbacks.

In order to solve this problem and ensure low compiling complexity, this paper presents a novel UEP LT coding scheme with feedback based on different degree distributions. The scheme starts from the standard LT coding process, applies different distributions to high priority and low priority data independently, and introduces a simple feedback when high priority data is recovered completely. Ultimately ensure the UEP property of high priority data in decoding performance and simulation time and increase the transmission efficiency of low priority data to some extent.

2 Review of LT Codes

2.1 Encoding and Decoding

Suppose LT encoder has K source packets to transmit, and randomly generates d packets called degree d through the function of degree distribution. Then gain an encoded packet by doing XOR operation with the selected packets. Encoder repeats the process constantly before decoding success.

For the sake of simplicity, we assume that the transmit channel is ideal and adopt Belief Propagation (BP) decoding algorithm [14]. LT decoder begins to work when the number of received encoded packets is equal or greater than K. Degree-1 packets are recovered primarily, because they are the same as source packets. Then release more degree-1 packets by performing XOR operations on their neighbors. Repeat this process until all source packets are known.

2.2 Degree Distributions

To have a better understanding on the new coding scheme, we briefly introduce some degree distributions at first.

To start BP decoding process as soon as possible, it is essential to produce many degree-1 encoded packets. BED can meet this requirement and the function is given as below:

$$\varphi(i)=\begin{cases} 1/2^{i}, & i=1,2,\dots,K-1 \\ 1/2^{K-1}, & i=K \end{cases} \tag{1}$$

$\varphi(i)$ is the probability of producing a degree-i encoded packet, when adopting BED to encode. We can see from Eq.1 that the probability of high degree encoded packets becomes low with the increasing of degree i, which results in the decrease of relevance and coverage between source packets. If BED is applied to short length information sequence [15], the effect of this problem on overhead and decoding efficiency will be diminished.

Compared to BED, RSD has stronger robustness with high degree encoded packets, which is suitable for long code length. RSD is modified on Ideal Soliton Distribution (ISD) and its expression is as follows:

$$\rho(i)=\begin{cases} 1/K, & i=1 \\ 1/i(i-1), & i=2,\dots,K \end{cases} \tag{2}$$

$$\tau(i)=\begin{cases} R/(i\cdot K), & i=1,2,\dots,K/R-1 \\ R\cdot\ln(R/\delta)/K, & i=K/R \\ 0, & i=K/R+1,\dots,K \end{cases} \tag{3}$$

$$\beta=\sum\nolimits_{i}(\rho(i)+\tau(i)) \tag{4}$$

$$\mu(i)=\frac{\rho(i)+\tau(i)}{\beta}, i=1,2,\dots,K \tag{5}$$

$\rho(i)$ is the probability of producing a degree-i encoded packet, when adopting ISD to encode. $\mu(i)$ is RSD. δ is the allowable failure probability of the decoder to recover source data, $0<c<1$ is a proper constant, $R=c\cdot\ln(K/\delta)\sqrt{K}$. Let c=0.03, δ=0.5 [13] here.

Combined the advantages of BED and RSD, SDD is designed in [6]. The function of the distribution is :

$$\omega_{i,K}=\begin{cases} \varphi(i), & i\le\alpha\cdot K \\ \mu(i), & i>\alpha\cdot K \end{cases} \tag{6}$$

$\omega_{i,K}$ is the probability of producing a degree-i encoded packet, when adopting SDD to encode, $\varphi(i)$ is BED, $\mu(i)$ is RSD. α=0.1 is the optimal switch point.

We can see form Eq.6 that SDD has the characteristics both BED and RSD, and a wider range of applicability. It is obvious to increase the number of encoded packets for starting BP decoding process and reduce the total number when recover completely.

3 Novel UEP LT coding Scheme

Assume two levels of priority on K source packets. The preceding $K_1=\alpha\cdot K$ $(0<\alpha<1)$ is high priority data, and the rest $K_2=K-K_1$ is low priority data.

In general, the ratio of high priority data is quite small and the majority of source packets are low priority data. Based on the analysis above, BED is suitable for short length information sequence and SDD is more flexible to apply. Therefore, we consider using BED to transmit high priority data and SDD to low priority data. To make sure of the UEP property of high priority data, it is necessary to decode these data at first and introduce a simple feedback after recovering all of them. And then adopt SDD to transmit low priority data until these data decode completely. The detail process is shown in Fig.1.

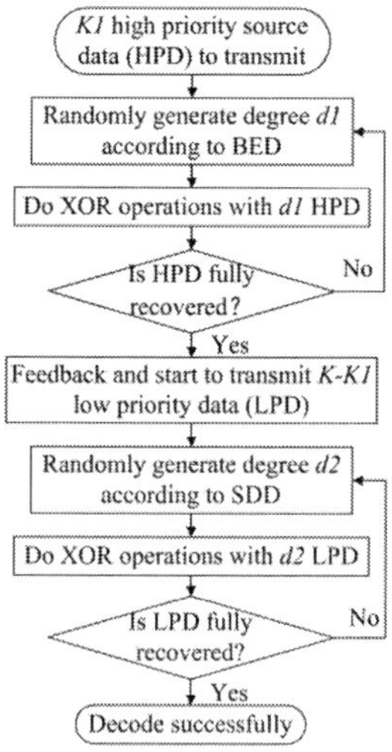

Figure 1. The encoding process of the novel scheme.

It can be seen from Figure 1 that high priority data utilizes a standard LT encoding method and low priority data does the same. Respectively generate $d1$ and $d2$ according to BED and SDD, and then produce enough encoded packets by doing XOR operations. These two transmission processes are separated and independent

 DOI: 10.1051/itmconf/20160709013

from each other, that is to say, there is no mutual influence between them, so that it can certainly overcome the disadvantage of sacrificing the decoding performance of low priority data in order to improve high priority data. The only feedback occurs when high priority data is completely recovered, and it is a simple confirmation message, thus the UEP property of high priority data will be guaranteed all the same. Moreover, there is no increase in compiling complexity.

4 Simulation Results

4.1 Analysis on Different degree Distributions

Simulations are implemented using MATALB 7.0 software in Windows system environment.

Figure 2 shows the probability of BED and RSD when source packets K=100. BED has half of probability to generate degree-1 encoded packets, which plays an important role at the beginning of BP decoding process. Though the probability of degree-1 is low in RSD, high degree especially $d=K/R$ is relatively large, which ensures the sustainable and effectiveness of the decoding process. SDD combines the advantages of BED and RSD, so it has a better decoding performance and applicability.

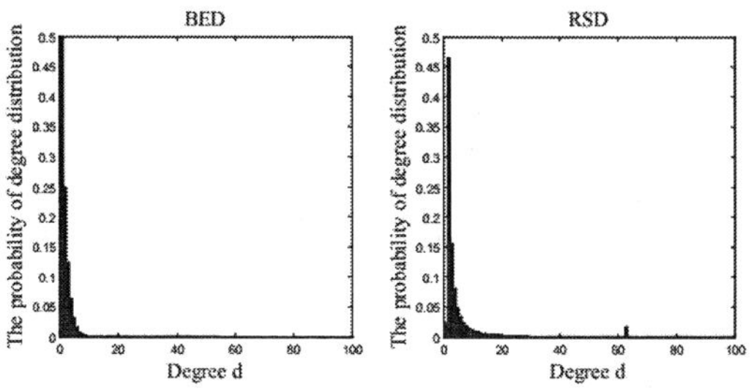

Figure 2. The probability of BED and RSD when source packets K=100.

Table 1 lists the number of received encoded packets and the average simulation time when K=100 source packets are recovered completely.

Table 1. The comparison of decoding performance with three degree distributions.

Degree distribution	BED	RSD	SDD
Number of received encoded packets	380	255	180
Simulation time on average [second]	0.479	1.235	1.219

Although BED requires the most of encoded packets when decoding success, its average simulation time is least and about a third of the other distributions. This is another reason why we apply BED to transmit high priority data, that is, to insure the UEP property in time. SDD needs the least of encoded packets when recovered completely and its average simulation time is less than RSD. After a comprehensive consideration, we select BED to transmit high priority data and SDD to transmit low priority data, for enhancing the coding efficiency further.

4.2 Comparison with Traditional UEP LT Codes

We assume lossless transmission and feedback channels, apply BP decoding method and set the parameters K=1000, $\alpha=K_1/K$=0.1. When running WUEP, its weighting factor km=6, 8 [13]. The first window selection probability is Γ_1=0.0065, 0.0084 [16] in EWF, and two RSD with the same parameters are applied to both windows for a better performance [16]. For the DWF scheme, we use RF_1=2, EF=4 [16] and RSD with the same parameters above.

Figure 3 and Figure 4 show the experiment results of our novel scheme in decoding efficiency comparing to three kinds of traditional UEP LT codes. It can be seen that our scheme outperforms others for both high priority and low priority data. With the increase of km in WUEP, the protection for high priority data is strengthened, but the property of low priority data degraded a lot. In addition, the UEP property of high priority data is not obvious in EWF and DWF codes.

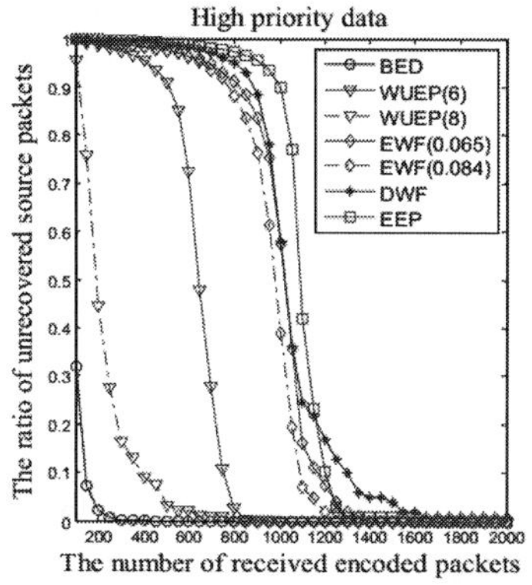

Figure 3. The comparison of high priority data between the novel scheme and traditional UEP LT codes.

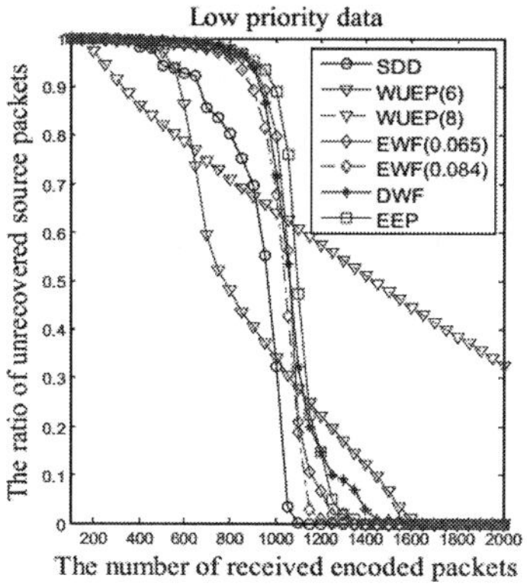

Figure 4. The comparison of low priority data between the novel scheme and traditional UEP LT codes.

As we can see, there are about 500 encoded packets required to recover all of 100 high priority source packets in our scheme, 850 in WUEP (*km*=8), 1350 in EWF (Γ_1=0.0084), and 1800 in DWF. Meanwhile, when the low priority data is recovered completely in our method, WUEP (*km*=6) remains about 22.3% unrecovered source packets, EWF (Γ_1=0.0065) remains 2.9%, and DWF remains 14.9%. In a word, our novel scheme not only has big superiority in the transmission of high priority data, but also markedly improves the decoding efficiency of low priority data.

4.3 Comparison with UEP LT Codes with Feedback

In this section, the novel scheme is compared with the multiple feedbacks and single feedback in [13]. These two schemes are based on WUEP (*km*=6), so the experiments only focus on the performance of low priority data.

Figure 5 demonstrates the simulation results of this section. Although the performance of single feedback scheme is lower than multiple feedbacks scheme, there is only a simple feedback during the whole decoding process, so single feedback scheme has a stronger applicability. Before about 70% low priority source packets are recovered, these two schemes are better in decoding property. However, when decoding success in the end, our novel scheme needs the least number of packets about 1150, multiple feedbacks scheme 1250 and single feedback scheme 1350. All in all, the proposed scheme inherits the advantages of single feedback scheme and promotes the decoding efficiency of low priority data from 8% to 14.8%.

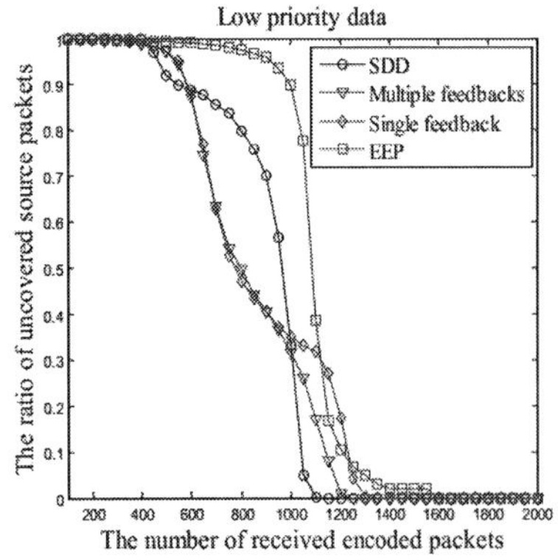

Figure 5. The comparison between the novel scheme and UEP LT codes with feedback.

Summary

In this paper, we propose a novel UEP LT coding scheme with a simple feedback based on BED and SDD. The novel coding scheme aims at the existing problems in traditional UEP LT coding methods, and overcomes their disadvantages with no increase in compiling complexity. The simulation results show that it has better performance in encoding and decoding comparing with others. For high priority data, this new scheme elevates its UEP property in decoding performance and simulation time. For low priority data, its overhead decreases about 2.9%-22.3%. What's more, there is only a simple feedback introduced, so the application of the novel scheme to multicast and broadcast environment is quite suitable.

References

1. H. Schwarz, D. Marpe, T. Wiegand, IEEE Trans Circuits Syst. Video Technol., 17, 1103-1120 (2007)
2. Jofina Jose, S. M Sameer, IEEE International Conference on Signal Processing, Informatics, Communication and Energy Systems (SPICES), 1-5 (2015)
3. B. Masnick, J. Wolf, IEEE Trans. Inf. Theory, 13, 600-607 (1967)
4. M.S. Zaman, G.R. Murthy, UKIWCWS, 1-5 (2009)
5. M. Luby, Proceedings of 43rd Annual IEEE symposium on the Fountains of Computer Science, 271-280 (2002)
6. Meng Zhang, Weijia Lei, Xianzhong Xie, IEEE Third International Conference on Information Science and Technology (ICIST), 1089-1092 (2013)
7. R. Nazanin, B.N. Vellambi, F. Fekri, IEEE Trans. Inf. Theory, 53, 1521-1532 (2007)
8. D. Sejdinovic, D. Vukobratovic, A. Doufexi, V. Senk, R.J. Piechocki, Conference Record of the Forty-First Asilomar Conference on Signals, Systems and Computers (ACSSC), 1020-1024 (2007)
9. S. Ahmad, R. Hamzaoui, M. Al-Akaidi, Proceedings of 9th Middle Eastern Simulation Multiconference, 104-108 (2008)
10. Yan Wang, Rongke Liu, IET Communications , 9, 33 -41 (2015)
11. J. H. Sorensen, P. Popovski, J. Ostergaard, IEEE Commun. Lett., 17, 1636-1639 (2013)
12. Jiaqi Yu, Jie Zhong, Miniian Zhao, Yulong Cai, Jie Wu, Conference on Wireless Communications and Signal Processing (WCSP), 1-5 (2012)
13. Meiling Chen, Weidang Zhang, Fangyuan Li, Science Technology and Engineering, 15, 100-104 (2015)
14. D. J. C. MacKay, Proceeding of IEEE Communications, 152, 1062-1068 (2005)
15. E. Bodine, M. Cheng, IEEE International Conference on Communications, 1195-1199 (2008)
16. Chunya Ni, Chunping Hou, Wei Xiang, IEEE Wireless Communications and Networking Conference (WCNC), 592-596 (2012)

DOI: 10.1051/itmconf/20160709014

A method to detect heart rate based on electrical bio-impedance

Kun-Yang LI[1,2,3],Wen-Hui CHEN[1,2,3],Lian-Rong ZHENG[1,2,3],Shan-Qing WANG[1,2,3],Xian-Ming LI[1,2,3],Guan-Zheng LIU[1,2,3*]

[1] *School of Engineering, Sun Yat-sen University, Guangzhou 510275,China*
[2]*Key Laboratory of Sensing Technology and Biomedical Instrument of Guangdong Province, School of Engineering, Sun Yat-sen University, Guangzhou 510275,China*
[3] *Guangdong Provincial Engineering and Technology Centre of Advanced and Portable Medical Device, Guangzhou 510275, China*
*Corresponding author: liugzh3@mail.sysu.edu.cn

Abstract. As a basic health indicator, heart rate has been widely used in clinical measurement and daily health care. Electrical bio-impedance (EBI) measurement provides non-invasive method for heart rate detection. Therefore, this paper proposed a method to detect heart rate based on EBI. With the BIOPAC EBI module, the signal can be de-noised in real-time. Finally, the de-noised EBI signal is used to compute heart rate. Four electrodes are located at radial artery of left upper limb in this method. The result proves that this method has high accuracy on heart rate measurement.

1. Introduction

Heart rate detection help in evaluating the state of the subject, especially in study of cardiovascular; heart rate is an independent risk factor of hypertension [1], coronary artery disease [2], and congestiveheart failure [3] and so on. In general, heart rate was measuring through Electrocardiogram(ECG) signal orPhotoplethysmography(PPG)signal[4]. As a novel method,EBI allow us to noninvasively obtain physical information from human body. In general, this measurement is performed on the limb by placing surface electrodes. The blood volume of the blood vessel changes resulting in the change of regional EBI, by measuring the variation of the electrical bio-impedance, the arterial pulse frequency can be collected to represent the heart rate.

EBI measurement with various types of electrodes and measuring systems has long been developed in past years[5 6]. In 2005, Kristiansen et.al using an handheld impedance plethysmograph to measure impedance heart rate, with a Pearson's of 1.00, the mean difference compare to the gold standard is -x beats/min, show no significance systemic error[7]. In 2008, Rafael et.al present a method from plantar bio-impedance measurement, compare with gold standard ECG derived RR, the mean bias of RR intervals was -0.2ms and the 95% confidence interval was about ±36ms, through the Bland-Altman analysis, there is only one point out of the 95% consistency limit[8]. In 2009, Cho et.al compared different measuring position of arm artery and find an appropriate position with the Pearson's correlation coefficient of 0.982 to the gold standard, and the RMSE (RootMean Square Error) is 1.817 beats/min[9].

We havedesigneda system to measure the electrical bio-impedance changes to detect the heart rate in motionless condition using multichannel physiologic recorder MP150 (BIOPAC, USA). Due to the low amplitude of the heart-related impedance variations, the collected signal's SNR (Signal- Noise ratio)is not very high, and need to be post process. The rest of this paper is organized as follows. Section II provides details of the methodology, including data acquisition and data process. The result is present in Section III and conclusion is drawn in Section IV.

2. Methodology

The designed system was consisted of hardware module and signal processing method. The ECG and EBI signal could be obtain through the data acquisition system. Figure1 shows the block diagram of the EBI based heart rate measurement system.

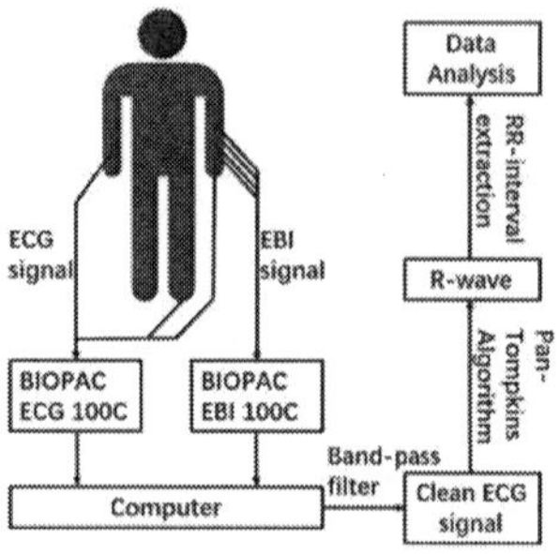

Figure1 the Block Diagram of The Ebi Based Heart Rate Measurement System

2.1 Data Acquisition

The data of this study consist of 5 minutes simultaneous ECG and EBI signal collected by multichannel physiologic recorder MP150 and its support software acknowledge 4.0, the subjects are 10 healthy people age between 18-25 years old. Here we choose ECG100C and EBI100C module to acquire ECG and EBI signal, respectively. Before paste the electrode, use sandpaper to exfoliating the surface, and then use the medical alcohol to disinfection. Then, paste electrode on lower left limbs, per left limb and right lower limb to composite standard lead of ECG measurement to acquire ECG signal. Paste four electrode E1~E4 on radial artery of arm as figure2, the space is 2cm, 3cm, 2cm. Electrode E1 and E2 is to generate input excitation current with the frequency of 50kHz,E3, E4 is using to receive the output voltage signal. After that, let the subject lie down, while the subject's physiological state is stable, open the MP150, and open the acknowledge 4.0 software on computer, issued a sound command to control subject's breathe regularly, this stage will last for 5 minutes. After that, save the data, close the MP150 and unload the electrode.

2.2 Data Process

Data processing is based on MATLAB R2010b (MATHWORKS, USA). After we obtained the origin signal, we use a band-pass filter with cut-off frequencies is comprised of 0.7and40 Hz, and the filtercould effectively remove the baseline driftand the interference signal such as respiration-related low frequencynoise and50Hz power-line interference[10].R-peaks are found using the Pan–Tompkins algorithm[11] that is properly for this study due to its high accuracy, and the R-peaks location are used to compute the RR interval time series.

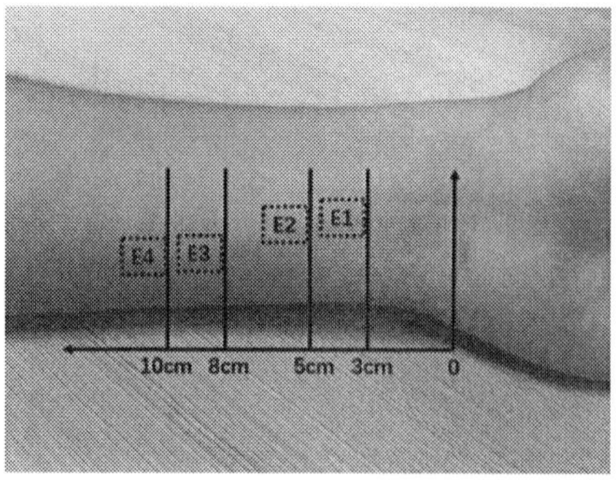

Figure2 The Electrode Position of The Ebi Method

3. Results

Figure 3 shows the ECG and the EBI signal from one of the volunteers. It can be observed that the peak of EBI is latter than the ECG signal in the same period. This may due to the closer of the position of the electrode can be faster to obtain the signal. The results of others subjects were similar and the baseline of the two signals were stable as long as the subjects keep quiet.

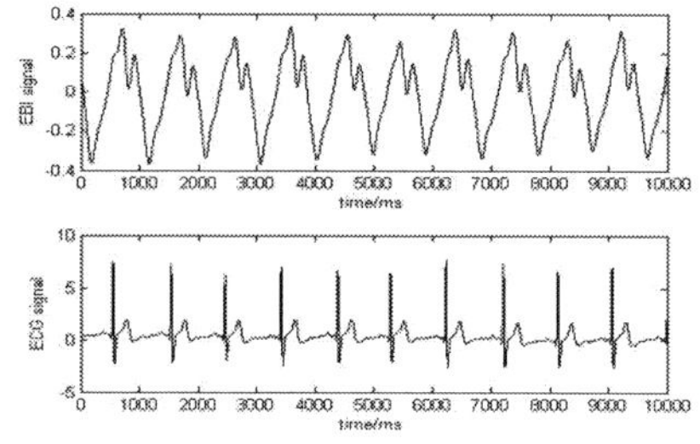

Figure3 ECG Signal and EBI Signal from One Volunteer

Figure 4 shows the EBI and ECG derived RR interval from one of the volunteers, it can be observed that they seemed very similar.

We choose the ECG derived heart rates the gold standard and the ECG derived heart rate is computed using 60/. In order to provide an agreement figure, we used a Bland-Altman plot[12]for each RR interval measured from the ECG and EBI signal in figure 5. The mean bias of RR intervals was -0.0065ms and the 95%

confidence interval was about ±0.04ms. It can be observedthat the RR interval derived from EBI signal essentiallyagrees with the RR intervalmeasuredfromECG.

In figure 6, eachECG derived RR interval is plotted versus the EBI derived RR interval. Pearson correlation coefficient was 0.9965 ($p<0.001$) with an RMSE of 0.0092ms/beat, indicating the EBI derived heart rate has a high accuracy.

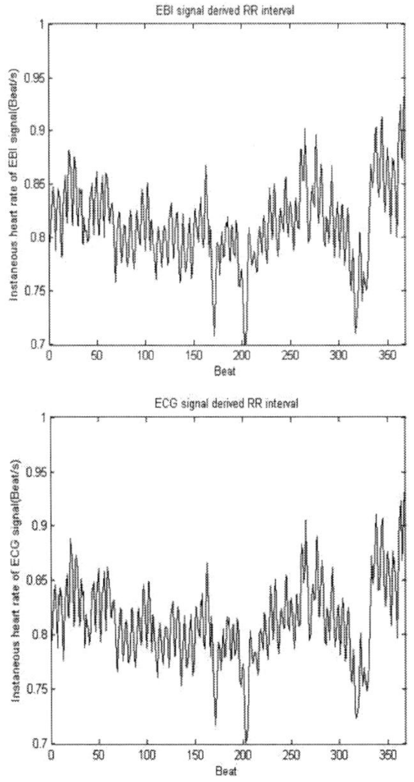

Figure4 EBI and ECG Derived Rr Interval from One of The Volunteers

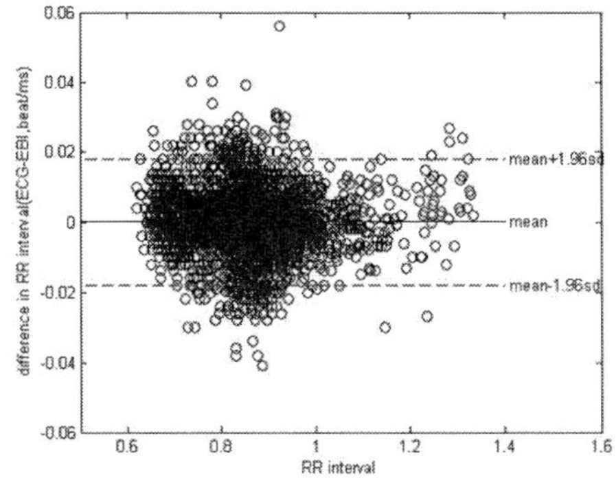

Figure5 Difference Plotted Against Average of Ebi and Ecg Measurements, with Mean and 95% Limits of Agreement.

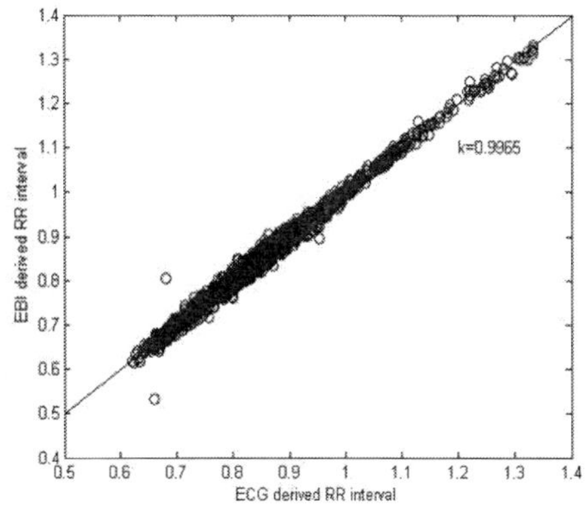

Figure6 The Measured Instantaneous heart Rate Using Ebi Signal Is Plotted Versus by the Reference Signal, the Plot is Fitted by Regression Method.

4. Discussion

A method to detect heart rate based on electrical bio-impedance have been presented ,after calculation and comparison, it is confirmed that the accuracy rate is up to 99.65%, indicate that in the motionless condition, the EBI based heart rate can be accurately reflected the subjects (normal person) heart rate. We also apply the EBI based method to analysis other physiological signal, such as respiratory signal - we designed an EBI based system to research the difference of the respiratory volume between different posture[13].We also concerned on BSN and mobile medical[14],in the future, we may try toapply the electrical bio-impedance on wearable device.

Acknowledgments

The authors would like to acknowledgment the support from the National Natural Science Foundation of China (61401521) and Natural Science Foundation of Guangdong province (2014A030310163).

References

1. M.G. William, W.B. Kannel, A. Belanger, R.B.D'Agostino,"Influence of heart rate on mortality among persons with hypertension: The Framingham Study", Am Heart J, 125, 4 (1993)
2. P. Palatini, "Heart rate: a strong predictor of mortality in subjects with coronary artery disease", Eur Heart J, 26, 10 (2005)
3. G.Z. Liu, L. Wang, Q. Wang, G.M. Zhou, Y. Wang, Q. Jiang, "A New Approach to Detect Congestive Heart Failure Using Short-Term Heart Rate Variability Measures", PLOS ONE, 9, 4 (2014)
4. C.G. Yu, Z.Q. Liu, T. McKenna,A.T. Reisner, J.Reifman, "A Method for Automatic Identification of Reliable Heart RatesCalculated from ECG and PPG Waveforms",Jamia, 13,3 (2006)

5. M.E. Valentinuzzi, "Bioelectrical impedance techniques in medicine: Bioimpedance measurement", Crit. Rev. Biomed. Eng,24,4(1996)
6. M.R. King, T.A. Anderson, et.al, "Age related incidence of desaturation events and the cardiac on stroke index, cardiac index, and heart rate measured by continuous bioimpedancenoninvasivecardiac output monitoring in infants and children undergoing general anaesthesia", j.jclinane, 32, 10 (2016)
7. N.K. Kristiansen, J. Fleischer, M.S. Jensen, K.S. Andersen, H. Nygaard,"Design and evaluation of a handheld impedance plethysmograph formeasuring heart rate variability", Medical&Biological Engineering & Computing, 43, 4(2005)
8. R. Gonzalez-Landaeta, O. Casas, R. Pallas-Areny, "Heart Rate Detection from Plantar Bioimpedance Measurements", TBME, 55, 3 (2008)
9. M.C. Cho, J.Y. Kim, S. Cho,"A Bio-Impedance Measurement System for Portable Monitoring of Heart Rate and Pulse Wave Velocity Using Small Body Area", ISCAS, IEEE (2009)
10. P. Kligfield, S.G. Leonard et.al, "Recommendations for the Standardization and Interpretation of the Electrocardiogram", J Am CollCardiol, 49, 10 (2007)
11. J.P. Pan, W.J. Tompkins, "A Real-Time QRS Detection Algorithm", TBME, 32, 3 (1985)
12. J.M. Bland,D.G. Altman, "Statistical methods for assessing agreement between two methods of clinical measurement", Lancet, 327, 8476 (1986)
13. G.Z. Liu, G.M. Zhou, W.H. Chen, Q. Jiang, "A Principal Component Analysis Based Data Fusion Method for Estimation of Respiratory Volume", JSEN, 15, 8 (2015)
14. G.Z. Liu, B.Y. Huang, L. Wang, "A Wearable Respiratory Biofeedback System Based on Generalized Body Sensor Network", tmj, 17, 5 (2011)

ITM Web of Conferences 7, 09015 (2016) DOI: 10.1051/itmconf/20160709015
ITA 2016

Java Performance Mysteries

Pranita Maldikar, San-Hong Li and Kingsum Chow

Pranita.maldikar@intel.com, {sanhong.lsh, kingsum.kc}@alibaba-inc.com

Abstract. While assessing software performance quality in the cloud, we noticed some significant performance variation of several Java applications. At a first glance, they looked like mysteries. To isolate the variation due to cloud, system and software configurations, we designed a set of experiments and collected set of software performance data. We analyzed the data to identify the sources of Java performance variation. Our experience in measuring Java performance may help attendees in selecting the trade-offs in software configurations and load testing tool configurations to obtain the software quality measurements they need.
The contributions of this paper are (1) Observing Java performance mysteries in the cloud, (2) Identifying the sources of performance mysteries, and (3) Obtaining optimal and reproducible performance data.

1 Introduction

Java is both a programming language and a platform. Java as a programming language follows object-oriented programming model and it requires Java Virtual Machine (Java Interpreter) to run Java programs. Java as a platform is an environment on which we can deploy Java applications. Java Enterprise Edition (Java EE) [1]is a platform which is used to run enterprise class workloads and applications. This platform provides API and runtime environment for developing and running multi-tiered, scalable, reliable enterprise applications. An Enterprise application is a business application that is complex, scalable, distributed and multi-tiered.

Java applications can be single tieredor multi-tiered. Single tier Java applications are self-contained applications that can perform certain operations. SPECjvm2008 [3]is an example of single tier Java benchmark. SPECjvm2008 benchmark comprises of dozens of Java applications. Some of these Java applications work on exercising encryption software like crypto.aes, crypto.rsa, crypto.signverify workloads while some of them are scientific mathematical algorithms like FFT, sparse matrix computation etc. that works with both large and small data set.

Multi-tier Java workload or enterprise Java application is a software application distributed over multiple machines. Such applications can be separated into multiple tiers like, client tier, middle-tier and data tier. For testing a Java EE workload theclient tier would be a load generator machine using load generator software like Faban [2]. This client tier will consist of users that will send the request to the application server or the middle tier.The middle tier contains the entire business logic for the enterprise application. Business logic is nothing but the code that gives functionality to the application. The data-tier is the data source for the application. It consists ofdatabase or the legacy data sources like mainframes.

2 Java Performance Monitoring

There are a number of factors that could affect the performance of Java program. Among them, garbage collection (GC) and just-in-time (JIT) compilation probably stand out as they are not present in native program performance monitoring.

Garbage collection is implemented by the Java Virtual Machine (JVM) for automatic memory management. Java HotSpotTM VM [8] (originally implemented by Sun, acquired by Oracle) supports several different garbage collection algorithms which were designed for serving different pause time and throughput requirements.For the multi-tier Java workloads running HotSpotTM in cloud, typically, we consider choosing one of these three collectors:throughput collector, CMS collector and G1 collector, the best choice dependson workload characteristics.

The parallel old collector (enabled by -XX:+UseParallelOldGC) is designed for maximizing the total throughput of an application, but some individual business transaction might be subjected to a long pause.

The CMS collector (enabled by -XX:+UseConcMarkSweepGC) can concurrently collect the objects in old generation while application threads are running. The CMS algorithm is designed to eliminate long pauses.It has two quick stop-the-world (STW) pauses per old generation collection. Compared with throughput collector, the CMS may increase the CPU usage due to its background processing.

The G1 collector (enabled by -XX:+UseG1GC) is designed for processing large heap with minimal pauses. The G1 divides the entire heap into equally-sized region and 'smartly' collects the regions with the least live data first (garbage first) [9]. Similar with CMS, the collection for old generation in G1 is also done in concurrent way.

We have the different GC collector choices as there is no one right algorithm for every workload, different GC collector optimizes for different user scenarios. In general, the parallel old collector is optimized for throughput. The CMS collector is optimized for pause time. The G1 collector is optimized for reducing pause time on large heaps more than 4GB.

Selecting the right GC algorithm can significantly help the application performance.As a rule of thumb: if the GC overhead is > 10%, the wrong GC algorithmmight be probably used.

The first important tuning for GC is the size of the application's heap. Smaller heap size means more frequent GC and not enough time for performing business logic. Larger heap size means less frequent GC, but the duration of each of GC pauses will be increased, as the time spent in GC pauses is generally proportional to the size of space being collected. Choosing proper heap size also depends on workloads. Heap occupancy is one important measure for heap size setting, as a rule of thumb: size the heap so that it is 30% occupied after a full GC[10].

The Just-In-Time compiler component in JVM is used to turn bytecode into much faster native code for accelerating Java programming language performance. There are a couple of typical tuning practices for JIT which can help the improvements in the performance of application.

The size of code cache is the first basic thing which we should pay more attention to. Generally, just make sure that the code cache is large enough otherwise the application might mysteriously slow down if it is running out of code cache space.

Inlining is one of important optimizations made by JIT to eliminate the overhead of method call. Thus small and frequently called methodsmight be good candidates for inlining.

To identify and resolve Java performance issues, the following methods might be considered. (1) Monitor the logs, e.g. GC or JIT log, (2) Use the diagnostics JVM parameters which will provide more useful information for your debug, and (3) Use profiling tools, likes VisualVM, JMC(shipped with OracleJDK as commercial feature set).

Logs are usually thekey to find possible performance bottleneck; there are some open source tools to visualize these logs, e.g. gcviewer[5] is a good tool for gc log analytics and jitwatch[6] provides visual insights into JIT compilation.

Diagnostics JVM parameters [7] is another good way to explore the performance related issues, e.g. enable inlining diagnostics output by adding -XX:+PrintInlining parameter and then check which method is failed to inline.

There are a lot of profiling tools for measuring application performance, technically speaking, the profiling can be made by either sampling or runtime instrumentation. Both instrumentation-based and sampling-based tools have different characteristics with their own advantages and disadvantages.Profiling does not come for free, we should pay close attention to the overhead introduced by profiling tool otherwise the results collected by them couldbe misleading for final conclusion.

3 Java Performance Mysteries

In a datacenter of a cloud service provider, before upgrading the hardware systems to a newer version it is very crucial to evaluate the goodness of the new hardware compared to the older ones. For evaluation we use multiple workloads/benchmarks to assess the performance [4]benefit it offers over the previous generation. In this paper we are evaluating two platforms called Platform A and Platform B using an Enterprise Javaworkload. We are using a two tier Java EE Web Application workload. The workload consists of a client tier which generates load using faban driver. Based on the injection rate the faban driver will start client users that send http request to the application server. The application server will process the request and send a response back to the client with appropriate web page. The web page is computed dynamically after processing the request from the client. When a user gets a response back from the application server it will immediately send another request. Advantage of this is, we can saturate the application server with very small number of clients to evaluate its maximum performance capability. This

 DOI: 10.1051/itmconf/20160709015

workload is useful in the test environment where we want to get quick performance numbers with high CPU saturation. We are running the workload on two platforms called Platform A and Platform B with fixed number of users. For this workload we are not sure of the optimal heap size and GC algorithm. So we are evaluating both the platforms with small and large heap sizes and two different GC algorithms called GC-1 and GC-2. The table below summarizes our findings on both the Platforms.

Table 1. Performance of Both Platforms at Higher Number of Users

config	web101.5W Platform A Small Heap GC-1	web101.5O Platform B Small Heap GC-1	web101.6F Platform A Large Heap GC-1	web101.6G Platform B Large Heap GC-1	web101.6B Platform A Small Heap GC-2	web101.6C Platform B Small Heap GC-2	web101.6I Platform A Large Heap GC-2	web101.6L Platform B Large Heap GC-2
Normalized Throughput	8.01	9.94	9.01	10.92	11.07	11.60	11.75	12.20
Performance Improvemen t		1.24		1.21		1.05		1.04
Network Utilization (Mbps)	6,344	7,839	7,108	8,609	8,730	9,089	9,263	9,611

3.1. Impact of GC-1 Garbage Collection Algorithm on Platform A and b

Based on Run ID web101.5W vs web101.6F and web101.5Ovs web101.6G we can infer that larger heap gives better throughput. Large heap results in less frequent GC. The JVM spends more time running the application and less time collecting garbage.For GC-1 garbage collection algorithm we can also say that Platform B produced 24% higher throughput than Platform A with small heap size. This performance delta is reduced to 21% with large heap.

3.2. Impact of GC-2 Garbage Collection Algorithm on Platform A and B

With runs web101.6B vs web101.6I and web101.6C vs web101.6L we see similar performance improvement with heap size. But if we look at platform comparison then we see only 5% performance improvement with Platform B over Platform A with small heap size and 4% performance improvement with large heap. After close inspection we realized that the performance impact with this GC algorithm is misleading because we are very close to saturate the network capacity. Hence these performance numbers should not be used to compare the two platforms.

3.3. Impact of Different Garbage Collection Algorithms on Platform A

For Platform A with small heap (web101.5W vs web101.6B) GC-2 algorithm provides 38% performance benefit over GC-1 algorithm and with large heap (web101.6F vs web101.6I)the performance delta reduced to 30%.

3.4. Impact of Different Garbage Collection Algorithms on Platform B

For Platform B with small heap GC-2 algorithm provides only 16% benefit over GC-1 algorithm and with larger heap this delta is decreased to 11%.

To characterize the behaviour of this Web Application workload the system level performance data is insufficient. We need information about the JVM behaviour, and the methods compiled on both the Platforms. We will have better understanding of the workload performance after looking at the JIT code and see how many resources were spent in the hot methods and GC methods for both the garbage collection algorithm on both the Platforms. For that we need to profile the application and collect JVM data.

3.5. Java Profiling

Data collected for performance evaluation does not come for free. It always comes at a cost of performance. Java profiling tools usually run in background, but every time a method is called or compiled the information gets logged in the tool. This has additional overhead. You should be very cautious when using such tools for performance testing.

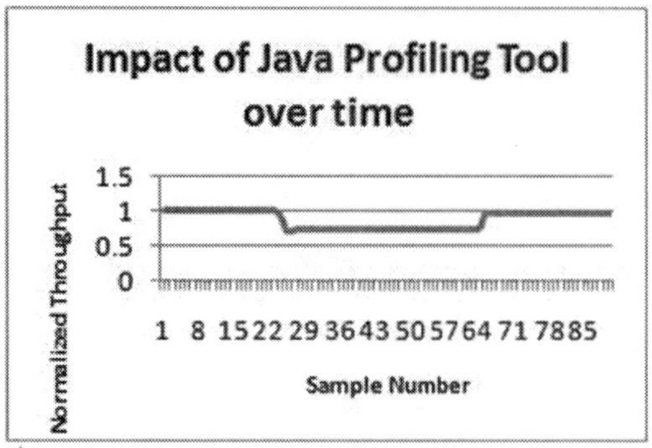

Figure 1. Performance Impact of a Java Profiling Tool

The overhead associated with the tools could be quite high. With one of the Java Profiling tool we saw 20% performance overhead. The throughput dropped down by 20% when the tool was collecting JVM information. Whenever such tools are used they might alter JVM behaviour and interfere with the workload performance.

Hence for performance testing one should always be careful when looking at the summary statistics for the workload. We should always look into the detail workload performance data. The overall summary data could be misleading. Figure 1demonstrates the impact of one such profiling tool used. We saw 20% performance dip when the JVM profiling tool was running. The workload summary reported the average throughput overrun time. It did not notify of thedrop in performance. Only after looking at the detail data we could see the performance impact of the tool.

Table 2. Performance of Both Platforms at Lower Number of Users

Config	web101. 7R Platform A Small Heap GC-1	web101.7C Platform B Small Heap GC-1	web101.7Q Platform A Large Heap GC-1	web101.7 B Platform B Large Heap GC-1	web101.7 V Platform A Small Heap GC-2	web101.7W Platform B Small Heap GC-2	web101.7 U Platform A Large Heap GC-2	web101.7X Platform B Large Heap GC-2
Normalizd Throughput	87.324	85.735	95.28	98.585	92.694	106.352	98.374	117.598
Performance Improvement		0.98		1.03		1.15		1.20
Network Utilization (Mbps)	6,896	6,764	7,522	7,766	7,326	8,391	7,769	9,275

With a low overhead tool we collected detailed data about the JIT code and we observed something really weird. There wasno change in performance when we moved to large heap on the same platform with same configuration.

When we looked into the Java JIT code we realized that between these two configurations the compiled code was different. In one of the runthe print methods got inlined. Whereas in the other run we saw lot of function calls to the print method.Just by method inlining we can observe significant performance difference.JVM is designed to make run time compilation and optimization decisions. Most of the times it will do the right thing, but then occasionally we do see such anomalies that may cause us to make wrong inferences.

With the previous number of users we were close tonetwork saturation.Hence for thenext set of experiments we reduced the number of users.

Table 2summarizes the performance of both the platforms with lower number of users. The strange thing is now when you look at the performance delta between the two platforms the picture that we saw with Table 1completely reverses. With GC-1 algorithm we see Platform A being better than Platform B by 2% for smaller heap and platform B being better than platform A by 3% for larger heap. On the other hand GC-2 algorithm shows 15% performance benefit on Platform B with small heap and 20% performance benefit with large heap. This configuration with lower users tells a completely different story.

4 Summary and Discussion

We showed a couple of examples of Java performance mysteries and identified the sources of those performance mysteries. Understanding Java performance mysteries would enable us to obtaining optimal and reproducible performance data that would in turn help us to make the right decisions in the data center.

References

1. http://docs.oracle.com/javaee/6/firstcup/doc/gcrky.html
2. https://java.net/projects/faban/
3. https://www.spec.org/jvm2008/
4. Khun Ban, Robert Scott, Huijun Yan and Kingsum Chow, "Delivering Quality in Software Performance and Scalability Testing", Pacific Northwest Software Quality Conference, October 2011, Portland, OR.

DOI: 10.1051/itmconf/20160709015

URL http://www.uploads.pnsqc.org/2011/papers/T-40_Ban_etal_paper.pdf

5. http://www.tagtraum.com/gcviewer.html
6. https://github.com/AdoptOpenJDK/jitwatch
7. https://docs.oracle.com/javase/7/docs/webnotes/tsg/TSG-VM/html/clopts.html
8. http://www.oracle.com/technetwork/java/whitepaper-135217.html
9. http://www.oracle.com/technetwork/articles/java/g1gc-1984535.html
10. Scott Oaks, "Java Performance: The Definitive Guide", Oreilly

Grasping Pattern Recognition and Grasping Force Estimation For Prosthetic Hands

Bing-Ke Zhang[1], Guo-Liang Zhong[1, 2, a] and Hua Deng[1, 2]

[1] *School of Mechanical and Electrical Engineering, Central South University 410083, Changsha, Hunan, China*
[2] *State Key Laboratory of High-Performance Complex Manufacturing, Central South University 410083, Changsha, Hunan, China*
[a] *Corresponding author: zhonggl2010@163.com*

Abstract. Human's movement can be decoded by surface electromyography (EMG), and the prosthetic hand can be controlled freely through EMG signal. This paper proposes a grasping pattern and force synchronized decoding method for prosthetic hands. Considering pattern recognition and force estimation simultaneously, this paper analyzes whether different muscle contraction levels affect pattern recognition and whether different grasping modes have impact on force estimation, then proposes two schemes to complete EMG simultaneously decoding. Experiments compare the accuracy of the two methods. The results show that there is no much difference between two methods in force estimation, the former's accuracy of pattern recognition is a little higher than the latter.

1 Introduction

In application, the prosthetic hand should be emphasized to the controllable grasping pattern and controllable force [1, 2]. In the prosthetic hand motion, not only need to recognize hand posture via the electromyographic (EMG) signal, but also need to analyze what should be the size of the grasping force .In actual work, pattern recognition and decoding should be done at the same time. Therefore, it is important to decode the EMG signal combined with pattern recognition and grasping force estimation.

Over the past decades, in order to improve grasping stability performance, synchronized decoding has been widely used in grasping force control and other aspects [3–5]. By imitating the method of grasping objects used by humans, it is possible to grasp any objects that the weight and friction coefficient are unknown [6–8]. A part of the researchers focus on the grasping used by human hands, try to find the grasping pattern recognition method and obtain the optimum value of grasping force. Wang et al. [9] proposed a method for controlling the grasping force by using finite element analysis based on human hand grasping when the weight of the grasped object is unknown. Besides, a lot of work has been done to estimate parameters by taking advantage of the EMG signal as it can be used to adjust the grasping force to the desired value when the prosthetic hand subjects to external disturbances [10].

In order to realize the stability of the prosthetic hand grasping, EMG signal need to decode for grasping mode and grasping force separately, that is, in the process of grasping, the prosthetic hand is not only able to correctly identify EMG signal of the grasping pattern and accurately estimate the size of the grasping force. Such as grasping an egg, excessive force may make eggs break, if the force is too small it will fall and broken. Therefore, an appropriate grasping force is a key factor to achieve excellent grasping performance. However, the existing studies almost focus on the pattern recognition for the prosthetic hand [11], few of them study the grasping pattern and grasping force synchronized decoding for prosthetic hands. This paper is aim to propose a method of grasping pattern and grasping force synchronized decoding for prosthetic hands.

2 Feature selection of grasping force estimation based on the EMG signal

In this paper, we choose the following characteristics that can represent the muscle contraction state in time-domain.

1)Mean Absolute Value (MAV). The mathematical formula can be defined as

$$MAV = \frac{1}{n}\sum_{k=1}^{n}|u(k)| \tag{1}$$

2)Integrated EMG (IEMG). The mathematical formula can be defined as

$$IEMG = \sum_{k=1}^{N}|u(k)| \tag{2}$$

3)Wave Length (WL). The mathematical formula can be defined as

DOI: 10.1051/itmconf/20160709016

$$WL = \sum_{k=1}^{N-1} |u(k+1) - u(k)| \quad (3)$$

4)V-order,(vOrder). The mathematical formula can be defined as

$$vOrder = \sqrt[v]{\frac{1}{N}\sum_{k=1}^{N} |u(k)|^{v}} \quad (4)$$

5)Willison Amplitude (WAMP). The mathematical formula can be defined as

$$WAMP = \sum_{k=1}^{N-1} \left[f(|u(k) - u(k+1)|) \right],$$
$$f(k) = \begin{cases} 1 & |u(k) - u(k+1)| > \varepsilon \\ 0 & else \end{cases} \quad (5)$$

6)Log Detector (log). The mathematical formula can be defined as

$$\log D = e^{\frac{1}{N}\sum_{k=1}^{N} \log(|u(k)|)} \quad (6)$$

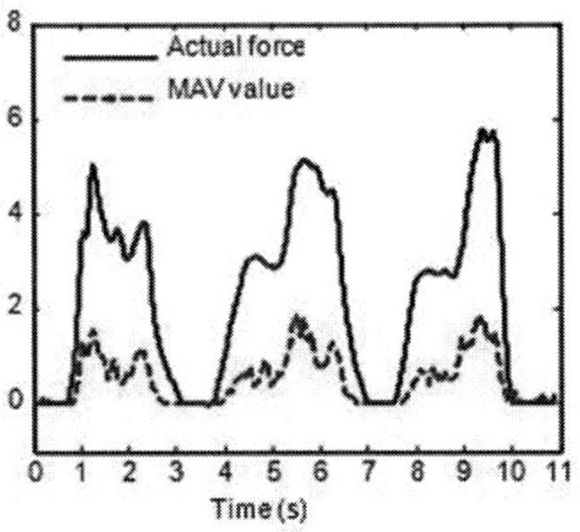

(a) The curves of actual value and MAV value

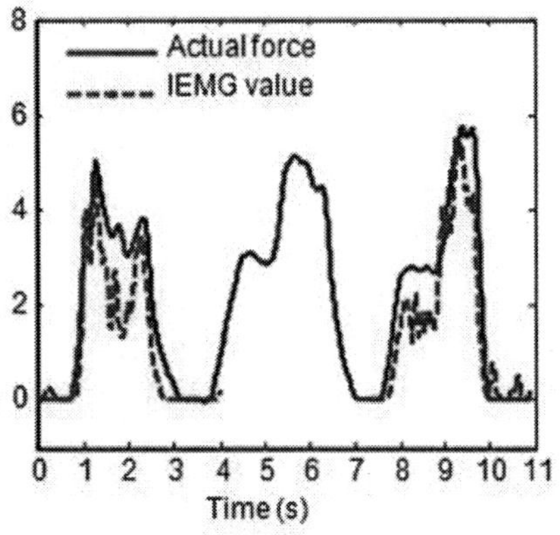

(b) The curves of actual value and IEMG value

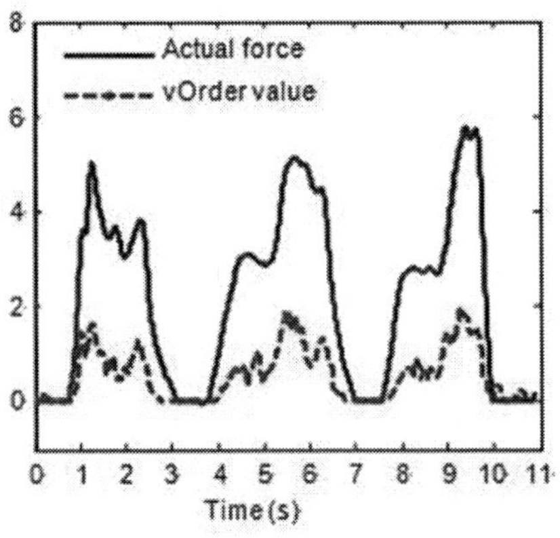

(c) The curves of actual value and WL value

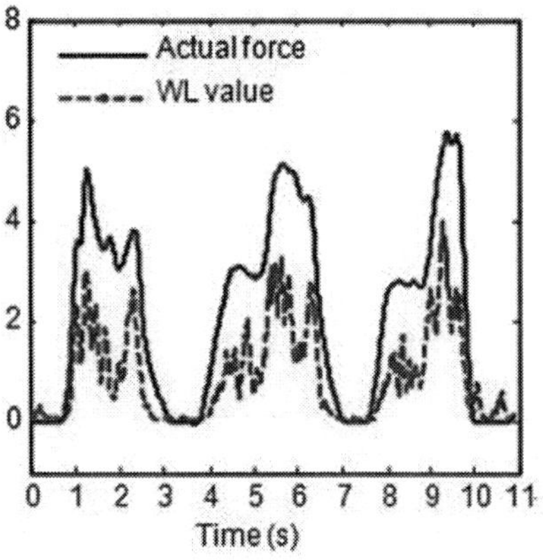

(d) The curves of actual value and vOrder value

 DOI: 10.1051/itmconf/20160709016

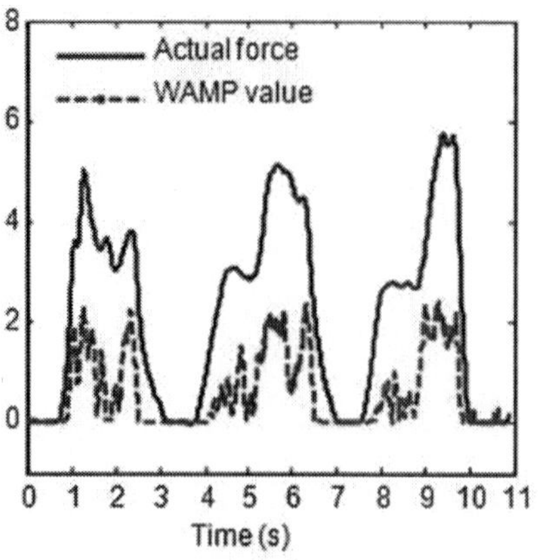

(e) The curves of actual value and WAMP value

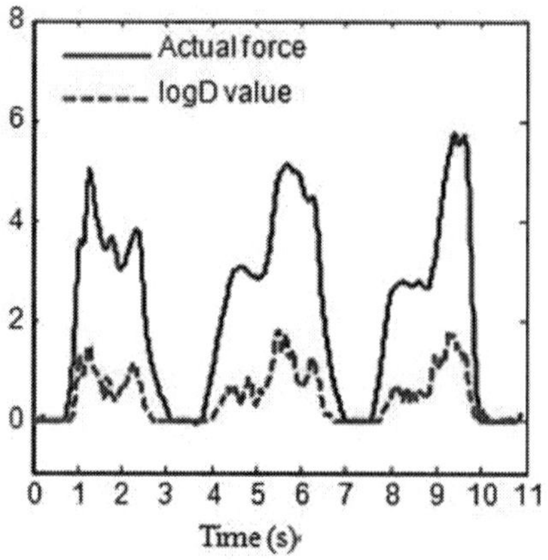

(f) The curves of actual value and logD value

Figure 1. The contrast between the Different Eigenvalues and Output Force.

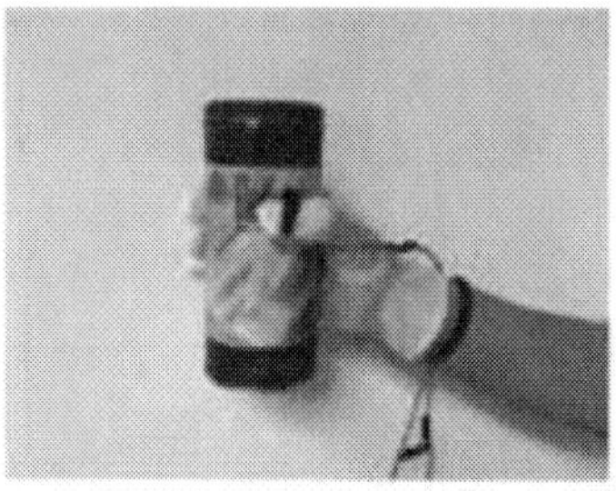

(a) Cylindrical grasping

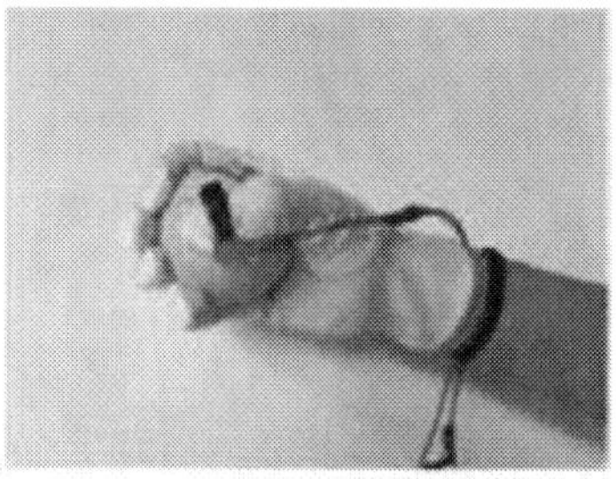

(b) Spherical grasping

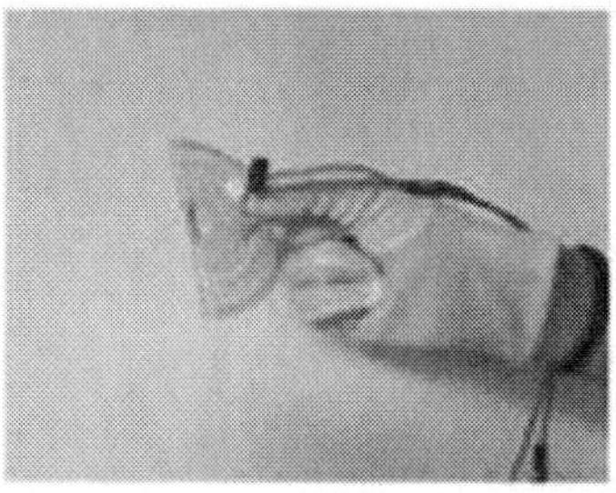

(c) Finger pinching

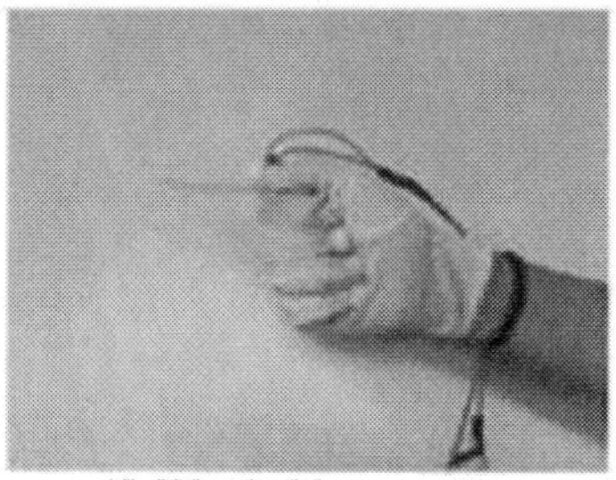

(d) Side pinching

Figure 2. Four Grasping Patterns.

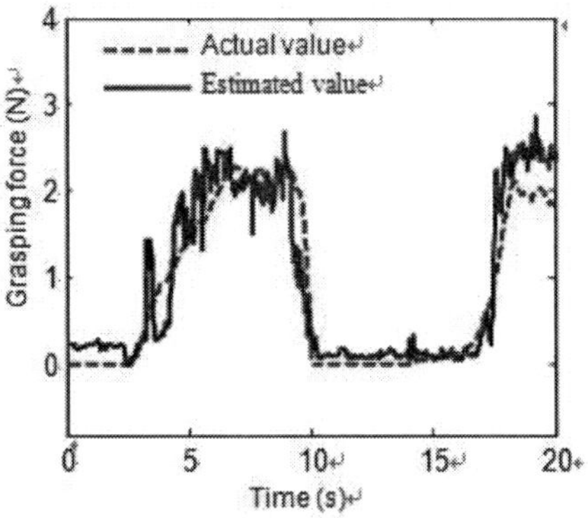

(a) Finger pinching

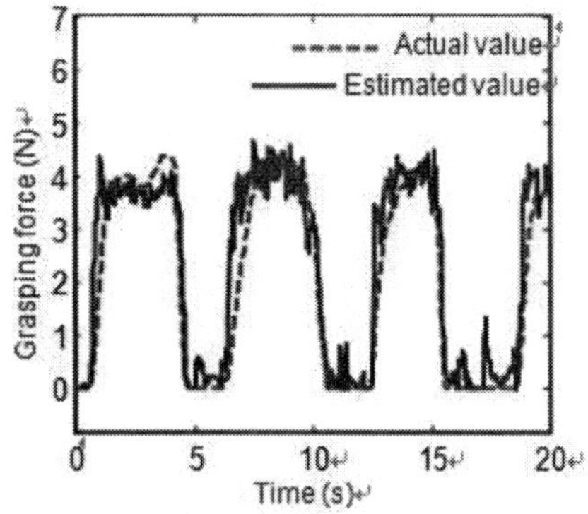

(b) Side pinching

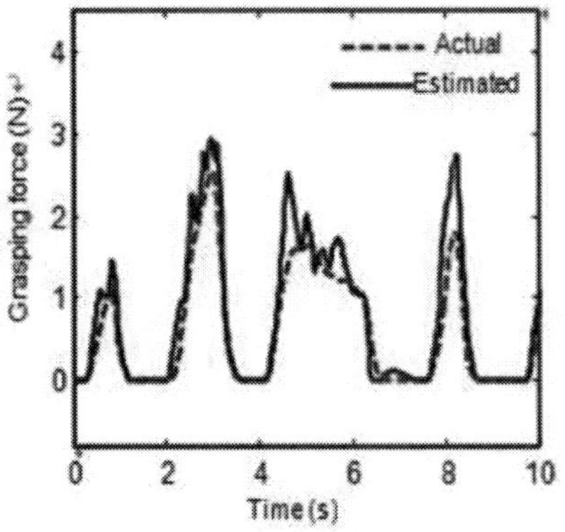

(c) Cylindrical grasping

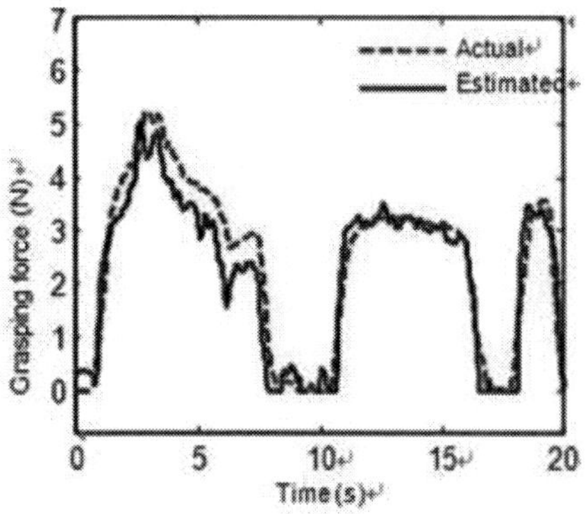

(d) Spherical grasping

Figure 3. Actual Value Estimated Value of Grasping Force Based on Bpnn Method.

Figure 1 shows the comparison between the eigenvalues of the input signal and output force, the EMG signal from the participant who uses side pinched posture for grasping, and the acquisition time for 10 s. The IEMG and WAMP characteristic value is in the range of 0-500. In order to compare the relationship between the characteristic value and the output value, Figure 1 is drew after the eigenvalues of IEMG and WAMP divided by 100, to make the two eigenvalues and the output force in an order of magnitude.

From Figure 1, we can see that the change trends of six kinds of characteristic value on the output force are the same. Because the EMG signal is muscle cells potential under the stimulation of nerve excitement action, the EMG signal and output force are not perfectly synchronized but has certain hysteresis theoretically. But in terms of EMG signal and the relation between grasping force, and EMG signal response is its excited state and the movement trend, not completely linear or polynomial relationship. Therefore, the regression analysis is needed.

3 Experimental results

3.1. Grasping force estimation

In order to measure the grasping force easily, this paper first discusses the relationship between grasping force and EMG signal under the four grasping patterns, i.e., the cylindrical grasping, spherical grasping, finger pinching, and side pinching, as shown in Figure 2. In the experiments, experimenter is wearing a FSR gloves in different grasping patterns, and the size of the grasping force is gradually changed in 15 s. After repeating 10 times, participants take 5 minutes to reduce muscle contraction effect on EMG signal.

Compared with the original measurements of smooth, there are different levels of fluctuations in two kinds of predict methods of predictive curves. Correspond to the input signal to a specific value when we make regression analysis. For the multi-channel input, each channel between numerical changes will affect the output signal, and the continuous input signal does not guarantee the continuity of the output value. Because the finger griping force is usually within the range 0 to 10 N, small fluctuation can not affect the trend of predictive value. In practice, it also can grasp the object stably through the

DOI: 10.1051/itmconf/20160709016

feedback information and reflex control. Therefore, in this case, if the predictive accuracy is within 20%, it can realize the force control of prosthetic hand.

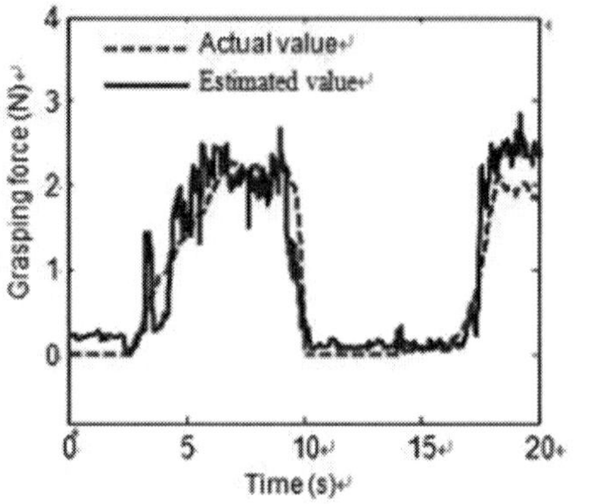

(a) Finger pinching

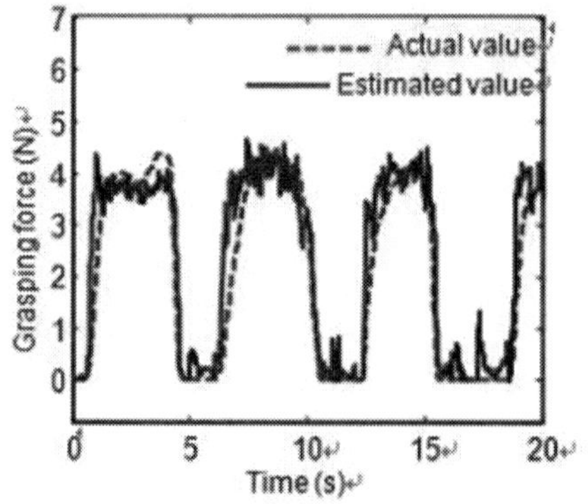

(b) Side pinching

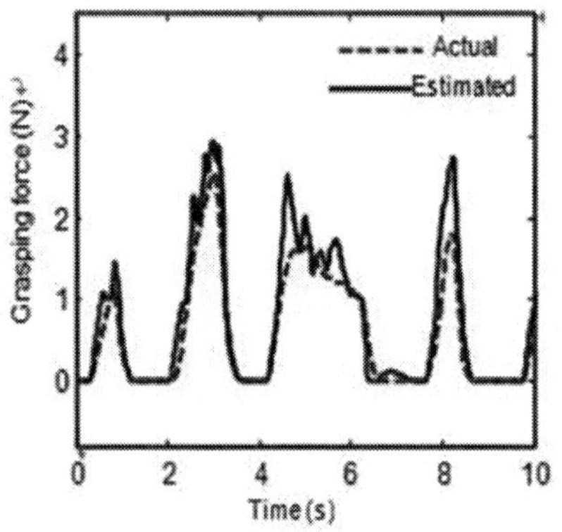

(c) Cylindrical grasping

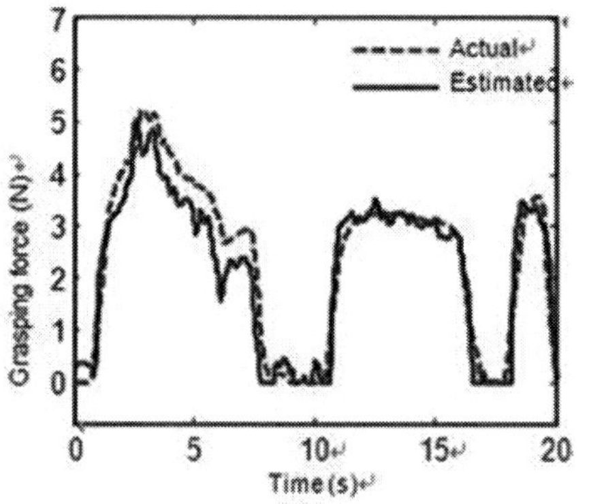

(d) Spherical grasping

Figure 4. Actual Value Estimated Value of Grasping Force Based on Svm Method.

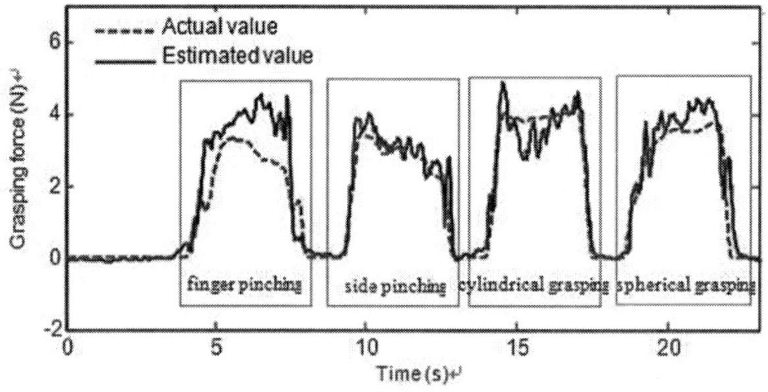

(a) With small force

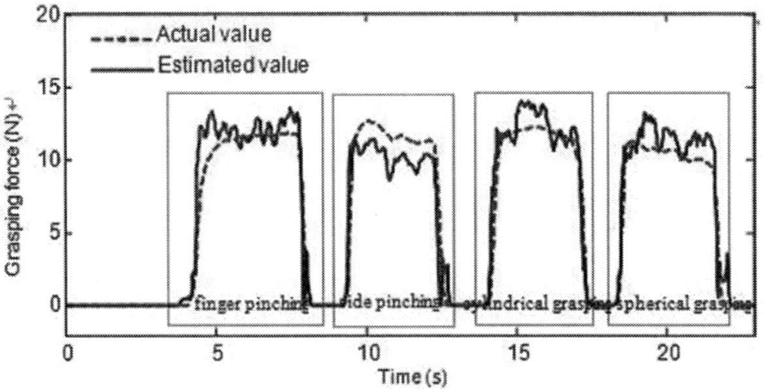

(b) With big force

Figure 5. the Actual Force and Estimated Force under Different Grasping Pattern for Grasping with Small and Big Force.

From Figures 3 and 4, we can see that all three methods can predict the change trend of grasping force, though the error size is slightly different under the correlation of different grasping mode. From the perspective of the evaluation index of MSE and SCC, MSE value becomes minimum while the SCC value becomes largest under the neural network method. That is to say, in three methods, the neural network prediction has the optimal comprehensive performance with minimum error. Under off-line analysis we find that, in the learning process the fitting degree of SVM training data is high, the SCC value is usually over 97% and MSE value is within 0.1 N. While in the testing, prediction data of SCC value decreases rapidly. The reasons are as follows: on the one hand, some error is existed in model, on the other hand, experience method are used to determine parameters may not be the optimal solution. Therefore, the prediction precision is lower than the SVM method.

3.2 Synchronized decoding

Figure 5 draws curves of the actual force and estimated force under different grasping pattern for grasping with small and large force. Due to the small grasping force, the EMG signal is relatively weak, so the precision of pattern recognition is the worst. By correlation coefficient and the MSE can be seen that when we use large grasping force to grasp the object the error is big reached about 20%. The reasons are as follows: on the one hand, due to the different grasp pattern by using the same neural network analysis, the error is bigger, on the other hand, the switch between different modes of action on the recognition accuracy.

Through these experimental results it can be seen that if we first recognize the grasping pattern and then estimate the griping force, precision of the grasping force estimation is higher. However, because the result of pattern recognition are greatly influenced by the degree of muscle contraction, the accuracy of the pattern recognition is low, which affect the invoking neural network. If we first obtain the interval of desired grasping force and then process pattern recognition, the pattern recognition accuracy is improved while precision of the grasping force estimation is reduced. Under this approach, since the initial griping force estimation is in a wide range of interval, we often can accurately determine grasping force interval to choose the right training data for pattern recognition.

4 Conclusions

This work studied the influence of different grasping patterns to the grasping force estimation. Experiments showed that the change of grasping pattern would lower the estimation precision of grasping force. In addition, the change of the degree of muscle contraction reduces the pattern recognition accuracy. This paper proposed two kinds of synchronized decoding method of the pattern recognition and grasping force focusing on the above reasons. Namely, one is invoking the corresponding pattern recognition model through the decoding of grasping force, and the other is invoking the corresponding neural network model through the decoding of grasping pattern. Experimental results show that the estimation precision for the two methods is not different, but the former pattern recognition accuracy is higher than the latter. Therefore, synchronized decoding method that invokes the corresponding pattern recognition model through the decoding of grasping force is the better one.

Acknowledgement

This work was supported by the "973" Program under Grant No. 2011CB013302.

References

1. R. Boostani, M. H. Moradi, Evaluation of the forearm EMG signal features for the control of a prosthetic hand, Physiological Measurement, **24**(2), 2003: 309-319

2. M. A. Oskoei, H. Hu, Myoelectric control systems– A survey, Biomed. Signal Proc. Control, **2**(4), 2007: 275-294
3. B. Hudgins, P. Parker, R. N. Scott, A new strategy for multifunction myoelectric control, IEEE Trans. Biomed. Eng., **40**(1), 1993: 82-94
4. Z. Kermani, M. Wheeler, B. C. Badie, R. M. Hashemi, EMG feature evaluation for movement control of upper extremity prostheses, IEEE Trans. Rehabilit. Eng., **3**(4), 1995: 324-333
5. M. Lei, Z. Wang, Z. Feng. Detecting nonlinearity of action surface EMG signal, Phys. Lett. A, **290** (5) 2001: 297-303
6. M. A. Oskoei, H. Hu, Support vector machine based classification scheme for myoelectric control applied to upper limb, IEEE Trans. Biomed. Eng., **55** (8), 2008: 1956-1965
7. D. Farina, R. Merletti, Comparison of algorithms for estimation of EMG variables during voluntary isometric contractions, J. Electromyography & Kinesiology, **10**(5), 2000: 337-349
8. A. Phinyomark Application of wavelet analysis in EMG feature extraction for pattern classificatio. Measurement Science Review, **11**, 2011: 45-52
9. G. Wang, Z. Yan, X. Hu, H. Xie, Z. Wang, Classification of surface EMG signals using harmonic wavelet packet transform, Institute of physics publishing physiological measurement, **27**, 2006:1255-1267
10. A.Starzacher, B. Rinner, K. N. N. Evaluating, LDA and QDA classification for embedded online feature fusion, International Conference on Sensor Networks and Information Processing, Dec. 2008: 85-90
11. P. Kaufmann, K. Englehart, M. Platzner, Fluctuating EMG signals: investigating long-term effects of pattern matching algorithms, Annual International Conference of the IEEE: Engineering in Medicine and Biology Society (EMBC), Aug. 2010: 6357-6360

Virtual Control of Prosthetic Hand Based on Grasping Patterns and Estimated Force from Semg

Gao-Ke ZHU, Li-Sha XU, Yi ZHANG and Hua DENG[a]

School of Mechanical & Electrical Engineering, Central South University, Changsha, 410083, China
[a] Corresponding author: Hua Deng: hdeng@csu.edu.cn

Abstract. Myoelectric prosthetic hands aim to serve upper limb amputees. The myoelectric control of the hand grasp action is a kind of real-time or online method. Thus it is of great necessity to carry on a study of online prosthetic hand electrical control. In this paper, the strategy of simultaneous EMG decoding of grasping patterns and grasping force was realized by controlling a virtual multi-degree-freedom prosthetic hand and a real one-degree-freedom prosthetic hand simultaneously. The former realized the grasping patterns from the recognition of the sEMG pattern. The other implemented the grasping force from sEMG force decoding. The results show that the control method is effective and feasible.

1 Introduction

Myoelectric prosthetic hand aims to serve people with upper limb amputation, whose myoelectric controlling process is a kind of real-time or online control. Thus it is of great necessity to carry on a study of online prosthetic hand electrical control, to verify the validity and feasibility of the EMG decoding algorithm.

Generally, only after being trained, can the myoelectric controlling hand, basing on pattern recognition, properly managing its movement or the power of gripping. During the training course, the disable is asked to take advantages of imagination or phantom limb sensation to carry out his willing action, which is a very complex process in which artificial limb user could easily have psychological pressure by excessive times of training or training time[1,2]. The emergence of virtual reality technology makes it possible for the disables easier to focus on training. The disables can interact with the virtual prosthetic hand via the EMG data, pattern recognition algorithms and 3D visual effect and enjoy the feeling of being in real environment. In addition, virtual reality(VR) technology can be used in muscle checking, rehabilitation training, and the man-machine interface performance validation[3-5].

In this paper, the recognition algorithm of grasping movement patterns in experiments will be verified constantly through the virtual multi-freedom prosthetic hand controlled by the surface EMG signal obtained from a normal person. movement patterns and synchronizing decoding of grasping force combine with virtual multi-freedom prosthetic hand and real unidirection prosthetic hand, will be online tested. Because the unidirection prosthetic hand has one limited action, different grasping patterns will be carried out by the virtual multi-freedom prosthetic hand; while the corresponding value of the gripping force can be synchronously realized by the unidirection prosthetic hand.

2 Building the virtual multi-freedom prosthetic hand system

VR technology is widely used in training disabled patients without limbs with great training improvement.. As shown in Figure1, virtual prosthetic hand system of electro myographic control, integrated with electro myographic signal acquisition system, virtual prosthetic hand model, electrical control algorithm, computer and user, is very convenient to verify and evaluate the EMG decoding algorithm. This paper, based on Virtual Reality Modeling Language(VRML)[6,7] and Simulink 3D Animation, establishes a virtual environment for multi-freedom prosthetic hand.

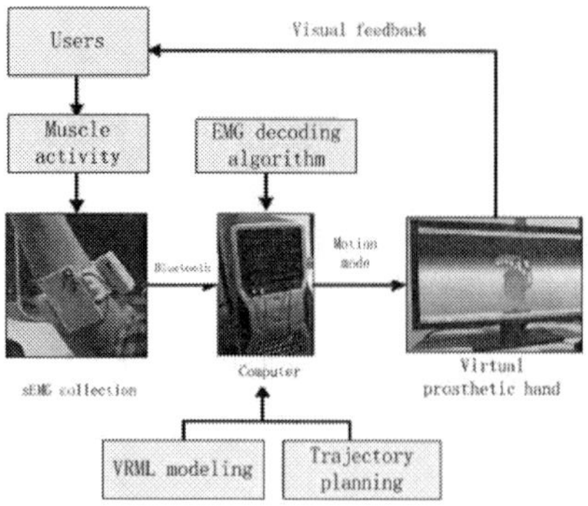

Figure.1 Soft and Hard Configuration Of Emg Control System Of Virtual Prosthetic Hand

Experimental platform of virtual prosthetic hands is shown in Figure 1. It can be seen from the picture that 8 wireless channels of the myoelectricity limb band collect EMG signal from the hand under the sampling frequency 1000HZ. The data then can be transmitted to a computer via Bluetooth in real-time, which uses the software developed by MS Visual Studio 2010 to achieve serial port communication with the Bluetooth device of the EMG control system,subsequently, the present sEMG data can be acquired by the serial communication protocol. At the same time, MATLAB calls the sEMG data in VS2010 and get the current pattern of movement according to sEMG data segmentation method and EMG decoding algorithm. The pattern is executed by virtual prosthetic hand in MATLAB/Simulink environment. This paper researches on the recognition of EMG signal patterns and the transmission of recognized signal of virtual prosthetic hand and mainly focuses on the 8 patterns of movements. (Natural state, spherical gripping, cylindrical gripping, tripod pinching, two fingers pinching, side pinching, hooking grasping, and cellphone fetching) According to the action code, the hand can perform the corresponding action patterns which include already made planning paths. In sum, VS collects the online sEMG data, shares the data with Matlab internal variables, and carry out online control of virtual prosthetic hand at the same time.

3 Experiment platform for EMG control of myoelectric prosthetic hand based on gripping pattern and synchronous force decoding

Limited by the experimental conditions, it is impossible to achieve the situation--applying the operation mode of electromyographic signals and the synchronous force decoding method to myoelectric control of artificial limb. The method adopted is to fulfill the myoelectric control of the virtual multi-DOF prosthetic hand and the single degree of freedom prosthetic hand in the meantime, so that virtual multi-DOF prosthetic hand is able to achieve various operation modes, while the single degree of freedom prosthetic hand attains the needed grasping force after EMG force decoding.

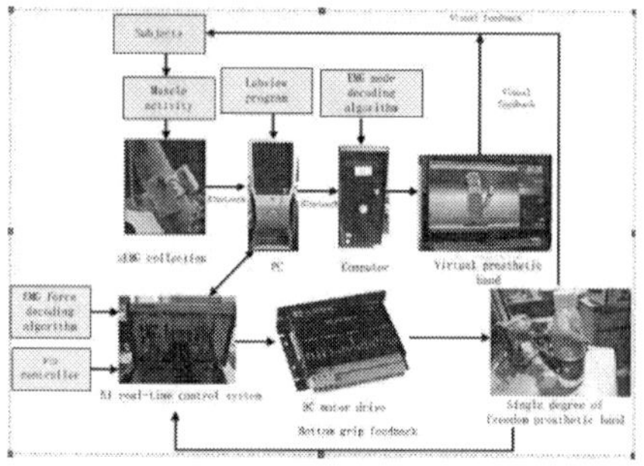

Figure 2 Soft and Hard Configuration of Emg Control System Of Virtual Prosthetic Hand Based on Movement Patterns and Synchronizing Decoding of Gripping Force

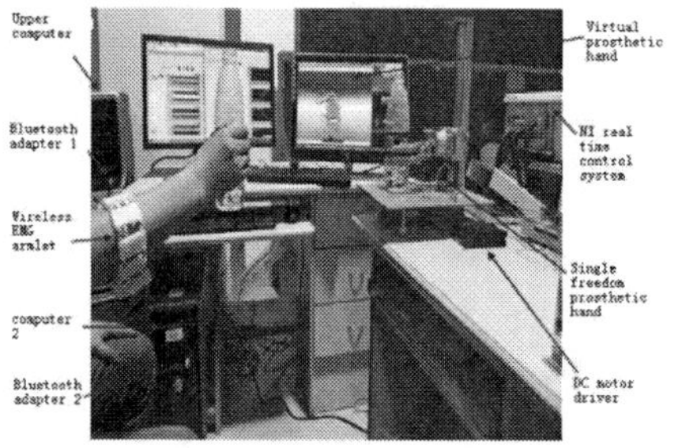

Figure 3 EMG Controlling Experiment Platform of Virtual Prosthetic Hand Based on Movement Patterns and Synchronizing Decoding of Gripping

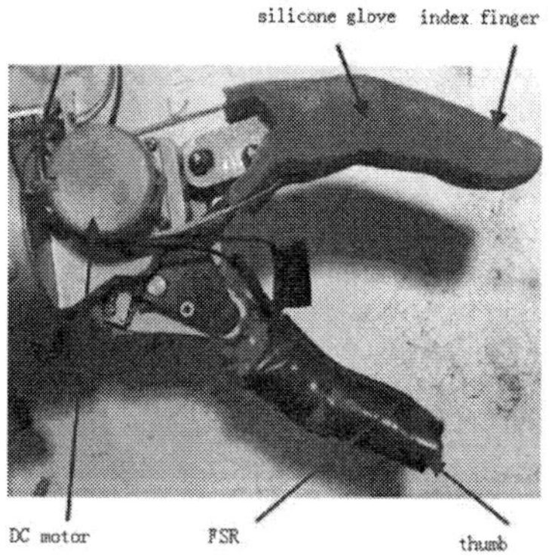

Figure.4 Unidirection Prosthetic Hand

As shown in Figure 2 and Figure 3, via serial port communication, the principal computer acquires wireless signal collected by myoelectricity limb band, and then transmits and shares data via local area network (TCP/IP protocol) with the NI real-time control system (NI PXIe-8144, based on high-performance embedded controller with Intel Core i7-820QM quad-core processer). The main tasks of the principal computer are to collect and share EMG data and code the main program in Labview. The NI real-time control system(slave computer) is mainly responsible for decoding EMG data force and controlling underlayer force of the unidirection prosthetic

DOI: 10.1051/itmconf/20160709017

hand. Meanwhile, the principal computer transmits the data to another computer via Bluetooth devices, which takes charge in decoding movement pattern of EMG data and controlling the prosthetic hand. As the three machines(principal computer, NI, slave computer) work together at the same time, EMG data transmits in real-time via Bluetooth(series port communication protocol) and local area network(TCP/IP protocol) and movement pattern of EMG data and force decoding in real-time can be carried out and controlling of virtual prosthetic hand and the unidirection prosthetic hand can be reached. Noticeably, NI real-time control system has integrated in a multi-function data acquisition card NI PXIe-6363, which could be used to collect the feedback of the actual gripping force from the force sensor of the thumb of the unidirection prosthetic hand and output the control voltage signal.

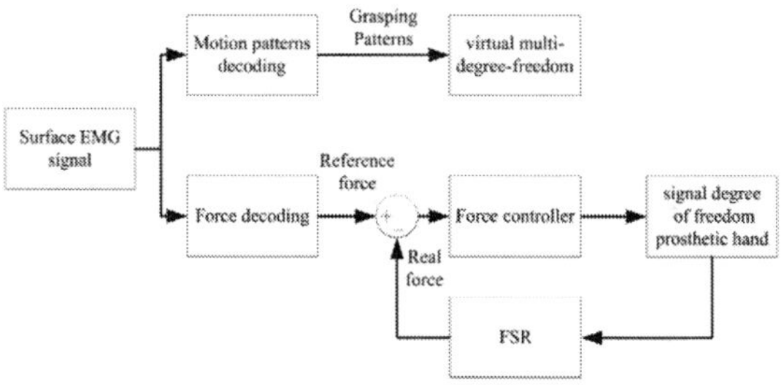

Figure 5 Prosthetic Hand Motion Modes and Grasping Force Separation and Synchronous Emg Control Methods

As shown in Figure 4, the thumb of single degree of freedom prosthetic hand has installed Force Sensing Resistor (FSR), which can gain pressure information by measuring the resistance value variation when under pressure. FSR, constant resistances and the constant DC electrical source are installed in series to measure the resistance value at both ends of FSR when single degree of freedom prosthetic hand grasps objects. As a result, the resistance value and the pressure match. 5th-order polynomial has been applied to correct the FSR pressure.

4 Gripping pattern and synchronous force decoding for EMG control of myoelectric prosthetic hand

In this paper, the method separates the myoelectric control of operation mode and grasping forces but operating both in the meantime to verify the synchronization myoelectric decoding algorithm of operation mode and grasping forces. As is shown in Figure 5, the operation mode of electromyogram signal decoded and the trainer control the grasping mode of virtual multi-DOF prosthetic hand. Meanwhile, grasping level after sEMG force decoding is regarded as the force for reference of single degree of freedom prosthetic hand and the grip can be handled by bottom force controller.

In Figure 5, after received the movement pattern by decoding the EMG data, virtual prosthetic hand will follow the already made path to do gripping, according to the corresponding pattern; The reference force of the unidirection prosthetic hand comes from the decoding of surface EMG data; when gripping, FSR is under pressure, and the actual gripping force will feedback to NI real-time control system; The deviation of reference force and actual force will be input into the force controller whose output data will be then transmit through driver to the DC motor of the unidirection prosthetic hand to adjust the gripping force. The trainer can control the virtual prosthetic hand and the unidirection prosthetic hand at the same time by EMG data.

Based on the feasibility of Linear Discriminant Analysis(LDA), Mel Frequency Cepstrum Coefficient, and ARC+SSC[8-10], the experiment asks the trainer to control the movement pattern of the virtual prosthetic hand and the actual gripping force of the unidirection prosthetic hand at the same time. The method of decoding EMG data is the judgement of threshold; the underlayer force controller of the unidirection prosthetic hand is PID controller; The trainer will grip under a comfortable and natural condition among all of the patterns; Other training samples of gripping are only for the three level of cylindrical gripping, in which the trainer act 10 times and the training time is 50s.

5 Verification and analysis of experiments

As shown in Figure 6, a trainer performed two kind of online EMG control experiment with different levels of gripping force----cylindrical gripping and spherical gripping. The experiment includes 8 stages: 10s for natural stage; 10s for small force gripping; 10s for moderate force gripping; 10s for large force gripping; another 10s for natural stage; 10s for small force gripping; 10s for moderate force gripping; and 10s for large force gripping. According to the training data set, the threshold of EMG signal decoding set to $\varepsilon_1 = 10$, $\varepsilon_2 = 20$ and $\varepsilon_3 = 40$. It is shown in Figure 7 and Figure 8 the result of EMG force control of unidirection prosthetic hand.

By analyzing the result of the experiment of gripping pattern and EMG force control, which are shown in Figure.7 and Figure.8, it is demonstrated that as soon as the virtual prosthetic hand acted its movement pattern, the EMG force control of unidirection prosthetic hand would be carried out. However, there still shows poor stability of decoding of gripping force: cylindrical gripping with large force was frequently misjudged to moderate one; decoding of spherical gripping with moderate force contained level of small force.

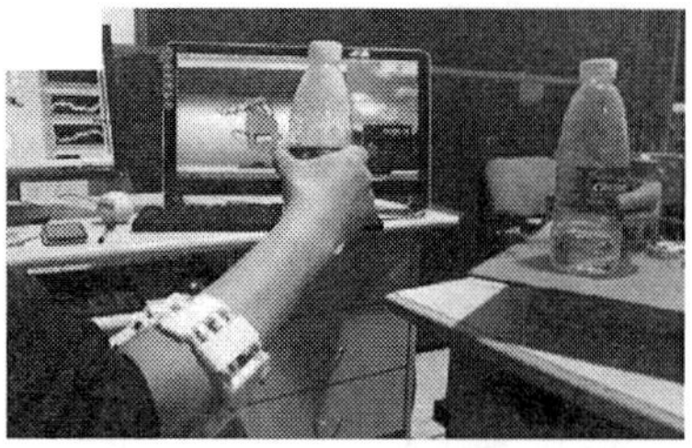

(a) cylindrical grasping

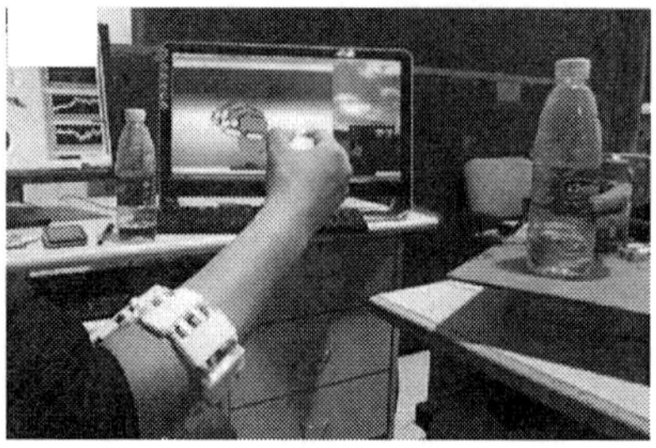

(b) spherical grasping

Figure.6 Experimental Scene of Emg Force Control of Prosthetic Hand Based on Movement Pattern and Real-Time Decoding of Grasping Force

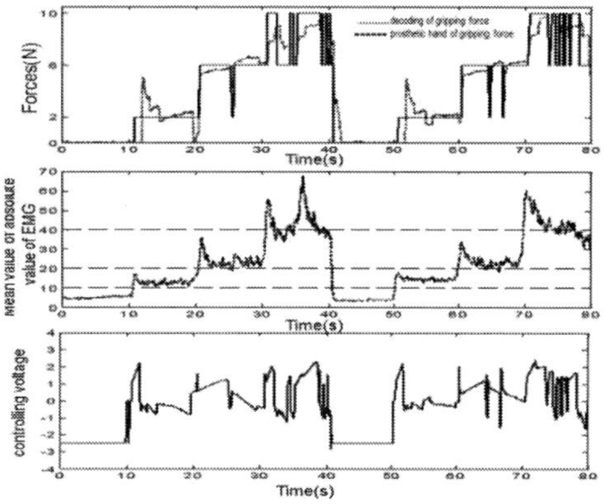

(a) variation of force of EMG decoding and grasping force of virtual prosthetic hand
(b) variation of Mean value of absolute value of EMG data.
(c) variation of controlling voltage of underlayer force of unidirection prosthetic hand

Figure 7 Result of Emg Control of Prosthetic Hand with Cylindrical Gripping

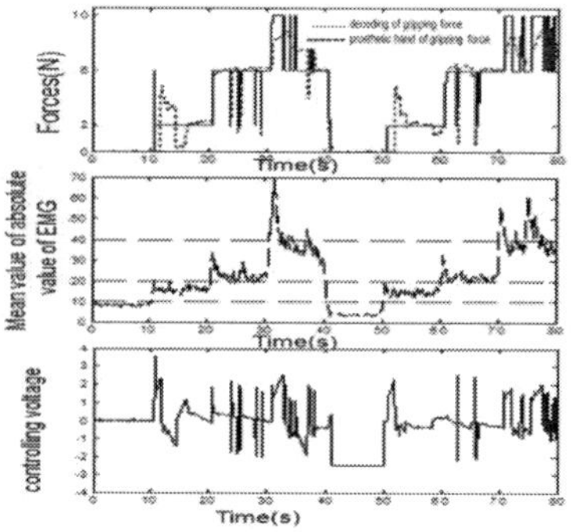

(a) variation of force of EMG decoding and grasping force of virtual prosthetic hand
(b) variation of Mean value of absolute value of EMG data.
(c) variation of controlling voltage of underlayer force of unidirection prosthetic hand

Figure 8. Result of EMG Control of Prosthetic Hand with Spherical Gripping

As shown in Figure 9, a trainer has successively performed 7 gripping patters: spherical gripping, cylindrical gripping, tripod pinching, two fingers pinching, side pinching, hooking grasping, and cellphone fetching. Every pattern has 140s in sum, including 4 cyclic stages: 5s for natural state; 5s for small force gripping; 5s for moderate force gripping; 5s for large force gripping. In the same way, the threshold of EMG signal decoding set to , and . Decoding algorithm of gripping pattern is the threshold method; underlayer force control of the unidirection prosthetic hand employs PID controller.

Accuracy of grasping patterns of EMG controlling virtual prosthetic hand is 21/28. Misjudged patterns are mainly side pinching (4), and cylindrical grasping (2). As shown in Figure 9 the result of EMG controlling unidirection prosthetic hand, generally, shows high misjudgment rate of gripping with large force, high accuracy rate of cylindrical gripping and spherical gripping, and side pinching with lowest accuracy rate.

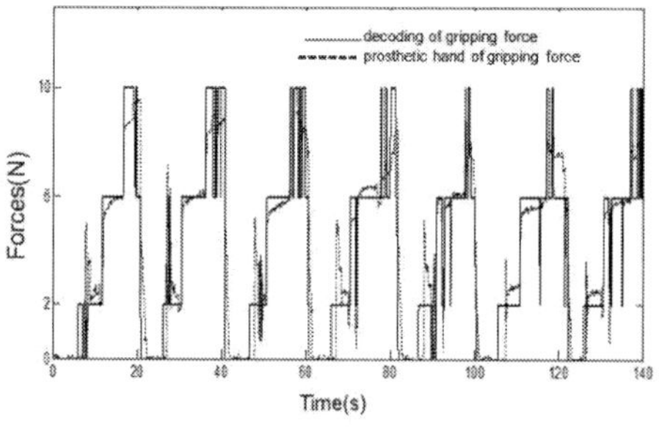

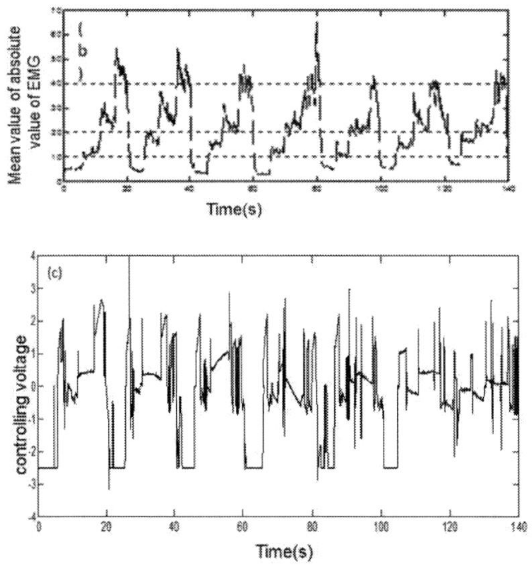

(a) variation of force of EMG decoding and grasping force of virtual prosthetic hand
(b) variation of Mean value of absolute value of EMG data.
(c) variation of controlling voltage of underlayer force of unidirection prosthetic hand

Figure.9 Result of Emg Control of Prosthetic Hand in Different Patterns

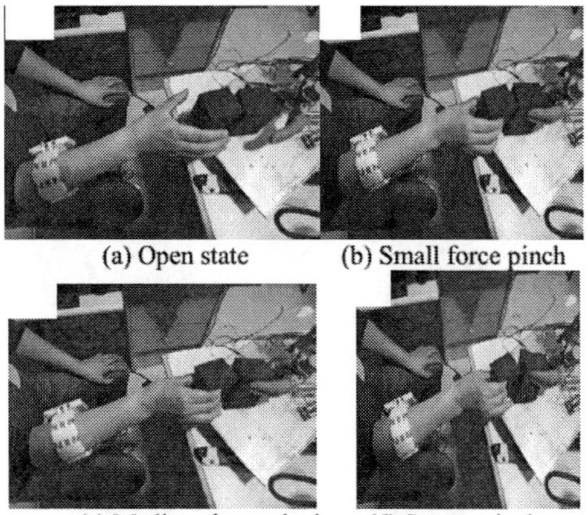

(a) Open state (b) Small force pinch
(c) Medium force pinch (d) Strong pinch

Figure 10 The EMG Control Experiment Scene of Single Dof Prosthetic Hand Grasping Force.

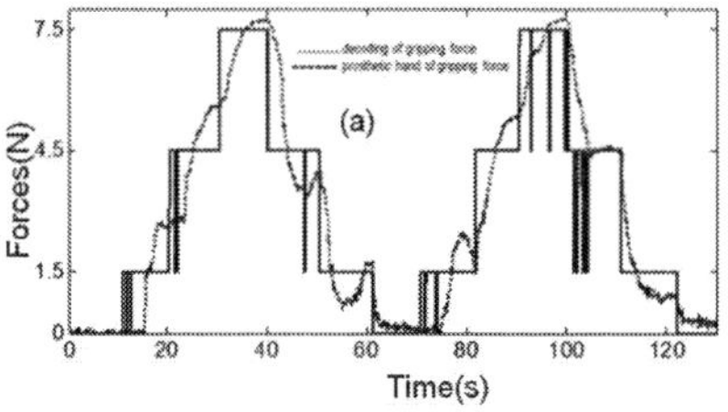

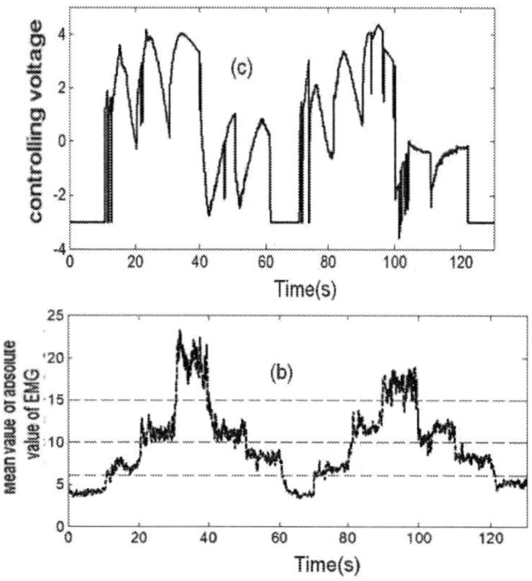

(a) variation of force of EMG decoding and grasping force of virtual prosthetic hand
(b) variation of Mean value of absolute value of EMG data.
(c) variation of controlling voltage of under layer force of unidirection prosthetic hand

Figure.11 Result Of Emg Control Of Prosthetic Hand When Grasping

By analyzing Figure 7, Figure 8 and Figure 9, it can be seen that force of EMG decoding shows poor stability and low accuracy. The reason for poor stability of force of EMG decoding is that under the same level of gripping force from the trainer, the MAV of EMG signal energy show drastic fluctuation as time passed, which is caused by the non-stationary characteristic of the EMG signal. What bring about the non-stationary characteristic are the initial stage unsteadiness of muscle contraction during the period of movement switch and the change of characteristic space of EMG signal over time, which leads to muscle fatigue in the end. Thus it will be easy to cause misjudgment if threshold value is set in the experiment.

As shown in Fig.10, the trainer grips a sponge by using EMG controlling unidirection prosthetic hand in the experiment. It can be qualitatively demonstrated that force level of the trainer's hand almost shares the same level of the prosthetic hand. To be more specific, result of EMG force control is shown in Fig.11. MAV characteristics of the threshold of EMG signal sets on $\varepsilon_1 = 5$, $\varepsilon_2 = 10$ and $\varepsilon_3 = 15$, section $[0, \varepsilon_1)$, $[\varepsilon_1, \varepsilon_2)$, $[\varepsilon_2, \varepsilon_3)$,and $[\varepsilon_3, +\infty)$ correspond to sEMG decoding force 0N, 1.5N, 4.5N and 7.5N respectively.

Fig.10 also shows that MAV feature fluctuates intensely under the identical grasping forces level, which means myoelectric signals have stronger non-stationary, especially in the initial stage, MAV feature fluctuates strongest, for the instability of muscle contraction at the moment, which easily causes the misjudgment during EMG force decoding. Besides, Fig.10 also reveals that the error rates of EMG force decoding, caused by the enhanced non-stationary and nonlinearity of sEMG in the process of muscle relaxation, become higher as the stronger grasping force shifted to a weaker one.

In a word, the on-line experiment for myoelectric control of artificial limb certifies the grip mode and forces synchronization decoding algorithm. The stability and recognition rate of grasping mode decoding perform well, with about 80% of on-line recognition under the condition of small training set and the changing level of muscle contraction. However, the grip myoelectric decoding is not stable enough, waiting a further improvement of the EMG force decoding method. Besides, the bottom forces control effect of single degree of freedom prosthetic hand, whose controller needs to be improved more, is unsatisfying.

6 Conclusion

In this paper, it has been built the experiment platform for simultaneously control of virtual prosthetic hand and real unidirection prosthetic hand. EMG gripping patterns and force synchronous decoding algorithm are used to control the gripping forces of the virtual and the real prosthetic hand. The control method has certain feasibility that has been tested by online experiments, and the decoding method of grasping pattern shows excellent stability and high recognition rate.

Acknowledgements

This work was supported by National Basic Research Program of China (2011CB013302)

References

1. Tkach D, Huang H, Kuiken T A. Study of stability of time-domain features for electromyographic pattern recognition [J]. J Neuroeng Rehabil, 2010, 7(21) :29
2. Nazarpour K, Sharafat A R, Firoozabadi S M P. Application of higher order statistics to surface electromyogram signal classification [J]. Biomedical Engineering, IEEE Transactions on, 2007, 54(10): 1762-1769.
3. Boostani R, Moradi M H. Evaluation of the forearm EMG signal features for the control of a prosthetic hand [J]. Physiological measurement, 2003, 24(2): 309.
4. Kang W-J, Shiu J-R, Cheng C-K, et al. The application of cepstral coefficients and maximum likelihood method in EMG pattern recognition [movements classification] [J]. Biomedical Engineering, IEEE Transactions on, 1995, 42(8): 777-785.
5. Oskoei M A, Hu H. GA-based feature subset selection for myoelectric classification [C]. Proceedings of the Robotics and Biomimetics, 2006 ROBIO'06 IEEE International Conference on: IEEE, 2006: 1465-1470.
6. Huang Y, Englehart K B, Hudgins B, et al. A Gaussian mixture model based classification scheme for myoelectric control of powered upper limb prostheses [J]. Biomedical Engineering, IEEE Transactions on, 2005, 52(11): 1801-1811.
7. Gibson W. Pattern Recognition.[2003] [M]. London: Penguin. 2004.
8. Jain A K, Duin R P W, Mao J. Statistical pattern recognition: A review [J]. Pattern Analysis and Machine Intelligence, IEEE Transactions on, 2000, 22(1): 4-37.
9. Chan A D, Englehart K B. Continuous myoelectric control for powered prostheses using hidden Markov models [J]. Biomedical Engineering, IEEE Transactions on, 2005, 52(1): 121-124.
10. Young A J, Hargrove L J, Kuiken T A. Improving myoelectric pattern recognition robustness to electrode shift by changing interelectrode distance and electrode configuration [J]. Biomedical Engineering, IEEE Transactions on, 2012, 59(3): 645-652.

Assessment of Ecosystem Water Conservation Value In The Beijing Four Seasons Flower Valley

Xiao-Na LIU and Hong LI[a]

Beijing Research & Development Center for Grass and Environment, Beijing 100097, China
[a] Corresponding author: lihsdf@sina.com

Abstract. Based on the data of field investigation and multi-source data analysis, Beijing Four Seasons Flower Valley declared in 2008 towards valley economy water conservation function and value was estimated by means of rainfall storage capacity as well as ecological economy. The results showed that: Landscape structure of FSFV was forest land-cultivated land-grassland. FSFV had the highest water conservation function in Beijing valleys, with the capacity of 1101.13 m^3/hm^2. Annual total amount of water conservation was 31.20×10^6 m^3, accounting for 10.07% of Beijing valleys, and the total value of water conservation was 3.61×10^8 Yuan. High water conservation capacity areas were mainly located in the eastern mountainous region with broadleaf forest centralized distribution. Low water conservation function areas were mainly occurred in the regions effected by human activities. Forest ecosystem had the highest capacity of water conservation of 1116 m^3/hm^2, while construction ecosystem had the lowest. Higher degree of human activities, lower capacity of water conservation. Shrub forest and broadleaf forest had the largest contribution on valley water conservation, with contribution rate of 36.35% and 35.62%. Ranking of water conservation capacity, broadleaf forest had the highest value of 1135 m^3/hm^2, followed by coniferous forest, shrub forest and mixed forest.

1 Introduction

With climate change and rapid socio-economic development, water demand is raising gradually and water environment is deteriorating sharply. Water shortage has become the focus of common concern, presented increasingly serious trend, especially in northern China. Beijing, as the national capital, has become one of metropolises facing the worst water scarcity in the world, with water resources less than 200 m^3 per capita, approximately 1/10 and 1/38 of the national and world per per capita level according to the newest Beijing water resources bulletin published in 2014. As ecological conservation area of the national capital, Beijing's mountainous area is the natural ecological barrier, water conservation region and bearing capacity of biodiversity. Restricted by tough geographical and natural conditions, it is also the region with economic underdevelopment. With the strength of human activities increasing, such as urbanization, industrialization and agricultural intensification, ecological environment and natural resources are faced with tremendous development pressure in those mountainous areas, such as mining, soil erosion, and destruction of vegetation. The contradiction between socio-economic development and ecological environment protection becomes relative prominent and acute, which prompting the gap between urban and rural significantly [1-2].

How to achieve supply equalization and benifits maximum of ecosystem services by means of combination of ecological protection and poverty alleviation on the basis of ecological construction and environmental protection? Ecological economization and economic ecologization is the hot issue currently [3]. With ecological protection as premise, aiming to drive local development, valley economy which was proposed officially in 2008 is industrial economic belt by unified development which takes natural valley of mountain as unit, and an important and effective way to break the bottleneck of the comprehensive arrangement and improvement rural and urban development in Beijing's mountainous areas [4-5]. Beijing has 179 valleys along with area more than 5 km^2 covering total area of 10418 km^2 with the percentage of 62% of total capital area. Beijing mountainous valley has a pivotal role in the capital water conservation, water environment security and socio-economic sustainable development. Ecosystem function in this region showed a decline trend for superimposed effects of human activities and its fragile ecological environment since implementation of valley economy in 2008, especially the funciton of water conservation in moutainous area. Water conservation function was influenced by many factors such as climate change, physical and chemical properties of soil, and topography [6]. Currently, the research of water conservation function was mainly focused on watershed

 DOI: 10.1051/itmconf/20160709018

and the large scale context, rarely on small-scale territorial unit like valley. Meanwhile, the relevant research was mainly for forest ecosystem, weakly for grass, shrub, and other ecosystmes. Differences of water conservation function among varied ecosystems were rarely mentioned, especially in small scale [7].

According to the investigation of Beijing Municipal Commission of Rural Affairs, Yanqing District as the host site of 2022 the winter Olympics has 17 valleys with development potential [5]. Ecological environment protection and ecological civilization construction becomes urgent and irreplaceable for regional sustainable development [8]. Four Seasons Flower Valley (FSFV), which is located in eastern mountainous region of Yanqing District, was listed as one of ten strategic growth pole construction of 'Demonstration Area of Green Beijing' in the 12th Five-Year Plan of Yanqing County. Meanwhile, it has also been listed as of seven key valleys in Beijing mountainous area in 2011. Based on the land use and land cover classification maps in 2013 extracted by SPOT5 images, forest ecosystem was major natural type with proportion of 81.27% in FSFV, followed by farmland and grassland ecosystem. Therefore, water conservation function of ecosystem in FSFV is the significant role. Effective assessment of water conservation function and its value is the basis for the establishment of long-term ecological compensation mechanism, for providing further natural vegetation protection and ecological construction, which meeting the construction of ecological civilization and ecological economy development in Beijing mountainous areas [9]. The value of water conservation function was assessed using method of ecological economics in FSFV in 2013, for the purpose of providing basic data for reasonable protection and exploration local natural resources, and serving in the ecological, economic and social sustainable development in Beijing mountainous areas.

2 Materials and methods

2.1 Study area

Four Seasons Flower Valley (FSFV) is located in the eastern part of Yanqing District in Beijing mountainous areas, including Liubinpu Town, Sihai Town and Zhenzhuquan Town (Figure 1).

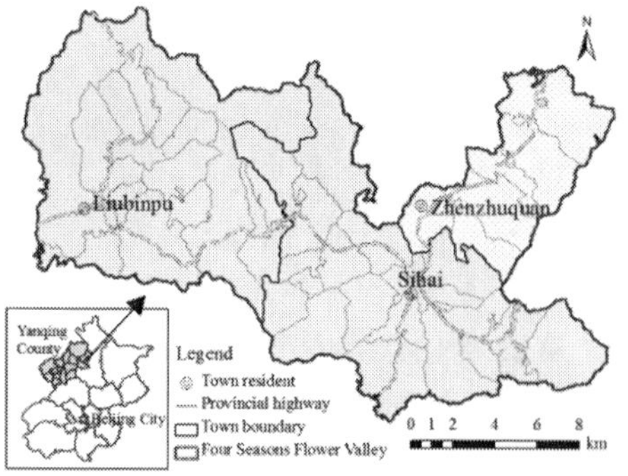

Figure 1. The Location of Study Area

The complex topography with altitude ranging from 385 m to 1482 m formed the typical vertical climate change, which brings out the significant vertical distribution of plant communities with warm temperate deciduous broad-leaved forest dominating. This region has a temperate continental monsoon climate, with annual mean temperature 8 °C and annual average precipitation ranged from 550 mm to 700 mm. The region cover 284.12 km^2 accounting for 14.25% of the total area of Yanqing District (2.73% of Beijing mountain areas) with ditch length of 47 km and a population of 16540 that has 45.88% of urbanization rate.

FSFV located in the middle mountainous area of Yanqing District has obvious artificial ecosystem features. Regional structure of land use and land cover in study area was forest land-cultivated land-grassland, while woodland was the major land cover type with proportion beyond 44% based on the land use and land cover classification maps in 2013 extracted by SPOT5 images (Figure 2). Farmland ecosystem was the dominant artificial type with proportion 12.23% mainly located in the relative low altitude areas and along the road regions, while forest ecosystem was major natural type with proportion of 81.27%. Orchard land was mainly occurred in the scope surrounding farmland and construction land. The primary forest types in FSFV are broadleaf forest, coniferous forest, mixed forest and shrub forest, the proportion respectively was 34.58%, 6.20%, 4.02% and 36.47% in 2013.

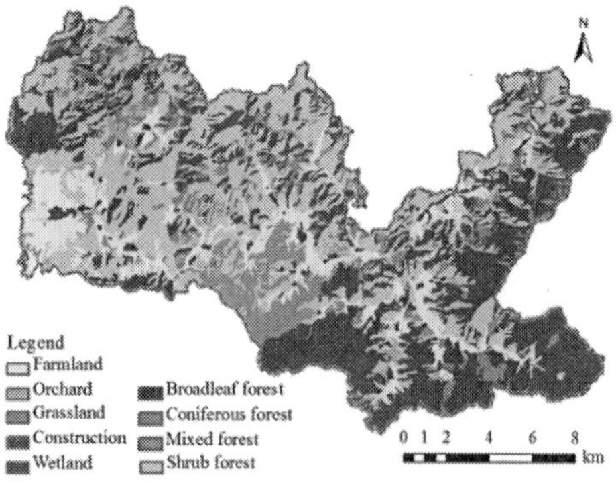

Figure 2. Land Cover Map of Fsfv In 2013

DOI: 10.1051/itmconf/20160709018

2.2 Methodology

Ecosystem water conservation funciton is consisted of water regulation and water purification. According to the similar essence between water regulation and reservoir storage, this study adopted the method of alternative cost of reservoir storage project to caculate the water regualtion value. Meanwhile, the value of water purification was evaluated through shadow project method with reference to the average price of residential water for the same principle of water purification. Currently, methods of regional water balance and rainfall storage are the common methods to evaluate water conservation funciton at home and abroad [10]. This study considered the water conservation as the increment of forest, grassland, waterbody, farmland, and desert ecosystem compared with bare land, that is the reduction of surface runoff. Quantization of water conservation function was used the method of rainfall storage. Formula is as follows:

$$Q_w = J \times R \times A = 0.55 \times J \times A \times VC \quad (1)$$

$$J = J_0 \times K \quad (2)$$

$$R = R_0 - R_g \quad (3)$$

$$VC = (NDVI - NDVIs) / (NDVIv - NDVIs) \quad (4)$$

$$NDVI = \frac{R_{nir} - R_{red}}{R_{nir} + R_{red}} \quad (5)$$

where Q_w is the annual rainfall storage of ecosystem, m^3/a; J is runoff from rainfall, mm; J_0 is the total rainfall, mm; K is the proportion rainfall runoff accounted for the total rainfall; R is efficiency coefficient of ecosystem runoff reduction, as ompared with bare land; R_0 is the rainfall runoff rate of bare land; R_g is the rainfall runoff rate of ecosystem; VC is the vegetation coverage, %; A is the acreage of region, m^2; $NDVI$ is normalized difference vegetation index; $NDVIv$ is the maximum of $NDVI$; $NDVIs$ is the minimum of $NDVI$; R_{nir} is the infrared spectral reflectance; R_{red} is the red spectral reflectance. K value is calculated based on daily rainfall data, this study used 0.4 based on the existing research results [11].

$$V_{cw} = Q_w \times c_r \quad (6)$$

where V_{cw} is the annual water regulation value, Yuan/a; Q_w is the annual rainfall storage of ecosystem, m^3/a;c_r is the unit capacity cost of reservoir construction, Yuan/m^3. According to China Water Conservation Yearbook from 1993 to 1999, the unit capacity cost of reservoir construction is 2.17 Yuan/t. In the light of Beijing's consumer fixed base Fixed price index, the c_r is 7.54 Yuan/t in 2013.

$$V_{pw} = Q_w \times p_w \quad (7)$$

where V_{pw} is the annual water purification value, Yuan/a; Q_w is the annual rainfall storage of ecosystem, m^3/a; p_w is the water purification cost, replaced with the average price of residential water in Beijing, that is 4 Yuan/m^3 in 2013.

$$V_w = V_{cw} + V_{pw} \quad (8)$$

where V_w is the annual water conservation value, Yuan/a; V_{cw} is the annual water regulation value, Yuan/a; V_{pw} is the annual water purification value, Yuan/a.

3 Results and analyses

FSFV has high vegetation coverage over 80%, which means that water conservation function is the vital ecosystem service in this valley. The average annual rainfall in this vally was 518.18 mm, close to the average of overall Beijing mountainous valleys. The water conservation capacity of FSFV in 2013 was 1101.13 m^3/hm^2, amount to 21.25% of annual average rainfall, higher than the capacity of overall mountainous valleys (1016.66 m^3/hm^2), which pointed that FSFV had the highest water conservation function in Beijing valleys. Annual total amount of water conservation was 31.20×10^6 m^3, accounting for 10.07% of Beijing mountainous valleys.

Water conservation function within the ditch showed significant spatial differences (Figure 3). High water conservation capacity areas were mainly located in the eastern mountainous region which was centralized distribution of broadleaf forest, followed by the northern and southern regions which mainly had shrub forest distribution. Low water conservation function areas were mainly in the western gently topography parts, regions along the road and the population concentrated areas. Those places was effected by human activities obviously, resulted in severely damaged vegetation and large intensity of land use which the land use types were farmland, orchard land and construction land with poor water conservation capacity. Other water conservation capacity areas had sparse vegetation coverage, low rainfall, with dominant land cover types of shrub forest and grassland.

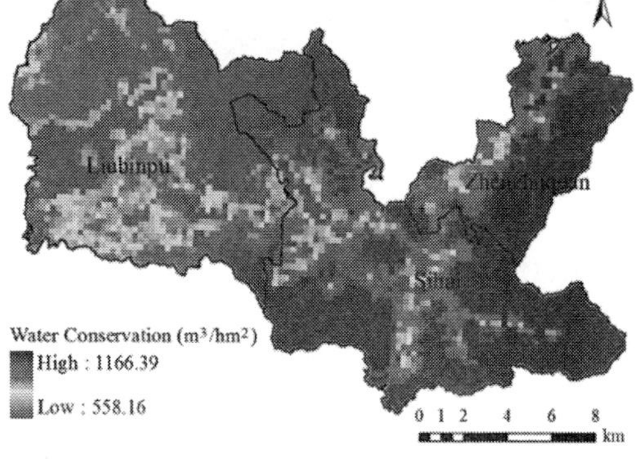

Figure 3. Spatial Distribution of Water Conservation Funciton Of Fsfv In 2013

Different ecosystem types had different water conservation capacity. Forest ecosystem had the highest capacity of water conservation, with the index value of 1116 m^3/hm^2, while construction ecosystem had the lowest capacity of 955 m^3/hm^2. The water conservation capacity showed apparent characteristics, that was natural ecosystem types were higher than artificial ecosystem types. Higher degree of human activities, lower capacity of water conservation. Although farmland ecosystem was dominant in FSFV for valley economy, but the capacity of ariticial ecosystem types was farmland > orchard > construction.

Toward to the forest ecosystem with highest water conservation capacity, different forest types varied obviously in water conservation funciton. Shrub forest and broadleaf forest had the largest constribution on valley water conservtion, with contribution rate of 36.35% and 35.62% (cumulative contribution rate of 71.97%), while the constribution rate of coniferous forest and mixed forest was 6.33% and 4.04%. In light of water conservation capacity, broadleaf forest had the highest value of 1135 m^3/hm^2, followed by coniferous forest of 1125 m^3/hm^2. Shrub forest had the lowest capacity with value of 1098 m^3/hm^2, but had the largest quantity of water conservation for the largest acreage.

The value of water conservation in FSFV was 3.61×10^8 Yuan in 2013, with 2.36×10^8 Yuan of water regulation value and 1.25×10^8 Yuan of water purification value accounting for 62.34% and 34.66% of the total water conservation value respectively. To the unit area value, the FSFV was 11991 Yuan/hm^2 of water conservation, 8303 Yuan/hm^2 of water regulaltion, and 4405 Yuan/hm^2 of water purification.

4 Conclusions

Water conservaiton funciton and value of Four Seasons Flower Valley (FSFV) was investigated and assessed by method of remote sensing, GIS integrated technology and ecological economy in 2013 after being listed as of seven key valleys in Beijing mountainous area in 2011 by Beijing Municipal Commission of Rural Affairs. The results showed that:

(1) Regional structure of land use and land cover in FSFV was forest land-cultivated land-grassland based on SPOT5 images in 2013. Farmland ecosystem was the dominant artificial type with proportion more 12%, while forest ecosystem was major natural type with proportion over 80%. The primary forest types in FSFV are broadleaf forest, coniferous forest, mixed forest and shrub forest, the proportion respectively was 34.58%, 6.20%, 4.02% and 36.47%.

(2) FSFV had the highest water conservation function in Beijing valleys, with the water conservation capacity of 1101.13 m^3/hm^2, higher than the overall valleys (1016.66 m^3/hm^2). Annual total amount of water conservation was 31.20×10^6 m^3, accounting for 10.07% of Beijing mountainous valleys. The value of water conservation in FSFV was 3.61×10^8 Yuan, with 2.36×10^8 Yuan of water regulation value and 1.25×10^8 Yuan of water purification value. Water conservation function showed significant spatial differences. High water conservation capacity areas were mainly located in the eastern mountainous region which was centralized distribution of broadleaf forest. Low water conservation function areas were mainly in the regions effected by human activities obviously, the land use types were farmland, orchard land and construction land.

(3) Different ecosystem types had different water conservation capacity. Forest ecosystem had the highest capacity of water conservation, with the index value of 1116 m^3/hm^2, while construction ecosystem had the lowest capacity of 955 m^3/hm^2. Natural ecosystem types were higher than artificial ecosystem types. Higher degree of human activities, lower capacity of water conservation. Different forest types varied obviously in water conservation funciton. Shrub forest and broadleaf forest had the largest constribution on valley water conservtion, with contribution rate of 36.35% and 35.62%. Ranking of water conservation capacity, broadleaf forest had the highest value of 1135 m^3/hm^2, followed by coniferous forest, shrub forest and mixed forest.

Acknowledgements

This work was financially supported by the Project funded by China Postdoctoral Science Foundation (2016M591112), the Project funded by Beijing Postdoctoral Science Foundation, the Project funded by Beijing Academy of Agricultural and Forestry Sciences Postdoctoral Science Foundation, and Beijing Municipal Science & Technology Plan Project (D131100000613002).

References

1. K.J. Yu, S.S. Wang, D.H. Li, et al. Ecological baseline for Beijing's urban sprawl: Basic ecosystem services and their security patterns. City Plann. Rev. 34(2), 19-24 (2010)
2. X.X. Yu, B. Zhou, X.Z. Lv, et al. Evaluation of water conservation function in mountain forest areas of Beijing based on InVEST model. Sci. Silvae Sin. 48(10), 1-5 (2012)
3. G.D. Xie and S.Y. Cao. Ecological economization and economic ecologization in succession progress of development. Resour. Sci. 32(4), 782-789 (2010)
4. Y.F. Zhang, D.M. Jia, J. Tan, et al. The spatial structure of valley economy development in the mountainous areas of Beijing. Acta Geog. Sin. 64(10), 1231-1242 (2009)
5. J.H. Chen, H. Li, and L.D. Zhou. Gully economy development's exploration and practice in Beijing mountain area. Ecol. Econ. (1), 57-62 (2010)
6. Y. Liu, W.B. Zhu, Y. Han, et al. Regionalization of water conservation function of Beijing-Tianjin-Hebei Area based on SOFM neural network. Res. Environ. Sci. 28(3), 369-376 (2015)
7. B. Fu, P. Xu, Y.K. Wang, et al. Spatial pattern of water retention in Dujiangyan County. Acta Ecol. Sin. 3(3), 789-797 (2013)

DOI: 10.1051/itmconf/20160709018

8. B.J. Yang, J.X. Gao, and C.X. Zou. The strategic significance of drawing the ecological protection red line. Chin. Dev. 14(1), 1-4 (2014)
9. J.M. Qin, W.Q. Yang, and J. Zhang. Assessment of ecosystem water conservation value in the Upper Minjiang River, Sichuan, China. Chin. J. Appl. Environ. Biol. 15(4), 453-458 (2009)
10. W.L. Jiang. Theory and method to accounting value of forest water conservative. J. Soil Water Conserv. 17(2), 34-36 (2003)
11. T.Q. Zhao, Z.Y. Ouyang, H. Zhen, et al. Forest ecosystem services and their valuation in China. J. Nat. Resour. 19(4), 480-491 (2004)

Genetic Circuit for the Early Warning of Lung Cancer using iBioSim

Xiang WANG [1,a], Xiao- Cui WANG[1], Jing- Bo JIANG[2], Jin- Jing SUN[1], Shu- Song PANG[1]
Han- Hong HE[1] and Wei- Ke WANG[1]

[1]*School of Electronic and Information Engineering, Beihang University, Beijing, 100191, China*
[2]*Honors College of Beihang University, Beihang University, Beijing, 100191, China*
[a] *Corresponding author: wxiang@buaa.edu.cn*

Abstract. With the development of molecular biology and gene-engineering technology, gene diagnosis has been an emerging approach for modern life sciences. Biological marker, recognized as the hot topic in the molecular and gene fields, has important values in early diagnosis, malignant tumour stage, treatment and therapeutic efficacy evaluation. The design of markers detection genetic circuit system for lung cancer is presented as a new method to provide basis for early warning and therapy. The system consists of three single-marker detection circuits and an integration circuit. The single-marker detection circuit provides an instantaneous low level when target marker's concentration reaches the threshold. The integration circuit uses gene and gate to complete the output data fusion from single-marker detection circuit through logic operations to finish the combined detection. All the structure is modelled and analyzed by iBioSim through the biochemical reactions of different gene circuits. The experimental result indicates that the whole lung cancer detection system can realize joint detection of tumor markers with good stability and sensitivity.

1. Introduction

Nowadays, lung cancer has become one of the most prevalent and deadly cancers worldwide, both the occurrence rate and the mortality rate remain at a high level. For instance, in China, it is estimated that there are as many as 650 thousand new lung cancer cases in 2012, occupying 22% of all cancer cases, according to recent published Cancer Fact Sheets by World Health Organization in Glob can project 2012 [1]. Especially in recent years, due to more and more serious air pollution, China's central and eastern regions faces some of the world's worst smog, which will increase the risk of lung cancer. Because symptoms of lung cancer resemble those of other diseases such as phthisis or pulmonary infection, it is possible to misdiagnose clinically and even to lose the optimal opportunity for the treatment. So far, conventional detecting methods includes chest CT examination, bronchoscope, lung puncture test and sputum cytology examination, requiring high testing costs and expensive apparatuses [2-3]. All these methods rely on doctors' judgment based on experiments, and are time and money consuming to some extent. This current situation calls for new technologies to realize more efficient and accurate lung cancer detection, and the development of genetic circuit meets this need.

Tumor Marker detection has become a hit idea in achieving early-stage prediction and treatment of cancer. It is an indicator of physiological and pathological state, produced by the cancer tissue itself or by the body in response to cancer growth. Compared to the traditional detection methods which usually have considerable experimental requirements and costs, tumor marker can not only explore the pathogenesis at the molecular level, but also have unique advantages in accurate and sensitive evaluation of early, low levels damage, which provides an early warning of cancer [4]. Many markers such as: CEA and CYFR21-1 have been found to play important roles in the diagnosis, treatment and prognosis of lung disease [5-6]. Thus, taking advantage of the genetic circuits inside cells, we can achieve more sensitive and economical tumor marker detection with good real-time performance.

The application of gene circuit has grown considerably and has chartered many notable achievements, offering new tools for the detection and prevention of lung cancer [7-8]. Researchers now have already constructed gate circuits, latch, and inverting amplifier in the gene circuit to build a complex regulation network to simulate the biochemical reactions in organisms [9-10]. Collins constructed a genetic toggle switch containing promoter that drives the expression of mutually inhibitory transcriptional repressors [11]. Anderson designed an AND logic gate based on the transcription of a gene, for which translation is dependent on the co-transcription of an engineered tRNA [12]. Tam sir and Moon finished comprehensive engineering of robust transcriptional logic including all 16 elementary logic gates, as well as the engineering of a multiple input logic network using a multitier transcriptional cascade

[13-14]. Chau used protein signalling circuits to produce spatial polarization in yeast by engineering circuits from components that can be self-organized into localized distributions [15]. We propose a genetic circuit network to realize the detection of breast cancer [16].

In this paper, we focus on constructing and simulating a genetic circuit in detecting lung cancer tumor markers so as to realize efficient and accuracy detection. The discussion is on cell level, so we only consider the chemical and biological reactions inside the cell, assuming no other interferences occur to react with reactants in our models. Our discussion contains mainly two parts: the single marker detection circuit and the combined detection circuit. The former part, basis of the whole circuit, detects the concentration of one certain target marker, and then outputs the result to the later part as its input with further logical operation and the emergence of the warning signal. Compared with our previous design on breast cancer, we innovatively present the influence of rRNA and mRNA concentration in the single marker detection circuit and threshold selection in the whole system to improve the detection accuracy and stability.

2. Single Marker Detection Circuit

The inverter genetic circuit is the core structure of single marker detection circuit, and is also used in the integration circuit. Generally, biochemical reactions in organisms include four types: transcription and translation process, regulation of protein multimerization process, regulation protein binding process and the deconstruction of different proteins and mRNA. Based on the biochemical reactions, we establish the iBioSim model of the inverter, shown in figure 1. In our design, we mainly use the inverter genetic circuit to detect the changes of the three markers' concentration. Since tumor markers are often RNA or have similar function, we assume the input signal is RNA.

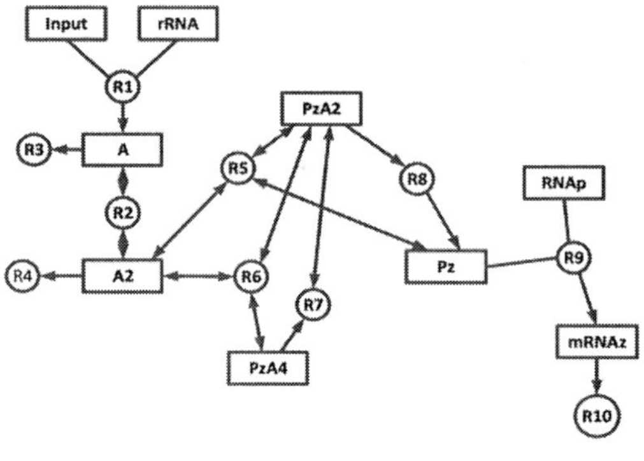

Figure 1. The SBML Model of The Genetic Inverter Constructed Using Ibiosim

In the single marker detection circuit, the input module is responsible for detecting input signal constantly and pass on the information. Specifically, we find out that the concentration of rRNA can influence the output response of single index detection module, which will change the threshold and affect the stability of the circuit. The whole system will be too sensitive and susceptible to interference if the rRNA concentration is too high; the next stage circuit cannot detect the input signal and be normally driven if the rRNA concentration is too low. And for this reason, we need to select the appropriate threshold in the final integration circuit.

3. Integration AND Gate Circuit

Different markers show varying sensitivity to the prediction of metastatic recurrence, so the integration circuit is put forward to build a multi-index monitor circuit network to implement the output data fusion of single-marker detection circuit through logic operations, just like the digital logic circuit. Once the integration circuit receives a signal from the single-index circuit, the genetic circuit in cells will be triggered, with green fluorescent protein (GFP) produced in large quantities to provide an early-warning of lung cancer. In our design, the integration circuit is implemented by AND logical operations constructed from a NAND gate followed by an inverter. In this case, GFP is produced only when both the two inputs of NAND gate are present. The main principle of the algorithm is shown as below. Similar to the inverter, an SBML model of the genetic and-gate is constructed using iBioSim, as shown in figure 2.

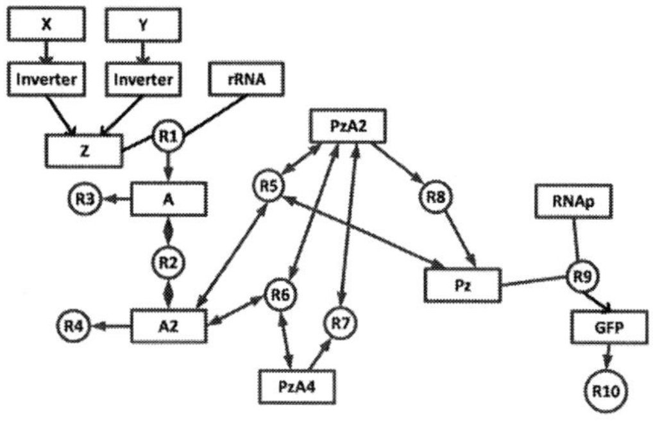

Figure 2. The SBML Model of The Genetic And-Gate Constructed Using Ibiosim

4. The Whole Joint Detection Circuit System

The novel complete design model for detecting lung cancer is a comprehensive system integrating of single-index circuit and the and-gate integration circuit, and includes two parts: the concentration test (measurement) and the logical operation. The whole structure is shown in figure 3. Combined detection of biomarkers associated with lung disease and cancer is proposed to increase the reliability and accuracy of the system. According to the clinical efficacy research, taking TPS > 80U/L, CEA > 5ng/mL and CYFR21-1 > 4ng/mL as the threshold value, the specificity of the combined measurement of the three markers can achieve high sensitivity and specificity. The diagnostic standard is expressed as TPS > 50pmol/L, CEA > 25pmol/mL and CYFR21-1 > 120pmol/L after concentration unit conversion in order to support the iBioSim simulation.

4.1 Threshold of TPS, CEA and CYFR21-1

For the digital circuit, efficient logic decision function relies on optimized selection of the threshold voltage of high and low level and other related circuit parameters, without which the function of the circuit can be inaccurate or interfered by noises. Similarly, the detection system needs research on how to optimize its threshold concentration as well. Appropriate input threshold can ensure accuracy of the results and certain anti-interference function. In the circuit we discuss in this paper, parameters of the input module of the single marker detection circuit needs to be adjusted, while the parameters of the output module also need to be adjusted to ensure the normal operation of the circuit and adjust the amplitude adjusting of the circuit. The simulation results are displayed in section 4.2.

Based on the simulation results, we can conclude that after modulation and optimization of the single marker detection circuit, the output amplitude of the three modules is relatively close and the output level to threshold input is also close, avoiding the situation that a single marker detection has too high or low output, which is more conducive to determine the judgment concentration levels, improve the accuracy of the results, and ameliorate the performance of the entire system.

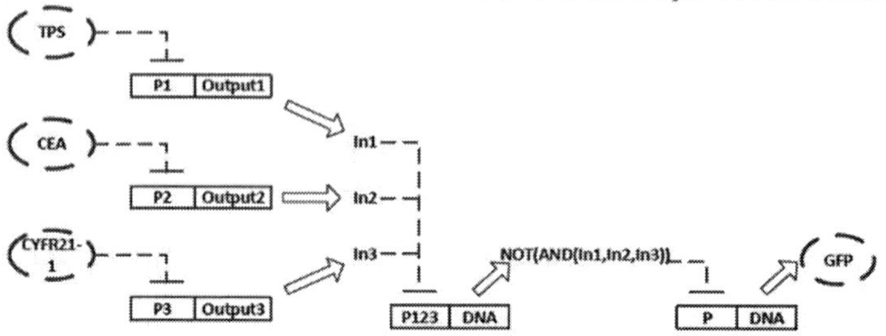

Figure 3. The Whole Design of The Detection Circuit

4.2 Experimental Result

First, we intend to prove the discussion about markers' threshold in section 4.1. In this design, we take TPS > 50pmol/L, CEA > 25pmol/mL and CYFR21-1 > 120pmol/L as the joint detection standard, which can achieve high sensitivity and specificity of the lung cancer detection. So we need to adjust parameters of each single-index circuit to ensure the output in the same level.

Figure 4 and Table 1 show the output results of this single-index circuit.

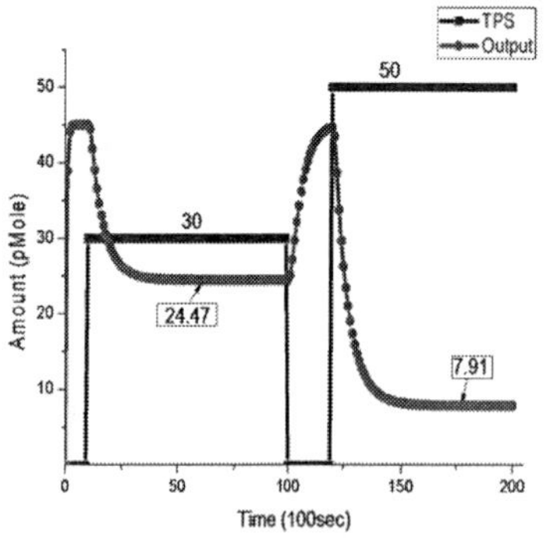

a)The single-index circuit output of TPS

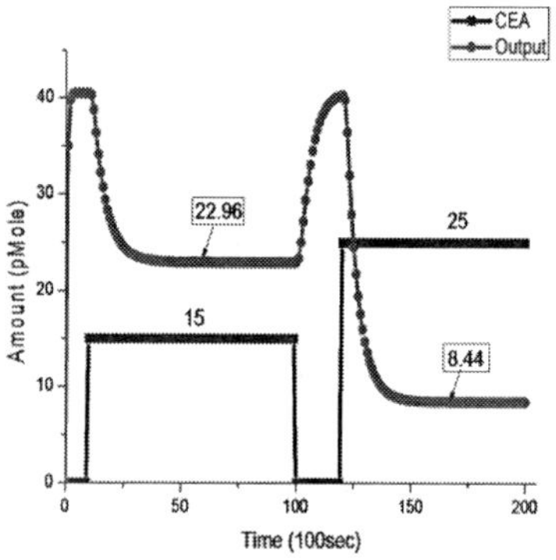

b) The single-index circuit output of CEA

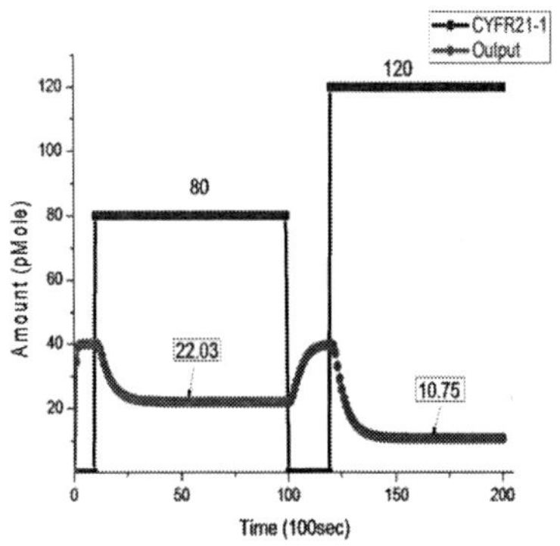

c) The single-index circuit output of CYFR21-1

Figure 4. Results For Threshold Selection of Tps, Cea and Cyfr21-1

Table 1. Results For The Threshold of Tps, Cea and Cyfr21-1

Tumor marker	Amount-of-substance concentration	Output value	Judgment
CEA	15	22.96	High
	25	8.44	Low
TPS	30	24.47	High
	50	7.91	Low
CYFR21-1	80	22.03	High
	120	10.75	Low

Based on the above discussion and analysis, experiment is designed to test the performance of the whole joint system under the condition that TPS > 50pmol/L, CEA > 25pmol/mL and CYFR21-1 > 120pmol/L are defined as the detection threshold. Figures 5 depict the experimental results of the whole design. Once a marker doesn't reach the threshold value, the output will get close to zero. The output GFP is produced and judged to be high only when all the three input markers TPS, CEA and CYFR21-1 are at high levels. Simulation results show that the type of circuit structure can achieve detection of the tumor markers of lung cancer with high veracity and real time quality. Compared to the relatively extensive detection method,uch as medical imaging technology, the genetic circuit we proposed can provide precise detection result at each stage of lung cancer. According to the simulation result, it has outstanding advantages in the treatment cost and reliability of the treatment, which can provide the real-time data of the markers related to the lung cancer.

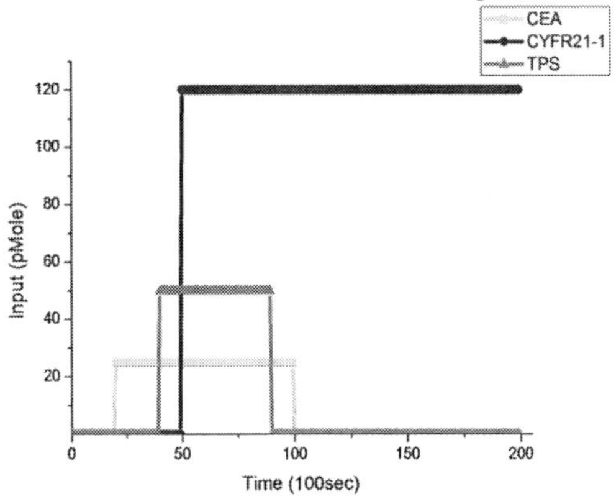

a) input

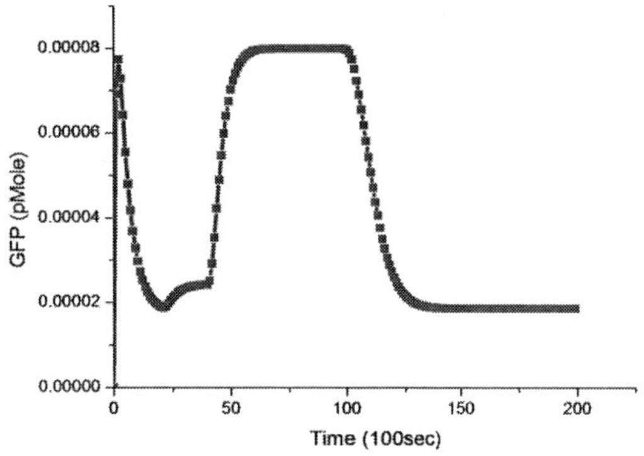

b)output

Figure 5. Simulation Result of The Whole Joint Detection Circuit

5. Conclusion

This paper introduces a novel system of gene circuit to achieve high efficiency and economical early-stage prediction of lung cancer. The design contains two parts: single marker detection circuit and integration detection circuit. Based on the SBML model of genetic gate, the whole system is modelled and simulated by iBioSim. Our design uses the inverter-based single-marker detection circuit to realize concentration detection of each marker, and presents the integration circuit to perform logic calculation of the three outputs from the single-marker circuits to finish the joint detection. The joint system innovatively introduces the analysis on the transmission properties in the single-index circuit and the threshold selection in the integration circuit to increase the whole system's accuracy and reliability. The simulation result shows that the whole system can implement the detection and early warning of lung cancer with good realtime performance and high accuracy. The design can also provide reference for further treatment.

Acknowledgment

This research is supported by the National Science Foundation of China (Grant No. 81571142), the National Science Key Foundation of China (Grant No. 61232009), the National Science Foundation of China (Grant No. 60973106), Astronautic support Fund (Grant No. 374007), and National 863 Project of China (Grant No. 2011AA010404), guidance and modification of Xia Li.

References

1. Organization: International Agency for Research on Cancer, GLOBOCAN 2012: Estimated Cancer Incidence, Mortality and Prevalence Worldwide in 2012. http://globocan.iarc.fr/Pages/fact_sheets_population.aspx
2. Amorín Kajatt E. Lung cancer: a review of current knowledge, diagnostic methods and therapeutic perspectives, Revista Peruana De Medicina Experimental Y Salud Pública, 30, 1: 85-92(2013)
3. Vansteenkiste J, Dooms C, Mascaux C, et al. Screening and early detection of lung cancer. Cancer Journal, 10, 1: 320-327 (2011)
4. Jimeno A, Hidalgo M. Molecular biomarkers: their increasing role in the diagnosis, characterization, and therapy guidance in pancreatic cancer. Molecular Cancer Therapeutics, 5, 4: 787-96 (2006)
5. Grunnet M, Sorensen J B. Carcinoembryonic antigen (CEA) as tumor marker in lung cancer. Lung Cancer, 76, 2: 138-143 (2012)
6. Okamura K, Takayama K, Izumi M, et al. Diagnostic value of CEA and CYFRA 21-1 tumor markers in primary lung cancer. Lung Cancer, 80, 1: 45-49 (2013)
7. De Rubertis G, Davies S W. Genetic circuit design from an electronics perspective. Molecular, Cellular and Tissue Engineering, 2002. Proceedings of the IEEE-EMBS Special Topic Conference on IEEE, 145-146 (2002)
8. Chen C, Sun W, Zheng B, Mao D, Liu W. An incremental approach to closest pair queries in spatial networks using best-first search. In International Conference on Database and Expert Systems Applications, Toulouse, France, 6861:136-143(2011)
9. Brophy J A, Voigt C A. Principles of genetic circuit design. Nature Methods, 11, 5: 508-520 (2014)
10. Weiss R, Basu S, Hooshangi S, et al. Genetic circuit building blocks for cellular computation, communications, and signal processing. Natural Computing, 2, 1: 47-84 (2003)
11. Gardner T S, Cantor C R, Collins J J. Construction of a genetic toggle switch in Escherichia coli. Nature, 403, 6767: 339-342 (2000)
12. Anderson J C, Voigt C A, Arkin A P. Environmental signal integration by a modular AND gate. Molecular Systems Biology, 3, 1: 133 (2007)
13. Tamsir A, Tabor J J, Voigt C A. Robust multicellular computing using genetically encoded NOR gates and chemical 'wires'. Nature, 469, 7329: 212-215 (2011)
14. Moon T S, Lou C, Tamsir A, et al. Genetic programs constructed from layered logic gates in single cells. Nature, 491, 7423: 249-253 (2012)
15. Chau A. H, Walter J M, Gerardin J, et al. Designing synthetic regulatory networks capable of self-organizing cell polarization. Cell, 151, 2: 320-332 (2012)
16. Wang X, Yuan GQ, Wang X, Zhao ZX, Wang K. Communication and Monitor of Breast Cancer Signal in the Pulse-Output Genetic Circuit Network. Science China, 57, 3: 1-10 (2014)

ITM Web of Conferences 7, 09020 (2016) DOI: 10.1051/itmconf/20160709020
ITA 2016

Investigation and Analysis of Agricultural Information Construction in the Economically Weak Rural Areas of Beijing

Wei-Wei ZHANG[1], Hong LI[1,a]

[1] *Beijing Academy of Agriculture and Forestry Sciences, No.9 Shu Gang Hua Yuan Middle Road, Beijing 100097, China*
[a] Corresponding author:lihsdf@sina.com

Abstract. The agricultural information construction in the economically weak rural areas of Beijing may promote mutual conversion between the informatization of traditional agricultural production elements and the factored information production, which provides the new opportunities and conditions for agricultural development. In the present study, the current status of the information construction, information personnel, the information operational capability of villagers and the reasons affecting their information utilization in the village was investigated and analyzed by questionnaire survey, which offers the targeted suggestions for advancing the agricultural information level in the economically weak rural areas of Beijing, including 1) establish effective internet environment within the village to supply effective access to the Internet for poor villagers; 2)emphasize the internet operational training for the villagers; 3) construct the internet platform to provide the communication platform and 4) reinforce the training of village level scientific and technical information personnel.

1. Introduction

Rural informatization is an important part of the national information construction, and it is also the essence of the construction of the new socialist countryside.

As the capital city of our country, Beijing has always attached great importance to the economic and social development of the economically weak area. The rural economy weak region in Beijing is relatively wide, the living area is relatively scattered, and the spendable income of the farmers is limited. The "Last kilometre" issue, as the biggest barrier of the rural informatization, is related to whether the achievement of information technology can really benefit ordinary people, as well as the process of constructing a new socialist countryside. In the present study, we explored the agricultural information construction and its popularizing status in Beijing rural region with weak economic development by questionnaire survey, which offers the targeted suggestions for improving the agricultural information level in the economically weak rural area of Beijing.

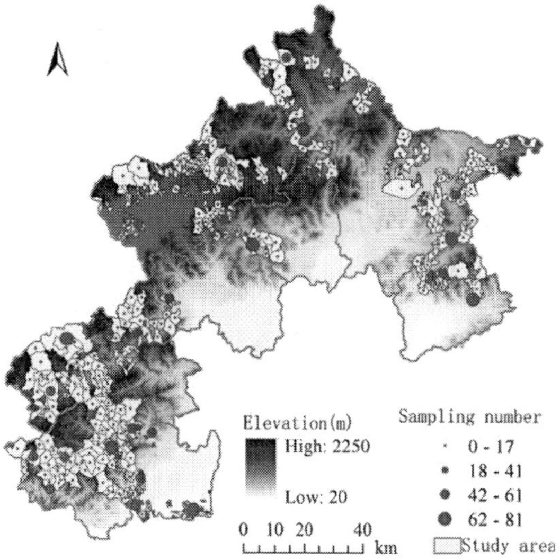

Figure 1. The Location of Study Area and The Questionnaire Sample Distribution

2. Research Methods

In the present study, questionnaire survey and interview were utilized to thoroughly mine the construction and popularization of agricultural information in the economically weak rural areas of Beijing. The current status of the information construction, information personnel, the information operational capability of villagers and the reasons affecting their information utilization in the village were investigated. The statistical analysis method was used to process data, and the Microsoft Excel software was used.

The research objects were divided into two levels, the village level and the peasant household. The village level objects was comprised of 393 villages in 32 townships, and the farmer level included 2210 rural household in 35 administrative villages in the economically weak rural areas of Beijing. Of these, 391 valid questionnaires were retrieved out of the 393 village level questionnaires, and 1851 out of 2210 were valid for the peasant household level. The general situation of the survey object is geographically isolated, small population size, old in age, low cultural level, single industrial structure with poor overall strength, and big proportion of young migrant workers.

3. The Current Developmental Status of Agricultural Informatization in The Economically Weak Rural Areas of Beijing

The statistical analysis was performed infrastructure construction of information in gully region, agricultural information system construction and personal information qualities of villagers.

3.1 The Status of the Information Infrastructure Construction

The information network infrastructure exhibited low level in the economically weak rural areas of Beijing with no optical fiber in any of the investigated village. However, telephone was available in every village, and it was convenient for villagers to install the telephone. In addition, cell phone was popularized with the rate over 95%, and even the poorest household possessed a cell phone. Convenient and fast was the main reason for the high rate of mobile phone, but the high cost inhibited the use rate of cell phones, which was about 45.4%. The penetration rate of TV was as high as 98% in the mountain region, but the rate was low for the cable. The broadcast and cable broadcast were available in all investigated villages. Moreover, the rural information stations were established in the townships, and the survey revealed that the ordinary operational effect, no effective service and never been to never heard of accounted for 49.4%, 15.2% and 25.2% respectively. Only 10.2% agreed on the desired effect of the station, which demonstrated that the insufficient self advertisement resulted in the lack of understanding and utilization of the station. Secondly, the service station did not play its due function because of the weak service ability.

3.2 The Status of Agricultural Information System Construction in the Village

By visiting the villages with the rural management system, the information management function of eight aspects was accomplished via the system, including rural population in the village, labor employment, the income of the farmers, rural finance, the party management, contract management, collective asset management and the publication of village affairs. The utilization of the system was under the superior guidance, but its main services in the government business needs cannot genuinely serve the villagers (Figure 2). On one hand, the government's initial investment is mainly to serve the level of government itself, but the lack of data foundation construction makes this service not exactly the best. On the other hand, the information service that cannot serve the rural areas certainly will not be valued in the village, so the data collection is not effectively guaranteed.

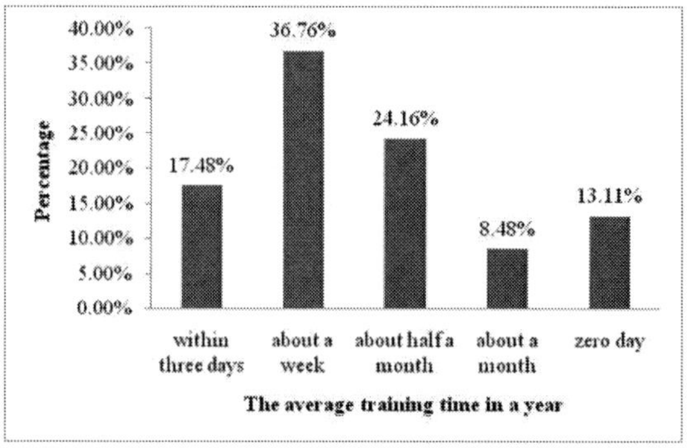

Figure 2. The Status of Village-Level Agricultural Information System Service

Currently, the survey on the service provided by agricultural information network indicated that redundant content with no novelty, weak pertinence, lack of interaction and poor design accounted for 26.4%, 28.4%, 24.5% and 3.5%, respectively. Therefore, as the social development and the improvement of farmer personal quality, the professional content of the website, the practicality of the content and the interaction of the website have been paid more attention.

As the most distal management organizations of administrative management, the village is the most effective sources of information entities. To break the "Last kilometre", government should adjust ideas to mine demand and strengthen the practicality and pertinence of information construction with village level as the construction unit.

3.3 The Status of Information Service Ability in the Village

The ability of village level information service depends on the level of village information officer. Overall, 391 villages of 32 townships and 391 information officers were involved in the investigation, one officers per village. From the perspective of age, officers born at 1960s, 1970s, 1980s and 1990s accounted for 23.14%,

52.44%, 15.95% and 8.48%, respectively. Officers born at 1970s are the largest proportion in the survey.

Secondly, from the perspective of training length, few opportunities are available for the officers to attend a whole training program, although many information trainings are held in Beijing each year, or the position personnel of village information officers is not fixed with substantial mobility, so the proportion of officers who can accomplish the whole training process to all the training attendee is only 8.48% (Figure 3). Thirdly, from the perspective of degree, most officers hold a high-school degree, and the officers born in the 80s and 90s hold associate degree and above, but their computer professional level is relatively low, so their professional skills are mainly dependent on self learning and government training.

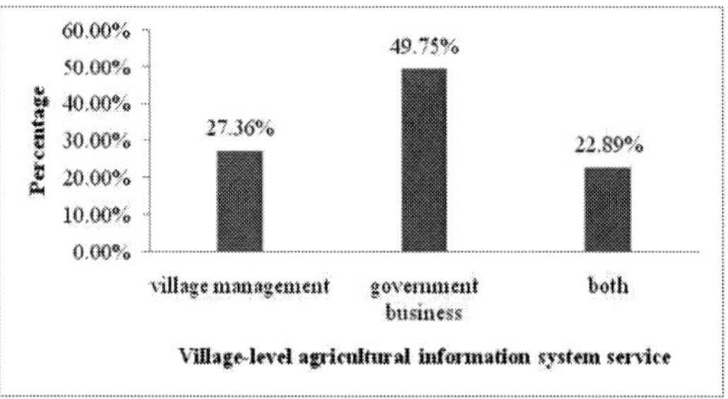

Figure 3. The Proportion of Officers Who Can Accomplish Training Process

Based on the age structure distribution and training time for the information officer, on one hand, the age structure is not reasonable, and their cultural level is low, suggesting the insufficient attention to rural information officers from the government. On the other hand, the information offers in the village is not properly organized, and their stipend is low (1000/year), therefore, the information staff is often temporarily part-timed by the relevant personnel with great mobility, leading to the cost increase of government training and unsatisfactory effect.

3.4 The Status of Villagers' Information Quality

For the 1851 investigated households, 304 households have computers, 933 do not, and the computer owner ship rate of 24.6%. In addition, all the computer owners initiatively connected to internet. Form the age perspective, the family with younger generation (80s) accounted for over 90% of the computer owners. From the aspect of the internet purpose, the production, education, obtaining information, recreation and entertainment accounted for 13.4%, 28.1%, 37.2% and 21.3%, respectively. Therefore, as the education level improvement of the villagers, their capability of information acquiring is also elevated. Our survey also showed reasons impacting the network utilization: do not know how to use internet (42.3%), do not need it (27.1%) and have no money for it (18.2%). The main reason would be that the cultural level is low for most villagers, and they are mainly involved in farming, resulting in a less prosperous life. However, they are all familiar with network, but have no convenient access to network. The major ways of obtaining information for farmers are TV, mobile phone and broadcast, accounting for 47.9%, 19.9% and 17.8%, respectively, followed by newspapers and periodicals 6.9%, home phone 5.5%, internet 4.2%, information station 2.7% and information machine 1.2%. The main measure of information distribution is text, accounting for 19.9%, then rural information station 11%, internet 4.2%, other ways 7.1% and the information machine 1.2%.

The main reason would be that the cultural level is low for most villagers, and they are mainly involved in farming, resulting in a less prosperous life. However, they are all familiar with network, but have no convenient access to network. In addition, information awareness of rural residents in mountainous areas is not strong. Although the prevalence level of TV, mobile and computer is high in mountainous area, the usage and understanding of information are deficient. Moreover, because of the young migrant workers, elder people and women are mainly involved in farming, which inhibits the development of rural information.

4. Related Suggestions

The investigation revealed the low prosperous level in the peasant households in the economically weak rural area of Beijing, low cultural level relatively low, low village management level and simple management methods, so desired measures and methods cannot be effectively implemented at the village level. Therefore, the following problems are needed to be resolved to promote the construction and development of economically weak rural areas of Beijing via information means:

4.1 Strengthen the Construction of Information Infrastructure in the Economically Weak Rural Areas of Beijing

To strengthen the construction of the information infrastructure in rural regions, the optical fiber should be available in the village to establish the effective network environment. The local network should be constructed at village level by the way of enterprise service and government purchase to provide the free and effective access to the Internet for poor villagers.

4.2 Reinforce the Education and Training of The Cultural and Scientific Knowledge

The function of various information engineering should be effectively elaborated by the education and training of the cultural and scientific knowledge. The overall personal quality of the villagers and the ability of the farmers to obtain and participate in market competition will be enhanced through the establishment and improvement of the pyramid training mechanism of the information officers, that is, county to township, township to village, and village to household.

DOI: 10.1051/itmconf/20160709020

4.3 Establish a Well-developed Information Service Platform

Based on the actual needs of the villagers, the market, technology, knowledge, life, work and other needs, establish highly efficient information service platform to achieve the collection, collation, publishing and trading of information resources by the connection to the logistics and financial system, so that the local villagers can easily get the production and living information they need.

4.4 Strengthen the Training of the Ability to Use Information Technology for Village Leaders to Improve their Awareness of Information Service

The understanding of information technology by village leaders directly affects the level of information construction in the village, so the government should strengthen the training of the ability to use information technology for village leaders to improve their awareness of information service.

5. Conclusions

Due to the backward information basis and low cultural level of the villages in the economically weak rural areas of Beijing, the information capability of the villagers should be improved gradually. As a science and technology service, it is the first to offer the construction service for the basic environment as much as possible. The information distribution can be used to influence, motivate and increase the information awareness and application capability, which services for the production and life and promotes the integrated development of all aspects of the industry.

References

1. C.L. Wang, J.R. Gai, C.P. Yang, Journal of Anhui Agri.Sci. 35, 4703 (2007)
2. Z.Z. Shu, H. Zhou, Y.Q. Wu, Anhui Agri. Sci. Bull. 19, 5 (2013)
3. Z.W. Fan, Journal of Intelligent 31, 151 (2012)
4. S.J. Wang, G.Z. Sun, Chin. Agric. Sci. Bull. 26, 393 (2010)
5. X.C. Zhang, X.Y. Qin, X.X. Zhang, Journal of Beijing Agricultural Vocation College 22, 42 (2008)
6. W.M. Liu, M.F. Rahman, S. Thirumuruganathan, N. Zhang, and G. Das. Proceedings of the VLDB Endowment. 8, 12 (2015)

The Influence of the Marine Culture on the Architecture in Jiaodong Peninsula

Juan XUE [1], Chao ZHAN[1], and Peng SUN [1]

[1] *Shandong Jianzhu University. FengMing Road ,Jinan city, Shandong Prov. China*

Abstract: With the arrival of the "Era of the Ocean", the coastal city ushered in an upsurge of the development and construction . In order to avoid being lack in the sense of belonging of the coastal city. Implant and deepen marine has become particularly important. This paper firstly has interpreted Marine culture, then analyzed Marine culture formation. Analysis of Marine culture to study the rural settlement. The paper has unearthed Marine culture connotation and characteristics thoroughly, on the basis of the knowledge of Marine culture before, in the Jiaodong building. The paper has carried about the Marine culture on the analysis emphatically to the settlement houses monomer and detail from layout to facade, from construction materials to decorative colors.This paper proposes the renovation of the building, it should carry out traditional marine culture with a view to building on the Jiaodong sustainable development to provide effective guidance, while research and rural settlements is a rich culture and complement. Meanwhile this would be a rich and supplement to research mention on the building.

1 Introduction

Shandong peninsula is one of the pivotal gateways on Sea Line of Communication of ancient eastern Asia. For thousands of years, Marine culture had got down into bone of the Jiaodong culture and become a main part of it.Residents of Jiaodong adjacent to the sea and rely on it, thus, it formed the unique geographical features and architecture. Wu Liangyong[Wu Liangyong[a], born in 1922 in Nanjing. Chinese Academy of Sciences and Chinese Academy of Engineering academician, Chinese architects, urban planning experts and educators, human settlements science creator.] once said: "culture is the crystallization of history, which retained in the building and together with life. Culture gradually influences the construction of cities and residential behaviors, it becomes the soul of city and architecture." Marine culture gives the unique style of building in Jiaodong area.

Marine culture of Shandong peninsula gives the Jiaodong people hard-working and competent personality. The houses they build combine exquisiteness with practical functions. The seaweed house with warmth and aesthetics is embodied with the wisdom of residents using local materials. Marine culture produces the Matsu culture which impacts on worship building in Jiao dong district. This article elaborates from the building material, building structure, building layout, architecture color, architectural decoration and construction category and other aspects and expounds the influences of Marine culture on architecture.

[a] Wu Liangyong, born in 1922 in Nanjing. Chinese Academy of Sciences and Chinese Academy of Engineering academician, Chinese architects, urban planning experts and educators, human settlements science creator.

2 Marine Culture and Architecture

2.1 The Influence on Architectural Materials

The selection of architectural materials can reflect local characteristics in the maximum degree. Jiao dong has a temperate and moist climate, encompasses a wealth of mineral resources and abundant flora. The local residents are skilled at selecting local materials and making the most of them. Jiaodong is rich in durable stone which can resist the wind waves. Therefore, stone serves as the common material of building in the Jiaodong area. Foundation is given priority to stone material, mostly, bases with macadam and fills the gap with sand. Walls are finished with stone or mixture brick, from plinth to the eaves is the thick stone walls. The grey tiles and grass are selected to construct roof. The kelp grass roof has the most distinct regional characteristics. Take the seaweed house in Rongcheng as an example to introduce.

The seaweed house Located in the eastern coastal Tianjintou (sky without horizon) in the easternmost end of Rongcheng City, seaweed house is an unique architectural form. Seaweed house is mainly distributed in the Jiaodong peninsula in Shandong coast, such as Weihai, Yantai, Qingdao. The largest quantity and best preserved sections of seaweed house is in Rongcheng area.

It gets its name by using seaweed grows along the coast of Shandong Peninsula to cover rooftops of the house, and with stones and grey bricks as the wall. Because the seaweed contains a large number of colloid and halogen which can prevent insect and mildew and is not easy to burn, it is the ideal building materials. All materials of traditional seaweed house are sourced locally. Main materials: seaweed, stone, wood, sorghum stalk, and yellow mud. Jiaodong peninsula has humid and rainy summer, fierce windy winter, and it snows a lot in Yantai and Weihai. After strong overlying, the seaweed has good heat preservation and strong wind resistance, it is significantly better than other kinds of tile-roofed houses.

2.1.1 The seaweed house

Located in the eastern coastal Tianjintou (sky without horizon) in the easternmost end of Rong cheng City, seaweed house is an unique architectural form. Seaweed house is mainly distributed in the Jiaodong peninsula in Shandong coast, such as Weihai, Yantai, Qingdao. The largest quantity and best preserved sections of seaweed house is in Rongcheng area.

It gets its name by using seaweed grows along the coast of Shandong Peninsula to cover rooftops of the house, and with stones and grey bricks as the wall. Because the seaweed which contains a large number of colloid and halogen can prevent insect and mildew and is not easy to burn, it is the ideal building materials. All materials of traditional seaweed house are sourced locally. Main materials: seaweed, stone, wood, sorghum stalk, and yellow mud. Jiaodong peninsula has humid and rainy summer, fierce windy winter, and it snows a lot in Yantai and Weihai. After strong overlying, the seaweed has good heat preservation and strong wind resistance, it is significantly better than other kinds of tile-roofed houses.

2.2 The Influence on Architectural Structure

Due to the affection of perennial damp Marine monsoon, air humidity in Jiaodong coastal areas is big, and it is the damp-proof which is very important to construction. The building is commonly built with high base and high threshold. To withstand wind and rain in summer Yingshan Roof is chosen, because its short depth and big slope is conducive to drainage. With gentle rolling hills local residents effectively use the natural resources to form the structure system of the mixture brick (stone) with wood.

2.3 The Influence on Architectural Layout

The main housing type in Jiaodong coastal area is courtyard whose core is the yard, and therefore courtyard residence has become the major kind of Jiaodong coastal residences. The courtyard in Jiaodong is very different from the courtyard in Beijing, houses instead of corridors are around the courtyard which save on the layout, there is only a yard in the middle without front yard and backyard. Due to the influence of the temperate zone monsoon climate, the dwelling houses in coastal area have closed wall and broad courtyard. Closed exterior wall is for escaping the seasonal winds, especially the north wind from the sea in cold winter. In the meantime, it is to strengthen security and construction strong privacy living environment. The open courtyard strives for sunshine as much as possible to resist the damp environment in the coastal areas.

2.4 The Influence on Architectural Color

Under the influence of sea cold color, the color of buildings in Jiaodong are black which is the characteristics of Marine culture. Black is the color of water in the Wuxing (five elements). It is clearly that the local people are advocate of the sea from this kind of color tendency. In addition to black, buildings mainly are in cold color. As the basic building material, brick reflects the decorous feeling of nature. At the same time, it always uses the nature color of the material, which includes white, grey and light brown.

2.5 The Influence of the Building Decoration

The ancient ancestors in the coastal areas lived by fish and hunt, relying on water draft. So formation of architectural decoration in the Jiaodong area and Marine culture are bound together inextricably. The adornments are fish, dragons etc, with obvious local characteristics.

It is often applied to the Kui dragon pattern in large houses and the corresponding Kui phoenix design. They are commonly used in the ridge, the end of vertical ridges, image wall etc. This kind of Kui dragon pattern which is abstract is very popular in Jiaodong coastal residents building.

What often appears in construction of decoration pattern is fish, turtle, shrimp, crab and other aquatic animals, as well as aquatic plants like seaweed. In a high level of construction, the dragon, fish, seaweed and other image in connection with the sea can be seen everywhere. It makes all kinds of image lifelike through the color processing. It all can reflect the Marin culture widespread influence of the building decoration in Jiaodong region. In addition to the applied animal and plant pattern, the myths and stories on eight immortals are also widely used which reflect the unique style and features of coastal areas.

3 Inheriting Marine Culture to Realize the Sustainable Development of Jiao dong Architecture

Nowadays, the sustainable development strategy has become a global program of action. At the same time, the globalization has created new opportunities and challenges for the development of architecture. However, the process of globalization is at the expense of the sacrifice. Fast-food culture is corroding national culture in people' s heart. Local characteristics are damaged. In gradually fading of particularity and losing of national tradition, we need to find a suitable architecture with the regional characteristic cultural ecology of the organic update strategy, in order to realize the sustainable development of regional architecture.

3.1 The Principle of Realizing the Sustainable Development of Jiao dong Architecture

Thus, how can architecture realize the development trend in today' s society? It relies on people, architecture and natural environment building a reasonable relationship of supplementing each other and mutual promotion, to achieve the harmony of the three. So we must follow certain principles:

3.1.1 The Principle of Continuity

The principle of continuity emphasizes the continuity of culture first of all. Usually, the development of economic in inland less rapid than coastal areas which echoes the profound history and culture. At the same time, the transportation is so convenient that the foreign cultural exchange frequently. In the local indigenous culture and foreign culture collision exchange, it gradually formed a composite, the freedom of open Marin culture. So, how does architecture in the coastal areas of Jiaodong explore and inherit the history in the process of organic update, how to protect and continue the Marine culture, how to guide, control and create maritime architectural form and symbol, all of them are the new task to build a new socialist countryside.

3.1.2 Ecologic Principle

We should take the concept of sustainable development in the sustainable development of architecture, promote the common development of both, create organic architecture which can be integrated with environment and put forward the "zero energy consumption". The purpose of architectural design is to adapt to the ecological environment. Architectural design not only has minimum assault to environment, but also can effectively utilize renewable resources and reduce energy consumption. Only in this way can we build a healthy, high-level and pleasant indoor environment. Therefore, environmental protection and the realization of sustainable development of architecture can' t be done without the concept of ecological architecture. It will become the inevitable trend of building development.

3.1.3 Characteristic Principle

The unique topography and climate conditions of Jiaodong region provide different natural and geographical backgrounds for the formation of characteristics of the coastal architecture in Jiaodong. Therefore, when we organically update coastal buildings of Jiaodong area, we should pay attention to excavate and shape their own characteristics, fully reflect and strengthen natural features of the sea, rather than copy the rigid design model of a new socialist countryside.

3.1.4 Re-use Principle

There is abundant marine cultural information in the coastal architecture of Jiaodong, which is to be used reasonably and updated in the process of buildings transformation. Certain building materials are energy which can be recycled and original, like adobe; tiles and rocks of masonry wall can be reused; wrack, as building materials of the roof, was taken from the nature and should be returned to nature and so on. The principle that we reasonably reuse them not only can save cost, but also can create unexpected results.

3.2 Positioning

Place the figure as close as possible after the point where it is first referenced in the text. If there is a large number of figures and tables it might be necessary to place some before their text citation. If a figure or table is too large to fit into one column, it can be cantered across both columns at the top or the bottom of the page.

3.3 Color illustrations

You are free to use color illustrations for the online version of the proceedings but any print version will be printed in black and white unless special arrangements have been made with the conference organizer. Please check with the conference organizer whether or not this is the case. If the print version will be black and white only, you should check your figure captions carefully and remove any reference to color in the illustration and text. In addition, some color figures will degrade or suffer loss of information when converted to black and white, and this should be taken into account when preparing them.

Conclusions

When a kind of culture is generally regarded as the "traditional culture", it means that it has gone through a long time and accumulated deep emotion. It becomes a kind of spirit being stationed in people's hearts and makes people admire, miss and even hard to forget. People develop and improve traditional architectural form by making the essence of national culture into it. This paper organically combines the Marine culture with the architectural features of Jiaodong coastal areas. By studying the influence of Marine culture of Jiaodong region on construction, this paper explores the sustainable

DOI: 10.1051/itmconf/20160709021

development of traditional buildings and the present situation of the Marine cultural heritage in the region, enriches and develops the traditional architectural culture and Marine culture.

Acknowledgements

First and foremost, I appreciate my country who give me a comfortable learning atmosphere. Second, I would like to show my deepest gratitude to my supervisor, Prof. Juan XUE, who has walked me through all the stages of the writing of this thesis. Without her illuminating instruction and patience, this thesis could not have reached its present form.

References

1. Qu Jinliang: A Marine Culture and Society, China Ocean University Press. (2003)
2. Sun Yun-long: Of Shandong House, Shandong Wenhua Yinxiang Press. (1999)
3. Luo Chunrong: The Matsu Legend Study—A Maritime Power of Myth, Tianjin Ancient Books Press. (2009)
4. Bo Xinhua, ZhaiXin and Li Longsen : Shandong Ocean Cultural Characteristics of the Formation and Development, Xi'an Jiaotong University Press. (2010)
5. M.A.Li Zheng: Jiaodong Traditional Tousesand Modern Interpretation, Tianjin University. (2003)
6. Zhao Gang: Regional Culture Return and Architectural Features of the Re-creation, Huazhong Architecture. (2001)
7. You Shaoping, Chang Xingzhao: Building, Shandong Friendship Press. (2002)
8. Sun Fenghua ,Wei Xiao: House, Shandong Friendship Press. (2004)

The Mechanism of Sharing Tacit Knowledge Based on Multi-Agent Systems

Qing-Nian WANG[1,a] , Yu-Jie QIN[2]

[1] *International Office, South China Univ. of Tech., Guangzhou 510641*
[2] *School of Environment and Energy, South China Univ. of Tech., Guangzhou, 510641*

Abstract. The effective application of knowledge management in organizations is an essential factor in their successful operation. Furthermore, it is more important that how people exploit tacit knowledge, how they make tacit knowledge beneficial to the organization. Sharing tacit knowledge within an organization is critical to the organization among the individuals and between the individuals. However, there is no approach based on multi-agent systems to analyze the sharing of tacit knowledge, and to discover what kinds of methods tacit knowledge can be shared and how organizations make themselves effective and efficient based on multi-agent systems. So this paper, based on multi-agent systems, aims to present for discussion the mechanism of sharing tacit knowledge within an organization. First of all, this paper describes three main characteristics of tacit knowledge; then expands to find the games between the individuals in the organization. Finally, some conclusions and further discussions are puts forward.

1 Introduction

The effective application of knowledge management in organizations is an essential factor in their successful operation. Furthermore, it is more important that how people exploit tacit knowledge, how they make individual knowledge and organizational knowledge easy to approach and how they make tacit knowledge beneficial to organizations.

Knowledge has been defined and has been classified into tacit knowledge (TK) and explicit knowledge (EK) [1], [2], [3], [4], [5], [6]. Knowledge is embedded in organizations and individuals [7]. Sharing tacit knowledge within an organization is critical to the cooperation among the individuals and between the individuals and the organization. However, there is no approach based on multi-agent systems to analyze the sharing of tacit knowledge and to think over how an organization creates a harmonious environment and exploit tacit knowledge, and to discover what kinds of mechanism can share tacit knowledge and how organizations make themselves effective and efficient based on multi-agent systems. So this paper, based on multi-agent systems, aims to present for discussion the mechanism of sharing tacit knowledge within an organization.

An organization is indeed a system. Most scholars who study tacit knowledge only focus on one or two key factors that affect knowledge creation, through some specific method to solve the problems occurring in tacit knowledge management, or using limited methods to apply to the organization without thinking of the values within it. Here, we apply the multi-agent systems in order to consider the games among the individuals and between the individuals and the organization based on their different payoffs.

First of all, this paper describes three main characteristics of tacit knowledge: 1) monopolization, which means that it is not automatic for the individuals to share tacit knowledge; 2) it is quite difficult for tacit knowledge to transform or flow among the individuals or groups and between the individual and the organization; 3) the instability of the subjective benefits is caused by the deeply individual tacit knowledge, because their values can not be simply accomplished by the network platform or cultural stimulation.

According to the situation whether the participators cooperate with each other, there are two kinds of games: the cooperative game and the un-cooperative game. Time and information are the main factors which affect the equivalence of the game. In the process of the game, the information communication between the participators judges their activity space and the choice of excellent strategy. At the same time, the sequence of the participators' activities directly affects the final equivalence of the game.

[a] Corresponding author: adqnwang@sina.com

Because all the games are consisted of basic games between individuals, we focus on analyzing two kinds of basic games, one is the cooperative game and the other is un-cooperative game between individuals with some illustrations which mark the payoffs of the participators. Then, we discuss four types of tacit knowledge flows and transformations in detail under the following conditions respectively: 1) between the individuals, 2) between the individuals and the group, 3) the individuals and the organization, 4) the groups and the organization. Finally, this paper gives some conclusions and puts forward some further discussions and the future work

2Tacit Knowledge and its Characteristics

2.1 Tacit Knowledge

According to what Polanyi analyzed, tacit knowledge refers to that "We can know more than we can tell" J.C. Spender defines tacit knowledge as "not yet explicated."[5]. Suchman observes that tacit knowledge enables us to take actions that are situated in particular social and physical circumstances, and then tacit knowledge is context bound [7]. While Polanyi addressed tacit knowledge at an individual level [3], others have suggested it exists in group settings. In fact, Richard Nedson and Sydney Winter suggested that organizations maintain their structure and coherency through tacit knowledge embedded in "organizational routines" that no single person understands completely. In this paper, tacit knowledge refers to the knowledge, which is hidden in social and physical circumstances, and which is the context bound imbedded in the individuals, groups and the organization.

2.2 Characteristics of Tacit Knowledge

2.2.1 The Monopolization of Tacit Knowledge

Because the sharing of tacit knowledge cannot be conducted freely and automatically by the knowledge subject, the monopolization of tacit knowledge has become apparent. People who possess of tacit knowledge would not transform their knowledge, particularly tacit knowledge which can take a lot of benefit to other people. In addition, the tacit knowledge subjects have no direct exchanges and contact among themselves without the order from the organization. Individuals cannot make face-to-face communications with the restriction of working positions. The more restrict the organizational management is, the more difficult the sharing of tacit knowledge between the individuals is.

2.2.2 The Difficulties to Transform Tacit Knowledge

The flows and transform of tacit knowledge includes knowledge flows between individuals, knowledge flows between individuals and the group, knowledge flow between groups, knowledge flow between group and organization. Therefore, knowledge transforming is obviously complex and difficult.

2.2.3 The Uncertainty of Subjective Benefit

One important reason for an organization to last forever is that both individuals and groups contribute to the organization or enterprise with their knowledge. The value of explicit knowledge can be calculated, but tacit knowledge owned by the individuals is very potential. It is not easy to gain value simply by establishing platform of network or stimulating organizational culture. If the tacit knowledge subjects share the knowledge, the monopolization is broken, the excess benefit and the feeling of achievement made by tacit knowledge will disappear.

2.3 Multi-Agent Systems

A multi-agent system (MAS) is a collection of software agents that work in conjunction with each other. They may cooperate or they may compete, or some combination of cooperation and competition, but there is some common infrastructure that results in the collection being a 'system', as opposed to simply being a disjoint set of autonomous agents.

A multi-agent system is either a closed multi-agent system or an open multi-agent system. A multi-agent system may or may not be a distributed multi-agent system. There is an alternative definition, that is: a multi-agent system (MAS) is a computational system where agents cooperate or compete with others to achieve some individual or collective task [8].

In the operation procedure, a proper way is to find out a multi-agent information system to run the systems and to achieve good performance. A multi-agent information system (IMAS) is generally composed of information agents that search, on the basis of requests that are sent to them (directly or indirectly through a database) for information on databases (local or distributed) or on Internet sites. Information agents' activities are often coordinated through coordinator agents. These agents own knowledge on information agents (such as their addresses, their search domains for example) to which they send requests (in a targeted way if they own knowledge on their competences or by broadcast techniques). Coordinator agents have to gather collected information, in order to check it, compare it or filter it. Most information multi-agents systems are directly in touch with the user, upstream (to receive new requests) and/or downstream (to display search results). In order to have a reactive interface and distribute to the users, some IMAS propose the use of interface agents acting as interfaces between the users and the system [9].

3 The Game Between The Agents

As an application of analyzing and solving conflicts and cooperation, the multi-agent systems study the maximization of the subjects' function at a certain information structure so as to balance the decisions of different subjects. The game includes three parts: one is decision subject, which means participators; the second is the certain information structure, that is the strategies and action space that the participators can choose; the third is payoff, which is the participator's benefit that can be defined and quantified. The participators, strategies and payoff function form a basic game.

According to the completeness of information, games can be divided into four types: complete information static game, complete information dynamic game, incomplete information static game and incomplete information dynamic game. They can also be divided into cooperative game and uncooperative game, and the difference rests with whether the participators reach a restricted agreement in the process of gaming. If no, the game is an uncooperative game that is the main research focus for modern game. In the uncooperative game, participators firstly consider how to sustain their own benefit. The cooperative game emphasizes the collectivism, group rationality, which is efficiency, fairness and justification. However, uncooperative game emphasizes individual rationality, individual optimized decision, and the result is that it is sometimes efficient, but sometimes not.

Multi-agent systems extremely emphasizes the time and information, and considers time and information are the main factors to affect equilibrium of the game. In the process of the game, the action space and the most optimized strategy selection are decided by the information transform between the participators; at the meantime, there exists a sequence of the game process, and the sequence of participator's action directly affect the final result of the game.

Because all the games are consisted of basic games between individuals, we focus on analyzing two kinds of basic games, one is the cooperative game and the other is uncooperative game between individuals with some illustrations of payoff matrix and payoff function.

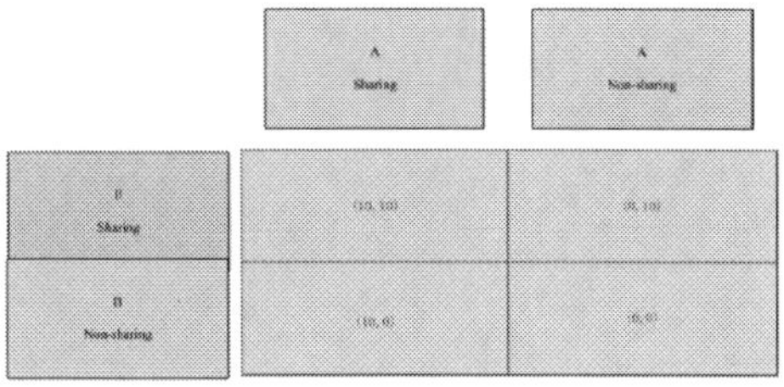

Fig. 1. Cooperative Game.

3.1 Cooperative Game

On the condition of good incentives, among all the individuals, there maintains basic cooperative game, and this makes knowledge sharing smoothly between individuals.

We establish the game as follows:

If individuals select sharing, then the benefit will be 10; otherwise, the benefit will be 0(without lose anything);

If A selects sharing, then B definitely selects sharing

If A selects not sharing, then B definitely selects not sharing;

If A knows that B will not select sharing, then A definitely selects not sharing.

Then we have the payoff matrix illustrated in figure 1. It is obvious that this cooperative game is not accord with daily motivated action. There must be something forcing people to behave "abnormal". This kind of thing could be a series of supporting systems, such as the organizational structure, organizational environment, and incentive mechanism. If there are no supporting systems, the game in organization is belonging to uncooperative game. We can see that in the situation of protecting individual benefit and making individuals competitive, the final result is that A and B share their own knowledge with each other because of the effect of various of factors.

3.2 Uncooperative Game

In the non-incentive situation, if people do share their own tacit knowledge with others in an organization, they will lose their competition and there exists some potential threat or crisis for the organization. Therefore, nobody will voluntarily share their special knowledge with others. Thus, in the organization, there is a harmful circulation; the more secret (tacit knowledge) people own, the more they can constrain others' development, the more they can plan only for themselves. This makes all the individuals not share knowledge with others and leads to the unfaithfulness of sharing knowledge or destructs the sharing environment. Eventually, it evolves to a long-term battle which makes the organization dysfunctional and loses their competition. The payoff matrix of uncooperative game is illustrated in figure 2.

 DOI: 10.1051/itmconf/20160709022

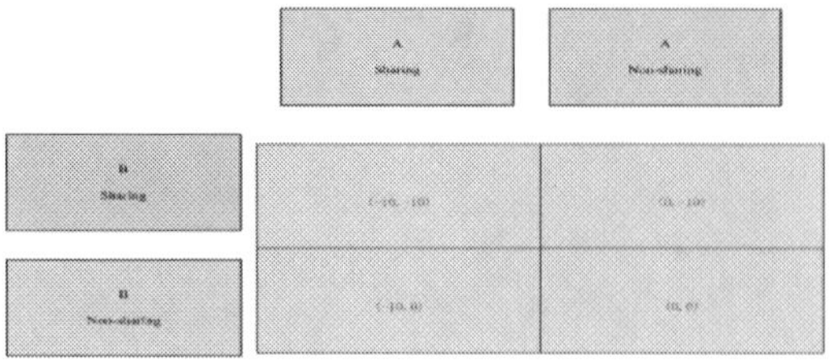

Fig. 2. Uncooperative Game

3.3 The Sharing Mechanism in Mathematic Support

In most interactive decision situations, organizations may have strong incentives to modify the information structure by sharing some of their knowledge. That is, when distributed knowledge is not common knowledge, predicted outcomes should be biased by communication possibilities. In this paper we use the model of strategic knowledge sharing presented in Koessler to investigate different classes of Bayesian games where it is possible to characterize endogenous information structures generated by voluntary and direct communication [8].

More precisely, we elaborate sufficient conditions for the initial game to become common knowledge or, on the contrary, for the information structure of the initial Bayesian game to remain unchanged, even if a first stage game of information revelation is added. Several examples and economic applications are also examined. In general terms, the idea is that a set of individuals are involved in a game with uncertain payoffs, where each individual has some piece of knowledge. An individual might perfectly know the game, another might completely ignore the real state of Nature, another might know who has some piece of knowledge that can complement his own knowledge, another might not know if others have some relevant information, etc.

We briefly define an equilibrium concept close to the sequential equilibrium, called knowledge equilibrium, for Bayesian games in which we add a first stage of strategic information revelation. Several useful definitions and properties of such equilibrium are also elaborated [9].

We consider an initial Bayesian game

$$G \equiv \langle N, \Omega, p, h, A, (u_i)_{i \in N} \rangle \qquad (1)$$

Where

$N = \{1,\ldots, n\}$ is a finite set of players;

Ω is a finite set of states of the world;

p is a full-support probability distribution on Ω;

$h = (hi)i \in N$ is the initial information structure on Ω;

Ai is player i's set of effective or payoff-relevant actions, and $A = \prod_{i \in N} A_i$;

$u_i : A \times \Omega \to R$ is player i's von Neumann Morgenstern utility function. The payoff- relevant partition P is the partition of Ω generated by the vector of utility functions $u = (u_i)i \in N$. Write $P(\omega)$ for the element of P containing ω.

For any information structure $h' = (h'i)i \in N$ on Ω, we denote by

$$G(h') \equiv \langle N, \Omega, p, h', A, (u_i)_{i \in N} \rangle \qquad (2)$$

Then, player i's expected utility when he is at his information set $h_i(\omega)$ and the strategy $\phi \in \Phi$ is used is given by

$$U_i(\phi | h_i(\omega)) \equiv E_p(u_i(\phi, \bullet) \,|h_i(\omega)) = \sum_{\omega' \in \Omega} p(\omega' | h_i(\omega)) u_i(\phi, \omega') \qquad (3)$$

For two individuals, the game can function can be very simple. However, for many individuals, the game becomes more and more complicated and complex.

4 The Analysis of Knowledge Flows and Transform

Because there are different levels and different groups in an organization and both the knowledge system and theorganization system are complicated, we mainly focus on four kinds of knowledge flows between the individuals, groups and the organization.

4.1 Tacit Knowledge Flows between Individuals

The tacit knowledge flows and transform between individuals are the base and creation source to form organizational knowledge. There are two kinds of approaches of tacit knowledge flows: one is the flows from tacit to tacit knowledge that is individuals can exchange and transform some tacit knowledge, such as technique, knack and the mode of thinker by social communication; The other is that flows from tacit knowledge to explicit knowledge, that is tacit knowledge can be externalized as explicit knowledge by mining, clearing up and concluding.

4.2 Tacit Knowledge Flow between Individuals and Group

The tacit knowledge flows between individuals and group is bidirectional. For the tacit knowledge flow from the individuals to the group, one approach is making individual tacit knowledge explicit to the group through social communication, such as technicians or experts instructing the group work; another approach is codifying some tacit knowledge; For the tacit knowledge flow from the group to the individuals, some tacit knowledge which is hard to be made explicit can be transformed into individual tacit

DOI: 10.1051/itmconf/20160709022

knowledge through the impact of the group and the feeling of individuals.

4.3 Tacit Knowledge Flows between the Individuals and the Organization

This individual tacit knowledge which is hard to be made explicit can be transformed to organizational tacit knowledge by socialization and effective integration. Some can be made organizational explicit knowledge, and some can be transformed into individual tacit knowledge, and eventually, forms organizational culture, view of valuation and the mode of thinker [10].

4.3 Tacit Knowledge Flows between the Groups and the Organization

For knowledge itself, there are four kinds of flows: from tacit to tacit, from tacit to explicit, from explicit to explicit, and from explicit to tacit. The game process is comparatively complicated when knowledge is hidden in the groups and the organization. It needs more and more cooperative works, highly ordered organizational structure and harmonious environment.

5 Discussion and Future Research

System focus is a philosophy rather than a specific technique, one that reinforces the importance of technology integration. The advantages of knowledge integration do not come without investment and commitment from top management. It also takes time to develop the skills of integrating teams. There exists value of system focus in an environment that is both complex and changeable. An integration team can build a solid and powerful base of knowledge about the interactions between the most critical decisions in new product design[11].

In knowledge-intensive organizations, one should expect randomness, chaos, and disorderliness that are inherent to innovation process. Those who accept chaos and try to manage it are likely to be far more successful that those who try to pretend it can be orderly if one can introduce more structure to the process. Knowledge-intensive organizations have to be driven by vision that attract superb people and motivate them to contribute in desired directions so that people are not "loose to innovate". Also, the organization has to capture its systematic and managerial knowledge in its information systems.

Knowledge-intensive organizations need not to follow blindly the competitive or partnership models, mixing cooperation and competition, trust and flexibility. An interesting agenda for future research should include how small and medium sized knowledge-intensive organizations and developing regions can react, where the focus is on imitation, absorption and incremental improvement rather than the development of radical new products or processes. Some disussions are as follows.

I. This paper mainly aims to establish managerial mechanism, which can develop the ability of public knowledge department. Therefore, based on transforming the organizational function, simplifying the institution, it is important to complete the operational rules and to execute strictly.

II. Rectifying the external effect. To the beneficial externality, it is necessary for the organization to encourage the individuals to share their knowledge by several of incentive policy, and to expand the effect to the most efficient
level to the organization by intellectual property right.

III. Improving the efficiency of the sharing of tacit knowledge. The effective way is to set up the competitive and incentive mechanism between the individuals, groups and the organization, and to introduce market competition to the organization. Another way is to form the inner knowledge sharing network, which can enhance the tacit knowledge exchange between individuals and organization, and maintain the organization efficient [12].

IV. Focusing on harmonious environment and relationship within the organization. To maintain competitiveness, organizations need both a sense of stability and continuity. At the same time, as there is a potential in human resource, tacit knowledge plays a crucial part in the successful process of continuous improvements. An emphasis on building bridge between colleagues and create suitable environment to promote this.

V. Focusing on social competence. Develop complementary relations within the company, based on apprenticeship, trust and a helping attitude. We have argued that organizing companies around process teams may be a viable solution. Effective systems for sharing tacit knowledge presuppose a focus on social competence.

VI. This paper based on the analysis of two kinds of basic game explains the tacit knowledge sharing mechanism between individuals and the organization. However, there are much more works to do in the near future, such as how to establish games for some other different level in the organization, how to simulate the knowledge flows, how to do some empirical research and so on.

Acknowledgment

This paper is sponsored by the fund of Humanities and Social Science of Ministry of Education, project No. 11YJA190149 and the Humanities and Social Science Fund of South China University of Technology. Great thinks to these two funds.

DOI: 10.1051/itmconf/20160709022

References

1. Davenport, T.H., Prusak, L., Working knowledge, Harvard Business School Press, Boston(1998)
2. Polanyi, M., The tacit Dimension, Routledge and Kegan Paul, London(1966) Polanyi, M., "The Tacit Dimension", In Prusak, L.
3. (Ed.) Knowledge in Organization, Butterworth-Heinemann, Boston, MA,(1998)
4. 4. Leonard, D., Sensiper, S., The Role of Tacit
5. Knowledge in Group Innovation [J].California Management Review,40(1998)
6. Spender, J. C. , Companies That Train Best, Fortune, 8 February(1993)
7. Spender ,J. C., Competitive Advantage from Tacit Knowledge? Unpacking the concept and its Strategic Implications, Sage Publications, London(1996)
8. Suchman, L.,Plans and Siruared Aerions: The Problem of Human- Machine Communication, Cambridge University Press, Cambridge, U.K. (1987)
9. Krupansky J., Defination: Multi-agent systems, Agtivity,(John W. Krupansky a Base Technology)(2005)
10. E. Adam and R. Mandiau, Bringing Multi-agent Systems into Human Organizations: Application to a Multi-agent Information System, working paper, University of Valenciennes(2003)
11. Koessler, F. "Strategic Knowledge Sharing in Bayesian Games: Application," Working Paper, BETA, Universit´e Louis Pasteur, Strasbourg(2002)
12. Arzaghi M., A Model of Knowledge Sharing and Network Formation among Advertising Agencies, working paper, Brown University(2004)
13. Stenmark D., Turning Tacit Knowledge Tangible, Proceedings of the 33rd Hawaii International Conference on System Sciences(2000)

ITM Web of Conferences 7, 09023 (2016) DOI: 10.1051/itmconf/20160709023
ITA 2016

Research On The Measure Method Of Oblique Pinhole Parameters

Yu-Zhen Ma[1,a], Xiao-Fang Xia[1] and Xue-Ren Dong[1]

[1] *School of Mechanical Engineering, University of Jinan, China*
[a] *Corresponding author:me-mayz@ujn.cn*

Abstract. There are many special advantages in measuring the diameter of blind and deep holes with a capacitive probe, there are still some challenges for the measurement of a oblique pinhole parameters because the measuring device is inconvenient to stretch into the oblique pinhole exactly. A five-dimensional measurement system was adopted in the paper which included a capacitive sensor probe and a three-coordinate measuring machine to accomplish the measurement for oblique pinholes. With the help of the three-dimensional coordinates measured from the pinhole axis, we put forward a comprehensive method of combining the projection method and the least squares method together for fitting spatial straight line to obtain the optimal equation of the spacial axis. Finally, a reliable and entire measurement system was set up.

1 Introduction

In a general way, the measurement of hole parts include the following parameters, the location of a hole on the part, the diameter or roundness of a hole on the part surface, the diameter or roundness in a certain depth of a hole, the orientation of a hole axis to the part surface, the straightness of axis and cylindricity[1-4].

When we do measure for a hole part, the operation space for the measuring instruments is restricted, then the adjusting operation is very inconvenience. We use a certain length of cylinder as a measuring probe of the capacitive sensor, which can form a capacitor with the inside surface of the hole. Due to the measurement area is a cylinder, the average effect of capacitance effectively overcome the influence of micro defects on the surface of the measured holes, it has obtained very good effect in the straight hole diameter measurement[5-6].

Some holes in a workpiece are special, the centerline of a hole named as axis is not necessarily vertical or parallel to the workpiece surface, but with a certain angle. In this paper, we will discuss a special workpiece with many oblique pinholes as shown in Figure 1.

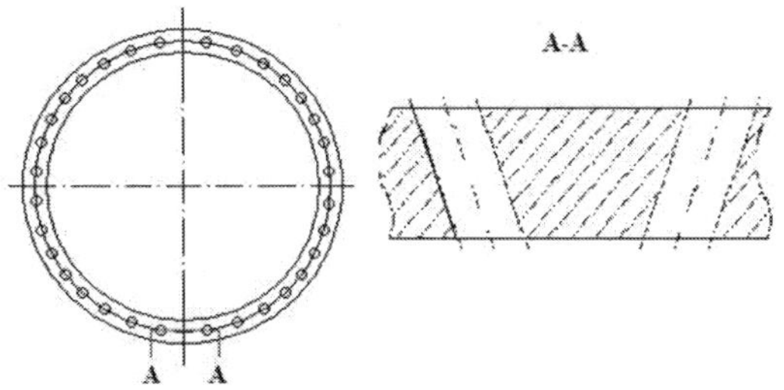

Figure 1. Drawing View of A Workpiece with Oblique Holes.

Many oblique holes with different angle were drilled in a annular metal workpiece with 3.5mm thickness, and the axis are at a certain angle between each pair of holes. For this kind of holes, not only should we get the diameter and axis position of single oblique pinhole, we should also get the position relationship namely impact height and impact error between two adjacent holes[7].

2 Measuring System Composition

To realize fast and automatic measurement for each pair of oblique holes on the annular workpiece, a five-dimension automatic adjustable measuring system is adopted to measure in high precision, the system composition is shown in Figure 2.

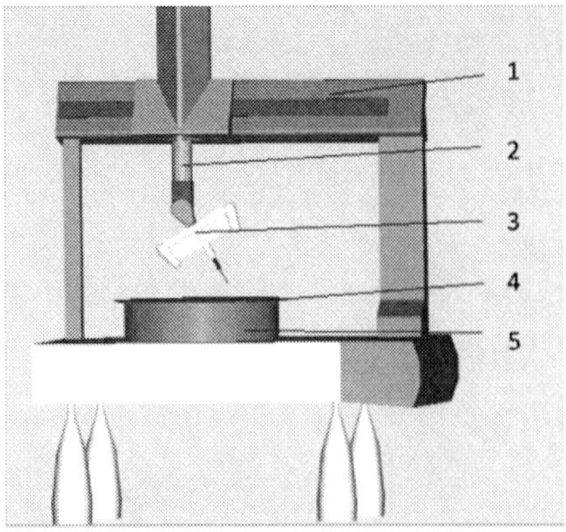

1-Three-coordinate measuring machine 2-Z axis
3-Intelligent guide measuring head 4-Annular work piece
5-Fixing and fastening bracket

Figure 2. Five-Dimension Measuring System for Annular Workpiece with Oblique Pinholes.

There are five parts in the entire measuring system, which are three-coordinate measuring machine, Z axis, intelligent guide measuring head, fixing and fastening bracket and annular workpiece to be tested. We regard the three-coordinate measuring machine as the main measuring unit to establish the main coordinate system to finish the coordinates measurement of oblique holes. A intelligent guide measuring head mounted with binocular vision camera is installed in Z axis of the three-coordinate measuring machine to realize the alignment of axis between the probe and hole, and the capacitive sensor is for the diameter measurement.

2.1 The Three-coordinate Measuring Machine

The precision of the coordinate converting in the entire system depends on that of the three-coordinate measuring machine. Considering the measuring requirement of the pinholes in the workpiece, a three-coordinate measuring machine produced in Hexagon company was adopted, the displacement measuring range for three coordinate axis is $X \times Y \times Z$=900mm × 1200mm × 800mm, and the indication error is [(1.4)+L/300]um.

2.2 The Fixing of Workpiece

To eliminate deformation in actual measurement, the fixing and fastening bracket with multifunction was used to compress the annular workpiece. Figure 3 shows the detailed structure. A one-dimension turntable with high angular resolution was installed on the workbench of three-coordinate measuring machine, a bracket was used to fix and fasten the annular part. The annular part to be tested (7) was placed at the center position which is concentric with centre pillar (9), compressed by external compressing plate (5) and internal compressing plate (8), several compressing screws (6) were fixed to tighten the plates.

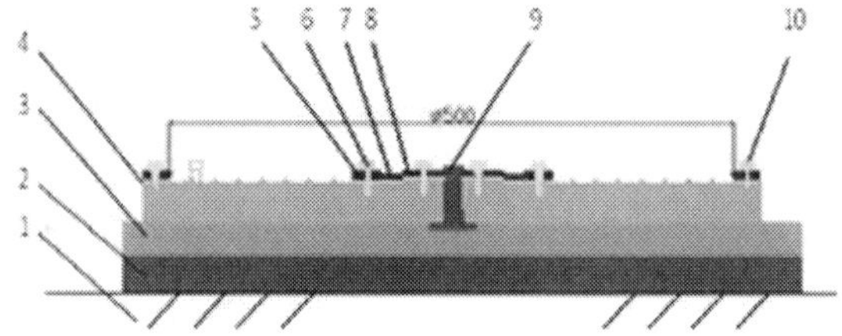

1-Workbench of three-coordinate measuring machine
2-Fixing base 3-Rotating table 4-Tooling table
5-External compressing plate 6-Compressing screw
7-Annular part to be tested 8-Internal compressing plate
9-Center pillar of the rotating table 10-Compression screw

Figure 3. Detailed Structure of A Multifunction Bracket.

2.3 The turning of workpiece

There is precise turntable under the workpiece, it can turn a desired small angle driven by a motor under the control of the program. Every time when we completed the measurement for a pinhole, the turntable turned with the workpiece to move the next pinhole to the measure position, then measurement continued. This can alleviate the inertial displacement of activating and stopping frequently when the three-coordinate measuring machine is looking for the target workpiece along the X axis and Y axis. Figure 4 shows the schematic diagram.

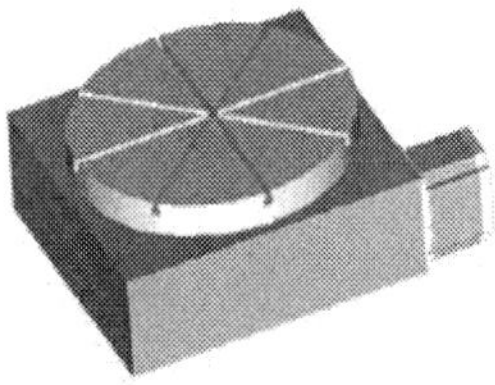

Figure 4. The Schematic Diagram of the Precise Turntable.

2.4 The Intelligent Measuring Head

The intelligent measuring head is composed of two parts, one part is a binocular vision camera which is used to find the centre point of the measured pinhole by the images captured from the surface of a pinhole. The recorded position coordinates of centre point will be helpful in the following step. Figure 5 shows the schematic diagram of the binocular vision camera.

 DOI: 10.1051/itmconf/20160709023

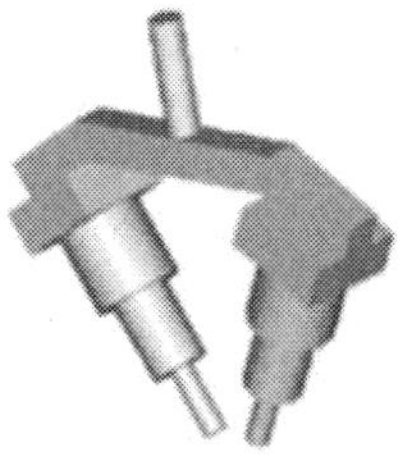

Figure 5. The Schematic Diagram Of the Binocular Vision Camera.

The other part is a capacitive probe or several probes mounted on the Z axis together. The capacitive probe is used to detect the inner diameter of the pinholes. If the parameter of the pinhole is fixed, one probe is enough. If the pinhole diameter changes in the workpiece, the diameter of capacitive probe has to change with that to make sure the measurement is available. Figure 6 shows the schematic diamatic of the capacitive probes.

Figure 6. The Schematic Diagram of The Capacitive Probes.

Obviously, when we do measurement with the capacitive probe, the most important is to make sure the alignment of the probe axis and the pinhole axis. The measured centre coordinates by binocular vision camera is useful for capacitive probe to find the right position in a shortest time.

3 Measuring Principle

When a part is reliably fixed on the workbench of three-coordinate measuring machine, the theoretical coordinate system is established accordingly and automatic measurement can start. While the three-coordinate measuring machine is moving under the program control, the intelligent measuring head with a binocular vision camera follows Z axis and moves to a hole, it first rotates an angle which is equal to the oblique hole axis angle, then the capacitive probe on the intelligent measuring head does the diameter measurement. By fitting the three-dimensional coordinate data obtained from three-coordinate measuring machine, we get the hole axis equation and complete a hole measurement. The intelligent measuring head rotates 180°around Z axis, and does the same measure for another hole. After we obtain the axis equations of a pair of holes, we can compute the position relationship between two adjacent holes.

4 The Coordinate Converting Principle

The entire coordinate system is composed of three-dimension displacement coordinates of three-coordinate measuring machine, one-dimension turning coordinate in horizontal direction from the precise turntable and one-dimension turning coordinate in vertical direction. It is a five-dimension coordinate system, the three-coordinate system is assigned as the main coordinate system, and the other coordinates will be normalized to the main coordinate system. This is the precondition for measuring accurately and correctly.

5 Fitting Algorithm of Axis Equation

The intelligent measuring head with capacitive probe is led by three-coordinate measuring machine to do measurement in a hole. To fit the equation of a axis, at least we should get two points along the axis of the hole. The axis of a oblique hole is a spatial line, it is necessary to measure the three-dimensional coordinates of each point.

Supposing there are a pair of oblique holes, their axis is named as Line A and Line B. We choose two points $M_1(x_1, y_1, z_1)$ and $M_2(x_2, y_2, z_2)$ in axis Line A, and two points $M_3(x_3, y_3, z_3)$ and $M_4(x_4, y_4, z_4)$ in axis Line B, based on the straight line equation, we get the equation for Line A and Line B,

$$\frac{x - x_1}{x_2 - x_1} = \frac{y - y_1}{y_2 - y_1} = \frac{z - z_1}{z_2 - z_1} \tag{1}$$

$$\frac{x - x_3}{x_4 - x_3} = \frac{y - y_3}{y_4 - y_3} = \frac{z - z_3}{z_4 - z_3} \tag{2}$$

In order to improve the accuracy of axis equation, we should get coordinate values in many cross sections of the hole, and adopt the points to fit the equation of the spacial line, which can eliminate the spacial distortion error greatly. Obviously, Line A and Line B are spacial three-dimensional straight line, there are six parameters in equation (1) and (2), which are not simple linear expression, we can't use the least squares fitting directly, but we can solve the problem by derivation.

Just as we know, a three-dimensional spacial line can be described with projective lines in three two-dimensional planes, vice versa, we can restore the original straight line in three-dimensional space by three projective lines. Based on this situation, we put forward a comprehensive method of combining the projection method and the least squares method together for fitting spatial straight line to obtain the optimal equation of the spacial axis.

First, we get some three-dimensional coordinate (x_i, y_i, z_i) points in the axis Line A by measurement, then we project the points to three orthogonal planes respectively, the two-dimensional coordinates on xoy plane are (x_i, y_i), xoz plane are (x_i, z_i) , and yoz plane are (y_i, z_i) , $i = 1 \cdots n$. Now we do fitting for the data (x_i, y_i) located in xoy plane with the least squares method, the fitting line is as follow,

$$y = a_1 + a_2 x \qquad (3)$$

By computing, the coefficient of a_1 and a_2 are got as,

$$a_1 = \frac{q_2 q_4 - q_1 q_3}{n q_2 - q_1^2}, \; a_2 = \frac{n q_3 - q_1 q_3}{n q_2 - q_1^2} \qquad (4)$$

$$q_1 = \sum_{i=1}^{n} x_i, q_2 = \sum_{i=1}^{n} x_i^2, q_3 = \sum_{i=1}^{n} x_i y_i \; q_4 = \sum_{i=1}^{n} y_i \qquad (5)$$

In the same way, we do fitting for the data (y_i, z_i) located in yoz plane with the least squares method, the fitting line is as follow,

$$z = a_1^{'} + a_2^{'} y \qquad (6)$$

We do fitting for the data (x_i, z_i) located in xoz plane with the least squares method, the fitting line is as follow,

$$z = a_1^{''} + a_2^{''} x \qquad (7)$$

So, the planar equation of a plane which contains the straight line (3) and is perpendicular to plane xoy is expressed as,

$$a_2 x + a_1 - y = 0 \qquad (8)$$

The planar equation of a plane which contains the straight line (6) and is perpendicular to plane yoz is expressed as,

$$a_2^{'} y + a_1^{'} - z = 0 \qquad (9)$$

The planar equation of a plane which contains the straight line (7) and is perpendicular to plane xoz is expressed as,

$$a_2^{''} y + a_1^{''} - z = 0 \qquad (10)$$

There is a common intersecting line between every two intersecting planes, so we can get three intersecting lines from the three planes. Next we compute the distance between the axis and three lines respectively with the three-dimensional coordintes in the axis, the line which has the least sum of distances is the optimal fitting spacial line. Also, we can get the axis equation of Line B in the same way.

6 Fitting Algorithm of Impact Parameters

As we have known that the axis of pinhole is a spacial line, so the axis between two adjacent holes is not sure to have a common point. After we get the two axis equations for a pair of holes, the shortest distance between two spacial axis can be computed, which is defined as imoact error, shown as figure 7.

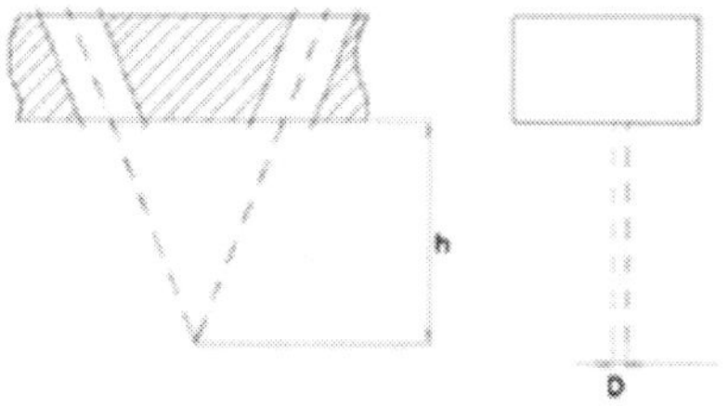

Figure 7. The Impact Height and Error.

Assuming that the point $M_0(x_0, y_0, z_0)$ in the axis line A, by computing the distance from that point to line B, we search the point which has the shortest distance, this is the impact error of two axis,

$$D = \sqrt{f_1(x, y, z) - f_2(x, y, z)} \qquad (11)$$

Here,

$$f_1(x, y, z) = (x_3 - x_0)^2 + (y_3 - y_0)^2 + (z_3 - z_0)^2 \qquad (12)$$

$$f_2(x, y, z) = \frac{l(x_3 - x_0) + m(y_3 - y_0) + n(z_3 - z_0)}{l^2 + m^2 + n^2} \qquad (13)$$

$$l = x_4 - x_3 \qquad (14)$$

$$m = y_4 - y_3 \qquad (15)$$

$$n = z_4 - z_3 \qquad (16)$$

DOI: 10.1051/itmconf/20160709023

Assuming that the equation of reference plane is as the following,

$$A_0x + B_0y + C_0z + D_0 = 0 \qquad (17)$$

Here, the reference plane is defined by at least three points in the same surface $P_1(x_1, y_1, z_1)$, $P_2(x_2, y_2, z_2)$ and $P_3(x_3, y_3, z_3)$, these point coordinates were got from the three-coordinate measuring machine, the plane is expressed as,

$$\begin{vmatrix} x - x_3 & y - y_3 & z - z_3 \\ x_1 - x_3 & y_1 - y_3 & z_1 - z_3 \\ x_2 - x_3 & y_2 - y_3 & z_2 - z_3 \end{vmatrix} = 0 \qquad (18)$$

Then the distance from point $M_0(x_0, y_0, z_0)$ to this reference plane can be obtained from the following expression,

$$h = \frac{|A_0x + B_0y + C_0z + D_0|}{\sqrt{A_0^2 + B_0^2 + C_0^2}} \qquad (19)$$

Here the h is defined as impact height of two axis.

7 Conclusion

We set up a five-dimensional measuring system in the paper. With the aid of three-dimensional measuring machine, we combine the advantages of capacitive sensor probe together to realize the measurement for oblique holes, this testing system can obtain the three-dimensional ordinates in the axis, by comprehensive fitting algorithm, the axis of a pair of oblique holes can be computed and the position relationship can also be figured out.

Acknowledgements

This work was financially supported by the Shandong Natural Science Foundation (ZR2013EEL004)

References

1. Ma Yuzhen, Wang Xinhua, Kang Yanhui, Roundness Measurement and Error Separation Technique, Applied Mechanics and Materials Vols. 303-306 (2013): 390-393
2. Yu Yongxin, Zhang Heng, Wang Zongchao, Chang Yizhe. Deep-Hole Inner Diameter Measuring System Based on Non-contact Capacitance Sensor, Transactions of Tianjin University, 2010, 16(6):447-451
3. Hrioshi MURAKAMI, Akio KATSUKI, Hiromichi ONIKURA. Development of a system for measuring micro hole accurary using an optical fiber probe, Journal of Advanced Mechanical Design, Systems and Manufacturing, 2010, 4(5): 995-1004
4. J Stone, B Muralikrishnan, C Sahay, Geometric Effects When Measuring Small Holes With Micro Contact Probes, Journal of Research of the National Institute of Standards and Technology, 2011, 116(2): 573-587
5. Ma Yu-zhen, Wang Xin-hua, Li Hong-min, A New Capacitive Sensing System for Roundness Measurement, Advanced Materials Research Vol. 662 (2013): 754-757
6. Yu-zhen Ma, Yong-xin Yu, Xin-hua Wang, Key technique for Inner Hole Diameter Measure with Capacitive Probe, Applied Mechanics and Materials Vols. 303-306 (2013): 827-830
7. Ma Yu-zhen, Yu Yong-xin, Wang Xin-hua, The diameter measuring technique based on capacitive probe for deep hole or oblique hole, Measurement, 47 (2014): 42-44

A Bayes Theory-Based Modeling Algorithm to End-to-end Network Traffic

Hong-hao Zhao[1], Fan-bo Meng[1,a], Si-wen Zhao[2], Si-hang Zhao[3], Yi Lu[4]

[1]*State Grid Liaoning Electric Power Company Limited, Shenyang 110006, China*
[2] *Shenyang China Resources Thermal Power Company Limited, Shenyang 110043, China*
[3] *State Grid Huludao Electric Power Supply Company, Huludao 125000, China*
[4]*State Grid Shenyang Electric Power Supply Company, Shenyang 110003, China*

Abstract. Recently, network traffic has exponentially increasing due to all kind of applications, such as mobile Internet, smart cities, smart transportations, Internet of things, and so on. the end-to-end network traffic becomes more important for traffic engineering. Usually end-to-end traffic estimation is highly difficult. This paper proposes a Bayes theory-based method to model the end-to-end network traffic. Firstly, the end-to-end network traffic is described as a independent identically distributed normal process. Then the Bases theory is used to characterize the end-to-end network traffic. By calculating the parameters, the model is determined correctly. Simulation results show that our approach is feasible and effective.

1 Introduction

With the quick development of network technology and new applications, network traffic exhibits new features. This leads to a new challenging for network engineering [1-2]. it is important to accurately characterize and model network traffic for improving network performance. The features of network traffic, such as self-similarity nature, auto-correlations, heavy-tailed distribution, have an important impact on network optimization and routing [3-4]. The end-to-end network traffic represents the network-wide behaviors from a global point of view. Hence, modeling the end-to-end network traffic has received an extensive attention from researchers, operators, and developer all around the world [5].

The end-to-end traffic behaviors embody the path-level feature in the network. It can be used to describe network status and nature, such as path loads, throughput, network utilization, and so on. The statistical methods are employed to denote the model of network traffic from the source node to the destination node [1,3]. The gravity model [4], generic evolvement [6-7], mix method [2], and compressive sensing are utilized to capture the properties of the end-to-end network traffic. These method can attain the better prediction and estimation of the end-to-end traffic by performing a modeling process. However, these methods need the additional information from link loads or a prior information about the end-to-end network traffic. This adds the computational complexity and overhead for attaining the model parameters. The time-frequency domain analysis can be used to capture the multi-scale features and dynamic nature [1,8]. The neural network is employed to model network traffic [7,9]. These approaches can build the model to denote the end-to-end network traffic, while it is very difficult to exactly capture and seize their features and to build the accurate and appropriate network traffic model for traffic engineering.

This paper proposes a end-to-end network traffic modeling method to accurately characterize their features. Generally, it is significantly impossible to directly build the model about them due to their complex properties. Different form previous methods, we use the Bayes theory to establish the model about the end-to-end network traffic. Firstly, we denote the end-to-end network traffic as a independent identically distributed normal process. In the random process, there are several parameters to be estimated accurately. This is very difficult for the limited traffic information. Secondly, to this end, we use the Bases theory to characterize the end-to-end network traffic. By calculating the parameters with statistical methods, the model is determined correctly. In such a case, the model about the end-to-end network traffic is correctly built. Thirdly, we propose a new algorithm to build the model. Simulation results show that our approach is feasible and effective.

The rest of this paper is organized as follows. Our method is derived in Section 2. Section 3 presents the simulation results and analysis. We then conclude our work in Section 4.

2 Problem Statement

The modeling problem of the end-to-end traffic is difficult. In the network, there exists a lot of many end-

[a] Corresponding author: amengfb@163.com

DOI: 10.1051/itmconf/20160709024

to-end network traffic. Without loss of generality, the end-to-end network traffic in the network is denoted as $x = \{x(1), x(2), \ldots\}$, where $x(i)$ (where $i = 1, 2, \ldots$) represents the value of traffic flow x at time slot i. Here, we assume that network traffic x follows the independent identically distributed normal process, which is denoted as:

$$X \sim N(\mu, \delta) \tag{1}$$

where μ and δ, respectively, denote the mean value and variance of the normal process X. Accordingly, the following equation can be attained:

$$P(X = x) = \frac{1}{\sqrt{2\pi}\delta} \exp(-\frac{(x-\mu)^2}{\delta^2}) \tag{2}$$

Here, parameters μ and δ describe the features of the end-to-end traffic x. However, Equations (1) and (2) only represent the statistical nature of the end-to-end traffic x. As mentioned in [10-12], the end-to-end network traffic holds the correlation property.

To capture the feature, we build the below model

$$x(k) = a_1 x(k-1) + \ldots + a_n x(k-n) + \varepsilon \tag{3}$$

where a_i (where $i = 1, 2, \ldots, n$) denotes parameters; ε represents the normal process $N(\alpha, \beta)$, which stands for the bias of the model in Equation (3); n indicates the number of time slots before the current time slot.

According to Equations (1) and (2), $x(i)$ (where $i = 1, 2, \ldots$) is an instance of the normal process X. From Equations (1)-(3), it is very clear that we have successfully characterize the statistical and correlation nature of the end-to-end network traffic. Equation (3) shows that given the end-to-end network traffic $x(k-1)$, $x(k-2)$, ..., $x(k-n)$ at time slots $k-1$, $k-2$, ..., $k-n$ and the bias distribution ε, we can get the end-to-end traffic $x(k)$ at time slot k. At each time slot, the end-to-end network traffic can be regarded as a random process. Thereby, according to the Bayes theory, Equation (3) can be denoted as:

$$P(X(k) \mid X(k-1), X(k-2), \ldots, X(k-n)) = \frac{P(X(k), X(k-1), X(k-2), \ldots, X(k-n))}{P(X(k-1), X(k-2), \ldots, X(k-n))} \tag{4}$$

Our experiments show that when $n = 3$, we can accurately capture the features of the end-to-end network traffic. In such case, Equations (3) and (4) can be simply denoted as:

$$x(k) = a_1 x(k-1) + a_2 x(k-2) + a_3 x(k-3) + \varepsilon \tag{5}$$

$$P(X(k) \mid X(k-1), X(k-2), X(k-3)) = \frac{P(X(k), X(k-1), X(k-2), X(k-3))}{P(X(k-1), X(k-2), X(k-3))} \tag{6}$$

Compared with Equations (3) and (4), Equations (5) and (6) use much simpler form to describe the end-to-end network traffic. Consequently, we can easily attain the model parameters. Due to the dynamic and random nature of the end-to-end network traffic, it is significantly difficult to directly determine the model in Equation (5).

To attain the parameters in Equation (5), we define the following loss function:

$$\begin{aligned}\Delta x(k) &= x(k) - \tilde{x}(k) \\ &= x(k) - (a_1 x(k-1) + a_2 x(k-2) + \\ &\quad a_3 x(k-3) + \varepsilon)\end{aligned} \tag{7}$$

Equation (7) show the model bias, which is a random process related with the parameters $a_1, a_2, a_3, \alpha, \beta, \mu$ and δ. Accordingly, the below equation is attained:

$$E(\Delta x(k) \mid a_1, a_2, a_3, \alpha, \beta, \mu, \delta) = \iint \Delta x(k) p(x, \varepsilon) dx d\varepsilon \tag{8}$$

where $p(x, \varepsilon)$ denotes the joint probability density function of the normal random processes X and ε. Generally, we wish Equation (8) to be equal to zero. Because of the time-varying and correlated nature, there always exists some bias in Equation (8). Only when the bias is minimum, can we attain the optimal model for the end-to-end network traffic.

Accordingly, to solve Equation (3), we build the below optimal equation:

$$\begin{cases} \min \quad E(\Delta x(k) \mid a_1, a_2, a_3, \alpha, \beta, \mu, \delta) \\ s.t. \quad \tilde{x}(k) = a_1 x(k-1) + \ldots + a_3 x(k-3) + \varepsilon \\ \qquad P(X = x) = \frac{1}{\sqrt{2\pi}\delta} \exp(-\frac{(x-\mu)^2}{\delta^2}) \\ \qquad \Delta x(k) = x(k) - \tilde{x}(k) \end{cases} \tag{9}$$

Equation (9) indicates a multi-constraint single object optimization problem. The first equation in Equation (9) denotes the object function, which minimizes the bias in the model in Equation (3); the second one represents the estimation of the end-to-end network traffic at time slot k according to Equation (3); the three one stands for the distribution of network traffic x; the four one indicates the model bias. Using the sample data to train and solve the model in Equation (9), we can correctly attain the model parameters. In such a case, we can perform the correct description for the end-to-end network traffic.

In the following, we propose our modeling algorithm, called Bayes theory Traffic Modeling Algorithm (BTMA), to the end-to-end network traffic according to the above analysis and derivation, namely:

Step 1: Give the h initial value of the end-to-end network traffic $x_{tr} = \{x(1), x(2), ..., x(h)\}$ in the network.

Step 2: According to statistical theory, use initial value x_{tr} to attain the experience distribution parameters $\tilde{\mu}$ and δ of the end-to-end network traffic in Equations (1)-(2). Accordingly, obtain the experience distribution probability $N(\tilde{\mu}, \delta)$.

Step 3: According to mathematical theory and signal processing theory, substitute initial value x_{tr} into Equation (5). Then determine the parameters $a_1, a_2, a_3, \alpha, \beta$. Accordingly, the experience model in Equation (3) is built.

Step 4: According to Equation (7), calculate the bias $\Delta x(k)$. Use Equation (8) to compute the statistical bias $E(\Delta x(k) \mid a_1, a_2, a_3, \alpha, \beta, \mu, \delta)$.

Step 5: According to Equation (9), minimize the statistical bias $E(\Delta x(k) \mid a_1, a_2, a_3, \alpha, \beta, \mu, \delta)$.

Step 6: Get the optimal parameters $a_1, a_2, a_3, \alpha, \beta, \mu, \delta$ in terms of Equation (9).

Step 7: If initial value x_{tr} has not been completely handled, go back to Step 4.

Step 8: The model of the end-to-end network traffic is correctly built. Then exit the modeling process.

3 Simulation Result and analysis

In this suction, we conduct some tests to demonstrate our algorithm BTMA. In order to verify the accuracy of our algorithm, we need to use real network data. The real data needed in the simulation experiment is collected by the network nodes; we use the real data from the real Abilene backbone network in the United States to validate BTMA. Matlab2010 is exploited performed the detailed simulation experiments. PCA [3], WABR [7], and HMPA [2] algorithms for the end-to-end network traffic modeling have been reported as the better performance. In this paper, we compare BTMA with them in detail. In the following, the prediction results of the end-to-end network traffic are analyzed for BTMA algorithm. The average relative errors for the end-to-end network traffic are indicated for four algorithms. Finally, we also evaluate the performance improvement of BTMA against PCA, WABR, and HMPA. In our simulation, the data of the first 500 time slots are used to train the models of four approaches, while other data are exploited to validate the performance of all algorithms.

Fig.1 shows the prediction results of end-to-end traffic flows 78 and 118, where end-to-end traffic flows 78 and 118 are selected randomly from the 144 end-to-end traffic pairs (or flows) in the Abilene backbone network. As our simulation experiments, other end-to-end traffic pairs holds similar results. Without loss of generality, we only discuss the end-to-end traffic flows 78 and 118 in this paper. Additionally, here we consider the end-to-end traffic flows equal to the Origin Destination (OD) pair. Fig. 1(a) indicates that BTMA can effectively capture the dynamic changes of the end-to-end traffic flow 78. For different time slots, the real end-to-end network traffic

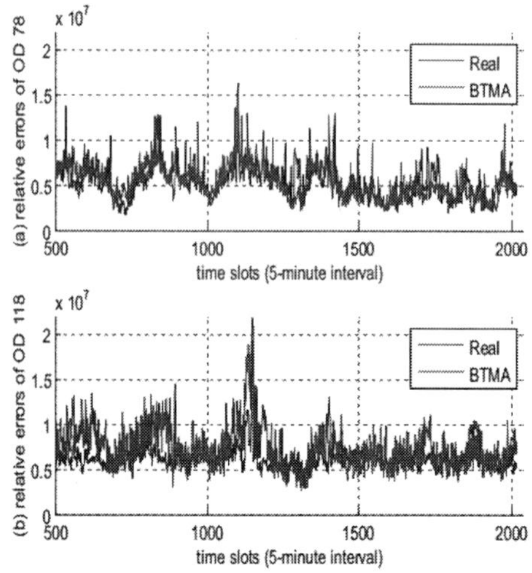

Figure 1. Prediction Results of End-to-End Traffic Flows 78 and 118.

exhibits the significant time-varying nature. From Fig. 1(a), we have seen that BTMA can seek the trend of the end-to-end traffic flow. Likewise, the end-to-end traffic flow 118 shows the irregular and dynamic changes over the time as indicated in Fig. 1(b). From Fig. 1(b), it is very clear that although BTMA holds the larger prediction errors for the end-to-end traffic flow 118, it can still capture its change trend. This further demonstrates that BTMA can effectively predict
the change of the end-to-end network traffic over the time.

Next, we discuss the predict errors of four algorithms. Generally, the time-varying nature of the end-to-end network traffic over the time is difficult to be captured only via the model. To further validate our algorithm, we compare the relative prediction errors over the time for all algorithms. To avoid the randomness in the simulation, we perform 500 runs to calculate the average relative prediction errors.

The average relative prediction errors over the time for the end-to-end network traffic are defined as:

$$e(t) = \frac{1}{N}\sum_{i=1}^{N} \frac{\| \hat{x}_i(t) - x_i(t) \|_2}{\| x_i(t) \|_2} \tag{10}$$

where $i = 1, 2, ..., N$, N is the number of runs in the simulation process, $\| \cdot \|_2$ is the norm of L_2, and $\hat{x}_i(t)$ indicates the end-to-end traffic prediction value of run i at time slot t.

Fig. 2 illustrates the average relative prediction errors of four algorithm over the time for end-to-end traffic flows 78 and 118. It is very interesting that for end-to-end traffic flows 78 and 118, WABR, HMPA, and BTMA exhibit the lower relative errors while PCA hold the larger prediction deviation. At the same time, Fig. 2 also indicates that BTMA holds the lowest relative errors. This tells us that in contrast to PCA, WABR, HMPA, and BTMA hold the better prediction ability for the end-to-end network traffic, while BTMA indeed has the best prediction ability. More importantly, WABR, HMPA, and BTMA exhibit the lower fluctuation over the time in terms of relative errors than PCA. This shows that compared with other three algorithms, BTMA can more effectively model the end-to-end network traffic with dynamic features.

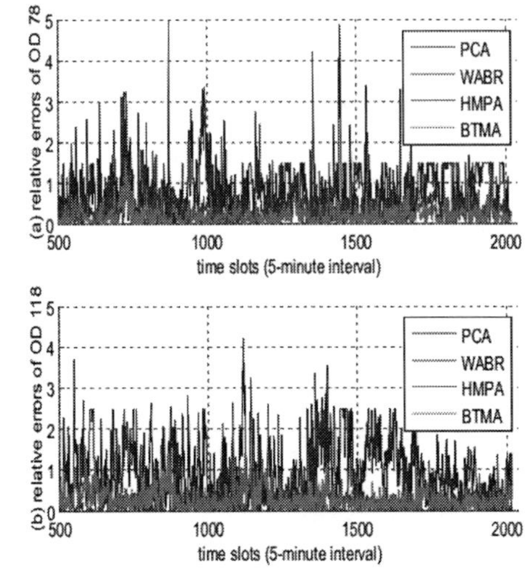

Figure 2. Average Relative Errors for End-to-End Traffic Flows 78 and 118.

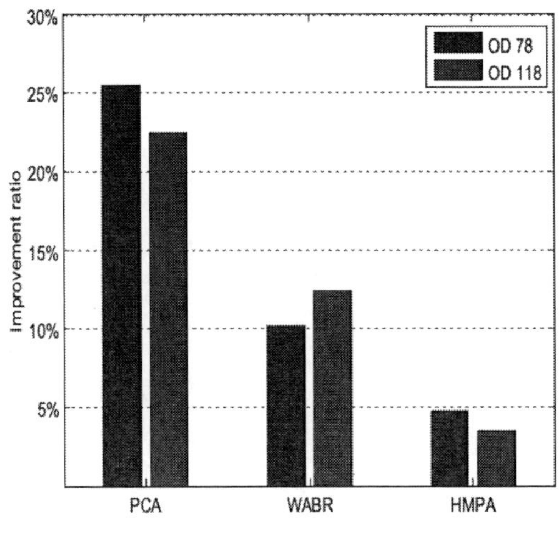

Figure 3. Improvement Ratio of End-to-End Traffic Flows 78 and 118.

Now, we analyze the improvement of BTMA to other three algorithms for the end-to-end network traffic. Fig. 3 plots the improvement ration of end-to-end traffic flow 78 and 118. For end-to-end traffic flow 78, BTMA attains the performance improvement of about 25.5%, 10.0%, and 4.0% against PCA, WABR, and HMPA, respectively. Similarly, For end-to-end traffic flow 118, BTMA obtains the performance improvement of about 22.8%, 12.5%, and 3.3% against PCA, WABR, and HMPA, respectively. This definitely demonstrates that in contrast to PCA, WABR, and HMPA, our algorithm BTMA can indeed model the end-to-end network traffic more effectively. From Fig. 3, we also see that relative to PCA, BTMA can reach the largest performance improvement. For WABR, BTMA only achieve the smaller improvement. However, BTMA holds the lowest improvement against HMPA, namely less than 5%. As mentioned in Fig. 2, this further shows that WABR, HMPA, and BTMA hold the better modeling capability for the end-to-end network traffic. Moreover, BTMA and HMPA hold the similar performance. Therefore, BTMA can correctly model the end-to-end traffic.

4. Conclusions

This paper proposes a Bayes theory-based method to model the end-to-end network traffic. Different from previous methods, the Bayes model is used to infer and establish the model parameters effectively. Firstly, the end-to-end network traffic is described as a independent identically distributed normal process. Secondly, the Bases method is exploited to capture the end-to-end network traffic. By calculating the parameters, we construct the corresponding network traffic model. Simulation results show that our approach is feasible and effective.

References

1. D. Jiang, Z. Xu, Z. Chen, et al. Joint time-frequency sparse estimation of large-scale network traffic. Computer Networks, 2011, 55(10): 3533-3547.
2. D. Jiang, Z. Xu, H. Xu. A novel hybrid prediction algorithm to network traffic. Annals of Telecommunications, 2015, 70(9): 427-439.
3. A. Soule, A. Lakhina, N. Taft, et al. Traffic matrices: balancing measurements, inference and modeling, In Proceedings of SIGMETRICS'05 2005, 33(1): 362-373.
4. Y. Zhang, M. Roughan, N. Duffield, et al. Fast accurate computation of large-scale IP traffic matrices from link loads, In Proceedings of SIGMETRICS'03, 2003, 31(3): 206-217.
5. T. Takeda, K. Shionoto. Traffic matrix estimation in large-scale IP networks, In Proceedings of LANMAN'10, 2010, pp: 1-6.
6. F Yingxun. The research and improvement of the genetic algorithm, Beijing, Beijing University of Posts and Telecommunications, 2010.
7. D. Jiang, Z. Zhao, Z. Xu, et al. How to reconstruct end-to-end traffic based on time-frequency analysis

and artificial neural network. AEU-International Journal of Electronics and Communications, 2014, 68(10): 915-925.

8. D. Jiang, Z. Yuan, P. Zhang, et al. A traffic anomaly detection approach in communication networks for applications of multimedia medical devices. Multimedia Tools and Applications, 2016, online available.
9. D. Jiang, Z. Xu, L. Nie, et al. An approximate approach to end-to-end traffic in communication networks. Chinese Journal of Electronics, 2012, 21(4): 705-710.
10. S. Vaton, J. Bedo. Network traffic matrix: How can one learn the prior distributions from the link counts only, In Proceedings of ICC'04, 2004, pp: 2138-2142.
11. M. Lad, R. Oliveira, D. Massey, et al. Inferring the origin of routing changes using link weights, In Proceedings of ICNP, 2007, pp: 93-102.
12. P. Tune, D. Veitch. Sampling vs sketching: An information theoretic comparison, In Proceedings of INFOCOM, 2011, pp: 2105-2113.

A Wavelet Analysis-Based Dynamic Prediction Algorithm to Network Traffic

Fan-Bo Meng[1,a], Hong-Hao Zhao[1], Si-Hang Zhao[2], Si-Wen Zhao[3], Zhong-Qiu Lin[4]

[1] *State Grid Liaoning Electric Power Company Limited, Shenyang 110006, China*
[2] *State Grid Huludao Electric Power Supply Company, Huludao 125000, China*
[3] *Shenyang China Resources Thermal Power Company Limited, Shenyang 110043, China*
[4] *State Grid Dandong Electric Power Supply Company, Dandong 118000, China*

Abstract. Network traffic is a significantly important parameter for network traffic engineering, while it holds highly dynamic nature in the network. Accordingly, it is difficult and impossible to directly predict traffic amount of end-to-end flows. This paper proposes a new prediction algorithm to network traffic using the wavelet analysis. Firstly, network traffic is converted into the time-frequency domain to capture time-frequency feature of network traffic. Secondly, in different frequency components, we model network traffic in the time-frequency domain. Finally, we build the prediction model about network traffic. At the same time, the corresponding prediction algorithm is presented to attain network traffic prediction. Simulation results indicates that our approach is promising.

1 Introduction

Network traffic is very significant for network management, traffic engineering, network monitoring, routing optimization, and network measurement activities [1-2]. Network traffic, special for end-to-end network traffic, represents the behavior features of network users' and network devices' activities. Network traffic denotes the volume of flows between nodes or between Origin-Destination (OD) pairs. Particularly, OD pairs can more effectively describe the behaviors of network activities from a network-wide or global perspective [3-4]. Hence, network traffic holds an important role in the normal network activities. However, network traffic, special for OD traffic pairs, is more difficult to be estimated and predicted due to their highly time-varying nature [5-7]. In this paper, we study the network-wide traffic prediction problem, that is, we model and predict the end-to-end network traffic or the traffic amount of OD node pairs. Despite the difficulty in predicting network traffic, it has been the hot topic and received the more attentions.

Tebaldi et al. proposed a new statistical approach which was based on the statistical model of the inversion method to build network source-destination traffic flow model and to predict network traffic [4]. Tune et al. used the information theoretic to describe network traffic [8]. Takeda et al used the partial measurement information to estimate the end-to-end traffic matrix and proposed the corresponding prediction algorithm [6]. Zhang et al. [9] managed to acquire prior information of traffic matrix based on gravity model and then proposed traffic matrix estimation method. Jiang et al used neural network to model the end-to-end network traffic and attain the accurate estimation [10]. Chen et al. studied the short-time network traffic prediction [11]. The expectation maximization algorithm was used to estimate traffic matrix via the assumption that traffic demands between OD pairs were independent of each other and obeyed Gaussian distribution [12]. Jiang et al. also exploited the compressive sensing theory to propose a joint time-frequency estimation of network traffic [13]. Some of these methods had relatively large estimation errors, while other were very sensitive to prior information [9,14]. Hence, the above models and methods are difficult to accurately capture network flow traffic, so it is still significantly necessary to find more accurate model to depict network flow traffic, to lower the complexity of algorithms, and to improve the prediction accuracy.

Different from the above algorithms, this paper proposes a new Wavelet Analysis-based Prediction Algorithm (WAPA) to predict network traffic in the network. Firstly, the signal analysis theory is exploited to transform network traffic from time domain to time-frequency domain. And then the time-frequency analysis approach is used to characterize the inherent property of network traffic. Secondly, in the time-frequency domain, we decompose network traffic into different frequency components, such as low-, medium-, and high-frequency components. The low-frequency part reflects the change trend of network traffic, medium-frequency one describes their slow change, but the high-frequency one reflects their quick change. Hence, we use the autoregressive model, period signal model, and Gaussian noise model to model the low-, medium-, and high-frequency

[a] Corresponding author: amengfb@163.com

components, respectively. Thirdly, the corresponding algorithm is proposed to predict network traffic. Simulation results show that our algorithm holds much lower prediction error than previous methods and thus it is promising.

The rest of this paper is organized as follows. Section II is problem statement. Section III is to derive our prediction approach. Section IV is simulation results and analysis. And finally our work in this paper is concluded in Section IV.

2 Problem Statement

The end-to-end traffic in the communication network can be expressed as $x=(x(1),x(2),...,x(m))$ for m observation time slots, where $x(t)$ (where $t=1,2,...,m$) represents the volume of network traffic x at moment t. To facilitate the processing, network traffic x is normalized as

$$z(t)=\frac{x(t)-\frac{1}{m}\sum_{i=1}^{m}x(i)}{h} \quad (1)$$

where

$$h=\max\{|x(1)-\frac{1}{m}\sum_{i=1}^{m}x(i)|,...,|x(m)-\frac{1}{m}\sum_{i=1}^{m}x(i)|\}$$

Accordingly, $z(t)$ satisfies the following constraint:

$$-1\le z(t)\le 1 \quad (2)$$

In such a case, the computational complex is reduced effectively. According the wavelet analysis theory, the new network traffic $z=\{z(1),z(2),...,z(m)\}$ is converted into:

$$\begin{cases} a_{i(j+1)}=Ha_{ij}, & j=0,1,2,...,I-1 \\ d_{i(j+1)}=Ga_{ij}, & j=0,1,2,...,I-1 \\ a_{i0}=z(t) \end{cases} \quad (3)$$

where H is the high-pass filter, G denotes the low-pass filter, $a_{i(j+1)}$ and $d_{i(j+1)}$ are, respectively, the time-frequency coefficients of z, and I represents the number of decomposition levels.

According to Equation (3), divide the time-domain signals of network traffic z into low-, medium-, and high-frequency components as follows:

$$\begin{cases} W(f,t)=Y(z_i(t)=W_l(f,t)+W_m(f,t)+W_h(f,t) \\ W_l(f,t)=a_I \\ W_m(f,t)=(d_1,d_2,...,d_k) \\ W_h(f,t)=(d_{k+1},d_{k+2},...,d_I) \end{cases} \quad (4)$$

where $W_l(f,t)$, $W_m(f,t)$, and $W_h(f,t)$, respectively, denote the low-, medium-, and high-frequency components in the time-frequency domain, and $W(f,t)$ represents the time-frequency signals of network traffic z at time t.

According to the inversion transformation of the wavelet, for the low-, medium-, and high-frequency components of z, the loss part is filled with zeros. Then the low-frequency coefficient in the time-frequency domain can be attained:

$$W_l(f,t)=(a_I,0,0,...,0) \quad (5)$$

The medium-frequency coefficient in the time-frequency domain can be expressed as:

$$W_m(f,t)=(0,d_1,d_2,...,d_k,0,...,0) \quad (6)$$

Similarly, the high-frequency coefficient in the time-frequency domain can be expressed as:

$$W_h(f,t)=(0,0,...,0,d_{k+1},d_{k+2},...,d_I) \quad (7)$$

Then we obtain the below equation:

$$\begin{cases} z_l(t)=Y^{-1}(W_l(f,t)) \\ z_m(t)=Y^{-1}(W_m(f,t)) \\ z_h(t)=Y^{-1}(W_h(f,t)) \end{cases} \quad (8)$$

where $z_l(t)$, $z_m(t)$, and $z_h(t)$, respectively, denote the reconstruction signals of the low-, medium-, and high-frequency signals $W_l(f,t)$, $W_m(f,t)$, and $W_h(f,t)$ of network traffic $z(t)$ at time t.

According to Equation (8), the low-frequency time-domain signal $z_l=\{z_l(1),z_l(2),...,z_l(m)\}$ is modeled as:

$$z_l(t)=b_1z_l(t-1)+b_2z_l(t-2)+...+b_pz_l(t-p)+\varepsilon \quad (9)$$

where p is the order number of the autoregressive model, ε represents the error, and $b=\{b_1,b_2,...,b_p\}$ stands for the parameters of the model. $b=\{b_1,b_2,...,b_p\}$ can be determined via the signal analysis. Accordingly, Equation (9) is decided correctly.

The medium-frequency signal $z_m=\{z_m(1),...,z_m(m)\}$ can be denoted as:

$$z_m(t)=u\sin(\omega t+\alpha)+v\sin(\omega t+\beta)+\eta \quad (10)$$

where u and v are the coefficients of the model; ω, α, and β denote the frequency and initial phase of the period signal, and η represents the error of the model. The model in Equation (10) is decided via the signal analysis theory.

The high-frequency signal $z_h = \{z_h(1),...,z_h(m)\}$ is modeled as:

$$z_h(t) = \frac{1}{\sqrt{2\pi\delta}}\exp(-\frac{(z_h(t)-\mu)}{2\delta^2}) + \lambda \qquad (11)$$

where δ and μ denote the variable and mean value of the Gaussian noise, and λ represents the error. Equation (11) is decided via the statistics theory.

According to the above discussion, the low-, medium-, and high-frequency signals corresponding to the time-frequency domain, respectively, are modeled as the autoregressive model, period signal, and Gaussian noise signal, as shown in Equations (9)-(11).

We can attain the time-domain signal as follows:

$$\hat{z}(t) = z_l(t) + z_m(t) + z_h(t) \qquad (12)$$

According to Equation (1), the resulting time-domain signal is obtained as follows:

$$\hat{x}(t) = h \times \hat{z}(t) + \frac{1}{m}\sum_{i=1}^{m} x(i) \qquad (13)$$

Accordingly, we can obtain the estimations of the end-to-end traffic by equation (13). The algorithm WAPA proposed can be described as follow:

Step 1: Give the initial data of the end-to-end network traffic data $x_0 = \{x_0(1), x_0(2),..., x_0(r)\}$, where r denotes the length of initial data.

Step 2: According to Equation (1), perform the transformation to attain a new sequence series about the end-to-end network traffic $z_0 = \{z_0(1), z_0(2),..., z_0(r)\}$.

Step 3: According to Equations (3), carry out the wavelet transformation, and then attain the time-frequency coefficients of $c_0 = \{a_J, d_1, d_2,..., d_J\}$ for time signals.

Step 4: According to Equations (4), divide the time-frequency signals into the low-, medium-, and high-frequency components of $W_l(f,t)$, $W_m(f,t)$, and $W_h(f,t)$ in the time-frequency domain, respectively.

Step 5: Fill the loss entries in the low-, medium-, and high-frequency components of $W_l(f,t)$, $W_m(f,t)$, and $W_h(f,t)$ with zeros according to Equations (5)-(7).

Step 6: According to Equation (8), perform the inversion transformation of the wavelet, and then attain the low-, medium-, and high-frequency signals of $z_l(t)$, $z_m(t)$, and $z_h(t)$ in the time domain.

Step 7: According to Equations (9)-(11), build the models corresponding to the low-, medium-, and high-frequency signals of $z_l(t)$, $z_m(t)$, and $z_h(t)$, respectively, using the signal analysis and statistics theories via the initial data.

Step 8: According Equations (9)-(11), attain the prediction value of the low-, medium-, and high-frequency signals of $z_l(t)$, $z_m(t)$, and $z_h(t)$.

Step 9 According to Equations (12), calculate the time-domain signal $\hat{z}(t)$.

Step 10: According to Equation (13), attain the prediction signal $\hat{x}(t)$ of the end-to-end network traffic at time t.

Step 11: If the process is over, then save the results to file and exit, or go back to Step 8.

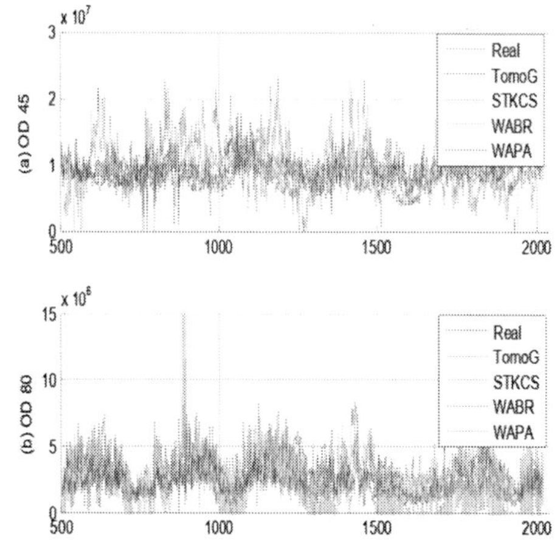

Figure 1. Prediction Results of Four Algorithms for Ods 45 and 80.

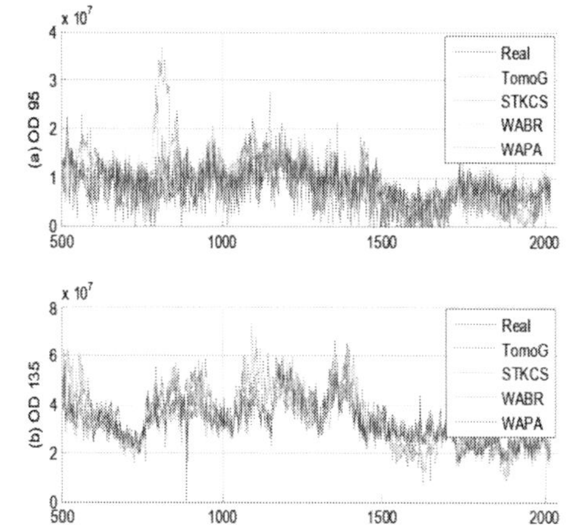

Figure 2. Prediction Results of Four Algorithms for Ods 95 and 135.

3 Simulation Result and analysis

Now we validate our algorithm WAPA. The real traffic data from the real Abilene backbone network in the United States are used to perform the simulation. STKCS [2], WABR[7], PCA [5], and TomoG [9] are reported as good prediction approaches for network traffic. In this paper, we will compare WAPA with them. at the same time, their prediction performance is analyzed in detail.

DOI: 10.1051/itmconf/20160709025

Figs. 1 and 2 plot the prediction results of four algorithms for ODs 45, 80, 95, and 135, respectively, where Real denotes the real network traffic. From Fig. 1, we can find that four algorithm can attain the good prediction results. In contrast to other three algorithms, WAPA holds the best prediction value

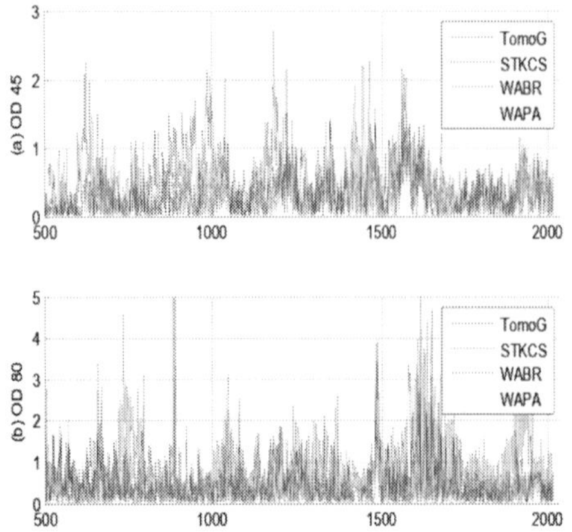

Figure 3. Relative Prediction Errors of Four Algorithms for Ods 45 and 80.

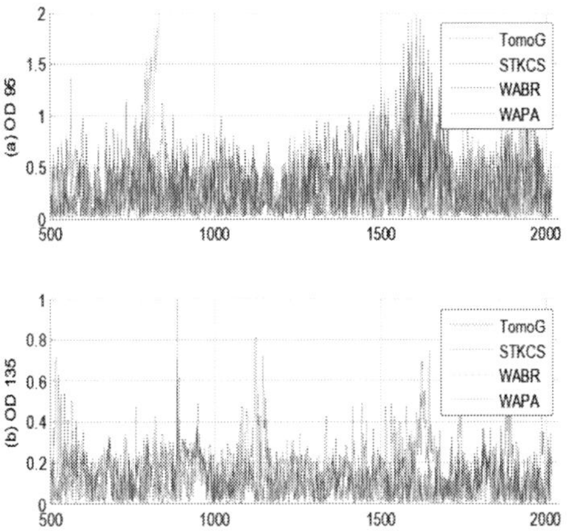

Figure 4. Relative Prediction Errors of Four Algorithms for Ods 95 And 135.

for ODs 45 and 80. TomoG has the larger prediction errors than other algorithm. Fig. 2 shows that four algorithms can also better predict the traffic of ODs 95 and 135. More importantly, when network traffic dynamically changes over time, four algorithms can capture the change trend of network traffic. Moreover, WAPA always can more accurately predict network traffic. This shows that WAPA holds the better prediction performance for network traffic.

Figs. 3 and 4 indicate the relative prediction errors of four algorithms for ODs 45, 80, 95, and 135, relative to the real network traffic. Fig. 3 shows that WAPA exhibits the lowest relative prediction errors in four algorithms for network traffic. In contrast to WAPA, TomoG holds the largest prediction errors, while STKCS and WABR illustrate the lower prediction. This demonstrates that WAPA holds the best prediction capacity for network traffic. From Figs. 3 and 4, it is clear that WAPA exhibits the more stationary prediction errors over the time than other three algorithm. This further indicates that WAPA holds the better prediction ability for network traffic.

4. Conclusions

This paper uses the wavelet analysis theory to model network traffic. By the wavelet transformation, we can correctly capture the dynamic and time-varying features in the time-frequency domain. Network traffic is converted into the time-frequency domain to capture time-frequency feature of network traffic. For different frequency components, we model network traffic in the time-frequency domain. Then network traffic signals are divided into the low-, medium-, and high-frequency signal. Accordingly we build the prediction model about network traffic. Finally, we propose the corresponding prediction algorithm to attain network traffic prediction. Simulation results indicates that our approach is promising and feasible.

References

1. D. Jiang, Z. Xu, J. Liu, et al. An optimization-based robust routing algorithm to energy-efficient networks for cloud computing. Telecommunication Systems, Sept., 2016, 63(1): 89-98.
2. T. Akgul, S. Baykut, M. Kantarci, S. Oktug. Periodicity-based anomalies in self-similar network traffic flow measurements, In Proceedings of TIM'11, 2011, 60(4): 1358-1366.
3. D. Jiang, L. Nie, Z. Lv, et al. Spatio-temporal Kronecker compressive sensing for traffic matrix recovery. IEEE Access, 2016, online available.
4. C. Tebaldi, M. West. Bayesian inference on network traffic using link count data, Journal of American Statistics Association, 1998, 93(442): 557-576.
5. A. Soule, A. Lakhina, N. Taft, et al. Traffic matrices: Balancing measurements, inference and modeling, ACM SIGMETRICS Performance Evaluation Review, 2005, 33(3): 362-373.
6. T. Takeda, K. Shionoto. Traffic matrix estimation in large-scale IP networks, In Proceedings of LANMAN'10, 2010, pp: 1-6.
7. D. Jiang, Z. Zhao, Z. Xu, et al. How to reconstruct end-to-end traffic based on time-frequency analysis and artificial neural network, AEU-International Journal of Electronics and Communications, 2014, 68(10): 915-925.
8. P. Tune, D. Veitch. Sampling vs sketching: An information theoretic comparison[C], In Proceedings of INFOCOM, 2011, pp: 2105-2113.
9. Y. Zhang, M Roughan, N. Duffield, et al. Fast accurate computation of large-scale IP traffic

DOI: 10.1051/itmconf/20160709025

matrices from link loads, ACM SIGMETRICS Performance Evaluation Review, 2003, 31(3): 206-217.

10. D. Jiang, Z. Xu, H. Xu, et al. An approximation method of origin-destination flow traffic from link load counts, Computers and Electrical Engineering, 2011, 37(6): 1106-1121.
11. C. Chen, J. Hu, et al. Short-time traffic flow prediction with ARIMA-GARCH model[C], In Proceedings of IV, 2011, pp: 607-612.
12. C. Hu. Online updating with a probability-based prediction model using expectation maximization algorithm for reliability forecasting. IEEE Transactions on Systems, Man and Cybernetics, Part A: Systems and Humans, 2011, 41(6): 1268-1277.
13. D. Jiang, Z. Xu, Z. Chen, et al. Joint time-frequency sparse estimation of large-scale network traffic, Computer Networks, 2011, 55(10): 3533-3547.
14. H. Singhal and G. Michailidis. Structural models for dual modality data with application to network tomography, IEEE Transactions on Information Theory, 2011, 57(8): 5054-5071.

AUTHOR INDEX

AUTHOR INDEX

AUTHOR INDEX